Microsoft
Computer
Dictionary
Fifth Edition

PUBLISHED BY
Microsoft Press
A Division of Microsoft Corporation
One Microsoft Way
Redmond, Washington 98052-6399

Library of Congress Cataloging-in-Publication Data
Microsoft Computer Dictionary.--5th ed.
      p. cm.
   ISBN 0-7356-1495-4
    1. Computers--Dictionaries.   2. Microcomputers--Dictionaries.

   AQ76.5. M52267 2002
   004'.03--dc21   200219714

Printed and bound in the United States of America.

2 3 4 5 6 7 8 9   QWT   7 6 5 4 3 2

Distributed in Canada by H.B. Fenn and Company Ltd.

A CIP catalogue record for this book is available from the British Library.

Microsoft Press books are available through booksellers and distributors worldwide. For further information about international editions, contact your local Microsoft Corporation office or contact Microsoft Press International directly at fax (425) 936-7329. Visit our Web site at www.microsoft.com/mspress. Send comments to *mspinput@microsoft.com*.

Acquisitions Editor: Alex Blanton
Project Editor: Sandra Haynes

Body Part No. X08-41929

Contributors

Peter Aiken

Bart Arenson

Janice Borzendowski

Jerome Colburn

Duane Hanson

Andrew Himes

Robert Howecton

Annette B. Jackson

Larry S. Jackson

Thomas A. Jackson

Chris Kinata

Ilana Kingsley

Robin Lombard

Thomas A. Long

William G. Madison

Thomas P. Magliery

David Mason

Terrence M. McLaren

Wallace Parker

Charles Petzold

Phil Rose

John Ross

David Rygmyr

Aimée Truchard

Michael Vose

Bruce Webster

Judson D. Weeks

Tom Winn

JoAnne Woodcock

Illustrators

Travis Beaven

David Holter

Alton Lawson

Rob Nance

Joel Panchot

Contents

Introduction

The *Microsoft Computer Dictionary, Fifth Edition* is designed to be a comprehensive and authoritative source of definitions for computer-related terms and abbreviations. The dictionary includes terms drawn from a wide variety of topics relevant to computer users, including software, hardware, networking, data storage, graphics, games, information processing, the Internet and the World Wide Web, gaming, history, jargon and slang, organizations, programming, and standards.

Although this book covers nearly every aspect of computing, it does not include entries on most companies or on most makes and models of computers, nor does it contain entries on most application software products. The few exceptions to this rule of thumb are key companies and products that have a historical or universal importance within the computing industry.

This dictionary emphasizes terminology that the average computer user will encounter in documentation, online help, computer manuals, marketing and sales materials, the popular media, and the computer trade press. Because most computer users operate personal computers and desktop systems at home, work, or both, the majority of the entries in this dictionary cover the terminology used in describing and working with these systems. However, some specialized or highly technical language is included that pertains to areas of industry, academia, software and hardware development, and research. These terms have been included because they have a bearing on more common computer terminology or because they are of historical significance.

Changes in the Fifth Edition

The fifth edition of the *Microsoft Computer Dictionary* has been revised and expanded to include over 10,000 entries, reflecting the many advances in the computer field and including several areas that have come into prominence in the public eye, such as networking, Web authoring, and new technologies, such as .NET. The content from the Year 2000 appendix has been integrated into the body of the dictionary and a new appendix on emoticons and instant messaging symbols has been added.

Order of Presentation

Entries are alphabetized by letter. Spaces are ignored, as are characters such as hyphens and slashes; for example, *Baudot code* falls between *baud* and *baud rate*, and *machine-independent* falls between *machine identification* and *machine instruction*. Numbers and symbols are located at the beginning of the book and are listed in ascending ASCII order. If an entry begins with a letter or letters but contains a number, it is listed alphabetically, according to the initial letter(s), and then according to ASCII order. Thus, V20 precedes V.2x, and both precede VAB.

Entries

Entries are of two types: main entries, which contain full definitions, and synonymous cross-references, which contain *See* references to the appropriate main entries. Synonymous cross-references are generally secondary or less common ways of referring to a main entry. The definition at the main entry can be substituted as a definition for the synonymous cross-reference.

Format

Information in each main entry is presented in a consistent format: entry name in boldface, spelling variants (if any), part of speech, definition, illustration or table reference (if any), acronym (if any), alternative names (if any), and cross-references (if any).

Main Entries

Entries that are acronyms or abbreviations for one or more words or concatenations of two or more words have those words spelled out at the beginning of the definition. The letters in these words or phrases that make up the acronym, abbreviation, or concatenation are in boldface.

When a main entry is spelled exactly the same as another main entry, the two entries are differentiated by the use of a superscript numeral after each term. These entries are called homographs, and they are generally different parts of speech. For example,

e-mail[1] *(noun)*
e-mail[2] *(verb)*

Spelling Variants

When a main entry has one or more variations in the way it is spelled, each spelling variant follows the main entry, after the word *or*.

Parts of Speech

Entries are broken down into four parts of speech, in addition to prefixes, abbreviated as follows:

n. noun
vb. verb
adj. adjective
adv. adverb

Definitions

Each of the more than 10,000 entries is written in clear, standard English. Many go beyond a simple definition to provide additional detail and to put the term in context for a typical computer user. When an entry has more than one sense or definition, the definitions are presented in a numbered list, to make it easier to distinguish the particular, sometimes subtle, variations in meaning.

Illustration and Table References

Some entries have affiliated illustrations or tables that aid in defining the entry. In most cases, illustrations and tables appear on the same page as the entries to which they apply.

In some instances, however, page layout requirements have forced them to a subsequent page. Entries with illustrations or tables usually have references at the end of the definition for an entry, in the following formats:

See the illustration.
See the table.

Acronyms

Some terminology in the computer field, particularly computer standards and Internet slang, can be shortened to form acronyms. Sometimes the acronym is the more common way to refer to the concept or object; in these cases, the acronym is the main entry. In other cases, the acronym is not as commonly used as the words or phrase for which it stands. In these cases, the words or phrase constitute the main entry. The acronym is given after the definition for these entries in the following format:

Acronym:

Alternative Names

Some items or concepts in the computer field can be referred to by more than one name. Generally, though, one way is preferred. The preferred terminology is the main entry. Alternative names are listed after any acronyms; otherwise they are listed after the definition in the following format:

Also called:

Cross-References

Cross-references are of three types: *See*, *See also*, and *Compare*. A *See* reference is used in an entry that is a synonymous cross-reference and simply points to another entry that contains the information sought. A *See also* reference points to one or more entries that contain additional or supplemental information about a topic and follows any acronyms or alternative names after the definition. A *Compare* reference points to an entry or entries that offer contrast and follows any *See also* references; otherwise it follows any acronyms or alternative names after the definition.

Future Printings and Editions

Every effort has been made to ensure the accuracy and
completeness of this book. If you find an error, think that
an entry does not contain enough information, or seek an
entry that does not appear in this edition, please let us
know. Address your letter to: Dictionary Editor, Microsoft
Press, One Microsoft Way, Redmond, WA 98052-6399. Or
send e-mail to mspcd@microsoft.com.

Numbers and Symbols

$0.02 *n. See* my two cents.

& *n.* **1.** UNIX command suffix for running the preceding command as a background process. *See also* background[1]. **2.** In UNIX, a root user command suffix for starting a daemon that is to remain running after logout. *See also* daemon. **3.** The default character used to designate a character entity (special character) in an HTML or SGML document. *See also* HTML, SGML. **4.** In spreadsheet programs, an operator for inserting text into a formula specifying the relationship between cells.

* *n.* **1.** A character used in applications and programming languages to signify multiplication. **2.** In Windows, MS-DOS, OS/2, and other operating systems, a wildcard character that can be used in place of one or more characters, as in *.*, which represents any combination of a filename and an extension. *See also* ?, *.*, wildcard character. **3.** In the C and C++ programming languages, the character used to dereference a pointer to a class or structure. *See also* dereference, pointer (definition 1).

. *n.* A file specification using the asterisk (star) wildcard, which means any combination of filename and extension in operating systems such as MS-DOS. *See also* asterisk (definition 2), wildcard character.

.. *n.* MS-DOS and UNIX syntax for the parent directory. A single dot refers to the current directory.

/ *n.* **1.** A character used to separate parts of a directory path in UNIX and FTP or parts of an Internet address (URL) in Web browsers. **2.** A character used to flag switches or parameters that control the execution of a program invoked through a command-line interface. *See also* command-line interface.

// *n.* Notation used with a colon to separate the URL protocol (such as http or ftp) from the URL host machine name, as in http://www.yahoo.com. *See also* URL.

: *n.* Colon, a symbol used after the protocol name (such as http or ftp) in a URL. *See also* URL.

<> *n.* **1.** Angle brackets, a pair of symbols used to enclose a keyword, comprising a tag in an HTML, SGML, or XML document. *See also* HTML, SGML, XML. **2.** In an Internet Relay Chat (IRC) or multiuser dungeon (MUD), a set of symbols used to designate some action or reaction, as in <chuckle>. *See also* emotag, IRC, MUD. **3.** A pair of symbols used to enclose a return address in an e-mail header.

> *n.* **1.** Right angle bracket, a symbol used in some operating systems, such as MS-DOS and UNIX, to direct the output resulting from some command into a file. **2.** A symbol commonly used in e-mail messages to designate text included from another message.

? *n.* In some operating systems and applications, a wildcard character often used to represent any other single character. The question mark is one of two wildcard characters supported by the MS-DOS, Windows NT, and OS/2 operating systems. *See also* *.

@ *n.* The separator between account names and domain names in Internet e-mail addresses. When spoken, @ is read as "at." Therefore, user@host.com would be read as "user at host dot com."

**** *n.* Back slash, a character used to separate directory names in MS-DOS and UNIX path specifications. When used as a leading character, it means that the path specification begins from the topmost level for that disk drive. *See also* path (definition 5).

0.07-micron *n.* A manufacturing technology with which 400 million transistors, with an effective channel length 1000 times thinner than a human hair, can be placed on a single chip. The extremely small sizes and faster speeds of 0.07-micron products can be used to create improved-performance microprocessors that may extend clock speeds beyond 10 GHz. Possible applications of 0.07-micron technology range from tiny hearing aids that can be implanted in the ear to hard disk drives that read gigabits of data per second.

0 wait state *n. See* zero wait state.

100Base-FX *n.* An Ethernet standard for baseband LANs (local area networks) using fiber optic cable carrying 100 Mbps (megabits per second). *Also called:* Fast Ethernet. *See also* Ethernet (definition 1).

100Base-T *n.* An Ethernet standard for baseband LANs (local area networks) using twisted-pair cable carrying 100 Mbps (megabits per second). The 100Base-T standard is comprised of 100Base-T4 (four pairs of medium-grade to high-grade twisted-pair cable) and 100Base-TX (two pairs of high-grade twisted-pair cable). *Also called:* Fast Ethernet. *See also* Ethernet (definition 1).

100Base-T4 *n. See* 100Base-T.

100Base-TX *n. See* 100Base-T.

100Base-VG *n.* An Ethernet standard for baseband LANs (local area networks) using voice-grade twisted-pair cable carrying 100 Mbps (megabits per second). Unlike other Ethernet networks, 100Base-VG relies on an access method called demand priority, in which nodes send requests to hubs, which in turn give permission to transmit based on the priority levels included with the requests. *Also called:* 100Base-VG-AnyLAN. *See also* Ethernet (definition 1).

100Base-VG-AnyLAN *n. See* 100Base-VG.

100Base-X *n.* Descriptor used for any of three forms of 100 Mbps Ethernet networks: 100Base-T4, 100Base-TX, or 100Base-FX. *Also called:* Fast Ethernet. *See also* 100Base-T, 100Base-FX, Ethernet (definition 1).

101-key keyboard *n.* A computer keyboard modeled after the enhanced keyboard; introduced by IBM for the IBM PC/AT. The 101-key keyboard and the enhanced keyboard are similar in the number and function of their keys; they may differ in the way the keys are laid out, the amount of tactile feedback expressed when a key is pressed, and the shape and feel of the keycaps. *See also* enhanced keyboard.

1024x768 *n.* A standard super VGA computer display having a resolution of 1024 columns of pixels by 768 rows of pixels. *See also* SVGA.

10Base2 *n.* The Ethernet and IEEE 802.3 standard for baseband LANs (local area networks) using a thin coaxial cable (3/16 inch) up to 200 meters long and carrying 10 Mbps (megabits per second) in a bus topology. A network node is connected to the cable by a BNC connector on the adapter card. *Also called:* Cheapernet, thin Ethernet, ThinNet, ThinWire. *See also* BNC connector, bus network, coaxial cable, Ethernet (definition 1), IEEE 802.x.

10Base5 *n.* The Ethernet and IEEE 802.3 standard for baseband LANs (local area networks) using a thick coaxial cable (3/8 inch) up to 500 meters long and carrying 10 Mbps (megabits per second) in a bus topology. A network node is equipped with a transceiver that plugs into a 15-pin AUI connector on the adapter card and taps into the cable. This form of Ethernet is generally used for network backbones. *Also called:* thick Ethernet, ThickNet, ThickWire. *See also* coaxial cable, Ethernet (definition 1), IEEE 802.x.

10Base-F *n.* The Ethernet standard for baseband LANs (local area networks) using fiber-optic cable carrying 10 Mbps (megabits per second) in a star topology. All nodes are connected to a repeater or to a central concentrator. A node is equipped with a fiber-optic transceiver that plugs into an AUI connector on the adapter card and attaches to the cable with an ST or SMA fiber-optic connector. The 10Base-F standard comprises 10Base-FB for a backbone, 10Base-FL for the link between the central concentrator and a station, and 10Base-FP for a star network. *See also* Ethernet (definition 1), fiber optics, star network.

10Base-FB *n. See* 10Base-F.

10Base-FL *n. See* 10Base-F.

10Base-FP *n. See* 10Base-F.

10Base-T *n.* The Ethernet standard for baseband LANs (local area networks) using twisted-pair cable carrying 10 Mbps (megabits per second) in a star topology. All nodes are connected to a central hub known as a multiport repeater. *See also* Ethernet (definition 1), star network, twisted-pair cable.

12-hour clock *n.* A clock that expresses the time within a 12-hour range, returning to 1:00 after 12:59 AM or PM. *Compare* 24-hour clock.

1.2M *adj.* Short for **1.2-m**egabyte. Refers to the storage capacity for high-density 5.25-inch floppy disks.

1394 *n. See* IEEE 1394.

14.4 *n.* A modem with a maximum data transfer rate of 14.4 Kbps (kilobits per second).

1.44M *adj.* Short for **1.44-m**egabyte. Refers to the storage capacity for high-density 3.5-inch floppy disks.

16-bit *adj. See* 8-bit, 16-bit, 32-bit, 64-bit.

16-bit application *n.* An application written to run on a computer with a 16-bit architecture or operating system, such as MS-DOS or Windows 3.*x*.

16-bit color *adj.* Of, pertaining to, or characteristic of a display that can produce 2^{16} (65,536) distinct colors. *Compare* 24-bit color, 32-bit color.

16-bit machine *n.* A computer that works with data in groups of 16 bits at a time. A computer may be considered a 16-bit machine either because its microprocessor operates internally on 16-bit words or because its data bus can transfer 16 bits at a time. The IBM PC/AT and similar models based on the Intel 80286 microprocessor are 16-bit machines in terms of both the word size of the microprocessor and the size of the data bus. The Apple Macintosh Plus and Macintosh SE use a microprocessor with a 32-bit word length (the Motorola 68000), but they have 16-bit data buses and are generally considered 16-bit machines.

16-bit operating system *n.* An operating system, now outdated, that can work with 2 bytes, or 16 bits, of information at one time. A 16-bit operating system, such as MS-DOS and Microsoft Windows 3.*x*, reflects the functionality of a 16-bit processor because the software and the chip must work together so closely. The main advantage of a 16-bit operating system over its earlier 8-bit predecessors (such as CP/M-80) was its ability to address more memory and use a larger (16-bit) bus. Sixteen-bit operating systems have since been eclipsed by 32-bit operating systems—such as the Macintosh operating system, Microsoft Windows NT, and Windows 9x—and by 64-bit operating systems, such as some versions of UNIX. *See also* 32-bit operating system.

/16 network *n.* IP address class B. This class has 16,382 networks available and more than sixty-five thousand hosts available. *See also* host, IP address classes, network.

1999 problem *n.* **1.** A variation on the Year 2000 problem in computer systems that have two-digit years in date fields and are used by companies and organizations in which the fiscal year 2000 begins before the end of calendar year 1999. These computer systems may interpret the fiscal year as the year 1900. **2.** A potential problem, if not corrected, with date fields in older code that were (sometimes) used to hold values with special meaning. For example, the date 9/9/99 was often used as an expiration date meaning "keep this information forever" or, worse, "destroy this document immediately."

1NF *n.* Short for **first n**ormal **f**orm. *See* normal form (definition 1).

2000 time problem *n. See* Year 2000 problem.

2038 limit *n.* A consideration in some PCs that use a signed 32-bit integer to represent date and time. Because such systems determine date and time as the number of seconds elapsed since midnight, January 1, 1970, they can handle a maximum of 2^{31} seconds, a number that will be reached at 3:14:07 a.m. on January 19, 2038. When the elapsed seconds exceed that maximum value, the clock will overflow, resulting in an incorrect date and time and, potentially, causing disruptions. Some organizations have defined Year 2000 compliant to mean a system that will have the correct date/time and do proper date handling up through the year 2038, although this is not universal. The extent of the potential problem, of course, is directly related to the number of such system solutions still in operation at the time. *See also* Year 2000 compliant.

24-bit color *n.* RGB color in which the level of each of the three primary colors in a pixel is represented by 8 bits of information. A 24-bit color image can contain over 16 million different colors. Not all computer monitors support 24-bit color, especially older models. Those that do not may use 8-bit color (256 colors) or 16-bit color (65,536 colors). *Also called:* true color. *See also* bit depth, pixel, RGB. *Compare* 16-bit color, 32-bit color.

24-hour clock *n.* A clock that expresses the time within a 24-hour range, from 0000 (midnight) to 2359 (one minute before the following midnight). *Compare* 12-hour clock.

2.4 kernel *n.* Update of the core of the Linux OS, released at the end of 2000. Features in the 2.4 kernel emphasize support for new buses, devices, and controllers; increased USB support; improved Web server performance; and increased symmetrical multiprocessing scalability.

/24 network *n.* IP address class A. This class has more than two million networks available and 254 hosts available. *See also* host, IP address classes, network.

256-bit *adj.* Having a data path that is 256 bits wide.

286 *n. See* 80286.

287 *n. See* 80287.

28.8 *n.* A modem with a maximum data transfer rate of 28.8 Kbps (kilobits per second).

2-digit year *n.* The capacity for storing only the last two digits of the year in a date. In such systems, the century for the date is not stored. *See also* two-digit date storage.

2G *n.* Acronym for **2**nd **G**eneration. The second generation of digital wireless technology, as defined by the International Telecommunications Union (ITU). Second generation technology delivers data transmission at speeds from 9.6 Kbps (kilobits per second) to 19.2 Kbps. Second generation technology provides greater data transmission capabilities and more efficient voice transmission than the analog technology first developed for wireless telecommunications.

2NF *n.* Short for **second n**ormal **f**orm. *See* normal form (definition 1).

2-nines availability *n. See* two-nines availability.

2.PAK *n.* An artificial intelligence programming language.

32-bit *adj. See* 8-bit, 16-bit, 32-bit, 64-bit.

32-bit application *n.* An application written to run on a computer with a 32-bit architecture or operating system, such as Mac OS or Windows 9x.

32-bit clean *adj.* **1.** Refers to Macintosh hardware designed to run in 32-bit mode, which can address up to 1 gigabyte of physical RAM under System 7. This includes all present Macintosh computers; some older models used 16-bit addressing. **2.** Refers to software written for 32-bit operation.

32-bit color *n.* RGB color that is similar to 24-bit color, with 8 additional bits used to allow for faster transfer of an image's color. *See also* bit depth, RGB. *Compare* 16-bit color, 24-bit color.

32-bit driver *n.* A software subsystem that controls either a hardware device (device driver) or another software subsystem. The 32-bit versions of this software take full advantage of the instruction sets of the 486 and Pentium processors for improved speed. *See also* driver, instruction set.

32-bit machine *n.* A computer that works with data in groups of 32 bits at a time. The Apple Macintosh II and higher models are 32-bit machines, in terms of both the word size of their microprocessors and the size of the data buses, as are computers based on the Intel 80386 and higher-level microprocessors.

32-bit operating system *n.* An operating system in which 4 bytes, or 32 bits, can be processed at one time.

Windows 95, Windows 98, Windows NT, Linux, and OS/2 are examples. *See also* instruction set, protected mode.

33.6 *n.* A modem with a maximum data transfer rate of 33.3 Kbps (kilobits per second).

34010, 34020 *n.* Graphics coprocessors from Texas Instruments (TI), used mainly in high-end PC graphics boards, which have become a de facto standard for programmable graphics processors. Although both chips use 32-bit registers, the 34010 uses a 16-bit data bus and the 34020 uses a 32-bit bus. The 34020 is compatible with the earlier 34010, and both chips work with TIGA (Texas Instruments Graphical Architecture), a TI standard that allows a single application driver to be used with all boards based on the standard. *See also* de facto standard, TIGA, video graphics board.

3.5-inch floppy disk *n.* Used with the Macintosh and with IBM and compatible microcomputers. A microfloppy disk is a round piece of polyester film coated with ferric oxide and encased in a rigid plastic shell equipped with a sliding metal cover. On the Macintosh, a single-sided 3.5-inch floppy disk can hold 400 kilobytes (KB); a double-sided (standard) disk can hold 800 KB; and a double-sided high-density disk can hold 1.44 megabytes (MB). On IBM and compatible machines, a microfloppy can hold either 720 KB or 1.44 MB of information. *See also* floppy disk.

360K *adj.* Short for **360-k**ilobyte. The storage capacity for standard 5.25-inch floppy disks.

.386 *n.* A file extension for virtual device drivers under Windows 3.1. *See also* virtual device driver.

386 *n. See* 80386DX.

386BSD *n.* A version of BSD UNIX, different from BSD386 from Berkeley Software Development, Inc. Freely distributable, 386BSD was released in 1992 and is available in two newer versions: NetBSD and FreeBSD. *See also* BSD UNIX, FreeBSD, NetBSD.

386DX *n. See* 80386DX.

386SL *n. See* 80386SL.

386SX *n. See* 80386SX.

387 *n. See* 80387.

387SX *n. See* 80387SX.

3-D or **3D** *adj.* **1.** Short for **three-d**imensional. Of, pertaining to, or being an object or image having or appearing to have all three spatial dimensions (length, width, and depth). **2.** Having the illusion of depth or varying distances, as in 3-D audio.

3-D array *n.* *See* three-dimensional array.

3-D audio *n.* Short for **three-d**imensional **audio**. Recorded as stereo sound, 3-D audio enables the listener to feel immersed in the sound and to determine its exact location (up, down, left, right, forward, or backward). This technology is commonly used in video games and virtual-reality systems, as well as in some Internet applications. *Also called:* 3-D sound, binaural sound.

3-D graphic *n.* Any graphical image that depicts one or more objects in three dimensions—height, width, and depth. A 3-D graphic is rendered on a two-dimensional medium; the third dimension, depth, is indicated by means of perspective and by techniques such as shading or gradient use of color.

3-D metafile *n.* A device-independent file for storing a 3-D display. *See also* metafile.

3DMF *n.* *See* QuickDraw 3-D.

3-D model *n.* *See* three-dimensional model.

3-D sound *n.* *See* 3-D audio.

3-finger salute *n.* *See* three-finger salute.

3G *n.* Acronym for **3rd G**eneration. The third generation of digital wireless technology, as defined by the International Telecommunications Union (ITU). Third generation technology is expected to deliver data transmission speeds between 144 Kbps (kilobits per second) and 2 Mbps (megabits per second), compared to the 9.6 Kbps to 19.2 Kbps offered by second generation technology. Western Europe and Japan lead the world in adoption of 3G technology and services.

3GL *n.* Short for **third**-generation **l**anguage. A high-level programming language that was designed to run on the third generation of computer processors, built on integrated circuit technology roughly from 1965 to 1970. C, FORTRAN, Basic, and Pascal are examples of third-generation languages still in use today. *See also* high-level language, integrated circuit. *Compare* 4GL, low-level language.

3NF *n.* Short for **third n**ormal **f**orm. *See* normal form (definition 1).

3-nines availability *n.* *See* three-nines availability.

3Station *n.* A diskless workstation developed by Bob Metcalfe at 3Com Corporation. *See also* diskless workstation.

400 *n.* HTTP status code—Bad Request. A Hypertext Transfer Protocol message from an HTTP server indicating that a client request cannot be completed because the syntax of the request is incorrect. *See also* HTTP server (definition 1), HTTP status codes.

401 *n.* HTTP status code—Unauthorized. A Hypertext Transfer Protocol message from an HTTP server indicating that a client request cannot be completed because the transaction requires an Authorization header, which was not supplied. *See also* HTTP server (definition 1), HTTP status codes.

402 *n.* HTTP status code—Payment Required. A Hypertext Transfer Protocol message from an HTTP server indicating that a client request cannot be completed because the transaction requires a payment, and no ChargeTo header was supplied. *See also* HTTP server (definition 1), HTTP status codes.

403 *n.* HTTP status code—Forbidden. A Hypertext Transfer Protocol message from an HTTP server indicating that a client request cannot be completed because access is restricted. *See also* HTTP server (definition 1), HTTP status codes.

404 *n.* HTTP status code—Not Found. A Hypertext Transfer Protocol message from an HTTP server indicating that a client request cannot be completed because the server is unable to find an address that matches the URL requested. *See also* HTTP server (definition 1), HTTP status codes, URL.

486 *n.* *See* i486DX.

486DX *n.* *See* i486DX.

486SL *n.* *See* i486SL.

486SX *n.* *See* i486SX.

4-digit year *n.* The capacity for storing all four digits of the year in a date in hardware or firmware products.

4GL *n.* Short for **fourth**-generation **l**anguage. A programming language designed to mimic human language. The designation is often used to specify languages used with relational databases and is intended to imply that such languages are a step up from standard high-level programming languages such as C, Pascal, and COBOL. *See also* application development language, high-level language. *Compare* 3GL, assembly language.

4GL architecture *n. See* two-tier client/server.

4mm tape *n. See* digital audio tape.

4NF *n.* Short for fourth normal form. *See* normal form (definition 1).

4-nines availability *n. See* four-nines availability.

5.25-inch floppy disk *n.* Used with the Macintosh and with IBM and compatible microcomputers. A microfloppy disk is a round piece of polyester film coated with ferric oxide and encased in a rigid plastic shell equipped with a sliding metal cover. A floppy disk 5.25 inches in diameter is encased in a flexible plastic jacket and has a large hole in the center, which fits around a spindle in the disk drive; such a disk can hold from a few hundred thousand to over one million bytes of data. *See* floppy disk.

56flex *n. See* K56flex.

56K[1] *adj.* Having 56 kilobits per second (Kbps) available for traffic on a communications circuit. One voice channel can carry up to 64 Kbps (called a T0 carrier); 8 Kbps are used for signaling, leaving 56 Kbps available for traffic. *See also* T-carrier.

56K[2] *n. See* 56-Kbps modem.

56-Kbps modem *n.* An asymmetric modem that operates over POTS (Plain Old Telephone Service) to deliver data downstream at 56 Kbps, with upstream speeds of 28.8 and 33.6 Kbps. Earlier, slower modems invoke a two-conversion transmission process: digital data from a computer is converted into analog form for transmission over the telephone wire and is then reconverted to digital data by the receiving modem. In contrast, 56-Kbps modems achieve faster speeds by converting analog data to digital data only once, typically at the telephone company's switching office near the beginning of the transmission's journey. Designed to improve download times for Internet users, 56-Kbps modems rely on a public phone network that allows for a single conversion and on the availability of a digital connection, such as ISDN or T1, at the ISP (Internet Service Provider) location that provides the actual connection to the Internet. *See also* analog data, digital data transmission, modem, POTS.

586 *n.* The unofficial name used by industry analysts and by the computer trade press to describe Intel's successor to the i486 microprocessor prior to its release. In the interest of using a name that could be trademarked, however, Intel decided to name the microprocessor Pentium. *See also* Pentium.

5NF *n.* Short for **fifth** **n**ormal **f**orm. *See* normal form (definition 1).

5-nines availability *n. See* five-nines availability.

5x86 *n.* Cyrix Corporation's clone of the Intel Pentium CPU. *See also* 586, 6x86, central processing unit, clone, Pentium.

601 *n. See* PowerPC 601.

603 *n. See* PowerPC 603.

604 *n. See* PowerPC 604.

64-bit *adj.* Of, pertaining to, or descriptive of the amount of data—64 bits, or 8 bytes—that certain computer systems or programs can process at one time.

64-bit machine *n.* A computer that works with data in groups of 64 bits at a time. A computer may be considered a 64-bit machine either because its CPU operates internally on 64-bit words or because its data bus can transfer 64 bits at a time. A 64-bit CPU thus has a word size of 64 bits, or 8 bytes; a 64-bit data bus has 64 data lines, so it ferries information through the system in sets of 64 bits at a time. Examples of 64-bit architecture include the Alpha AXP from Digital Equipment Corporation, the Ultra workstation from Sun Microsystems, Inc., and the PowerPC 620 from Motorola and IBM.

64-bit operating system *n.* An operating system in which 8 bytes, or 64 bits, can be processed at one time. For Microsoft Windows, the 64-bit operating systems are Windows XP 64-Bit Edition, the 64-bit versions of Windows .NET Enterprise Server, and Windows .NET Datacenter Server. The IBM AS/400 uses a 64-bit operating system.

6502 *n.* The 8-bit microprocessor, developed by Rockwell International, that was used in the Apple II and Commodore 64 microcomputers.

65816 *n.* A 16-bit microprocessor from Western Digital Design used in the Apple IIGS. It can emulate the 6502, providing compatibility with all old Apple II software. *See also* 6502.

6800 *n.* An 8-bit microprocessor developed by Motorola in the early 1970s. It failed to gain wide acceptance.

68000 *n.* The original microprocessor in the 680x0 family from Motorola, introduced in 1979 and used in the first Apple Macintosh computers as well as the Apple LaserWriter IISC and Hewlett-Packard's LaserJet printers. The 68000 has 32-bit internal registers but transfers data over a

16-bit data bus. With 24-bit physical addressing, the 68000 can address 16 megabytes of memory—16 times as much memory as does the Intel 8088 found in the IBM PC. In addition, the 68000's architecture, in which addressing is linear (as opposed to the 8088's segmented addressing) and in which all address registers work the same way and all data registers work the same way, makes programming more straightforward. *See also* linear addressing architecture, segmented addressing architecture.

68020 *n.* A microprocessor in the 680x0 family from Motorola, introduced in 1984. This chip has 32-bit addressing and a 32-bit data bus and is available in speeds from 16 MHz to 33 MHz. The 68020 is found in the original Macintosh II and the LaserWriter IINT from Apple.

68030 *n.* A microprocessor in the 680x0 microprocessor family from Motorola, introduced in 1987. This chip has 32-bit addressing and a 32-bit data bus and is available in speeds from 20 MHz to 50 MHz. The 68030 has built-in paged memory management, precluding the need for supplemental chips to provide that function.

68040 *n.* A microprocessor in the 680x0 family from Motorola, introduced in 1990, with 32-bit addressing and a 32-bit data bus. The 68040 runs at 25 MHz and includes a built-in floating-point unit and memory management units, including independent 4-KB instruction and data caches, which eliminate the need for supplemental chips to provide these functions. In addition, the 68040 is capable of parallel instruction execution by means of multiple independent instruction pipelines, multiple internal buses, and separate caches for both data and instructions.

68060 *n.* The latest and fastest of the 680x0 microprocessors from Motorola, introduced in 1995. This chip has 32-bit addressing and a 32-bit data bus and is available in speeds from 50 MHz to 75 MHz. There was no 68050. The 68060 is probably the last in the 680x0 series from Motorola.

6845 *n.* A programmable video controller from Motorola used in IBM's Monochrome Display Adapter (MDA) and Color/Graphics Adapter (CGA). The 6845 became such an integral part of the IBM PC and compatibles that later generations of video adapters, such as EGA and VGA, continue to support the operations of the 6845. *See also* CGA, EGA, MDA, VGA.

68881 *n.* The floating-point coprocessor from Motorola for use with the 68000 and the 68020. The 68881 provides instructions for high-performance floating-point arithmetic, a set of floating-point data registers, and 22 built-in constants including p and powers of 10. The 68881 conforms to the ANSI/IEEE 754-1985 standard for binary floating-point arithmetic. The 68881 can produce a dramatic improvement in system performance when software takes advantage of it. *See also* floating-point processor.

68K *n. See* 68000.

6x86 *n.* An 8086-compatible microprocessor designed by Cyrix Corporation. It is socket-compatible with some Pentium microprocessors from Intel and can be used in their place. *See also* 8086, microprocessor, Pentium.

740 *n. See* PowerPC 740.

750 *n. See* PowerPC 750.

7-bit ASCII *n.* A 7-bit ASCII character set used for standard UNIX mail messages. The leftover eighth bit is a parity bit used for error correction. *See also* ASCII, parity bit.

7-track *n.* A tape storage scheme that places data on seven separate, parallel tracks on 1/2-inch reel-to-reel magnetic tape. This is an old recording format used with computers that transfer data 6 bits at a time. Data is recorded as 6 data bits and 1 parity bit. Some personal computers now use the 9-track tape storage scheme. *See also* 9-track.

80286 *n.* A 16-bit microprocessor from Intel, introduced in 1982 and included in the IBM PC/AT and compatible computers in 1984. The 80286 has 16-bit registers, transfers information over the data bus 16 bits at a time, and uses 24 bits to address memory locations. The 80286 operates in two modes: real mode, which is compatible with the 8086 and supports MS-DOS, and protected mode, which enables the CPU to access 16 megabytes of memory and protects the operating system from incorrect memory accesses by ill-behaved applications, which could crash a system in real mode. *Also called:* 286. *See also* protected mode, real mode.

80287 *n.* A floating-point coprocessor from Intel for use with the 80286 family of microprocessors. Available in speeds from 6 MHz to 12 MHz, the 80287 offers the same mathematical capabilities that the 8087 coprocessor provides to an 8086-based system. Because the 80287 conforms to the 80286 memory management and protection schemes, it can be used in both the real and protected modes of the 80286. Also, if the computer manufacturer implements support for it in the motherboard design, the 80287 can be used in a system with an 80386 microprocessor. *See also* floating-point processor.

802.x standards *n. See* IEEE 802.x.

802.11 standards *n. See* IEEE 802.11.

80386 *n. See* 80386DX.

80386DX *n.* A 32-bit microprocessor from Intel, introduced in 1985. The 80386 is a full 32-bit microprocessor; that is, it has 32-bit registers, it can transfer information over its data bus 32 bits at a time, and it can use 32 bits to address memory. Like the earlier 80286, the 80386 operates in two modes: real mode, which is compatible with the 8086 chip and supports MS-DOS, and protected mode, which allows the CPU to access 4 GB of memory directly, supports multitasking, and protects the operating system from crashing as a result of an incorrect memory access caused by an application program error. The 80386 also includes a virtual 8086 mode (also called virtual real mode), which appears to software as an 8086 but whose 1-MB effective address space can be located anywhere in physical memory under the same safeguards as in protected mode. The virtual 8086 mode is the basis for the MS-DOS prompt available inside Windows. *Also called:* 386, 386DX, 80386. *See also* protected mode, real mode, virtual real mode.

80386SL *n.* A microprocessor from Intel intended for use in laptop computers. The 80386SL has similar features to the 80386SX, but it also has capabilities for reducing its power consumption. In particular, the 80386SL can reduce its clock speed to zero when not in use and return to full speed, with the contents of all its registers intact, when called on to perform another task. *Also called:* 386SL. *See also* 80386SX, green PC, i486SL.

80386SX *n.* A microprocessor from Intel, introduced in 1988 as a low-cost alternative to the 80386DX. The 80386SX is basically an 80386DX processor limited by a 16-bit data bus. The 16-bit design allows 80386SX systems to be configured from less expensive AT-class parts, resulting in a much lower total system price. The 80386SX offers improved performance over the 80286 and access to software designed for the 80386DX. The 80386SX also offers 80386DX features such as multitasking and virtual 8086 mode. *Also called:* 386SX. *See also* 80386DX.

80387 *n.* The floating-point coprocessor introduced by Intel for use with the 80386 microprocessors. Available in speeds from 16 MHz to 33 MHz, the 80387 offers the same mathematical capabilities that the 8087 provides for an 8086-based system, as well as transcendental operations for sine, cosine, tangent, arctangent, and logarithm calculations. The 80387 conforms to the ANSI/IEEE 754-1985 standard for binary floating-point arithmetic. The 80387 operates independently of the 80386's mode, and it performs as expected regardless of whether the 80386 is running in real, protected, or virtual 8086 mode. *Also called:* 387. *See also* 80386DX, floating-point processor.

80387SX *n.* The floating-point coprocessor from Intel for use with the 80386SX microprocessor. It provides the same capabilities that the 80387 does for an 80386-based system, but it is available only in a 16-MHz version. *Also called:* 387SX. *See also* 80386SX, floating-point processor.

80486 *n. See* i486DX.

80486SL *n. See* i486SL.

80486SX *n. See* i486SX.

8080 *n.* One of the first chips capable of serving as the basis of a personal computer, introduced by Intel in 1974 and used in the Altair 8800. The 8080 provided 8-bit data operations and 16-bit addressing and influenced the design of the Z80. Furthermore, the microprocessors of the 80x86 line, which serve as the foundation for the IBM PC and all its successors and compatibles, are all based on a set of registers organized similarly to the 8080's. *See also* Altair 8800, Z80.

8086 *n.* The original microprocessor in the 80x86 family from Intel, introduced in 1978. The 8086 has 16-bit registers, a 16-bit data bus, and 20-bit addressing, allowing access to 1 megabyte of memory. Its internal registers include a set that is organized in the same way as those of the 8080. Speeds range from 4.77 MHz to 10 MHz. *See also* 8080.

8087 *n.* A floating-point coprocessor from Intel for use with the 8086/8088 and 80186/80188 microprocessors. Available in speeds from 5 MHz to 10 MHz, the 8087 offers instructions, not found in the 8086/8088 instruction sets, for performing arithmetic, trigonometric, exponential, and logarithmic operations on 16-, 32-, and 64-bit integers; 32-, 64-, and 80-bit floating-point numbers; and 18-digit BCD (binary-coded decimal) operands. With application software that takes advantage of these instructions, the 8087 can dramatically improve system performance. The 8087 conforms to the proposed IEEE 754 standard for binary floating-point arithmetic. *See also* 8086, 8088, floating-point processor.

8088 *n.* The microprocessor on which the original IBM PC was based. Released by Intel in 1978, the 8088 is identical to the 8086 but transfers information 8 bits at a time (through an 8-bit data bus) rather than 16 bits at a time (through a 16-bit data bus). *See also* 8086, bus.

80-character line length *n.* A standard line length for text mode displays. This length, found in the earliest IBM PCs and in professional terminals of the 1970s and 1980s, is a legacy of the punched card and of mainframe operating systems in which each line in a file as displayed on a terminal appeared to the computer as a card in a deck. Graphical user interfaces support longer or shorter lines depending on the fonts chosen. A message composed with longer lines using a graphical e-mail program appears broken up and difficult to read when viewed by a user with only a terminal emulation program and a shell account.

80x86 *n.* See 8086.

82385 *n.* A cache controller chip by Intel that allows modified cache blocks to be restored to main memory in parallel with cache accesses by the CPU (or DMA). *See also* cache, central processing unit, controller, direct memory access.

8.3 *n.* The standard format for filenames in MS-DOS/Windows 3.*x*: a filename with eight or fewer characters, followed by a period ("dot"), followed by a three-character file extension. *See also* extension. *Compare* long filenames.

8514/A *n.* A graphics adapter introduced by IBM in April 1987 and withdrawn in October 1991. The 8514/A was designed to increase the capability of the VGA adapter in some of IBM's PS/2 computers from a resolution of 640 by 480 pixels with 16 simultaneous colors to a resolution of 1024 by 768 pixels (almost quadrupling the amount of information displayed on the screen) with 256 simultaneous colors. The 8514/A worked only in Micro Channel Architecture-based PS/2 computers, and it used the interlacing method for display, which can cause a perceptible flicker at higher resolutions. Therefore, it never gained widespread popularity; the SVGA (Super VGA) adapter prevailed because it was designed to work with the more prevalent ISA and EISA bus architectures. *See also* EISA, interlacing, ISA, Micro Channel Architecture, non-interlaced, SVGA, VGA.

88000 *n.* A reduced instruction set computing (RISC) chip set from Motorola, introduced in 1988 and based on the Harvard architecture. The 20-MHz 88000 set includes one 88100 CPU and at least two 88200 CMMUs (cache memory management units)—one for data memory and one for instruction memory. The 88100 RISC CPU includes both integer and floating-point processors and has thirty-two 32-bit general-purpose registers, 21 control registers, and 32-bit data paths and addresses. The 88100 is capable of addressing 4 gigabytes of external data and 1 gigabyte of 32-bit instructions in memory space. Up to four chip sets can be set up to work with the same memory in a multiprocessing configuration. *See also* central processing unit, floating-point processor, Harvard architecture, RISC.

88100 *n. See* 88000.

88200 *n. See* 88000.

8-bit, 16-bit, 32-bit, 64-bit *adj.* **1.** Capable of transferring 8, 16, 32, or 64 bits, respectively, on data bus lines. For example, the IBM Micro Channel Architecture includes one or more 32-bit data buses with additional 16-bit and 8-bit data lines. *See also* 16-bit machine, 32-bit machine, 64-bit machine, 8-bit machine. **2.** Capable of transferring 8, 16, 32, or 64 bits, respectively, on the data path of a video adapter. An n-bit video adapter can display up to 2^n colors. For example, an 8-bit video adapter is capable of displaying up to 256 colors; a 16-bit adapter can display up to 65,536 colors; and a 24-bit adapter can display over 16 million colors. (A 24-bit video adapter has a 32-bit data path, although the upper 8 bits are not used directly to generate color.) *See also* alpha channel.

8-bit color *n.* A display setting that holds up to 256 specific color entries. Any color palette attached to a picture is by definition an 8-bit palette.

8-bit machine *n.* A computer that works with data in groups of 8 bits at a time. A computer may be considered an 8-bit machine either because its microprocessor operates internally on 8-bit words or because its data bus can transfer 8 bits at a time. The original IBM PC was based on a microprocessor (the 8088) that worked internally on 16-bit words but transferred them 8 bits at a time. Such machines are generally called 8-bit machines because the size of the data bus limits the machine's overall speed.

8mm tape *n.* A tape cartridge format used for data back-ups, similar to that used for some video cameras except that the tape is rated for data storage. The capacity is 5 GB (gigabytes) or more of (optionally compressed) data.

8-N-1 *n.* Short for **8** bits, **N**o parity, **1** stop bit. Typical default settings for serial communications, such as modem transmissions.

/8 network *n.* IP address class C. This class has 126 networks available and more than sixteen million hosts available. *See also* host, IP address classes, network.

9600 *n.* A modem with a maximum data transfer rate of 9600 bps (bits per second).

99 or **9999** *n.* A number sometimes given special meaning in older programs—for example, as an end-of-file indicator or as an expiration date that actually meant "do not allow to expire." Uncorrected programs may interpret that date as an end-of-file indicator or expiration date and cause problems. *See also* 1999 problem.

9/9/99 *n. See* 99 or 9999.

9-track *n.* A tape storage scheme that places data on nine separate parallel tracks (one track for each of 8 data bits of a byte and 1 parity bit) on 1/2-inch reel-to-reel magnetic tape. *See also* 7-track.

Å *n. See* angstrom.

Å *n. See* angstrom.

A or **a** *n. See* ampere.

A: or **a:** *n.* In Windows and some other operating systems, the identifier used for the first, or primary, floppy disk drive. Unless otherwise specified by changing the CMOS startup instructions, this is the drive the operating system checks first for startup instructions.

AAL *n. See* ATM Adaptation Layer.

abandonware *n.* Discontinued video or computer games. Abandonware is often collected and played by computer game enthusiasts on refurbished systems or on PCs running emulator software. *See also* arcade game, emulator, MAME.

ABC *n.* **1.** Acronym for **A**tanasoff-**B**erry **C**omputer. The first electronic digital computer, created by John Atanasoff and Clifford Berry of Iowa State University in 1942. **2.** Acronym for **a**utomatic **b**rightness **c**ontrol. A circuit that changes the luminance of a monitor to compensate for ambient lighting conditions. **3.** An imperative language and programming environment from CWI, Netherlands. This interactive, structured, high-level language is easy to learn and use. It is not a systems-programming language, but it is good for teaching or prototyping.

Abeline *n.* A high-performance network developed by Qwest Communications, Nortel, and Cisco Systems to provide a backbone network for the Internet2 project. Abeline interconnects the gigaPoPs created by the Internet2 project and its member institutions, enabling connected institutions to develop advanced network services and applications. *See also* gigaPoP, Internet2.

abend or **ABEND** *n.* Short for **ab**normal **end**. The premature ending of a program because of program error or system failure. *See also* abort, crash[1].

ABI *n. See* application binary interface.

ABIOS *n.* Acronym for **A**dvanced **B**asic **I**nput/**O**utput **S**ystem. A set of input/output service routines designed to support multitasking and protected mode that were built into IBM PS/2 PCs. *See also* BIOS.

abnormal end *n. See* abend.

A-Bone *n.* The Asian-Pacific Internet backbone that connects users in East and South Asian countries and Australia at T1 speeds or better, without the need to send data through North American facilities. The A-Bone was launched by Asia Internet Holding Co., Ltd. in 1996. By 1998, a total of 13 countries were connected to the A-Bone's hub in Japan. A-Bone also includes links to both Europe and the United States. *See also* backbone.

abort *vb.* To terminate abruptly, often used in reference to a program or procedure in progress.

absolute address *n.* A means of specifying a precise memory location in a program by using its address (number) rather than an expression to calculate the address. *Also called:* direct address, machine address, real address. *See also* absolute coding. *Compare* relative address, virtual address.

absolute coding *n.* Program code that uses absolute addressing rather than indirect addressing. *See also* absolute address, relative address.

absolute coordinates *n.* Coordinates that are defined in terms of their distance from the origin, the point where the axes intersect. Graphs and computer graphics use absolute coordinates to locate points on a chart or display grid—for example, points in relation to the x- and y-axes on a graph or the x-, y-, and z-axes used to specify the location of a three-dimensional graphic object on the screen. See the illustration. *See also* Cartesian coordinates.

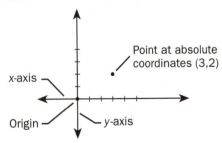

Absolute coordinates.

absolute link *n.* A hyperlink to the exact location of a file on a file server, the World Wide Web, or a company intranet. Absolute links use an exact path; if you move the file containing the hyperlink or a hyperlink destination, the link breaks.

absolute path *n.* A path to a file that begins with the drive identifier and root directory or with a network share and ends with the complete file name (for example, C:\docs\work\contract.txt or \\netshare\docs\work\contract.txt). *Also called:* full path. *See also* path (definition 2). *Compare* relative path.

absolute pointing device *n.* A mechanical or physical pointing device whose location is associated with the position of the on-screen cursor. For example, if the user of a graphics tablet places the pen on the upper right corner of the tablet, the cursor moves to the upper right corner of the screen or on-screen window associated with the pen. *See also* absolute coordinates. *Compare* relative pointing device.

absolute URL *n.* The full Internet address of a page or other World Wide Web resource. The absolute URL includes a protocol, such as "http," network location, and optional path and file name—for example, http://example.microsoft.com/.

absolute value *n.* The magnitude of a number, irrespective of its sign (+ or –). An absolute value is always greater than or equal to zero. For example, 10 is the absolute value of 10 and of –10. Programming languages and spreadsheet programs commonly include functions that return the absolute value of a number.

abstract[1] *adj.* **1.** In character recognition systems, of, pertaining to, or being a type of symbol that, unlike a letter or numeral, has no intrinsic meaning and must be defined before it can be interpreted. **2.** In programming, of, pertaining to, or being a data type defined by the operations that can be performed on objects of that type rather than by the properties of the objects themselves. *See also* abstract data type.

abstract[2] *n.* In information processing and library science, a summary typically consisting of a paragraph or a few paragraphs at the beginning of an investigative document, such as a scientific paper.

abstract class *n.* **1.** In object-oriented programming, a class in which no objects can be created. It is, however, used to defined subclasses, and objects are created from the subclasses. *See also* object (definition 2). *Compare* concrete class. **2.** In Java programming, a class that contains one or more abstract methods and therefore can never be instantiated. Abstract classes are defined so that other classes can extend them and make them concrete by implementing the abstract methods. *See also* class, instantiate, Java, method, object (definition 2). *Compare* concrete class.

abstract data type *n.* In programming, a data set defined by the programmer in terms of the information it can contain and the operations that can be performed with it. An abstract data type is more generalized than a data type constrained by the properties of the objects it contains—for example, the data type "pet" is more generalized than the data types "pet dog," "pet bird," and "pet fish." The standard example used in illustrating an abstract data type is the stack, a small portion of memory used to store information, generally on a temporary basis. As an abstract data type, the stack is simply a structure onto which values can be pushed (added) and from which they can be popped (removed). The type of value, such as integer, is irrelevant to the definition. The way in which the program performs operations on abstract data types is encapsulated, or hidden, from the rest of the program. Encapsulation enables the programmer to change the definition of the data type or its operations without introducing errors to the existing code that uses the abstract data type. Abstract data types represent an intermediate step between traditional programming and object-oriented programming. *See also* data type, object-oriented programming.

abstraction *n.* **1.** Broadly, the use of specialized software, such as an application programming interface (API), as a means of shielding software from device dependencies or the complexities of underlying software. For instance, hardware abstraction enables programs to focus on a task, such as communications, instead of on individual differences between communications devices. **2.** In object-oriented programming, the process of reducing an object to its essence so that only the necessary elements are represented. Abstraction defines an object in terms of its properties (attributes), behaviors (functionality), and interface (means of communicating with other objects).

abstract machine *n.* A design for a processor that is not meant for implementation but that represents a model for processing abstract machine language. Its instruction set can use instructions that more closely resemble the compiled language than the instructions used by an actual computer. It can also be used to make the implementation of the language more portable to other platforms.

abstract machine language *n.* **1.** An intermediate programming language used by an interpreter or compiler. **2.** *See* pseudocode (definition 1).

abstract syntax *n.* A data structure description that is independent of hardware structures and encodings.

Abstract Syntax Notation One *n.* The ISO standard notation for independent specification of data types and structures for syntax conversion. *Acronym:* ASN.1.*See also* data type, ISO, syntax.

abstract syntax tree *n.* A treelike representation of programs used in many integrated programming environments and structure-oriented editors.

Abstract Window Toolkit *n.* A library of Java GUIs (graphical user interfaces) that provides the connections between a Java application and the native GUI of the computer on which the application runs. *Also called:* AWT.

A/B switch box *n.* A switch box with two outputs. By flipping the switch, the user can select which to use. *See also* switch (definition 1), switch box.

AC *n. See* alternating current.

AC adapter *n.* An external power supply that converts from a 110 VAC or 220 VAC domestic electric supply ("house current" or "main power") to low-voltage DC, which is required to operate solid-state electronic equipment (such as a laptop computer) that does not include an internal power supply.

Accelerated Graphics Port *n. See* AGP.

accelerator *n.* **1.** In applications, a key or key combination used to perform a defined function. *Also called:* shortcut key. **2.** In hardware, a device that speeds or enhances the operation of one or more subsystems, leading to improved program performance. *See also* accelerator card, Windows-based accelerator.

accelerator board *n. See* accelerator card.

accelerator card *n.* A printed circuit board that replaces or augments the computer's main microprocessor, resulting in faster performance. *Also called:* accelerator board. *See also* expansion board, graphics accelerator.

acceptable use policy *n.* A statement issued by an ISP (Internet service provider) or an online information service that indicates what activities users may or may not engage in while logged into the service. For example, some providers prohibit users from engaging in commercial activity on the network. *Acronym:* AUP.*See also* ISP, online information service.

acceptance test *n.* A formal evaluation of a hardware product performed by the customer, usually at the factory, to verify that the product is performing according to specifications.

access[1] *n.* **1.** The act of reading data from or writing data to memory. **2.** Connection to the Internet or other network or system.

access[2] *vb.* To gain entry to memory in order to read or write data.

Access *n.* Microsoft's relational database–management software for the Windows desktop platform. Part of the family of Microsoft Office products, Access in its most recent version (Access 2002) supports Web technology for building, managing, and sharing data. Access 2002 also includes new and improved tools for accessing and viewing information and offers integration with Microsoft's BackOffice database product, SQL Server. *See also* Office.

access arm *n.* A mechanical arm that moves the read/write head(s) over the surface of a disk in a disk drive. See the illustration. *Also called:* head arm.

Access arm

Access arm.

ACCESS.bus *n.* A bidirectional bus for connecting peripherals to a PC. The ACCESS.bus can connect up to 125 low-speed peripherals, such as printers, modems, mice, and keyboards, to the system through a single, general-purpose port. Peripherals that support the ACCESS.bus provide a connector or port connection that is similar to a phone-jack connector and are daisy-chained together. However, the PC communicates directly with each peripheral and vice versa. Connecting an ACCESS.bus device (for example, a printer) to a system results in the system automatically identifying and configuring it for optimum performance. Peripherals can be connected while the computer is running (*hot plugging*) and are automatically assigned a unique address (auto-addressing). Developed from the l2 architecture designed jointly by Philips and Digital Equipment Corporation, the ACCESS.bus specification is controlled by the ACCESS.bus Industry Group and competes with Intel's USB. *See also* bidirectional, bus, daisy chain[1], hot plugging, input/output port, peripheral. *Compare* USB.

access code *n. See* password.

access control *n.* The mechanisms for limiting access to certain items of information or to certain controls based on users' identities and their membership in various predefined groups. Access control is typically used by system administrators for controlling user access to network resources, such as servers, directories, and files. *See also* access privileges, system administrator.

access control list *n.* A list associated with a file or a resource that contains information about which users or groups have permission to access a resource or modify the file. *Acronym:* ACL.

accessibility *n.* A quality of software, hardware, or a complete computer system that makes it usable by people with one or more physical disabilities, such as restricted mobility, blindness, or deafness.

accessibility aids *n.* Utilities that make computers easier to use for people with disabilities. Examples of accessibility aids include screen readers, speech recognition programs, and on-screen keyboards.

access key *n.* A key combination, such as ALT+F, that moves the focus to a menu, a command, or a control, without using the mouse.

access mechanism *n.* **1.** The disk drive components that move the read/write head(s) to the proper track of a magnetic disk or optical disc. *See also* disk controller. **2.** A circuit that allows one part of a computer system to send signals to another part. **3.** In programming, the means by which an application can read from or write to a resource. *Also called:* access method.

access method *n. See* access mechanism.

access number *n.* The telephone number used by a subscriber to gain access to an online service.

accessory *n. See* peripheral.

access path *n. See* search path.

access permission *n. See* permission.

access point *n.* In a wireless LAN (local area network), a transceiver that connects the LAN to a wired network. *See also* wireless LAN.

access privileges *n.* The type of operations permitted a given user for a certain system resource on a network or a file server. A variety of operations, such as the ability to access a server, view the contents of a directory, open or transfer files, and create, modify, or delete files or directories, can be allowed or disallowed by the system administrator. Assigning access privileges to users helps the system administrator to maintain security on the system, as well as the privacy of confidential information, and to allocate system resources, such as disk space. *Also called:* access rights. *See also* file protection, file server, permission, system administrator, write access.

access provider *n. See* ISP.

access rights *n. See* access privileges.

access speed *n. See* access time.

access time *n.* **1.** The amount of time it takes for data to be delivered from memory to the processor after the address for the data has been selected. **2.** The time needed for a read/write head in a disk drive to locate a track on a disk. Access time is usually measured in milliseconds and is used as a performance measure for hard disks and CD-ROM drives. *See also* read/write head, seek time, settling time, wait state. *Compare* cycle time.

account *n.* **1.** A record-keeping arrangement used by the vendor of an online service to identify a subscriber and to maintain a record of customer usage for billing purposes. **2.** The record-keeping mechanism used by networks and multiuser operating systems for keeping track of authorized users. Network accounts are created by network administrators and are used both to validate users and to administer policies—for example, permissions—related to each user.

accounting file *n.* A file generated by a printer controller that keeps track of the number of pages printed per job as well as the user that requested the print job.

accounting machine *n.* **1.** One of the earliest applications of automatic data processing, used in business accounting primarily during the 1940s and 1950s. The first accounting machines were nonelectronic and used punched cards and wires arranged in plugboard panels. **2.** A computer in which an accounting software package starts up whenever the machine is turned on, the computer thus becoming a dedicated machine with accounting as its sole function.

account lockout *n.* A security feature in Windows XP that locks a user account if a number of failed logon attempts occur within a specified amount of time, based on security policy lockout settings. Locked accounts cannot log on.

account name *n.* The part of an e-mail address that identifies a user or an account on an e-mail system. An e-mail address on the Internet typically consists of an account name, followed by the @ (at) symbol, a host name, and a domain name. *See also* account (definition 2), domain name, e-mail address.

account policy *n.* On local area networks and multi-user operating systems, a set of rules governing whether a new user is allowed access to the system and whether an existing user's rights are expanded to include additional system resources. An account policy also generally states the rules with which the user must comply while using the system in order to maintain access privileges.

ACCU *n. See* Association of C and C++ Users.

accumulator *n.* A register used for logic or arithmetic, usually to count items or accumulate a sum. *See also* register.

accuracy *n.* The degree to which the result of a calculation or measurement approximates the true value. *Compare* precision (definition 1).

ACID *n.* Short for **A**tomicity, **C**onsistency, **I**solation, **D**urability. The four essential properties of an electronic transaction. Atomicity requires that a transaction be fully completed or else fully canceled. Consistency requires that resources used are transformed from one consistent state to another. Isolation requires all transactions to be independent of each other. Durability requires that the completed transaction be permanent, including survival through system failure. *See also* transaction.

ACIS *n.* Acronym for **A**ndy, **C**harles, **I**an's **S**ystem. An object-oriented geometric modeling toolkit owned by Spatial Technology. Designed for use as a "geometry engine" within 3-D modeling applications, ACIS provides an open architecture framework for wire-frame, surface, and solid modeling from a common, unified data structure. ACIS is generally considered the de facto standard for solids modeling in the CAM/CAE industries.

ACK *n.* Short for **ack**nowledgment. A message sent by the receiving unit to the sending station or computer indicating either that the unit is ready to receive transmission or that a transmission was received without error. *Compare* NAK.

ACL *n. See* access control list.

ACM *n. See* Association for Computing Machinery.

acoustic coupler *n.* An archaic device once used in computer communications. The coupler was a cradle-like instrument into which the headset of a telephone was placed. Its function was somewhat similar to the job now done by modems.

ACPI *n.* Acronym for **A**dvanced **C**onfiguration and **P**ower **I**nterface. An open specification developed jointly by Microsoft, Intel, and Toshiba for managing power consumption on mobile, desktop, and server computers. Unlike earlier, BIOS-based management solutions, ACPI provides a means of integrating power management through all parts of a PC, including applications, hardware, and the operating system (OS). ACPI enables an OS to control a computer's power state in response to input from the user, from an application, or from a device driver. For example, an ACPI-enabled OS could turn a CD-ROM drive, a printer, or even a television on or off as needed. ACPI is part of the industry-wide OnNow initiative that allows system manufacturers to deliver computers that start at the touch of a keyboard. *See also* plug and play, power management. *Compare* Advanced Power Management.

Acrobat *n.* A program from Adobe Systems, Inc., that converts a fully formatted document created on a Windows, Macintosh, MS-DOS, or UNIX platform into a Portable Document Format (PDF) file that can be viewed on several different platforms. Acrobat enables users to send documents that contain distinctive typefaces, color, graphics, and photographs electronically to recipients, regardless of the application used to create the originals. Recipients need the Acrobat Reader, which is available free, to view the files. Depending on version and platform, it also includes tools such as Distiller (which creates PDF files from PostScript files), Exchange (which is used for links, annotations, and security-related matters), and PDF Writer (which creates PDF files from files created with business software).

Acrobat Reader *n.* A free program produced and distributed by Adobe Systems, Inc., for displaying and printing documents that are in Portable Document Format (PDF).

ACSE *n. See* Association Control Service Element.

action query *n.* In Microsoft Access, a query that copies or changes data. Action queries include append, delete, make-table, and update queries. They are identified by an exclamation point (!) next to their name in the Database window.

action statement *n. See* statement.

activation *n.* In Sun Microsystem's J2EE network platform, the process of transferring an enterprise java bean (EJB) from secondary storage to memory. *See also* EJB, J2EE. *Compare* passivation.

activation record *n.* A data structure that represents the state of some construct (such as a procedure, a function, a block, an expression, or a module) of a running program. An activation record is useful for the run-time management of both data and sequencing. *See also* data structure.

active *adj.* Pertaining to the device, program, file, or portion of the screen that is currently operational or subject to command operations. Usually the cursor or a highlighted section shows the active element on the display screen.

Active Accessibility *n.* A Microsoft initiative, introduced in 1997, that consists of program files and conventions that make it easier for software developers to integrate accessibility aids, such as screen magnifiers or text-to-voice converters, into their application's user interface to make software easier for users with limited physical abilities to use. Active Accessibility is based on COM technologies and is supported by Windows 9x, Windows XP, Windows NT 4.0 and above, Internet Explorer 3 and above, and Office 2000 and above. *Acronym:* MSAA. *Also called:* Microsoft Active Accessibility.

active cell *n.* The highlighted cell on a spreadsheet display that is the current focus of operation. *Also called:* current cell, selected cell. *See also* range.

Active Channel *n.* A Web site described by a Channel Definition Format (CDF) file. Developers can use Active Channels to automatically download content to a user on a subscription basis, to send content to users on a regular schedule, to deliver personalized content to individual users, and to provide content to a Windows screen saver. Active Channels were introduced in Microsoft Internet Explorer 4 and can be used to deliver information through either the Internet or an intranet. *See also* pull, webcasting.

Active Client *n.* The client-side set of technologies in Microsoft's Active Platform for Web-oriented, cross-platform distributed computing. The chief features of the Active Client include support for HTML and dynamic HTML, language-independent scripting, Java applets, and ActiveX objects. Active Client is operating system–independent, so it runs on multiple platforms, including Microsoft Windows, UNIX, and Apple Macintosh. *See also* Active Platform, Active Server.

active content *n.* Material on a Web page that changes on the screen with time or in response to user action. Active content is implemented through ActiveX controls. *See also* ActiveX control.

Active data object *n.* An application programming interface (API) developed by Microsoft for applications that access databases. ADO is an easy-to-use interface to OLE Database (OLE DB), an API that accesses the data directly from a database. *Also called:* ActiveX data object.

Active Desktop *n.* The feature introduced with Microsoft's Internet Explorer 4 that enables end users to display active—that is, updateable, customizable—HTML content on the Windows desktop. Active content includes such items as channels, Web pages, ActiveX controls, and Java applets. *See also* Active Channel, ActiveX, HTML, Internet Explorer, Java.

Active Directory *n.* A Microsoft technology, part of the Active Platform, that is designed to enable applications to find, use, and manage directory resources (for example, user names, network printers, and permissions) in a distributed computing environment. Distributed environments are usually heterogeneous collections of networks that often run proprietary directory services from different providers. To simplify directory-related activities associated with locating and administering network users and resources, Active Directory presents applications with a single set of interfaces that eliminates the need to deal with differences between and among these proprietary services. Active Directory is a component of the Windows Open Services Architecture (WOSA). *See also* directory service, WOSA.

Active Directory Services Interface *n.* An administrative tool known as a Microsoft Management Console (MMC) snap-in that allows administrators to manage objects in the domain. *Acronym:* ADSI.

active file *n.* The file affected by a current command—typically a data file.

Active Framework for Data Warehousing *n.* A data warehousing solution developed by Microsoft and Texas Instruments that represents Microsoft's standard for managing metadata. *Acronym:* AFDW. *See also* ActiveX, metadata.

active hub *n.* **1.** The central computer that regenerates and retransmits all signals in an active star network. *See also* active star. **2.** A type of hub used on ARCnet networks that both regenerates (boosts) signals and passes them along. *Compare* intelligent hub, passive hub.

active-matrix display *n.* A liquid crystal display (LCD) made from a large array of liquid crystal cells using active-matrix technology. The active matrix is a method of addressing an array of simple LC cells—one cell per pixel. In its simplest form there is one thin-film transistor (TFT) for each cell. Voltage applied selectively to these cells produces the viewable image. Active-matrix displays are often used in laptop and notebook computers because of their shallow depth and are notable for their high-quality color displays, which are viewable from wider angles than images produced by most passive-matrix displays. *Also called:* TFT, TFT display, TFT LCD. *See also* liquid crystal display, TFT. *Compare* passive-matrix display.

ActiveMovie *n.* Former name for the DirectX component now known as DirectShow. *Also called:* DirectShow. *See also* DirectX.

Active Platform *n.* A Microsoft development platform that offers a standardized approach to incorporating Internet and distributed computing technologies in client/server applications. Microsoft Windows 9x, Microsoft Windows NT, and Microsoft Internet Explorer 4.*x* (and later) provide the basis for the Active Platform. On the client side, users are given a consistent interface that enables them to easily access both local and remote information. On the server side, developers can take advantage of the tools and technologies that span the client and the server. Active Platform supports development of the modular object-oriented programs known as component software and allows creation of cross-platform applications that can run on multiple chips and operating systems. Active Platform includes support for HTML and the creation of small programs in several languages through client-side scripting. *See also* Active Desktop, Active Server, ActiveX.

active program *n.* The program currently in control of a microprocessor.

Active Server *n.* The server-based component of Microsoft's Active Platform. Comprised of a set of technologies that includes DCOM (distributed component object model), Active Server Pages, Microsoft Transaction Server, and message queues, Active Server provides support for developing component-based, scalable, high-performance Web applications on Microsoft Windows NT servers. Active Server is designed to allow developers to concentrate on creating Internet and intranet software in a variety of languages without having to focus on the intricacy of the network itself. *See also* Active Desktop, Active Platform, Active Server Pages, ActiveX.

Active Server Pages *n.* A Web-oriented technology developed by Microsoft that is designed to enable server-side (as opposed to client-side) scripting. Active Server Pages are text files that can contain not only text and HTML tags as in standard Web documents, but also commands written in a scripting language (such as VBScript or JavaScript) that can be carried out on the server. This server-side work enables a Web author to add interactivity to a document or to customize the viewing or delivery of information to the client without worrying about the platform the client is running. All Active Server Pages are saved with an .asp extension and can be accessed like standard URLs through a Web browser, such as Microsoft Internet Explorer or Netscape Navigator. When an Active Server Page is requested by a browser, the server carries out any script commands embedded in the page, generates an HTML document, and sends the document back to the browser for display on the requesting (client) computer. Active Server Pages can also be enhanced and extended with ActiveX components. *Acronym:* ASP. *See also* Active Server, ActiveX.

active star *n.* A form of the star network topology in which the central computer actively regenerates and retransmits all signals. *See also* star network.

ActiveStore *n.* A Microsoft initiative, introduced in 1998, for supporting integration of applications used in retail environments regardless of the developing vendor. ActiveStore provides a common user interface, base system services (such as security and crash recovery), common access to data across applications, and communication between applications.

ActiveSync *n.* A Microsoft program that manages synchronization of information, including e-mail, schedules, and application files, between a handheld PC and a desktop computer.

active vision *n.* A branch of computer vision research that believes robotic vision problems can be solved by allowing a robot to collect and analyze a sequence of images dynamically from changing viewpoints. Not unlike human or animal vision, active vision uses the information derived from multiple viewpoints to gain a greater depth of perception, resolve haziness, and establish relationships between the visual representation of an action and the action itself. Active vision systems may be characterized by simple image-processing algorithms, little or no calibration, and fast real-time hardware. *See also* artificial intelligence, computer vision, robotics.

active window *n.* In an environment capable of displaying multiple on-screen windows, the window containing the display or document that will be affected by current cursor movements, commands, and text entry. *See also* graphical user interface. *Compare* inactive window.

ActiveX *n.* A set of technologies that enables software components to interact with one another in a networked environment, regardless of the language in which the components were created. ActiveX, which was developed by Microsoft in the mid 1990s and is currently administered by the Open Group, is built on Microsoft's Component Object Model (COM). Currently, ActiveX is used primarily to develop interactive content for the World Wide Web, although it can be used in desktop applications and other programs. ActiveX controls can be embedded in Web pages to produce animation and other multimedia effects, interactive objects, and sophisticated applications. *See also* ActiveX control, COM. *Compare* applet, plug-in (definition 2).

ActiveX control *n.* A reusable software component based on Microsoft's ActiveX technology that is used to add interactivity and more functionality, such as animation or a popup menu, to a Web page, applications, and software development tools. An ActiveX control can be written in any of a number of languages, including Java, C++, and Visual Basic. *See also* ActiveX. *Compare* helper program.

activity ratio *n.* The number of records in use compared with the total number of records in a database file. *See also* database, record[1].

ACTOR *n.* An object-oriented language developed by The Whitewater Group, Ltd., designed primarily to facilitate Microsoft Windows programming. *See also* object-oriented programming.

actuator *n.* A disk drive mechanism for moving the read/write head(s) to the location of the desired track on a disk. See the illustration. *See also* disk drive, stepper motor, voice coil.

Actuator

Actuator.

Ada *n.* A high-level programming language designed under the direction of the U.S. Department of Defense (DoD) in the late 1970s and intended to be the primary language for DoD software development. Originally based on Pascal, Ada supports real-time operations and multitasking. The language was named after Augusta Ada Byron, who assisted Charles Babbage in developing programs for his Analytical Engine, the first mechanical computer, in the nineteenth century. *See also* multitasking, Pascal, real-time.

adapter or **adaptor** *n.* A printed circuit board that enables a personal computer to use a peripheral device, such as a CD-ROM drive, modem, or joystick, for which it does not already have the necessary connections, ports, or circuit boards. Commonly, a single adapter card can have more than one adapter on it. *Also called:* interface card. *See also* controller, expansion board, network adapter, port[1], video adapter.

adapter card or **adaptor card** *n. See* adapter.

adaptive answering *n.* The ability of a modem to detect whether an incoming call is a fax or a data transmission and respond accordingly. *See also* modem.

adaptive delta pulse code modulation *n.* A class of compression encoding and decoding algorithms used in audio compression and other data compression applications. These algorithms store digitally sampled signals as a series of changes in value, adapting the range of the change with each sample as needed, thus increasing the effective bit resolution of the data. *Acronym:* ADPCM. *See also* pulse code modulation. *Compare* adaptive differential pulse code modulation.

adaptive differential pulse code modulation *n.* A digital audio compression algorithm that stores a sample as the difference between a linear combination of previous samples and the actual sample, rather than the measurement itself. The linear combination formula is modified every few samples to minimize the dynamic range of the output signal, resulting in efficient storage. *See also* pulse code modulation. *Compare* adaptive delta pulse code modulation.

adaptive load balancing *n.* *See* load balancing.

adaptive routing *n.* *See* dynamic routing.

adaptive system *n.* An artificial intelligence system that is capable of altering its behavior based on certain features of its experience or environment. *See also* expert system.

ADB *n.* *See* Apple Desktop Bus.

ADC *n.* *See* analog-to-digital converter.

A-D converter *n.* *See* analog-to-digital converter.

adder *n.* **1.** A component of the CPU (central processing unit) that adds two numbers sent to it by processing instructions. *See also* central processing unit. **2.** A circuit that sums the amplitudes, or strength, of two input signals. *See also* full adder, half adder.

add-in *n.* *See* add-on.

addition record *n.* **1.** A file that describes new record entries (such as a new customer, employee, or product) in a database so that they can later be scrutinized and posted. **2.** A record in a change file specifying a new entry. *See also* change file.

add-on *n.* **1.** A hardware device, such as an expansion board or chip, that can be added to a computer to expand its capabilities. *Also called:* add-in. *See also* open archi-

tecture (definition 2). **2.** A supplemental program that can extend the capabilities of an application program. *See also* utility program.

address[1] *n.* **1.** A number specifying a location in memory where data is stored. *See also* absolute address, address space, physical address, virtual address. **2.** A name or token specifying a particular computer or site on the Internet or other network. **3.** A code used to specify an e-mail destination.

address[2] *vb.* To reference a particular storage location.

addressable cursor *n.* A cursor programmed so that it can be moved to any location on the screen, by means of the keyboard or a mouse.

address book *n.* **1.** In an e-mail program, a reference section listing e-mail addresses and individuals' names. **2.** As a Web page, an informal e-mail or URL phone book.

address bus *n.* A bus consisting of 20 to 64 separate hardware lines that is used to carry the signals specifying memory locations for data. *See also* bus.

address classes *n.* Predefined groupings of Internet addresses with each class defining networks of a certain size. The range of numbers that can be assigned for the first octet in the IP address is based on the address class. Class A networks (values 1 to 126) are the largest, with more than 16 million hosts per network. Class B networks (128 to 191) have up to 65,534 hosts per network, and Class C networks (192 to 223) can have up to 254 hosts per network.

address decoder *n.* An electronic device that converts a numeric address to the electrical signals needed to select a specific memory location on one or more RAM chips.

addressing *n.* The process of assigning or referring to an address. In programming, the address is typically a value specifying a memory location. *See also* address[1].

address mapping table *n.* A table used by routers or DNS (Domain Name System) servers to obtain the corresponding IP (Internet Protocol) address of a text name of a computer resource, such as the name of a host computer on the Internet. *Acronym:* AMT. *See also* DNS server, IP address, router.

address mark *n.* *See* index mark.

address mask *n.* A number that, when compared by the computer with a network address number, will block out all but the necessary information. For example, in a network that uses XXX.XXX.XXX.YYY and where all computers within the network use the same first address numbers, the mask will block out XXX.XXX.XXX and use only the significant numbers in the address, YYY. *See also* address[1] (definition 2).

address mode *n.* The method used to indicate an address in memory. *See also* absolute address, indexed address, paged address, relative address.

address modification *n.* The process of updating an address of a location in memory during computation.

address munging *n.* The practice of modifying an e-mail address in posts to newsgroups or other Internet forums to foil computer programs that gather e-mail addresses. The host name in an e-mail address is altered to create a fictitious address in such a way that a human can still easily determine the correct address. For example, a person with an e-mail address of Jane@myispoffers-usersfreeemail.com could modify, or "mung," her address to read Jane@remove-this-to-reply-myispoffersusers-freeemail.com. Address munging is generally used to prevent delivery of unsolicited junk e-mail or spam. *Also called:* munging. *See also* address[1] (definition 2), host name, mung, spam.

address register *n.* A register (a high-speed memory circuit) that holds an address where specific data can be found for the transfer of information. *See also* register.

address resolution *n.* The identification of a computer's IP (Internet Protocol) address by finding the corresponding match in an address mapping table. *See also* address mapping table.

Address Resolution Protocol *n. See* ARP.

address space *n.* The total range of memory locations addressable by a computer.

address translation *n.* The process of converting one kind of address to another, such as a virtual address to a physical address.

ad-hoc network *n.* A temporary network formed by communicating stations or computers in a wireless LAN. *See also* wireless LAN.

ADJ *n.* Short for **adj**acent. A Boolean qualifier to indicate cases where two instances are adjacent to each other. In the case of a search string, "Microsoft ADJ Word" would

return only instances where "Microsoft" and "Word" are adjacent in the string.

administrative alerts *n.* Alerts that relate to server and resource use. They notify users about problems in areas such as security and access, user sessions, server shutdown due to power loss (when an uninterruptible power supply is available), directory replication, and printing. When a computer generates an administrative alert, a message is sent to a predefined list of users and computers. *See also* Alerter service.

ADN *n. See* Advanced Digital Network.

ADO *n. See* Active data object.

Adobe Type Manager *n.* Software from Adobe Systems, Inc., that manages PostScript fonts on a system. *Acronym:* ATM. *See also* PostScript.

ADO.NET *n.* The suite of data access technologies included in the .NET Framework class libraries that provide access to relational data and XML. ADO.NET consists of classes that make up the DataSet (such as tables, rows, columns, relations, and so on), .NET Framework data providers, and custom type definitions (such as SqlTypes for SQL Server).

ADP *n. See* data processing.

ADPCM *n. See* adaptive delta pulse code modulation.

ADSL *n.* Acronym for **a**symmetric **d**igital **s**ubscriber **l**ine. Technology and equipment allowing high-speed digital communication, including video signals, across an ordinary twisted-pair copper phone line, with speeds up to 8 Mbps (megabits per second) downstream (to the customer) and up to 640 Kbps (kilobits per second) upstream. ADSL access to the Internet is offered by some regional telephone companies, offering users faster connection times than those available through connections made over standard phone lines. *Also called:* asymmetric digital subscriber loop. *Compare* SDSL.

Advanced Configuration and Power Interface *n. See* ACPI.

Advanced Digital Network *n.* A dedicated line service capable of transmitting data, video, and other digital signals with exceptional reliability, offered as a premier service by communications companies. Usually Advanced Digital Network refers to speeds at or above 56 kilobits per second (Kbps). *See also* dedicated line.

Advanced Encryption Standard *n. See* AES.

Advanced Interactive Executive *n. See* AIX.

Advanced Mobile Phone Service *n. See* AMPS.

Advanced Power Management *n.* An older power management technology used in mobile PCs before the implementation of Advanced Configuration and Power Interface (ACPI). Advanced Power Management is a software interface that functions between the BIOS power-management software that is specific to the hardware and a power-management policy driver that is run by the operating system. *Acronym:* APM.

Advanced Program-to-Program Communication *n. See* APPC.

Advanced Research Projects Agency Network *n. See* ARPANET.

Advanced RISC *n.* Short for **Advanced r**educed **i**nstruction **s**et **c**omputing. A specification for a RISC microchip architecture and system environment designed by MIPS Computer Systems to provide binary compatibility among software applications. *See also* RISC.

Advanced RISC Computing Specification *n.* The minimum hardware requirements enabling a RISC-based system to comply with the Advanced Computing Environment standard. *See also* Advanced RISC.

Advanced RISC Machines *n. See* ARM.

Advanced SCSI Programming Interface *n.* An interface specification developed by Adaptec, Inc., for sending commands to SCSI host adapters. The interface provides an abstraction layer that insulates the programmer from considerations of the particular host adapter used. *Acronym:* ASPI. *See also* adapter, SCSI.

Advanced Streaming Format *n.* An open file format specification for streaming multimedia files containing text, graphics, sound, video, and animation. Advanced Streaming Format (ASF) does not define the format for any media streams within the file. Rather, it defines a standardized, extensible file "container" that is not dependent on a particular operating system or communication protocol, or on a particular method (such as HTML or MPEG-4) used to compose the data stream in the file. An ASF file consists of three objects: a Header object containing information about the file itself, a Data object containing the media streams, and an optional Index object that can help support random access to data within the file. The ASF

specification has been submitted to the ISO (International Organization for Standardization) for consideration. *Acronym:* ASF. *See also* streaming.

adventure game *n.* A role-playing computer game in which the player becomes a character in a narrative. In order to complete the game, the player must solve problems and avoid or overcome attacks and other forms of interference from the game's environment and other characters. The first adventure game was called "Adventure." It was developed in 1976 by Will Crowther of Bolt, Baranek & Newman. *See also* arcade game, computer game, role-playing game.

AE *n.* Acronym for **a**pplication **e**ntity. In the ISO/OSI reference model, one of the two software parties involved in a communications session. *See also* ISO/OSI reference model.

A/E/C SYSTEMS conference *n.* Annual conference of the architecture, engineering, and construction industry. The conference promotes the exchange of information on new techniques and technologies used by these industries.

.aero *n.* One of seven new top-level domain names approved in 2000 by the Internet Corporation for Assigned Names and Numbers (ICANN). .aero is meant for use with air-transport industry-related Web sites. The seven new domain names became available for use in the spring of 2001.

AES *n.* Acronym for **A**dvanced **E**ncryption **S**tandard. A cryptographic algorithm specified by the National Institute of Standards and Technology (NIST) to protect sensitive information. AES is specified in three key sizes: 128, 192, and 256 bits. AES replaces the 56-bit key Data Encryption Standard (DES), which was adopted in 1976. *See also* DES.

AFC *n. See* Application Foundation Classes.

AFDW *n. See* Active Framework for Data Warehousing.

affinity *n.* For Network Load Balancing, the method used to associate client requests to cluster hosts. When no affinity is specified, all network requests are load balanced across the cluster without respect to their source. Affinity is implemented by directing all client requests from the same IP address to the same cluster host. *See also* client request, IP address.

AFIPS *n.* Acronym for **A**merican **F**ederation of **I**nformation **P**rocessing **S**ocieties. An organization formed in 1961 for the advancement of computing and information-related concerns. The U.S. representative of the International Federation of Information Processing, AFIPS was replaced by the Federation on Computing in the United States (FOCUS) in 1990.

AFK *adv.* Acronym for **a**way **f**rom **k**eyboard. A phrase occasionally seen in live chat services on the Internet and online information services as an indication that one is momentarily unable to answer. *See also* chat[1] (definition 1).

AFP *n.* Acronym for **A**ppleTalk **F**iling **P**rotocol. A remote filing system protocol that provides a standard means for a workstation on an AppleTalk network to access and manipulate files on an AFP-implemented server. *Also called:* AppleShare File Server.

AFS *n.* Acronym for **A**ndrew **F**ile **S**ystem. A distributed file system that allows clients and servers to share resources through local-area and wide-area networks. AFS is based on a distributed file system developed at Carnegie-Mellon University, and is named for the university's founders—Andrew Carnegie and Andrew Mellon. AFS is now maintained and supplied by Transarc Corporation. *See also* distributed file system.

agent *n.* **1.** A program that performs a background task for a user and reports to the user when the task is done or some expected event has taken place. **2.** A program that searches through archives or other repositories of information on a topic specified by the user. Agents of this sort are used most often on the Internet and are generally dedicated to searching a single type of information repository, such as postings on Usenet groups. Spiders are a type of agent used on the Internet. *Also called:* intelligent agent. *See also* spider. **3.** In client/server applications, a process that mediates between the client and the server. **4.** In Simple Network Management Protocol (SNMP), a program that monitors network traffic. *See also* SNMP.

aggregated links *n. See* link aggregation.

aggregation of links *n. See* link aggregation.

AGP *n.* Acronym for **A**ccelerated **G**raphics **P**ort. A high-performance bus specification designed for fast, high-quality display of 3-D and video images. Developed by Intel Corporation, AGP uses a dedicated point-to-point connection between the graphics controller and main system memory. This connection enables AGP-capable display adapters and compatible chip sets to transfer video data directly between system memory and adapter memory, to display images more quickly and smoothly than they can be displayed when the information must be transferred over the system's primary (PCI) bus. AGP also allows for storing complex image elements such as texture maps in system memory and thus reduces the need for large amounts of memory on the adapter itself. AGP runs at 66 MHz—twice as fast as the PCI bus—and can support data transfer speeds of up to 533 Mbps. *See also* PCI local bus.

AH *n.* **A**uthentication **H**eader. A form of IP packet authentication included in the IPSec security standard. AH attaches a header to the packet with authentication information but does not encrypt the packet data, which allows its use in cases where encryption is not allowed. *See also* ESP, IPSec.

AI *n. See* artificial intelligence.

.aiff *n.* The file extension that identifies audio files in the sound format originally used on Apple and Silicon Graphics (SGI) computers.

AIFF *n.* The sound format originally used on Apple and Silicon Graphics (SGI) computers. AIFF stores waveform files in an 8-bit monaural format. *See also* waveform.

AIM *n.* Acronym for **A**merica Online **I**nstant **M**essenger. A popular instant-messaging service provided for free by America Online. With the AIM service, instant messages can be sent over an Internet connection using the AIM software or directly from a Web browser using AIM Express. *See also* America Online, instant messaging. *Compare* ICQ, .NET Messenger Service, Yahoo! Messenger.

AirPort *n.* A wireless connectivity option introduced by Apple in 1999. AirPort provides wireless network and Internet communications to all AirPort card–equipped Macintosh computers within 150 feet of an AirPort base station. AirPort was developed around the IEEE 802.11 Direct Sequence Spectrum (DSSS) industry standard and is interoperable with other 802.11-based equipment.

AirSnort *n.* A hacking tool used to gather and decrypt passwords in data sent over wireless networks. AirSnort monitors wireless transmissions and collects packets of data. When it has collected enough data, AirSnort is able to compute the encryption key used in the transmission. AirSnort takes advantage of security flaws in the Wired Equivalent Protocol (WEP) standard. *See also* password sniffing.

AIX *n.* Acronym for **A**dvanced **I**nteractive **E**xecutive. A version of the UNIX operating system developed and maintained by IBM for its UNIX workstations and PCs.

alarm *n.* A visual or auditory signal from a computer alerting the user to an error or a hazardous situation.

ALB *n. See* load balancing.

alert *n.* **1.** In many operating systems with GUIs (graphical user interfaces), an audible or visual alarm that signals an error or represents a warning of some sort. *See also* alert box. **2.** In programming, an asynchronous notification sent by one thread to another. The alert interrupts the recipient thread at defined points in its execution and causes it to execute an asynchronous procedure call. *See also* asynchronous procedure call, thread (definition 1).

alert box *n.* An on-screen box in a GUI (graphical user interface) that is used to deliver a message or warning. *Compare* dialog box.

Alerter service *n.* A service used by the server and other services to notify selected users and computers of administrative alerts that occur on a computer. The Alerter service requires the Messenger service. *See also* administrative alerts, Messenger service, service.

ALGOL *n.* Acronym for **Alg**orithmic **L**anguage. The first structured procedural programming language, developed in the late 1950s and once widely used in Europe.

algorithm *n.* A finite sequence of steps for solving a logical or mathematical problem or performing a task.

algorithmic language *n.* A programming language, such as Ada, Basic, C, or Pascal, that uses algorithms for problem solving.

Algorithmic Language *n. See* ALGOL.

alias *n.* **1.** An alternative label for some object, such as a file or data collection. **2.** A name used to direct e-mail messages to a person or group of people on a network. **3.** A false signal that results from the digitization of an analog audio sample.

aliasing *n.* In computer graphics, the jagged appearance of curves or diagonal lines on a display screen, which is caused by low screen resolution. See the illustration.

Aliasing. *The lower resolution of the image on the right reveals the aliasing effect.*

aliasing bug *n.* A class of subtle programming errors that can arise in code that performs dynamic allocation. If sev-

eral pointers address the same chunk of storage, the program may free the storage using one of the pointers but then attempt to use another one (an alias), which would no longer be pointing to the desired data. This bug is avoidable by the use of allocation strategies that never use more than one copy of a pointer to allocated core memory, or by the use of higher-level languages, such as LISP, which employ a garbage collection feature. *Also called:* stale pointer bug. *See also* alias, dynamic allocation, garbage collection.

align *vb.* **1.** In an application such as a word processor, to position lines of type relative to some point, such as the page margin. The most common types of alignment are left- and right-aligned and centered. See the illustration. **2.** To adjust some device to position it within specified tolerances, such as the read/write head relative to a track on a disk. **3.** In data handling, to store multiple-byte data units so that the respective bytes fall in corresponding locations of memory.

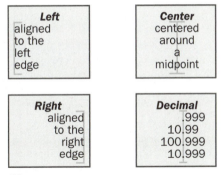

Align.

alignment *n.* The arrangement of objects in fixed or predetermined positions, rows, or columns. For example, the Macintosh Finder can do automatic alignment of icons in a folder or on the desktop.

Allegro *n.* Ported to a number of operating systems, Allegro is a freeware library of functions for use in programming computer games and graphics programs. It is written for the DJGPP compiler in a mixture of C and assembly language. The most recent release version is 4.0.0. *See also* assembly language, DJGPP.

allocate *vb.* To reserve a resource, such as sufficient memory, for use by a program. *Compare* deallocate.

allocation *n.* In operating systems, the process of reserving memory for use by a program.

allocation block size *n.* The size of an individual block on a storage medium, such as a hard drive, which is determined by factors such as total disk size and partitioning options.

allocation unit *n. See* cluster.

all points addressable *n.* The mode in computer graphics in which all pixels can be individually manipulated. *Acronym:* APA. *See also* graphics mode.

ALOHA *n. See* ALOHAnet.

ALOHAnet *n.* The first wireless packet-switched network and the first large network to be connected to the ARPANET. ALOHAnet was built in 1970 at the University of Hawaii by Norm Abramson and was funded by Larry Roberts. ALOHAnet enabled computers at seven campuses on four different islands to communicate bidirectionally with the central computer on Oahu using a network of radio transmitters. The ALOHA protocol was the basis for Ethernet. *See also* ARPANET, Ethernet, network.

alpha[1] *adj.* Of or pertaining to software that is ready for initial testing.

alpha[2] *n.* A software product that is under development and has enough functionality to begin testing. An alpha is usually unstable and does not have all the features or functionality that the released product is to have. *Compare* beta[2].

Alpha *n.* **1.** Digital Equipment Corporation's (DEC) line of computers built on its 64-bit RISC-based microprocessor (Alphachip). **2.** DEC's internal name for a microprocessor product introduced in February 1992 as the DECchip 21064, which evolved into DEC's current Alphachips. *See also* Alphachip, DECchip 21064.

Alpha AXP *adj.* Of, pertaining to, or characteristic of Digital Equipment Corporation's 64-bit RISC-based microprocessor technology implemented in its DECchip product. The designation AXP is used by DEC in its personal computer products to indicate that a product has a DECchip microprocessor. *See also* Alpha, DECchip 21064, RISC.

alphabet *n.* In communications and data processing, the subset of a complete character set, including letters, numerals, punctuation marks, and other common symbols as well as the codes used to represent them. *See also* ASCII, CCITT, character set, EBCDIC, ISO.

alpha blending *n.* In 3-D computer game rendering and other digital animation applications, a graphics technique for creating realistic transparent and semi-transparent images. Alpha blending combines a transparent source color with a translucent destination color to realistically simulate effects such as smoke, glass, and water.

Alpha box *n.* A computer built around the DEC's DECchip 21064 processor (called Alpha internally at Digital Equipment Corporation). *See also* DECchip 21064.

alpha channel *n.* The high-order 8 bits of a 32-bit graphics pixel used to manipulate the remaining 24 bits for purposes of coloring or masking.

Alphachip *n.* A 64-bit RISC-based microprocessor from Digital Equipment Corporation. *See also* DECchip 21064, RISC.

alphageometric *adj.* In reference to computer graphics, especially videotext and teletext systems, pertaining to or being a display method that uses codes for alphanumeric characters and creates graphics using geometric primitives. Shapes such as horizontal and vertical lines and corners are alphageometric. *See also* alphamosaic.

alphamosaic *adj.* In reference to computer graphics, especially videotext and teletext systems, pertaining to or being a display technique that uses codes for alphanumeric characters and creates graphics using rectangular arrangements of elements to form a mosaic. *See also* alphageometric.

alphanumeric *adj.* Consisting of letters or digits, or both, and sometimes including control characters, space characters, and other special characters. *See also* ASCII, character set, EBCDIC.

alphanumeric display *n.* Electronic display on a wireless phone, pager, or handheld device capable of showing both text and numbers.

alphanumeric display terminal *n.* A terminal capable of displaying characters but not graphics.

alphanumeric messaging *n.* Ability to receive messages containing text and numbers on a pager or digital wireless phone. Also known as short message service (SMS).

alphanumeric mode *n. See* text mode.

alphanumeric sort *n.* A method of sorting data, such as a set of records, that typically uses the following order: punctuation marks, numerals, alphabetic characters (with capitals preceding lowercase letters), and any remaining symbols.

alpha test *n.* The process of user testing that is carried out on a piece of alpha software.

Altair 8800 *n.* A small computer introduced in 1975 by Micro Instrumentation Telemetry Systems (MITS) of New Mexico and sold primarily in kit form. The Altair was based on the 8-bit Intel 8080 microprocessor, had 256 bytes of random access memory, received input through a bank of switches on the front panel, and displayed output via a row of light-emitting diodes. Although it was short-lived, the Altair is considered the first successful personal computer, which was then called a home computer.

AltaVista *n.* A World Wide Web search site and portal hosted by Digital Equipment Corporation. *See also* portal.

alternate circuit-switched voice/circuit-switched data *n.* A configuration option for ISDN B (bearer) channels that enables the digital transmission of either voice or data communications between two users for the duration of a call. *Acronym:* CSV/CSD.*See also* B channel, circuit-switched data, circuit-switched voice, ISDN.

alternate key *n.* **1.** Any candidate key in a database not designated as the primary key. **2.** *See* Alt key.

alternating current *n.* Electric current that reverses its direction of flow (polarity) periodically according to a frequency measured in hertz, or cycles per second. *Acronym:* AC.*Compare* direct current.

Alt key *n.* A key included on PC and other standard keyboards that is used in conjunction with another key to produce some special feature or function and is typically marked with the letters Alt.

alt. newsgroups *n.* Internet newsgroups that are part of the alt. ("alternative") hierarchy and have the prefix alt. Unlike the seven Usenet newsgroup hierarchies (comp., misc., news., rec., sci., soc., talk.) that require formal votes among users in the hierarchy before official newsgroups can be established, anybody can create an alt. newsgroup. Therefore, newsgroups devoted to discussions of obscure or bizarre topics are generally part of the alt. hierarchy.

ALU *n.* *See* arithmetic logic unit.

always on *n.* An Internet connection that is maintained continuously, whether or not the computer user is on line. Always-on connections provide convenience to users who don't need to dial in or log on to access the Internet, but

also provide more opportunities for hackers to attempt to access the system or use the computer to spread malicious programs.

AM *n.* *See* amplitude modulation.

AMD-K6 *n.* Family of x86-compatible processors introduced by Advanced Micro Devices, Inc. (AMD) in 1997. Comparable in performance to the Intel Pentium II, the AMD-K6 family is composed of Windows-compatible processors with MMX support that run 32-bit programs. They have 8.8 million transistors, include 64-KB (AMD-K6) L1 caches for faster execution, and are based on a technology known as RISC86 that converts x86 program instructions into RISC operations for execution. The AMD-K6 family ranges in speed from 166 to over 500 MHz. *See also* MMX, Pentium, RISC.

AMD-K7 *n.* *See* Athlon.

American Federation of Information Processing Societies *n.* *See* AFIPS.

American National Standards Institute *n.* *See* ANSI.

American Registry for Internet Numbers *n.* *See* ARIN.

American Standard Code for Information Interchange *n.* *See* ASCII.

America Online *n.* An online information service, based in Vienna, Virginia, that provides e-mail, news, educational and entertainment services, and Internet access. America Online is one of the largest American ISPs (Internet service providers). In 2000 America Online merged with media giant Time Warner Inc. to become AOL Time Warner Inc. Intended for mass-market delivery of branded content and communication services, the merged companies form a communication and media conglomerate with the Internet's largest user base and a wide range of entertainment, publishing, and cable properties. *Acronym:* AOL.

America Online Instant Messenger *n.* *See* AIM.

AMI BIOS *n.* A ROM BIOS developed and marketed by American Megatrends, Inc. (AMI), for use in IBM-compatible computers. A popular feature is that its configuration software is stored in the ROM chip along with the BIOS routines, so the user does not need a separate configuration disk to modify system settings, such as amount of memory installed and number and types of disk drives. *See also* BIOS, Phoenix BIOS, ROM BIOS.

Amiga *n.* An operating system owned by Amiga, Inc. The Amiga model of desktop computer, which featured the Amiga operating system, was introduced by Commodore in 1985. The Amiga was especially strong in its ability to support sound and video, which made it popular among broadcast and multimedia producers, but it was overshadowed by the IBM Personal Computer (and its clones) and the Apple Macintosh. The ownership of the Amiga design has been through the hands of several companies in the United States and Germany.

amp *n. See* ampere.

ampere *n.* The basic unit of electric current. One ampere is equivalent to a flow of 1 coulomb per second. *Abbreviation:* a, A, amp.

amplitude *n.* A measure of the strength of a signal, such as sound or voltage, determined by the distance from the baseline to the peak of the waveform. *See also* waveform.

amplitude modulation *n.* A method of encoding information in a transmission, such as radio, using a carrier wave of constant frequency but of varying amplitude. See the illustration. *Acronym:* AM. *Compare* frequency modulation.

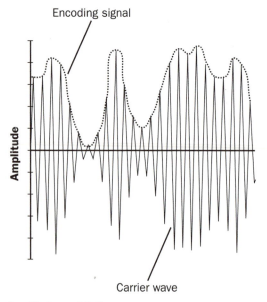

Amplitude modulation.

amplitude shift keying *n.* A form of amplitude modulation that uses two different wave heights to represent the binary values 1 and 0. *See also* amplitude modulation.

AMPS *n.* Acronym for **A**dvanced **M**obile **P**hone **S**ervice. The standard for analog cellular phone service, widely used in the United States and many other countries around the world. AMPS was introduced by AT&T in 1983. It relies on frequency division multiple access (FDMA) to divide frequencies in the 800 MHz to 900 MHz range into 30 KHz channels for sending and receiving calls. A form of AMPS based on a narrower bandwidth is known as N-AMPS. The comparable standard for digital cellular phones is known as D-AMPS. *See also* D-AMPS, N-AMPS.

AMPS/D-AMPS/N-AMPS *n. See* AMPS, D-AMPS, N-AMPS.

AMT *n. See* address mapping table.

Anaglyph *n.* A 3-D effect obtained by creating two overlapping images that appear as a single three dimensional image when viewed through special lenses. Anaglyph 3-D technologies are used on the Web to produce 3-D images for a variety of virtual reality, teaching, and research applications.

analog *adj.* Pertaining to or being a device or signal that is continuously varying in strength or quantity, such as voltage or audio, rather than based on discrete units, such as the binary digits 1 and 0. A lighting dimmer switch is an analog device because it is not based on absolute settings. *Compare* digital (definition 2).

analog channel *n.* A communications channel, such as a voice-grade telephone line, carrying signals that vary continuously and can assume any value within a specified range.

analog computer *n.* A computer that measures data varying continuously in value, such as speed or temperature.

analog data *n.* Data that is represented by continuous variations in some physical property, such as voltage, frequency, or pressure. *Compare* digital data transmission.

analog display *n.* A video display capable of depicting a continuous range of colors or shades rather than discrete values. *Compare* digital display.

analog line *n.* A communications line, such as a standard telephone line, that carries continuously varying (analog) signals.

analog modem *n. See* modem.

analog signal generator *n.* A device that generates continuously variable signals and is sometimes used to activate an actuator in a disk drive. *See also* actuator.

analog-to-digital converter *n.* A device that converts a continuously varying (analog) signal, such as sound or voltage, from a monitoring instrument to binary code for use by a computer. See the illustration. *Acronym:* ADC. Also called: A-D converter. *See also* modem. *Compare* digital-to-analog converter.

Analog input — Digital output

Analog-to-digital converter.

analysis *n.* The evaluation of a situation or problem, including review from various aspects or points of view. In computing, analysis commonly involves such features as flow control, error control, and evaluation of efficiency. Often the overall problem is divided into smaller components that can be more easily dealt with. *See also* flow analysis, numerical analysis, systems analysis. *Compare* synthesis.

analysis graphics *n. See* presentation graphics.

Analytical Engine *n.* A mechanical calculating machine designed by British mathematician Charles Babbage in 1833 but never completed. It was the first general-purpose digital computer. *See also* Difference Engine.

anchor *n.* **1.** A format code in a desktop publishing or word processing document that keeps an element in the document, such as a figure or a caption or a label associated with the figure, in a certain position in the document. The anchored object is generally attached to another element in the document such as a piece of text (often a paragraph), a graphic, or a particular place in the document. As text and other objects are added to the document, the anchored object moves relative to the object to which it is anchored or remains stationary. **2.** A tag in an HTML document that defines a section of text, an icon, or other element as a link to another element in the document or to another document or file. *See also* hyperlink.

ancillary equipment *n. See* peripheral.

AND *n.* A logical operation combining the values of two bits (0, 1) or two Boolean values (false, true) that returns a value of 1 (true) if both input values are 1 (true) and returns a 0 (false) otherwise. See the table.

Table A.1   The Possible Combinations with a Boolean AND.

a	*b*	*a AND b*
0	0	0
0	1	0
1	0	0
1	1	1

AND gate *n.* A digital circuit whose output is a value of 1 only when all input values are 1. See the illustration. *See also* truth table.

Input 1 — Input 2 — Output

AND gate.

Andrew File System *n. See* AFS.

angle bracket *n. See* <>.

angstrom *n.* A unit of measure equal to one 10-billionth (10^{-10}) of a meter or one 250-millionth of an inch. Light wavelength, for example, is commonly measured in angstroms. *Abbreviation:* Å.

animated cursors *n.* A Windows 95 and Windows NT feature that allows a series of frames, one after another, to appear at the mouse pointer location instead of a single image, thus producing a short loop of animation. The animated cursors feature is designated by the .ani suffix.

animated GIF *n.* A series of graphic images in GIF format, displayed sequentially in a single location to give the appearance of a moving picture. *See also* GIF.

animation *n.* The illusion of movement created by using a succession of static images. In computer graphics, the images can all be drawn separately, or starting and ending points can be drawn with the intervening images provided by software. *See also* 3-D graphic, surface modeling, tween, wire-frame model.

ANN *n. See* artificial neural network.

annotation *n.* A note or comment attached to some part of a document to provide related information. Some applications support voice annotations or annotations accessible by icons. *See also* comment.

annoybot *n.* A bot on an Internet Relay Chat (IRC) channel or a multiuser dungeon (MUD) that interacts with the user in an obnoxious manner. *See also* bot, IRC, MUD.

anode *n.* In electronics, the positively charged terminal or electrode toward which electrons flow. *Compare* cathode.

anonymity *n.* The ability to send an e-mail message or an article to a newsgroup without one's identity becoming known. Ordinarily, the e-mail address of the sender appears automatically in a message's header, which is created by the client software. To achieve anonymity, a message must be sent through an anonymous remailer— which, however, maintains a record of the sender's identity to enable replies. *See also* anonymous remailer.

anonymous *n.* On the Internet, the standard login name used to obtain access to a public FTP file archive. *See also* anonymous FTP.

anonymous FTP *n.* The ability to access a remote computer system on which one does not have an account, via the Internet's File Transfer Protocol (FTP). Users have restricted access rights with anonymous FTP and usually can only copy files to or from a public directory, often named */pub*, on the remote system. Users can also typically use FTP commands, such as listing files and directories. When using anonymous FTP, the user accesses the remote computer system with an FTP program and generally uses *anonymous* or *ftp* as a logon name. The password is usually the user's e-mail address, although a user can often skip giving a password or give a false e-mail address. In other cases, the password can be the word *anonymous*. Many FTP sites do not permit anonymous FTP access in order to maintain security. Those that do permit anonymous FTP sometimes restrict users to only downloading files for the same reason. *See also* FTP[1] (definition 1), logon, /pub.

anonymous post *n.* A message in a newsgroup or mailing list that cannot be traced to its originator. Generally this is accomplished by using an anonymous server for newsgroup posts or an anonymous remailer for e-mail. *See also* anonymous remailer.

anonymous remailer *n.* An e-mail server that receives incoming messages, replaces the headers that identify the original sources of the messages, and sends the messages to their ultimate destinations. The purpose of an anonymous remailer is to hide the identities of the senders of the e-mail messages.

anonymous server *n.* **1.** The software used by an anonymous remailer. *See also* anonymous remailer. **2.** Software that provides anonymous FTP service. *See also* anonymous FTP.

ANSI *n.* **1.** Acronym for **A**merican **N**ational **S**tandards **I**nstitute. A voluntary, nonprofit organization of business and industry groups formed in 1918 for the development and adoption of trade and communication standards in the United States. ANSI is the American representative of ISO (the International Organization for Standardization). Among its many concerns, ANSI has developed recommendations for the use of programming languages including FORTRAN, C, and COBOL, and various networking technologies. *See also* ANSI C, ANSI.SYS, SCSI. **2.** The Microsoft Windows ANSI character set. This set is includes ISO 8859/x plus additional characters. This set was originally based on an ANSI draft standard. The MS-DOS operating system uses the ANSI character set if ANSI.SYS is installed.

ANSI C *n.* A version of the C programming language standardized by ANSI. *See also* ANSI, K&R C.

ANSI/SPARC *n.* Acronym for **A**merican **N**ational **S**tandards **I**nstitute **S**tandards **P**lanning **a**nd **R**equirements **C**ommittee. The ANSI committee that, in the 1970s, proposed a generalized, three-schema architecture that is used as the foundation for some database management systems.

ANSI.SYS *n.* An installable device driver for MS-DOS computers that uses ANSI commands (escape sequences) to enhance the user's control of the console. *See also* ANSI, driver, escape sequence, install.

ANSI X3.30-1997 *n.* A standard entitled "Representation for Calendar Date and Ordinal Date for Information Interchange" from the American National Standards Institute (ANSI) that covers date formats. Many organizations, including the U.S. federal government, have standardized date formats using this standard to facilitate work on the Year 2000 problem.

answer mode *n.* A setting that allows a modem to answer an incoming call automatically. It is used in all fax machines. *Also called:* auto answer.

answer-only modem *n.* A modem that can receive but not originate calls.

answer/originate modem *n.* A modem that can both send and receive calls—the most common type of modem in use.

antialiasing *n.* A software technique for smoothing the jagged appearance of curved or diagonal lines caused by poor resolution on a display screen. Methods of anti-aliasing include surrounding pixels with intermediate shades and manipulating the size and horizontal alignment of pixels. See the illustration. *See also* dithering. *Compare* aliasing.

Antialiasing. *The image on the right shows the result of antialiasing through the use of higher resolution.*

antiglare or **anti-glare** *adj.* Pertaining to any measure taken to reduce reflections of external light on a monitor screen. The screen may be coated with a chemical (which may reduce its brightness), covered with a polarizing filter, or simply rotated so that external light is not reflected into the user's eye.

anti-replay *n.* An IP packet–level security feature that prevents packets that have been intercepted and changed from being inserted into the data stream. Anti-replay creates a security association between a source and destination computer, with each agreeing on a numbering sequence for transmitted packets. The anti-replay mechanism detects packets tagged with numbers that fall outside the accepted sequence, discards them, sends an error message, and logs the event. The anti-replay protocol is included as part of the IPSec standard. *See also* IPSec.

antistatic device *n.* A device designed to minimize shocks caused by the buildup of static electricity, which can disrupt computer equipment or cause data loss. An antistatic device may take the form of a floor mat, a wristband with a wire attached to the workstation, a spray, a lotion, or other special-purpose device. *See also* static[2], static electricity.

antivirus program *n.* A computer program that scans a computer's memory and mass storage to identify, isolate, and eliminate viruses, and that examines incoming files for viruses as the computer receives them.

anti-worm *n. See* automatic patching, do-gooder virus.

anycasting *n.* Communication between a single sender and the nearest receiver in a group. In IPv6, anycasting enables one host to initiate the updating of routing tables for a group of hosts. *See also* IPv6. *Compare* multicasting, unicast.

any key *n.* Any random key on a computer keyboard. Some programs prompt the user to "press any key" to continue. It does not matter which key the user presses. There is no key on the keyboard called Any.

any-to-any connectivity *n.* The property of an integrated computer network environment where it is possible to share data across multiple protocols, host types, and network topologies.

AOL *n. See* America Online.

AOL Instant Messenger *n. See* AIM.

AOL NetFind *n.* Resident Web-finding tool of America Online (AOL) information service. Searches by keyword and concept. Using Intelligent Concept Extraction (ICE) and Excite technology, this tool finds relationships between words and ideas; for example, between "elderly people" and "senior citizen." *See also* Excite, Intelligent Concept Extraction.

APA *n. See* all points addressable.

Apache *n.* A free open-source HTTP (Web) server introduced in 1995 by the Apache Group as an extension to, and improvement of, the National Center for Supercomputing Applications' earlier HTTPd (version 1.3). Apache is popular on UNIX-based systems, including Linux, and also runs on Windows NT and other operating systems, such as BeOS. Because the server was based on existing code with a series of patches, it became known as "A Patchy server," which led to the official name Apache. *See also* HTTPd.

Apache Group *n.* A non-profit organization of volunteers from around the world that operates and contributes to the Apache HTTP Server Project.

Apache HTTP Server Project *n.* A collaborative effort by the members of the Apache Group to design, develop, and maintain the Apache HTTP (Web) server. *See also* Apache, Apache Group.

Apache project *n. See* Apache HTTP Server Project.

APC *n. See* asynchronous procedure call.

aperture grill *n.* A type of CRT (cathode ray tube) used in computer monitors that uses thin, closely-spaced vertical wires to isolate the individual pixels. The first aperture grill CRT was the Sony Trinitron, but several other manufacturers also produce aperture grill CRTs. *See also* CRT.

APEX *n.* Acronym for **A**ssembly **P**rocess **Ex**hibition and Conference. Exhibition and conference for members of the electronics manufacturing industry. APEX features product exhibits, speeches, technical conferences, and forums on issues that affect the industry.

API *n. See* application programming interface.

APL *n.* Acronym for **A P**rogramming **L**anguage. A high-level language introduced in 1968 for scientific and mathematical applications. APL is a subprogram-based interpreted language that uses a large set of special characters and terse syntax and is available for use on PC-compatible machines. *See also* interpreted language.

APM *n. See* Advanced Power Management.

APNIC *n.* Acronym for **A**sian-**P**acific **N**etwork **I**nformation **C**enter, a nonprofit, voluntary membership organization covering the Asia/Pacific Rim region. APNIC, like its European counterpart RIPE and its American counterpart ARIN, devotes itself to matters related to the Internet, among them such tasks as registering new members, allocating IP addresses, and maintaining database information. *See also* ARIN, RIPE.

app *n. See* application.

APPC *n.* Acronym for **A**dvanced **P**rogram-to-**P**rogram Communication. A specification developed as part of IBM's SNA (Systems Network Architecture) model and designed to enable applications programs running on different computers to communicate and exchange data directly. APPC extends SNA to include minicomputers and PCs.

append *vb.* To place or insert as an attachment by adding data to the end of a file or database or extending a character string. *See also* file, string. *Compare* truncate.

Apple II *n.* The second computer introduced by the Apple Computer Corporation, in April 1977. The Apple II featured 4 K dynamic RAM, expandable to 48 K (with 16 K chips), and used the 6502 microprocessor. The Apple II was the first computer to offer a TV video adapter as an optional alternative to a color computer monitor. It also featured sound and eight expansion slots. *See also* 6502.

Apple Desktop Bus *n.* A serial communications pathway built into Apple Macintosh and Apple IIGS computers. Typically a flexible cord, it enables low-speed input devices, such as a keyboard or mouse, to communicate with the computer. The bus functions like a simple local area network that can connect up to 16 devices, such as light pens, trackballs, and graphics tablets, to the computer. Although there are only two external ports, more than two devices can be linked in a series called a daisy chain. *Acronym:* ADB. *See also* bus, daisy chain[2], device driver, input/output port, serial communication.

AppleDraw *n.* A shareware drawing application for Macintosh computers.

Apple Events *n.* A feature added to Mac OS System 7 that enables one application to send a command, such as save or open, to another application. *See also* Mac OS.

Apple Extended Keyboard *n.* A 105-key keyboard that works with the Macintosh SE, Macintosh II, and Apple IIGS computers. This keyboard marks Apple's first inclusion of function (F) keys, whose absence was long cited as a shortcoming of the Macintosh compared with IBM PCs and compatibles. This feature, along with other layout changes and the addition of new keys and lights, makes the Apple Extended Keyboard quite similar in form to the IBM enhanced keyboard. See the illustration. *See also* enhanced keyboard.

Apple Extended Keyboard.

Apple Filing Protocol *n. See* AFP.

Apple key *n.* A key on Apple keyboards labeled with an outline of the Apple logo. On the Apple Extended Keyboard, this key is the same as the Command key, which functions similarly to the Control key on IBM and compatible keyboards. It is generally used in conjunction with a character key as a shortcut to making menu selections or starting a macro.

Apple Macintosh *n. See* Macintosh.

Apple Newton *n. See* Newton.

AppleScript *n.* A script language developed by Apple Computer, Inc., for Macintosh computers running under the Mac OS to execute commands and automate functions. *See also* script.

AppleShare *n.* A file server software developed by Apple Computer, Inc., that works with the Mac OS and allows one Macintosh computer to share files with another on the same network. *See also* file server, Mac OS.

applet *n.* A program that can be downloaded over the Internet and executed on the recipient's machine. Applets are often written in the Java programming language and run within browser software, and they are typically used to customize or add interactive elements to a Web page.

AppleTalk *n.* An inexpensive local area network developed by Apple Computer, Inc., for Macintosh computers that can be used by Apple and non-Apple computers to communicate and share resources such as printers and file servers. Non-Apple computers must be equipped with AppleTalk hardware and suitable software. The network uses a layered set of protocols similar to the ISO/OSI reference model and transfers information in the form of packets called frames. AppleTalk supports connections to other AppleTalk networks through devices known as bridges, and it supports connections to dissimilar networks through devices called gateways. *See also* bridge, frame (definition 2), gateway.

AppleTalk Phase 2 *n.* The extended AppleTalk Internet model designed by Apple Computer, Inc., that supports multiple zones within a network and extended addressing capacity.

AppleWorks *n.* A suite of productivity applications, formerly known as ClarisWorks, distributed by Apple Computer, Inc., and shipped on the iMac computer. AppleWorks/ClarisWorks is an integrated product that includes support for word processing, spreadsheets, databases, drawing, painting, charting, and the Internet.

appliance *n.* **1.** *See* server appliance. **2.** *See* information appliance. **3.** A device with a single or limited purpose with functionality. This functionality is similar to a simple consumer appliance.

appliance server *n.* **1.** An inexpensive computing device used for specific tasks including Internet connectivity or file-and-print services. The server is usually easy to use but does not possess the capabilities or software of a typical server for general office use. **2.** *See* server appliance.

application *n.* A program designed to assist in the performance of a specific task, such as word processing, accounting, or inventory management. *Compare* utility.

application binary interface *n.* A set of instructions that specifies how an executable file interacts with the hardware and how information is stored. *Acronym:* ABI.*Compare* application programming interface.

application-centric *adj.* Of, pertaining to, or characteristic of an operating system in which a user invokes an application to open or create documents (such as word processing files or spreadsheets). Command-line interfaces and some graphical user interfaces such as the Windows 3.*x* Program Manager are application-centric. *Compare* document-centric.

application developer *n.* An individual who designs and analyzes the appearance and operation of an application program.

application development environment *n.* An integrated suite of programs for use by software developers. Typical components of application development environments include a compiler, file browsing system, debugger, and text editor for use in creating programs.

application development language *n.* A computer language designed for creating applications. The term is usually restricted to refer to languages with specific high-level constructs geared toward record design, form layout, database retrieval and update, and similar tasks. *See also* 4GL, application, application generator.

application development system *n.* A programming environment designed for the development of an application, typically including a text editor, compiler, and linker, and often including a library of common software routines for use in the developed program.

application entity *n. See* AE.

application file *n. See* program file.

Application Foundation Classes *n.* A set of Java class libraries developed by Microsoft that provides developers with user-interface controls and graphics tools for creating and manipulating elements such as text and fonts. The Application Foundation Classes extend the capabilities of Java's Abstract Windowing Toolkit (AWT) and are used to facilitate and expedite the creation of Java applets and applications through the use of prebuilt, customizable development components. *Acronym:* AFC.*See also* Internet Foundation Classes, Java, Java Foundation Classes, Microsoft Foundation Classes.

application gateway *n.* Software running on a machine that is intended to maintain security on a secluded network

yet allow certain traffic to go between the private network and the outside world. *See also* firewall.

application generator *n.* Software for generating source or machine code for running an application based on a description of the desired functionality. Limited in scope, application generators are included with some database programs and use built-in instruction sets to generate program code. *See also* application.

application heap *n.* A block of RAM used by an application to store its code, resources, records, document data, and other information. *See also* heap (definition 1), RAM.

application layer *n.* The highest layer of standards in the Open Systems Interconnection (OSI) reference model. The application layer contains signals that perform useful work for the user, such as file transfer or remote access to a computer, as opposed to lower levels, which control the exchange of data between transmitter and receiver. See the illustration. *See also* ISO/OSI reference model.

ISO/OSI MODEL	
ISO/OSI Layer	**Focus**
Application (highest level)	Program-to-program transfer of information
Presentation	Text formatting and display, code conversion
Session	Establishing, maintaining, and coordinating communication
Transport	Accurate delivery, service quality
Network	Transport routes, message handling and transfer
Data-link	Coding, addressing, and transmitting information
Physical	Hardware connections

Application layer. *The highest layer in the ISO/OSI reference model.*

application notification *n.* An application notification starts an application at a specified time or when a system event occurs. When an application starts as the result of a notification, the system specifies a command-line parameter that identifies the event that has occurred. *See also* Class A IP address, Class B IP address, Class C IP address.

application processor *n.* A processor dedicated to a single application.

application program *n. See* application.

application program interface. *n. See* application programming interface.

application programming interface *n.* A set of routines used by an application program to direct the performance of procedures by the computer's operating system. *Acronym:* API. *Also called:* application program interface.

application server *n.* **1.** A server program on a computer in a distributed network that handles the business logic between users and backend business applications or databases. Application servers also can provide transaction management, failover, and load balancing. An application server is often viewed as part of a three-tier application consisting of a front-end GUI server such as an HTTP server (first tier), an application server (middle tier), and a backend database and transaction server (third tier). *Also called:* appserver. *Compare* HTTP server (definition 1). **2.** Any machine on which an application-server program is running. *Also called:* appserver.

application service provider *n.* A third-party company or organization that hosts applications or services for individuals or business customers. The customer connects to a data center maintained by the application service provider (ASP) through Internet or private lines to access applications that would otherwise need to be housed on the customer's local servers or individual PCs. This arrangement allows the customer to free up disk space that would otherwise be taken by applications, as well as to access the most recent software updates. ASPs deliver solutions ranging from high-end applications to services for small and medium-sized businesses. *Acronym:* ASP.

application shortcut key *n.* A key or combination of keys that when pressed will quickly perform an action within an application that would normally require several user actions, such as menu selections. *Also called:* keyboard shortcut.

application software *n. See* application.

application-specific integrated circuit *n. See* gate array.

application suite *n. See* suite (definition 1).

appserver *n. See* application server.

Aqua *n.* The graphical user interface (GUI) of Macintosh OS X. Aqua was designed to maintain familiarity and a comfort level for users of the earlier Macintosh system while allowing access to newer Macintosh OS X capabilities. The Aqua GUI features updated versions of Macintosh staples such as the Finder alongside new features like the Dock, a new type of organizational tool. *See also* Dock, Macintosh OS X.

arbitration *n.* A set of rules for resolving competing demands for a machine resource by multiple users or processes. *See also* contention.

.arc *n.* The file extension that identifies compressed archive files encoded using the Advanced RISC Computing Specification (ARC) format. *See also* compressed file.

arcade game *n.* **1.** A coin-operated computer game for one or more players that features high-quality screen graphics, sound, and rapid action. **2.** Any computer game designed to mimic the style of a coin-operated arcade game, such as games marketed for the home computer. *See also* computer game.

Archie *n.* An Internet utility for finding files in public archives obtainable by anonymous FTP. The master Archie server at McGill University in Montreal downloads FTP indexes from participating FTP servers, merges them into a master list, and sends updated copies of the master list to other Archie servers each day. Archie is a shortened form of *archive. See also* anonymous FTP, FTP[1] (definition 1). *Compare* Jughead, Veronica.

Archie client *n. See* Archie.

Archie server *n.* On the Internet, a server that contains Archie indexes to the names and addresses of files in public FTP archives. *See also* Archie, FTP[1] (definition 1), server (definition 2).

architecture *n.* **1.** The physical construction or design of a computer system and its components. *See also* cache, CISC, closed architecture, network architecture, open architecture, pipelining, RISC. **2.** The data-handling capacity of a microprocessor. **3.** The design of application software incorporating protocols and the means for expansion and interfacing with other programs.

archive[1] *n.* **1.** A tape or disk containing files copied from another storage device and used as backup storage. **2.** A compressed file. **3.** A file directory on the Internet that is available by File Transfer Protocol (FTP) or an Internet directory established for dissemination of stored files.

archive[2] *vb.* **1.** To copy files onto a tape or disk for long-term storage. **2.** To compress a file.

archive bit *n.* A bit that is associated with a file and is used to indicate whether the file has been backed up. *See also* back up, bit.

archive file *n.* A file that contains a set of files, such as a program with its documentation and example input files, or collected postings from a newsgroup. On UNIX systems, archive files can be created using the tar program; they can then be compressed using compress or gzip. PKZIP under MS-DOS and Windows and StuffIt under Mac OS create archive files that are already compressed. *See also* compress[1], gzip, PKZIP, StuffIt, tar[1].

archive site *n.* A site on the Internet that stores files. The files are usually accessed through one of the following ways: downloaded through anonymous FTP, retrieved through Gopher, or viewed on the World Wide Web. *See also* anonymous FTP, Gopher.

ARCnet *n.* Short for **A**ttached **R**esource **C**omputer **Net**work. A form of token bus network architecture for PC-based LANs developed by Datapoint Corporation. ARCnet relies on a bus or star topology and can support up to 255 nodes. Different versions run at speeds of 1.5 Mbps, 20 Mbps (ARCnet Plus), and 100 Mbps.

ARCnet Plus *n. See* ARCnet.

area chart *n.* A graphical presentation, such as of quarterly sales figures, that uses shading or coloring to emphasize the difference between the line representing one set of data points and the line representing a separate but related set of data points. See the illustration.

Quarterly Sales Summary

Area chart.

area search *n.* In information management, the examination of a group of documents for the purpose of identifying those that are relevant to a particular subject or category.

arg *n. See* argument.

argument *n.* An independent variable, used with an operator or passed to a subprogram that uses the argument to carry out specific operations. *See also* algorithm, operator (definition 1), parameter, subprogram.

ARIN *n.* Acronym for **A**merican **R**egistry for **I**nternet **N**umbers. A nonprofit organization formed to register and administer Internet Protocol (IP) addresses in North and South America. The American Registry for Internet Numbers separates the allocation of IP addresses from the administration of top-level Internet domains, such as .com and .edu. Both of these tasks were previously managed by Network Solutions, Inc., as part of the InterNIC consortium. Its international counterparts are RIPE, in Europe, and APNIC, in Asia and the Pacific Rim. *See also* APNIC, InterNIC, IP address, RIPE.

arithmetic[1] *adj.* Pertaining to the mathematical operations of addition, subtraction, multiplication, and division.

arithmetic[2] *n.* The branch of mathematics dealing with the addition, subtraction, multiplication, and division of real numbers.

arithmetic expression *n.* A series of elements, including data labels and constants as well as numbers, that are joined by arithmetic operators, such as + and −, and can be calculated to produce a value.

arithmetic logic unit *n.* A component of a microprocessor chip used for arithmetic, comparative, and logical functions. *Acronym:* ALU. *See also* gate (definition 1).

arithmetic operation *n.* Any of the standard calculations performed in arithmetic—addition, subtraction, multiplication, or division. The term is also used in reference to negative numbers and absolute values.

arithmetic operator *n.* An operator that performs an arithmetic operation: +, −,*, or /. An arithmetic operator usually takes one or two arguments. *See also* argument, binary[1], logical operator, operator (definition 1), unary.

.arj *n.* The MS-DOS file extension used with archive files created with the ARJ compression program.

ARM *n.* Short for **A**dvanced **RISC** **M**achines. A name for any of a group of small, high-performance 32-bit RISC-based microprocessors licensed to various semiconductor manufacturers by designer ARM Limited. ARM chips are notable for their low cost and efficient use of power. They are used in a wide variety of products, including mobile phones, handheld computers, automotive and embedded solutions, and consumer electronics, including digital cameras and game systems. *See also* StrongARM.

ARP *n.* Acronym for **A**ddress **R**esolution **P**rotocol. A TCP/IP protocol for determining the hardware address (or physical address) of a node on a local area network connected to the Internet, when only the IP address (or logical address) is known. An ARP request is sent to the network, and the node that has the IP address responds with its hardware address. Although ARP technically refers only to finding the hardware address, and RARP (for Reverse ARP) refers to the reverse procedure, ARP is commonly used for both senses. *See also* IP address, TCP/IP.

ARPANET *n.* A large wide area network created in the 1960s by the U.S. Department of Defense Advanced Research Projects Agency (ARPA, renamed DARPA in the 1970s) for the free exchange of information between universities and research organizations, although the military also used this network for communications. In the 1980s MILNET, a separate network, was spun off from ARPANET for use by the military. ARPANET was the network from which the Internet evolved. *See also* ALOHAnet, Internet, MILNET.

ARP request *n.* Short for **A**ddress **R**esolution **P**rotocol **request**. An ARP packet containing the Internet address of a host computer. The receiving computer responds with or passes along the corresponding Ethernet address. *See also* ARP, Ethernet, IP address, packet.

array *n.* In programming, a list of data values, all of the same type, any element of which can be referenced by an expression consisting of the array name followed by an indexing expression. Arrays are part of the fundamentals of data structures, which, in turn, are a major fundamental of computer programming. *See also* array element, index[1], record[1], vector.

array element *n.* A data value in an array.

array processor *n.* A group of interconnected, identical processors operating synchronously, often under the control of a central processor.

arrow key *n.* Any of four keys labeled with arrows pointing up, down, left, and right, used to move the cursor vertically or horizontally on the display screen or, in some programs, to extend the highlight. See the illustration.

Arrow Keys
(when Num Lock is off)

Arrow Keys

Arrow key. *When Num Lock is off, the arrow keys on the number keypad can be used.*

ART *n.* Acronym for **A**daptive **R**esonance **T**heory. First introduced as a theory of human information processing by Stephen Grossberg, ART has evolved into several classes of self-organizing neural networks that use two layers of ideal cases to predict outcome. It is a form of cluster analysis where data is classified or matched to the previously stored pattern it most closely resembles. This data is said to *resonate* with the ideal case layer, which is then updated to reflect the new information. The constant recategorization of input results in a powerful autonomous neural network. *See also* artificial intelligence, cluster analysis, neural network.

article *n.* A message that appears in an Internet newsgroup. *Also called:* post. *See also* newsgroup.

articulation *n.* A series of adjustments applied by a synthesizer to the pitch, volume, and other parameters of an instrument sound to make it more realistic.

artifact *n.* A visible imperfection or distortion in a digital image. Artifacts may be caused by hardware/software limitations or may be a byproduct of compression.

artificial intelligence *n.* The branch of computer science concerned with enabling computers to simulate such aspects of human intelligence as speech recognition, deduction, inference, creative response, the ability to learn from experience, and the ability to make inferences given incomplete information. Two common areas of artificial-intelligence research are expert systems and natural-language processing. *Acronym:* AI. *See also* expert system, natural-language processing.

artificial life *n.* The study of computer systems that simulate some aspects of the behavior of living organisms. Artificial life includes systems in which programs intended to perform some particular task compete for survival and reproduction based on their performance; the offspring can combine pieces of code and undergo random variations, and the programs so modified compete in turn, until an optimal solution is found.

artificial neural network *n.* A form of computer artificial intelligence that uses software based on concepts understood from biological neural networks to adaptively perform a task. *Acronym:* ANN.

AS *n. See* autonomous system.

.asc *n.* A file name extension most commonly indicating that the file contains ASCII text that can be processed by all types of word processing software, including MS-DOS Edit, Windows Notepad, Windows 9x or Windows NT WordPad, and Microsoft Word. Some systems may use this extension to indicate that a file contains image information. *See also* ASCII.

ascender *n.* The portion of a lowercase letter that extends above the main body (x-height) of the letter. See the illustration. *See also* base line, x-height. *Compare* descender.

Ascender.

ascending order *n.* The arrangement of a sequence of items from lowest to highest, such as from 1 to 10 or from A to Z. The rules for determining ascending order in a particular application can be very complicated: capital letters before lowercase letters, extended ASCII characters in ASCII order, and so on.

ascending sort *n.* A sort that results in the arrangement of items in ascending order. *See also* alphanumeric sort, ascending order. *Compare* descending sort.

ascii *n.* In an FTP client program, the command that instructs the FTP server to send or receive files as ASCII text. *See also* ASCII, FTP client. *Compare* binary[2].

ASCII *n.* Acronym for **A**merican **S**tandard **C**ode for **I**nformation **I**nterchange. A coding scheme using 7 or 8 bits that assigns numeric values to up to 256 characters, including letters, numerals, punctuation marks, control characters, and other symbols. ASCII was developed in 1968 to standardize data transmission among disparate hardware and software systems and is built into most minicomputers and all PCs. ASCII is divided into two sets: 128 characters (standard ASCII) and an additional 128 (extended ASCII). *See also* ASCII file, character, character code, control character, extended ASCII, standard ASCII. *Compare* EBCDIC.

ASCII character set *n.* A standard 7-bit code for representing ASCII characters using binary values; code values range from 0 to 127. Most PC-based systems use an 8-bit extended ASCII code, with an extra 128 characters used to represent special symbols, foreign-language characters, and graphic symbols. *See also* ASCII, character, EBCDIC, extended ASCII, standard ASCII.

ASCII EOL value *n.* The sequence of bytes that indicates the end of a line of text. For Windows and MS-DOS systems, this is the hexadecimal sequence 0D 0A or the decimal sequence 13 10. Data files imported from other kinds of computers might not display correctly if the software used is not capable of recognizing these differences and adjusting for them. *See also* ASCII, EOL.

ASCII file *n.* A document file in ASCII format, containing characters, spaces, punctuation, carriage returns, and sometimes tabs and an end-of-file marker, but no formatting information. *Also called:* ASCII file, text file, text-only file. *See also* ASCII, text file. *Compare* binary file.

ASCII transfer *n.* The preferred mode of electronic exchange for text files. In ASCII mode, character conversions to and from the network-standard character set are performed. *See also* ASCII. *Compare* binary transfer.

ASCIIZ string *n.* In programming, an ASCII string terminated by the NULL character (a byte containing the character whose ASCII value is 0). *Also called:* null-terminated string.

ASF *n. See* Advanced Streaming Format.

Asian-Pacific Network Information Center *n. See* APNIC.

ASIC *n.* Acronym for **a**pplication-**s**pecific **i**ntegrated **c**ircuit. *See also* gate array.

ASK *n. See* amplitude shift keying.

ASN *n.* Acronym for **a**utonomous-**s**ystem **n**umber. *See* autonomous system.

ASN.1 *n. See* Abstract Syntax Notation One.

.asp *n.* A file extension that identifies a Web page as an Active Server Page.

ASP *n.* **1.** *See* Active Server Pages. **2.** *See* application service provider.

aspect ratio *n.* In computer displays and graphics, the ratio of the width of an image or image area to its height. An aspect ratio of 2:1, for example, indicates that the image is twice as wide as it is high. The aspect ratio is an important factor in maintaining correct proportions when an image is printed, rescaled, or incorporated into another document.

ASPI *n. See* Advanced SCSI Programming Interface.

ASP.NET *n.* A set of technologies in the Microsoft .NET Framework for building Web applications and XML Web services. ASP.NET pages execute on the server and generate markup (such as HTML, WML, or XML) that is sent to a desktop or mobile browser. ASP.NET pages use a compiled, event-driven programming model that improves performance and enables the separation of application logic and user interface. ASP.NET pages and XML Web services files created using ASP.NET contain server-side (rather than client-side) logic written in Visual Basic .NET, C# .NET, or any .NET-compatible language. Web applications and XML Web services take advantage of the features of the common language runtime, such as type safety, inheritance, language interoperability, versioning, and integrated security.

ASP.NET server control *n.* A server-side component that encapsulates user-interface and related functionality. An ASP.NET server control derives directly or indirectly from the System.Web.UI.Control class. The superset of ASP.NET server controls includes Web server controls, HTML server controls, and mobile controls. The page syntax for an ASP.NET server control includes a runat="server" attribute on the control's tag. See also Web server control, HTML server control, validation server controls.

ASP.NET Web application *n.* An application that processes HTTP requests (Web requests) and executes on top of the ASP.NET runtime. An ASP.NET application can include ASP.NET pages, XML Web services, HTTP handlers, and HTTP modules.

ASR *n.* **1.** *See* automatic system reconfiguration. **2.** Acronym for **A**utomatic **S**peech **R**ecognition. Technology which allows machines to recognize and respond to human voice commands. ASR systems may be used to control a computer or to operate word processing and similar applications. Many ASR products are designed for use by users with disabilities who might have difficulty using a keyboard or mouse.

assemble *vb.* In programming, to convert an assembly language program to equivalent machine language instructions called object code. *See also* assembler, assembly language, linker, object code.

assembler *n.* A program that converts assembly language programs, which are understandable by humans, into executable machine language. *See also* assemble, assembly language, assembly listing, compiler (definition 2), machine code.

assembly *n.* A collection of one or more files that are versioned and deployed as a unit. An assembly is the primary building block of a .NET Framework application. All managed types and resources are contained within an assembly and are marked either as accessible only within the assembly or as accessible from code in other assemblies. Assemblies also play a key role in security. The code access security system uses information about the assembly to determine the set of permissions that code in the assembly is granted.

assembly cache *n.* A machine-wide code cache used for side-by-side storage of assemblies. There are two parts to the cache: the global assembly cache contains assemblies that are explicitly installed to be shared among many applications on the computer; the download cache stores code downloaded from Internet or intranet sites, isolated to the application that triggered the download so that code downloaded on behalf of one application/page does not impact other applications. *See also* global assembly cache.

assembly language *n.* A low-level programming language using abbreviations or mnemonic codes in which each statement corresponds to a single machine instruction. An assembly language is translated to machine language by the assembler and is specific to a given processor. Advantages of using an assembly language include increased execution speed and direct programmer interaction with system hardware. *See also* assembler, compiler, high-level language, low-level language, machine code.

assembly listing *n.* A file created by an assembler that includes the statements of an assembly language program, the machine language generated by the assembler, and a list of the symbols used in the program. *See also* assembler, assembly language.

assertion *n.* A Boolean statement used in a program to test a condition that, if the program is operating correctly, should always evaluate as true; otherwise the program will typically terminate with an appropriate error message. Assertions are used for debugging programs and for documenting how a program should operate.

assignment operator *n.* An operator used to assign a value to a variable or data structure. *See also* assignment statement, operator (definition 1).

assignment statement *n.* A programming language statement used to assign a value to a variable. It usually consists of three elements: an expression to be assigned, an assignment operator (typically a symbol such as = or :=), and a destination variable. On execution of the assignment statement, the expression is evaluated and the resulting value is stored in the specified destination. *See also* assignment operator, expression, variable.

associate *vb.* To inform the operating system that a particular file name extension is linked to a specific application. When a file is opened that has an extension associated with a given application, the operating system automatically starts the application and loads the file.

Association Control Service Element *n.* An Open Systems Interconnection (OSI) method to establish a call between two applications by checking the identities and contexts of the application entities and performing an authentication security check. *Acronym:* ACSE. *See also* ISO/OSI reference model.

Association for Computing Machinery *n.* A membership society founded in 1947 and devoted to the advancement of knowledge and technical proficiency of information processing professionals. *Acronym:* ACM.

Association of C and C++ Users *n.* An organization of people interested in the programming language C and its variants. Members of the association include professional

programmers, manufacturers and vendors of compilers, and nonprofessional programming enthusiasts. *Acronym:* ACCU.

associative storage *n.* A memory-based storage method in which data items are accessed not on the basis of a fixed address or location but by analysis of their content. *Also called:* content-addressed storage.

associativity *n. See* operator associativity.

asterisk *n. See* *.

asymmetrical transmission *n.* A form of transmission used by high-speed modems, typically those that operate at rates of 9600 bps or more, that allows simultaneous incoming and outgoing transmission by dividing a telephone line bandwidth into two channels: one in the range of 300 to 450 bps and one at a speed of 9600 bps or more.

asymmetric digital subscriber line *n. See* ADSL.

asymmetric digital subscriber loop *n. See* ADSL.

asymmetric modem *n.* A modem that transmits data to the telephone network and receives data from the network at different speeds. Most commonly, an asymmetric modem will have a maximum download speed substantially higher than its upload speed. *See also* modem.

asynchronous *adj.* Pertaining to, being, or characteristic of something that is not dependent on timing. For example, asynchronous communications can start and stop at any time instead of having to match the timing governed by a clock.

asynchronous chip *n.* A microprocessor chip that does not need to operate in sync with a system clock. Asynchronous chip operations do not need to be timed to clock speed and draw power only when operations are in progress. This allows asynchronous chips the potential for greater computational speed and lower power consumption than traditional chips.

asynchronous communications *n.* Computer-to-computer communications in which the sending and receiving computers do not rely on timing as a means of determining where transmissions begin and end. *Compare* synchronous communications.

asynchronous device *n.* A device whose internal operations are not synchronized with the timing of any other part of the system.

asynchronous operation *n.* An operation that proceeds independently of any timing mechanism, such as a clock.

For example, two modems communicating asynchronously rely upon each sending the other start and stop signals in order to pace the exchange of information. *Compare* synchronous operation.

asynchronous procedure call *n.* A function call that executes separately from an executing program when a set of enabling conditions exist. After the conditions have been met, the operating system's kernel issues a software interrupt and directs the executing program to execute the call. *Acronym:* APC. *See also* function call.

Asynchronous Protocol Specification *n.* The X.445 standard. *See also* X series.

asynchronous static RAM *n.* A type of static RAM (SRAM) that is not synchronized with the system clock. Like static RAM in general, asynchronous static RAM, or async SRAM, is used in a computer's L2 cache—the special portion of memory used for storing frequently accessed information. Because this type of static RAM is not synchronized with the clock, the CPU must wait for data requested from the L2 cache. Asynchronous static RAM is faster than main memory but not as fast as synchronous burst static RAM or pipeline burst static RAM. *Also called:* async SRAM. *See also* L2 cache, static RAM. *Compare* dynamic RAM, pipeline burst static RAM, synchronous burst static RAM.

Asynchronous Transfer Mode *n. See* ATM (definition 1).

asynchronous transmission *n.* In modem communication, a form of data transmission in which data is sent intermittently, one character at a time, rather than in a steady stream with characters separated by fixed time intervals. Asynchronous transmission relies on the use of a start bit and stop bit(s), in addition to the bits representing the character (and an optional parity bit), to distinguish separate characters. See the illustration.

Asynchronous transmission. *The coding of a typical character sent in asynchronous transmission.*

async SRAM *n. See* asynchronous static RAM.

AT&T System V *n. See* System V.

ATA *n.* Acronym for **A**dvanced **T**echnology **A**ttachment. ANSI group X3T10's official name for the disk drive interface standard for integrating drive controllers directly on disk drives. The original ATA standard is commonly known as Integrated Drive Electronics (IDE). Later ATA versions include ATA-2, ATA-3, and Ultra-ATA. See the table. *Also called:* AT attachment. *See also* direct memory access, EIDE, IDE, logical block addressing, PIO, SMART system.

Table A.2 **ATA Specifications.**

ATA Specification	Also Called	Features
ATA	IDE	Supports PIO (Programmed Input/Output), which transfers data through the CPU. Data transfer rates are 3.3 mbps, 5.2 mbps, and 8.3 mbps.
ATA-2	Fast ATA, Enhanced IDE (EIDE)	Supports faster PIO rates and DMA (direct memory access), which bypasses the CPU. Data transfer rates are between 4 mbps and 16.6 mbps. It also supports LBA (logical block addressing), which allows support for drives larger than 528 MB.
ATA-3		Revision of ATA-2 with SMART (self-monitoring analysis and reporting technology) for greater reliability.
Ultra-ATA	ATA-33, DMA-33, Ultra-DMA, UDMA	Supports DMA burst mode (roughly, all-at-once) data transfers of 33.3 mbps.

ATA hard disk drive card *n.* Expansion card used to control and interface with an ATA hard disk drive. These cards are usually ISA cards. *See also* ATA, ISA.

ATA/IDE hard disk drive *n.* ATA (Advanced Technology Attachment) and IDE (Integrated Drive Electronics—or numerous other interpretations) are one and the same thing: a disk drive implementation designed to integrate the controller onto the drive itself, thereby reducing interface costs and making firmware implementations easier.

ATAPI *n.* The interface used by the IBM PC AT system for accessing CD-ROM devices.

AT Attachment *n. See* ATA.

AT bus *n.* The electric pathway used by IBM AT and compatible computers to connect the motherboard and peripheral devices. The AT bus supports 16 bits of data, whereas the original PC bus supports only 8 bits. *Also called:* expansion bus. *See also* EISA, ISA, Micro Channel Architecture.

aTdHvAaNnKcSe *n. See* TIA.

ATDP *n.* Acronym for **At**tention **D**ial **P**ulse, a command that initiates pulse (as opposed to touch-tone) dialing in Hayes and Hayes-compatible modems. *Compare* ATDT.

ATDT *n.* Acronym for **At**tention **D**ial **T**one, a command that initiates touch-tone (as opposed to pulse) dialing in Hayes and Hayes-compatible modems. *Compare* ATDP.

Athlon *n.* Family of x86-compatible processors introduced by Advanced Micro Devices, Inc. (AMD) in 1999. Athlon, which was code-named AMD-K7, is a successor to the AMD-K6 family. Comparable to upper-end Intel Pentium III processors in performance, Athlon is distinguished by over 22 million transistors; a fully pipelined, superscalar floating-point engine, which enhances performance of graphics and multimedia programs, Internet streaming applications, and games; a 200-MHz system bus; and a 128-KB L1 cache. Although the L2 cache is 512 KB in size, the Athlon can support L2 cache sizes up to 8 MB. The first Athlon releases featured clock speeds of 500 to 650 MHz; 800-MHz and faster versions are now available. Athlon, which runs 32-bit programs, is compatible with most PC operating systems, including Microsoft Windows, Linux, OS/2 Warp, and NetWare. *See also* AMD-K6.

ATM *n.* **1.** Acronym for **A**synchronous **T**ransfer **M**ode. A network technology capable of transmitting data, voice, audio, video, and frame relay traffic in real time. Data, including frame relay data, is broken into packets containing 53 bytes each, which are switched between any two nodes in the system at rates ranging from 1.5 Mbps to 622 Mbps (over fiber optic cable). The basic unit of ATM transmission is known as a cell, a packet consisting of 5 bytes routing information and a 48-byte payload (data). These

cells are transmitted to their destination, where they are reassembled into the original traffic. During transmission, cells from different users may be intermixed asynchronously to maximize utilization of network resources. ATM is defined in the broadband ISDN protocol at the levels corresponding to levels 1 and 2 of the ISO/OSI reference model. It is currently used in LANs (local area networks) involving workstations and personal computers, but it is expected to be adopted by the telephone companies, which will be able to charge customers for the data they transmit rather than for their connect time. *See also* broadband, ISDN, ISO/OSI reference model. **2.** Acronym for **auto**mated **t**eller **m**achine. A special-purpose terminal that bank customers can use to make deposits, obtain cash, and perform other transactions. **3.** *See* Adobe Type Manager.

ATM Adaptation Layer *n.* The ATM layer that mediates between higher-level and lower-level services, converting different types of data (such as audio, video, and data frames) to the 48-byte payloads required by ATM. *Acronym:* AAL. *See also* ATM (definition 1).

ATM Forum *n.* Forum created in 1991 and including more than 750 companies related to communications and computing, as well as government agencies and research groups. The forum aims to promote Asynchronous Transfer Mode for data communication. *See also* ATM (definition 1).

Atomicity, Consistency, Isolation, Durability *n. See* ACID.

atomic operation *n.* An operation considered or guaranteed to be indivisible (by analogy with an atom of matter, once thought to be indivisible). Either the operation is uninterruptible or, if it is aborted, a mechanism is provided that ensures the return of the system to its state prior to initiation of the operation.

atomic transaction *n.* A set of operations that follow an "all or nothing" principle, in which either all of the operations are successfully executed or none of them is executed. Atomic transactions are appropriate for order entry and fulfillment or for money transfers to ensure that information is fully updated. For example, if funds are transferred between accounts on two databases, one account cannot be credited if the other is not debited by the same amount. An atomic transaction would involve both recording the credit in one database and recording the corresponding debit in the other. If any operation in the transaction fails, the transaction is aborted and any information changes are undone. *See also* Distributed Computing Environment, TP monitor, transaction processing.

at sign *n. See* @.

attach *vb.* To include an external document, a file, or an executable program with an e-mail message.

attached document *n.* An ASCII text file or a binary file, such as a document created in a word processing system, that is included with an e-mail message as an attachment. *See also* ASCII, attachment, binary file, BinHex[1], MIME, uuencode.

attached file *n. See* attachment.

attached processor *n.* A secondary processor attached to a computer system, such as a keyboard or video subsystem processor.

Attached Resource Computer Network *n. See* ARCnet.

attachment *n.* A file that accompanies an e-mail message. As transmitted, an attached file is an exact copy of the original file located on the sender's computer. The file can be a document, an executable program, or a compressed file containing more than one item, among other types of files. The file is not part of the actual e-mail message, and it is generally encoded using uuencoding, MIME, or BinHex. Most e-mail programs automatically encode an attached document for transmission with a message. The recipient of the message must have an e-mail program capable of decoding the attached document or use a separate utility to decode it in order to read the document. Some gateways prohibit transmission of files over a certain size. Most e-mail systems permit more than one file to be attached to an e-mail message at a time.

attachment unit interface *n. See* AUI.

attenuation *n.* The weakening of a transmitted signal, such as the distortion of a digital signal or the reduction in amplitude of an electrical signal, as it travels farther from its source. Attenuation is usually measured in decibels and is sometimes desirable, as when signal strength is reduced electronically, for example, by a radio volume control, to prevent overloading.

atto- *prefix* Metric prefix meaning 10^{-18} (one quintillionth).

attract mode *n.* In commercial arcade games, when a coin-operated game is not in use, the screen will rotate through "attract mode." The aim is to both tempt prospective players and demonstrate game play or rules. Also, by constantly changing the screen image, attract mode avoids screen burn in. *See also* arcade game, burn in.

attribute *n.* **1.** In a database record, the name or structure of a field. For example, the files LASTNAME, FIRST-NAME, and PHONE would be attributes of each record in a PHONELIST database. The size of a field or the type of information it contains would also be attributes of a database record. **2.** In screen displays, an element of additional information stored with each character in the video buffer of a video adapter running in character mode. Such attributes control the background and foreground colors of the character, underlining, and blinking. **3.** In markup languages such as SGML and HTML, a name-value pair within a tagged element that modifies certain features of that element. *See also* HTML, SGML.

attribution line *n.* In newsgroups, e-mail, and other Internet-based communications, an identification line added to material quoted from earlier postings. Some mail and messaging software will add an attribution line automatically, which might read something like "News King wrote:" and usually appears immediately before the quoted text.

ATX *n.* A specification for PC motherboard architectures with built-in audio and video capabilities, introduced by Intel in 1995. ATX supports USB and full-length boards in all sockets. *See also* board, motherboard, specification, USB.

audio *adj.* Relating to frequencies within the range of perception by the human ear—from about 15 to 20,000 hertz (cycles per second). *See also* audio response, synthesizer.

audio board *n. See* sound card.

audio card *n. See* sound card.

audiocast *n.* The transmission of an audio signal using IP protocols. *See also* IP.

audio compression *n.* A method of reducing the overall loudness of an audio signal. This is accomplished by limiting the amount of apparent distortion when the signal is played back through a speaker or transmitted through a communications link.

audio output *n. See* audio response.

audio output port *n.* A circuit consisting of a digital-to-analog converter that transforms signals from the computer to audible tones. It is used in conjunction with an amplifier and a speaker. *See also* digital-to-analog converter.

audio response *n.* Any sound produced by a computer; specifically, spoken output produced by a computer in response to some specific type of input. Such output may be generated using a combination of words from a digitized vocabulary or through the synthesis of words from tables of phonemes. *See also* frequency response, phoneme.

audiotex *n.* An application allowing users to send and receive information by telephone. Users typically call an audiotex system and are presented with a series of choices or a series of questions through a voice mail system. When users select choices by pressing the buttons on the phone (rotary dial phones cannot be used for audiotex) or by speaking aloud, a database host responds by sending information to the voice mail system, which then converts the data to a spoken message for the user, or it responds by receiving and storing the information entered by the user. *Also called:* audiotext. *See also* voice mail.

audiotext *n. See* audiotex.

Audio Video Interleaved *n. See* AVI.

audiovisual *adj.* Relating to or being any material that uses a combination of sight and sound to present information.

audit *n.* In reference to computing, an examination of equipment, programs, activities, and procedures to determine how efficiently the overall system is performing, especially in terms of ensuring the integrity and security of data.

auditing *n.* The process an operating system uses to detect and record security-related events, such as an attempt to create, to access, or to delete objects such as files and directories. The records of such events are stored in a file known as a security log, whose contents are available only to those with the proper clearance. *See also* security log.

audit policy *n.* A policy that determines the security events to be reported to the network administrator.

audit trail *n.* In reference to computing, a means of tracing all activities affecting a piece of information, such as a data record, from the time it is entered into a system to the time it is removed. An audit trail makes it possible to document, for example, who made changes to a particular record and when.

AUI *n.* **1.** Acronym for **a**ttachment **u**nit **i**nterface. A 15-pin (DB-15) connector commonly used to connect a net-work interface card to an Ethernet cable. **2.** *See* aural user interface.

AUI cable *n.* Short for **A**ttachment **U**nit **I**nterface **cable**. A transceiver cable used to connect a host adapter within a computer to an Ethernet (10base5 or 10BaseF) network. *See also* 10Base5, 10Base-F, Ethernet (definition 1), transceiver cable.

AUP *n. See* acceptable use policy.

aural user interface *n.* Voice-activated interface that allows users to issue spoken commands to electronic devices. The aural user interface is used with features such as voice recognition for computers and voice-activated dialing for wireless phones. *Acronym:* AUI.

authentication *n.* In a multiuser or network operating system, the process by which the system validates a user's logon information. A user's name and password are compared against an authorized list, and if the system detects a match, access is granted to the extent specified in the permission list for that user. *See also* logon, password, permission, user account, user name.

authentication center *n.* Secure database used to identify and prevent wireless phone fraud. Authentication centers verify whether a wireless phone is registered with a wireless carrier's network.

Authentication Header *n. See* AH.

Authenticode *n.* A security feature of Microsoft Internet Explorer. Authenticode allows vendors of downloadable executable code (plug-ins or ActiveX controls, for example) to attach digital certificates to their products to assure end users that the code is from the original developer and has not been altered. Authenticode lets end users decide for themselves whether to accept or reject software components posted on the Internet before downloading begins. *See also* ActiveX control, Internet Explorer, security.

author¹ *vb.* **1.** To create a product for implementation via computer technology. **2.** To write a computer program. **3.** To assemble multimedia components, such as graphics, text, audio, and animation, in a publication or product, for delivery on a CD-ROM or DVD or on line, to be viewed on a computer. **4.** To create Web pages. Traditionally, to author meant to write a literary work or journalistic piece; in the cyberworld, to write is "to provide content"; thus, to author in the traditional sense is to be a "content provider."

author² *n. See* Web author.

authoring language *n.* A computer language or application development system designed primarily for creating programs, databases, and materials for computer-aided instruction (CAI). A familiar example in relation to microcomputers is PILOT, a language used to create lessons. *See also* CAI, PILOT.

authoring software *n.* A type of computer program used for creating Web pages and other hypertext and multimedia applications. Authoring software provides a way to define relationships between different types of objects, including text, graphics, and sound, and to present them in a desired order. This type of program is sometimes known as authorware, although the latter name is generally associated with a specific product from Macromedia. *Also called:* authoring tool.

authoring system *n.* Application software that enables the operator to create and format a document for a specific kind of computer environment. An authoring system, especially for multimedia work, often consists of several applications within the framework of a single, controlling application. *See also* authoring language.

authority *n.* A DNS server responsible for resolving names and IP addresses of sites and resources on the Internet at a particular level of authority: top-level domain, second-level domain, or subdomain.

authorization *n.* In reference to computing, especially remote computers on a network, the right granted an individual to use the system and the data stored on it. Authorization is typically set up by a system administrator and verified by the computer based on some form of user identification, such as a code number or password. *Also called:* access privileges, permission. *See also* network, system administrator.

authorization code *n. See* password.

autoanswer *n. See* answer mode.

autoassociative *adj.* In data reduction or clustering, autoassociative models use the same set of variables as both predictors and targets. In autoassociative neural networks, each pattern presented serves as both the input and output pattern. Autoassociative networks are typically used for tasks involving pattern completion. *See also* artificial intelligence, cluster analysis, neural networks, operator associativity, pattern recognition.

autoattendant *adj.* A term used to describe a store-and-forward computer system that replaces the traditional switchboard operator, directing telephone calls to their correct extensions or voice mail. Autoattendant systems may implement voice prompts, touch-tone menus, or voice recognition features to send calls to their proper destinations. *Compare* interactive voice response systems.

AutoCorrect *n.* A function in Microsoft Word for Windows that automatically corrects errors and makes other substitutions as soon as a user types text. For example, AutoCorrect can be set up to fix misspellings, such as *teh* for *the*, or to change "straight" (" ") quotation marks to "smart" (" ") quotation marks. The user can select which AutoCorrect features to enable. *See also* smart quotes.

autodial *n.* A feature enabling a modem to open a telephone line and initiate a call by transmitting a stored telephone number as a series of pulses or tones.

AUTOEXEC.BAT *n.* A special-purpose batch file (set of commands) that is automatically carried out by the MS-DOS operating system when the computer is started or restarted. Created by the user or (in later versions of MS-DOS) by the operating system at system installation, the file contains basic startup commands that help configure the system to installed devices and to the user's preferences.

AutoIP *n.* Short for **auto**matic **I**nternet **P**rotocol addressing. A technique used by a device to obtain a valid IP address without a DHCP server or other IP-configuration authority. With AutoIP, a device randomly chooses an IP address from a set of reserved addresses and queries the local network to determine whether another client already is using that address. The device repeats the steps of picking and verifying until an unused address is found. AutoIP, based on an Internet Engineering Task Force (IETF) Internet Draft, is used in Universal Plug and Play (UPnP) networking. *See also* UPnP networking.

autokey *n. See* typematic.

autoload *vb.* To make some type of resource available without it having to be specifically requested. A program, for example, might autoload fonts or files as they are needed. Similarly, a CD-ROM drive might autoload audio discs or automatically start a setup program on a software CD-ROM. *See also* AutoPlay.

autoloader *n.* A device that automatically prepares a diskette, CD, or other storage medium for use.

automagic *adj.* Slang for a process performed in some unexplained (but not inexplicable) way by a computer. An automagic process might either be too complicated to explain (such as a complex spreadsheet calculation), or it might be a complex process made to appear simple to the user (such as clicking on a heading to arrange the items in a list in alphabetical or chronological order). *Compare* black box.

automata theory *n.* **1.** The study of computing processes and their capabilities and limitations; that is, how systems receive and process input and produce output. *See also* cellular automata. **2.** The study of the relationship between behavioral theories and the operation of automated devices.

automated home *n. See* smart home.

automated office *n.* A broad term used to refer to an office where work is carried out with the aid of computers, telecommunications facilities, and other electronic devices.

automated teller machine *n. See* ATM (definition 2).

automatic answering *n. See* answer mode.

automatic data processing *n. See* data processing.

automatic dialing *n. See* auto dial.

automatic error correction *n.* A process that, upon detection of an internal processing or data transmission error, invokes a routine designed to correct the error or retry the operation.

automatic IP addressing *n. See* AutoIP.

automatic patching *n.* A process in which vulnerabilities caused by a destructive computer virus infection are tracked down and corrected by a do-gooder virus or other anti-virus program. Automatic patching may be initiated by the user, or may be done by a virus entering a back door left by a malicious virus, without the consent of the user. *See also* anti-worm, do-gooder virus.

Automatic Private IP Addressing *n.* A feature of Windows XP TCP/IP that automatically configures a unique IP address from the range 169.254.0.1 through 169.254.255.254 and a subnet mask of 255.255.0.0 when the TCP/IP protocol is configured for dynamic addressing and Dynamic Host Configuration Protocol (DHCP) is not available. *Acronym:* APIPA.*See also* DHCP server,

Dynamic Host Configuration Protocol (DHCP), IP address, Transmission Control Protocol/Internet Protocol (TCP/IP).

Automatic Sequence Controlled Calculator *n. See* Mark I.

automatic speech recognition *n. See* ASR (definition 2).

automatic system reconfiguration *n.* Automation of configuration by the system to accommodate some change in either the software or the hardware. *Acronym:* ASR.

Automation *n.* **1.** The implementation of a mechanical or electronic system or tool to automatically complete a task, thereby reducing or eliminating human intervention. **2.** Formerly known as OLE Automation, a Microsoft-designed technology that enables an application to expose objects and their properties for use by other applications. This allows a word processor to display and manipulate a spreadsheet program, for instance. The application that exposes an object for use is called the server; the application that manipulates the object is called the client. Automation can be either local or remote (on a computer elsewhere on a network). It is intended primarily for use by high-level languages such as Microsoft Visual Basic and Microsoft Visual C++. *See also* ActiveX control, OLE.

automonitor *n.* A process or system feature capable of assessing the status of its own internal environment.

autonomous agent *n.* A software or robotic entity that is capable of independent action in open, unpredictable environments. Often referred to as an intelligent agent, or simply agent, autonomous agents complete some kind of automatic process that can communicate with other agents or perform different kinds of directed tasks. Autonomous agents are currently being applied in areas as diverse as computer games, interactive cinema, information retrieval and filtering, user interface design, electronic commerce, auto piloting of vehicles and spacecraft, and industrial process control. *Also called:* intelligent agent. *See also* agent (definition 2).

autonomous-system number *n. See* autonomous system.

autonomous system *n.* A group of routers or networks controlled by a single administrative authority using a common Interior Gateway Protocol (IGP) for routing packets. Each autonomous system is assigned a globally unique number called an autonomous-system number (ASN). *Acronym:* AS. *Also called:* routing domain. *See also* IGP.

Auto PC *n.* An information and entertainment system for use in automobiles. Developed by Microsoft and powered by Microsoft Windows CE (a Windows-compatible operating system designed for embedded applications), Auto PC implements speech-recognition technology to enable individuals to rely on hands-free, spoken commands for tasks such as accessing a contact database (names, addresses, numbers), calling up e-mail or traffic reports, controlling an audio system, or obtaining destination directions. The Auto PC fits into the dashboard, in the space normally occupied by a radio. *See also* voice recognition, Windows.

AutoPlay *n.* A feature in Windows 9x and later that allows it to automatically operate a CD-ROM. When a CD is inserted into a CD-ROM drive, Windows looks for a file called AUTORUN.INF on the CD. If the file is found, Windows will open it and carry out its instructions, which are usually to set up an application from the CD-ROM on the computer's hard disk or to start the application once it has been installed. If an audio CD is inserted into the drive, Windows will automatically launch the CD Player application and play it.

autopolling *n.* The process of periodically determining the status of each device in a set so that the active program can process the events generated by each device, such as whether a mouse button was pressed or whether new data is available at a serial port. This can be contrasted with event-driven processing, in which the operating system alerts a program or routine to the occurrence of an event by means of an interrupt or message rather than having to check each device in turn. *Also called:* polling. *Compare* event-driven processing, interrupt-driven processing.

autorepeat *n. See* typematic.

autoresponder *n.* E-mail utility that replies automatically to an incoming e-mail. Typically, an autoresponder sends a standard, pre-written message confirming the receipt of the original e-mail.

autorestart *n.* A process or system feature that can automatically restart the system after the occurrence of certain type of errors or a power system failure.

AUTORUN.INF *n.* A file that when present on removable media, such as CD-ROMs, triggers the AutoPlay feature in Windows 9x and Windows NT. The file, located in the root directory of the inserted medium, contains information on what action the operating system is to take on the CD-ROM—generally, an instruction to run an installation program.

autosave *n.* A program feature that automatically saves an open file to a disk or other medium at defined intervals or after a certain number of keystrokes to ensure that changes to a document are periodically saved.

autosizing *n.* The ability of a monitor to accept signals at one resolution and display the image at a different resolution. A monitor capable of autosizing maintains the aspect ratio of an image but enlarges or reduces the image to fit in the space available. *See also* monitor, resolution (definition 1).

autostart routine *n.* A process by which a system or device is automatically prepared for operation with the occurrence of powering up, or turning the system on, or some other predetermined event. *See also* AUTOEXEC.BAT, autorestart, boot^2, power up.

autostereogram *n.* A computer-generated image, popularized in books and posters, that looks like an abstract design, but which emerges as a three-dimensional picture when the user looks beyond the image, without trying to focus on the hidden picture itself. Autostereograms in which the overlying design consists of a repetitive pattern are known as Single Image Stereograms (SIS). Those in which the design looks like a random pattern of colored dots are called Single Image Random Dot Stereograms, or SIRDS. *Also called:* stereogram.

autotrace *n.* A drawing program feature that draws lines along the edges of a bitmapped image to convert the image to an object-oriented one. *See also* bitmapped graphics, object-oriented graphics.

AUX *n.* The logical device name reserved by MS-DOS for an auxiliary device, or peripheral. AUX usually refers to a system's first serial port, also known as COM1.

A/UX *n.* A version of the multiuser, multitasking UNIX operating system provided by Apple Computer for various Macintosh computers and based on the AT&T System V, release 2.2 of UNIX with some enhancements. A/UX incorporates a number of Apple features, including support for the Macintosh Toolbox, so that applications can provide users with the graphics-based interface characteristic of that computer. *See also* System V.

auxiliary device *n. See* peripheral.

auxiliary equipment *n. See* peripheral.

auxiliary storage *n.* Any storage medium, such as disk or tape, not directly accessed by a computer's microprocessor, as is random access memory (RAM). In current usage, such media are typically referred to as *storage* or *permanent storage*, and the RAM chips that the microprocessor uses directly for temporary storage are referred to as *memory*.

availability *n.* **1.** In processing, the accessibility of a computer system or resource, such as a printer, in terms of usage or of the percentage of the total amount of time the device is needed. **2.** A measure of the fault tolerance of a computer and its programs. A highly available computer runs 24 hours a day, 7 days a week. *See also* fault tolerance.

available time *n. See* uptime.

avalanche ad *n.* One of several larger formats for online ads developed to replace traditional banner ads on the Internet. Avalanche ads are generally 120 x 800 pixels in size. *See also* skyscraper ad.

avatar *n.* In virtual-reality environments such as certain types of Internet chat rooms, a graphical representation of a user. An avatar typically is a generic picture or animation of a human of either gender, a photograph or caricature of the user, a picture or animation of an animal, or an object chosen by the user to depict his or her virtual-reality "identity." *See* superuser.

.avi *n.* The file extension that identifies an audiovisual interleaved data file in the Microsoft RIFF format.

AVI *n.* Acronym for **A**udio **V**ideo **I**nterleaved. A Windows multimedia file format for sound and moving pictures that uses the Microsoft RIFF (Resource Interchange File Format) specification.

awk *n.* A UNIX-based language designed for file processing applications, awk is a part of the POSIX Command Language and Utilities standard. It is considered a subset of PERL.

AWT *n. See* Abstract Window Toolkit.

axis *n.* In a chart or other two-dimensional system using coordinates, the horizontal line (x-axis) or vertical line (y-axis) that serves as a reference for plotting points. In a three-dimensional coordinate system, a third line (z-axis) is used to represent depth. See the illustration. *See also* Cartesian coordinates.

Axis.

b¹ *adj.* Short for **b**inary.

b² *n.* **1.** Short for **b**it. **2.** Short for **b**aud.

B *n.* Short for **b**yte.

B: or **b:** *n.* **1.** Identifier for a second floppy disk drive on MS-DOS and other operating systems. **2.** Identifier for a single disk drive when used as the secondary drive.

B1FF *n.* Slang for a new online user who is prone to making mistakes in e-mail, newsgroup articles, or chats that show his or her inexperience. Examples of typical mistakes made by B1FFs include sentences ending with multiple exclamation points (!!!!) and messages typed in ALL CAPS. Although it's spelled B-1(one)-F-F, the term is pronounced "bif."

B2B *n.* Short for **b**usiness-**to**-**b**usiness. The electronic exchange of products and services between businesses without the direct involvement of consumers. B2B's effects on business include streamlining purchasing, accounting, and other administrative functions; lowering transaction costs; and simplifying the sale of excess inventory. Related businesses have collaborated on the creation of Internet-based supply-chain networks.

B2C *n.* Short for **b**usiness-**to**-**c**onsumer. The direct electronic exchange of products and services between businesses and consumers. B2C's effects on business include improving the efficiency in delivering goods and services to consumers.

backbone *n.* **1.** A network of communication transmission that carries major traffic between smaller networks. The backbones of the Internet, including communications carriers such as Sprint and MCI, can span thousands of miles using microwave relays and dedicated lines. **2.** The smaller networks (compared with the entire Internet) that perform the bulk of the packet switching of Internet communication. Today these smaller networks still consist of the networks that were originally developed to make up the Internet—the computer networks of the educational and research institutions of the United States—especially NSFnet, the computer network of the National Science Foundation in Oak Ridge, Tennessee. *See also* NSFnet, packet switching. **3.** The wires that carry major communications traffic within a network. In a local area network, a backbone may be a bus. *Also called:* collapsed backbone.

backbone cabal *n.* On the Internet, a term for the group of network administrators responsible for naming the hierarchy of Usenet newsgroups and devising the procedures for creating new newsgroups. The backbone cabal no longer exists.

back door *n.* A means of gaining access to a program or system by bypassing its security controls. Programmers often build back doors into systems under development so that they can fix bugs. If the back door becomes known to anyone other than the programmer, or if it is not removed before the software is released, it becomes a security risk. *Also called:* trapdoor.

back end *n.* **1.** In a client/server application, the part of the program that runs on the server. *See also* client/server architecture. *Compare* front end. **2.** In networking, a server computer or the processing that takes place on it. **3.** The part of a compiler that transforms source code (human-readable program statements) into object code (machine-readable code). *See also* compiler (definition 2), object code, source code.

back-end processor *n.* **1.** A slave processor that performs a specialized task such as providing rapid access to a database, freeing the main processor for other work. Such a task is considered "back-end" because it is subordinate to the computer's main function. **2.** A processor that manipulates data sent to it from another processor; for example, a high-speed graphics processor dedicated to painting images on a video display operates in response to commands passed "back" to it by the main processor. *Compare* coprocessor.

background¹ *adj.* In the context of processes or tasks that are part of an operating system or program, operating without interaction with the user while the user is working on another task. Background processes or tasks are

B

assigned a lower priority in the microprocessor's allotment of time than foreground tasks and generally remain invisible to the user unless the user requests an update or brings the task to the foreground. Generally, only multitasking operating systems are able to support background processing. However, some operating systems that do not support multitasking may be able to perform one or more types of background tasks. For example, in the Apple Macintosh operating system running with multitasking turned off, the Background Printing option can be used to print documents while the user is doing other work. *See also* multitasking. *Compare* foreground[1].

background[2] *n.***1.** The color against which characters and graphics are displayed, such as a white background for black characters. *Compare* foreground[2] (definition 1). **2.** The colors, textures, patterns, and pictures that comprise the surface of the desktop, upon which icons, buttons, menu bars, and toolbars are situated. *See also* wallpaper. **3.** The colors, textures, patterns, and pictures that comprise the surface of a Web page, upon which text, icons, graphics, buttons, and other items are situated. *See also* wallpaper. **4.** The condition of an open but currently inactive window in a windowing environment. *See also* inactive window. *Compare* foreground[2] (definition 2).

background noise *n.* The noise inherent in a line or circuit, independent of the presence of a signal. *See also* noise.

background printing *n.* The process of sending a document to a printer at the same time that the computer is performing one or more other tasks.

background processing *n.* The execution of certain operations by the operating system or a program during momentary lulls in the primary (foreground) task. An example of a background process is a word processor program printing a document during the time that occurs between the user's keystrokes. *See also* background[1].

background program *n.* A program that can run or is running in the background. *See also* background[1].

background task *n. See* background[1].

back-lit or **backlit** *adj.* Having a source of light, such as a lamp or LED behind a (usually translucent) viewing surface, in order to illuminate the surface.

back-lit display or **backlit display** *n.* Something illuminated from behind, rather than by a light source above or to the front.

BackOffice *n.* A suite of software developed by Microsoft that provides certain network services.

Designed to work with Windows NT and Windows 2000, BackOffice includes such services as e-mail (Exchange), intranet capabilities (Site Server), network management (Systems Management Server), and high-end database development (SQL Server), among others.

Back Orifice *n.* A hostile application tool used by hackers to gain control of a remote computer. Back Orifice consists of client and server applications. The client application is used to control a computer running the server application. A target computer is taken over after an executable file, typically delivered by an e-mail attachment or a removable disk, is opened. Back Orifice then copies itself to the Windows System directory and transfers control to the machine running the client application. Back Orifice first appeared in the summer of 1998 and was quickly contained through updated security software. Its name is a play on words for the Microsoft BackOffice suite of servers.

back panel *n.* The panel at the rear of a computer cabinet through which most of the connections to outside power sources and peripherals are made. See the illustration.

Back panel

Back panel.

backplane *n.* A circuit board or framework that supports other circuit boards, devices, and the interconnections among devices, and provides power and data signals to supported devices.

backslash *n. See* \.

Backspace key *n.* **1.** A key that, on IBM and compatible keyboards, moves the cursor to the left, one character at a time, usually erasing each character as it moves. **2.** On Macintosh keyboards, a key (called the Delete key on some Macintosh keyboards) that erases currently selected text or, if no text is selected, erases the character to the left of the insertion point (cursor). See the illustration.

Backspace key.

backtracking *n.* The ability of an expert system to try alternative solutions in an attempt to find an answer. The various alternatives can be viewed as branches on a tree: in backtracking, the program follows one branch and, if it reaches the end without finding what it seeks, backs up and tries another branch.

back up *vb.* **1.** To make a duplicate copy of a program, a disk, or data. *See also* backup. **2.** To return to a previous stable state, such as one in which a database is known to be complete and consistent.

backup *n.* A duplicate copy of a program, a disk, or data, made either for archiving purposes or for safeguarding valuable files from loss should the active copy be damaged or destroyed. A backup is an "insurance" copy. Some application programs automatically make backup copies of data files, maintaining both the current version and the preceding version on disk. *Also called:* backup copy, backup file.

backup and recovery *n.* A strategy available in many database management systems that allows a database to be restored to the latest complete unit of work (transaction) after a software or hardware error has rendered the database unusable. The process starts with the latest backup copy of the database. The transaction log, or change file, for the database is read, and each logged transaction is recovered through the last checkpoint on the log. *See also* backup, checkpoint, log (definition 1).

backup and restore *n.* The process of maintaining backup files and putting them back onto the source medium if necessary.

backup copy *n. See* backup.

backup file *n. See* backup.

Backus-Naur form *n.* A metalanguage used for defining the syntax of formal languages, both for the developer of the language and for the user. A language is defined by a set of statements, in each of which a language element known as a metavariable, written in angle brackets, is defined in terms of actual symbols (called terminals) and other metavariables (including itself if necessary). See the illustration. *Acronym:* BNF. *See also* metalanguage, normal form (definition 2).

```
<number>::=<unsigned number> |
          <sign> <unsigned number>
<unsigned    number>::=<digit>|<digit>
<unsigned
              number>
<digit>::=0|1|2|3|4|5|6|7|8|9
<sign>::=+|-
```
Backus-Naur form.

backward chaining *n.* In expert systems, a form of problem solving that starts with a statement and a set of rules leading to the statement and then works backward, matching the rules with information from a database of facts until the statement can be either verified or proved wrong. *Compare* forward chaining.

bacterium *n.* A type of computer virus that repeatedly replicates itself, eventually taking over the entire system. *See also* virus.

BAD *adj.* Acronym for **b**roken **a**s **d**esigned. Derogatory jargon for a product or device that consistently fails to work.

bad block *n.* A faulty memory location. A bad block is identified by the computer's memory controller in the self-test procedure when the computer is turned on or is rebooted. *See* bad sector.

bad sector *n.* A disk sector that cannot be used for data storage, usually because of media damage or imperfections. Finding, marking, and avoiding bad sectors on a disk is one of the many tasks performed by a computer's operating system. A disk-formatting utility can also find and mark the bad sectors on a disk.

bad track *n.* A track on a hard disk or floppy disk that is identified as containing a faulty sector and consequently is bypassed by the operating system. *See also* bad sector.

.bak *n.* An auxiliary file, created either automatically or upon command, that contains the second-most-recent version of a file and that bears the same file name, with the extension .bak. *See also* backup.

B

balanced line *n.* A transmission line, such as twisted-pair cabling, that contains two conductors capable of carrying equal voltages and currents of opposite polarity and direction.

Balloon Help *n.* An on-screen help feature in the form of a cartoon dialog balloon on the Mac OS developed by Apple Computer, Inc. After activating this feature by clicking on the balloon icon on the toolbar, the user can position the cursor over an icon or other item, and a dialog balloon will appear that describes the function of the item.

balloons *n.* In print layout view or Web layout view, markup balloons show markup elements, such as comments and tracked changes, in the margins of your document. Use these balloons to easily see and respond to reviewers' changes and comments.

ball printer *n.* An impact printer that uses a small ball-shaped print head that bears fully formed characters in raised relief on its surface. The printer rotates and tilts the ball to line up characters and then strikes the ball against a ribbon. This method was used in the IBM Selectric typewriter.

band *n.* **1.** In printing graphics, a rectangular portion of a graphic sent by the computer to a printer. The technique of dividing a graphic into bands prevents a printer from having to reconstruct an entire image in memory before printing it. **2.** In communications, a contiguous range of frequencies used for a particular purpose, such as radio or television broadcasts.

bandpass filter *n.* An electronic circuit that passes signals that are within a certain frequency range (band) but blocks or attenuates signals above or below the band. *See also* attenuation. *Compare* highpass filter, lowpass filter.

bandwidth *n.* **1.** The difference between the highest and lowest frequencies that an analog communications system can pass as measured in Hertz (Hz) or cycles per second. For example, a telephone accommodates a bandwidth of 3000 Hz: the difference between the lowest (300 Hz) and highest (3300 Hz) frequencies it can carry. **2.** The data transfer capacity, or speed of transmission, of a digital communications system as measured in bits per second (bps).

bandwidth allocation *n. See* bandwidth reservation.

bandwidth brokerage *n. See* bandwidth trading.

bandwidth exchange *n. See* bandwidth trading.

bandwidth management *n.* The analysis and control of traffic on WAN (wide area network) and Internet links to prioritize bandwidth and improve quality of service (QoS). *See also* quality of service (definition 2), traffic shaping.

bandwidth on demand *n.* In telecommunications, the capability of increasing throughput, in increments, as required by the channel to be serviced. *See also* bandwidth, channel (definition 2), throughput.

bandwidth reservation *n.* Process of assigning in advance a percentage of bandwidth to each user or application served by a network. Bandwidth reservation optimizes the use of available traffic by prioritizing time-critical packets. *Also called:* bandwidth allocation, custom queuing. *See also* bandwidth management, traffic shaping.

bandwidth shaping *n. See* traffic shaping.

bandwidth test *n.* A benchmark test that determines the speed of a network connection. Bandwidth tests estimate the downstream and upstream speeds by sending a series of packets over the network and measuring how many packets are received in a given amount of time. *Also called:* throughput test. *See also* benchmark[1], throughput (definition 1).

bandwidth trading *n.* The exchange of excess bandwidth capacity. Although considered a possible commodity market, bandwidth trading currently lacks standardized contracts and instantaneous provisioning needed to simplify the trading process. *Also called:* bandwidth brokerage, bandwidth exchange.

bang *n.* The pronunciation for an exclamation point, particularly when the exclamation point is used in a file name or in a path on UNIX systems. *See also* bang path.

bang path *n.* Slang for an older form of e-mail address used in UUCP (UNIX-to-UNIX copy). A bang address supplies the path that the message needs to take to reach its destination, including the name of each host through which the message is to be passed. Exclamation points called "bangs" separate the elements of the e-mail address, such as the user account and host names. The address name!location, where "name" is the user account and "location" is the host name, would be spoken as "name bang location."

bank *n.***1.** Any group of similar electrical devices connected together for use as a single device. For example, transistors may be connected in a row/column array inside a chip to form memory, or several memory chips may be connected together to form a memory module such as a SIMM. *See also* SIMM. **2.** A section of memory, usually of a size convenient for a CPU to address. For example, an 8-bit processor can address 65,536 bytes of memory; therefore, a 64-kilobyte (64-KB) memory bank is the largest that the processor can address at once. To address another 64-KB bank of memory requires circuitry that fools the CPU into looking at a separate block of memory. *See also* bank switching, page (definition 2).

bank switching *n.* A method of expanding a computer's available random access memory (RAM) by switching between banks of RAM chips that share a range of memory addresses, which is set aside before switching begins. Only one bank is directly accessible at a time; when a bank is not active, it retains whatever is stored in it. Before another bank can be used, the operating system, driver, or program must explicitly issue a command to the hardware to make the switch. Because switching between banks takes time, memory-intensive operations take longer with bank-switched memory than with main memory. Bank-switched memory typically takes the form of an expansion card that plugs into a slot on the motherboard.

banner *n.* A section of a Web page containing an advertisement that is usually an inch or less tall and spans the width of the Web page. The banner contains a link to the advertiser's Web site. *See also* Web page, Web site.

banner page *n.***1.** The title page that may be added to printouts by most print spoolers. Such a page typically incorporates account ID information, job length, and print spooler information, and is used primarily to separate one print job from another. *See also* print spooler. **2.** In software, an initial screen used to identify a product and credit its producers.

bar chart *n.* A type of graphic in which data items are shown as rectangular bars. The bars may be displayed either vertically or horizontally and may be distinguished from one another by color or by some type of shading or pattern. Positive and negative values may be shown in relation to a zero baseline. Two types of bar charts are common: a standard bar chart, in which each value is represented by a separate bar, and a stacked bar chart, in which several data points are "stacked" to produce a single bar. See the illustration. *Also called:* bar graph.

Quarterly Sales Summary

Vertical bar chart

Stacked bar chart

Bar chart. *Two common types of bar chart.*

bar code *n.* The special identification code printed as a set of vertical bars of differing widths on books, grocery products, and other merchandise. Used for rapid, error-free input in such facilities as libraries, hospitals, and grocery stores, bar codes represent binary information that can be read by an optical scanner. The coding can include numbers, letters, or a combination of the two; some codes include built-in error checking and can be read in either direction.

bar code reader *n. See* bar code scanner.

bar code scanner *n.* An optical device that uses a laser beam to read and interpret bar codes, such as the Universal Product Codes found on grocery products and other retail items. *See also* bar code, Universal Product Code.

bare board *n.* A circuit board with no chips on it; most commonly, a memory board not populated with memory chips.

bare bones[1] *adj.* Purely functional; stripped or otherwise clean of features. Bare bones applications provide only the most basic functions necessary to perform a given task. By

B

the same token, a bare bones computer provides a minimal amount of hardware or is sold at retail with no peripherals and just the operating system (and no other software).

bare bones[2] *n.* **1.** An application that provides only the most basic functions necessary to perform a given task. **2.** A computer consisting only of motherboard (equipped with CPU and RAM), cabinet, power supply, floppy disk drive, and keyboard, to which the user must add hard disk, video adapter, monitor, and any other peripherals. *See also* motherboard, peripheral.

bar graph *n. See* bar chart.

base *n.* **1.** In mathematics, a number that is raised to the power specified by an exponent. For example, in $2^3 = 2 \times 2 \times 2 = 8$, the base is 2. **2.** In mathematics, the number of digits in a particular numbering system. With microcomputers, four numbering systems are commonly used or referred to—binary, octal, decimal, and hexadecimal—and each is based on a different number of digits. The binary, or base-2, numbering system, which is used to discuss the states of a computer's logic, has two digits, 0 and 1. Octal, or base-8, has eight digits, 0 through 7. The familiar decimal, or base-10, numbering system has ten digits, 0 through 9. Hexadecimal, or base-16, has sixteen digits, 0 through 9 and A through F. When numbers are written in a particular base, the base is often subscripted and enclosed in parentheses after the number, as in $24AE(16) = 9,390$. *Also called:* radix. *See also* binary[1], decimal, hexadecimal, octal. **3.** One of three terminals (emitter, base, and collector) in a bipolar transistor. The current through the base controls the current between the emitter and the collector. *See also* transistor. **4.** The insulating foundation of a printed circuit board. *See also* circuit board.

base 10 *adj. See* decimal.

base 16 *adj. See* hexadecimal.

base 2 *adj. See* binary[1].

base 8 *adj. See* octal.

base address *n.* The part of a two-part memory address that remains constant and provides a reference point from which the location of a byte of data can be calculated. A base address is accompanied by an offset value that is added to the base to determine the exact location (the absolute address) of the information. The concept is similar to a street address system. For example, "2010 Main Street" consists of a base (the 2000 block of Main Street) plus an offset (10 from the beginning of the block). Base addresses are known as segment addresses in IBM PCs

and compatibles; data in these computers is identified by its position as a relative offset from the start of the segment. *See also* absolute address, offset, relative address, segment.

baseband *adj.* Of or relating to communications systems in which the medium of transmission (such as a wire or fiber-optic cable) carries a single message at a time in digital form. Baseband communication is found in local area networks such as Ethernet and Token Ring. *See also* Ethernet, fiber optics, Token Ring network. *Compare* broadband.

baseband network *n.* A type of local area network in which messages travel in digital form on a single transmission channel between machines connected by coaxial cable or twisted-pair wiring. Machines on a baseband network transmit only when the channel is not busy, although a technique called *time-division multiplexing* can enable channel sharing. Each message on a baseband network travels as a packet that contains information about the source and destination machines as well as message data. Baseband networks operate over short distances at speeds ranging from about 50 kilobits per second (50 Kbps) to 16 megabits per second (16 Mbps). Receiving, verifying, and converting a message, however, add considerably to the actual time, reducing throughput. The maximum recommended distance for such a network is about 2 miles, or considerably less if the network is heavily used. *See also* coaxial cable, multiplexing, packet (definition 2), throughput, time-division multiplexing, twisted-pair cable. *Compare* broadband network.

base class *n.* In C++, a class from which other classes have been or can be derived by inheritance. *See also* class, derived class, inheritance, object-oriented programming.

base line or **baseline** *n.* In the printing and display of characters on the screen, an imaginary horizontal line with which the base of each character, excluding descenders, is aligned. See the illustration. *See also* ascender, descender, font.

Descender   Base line

Base line.

base memory *n. See* conventional memory.

base RAM *n. See* conventional memory.

B

base station *n.* Transmission tower for wireless phone signals. Commonly known as cell towers, base stations also encompass the radio antennas and electronics that handle wireless calls. Base stations relay conversations into and out of the wired phone network and between wireless phones. Each base station covers a limited area known as a cell.

base style *n.* The underlying or original style on which other styles in a document are dependent. When you change a formatting element of the base style in a document, all other styles that originate from the base style will also reflect the change.

Basic or **BASIC** *n.* Acronym for **B**eginner's **A**ll-purpose **S**ymbolic **I**nstruction **C**ode, a high-level programming language developed in the mid-1960s by John Kemeny and Thomas Kurtz at Dartmouth College. It is widely considered one of the easiest programming languages to learn. *See also* True BASIC, Visual BASIC.

Basic Rate Interface *n. See* BRI.

Basic Service Set *n.* The communicating stations, or nodes, on a wireless LAN. *See also* wireless LAN,

bastion host *n.* A computer which provides security by serving as a gateway between an internal network and external systems. All outside traffic attempting to connect to the internal network is routed through the bastion host, which defends against potential attacks by intercepting and screening incoming packets. The bastion host may be part of a larger security system providing multiple layers of protection.

.bat *n.* The file extension that identifies a batch program file. In MS-DOS, .bat files are executable files that contain calls to other program files. *See also* batch file.

batch *n.* A group of documents or data records that are processed as a unit. *See also* batch job, batch processing.

batch file *n.* An ASCII text file containing a sequence of operating-system commands, possibly including parameters and operators supported by the batch command language. When the user types a batch file name at the command prompt, the commands are processed sequentially. *Also called:* batch program. *See also* AUTOEXEC.BAT, .bat.

batch file transmission *n.* The transmission of multiple files as the result of a single command. *Acronym:* BFT.

batch job *n.* A program or set of commands that runs without user interaction. *See also* batch processing.

batch processing *n.* **1.** Execution of a batch file. *See also* batch file. **2.** The practice of acquiring programs and data sets from users, running them one or a few at a time, and then providing the results to the users. **3.** The practice of storing transactions for a period of time before they are posted to a master file, typically in a separate operation undertaken at night. *Compare* transaction processing.

batch program *n.* A program that executes without interacting with the user. *See also* batch file. *Compare* interactive program.

batch system *n.* A system that processes data in discrete groups of previously scheduled operations rather than interactively or in real time.

batch total *n.* A total calculated for an element common to a group (batch) of records, used as a control to verify that all information is accounted for and has been entered correctly. For example, the total of a day's sales can be used as a batch total to verify the records of all individual sales.

battery *n.* Two or more cells in a container that produce an electrical current when two electrodes within the container touch an electrolyte. In personal computers, batteries are used as an auxiliary source of power when the main power is shut off, as a power source for laptop and notebook computers (rechargeable batteries, such as nickel cadmium, nickel metal hydride, and lithium ion, are used), and as a method to keep the internal clock and the circuitry responsible for the part of RAM that stores important system information always powered up. *See also* lead ion battery, lithium ion battery, nickel cadmium battery, nickel metal hydride battery, RAM.

battery backup *n.* **1.** A battery-operated power supply used as an auxiliary source of electricity in the event of a power failure. **2.** Any use of a battery to keep a circuit running when the main power is shut off, such as powering a computer's clock/calendar and the special RAM that stores important system information between sessions. *See also* UPS.

battery meter *n.* A device used to measure the current (capacity) of an electrical cell.

baud *n.* One signal change per second, a measure of data transmission speed. Named after the French engineer and telegrapher Jean-Maurice-Emile Baudot and originally used to measure the transmission speed of telegraph equipment, the term now most commonly refers to the data transmission speed of a modem. *See also* baud rate.

B

Baudot code *n.* A 5-bit coding scheme used principally for telex transmissions, originally developed for telegraphy by the French engineer and telegrapher Jean-Maurice-Emile Baudot. Sometimes it is equated, although inaccurately, with the International Alphabet Number 2 proposed by the Comité Consultatif Internationale Télégraphique et Téléphonique (CCITT).

baud rate *n.* The speed at which a modem can transmit data. The baud rate is the number of events, or signal changes, that occur in one second—not the number of bits per second (bps) transmitted. In high-speed digital communications, one event can actually encode more than one bit, and modems are more accurately described in terms of bits per second than baud rate. For example, a so-called 9600-baud modem actually operates at 2400 baud but transmits 9600 bits per second by encoding 4 bits per event (2400 x 4 = 9600) and thus is a 9600-bps modem. *Compare* bit rate, transfer rate.

bay *n.* A shelf or opening used for the installation of electronic equipment—for example, the space reserved for additional disk drives, CD-ROM drives, or other equipment in the cabinets of microcomputers. *See also* drive bay.

bayonet-Neill-Concelman *n. See* BNC.

BBL *n.* Acronym for **b**e **b**ack **l**ater. An expression used commonly on live chat services on the Internet and online information services to indicate that a participant is temporarily leaving the discussion forum but intends to return at a later time. *See also* chat[1] (definition 1).

BBS *n.* **1.** Acronym for **b**ulletin **b**oard **s**ystem. A computer system equipped with one or more modems or other means of network access that serves as an information and message-passing center for remote users. Often BBSs are focused on special interests, such as science fiction, movies, Windows software, or Macintosh systems, and can have free or fee-based access, or a combination. Users dial into a BBS with their modems and post messages to other BBS users in special areas devoted to a particular topic, in a manner reminiscent of the posting of notes on a cork bulletin board. Many BBSs also allow users to chat online with other users, send e-mail, download and upload files that include freeware and shareware software, and access the Internet. Many software and hardware companies run proprietary BBSs for customers that include sales information, technical support, and software upgrades and patches. **2.** Acronym for **b**e **b**ack **s**oon. A shorthand expression often seen in Internet discussion groups by a participant leaving the group who wishes to bid a temporary farewell to the rest of the group.

bcc *n.* Acronym for **b**lind **c**ourtesy **c**opy. A feature of e-mail programs that allows a user to send a copy of an e-mail message to a recipient without notifying other recipients that this was done. Generally, the recipient's address is entered into a field called "bcc:" in the mail header. *Also called:* blind carbon copy. *See also* e-mail[1] (definition 1), header (definition 1). *Compare* cc.

BCD *n. See* binary-coded decimal.

bCentral *n.* A Web site for small businesses that provides online subscription services for customer management, financial management, and e-commerce. BCentral is part of the Microsoft .NET initiative. *See also* MSN, .NET.

B channel *n.* Short for **b**earer **channel**. One of the 64-Kbps communications channels that carry data on an ISDN circuit. A BRI (Basic Rate Interface) ISDN line has two B channels and one D (data) channel. A PRI (Primary Rate Interface) ISDN line has 23 B channels (in North America) or 30 B channels (in Europe) and one D channel. *See also* BRI, D channel, ISDN.

BCNF *n.* Acronym for **B**oyce-**C**odd **n**ormal **f**orm. *See* normal form (definition 1).

beacon *n.* On an FDDI network, a special frame generated and passed along when a node detects a problem. *See also* frame (definition 2).

beam *vb.* To transfer information from one device to another through an infrared wireless connection. The term typically refers to data sharing using handheld devices such as Palm organizers, Pocket PCs, mobile phones, and pagers.

bearer channel *n. See* B channel.

BeBox *n.* A high-performance multiprocessor computer (RISC-based PowerPC) made by Be, Inc., and loaded with Be's operating system, BeOS. Be discontinued production of the BeBox in January 1997 in order to focus on software (BeOS) development. *See also* BeOS, PowerPC, RISC.

BEDO DRAM *n.* Acronym for **B**urst **E**xtended **D**ata **O**ut **D**ynamic **RAM**. A type of EDO (extended-data-out) dynamic RAM (DRAM) that handles memory transfers in bursts of four items in order to speed the process of returning data to a computer's CPU. BEDO DRAM takes advantage of the fact that memory requests typically refer to sequential addresses. BEDO DRAM does not function well with bus speeds above 66 MHz. However, once it has accessed the first memory address, it can process the remaining three items in the burst at 10 ns (nanoseconds) each. *Also called:* BEDO RAM. *See also* dynamic RAM, EDO DRAM.

Beginner's All-purpose Symbolic Instruction Code *n. See* Basic.

beginning-of-file *n.* **1.** A code placed by a program before the first byte in a file, used by the computer's operating system to keep track of locations within a file with respect to the first byte (character) in it. **2.** The starting location of a file on a disk relative to the first storage location on the disk. A data directory or catalog contains this location. *Acronym:* BOF. *Compare* end-of-file.

Bell communications standards *n.* A series of data transmission standards originated by AT&T during the late 1970s and early 1980s that, through wide acceptance in North America, became de facto standards for modems. Bell 103, now mostly obsolete, governed transmission at 300 bits per second (bps) with full-duplex, asynchronous communications over dial-up telephone lines using frequency-shift keying (FSK). Bell 212A governed modem operations at 1200 bps with full-duplex, asynchronous communications over dial-up telephone lines using phase-shift keying (PSK). An international set of transmission standards, known as the CCITT recommendations, has become generally accepted as the primary source of standardization, especially for communications at speeds greater than 1200 bps. *See also* CCITT V series, FSK, phase-shift keying.

Bell-compatible modem *n.* A modem that operates according to the Bell communications standards. *See also* Bell communications standards.

Bellman-Ford distance-vector routing algorithm *n.* An algorithm that helps to determine the shortest route between two nodes on a network. The Routing Information Protocol (RIP) is based on the Bellman-Ford distance-vector routing algorithm. *See also* RIP (definition 2).

bells and whistles *n.* Attractive features added to hardware or software beyond basic functionality, comparable to accessories such as electric door locks and air conditioning added to an automobile. Products, especially com-

puter systems, without such adornments are sometimes called "plain vanilla."

benchmark[1] *n.* A test used to measure hardware or software performance. Benchmarks for hardware use programs that test the capabilities of the equipment—for example, the speed at which a CPU can execute instructions or handle floating-point numbers. Benchmarks for software determine the efficiency, accuracy, or speed of a program in performing a particular task, such as recalculating data in a spreadsheet. The same data is used with each program tested, so the resulting scores can be compared to see which programs perform well and in what areas. The design of fair benchmarks is something of an art, because various combinations of hardware and software can exhibit widely variable performance under different conditions. Often, after a benchmark has become a standard, developers try to optimize a product to run that benchmark faster than similar products run it in order to enhance sales. *See also* sieve of Eratosthenes.

benchmark[2] *vb.* To measure the performance of hardware or software.

benign virus *n.* A program that exhibits properties of a virus, such as self-replication, but does not otherwise do harm to the computer systems that it infects.

BeOS *n.* An operating system developed by Be, Inc., that runs on PowerPC systems and, until they were discontinued, the company's original BeBox computers. Designed as a "media OS," the BeOS was created to support the large file sizes and high-performance processing demands of digital media and the Internet. It is an object-oriented, multithreaded operating system and can be run on symmetric multiprocessing systems containing two or more processors. Like many other operating systems, the BeOS provides preemptive multitasking, virtual memory, and memory protection. It also provides high-performance input/output capabilities, a 64-bit file system that can support terabyte-sized files, and a number of Internet-related features including built-in mail and Web services. *See also* BeBox.

Beowulf *n.* Name for a class of virtual supercomputer created by linking numerous PCs through network connections into a single high-performance unit based on inexpensive, x86-based hardware and publicly available software, such as some versions of UNIX. This clustering technique can provide performance comparable to a traditional supercomputer at approximately 10 percent of the cost. The first Beowulf cluster was assembled at NASA's Goddard Space Flight Center in 1994. The origin of the name comes from Beowulf, the hero who fought and killed the monster Grendel in an eighth-century Old English saga.

Beowulf-class computing *n. See* Beowulf.

Berkeley Internet Name Domain *n. See* BIND.

Berkeley Sockets API *n. See* sockets API.

Bernoulli box *n.* A removable floppy disk drive for personal computers that uses a nonvolatile cartridge and has high storage capacity. Named after Daniel Bernoulli, an eighteenth-century physicist who first demonstrated the principle of aerodynamic lift, the Bernoulli box uses high speed to bend the flexible disk close to the read/write head in the disk drive. *See also* read/write head.

Bernoulli distribution *n. See* binomial distribution.

Bernoulli process *n.* A mathematical process involving the Bernoulli trial, a repetition of an experiment in which there are only two possible outcomes, such as success and failure. This process is used mostly in statistical analysis. *See also* Bernoulli sampling process, binomial distribution.

Bernoulli sampling process *n.* In statistics, a sequence of *n* independent and identical trials of a random experiment, with each trial having one of two possible outcomes. *See also* Bernoulli process, binomial distribution.

best of breed *adj.* A term used to describe a product that is the best in a particular category of products.

beta[1] *adj.* Of or relating to software or hardware that is a beta. *See also* beta[2]. *Compare* alpha[1].

beta[2] *n.* A new software or hardware product, or one that is being updated, that is ready to be released to users for beta testing in real-world situations. Usually betas have most or all of the features and functionality implemented that the finished product is to have. *See also* beta test. *Compare* alpha[2].

beta site *n.* An individual or an organization that tests software before it is released to the public. The company producing the software usually selects these beta sites from a pool of established customers or volunteers. Most beta sites perform this service free of charge, often to get a

first look at the software and to receive free copies of the software once it is released to the public.

beta test *n.* A test of software that is still under development, accomplished by having people actually use the software. In a beta test, a software product is sent to selected potential customers and influential end users (known as beta sites), who test its functionality and report any operational or utilization errors (bugs) found. The beta test is usually one of the last steps a software developer takes before releasing the product to market; however, if the beta sites indicate that the software has operational difficulties or an extraordinary number of bugs, the developer may conduct more beta tests before the software is released to customers.

betweening *n. See* tween.

bezel *n.* In arcade games, the bezel refers to the glass located around the monitor. It is often silk-screened with artwork relating to the game. *See also* arcade game.

Bézier curve *n.* A curve that is calculated mathematically to connect separate points into smooth, free-form curves and surfaces of the type needed for illustration programs and CAD models. Bézier curves need only a few points to define a large number of shapes—hence their usefulness over other mathematical methods for approximating a given shape. See the illustration. *See also* CAD.

Bézier curve.

BFT *n. See* batch file transmission, binary file transfer.

BGP *n. See* Border Gateway Protocol.

bias *n.* **1.** A uniform or systematic deviation from a point of reference. **2.** In mathematics, an indication of the amount by which the average of a group of values deviates from a reference value. **3.** In electronics, a voltage applied to a transistor or other electronic device to establish a reference level for its operation. **4.** In communications, a type of distortion in the length of transmitted bits, caused by a lag that occurs as voltage builds up or falls off each time the signal changes from 0 to 1 or vice versa.

bidirectional *adj.* Operating in two directions. A bidirectional printer can print from left to right and from right to left; a bidirectional bus can transfer signals in both directions between two devices.

bidirectional parallel port *n.* An interface that supports two-way parallel communication between a device, such as a printer, and a computer. *See also* interface (definition 3), parallel port.

bidirectional printing *n.* The ability of an impact or ink-jet printer to print from left to right and from right to left. Bidirectional printing improves speed substantially because no time is wasted returning the print head to the beginning of the next line, but it may lower print quality.

bi-endian *adj.* Of, pertaining to, or characteristic of processors and other chips that can be switched to work in big endian or little endian mode. The PowerPC chip has this ability, which allows it to run the little endian Windows NT or the big endian MacOS/PPC. *See also* big endian, little endian, PowerPC.

BIFF *n.* Short for **B**inary **I**nterchange **F**ile **F**ormat. The native file format used by Microsoft Excel.

biff *n.* **1.** A BSD utility that issues a signal when new mail has arrived. Biff was named after a University of California graduate student's dog who had a habit of barking at the mailman at the time the utility was developed. **2.** *See* B1FF.

biff *vb.* To provide notification of new (incoming) e-mail.

bifurcation *n.* A split that results in two possible outcomes, such as 1 and 0 or on and off.

Big 5 *n.* Traditional Chinese encoding.

Big Blue *n.* The International Business Machines (IBM) Corporation. This nickname comes from the corporate color used on IBM's early mainframes and still used in the company logo.

big endian *adj.* Storing numbers in such a way that the most significant byte is placed first. For example, given the hexadecimal number A02B, the big endian method would cause the number to be stored as A02B, and the little endian method would cause the number to be stored as

2BA0. The big endian method is used by Motorola microprocessors; Intel microprocessors use the little endian method. The term *big endian* is derived from Jonathan Swift's *Gulliver's Travels*, in which the Big-Endians were a group of people who opposed the emperor's decree that eggs should be broken at the small end before they were eaten. *Compare* little endian.

bigint data type *n.* In an Access project, a data type of 8 bytes (64 bits) that stores whole numbers in the range of -2^{63} ($-9,223,372,036,854,775,808$) through $2^{63}-1$ ($9,223,372,036,854,775,807$).

big iron *n.* One or more large, fast, and expensive computers, such as a Cray supercomputer or a room-filling mainframe system.

big red switch *n.* The power on/off switch of a computer, thought of as a kind of interrupt or last resort. On the original IBM PC and many other computers, it was indeed big and red. Using the switch is an interrupt of last resort because it deletes all the data in RAM and can also damage the hard drive. *Acronym:* BRS.

billboard *n.* A primitive inserted into a 3-D scene that is oriented so that one face is toward the viewer. A texture, usually an animated sprite, is applied to the billboard to give the appearance of a 3-D object in the scene.

billion *n.* **1.** In American usage (as is usual with microcomputers), a thousand million, or 10^9. Computer terminology uses the prefixes *giga-* for 1 billion and *nano-* for 1 billionth. **2.** In British usage, a million million, or 10^{12}, which is a *trillion* in American usage.

billisecond *n. See* nanosecond.

bimodal virus *n. See* multipartite virus.

.bin *n.* A file name extension for a file encoded with MacBinary. *See also* MacBinary.

binary[1] *adj.* Having two components, alternatives, or outcomes. The binary number system has 2 as its base, so values are expressed as combinations of two digits, 0 and 1. These two digits can represent the logical values *true* and *false* as well as numerals, and they can be represented in an electronic device by the two states *on* and *off*, recognized as two voltage levels. Therefore, the binary number system is at the heart of digital computing. Although ideal for computers, binary numbers are usually difficult for people to interpret because they are repetitive strings of 1s and 0s. To ease translation, programmers and others who habitually work with the computer's internal processing abilities use hexadecimal (base-16) or octal (base-8) numbers. See Appendix E. *See also* base (definition 2), binary-coded decimal, binary number, bit, Boolean algebra, byte, cyclic binary code, digital computer, dyadic, logic circuit. *Compare* ASCII, decimal, hexadecimal, octal.

binary[2] *n.* In an FTP client program, the command that instructs the FTP server to send or receive files as binary data. *See also* FTP client, FTP server. *Compare* ascii.

binary chop *n. See* binary search.

binary-coded decimal *n.* A system for encoding decimal numbers in binary form to avoid rounding and conversion errors. In binary-coded decimal coding, each digit of a decimal number is coded separately as a binary numeral. Each of the decimal digits 0 through 9 is coded in 4 bits, and for ease of reading, each group of 4 bits is separated by a space. This format is also called 8-4-2-1, after the weights of the four bit positions, and uses the following codes: 0000 = 0; 0001 = 1; 0010 = 2; 0011 = 3; 0100 = 4; 0101 = 5; 0110 = 6; 0111 = 7; 1000 = 8; 1001 = 9. Thus, the decimal number 12 is 0001 0010 in binary-coded decimal notation. *Acronym:* BCD. *See also* base (definition 2), binary[1], binary number, decimal, EBCDIC, packed decimal, round.

binary compatibility *n.* Portability of executable programs (binary files) from one platform, or flavor of operating system, to another. *See also* flavor, portable (definition 1).

binary conversion *n.* The conversion of a number to or from the binary number system. See Appendix E. *See also* binary[1].

binary device *n.* Any device that processes information as a series of on/off or high/low electrical states. *See also* binary[1].

binary digit *n.* Either of the two digits in the binary number system, 0 and 1. *See also* bit.

binary file *n.* A file consisting of a sequence of 8-bit data or executable code, as distinguished from files consisting of human-readable ASCII text. Binary files are usually in a form readable only by a program, often compressed or

structured in a way that is easy for a particular program to read. *Compare* ASCII file.

binary file transfer *n.* Transfer of a file containing arbitrary bytes or words, as opposed to a text file containing only printable characters (for example, ASCII characters with codes 10, 13, and 32–126). On modern operating systems a text file is simply a binary file that happens to contain only printable characters, but some older systems distinguish the two file types, requiring programs to handle them differently. *Acronym:* BFT.

binary format *n.* Any format that structures data in 8-bit form. Binary format is generally used to represent object code (program instructions translated into a machine-readable form) or data in a transmission stream. *See also* binary file.

binary notation *n.* Representation of numbers using the binary digits, 0 and 1. *Compare* floating-point notation.

binary number *n.* A number expressed in binary form, or base 2. Binary numbers are composed of zeros and ones. See Appendix E. *See also* binary[1].

binary search *n.* A type of search algorithm that seeks an item, with a known name, in an ordered list by first comparing the sought item to the item at the middle of the list's order. The search then divides the list in two, determines in which half of the order the item should be, and repeats this process until the sought item is found. *Also called:* binary chop, dichotomizing search. *See also* search algorithm. *Compare* hash search, linear search.

binary synchronous protocol *n. See* BISYNC.

binary transfer *n.* The preferred mode of electronic exchange for executable files, application data files, and encrypted files. *Compare* ASCII transfer.

binary tree *n.* In programming, a specific type of tree data structure in which each node has at most two subtrees, one left and one right. Binary trees are often used for sorting information; each node of the binary search tree contains a key, with values less than that key added to one subtree and values greater than that key added to the other. See the illustration. *See also* binary search, tree.

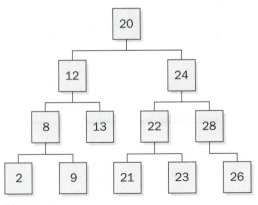

Binary tree.

binaural sound *n. See* 3-D audio.

bind *vb.* To associate two pieces of information with one another. The term is most often used with reference to associating a symbol (such as the name of a variable) with some descriptive information (such as a memory address, a data type, or an actual value). *See also* binding time, dynamic binding, static binding.

BIND *n.* Acronym for **B**erkeley **I**nternet **N**ame **D**omain. A domain name server originally written for the BSD version of UNIX developed at the Berkeley campus of the University of California but now available for most versions of UNIX. As a domain name server, BIND translates between human-readable domain names and Internet-friendly, numeric IP addresses. It is widely used on Internet servers. *See also* DNS, DNS server, IP address.

Binder *n.* A Microsoft Office program that you can use to organize related documents. You can check spelling, number pages consecutively across all documents in the binder, and print the documents.

binding *n.* The process by which protocols are associated with one another and the network adapter to provide a complete set of protocols needed for handling data from the application layer to the physical layer. *See also* ISO/OSI reference model.

binding time *n.* The point in a program's use at which binding of information occurs, usually in reference to program elements being bound to their storage locations and values. The most common binding times are during compilation (compile-time binding), during linking (link-time binding), and during program execution (run-time binding). *See also* bind, compile-time binding, link-time binding, run-time binding.

BinHex[1] *n.* **1.** Short for **bin**ary to **hex**adecimal. A format for converting binary data files into ASCII text so they can be transmitted via e-mail to another computer or in a newsgroup post. This method can be used when standard ASCII characters are needed for transmission, as they are on the Internet. BinHex is used most frequently by Mac users. *See also* MIME. **2.** An Apple Macintosh program for converting binary data files into ASCII text and vice versa using the BinHex format. *Compare* uudecode[1], uuencode[1].

BinHex[2] *vb.* To convert a binary file into printable 7-bit ASCII text or to convert the resulting ASCII text file back to binary format using the BinHex program. *Compare* uudecode[2], uuencode[2].

binomial distribution *n.* In statistics, a list or a function that describes the probabilities of the possible values of a random variable chosen by means of a Bernoulli sampling process. A Bernoulli process has three characteristics: each trial has only two possible outcomes—success or failure; each trial is independent of all other trials; and the probability of success for each trial is constant. A binomial distribution can be used to calculate the probability of getting a specified number of successes in a Bernoulli process. For example, the binomial distribution can be used to calculate the probability of getting a 7 three times in 20 rolls of a pair of dice. *Also called:* Bernoulli distribution.

BioAPI *n.* An open system specification for use in biometric security and authentication technologies. BioAPI supports a wide range of biometric technology, from handheld devices to large-scale networks, and applications include fingerprint identification, facial recognition, speaker verification, dynamic signatures, and hand geometry. BioAPI was developed for the BioAPI Consortium, a group of organizations with ties to biometrics. BioAPI incorporates compatibility with existing biometric standards such as HA-API, which allows applications to operate BioAPI-compliant technologies without modification.

biometrics *n.* Traditionally, the science of measuring and analyzing human biological characteristics. In computer technology, biometrics relates to authentication and secu-

B

rity techniques that rely on measurable, individual biological stamps to recognize or verify an individual's identity. For example, fingerprints, handprints, or voice-recognition might be used to enable access to a computer, to a room, or to an electronic commerce account. Security schemes are generally categorized into three levels: level 1 relies on something the person carries, such as an ID badge with a photo or a computer cardkey; level 2 relies on something the person knows, such as a password or a code number; and level 3, the highest level, relies on something that is a part of the person's biological makeup or behavior, such as a fingerprint, the pattern of blood vessels in a retina, or a signature. *See also* fingerprint reader, handwriting recognition (definition 1), voice recognition.

bionics *n.* The study of living organisms, their characteristics, and the ways they function, with a view toward creating hardware that can simulate or duplicate the activities of a biological system. *See also* cybernetics.

BIOS *n.* Acronym for **b**asic **i**nput/**o**utput **s**ystem. On PC-compatible computers, the set of essential software routines that tests hardware at startup, starts the operating system, and supports the transfer of data among hardware devices, including the date and time. The operating system date is initialized from the BIOS or Real Time Clock date when the machine is booted. Many older PCs, particularly those dating before 1997, have BIOSs that store only 2-digit years and thus may have suffered from Year 2000 problems. The BIOS is stored in read-only memory (ROM) so that it can be executed when the computer is turned on. Although critical to performance, the BIOS is usually invisible to computer users. *See also* AMI BIOS, CMOS setup, Phoenix BIOS, ROM BIOS. *Compare* Toolbox.

BIOS test *n.* A test to see if a PC will make the transition to the year 2000 and keep the correct date. The test can range from resetting the system time in the BIOS and

rebooting to running a program or software routine specially designed to uncover Year 2000 problems.

bipartite virus *n. See* multipartite virus.

bipolar *adj.* **1.** Having two opposite states, such as positive and negative. **2.** In information transfer and processing, pertaining to or characteristic of a signal in which opposite voltage polarities represent on and off, true and false, or some other pair of values. *See also* nonreturn to zero. *Compare* unipolar. **3.** In electronics, pertaining to or characteristic of a transistor having two types of charge carriers. *See also* transistor.

BIS *n. See* business information system.

BISDN *n. See* broadband ISDN.

bistable *adj.* Of, pertaining to, or characteristic of a system or device that has two possible states, such as on and off. *See also* flip-flop.

bistable circuit *n.* Any circuit that has only two stable states. The transition between them must be initiated from outside the circuit. A bistable circuit is capable of storing 1 bit of information.

bistable multivibrator *n. See* flip-flop.

BISYNC *n.* Short for **binary sync**hronous communications protocol. A communications standard developed by IBM. BISYNC transmissions are encoded in either ASCII or EBCDIC. Messages can be of any length and are sent in units called frames, optionally preceded by a message header. BISYNC uses synchronous transmission, in which message elements are separated by a specific time interval, so each frame is preceded and followed by special characters that enable the sending and receiving machines to synchronize their clocks. STX and ETX are control characters that mark the beginning and end of the message text; BCC is a set of characters used to verify the accuracy of transmission. See the illustration. *Also called:* BSC.

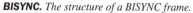

BISYNC. *The structure of a BISYNC frame.*

bit *n.* Short for **bi**nary digi**t**. The smallest unit of information handled by a computer. One bit expresses a 1 or a 0 in a binary numeral, or a true or false logical condition, and is represented physically by an element such as a high or low voltage at one point in a circuit or a small spot on a disk magnetized one way or the other. A single bit conveys little information a human would consider meaningful. A group of 8 bits, however, makes up a byte, which can be used to represent many types of information, such as a letter of the alphabet, a decimal digit, or other character. *See also* ASCII, binary[1], byte.

bit block *n.* In computer graphics and display, a rectangular group of pixels treated as a unit. Bit blocks are so named because they are, literally, blocks of bits describing the pixels' display characteristics, such as color and intensity. Programmers use bit blocks and a technique called bit block transfer (bitblt) to display images rapidly on the screen and to animate them. *See also* bit block transfer.

bit block transfer *n.* In graphics display and animation, a programming technique that manipulates blocks of bits in memory that represent the color and other attributes of a rectangular block of pixels forming a screen image. The image described can range in size from a cursor to a cartoon. Such a bit block is moved through a computer's video RAM as a unit so that its pixels can be rapidly displayed in a desired location on the screen. The bits can also be altered; for example, light and dark portions of an image can be reversed. Successive displays can thus be used to change the appearance of an image or to move it around on the screen. Some computers contain special graphics hardware for manipulating bit blocks on the screen independently of the contents of the rest of the screen. This speeds the animation of small shapes, because a program need not constantly compare and redraw the background around the moving shape. *Also called:* bitblt. *See also* sprite.

bitblt *n. See* bit block transfer.

bit bucket *n.* An imaginary location into which data can be discarded. A bit bucket is a null input/output device from which no data is read and to which data can be written without effect. The NUL device recognized by MS-DOS is a bit bucket. A directory listing, for example, simply disappears when sent to NUL.

bit data type *n.* In an Access project, a data type that stores either a 1 or 0 value. Integer values other than 1 or 0 are accepted, but are always interpreted as 1.

bit density *n.* A measure of the amount of information per unit of linear distance or surface area in a storage medium or per unit of time in a communications pipeline.

bit depth *n.* The number of bits per pixel allocated for storing indexed color information in a graphics file.

bit flipping *n.* A process of inverting bits—changing 1s to 0s and vice versa. For example, in a graphics program, to invert a black-and-white bitmapped image (to change black to white and vice versa), the program could simply flip the bits that compose the bit map.

bit image *n.* A sequential collection of bits that represents in memory an image to be displayed on the screen, particularly in systems having a graphical user interface. Each bit in a bit image corresponds to one pixel (dot) on the screen. The screen itself, for example, represents a single bit image; similarly, the dot patterns for all the characters in a font represent a bit image of the font. In a black-and-white display each pixel is either white or black, so it can be represented by a single bit. The "pattern" of 0s and 1s in the bit image then determines the pattern of white and black dots forming an image on the screen. In a color display the corresponding description of on-screen bits is called a pixel image because more than one bit is needed to represent each pixel. *See also* bitmap, pixel image.

bit manipulation *n.* An action intended to change only one or more individual bits within a byte or word. Manipulation of the entire byte or word is much more common and generally simpler. *See also* mask.

bitmap *n.* A data structure in memory that represents information in the form of a collection of individual bits. A bit map is used to represent a bit image. Another use of a bit map in some systems is the representation of the blocks of storage on a disk, indicating whether each block is free (0) or in use (1). *See also* bit image, pixel image.

bitmapped font *n.* A set of characters in a particular size and style in which each character is described as a unique bit map (pattern of dots). Macintosh screen fonts are examples of bitmapped fonts. See the illustration. *See also*

B

downloadable font, outline font, TrueType. *Compare* Post-Script font, vector font.

Bitmapped font. *Each character is composed of a pattern of dots.*

bitmapped graphics *n.* Computer graphics represented as arrays of bits in memory that represent the attributes of the individual pixels in an image (one bit per pixel in a black-and-white display, multiple bits per pixel in a color or gray-scale display). Bitmapped graphics are typical of paint programs, which treat images as collections of dots rather than as shapes. *See also* bit image, bit map, pixel image. *Compare* object-oriented graphics.

bit mask *n.* A value used with bit-wise operators (And, Eqv, Imp, Not, Or, and Xor) to test, set, or reset the state of individual bits in a bit-wise field value.

BITNET *n.* Acronym for **B**ecause **I**t's **T**ime **Net**work. A WAN (wide area network) founded in 1981 and operated by the Corporation for Research and Educational Networking (CREN) in Washington, D.C. Now defunct, BIT-NET provided e-mail and file transfer services between mainframe computers at educational and research institutions in North America, Europe, and Japan. BITNET used the IBM Network Job Entry (NJE) protocol rather than TCP/IP, but it could exchange e-mail with the Internet. The listserv software for maintaining mailing lists was originated on BITNET.

bit. newsgroups *n.* A hierarchy of Internet newsgroups that mirror the content of some BITNET mailing lists. *See also* BITNET.

bit-oriented protocol *n.* A communications protocol in which data is transmitted as a steady stream of bits rather than as a string of characters. Because the bits transmitted have no inherent meaning in terms of a particular character set (such as ASCII), a bit-oriented protocol uses special sequences of bits rather than reserved characters for control purposes. The HDLC (high-level data link control) defined by ISO is a bit-oriented protocol. *Compare* byte-oriented protocol.

bit parallel *adj.* Transmitting simultaneously all bits in a set (such as a byte) over separate wires in a cable. *See also* parallel transmission.

bit pattern *n.* **1.** A combination of bits, often used to indicate the possible unique combinations of a specific number of bits. For example, a 3-bit pattern allows 8 possible combinations and an 8-bit pattern allows 256 combinations. **2.** A pattern of black and white pixels in a computer system capable of supporting bitmapped graphics. *See also* pixel.

bitplane *n.* **1.** One of a set of bit maps that collectively make up a color image. Each bit plane contains the values for one bit of the set of bits that describe a pixel. One bit plane allows two colors (usually black and white) to be represented; two bit planes, four colors; three bit planes, eight colors; and so on. These sections of memory are called bit planes because they are treated as if they were separate layers that stack one upon another to form the complete image. By contrast, in a chunky pixel image, the bits describing a given pixel are stored contiguously within the same byte. The use of bit planes to represent colors is often associated with the use of a color look-up table, or color map, which is used to assign colors to particular bit patterns. Bit planes are used in the EGA and VGA in 16-color graphics modes; the four planes correspond to the 4 bits of the IRGB code. *See also* color look-up table, color map, EGA, IRGB, layering, VGA. *Compare* color bits. **2.** Rarely, one level of a set of superimposed images (such as circuit diagrams) to be displayed on the screen.

bit rate *n.* **1.** The speed at which binary digits are transmitted. *See also* transfer rate. **2.** The streaming speed of digital content on a network. Bit rate is usually measured in kilobits per second (Kbps).

bit serial *n.* The transmission of bits in a byte one after another over a single wire. *See also* serial transmission.

bit slice microprocessor *n.* A building block for microprocessors that are custom-developed for specialized uses. These chips can be programmed to handle the same tasks as other CPUs but they operate on short units of information, such as 2 or 4 bits. They are combined into processors that handle the longer words.

bits per inch *n.* A measure of data storage capacity; the number of bits that fit into an inch of space on a disk or a tape. On a disk, bits per inch are measured based on inches of circumference of a given track. *Acronym:* BPI. *See also* packing density.

bits per pixel *n.* Also known as color depth or bit depth. The term refers to the number of bits (8, 16, 24, or 32) used to store and display the color data for a single pixel. The number of bits per pixel determines the range of color available to an image. *Acronym:* bpp.

bits per second *n.* See bps.

bit stream *n.* **1.** A series of binary digits representing a flow of information transferred through a given medium. **2.** In synchronous communications, a continuous flow of data in which characters in the stream are separated from one another by the receiving station rather than by markers, such as start and stop bits, inserted into the data.

bit stuffing *n.* The practice of inserting extra bits into a stream of transmitted data. Bit stuffing is used to ensure that a special sequence of bits appears only at desired locations. For example, in the HDLC, SDLC, and X.25 communications protocols, six 1 bits in a row can appear only at the beginning and end of a frame (block) of data, so bit stuffing is used to insert a 0 bit into the rest of the stream whenever five 1 bits appear in a row. The inserted 0 bits are removed by the receiving station to return the data to its original form. *See also* HDLC, SDLC, X.25.

bit transfer rate *n.* See transfer rate.

bit twiddler *n.* Slang for someone devoted to computers, particularly one who likes to program in assembly language. *See also* hacker.

BIX *n.* Acronym for **BYTE** **I**nformation **E**xchange. An online service originated by *BYTE* magazine, now owned and operated by Delphi Internet Services Corporation. BIX offers e-mail, software downloads, and conferences relating to hardware and software.

.biz *n.* One of seven new top-level domain names approved in 2000 by the Internet Corporation for Assigned Names and Numbers (ICANN), .biz is meant for use in business-related Web sites.

biz. news groups *n.* Usenet newsgroups that are part of the biz. hierarchy and have the prefix of biz. These newsgroups are devoted to discussions related to business. Unlike most other newsgroup hierarchies, biz. newsgroups permit users to post advertisement and other marketing material. *See also* newsgroup, traditional newsgroup hierarchy.

BizTalk Server *n.* An application developed by Microsoft Corporation to streamline business processes within a large company's internal network and between business partners over the Internet. BizTalk Server enables the integration of business applications written in different computer languages and running on various operating systems.

BlackBerry *n.* A wireless handheld device that allows mobile users to send and receive e-mail, as well as view appointment calendars and contact lists. The BlackBerry features a display screen and a built-in keyboard operated by pressing the keys with the thumbs. BlackBerry's ease of use and its ability to send and receive messages silently have made it a popular device for wireless text messaging in a business environment.

black box *n.* A unit of hardware or software whose internal structure is unknown but whose function is documented. The internal mechanics of the function do not matter to a designer who uses a black box to obtain that function. For example, a memory chip can be viewed as a black box. Many people use memory chips and design them into computers, but generally only memory chip designers need to understand their internal operation.

black box testing *n.* An approach to testing software in which the tester treats the software as a black box—that is, the testing focuses on the program's functionality rather than on its internal structure. Black box testing is thus user oriented, in that the primary concern is whether the program works, not how it is constructed. Black box testing is generally performed on software that is under development. *Compare* white box testing.

black hat *n.* A hacker who operates with malicious or criminal intent. A black hat will break into a system to alter or damage data or to commit theft. *Compare* white hat.

black hole *n.* A mysterious "place" on a computer network where messages, such as e-mail and news items, disappear without a trace. The usage is derived from stellar black holes, which have such strong gravitational fields that even light cannot escape them. The term is sometimes also used to refer to projects that consume vast amounts of time with no apparent product.

blackout *n.* A condition in which the electricity level drops to zero; a complete loss of power. A number of factors cause a blackout, including natural disasters, such as a storm or an earthquake, or a failure in the power company's equipment, such as a transformer or a power line. A blackout might or might not damage a computer, depending on the state of the computer when the blackout occurs. As with switching a computer off before saving any data, a blackout will cause all unsaved data to be irretrievably lost. The most potentially damaging situation is one in which a blackout occurs while a disk drive is reading information from or writing information to a disk. The information being read or written will probably become corrupted, causing the loss of a small part of a file, an entire file, or the entire disk; the disk drive itself might suffer damage as a result of the sudden power loss. The only reliable means of preventing damage caused by a blackout is to use a battery-backed uninterruptible power supply (UPS). *See also* UPS. *Compare* brownout.

blank[1] *n.* The character entered by pressing the spacebar. *See also* space character.

blank[2] *vb.* To not show or not display an image on part or all of the screen.

blanking *n.* The brief suppression of a display signal as the electron beam in a raster-scan video monitor is moved into position to display a new line. After tracing each scan line, the beam is at the right edge of the screen and must return to the left (horizontal retrace) to begin a new line. The display signal must be turned off during the time of the retrace (horizontal blanking interval) to avoid overwriting the line just displayed. Similarly, after tracing the bottom scan line, the electron beam moves to the top left corner (vertical retrace), and the beam must be turned off during the time of this retrace (vertical blanking interval) to avoid marking the screen with the retrace path.

blast *vb. See* burn (definition 1).

bleed *n.* In a printed document, any element that runs off the edge of the page or into the gutter. Bleeds are often used in books to mark important pages so they are easier to find. *See also* gutter.

blend[1] *n.* A photo or graphic created with a software blending process.

blend[2] *vb.* In illustration and other graphics software, to create a new combined graphic from two or more separate graphic elements. Photos, art, colors, shapes, and text may be blended together digitally. Graphic elements may be blended for artistic effect, or may be realistic enough to appear as a single photo or graphic.

blind carbon copy *n. See* bcc.

blind courtesy copy *n. See* bcc.

blind search *n.* A search for data in memory or on a storage device with no foreknowledge as to the data's order or location. *See also* linear search. *Compare* binary search, indexed search.

blink *vb.* To flash on and off. Cursors, insertion points, menu choices, warning messages, and other displays on a computer screen that are intended to catch the eye are often made to blink. The rate of blinking in a graphical user interface can sometimes be controlled by the user.

blink speed *n.* The rate at which the cursor indicating the active insertion point in a text window, or other display element, flashes on and off.

blip *n.* A small, optically sensed mark on a recording medium, such as microfilm, that is used for counting or other tracking purposes.

blit *vb.* To render a glyph/bitmap to the display. *Also called:* blitting. *See also* bit block transfer.

blitter *n.* A function that copies a bitmap from memory onto the screen.

bloatware *n.* Software whose files occupy an extremely large amount of storage space on a user's hard disk, especially in comparison with previous versions of the same product.

block[1] *n.* **1.** Generally, a contiguous collection of similar things that are handled together as a whole. **2.** A section of random access memory temporarily assigned (allocated) to a program by the operating system. **3.** A group of statements in a program that are treated as a unit. For example, if a stated condition is true, all of the statements in the block are executed, but none are executed if the condition is false. **4.** A unit of transmitted information consisting of identification codes, data, and error-checking codes. **5.** A collection of consecutive bytes of data that are read from or written to a device (such as a disk) as a group. **6.** A rectangular grid of pixels that are handled as a unit. **7.** A segment of text that can be selected and acted upon as a whole in an application. **8.** In the Java programming language, any code between matching braces constitutes a block. For example, { x = 1; }. *See also* code, Java.

block[2] *vb.* **1.** To distribute a file over fixed-size blocks in storage. **2.** To prevent a signal from being transmitted.

3. To select a segment of text, by using a mouse, menu selection, or cursor key, to be acted upon in some way, such as to format or to delete the segment.

block cipher *n.* A private key encryption method that encrypts data in blocks of a fixed size (usually 64 bits). The encrypted data block contains the same number of bits as the original. *See also* encryption, private key.

block cursor *n.* An on-screen cursor that has the same width and height in pixels as a text-mode character cell. A block cursor is used in text-based applications, especially as the mouse pointer when a mouse is installed in the system. *See also* character cell, cursor (definition 1), mouse pointer.

block device *n.* A device, such as a disk drive, that moves information in blocks—groups of bytes—rather than one character (byte) at a time. *Compare* character device.

block diagram *n.* A chart of a computer or other system in which labeled blocks represent principal components and lines and arrows between the blocks show the pathways and relationships among the components. A block diagram is an overall view of what a system consists of and how it works. To show the various components of such a system in more detail, different types of diagrams, such as flowcharts or schematics, are used. See the illustration. *Compare* bubble chart, flowchart.

Block diagram.

block gap *n.* The unused physical space that separates blocks of data or physical records on a tape or formatted sectors on a disk. *Also called:* IBG, interblock gap.

block header *n.* Information that appears at the beginning of a block of data and serves such purposes as signaling the beginning of the block, identifying the block, providing error-checking information, and describing such characteristics as the block length and the type of data contained in the block. *See also* header (definition 2).

blocking factor *n.* **1.** The size of the chunks in which data is transferred to or from a block device such as a disk. If fewer bytes are requested, the disk drive will still read the whole block. Common blocking factors on personal computers are 128, 256, and 512 bytes. **2.** The number of file records in one disk block. If the record length for a file is 170 bytes, a block on the disk contains 512 bytes, and records do not span blocks, then the blocking factor is 3, and each block contains 510 (170 x 3) bytes of data and 2 unused bytes.

block length *n.* The length, usually in bytes, of a block of data. Block length typically ranges from 512 bytes through 4096 kilobytes (KB), depending on the purpose for which the block is used.

block move *n.* Movement of a number of items of data together to a different location, as in reorganizing documents with a word processor or moving the contents of cell ranges in a spreadsheet. Most CPUs have instructions that easily support block moves.

block size *n.* The declared size of a block of data transferred internally within a computer, via FTP, or by modem. The size is usually chosen to make the most efficient use of all the hardware devices involved. *See also* FTP[1] (definition 1).

block structure *n.* The organization of a program into groups of statements called *blocks*, which are treated as units. Programming languages such as Ada, C, and Pascal were designed around block structure. A block is a section of code surrounded by certain delimiters (such as BEGIN and END or { and }), which signify that the intervening code can be treated as a related group of statements. For example, in C, each function is a separate block. Block structure also limits the scope of constants, data types, and variables declared in a block to that block. *See also* function (definition 2), procedure, scope (definition 1).

block transfer *n.* The movement of data in discrete blocks (groups of bytes).

blog[1] *n. See* weblog.

blog[2] *vb.* To create or maintain a weblog.

blogger *n.* One who creates or maintains a weblog.

blow *vb. See* burn (definition 1).

blow up *vb.* To terminate abnormally, as when a program crosses some computational or storage boundary and cannot handle the situation on the other side, as in, "I tried to

B

draw outside the window, and the graphics routines blew up." *See also* abend, abort.

blue screen *n.* A technique used in film matte special effects, in which one image is superimposed on another image. Action or objects are filmed against a blue screen. The desired background is filmed separately, and the shot containing the action or objects is superimposed onto the background. The result is one image where the blue screen disappears.

Blue Screen of Death *n.* In a Microsoft Windows computer environment, a semi-humorous reference to the result of a fatal error in which the screen turns blue and the computer crashes. Recovery from a Blue Screen of Death error typically requires the user to reboot the computer. *Acronym:* BSOD. *Also called:* blue-screen error. *See also* fatal error.

Bluetooth *n.* Technology protocol developed to wirelessly connect electronic devices such as wireless phones, personal digital assistants (PDAs), and computers. Devices equipped with Bluetooth chips can exchange information within about a 30-foot range via radio waves in the 2.45 gigahertz (GHz) spectrum. Bluetooth was developed by the Bluetooth Special Interest Group, a consortium of telecommunications, computing, consumer electronics, and related industry groups.

Bluetooth Special Interest Group *n.* A group of companies from the telecommunications, computing, and networking industries that promotes the development and deployment of Bluetooth technology. *See also* Bluetooth.

Bluetooth wireless technology *n.* A specification for radio links between mobile PCs, mobile phones, and other portable devices. These radio links are small-form factor, low cost, and short range.

.bmp *n.* The file extension that identifies raster graphics stored in bit map file format. *See also* bit map.

BNC *n.* Acronym for **b**ayonet-**N**eill-**C**oncelman. Named for Paul Neill of Bell Labs and Carl Concelman (affiliation unknown), who developed two earlier types of coaxial connectors known as the N connector and C connector, BNC is a type of connector used to join segments of coaxial cable. When one connector is inserted into another and rotated 90 degrees, they lock. BNC connectors are often used with closed-circuit television. The letters BNC are sometimes also considered an acronym for British Naval Connector. See the illustration. *Also called:* BNC connector. *See also* coaxial cable.

BNC connector. *Male (left) and female (right) BNC connector.*

BNC connector *n. See* BNC.

board *n.* An electronic module consisting of chips and other electronic components mounted on a flat, rigid substrate on which conductive paths are laid between the components. A personal computer contains a main board, called the motherboard, which usually has the microprocessor on it and slots into which other, smaller boards, called cards or adapters, can be plugged to expand the functionality of the main system, allowing connections to monitors, disk drives, or a network. *See also* adapter, card (definition 1), motherboard.

board computer *n. See* single-board.

board level *n.* A level of focus in troubleshooting and repair that involves tracking down a problem in a computer to a circuit board and replacing the board. This is in contrast to the component level, which involves repairing the board itself. In many cases board-level repairs are made in order to quickly restore the device to working condition; the boards replaced are then repaired and tested for use in later board-level repairs. *See also* circuit board.

body *n.* **1.** In e-mail and Internet newsgroups, the content of a message. The body of a message follows the header, which contains information about the sender, origin, and destination of the message. *See also* header (definition 1). **2.** In HTML, SGML, and XML, a section of a document that contains the content of the document, along with tags describing characteristics of the content—for example, format. **3.** A segment of a data packet containing the actual data.

body face *n.* A typeface suitable for the main text in a document rather than for headings and titles. Because of their readability, fonts having serifs, such as Times and Palatino, are good body faces, although sans serif faces can also be used as body text. *See also* sans serif, serif. *Compare* display face.

BOF *n.* Acronym for **b**irds **o**f a **f**eather. Meetings of special interest groups at trade shows, conferences, and conventions. BOF sessions provide an opportunity for people boilerplate   Boolean algebra

B

working on the same technology at different companies or research institutions to meet and exchange their experiences. *See* beginning-of-file.

boilerplate *n.* Recyclable text; a piece of writing or code, such as an organization's mission statement or the graphics code that prints a software company's logo, which can be used over and over in many different documents. The size of boilerplate text can range from a paragraph or two to many pages. It is, essentially, generic composition that can be written once, saved on disk, and merged, either verbatim or with slight modification, into whatever documents or programs later require it.

boldface *n.* A type style that makes the text to which it is applied appear darker and heavier than the surrounding text. Some applications allow the user to apply a "Bold" command to selected text; other programs require that special codes be embedded in the text before and after words that are to be printed in boldface. **This sentence appears in boldface.**

bomb[1] *n.* A program planted surreptitiously, with intent to damage or destroy a system in some way—for example, to erase a hard disk or cause it to be unreadable to the operating system. *See also* Trojan horse, virus, worm.

bomb[2] *vb.* To fail abruptly and completely, without giving the user a chance to recover from the problem short of restarting the program or system. *See also* abend, bug (definition 1), crash[2] (definition 1), hang.

bonding *n.* **1.** Acronym for **B**andwidth **On D**emand **I**nteroperability **G**roup. **2.** The process of combining two or more ISDN B (bearer) channels to form a single channel with a bandwidth greater than the standard B channel bandwidth of 64 Kbps. Bonding two B channels, for example, provides a bandwidth of 128 Kbps, which is four times faster than a 28.8 Kbps modem. Such high-speed channels are ideal for video conferencing, imaging, and transferring large-scale data. *See also* B channel, BRI, ISDN.

bonding *vb. See* link aggregation.

bookmark *n.* **1.** A marker inserted at a specific point in a document to which the user may wish to return for later reference. **2.** In Netscape Navigator, a link to a Web page

or other URL that a user has stored in a local file in order to return to it later. *See also* Favorites folder, hotlist, URL.

bookmark file *n.* **1.** A Netscape Navigator file containing the addresses of preferred Web sites. It is synonymous with the Favorites folder in Internet Explorer and the hotlist in Mosaic. *See also* Favorites folder, hotlist, Internet Explorer, Mosaic. **2.** A rendering of such a file in HTML format, generally posted on a Web page for the benefit of other people. *See also* HTML.

Boolean *adj.* Of, pertaining to, or characteristic of logical (true, false) values. Many languages directly support a Boolean data type, with predefined values for true and false; others use integer data types to implement Boolean values, usually (although not always) with 0 equaling false and "not 0" equaling true. *See also* Boolean algebra, Boolean operator.

Boolean algebra *n.* An algebra, fundamental to computer operations but developed in the mid-nineteenth century by English mathematician George Boole, for determining whether logical propositions are true or false rather than for determining the values of numerical expressions. In Boolean algebra, variables must have one of only two possible values, *true* or *false*, and relationships between these variables are expressed with logical operators, such as AND, OR, and NOT. Given these two-state variables and the relationships they can have to one another, Boolean algebra produces such propositions as $C = A$ AND B, which means that C is *true* if and only if both A is *true* and B is *true*; thus, it can be used to process information and to solve problems. Furthermore, Boolean logic can be readily applied to the electronic circuitry used in digital computing. Like the binary numbers 1 and 0, *true* and *false* are easily represented by two contrasting physical states of a circuit, such as voltages, and computer circuits known as logic gates control the flow of electricity (bits of data) so as to represent AND, OR, NOT, and other Boolean operators. Within a computer, these logic gates are combined, with the output from one becoming the input to another so that the final result (still nothing more than sets of 1s and 0s) is meaningful data, such as the sum of two numbers. See the illustration. *See also* adder (definition 1), binary[1], Boolean operator, gate (definition 1), logic circuit, truth table.

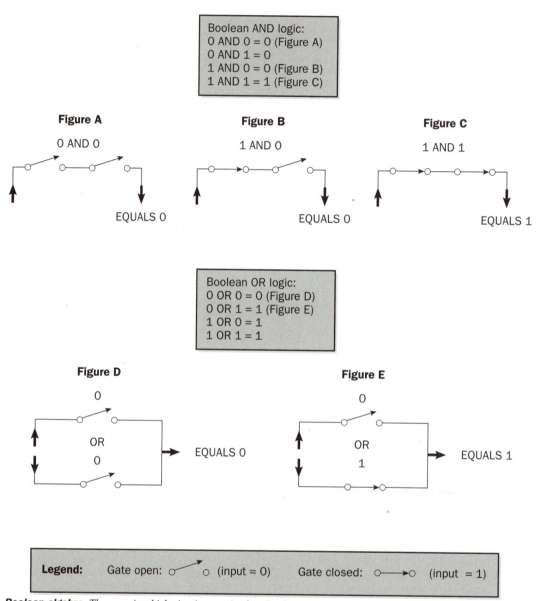

Boolean algebra. *The ways in which circuits can simulate Boolean operations. The boxed tables show the possible results of various input combinations.*

Boolean expression *n.* An expression that yields a Boolean value (*true* or *false*). Such expressions can involve comparisons (testing values for equality or, for non-Boolean values, the < [less than] or > [greater than] relation) and logical combination (using Boolean operators such as AND, OR, and XOR) of Boolean expressions. *Also called:* conditional expression, logical expression. *See also* Boolean, Boolean algebra, Boolean operator, relational operator.

Boolean logic *n. See* Boolean algebra.

Boolean operator *n.* An operator designed to work with Boolean values. The four most common Boolean operators in programming use are AND (logical conjunction), OR (logical inclusion), XOR (exclusive OR), and NOT (logical negation). Boolean operators are often used as qualifiers in database searches—for example, *find all records where DEPARTMENT = "marketing" OR DEPARTMENT = "sales" AND SKILL = "word processing"*. *Also called:* logical operator. *See also* AND, exclusive OR, NOT, OR.

Boolean search *n.* A database search that uses Boolean operators. *See also* Boolean operator.

boost *vb.* To strengthen a network signal before it is transmitted further.

boot[1] *n.* The process of starting or resetting a computer. When first turned on (*cold boot*) or reset (*warm boot*), the computer executes the software that loads and starts the computer's more complicated operating system and prepares it for use. Thus, the computer can be said to pull itself up by its own bootstraps. *Also called:* bootstrap. *See also* BIOS, bootstrap loader, cold boot, warm boot.

boot[2] *vb.* **1.** To start or reset a computer by turning the power on, by pressing a reset button on the computer case, or by issuing a software command to restart. *Also called:* bootstrap, boot up. *See also* reboot. **2.** To execute the bootstrap loader program. *Also called:* bootstrap. *See also* bootstrap loader.

bootable *adj.* Containing the system files necessary for booting a PC and running it. *See also* boot[2].

bootable disk *n. See* boot disk.

boot block *n.* A portion of a disk that contains the operating-system loader and other basic information that enables a computer to start up. *See also* block[1] (definition 5).

boot disk *n.* A floppy disk that contains key system files from a PC-compatible operating system and that can boot, or start, the PC. A boot disk must be inserted in the primary floppy disk drive (usually drive A:) and is used when there is some problem with starting the PC from the hard disk, from which the computer generally boots. *Also called:* bootable disk. *See also* A:, boot[2], boot drive, hard disk.

boot drive *n.* In a PC-compatible computer, the disk drive that the BIOS uses to automatically load the operating system when the computer is turned on. Generally, the default boot drive is the primary floppy disk drive A: in PC-compatible computers with MS-DOS, Windows 3*x*, or Windows 9x operating systems. If a floppy disk is not found in that drive, the BIOS will check the primary hard disk next, which is drive C:. The BIOS for these operating systems can be reconfigured to search drive C: first by using the BIOS setup program. *See also* A:, BIOS, disk drive, hard disk.

boot failure *n.* The inability of a computer to locate or activate the operating system and thus boot, or start, the computer. *See also* boot[2].

boot files *n.* The system files needed to start Microsoft Windows. The boot files include Ntldr and Ntdetect.com. *See also* partition boot sector.

boot loader *n. See* bootstrap loader.

BOOTP *n. See* Bootstrap Protocol.

boot partition *n.* The partition on a hard disk that contains the operating system and support files that the system loads into memory when the computer is turned on or restarted.

boot record *n.* The section of a disk that contains the operating system.

boot sector *n.* The portion of a disk reserved for the bootstrap loader (the self-starting portion) of an operating system. The boot sector typically contains a short machine language program that loads the operating system.

bootstrap[1] *n. See* boot[1].

bootstrap[2] *vb. See* boot[2].

bootstrap loader *n.* A program that is automatically run when a computer is switched on (booted). After first performing a few basic hardware tests, the bootstrap loader loads and passes control to a larger loader program, which typically then loads the operating system. The bootstrap loader typically resides in the computer's read-only memory (ROM).

Bootstrap Protocol *n.* A protocol used primarily on TCP/IP networks to configure diskless workstations. RFCs 951 and 1542 define this protocol. DHCP is a later boot configuration protocol that uses this protocol. The

Microsoft DGCP service provided limited support for BOOTP service. *Acronym:* BOOTP. *Also called:* Boot Protocol. *See also* boot[2], DHCP, RFC, TCP/IP.

boot up *vb. See* boot[2].

border *n.* **1.** In programs and working environments that feature on-screen windows, the edge surrounding the user's workspace. Window borders provide a visible frame around a document or graphic. Depending on the program and its requirements, they can also represent an area in which the cursor or a mouse pointer takes on special characteristics. For example, clicking the mouse on a window border can enable the user to resize the window or split the window in two. **2.** In printing, a decorative line or pattern along one or more edges of a page or illustration.

Border Gateway Protocol *n.* A protocol used by NSFnet that is based on the External Gateway Protocol. *Acronym:* BGP. *See also* External Gateway Protocol, NSFnet.

boss screen *n.* A false display screen usually featuring business-related material that can be substituted for a game display when the boss walks by. Boss screens were popular with MS-DOS games, where it was difficult to switch to another application quickly. However, games designed for the Mac or Windows 9x generally don't need them because it is easy to switch to a different screen or application to hide the fact that one is playing a game.

bot *n.* **1.** Short for ro**bot**. A displayed representation of a person or other entity whose actions are based on programming. **2.** A program that performs some task on a network, especially a task that is repetitive or time consuming. **3.** On the Internet, a program that performs a repetitive or time-consuming task, such as searching Web sites and newsgroups for information and indexing them in a database or other record-keeping system (called *spiders*); automatically posting one or more articles to multiple newsgroups (often used in spamming and called *spambots*); or keeping IRC channels open. *Also called:* Internet robot. *See also* IRC, newsgroup, spam, spambot, spider.

bottom-up design *n.* A program development design methodology in which the lower-level tasks of a program are defined first; the design of the higher-level functions proceeds from the design of the lower-level ones. *See also* bottom-up programming, top-down programming. *Compare* top-down design.

bottom-up programming *n.* A programming technique in which lower-level functions are developed and tested first; higher-level functions are then built using the lower-level functions. Many program developers believe that the ideal combination is top-down design and bottom-up programming. *See also* top-down design. *Compare* object-oriented programming, top-down programming.

bounce *vb.* To return to the sender, used in reference to undeliverable e-mail.

BounceKeys *n.* A feature in Windows 9x that instructs the processor to ignore double strokes of the same key and other unintentional keystrokes.

bound[1] *adj.* Limited in performance or speed; for example, an input/output-bound system is limited by the speed of its input and output devices (keyboard, disk drives, and so on), even though the processor or program is capable of performing at a higher rate.

bound[2] *n.* The upper or lower limit in a permitted range of values.

bounding box *n. See* graphic limits.

Bourne shell *n.* The first major shell, or command interpreter, for UNIX and part of the AT&T System V release. The Bourne shell scripting language, developed at AT&T Bell Laboratories by Steve Bourne in 1979, was one of the original command languages for the UNIX operating system. While the Bourne shell lacks some features common in other UNIX shells, such as command-line editing and recall of previously issued commands, it is the one that the majority of shell scripts adhere to. *Also called:* sh. *See also* shell[1], shell script, System V, UNIX. *Compare* C shell, Korn shell.

boutique reseller *n.* A type of VAR (value-added reseller) that specializes in providing customized software, hardware, and services to vertical, or niche, markets. In the VAR environment, boutique resellers are distinguished from master resellers, or systems integrators, which offer a much wider variety of products and services. *See also* value-added reseller.

box *n.* **1.** Container for a piece of electronic equipment. **2.** Slang term for a computer; more specifically the unit holding the central processing unit, or CPU, and other "guts" of the system, as in "bet that new high-performance box really screams." *See also* central processing unit.

B

3. An IBM front-end processor. **4.** A rectangular—actually, diamond-shaped—symbol, usually called a decision box, used in flowcharting to represent a point at which a process branches into more than one possible outcome, as in a yes/no situation. *See also* decision box. **5.** The boundary around a graphic image on screen. *See also* graphic limits.

box-top license *n. See* shrinkwrap agreement.

Boyce-Codd normal form *n. See* normal form (definition 1).

bozo *n.* A slang term used frequently on the Internet, particularly in newsgroups, for a foolish or eccentric person.

bozo filter *n.* On the Internet, slang for a feature in some e-mail clients and newsgroup readers or a separate utility that allows the user to block, or filter out, incoming e-mail messages or newsgroup articles from specified individuals. Generally these individuals are ones that the user does not want to hear from, such as bozos. *Also called:* kill file. *See also* bozo.

BPI *n. See* bits per inch, bytes per inch.

bpp *n. See* bits per pixel.

bps *n.* Short for **b**its **p**er **s**econd. The measure of transmission speed used in relation to networks and communication lines. Although bps represents the basic unit of measure, networks and communications devices, such as modems, are so fast that speeds are usually given in multiples of bps—Kbps (kilobits, or thousands of bits, per second), Mbps (megabits, or millions of bits, per second), and Gbps (gigabits, or billions of bits, per second). Speed in bps is not the same as the baud rate for a modem. *See also* baud rate.

braindamaged *adj.* Performing in an erratic or destructive manner. A braindamaged application or utility program is characterized by some or all of the following traits: a mysterious and unintuitive user interface, failure to respond predictably to commands, failure to release unused memory, failure to close open files, and use of "reserved" elements of the operating system that can result in a fatal error in a program or the operating system. Braindamaged programs are also often responsible for causing problems across local area networks. *Compare* kludge.

brain dump *n.* A large, unorganized mass of information, presented in response to a query via e-mail or a newsgroup article, that is difficult to digest or interpret.

branch *n.* **1.** A node intermediate between the root and the leaves in some types of logical tree structure, such as the directory tree in Windows or a tape distribution organization. **2.** Any connection between two items such as blocks in a flowchart or nodes in a network. *See* branch instruction.

branch instruction *n.* An assembly- or machine-level instruction that transfers control to another instruction, usually based on some condition (that is, it transfers if a specific condition is true or false). Branch instructions are most often relative transfers, jumping forward or backward by a certain number of bytes of code. *See also* GOTO statement, jump instruction.

branchpoint *n.* The location at which a given branch instruction occurs if the attendant condition (if any) is true. *See also* branch instruction.

branch prediction *n.* A technique used in some processors with an instruction called prefetch to guess whether or not a branch will be taken in a program, and to fetch executable code from the appropriate location. When a branch instruction is executed, it and the next instruction executed are stored in a buffer. This information is used to predict which way the instruction will branch the next time it is executed. When the prediction is correct (as it is over 90 percent of the time), executing a branch does not cause a pipeline break, so the system is not slowed down by the need to retrieve the next instruction. *See also* branch instruction, buffer[1], central processing unit, pipeline processing.

BRB *n.* Acronym for (I'll) **b**e **r**ight **b**ack. An expression used commonly on live chat services on the Internet and online information services by participants signaling their temporary departure from the group. *See also* chat[1] (definition 1).

breadboard *n.* A blank, perforated board used to support prototype electronic circuits. Experimenters would put components on one side of the board and run the leads through the perforations to be connected by wires running along the underside. Today a circuit designer's breadboard is made of plastic. Its holes are small and closely spaced to accommodate the pins of chips, and connections are made by metal strips plugged into the holes. See the illustration. *Compare* wire-wrapped circuits.

Breadboard.

break[1] *n.* **1.** Interruption of a program caused by the user pressing the Break key or its equivalent. **2.** Interruption of a communications transmission that occurs when the receiving station interrupts and takes over control of the line or when the transmitting station prematurely halts transmission. **3.** In the Java programming language, a keyword used to resume program execution at the next statement following the current statement. If the keyword is followed by a label, the program resumes at the indicated labeled statement. *See also* execute, statement.

break[2] *vb.* **1.** To interrupt execution at a given spot, usually for the purpose of debugging. *See also* breakpoint. **2.** To cause a routine, module, or program that had previously worked to cease working correctly.

Break key *n.* A key or combination of keys used to tell a computer to halt, or break out of, whatever it is doing. On IBM PCs and compatibles under DOS, pressing the Pause/Break or Scroll Lock/Break key while holding down the Ctrl key issues the break command (as does Ctrl-C). On Macintosh computers, the key combination that sends a break code is Command-period. See the illustration.

Break key.

break mode *n.* A temporary suspension of program execution while in the development environment. In break mode, you can examine, debug, reset, step through, or continue program execution.

breakout box *n.* A small hardware device that can be attached between two devices normally connected by a cable (such as a computer and a modem) to display and, if necessary, change the activity through individual wires of the cable.

breakpoint *n.* A location in a program at which execution is halted so that a programmer can examine the program's status, the contents of variables, and so on. A breakpoint is set and used within a debugger and is usually implemented by inserting at that point some kind of jump, call, or trap instruction that transfers control to the debugger. *See also* debug, debugger.

BRI *n.* Acronym for **B**asic **R**ate **I**nterface. An ISDN subscriber service that uses two B (64 Kbps) channels and one D (64 Kbps) channel to transmit voice, video, and data signals. *See also* ISDN.

bridge *n.* In terms of the Year 2000 problem, a program, routine, or other conversion mechanism that converts date formats from 2-digit years to 4-digit years and vice versa. A bridge is used as a remedy for literally bridging the 2-digit/4-digit format gap between programs or systems.

bridge *n.* **1.** A device that connects networks using the same communications protocols so that information can be passed from one to the other. *Compare* gateway. **2.** A device that connects two LANs (local area networks), whether or not they use the same protocols, and allows information to flow between them. The bridge operates at the ISO/OSI data-link layer. *Also called:* layer switch. *See also* data-link layer. *Compare* router.

bridge page *n. See* doorway page.

bridge router *n.* A device that supports the functions of both a bridge and router. A bridge router links two segments of a local or wide area network, passing packets of data between the segments as necessary, and uses Level 2 addresses for routing. *Also called:* Brouter. *See also* bridge (definition 2), router.

bridgeware *n.* Hardware or software designed to convert application programs or data files to a form that can be used by a different computer.

B

Briefcase *n.* A system folder in Windows 9x used for synchronizing files between two computers, usually between desktop and laptop computers. The Briefcase can be transferred to another computer via disk, cable, or network. When files are transferred back to the original computer, the Briefcase updates all files to the most recent version.

brightness *n.* The perceived quality of radiance or luminosity of a visible object. Brightness is literally in the eye (and mind) of the beholder; a candle in the night appears brighter than the same candle under incandescent lights. Although its subjective value cannot be measured with physical instruments, brightness can be measured as luminance (radiant energy). The brightness component of a color is different from its color (the hue) and from the intensity of its color (the saturation). *See also* color model, HSB.

British Naval Connector *n. See* BNC.

broadband *adj.* Of or relating to communications systems in which the medium of transmission (such as a wire or fiber-optic cable) carries multiple messages at a time, each message modulated on its own carrier frequency by means of modems. Broadband communication is found in wide area networks. *Compare* baseband.

broadband ISDN *n.* Next-generation ISDN based on ATM (Asynchronous Transfer Mode) technology. Broadband ISDN divides information into two categories: interactive services, which are controlled by the user, and distributed (or distribution) services that can be broadcast to the user. *Acronym:* BISDN. *See also* ATM (definition 1), ISDN.

broadband modem *n.* A modem for use on a broadband network. Broadband technology allows several networks to coexist on a single cable. Traffic from one network does not interfere with traffic from another, since the conversations happen on different frequencies, rather like the commercial radio system. *See also* broadband network.

broadband network *n.* A local area network on which transmissions travel as radio-frequency signals over separate inbound and outbound channels. Stations on a broadband network are connected by coaxial or fiber-optic cable, which can carry data, voice, and video simultaneously over multiple transmission channels that are distinguished by frequency. A broadband network is capable of high-speed operation (20 megabits or more), but it is more expensive than a baseband network and can be difficult to install. Such a network is based on the same technology used by cable television (CATV). *Also called:* wideband transmission. *Compare* baseband network.

broadcast¹ *adj.* Sent to more than one recipient. In communications and on networks, a broadcast message is one distributed to all stations. *See also* e-mail¹ (definition 1).

broadcast² *n.* As in radio or television, a transmission sent to more than one recipient.

broadcast publishing point *n.* A type of publishing point that streams content in such a way that the client cannot control (start, stop, pause, fast forward, or rewind) the content. Content streamed from a broadcast publishing point can be delivered as a multicast or unicast stream. Formerly called a station.

broadcast storm *n.* A network broadcast that causes multiple hosts to respond simultaneously, overloading the network. A broadcast storm may occur when old TCP/IP routers are mixed with routers that support a new protocol. *See also* communications protocol, router, TCP/IP.

broken as designed *adj. See* BAD.

Brouter *n. See* bridge router.

brownout *n.* A condition in which the electricity level is appreciably reduced for a sustained period of time. In contrast to a blackout, or total loss of power, a brownout continues the flow of electricity to all devices connected to electrical outlets, although at lower levels than the normally supplied levels (120 volts in the United States). A brownout can be extremely damaging to sensitive electronic devices, such as computers, because the reduced and often fluctuating voltage levels can cause components to operate for extended periods of time outside the range they were designed to work in. On a computer, a brownout is characterized by a smaller, dimmer, and somewhat fluctuating display area on the monitor and potentially erratic behavior by the system unit. The only reliable means of preventing damage caused by a brownout condition is to use a battery-backed uninterruptible power supply (UPS). *See also* UPS. *Compare* blackout.

browse *vb.* To scan a database, a list of files, or the Internet, either for a particular item or for anything that seems to be of interest. Generally, browsing implies observing, rather than changing, information. In unauthorized computer hacking, browsing is a (presumably) nondestructive

B

means of finding out about an unknown computer after illegally gaining entry.

browser *n. See* Web browser.

browser box *n. See* WebTV.

browser CLUT *n.* A color look-up table consisting of the 216 colors deemed safe when viewed with most Web browsers on most computer operating systems. *See also* CLUT, Web safe palette.

BRS *n. See* big red switch.

brush *n.* A tool used in paint programs to sketch or fill in areas of a drawing with the color and pattern currently in use. Paint programs that offer a variety of brush shapes can produce brushstrokes of varying width and, in some cases, shadowing or calligraphic effects.

brute force *adj.* In general, any process that essentially involves "doing it the hard way." In computer technology, however, brute force typically refers to a programming style that relies on the computer's processing power rather than on skill and planning to create or find a more elegant solution to a problem. Brute-force programming also ignores available information on how similar situations were handled in the past and might depend on outmoded design methodologies. For example, a program using brute force to crack passwords might try all the words in a dictionary (which would require huge amounts of computing power). Instead, more elegant programming would involve using special rules, history, statistics, and other available techniques or information to limit the number and types of words to try first.

BSC *n. See* BISYNC.

BSD/OS *n.* A version of the UNIX operating system based on BSD UNIX and sold by Berkeley Software Design, Inc. *See also* BSD UNIX.

BSD UNIX *n.* Acronym for **B**erkeley **S**oftware **D**istribution **UNIX**. A UNIX version developed at the University of California at Berkeley, providing additional capabilities such as networking, extra peripheral support, and use of extended filenames. BSD UNIX was instrumental in gaining widespread acceptance of UNIX and in getting academic institutions connected to the Internet. BSD UNIX is now being developed by Berkeley Software Design, Inc. *Also called:* Berkeley UNIX. *See also* BSD/OS, UNIX.

BSOD *n. See* Blue Screen of Death.

BSS *n. See* Basic Service Set.

B-tree or **btree** *n.* A tree structure for storing database indexes. Each node in the tree contains a sorted list of key values and links that correspond to ranges of key values between the listed values. To find a specific data record given its key value, the program reads the first node, or root, from the disk and compares the desired key with the keys in the node to select a subrange of key values to search. It repeats the process with the node indicated by the corresponding link. At the lowest level, the links indicate the data records. The database system can thus rapidly skip down through the levels of the tree structure to find the simple index entries that contain the location of the desired records or rows. See the illustration.

B-tree. *A B-tree index structure.*

BTW or **btw** *n.* Acronym for **by the way.** An expression often used to preface remarks in e-mail and Internet newsgroup articles.

bubble chart *n.* A chart in which annotated ovals (bubbles) representing categories, operations, or procedures are connected by lines or arrows that represent data flows or other relationships among the items represented by bubbles. In systems analysis, bubble charts, rather than block diagrams or flowcharts, are used to describe the connections between concepts or parts of a whole, without emphasizing a structural, sequential, or procedural relationship between the parts. See the illustration. *Compare* block diagram, flowchart.

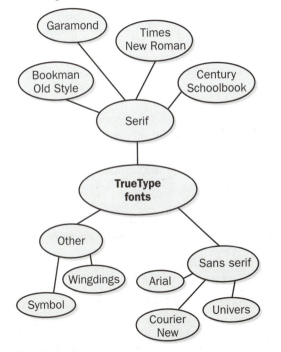

Bubble chart.

bubble-jet printer *n.* A form of nonimpact printer that uses a mechanism similar to that used by an ink-jet printer to shoot ink from nozzles to form characters on paper. A bubble-jet printer uses special heating elements to prepare the ink, whereas an ink-jet printer uses piezoelectric crystals. *See also* ink-jet printer, nonimpact printer. *Compare* laser printer.

bubble memory *n.* Memory formed by a series of persistent magnetic "bubbles" in a thin film substrate. In contrast to ROM, information can be written to bubble memory. In contrast to RAM, data written to bubble memory remains there until it is changed, even when the computer is turned off. For this reason, bubble memory has had some application in environments in which a computer system must be able to recover with minimal data loss in the event of a power failure. The use of and demand for bubble memory has all but disappeared because of the introduction of flash memory, which is less expensive and easier to produce. *See also* flash memory, nonvolatile memory.

bubble sort *n.* A sorting algorithm that starts at the end of a list with n elements and moves all the way through, testing the value of each adjacent pair of items and swapping them if they aren't in the right order. The entire process is then repeated for the remaining $n - 1$ items in the list, and so on, until the list is completely sorted, with the largest value at the end of the list. A bubble sort is so named because the "lightest" item in a list (the smallest) will figuratively "bubble up" to the top of the list first; then the next-lightest item bubbles up to its position, and so on. See the illustration. *Also called:* exchange sort. *See also* algorithm, sort. *Compare* insertion sort, merge sort, quicksort.

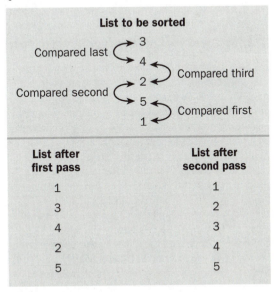

Bubble sort.

bubble storage *n. See* bubble memory.

bucket *n.* A region of memory that is addressable as an entity and can be used as a receptacle to hold data. *See also* bit bucket.

bucket brigade attack *n. See* man-in-the-middle attack.

buffer[1] *n.* A region of memory reserved for use as an intermediate repository in which data is temporarily held while waiting to be transferred between two locations or devices. For instance, a buffer is used while transferring data from an application, such as a word processor, to an input/output device, such as a printer.

buffer[2] *vb.* To use a region of memory to hold data that is waiting to be transferred, especially to or from input/output (I/O) devices such as disk drives and serial ports.

buffer pool *n.* A group of memory or storage-device locations that are allocated for temporary storage, especially during transfer operations.

buffer storage *n.* **1.** The use of a special area in memory to hold data temporarily for processing until a program or operating system is ready to deal with it. **2.** An area of storage that is used to hold data to be passed between devices that are not synchronized or have different bit transfer rates.

bug *n.* **1.** An error in coding or logic that causes a program to malfunction or to produce incorrect results. Minor bugs, such as a cursor that does not behave as expected, can be inconvenient or frustrating, but do not damage information. More severe bugs can require the user to restart the program or the computer, losing whatever previous work had not been saved. Worse yet are bugs that damage saved data without alerting the user. All such errors must be found and corrected by the process known as *debugging*. Because of the potential risk to important data, commercial application programs are tested and debugged as completely as possible before release. After the program becomes available, further minor bugs are corrected in the next update. A more severe bug can sometimes be fixed with a piece of software called a *patch*, which circumvents the problem or in some other way alleviates its effects. *See also* beta test, bomb[2], crash[2] (definition 1), debug, debugger, hang, inherent error, logic error, semantic error, syntax error. **2.** A recurring physical problem that prevents a system or set of components from working together properly. While the origin of this defini-

tion is in some dispute, computer folklore attributes the first use of bug in this sense to a problem in the Harvard Mark I or the Army/University of Pennsylvania ENIAC that was traced to a moth caught between the contacts of a relay in the machine (although a moth is not entomologically a true bug).

buggy *adj.* Full of flaws, or bugs, in reference to software. *See also* bug (definition 1).

building-block principle *n. See* modular design.

built-in check *n. See* hardware check, power-on self test.

built-in font *n. See* internal font.

built-in groups *n.* The default groups provided with Microsoft Windows NT and Windows NT Advanced Server. A group defines a collection of rights and permissions for the user accounts that are its members. Built-in groups are therefore a convenient means of providing access to commonly used resources. *See also* group[1].

bulk eraser *n.* A device for eliminating all information from a storage medium, such as a floppy disk or a tape, by generating a strong magnetic field that scrambles the alignment of the ferrous materials in the media that encode stored data.

bulk storage *n.* Any medium capable of containing large quantities of information, such as tape, fixed disk, or optical disc.

bullet *n.* A typographical symbol, such as a filled or empty circle, diamond, box, or asterisk, used to set off a small block of text or each item in a list. Round and square bullets are used to set off different levels of information. *See also* dingbat.

bulletin board system *n. See* BBS.

bulletproof *adj.* Capable of overcoming hardware problems that, in another system, could lead to interruption of the task in progress.

bump mapping *n.* In 3D computer game rendering and other digital animation applications, a graphic technique in which a texture is added to the surface of an image to increase the perceived detail of the object. Bump mapping gives each pixel a texture, which is calculated by the computer's video card to respond to changes in surroundings, allowing a more realistic interpretation of objects. See the illustration.

**3-D–rendered
sphere**

**3-D–rendered sphere
with bump mapping**

Bump mapping. *A 3-D–rendered sphere showing bump mapping.*

bundle *vb.* To combine products for sale as a lot. Frequently, operating system software and some widely used applications are bundled with a computer system for sale.

bundled software *n.* **1.** Programs sold with a computer as part of a combined hardware/software package. **2.** Smaller programs sold with larger programs to increase the latter's functionality or attractiveness.

burn *vb.* **1.** To write data electronically into a programmable read-only memory (PROM) chip by using a special programming device known variously as a PROM programmer, PROM blower, or PROM blaster. *Also called:* blast, blow. *See also* PROM. **2.** To create read-only memory compact discs (CD-ROMs). **3.** To write data electronically on a flash memory chip or a PC Card Type III. Unlike PROM chips or CD-ROM, flash memory media can be burned, or flashed, repeatedly with new information. *Also called:* flash.

burn in *vb.* **1.** To keep a new system or device running continuously so that any weak elements or components will fail early and can be found and corrected before the system becomes an integral part of the user's work routine. Such a test is often performed at the factory before a device is shipped. **2.** To make a permanent change in the phosphor coating on the inside of a monitor screen by leaving the monitor on and keeping a bright, unchanging image on the screen for extended periods. Such an image will remain visible after the monitor is turned off. Burning in was a danger with older PC monitors; it is no longer a concern with most new PC monitors. *Also called:* ghosting.

burst¹ *n.* Transfer of a block of data all at one time without a break. Certain microprocessors and certain buses have features that support various types of burst transfers. *See also* burst speed (definition 1).

burst² *vb.* To break fanfold continuous-feed paper apart at its perforations, resulting in a stack of separate sheets.

burster *n.* A device used to burst, or break apart at the perforations, fanfold continuous-feed paper.

burst extended-data-out RAM *n. See* BEDO DRAM.

burst mode *n.* A method of data transfer in which information is collected and sent as a unit in one high-speed transmission. In burst mode, an input/output device takes control of a multiplexer channel for the time required to send its data. In effect, the multiplexer, which normally merges input from several sources into a single high-speed data stream, becomes a channel dedicated to the needs of one device until the entire transmission has been sent. Burst mode is used both in communications and between devices in a computer system. *See also* burst¹.

burst rate *n. See* burst speed (definition 1).

burst speed *n.* **1.** The fastest speed at which a device can operate without interruption. For example, various communications devices (as on networks) can send data in bursts, and the speed of such equipment is sometimes measured as the burst speed (the speed of data transfer while the burst is being executed). *Also called:* burst rate. **2.** The number of characters per second that a printer can print on one line without a carriage return or linefeed. Burst speed measures the actual speed of printing, without consideration of the time taken to advance paper or to move the print head back to the left margin. Almost always, the speed claimed by the manufacturer is the burst speed. By contrast, *throughput* is the number of characters per second when one or more entire pages of text are being printed and is a more practical measurement of printer speed in real-life situations.

bursty *adj.* Transmitting data in spurts, or bursts, rather than in a continuous stream.

bus *n.* A set of hardware lines (conductors) used for data transfer among the components of a computer system. A bus is essentially a shared highway that connects different parts of the system—including the processor, disk-drive controller, memory, and input/output ports—and enables them to transfer information. The bus consists of specialized groups of lines that carry different types of information. One group of lines carries data; another carries memory addresses (locations) where data items are to be found; yet another carries control signals. Buses are characterized by the number of bits they can transfer at a single

B

time, equivalent to the number of wires within the bus. A computer with a 32-bit address bus and a 16-bit data bus, for example, can transfer 16 bits of data at a time from any of 2^{32} memory locations. Most PCs contain one or more expansion slots into which additional boards can be plugged to connect them to the bus.

bus enumerator *n.* A device driver that identifies devices located on a specific bus and assigns a unique identification code to each device. The bus enumerator is responsible for loading information about the devices onto the hardware tree. *See also* bus, device driver, hardware tree.

bus extender *n.* **1.** A device that expands the capacity of a bus. For example, IBM PC/AT computers used a bus extender to add onto the earlier PC bus and allow the use of 16-bit expansion boards in addition to 8-bit boards. *See also* bus. **2.** A special board used by engineers to raise an add-on board above the computer's cabinet, making it easier to work on the circuit board.

business graphics *n. See* presentation graphics.

business information system *n.* A combination of computers, printers, communications equipment, and other devices designed to handle data. A completely automated business information system receives, processes, and stores data; transfers information as needed; and produces reports or printouts on demand. *Acronym:* BIS. *See also* management information system.

business logic *n.* A set of rules and calculations built into a business information application. The application uses business logic to sort incoming information and respond accordingly. Business logic functions as a set of guidelines that ensure the application's actions conform to the specific needs of a business.

business software *n.* Any computer application designed primarily for use in business, as opposed to scientific use or entertainment. In addition to the well-known areas of word processing, spreadsheets, databases, and communications, business software for microcomputers also encompasses such applications as accounting, payroll, financial planning, project management, decision and support systems, personnel record maintenance, and office management.

Business Software Alliance *n.* International organization of computer software companies that promotes the interests of the software industry. This alliance focuses on educating the public on the importance of software, advancing free and open world trade, and supporting legislation opposing software piracy and Internet theft. The Business Software Alliance has offices in the United States, Europe, and Asia, with members in more than 60 nations around the world. *Acronym:* BSA.

business-to-business *n. See* B2B.

business-to-consumer *n. See* B2C.

bus mastering *n.* In modern bus architectures, the ability of a device controller card—a network adapter or a disk controller, for example—to bypass the CPU and work directly with other devices to transfer data into and out of memory. Enabling devices to take temporary control of the system bus for data transfer and bus mastering frees the CPU for other work. This in turn improves performance in tasks, such as video replay and multiple-user queries to large databases, that require simultaneous data access and intensive processing. The technology known as direct memory access (DMA) is a well-known example of bus mastering. *See also* bus, controller, direct memory access. *Compare* PIO.

bus mouse *n.* A mouse that attaches to the computer's bus through a special card or port rather than through a serial port. *See also* mouse. *Compare* serial mouse.

bus network *n.* A topology (configuration) for a LAN (local area network) in which all nodes are connected to a main communications line (bus). On a bus network, each node monitors activity on the line. Messages are detected by all nodes but are accepted only by the node(s) to which they are addressed. A malfunctioning node ceases to communicate but does not disrupt operation (as it might on a ring network, in which messages are passed from one node to the next). To avoid collisions that occur when two or more nodes try to use the line at the same time, bus networks commonly rely on collision detection or token passing to regulate traffic. See the illustration. *Also called:* bus topology, linear bus. *See also* collision detection, contention, CSMA/CD, token bus network, token passing. *Compare* ring network, star network.

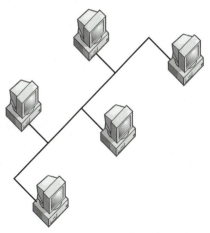

Bus network. *A bus network configuration.*

bus system *n.* The interface circuitry that controls the operations of a bus and connects it with the rest of the computer system. *See also* bus.

bus topology *n. See* bus network.

button *n.* **1.** A graphic element in a dialog box that, when activated, performs a specified function. The user activates a button by clicking on it with a mouse or, if the button has the focus, by hitting the Return or Enter key. **2.** On a mouse, a movable piece that is pressed to activate some function. Older mouse models have only one button; newer models typically have two or more buttons.

button bomb *n.* A button on Web pages with the image of a bomb.

button help *n.* Help information displayed via the selection of buttons or icons. Applications such as the World Wide Web, multimedia kiosks, and computer-aided instruction often use button help icons to ease system navigation.

bypass *n.* In telecommunications, the use of communication pathways other than the local telephone company, such as satellites and microwave systems.

byte *n.* Short for **bi**nary **te**rm. A unit of data, today almost always consisting of 8 bits. A byte can represent a single character, such as a letter, a digit, or a punctuation mark. Because a byte represents only a small amount of information, amounts of computer memory and storage are usually given in kilobytes (1024 bytes), megabytes (1,048,576 bytes), or gigabytes (1,073,741,824 bytes). *Abbreviation:* B. *See also* bit, gigabyte, kilobyte, megabyte. *Compare* octet, word.

bytecode *n.* An encoding of a computer program that a compiler produces when the original source code is processed. This encoding is in an abstract, processor-independent form that cannot be directly executed by most CPUs but is highly suitable for further analysis (for example, compiler optimization), for processing by interpreters (for example, executing Java applets within Web browsers), or for use in generation of binary instructions for the target computer's CPU. Intermediate bytecode production is a feature of the compilers for the Pascal and Java programming languages. *See also* central processing unit, compiler (definition 2), interpreter, Java, Java applet, Pascal.

BYTE Information Exchange *n. See* BIX.

byte-oriented protocol *n.* A communications protocol in which data is transmitted as a string of characters in a particular character set, such as ASCII, rather than as a stream of bits as in a bit-oriented protocol. To express control information, a byte-oriented protocol relies on control characters, most of which are defined by the coding scheme used. The asynchronous communications protocols commonly used with modems and IBM's BISYNC protocol are byte-oriented protocols. *Compare* bit-oriented protocol.

bytes per inch *n.* The number of bytes that fit into an inch of length on a disk track or a tape. *Acronym:* BPI.

C *n.* A programming language developed by Dennis Ritchie at Bell Laboratories in 1972. It is so named because its immediate predecessor was the B programming language. Although C is considered by many to be more a machine-independent assembly language than a high-level language, its close association with the UNIX operating system, its enormous popularity, and its standardization by the American National Standards Institute (ANSI) have made it perhaps the closest thing to a standard programming language in the microcomputer/workstation marketplace. C is a compiled language that contains a small set of built-in functions that are machine dependent. The rest of the C functions are machine independent and are contained in libraries that can be accessed from C programs. C programs are composed of one or more functions defined by the programmer; thus C is a structured programming language. *See also* C++, compiled language, library, Objective-C, structured programming.

C++ *n.* An object-oriented version of the C programming language, developed by Bjarne Stroustrup in the early 1980s at Bell Laboratories and adopted by a number of vendors, including Apple Computer, Inc. and Sun Microsystems, Inc. *See also* C, Objective-C, object-oriented programming.

C2 *n.* A security class of the U.S. Department of Defense Trusted Computer System Evaluation Criteria (DOD 4200.28.STD). C2 is the lowest level of security in the U.S. National Computer Security Center's hierarchy of criteria for trusted computer systems, requiring user logon with password and a mechanism for auditing. The C2 level is outlined in the Orange Book. *See also* Orange Book (definition 1).

CA *n. See* certificate authority.

.cab *n.* File extension for cabinet files, which are multiple files compressed into one and extractable with the extract.exe utility. Such files are frequently found on Microsoft software (for example, Windows 9x) distribution disks.

cabinet *n.* The box in which the main components of a computer (CPU, the hard drive, floppy and CD-ROM drives, and expansion slots for peripheral devices, such as monitors) are located. *See also* CPU, expansion slot.

cable¹ *n.* A collection of wires shielded within a protective tube, used to connect peripheral devices to a computer. A mouse, a keyboard, and a printer might all be connected to a computer with cables. Printer cables typically implement a serial or a parallel path for data to travel along. See the illustration.

Cable.

cable² *adj.* Pertaining to the cable television (CATV) distribution system. For example, a cable modem is a modem that sends and receives digital data through a connection to a cable TV system. Because cable TV is a broadband service, it can carry data (such as an Internet connection) at a very high speed. *See also* CATV.

cable connector *n.* The connector on either end of a cable. *See also* DB connector, DIN connector, RS-232-C standard, RS-422/423/449.

cable matcher *n.* A device that allows the use of a cable that has slightly different wire connections from those required by the devices to which it is attached.

cable modem *n.* A modem that sends and receives data through a coaxial cable television network instead of telephone lines, as with a conventional modem. Cable modems, which have speeds of 500 kilobits per second (Kbps), can generally transmit data faster than current conventional modems. However, cable modems do not operate at the same rate upstream (when sending information) and downstream (when receiving information). Upstream rates vary from about 2 Mbps to 10 Mbps, downstream rates from about 10 Mbps to 36 Mbps. *See also* coaxial cable, modem.

cable telephony *n.* Telephone service provided over a cable TV connection rather than over traditional telephone lines. Although service is delivered over cable rather than telephone wire, the end user perceives no difference between cable telephony and normal telephone service. Proponents of cable telephony see it as part of the eventual integration of Internet, television, and telephone services into a single communication/entertainment unit.

cable television *n. See* CATV.

cabling diagram *n.* A plan that shows the path of cables that attach computer system components or peripherals. Cabling diagrams are particularly important for explaining the connection of disk drives to a disk controller.

cache *n.* A special memory subsystem in which frequently used data values are duplicated for quick access. A memory cache stores the contents of frequently accessed RAM locations and the addresses where these data items are stored. When the processor references an address in memory, the cache checks to see whether it holds that address. If it does hold the address, the data is returned to the processor; if it does not, a regular memory access occurs. A cache is useful when RAM accesses are slow compared with the microprocessor speed because cache memory is always faster than main RAM memory. *See also* disk cache, wait state.

cache card *n.* An expansion card that increases a system's cache memory. *See also* cache, expansion board.

Cache-Coherent Non-Uniform Memory Access *n. See* ccNUMA.

cache farm *n.* A group of servers that save copies of Web pages to caches to fulfill successive requests without calling the pages up repeatedly from the Web server. In essence, the servers are dedicated to caching. By saving Web pages where they can be accessed without increasing traffic on the Web site, the cache farm allows higher-performance Web access for the end user and a reduction in network congestion and volume. *See also* cache.

cache memory *n. See* cache.

cache poisoning *n.* Deliberate corruption of Internet Domain Name System (DNS) information through alteration of data that equates host names with their IP addresses. Misleading information of this type, when cached (saved) by one DNS server and later passed to another, exposes DNS servers to attacks in which data sent from one host to another can be accessed or corrupted. Cache poisoning has been used to redirect network requests from a legitimate server to an alternate Web site. *See also* DNS.

CAD *n.* Acronym for **c**omputer-**a**ided **d**esign. A system of programs and workstations used in designing engineering, architectural, and scientific models ranging from simple tools to buildings, aircraft, integrated circuits, and molecules. Various CAD applications create objects in two or three dimensions, presenting the results as wire-frame "skeletons," as more substantial models with shaded surfaces, or as solid objects. Some programs can also rotate or resize models, show interior views, generate lists of materials required for construction, and perform other allied functions. CAD programs rely on mathematics, often requiring the computing power of a high-performance workstation. *See also* CAD/CAM, I-CASE.

CAD/CAM *n.* Acronym for **c**omputer-**a**ided **d**esign/**c**omputer-**a**ided **m**anufacturing. The use of computers in both the design and manufacture of a product. With CAD/CAM, a product, such as a machine part, is designed with a CAD program and the finished design is translated into a set of instructions that can be transmitted to and used by the machines dedicated to fabrication, assembly, and process control. *See also* CAD, I-CASE.

CADD *n.* A system of hardware and software similar to CAD but with additional features related to engineering conventions, including the ability to display dimension specifications and other notes. *Acronym:* CADD. *See also* CAD.

caddy *n.* A plastic carrier that holds a CD-ROM and is inserted into a CD-ROM drive. Some PCs, especially older models, have CD-ROM drives that require the use of a caddy. Most current CD-ROM drives do not require a caddy.

CAE *n.* Acronym for **c**omputer-**a**ided **e**ngineering. An application that enables the user to perform engineering tests and analyses on designs created with a computer. In some instances, capabilities such as logic testing that are generally attributed to CAE applications are also part of CAD programs, so the distinction between CAD and CAE is not a hard-and-fast one. *See also* CAD, I-CASE.

C

CAI *n.* Acronym for **c**omputer-**a**ided (or **c**omputer-**a**ssisted) **i**nstruction. An educational program designed to serve as a teaching tool. CAI programs typically use tutorials, drills, and question-and-answer sessions to present a topic and to test the student's comprehension. CAI programs are excellent aids for presenting factual material and for allowing students to pace their learning speed. Subjects and complexity range from beginning arithmetic to advanced mathematics, science, history, computer studies, and specialized topics. *Also called:* CAL, CAT, computer-aided learning, computer-aided teaching, computer-assisted learning, computer-assisted teaching, computer-augmented learning. *See also* I-CASE. *Compare* CBT, CMI.

CAL *n.* **1.** Acronym for **c**omputer-**a**ssisted (or **c**omputer-**a**ugmented) **l**earning. *See* CAI. **2.** Acronym for **C**ommon **A**pplication **L**anguage. An object-oriented communications language for controlling home-networking products. CAL, originally part of the CEBus (Consumer Electronic Bus) standard for home automation, can be implemented with various communication protocols, home-networking standards, and home electronic products. *See also* CEBus, home automation.

calculator *n.* Broadly, any device that performs arithmetic operations on numbers. Sophisticated calculators can be programmed for certain functions and can store values in memory, but they differ from computers in several ways: they have a fixed set of commands, they do not recognize text, they cannot retrieve values stored in a data file, and they cannot find and use values generated by a program such as a spreadsheet.

calendar program *n.* An application program in the form of an electronic calendar, commonly used for highlighting dates and scheduling appointments. Some calendar programs resemble wall calendars, displaying dates in blocks labeled with the days of the week; others display dates day by day and enable the user to enter appointments, notes, and other memoranda. A day-of-the-week type of calendar program could, for example, be used to find out that Christmas 2003 will be on a Saturday. Depending on its capabilities, such a program might cover only the current century, or it might cover hundreds of years and even allow for the change (in 1582) from the Julian to the Gregorian calendar. A calendar/scheduler program might show blocks of dates or, like an appointment book, single days divided into hours or half hours, with room for notes. Some programs allow the user to set an alarm to go off at an important point in the schedule. Other programs can coordinate the calendars of different people on the same network so that a person entering an appointment into his or her calendar also enters the appointment into a colleague's calendar.

call[1] *n.* In a program, an instruction or statement that transfers program execution to some section of code, such as a subroutine, to perform a specific task. Once the task is performed, program execution resumes at the calling point in the program. *See also* calling sequence.

call[2] *vb.* **1.** To establish a connection through a telecommunications network. **2.** To transfer program execution to some section of code (usually a subroutine) while saving the necessary information to allow execution to resume at the calling point when the called section has completed execution. Some languages (such as FORTRAN) have an explicit CALL statement; others (such as C and Pascal) perform a call when the name of a procedure or function appears. In assembly language, there are various names for a CALL instruction. When a subroutine call occurs in any language, one or more values (known as arguments or parameters) are often passed to the subroutine, which can then use and sometimes modify these values. *See also* argument, parameter.

callback or **callback security** *n.* A security feature used to authenticate users calling in to a network. During callback, the network validates the caller's username and password, hangs up, and then returns the call, usually to a preauthorized number. This security measure usually prevents unauthorized access to an account even if an individual's logon ID and password have been stolen. *See also* authentication, preset-to callback, remote access server.

callback modem *n.* A modem that, instead of answering an incoming call, requires the caller to enter a touch-tone code and hang up so that the modem can return the call. When the modem receives the caller's code, it checks the code against a stored set of phone numbers. If the code matches an authorized number, the modem dials the number and then opens a connection for the original caller. Callback modems are used when communications lines must be available to outside users but data must be protected from unauthorized intruders.

calling sequence *n.* In a program when a subroutine call occurs, an agreement between the calling routine and the called routine on how arguments will be passed and in what order, how values will be returned, and which routine will handle any necessary housekeeping (such as cleaning up the stack). The calling sequence becomes important when the calling and called routines were created with different compilers or if either was written in assembly language. Two common calling sequences are the C calling sequence and the Pascal calling sequence. In the C calling sequence, the calling routine pushes any arguments included in the call on the stack in reverse order (right to left) and performs any stack cleanup; this permits a varying number of arguments to be passed to a given routine. In the Pascal calling sequence, the calling routine pushes any included arguments on the stack in the order in which they appear (left to right), and the called routine is expected to clean up the stack. *See also* argument, call[1], stack.

CALL instruction *n.* A type of programming instruction that diverts program execution to a new area in memory (sequence of directives) and also allows eventual return to the original sequence of directives.

CALS *n.* Acronym for **C**omputer-**A**ided **A**cquisition and **L**ogistics **S**upport. A U.S. Department of Defense standard for electronic exchange of data with commercial suppliers.

CAM *n.* **1.** Acronym for **c**omputer-**a**ided **m**anufacturing. The use of computers in automating the fabrication, assembly, and control aspects of manufacturing. CAM applies to the manufacture of products ranging from small-scale production to the use of robotics in full-scale assembly lines. CAM relates more to the use of specialized programs and equipment than it does to the use of microcomputers in a manufacturing environment. *See also* CAD/CAM, I-CASE. **2.** *See* Common Access Method.

camera-ready *adj.* In publishing, of or pertaining to the stage at which a document, with all typographic elements and graphics in place, is suitably prepared to be sent to a printing service. The printing service photographs the camera-ready copy and then uses the photograph to make plates for printing. Some applications are advertised as being able to bring documents to the camera-ready stage, eliminating the need for manual layout and pasteup of elements onto boards.

campuswide information system *n.* Information and services distributed on a college or university campus through computer networks. Campuswide information system services typically include student and faculty directories, calendars of campus events, and access to databases. *Acronym:* CWIS.

cancel *n.* A control character used in communication with printers and other computers, commonly designated as CAN. It usually means that the line of text being sent should be canceled. In ASCII, which is the basis of character sets used by most microcomputers, this is represented internally as character code 24.

cancelbot *n.* Short for **cancel** ro**bot**. A program that identifies articles in newsgroups based on a set of criteria and cancels the distribution of those articles. Although the criteria for cancellation is set by the owner of the cancelbot, most cancelbots exist to identify and eliminate spam messages posted to dozens or hundreds of newsgroups. *See also* spam.

cancel message *n.* A message sent to Usenet news servers indicating that a certain article is to be canceled, or deleted, from the server. *See also* article, news server, Usenet.

candidate key *n.* A unique identifier for a tuple (row) within a relation (database table). The candidate key may be either simple (a single attribute) or composite (two or more attributes). By definition, every relation must have at least one candidate key, but it is possible for a relation to have more than one candidate key. If there is only one candidate key, it automatically becomes the primary key for the relation. If there are multiple candidate keys, the designer must designate one as the primary key. Any candidate key that is not the designated primary key is an alternate key. *See also* key (definition 2), primary key.

canned program *n.* *See* canned software.

canned routine *n.* A previously written routine that is copied into a program and used as is, without modification. *See also* library routine.

canned software *n.* Off-the-shelf software, such as word processors and spreadsheet programs.

canonical form *n.* In mathematics and programming, the standard or prototypical form of an expression or a statement.

canonical name *n.* An object's distinguished name presented with the root first and without the LDAP attribute tags (such as: CN=, DC=). The segments of the name are delimited with forward slashes (/). For example, CN=MyDocuments,OU=MyOU,DC=Microsoft,DC=Com is presented as microsoft.com/MyOU/MyDocuments in canonical form. *See also* Lightweight Directory Access Protocol.

capacitance *n.* The ability to store an electric charge. Capacitance is measured in farads. A capacitance of 1 farad will hold 1 coulomb of charge at a potential of 1 volt. In practical use, a farad is an extremely large amount of capacitance; typical capacitors have values of microfarads (10^{-6}) or picofarads (10^{-12}). *See also* capacitor.

capacitor *n.* A circuit component that provides a known amount of capacitance (ability to store an electric charge). A capacitor typically consists of two conductive plates separated by an insulating (dielectric) material. If other factors remain constant, capacitance increases as the plates are made larger or brought closer together. A capacitor blocks direct current but passes alternating current to an extent that depends on its capacitance and on the frequency of the current. *See also* capacitance.

capacity *n.* The amount of information a computer or an attached device can process or store. *See also* computer.

caps *n.* Short for **cap**ital letter**s**. *Compare* lowercase.

Caps Lock key *n.* A toggle key that, when on, shifts the alphabetic characters on the keyboard to uppercase. The Caps Lock key does not affect numbers, punctuation marks, or other symbols. See the illustration.

Caps Lock key.

capstan *n.* On a tape recorder, a polished metal post against which a turning rubber wheel (called a pinch roller) presses to move a length of magnetic tape placed between the wheel and the post. The capstan controls the speed of the tape as it moves past the recording head. *See also* pinch roller.

capture *vb.* In communications, to transfer received data into a file for archiving or later analysis.

capture board *n.* *See* video capture card.

capture card *n.* *See* video capture card.

Carbon *n.* Code name for the Application Program Interfaces (API) and shared libraries used to write applications for Macintosh OS X. Since Macintosh OS X is an entirely different system rather than an update of the previous

Macintosh OS, Carbon bridges the gap between the systems, allowing developers to rewrite their programs to OS X without rewriting the code for the entire application. Carbon allows OS X native applications to run under earlier versions of the Macintosh OS without modification but with OS X advantages.

carbon copy *n.* *See* cc.

carbonize *vb.* To update a Macintosh application for OS X. Although older versions of Macintosh applications will run under OS X, only those that have been carbonized will be able to use OS X–specific advantages.

carbon ribbon *n.* A ribbon used with impact printers, especially daisy-wheel printers, and with typewriters for highest-quality output. A carbon ribbon is made of a thin strip of Mylar coated on one side with a carbon film. Characters printed with a carbon ribbon are extremely crisp and free from the fuzziness that can be associated with an inked cloth ribbon. *Also called:* film ribbon, Mylar ribbon. *See also* daisy-wheel printer. *Compare* cloth ribbon.

card *n.* **1.** A printed circuit board or adapter that can be plugged into a computer to provide added functionality or new capability. These cards provide specialized services, such as mouse support and modem capabilities, that are not built into the computer. *See also* adapter, board, printed circuit board. **2.** In programs such as the HyperCard hypertext program, an on-screen representation of an index card on which information can be stored and "filed" (saved) for future reference. *See also* hypertext. **3.** A manila card about 3 inches high by 7 inches long on which 80 columns of data could be entered in the form of holes punched with a keypunch machine. The punched holes corresponded to numbers, letters, and other characters and could be read by a computer that used a punched-card reader. *Also called:* punched card. *See also* card reader (definition 2).

card cage *n.* An enclosure area for holding printed circuit boards (cards). Most computers have area with protective metal and mounting brackets where cards are installed. The term originally came from an external box that held rack-mounted cards or peripherals and resembled a cage.

carder *n.* A person who engages in online credit card fraud. Specifically, a carder steals credit card numbers, either to purchase merchandise (often computer-related) from Web-based stores or to trade the stolen numbers with like-minded individuals—again, over the Internet. Carders generally obtain credit card numbers through conventional means, such as "trashing" (searching through trash) or calling individuals and posing as bank officers. *See also* hacker (definition 2).

cardinal number *n.* A number that indicates how many items there are in a set—for example, "There are 27 names on that list." *Compare* ordinal number.

card punch *n. See* keypunch.

card reader *n.* **1.** An input device used chiefly for identification purposes that reads information that has been magnetically encoded, usually in two tracks, on a plastic card, such as a credit card or an employee badge. **2.** A mechanical apparatus that reads computer data from punched cards. No longer in widespread use, card readers allow computer data to be created off line and then input to the computer for processing. This need for offline data creation was because of limited CPU resources. Reading batches of punched cards was a better use of CPU time than waiting for a human operator to key data directly into the computer's memory. *Also called:* punched-card reader.

caret *n.* The small, upward-pointing symbol (^) typically found over the 6 key on the top row of a microcomputer keyboard. In some programming languages, the caret is used as an exponentiation operator. For example, the expression 3 ^ 2 represents the number 3 raised to the second power. The caret is also used to represent the Control key on the keyboard. For example, ^Z means "hold the Control key down and press the Z key."

careware *n.* Software developed by an individual or a small group and distributed freely, with the proviso that users make a donation to a charity if they continue to use the software after trying it out. The charity is one usually designated by the software creator.

Carnivore *n.* Digital wiretap technology developed by the U.S. Federal Bureau of Investigation. Carnivore's purpose is to track and capture e-mail and other Internet-based communications sent from and received by a suspect. Carnivore copies all of an ISP's network traffic into a collection system where a filter sifts through all communications, disregarding all data but that related to the suspect.

carpal tunnel syndrome *n.* A form of repetitive strain injury to the wrist and hand. Making the same small motions over and over can cause swelling and scarring of the soft tissue of the wrist, which then compresses the main nerve leading to the hand. Symptoms of carpal tunnel syndrome include pain and tingling in the fingers, and in advanced cases, carpal tunnel syndrome can lead to loss of functionality of the hands. Typing at a computer keyboard without proper wrist support is a common cause of carpal tunnel syndrome. *Acronym:* CTS. *See also* repetitive strain injury, wrist support.

carriage *n.* The assembly that holds the platen of a typewriter or a typewriterlike printer. On a standard typewriter, the platen and carriage move past a fixed position within the typewriter housing, where the keys strike the paper; the platen rotates to advance the paper held in the carriage. On most impact printers for computers, however, the print head moves back and forth across a platen, which rotates but does not move horizontally; in such machines, the assembly that carries the print head is often called the print-head carriage assembly. *See also* carriage return, platen.

carriage return *n.* A control character that tells a computer or printer to return to the beginning of the current line. A carriage return is similar to the return on a typewriter but does not automatically advance to the beginning of a new line. For example, a carriage-return character alone, received at the end of the words *This is a sample line of text* would cause the cursor or printer to return to the first letter of the word *This*. In the ASCII character set, the carriage-return character has the decimal value of 13 (hexadecimal 0D). See the illustration.

Carriage return.

carrier *n.* **1.** In communications, a specified frequency that can be modulated to convey information. **2.** A company that provides telephone and other communications services to consumers.

Carrier Detect *n. See* CD (definition 2).

carrier frequency *n.* A radio-frequency signal, such as those used with modems and on networks, used to transmit information. A carrier frequency is a signal that vibrates at a fixed number of cycles per second, or hertz (Hz), and is modulated (changed) in either frequency or amplitude to enable it to carry intelligible information.

carrier sense multiple access with collision detection *n. See* CSMA/CD.

carrier signal *n. See* carrier frequency.

carrier system *n.* A communications method that uses different carrier frequencies to transfer information along multiple channels of a single path. Transmission involves modulating the signal on each frequency at the originating station and demodulating the signal at the receiving station.

carry *n.* In arithmetic, the process of moving a digit to the next higher position when the sum of two numbers is greater than the largest digit in the number system being used. Computers, based on logic circuits, and often able to add all digits in two numbers simultaneously (do parallel addition), perform carries in several exotic ways. For example, they perform complete carries, in which one carry is allowed to propagate—that is, to generate other carries in other digit positions. They can also perform partial carries, in which carries resulting from parallel addition are stored temporarily.

carry bit *n.* The bit, associated with an adder circuit, that indicates that an addition operation has produced a carry (as in 9 + 7). *Also called:* carry flag.

carry flag *n. See* carry bit.

Cartesian coordinates *n.* Points on a plane (two dimensions) or in space (three dimensions) that are located by their positions in relation to intersecting axes; named after the French mathematician René Descartes, who introduced the system in the seventeenth century. In two dimensions, points are described by their positions in relation to the two familiar axes, x (usually horizontal) and y (usually vertical). In three dimensions, a third axis, z, is added to the x- and y-axes. See the illustration. *See also* x-y-z coordinate system. *Compare* polar coordinates.

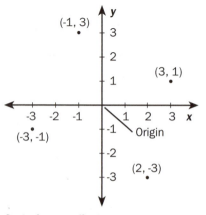

Cartesian coordinates.

Cartesian product *n. See* product (definition 1).

cartridge *n.* Any of various container devices that usually consist of some form of plastic housing. *See also* disk cartridge, ink cartridge, memory cartridge, ribbon cartridge, ROM cartridge, tape cartridge, toner cartridge.

cartridge font *n.* A font contained in a plug-in cartridge and used to add fonts to laser, ink-jet, or high-end dot-matrix printers. Cartridge fonts are distinguished both from internal fonts, which are contained in ROM in the printer and are always available, and from downloadable (soft) fonts, which reside on disk and which can be sent to the printer as needed. *See also* font cartridge. *Compare* internal font.

cascade *n.* **1.** Additional elements displayed by a menu item or list box from which the user can choose in order to interact with other screen elements. See the illustration. **2.** In newsgroup articles, the accumulation of quotation marks (often angle brackets) added by newsgroup readers each time an article is replied to. Most newsgroup readers will copy the original article in the body of the reply; after several replies, the original material will have several quotation marks. *See also* article, newsgroup, newsreader.

Cascade.

cascade connection *n. See* pipe (definition 1).

cascaded star topology *n.* A star network in which nodes connect to hubs and hubs connect to other hubs in a hierarchical (cascaded) parent/child relationship. This topology is characteristic of 100Base-VG networks.

cascading hubs *n.* A network configuration in which hubs are connected to other hubs. *See also* hub.

cascading menu *n.* A hierarchical graphical menu system in which a side menu of subcategories is displayed when the pointer is placed on the main category.

Cascading Style Sheet mechanism *n. See* cascading style sheets.

cascading style sheets *n.* A Hypertext Markup Language (HTML) specification developed by The World Wide Web Consortium (W3C) that allows authors of HTML documents and users to attach style sheets to HTML documents. The style sheets include typographical information on how the page should appear, such as the font of the text in the page. This specification also directs the way in which the style sheets of the HTML document and the user's style will blend. Cascading style sheets have been proposed for the HTML 3.2 standard. *Acronym:* CSS. *Also called:* Cascading Style Sheet mechanism, CSS1. *See also* HTML, style sheet (definition 2).

cascading windows *n.* A sequence of successive, overlapping windows in a graphical user interface, displayed so that the title bar of each is visible. *Also called:* overlaid windows.

case *n.* In text processing, an indication of whether one or more alphabetic characters are capitalized (uppercase) or not (lowercase). A case-sensitive program or routine distinguishes between uppercase and lowercase letters and treats the word *cat* as totally distinct from either *Cat* or *CAT*. A case-sensitive program that also separates capitalized and lowercased words would list *Arkansas* before *aardvark* or *antimony*, even though its alphabetic position follows both lowercased words.

CASE *n.* Acronym for **c**omputer-**a**ided **s**oftware **e**ngineering. A comprehensive label for software designed to use computers in all phases of computer program development, from planning and modeling through coding and documentation. CASE represents a working environment consisting of programs and other development tools that help managers, systems analysts, programmers, and others to automate the design and implementation of programs and procedures for business, engineering, and scientific computer systems.

case-sensitive search *n.* A search in a database in which capitalization of key words must exactly match the capitalization of words in the database. A case-sensitive search for "north and south" would fail to find a database entry for "North and South."

case sensitivity *n.* Discrimination between lowercase and uppercase characters in a program or a programming language. *See also* case.

case statement *n.* In programming languages such as Ada, Pascal, and C, a type of control statement that executes one of several sets of instructions based on some key value. Case statements are used in evaluating situations that can have a number of different results. "Case" in this sense refers to a refinement of a basic IF-THEN type of conditional statement (if A is true, then do B), but a case statement functions more like a series of nested IFs (if A, then do this; else if B, then do that; else . . .). In a case evaluation, a variable (such as a number or a string of characters) is compared against one after another of a series of constants assigned by the programmer. Each constant represents a different case and defines an action to be carried out. When the program finds a constant that matches the variable, it carries out whatever action is dictated by the case in which the match occurs. *See also* constant, control statement, variable.

cassette *n.* The unit consisting of both the plastic case and the magnetic tape it contains. Cassette tapes are used for backing up large amounts of computer data.

cassette tape *n.* **1.** The tape within a cassette. **2.** The unit consisting of both the plastic cassette case and the tape it contains.

cast *n.* A programmer-specified data conversion from one type to another, such as a conversion from integer to floating point. *Also called:* coercion. *See also* data type.

CAT *n.* **1.** Acronym for **c**omputer-**a**ided **t**esting. A procedure used by engineers for checking or analyzing designs, especially those created with CAD programs. Computer-aided testing is also used by software developers for automated regression testing. **2.** Acronym for **c**omputer-**a**ssisted **t**eaching or **c**omputer-**a**ided **t**eaching. *See* CAI. **3.** Acronym for **c**omputerized **a**xial **t**omography. A medical procedure in which a computer is used to generate a three-dimensional image of a body part from a series of X-rays taken as cross sections along a single axis. *See* CAI.

catalog *n.* **1.** In a computer, a list containing specific information, such as name, length, type, and location of files or of storage space. **2.** In a database, the data dictionary. *See also* data dictionary.

catch *n.* A keyword in the Java programming language used to declare a block of statements to be executed in the event that a Java exception or runtime error occurs in a preceding "try" block. *See also* block, exception, keyword, runtime, try.

C

Category 3 cable *n.* Network cable that supports frequencies up to 16 MHz and transmission speeds up to 10 Mbps (standard Ethernet). Category 3 cable has four unshielded twisted pairs (UTPs) of copper wire and RJ-45 connectors, and is used in voice and 10Base-T applications. *Also called:* Cat 3 cable.

Category 4 cable *n.* Network cable that supports frequencies up to 20 MHz and transmission speeds up to 16 Mbps. Category 4 cable has four unshielded twisted pairs (UTPs) of copper wire and RJ-45 connectors. Less popular than Category 3 and Category 5 cables, it is used primarily for token ring networks. *Also called:* Cat 4 cable.

Category 5 cable *n.* Network cable that supports frequencies up to 100 MHz and transmission speeds up to 100 Mbps (using two pairs) or 1000 Mbps (using four pairs and called gigabit over copper). Category 5 cable has four unshielded twisted pairs (UTPs) of copper wire and RJ-45 connectors, and is used for 10/100/1000 Base-T, ATM, and token ring networks. *Also called:* Cat 5 cable.

Category 5e cable *n.* Network cable that supports frequencies up to 100 MHz and transmission speeds up to 1000 Mbps (half-duplex mode) or 2000 Mbps (full-duplex mode). Category 5e cable has four unshielded twisted pairs (UTPs) of copper wire, RJ-45 connectors, and enhanced shielding to prevent signal degradation. Category 5e cable can be used for 10/100/1000 Base-T, ATM, and token ring networks. *Also called:* Cat 5e cable. *See also* duplex[2] (definition 1), half-duplex transmission.

catena *n.* A series of items in a chained list—that is, a list in which one item points to the next in sequence. *See also* linked list.

cathode *n.* **1.** The terminal or electrode that is negatively charged and from which electrons flow. **2.** The electron-emitting electrode in a vacuum tube. **3.** The negative terminal of a battery. *Compare* anode.

cathode-ray oscilloscope *n. See* oscilloscope.

cathode-ray tube *n. See* CRT.

CATV *n.* Acronym for **c**ommunity **a**ntenna **t**elevision or **ca**ble **t**elevision. A television broadcasting system that uses coaxial or fiber-optic cable to distribute a broadband signal containing many separate television program channels. CATV systems are also increasingly being used to carry digital data—for example, Internet connections—to and from subscribers.

CatXML *n.* Acronym for **Cat**alogue **XML**. An open standard for using XML in catalogue information exchanges over the Internet. CatXML uses a flexible XML schema with multiple profiles that can be adapted to meet the needs of individual businesses. CatXML supports existing information structures and provides distributed query information grid models and dynamic output formats.

cavity virus *n.* A type of virus that overwrites and hides within a section of the file it has infected. A cavity virus overwrites only a part of the host file filled with a constant, allowing the file to continue to function.

CBEMA *n.* Acronym for **C**omputer and **B**usiness **E**quipment **M**anufacturers **A**ssociation. An organization of hardware vendors and manufacturers in the United States involved in standardizing information processing and related equipment.

CBL *n.* Acronym for **c**omputer-**b**ased **l**earning. Applies to either computer-aided instruction (CAI), which focuses primarily on education, or computer-based training (CBT), which is application-specific or job-oriented teaching. *See also* CAI, CBT.

CBT *n.* Acronym for **c**omputer-**b**ased **t**raining. The use of computers and specially developed tutorial programs for teaching. CBT uses color, graphics, and other attention-getting aids to help maintain interest, and it has both simple and sophisticated applications. A software developer, for example, might include a series of CBT lessons with an application to give new users a hands-on feel for the program; a consultant might use a longer and more detailed CBT program as a tool in a management-training seminar.

cc *n.* Acronym for **c**ourtesy **c**opy. A directive to an e-mail program to send a complete copy of a given piece of mail to another individual. The use of cc mail addressing, as opposed to directly addressing the mail to a person, generally implies that the recipient is not required to take any action; the message is for informational purposes only. In a cc directive, the fact that this recipient received the mail is printed in the mail header and is thus known to all other recipients. *Also called:* carbon copy. *See also* e-mail[1] (definition 1), header. *Compare* bcc.

CCC *n.* Acronym for **C**omputer **C**ontrolled **C**haracter. CCC is generally used in role-playing computer games like MUD. It refers to a character that is not played by a human player but is actually a computer-generated character built into the game itself. *See also* computer game, MUD, role-playing game.

CCD *n. See* charge-coupled device.

CCI *n. See* Common Client Interface.

CCITT *n.* Acronym for **C**omité **C**onsultatif **I**nternational **T**élégraphique et **T**éléphonique, now called the International Telecommunication Union-Telecommunication Standardization Sector (ITU-TSS, often abbreviated as ITU-T). CCITT was the organization that performed the standardization functions for the International Telecommunication Union (ITU). Following a reorganization of the ITU in 1992, CCITT ceased to exist as a separate body, although several standards are still known by the CCITT prefix. *See also* ITU.

CCITT Groups 1–4 *n.* A set of four standards recommended by the Comité Consultatif International Télégraphique et Téléphonique (International Telegraph and Telephone Consultative Committee) for the encoding and transmission of images over fax machines. Groups 1 and 2 relate to analog devices and are generally out of use. Groups 3 and 4, which deal with digital devices, are outlined below. Group 3 is a widespread standard that supports standard images of 203 horizontal dots per inch (dpi) by 98 vertical dpi and fine images of 203 horizontal dpi by 198 vertical dpi; supports two methods of data compression, one (based on the Huffman code) reducing an image to 10 to 20 percent of the original, the second (READ, for relative element address designate) compressing images to 6 to 12 percent of the original; and provides for password protection and for polling so that a receiving machine can request transmission as appropriate. Group 4, a newer standard, supports images of up to 400 dpi; supports data compression based on a beginning row of white pixels (dots), with each succeeding line encoded as a series of changes from the line before, compressing images to 3 to 10 percent of the original; does not include error-correction information in the transmission; and requires an Integrated Services Digital Network (ISDN) phone line rather than a dial-up line.

CCITT V series *n. See* V series.

CCITT X series *n. See* X series.

cc:Mail *n.* An e-mail program originally introduced by cc:mail, Inc., and currently produced by the Lotus Development Corporation. Lotus cc:Mail runs on multiple networking platforms and the Internet and is closely integrated with Lotus Notes collaborative software.

ccNUMA *n.* Acronym for **C**ache-**C**oherent **N**on-Uniform **M**emory **A**ccess. A technology that enables many symmetric multiprocessing systems to be connected by high-speed/wide-bandwidth interconnect hardware so that they function as one machine. *See also* symmetric multiprocessing.

CCP *n.* Acronym for **C**ertificate in **C**omputer **P**rogramming. A senior-level programming credential awarded by the Institute for Certification of Computer Professionals to individuals who pass an extensive set of programming examinations.

cd *n.* Acronym for **c**hange **d**irectory. In MS-DOS, UNIX, and FTP client programs, the command that changes the current directory to the directory whose path follows *cd* in the command. *See also* directory, path (definition 5).

CD *n.* **1.** An individual compact disc, such as a CD-ROM. *See also* CD-ROM, compact disc (definition 2). **2.** Acronym for **C**arrier **D**etect, a signal sent from a modem to the attached computer to indicate that the modem is on line. *See also* DCD.

CD burner *n. See* CD recorder.

CD drive *n. See* CD-ROM drive.

CD-E *n.* Acronym for **c**ompact **d**isc-**e**rasable. A technological improvement in CDs (compact discs) whereby information can be repeatedly changed on the CD. Contemporary CDs are "write once, read many," in that the information originally written cannot be changed.

cdev *n.* Short for **c**ontrol panel **dev**ice. A Macintosh utility that allows basic system settings to be customized. In Macintosh computers running System 6, a cdev is a utility program placed in the system folder. Keyboard and mouse cdevs are preinstalled. Other cdevs are provided with software packages and utilities. In System 7, cdevs are called control panels. *See also* control panel, system folder. *Compare* INIT.

CDF *n. See* Channel Definition Format.

CDFS *n.* **1.** Acronym for **CD-ROM** **F**ile **S**ystem. A 32-bit protected-mode file system that controls access to the contents of CD-ROM drives in Windows 9x. *See also* protected mode. **2.** A designation used with UNIX computers to indicate that a file system resides on a read-only removable medium (that is a CD-ROM). This usually implies

C

that the compact disc is compliant with the ISO 9660 standard. CDFS is also used as a part of commands that mount media (hard drives, tape drives, remote networked drives, and CD-ROMs) for use on a computer. *See also* CD-ROM, ISO 9660.

CD-I *n.* Acronym for **c**ompact **d**isc-**i**nteractive. A hardware and software standard for a form of optical disc technology that can combine audio, video, and text on high-capacity compact discs. CD-I includes such features as image display and resolution, animation, special effects, and audio. The standard covers methods of encoding, compressing, decompressing, and displaying stored information. *See also* CD-ROM.

CDMA *n. See* Code Division Multiple Access.

CDN *n.* Acronym for **c**ontent **d**elivery **n**etwork. A service that caches the pages of a Web site on geographically dispersed servers to enable faster delivery of Web pages. When a page is requested at a URL that is content delivery–enabled, the content delivery network routes the user's request to a cache server close to the user. *See also* content delivery.

CDP *n.* Acronym for **C**ertificate in **D**ata **P**rocessing. A certificate awarded by the Institute for Certification of Computer Professionals to individuals who pass a set of examinations on computers and related areas, including programming, software, and systems analysis.

CDPD *n. See* Cellular Digital Packet Data.

CD player *n.* Short for **c**ompact **d**isc **p**layer. A device that reads the information stored on a CD. A CD player contains the optical equipment necessary for reading a disc's contents and the electronic circuitry for interpreting the data as it is read.

CD Plus *n.* A compact disc encoding format that allows mixing of audio recordings and computer data on the same CD, without the possibility of audio equipment becoming damaged by attempting to play the data sections.

CD-R *n.* Acronym for **c**ompact **d**isc-**r**ecordable. A type of CD-ROM that can be written on a CD recorder and read on a CD-ROM drive. *See also* CD recorder, CD-ROM.

CD-R/E *adj.* Acronym for **c**ompact **d**isc-**r**ecordable and **e**rasable. Of or pertaining to hardware and software for interfacing computers with both CD-R (compact disc-recordable) and CD-E (compact disc-erasable) devices. *See also* CD-R.

CD recorder *n.* A device used to write CD-ROMs. Because a disc can be written only once on these machines, they are used most commonly to create CD-ROMs for data archives or to produce CD-ROM masters that can be duplicated for mass distribution. *Also called:* CD-R machine, CD-ROM burner. *See also* CD-ROM.

CD-R machine *n. See* CD recorder.

CD-ROM *n.* **1.** Acronym for **c**ompact **d**isc **r**ead-**o**nly **m**emory. A form of storage characterized by high capacity (roughly 650 megabytes) and the use of laser optics rather than magnetic means for reading data. Although CD-ROM drives are strictly read-only, they are similar to CD-R drives (write once, read many), optical WORM devices, and optical read-write drives. *See also* CD-I, CD-R, WORM. **2.** An individual CD (compact disc) designed for use with a computer and capable of storing up to 650 megabytes of data. *See also* CD, disc.

CD-ROM burner *n. See* CD recorder.

CD-ROM drive *n.* An electromechancial device that reads data on CD-ROMs. Most CD-ROM drives have a SCSI interface, although some are connected to a PC via a controller for a disk drive. Data is read through a small laser that is focused on the surface of the CD-ROM through optical mirrors in the read/write head. A spindle and drive motor revolve the CD-ROM, so all data, which is stored in spirals from the center, can be read. CD-ROM drives vary in the access time to locate a track on the CD-ROM and the seek time to move the read/write head. See the illustration. *Also called:* CD drive. *See also* CD-ROM, compact disc.

CD-ROM drive

CD-ROM drive.

CD-ROM Extended Architecture *n. See* CD-ROM/XA.

CD-ROM File System *n. See* CDFS (definition 1).

CD-ROM jukebox *n.* A CD-ROM player that can contain up to 200 CD-ROMs and is connected to a CD-ROM drive in a personal computer or workstation. A user can request data from any of the CD-ROMs in the jukebox, and the device will locate and play the disk that contains the data. Although only one CD-ROM can be played at a time, if multiple CD-ROM jukeboxes are each connected to separate CD-ROM drives that are daisy-chained together to the computer, more than one CD-ROM can be used at a time. *See also* CD-ROM, CD-ROM drive, daisy chain.

CD-ROM/XA *n.* Short for **CD-ROM E**xtended **A**chitecture. An extended CD-ROM format developed by Philips, Sony, and Microsoft. CD-ROM/XA is consistent with the ISO 9660 (High Sierra) standard, with further specification of ADPCM (adaptive differential pulse code modulation) audio, images, and interleaved data. *See also* adaptive differential pulse code modulation, CD-ROM, High Sierra specification.

CD-RW *n.* Acronym for **c**ompact **d**isc-**rew**ritable. The technology, equipment, software, and media used in the production of multiple-write CDs (compact discs).

CDS *n. See* Circuit Data Services.

CDV *n.* **1.** Acronym for **c**ompressed **d**igital **v**ideo. The compression of video images for high-speed transmission. **2.** Acronym for **c**ompact **d**isc video. A 5-inch videodisc. *See also* videodisc.

CD Video *n. See* CDV (definition 2).

CeBIT *n.* One of the world's leading tradeshows for the information technology, telecommunications, and office automation industries. Held annually in Hannover, Germany, CeBIT attracts hundreds of thousands of visitors and exhibitors from more than 60 countries.

CEBus *n.* Short for **C**onsumer **E**lectronic **Bus**. CEBus is an open architecture set of specification documents that define protocols for how to make products communicate through power line wires, low voltage twisted pairs, coax, infrared, RF, and fiber optics. Anyone, anywhere can get a copy of the plans and develop products that work with the CEBus standard.

Celeron *n.* Intel's family of budget-priced microprocessors introduced in 1998. Celeron chips are based on the same P6 microarchitecture as the Pentium II processor. They include an integrated 128-KB L2 cache and support Intel's MMX technology. Celeron chips have speeds of up to 1.3 GHz in early 2002. *See also* Pentium.

cell *n.* **1.** The intersection of a row and a column in a spreadsheet. Each row and column in a spreadsheet is unique, so each cell can be uniquely identified—for example, cell B17, at the intersection of column B and row 17. Each cell is displayed as a rectangular space that can hold text, a value, or a formula. **2.** An addressable (named or numbered) storage unit for information. A binary cell, for example, is a storage unit that can hold 1 bit of information—that is, it can be either on or off. **3.** A fixed-length packet, the basic transmission unit on high-speed networks, such as ATM. *See also* ATM. **4.** Coverage area for wireless phones served by a single base station (cell tower), usually surrounded by six other cells. As a wireless phone moves across the boundary between cells, the conversation is handed from one cell to the next. Cells may be less than a half mile or more than 15 miles in radius, depending on the volume of wireless calls or the presence of large buildings or terrain that might interfere with signals.

cell animation or **cel animation** *n.* A process performed by software that emulates traditional cell animation, which uses transparent celluloid sheets ("cells" or "cels" for short) to overlay active elements in an animation frame onto a static background. Computer cell animation is quite efficient because images can be quickly reproduced and manipulated.

cell padding *n.* The space between the contents and the inside edges of a table cell.

cell reference *n.* The set of coordinates that a cell occupies on a worksheet. For example, the reference of the cell that appears at the intersection of column B and row 3 is B3.

cell relay *n.* A form of packet switching in which information is multiplexed onto a carrier and transferred in fixed-length packets (cells).

cellular automata *n.* **1.** In computer science, theoretical models of parallel computers. They enable the investigation of parallel computers without the need to actually build them. The cellular automaton is composed of a network of multiple cells, each representing a processor in the parallel computer. The cells must be identical, and they must have a finite amount of available memory. Each cell outputs a value calculated from the input values it

C

receives from its neighboring cells, and all cells output their values simultaneously. **2.** Systems in which rules are applied to multiple cells and their neighbors in a regular spatial lattice or grid that advances through time. Usually, each cell in a cellular automaton has any one state out of a finite number of states. The state changes discretely in time according to rules that depend on the condition of the individual cell and its neighbors. Thus, an individual cell in a cellular automaton takes a neighbor cell's state as input before outputting its own state. Additionally, all the cells in the lattice are updated simultaneously, while the state of the entire lattice also advances discretely in time. Many computer simulations of cellular automata are demonstrated on Web sites; the best known Web example is J.H. Conway's Game of Life.

Cellular Digital Packet Data *n.* A wireless standard providing two-way, 19.2-Kbps packet data transmission over existing cellular telephone channels. *Acronym:* CDPD. *See also* packet, wireless.

Cellular Telecommunications and Internet Association *n.* Association based in Washington, D.C. that represents the wireless telecommunications industry and its equipment manufacturers. *Acronym:* CTIA.

censorship *n.* The action of preventing material that a party considers objectionable from circulating within a system of communication over which that party has some power. The Internet as a whole is not censored, but some parts of it come under varying degrees of control. A news server, for example, often is set to exclude any or all of the alt. newsgroups, such as alt.sex.* or alt.music.white-power, which are unmoderated and tend to be controversial. A moderated newsgroup or mailing list might be considered to be "censored" because the moderator will usually delete highly controversial and obscene content or content that is on a different topic from that followed by the newsgroup. Online services have identifiable owners, who often take some share of responsibility for what reaches their users' computer screens. In some countries, censorship of certain political or cultural Web sites is a matter of national policy.

censorware *n.* Software that imposes restrictions on what Internet sites, newsgroups, or files may be accessed by the user.

center *vb.* To align characters around a point located in the middle of a line, page, or other defined area; in effect, to place text an equal distance from each margin or border. *See also* align (definition 1).

centi- *prefix* **1.** One hundred. **2.** One hundredth, as in *centimeter*—one hundredth of a meter.

centralized network *n.* A network in which nodes connect to and use resources on a single central computer, typically a mainframe.

centralized processing *n.* The location of computer processing facilities and operations in a single (centralized) place. *Compare* decentralized processing, distributed processing.

central office *n.* In communications, the switching center where interconnections between customers' communications lines are made.

central office exchange service *n. See* Centrex.

central processing unit *n. See* CPU.

Centrex *n.* An option offered by some phone companies in which up-to-date phone facilities are available to business customers, giving the customer access to a complete range of phone services without having to purchase or maintain the necessary equipment. Customers can purchase just the lines and services they will use. The name *central office exchange* refers to the fact that the phone facilities for Centrex services, particularly switching services, are generally maintained at the offices of the local or central phone company. Since Centrex offers a wider range of services, it is replacing PBX for businesses. *See also* switching. *Compare* PBX.

Centronics parallel interface *n.* A de facto standard for parallel data exchange paths between computers and peripherals, originally developed by the printer manufacturer Centronics, Inc. The Centronics parallel interface provides eight parallel data lines plus additional lines for control and status information. *See also* parallel interface.

CERN *n.* Acronym for **C**onseil **E**uropéen pour la **R**echerche **N**ucléaire (the European Laboratory for Particle Physics). CERN, a physics research center located in Geneva, Switzerland, is where the original development of the World Wide Web took place by Tim Berners-Lee in 1989 as a method to facilitate communication among members of the scientific community. *See also* NCSA (definition 1).

CERN server *n.* One of the first Hypertext Transfer Protocol (HTTP) servers, developed at CERN by Tim Berners-Lee. The CERN server is still in wide use and is free of charge. *See also* CERN, HTTP server (definition 1).

CERT *n.* Acronym for **C**omputer **E**mergency **R**esponse **T**eam. An organization that provides a round-the-clock security consultation service for Internet users and provides advisories whenever new virus programs and other computer security threats are discovered.

certificate *n.* A certificate is sent when a message is digitally signed. The certificate proves the sender's identity and supplies the recipient with a public key with which to decrypt the sender's encrypted messages. *Also called:* digital certificate.

certificate authority *n.* An issuer of digital certificates, the cyberspace equivalent of identity cards. A certificate authority may be an external issuing company (such as VeriSign) or an internal company authority that has installed its own server (such as the Microsoft Certificate Server) for issuing and verifying certificates. A certificate authority is responsible for providing and assigning the unique strings of numbers that make up the "keys" used in digital certificates for authentication and to encrypt and decrypt sensitive or confidential incoming and outgoing online information. *Acronym:* CA. *See also* digital certificate, encryption.

Certificate in Computer Programming *n. See* CCP.

Certificate in Data Processing *n. See* CDP.

certificate revocation list *n.* A document maintained and published by a certification authority that lists certificates that have been revoked. *Acronym:* CRL. *See also* certificate, certification authority.

certificate trust list *n.* A signed list of root certification authority certificates that an administrator considers reputable for designated purposes, such as client authentication or secure e-mail. *Acronym:* CTL. *See also* certificate, certificate authority, root certificate.

certification *n.* **1.** The act of awarding a document to demonstrate a computer professional's competence in a particular field. Some hardware and software suppliers, such as Microsoft and Novell, offer certification in the use of their products; other organizations, such as the Institute for Certification of Computer Professionals (ICCP) and the Computing Technology Industry Association (Comp-TIA), offer more general certification. **2.** The act of awarding a document to demonstrate that a hardware or software product meets some specification, such as being able to work with a certain other hardware or software product. **3.** The issuance of a notice that a user or site is trusted for the purpose of security and computer authentication. Often certification is used with Web sites.

certification authority *n.* An organization that assigns encryption keys. *See also* certificate authority.

CFML *n.* Acronym for **C**old **F**usion **M**arkup **L**anguage. A programming environment and proprietary, tag-based markup language for server-side processing.

CGA *n.* Acronym for **C**olor/**G**raphics **A**dapter. A video adapter board introduced by IBM in 1981. The CGA is capable of several character and graphics modes, including character modes of 40 or 80 horizontal characters (columns) by 25 vertical lines with 16 colors, and graphics modes of 640 horizontal pixels by 200 vertical pixels with 2 colors, or 320 horizontal pixels by 200 vertical pixels with 4 colors. *See also* graphics adapter, video adapter.

CGI *n.* **1.** Acronym for **C**ommon **G**ateway **I**nterface. The specification that defines communications between information servers (such as HTTP servers) and resources on the server's host computer, such as databases and other programs. For example, when a user submits a form through a Web browser, the HTTP server executes a program (often called a CGI script) and passes the user's input information to that program via CGI. The program then returns information to the server via CGI. Use of CGI can make a Web page much more dynamic and add interactivity for the user. *See also* CGI script, HTTP server (definition 1). **2.** *See* Computer Graphics Interface.

cgi-bin *n.* Short for **C**ommon **G**ateway **I**nterface-**bin**aries. A file directory that holds external applications to be executed by HTTP servers via CGI. *See also* CGI (definition 1).

CGI program *n. See* CGI script.

CGI script *n.* Short for **C**ommon **G**ateway **I**nterface script. An external application that is executed by an HTTP server machine in response to a request by a client, such as a Web browser. Generally, the CGI script is invoked when the user clicks on some element in a Web page, such as a link or an image. Communication between the CGI script and the server is carried out via the CGI specification. CGI scripts can be written in many programming languages, including C, C++, and Visual Basic. However, the most commonly used language for CGI scripts is Perl because it is a small but robust language and it is common on UNIX, which is the platform on which the majority of Web sites run. CGI scripts don't necessarily need to be scripts; they can also be batch programs or compiled programs. CGI scripts are used to provide interactivity on a

C

Web page, including such features as providing a form that users can fill out, image maps that contain links to other Web pages or resources, and links that users can click on to send e-mail to a specified address. ActiveX controls and Java applets can provide much the same functionality as CGI scripts, through different means. *See also* CGI (definition 1), cgi-bin, image map, Perl. *Compare* ActiveX control, Java applet.

CGM *n. See* Computer Graphics Metafile.

chad *n.* The paper removed when a hole is punched in a card, in a tape, or at the perforated edge of continuous-form paper—the computer equivalent of a doughnut hole.

chaining *n.* **1.** In computers, the linking of two or more entities so that they are dependent upon one another for operation. **2.** In programming, the linking of two or more programs so that the first program causes the second program to begin executing. **3.** In programming, linking program statements so that each statement, except for the first, relies on the previous statement for input. **4.** With batch files, linking two or more batch files so that the completion of the first batch file causes the second batch file to begin executing. **5.** With data storage, linking two or more individual units of storage. For example, a single file on a disk may actually be stored on several different sectors of the disk, each of which points to the next sector containing a piece of that file. These sectors are said to be chained together, or, more literally, to be a chain of clusters. **6.** *See* daisy chaining.

chain printer *n. See* line printer.

chalkware *n. See* vaporware.

Challenge Handshake Authentication Protocol *n.* An authentication scheme used by PPP servers to validate the identity of the originator of a connection, upon connection or any time later. *Acronym:* CHAP. *See also* authentication, PPP.

change directory *n. See* cd.

change file *n.* A file that records transactional changes occurring in a database, providing a basis for updating a master file and establishing an audit trail. *Also called:* transaction log. *See also* addition record.

change management *n.* **1.** The process of tracking and controlling updates, revisions, and other changes to a hardware or software product or project. **2.** The process of managing change during a company's restructuring or reengineering.

channel *n.* **1.** A path or link through which information passes between two devices. A channel can be either internal or external to a microcomputer. **2.** In communications, a medium for transferring information. Depending on its type, a communications channel can carry information (data, sound, and/or video) in either analog or digital form. A communications channel can be a physical link, such as the cable connecting two stations in a network, or it can consist of some electromagnetic transmission on one or more frequencies within a bandwidth in the electromagnetic spectrum, as in radio and television, or in optical, microwave, or voice-grade communication. *Also called:* circuit, line. *See also* analog, band, bandwidth, digital, electromagnetic spectrum, frequency. **3.** A single color within a digital color space. For example, the RGB color space contains three channels—red, green, and blue—and all colors within the RGB color space are created with a combination of one or more of those three color channels. In CMYK there are four channels—cyan, magenta, yellow, and black. Color management and graphics applications rely on control and manipulation of individual color channels. *See also* color space.

channel access *n.* **1.** A method used in networked systems to gain access to the data communication channel that links two or more computers. Common methods of channel access are contention, polling, and the token ring network. *See also* channel, contention, polling, token ring network. **2.** In wireless technology, an access method such as CDMA (Code Division Multiple Access). *See also* Code Division Multiple Access.

channel adapter *n.* A device that enables hardware using two different types of communications channels to communicate.

channel aggregator *n. See* content aggregator.

channel capacity *n.* The speed at which a communications channel can transfer information, measured in bits per second (bps) or in baud.

Channel Definition Format *n.* A file format based on XML that describes a channel—a collection of Web pages—on a server. The Channel Definition Format is used with the Active Channel feature in Microsoft Internet Explorer to deliver selected, often personalized, information to individuals on a subscription basis. *See also* Active Channel, webcasting.

channel hop *vb.* To switch repeatedly from one IRC channel to another. *See also* IRC.

channel op *n.* Short for **channel op**erator. A user on an IRC channel who has the privilege of expelling undesirable participants. *See also* IRC.

channel operator *n. See* channel op.

Channel Service Unit *n. See* DDS.

CHAP *n. See* Challenge Handshake Authentication Protocol.

character *n.* A letter, number, punctuation mark, or other symbol or control code that is represented to a computer by one unit—1 byte—of information. A character is not necessarily visible, either on the screen or on paper; a space, for example, is as much a character as is the letter *a* or any of the digits 0 through 9. Because computers must manage not only so-called printable characters but also the look (formatting) and transfer of electronically stored information, a character can additionally indicate a carriage return or a paragraph mark in a word-processed document. It can be a signal to sound a beep, begin a new page, or mark the end of a file. *See also* ASCII, control character, EBCDIC.

character cell *n.* A rectangular block of pixels that represents the space in which a given character is drawn on the screen. Computer displays use different numbers of pixels as character cells. Character cells are not always the same size for a given font, however; for proportionally spaced fonts, such as those commonly displayed on the Apple Macintosh, the height within a given font remains the same, but the width varies with each character.

character code *n.* A specific code that represents a particular character in a set, such as the ASCII character set. The character code for a given key depends on whether another key, such as Shift, is pressed at the same time. For example, pressing the A key alone normally generates the character code for a lowercase *a*. Pressing Shift plus the A key normally generates the character code for an uppercase *A. Compare* key code.

character definition table *n.* A table of patterns that a computer can hold in memory and use as a reference for determining the arrangement of dots used to create and display bitmapped characters on the screen. *See also* bitmapped font.

character density *n.* In printing or screen display, a measure of the number of characters per unit of area or of linear distance. *See also* pitch (definition 1).

character device *n.* **1.** A computer device, such as a keyboard or printer, that receives or transmits information as a stream of characters, one character at a time. The characters can be transferred either bit by bit (serial transmission) or byte by byte (parallel transmission) but are not moved from place to place in blocks (groups of bytes). *Compare* block device. **2.** In reference to video displays, a device that handles text but not graphics. *See also* text mode.

character entity *n.* In HTML and SGML, the notation for a special character. A character entity begins with an & (ampersand), followed by either a string of letters or of numbers, and ends with a semicolon. The special characters represented by character entities include acute and grave accents, the tilde, and Greek letters, among others. *Also called:* named entity.

character generator *n.* A program or a hardware device that translates a given character code, such as an ASCII code, into a matching pixel pattern for display on the screen. Such devices are typically limited in the number and range of styles of fonts they support, as compared to machines that support bitmapped characters. *Compare* bitmapped font.

character image *n.* A set of bits arranged in the shape of a character. Each character image exists within a rectangular grid, or *character rectangle*, that defines its height and width. *See also* bitmapped font.

characteristic *n.* In mathematics, the exponent of a floating-point number (the portion following the *E* that indicates the position of the decimal point) or the integer portion of a logarithm. *See also* floating-point notation, logarithm.

character map *n.* In text-based computer graphics, a block of memory addresses that correspond to character spaces on a display screen. The memory allocated to each character space is used to hold the description of the character to be displayed in that space. *See also* alphageometric.

character mode *n. See* text mode.

character-oriented protocol *n. See* byte-oriented protocol.

character printer *n.* **1.** A printer that operates by printing one character at a time, such as a standard dot-matrix printer or a daisy-wheel printer. *Compare* line printer, page printer. **2.** A printer that cannot print graphics, such as a daisy-wheel printer or even a dot-matrix or laser printer that lacks a graphics mode. Such a printer simply receives character codes from the controlling system and prints the appropriate characters. *Compare* graphics printer.

character recognition *n.* The process of applying pattern-matching methods to character shapes that have been read into a computer to determine which alphanumeric characters or punctuation marks the shapes represent. Because different typefaces and text treatments, such as bold and italic, can make big differences in the way characters are shaped, character recognition can be prone to error. Some systems work only with known typefaces and sizes, with no text treatments. These systems achieve very high accuracy levels, but they can work only with text specifically printed for them. Other systems use extremely sophisticated pattern-matching techniques to learn new typefaces and sizes, achieving fairly good accuracy. *See also* magnetic-ink character recognition, optical character recognition, pattern recognition (definition 1).

character rectangle *n.* The space taken up by the graphical representation (bit map) of a character. See the illustration. *See also* bit map.

Character rectangle.

character set *n.* A grouping of alphabetic, numeric, and other characters that have some relationship in common. For example, the standard ASCII character set includes letters, numbers, symbols, and control codes that make up the ASCII coding scheme.

characters per inch *n.* A measurement for the number of characters of a particular size and font that can fit into a line one inch long. This number is affected by two attributes of the type: its point size and the width of the letters in the particular font being measured. In monospace fonts, characters have a constant width; in proportional fonts, characters have varying widths. Thus, measurements of the number of characters per inch must be averaged. *Acronym:* cpi. *See also* monospace font, pitch (definition 1), proportional font.

characters per second *n.* **1.** A measure of the speed of a nonlaser printer, such as a dot-matrix or an ink-jet printer. **2.** A measure of the rate at which a device, such as a disk drive, can transfer data. In serial communications, the speed of a modem in bits per second can generally be divided by 10 for a rough determination of the number of characters per second transmitted. *Acronym:* CPS.

character string *n.* A set of characters treated as a unit and interpreted by a computer as text rather than numbers. A character string can contain any sequence of elements from a given character set, such as letters, numbers, control characters, and extended ASCII characters. *Also called:* string. *See also* ASCII, control character, extended ASCII.

character style *n.* Any attribute, such as boldface, italic, underline, or small caps, applied to a character. Depending on the operating system or program considered, the range of character styles of text might or might not include the font, which refers to the design of a group of characters in a given size. *See also* font family.

character user interface *n.* A user interface that displays only text characters. *Acronym:* CUI. *See also* user interface. *Compare* graphical user interface.

charge *n.* A property of subatomic particles, which can have either a negative charge or a positive charge. In electronics, a charge consists of either an excess of electrons (a negative charge) or a deficiency of electrons (a positive charge). The unit of charge is the *coulomb*, which corresponds to 6.26×10^{18} electrons.

charge-coupled device *n.* A device in which individual semiconductor components are connected so that the electrical charge at the output of one device provides the input to the next. The light-detecting component of digital cameras and many video cameras is a charge-coupled device. *Acronym:* CCD.

chart *n.* A graphic or diagram that displays data or the relationships between sets of data in pictorial rather than numeric form.

chassis *n.* A metal frame on which electronic components, such as printed circuit boards, fans, and power supplies, are mounted. See the illustration.

Chassis.

chat¹ *n.* **1.** Real-time conversation via computer. When a participant types a line of text and then presses the Enter key, that participant's words appear on the screens of the other participants, who can then respond in kind. Most online services support chat; on the Internet, IRC is the usual system. *See also* IRC. **2.** An Internet utility program that supports chat. IRC has largely superseded it.

chat² *vb.* To carry on a real-time conversation with other users by computer. *See also* IRC.

chat room *n.* The informal term for a data communication channel that links computers and permits users to "converse" by sending text messages to one another in real time. Similar to the channels provided by IRC (Internet Relay Chat), chat rooms are available through online services and some electronic bulletin board systems (BBSs). Chat rooms are often devoted to a particular subject or are conducted on a certain schedule. *See also* BBS, chat, IRC, room.

Cheapernet *n. See* 10Base2.

cheat code *n.* In computer games, a secret keyboard sequence or code that gives a player an advantage in the game. For example, cheat codes often confer more ammunition, lives, or the ability to fly or walk through obstacles. *See also* adventure games, computer games.

check bit *n.* One of a set of bits that are added to a data message at its origin and scrutinized by the receiving process to determine whether an error has occurred during transmission. The simplest example is a parity bit. *See also* data integrity, parity bit.

check box *n.* An interactive control often found in graphical user interfaces. Check boxes are used to enable or disable one or more features or options from a set. When an option is selected, an x or a check mark appears in the box. *See also* control (definition 2). *Compare* radio button.

check digit *n.* A digit added to an account number or other identifying key value and then recomputed when the number is used. This process determines whether an error occurred when the number was entered. *See also* checksum.

checkpoint *n.* **1.** A processing juncture at which the normal operation of a program or system is momentarily suspended in order to determine its environmental status. **2.** A file containing information that describes the state of the system (the environment) at a particular time.

checksum *n.* A calculated value that is used to test data for the presence of errors that can occur when data is transmitted or when it is written to disk. The checksum is calculated for a given chunk of data by sequentially combining all the bytes of data with a series of arithmetic or logical operations. After the data is transmitted or stored, a new checksum is calculated in the same way using the (possibly faulty) transmitted or stored data. If the two checksums do not match, an error has occurred and the data should be transmitted or stored again. Checksums cannot detect all errors, and they cannot be used to correct erroneous data. *See also* error-correction coding.

Cheese worm *n.* An Internet worm that patches security holes created by the Lion worm. The Cheese worm searches out and infects Linux-based systems that were previously compromised by the Lion worm, repairing vulnerabilities and closing a back door left by the earlier infection. It then uses the healed computer to scan for other vulnerable computers connected to the Internet and sends itself to them.

Chernobyl packet *n.* A form of network attack in which a data packet sent by a hacker activates every available option for the protocol in use on the receiving system. The Chernobyl packet will cause a packet storm that will eventually overload and crash the network. *Also called:* kamikaze packet.

Chernobyl virus *n. See* CIH virus.

chiclet keyboard *n.* A microcomputer keyboard used on the first version of the IBM PCjr home computer. Chiclet keys are small and square, resembling the chewing gum pieces, and they act like pushbuttons, without the resistance and clear feedback of traditional keys. They are also much smaller and typically are spread out, so touch typing is more difficult than on a conventional keyboard.

child *n.* **1.** A process initiated by another process (the parent). This initiating action is frequently called a *fork.* The parent process often sleeps (is suspended) until the child process stops executing. **2.** In a tree structure, the relationship of a node to its immediate predecessor. *See also* generation (definition 2), tree structure.

child directory *n. See* subdirectory.

child menu *n. See* submenu.

child process *n. See* child (definition 1).

Children's Online Privacy Protection Act *n. See* COPPA.

chimes of doom *n.* In Macintosh computers, a series of chimes that sound as a result of serious system failure.

chip *n. See* integrated circuit.

chip card *n. See* smart card.

chip set or **chipset** *n.* A collection of chips designed to function as a unit in the performance of some common task. The term is most commonly used to refer to the set of integrated circuits, such as the programmable interrupt controller, that support a CPU together with the CPU itself. Often a chip set will fit on one chip. *See also* CPU, integrated circuit, programmable interrupt controller.

choke *n. See* inductor.

choose *vb.* To pick a command or an option from within a graphical user interface, as by clicking a button in a dialog box or pulling down a menu and then releasing the mouse button on one of its options. Although *select* is often used instead of *choose* to describe the same action, *choose* is the preferred term because *select* has specific connotations within computing. *See also* select.

Chooser *n.* On the Apple Macintosh, a desk accessory that allows the user to select a printer or a device on a network, such as a file server or a printer.

Chooser extension *n.* A program that adds items to the Macintosh Chooser desk accessory. At system startup, Chooser adds to its menu of options from the extensions available in the system extensions folder. For example, if you want to use a particular printer with your Mac OS, you must have the right Chooser extension for that printer

in the extensions folder when the computer is turned on. *See also* Chooser, extension (definition 4).

chroma *n.* The quality of a color that combines hue and saturation. *See also* hue, saturation.

CHRP *n. See* Common Hardware Reference Platform.

churn rate *n.* The rate of customer subscription turnover. In beeper, cell phone, and online businesses, it is common for customers to drop their monthly subscriptions, creating a churn rate as high as 2 or 3 percent per month. High churn rates are costly to companies because attracting new subscribers through advertising and promotion is expensive.

CIDR *n. See* classless interdomain routing.

CIFS *n. See* Common Internet File System.

CIH virus *n.* A highly destructive virus that first appeared in early 1998. When activated, the CIH virus code will attempt to overwrite the flash BIOS of infected machines, rendering the computer unbootable. The CIH virus is also known as the Chernobyl virus because in its original form it was set to activate on the anniversary of the Chernobyl nuclear accident. Although the CIH virus lacks stealth or sophisticated replication capabilities and is easily detected by current virus security programs, it continues to appear regularly. *Also called:* Chernobyl virus. *See also* virus.

CIM *n.* **1.** Acronym for **C**ommon **I**nformation **Mo**del. A conceptual specification supported by the Desktop Management Task Force (DMTF) for applying an object-oriented, Web-based model to describing management data in an enterprise network. Part of the DMTF's Web-Based Enterprise Management initiative, CIM is a system-independent and application-independent common framework for describing and sharing management information. It is based on a three-tiered model based on schemas—sets of classes: the Core Schema covers all areas of management; Common Schemas cover specific management areas, such as networks, applications, and devices; and Extension Schemas cover specific technologies, such as operating systems and applications. CIM is supported by a number of industry vendors, including Sun, IBM, Microsoft, and Cisco. *See also* DMTF, WBEM. **2.** Acronym for **c**omputer-**i**ntegrated **m**anufacturing. The use of computers, communication lines, and specialized software to automate both the managerial functions and the operational activities involved in the manufacturing process. A common database is used in all aspects of the process, from design through assembly, accounting, and resource management. Advanced CIM systems integrate computer-aided design and engineering (CAD/CAE), material requirements planning (MRP), and robotic assembly control to provide "paperless" management of the entire manufacturing process. **3.** Acronym for **c**omputer-**i**nput **m**icrofilm. A process in which information stored on microfilm is scanned and the data (both text and graphics) converted into codes that can be used and manipulated by a computer. Computer-input microfilm is similar to processes such as optical character recognition, in which images on paper are scanned and converted to text or graphics. *Compare* COM (definition 4).

CIP *n.* **1.** Short for **C**ommerce **I**nterchange **P**ipeline. A Microsoft technology that provides for secure routing of business data between applications over a public network such as the Internet. CIP is independent of data format and supports encryption and digital signatures, as well as various transport protocols including SMTP, HTTP, DCOM, and EDI value-added networks. Typically, data such as invoices and purchase orders travel over a network through a transmit pipeline and are read from the network by a receive pipeline that decodes and prepares the data for the receiving application. **2.** Short for **C**ommon **I**ndexing **P**rotocol. A protocol defined by the Internet Engineering Task Force (IETF) for enabling servers to share indexing information. CIP was developed to provide servers with a standard means of sharing information about the contents of their databases. With such sharing, a server unable to resolve a particular query would be able to route the query to other servers that might contain the desired information—for example, to find the e-mail address of a particular user on the Web.

cipher *n.* **1.** A code. **2.** An encoded character. **3.** A zero.

ciphertext *n.* The scrambled or otherwise encoded text of an encrypted message. *See also* encryption.

circuit *n.* **1.** Any path that can carry electrical current. **2.** A combination of electrical components interconnected to perform a particular task. At one level, a computer consists of a single circuit; at another, it consists of hundreds of interconnected circuits.

circuit analyzer *n.* Any device for measuring one or more characteristics of an electrical circuit. Voltage, current, and resistance are the characteristics most commonly measured. Oscilloscopes are circuit analyzers.

circuit board *n.* A flat piece of insulating material, such as epoxy or phenolic resin, on which electrical components are mounted and interconnected to form a circuit.

Most modern circuit boards use patterns of copper foil to interconnect the components. The foil layers may be on one or both sides of the board and, in more advanced designs, in several layers within the board. A printed circuit board is one in which the pattern of copper foil is laid down by a printing process such as photolithography. See the illustration. *See also* board, printed circuit board.

Circuit board.

circuit breaker *n.* A switch that opens and cuts off the flow of current when the current exceeds a certain level. Circuit breakers are placed at critical points in circuits to protect against damage that could result from excessive current flow, which is typically caused by component failure. Circuit breakers are often used in place of fuses because they need only to be reset rather than replaced. *Compare* surge protector.

circuit card *n. See* circuit board.

Circuit Data Services *n.* A GTE service that uses circuit switching technology to provide fast data transfer using a laptop computer and cellular telephone. *Acronym:* CDS. *See also* circuit switching.

circuit-switched data *n.* An ISDN option that can be specified for B (bearer) channels that enables an ISDN user to transmit digital data over the channel at 64 Kbps along a point-to-point, dedicated connection for the duration of a call. *Acronym:* CSD. *See also* alternate circuit-switched voice/circuit-switched data, B channel, ISDN. *Compare* circuit-switched voice.

circuit-switched voice *n.* An ISDN option that can be specified for B (bearer) channels that uses the channel to set up a point-to-point, dedicated connection for the digital transmission of voice communications for the duration of a call. *Acronym:* CSV. *See also* alternate circuit-switched

C

voice/circuit-switched data, B channel, ISDN. *Compare* circuit-switched data.

circuit switching *n.* A method of opening communications lines, as through the telephone system, by creating a physical link between the initiating and receiving parties. In circuit switching, the connection is made at a switching center, which physically connects the two parties and maintains an open line between them for as long as needed. Circuit switching is typically used on the dial-up telephone network, and it is also used on a smaller scale in privately maintained communications networks. Unlike other methods of transmission, such as packet switching, it requires the link to be established before any communication can take place. *Compare* message switching, packet switching.

circular list *n.* A linked or chained list in which processing continues through all items, as in a ring, and returns to the starting point, no matter where that point is located in the list. *See also* linked list.

CIS *n.* **1.** Acronym for **C**ompuServe **I**nformation **S**ervice *See* CompuServe. **2.** Short for **c**ontact **i**mage **s**ensor. A light-sensitive mechanism used in scanners and fax machines. A CIS scanner reflects light from a row of light-emitting diodes (LEDs) onto a document or other object and converts the reflected light to digital images. CIS sensors are smaller and lighter than the charge-coupled devices (CCDs) traditionally used in scanners, but the image quality they produce is not as good as the image quality produced by CCDs. *See also* light-emitting diode, scanner. *Compare* charge-coupled device.

CISC *n.* Acronym for **c**omplex **i**nstruction **s**et **c**omputing. The implementation of complex instructions in a microprocessor design so that they can be invoked at the assembly language level. The instructions can be very powerful, allowing for complicated and flexible ways of calculating such elements as memory addresses. All this complexity, however, usually requires many clock cycles to execute each instruction. *Compare* RISC.

CIX *n.* *See* Commercial Internet Exchange.

CKO *n.* Acronym for **C**hief **K**nowledge **O**fficer. A corporate executive in charge of management and distribution of all the business and technical knowledge of a company. The CKO maximizes the value of stored knowledge by ensuring that employees have access, and by avoiding knowledge loss caused by technology-based changes and upgrades in databases and other storage.

ClariNet *n.* A commercial service that distributes news articles from United Press International (UPI) and other news agencies in newsgroups that are part of the clari. hierarchy. Unlike most other newsgroups, access to the clari. newsgroups is restricted to Internet service providers who pay a subscription fee to ClariNet.

clari. newsgroups *n.* Internet newsgroups maintained by ClariNet Communications, Inc. ClariNet newsgroups contain news articles obtained from the Reuters and United Press International wire services, SportsTicker, Commerce Business Daily, and other sources. Unlike most other newsgroups, ClariNet groups are only accessible through Internet service providers who purchase the service. *See also* ClariNet, ISP, newsgroup.

ClarisWorks *n.* *See* AppleWorks.

class *n.* **1.** In object-oriented programming, a generalized category that describes a group of more specific items, called *objects*, that can exist within it. A class is a descriptive tool used in a program to define a set of attributes or a set of services (actions available to other parts of the program) that characterize any member (object) of the class. Program classes are comparable in concept to the categories that people use to organize information about their world, such as *animal*, *vegetable*, and *mineral*, that define the types of entities they include and the ways those entities behave. The definition of classes in object-oriented programming is comparable to the definition of types in languages such as C and Pascal. *See also* object-oriented programming. **2.** For hardware, the method for grouping particular types of devices and buses according to the basic ways that they can be installed and managed by the operating system. The hardware tree is organized by device class, and Windows uses class installers to install drivers for all hardware classes.

Class A IP address *n.* A unicast IP address that ranges from 1.0.0.1 through 126.255.255.254. The first octet indicates the network, and the last three octets indicate the host on the network. *See also* Class B IP address, Class C IP address, IP address classes.

Class A network *n.* An Internet network that can define a maximum of 16,777,215 hosts. Class A networks use the first byte of an IP address to designate the network, with the first (high-order) bit set to 0. The host is designated by the last 3 bytes. Class A addressing currently allows for a maximum of 128 networks. Class A networks are best suited for sites with few networks but numerous hosts and are usually designated for use by large government or educational institutions. *See also* host, IP address.

Class B IP address *n.* A unicast IP address that ranges from 128.0.0.1 through 191.255.255.254. The first two octets indicate the network, and the last two octets indicate the host on the network. *See also* Class A IP address, Class C IP address, IP address classes.

Class C IP address *n.* A unicast IP address that ranges from 192.0.0.1 to 223.255.255.254. The first three octets indicate the network, and the last octet indicates the host on the network. *See also* Class A IP address, Class B IP address, IP address classes.

classful IP addressing *n.* An IP addressing scheme where IP addresses are organized into classes: Class A, Class B, and Class C. *See also* IP address classes.

Classic *n.* An environment within Mac OS X that allows a user to run legacy software. Classic emulates the earlier Macintosh operating system chosen by the user and provides support for programs that aren't compatible with Mac OS X architecture. *See also* Carbon, Cocoa, Mac OS X.

classless interdomain routing *n.* An address scheme that uses aggregation strategies to minimize the size of top-level Internet routing tables. Routes are grouped with the objective of minimizing the quantity of information carried by core routers. The main requirement for this scheme is the use of routing protocols that support it, such as Border Gateway Protocol (BGP) version 4 and RIP version 2. *Acronym:* CIDR. *See also* Border Gateway Protocol, communications protocol, RIP, router, supernetting.

class library *n.* A collection of standard routines and sub-programs that a programmer can use in object-oriented programs. A typical class library for a graphical user interface might include routines for buttons and scroll bars; or a class library for a communications program might include a routine for dialing a telephone line through a modem. *See also* class, object-oriented programming.

classpath *n.* In Java programming, a classpath is an environmental variable that tells the Java Virtual Machine (JVM) and Java programs where to find class libraries, including user-defined class libraries. *See also* class, class library, Java Virtual Machine.

clean boot *n.* Booting or starting a computer using the minimum system files in the operating system. The clean boot is used as a troubleshooting method for isolating

problems associated with software that may be calling on the same system resources at the same time, causing conflicts that lower the performance of the system, make some programs inoperable, or crash the computer. *See also* boot[1], crash[1] (definition 1), operating system.

clean install *n.* Reinstallation of software in a manner that ensures that no application or system files from a previous installation will remain. The procedure prevents smart installer programs from skipping file installations where a file already exists, which could potentially keep a problem from being removed.

clean interface *n.* A user interface with simple features and intuitive commands. *See also* user interface.

clean room *n.* A room in which dust and other small particles are filtered from the air and in which protective clothing is worn to avoid contaminating electronic components and other delicate, sensitive equipment.

Clear key *n.* A key in the upper left corner of the numeric keypad on some keyboards. In many applications, it clears the currently selected menu choice or deletes the current selection. See the illustration.

Clear key.

clear memory *vb.* A process that erases all data stored in RAM.

Clear To Send *n.* *See* CTS.

ClearType *n.* A Microsoft font technology that improves the resolution of text on LCD displays, such as those used on laptop computers. ClearType technology uses proprietary signal processing and the properties of LCD displays to produce clearer, more detailed characters and spacing, and thus significantly increase readability.

CLEC *n.* Acronym for Competitive Local Exchange Carrier. A company that sells access to the public switched telephone network, or other last mile network connections, in competition with a traditional telephone company. *See also* ILEC, last mile.

C

click *vb.* To press and release a mouse button once without moving the mouse. Clicking is usually performed to select or deselect an item or to activate a program or program feature. *See also* right click. *Compare* double-click, drag.

clickable maps *n. See* image map.

click rate *n. See* clickthrough rate.

clicks and mortar *n.* A business that combines an online presence with traditional "bricks and mortar" outlets.

click speed *n.* The maximum interval between the first and second time a user presses a button on a mouse or other pointing device that will still identify these actions as a double-click to the computer as opposed to two single-clicks. *See also* double-click, mouse, pointing device.

clickstream *n.* The path a user takes while browsing a Web site. Each distinct selection made on a Web page adds one click to the stream. The further down the clickstream the user goes without finding the sought item, the more likely he or she is to depart to another Web site. Analysis of usage patterns helps Web site designers create user-friendly site structures, links, and search facilities. *See also* Web site.

clickthrough *n.* The number of times that visitors to a Web site click on an advertising banner within a specified period of time. Clickthrough is one of the elements that Web site producers use to decide how much to charge advertisers. *See also* clickthrough rate.

clickthrough rate *n.* The proportion of visitors to a Web site who click on a banner advertisement there, expressed as a percentage of total visitors to the Web site. *Also called:* click rate. *See also* clickthrough.

clickwrap agreement *n.* A contract or license in software or on a Web site that sets forth conditions for use of the software or for goods and services distributed through the Web site. Users must agree to the terms in a clickwrap agreement—typically by clicking on a button that states "I Agree" or "Agree"—before they can install the software or utilize goods or services. A clickwrap agreement is an electronic version of an End-User License Agreement. *Also called:* clickwrap license. *See also* End-User License Agreement. *Compare* shrinkwrap agreement.

clickwrap license *n. See* clickwrap agreement.

client *n.* **1.** In object-oriented programming, a member of a class (group) that uses the services of another class to which it is not related. *See also* inheritance (definition 1). **2.** A process, such as a program or task, that requests a service provided by another program—for example, a word processor that calls on a sort routine built into another program. The client process uses the requested service without having to "know" any working details about the other program or the service itself. *Compare* child (definition 1), descendant (definition 2). **3.** On a local area network or the Internet, a computer that accesses shared network resources provided by another computer (called a *server*). *See also* client/server architecture, server.

client error *n.* A problem reported by the Hypertext Transfer Protocol (HTTP) client module as the result of difficulty in interpreting a command or the inability to connect properly to a remote host.

client/server architecture *n.* An arrangement used on LANs (local area networks) that makes use of distributed intelligence to treat both the server and the individual workstations as intelligent, programmable devices, thus exploiting the full computing power of each. This is done by splitting the processing of an application between two distinct components: a "front-end" client and a "back-end" server. The client component is a complete, standalone personal computer (not a "dumb" terminal), and it offers the user its full range of power and features for running applications. The server component can be a personal computer, a minicomputer, or a mainframe that provides the traditional strengths offered by minicomputers and mainframes in a time-sharing environment: data management, information sharing between clients, and sophisticated network administration and security features. The client and server machines work together to accomplish the processing of the application being used. Not only does this increase the processing power available over older architectures but it also uses that power more efficiently. The client portion of the application is typically optimized for user interaction, whereas the server portion provides the centralized, multiuser functionality. *See also* distributed intelligence. *Compare* peer-to-peer network.

client/server network *n. See* client/server architecture.

client-side image maps *n.* An image map that performs the processing completely within the client program (i.e., Web browser) itself. Early Web implementations of image maps (circa 1993) transmitted user mouse click coordinates to the Web server for processing. Generally client-side image maps improve the speed of response to the user. *See also* image map.

client-side program *n.* On the Internet, a program that is run on a client computer rather than on a server computer.

clip *vb.* **1.** To cut off the portion of a displayed image that lies beyond a certain boundary, such as the edge of a window. Certain graphics programs also support clipping as a means of masking everything but a certain object so that painting tools, for example, can be applied to the object alone. **2.** To cut a photograph, drawing, or other illustration from a clip art collection—either in a book or on a disk. *See also* clip art. **3.** To cut off the peaks of a signal in an electronic circuit.

clip art *n.* A collection—either in a book or on a disk—of proprietary or public-domain photographs, diagrams, maps, drawings, and other such graphics that can be "clipped" from the collection and incorporated into other documents.

clipboard *n.* **1.** A special memory resource maintained by windowing operating systems. The clipboard stores a copy of the last information that was copied or cut. A paste operation passes data from the clipboard to the current program. A clipboard allows information to be transferred from one program to another, provided the second program can read data generated by the first. Data copied using the clipboard is static and will not reflect later changes. *See also* cut and paste, DDE. *Compare* scrap. **2.** A computer that uses a pen as the primary input device. *See also* clipboard computer, pen computer.

clipboard computer *n.* A portable computer whose overall appearance and operation resembles that of a traditional clipboard. A clipboard computer has an LCD or similar flat display and has a pen for user input instead of a keyboard, mouse, or other input device; the user operates the computer by touching the pen to the display. Data entered in a clipboard computer is generally transferred to another computer via a cable or a modem. A clipboard computer is used as a traditional clipboard is used, as in field work, data collection, or meetings. *See also* pen computer, portable computer.

Clipper Chip *n.* An integrated circuit that implements the SkipJack algorithm, an encryption algorithm created by the National Security Agency that encrypts 64-bit blocks of data with an 80-bit key. The Clipper Chip is manufactured by the U.S. government to encrypt telephone data. It has the added feature that it can be decrypted by the U.S. government, which has tried unsuccessfully to make the chip compulsory in the United States. *See also* encryption.

clipping path *n.* A polygon or curve that is used to mask an area in a document. Only what is inside the clipping path appears when the document is printed. *See also* PostScript.

clip source tag *n.* Computer coding tag that locates a streaming digital media image for use on a Web page. The clip source tag includes the pathway to the image, which may be stored on a Web server, a Web site, or on the computer where the Web page is displayed.

clobber *vb.* To destroy data, generally by inadvertently writing other data over it.

clock *n.* **1.** The electronic circuit in a computer that generates a steady stream of timing pulses—the digital signals that synchronize every operation. The system clock signal is precisely set by a quartz crystal, typically at a specific frequency between 1 and 50 megahertz. The clock rate of a computer is one of the prime determinants of its overall processing speed, and it can go as high as the other components of the computer allow. *Also called:* system clock. **2.** The battery-backed circuit that keeps track of the time and date in a computer—not the same as the system clock. *Also called:* clock/calendar.

clock/calendar *n.* An independent timekeeping circuit used within a microcomputer to maintain the correct time and calendar date. A clock/calendar circuit is battery powered, so it continues running even when the computer is turned off. The time and date kept by the clock/calendar can be used by the operating system (for example, to "stamp" files with the date and time of creation or revision) and by application programs (for example, to insert the date or time in a document). *Also called:* clock, internal clock.

clock doubling *n.* A technology employed by some Intel microprocessors that enables the chip to process data and instructions at twice the speed of the rest of the system. *See also* i486DX2.

clocking *n. See* synchronization (definition 3).

clockless chip *n. See* asynchronous chip.

clock pulse *n.* An electronic pulse generated periodically by a crystal oscillator to synchronize the actions of a digital device.

clock rate *n.* The speed at which the internal clock in an electronic device oscillates. In computers, each tick (oscillation) of the clock is called a cycle, and the clock rate is measured in megahertz, or millions of cycles per second. Also called clock speed, the clock rate determines how quickly the CPU can execute basic instructions, such as adding two numbers, and it is used to synchronize the activities of various components in the system. Between 1981, when the IBM PC was released, and early 2002, typical clock rates for personal computers increased about 1000-fold, from 4.77 MHz to 2 GHz and faster. *Also called:* clock speed, hertz time. *See also* clock (definition 1).

clock speed *n.* *See* clock rate.

clock tick *n.* *See* CPU cycle (definition 2).

clone[1] *n.* A copy; in microcomputer terminology, a look-alike, act-alike computer that contains the same microprocessor and runs the same programs as a better-known, more prestigious, and often more expensive machine.

clone[2] *vb.* To copy or replicate the entire contents of a hard disk drive, including the operating system, configuration settings, and programs, by creating an image of the hard disk drive. Hard disk drives are often cloned for batch installation on other computers, particularly those on a network, or for use as backups.

close[1] *n.* An FTP command that instructs the client to close the current connection with a server. *See also* FTP[1] (definition 1), Web site.

close[2] *vb.* **1.** To end an application's relationship with an open file so that the application will no longer be able to access the file without opening it again. **2.** To end a computer's connection with another computer on a network.

close box *n.* In the Macintosh graphical user interface, a small box in the left corner of a window's title bar. Clicking on the box closes the window. *Compare* close button.

close button *n.* In the graphical user interface for Windows 9x, Windows NT, and the X Window System, a square button in the right corner (left corner in X Windows) of a window's title bar with an x mark on it. Clicking on the button closes the window. *Also called:* X button. *Compare* close box.

closed architecture *n.* **1.** Any computer design whose specifications are not freely available. Such proprietary specifications make it difficult or impossible for third-party vendors to create ancillary devices that work correctly with a closed-architecture machine; usually only its original maker can build peripherals and add-ons for such a machine. *Compare* open architecture (definition 1). **2.** A computer system that provides no expansion slots for adding new types of circuit boards within the system unit. The original Apple Macintosh was an example of a closed architecture. *Compare* open architecture (definition 2).

closed file *n.* A file not being used by an application. An application must open such a file before reading or writing to it and must close it afterward. *Compare* open file.

closed shop *n.* A computer environment in which access to the computer is restricted to programmers and other specialists. *Compare* open shop.

closed system *n.* *See* closed architecture (definition 2).

cloth ribbon *n.* An inked ribbon generally used with impact printers and typewriters. The print element strikes the ribbon and drives it against the paper so as to transfer ink; then the ribbon advances slightly to make fresh ink available. A cloth ribbon is wrapped onto a spool or loaded into a cartridge that is made to fit the printer used. Cloth ribbon, although adequate for most tasks, is sometimes replaced by film ribbon when the crispest possible output is called for. However, a cloth ribbon, which re-inks itself by capillary action, is usable for multiple impressions, unlike a film ribbon. *Compare* carbon ribbon.

CLS *n.* Acronym for **C**ommon **L**anguage **S**pecification. A subset of language features supported by the .NET common language runtime, comprised of features common to several object-oriented programming languages. CLS-compliant components and tools are guaranteed to interoperate with other CLS-compliant components and tools.

cluster *n.* **1.** An aggregation, such as a group of data points on a graph. **2.** A communications computer and its associated terminals. **3.** In data storage, a disk-storage unit consisting of a fixed number of sectors (storage segments on the disk) that the operating system uses to read or write information; typically, a cluster consists of two to eight sectors, each of which holds a certain number of bytes (characters). **4.** A group of independent network servers that operate—and appear to clients—as if they were a single unit. A cluster network is designed to improve network capacity by, among other things, enabling the servers within a cluster to shift work in order to balance the load. By enabling one server to take over for another, a cluster network also enhances stability and minimizes or eliminates downtime caused by application or system failure. *See also* client/server architecture.

cluster analysis *n.* A technique used in data mining and knowledge discovery to group observations by identifying and extracting like or similar group conditions. Cluster analysis aims to describe the structure of a complex data set. *See also* ART, data mining.

C

cluster controller *n.* An intermediary device that is situated between a computer and a group (cluster) of subsidiary devices, such as terminals on a network, and is used to control the cluster.

clustering *n.* The grouping of multiple servers in a way that allows them to appear to be a single unit to client computers on a network. Clustering is a means of increasing network capacity, providing live backup in case one of the servers fails, and improving data security. *See also* cluster (definition 4), server.

cluster network *n. See* cluster (definition 4).

cluster virus *n.* A type of virus that infects once but gives the appearance of infecting every application launched. A cluster virus modifies the file system so that it is loaded before any application that the user attempts to open. Because the virus is also run when running any program, it appears that every program on the disk is infected.

CLUT *n.* Acronym for **C**olor **L**ook **U**p **T**able. In digital graphics applications, a specific set of colors used in the creation of graphics. When a graphic is created or edited, the user may specify a CLUT that corresponds with the needs of print, Web, or other destination media. In Web design, a specific CLUT of browser-safe colors is used to be certain graphics and designs will display consistently across different platforms and with different browsers. *See also* browser CLUT, websafe palette.

CMI *n.* Acronym for **c**omputer-**m**anaged **i**nstruction. Any type of teaching that uses computers as educational tools. *See also* CAI, CBT.

CMOS *n.* **1.** Acronym for **c**omplementary **m**etal-**o**xide **s**emiconductor. A semiconductor technology in which pairs of metal-oxide semiconductor field-effect transistors (MOSFETs), one N-type and one P-type, are integrated on a single silicon chip. Generally used for RAM and switching applications, these devices have very high speed and extremely low power consumption. They are, however, easily damaged by static electricity. *See also* MOSFET, N-type semiconductor, P-type semiconductor. **2.** The battery-backed memory used to store parameter values needed to boot PCs, such as the type of disks and the amount of memory, as well as the clock/calendar time.

CMOS RAM *n.* Short for **r**andom **a**ccess **m**emory made using **c**omplementary **m**etal-**o**xide **s**emiconductor technology. CMOS chips consume extremely little power and have high tolerance for noise from the power supply. These characteristics make CMOS chips, including

CMOS RAM chips, very useful in hardware components that are powered by batteries, such as most microcomputer clocks and certain types of scratchpad RAM that are maintained by the operating system. *See also* CMOS (definition 1), parameter RAM, RAM.

CMOS setup *n.* A system configuration utility, accessible at boot time, for setting up certain system options, such as the date and time, the kind of drives installed, and port configuration. *See also* CMOS (definition 2).

CMS *n. See* color management system.

CMY *n.* Acronym for **c**yan-**m**agenta-**y**ellow. A model for describing colors that are produced by absorbing light, as by ink on paper, rather than by emitting light, as on a video monitor. The three kinds of cone cells in the eye respond to red, green, and blue light, which are absorbed (removed from white light) by cyan, magenta, and yellow pigments, respectively. Percentages of pigments in these subtractive primary colors can therefore be mixed to get the appearance of any desired color. Absence of any pigment leaves white unchanged; adding 100 percent of all three pigments turns white to black. *Compare* CMYK, RGB.

CMYK *n.* Acronym for **c**yan-**m**agenta-**y**ellow-blac**k**. A color model that is similar to the CMY color model but produces black with a separate black component rather than by adding 100 percent of cyan, magenta, and yellow. *See also* CMY.

coaxial cable *n.* A round, flexible, two-conductor cable consisting of—from the center outwards—a copper wire, a layer of protective insulation, a braided metal mesh sleeve, and an outer shield, or jacket of PVC or fire-resistant material. The shield prevents signals transmitted on the center wire from affecting nearby components and prevents external interference from affecting the signal carried on the center wire. Coaxial cable is widely used in networks. It is the same type of wiring as that used for cable television. See the illustration. *Compare* fiberoptic cable, twisted-pair wiring.

Central wire

Insulated material

Braided shield

Outer insulating sheath

Coaxial cable.

COBOL *n.* Acronym for **Co**mmon **B**usiness-**O**riented **L**anguage. A verbose, English-like compiled programming language developed between 1959 and 1961 and still in widespread use today, especially in business applications typically run on mainframes. A COBOL program consists of an Identification Division, which specifies the name of the program and contains any other documentation the programmer wants to add; an Environment Division, which specifies the computers being used and the files used in the program for input and output; a Data Division, which describes the format of the data structures used in the program; and a Procedure Division, which contains the procedures that dictate the actions of the program. *See also* compiled language.

cobweb site *n.* A Web site that is far out of date. *See also* Web site.

Cocoa *n.* A set of object-oriented development tools and interfaces available on Mac OS X. Cocoa contains a set of frameworks, software components, and development tools used to construct applications for Mac OS X and provides programming interfaces in Java and Objective-C. Cocoa is based on NeXT's OpenStep and is integrated with Apple technologies.

CODASYL *n.* Acronym for **Co**nference on **Da**ta **Sy**stems **L**anguages. An organization founded by the U.S. Department of Defense. CODASYL is dedicated to the development of data-management systems and languages, among them the widely used COBOL.

code[1] *n.* **1.** Program instructions. Source code consists of human-readable statements written by a programmer in a programming language. Machine code consists of numerical instructions that the computer can recognize and execute and that were converted from source code. *See also* data, program. **2.** A system of symbols used to convert information from one form to another. A code for converting information in order to conceal it is often called a *cipher*. **3.** One of a set of symbols used to represent information.

code[2] *vb.* To write program instructions in a programming language. *See also* program.

code access security *n.* A mechanism provided by the runtime whereby managed code is granted permissions by security policy and these permissions are enforced, limiting what operations the code will be allowed to perform. To prevent unintended code paths from exposing a security vulnerability, all callers on the call stack must be granted the necessary permissions (possibly subject to override by assertion or denial).

codec *n.* **1.** Short for **co**der/**dec**oder. Hardware that can convert audio or video signals between analog and digital forms. **2.** Short for **co**mpressor/**dec**ompressor. Hardware or software that can compress and uncompress audio or video data. *See also* compress[2], uncompress. **3.** Hardware that combines the functions of definitions 1 and 2.

code conversion *n.* **1.** The process of translating program instructions from one form into another. Code may be converted at the source-language level (for example, from C to Pascal), at the hardware-platform level (for example, from working on the IBM PC to working on the Apple Macintosh), or at the language level (for example, from source code in C to machine code). *See also* code[1] (definition 1). **2.** The process of transforming data from one representation to another, such as from ASCII to EBCDIC or from two's complement to binary-coded decimal.

Code Division Multiple Access *n.* A form of multiplexing in which the transmitter encodes the signal, using a pseudo-random sequence that the receiver also knows and can use to decode the received signal. Each different random sequence corresponds to a different communication channel. Motorola uses Code Division Multiple Access for digital cellular phones. *Acronym:* CDMA. *Also called:* spread spectrum. *See also* multiplexing, transmitter.

code page *n.* In MS-DOS versions 3.3 and later, a table that relates the binary character codes used by a program to keys on the keyboard or to the appearance of characters on the display. Code pages are a means of providing support for character sets and keyboard layouts used in different countries. Devices such as the display and the keyboard can be configured to use a specific code page and to switch from one code page (such as United States) to another (such as Portugal) at the user's request.

code profiler *n.* A tool designed to aid developers in identifying and eliminating the code inefficiencies that cause bottlenecks and degrade performance in their applications. Code profilers analyze an executing application to determine both how long functions take to execute and how often they are called. Using a code profiler is a repetitive process in that the tool must be reused after each section of inefficient code has been found and corrected.

coder *n. See* programmer.

Code Red worm *n.* A fast-spreading and pernicious Internet worm first discovered in mid-2001. The Code Red worm propagates quickly, and any machine that was infected once is potentially vulnerable to re-infection. The Code Red worm is time sensitive, spreading in propagation mode from the 1st to the 19th of each month, attacking in flood mode from the 20th to the 27th, and finally hiding in hibernation mode until the 1st of the next month when the cycle begins again. The worm maintains a list of all computers previously infected, and all these computers will be attacked each month by every newly infected machine. This makes total eradication of the worm difficult because a single machine remaining infected from earlier propagation/attack cycles can potentially re-infect every machine on the list, and each computer might be subject to multiple attacks. At least three versions of the Code Red worm are known to exist. The Code Red worm was named for a caffeinated soft drink by the security team that first tracked the worm.

code segment *n.* **1.** A memory segment containing program instructions. **2.** A named and segregated portion of a program's code typically performing a specific class of operations. Code segments in this sense are often loaded into memory as memory segments. The main program segment is kept in memory, and auxiliary segments are loaded only when they are required.

code signing *n.* The process of adding a digital signature to additions and updates made to source code and applications published on the Internet. Code signing is intended to provide a level of security and trust to Internet software distribution. *See also* digital signature.

code snippet *n.* **1.** In a graphical user interface, programming instructions embedded in a menu option or button defined by the user. The snippet—consisting of one or more lines of source code—determines what the option or button does when chosen or clicked. **2.** A small piece of programming code that is part of a larger program. Usually the code snippet performs a specific function or task.

coding form *n.* A sheet of paper ruled with horizontal and vertical lines to aid in writing source code for older languages that have position-dependent syntax (such as FORTRAN). Most programmers now use graph paper if they use paper at all.

coercion *n. See* cast.

Coffee Pot Control Protocol *n. See* HTCPCP.

coherence *n.* **1.** In raster-scan technology, the assignment of the value of one pixel to the pixel next to it. **2.** In optics,

the property of some electromagnetic waves of being in phase with one another, as in light from a laser.

cold boot *n.* A startup process that begins with turning on the computer's power. Typically, a cold boot involves some basic hardware checking by the system, after which the operating system is loaded from disk into memory. *See also* boot[1]. *Compare* warm boot.

cold fault *n.* A fatal error that occurs immediately upon or shortly after startup as a result of the misalignment of components in the system. The process of running and shutting down any computer induces a series of thermal expansions and contractions in its internal components. Over time, these changes in the dimensions of components can create a microscopic crack in a chip or loosen a pin in a socket; thus, the system crashes when cold, but the problem seems to disappear after the machine is warm. For this reason, some users leave the system unit (but not the monitor) of a computer running from day to day, rather than turn the machine on only when needed.

cold link *n.* A link established upon a request for data. Once the request is filled, the link is broken. The next time data is required, a link from the client to the server must be reestablished. In a client/server architecture, cold links are useful when the linked item consists of a large amount of data. Dynamic Data Exchange (DDE), used in applications such as Microsoft Excel, uses cold links for data exchange. *See also* client/server architecture, DDE. *Compare* hot link.

cold start *n. See* cold boot.

collaboration data object *n.* Microsoft Exchange Server technology for creating messaging and collaboration applications. A collaboration data object consists of a scripting interface added to Microsoft Messaging Application Programming Interface (MAPI). *Acronym:* CDO.

collaborative filtering *n.* A means of deriving information from the experiences and opinions of a number of people. The term was coined by Doug Terry at Xerox PARC, who first used the technique by allowing users to annotate documents as they read them and to choose which documents to read next based not only on their content but also on what others wrote about them. A common use of collaborative filtering is the creation of lists of World Wide Web pages of interest to particular people; by documenting the experiences of several people, a list of interesting Web sites can be "filtered." Collaborative filtering is also used as a marketing research tool; by keeping a

C

database of opinions and ratings regarding several products, researchers can predict which new products the people contributing to the database will like.

collapsed backbone *n. See* backbone (definition 3).

collate *vb.* In data handling, to merge items from two or more similar sets to create a combined set that maintains the order or sequence of items in the original sets.

collating sort *n.* A sort that proceeds by continuous merging of two or more files to produce a certain sequence of records or data items.

collation sequence *n.* The ordering relationship (sequence) among objects that is to be established by a collating sort. *See also* collating sort.

collector *n.* The region of a bipolar transistor into which charge carriers flow under normal operating conditions. The output of the transistor is usually taken from the collector. With respect to the base and emitter, the collector is positive in an NPN transistor and negative in a PNP transistor. *See also* NPN transistor, PNP transistor. *Compare* base (definition 3), emitter.

collision *n.* The result of two devices or network workstations trying to transmit signals at the exact same time on the same channel. The typical outcome is a garbled transmission.

collision detection *n.* **1.** The process by which a node on a local area network monitors the communications line to determine when a collision has occurred; that is, when two nodes have attempted to transmit at the same time. Although network stations usually avoid collisions by monitoring the line and waiting for it to clear before transmitting, the method is not foolproof. When a collision does occur, the two nodes involved usually wait a random amount of time before attempting to retransmit. *See also* contention, CSMA/CD. **2.** The process by which a game or simulation program determines whether two objects on the screen are touching each other. This is a time-consuming, often complicated procedure; some computers optimized for graphics and games, such as the Amiga, have special hardware built in specifically to detect collisions.

colocation or **co-location** *n.* The operation of a server, router, or other device in a facility that provides a dedicated Internet connection, physical space in a secured cage, and regulated power. Colocation services often include fire detection and extinguishing, backup power, technical support, and additional security measures to ensure high availability.

color *n.* In physics, the component of the human perception of light that depends on frequency. For light of a single frequency, color ranges from violet at the high-frequency end of the visible-light band (a small portion of the total electromagnetic spectrum) to red at the low-frequency end. In computer video, color is produced by a combination of hardware and software. Software manipulates combinations of bits that represent the distinct shades of color that are destined for particular positions on the screen (characters or individual dots, called pixels). The video adapter hardware translates these bits into electrical signals, which in turn control the brightnesses of different-colored phosphors at the corresponding positions on the screen of the monitor CRT. The user's eye unites the light from the phosphors to perceive a single color. *See also* color model, color monitor, CRT, HSB, monitor, RGB, video, video adapter.

color bits *n.* A predetermined number of bits assigned to each displayable pixel that determine the pixel's color when it is displayed on a monitor. For example, two color bits are required for four colors; eight color bits are required for 256 colors. *See also* pixel image. *Compare* bit plane.

color box *n.* In the Windows NT and Windows 9x Paint accessory, a graphic screen element in the form of a paint box that is used to select foreground and background colors.

color burst *n.* A technique used to encode color in a composite video signal, originally developed so that black-and-white television monitors could display programs broadcast in color. The color burst consists of a combination of the red, green, and blue intensities (used by black-and-white displays) and two color-difference signals that determine separate red, green, and blue intensities (used by color displays). *See also* color look-up table.

color cycling *n.* A technique used in computer graphics for changing the color of one or more pixels on the screen by changing the color palette used by the video adapter rather than by changing the color bits for each pixel. For example, to cause a red circle to fade away to a black background color, the program need only change the set of signal values corresponding to "red" in the video adapter's color look-up table, periodically making it darker until it matches the black background. At each step, the apparent color of the whole circle changes instantly; it appears to fade rather than to be painted over and over. The speed at which and the degree to which the circle fades are entirely up to the programmer.

color depth *n.* The number of color values that can be assigned to a single pixel in an image. Also known as bit depth, color depth can range from 1 bit (black and white) to 32 bits (over 16.7 million colors). *See also* bit depth.

color gamut *n.* The particular range of colors that a device is able to produce. A device such as a scanner, monitor, or printer can produce a unique range of colors, which is determined by the characteristics of the device itself. *See also* rendering intent.

Color/Graphics Adapter *n. See* CGA.

colorimeter *n.* A device that evaluates and identifies colors in terms of a standard set of synthesized colors.

color look-up table *n.* A table stored in a computer's video adapter, containing the color signal values that correspond to the different colors that can be displayed on the computer's monitor. When color is displayed indirectly, a small number of color bits are stored for each pixel and are used to select a set of signal values from the color look-up table. *Also called:* color map, color table, video look-up table. *See also* color bits, palette (definition 2), pixel.

Color Look Up Table *n. See* CLUT.

color management *n.* The process of producing or reproducing accurate, consistent color across any of a variety of color input, output, and display devices. Color management includes, but is not limited to, accurate conversion of RGB input from input devices such as a scanner or a camera or from display devices such as a monitor to CMYK output for an output device such as a printer. Color management also encompasses application of a device profile, which contains information on color behavior for the printer or other device on which the image will be reproduced, and allowance for environmental variations such as humidity and lighting. *See also* CMYK, RGB.

color management system *n.* A technology designed to calibrate, characterize, and process color production and reproduction across a variety of color input, output, and display devices. *See also* color management.

color map *n. See* color look-up table.

color model *n.* Any method or convention for representing color in desktop publishing and graphic arts. In the graphic arts and printing fields, colors are often specified with the Pantone system. In computer graphics, colors can be described using any of several different color systems: HSB (hue, saturation, and brightness), CMY (cyan, magenta, and yellow), and RGB (red, green, and blue). *See also* CMY, HSB, Pantone Matching System, process color, RGB, spot color.

color monitor *n.* A video display device designed to work with a video card or an adapter to produce text or graphics images in color. A color monitor, unlike a monochrome display, has a screen coated internally with patterns of three phosphors that glow red, green, and blue when struck by an electron beam. To create colors such as yellow, pink, and orange, the three phosphors are lighted together in varying degrees. A video card that uses large groups of bits (6 or more) to describe colors and that generates analog (continuously variable) signals is capable of generating an enormous potential range of colors on a color monitor. *See also* color, color model, Cycolor.

color palette *n. See* palette (definition 1).

color plane *n. See* bit plane.

color printer *n.* A computer printer that can print fullcolor output. Most color printers can also produce blackand-white output.

color saturation *n.* The amount of a hue contained in a color; the more saturation, the more intense the color. *See also* color model, HSB.

color scanner *n.* A scanner that converts images to a digitized format and is able to interpret color. Depth of color depends on the scanner's bit depth—its ability to transform color into 8, 16, 24, or 32 bits. High-end color scanners, commonly used when output is to be printed, are able to encode information at a high resolution or number of dots per inch (dpi). Low-end color scanners encode information at a resolution of 72 dpi and are commonly used for computer screen images not intended for printing. *See also* resolution (definition 1), scanner.

color separation *n.* **1.** The process of printing the colors in a document as separate output files, each of which is to be printed using a different-colored ink. There are two types of color separation: spot color separation and process color separation. *See also* color model, process color, spot color. **2.** One of the output files produced by a color document, to be printed in its own color of ink.

color space *n.* A means of describing color in digital environments. RGB is the most common color space on the Web, and with other color, the most common color space viewed on computer displays, while CMYK is the main color space for desktop publishing and other digital print media.

C

color supertwist nematic display *n. See* supertwist display.

color table *n. See* color look-up table.

column *n.* **1.** A series of items arranged vertically within some type of framework—for example, a continuous series of cells running from top to bottom in a spreadsheet, a set of lines of specified width on a printed page, a vertical line of pixels on a video screen, or a set of values aligned vertically in a table or matrix. *Compare* row. **2.** In a relational database management system, the name for an attribute. The collection of column values that form the description of a particular entity is called a *tuple* or *row*. A column is equivalent to a field in a record in a nonrelational file system. *See also* entity, field (definition 1), row, table (definition 2).

column chart *n.* A bar chart in which values are displayed and printed as vertical bars. See the illustration. *See also* bar chart.

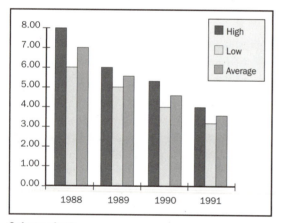

Column chart.

.com *n.* **1.** In the Internet's Domain Name System, the top-level domain that identifies addresses operated by commercial organizations. The domain name .com appears as a suffix at the end of the address. *See also* DNS (definition 1), domain (definition 3). *Compare* .edu, .gov, .mil, .net, .org. **2.** In MS-DOS, the file extension that identifies a command file. *See also* COM (definition 3).

COM *n.* **1.** A name reserved by the MS-DOS operating system for serial communications ports. For example, if a modem is connected to one serial port and a serial printer to another, the devices are identified as COM1 and COM2 by the operating system. **2.** Acronym for **C**omponent

Object **M**odel. A specification developed by Microsoft for building software components that can be assembled into programs or add functionality to existing programs running on Microsoft Windows platforms. COM components can be written in a variety of languages, although most are written in C++, and can be unplugged from a program at runtime without having to recompile the program. COM is the foundation of the OLE (object linking and embedding), ActiveX, and DirectX specifications. *See also* ActiveX, component (definition 2), DirectX, OLE. **3.** The extension reserved by MS-DOS for a type of executable binary (program) file limited to a single 64-kilobyte (KB) segment. COM files are often used for utility programs and short routines. They are not supported in OS/2. **4.** Acronym for **c**omputer-**o**utput **m**icrofilm. Microfilm that can record data from a computer.

COM1 *n.* A serial communications port in Wintel systems. COM1 is usually specified by the I/O range 03F8H, is usually associated with interrupt request line IRQ4, and in many systems is used to connect an RS232 serial mouse. *See also* IRQ.

COM2 *n.* A serial communications port in Wintel systems. COM2 is usually specified by the I/O range 02F8H, is usually associated with interrupt request line IRQ3, and in many systems is used to connect a modem. *See also* IRQ.

COM3 *n.* A serial communications port in Wintel (Windows running on an Intel chip) systems. COM3 is usually specified by the I/O range 03E8H, is usually associated with interrupt request line IRQ4, and in many systems is used as an alternative to COM1 or COM2 if the latter is being used by some other peripheral. *See also* IRQ, port, Wintel.

combinatorial explosion *n.* A condition inherent in certain types of mathematical problems in which small increases in the problem's size (number of data items or parameters of the operation) lead to enormous increases in the time required to obtain a solution. *See also* combinatorics.

combinatorics *n.* A branch of mathematics related to probability and statistics, involving the study of counting, grouping, and arrangement of finite sets of elements. Combinatorics involves the two concepts of combinations and permutations. A combination is the grouping of elements taken from a larger set without regard to the order of the elements in each group; for example, taking two elements at a time from a set of four objects (A, B, C, and D) creates six combinations of objects: AB, AC, AD, BC, BD, and

CD. A permutation is a grouping of elements taken from a larger set with regard to the order of the elements. For example, in making permutations of two objects from the same set of four objects, there would be four candidates to choose from for the first selection (A), and three left over to choose from for the second selection (B), or 12 permutations in all: AB, AC, AD, BA, BC, BD, CA, CB, CD, DA, DB, DC. *See also* combinatorial explosion.

COM callable wrapper *n.* A proxy object generated by the runtime so that existing COM applications can use managed classes, including .NET Framework classes, transparently. *Acronym:* CCW.

COMDEX *n.* Any of a series of annual computer trade shows operated by Softbank COMDEX, Inc. One of these shows takes place in Las Vegas each November and is the largest computer trade show in the United States.

Comité Consultatif International Télégraphique et Téléphonique *n. See* CCITT.

comma-delimited file *n.* A data file consisting of fields and records, stored as text, in which the fields are separated from each other by commas. Use of comma-delimited files allows communication between database systems that use different formats. If the data in a field contains a comma, the field is further surrounded with quotation marks.

command *n.* An instruction to a computer program that, when issued by the user, causes an action to be carried out. Commands are usually either typed at the keyboard or chosen from a menu.

command buffer *n.* An area in memory in which commands entered by the user are kept. A command buffer can enable the user to repeat commands without retyping them completely, edit past commands to change some argument or correct a mistake, undo commands, or obtain a list of past commands. *See also* history, template (definition 4).

command button *n.* A control shaped like a pushbutton in a dialog box in a graphical user interface. By clicking a command button, the user causes the computer to perform some action, such as opening a file that has just been selected using the other controls in the dialog box.

COMMAND.COM *n.* The command interpreter for MS-DOS. *See also* command interpreter.

command-driven *adj.* Accepting commands in the form of code words or letters, which the user must learn. *Compare* menu-driven.

command-driven system *n.* A system in which the user initiates operations by a command entered from the console. *Compare* graphical user interface.

command interpreter *n.* A program, usually part of the operating system, that accepts typed commands from the keyboard and performs tasks as directed. The command interpreter is responsible for loading applications and directing the flow of information between applications. In OS/2 and MS-DOS, the command interpreter also handles simple functions, such as moving and copying files and displaying disk directory information. *See also* shell[1].

Command key *n.* On the original Macintosh keyboard, a key labeled with the special symbol, sometimes called the propeller or puppy foot. This key is found on one or both sides of the Spacebar, depending on the version of the Apple keyboard. The key serves some of the same functions as the Control key on IBM keyboards. *See also* Control key.

command language *n.* The set of keywords and expressions that are accepted as valid by the command interpreter. *See also* command interpreter.

command line *n.* A string of text written in the command language and passed to the command interpreter for execution. *See also* command language.

command-line interface *n.* A form of interface between the operating system and the user in which the user types commands, using a special command language. Although systems with command-line interfaces are usually considered more difficult to learn and use than those with graphical interfaces, command-based systems are usually programmable; this gives them flexibility unavailable in graphics-based systems that do not have a programming interface. *Compare* graphical user interface.

command mode *n.* A mode of operation in which a program waits for a command to be issued. *Compare* edit mode, insert mode.

command processing *n. See* command-driven system.

command processor *n. See* command interpreter.

command prompt window *n.* A window displayed on the desktop used to interface with the MS-DOS operating

C

system. MS-DOS commands are typed at an entry point identified by a blinking cursor. *See also* MS-DOS.

command shell *n. See* shell[1].

command state *n.* The state in which a modem accepts commands, such as a command to dial a telephone number. *Compare* online state.

comment *n.* Text embedded in a program for documentation purposes. Comments usually describe what the program does, who wrote it, why it was changed, and so on. Most programming languages have a syntax for creating comments so that they can be recognized and ignored by the compiler or assembler. *Also called:* remark. *See also* comment out.

comment out *vb.* To disable one or more lines of code from a program temporarily by enclosing them within a comment statement. *See also* comment, conditional compilation, nest.

Commerce Interchange Pipeline *n. See* CIP.

commerce server *n.* An HTTP server designed for conducting online business transactions. Data is transferred between the server and Web browser in an encrypted form to keep information such as credit card numbers reasonably secure. Commerce servers are typically used by online stores and companies that are set up for mail order business. The wares or services offered by the store or company are described and displayed in photographs on the store or company Web site and users can order directly from the site using their Web browser. A number of companies market commerce servers, including Netscape, Microsoft, and Quarterdeck. *See also* HTTP server (definition 1), Secure Sockets Layer, Web browser.

commercial access provider *n. See* ISP.

Commercial Internet Exchange *n.* A nonprofit trade organization of public Internet service providers. In addition to the usual representational and social activities, the organization also operates an Internet backbone router that is accessible to its members. *Acronym:* CIX. *See also* backbone (definition 1), ISP, router.

commercial off-the-shelf board *n.* A hardware board or platform that is readily available in the industry for purchase and can be used for development or test purposes. *Also called:* COTS board.

Common Access Method *n.* A standard developed by Future Domain and other SCSI vendors allowing SCSI adapters to communicate with SCSI peripherals regardless of the particular hardware used. *See also* SCSI.

Common Application Language *n. See* CAL.

common carrier *n.* A communications company (e.g., a telephone company) that provides service to the public and is regulated by governmental organizations.

Common Client Interface *n.* A control interface begun with the X Windows version of NCSA Mosaic whereby other programs can control the local copy of a Web browser. The X Windows and Windows versions of NCSA Mosaic can communicate with other programs via TCP/IP. The Windows version is also capable of OLE communication. *Acronym:* CCI. *See also* Mosaic, OLE, TCP/IP, X Window System.

Common Gateway Interface *n. See* CGI (definition 1), CGI script.

Common Hardware Reference Platform *n.* A specification describing a family of machines, based on the PowerPC processor, that are capable of booting multiple operating systems, including Mac OS, Windows NT, AIX, and Solaris. *Acronym:* CHRP. *See also* PowerPC.

Common Indexing Protocol *n. See* CIP.

Common Information Model *n. See* CIM (definition 1).

Common Internet File System *n.* A standard proposed by Microsoft that would compete directly with Sun Microsystems' Web Network File System. A system of file sharing of Internet or intranet files. *Acronym:* CIFS.

common language runtime *n.* The engine at the core of managed code execution. The runtime supplies managed code with services such as cross-language integration, code access security, object lifetime management, and debugging and profiling support.

common language runtime host *n.* An unmanaged application that uses a set of APIs, called the hosting interfaces, to integrate managed code into the application. Common language runtime hosts often require a high degree of customization over the runtime that is loaded into the process. The hosting interfaces allow common language runtime hosts to specify settings that configure the garbage collector, select the appropriate build for their environment (server versus workstation), and so on. Common language runtime hosts often support an extensibility model that allows the end user to dynamically add new pieces of functionality, such as a new control or a user-written function. These extensions are typically isolated from each other in the process using application domains and custom security settings. Examples of common language runtime hosts include ASP.NET, Microsoft Internet Explorer, and a host to run executables launched from the Windows Shell.

Common Language Specification *n. See* CLS.

Common LISP *n.* Short for **Common List P**rocessing. A formalized and standardized version of the LISP programming language. Because LISP is in the public domain, a number of different versions of the language have evolved, and Common LISP was made a standard to give programmers a definitive source for LISP. *See also* LISP, programming language, standard (definition 1).

Common Object Request Broker Architecture *n. See* CORBA.

common type system *n.* The specification that determines how the runtime defines, uses, and manages types.

Common User Access *n.* A set of standards for management of user interfaces as part of IBM's Systems Application Architecture (SAA). Common User Access is designed to facilitate development of applications that are compatible and consistent across different platforms. *Acronym:* CUA. *See also* standard (definition 1), user interface.

communications *n.* The vast discipline encompassing the methods, mechanisms, and media involved in information transfer. In computer-related areas, communications involves data transfer from one computer to another through a communications medium, such as a telephone, microwave relay, satellite link, or physical cable. Two primary methods of computer communications exist: temporary connection of two computers through a switched network, such as the public telephone system, and permanent or semipermanent linking of multiple workstations or computers in a network. The line between the two is indistinct, however, because microcomputers equipped with modems are often used to access both privately owned and public-access network computers. *See also* asynchronous transmission, CCITT, channel (definition 2), communications protocol, IEEE, ISDN, ISO/OSI model, LAN,

modem, network, synchronous transmission. *Compare* data transmission, telecommunications, teleprocess.

Communications Act of 1934 *n. See* FCC.

Communication Satellite Corporation *n.* Corporation created by the U.S. government to provide international satellite services for telecommunications. *Acronym:* COMSAT.

communications channel *n. See* channel (definition 2).

communications controller *n.* A device used as an intermediary in transferring communications to and from the host computer to which it is connected. By relieving the host computer of the actual tasks of sending, receiving, deciphering, and checking transmissions for errors, a communications controller helps to make efficient use of the host computer's processing time—time that might be better used for noncommunications tasks. A communications controller can be either a programmable machine in its own right or a nonprogrammable device designed to follow certain communications protocols. *See also* front-end processor (definition 2).

communications link *n.* The connection between computers that enables data transfer.

communications network *n. See* network.

communications parameter *n.* Any of several settings required in order to enable computers to communicate. In asynchronous communications, for example, modem speed, number of data bits and stop bits, and type of parity are parameters that must be set correctly to establish communication between two modems.

communications port *n. See* COM.

communications program *n.* A software program that enables a computer to connect with another computer and to exchange information. For initiating communications, communications programs perform such tasks as maintaining communications parameters, storing and dialing phone numbers automatically, recording and executing logon procedures, and repeatedly dialing busy lines. Once a connection is made, communications programs can also be instructed to save incoming messages on disk or to find and transmit disk files. During communication, these types of programs perform the major, and usually invisible, tasks of encoding data, coordinating transmissions to and from the distant computer, and checking incoming data for transmission errors.

communications protocol *n.* A set of rules or standards designed to enable computers to connect with one another and to exchange information with as little error as possible. The protocol generally accepted for standardizing overall computer communications is a seven-layer set of hardware and software guidelines known as the OSI (Open Systems Interconnection) model. A somewhat different standard, widely used before the OSI model was developed, is IBM's SNA (Systems Network Architecture). The word *protocol* is often used, sometimes confusingly, in reference to a multitude of standards affecting different aspects of communication, such as file transfer (for example, XMODEM and ZMODEM), handshaking (for example, XON/XOFF), and network transmissions (for example, CSMA/CD). *See also* ISO/OSI model, SNA.

communications satellite *n.* A satellite stationed in geosynchronous orbit that acts as a microwave relay station, receiving signals sent from a ground-based station (earth station), amplifying them, and retransmitting them on a different frequency to another ground-based station. Initially used for telephone and television signals, communications satellites can also be used for high-speed transmission of computer data. Two factors affecting the use of satellites with computers, however, are propagation delay (the time lag caused by the distance traveled by the signal) and security concerns. *See also* downlink, uplink.

communications server *n.* A gateway that translates packets on a local area network (LAN) into asynchronous signals, such as those used on telephone lines or in RS-232-C serial communications, and allows all nodes on the LAN access to its modems or RS-232-C connections. *See also* gateway, RS-232-C standard.

communications slot *n.* On many models of the Apple Macintosh, a dedicated expansion slot for network interface cards. *Acronym:* CS.

communications software *n.* The software that controls the modem in response to user commands. Generally such software includes terminal emulation as well as file transfer facilities. *See also* modem, terminal emulation.

communications system *n.* The combination of hardware, software, and data transfer links that make up a communications facility.

Communications Terminal Protocol *n.* A terminal protocol that enables a user at a remote location to access a computer as if the remote computer were directly connected (hardwired) to the computer. *Acronym:* CTERM.

community antenna television *n. See* CATV.

COMNET Conference & Expo *n.* Conference and exposition for the communications networking industry. The conference features educational sessions and exhibitions on technical and business issues affecting communications networks.

compact disc *n.* **1.** An optical storage medium for digital data, usually audio. A compact disc is a nonmagnetic, polished metal disc with a protective plastic coating that can hold up to 74 minutes of high-fidelity recorded sound. The disk is read by an optical scanning mechanism that uses a high-intensity light source, such as a laser, and mirrors. *Also called:* optical disc. **2.** A technology that forms the basis of media such as CD-ROM, CD-ROM/XA, CD-I, CD-R, DVI, and PhotoCD. These media are all compact disc–based but store various types of digital information and have different read/write capabilities. Documentation for compact disc formats can be found in books designated by the color of their covers. For example, documentation for audio compact discs is found in the Red Book. *See also* CD-I, CD-R, CD-ROM, CD-ROM/XA, DVI, Green Book (definition 2), Orange Book (definition 2), PhotoCD, Red Book (definition 2). **3.** *See* CD.

compact disc-erasable *n. See* CD-E.

compact disc-interactive *n. See* CD-I.

compact disc player *n. See* CD player.

compact disc-recordable *n. See* CD-R.

compact disc-recordable and erasable *adj. See* CD-R/E.

compact disc-rewritable *n. See* CD-RW.

CompactFlash *n.* Plug-in memory devices designed by the CompactFlash Association for use in digital cameras and, eventually, other devices for storing and transporting digital data, sound, images, and video. CompactFlash devices are small cards 1.7 x 1.4 x 0.13 inches (43 x 36 x 3.3 mm) in size. They are based on nonvolatile flash technology, so they do not rely on batteries or other power to retain information. *See also* digital camera.

CompactFlash Association *n.* A nonprofit association that developed and promotes the CompactFlash specification. Founded in October 1995, it has a membership that includes 3COM, Eastman Kodak Company, Hewlett-Packard, IBM, and NEC, among other corporations. *See also* CompactFlash.

compaction *n.* The process of gathering and packing the currently allocated regions of memory or auxiliary storage into as small a space as possible, so as to create as much continuous free space as possible. *Compare* dispersion, file fragmentation (definition 1).

compact model *n.* A memory model of the Intel 80x86 processor family. The compact model allows only 64 kilobytes (KB) for the code of a program but up to 1 megabyte (MB) for the program's data. *See also* memory model.

CompactPCI *n.* An open bus specification for industrial computing needs developed by the PCI Industrial Computer Manufacturers Group (PICMG). CompactPCI is based on the desktop-computing PCI bus but differs in a number of respects, including a pin-and-socket connector and a design that allows for front loading and removal of cards. CompactPCI is intended for applications such as industrial automation, military systems, and real-time data acquisition. It is suitable for high-speed communications devices, such as routers, and allows for hot-plugging. *See also* hot plugging, PCI local bus.

comparator *n.* A device for comparing two items to determine whether they are equal. In electronics, for example, a comparator is a circuit that compares two input voltages and indicates which is higher.

compare *vb.* To check two items, such as words, files, or numeric values, so as to determine whether they are the same or different. In a program, the outcome of a compare operation often determines which of two or more actions is taken next.

comparison criteria *n.* A set of search conditions that is used to find data. Comparison criteria can be a series of characters that you want to match, such as "Northwind Traders", or an expression, such as ">300".

compatibility *n.* **1.** The degree to which a computer, an attached device, a data file, or a program can work with or understand the same commands, formats, or language as another. True compatibility means that any operational differences are invisible to people and programs alike. **2.** The extent to which two machines can work in harmony. Compatibility (or the lack thereof) between two machines indicates whether, and to what degree, the computers can communicate, share data, or run the same programs. For example, an Apple Macintosh and an IBM PC are generally incompatible because they cannot communicate freely or share data without the aid of hardware and/or software that functions as an intermediary or a con-

verter. **3.** The extent to which a piece of hardware conforms to an accepted standard (for example, IBM-compatible or Hayes-compatible). In this sense, compatibility means that the hardware ideally operates in all respects like the standard on which it is based. **4.** In reference to software, harmony on a task-oriented level among computers and computer programs. Computers deemed software-compatible are those that can run programs originally designed for other makes or models. Software compatibility also refers to the extent to which programs can work together and share data. In another area, totally different programs, such as a word processor and a drawing program, are compatible with one another if each can incorporate images or files created using the other. All types of software compatibility become increasingly important as computer communications, networks, and program-to-program file transfers become near-essential aspects of microcomputer operation. *See also* downward compatibility, upward-compatible.

compatibility box *n. See* DOS box (definition 1).

compatibility mode *n.* A mode in which hardware or software in one system supports operations of software from another system. The term often refers to the ability of advanced operating systems designed for Intel microprocessors (for example, OS/2 and Windows NT) to run MS-DOS software or to the ability of some UNIX workstations and of some Apple Macintosh systems to run MS-DOS software.

Competitive Local Exchange Carrier *n. See* CLEC.

compile *vb.* To translate all the source code of a program from a high-level language into object code prior to execution of the program. Object code is executable machine code or a variation of machine code. More generally, *compiling* is sometimes used to describe translating any high-level symbolic description into a lower-level symbolic or machine-readable format. A program that performs this task is known as a *compiler*. *See also* compiler (definition 2), compile time, high-level language, machine code, source code. *Compare* interpret.

compile-and-go *adj.* Of, pertaining to, or characteristic of a development environment that automatically runs a program after compiling it. *See also* compile, execute.

compiled Basic *n.* Any version of Basic that is translated into machine code prior to execution by a compiler. Basic has traditionally been an interpreted language (translated and executed statement by statement); because compiled

C

Basic generally produces faster-executing programs, it is the technology of choice for professional Basic programmers. *See also* Basic, compiled language, interpreted language.

compiled language *n.* A language that is translated into machine code prior to any execution, as opposed to an interpreted language, which is translated and executed statement by statement. *See also* compiler (definition 2). *Compare* interpreted language.

compiler *n.* **1.** Any program that transforms one set of symbols into another by following a set of syntactic and semantic rules. **2.** A program that translates all the source code of a program written in a high-level language into object code prior to execution of the program. *See also* assembler, compile, high-level language, interpreted language, language processor, object code.

compile time *n.* **1.** The amount of time required to perform a compilation of a program. Compile time can range from a fraction of a second to many hours, depending on the size and complexity of the program, the speed of the compiler, and the performance of the hardware. *See also* compiler (definition 2). **2.** The point at which a program is being compiled (i.e., most languages evaluate constant expressions at compile time but evaluate variable expressions at run time). *See also* link time, run time.

compile-time binding *n.* Assignment of a meaning to an identifier (such as a function name or a constant) in a program at the time the program is compiled rather than at the time it is run. *Compare* run-time binding.

complement *n.* Loosely, a number that can be thought of as the mirror image of another number written to the same base, such as base 10 or base 2. Complements are commonly used to represent negative numbers. Two types of complements are encountered in computer-related contexts: radix-minus-1 complements and true complements. A radix-minus-1 complement is known in the decimal system as a nine's complement and in the binary system as a one's complement. True complements are known in the decimal system as ten's complement and in binary as two's complement—a form commonly used to represent negative numbers in processing. *See also* complementary operation, nine's complement, one's complement, ten's complement, two's complement.

complementary metal-oxide semiconductor *n. See* CMOS.

complementary operation *n.* In Boolean logic, an operation that produces the opposite result from that of another operation performed on the same data. For example, if A is true, NOT A (its complement) is false. *See also* Boolean algebra.

completeness check *n.* A survey to determine that all data required in a record is present. *Compare* consistency check.

complex instruction set computing *n. See* CISC.

complex number *n.* A number of the form $a + bi$, where a and b are real numbers and i is the square root of -1, called the imaginary unit. Complex numbers can be plotted as points on a two-dimensional plane called the complex plane. The a number is plotted along the plane's horizontal axis (the real axis), and the b number is plotted along the vertical axis (the imaginary axis). *Compare* real number.

comp. newsgroups *n.* Usenet newsgroups that are part of the comp. hierarchy and have the prefix comp. These newsgroups are devoted to discussions of computer hardware, software, and other aspects of computer science. Comp. newsgroups are one of the seven original Usenet newsgroup hierarchies. The other six are misc., news., rec., sci., soc., and talk. *See also* newsgroup, traditional newsgroup hierarchy, Usenet.

component *n.* **1.** A discrete part of a larger system or structure. **2.** An individual modular software routine that has been compiled and dynamically linked, and is ready to use with other components or programs. *See also* compile, component software, link (definition 1), program, routine. **3.** In Sun Microsystem's J2EE network platform, an application-level software unit supported by a container. Components are configurable at deployment time. The J2EE platform defines four types of components: enterprise java beans, Web components, applets, and application clients. *See also* applet, container (definition 3), Enterprise Java-Beans, J2EE.

Component Object Model *n. See* COM (definition 2).

Component Pascal *n.* A Pascal derivative designed for programming software components for .NET and JVM platforms. *See also* Oberon, Pascal.

component software *n.* Modular software routines, or components, that can be combined with other components to form an overall program. A programmer can use and reuse an existing component and not have to understand its inner workings, just how to have another program or component call it and pass data to and from it. *Also called:* componentware. *See also* component, program, routine.

C

componentware *n. See* component software.

COM port or **comm port** *n.* Short for **com**munications **port**, the logical address assigned by MS-DOS (versions 3.3 and later) and Microsoft Windows (including Windows 9x and Windows NT) to each of the four serial ports on an IBM Personal Computer or a PC compatible. COM ports also have come to be known as the actual serial ports on a PC's CPU where peripherals, such as printers, scanners, and external modems, are plugged in. See the illustration. *See also* COM (definition 1), input/output port, serial port.

— COM port

COM port.

composite display *n.* A display, characteristic of television monitors and some computer monitors, that is capable of extracting an image from a composite signal (also called an *NTSC signal*). A composite display signal carries on one wire not only the coded information required to form an image on the screen but also the pulses needed to synchronize horizontal and vertical scanning as the electron beam sweeps back and forth across the screen. Composite displays can be either monochrome or color. A composite color signal combines the three primary video colors (red, green, and blue) in a color burst component that determines the shade of color displayed on the screen. Composite color monitors are less readable than either monochrome monitors or the RGB color monitors that use separate signals (and wires) for the red, green, and blue components of the image. *See also* color burst, color monitor, monochrome display, NTSC, RGB monitor.

composite key *n.* A key whose definition consists of two or more fields in a file, columns in a table, or attributes in a relation.

composite video display *n.* A display that receives all encoded video information (including color, horizontal synchronization, and vertical synchronization) in one signal. A composite video signal under NTSC (National Television System Committee) standards is generally required for television sets and videotape recorders. *See also* NTSC. *Compare* RGB monitor.

compound document *n.* A document that contains different types of information, each type created with a different application; for example, a report containing both charts (created with a spreadsheet) and text (created with a word processor) is a compound document. Although a compound document is visually a single, seamless unit, it is actually formed of discrete objects (blocks of information) that are created in their own applications. These objects can either be physically *embedded* in the destination document, or they can be *linked* to it while remaining in the originating file. Both embedded and linked objects can be edited. Linked objects, however, can be updated to reflect changes made to the source file. *See also* ActiveX, OLE, OpenDoc.

compound statement *n.* A single instruction composed of two or more individual instructions.

compress[1] *n.* A proprietary UNIX utility for reducing the size of data files. Files compressed with this utility have the extension .Z added to their names.

compress[2] *vb.* To reduce the size of a set of data, such as a file or a communications message, so that it can be stored in less space or transmitted with less bandwidth. Data can be compressed by removing repeated patterns of bits and replacing them with some form of summary that takes up less space; restoring the repeated patterns decompresses the data. Lossless compression methods must be used for text, code, and numeric data files; lossy compression may be used for video and sound files. *See also* lossless compression, lossy compression.

compressed digital video *n. See* CDV (definition 1).

compressed disk *n.* A hard disk or floppy disk whose apparent capacity to hold data has been increased through the use of a compression utility, such as Stacker or Double Space. *See also* data compression.

compressed drive *n.* A hard disk whose apparent capacity has been increased through the use of a compression utility, such as Stacker or Double Space. *See also* compressed disk, data compression.

compressed file *n.* A file whose contents have been compressed by a special utility program so that it occupies less space on a disk or other storage device than in its uncompressed (normal) state. *See also* installation program, LHARC, PKUNZIP, PKZIP, utility program.

Compressed Read-Only File System *n. See* cramfs.

C

Compressed SLIP *n.* Short for **Compressed S**erial **L**ine **I**nternet **P**rotocol. A version of SLIP using compressed Internet address information, thereby making the protocol faster than SLIP. *Acronym:* CSLIP. *See also* SLIP.

compression *n. See* data compression.

compressor *n.* A device that limits some aspect of a transmitted signal, such as volume, in order to increase efficiency.

CompuServe *n.* An online information service that is a subsidiary of America Online. CompuServe provides information and communications capabilities, including Internet access. It is primarily known for its technical support forums for commercial hardware and software products and for being one of the first large commercial online services. CompuServe also operates various private network services.

computational intelligence *n.* The study of the design of intelligent agents whose reasoning is based on computational methods. The central scientific goal of computational intelligence is to understand the principles that make intelligent behavior possible, in natural or artificial systems. An intelligent agent is flexible to changing environments and changing goals—it learns from experience, and it makes appropriate choices given perceptual limitations and finite computation. The central engineering goal of computational intelligence is to specify methods for the design of useful, intelligent artifacts. *See also* agents (definition 2), artificial intelligence, autonomous agent.

computation-bound *adj.* Of, pertaining to, or characteristic of a situation in which the performance of a computer is limited by the number of arithmetic operations the microprocessor must perform. When a system is computation-bound, the microprocessor is overloaded with calculations. *Also called:* CPU-bound.

compute *vb.* **1.** To perform calculations. **2.** To use a computer or cause it to do work.

computer *n.* Any device capable of processing information to produce a desired result. No matter how large or small they are, computers typically perform their work in three well-defined steps: (1) accepting input, (2) processing the input according to predefined rules (programs), and (3) producing output. There are several ways to categorize computers, including class (ranging from microcomputers to supercomputers), generation (first through fifth generation), and mode of processing (analog versus digital). See the table. *See also* analog, digital (definition

2), integrated circuit, large-scale integration, very-large-scale integration.

Table C.1   Ways to Categorize Computers

Class	Computers can be classified as super-computers, mainframes, superminicomputers, minicomputers, workstations, microcomputers, or PDAs. All other things (for example, the age of the machine) being equal, such a categorization provides some indication of the computer's speed, size, cost, and abilities.
Generation	First-generation computers of historic significance, such as UNIVAC, introduced in the early 1950s, were based on vacuum tubes. Second-generation computers, appearing in the early 1960s, were those in which transistors replaced vacuum tubes. Third-generation computers, dating from the 1960s, were those in which integrated circuits replaced transistors. Fourth-generation computers, appearing in the mid-1970s, are those, such as microcomputers, in which large-scale integration (LSI) enabled thousands of circuits to be incorporated on one chip. Fifth-generation computers are expected to combine very-large-scale integration (VLSI) with sophisticated approaches to computing, including artificial intelligence and true distributed processing.
Mode of processing	Computers are either analog or digital. Analog computers, generally used in scientific pursuits, represent values by continuously variable signals that can have any of an infinite number of values within a limited range at any particular time. Digital computers, the type most people think of as computers, represent values by discrete signals—the bits representing the binary digits 0 and 1.

computer-aided design *n. See* CAD.

computer-aided design and drafting *n. See* CADD.

computer-aided design/computer-aided manufacturing *n. See* CAD/CAM.

computer-aided engineering *n. See* CAE.

computer-aided instruction *n. See* CAI.

computer-aided learning *n. See* CAL.

computer-aided manufacturing *n. See* CAM (definition 1).

computer-aided testing *n. See* CAT (definition 1).

Computer and Business Equipment Manufacturers Association *n. See* CBEMA.

computer art *n.* A broad term that can refer either to art created on a computer or to art generated by a computer, the difference being whether the artist is human or electronic. When created by human beings, computer art is done with painting programs that offer a range of line-drawing tools, brushes, shapes, patterns, and colors. Some programs also offer predrawn figures and animation capabilities.

computer-assisted diagnosis *n.* The use of computers by physicians in diagnosing patient conditions. Medical application programs can help to determine the cause, symptoms, and treatment of a problem as well as to maintain a record of a patient's medical history and test results. *See also* expert system.

computer-assisted instruction *n. See* CAI.

computer-assisted learning *n. See* CAL.

computer-assisted teaching *n. See* CAI.

computer-augmented learning *n. See* CAL.

computer-based learning *n. See* CBL.

computer-based training *n. See* CBT.

computer center *n.* A centralized location that contains computers, such as mainframes or minicomputers, along with associated equipment for providing data processing services to a group of people.

computer conferencing *n.* Person-to-person interaction through the use of computers located in different places but connected through communications facilities.

computer control console *n. See* system console.

computer crime *n.* The illegal use of a computer by an unauthorized individual, either for pleasure (as by a computer hacker) or for profit (as by a thief). *See also* hacker (definition 2).

computer-dependent *adj. See* hardware-dependent.

Computer Emergency Response Team *n. See* CERT.

computer engineering *n.* The discipline that involves the design and underlying philosophies involved in the development of computer hardware.

computer family *n.* A term commonly used to indicate a group of computers that are built around the same microprocessor or around a series of related microprocessors and that share significant design features. For example, the Apple Macintosh computers, from the original Macintosh (introduced in 1984) to the Quadra, represent a family designed by Apple around the Motorola 68000, 68020, 68030, and 68040 microprocessors. Computer families tend to parallel microprocessor families, but this is not always the case. For instance, Macintoshes are no longer made with 680x0 processors, and the Macintosh family has "extended" to another generation: the Power Macs, based on the PowerPC microprocessor.

computer game *n.* A class of computer program in which one or more users interacts with the computer as a form of entertainment. Computer games run the gamut from simple alphabet games for toddlers to chess, treasure hunts, war games, and simulations of world events. The games are controlled from a keyboard or with a joystick or other device and are supplied on disks, on CD-ROMs, as game cartridges, on the Internet, or as arcade devices.

computer graphics *n.* The display of "pictures," as opposed to only alphabetic and numeric characters, on a computer screen. Computer graphics encompasses different methods of generating, displaying, and storing information. Thus, computer graphics can refer to the creation of business charts and diagrams; the display of drawings, italic characters, and mouse pointers on the screen; or the way images are generated and displayed on the screen. *See also* graphics mode, presentation graphics, raster graphics, vector graphics.

Computer Graphics Interface *n.* A software standard applied to computer graphics devices, such as printers and plotters. Computer Graphics Interface is an offshoot of a widely recognized graphics standard called GKS (Graphical Kernel System), which provides applications programmers with standard methods of creating, manipulating, and displaying or printing computer graphics. *Acronym:* CGI. *See also* Graphical Kernel System.

Computer Graphics Metafile *n.* A software standard related to the widely recognized GKS (Graphical Kernel

C

System) that provides applications programmers with a standard means of describing a graphic as a set of instructions for re-creating it. A graphics metafile can be stored on disk or sent to an output device; Computer Graphics Metafile provides a common language for describing such files in relation to the GKS standard. *Acronym:* CGM. *See also* Graphical Kernel System.

computer-independent language *n.* A computer language designed to be independent of any given hardware platform. Most high-level languages are intended to be computer-independent; actual implementations of the languages (in the form of compilers and interpreters) tend to have some hardware-specific features and aspects. *See also* computer language.

computer-input microfilm *n. See* CIM (definition 2).

computer instruction *n.* **1.** An instruction that a computer can recognize and act on. *See also* machine instruction. **2.** The use of a computer in teaching. *See also* CAI.

computer-integrated manufacturing *n. See* CIM (definition 1).

computer interface unit *n. See* interface (definition 3).

computerized axial tomography *n. See* CAT (definition 3).

computerized mail *n. See* e-mail[1].

computer language *n.* An artificial language that specifies instructions to be executed on a computer. The term covers a wide spectrum, from binary-coded machine language to high-level languages. *See also* assembly language, high-level language, machine code.

computer letter *n. See* form letter.

computer literacy *n.* Knowledge and an understanding of computers combined with the ability to use them effectively. On the least specialized level, computer literacy involves knowing how to turn on a computer, start and stop simple application programs, and save and print information. At higher levels, computer literacy becomes more detailed, involving the ability of power users to manipulate complex applications and, possibly, to program in languages such as Basic or C. At the highest levels, computer literacy leads to specialized technical knowledge of electronics and assembly language. *See also* power user.

computer-managed instruction *n. See* CMI.

computer name *n.* In computer networking, a name that uniquely identifies a computer to the network. A computer's name cannot be the same as any other computer or domain name on the network. It differs from a user name in that the computer name is used to identify a particular computer and all its shared resources to the rest of the system so that they can be accessed. *Compare* alias (definition 2), user name.

computer network *n. See* network.

computer-output microfilm *n. See* COM (definition 4).

computerphile *n.* A person who is immersed in the world of computing, who collects computers, or whose hobby involves computing.

computer power *n.* The ability of a computer to perform work. If defined as the number of instructions the machine can carry out in a given time, computer power is measured in millions of instructions per second (MIPS) or millions of floating-point operations per second (MFLOPS). Power is measured in other ways too, depending on the needs or objectives of the person evaluating the machine. By users or purchasers of computers, power is often considered in terms of the machine's amount of random access memory (RAM), the speed at which the processor works, or the number of bits (8, 16, 32, and so on) handled by the computer at one time. Other factors enter into such an evaluation, however; two of the most important are how well the components of the computer work together and how well they are matched to the tasks required of them. For example, no matter how fast or powerful the computer, its speed will be hampered during operations involving the hard disk if the hard disk is slow (for example, with an access time of 65 milliseconds or higher). *See also* access time (definition 2), benchmark[1], MFLOPS, MIPS.

Computer Press Association *n.* A trade organization of journalists, broadcasters, and authors who write or report about computer technology and the computer industry.

Computer Professionals for Social Responsibility *n. See* CPSR.

computer program *n.* A set of instructions in some computer language intended to be executed on a computer so as to perform some task. The term usually implies a self-contained entity, as opposed to a routine or a library. *See also* computer language. *Compare* library (definition 1), routine.

computer-readable *adj.* Of, pertaining to, or characteristic of information that can be interpreted and acted on by a computer. Two types of information are referred to as computer-readable: bar codes, magnetic tape, magnetic-ink characters, and other formats that can be scanned in some way and read as data by a computer; and machine code, the form in which instructions and data reach the computer's microprocessor.

computer revolution *n.* The societal and technological phenomenon involving the swift development and widespread use and acceptance of computers—specifically single-user personal computers. The impact of these machines is considered revolutionary for two reasons. First, their appearance and success were rapid. Second, and more important, their speed and accuracy produced a change in the ways in which information can be processed, stored, and transferred.

computer science *n.* The study of computers, including their design, operation, and use in processing information. Computer science combines both theoretical and practical aspects of engineering, electronics, information theory, mathematics, logic, and human behavior. Aspects of computer science range from programming and computer architecture to artificial intelligence and robotics.

computer security *n.* The steps taken to protect a computer and the information it contains. On large systems or those handling financial or confidential data, computer security requires professional supervision that combines legal and technical expertise. On a microcomputer, data protection can be achieved by backing up and storing copies of files in a separate location, and the integrity of data on the computer can be maintained by assigning passwords to files, marking files read-only to avoid changes to them, physically locking a hard disk, storing sensitive information on floppy disks kept in locked cabinets, and installing special programs to protect against viruses. On a computer that many people have access to, security can be maintained by requiring personnel to use passwords and by granting only approved users access to sensitive information. *See also* bacterium, encryption, virus.

computer simulation *n. See* simulation.

computer system *n.* The configuration that includes all functional components of a computer and its associated hardware. A basic microcomputer system includes a console, or system unit, with one or more disk drives, a monitor, and a keyboard. Additional hardware, called *peripherals*, can include such devices as a printer, a modem, and a mouse. Software is usually not considered part of a computer system, although the operating system that runs the hardware is known as system software.

computer telephone integration *n.* A process allowing computer applications to answer incoming calls, provide database information on-screen at the same time the call comes in, automatically route and reroute calls by drag-and-drop, automatically dial and speed-dial outgoing calls from a computer-resident database, and identify incoming customer calls and transfer them to predetermined destinations. *See also* drag-and-drop.

Computer Telephony Expo *n. See* CT Expo.

computer typesetting *n.* Typesetting operations that are partially or totally controlled by computers. Partial control can involve the transmittal of text directly from the source to the typesetter, without a paste-up stage. Full computerization can include the digitization of all graphics, which would then also be transmitted directly to the typesetter and regenerated without paste-up.

computer users' group *n. See* user group.

computer utility *n. See* utility.

computer virus *n. See* virus.

computer vision *n.* The processing of visual information by a computer. Computer vision is a form of artificial intelligence that creates a symbolic description of images that are generally input from a video camera or sensor in order to convert the images to digital form. Computer vision is often associated with robotics. *Acronym:* CV. *See also* artificial intelligence, robotics.

Computer Vision Syndrome *n.* A change in a user's vision caused by prolonged exposure to computer monitors. Symptoms of Computer Vision Syndrome (CVS) can include blurred vision, dry, burning eyes, focusing problems, and headaches. CVS may be controlled with regular breaks from the computer, use of monitor filters or color adjustments, or adjustments to eyeglass prescriptions. *Acronym:* CVS.

COM recorder *n.* Short for **c**omputer **o**utput **m**icrofilm **recorder**. A device that records computer information on microfilm.

COMSAT *n. See* Communication Satellite Corporation.

CON *n.* The logical device name for *console*; reserved by the MS-DOS operating system for the keyboard and the screen. The input-only keyboard and the output-only

C

screen together make up the console and represent the primary sources of input and output in an MS-DOS computer system.

concatenate *vb.* To join sequentially (for example, to combine the two strings "hello" and "there" into the single string "hello there"). *See also* character string.

concatenated data set *n.* A group of separate sets of related data treated as a single unit for processing.

concentrator *n.* A communications device that combines signals from multiple sources, such as terminals on a network, into one or more signals before sending them to their destination. *Compare* multiplexer (definition 2).

conceptual schema *n.* In a database model that supports a three-schema architecture (such as that described by ANSI/X3/SPARC), a description of the information contents and structure of a database. A conceptual schema (also known as a *logical schema*) provides a model of the total database, thus acting as an intermediary between the two other types of schemas (internal and external) that deal with storing information and presenting it to the user. Schemas are generally defined using commands from a DDL (data definition language) supported by the database system. *See also* internal schema, schema.

concordance *n.* A list of words that appear in a document, along with the contexts of the appearances.

concrete class *n.* In object-oriented programming, a class in which objects can be created. *See also* class (definition 1). *Compare* abstract class.

concurrent *adj.* Of, pertaining to, or characteristic of a computer operation in which two or more processes (programs) have access to the microprocessor's time and are therefore carried out nearly simultaneously. Because a microprocessor can work with much smaller units of time than people can perceive, concurrent processes appear to be occurring simultaneously but in reality are not.

concurrent execution *n.* The apparently simultaneous execution of two or more routines or programs. Concurrent execution can be accomplished on a single process or by using time-sharing techniques, such as dividing programs into different tasks or threads of execution, or by using multiple processors. *Also called:* parallel execution. *See also* parallel algorithm, processor, sequential execution, task, thread (definition 1), time-sharing.

concurrent operation *n. See* concurrent.

concurrent processing *n. See* concurrent.

concurrent program execution *n. See* concurrent.

Concurrent Versions System *n. See* CVS (definition 2).

condensed *adj.* Of, pertaining to, or characteristic of a font style, supported in some applications, that reduces the width of each character and then sets the characters closer together than their normal spacing. Many dot-matrix printers have a feature that causes the printer to reduce the width of each character and print them closer together, resulting in more characters fitting on a single line. *Compare* expanded.

condition *n.* The state of an expression or a variable (for example, when a result can be either true or false, or equal or not equal).

conditional *adj.* Of, pertaining to, or characteristic of an action or operation that takes place based on whether or not a certain condition is true. *See also* Boolean expression, conditional statement.

conditional branch *n.* In a program, a branch instruction that occurs when a particular condition code is true or false. The term is normally used in relation to low-level languages. *See also* branch instruction, condition code.

conditional compilation *n.* Selective compilation or translation of source code of a program based on certain conditions or flags; for example, sections of a program specified by the programmer might be compiled only if a DEBUG flag has been defined at compilation time. *See also* comment out.

conditional expression *n. See* Boolean expression.

conditional jump *n.* In a program, a jump instruction that occurs when a particular condition code is true or false. The term is normally used in relation to low-level languages. *See also* condition code, jump instruction.

conditional statement *n.* A programming-language statement that selects an execution path based on whether some condition is true or false (for example, the IF statement). *See also* case statement, conditional, IF statement, statement.

conditional transfer *n.* A transfer of the flow of execution to a given location in a program based on whether a particular condition is true. The term is usually used in relation to high-level languages. *See also* conditional statement.

condition code *n.* One of a set of bits that are set *on* (1, or true) or *off* (0, or false) as the result of previous machine instructions. The term is used primarily in assembly or machine language situations. Condition codes are hardware-specific but usually include carry, overflow, zero result, and negative result codes. *See also* conditional branch.

conditioning *n.* The use of special equipment to improve the ability of a communications line to transmit data. Conditioning controls or compensates for signal attenuation, noise, and distortion. It can be used only on leased lines, where the path from sending to receiving computer is known in advance.

conductor *n.* A substance that conducts electricity well. Metals are good conductors, with silver and gold being among the best. The most commonly used conductor is copper. *Compare* insulator, semiconductor.

Conference on Data Systems Languages *n. See* CODASYL.

CONFIG.SYS *n.* A special text file that controls certain aspects of operating-system behavior in MS-DOS and OS/2. Commands in the CONFIG.SYS file enable or disable system features, set limits on resources (for example, the maximum number of open files), and extend the operating system by loading device drivers that control hardware specific to an individual computer system.

configuration *n.* **1.** In reference to a single microcomputer, the sum of a system's internal and external components, including memory, disk drives, keyboard, video, and generally less critical add-on hardware, such as a mouse, modem, or printer. Software (the operating system and various device drivers), the user's choices established through configuration files such as the AUTOEXEC.BAT and CONFIG.SYS files on IBM PCs and compatibles, and sometimes hardware (switches and jumpers) are needed to "configure the configuration" to work correctly. Although system configuration can be changed, as by adding more memory or disk capacity, the basic structure of the system—its architecture—remains the same. *See also* AUTOEXEC.BAT, CONFIG.SYS. **2.** In relation to networks, the entire interconnected set of hardware, or the way in which a network is laid out—the manner in which elements are connected.

configuration file *n.* A file that contains machine-readable operating specifications for a piece of hardware or software or that contains information on another file or on a specific user, such as the user's logon ID.

congestion *n.* The condition of a network when the current load approaches or exceeds the available resources and bandwidth designed to handle that load at a particular location in the network. Packet loss and delays are associated with congestion.

connect charge *n.* The amount of money a user must pay for connecting to a commercial communications system or service. Some services calculate the connect charge as a flat rate per billing period. Others charge a varying rate based on the type of service or the amount of information being accessed. Still others base their charges on the number of time units used, the time or distance involved per connection, the bandwidth of each connected session, or some combination of the preceding criteria. *See also* connect time.

connection *n.* A physical link via wire, radio, fiberoptic cable, or other medium between two or more communications devices.

connection-based session *n.* A communications session that requires a connection to be established between hosts prior to an exchange of data.

connectionism *n.* A model in artificial intelligence that advocates using highly parallel, specialized processes that compute simultaneously and are massively connected. Thus, the connectionist approach would not use a single high-speed processor to compute an algorithm, but would break out many simple specialized processing elements that are highly connected. Neural networks are classic examples of connectionism in that each "neuron" in the network may be assigned to a single processor. *See also* algorithm, artificial intelligence, neural network.

connectionless *adj.* In communications, of, pertaining to, or characteristic of a method of data transmission that does not require a direct connection between two nodes on one or more networks. Connectionless communication is achieved by passing, or routing, data packets, each of which contains a source and destination address, through the nodes until the destination is reached. *See also* node (definition 2), packet (definition 2). *Compare* connection-oriented.

connectionless session *n.* A communications session that does not require a connection to be established between hosts prior to an exchange of data.

connection-oriented *adj.* In communications, of, pertaining to, or characteristic of a method of data transmission that requires a direct connection between two nodes on one or more networks. *Compare* connectionless.

connection pooling *n.* A resource optimization feature of ODBC (Open Database Connectivity) 3 that results in

C

more efficient sharing of database connections and objects. Connection pooling maintains open collections (pools) of database connections that can be used and reused by applications without the need to open and close a connection for each request. This is particularly important for Web-based applications. Connection pooling enables sharing among different components, maximizes performance, and minimizes the number of idle connections. *See also* ODBC.

connectivity *n.* **1.** The nature of the connection between a user's computer and another computer, such as a server or a host computer on the Internet or a network. This may describe the quality of the circuit or telephone line, the degree of freedom from noise, or the bandwidth of the communications devices. **2.** The ability of hardware devices or software packages to transmit data between other devices or packages. **3.** The ability of hardware devices, software packages, or a computer itself to work with network devices or with other hardware devices, software packages, or a computer over a network connection.

connectoid *n.* In Windows 9x and Windows NT, an icon representing a dial-up networking connection that will also execute a script for logging onto the network dialed.

connector *n.* **1.** In hardware, a coupler used to join cables or to join a cable to a device (for example, an RS-232-C connector used to join a modem cable to a computer). Most connector types are available in one of two genders—male or female. A male connector is characterized by one or more exposed pins; a female connector is characterized by one or more receptacles—sockets or jacks—designed to accept the pins on the male connector. *See also* DB connector, DIN connector. **2.** In programming, a circular symbol used in a flowchart to indicate a break, as to another page.

connect time *n.* The amount of time during which a user is actively connected to a remote computer. On commercial systems, the connect time is one means of calculating how much money the user must pay for using the system. *See also* connect charge.

consistency check *n.* A survey to verify that items of data conform to certain formats, bounds, and other parameters and are not internally contradictory. *Compare* completeness check.

console *n.* **1.** A control unit, such as a terminal, through which a user communicates with a computer. In microcomputers, the console is the cabinet that houses the main components and controls of the system, sometimes includ-

ing the screen, the keyboard, or both. With the MS-DOS operating system, the console is the primary input (keyboard) and primary output device (screen), as evidenced by the device name CON. *See also* CON, system console. **2.** *See* game console.

console game *n.* A special-purpose computer system designed specifically for the home user to play video games. A game console typically includes a CPU, one or more game controllers, audio output, and a video output that connects to a television set. Individual games and memory cards are supplied on plug-in cartridges or compact discs. Many recent versions are 128-bit systems and also include a modem for online gaming over the Internet. Well-known console games include Microsoft Xbox, Sony PlayStation 2, Nintendo GameCube, and Sega Dreamcast. *Also called:* game console. *Compare* arcade game. *See also* computer game, Dreamcast, GameCube, PlayStation, Xbox.

constant *n.* A named item that retains a consistent value throughout the execution of a program, as opposed to a variable, which can have its value changed during execution. *Compare* variable.

constant expression *n.* An expression that is composed only of constants and, hence, whose value does not change during program execution. *Compare* variable expression.

constellation *n.* In communications, a pattern representing the possible states of a carrier wave, each of which is associated with a particular bit combination. A constellation shows the number of states that can be recognized as unique changes in a communications signal and thus the maximum number of bits that can be encoded in a single change (equivalent to 1 baud, or one event). See the illustration.

0111	0110	0010	0001
●	●	●	●
0100	0101	0011	0000
●	●	●	●
1100	1111	1001	1000
●	●	●	●
1101	1110	1010	1011
●	●	●	●

Constellation.

constraint *n.* In programming, a restriction on the solutions that are acceptable for a problem.

consultant *n.* A computer professional who deals with client firms as an independent contractor rather than as an employee. Consultants are often engaged to analyze user needs and develop system specifications.

Consumer Electronics Show *n.* Annual tradeshow of the consumer electronics industry, held in Las Vegas, Nevada. CES features exhibits of the latest consumer electronics products and conference events that focus on consumer trends and business strategies. *Acronym:* CES.

contact manager *n.* A type of specialized database that allows a user to maintain a record of personal communication with others. Contact managers are widely used by salespeople and others who want to keep track of conversations, e-mail, and other forms of communication with a large number of current and prospective customers or clients. *See also* database.

container *n.* **1.** In OLE terminology, a file containing linked or embedded objects. *See also* OLE. **2.** In SGML, an element that has content as opposed to one consisting solely of the tag name and attributes. *See also* element, SGML, tag. **3.** In Sun Microsystem's J2EE network platform, an entity that provides life cycle management, security, deployment, and runtime services to components such as beans, Web components, applets, and application clients. Each type of container created (for example, EJB, Web, JSP, servlet, applet, and application client) also provides component-specific services. *See also* applet, component (definition 3), enterprise java bean, JSP, servlet.

container object *n.* An object that can logically contain other objects. For example, a folder is a container object. *See also* noncontainer object, object.

content *n.* **1.** The data that appears between the starting and ending tags of an element in an SGML, XML, or HTML document. The content of an element may consist of plain text or other elements. *See also* element (definition 2), HTML, SGML, tag (definition 3). **2.** The message body of a newsgroup article or e-mail message. **3.** The "meat" of a document, as opposed to its format or appearance.

content-addressed storage *n.* *See* associative storage.

content aggregator *n.* **1.** Broadly, an organization or business that groups Internet-based information by topic or area of interest—for example, sports scores, business news, or online shopping—to provide users with a means of accessing that content from a single location. **2.** In

terms of push technology and multicasting, a service business that mediates between subscribers ("customers") and content providers by gathering and organizing information for broadcast over the Internet. Content aggregators supply subscribers with client software through which content providers broadcast (push) information via "channels" that allow users both to choose the kind of information they receive and to decide when they want it updated. *Also called:* channel aggregator. *See also* push, webcasting. *Compare* content provider.

content caching *n.* *See* content delivery.

content delivery *n.* The process of caching the pages of a Web site on geographically dispersed servers to enable faster delivery of Web pages. When a page is requested at a URL that is content-delivery enabled, the content-delivery network routes the user's request to a cache server closer to the user. Content delivery frequently is used for high-traffic Web sites or for specific high-traffic events. *Also called:* content distribution, content caching.

content distribution *n.* *See* content delivery.

contention *n.* On a network, competition among nodes for the opportunity to use a communications line or network resource. In one sense, contention applies to a situation in which two or more devices attempt to transmit at the same time, thus causing a collision on the line. In a somewhat different sense, contention also applies to a free-for-all method of controlling access to a communications line, in which the right to transmit is awarded to the station that wins control of the line. *See also* CSMA/CD. *Compare* token passing.

Content Management Server *n.* Automated software application developed by Microsoft Corporation to assist nontechnical users in creating, tracking, and publishing content for Web sites. A workflow system delineates the tasks each user can perform, assigns content to individuals or groups, and allows users to monitor the status of content with which they are associated.

Content Protection for Recordable Media *n.* *See* CPRM.

content provider *n.* **1.** Broadly, an individual, group, or business that provides information for viewing or distribution on the Internet or on private or semiprivate intranets or extranets. Content in this sense includes not only information but also video, audio, software, listings of Web sites, and product-specific materials such as online catalogs. **2.** A service business that makes Internet information

C

resources available to users. Content providers include online services such as America Online and CompuServe, Internet service providers (ISPs), and an increasing number of media companies representing television, long-distance telephone, and publishing industries. *See also* ISP, online information service. *Compare* content aggregator.

Content Scrambling System *n. See* CSS.

contents directory *n.* A series of queues that contain the descriptors and addresses of routines located within a region of memory.

context-dependent *adj.* Of, pertaining to, or characteristic of a process or a set of data characters whose meaning depends on the surrounding environment.

context-sensitive help *n.* A form of assistance in which a program that provides on-screen help shows information to the user concerning the current command or operation being attempted.

context-sensitive menu *n.* A menu that highlights options as available or unavailable depending on the context in which the option is called. The menus on Windows' menu bar, for example, are context sensitive; options such as copy are grayed out if nothing is selected.

context switching *n.* A type of multitasking; the act of turning the central processor's "attention" from one task to another, rather than allocating increments of time to each task in turn. *See also* multitasking, time slice.

contextual search *n.* A search operation in which the user can direct a program to search specified files for a particular set of text characters.

contiguous *adj.* Having a shared boundary; being immediately adjacent. For example, contiguous sectors on a disk are data-storage segments physically located next to one another.

contiguous data structure *n.* A data structure, such as an array, that is stored in a consecutive set of memory locations. *See also* data structure. *Compare* noncontiguous data structure.

continuous carrier *n.* In communications, a carrier signal that remains on throughout the transmission, whether or not it is carrying information.

continuous-form paper *n.* Paper in which each sheet is connected to the sheets before and after it, for use with most impact and ink-jet printers and some other printing devices designed with an appropriate paper-feed mechanism. The paper usually has holes punched along each side

so that it can be pulled by a tractor-feed device. See the illustration. *See also* pin feed, sprocket feed, tractor feed.

Continuous-form paper.

continuous processing *n.* The processing of transactions as they are input to the system. *Compare* batch processing (definition 3).

continuous speech recognition *n.* A type of automatic speech recognition (ASR) technology that responds to strings of words. Continuous speech recognition allows a user to speak in a natural voice without the need to slow down and enunciate each word separately. Continuous speech recognition software takes advantage of context in recognizing words, and thus will not operate at full efficiency if each word is spoken with distinct separation. *See also* ASR (definition 2).

continuous-tone image *n.* An image, such as a photograph, in which color or varying shades of gray are reproduced as gradients rather than as clustered or variably sized dots, as in traditional book or newspaper printing. Continuous-tone images can be viewed on an analog monitor (such as a television monitor), which accepts input as a continuously variable signal. They cannot be viewed on a digital monitor, which requires input broken into discrete units, nor can they be printed in books or newspapers, which represent illustrations as groups of dots. *See also* scan (definition 2), video digitizer. *Compare* halftone.

continuous-tone printer *n.* A printer that produces an image using smoothly blended levels of continuous ink for gradations of gray or color. *Compare* dithering.

contouring *n.* **1.** In computer graphics, such as CAD models, the representation of the surface of an object—its bumps and crannies. See the illustration. **2.** In image processing, the loss of detail that occurs in a shaded image when too few gradations of gray are used to reproduce a graphic, such as a photograph. In photography and graphic arts, this phenomenon is sometimes called *posterization*.

Contouring.

contrast *n.* **1.** The degree of difference between light and dark extremes of color on a monitor or on printed output. **2.** The control knob by which the contrast of a monitor is changed.

control *n.* **1.** Management of a computer and its processing abilities so as to maintain order as tasks and activities are carried out. Control applies to measures designed to ensure error-free actions carried out at the right time and in the right order relative to other data-handling or hardware-based activities. In reference to hardware, control of system operations can reside in a data pathway called a *control bus.* In reference to software, *control* refers to program instructions that manage data-handling tasks. **2.** In a graphical user interface, an object on the screen that can be manipulated by the user to perform an action. The most common controls are buttons, which allow the user to select options, and scroll bars, which allow the user to move through a document or position text in a window.

control break *n.* A transition in control of the computer that typically gives control of the CPU (central processing unit) to the user console or to some other program.

Control-Break *n. See* Break key.

control bus *n.* The set of lines (conductors) within a computer that carry control signals between the CPU (central processing unit) and other devices. For example, a control bus line is used to indicate whether the CPU is attempting to read from memory or to write to it; another control bus line is used by memory to request an interrupt in case of a memory error.

control character *n.* **1.** Any of the first 32 characters in the ASCII character set (0 through 31 in decimal representation), each of which is defined as having a standard control function, such as carriage return, linefeed, or backspace. **2.** Any of the 26 characters Control-A through Control-Z (1 through 26 in decimal representation) that can be typed

at the keyboard by holding the Control key down and typing the appropriate letter. The six remaining characters with control functions, such as Escape (ASCII 27), cannot be typed using the Control key. *Compare* control code.

control code *n.* One or more nonprinting characters used by a computer program to control the actions of a device, used in printing, communications, and management of display screens. Control codes are mainly employed by programmers or by users to control a printer when an application program does not support the printer or one of its specialized features. In video, control codes are sent from a computer to a display unit to manipulate the appearance of text or a cursor on the screen. Popular video control code sets are ANSI and VT-100. *Also called:* escape sequence, setup string. *See also* control character.

control console *n. See* console.

control data *n.* Data that consists of information about timing and switching, used to synchronize and route other data or to manage the operation of a device such as a bus or a port.

control flow *n.* The tracing of all possible execution paths in a program, often represented in the form of a diagram. See the illustration.

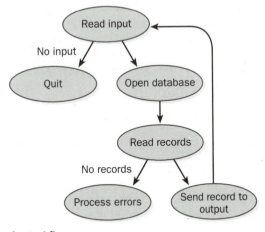

Control flow.

Control key *n.* A key that, when pressed in combination with another key, gives the other key an alternative meaning. In many application programs, Control (labeled CTRL or Ctrl on a PC keyboard) plus another key is used as a command for special functions. See the illustration. *See also* control character (definition 2).

Control key.

controller *n.* A device that other devices rely on for access to a computer subsystem. A disk controller, for example, controls access to one or more disk drives, managing physical and logical access to the drive or drives.

control logic *n.* The electronic circuitry that generates, interprets, and uses control data.

control panel *n.* In Windows and Macintosh systems, a utility that allows the user to control aspects of the operating system or hardware, such as system time and date, keyboard characteristics, and networking parameters.

control panel device *n. See* cdev.

control sequence *n. See* control code.

control signal *n.* An electronic signal used to control internal or external devices or processes.

control statement *n.* A statement that affects the flow of execution through a program. Control statements include conditional statements (CASE, IF-THEN-ELSE), iterative statements (DO, FOR, REPEAT, WHILE), and transfer statements (GOTO). *See also* conditional statement, iterative statement, statement, transfer statement.

control strip *n.* **1.** An equipment calibration tool used to determine the corrections needed to restore accuracy by comparing recorded data against known values. **2.** A utility that groups shortcuts to commonly used items or information, such as time, battery power level, desktop items, and programs, in an easily accessible place. *See also* shortcut.

control structure *n.* A portion of a program defined by the relationship between the statements, used in structured programming. There are three basic control structures: sequence, where one statement simply follows another; selection, where program flow depends on which criteria are met; and iteration, where an action is repeated until some condition occurs.

control unit *n.* A device or circuit that performs an arbitrating or regulating function. For example, a memory controller chip controls access to a computer's memory and is the control unit for that memory.

control variable *n.* In programming, the variable in a control statement that dictates the flow of execution. For example, the index variable in a FOR loop controls the number of times a group of statements are executed. *See also* control statement.

convenience adapter *n. See* port replicator.

convention *n.* Any standard that is used more or less universally in a given situation. Many conventions are applied to microcomputers. In programming, for example, a language such as C relies on formally accepted symbols and abbreviations that must be used in programs. Less formally, programmers usually adopt the convention of indenting subordinate instructions in a routine so that the structure of the program is more easily visualized. National and international committees often discuss and arbitrate conventions for programming languages, data structures, communication standards, and device characteristics. *See also* CCITT, ISO, NTSC, standard (definition 1).

conventional memory *n.* The amount of RAM addressable by an IBM PC or compatible machine operating in real mode. This is typically 640 kilobytes (KB). Without the use of special techniques, conventional memory is the only kind of RAM accessible to MS-DOS programs. *See also* protected mode, real mode. *Compare* expanded memory, extended memory.

convergence *n.* A coming together. Convergence can occur between different disciplines and technologies, as when telephone communications and computing converge in the field of telecommunications. It can also occur within a program, such as a spreadsheet, when a circular set of formulas are repeatedly recalculated (iterated), with the results of each iteration coming closer to a true solution.

conversational *adj.* Of, pertaining to, or characteristic of the mode of operation, typical of microcomputers, in which the computer user and the system engage in a dialogue of commands and system responses. *See also* interactive.

conversational interaction *n.* Interaction in which two or more parties alternately transmit and receive messages from each other. *See also* interactive processing.

conversational language *n.* Any programming language that allows the programmer to instruct the computer in a conversational mode, as opposed to more formal, structured languages. For example, in a COBOL program, in order to execute a procedure called CHECK 10 times, a program would use the following statement: PERFORM CHECK 10 TIMES.

conversational mode *n.* *See* conversational.

conversion *n.* The process of changing from one form or format to another; where information is concerned, a changeover that affects form but not substance. Types of conversion include data (changing the way information is represented), file (changing a file from one format to another), hardware (changing all or part of a computer system), media (transferring data from one storage media to another), software (changing a program designed for one platform so that it runs on another), and system (changing from one operating system to another).

conversion table *n.* A table listing a set of characters or numbers and their equivalents in another coding scheme. Common examples of conversion tables include ASCII tables, which list characters and their ASCII values, and decimal-to-hexadecimal tables. Several conversion tables are in Appendixes A-E.

converter *n.* Any device that changes electrical signals or computer data from one form to another. For example, an analog-to-digital converter translates analog signals to digital signals.

converter box *n.* *See* converter.

cookbook¹ *adj.* Of, pertaining to, or characteristic of a book or manual that presents information using a step-by-step approach. For example, a cookbook approach to programming might present a series of sample programs that the reader could analyze and adapt to his or her own needs.

cookbook² *n.* A computer book or manual that presents information using a step-by-step approach. Most often, *cookbook* refers to a programming guide, but it can refer to a book that shows how to accomplish specialized tasks in an application.

cooked mode *n.* One of two forms (the other being raw mode) in which an operating system such as UNIX or MS-DOS "sees" the handle, or identifier, for a character-based device. If the handle is in cooked mode, the operating system stores each character in a buffer and gives special treatment to carriage returns, end-of-file markers, and linefeed and tab characters, sending a line of data to a device, such as the screen, only after it reads a carriage-return or end-of-file character. In cooked mode, characters

read from standard input are often automatically echoed (displayed) on the screen. *Compare* raw mode.

cookie *n.* **1.** A block of data that a server returns to a client in response to a request from the client. **2.** On the World Wide Web, a block of data that a Web server stores on a client system. When a user returns to the same Web site, the browser sends a copy of the cookie back to the server. Cookies are used to identify users, to instruct the server to send a customized version of the requested Web page, to submit account information for the user, and for other administrative purposes. **3.** Originally an allusion to fortune cookie, a UNIX program that outputs a different message, or "fortune," each time it is used. On some systems, the cookie program is run during user logon.

cookie filtering tool *n.* A utility that prevents a cookie on a Web browser from relaying information about the user requesting access to a Web site. *See also* cookie (definition 2).

cookies policy *n.* A statement that describes a Web site's policy regarding cookies. The policy usually defines a cookie, explains the types of cookies used by the Web site, and describes how the Web site uses the information stored in the cookies.

.coop *n.* One of seven new top-level domain names approved in 2000 by the Internet Corporation for Assigned-Names and Numbers (ICANN), .coop is meant for use with the Web sites of nonprofit cooperatives. The seven new domain names became available for use in the spring of 2001.

cooperative multitasking *n.* A type of multitasking in which one or more background tasks are given processing time during idle times in the foreground task only if the foreground task allows it. This is the primary mode of multitasking in the Macintosh operating system. *See also* background¹, context switching, foreground¹, multitasking, time slice. *Compare* preemptive multitasking.

cooperative processing *n.* A mode of operation characteristic of distributed systems in which two or more computers, such as a mainframe and a microcomputer, can simultaneously carry out portions of the same program or work on the same data. *Compare* distributed processing.

coordinate *n.* Any element in a group of references to a particular location, such as the intersection of a certain row and column. In computer graphics and displays,

C

coordinates specify such elements as points on a line, the corners of a square, or the location of a pixel on the screen. In other computer applications, coordinates specify cells on a spreadsheet, data points on a graph, locations in memory, and so on. *See also* Cartesian coordinates, polar coordinates.

coordinate dimensioning *n.* A form of spatial positioning in which a point is described, relative to a fixed reference, in terms of its distance and direction along predefined axes. *See also* Cartesian coordinates, three-dimensional model, two-dimensional model.

coordinated universal time format *n. See* Universal Time Coordinate.

coordinate pair *n.* A pair of values representing the x-coordinate and y-coordinate of a point that are stored in a two-dimensional array that can contain coordinates for many points.

COPPA *n.* Acronym for **C**hildren's **O**nline **P**rivacy **P**rotection **A**ct. A U.S. federal law enacted in April 2000 and designed to protect the online privacy of children under the age of 13. COPPA requires Web sites that collect personal information from children under 13 to receive permission from parents or guardians first, and to monitor and supervise children's experiences with interactive Web elements such as chat rooms and e-mail.

copper chip *n.* A microprocessor that uses copper (rather than the more common aluminum) to connect transistors in a computer chip. Copper chip technology, which was developed by IBM and introduced in 1997, can be expected to boost the speed of a microprocessor by as much as 33 percent.

coprocessor *n.* A processor, distinct from the main microprocessor, that performs additional functions or assists the main microprocessor. The most common type of coprocessor is the floating-point coprocessor, also called a numeric or math coprocessor, which is designed to perform numeric calculations faster and better than the general-purpose microprocessors used in personal computers. *See also* floating-point processor.

copy *vb.* To duplicate information and reproduce it in another part of a document, in a different file or memory location, or in a different medium. A copy operation can affect data ranging from a single character to large segments of text, a graphics image, or from one to many data files. Text and graphics, for example, can be copied to another part of a document, to the computer's memory (by means of a temporary storage facility such as the Windows or Macintosh Clipboard), or to a different file. Similarly, files can be copied from one disk or directory to another, and data can be copied from the screen to a printer or to a data file. In most cases, a copy procedure leaves the original information in place. *Compare* cut and paste, move.

copy disk *n.* An MS-DOS command to duplicate the contents of a floppy disk on a second disk. *See also* floppy disk, MS-DOS.

copy holder *n.* An inclined clipboard or other such device designed to hold printed material so that it can be easily viewed by someone working at a computer keyboard.

copyleft *n. See* General Public License.

copy program *n.* **1.** A program designed to duplicate one or more files to another disk or directory. **2.** A program that disables or circumvents the copy-protection device on a computer program so that the software can be copied, often illegally, to another disk. *See also* copy protection.

copy protection *n.* A software lock placed on a computer program by its developer to prevent the product from being copied and distributed without approval or authorization.

copyright *n.* A method of protecting the rights of an originator of a creative work, such as a text, a piece of music, a painting, or a computer program, through law. In many countries the originator of a work has copyright in the work as soon as it is fixed in a tangible medium (such as a piece of paper or a disk file); that rule applies in the United States for works created after 1977. Registration of a copyright, or the use of a copyright symbol, is not needed to create the copyright but does strengthen the originator's legal powers. Unauthorized copying and distribution of copyrighted material can lead to severe penalties, whether done for profit or not. Copyrights affect the computer community in three ways: the copyright protection of software, the copyright status of material (such as song lyrics) distributed over a network such as the Internet, and the copyright status of original material distributed over a network (such as a newsgroup post). The latter two involve electronic media that are arguably not tangible, and legislation protecting the information disseminated through electronic media is still evolving. *See also* fair use, General Public License.

CORBA *n.* Acronym for **C**ommon **O**bject **R**equest **B**roker **A**rchitecture. A specification developed by the Object Management Group in 1992 in which pieces of programs (objects) communicate with other objects in other programs, even if the two programs are written in different programming languages and are running on different platforms. A program makes its request for objects through an *object request broker*, or *ORB*, and thus does not need to know the structure of the program from which the object comes. CORBA is designed to work in object-oriented environments. *See also* IIOP, object (definition 2), Object Management Group, object-oriented.

core *n.* One of the types of memory built into computers before random access memory (RAM) was available or affordable. Some people still use the term to refer to the main memory of any computer system, as in the phrase *core dump*—a listing of the raw contents of main memory at the moment of a system crash. *Compare* RAM.

core class *n.* In the Java programming language, a public class or interface that is a standard member of the language. Core classes, at minimum, are available on all operating systems where the Java platform runs. A program written entirely in the Java programming language relies only on core classes. *See also* class (definition 1), object, object-oriented programming.

core program *n.* A program or program segment that is resident in random access memory (RAM).

coresident *adj.* Of or pertaining to a condition in which two or more programs are loaded in memory at the same time.

corona wire *n.* In laser printers, a wire though which high voltage is passed to ionize the air and transfer a uniform electrostatic charge to the photosensitive medium in preparation for the laser.

coroutine *n.* A routine that is in memory at the same time as, and frequently executed concurrently with, another.

corrective maintenance *n.* The process of diagnosing and correcting computer problems after they occur. *Compare* preventive maintenance.

correspondence quality *n. See* print quality.

corruption *n.* A process wherein data in memory or on disk is unintentionally changed, with its meaning thereby altered or obliterated.

cost-benefit analysis *n.* The comparison of benefits to costs for a particular item or action. Cost-benefit analysis is often used in MIS or IS departments to determine such things as whether purchasing a new computer system is a good investment or whether hiring more staff is necessary. *See also* IS, MIS.

coulomb *n.* A unit of electrical charge equivalent to roughly 6.26×10^{18} electrons, with a negative charge being an excess of electrons and a positive charge being a deficiency of electrons.

counter *n.* **1.** In programming, a variable used to keep count of something. **2.** In electronics, a circuit that counts a specified number of pulses before generating an output. **3.** A device that keeps track of the number of visitors to a World Wide Web site.

counting loop *n.* In a program, a group of statements that are repeated, thereby incrementing a variable used as a counter (for example, a program might repeat a counting loop that adds 1 to its counter until the counter equals 10). *See also* loop[1] (definition 1).

country code *n. See* major geographic domain.

country-specific *adj.* Of, pertaining to, or characteristic of hardware or software that uses characters or conventions unique to a particular country or group of countries. *Country-specific* does not necessarily refer to spoken languages, although it does allow for special characters (such as accent marks) that are language-specific. Generally, the features considered country-specific include keyboard layout (including special-character keys), time and date conventions, financial and monetary symbols, decimal notation (decimal point or comma), and alphabetic sorting order. Such features are handled either by a computer's operating system (for example, by the Keyboard and Country commands in MS-DOS) or by application programs that offer options for tailoring documents to a particular set of national or international conventions.

courseware *n.* Software dedicated to education or training.

courtesy copy *n. See* cc.

CPA *n. See* Computer Press Association.

CPCP *n. See* HTCPCP.

cpi *n. See* characters per inch.

CP/M *n.* Acronym for **C**ontrol **P**rogram/**M**onitor. A line of operating systems from Digital Research, Inc. (DRI), for microcomputers based on Intel microprocessors. The first system, CP/M-80, was the most popular operating system for 8080- and Z80-based microcomputers. Digital Research also developed CP/M-86 for 8086/8088-based computers, CP/M-Z8000 for Zilog Z8000-based computers, and CP/M-68K for Motorola 68000-based computers. When the IBM PC and MS-DOS were introduced, common use of CP/M by end users dwindled. DRI continues to enhance the CP/M line, supporting multitasking with the Concurrent CP/M and MP/M products. *See also* MP/M.

CPM *n. See* critical path method.

CPRM *n.* Acronym for **C**ontent **P**rotection for **R**ecordable **M**edia. Technology developed to control the use of copyrighted digital music and video material by blocking the transfer of protected files to portable media such as zip disks and smart cards. CPRM would be added to storage devices and provide data scrambling and identification codes to block the copying of copyrighted files.

cps *n. See* characters per second.

CPSR *n.* Acronym for **C**omputer **P**rofessionals for **S**ocial **R**esponsibility. A public advocacy organization of computer professionals. CPSR was originally formed out of concern over the use of computer technology for military purposes but has extended its interest to such issues as civil liberties and the effect of computers on workers.

CPU *n.* Acronym for **c**entral **p**rocessing **u**nit. The computational and control unit of a computer. The CPU is the device that interprets and executes instructions. Mainframes and early minicomputers contained circuit boards full of integrated circuits that implemented the CPU. Single-chip central processing units, called *microprocessors*, made possible personal computers and workstations. Examples of single-chip CPUs are the Motorola 68000, 68020, and 68030 chips and the Intel 8080, 8086, 80286, 80386, and i486 chips. The CPU—or microprocessor, in the case of a microcomputer—has the ability to fetch, decode, and execute instructions and to transfer information to and from other resources over the computer's main data-transfer path, the bus. By definition, the CPU is the chip that functions as the "brain" of a computer. In some instances, however, the term encompasses both the processor and the computer's memory or, even more broadly, the main computer console (as opposed to peripheral equipment). See the illustration. *See also* microprocessor.

CPU.

CPU-bound *adj. See* computation-bound.

CPU cache *n.* A section of fast memory linking the CPU (central processing unit) and main memory that temporarily stores data and instructions the CPU needs to execute upcoming commands and programs. Considerably faster than main memory, the CPU cache contains data that is transferred in blocks, thereby speeding execution. The system anticipates the data it will need through algorithms. *Also called:* cache memory, memory cache. *See also* cache, CPU, VCACHE.

CPU cycle *n.* **1.** The smallest unit of time recognized by the CPU (central processing unit)—typically a few hundred-millionths of a second. **2.** The time required for the CPU to perform the simplest instruction, such as fetching the contents of a register or performing a no-operation instruction (NOP). *Also called:* clock tick.

CPU fan *n.* An electric fan usually placed directly on a CPU (central processing unit) or on the CPU's heat sink to help dissipate heat from the chip by circulating air around it. *See also* CPU, heat sink.

CPU speed *n.* A relative measure of the data-processing capacity of a particular CPU (central processing unit), usually measured in megahertz. *See also* CPU.

CPU time *n.* In multiprocessing, the amount of time during which a particular process has active control of the CPU (central processing unit). *See also* CPU, multiprocessing.

CR *n. See* carriage return.

crack *vb.* **1.** To gain unauthorized access to a network by breaching its security. **2.** To decipher encrypted information.

cracker *n.* A person who overcomes the security measures of a computer system and gains unauthorized access. The goal of some crackers is to obtain information illegally from a computer system or use computer resources. However, the goal of the majority is only to break into the system. *See also* hacker (definition 2).

cradle *n.* A receptacle used to recharge the batteries in some handheld or palm-size PCs or PDAs (personal digital assistants). Some cradles also serve as a means to connect these smaller devices with a desktop PC. Not all of these devices require a cradle to recharge or connect to a desktop system. *Also called:* dock, docking station.

cramfs *n.* Short for **C**ompressed **R**ead-**O**nly **F**ile **S**ystem and **cram** a **f**ilesystem onto a small ROM. A filesystem feature available with Linux version 2.4 systems. Cramfs are used in handheld Linux devices to compress and write applications to ROM or Flash memory.

crash[1] *n.* The failure of either a program or a disk drive. A program crash results in the loss of all unsaved data and can leave the operating system unstable enough to require restarting the computer. A disk drive crash, sometimes called a disk crash, leaves the drive inoperable and can cause loss of data. *See also* abend, head crash.

crash[2] *vb.* **1.** For a system or program, to fail to function correctly, resulting in the suspension of operation. *See also* abend. **2.** For a magnetic head, to hit a recording medium, with possible damage to one or both.

crash recovery *n.* The ability of a computer to resume operation after a disastrous failure, such as the failure of a hard drive. Ideally, recovery can occur without any loss of data, although usually some, if not all, data is lost. *See also* crash[1].

crawl *vb.* To compile and organize entries for a search engine by reading Web pages and related information. Crawling is typically performed by programs called "spiders."

crawler *n. See* spider, Web browser.

Cray-1 *n.* An early supercomputer developed in 1976 by Seymour Cray. Extremely powerful in its day, the 64-bit Cray-1 ran at 75 MHz and was capable of executing 160 million floating-point operations per second. *See also* supercomputer.

CRC *n.* Acronym for **c**yclical (or **c**yclic) **r**edundancy check. A procedure used in checking for errors in data transmission. CRC error checking uses a complex calculation to generate a number based on the data transmitted. The sending device performs the calculation before transmission and includes it in the packet that it sends to the receiving device. The receiving device repeats the same calculation after transmission. If both devices obtain the same result, it is assumed that the transmission was error free. The procedure is known as a redundancy check because each transmission includes not only data but extra (redundant) error-checking values. Communications protocols such as XMODEM and Kermit use cyclical redundancy checking.

create method *n.* In Java programming, a method defined in the home interface and invoked by a client to create an enterprise java bean. *See also* enterprise java bean, method.

creator *n.* On the Apple Macintosh, the program that creates a file. Files are linked to their creators by creator codes; this link enables the operating system to open the creator application when a document file is opened.

credentials *n.* A set of information that includes identification and proof of identification that is used to gain access to local and network resources. Examples of credentials are user names and passwords, smart cards, and certificates.

creeping featurism *n.* The process by which features are added to a new version of a program by software developers until the program becomes unduly cumbersome and difficult to use. Generally, creeping featurism occurs as developers attempt to enhance the competitiveness of the program with each new release by adding new features.

crippled version *n.* A scaled-down or functionally reduced version of hardware or software, distributed for demonstration purposes. *See also* demo.

critical error *n.* An error that suspends processing until the condition can be corrected either by software or by user intervention (for example, an attempt to read to a nonexistent disk, an out-of-paper condition on the printer, or a checksum fault in a data message).

critical-error handler *n.* A software routine that attempts to correct or achieve a graceful exit from a critical or threatening error. *See also* critical error, graceful exit.

critical path method *n.* A means of evaluating and managing a large project by isolating tasks, milestone events, and schedules and by showing interrelationships among them. The critical path for which this method is named is a line connecting crucial events, any of which, if delayed, affects subsequent events and, ultimately, completion of the project. *Acronym:* CPM.

C

crop *vb.* In computer graphics, to cut off part of an image, such as unneeded sections of a graphic or extra white space around the borders. As in preparing photographs or illustrations for traditional printing, cropping is used to refine or clean up a graphic for placement in a document.

crop marks *n.* **1.** Lines drawn at the edges of pages to mark where the paper will be cut to form pages in the final document. See the illustration. *See also* registration marks. **2.** Lines drawn on photographs or illustrations to indicate where they will be cropped, or cut. *See also* crop.

Crop marks.

cross-assembler *n.* An assembler that executes on one hardware platform but generates machine code for another. *See also* assembler, compiler, cross-compiler, cross development.

cross-check *vb.* To check the accuracy of a calculation by using another method to verify the result. *Compare* cross-foot.

cross-compiler *n.* A compiler that executes on one hardware platform but generates object code for another. *See also* assembler, compiler (definition 2), cross-assembler, cross development.

cross development *n.* The use of one system to develop programs for a different type of system, often because the software development tools of the development system are superior to those of the target system.

cross-foot *vb.* To check the accuracy of a total, as on a ledger sheet, by adding across columns and down rows, all figures contributing to the total.

cross hairs *n.* Intersecting lines used by some computer input devices to locate a particular *x-y*-coordinate.

cross-hatching *n.* Shading made up of regularly spaced, intersecting lines. Cross-hatching is one of several methods for filling in areas of a graphic. See the illustration.

            — Cross-hatching

Cross-hatching.

cross-linked files *n.* In Windows 9x, Windows 3.*x*, and MS-DOS, a file-storage error occurring when one or more sections, or *clusters*, of the hard drive or a floppy disk have been erroneously allocated to more than one file in the file allocation table. Like lost clusters, cross-linked files can result from the ungraceful exit (messy or abrupt termination) of an application program. *See also* file allocation table, lost cluster.

crossover cable *n.* A cable used to connect two computers together for file sharing and personal networking. Crossover cables may be connected to Ethernet or FireWire ports.

cross-platform *adj.* Of, pertaining to, or characteristic of a software application or hardware device that can be run or operated on more than one system platform.

cross-post *vb.* To copy a message or news article from one newsgroup, conference topic, e-mail system, or other communications channel to another—for example, from a Usenet newsgroup to a CompuServe forum or from e-mail to a newsgroup.

cross-site scripting *n.* A security vulnerability of dynamic Web pages generated from a database in response to user input. With cross-site scripting, a malicious user introduces unwanted executable script or code into another user's Web session. Once running, this script could allow others to monitor the user's Web session, change what is displayed on the screen, or shut down the Web browser. Web sites that allow visitors to add comments or make other additions or changes to the pages are the most vulnerable to this flaw. Cross-site scripting is not restricted to the products of a particular vendor or a particular operating system. *See also* script.

crosstab query *n.* A query that calculates a sum, an average, a count, or other type of total on records, and then groups the result by two types of information—one down the left side of the datasheet and the other across the top.

crosstalk *n.* Interference caused by a signal transferring from one circuit to another, as on a telephone line.

CRT *n.* Acronym for **c**athode-**r**ay **t**ube. The basis of the television screen and the standard microcomputer display screen. A CRT display is built around a vacuum tube containing one or more electron guns whose electron beams rapidly sweep horizontally across the inside of the front surface of the tube, which is coated with a material that glows when irradiated. Each electron beam moves from left to right, top to bottom, one horizontal scan line at a time. To keep the screen image from flickering, the electron beam refreshes the screen 30 times or more per second. The clarity of the image is determined by the number of pixels on the screen. See the illustration. *See also* pixel, raster, resolution (definition 1).

CRT. *Cutaway view of a CRT.*

CRT controller *n.* The part of a video adapter board that generates the video signal, including the horizontal and vertical synchronization signals. *See also* video adapter.

cruise *vb. See* surf.

crunch *vb.* To process information. *See also* number crunching.

cryoelectronic *adj.* Involving the use of superconducting electronics kept in a cryogenic environment at very low temperatures.

crypto *n. See* cryptography.

cryptoanalysis *n.* The decoding of electronically encrypted information for the purpose of understanding encryption techniques. *See also* cryptography, encryption.

CryptoAPI *n.* An application programming interface (API) that is provided as part of Microsoft Windows. CryptoAPI provides a set of functions that allows applications to encrypt or digitally sign data in a flexible manner while providing protection for the user's sensitive private key data. Actual cryptographic operations are performed by independent modules known as cryptographic service providers (CSPs). *See also* application programming interface (API), cryptographic service provider, private key.

cryptographic service provider *n.* An independent module that performs cryptographic operations, such as creating and destroying keys. A cryptographic service provider consists of, at a minimum, a DLL and a signature file. *Acronym:* CSP.

cryptography *n.* The use of codes to convert data so that only a specific recipient will be able to read it using a key. The persistent problem of cryptography is that the key must be transmitted to the intended recipient and may be intercepted. Public key cryptography is a recent significant advance. *Also called:* crypto. *See also* code[1] (definition 2), encryption, PGP, private key, public key.

CSD *n. See* circuit-switched data.

C shell *n.* One of the command-line interfaces available under UNIX. The C shell is very usable but is not on every system. *Compare* Bourne shell, Korn shell.

CSLIP *n. See* Compressed SLIP.

CSMA/CA *n.* Acronym for **C**arrier **S**ense **M**ultiple **A**ccess with **C**ollision **A**voidance, a protocol for controlling network access similar to CSMA/CD, in that nodes (stations) listen to the network and transmit only when it is free. But in CSMA/CA, nodes avoid data collisions by signaling their intention with a brief Request to Send (RTS) signal and then waiting for acknowledgment before actually transmitting.

CSMA/CD *n.* Acronym for **C**arrier **S**ense **M**ultiple **A**ccess with **C**ollision **D**etection. A network protocol for handling situations in which two or more nodes (stations) transmit at the same time, thus causing a collision. With CSMA/CD, each node on the network monitors the line and transmits when it senses that the line is not busy. If a collision occurs because another node is using the same

C

opportunity to transmit, both nodes stop transmitting. To avoid another collision, both then wait for differing random amounts of time before attempting to transmit again. *Compare* token passing.

CSO *n.* Acronym for **C**omputing **S**ervices **O**ffice. An Internet directory service that matches users' own names with e-mail addresses, generally at colleges and universities. The CSO service, which can be reached through Gopher, was originally developed at the Computing Services Office at the University of Illinois.

CSO name server *n.* A facility that provides e-mail directory information through the CSO system. *See also* CSO.

CSR *n. See* continuous speech recognition.

CSS *n.* **1.** *See* cascading style sheets. **2.** Acronym for **C**ontent **S**crambling **S**ystem. An encryption feature added to DVDs distributed with approval of the MPAA. CSS looks for a matching region code on the DVD and the playback device. If the codes do not match (such as for a DVD purchased in Japan and a DVD player purchased in the United States), CSS will not allow the DVD to play. CSS also will not allow a DVD to be played on playback equipment not approved by the MPAA. *See also* deCSS, region code.

CSS1 *n. See* cascading style sheets.

CSTN display *n. See* supertwist display.

CSU *n. See* DDS.

.csv *n.* The file extension for a comma-delimited text file.

CSV *n.* **1.** *See* circuit-switched voice. **2.** *See* alternate circuit-switched voice/circuit-switched data. **3.** Acronym for **c**omma **s**eparated **v**alues. Filename extension assigned to text files containing tabular data of the sort stored in database fields. As the name indicates, individual data entries are separated by commas. *Compare* TSV.

CTERM *n. See* Communications Terminal Protocol.

CT Expo *n.* Acronym for **C**omputer **T**elephony **Expo**. Annual exposition on data and communications issues involving the computer, telecommunications, and Internet industries. Held in Los Angeles, California, CT Expo features exhibits by hundreds of companies displaying their latest products and services, as well as conferences on a range of subjects affecting computer telephony.

CTI *n.* Acronym for **c**omputer-**t**elephony **i**ntegration. The practice of using a computer to control one or more telephone and communications functions.

CTIA *n. See* Cellular Telecommunications and Internet Association.

CTIA Wireless *n.* Annual conference of the wireless data, mobile Internet, and handheld computing industries. Sponsored by the Cellular Telecommunications and Internet Association, CTIA Wireless showcases products and technical developments in the field of wireless communications and data.

CTL *n.* Short for **control**. *See* control character (definition 2), Control key.

CTO *n.* Acronym for **C**hief **T**echnology **O**fficer. A corporate executive in charge of managing a company's information technology (IT) architecture and other technological assets. The CTO's responsibilities may include oversight of IT centers, networks and intranet, applications, databases, Web presence, and other technological resources.

CTRL or **Ctrl** *n.* Short for **control**. A designation used to label the Control key on computer keyboards. *See also* control character (definition 2), Control key.

Ctrl+Alt+Delete *n.* A three-key combination used with IBM and compatible computers to restart (reboot) the machine. Pressing Ctrl+Alt+Delete (Control+Alternate+ Delete) causes a warm boot in MS-DOS—the computer restarts but does not go through all of the internal checks involved when power to the system is switched on (cold boot). In Windows 9x and Windows NT, Ctrl+Alt+Delete provides a dialog box from which the user may choose to shut down the computer or end any current tasks.

Ctrl+C *n.* **1.** In UNIX, the key combination used to break out of a running process. **2.** The keyboard shortcut recognized by many programs (as in Windows) as an instruction to copy the currently selected item.

Ctrl+S *n.* **1.** On systems in which a software handshake is used between terminals and a central computer, the key combination used to suspend output. Ctrl+Q will resume output after a Ctrl-S suspension. *See also* software handshake, XON/XOFF. **2.** A keyboard shortcut recognized by many programs as an instruction to save the current document or file.

CTS *n.* Acronym for **C**lear **T**o **S**end. In serial communications, a signal sent, as from a modem to its computer, to indicate that transmission can proceed. CTS is a hardware signal sent over line 5 in RS-232-C connections. *Compare* RTS.

CUA *n. See* Common User Access.

C

cube *n.* An OLAP data structure. A cube contains dimensions (like Country/Region/City) and data fields (like Sales Amount). Dimensions organize types of data into hierarchies with levels of detail, and data fields measure quantities.

Cube *n.* A personal computer design introduced by Apple in 2000. The Cube featured a unique 8-by-8-by-8-inch transparent curved cube shape with the power supply outside the chassis to create a small and extremely quiet computer. The Cube offered the same G4 processor and features available on other Macintosh computers, but with fewer expansion options. Although the unique design drew notice for innovation, Apple discontinued manufacture of the Cube in 2001 after only one year of production.

CUI *n.* *See* character user interface.

CUL8R *n.* A fanciful shorthand notation meaning "See you later," sometimes seen in Internet discussion groups as a farewell by a participant temporarily leaving the group.

curly quotes *n.* *See* smart quotes.

current *n.* The flow of electric charge through a conductor, or the amount of such flow. Current is measured in amperes. *See also* ampere, coulomb. *Compare* volt.

current cell *n.* *See* active cell.

current directory *n.* The disk directory at the end of the active directory path—the directory that is searched first for a requested file, and the one in which a new file is stored unless another directory is specified. *See also* path (definition 2).

current drain *n.* **1.** The current taken from a voltage source by its load (the object receiving the current). *Also called:* drain. **2.** The load itself. For example, a flashlight bulb takes current from the battery; this current is the drain on the battery, and the bulb itself may also be called the drain.

current location counter *n.* *See* program counter.

current-mode logic *n.* A type of circuit design in which the transistors operate in unsaturated (amplifying) mode.

cursor *n.* **1.** A special on-screen indicator, such as a blinking underline or rectangle, that marks the place at which a keystroke will appear when typed. **2.** In reference to digitizing tablets, the stylus (pointer or "pen"). **3.** In applications and operating systems that use a mouse, the arrow or other on-screen icon that moves with movements of the mouse.

cursor blink speed *n.* The rate at which a cursor on a screen flashes on and off. *See also* cursor (definition 1).

cursor control *n.* The ability of a computer user to move the cursor to a specified location on the screen. Keys dedicated to cursor control include the left, right, up, and down arrow keys and certain others, such as Backspace, Home, and End. Pointing devices such as the mouse can also control cursor movements, often helping the user move the cursor long distances from place to place in a document.

cursor key *n.* *See* arrow key.

CUSeeMe *n.* A video conferencing program developed at Cornell University. It was the first program to give Windows and Mac OS users the ability to engage in real-time video conferencing over the Internet, but it requires a lot of bandwidth (at least 128 Kbps speed) to function properly.

custom control *n.* A control authored by a user or a third-party software vendor that does not belong to the .NET Framework class library. This is a generic term that includes user controls. A custom server control is used in Web Forms (ASP.NET pages). A custom client control is used in Windows Forms applications.

customize *vb.* To modify or assemble hardware or software to suit the needs or preferences of the user. Traditionally, hardware customizing ranges from designing an electronic circuit for a particular customer to putting together a computer facility tailored to a customer's special need. Software customizing usually means modifying or designing software for a specific customer.

custom queuing *n.* A form of queuing on Cisco routers where the wide area network (WAN) link is divided into micropipes based on a percentage of the total bandwidth available on the pipe. *See also* bandwidth reservation.

custom software *n.* Any type of program developed for a particular client or to address a special need. Certain products, such as dBASE and Lotus 1-2-3, are designed to provide the flexibility and tools required for producing tailor-made applications. *See also* CASE.

cut *vb.* To remove part of a document, usually placing it temporarily in memory so that the cut portion can be inserted (pasted) elsewhere. *Compare* delete.

cut and paste *n.* A procedure in which the computer acts as an electronic combination of scissors and glue for reorganizing a document or for compiling a document from different sources. In cut and paste, the portion of a document

C

to be moved is selected, removed to storage in memory or on disk, and then reinserted into the same or a different document.

cut-through switch *n.* A network switch that routes packets immediately to the port associated with the packet's recipient. *See also* packet.

CV *n. See* computer vision.

CVS *n.* **1.** *See* Computer Vision Syndrome. **2.** Acronym for **C**oncurrent **V**ersions **S**ystem. An open-source network-transparent version control system which allows multiple developers to view and edit code simultaneously. Popular because the client-server function allows operation over the Internet. CVS maintains a single copy of the source code with a record of who initiated changes and when the changes were made. CVS was developed for the UNIX operating system and is commonly used by programmers working with Linux, Mac OS X, and other UNIX-based environments.

CWIS *n. See* campuswide information system.

cXML *n.* Acronym for **c**ommerce **XML**. A set of document definitions for Extensible Markup Language (XML) developed for use in business-to-business e-commerce. cXML defines standards for product listings, allows for electronic requests and responses between procurement applications and suppliers, and provides for secure financial transactions via the Internet.

cyber- *prefix* A prefix attached to "everyday" words in order to give them a computer-based or online meaning, as in cyberlaw (the practice of law either in relation to or through the use of the Internet) and cyberspace (the virtual online world). The prefix is derived from the word *cybernetics*, which refers to the study of mechanisms used to control and regulate complex systems, either human or machine.

cyberart *n.* The artwork of artists who use computers to create or distribute their efforts.

cybercafe or **cyber café** *n.* **1.** A coffee shop or restaurant that offers access to PCs or other terminals that are connected to the Internet, usually for a per-hour or per-minute fee. Users are encouraged to buy beverages or food to drink or eat while accessing the Internet. **2.** A virtual café on the Internet, generally used for social purposes. Users interact with each other by means of a chat program or by posting messages to one another through a bulletin board system, such as in a newsgroup or on a Web site.

cybercash *n. See* e-money.

cyberchat *n. See* IRC.

cybercop *n.* A person who investigates criminal acts committed on line, especially fraud and harassment.

cyberculture *n.* The behavior, beliefs, customs, and etiquette that characterize groups of individuals who communicate or socialize over computer networks, such as the Internet. The cyberculture of one group can be vastly different from the cyberculture of another.

Cyberdog *n.* Apple's Internet suite for Web browsing and e-mail, based on OpenDoc for easy integration with other applications. *See also* OpenDoc.

cyberlawyer *n.* **1.** An attorney whose practice involves the law related to computers and online communication, including elements of communications law, intellectual property rights, privacy and security issues, and other specialties. **2.** An attorney who advertises or distributes information over the Internet and the World Wide Web.

cyberlife *n.* In the gaming world, a technology that mimics biological DNA. *See also* digital DNA.

cybernaut *n.* One who spends copious time on line, exploring the Internet. *Also called:* Internaut. *See also* cyberspace.

cybernetics *n.* The study of control systems, such as the nervous system, in living organisms and the development of equivalent systems in electronic and mechanical devices. Cybernetics compares similarities and differences between living and nonliving systems (whether those systems comprise individuals, groups, or societies) and is based on theories of communication and control that can be applied to either living or nonliving systems or both. *See also* bionics.

cyberpunk *n.* **1.** A genre of near-future science fiction in which conflict and action take place in virtual-reality environments maintained on global computer networks in a worldwide culture of dystopian alienation. The prototypical cyberpunk novel is William Gibson's *Neuromancer* (1982). **2.** A category of popular culture that resembles the ethos of cyberpunk fiction. **3.** A person or fictional character who resembles the heroes of cyberpunk fiction.

cybersex *n.* Communication via electronic means, such as e-mail, chat, or newsgroups, for the purpose of sexual stimulation or gratification. *See also* chat[1] (definition 1), newsgroup.

cyberspace *n.* **1.** The advanced shared virtual-reality network imagined by William Gibson in his novel *Neuromancer* (1982). **2.** The universe of environments, such as the Internet, in which persons interact by means of connected computers. A defining characteristic of cyberspace is that communication is independent of physical distance.

cyberspeak *n.* Terminology and language (often jargon, slang, and acronyms) relating to the Internet (computer-connected) environment, that is, cyberspace. *See also* cyberspace.

cybersquatter *n.* A person who registers company names and other trademarks as Internet domain names in order to force the named companies or owners of the trademarks to buy them at an inflated price.

cyberwidow *n.* The spouse of a person who spends inordinate amounts of time on the Internet.

cybrarian *n.* Software used at some libraries that allows one to query a database through the use of an interactive search engine.

cycle power *vb.* To turn the power to a machine off and back on in order to clear something out of memory or to reboot after a hung or crashed state.

cycle time *n.* The amount of time between a random access memory (RAM) access and the earliest time a new access can occur. *See also* access time (definition 1).

cyclical redundancy check *n.* *See* CRC.

cyclic binary code *n.* A binary representation of numbers in which each number differs from the one that precedes it by one unit (bit), in one position. Cyclic binary numbers differ from "plain" binary numbers, even though both are based on two digits, 0 and 1. The numbers in the cyclic binary system represent a code, much like Morse code, whereas "plain" binary numbers represent actual values in the binary number system. Because sequential numbers differ by only 1 bit, cyclic binary is used to minimize errors in representing unit measurements. See the table.

Table C.2 Cyclic Binary Code Compared to Other Numeral Systems

Cyclic binary	"Plain" binary	Decimal
0000	0000	0
0001	0001	1
0011	0010	2
0010	0011	3
0110	0100	4
0111	0101	5
0101	0110	6
0100	0111	7
1100	1000	8
1101	1001	9

Cycolor *n.* A color printing process that uses a special film embedded with millions of capsules filled with cyan, magenta, and yellow dyes. When exposed to red, green, or blue light, the respective capsules become hard and unbreakable. The film is then pressed against specially treated paper, and the capsules that have not hardened in the previous process break, releasing their colors onto the paper. *See also* CMY.

DA *n. See* desk accessory.

DAC *n. See* digital-to-analog converter.

DACL *n. See* discretionary access control list.

daemon *n.* A program associated with UNIX systems that performs a housekeeping or maintenance utility function without being called by the user. A daemon sits in the background and is activated only when needed, for example, to correct an error from which another program cannot recover.

daisy chain[1] *n.* A set of devices connected in series. In order to eliminate conflicting requests to use the channel (bus) to which all the devices are connected, each device is given a different priority. SCSI (**S**mall **C**omputer **S**ystem **I**nterface) and the newer USB (**U**niversal **S**erial **B**us) both support daisy-chained devices. *See also* SCSI, USB.

daisy chain[2] *vb.* To connect a series of devices, one to another, like daisies in a chain of flowers.

daisy wheel *n.* A print element consisting of a set of formed characters with each character mounted on a separate type bar, all radiating from a center hub. *See also* daisy-wheel printer, thimble, thimble printer.

daisy-wheel printer *n.* A printer that uses a daisy-wheel type element. Daisy-wheel output is crisp and slightly imprinted, with fully formed characters resembling typewriter quality. Daisy-wheel printers were standard for high-quality printing until being superseded by laser printers. *See also* daisy wheel, thimble, thimble printer.

damping *n.* A technique for preventing overshoot (exceeding the desired limit) in the response of a circuit or device.

D-AMPS *n.* Acronym for **D**igital **A**dvanced **M**obile **P**hone Service. The digital form of the analog AMPS cellular phone service. D-AMPS, sometimes spelled DAMPS, differs from AMPS in being digital and in tripling the number of available channels by using time division multiple access (TDMA) to divide each of the 30 AMPS channels into three separate channels. *See also* AMPS, FDMA, TDMA.

DAO *n. See* Data Access Objects.

DAP *n. See* Directory Access Protocol.

DaratechSUMMIT *n.* Conference on emerging engineering and technology developments in the information technology industry. The DaratechSUMMIT focuses on how information technology affects business practices and assists in manufacturing and production.

dark fiber *n.* Unused capacity in fiber-optic communications.

Darlington circuit *n.* An amplifier circuit made of two transistors, often mounted in the same housing. The collectors of the two transistors are connected, and the emitter of the first is connected to the base of the second. Darlington circuits provide high-gain amplification. *Also called:* Darlington pair.

Darlington pair *n. See* Darlington circuit.

DARPA *n. See* Defense Advanced Research Projects Agency.

DARPANET *n.* Short for **D**efense **A**dvanced **R**esearch **P**rojects **A**gency **Net**work. *See* ARPANET.

Darwin *n.* Apple Computer's open-source operating system, which forms the core of Mac OS X. Darwin is a processor-independent BSD UNIX operating system based on FreeBSD and Mach 3.0 technologies. Darwin offers advanced networking, protected memory, preemptive multitasking, and support for Macintosh and UNIX file systems. Darwin can be run on both the Power PC Macintosh and Intel processor–based computers. *See also* Mac OS X.

DAS *n. See* dual attachment station.

DASD *n.* Acronym for **d**irect **a**ccess **s**torage **d**evice. A data storage device by which information can be accessed directly, instead of by passing sequentially through all storage areas. For example, a disk drive is a DASD, but a tape unit is not, because, with a tape unit, the data is stored as a linear sequence. *See also* direct access. *Compare* sequential access.

.dat *n.* A generic file extension for a data file.

DAT *n. See* digital audio tape, dynamic address translation.

D

data *n.* Plural of the Latin *datum*, meaning an item of information. In practice, *data* is often used for the singular as well as the plural form of the noun. *See also* datum. *Compare* information.

Data Access Objects *n.* A data access interface that communicates with Microsoft Jet and ODBC-compliant data sources to connect to, retrieve, manipulate, and update data and the database structure. *Acronym:* DAO.

data acquisition *n.* The process of obtaining data from another source, usually one outside a specific system.

data aggregate *n.* A collection of data records. It usually includes a description of the placement of the data blocks and their relation to the entire set.

data attribute *n.* Structural information about data that describes its context and meaning.

data bank *n.* Any substantial collection of data.

database *n.* A file composed of records, each containing fields together with a set of operations for searching, sorting, recombining, and other functions. *Acronym:* DB.

database administrator *n.* One who manages a database. The administrator determines the content, internal structure, and access strategy for a database, defines security and integrity, and monitors performance. *Acronym:* DBA. *Also called:* database manager.

database analyst *n.* One who provides the analytic functions needed to design and maintain applications requiring a database.

database designer *n.* One who designs and implements functions required for applications that use a database.

database engine *n.* The program module or modules that provide access to a database management system (DBMS).

database machine *n.* **1.** A peripheral that executes database tasks, thereby relieving the main computer from performing them. **2.** A database server that performs only database tasks.

database management system *n.* A software interface between the database and the user. A database management system handles user requests for database actions and allows for control of security and data integrity requirements. *Acronym:* DBMS. *Also called:* database manager. *See also* database engine.

database manager *n. See* database administrator, database management system.

database publishing *n.* The use of desktop publishing or Internet technology to produce reports containing information obtained from a database.

database server *n.* A network node, or station, dedicated to storing and providing access to a shared database. *Also called:* database machine.

database structure *n.* A general description of the format of records in a database, including the number of fields, specifications regarding the type of data that can be entered in each field, and the field names used.

data bit *n.* In asynchronous communications, one of a group of from 5 to 8 bits that represents a single character of data for transmission. Data bits are preceded by a start bit and followed by an optional parity bit and one or more stop bits. *See also* asynchronous transmission, bit, communications parameter.

data buffer *n.* An area in memory where data is temporarily stored while being moved from one location to another. *See also* buffer[1].

data bus *n. See* bus.

data cable *n.* Fiber-optic or wire cable used to transfer data from one device to another.

data capture *n.* **1.** The collection of information at the time of a transaction. **2.** The process of saving on a storage medium a record of interchanges between a user and a remote information utility.

data carrier *n. See* carrier (definition 1).

Data Carrier Detected *n. See* DCD (definition 1).

data chaining *n.* The process of storing segments of data in noncontiguous locations while retaining the ability to reconnect them in the proper sequence.

data channel *n. See* channel (definition 1).

data closet *n. See* wiring closet.

data collection *n.* **1.** The process of acquiring source documents or data. **2.** The grouping of data by means of classification, sorting, ordering, and other organizing methods.

datacom *n.* Short for **data com**munications. *See* communications.

data communications *n. See* communications.

data compaction *n. See* data compression.

data compression *n.* A means of reducing the amount of space or bandwidth needed to store or transmit a block of data, used in data communications, facsimile transmission, file storage and transfer, and CD-ROM publishing. *Also called:* data compaction.

data conferencing *n.* Simultaneous data communication among geographically separated participants in a meeting. Data conferencing involves whiteboards and other software that enable a single set of files at one location to be accessed and modified by all participants. See the illustration. *See also* desktop conferencing, whiteboard. *Compare* video conferencing.

Data conferencing.

data control *n.* The aspect of data management concerned with tracking how and by whom data is used, accessed, altered, owned, and reported on.

data conversion *n.* Changing the way information is represented in a document or file—for instance, changing binary representation to decimal or hexadecimal.

data corruption *n. See* corruption.

data declaration *n.* A statement in a program that specifies the characteristics of a variable. The requirements for data declarations vary among different programming languages but can include such values as variable name, data type, initial value, and size specification. *See also* array, data type, record[1], variable.

data definition language *n.* A language that defines all attributes and properties of a database, especially record layouts, field definitions, key fields, file locations, and storage strategy. *Acronym:* DDL.

data description language *n.* A language designed specifically for declaring data structures and files. *See also* data definition language.

data dictionary *n.* A database containing data about all the databases in a database system. Data dictionaries store all the various schema and file specifications and their locations. They also contain information about which programs use which data and which users are interested in which reports.

data directory *n. See* catalog, data dictionary.

data-driven attack *n.* A form of attack in which malicious code is hidden in a program or other innocuous data. When the data is executed, the virus or other destructive code is activated. A data-driven attack is typically used to bypass a firewall or other security measures.

data-driven processing *n.* A form of processing where the processor or program must wait for data to arrive before it can advance to the next step in a sequence. *Compare:* demand-driven processing.

data element *n.* A single unit of data. *Also called:* data item. *See also* data field.

data encapsulation *n.* A method of dealing with computers with Year 2000 problems that entailed modifying the input and output logic of a program, leaving the actual data unchanged as it was processed. The input logic was modified to reflect a date in the past that the computer could handle that paralleled the current calendar. When output was generated, the output logic changed the data to reflect the correct date.

data encryption *n. See* encryption.

data encryption key *n.* A sequence of secret information, such as a string of decimal numbers or binary digits, that is used to encrypt and decrypt data. *Acronym:* DEK. *See also* decryption, encryption, key (definition 3).

data encryption standard *n. See* DES.

data entry *n.* The process of writing new data to computer memory.

data/fax modem *n.* A modem that can handle both serial data and facsimile images to either send or receive transmissions.

data field *n.* A well-defined portion of a data record, such as a column in a database table.

data field masking *n.* The process of filtering or selecting part of a data field to control the way it is returned and displayed.

data file *n.* A file consisting of data in the form of text, numbers, or graphics, as distinct from a program file of commands and instructions. *Compare* program file.

data flow or **dataflow** *n.* **1.** The movement of data through a system, from entry to destination. **2.** In parallel processing, a design in which a calculation is made either when all necessary data is available (data-driven processing) or when other processors request the data (demand-driven processing). *See also* parallel processing.

data fork *n.* In Macintosh files, the part of a stored document that contains user-supplied information, such as the text of a word-processing document. A Macintosh file can have a data fork, a resource fork (which contains information such as program code, font data, digitized sound, or icons), and a header. All three parts are used by the operating system in file management and storage. *See also* resource (definition 2), resource fork.

data format *n.* The structure applied to data by an application program to provide a context in which the data can be interpreted.

data frame *n.* A packet of information transmitted as a unit on a network. Data frames are defined by the network's data-link layer and exist only on the wire between network nodes. *See also* data-link layer, frame (definition 2).

data glove *n.* A data input device or controller in the form of a glove fitted with sensors that convert movement of the hand and fingers into commands. *See also* virtual reality.

datagram *n.* One packet, or unit, of information, along with relevant delivery information such as the destination address, that is sent through a packet-switching network. *See also* packet switching.

data independence *n.* The separation of data in a database from the programs that manipulate it. Data independence makes stored data as accessible as possible.

data integrity *n.* The accuracy of data and its conformity to its expected value, especially after being transmitted or processed.

data interchange format *n.* A format consisting of ASCII codes in which database, spreadsheet, and similar documents can be structured to facilitate their use by and transfer to other programs. *Acronym:* DIF. *See also* ASCII.

data item *n. See* data element.

data library *n.* A cataloged collection of data files on disk or in another storage medium.

data link *n.* A connection between any two devices capable of sending and receiving information, such as a computer and a printer or a main computer and a terminal. Sometimes the term is extended to include equipment, such as a modem, that enables transmission and receiving. Such devices follow protocols that govern data transmission. *See also* communications protocol, data-link layer, DCE (definition 1), DTE.

Data Link Connection Identifier *n.* A virtual circuit on frame relay networks that permanently identifies the path to a particular destination. *See also* frame relay, virtual circuit.

Data Link Control *n. See* DLC.

data link escape *n.* In data transmission, a control character that changes the meaning of the characters immediately following it.

data-link layer *n.* The second of seven layers in the ISO/OSI reference model for standardizing computer-to-computer communications. The data-link layer is one layer above the physical layer. Its concern is packaging and addressing data and managing the flow of transmissions. It is the lowest of the three layers (data-link, network, and transport) involved in actually moving data between devices. See the illustration. *See also* ISO/OSI reference model.

ISO/OSI MODEL	
ISO/OSI Layer	***Focus***
Application *(highest level)*	Program-to-program transfer of information
Presentation	Text formatting and display, code conversion
Session	Establishing, maintaining, and coordinating communication
Transport	Accurate delivery, service quality
Network	Transport routes, message handling and transfer
Data-link	Coding, addressing, and transmitting information
Physical	Hardware connections

Data-link layer on ISO/OSI reference model.

data management *n.* The control of data from acquisition and input through processing, output, and storage. In microcomputers, hardware manages data by gathering it, moving it, and following instructions to process it. The operating system manages the hardware and ensures that

D

the parts of the system work in harmony so that data is stored safely and accurately. Application programs manage data by receiving and processing input according to the user's commands, and sending results to an output device or to disk storage. The user also is responsible for data management by acquiring data, labeling and organizing disks, backing up data, archiving files, and removing unneeded material from the hard disk.

data manipulation *n.* The processing of data by means of programs that accept user commands, offer ways to handle data, and tell the hardware what to do with the data.

data manipulation language *n.* In database management systems, a language that is used to insert data in, update, and query a database. Data manipulation languages are often capable of performing mathematical and statistical calculations that facilitate generating reports. *Acronym:* DML. *See also* structured query language.

data mart *n.* A scaled-down version of a data warehouse that is tailored to contain only information likely to be used by the target group. *See also* data warehouse.

data medium *n.* The physical material on which computer data is stored.

data migration *n.* **1.** The process of moving data from one repository or source, such as a database, to another, usually via automated scripts or programs. Often data migration involves transferring data from one type of computer system to another. **2.** In supercomputing applications, the process of storing large amounts of data off line while making them appear to be on line as disk-resident files.

data mining *n.* The process of identifying commercially useful patterns, problems, or relationships in a database, a Web server, or other computer repository through the use of advanced statistical tools. Some Web sites use data mining to monitor the efficiency of site navigation and to determine changes in the Web site's design based on how consumers are using the site.

data model *n.* A collection of related object types, operators, and integrity rules that form the abstract entity supported by a database management system (DBMS). Thus, one speaks of a relational DBMS, a network DBMS, and so on, depending on the type of data model a DBMS supports. In general, a DBMS supports only one data model as a practical rather than a theoretical restriction.

data network *n.* A network designed for transferring data encoded as digital signals, as opposed to a voice network, which transmits analog signals.

Data Over Cable Service Interface Specification *n.* *See* DOCSIS.

data-overrun error *n.* An error that occurs when more data is being acquired than can be processed. *See also* bps.

data packet *n. See* packet.

data path *n.* The route that a signal follows as it travels through a computer network.

data point *n.* Any pair of numeric values plotted on a chart.

data processing *n.* **1.** The general work performed by computers. **2.** More specifically, the manipulation of data to transform it into some desired result. *Acronym:* DP. *Also called:* ADP, automatic data processing, EDP, electronic data processing. *See also* centralized processing, decentralized processing, distributed processing.

Data Processing Management Association *n. See* DPMA.

data projector *n.* A device, similar to a slide projector, that projects the video monitor output of a computer onto a screen.

data protection *n.* The process of ensuring the preservation, integrity, and reliability of data. *See also* data integrity.

data rate *n.* The speed at which a circuit or communications line can transfer information, usually measured in bits per second (bps).

data record *n. See* record[1].

data reduction *n.* The process of converting raw data to a more useful form by scaling, smoothing, ordering, or other editing procedures.

data segment *n.* The portion of memory or auxiliary storage that contains the data used by a program.

Data Service Unit *n. See* DDS.

data set *n.* **1.** A collection of related information made up of separate elements that can be treated as a unit in data handling. **2.** In communications, a modem. *See also* modem.

Data Set Ready *n. See* DSR.

data sharing *n.* The use of a single file by more than one person or computer. Data sharing can be done by physically transferring a file from one computer to another, or, more commonly, by networking and computer-to-computer communications.

data signal *n.* The information transmitted over a line or circuit. It consists of binary digits and can include actual information or messages and other elements such as control characters or error-checking codes.

data sink *n.* **1.** Any recording medium where data can be stored until needed. **2.** In communications, the portion of a Data Terminal Equipment (DTE) device that receives transmitted data.

data source *n.* **1.** The originator of computer data, frequently an analog or digital data collection device. **2.** In communications, the portion of a Data Terminal Equipment (DTE) device that sends data.

data stream *n.* An undifferentiated, byte-by-byte flow of data.

data structure *n.* An organizational scheme, such as a record or array, that can be applied to data to facilitate interpreting the data or performing operations on it.

data switch *n.* A device in a computer system that routes incoming data to various locations.

Data Terminal Equipment *n.* See DTE.

Data Terminal Ready *n.* See DTR.

data traffic *n.* The exchange of electronic messages—control and data—across a network. Traffic capacity is measured in bandwidth; traffic speed is measured in bits per unit of time.

data transfer *n.* The movement of information from one location to another, either within a computer (as from a disk drive to memory), between a computer and an external device (as between a file server and a computer on a network), or between separate computers.

data transfer rate *n.* See data rate.

data transmission *n.* The electronic transfer of information from a sending device to a receiving device.

data type *n.* In programming, a definition of a set of data that specifies the possible range of values of the set, the operations that can be performed on the values, and the way in which the values are stored in memory. Defining the data type allows a computer to manipulate the data appropriately. Data types are most often supported in high-level languages and often include types such as real, integer, floating point, character, Boolean, and pointer. How a language handles data typing is one of its major characteristics. *See also* cast, constant, enumerated data type, strong typing, type checking, user-defined data type, variable, weak typing.

data validation *n.* The process of testing the accuracy of data.

data value *n.* The literal or interpreted meaning of a data item, such as an entry in a database, or a type, such as an integer, that can be used for a variable.

data warehouse[1] *n.* A database, frequently very large, that can access all of a company's information. While the warehouse can be distributed over several computers and may contain several databases and information from numerous sources in a variety of formats, it should be accessible through a server. Thus, access to the warehouse is transparent to the user, who can use simple commands to retrieve and analyze all the information. The data warehouse also contains data about how the warehouse is organized, where the information can be found, and any connections between data. Frequently used for decision support within an organization, the data warehouse also allows the organization to organize its data, coordinate updates, and see relationships between information gathered from different parts of the organization. *See also* database, decision support system, server (definition 1), transparent (definition 1).

data warehouse[2] *vb.* To acquire, collect, manage, and disseminate information gathered from various sources into a single location; or to implement an informational database used to store sharable data. Data warehousing is a four-step process: gathering data; managing the data in a centralized location; providing access to the data along with tools for interpreting, analyzing, and reporting on the data; and producing reports on the data to be used for decision making. *See also* downflow, inflow, metaflow, upflow.

date and time stamp *n.* See time stamp.

date counter overflow *n.* A problem that may occur in systems or programs when the value in a date variable exceeds allowable values. A date counter overflow can occur when an incremental date produces a number that the system interprets as zero or a negative number. This is likely to cause the system or program to post an error message in turn or to revert to the original starting point. Although this was largely considered a Year 2000 problem, such an error is not necessarily confined to the year 2000.

date dependency *n.* In terms of the Year 2000 problem, the need many programs have for date-related input or output data and the way dates are represented in that data. This dependency affects whether the program can run correctly when the turn of the century is reached.

D

date expansion *n*. A method of dealing with programs with Year 2000 problems that entails changing data, data descriptions, and (if necessary) program logic that pertains to dates by expanding date fields from two digits to four digits—for example, from DDMMYY to DDMMYYYY.

date format *n*. The manner in which dates are formatted in a computer system or program. While some organizations require that the same format be used throughout their systems and programs, many organizations have not, which can make tracking down potential date problems, such as the Year 2000 problem, difficult. In addition, date formats can vary widely from organization to organization, although many have opted to standardize on formats specified in ANSI X3.30-1997 or ISO8601:1988.

date horizon *n*. A period of time that a program uses to determine the beginning or ending point in performing its functions. A program that tracks inventory may have one date horizon that trails the current date by two months (a trailing date horizon) to process returned merchandise and another that precedes it by another two months (a leading date horizon) for planning purposes. If the program logic doesn't account for any date horizons it may have, for example, if the year was 1999, the program could experience Year 2000 problems when the leading date horizon enters January 1, 2000. *See also* event horizon.

date-in-key problem *n*. A potential problem in computer systems that depend on indexed files using a two-digit date as part of the key, such as certain databases. If the files need to be in chronological order, the files beginning with the year 2000 will be out of sequence—for example, (19)99 would be interpreted as more recent than (20)00.

date rollover *n*. *See* Year 2000 rollover.

date stamp *n*. *See* time stamp.

date stamping *n*. A software feature that automatically inserts the current date into a document.

datum *n*. Singular of *data*; a single item of information. *See also* data.

daughterboard *n*. A circuit board that attaches to another, such as the main system board (motherboard), to add extra capabilities. *See also* motherboard.

DAV connector *n*. *See* digital audio/video connector.

day-of-the-week problem *n*. A reference to an inaccuracy that may occur after the Year 2000 in computers that calculate the day of the week based on the last two digits of the year, assuming that the dates they calculate fall in the 1900s. Because January 1, 1900 was a Monday, but January 1, 2000 will be a Saturday, those computers may not be able to correctly determine the day of the week. This is particularly problematic in computers that regulate timed systems based on the business week, such as a door or vault that unlocks during business hours.

DB *n*. *See* database.

dB *n*. *See* decibel.

DBA *n*. *See* database administrator.

DB connector *n*. Any of various connectors that facilitate parallel input and output. The initials DB (for data bus) are followed by a number that indicates the number of lines (wires) within the connector. For example, a DB-9 connector has nine pins and supports up to nine lines, each of which can connect to a pin on the connector.

.dbf *n*. A file extension for a dBASE database file.

DBMS *n*. *See* database management system.

DBS *n*. *See* direct broadcast satellite.

dbXML *n*. Acronym for **d**ata**b**ase **XML**. A native XML database server designed to manage large collections of XML documents. dbXML may be embedded in custom applications or run as a stand-alone database.

DC *n*. *See* direct current.

DCA *n*. **1.** Acronym for **D**ocument **C**ontent **A**rchitecture. A formatting guideline used in IBM's Systems Network Architecture (SNA) that enables the exchange of text-only documents between differing types of computers. DCA provides for two types of document formatting: Revisable-Form-Text DCA (RFTDCA), which allows for modification of formatting, and Final-Form-Text DCA (FFTDCA), which cannot be modified. *See also* DIA, SNA. **2.** Acronym for **D**irectory **C**lient **A**gent. *See* DUA.

DCD *n*. **1.** Acronym for **D**ata **C**arrier **D**etected. A signal in serial communications that is sent from a modem to its computer to indicate that the modem is ready for transmitting. *Also called:* RLSD. *See also* RS-232-C standard. **2.** Acronym for **D**ocument **C**ontent **D**escription. A specification governing the rules for defining the structure and content of XML documents. The specification was created by IBM and Microsoft in 1998 and was submitted to the World Wide Web Consortium for approval. *See also* XML.

DCE *n.* **1.** Acronym for **D**ata **C**ommunications **E**quipment. The term used in RS-232 and X.25 specifications for a device, such as a modem, that provides another device (known as the Data Terminal Equipment or DTE) with access to a communications line. A DCE is an intermediary device that often transforms input from a DTE before sending it to a recipient. *See also* RS-232-C standard, X series. *Compare* DTE. **2.** *See* Distributed Computing Environment.

D channel *n.* Short for **data channel**. In the ISDN communications architecture, the channel dedicated to carrying control signals, such as packet-switching information; and user-related data, such as phone numbers. The basic ISDN connection, called the Basic Rate Interface (BRI), is composed of two B (bearer) channels, which carry as much as 64 Kbps of actual data each, and one D channel, which transmits at either 16 Kbps or 64 Kbps. The faster Primary Rate Interface (PRI) is composed of one 64-Kbps D channel and either 23 or 30 B channels operating at 64 Kbps. *See also* B channel, BRI, ISDN.

DCOM *n.* Acronym for **D**istributed **C**omponent **O**bject **M**odel. The version of Microsoft's Component Object Model (COM) specification that stipulates how components communicate over Windows-based networks. It permits the distribution of different components for a single application across two or more networked computers, running an application distributed across a network so that the distribution of components is not apparent to the user, and remotely displaying an application. *Also called:* Distributed COM. *See also* COM (definition 2), component (definition 2).

DCS *n.* Acronym for **D**esktop **C**olor **S**eparation. The primary format for preparing digital publication text and graphics for printing. DCS layouts consist of five files, one for each of the CMYK colors, and a master file which, includes the display version of the page and information on the other four files. *See also* OPI.

DCTL *n. See* direct-coupled transistor logic.

DDBMS *n. See* distributed database management system.

DDC *n.* Acronym for **D**isplay **D**ata **C**hannel. A VESA standard that allows software control of graphical computer monitors. Under DDC, monitor characteristics are provided to the graphics subsystem, which uses the data to configure the display and provide a bidirectional communication channel between the monitor and computer. *Also called:* VESA DDC. *See also* VESA[2].

DDCP *n. See* direct digital color proof.

DDE *n.* Acronym for **D**ynamic **D**ata **E**xchange. An interprocess communication method featured in Microsoft Windows and OS/2. DDE allows two or more programs that are running simultaneously to exchange data and commands. In Windows 3.1, DDE was largely supplanted by OLE, which is an extension of DDE. In Windows 95 and Windows NT, OLE and ActiveX are more commonly used. *See also* ActiveX, interprocess communication, OLE.

DDK *n.* Acronym for **D**river **D**evelopment **K**it. A set of tools used to create software that enables an operating system to work with hardware devices. With a DDK, a software developer can build drivers to support network, storage, print, sound, video, input, and other devices. *Also called:* Device Driver Kit, Device Driver Developer Kit. *See also* driver.

DDL *n. See* data definition language.

DDoS *n.* Acronym for **d**istributed **d**enial of **s**ervice attack. A form of denial of service attack (DoS) originating from several computers that seeks to disrupt Web access by overwhelming a target with connection requests that cannot be completed. A DDoS attack involves cracking into a number of computers and planting programs that lie dormant until sent a signal to attack. At that point the computers send a steady stream of data packets to the targeted Web site, overwhelming the ability of the Web server to respond. Because the attack is coming from many computers, security features that might otherwise recognize the attack and stop accepting data packets from a single source are unable to shut down connections to all the attackers. *See also* DoS, packet, zombie.

DDR SDRAM *n.* Short for **D**ouble **D**ata **R**ate **S**ynchronous **D**ynamic **RAM** (SDRAM). A form of SDRAM that essentially doubles memory throughput to 200 megahertz or better. DDR SDRAM gets a boost in data transfer rates by producing output on both the rising and falling of the system clock—that is, twice for each clock cycle. *See also* SDRAM.

DDS *n.* Acronym for **d**igital **d**ata **s**ervice, a dedicated communications line that provides transmission at speeds up to 56 Kbps. DDS lines use a device known as a CSU/DSU rather than a modem for connecting two networks. The CSU, or Channel Service Unit, connects the network to the transmission line; the DSU, or Data Service Unit, converts data for transmission by the CSU and controls data flow.

D

dead code *n.* Program code that never gets executed, possibly because the programmer has eliminated all references to it, or possibly because the program is written in such a way that the instruction(s) will never be needed—for example, an ELSE statement would never be needed in an IF condition that always proved to be true. Dead code can slow program execution and increase the size of the program in memory. *Also called:* grunge, software rot.

dead halt *n.* A machine stop with no hope of recovery by either the program or the operating system. The only choice after a dead halt is to reboot. *Also called:* drop-dead halt. *See also* hang. *Compare* reboot.

dead key *n.* A key used with another key to create an accented character. When pressed, a dead key produces no visible character (hence its name) but indicates that the accent mark it represents is to be combined with the next key pressed. *See also* key (definition 1).

dead-letter box *n.* In e-mail or message systems, a file to which undeliverable messages are sent.

deadlock *n.* **1.** A situation that occurs when two programs or devices are each waiting for a response from the other before continuing. *Also called:* deadly embrace. **2.** In operating systems, a situation in which two or more processes are prevented from continuing while each waits for resources to be freed by the continuation of the other. **3.** In computer games, a deadlock occurs when the resources needed to continue the game become unavailable to the player. The deadlock condition could be intentional, such as a loss condition, or a design error on the part of the game developer. *See also* computer games.

deadly embrace *n. See* deadlock.

deallocate *vb.* To free previously allocated memory. *See also* pointer. *Compare* allocate.

deblock *vb.* To remove one or more logical records (units of stored information) from a block. Application or database systems must often deblock information to make specific units of information available for processing. *Compare* block² (definition 1).

debounce algorithm *n.* A set of instructions that makes an assumption about how fast a user can press and release a switch and then ensures that only one press is registered in the time specified.

debug *vb.* To detect, locate, and correct logical or syntactical errors in a program or malfunctions in hardware. In hardware contexts, the term *troubleshoot* is the term more often used, especially when the problem is a major one. *See also* bug, debugger.

debugger *n.* A program designed to aid in debugging another program by allowing the programmer to step through the program, examine the data, and monitor conditions such as the values of variables. *See also* bug (definition 1), debug.

deca- *prefix* Metric prefix meaning 10—that is, 10 to the first power, or 10^1.

decay *n.* A decrease in the amplitude of a signal over time.

DECchip 21064 *n.* A Digital Equipment Corporation microprocessor introduced in February 1992. The DECchip 21064 is a 64-bit, RISC-based, superscalar, superpipelined chip with 64-bit registers, a 64-bit data bus, a 64-bit address bus, and a 128-bit data path between the microprocessor and memory. It also has a built-in 8-KB instruction cache, a built-in 8-KB data cache, and a floating-point processor. The DECchip 21064 contains 1.7 million transistors and operates at 3.3 volts. The 200-MHz version runs at a peak rate of 400 MPS. The chip's architecture is SMP compliant, so that several chips can be used in a parallel (multiprocessor) configuration. *See also* floating-point processor, MIPS, pipelining (definition 1), RISC, superpipelining, superscalar.

deceleration time *n.* The time required for an access arm to come to a stop as it approaches the desired portion of a disk. The faster the arm moves, the more momentum it gains and the greater the deceleration time.

decentralized processing *n.* The distribution of computer processing facilities in more than one location. Decentralized processing is not the same as distributed processing, which assigns multiple computers to the same task to increase efficiency.

deci- *prefix* Metric prefix meaning 10^{-1} (one-tenth).

decibel *n.* One tenth of a bel (named after Alexander Graham Bell), a unit used in electronics and other fields to measure the strength of a sound or signal. Decibel measurements fall on a logarithmic scale and compare the measured quantity against a known reference. The following formula gives the number of decibels between two values: dB = n log (x/r) where x is the measured quantity, r is the reference quantity, and n is 10 for voltage and current measurements and 20 for power measurements. *Abbreviation:* dB.

decimal *n.* The base-10 numbering system. *See also* base (definition 2).

decision box *n.* A diamond-shaped flowchart symbol denoting a decision that results in a branching in the process being considered. See the illustration.

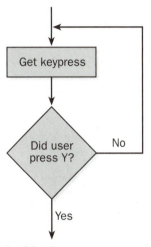

Decision box.

decision support system *n.* A set of programs and related data designed to help with analysis and decision making. A decision support system provides more help in formulating decisions than a management information system (MIS) or an executive information system (EIS). It includes a database, a body of knowledge about the subject area, a "language" used to formulate problems and questions, and a modeling program for testing alternative decisions. *Acronym:* DSS. *Compare* executive information system, management information system.

decision table *n.* A tabular listing of possible conditions (inputs) and the desired result (output) corresponding to each condition. A decision table may be used in the preliminary analysis of program flow, or it may be converted and incorporated into the program itself.

decision tree *n.* Similar to a decision table, an analysis instrument where possible outcomes of some condition are represented as branches, which may in turn generate other branches. See the illustration. *See also* branch, tree structure.

Decision tree.

deck *n.* A storage device, such as a tape deck, or a group of such devices.

declaration *n.* A binding of an identifier to the information that relates to it. For example, to make a declaration of a constant means to bind the name of the constant with its value. Declaration usually occurs in a program's source code; the actual binding can take place at compile time or run time. *See also* bind, constant, data declaration, data type, identifier, instruction, routine, type declaration, variable.

declarative markup language *n.* In text processing, a system of text-formatting codes that indicates only that a unit of text is a certain part of a document. Document formatting is then done by another program, called a parser. SGML and HTML are examples of declarative markup languages. *Acronym:* DML. *Also called:* data manipulation language. *See also* HTML, SGML.

declare *vb.* To specify the name and type of a variable that will be used in a program. In most high-level programming languages, variables are declared at the beginning of sections of code. *See also* variable.

DECnet *n.* A hardware, software, and protocol stack designed by Digital Equipment Corporation for its Digital Network Architecture (DNA).

decoder *n.* **1.** A device or program routine that converts coded data back to its original form. This can mean changing unreadable or encrypted codes into readable text or changing one code to another, although the latter type of decoding is usually referred to as conversion. *Compare* conversion. **2.** In electronics and hardware, a type of circuit that produces one or more selected output signals based on the combination of input signals it receives.

decollate *vb.* To separate copies in a multipart continuous paper form.

decompiler *n.* A program that attempts to generate high-level source code from assembly language code or machine code. This can be a difficult task, as some assembly language code has no corresponding high-level source code. *See also* disassembler. *Compare* compiler (definition 2).

decompress *vb. See* uncompress.

decrement[1] *n.* The amount by which a number is decreased. *Compare* increment[1].

decrement[2] *vb.* To decrease a number by a given amount. *Compare* increment[2].

decryption *n.* The process of restoring encrypted data to its original form. *See also* data encryption key. *Compare* encryption.

deCSS *n.* Decrypt CSS. A utility capable of cracking the CSS encryption system used on DVD discs. By decrypting the CSS code, DVD movies and other copyrighted material can be used with any DVD playback device without regard to license or region coding. The origin of deCSS can be traced to a number of individuals interested in creating a DVD player for the Linux OS. The term deCSS is sometimes used generically for any software capable of defeating CSS technology. *See also* CSS, region code.

DECstation *n.* **1.** A small computer system used primarily for word processing, introduced by Digital Equipment Corporation in 1978. **2.** A personal computer, part of a series, introduced by Digital Equipment Corporation in 1989. **3.** A single-user UNIX workstation introduced by Digital Equipment Corporation in 1989 and based on RISC processors. *See also* RISC.

dedicated *adj.* Of, pertaining to, or being a device, program, or procedure devoted to a single task or function.

dedicated channel *n.* A communications link reserved for a particular use or a particular user.

dedicated circuit *n. See* dedicated line.

dedicated connection *n. See* dedicated line.

dedicated line *n.* **1.** A communications channel that permanently connects two or more locations. Dedicated lines are private or leased lines, rather than public ones. T1 lines, which are used by many organizations for Internet connectivity, are examples of dedicated lines. *Also called:* dedicated connection, leased line, private line. *Compare* switched line. **2.** A telephone line that is used for one purpose only, such as to receive or send faxes or to serve as a modem line.

dedicated server *n.* A computer—usually quite powerful—that is used solely as a network server. *See also* server. *Compare* nondedicated server.

deep copy *n.* A copy of the contents of a data structure, including all its substructures.

deep hack *n.* A state of total concentration on and preoccupation with a programming effort. *Also called:* deep hack mode.

de facto standard *n.* A design, program, or language that has become so widely used and imitated that it has little competition, but whose status has not been officially recognized as standard by an organization such as the American National Standards Institute (ANSI) or the International Organization for Standardization (ISO). *See also* standard. *Compare* de jure standard.

default[1] *n.* A choice made by a program when the user does not specify an alternative. Defaults are built into a program when a value or option must be assumed for the program to function.

default[2] *vb.* In reference to programs, to make a choice when the user does not specify an alternative.

default button *n.* The control that is automatically selected when a window is introduced by an application or operating system, typically activated by pressing the Enter key.

default drive *n.* The disk drive that an operating system reads to and writes from when no alternative is specified.

default home page *n.* On a Web server, the file that is returned when a directory is referenced without a specific filename. This is specified by the Web server software and is typically the file called index.html or index.htm.

default printer *n.* The printer to which a computer sends documents for printing unless an alternative is specified.

Defense Advanced Research Projects Agency *n.* The U.S. government agency that provided the original support for the development of the interconnected networks that later grew into the Internet. *Acronym:* DARPA. *See also* ARPANET.

deferral time *n.* The length of time that nodes on a CSMA/CD network wait before trying to retransmit after a collision. *See also* CSMA/CD.

D

deferred address *n.* An indirect address (memory location) whose calculation is delayed until a program is run. *See also* relative address.

deferred processing *n.* Processing of data after it has been received and stored in blocks. *Compare* direct processing.

deflection coils *n. See* yoke.

deflection routing *n. See* hot potato routing.

deformation *n.* In multimedia and computer-aided design applications, the process of altering a model via certain tools, such as stretch, shatter, bend, and twist. *See also* CAD, multimedia.

defrag *vb.* Slang for defragment. To rearrange data on a disk drive so that whole files are stored in contiguous sectors and the drive heads do not have to travel to scattered locations on the disk in order to read or write portions of a particular file. *See also* defragmentation.

defragger *n.* A software utility for reuniting parts of a file that have become fragmented through rewriting and updating. A defragger physically restores the file to contiguous sectors on a hard disk to speed up access as much as 75 percent. *See also* defragmentation, fragmentation, optimizer.

defragmentation *n.* The process of rewriting parts of a file to contiguous sectors on a hard disk to increase the speed of access and retrieval. When files are updated, the computer tends to save these updates on the largest continuous space on the hard disk, which is often on a different sector than the other parts of the file. When files are thus "fragmented," the computer must search the hard disk each time the file is accessed to find all of the file's parts, which slows down response time. *See also* optimization (definition 1). *Compare* fragmentation.

degausser *n.* A device used to remove magnetization from a video monitor or tape recorder head and to erase information from magnetic storage media, such as tapes and disks.

degradation *n.* **1.** In communications, a deterioration of signal quality, as from line interference. **2.** In computer systems, a reduction in level of performance or service. Degradation in microcomputer performance is indicated by slow response times or frequent pauses for disk access because memory is insufficient to hold an entire program plus the data the program is using.

deinstall *vb. See* uninstall.

deinterlace *n.* To combine two interlaced fields into a single frame that is not interlaced. Deinterlacing is done to remove artifacts and improve the quality of encoded video.

dejagging *n.* Smoothing of the jagged, "stairstep" appearance of diagonal lines and curves in graphical images. *Also called:* anti-aliasing. *Compare* aliasing.

de jure standard *n.* A standard for hardware or software development that has been issued or approved through a formal process by a standards organization. *See also* standard. *Compare* de facto standard.

DEK *n. See* data encryption key.

deka- *prefix See* deca-.

delay distortion *n. See* envelope delay.

delete *vb.* To eliminate text, a file, or part of a document with the intention of removing the information permanently. There are several ways to delete. On-screen characters and parts of documents can be deleted with the Delete key, the Backspace key, or with a program's Delete command. Files can be deleted through a command to the operating system.

Delete key *n.* **1.** On IBM and PC-compatible computers, a key whose function changes depending on the application program. Usually it erases the character under the cursor, although in some applications it can erase selected text or graphics. See the illustration. *Also called:* Del key. **2.** On Apple Macintosh computers, a key on the ADB and Extended keyboards that erases the character preceding the insertion point or erases highlighted text or graphics.

Delete key.

deletia *n.* Omitted material. The term is used in responses to Usenet or mailing list messages to indicate that some unnecessary material has been excluded from the incorporated message being answered.

D

delimit *vb.* To set the limits of some entity, generally by using a special symbol called a delimiter. Programming languages typically delimit such variable-length elements as comments, strings, and program blocks. *See also* delimiter.

delimiter *n.* A special character that sets off, or separates, individual items in a program or set of data. Special characters often used include commas, semi-colons, tabs, and paragraph marks. *See also* delimit, field (definition 1), record[1].

Del key *n. See* Delete key.

delta channel *n. See* ISDN.

demand-driven processing *n.* The processing of data immediately as it becomes available or ready. Such real-time processing avoids the need to store data that has not been processed. *Compare* data-driven processing.

demand paging *n.* The most common implementation of virtual memory, in which pages of data are read into main memory from an auxiliary storage device only in response to interrupts that result when software requests a memory location that the system has saved to auxiliary storage and reused for other purposes. *See also* paging, swap (definition 2), virtual memory.

demand priority *n.* A network access method in which hubs control network access; a feature of 100Base-VG Ethernet networks. With demand priority, nodes send requests to hubs and the hubs give permission to transmit based on priority levels assigned to the requests by the nodes. *See also* 100Base-VG.

demand publishing *n.* Producing print copies of publications on an as-needed basis rather than in a single long press run. Demand publishing is a by-product of desktop publishing and advancements in printer capabilities.

demo *n.* **1.** Short for **demo**nstration. A partial or limited version of a software package distributed free of charge for advertising purposes. Demos often consist of animated presentations that describe or demonstrate the program's features. *See also* crippled version. **2.** A computer in a store that is available for customers to test, to see if they wish to buy it.

demodulation *n.* In communications, the means by which a modem converts data from modulated carrier frequencies (waves that have been modified in such a way that variations in amplitude and frequency represent meaningful information) over a telephone line. Data is converted to the digital form needed by a computer to

which the modem is attached, with as little distortion as possible. *Compare* modulation (definition 1).

demon dialer *n. See* war dialer.

demonstration program or **demo program** *n.* **1.** A prototype that shows the on-screen look and sometimes the proposed capabilities of a program under development. *See also* prototyping. **2.** A scaled-down version of a proprietary program offered as a marketing tool.

denial of service attack *n. See* DoS.

denizen *n.* A participant in a Usenet newsgroup.

dense wavelength division multiplexing *n.* A data transmission technique in which multiple optical signals, each assigned to a separate color (wavelength frequency), are multiplexed onto a single strand of optical fiber. Because each signal travels separately in its own color band on the fiber, dense wavelength division multiplexing allows for the simultaneous transmission of different types of signals, such as SONET and ATM, each traveling at its own rate of speed. Dense wavelength division multiplexing can greatly increase the carrying capacity of a single optical fiber. Depending on the number, type, and rate of the signals involved, bandwidth can range from more than 40 Gbps to projected highs of 200 Gbps or more. *Acronym:* DWDM. *Also called:* wave divisision multiplexing, WDM. *Compare* time division multiple access.

dependence *n.* The state in which one entity relies upon specific hardware, software, or specific events for its own definition or functionality. *See also* context-dependent, dependent variable, device dependence, hardware-dependent, software-dependent.

dependent variable *n.* A variable in a program whose value relies on the outcome of another operation.

deployment descriptor *n.* In the Java J2EE network platform, a deployment descriptor is an XML file provided for each module or application describing how it should be deployed. The deployment descriptor directs a deployment tool to deploy a module or application with specific container options. It also describes the specific configuration requirements that an administrator must resolve when installing modules and J2EE applications into an operational environment. *See also* container, J2EE, module, XML.

depth queuing *vb.* **1.** In computer graphics and modeling, giving a two-dimensional object a three-dimensional appearance through such techniques as shading and hidden-line removal. **2.** Drawing objects from background to foreground to ease in the task of hidden-line removal.

deque *n.* Short for **d**ouble-**e**nded **que**. A form of the queue data structure that can have elements added to or removed from either end of the list. *See also* queue.

dequeue *vb.* To remove from a queue. *See also* queue.

dereference *vb.* In programming, to access information at the address contained by a pointer. The syntax for dereferencing varies among computer languages. *See also* double-dereference, handle (definition 1), pointer.

derived class *n.* In object-oriented programming, a class created from another class, called the base class. A derived class inherits all the features of its base class. It can then add data elements and routines, redefine routines from the base class, and restrict access to base-class features. *See also* base class, class, inheritance (definition 1), object-oriented programming.

derived font *n.* A font that has been scaled or modified from a previously existing font. For example, the Macintosh operating system can generate characters in font sizes other than the installed range of sizes. *See also* font. *Compare* intrinsic font.

derived relation *n.* A relation produced as the result of one or more relational-algebra operations on other relations. *See also* relational algebra, view[1] (definition 2).

DES *n.* Acronym for **D**ata **E**ncryption **S**tandard. A specification for encryption of computer data developed by IBM and adopted by the U.S. government as a standard in 1976. DES uses a 56-bit key. *See also* encryption, key (definition 3).

descendant *n.* **1.** In object-oriented programming, a class (group) that is a more specialized form of another, higher-level class. *See also* class, object-oriented programming. **2.** In computing, a process (roughly, a program or task) that is called by another process and inherits certain of the originator's properties, such as open files. *See also* child (definition 1), inheritance (definition 2). *Compare* client (definition 2).

descendent key *n.* All the subkeys that appear when a key in the registry is expanded. A descendent key is the same as a subkey. *Also called:* descendant key. *See also* key, subkey.

descender *n.* The portion of a lowercase letter that falls below the baseline. See the illustration. *See also* baseline, x-height. *Compare* ascender.

xylem

Descender   Baseline

Descender.

descending sort *n.* A sort that arranges items in descending order—for example, with Z preceding A and higher numbers preceding lower ones. *See also* alphanumeric sort. *Compare* ascending sort.

descriptor *n.* **1.** In information retrieval, a word, similar to an index entry in a book, that identifies a significant topic or element in a stored document or group of documents. It is used as a key in rapid search and retrieval of information. *See also* keyword (definition 1). **2.** In programming, a piece of stored information used to describe something else, often in terms of structure, content, or some other property. *Compare* identifier.

deselect *vb.* To reverse the action of selecting an option, a range of text, a collection of graphical objects, and so on. *Compare* select.

deserialize *vb.* To change from serial (by bit) to parallel (by byte); to convert a single (serial) stream of bits to parallel streams representing the same information. *Compare* serialize.

Design by Contract *n.* An approach to building reusable systems where a software system is viewed as a set of communicating components whose interaction is based on precisely defined specifications of the mutual obligations, also known as contracts.

design cycle *n.* All the phases involved in developing and producing new hardware or software, including product specification, creation of prototypes, testing, debugging, and documentation.

desk accessory *n.* A type of small program on Macintosh computers and in windowing programs for IBM and PC-compatible machines that acts as the electronic equivalent of a clock, calendar, calculator, or other small appliance found on a typical desktop. Desk accessories are conveniences that can be activated when needed and then either put away or moved to a small part of the screen. A special type of desk accessory, a control panel, provides the user with the ability to change the date and time as well as to control screen colors, mouse movements, and other parameters. *Acronym:* DA. *Also called:* desktop accessory. *See also* control panel.

desktop *n.* An on-screen work area that uses icons and menus to simulate the top of a desk. A desktop is characteristic of the Apple Macintosh and of windowing programs such as Microsoft Windows. Its intent is to make a computer easier to use by enabling users to move pictures of objects and to start and stop tasks in much the same way as they would if they were working on a physical desktop. *See also* graphical user interface.

desktop accessory *n. See* desk accessory.

Desktop Color Separation *n. See* DCS.

desktop computer *n.* A computer that fits conveniently on the surface of a business desk. Most personal computers as well as some workstations can be considered desktop computers. *Compare* portable computer.

desktop conferencing *n.* The use of computers for simultaneous communication among geographically separated participants in a meeting. This communication may include input to and display from application programs as well as audio and video communication. *See also* data conferencing, teleconferencing, video conferencing.

desktop enhancer *n.* Software that adds functionality to a windows-based operating system such as Microsoft Windows or Mac OS—for example, an enhanced file browser, clipboard, or multimedia player.

desktop environment *n.* The appearance and user interface of a computer operating system (OS). An OS may offer the user opportunities to customize the desktop environment, or sometimes a choice of alternate desktop environments, with the OS underneath remaining the same.

Desktop file *n.* A hidden file maintained on a particular volume (roughly equivalent to a disk) by the Macintosh operating system for storing information about the files on it, such as version data, lists of icons, and file references.

Desktop Management Interface *n. See* DMI.

desktop publishing *n.* The use of a computer and specialized software to combine text and graphics to create a document that can be printed on either a laser printer or a typesetting machine. Desktop publishing is a multiple-step process involving various types of software and equipment. The original text and illustrations are generally produced with software such as word processors and drawing and painting programs and with photograph-scanning

equipment and digitizers. The finished product is then transferred to a page-makeup program, which is the software most people think of as the actual desktop publishing software. This type of program enables the user to lay out text and graphics on the screen and see what the results will be; for refining parts of the document, these programs often include word processing and graphics features in addition to layout capabilities. As a final step, the finished document is printed either on a laser printer or, for the best quality, by typesetting equipment.

desktop video *n.* The use of a personal computer to display video images. The video images may be recorded on video tape or on a laser disc or may be live footage from a video camera. Live video images can be transmitted in digital form over a network in video conferencing. *Acronym:* DTV.

destination *n.* The location (drive, folder, or directory) to which a file is copied or moved. *Compare* source.

destructive read *n.* An attribute of certain memory systems, notably core systems. In a destructive read of a memory location, the data is passed on to the processor, but the copy in memory is destroyed by the process of reading. Destructive memory systems require special logic to rewrite data back to a memory location after it is read. *Also called:* destructive readout. *See also* core. *Compare* nondestructive readout.

detail file *n. See* transaction file.

detection *n.* Discovery of a certain condition that affects a computer system or the data with which it works.

determinant *n.* In database design theory, any attribute or combination of attributes on which any other attribute or combination of attributes is functionally dependent.

determinism *n.* In computing, the ability to predict an outcome or to know in advance how data will be manipulated by a processing system. A deterministic simulation, for example, is one in which a certain input always produces the same output.

developer *n.* **1.** One who designs and develops software. **2.** *See* programmer.

developer's toolkit *n.* A set of routines (usually in one or more libraries) designed to allow developers to more easily write programs for a given computer, operating system, or user interface. *See also* library (definition 1), toolbox.

development cycle *n.* The process of application development from definition of requirements to finished product, including the following stages: analysis, design and prototyping, software coding and testing, and implementation.

device *n.* A generic term for a computer subsystem. Printers, serial ports, and disk drives are often referred to as devices; such subsystems frequently require their own controlling software, called device drivers. *See also* device driver.

device address *n.* A location within the address space of a computer's random access memory (RAM) that can be altered either by the microprocessor or by an external device. Device addresses are different from other locations in RAM, which can be altered only by the microprocessor. *See also* device, input/output, RAM.

device control character *n. See* control character.

device controller *n. See* input/output controller.

device dependence *n.* The requirement that a particular device be present or available for the use of a program, interface, or protocol. Device dependence in a program is often considered unfortunate because the program either is limited to one system or requires adjustments for every other type of system on which it is to run. *Compare* device independence.

device driver *n.* A software component that permits a computer system to communicate with a device. In most cases, the driver also manipulates the hardware in order to transmit the data to the device. However, device drivers associated with application packages typically perform only the data translation; these higher-level drivers then rely on lower-level drivers to actually send the data to the device. Many devices, especially video adapters on PC-compatible computers, will not work properly—if at all—without the correct device drivers installed in the system.

Device Driver Developer Kit *n. See* DDK.

Device Driver Kit *n. See* DDK.

device independence *n.* A characteristic of a program, interface, or protocol that supports software operations that produce similar results on a wide variety of hardware. For example, the PostScript language is a device-independent page description language because programs issuing PostScript drawing and text commands need not be customized for each potential printer. *Compare* device dependence.

device-independent bitmap *n. See* DIB.

device manager *n.* A software utility that allows viewing and changing hardware configuration settings, such as

interrupts, base addresses, and serial communication parameters.

Device Manager *n.* In Windows 95, a function within the System Properties utility that indicates device conflicts and other problems and allows a user to change the properties of the computer and each device attached to it. *See also* property, property sheet.

device name *n.* The label by which a computer system component is identified by the operating system. MS-DOS, for example, uses the device name COM1 to identify the first serial communications port.

device partnership *n.* A registry key, stored on the Windows CE device, that a desktop computer uses to identify that Windows CE device when it is connected to the desktop. The key defines values for synchronization, file conversions, and backup and restore information, which enable multiple Windows CE devices to connect to the same desktop computer. A device partnership is created the first time you connect a Windows CE device to a desktop computer.

device resolution *n. See* resolution (definition 1).

DFP *n. See* digital flat panel port.

DFS *n. See* distributed file system.

DGIS *n.* Acronym for **D**irect **G**raphics **I**nterface **S**pecification. An interface developed by Graphics Software Systems. DGIS is firmware (generally implemented in ROM on a video adapter) that allows a program to display graphics on a video display through an extension to the IBM BIOS Interrupt 10H interface.

DHCP *n.* Acronym for **D**ynamic **H**ost **C**onfiguration **P**rotocol. A TCP/IP protocol that enables a network connected to the Internet to assign a temporary IP address to a host automatically when the host connects to the network. *See also* IP address, TCP/IP. *Compare* dynamic SLIP.

Dhrystone *n.* A general-performance benchmarking test, originally developed by Rheinhold Weicker in 1984 to measure and compare computer performance. The test reports general system performance in dhrystones per second. It is intended to replace the older and less reliable Whetstone benchmark. The Dhrystone benchmark, like most benchmarks, consists of standard code revised periodically to minimize unfair advantages to certain combinations of hardware, compiler, and environment. Dhrystone concentrates on string handling and uses no floating-point operations. Like most benchmarking tests, it is heavily influenced by hardware and software design, such as compiler and linker options, code optimizing, cache memory, wait states, and integer data types. *See also* benchmark[2]. *Compare* sieve of Eratosthenes, Whetstone.

DHTML *n. See* dynamic HTML.

DIA *n.* Acronym for **D**ocument **I**nterchange **A**rchitecture. A document exchange guideline used in IBM's Systems Network Architecture (SNA). DIA specifies methods of organizing and addressing documents for transmission between computers of different sizes and models. DIA is supported by IBM's Advanced Program-to-Program Communication (APPC) and by Logical Unit (LU) 6.2, which establish the capabilities and types of interactions possible in an SNA environment. *See also* DCA (definition 1), SNA.

diacritical mark *n.* An accent mark above, below, or through a written character—for example, the acute (´) and grave (`) accents.

dialect *n.* A variant of a language or protocol. For example, Transact-SQL is a dialect of structured query language (SQL).

dialog *n.* **1.** In computing, the exchange of human input and machine responses that forms a "conversation" between an interactive computer and the person using it. **2.** The exchange of signals by computers communicating on a network.

dialog box *n.* In a graphical user interface, a special window displayed by the system or application to solicit a response from the user. *See also* windowing environment. *Compare* integrator.

dial-up *adj.* Of, pertaining to, or being a connection that uses the public switched telephone network rather than a dedicated circuit or some other type of private network.

dial-up access *n.* Connection to a data communications network through a public switched telecommunication network.

dial-up boot loader *n.* A tool for upgrading a version of an operating system on a target device. *Acronym:* DUB.

dial-up networking *n.* Connection to a remote network through use of a modem. Dial-up networking is typically used in reference to telecommuting, although the term is equally applicable to connecting to the Internet.

dial-up service *n.* A telephone connection provider for a local or worldwide public switched telephone network that provides Internet or intranet access, advertisement via a Web page, access to news services, or access to the stock market and other resources.

DIB *n.* **1.** Acronym for **d**evice-**i**ndependent **b**itmap. A file format designed to ensure that bitmapped graphics created using one application can be loaded and displayed in another application exactly the way they appeared in the originating application. *See also* bitmapped graphics. **2.** Acronym for **D**irectory **I**nformation **B**ase. A directory of user and resource names in an X.500 system. The DIB is maintained by a Directory Server Agent (DSA). *Also called:* white pages.

DIBengine *n.* Software, or a combination of hardware and software, that produces DIB files. *See also* DIB (definition 1).

dibit *n.* A set of 2 bits representing one of four possible combinations: 00, 01, 10, and 11. In communications, a dibit is a kind of transmission unit made possible by the modulation technique known as differential phase-shift keying, which encodes data by using four different states (phase shifts) in the transmission line to represent each of the four dibit combinations. *See also* phase-shift keying.

dichotomizing search *n. See* binary search.

dictation software *n.* Computer programs that can recognize spoken words as input. Used as an alternative to keyboard input, dictation software cannot comprehend the spoken language; it can only convert and transmit the sounds to the computer. Speaker-dependent dictation software requires the user to "train" the computer to become familiar with his or her voice patterns and accent. First-generation discrete speech systems require the user to speak slowly and distinctly, with pauses between words. Next-generation continuous speech systems can interpret natural speech patterns and speeds. *See also* voice recognition.

dictionary attack *n.* Originally a method of guessing a user's password or PIN by trying every word in the dictionary until successful. Currently used to identify any attack that tries known words or alphanumeric character strings to break a simple password.

dielectric *n.* Insulating material, such as rubber or plastic, that does not conduct electricity.

DIF *n. See* data interchange format.

difference *n.* **1.** The amount by which two values differ. In electronics, differences in physical elements, such as waveforms or voltages, are used in the operation of circuits, amplifiers, multiplexers, communications equipment, and so on. **2.** In database management, it is an operator in relational algebra that is used in sorting record sets (tuples). For example, given two relational tables, A and B, that are union-compatible (contain the same number of fields, with corresponding fields containing the same types of values), the statement *DIFFERENCE A, B* builds a third relation containing all those records that appear in A but not in B. *See also* relational algebra, tuple. *Compare* intersect, union.

Difference Engine *n.* An early computerlike mechanical device designed by British mathematician and scientist Charles Babbage in the early 1820s. The Difference Engine was intended to be a machine with a 20-decimal capacity capable of solving mathematical problems. The concept of the Difference Engine was enhanced by Babbage in the 1830s in the design of his more famous Analytical Engine, a mechanical precursor of the electronic computer. *See also* Analytical Engine.

differential *adj.* In electronics, a reference to a type of circuit that makes use of the difference between two signals rather than the difference between one signal and some reference voltage.

differential backup *n.* A backup that copies files created or changed since the last normal or incremental backup. It does not mark files as having been backed up (in other words, the archive attribute is not cleared). If you are performing a combination of normal and differential backups, restoring files and folders requires that you have the last normal, as well as the last differential, backup.

differential phase-shift keying *n. See* phase-shift keying.

differentiator *n.* A circuit whose output is the differential (first derivative) of the input signal. The differential measures how fast a value is changing, so the output of a differentiator is proportional to the instantaneous rate of change of the input signal. See the illustration. *Compare* integrator.

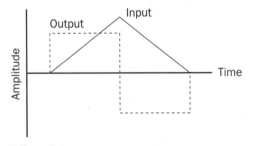

Differentiator.

Diffie-Hellman *n.* Diffie-Hellman key agreement protocol. A public-key cryptography method that allows two

hosts to create and share a secret key. Diffie-Hellman is used for key management by virtual private networks (VPNs) operating on the IPSec standard. *See also* IPSec.

digerati *n.* Cyberspace populace that can be roughly compared to *literati*. Digerati are people renowned as or claiming to be knowledgeable about topics and issues related to the digital revolution; more specifically, they are people "in the know" about the Internet and online activities. *See also* guru, techie, wizard (definition 1).

digest *n.* **1.** An article in a moderated newsgroup that summarizes multiple posts submitted to the moderator. *See also* moderator, newsgroup. **2.** A message in a mailing list that is sent to subscribers in place of the multiple individual posts that the digest contains. If the mailing list is moderated, the digest may be edited. *See also* moderated.

digicash *n. See* e-money.

digit *n.* One of the characters used to indicate a whole number (unit) in a numbering system. In any numbering system, the number of possible digits is equal to the base, or radix, used. For example, the decimal (base-10) system has 10 digits, 0 through 9; the binary (base-2) system has 2 digits, 0 and 1; and the hexadecimal (base-16) system has 16 digits, 0 through 9 and A through F.

digital *adj.* **1.** A reference to something based on digits (numbers) or their representation. **2.** In computing, analogous in use, though not in meaning, to *binary* because the computers familiar to most people process information coded as different combinations of the binary digits (bits) 0 and 1. *Compare* analog.

Digital Advanced Mobile Phone Service *n. See* D-AMPS.

digital audio disc *n.* An optical storage medium for recording digitally encoded audio information. *See also* compact disc (definition 1).

digital audio tape *n.* A magnetic tape storage medium for recording digitally encoded audio information. *Acronym:* DAT.

digital audio/video connector *n.* An interface on some high-end video cards or TV tuner cards that allows the simultaneous transmission of digital audio and video signals. *Also called:* DAV connector. *See also* interface (definition 3), video adapter.

digital broadcast satellite *n. See* direct broadcast satellite.

D

digital camera *n.* A type of camera that stores photographed images electronically instead of on traditional film. A digital camera uses a CCD (charge-coupled device) element to capture the image through the lens when the operator releases the shutter in the camera; circuitry within the camera then stores the image captured by the CCD in a storage medium such as solid-state memory or a hard disk. After the image has been captured, it is downloaded by cable to the computer using software supplied with the camera. Once stored in the computer, the image can be manipulated and processed much like the image from a scanner or related input device. *See also* charge-coupled device, digital photography.

digital cash *n. See* e-money.

digital certificate *n.* **1.** An assurance that software downloaded from the Internet comes from a reputable source. A digital certificate provides information about the software—such as the identity of the author and the date on which the software was registered with a certificate authority (CA), as well as a measure of tamper-resistance. **2.** A user identity card or "driver's license" for cyberspace. Issued by a certificate authority (CA), a digital certificate is an electronic credential that authenticates a user on the Internet and intranets. Digital certificates ensure the legitimate online transfer of confidential information, money, or other sensitive materials by means of public encryption technology. A digital certificate holder has two keys (strings of numbers): a private key held only by the user, for "signing" outgoing messages and decrypting incoming messages; and a public key, for use by anyone, for encrypting data to send to a specific user. *See also* certificate authority, encryption, private key, public key.

digital communications *n.* Exchange of communications in which all information is transmitted in binary-encoded (digital) form.

digital computer *n.* A computer in which operations are based on two or more discrete states. Binary digital computers are based on two states, logical "on" and "off," represented by two voltage levels, arrangements of which are used to represent all types of information—numbers, letters, graphics symbols, and program instructions. Within such a computer, the states of various circuit components change continuously to move, operate on, and save this information. *Compare* analog computer.

Digital Darkroom *n.* A Macintosh program developed by Silicon Beach Software for enhancement of black-and-white photographs or scanned images.

digital data service *n. See* DDS.

digital data transmission *n.* The transfer of information encoded as a series of bits rather than as a fluctuating (analog) signal in a communications channel.

digital display *n.* A video display capable of rendering only a fixed number of colors or gray shades. Examples of digital displays are IBM's Monochrome Display, Color/Graphics Display, and Enhanced Color Display. *See also* CGA, EGA, MDA. *Compare* analog display.

digital divide *n.* The gap between those who have the opportunity to take advantage of the Internet and related information resources, and those who do not. Differences in income, education, and comfort levels with technology are contributing factors to the separation between those with access to technological resources and those without.

digital DNA *n.* **1.** Broadly, a reference to the bits that comprise digital information. **2.** In the gaming world, a technology called "Cyberlife" that mimics biological DNA in the creation and development of trainable creatures known as Norns. Like real DNA, digital DNA is passed from parent to offspring and determines the artificial creature's characteristics and adaptability.

digital fingerprinting *n. See* digital watermark.

digital flat panel port *n.* An interface designed to allow direct connection between a flat panel monitor and a computer without requiring an analog-to-digital conversion. *Acronym:* DFP.

digital home *n. See* smart home.

digital light processing projector *n. See* DLP.

digital line *n.* A communications line that carries information only in binary-encoded (digital) form. To minimize distortion and noise interference, a digital line uses repeaters to regenerate the signal periodically during transmission. *See also* repeater. *Compare* analog line.

digital linear tape *n.* A magnetic storage medium used to back up data. Digital linear tape allows for faster transfer of data compared with other tape technologies. *Acronym:* DLT.

Digital Micromirror Device *n.* The circuit technology behind Texas Instruments' Digital Light Processing, used in image projectors. A Digital Micromirror Device, or DMD, consists of an array of individually addressable, hinged mirrors on a chip. Each chip, which is less than 0.002 mm wide, rotates in response to a digital signal to reflect light into the lens of the projection system and thus create a bright, full-color display. Displays can be combined to create high-definition systems of 1920 × 1035 (1,987,200) pixels with 64 million colors. *Acronym:* DMD.

digital modem *n.* **1.** A communications device that acts as the intermediary between a digital device such as a computer or terminal and a digital communications channel, such as a high-speed network line, an ISDN circuit, or a cable TV system. Although a digital modem supports standard (analog) modem protocols, it is not a "typical" modem in the sense of being a device whose primary function is to modulate (convert digital to analog) before transmission and demodulate (convert analog to digital) after transmission. It uses advanced digital modulation techniques for changing data frames into a format suitable for transmission over a digital line. *See also* terminal adapter. *Compare* modem. **2.** A 56 Kbps modem. Such a modem is not purely digital but does eliminate the traditional digital-to-analog conversion for downstream transmissions—that is, transmissions moving from the Internet to the end user. A 56 Kbps modem is also digital in that it requires a digital connection, such as T1, between the telephone company and the user's Internet Service Provider (ISP) in order to achieve its highest speed. *See also* 56-Kbps modem. **3.** A term used to distinguish all-digital communications devices, such as ISDN and cable "modems" from the more traditional analog-to-digital, phone-based modems.

Digital Network Architecture *n.* A multilayered architecture and set of protocol specifications for networks. Designed by the Digital Equipment Corporation, Digital Network Architecture is implemented in the set of products known by the name *DECnet. Acronym:* DNA. *See also* DECnet.

digital photography *n.* Photography by means of a digital camera. Digital photography differs from conventional photography in that a digital camera does not use a silver halide–based film to capture an image. Instead, a digital camera captures and stores each image electronically. *See also* digital camera.

digital picture frame *n.* Electronic device used in displaying digital photos and graphics while giving the outward appearance of a traditional picture frame. Digital picture frames allow users to rotate photos within the frame at specified intervals, display a series of photos as a slide show, or use an Internet connection to download photos, order prints, or send customized photo sets to others.

Digital Print Order Format *n. See* DPOF.

digital proof *n. See* direct digital color proof.

digital recording *n.* The storage of information in binary-encoded (digital) format. Digital recording converts information—text, graphics, sound, or pictures—to strings of 1s and 0s that can be physically represented on a storage medium. Digital recording media include computer disks and tapes, optical (or compact) discs, and ROM cartridges of the type used for some software and many computer games.

Digital Rights Management *n. See* DRM.

digital satellite system *n.* A high-powered satellite system with the capability to deliver high-quality transmissions of hundreds of channels directly to television receivers. A DSS broadcast begins as a digital signal sent from a service provider's station to a satellite. From there, it is directed to a satellite dish (typically 18 inches) at the user's premises. The dish next transmits the signal to a converter box, which changes it to an analog signal before sending it to the television set. *Acronym:* DSS.

Digital Services *n. See* DS.

digital signal *n.* A signal, such as one transmitted within or between computers, in which information is represented by discrete states—for example, high and low voltages—rather than by fluctuating levels in a continuous stream, as in an analog signal.

Digital Signal *n. See* DS.

digital signal processor *n.* An integrated circuit designed for high-speed data manipulation and used in audio, communications, image manipulation, and other data acquisition and data control applications. *Acronym:* DSP.

digital signature *n.* A security mechanism used on the Internet that relies on two keys, one public and one private, that are used to encrypt messages before transmission and to decrypt them on receipt.

Digital Signature Algorithm *n.* The U.S. government standard for digital signatures, as specified by the National Institute of Standards and Technology, in FIPS 186, Digital Signature Standard. DSA is based on signature encryption based on a public and a private key. *Acronym:* DSA. *See also* digital signature.

Digital Signature Standard *n.* A public key cryptographic standard issued in 1994 by the United States National Institute of Standards and Technology (NIST) to authenticate electronic documents. The DSS uses a Digital Signature Algorithm (DSA) to generate and verify digital

D

signatures based on a public key, which is not secret, and a private key, which is known or held only by the person generating the signature. A digital signature serves to authenticate both the identity of the signer and the integrity of the transmitted information. *Acronym:* DSS. *See also* public key encryption.

Digital Simultaneous Voice and Data *n.* A modem technology by Multi-Tech Systems, Inc., that allows a single telephone line to be used for conversation together with data transfer. This is accomplished by switching to packet-mode communications when the need for voice transfer is detected; digitized voice packets are then transferred along with data and command packets. *Acronym:* DSVD.

digital sort *n.* A type of ordering process in which record numbers or their key values are sorted digit by digit, beginning with the least significant (rightmost) digit. *Also called:* radix sort.

digital speech *n. See* speech synthesis.

digital subscriber line or **Digital Subscriber Line** *n. See* DSL.

Digital Subscriber Line Access Multiplexer or **Digital Subscriber Line Multiplexer** *n. See* DSLAM.

digital-to-analog converter *n.* A device that translates digital data to an analog signal. A digital-to-analog converter takes a succession of discrete digital values as input and creates an analog signal whose amplitude corresponds, moment by moment, to each digital value. See the illustration. *Acronym:* DAC. *Compare* analog-to-digital converter.

Digital
input

Analog
output

Digital-to-analog converter.

digital versatile disc *n. See* digital video disc.

digital video *n.* Video images and sound stored in a digital format. *Acronym:* DV.

digital TV or **digital television** *n.* The transmission of television signals using digital rather than the conventional analog signals. A digital TV standard for the United States was approved by the FCC in 1996. Digital TV provides a better television experience and new information services. Digital signals produce higher quality pictures and CD-

quality sound, compared to the analog signals used with today's television. Digital TV can support interactive television, electronic program guides, and a variety of digital services, such as Internet channel broadcasting and data services. *Acronym:* DTV. *Compare* HDTV.

digital video disc *n.* The next generation of optical disc storage technology. With digital video disc technology, video, audio, and computer data can be encoded onto a compact disc (CD). A digital video disc can store greater amounts of data than a traditional CD. A standard single-layer, single-sided digital video disc can store 4.7 GB of data; a two-layer standard increases the single-sided disc capacity to 8.5 GB. Digital video discs can be double-sided with a maximum storage of 17 GB per disc. A digital video disc player is needed to read digital video discs; this player is equipped to read older optical storage technologies. Advocates of the digital video disc intend to replace current digital storage formats, such as laser disc, CD-ROM, and audio CD, with the single digital format of the digital video disc. *Acronym:* DVD. *Also called:* digital versatile disc. *See also* digital video disc–ROM.

digital video disc–erasable *n.* A proposed extension to the digital video disc recording format to allow multiple re-recording by a consumer. *Acronym:* DVD-E. *Also called:* digital video disc–ROM.

digital video disc–recordable *n.* A proposed extension to the digital video disc recording format to allow one-time recording by a consumer. *Acronym:* DVD-R.

digital video disc–ROM *n.* A computer-readable version of a digital video disc containing either 4.7 or 8.5 GB of storage per side, the larger if 3M's dual-layer "2P" technology is used. *Acronym:* DVD-ROM. *Also called:* digital video disc–erasable. *See also* digital video disc.

Digital Video–Interactive *n.* A hardware/software system developed by RCA, General Electric, and Intel that implements compression of digital video and audio for microcomputer applications. *Acronym:* DV-I.

Digital Video Interface *n. See* DVI.

digital video recording *n. See* DVR.

digital watermark *n.* A unique identifier embedded in a file to deter piracy and prove file ownership and quality. Digital watermarking is often used with graphics and audio files to identify the owner's rights to these works. *See also* fingerprint (definition 2).

digiterati *n. See* digerati.

digitize *vb.* To convert any continuously varying (analog) source of input, such as the lines in a drawing or a sound signal, to a series of discrete units represented in a computer by the binary digits 0 and 1. Analog-to-digital converters are commonly used to perform this translation. *See also* aliasing, analog-to-digital converter.

digitizing tablet *n. See* graphics tablet.

DikuMUD *n.* **1.** Multiuser dungeon (MUD) software developed by five individuals at the Computer Science Institute at Copenhagen University (whose acronym in Danish is DIKU). DikuMUD uses multimedia and is object-oriented, but the classes are hard-coded. The software is covered by a license agreement that forbids its distribution for money. *See also* MUD, multimedia, object-oriented. **2.** A game that uses the DikuMUD software.

dimensioning *n.* In CAD programs, a means of specifying and possibly controlling the measurements and spatial relationships of elements in a modeled object, such as using lines, arrows, and text (that is, measurements) to indicate the length, height, and thickness of each of the walls in a modeled room or house. *See also* CAD.

DIMM *n.* Acronym for **d**ual **i**nline **m**emory **m**odule. A type of memory board comprised of RAM chips mounted on a circuit board, similar to the more commonly used SIMM (Single Inline Memory Module). DIMMs are characterized by a 64-bit data path and pins (connectors) on each side that are on different circuits and that respond to different signals. SIMMs, in contrast, have a 32-bit data path, and their connectors are on the same circuit and respond to the same signal. While SIMMs must be added in pairs, DIMMs can be added to a computer one at a time. *See also* memory chip. *Compare* SIMM.

dimmed *adj.* Shown on the screen in gray characters instead of black characters on white or white characters on black. Menu options appear dimmed in a graphical user interface to indicate that under current circumstances they are not available—for example, "Cut" when no text has been highlighted or "Paste" when there is no text in the clipboard.

DIN connector *n.* A multipin connector conforming to the specification of the German national standards organization (Deutsch Industrie Norm). DIN connectors are used to link various components in personal computers.

dingbat *n.* A small graphical element used for decorative purposes in a document. Some fonts, such as Zapf Dingbats, are designed to present sets of dingbats. *See also* font. *Compare* bullet.

diode *n.* A device that passes current in only one direction. A diode is usually a semiconductor. See the illustration. *See also* semiconductor.

Diode. *The drawings (top) show two of the many types of diode packages. The band on the right end of each indicates polarity. At bottom is a schematic representation of a diode.*

diode-transistor logic *n.* A type of circuit design that employs diodes, transistors, and resistors to perform logic functions. *Acronym:* DTL.

DIP *n.* Acronym for **d**ual **i**nline **p**ackage. A standard for packaging integrated circuits in which the microminiature electronic circuits etched on a silicon wafer are enclosed in a rectangular housing of plastic or ceramic and connected to downward-pointing pins protruding from the longer sides of the chip. Designed to facilitate circuit board manufacturing, this design does not work well for modern chips requiring very large numbers of connections. *See also* document image processing. *Compare* leadless chip carrier, pin grid array, SIP, surface-mount technology.

dipole *n.* A pair of opposite electric charges or magnetic poles of opposite sign separated by a small distance.

DIP switch *n.* Short for **D**ual **I**nline **P**ackage **switch**. One or more small rocker- or sliding-type toggle switches contained in the plastic or ceramic housing of a dual inline package (DIP) connected to a circuit board. Each switch on a DIP switch can be set to one of two positions, closed or open, to control options on the circuit board. *See also* DIP.

dir *n.* An MS-DOS command that instructs a computer to display a list of files and subdirectories in the current directory or folder. If the command is followed by a path, the computer displays a list of files and subdirectories in the specified directory or folder. *See also* command, MS-DOS, path (definition 2).

Direct3D *n. See* DirectX.

direct access *n.* The ability of a computer to find and go straight to a particular storage location in memory or on disk to retrieve or store an item of information. Note that direct access is not the same as direct memory access (DMA), which is the ability to transfer information

D

directly between an input/output channel and memory rather than taking the longer and more circuitous route of I/O channel to microprocessor to memory. *See also* random access. *Compare* direct memory access.

direct access storage device *n. See* DASD.

direct address *n. See* absolute address.

DirectAnimation *n. See* DirectX.

direct broadcast satellite *n.* A digital telecommunications service that delivers television programming via the Digital Satellite System (DSS). Direct broadcast satellite technology uses a geostationary orbit satellite (GEO) to receive digitized signals sent by ground-based uplink centers; the satellite then beams the signal across a wide swath on Earth. Subscribers within that swath use small (18-inch) satellite dishes to bring the signal into a set-top box decoder for playback. Although primarily used for television broadcasts, the technology is seen as having potential to also deliver high-quality, digital communications and multimedia content in the future. *Acronym:* DBS. *Also called:* digital broadcast satellite. *See also* digital satellite system, geostationary orbit satellite, webcasting.

direct cable connection *n.* A link between the I/O ports of two computers that uses a single cable rather than a modem or other active interface device. In most cases, a direct cable connection requires a null modem cable.

direct-connect modem *n.* A modem that uses standard telephone wire and connectors and that plugs directly into a telephone jack, eliminating the need for an intermediary telephone. *Compare* acoustic coupler.

direct-coupled transistor logic *n.* A circuit design that uses transistors and resistors only, with the transistors directly connected to each other. This design was used in the earliest commercial integrated circuits. The switching speed and power consumption of such circuits are about average. *Acronym:* DCTL.

direct current *n.* Electrical current whose direction of flow does not reverse. The current may stop or change amplitude, but it always flows in the same direction. *Acronym:* DC. *Compare* alternating current.

direct digital color proof *n.* A test sheet produced by a lower-cost output device, such as a color laser printer, to serve as an approximation of what the final image will look like when produced on professional-quality printing equipment. A direct digital color proof does not involve color separation, as in traditional proofs. Instead, a direct digital color proof is printed in all colors at one time on a single page, resulting in somewhat lower quality compared with traditional separation methods but having the advantages of increased speed and reduced cost. *Acronym:* DDCP. *Also called:* digital proof. *See also* color separation (definition 1).

DirectDraw *n. See* DirectX.

Direct Graphics Interface Specification *n. See* DGIS.

DirectInput *n.* An API (application programming interface) developed by Microsoft for joysticks and similar pointing devices in Windows 9x. *See also* DirectX.

direction key *n. See* arrow key.

direct memory access *n.* Memory access that does not involve the microprocessor and is frequently used for data transfer directly between memory and an "intelligent" peripheral device, such as a disk drive. *Acronym:* DMA. *Compare* PIO.

DirectMusic *n. See* DirectX.

directory *n.* **1.** A catalog for filenames and other directories stored on a disk. A directory is a way of organizing and grouping the files so that the user is not overwhelmed by a long list of them. The uppermost directory is called the *root directory*; the directories within a directory are called *subdirectories*. Depending on how an operating system supports directories, filenames in a directory can be viewed and ordered in various ways—for example, alphabetically, by date, by size, or as icons in a graphical user interface. What the user views as a directory is supported in the operating system by tables of data, stored on the disk, that indicate characteristics and the location of each file. In the Macintosh and Windows 9x operating systems, directories are called *folders*. **2.** On a network, an index of names and pertinent information related to authorized users and network resources.

Directory Access Protocol *n.* The protocol that governs communications between X.500 clients and servers. *See also* CCITT X series.

Directory Client Agent *n. See* DUA.

Directory Information Base *n. See* DIB (definition 2).

Directory Mozilla *n. See* Open Directory Project.

directory path *n. See* pathname.

directory replication *n.* The copying of a master set of directories from a server (called an *export server*) to specified servers or workstations (called *import computers*) in the same or other domains. Replication simplifies the task of maintaining identical sets of directories and files on

D

multiple computers because only a single master copy of the data must be maintained. *See also* directory, server.

Directory Server Agent *n. See* DSA.

directory service *n.* A service on a network that returns mail addresses of other users or enables a user to locate hosts and services.

Directory System Agent *n. See* DSA.

directory tree *n.* A graphic display listing the directories and subdirectories on a hard disk in tree form, with subdirectories shown as branches of the main directory. *See also* branch (definition 1), directory, tree structure.

Directory User Agent *n. See* DUA.

DirectPlay *n. See* DirectX.

direct processing *n.* Processing of data as it is received by the system, as opposed to deferred processing, in which data is stored in blocks before processing. *Compare* deferred processing.

direct read after write *n. See* DRAW.

direct read during write *n. See* DRDW.

direct sequence *n.* In spread spectrum communication, a form of modulation in which a carrier is modulated by a series of binary pulses. *See also* modulation (definition 1), spread spectrum.

DirectShow *n. See* DirectX.

DirectSound *n. See* DirectX.

direct view storage tube *n.* A type of cathode-ray tube (CRT) in which the screen can retain images for a long time and in which a beam of electrons from an electron gun can be moved arbitrarily across the screen surface (as opposed to a standard cathode-ray tube, in which the electron beam is moved in a specific pattern). This type of CRT is capable of displaying a precise, detailed image without requiring any screen refresh. However, once the image is drawn, it cannot be changed without a complete erasing of the screen. *Acronym:* DVST. *Also called:* storage tube. *Compare* CRT.

DirectX *n.* A set of Microsoft technologies that provide developers with the tools needed to create sophisticated multimedia applications on Windows-based computers. DirectX consists of components making up two integrated layers. The Foundation layer provides low-level functions, such as support for input devices, designed to ensure that

applications can run on—and take full advantage of—Windows-based hardware. The Media layer, above the Foundation layer, provides high-level services, such as support for media streaming and animation, that are needed in creating applications incorporating such features as surround sound, video, and 3-D animation. Direct-Animation, DirectSound, and other similarly named application programming interfaces (APIs) are members of the DirectX family. See the table. *See also* application programming interface.

Table D.1 **ATA Specifications.**

DirectX Component	Part Of	Supports
Direct3D Immediate Mode	Foundation layer	Access to 3-D video hardware
Direct3D Retained Mode	Media layer	Creation and animation of onscreen 3-D worlds
Direct-Animation	Media layer	Interactive animation and integration of different multimedia types
DirectDraw	Foundation layer	Access to display memory and hardware capabilities
DirectInput	Foundation layer	Direct access to various input devices, including force-feedback joysticks
DirectMusic	Foundation layer	Real-time music composition
DirectPlay	Foundation layer	Multiplayer online gaming and other networked applications
DirectShow	Media layer	Capture and playback of streaming multimedia
DirectSound	Foundation layer	Direct access to sound cards; wave sound capture and playback
Direct-Sound3D	Foundation layer	3-D sound positioning
DirectX Transform	Media layer	Extensibility of the DirectX platform to include value-added products

DirectX Transform *n. See* DirectX.

dirty *adj.* Of, pertaining to, or characteristic of a communications line that is hampered by excessive noise, degrading the quality of the signal. *See also* noise (definition 2).

dirty bit *n.* A bit used to mark modified data in a cache so that the modifications may be carried over to primary memory. *See also* bit, cache.

dirty power *n.* A power source that can cause damage to electronic components, due to noise, voltage spikes, or incorrect voltage levels.

dirty ROM *n.* Short for **dirty r**ead-**o**nly **m**emory. In the earlier versions of the Macintosh (Mac II, IIx, SE/30, and IIcx), a memory system that simulates a 32-bit system but is not a true (clean) 32-bit system. Among other flaws, a dirty ROM machine can access only 8 megabytes of memory under Mac OS System 7. System extensions such as MODE32 and the 32-bit enabler are available to allow a dirty ROM machine to function like a true, 32-bit clean machine.

disable *vb.* To suppress something or to prevent it from happening. Disabling is a method of controlling system functions by disallowing certain activities. For example, a program might temporarily disable nonessential interrupts (requests for service from system devices) to prevent interruptions during a critical point in processing. *Compare* enable.

disabled folders *n.* In the Mac OS, several folders in the System folder that contain system extensions, control panels, and other items that have been removed from the system by the extension manager. Items currently in disabled folders will not be installed upon system startup; they may, however, later be moved back to their regular folders automatically by the extension manager. *See also* extension manager, System folder.

disassembler *n.* A program that converts machine code to assembly language source code. Most debuggers have some kind of built-in disassembler that allows the programmer to view an executable program in terms of human-readable assembly language. *See also* decompiler. *Compare* assembler.

disassociate *vb.* In Windows 95 and Windows NT, to remove an association between a file and some application. *Compare* associate.

disaster dump *n.* A dump (transfer of memory contents to a printer or other output device) made when a program fails without hope of recovery.

disc *n.* A round, flat piece of nonmagnetic, shiny metal encased in a plastic coating, designed to be read from and written to by optical (laser) technology. It is now standard practice to use the spelling *disc* for optical discs and *disk* in all other computer contexts, such as floppy disk, hard disk, and RAM disk. *See also* compact disc.

disconnect *vb.* To break a communications link.

discrete *adj.* Separate; individual; identifiable as a unit. For example, bits are discrete elements of data processed by a computer.

discrete multitone *n.* In telecommunications, a technology that uses digital signal processors to split available bandwidth into a number of subchannels, allowing over 6 Mbps of data to be carried over one copper twisted-pair wire. *Acronym:* DMT.

discrete speech recognition *n.* Computer speech recognition format in which each word is recognized as a distinct individual unit, requiring a pause between each word spoken.

discretionary access control list *n.* The part of an object's security descriptor that grants or denies specific users and groups permission to access the object. Only the owner of an object can change permissions granted or denied in a DACL; thus, access to the object is at the owner's discretion. *Acronym:* DACL. *See also* distribution group.

discretionary hyphen *n. See* hyphen.

discussion group *n.* Any of a variety of online forums in which people communicate about subjects of common interest. Forums for discussion groups include electronic mailing lists, Internet newsgroups, and IRC channels.

dish *n. See* satellite dish.

disk *n.* **1.** A round, flat piece of flexible plastic coated with a magnetic material that can be electrically influenced to hold information recorded in digital (binary) form and encased in a protective plastic jacket to protect the disk from damage and contamination. *Also called:* floppy, floppy disk, microfloppy disk. *Compare* compact disc, disc. **2.** *See* hard drive.

disk access time *n. See* access time (definition 2).

disk buffer *n.* A small amount of memory set aside for the purpose of storing data read from, or soon to be written

D

to, a disk. Because disk devices are slow compared with the CPU, it is not efficient to access the disk for only one or two bytes of data. Instead, during a read, a large chunk of data is read and stored in the disk buffer. When the program wants information, it is copied from the buffer. Many requests for data can be satisfied by a single disk access. The same technique can be applied to disk writes. When the program has information to store, it writes it into the disk buffer area in memory. When the buffer has been filled, the entire contents of the buffer are written to the disk in a single operation.

disk cache *n.* A portion of a computer's random access memory (RAM) set aside for temporarily holding information read from disk. A disk cache does not hold entire files, as does a RAM disk (a portion of memory that acts as if it were a disk drive). Instead, a disk cache is used to hold information that either has recently been requested from disk or has previously been written to disk. If the required information remains in a disk cache, access time is considerably faster than if the program must wait for the disk drive mechanism to fetch the information from disk. *See also* cache. *Compare* disk buffer.

disk cartridge *n.* A removable disk enclosed in a protective case. A disk cartridge can be used by certain types of hard disk drives and related devices, such as the external data storage units known as Bernoulli boxes.

disk controller *n.* A special-purpose chip and associated circuitry that directs and controls reading from and writing to a computer's disk drive. A disk controller handles such tasks as positioning the read/write head, mediating between the drive and the microprocessor, and controlling the transfer of information to and from memory. Disk controllers are used with floppy disk drives and hard disks and can either be built into the system or be part of a card that plugs into an expansion slot.

disk copy *n.* The process of duplicating a source disk's data and the data's organizational structure onto a target disk. *See also* backup.

disk crash *n.* The failure of a disk drive. *See also* crash[1].

disk directory *n.* An index of the files on a disk, analogous to a card catalog. A disk directory includes information about the files, such as their names, sizes, dates of creation, and physical locations on the disk. *See also* directory.

disk drive *n.* An electromechanical device that reads from and writes to disks. The main components of a disk drive include a spindle on which the disk is mounted, a drive motor that spins the disk when the drive is in operation, one or more read/write heads, a second motor that positions the read/write heads over the disk, and controller circuitry that synchronizes read/write activities and transfers information to and from the computer. Two types of disk drives are in common use: floppy disk drives and hard disk drives. Floppy disk drives are designed to accept removable disks in either 5.25-inch or 3.5-inch format; hard disk drives are faster, high-capacity storage units that are completely enclosed in a protective case.

disk driver *n.* A device driver that is added to a system to support a specific manufacturer's disk device. *See also* device driver.

disk duplexing *n. See* disk mirroring.

disk envelope *n.* The paper container that holds a 5.25-inch floppy disk and its attached jacket. The disk envelope protects exposed surfaces of the disk from dust and other foreign material that can scratch and otherwise damage the surface, resulting in the loss of recorded data. *See also* disk jacket.

diskette *n. See* floppy disk.

disk farm *n.* A number of disk drives in a single location used together to store or process vast quantities of information, such as scientific data, years' worth of corporate sales figures, large numbers of graphic images, or telephone company billing records. Current disk farms consist of magnetic or optical disks and can hold terabytes of information. In older usage, disk farms were sometimes known as "Laundromats" because they contained large drives referred to in jargon as "washing machines." *See also* server farm.

disk interface *n.* **1.** The circuitry that connects a disk drive to a computer system. **2.** A standard for connecting disk drives and computers. For example, the ST506 standard for connecting hard disks to computers is a disk interface standard.

disk jacket *n.* The protective plastic sheath that covers a floppy disk.

diskless workstation *n.* A station on a computer network that is not equipped with a disk drive and that uses files stored in a file server. *See also* file server.

disk memory *n. See* virtual memory.

disk mirroring *n.* A technique in which all or part of a hard disk is duplicated onto one or more other hard disks,

D

each of which ideally is attached to its own controller. With disk mirroring, any change made to the original disk is simultaneously made to the other disks so that if the original disk becomes damaged or corrupted, the mirror disks will contain a current, undamaged collection of the data from the original disk. *Also called:* disk duplexing. *See also* fault tolerance.

disk operating system *n. See* DOS.

disk pack *n.* A collection of disks in a protective container. Used primarily with minicomputers and mainframe computers, a disk pack is a removable medium, generally a stack of 14-inch disks in a plastic housing.

disk partition *n.* A logical compartment on a physical disk drive. A single disk might have two or more logical disk partitions, each of which would be referenced with a different disk drive name. Multiple partitions are divided into a primary (boot) partition and one or more extended partitions.

disk server *n.* A node on a local area network that acts as a remote disk drive shared by network users. Unlike a file server, which performs the more sophisticated tasks of managing network requests for files, a disk server functions as a storage medium on which users can read and write files. A disk server can be divided into sections (volumes), each of which appears to be a separate disk. *Compare* file server.

disk striping *n.* The procedure of combining a set of same-size disk partitions that reside on separate disks (from 2 to 32 disks) into a single volume, forming a virtual stripe across the disks that the operating system recognizes as a single drive. Disk striping enables multiple I/O operations in the same volume to proceed concurrently, thus offering enhanced performance. *See also* disk striping with parity, input/output.

disk striping with parity *n.* The technique of maintaining parity information across a disk stripe so that if one disk partition fails, the data on that disk can be re-created using the information stored across the remaining partitions in the disk stripe. *See also* disk striping, fault tolerance, parity.

disk unit *n.* A disk drive or its housing.

dispatcher *n.* In some multitasking operating systems, the set of routines responsible for allocating CPU (central processing unit) time to various applications.

dispatch table *n.* A table of identifiers and addresses for a certain class of routines such as interrupt handlers (routines carried out in response to certain signals or conditions). *Also called:* interrupt vector table, jump table, vector table. *See also* interrupt handler.

disperse *vb.* To break up and place in more than one location—for example, to disperse results among several sets of data or to disperse items (such as fields in records) so that they appear in more than one place in the output. *Compare* distribute.

dispersion *n.* The degree to which, at any given time, data in a distributed (interconnected) system of computers is stored at different locations or on different devices.

display *n.* The visual output device of a computer, which is commonly a CRT-based video display. With portable and notebook computers, the display is usually an LCD-based or a gas plasma–based flat-panel display. *See also* flat-panel display, liquid crystal display, video adapter, video display.

display adapter *n. See* video adapter.

display attribute *n.* A quality assigned to a character or an image displayed on the screen. Display attributes include such features as color, intensity, and blinking. Users of applications can control display attributes when programs allow them to change color and other screen elements.

display background *n.* In computer graphics, the portion of an on-screen image that remains static while other elements change; for example, window borders on a screen, or a palette of shapes or patterns in a drawing program.

display board *n. See* video adapter.

display card *n. See* video adapter.

display cycle *n.* The complete set of events that must occur in order for a computer image to be displayed on the screen, including both the software creation of an image in a computer's video memory and the hardware operations required for accurate on-screen display. *See also* refresh cycle.

Display Data Channel *n. See* DDC.

display device *n. See* display.

display element *n. See* graphics primitive.

display entity *n. See* entity, graphics primitive.

display face *n.* A typeface suitable for headings and titles in documents, distinguished by its ability to stand out from

D

other text on the page. Sans serif faces such as Helvetica and Avant Garde often work well as display faces. *See also* sans serif. *Compare* body face.

display frame *n.* One image in an animation sequence. *See also* frame (definition 3).

display image *n.* The collection of elements displayed together at a single time on a computer screen.

display page *n.* One screenful of display information stored in a computer's video memory. Computers can have enough video memory to hold more than one display page at a time. In such instances, programmers, especially those concerned with creating animation sequences, can update the screen rapidly by creating or modifying one display page while another is being viewed by the user. *See also* animation.

display port *n.* An output port on a computer that provides a signal for a display device such as a video monitor. See the illustration. *Also called:* monitor port.

— Display port

Display port.

Display PostScript *n.* An extended version of the PostScript language intended to provide a device-independent language for displaying images and text on bitmapped displays. *See also* PostScript.

Display Power Management Signaling *n. See* DPMS.

display screen *n.* The part of a video unit on which images are shown. *See also* CRT.

display terminal *n. See* terminal (definition 1).

distance learning *n.* Broadly, any educational or learning process or system in which the teacher/instructor is separated geographically or in time from his or her students, or in which students are separated from other students or educational resources. Contemporary distance learning is effected through the implementation of computer and electronics technology to connect teacher and student in either real or delayed time or on an as-needed basis. Content delivery may be achieved through a variety of technologies, including satellites, computers, cable television, interactive video, electronic transmissions via telephone lines, the World Wide Web and other Internet technology, and others. Distance learning does not preclude traditional learning processes; frequently it is used in conjunction with in-person classroom or professional training procedures and practices.

Distance Vector Multicast Routing Protocol *n.* An Internet routing protocol that provides an efficient mechanism for connectionless datagram delivery to a group of hosts across an Internet network. It is a distributed protocol that dynamically generates IP multicast delivery trees using a technique called Reverse Path Multicasting (RPM). *Acronym:* DVMRP.

distance-vector routing algorithm *n. See* Bellman-Ford distance-vector routing algorithm.

distortion *n.* An undesirable change in the waveform of a signal. Distortion can occur during signal transmission, as when a radio broadcast becomes garbled, or when a signal passes through a circuit, as when a stereo system is turned up too loud. Distortion often results in loss of information. It is mainly a problem in analog signals; digital signals are not affected by moderate distortion.

distribute *vb.* To allocate among locations or facilities, as in a data-processing function that is performed by a collection of computers and other devices linked together by a network.

distributed bulletin board *n.* A collection of newsgroups distributed to all computers in a wide area network. *See also* newsgroup, Usenet.

Distributed COM *n. See* DCOM.

Distributed Component Object Model *n. See* DCOM.

distributed computing *n. See* distributed processing.

Distributed Computing Environment *n.* A set of standards from the Open Group (formerly the Open Software Foundation) for development of distributed applications that can operate on more than one platform. *Acronym:* DCE. *See also* distributed processing.

distributed database *n.* A database implemented on a network. The component partitions are distributed over various nodes (stations) of the network. Depending on the specific update and retrieval traffic, distributing the database can significantly enhance overall performance. *See also* partition (definition 2).

D

distributed database management system *n.* A database management system capable of managing a distributed database. *Acronym:* DDBMS. *See also* distributed database.

distributed denial of service attack *n. See* DDoS.

distributed file system *n.* A file management system in which files may be located on multiple computers connected over a local or wide area network. *Acronym:* DFS.

distributed intelligence *n.* A system in which processing ability (intelligence) is distributed among multiple computers and other devices, each of which can work independently to some degree but can also communicate with the other devices to function as part of the larger system. *See also* distributed processing.

distributed network *n.* A network in which processing, storage, and other functions are handled by separate units (nodes) rather than by a single main computer.

distributed processing *n.* A form of information processing in which work is performed by separate computers linked through a communications network. Distributed processing is usually categorized as either plain distributed processing or true distributed processing. Plain distributed processing shares the workload among computers that can communicate with one another. True distributed processing has separate computers perform different tasks in such a way that their combined work can contribute to a larger goal. The latter type of processing requires a highly structured environment that allows hardware and software to communicate, share resources, and exchange information freely.

distributed services *n. See* BISDN.

distributed system *n.* A noncentralized network consisting of numerous computers that can communicate with one another and that appear to users as parts of a single, large, accessible "storehouse" of shared hardware, software, and data.

Distributed System Object Model *n.* IBM's System Object Model (SOM) in a shared environment, where binary class libraries can be shared between applications on networked computers or between applications on a given system. The Distributed System Object Model complements existing object-oriented languages by allowing SOM class libraries to be shared among applications written in different languages. *Acronym:* DSOM. *See also* SOM (definition 1).

distributed transaction processing *n.* Transaction processing that is shared by one or more computers communicating over a network. *Acronym:* DTP. *See also* distributed processing, transaction processing.

distributed workplace *n.* An environment other than the traditional office or factory, in which work is carried out on a regular basis. The flexibility afforded by the combination of communications and computing technologies enables many workers to conduct business anywhere the appropriate computer and data communications infrastructure has been set up. *See also* SOHO, telecommute.

distribution group *n.* A group that is used solely for e-mail distribution and that is not security-enabled. Distribution groups cannot be listed in discretionary access control lists (DACLs) used to define permissions on resources and objects. Distribution groups can be used only with e-mail applications (such as Microsoft Exchange) to send e-mail messages to collections of users. If you do not need a group for security purposes, create a distribution group instead of a security group. *See also* discretionary access control list, security group.

distribution list *n.* A list of recipients on an e-mail mailing list. This can be in the form of either a mailing list program, such as LISTSERV, or an alias in an e-mail program for all recipients of an e-mail message. *See also* alias (definition 2), LISTSERV, mailing list.

distribution services *n. See* BISDN.

distributive sort *n.* An ordering process in which a list is separated into parts and then reassembled in a particular order. *See also* sort algorithm. *Compare* bubble sort, insertion sort, merge sort, quicksort.

distro[1] *n.* **1.** A distribution of software (usually a version of Linux), digital music, or an online magazine or e-zine. *See also* e-zine, Linux. **2.** A company or individual that sells items, typically software, music CDs, or books, via the Web.

distro[2] *vb.* To distribute or sell software releases, digital music, or text items via the Web.

dithering *n.* A technique used in computer graphics to create the illusion of varying shades of gray on a monochrome display or printer, or additional colors on a color display or printer. Dithering relies on treating areas of an image as groups of dots that are colored in different patterns. Akin to the print images called *halftones*, dithering takes advantage of the eye's tendency to blur spots of different colors by averaging their effects and merging them into a single perceived shade or color. Depending on the ratio of black dots to white dots within a given area, the overall effect is of a particular shade of gray. Dithering is used to add realism to computer graphics and to soften jagged edges in curves and diagonal lines at low resolutions. See the illustration. *See also* aliasing, halftone.

Not dithered   Dithered

Dithering. *A halftone image (left) and a dithered image (right) both at 72 cells per inch.*

divergence *n.* A moving apart or separation. On computer displays, divergence occurs when the red, green, and blue electron beams in a color monitor do not collectively light the same spot on the screen. Within a program, such as a spreadsheet, divergence can occur when a circular set of formulas is repeatedly recalculated (iterated), with the results of each iteration moving further from a stable solution. *Compare* convergence.

divide overflow *n. See* overflow error.

division by zero *n.* An error condition caused by an attempt to divide a number by zero, which is mathematically undefined, or by a number that is sufficiently near to zero that the result is too large to be expressed by the machine. Computers do not allow division by zero, and software must provide some means of protecting the user from program failure on such attempts.

DIX *n.* Acronym for **D**igital **I**ntel **X**erox, the companies that developed the AUI connector for thicknet Ethernet cable. *See also* AUI.

DJGPP *n.* A compiler and a set of tools used by some game programmers to produce 32-bit protected-mode programs that run on Windows operating systems. DJGPP is a complete 32-bit C/C++ development system for PCs running MS-DOS; it includes ports of many GNU development utilities. In most cases, programs produced using DJGPP can be sold commercially without license or royalties. *See also* 32-bit, Allegro, GNU.

djinn *n.* A group of devices, resources, and users joined by Sun Microsystem's JINI technology. The group, controlled by the JINI technology infrastructure, agrees on basic specifications for administration, trust, identification, and policy. *See also* JINI.

DLC *n.* Acronym for **D**ata **L**ink **C**ontrol. An error-correction protocol in the Systems Network Architecture (SNA) responsible for transmission of data between two nodes over a physical link. Supported by Microsoft Windows NT and Windows 2000, DLC is designed to provide access to IBM mainframe computers and to Hewlett-Packard printers connected to the network. *See also* HDLC, SNA.

DLCI *n. See* Data Link Connection Identifier.

.dll *n.* A file extension for a dynamic-link library. *See also* dynamic-link library.

DLL *n. See* dynamic-link library.

DLL hell *n.* A problem occurring in versions of Microsoft Windows prior to Windows Me and Windows 2000 in which a newly installed application overwrites shared dynamic-link library (DLL) files with the (older or newer) versions it needs in order to run. If the replaced files are incompatible with those needed by other applications, those applications may exhibit buggy behavior or crash when they access the incompatible DLL files. The latest versions of the Windows operating system, Windows 2000 and Windows XP, incorporate a feature called Windows File Protection that eliminates this situation by monitoring and correcting installation and replacement of DLL files. *See also* dynamic-link library.

DLP *n.* Short for **D**igital **L**ight **P**rocessing, a digital projection technology developed by Texas Instruments in which a signal sent from a computer to a DLP projector is projected onto a screen by means of light reflected from a Digital Micromirror Device, or DMD, that consists of thousands of tiny hinged mirrors, each representing one pixel, attached to a chip. The chip acts as a bank of switches, one switch per mirror. These switches, in turn, rotate the mirrors in response to the digital signal to reflect light through a projection lens to create the image. DLP projectors represent a newer technology than the LCD projectors also used to display images on screen. *See also* Digital Micromirror Device.

DLS *n. See* Downloadable Sounds.

D

DLT *n. See* digital linear tape.

DMA *n. See* direct memory access, document management system.

DMD *n. See* Digital Micromirror Device.

DMI *n.* Acronym for **D**esktop **M**anagement **I**nterface. A system for managing the configurations and status of PCs on a network from a central computer. In DMI an agent program runs in the background on each machine and returns information or performs some action (as specified by a file on that machine) in response to a query received from the central computer. The actions to be performed by the agent might include watching for errors and reporting them to the central computer as they occur; for example, a printer might be set up to report to the central computer when paper runs out or jams. DMI was developed by the DMTF (Desktop Management Task Force), a consortium of computer equipment manufacturers, and competes with SNMP (although the two can coexist on the same system). *See also* agent (definition 1), DMTF. *Compare* SNMP.

DML *n. See* data manipulation language, declarative markup language.

DMOZ *n. See* Open Directory Project.

DMQL *n.* Acronym for **D**ata **M**ining **Q**uery **L**anguage. Any query language developed and used for data mining relational databases. DMQLs provide a syntax for specifying the kind of knowledge to be mined, pattern presentation and visualization, conceptual hierarchies, and task relevant data. *See also* data mining. *Compare* structured query language (SQL).

DMS *n. See* document management system.

DMT *n. See* discrete multitone.

DMTF *n.* Acronym for **D**esktop **M**anagement **T**ask **F**orce. A consortium formed in 1992 to develop standards for PC-based stand-alone and networked systems based on user and industry needs.

DNA *n. See* digital DNA, Digital Network Architecture, distributed network, Windows DNA.

DNS *n.* **1.** Acronym for **D**omain **N**ame **S**ystem. The hierarchical system by which hosts on the Internet have both domain name addresses (such as bluestem.prairienet.org) and IP addresses (such as 192.17.3.4). The domain name address is used by human users and is automatically translated into the numerical IP address, which is used by the packet-routing software. DNS names consist of a top-level domain (such as .com, .org, and .net), a second-level

domain (the site name of a business, an organization, or an individual), and possibly one or more subdomains (servers within a second-level domain). *See also* domain name address, IP address. **2.** Acronym for **D**omain **N**ame **Se**rvice. The Internet utility that implements the Domain Name System. DNS servers, also called name servers, maintain databases containing the addresses and are accessed transparently to the user. *See also* Domain Name System (definition 1), DNS server.

DNS name server *n. See* DNS server.

DNS server *n.* Short for **D**omain **N**ame **S**ystem **server**, a computer that can answer Domain Name System (DNS) queries. The DNS server keeps a database of host computers and their corresponding IP addresses. Presented with the name apex.com, for example, the DNS server would return the IP address of the hypothetical company Apex. *Also called:* name server. *See also* DNS (definition 2), IP address.

DNS zone transfer *n. See* zone transfer.

.doc *n.* A file extension that identifies document files formatted for a word processor. This is the default file extension for Microsoft Word document files.

dock *vb.* **1.** To connect a laptop or notebook computer to a docking station. *See also* docking station, laptop, portable computer. **2.** To move a toolbar to the edge of an application window so that it attaches to and becomes a feature of the application window.

Dock *n.* An organizational feature of Mac OS X that keeps track of frequently used applications, documents, and windows. Users can drag icons to the dock for easy access or can minimize an active window to the Dock and still see the application running while working with other windows. The Dock can run along the bottom or either side of the screen. *See also* Mac OS X.

docking mechanism *n.* The portion of a docking station that physically connects the portable computer with the station. *See also* docking station.

docking station *n.* A unit for housing a laptop or notebook computer that contains a power connection, expansion slots, and connections to peripherals, such as a monitor, printer, full-sized keyboard, and mouse. The purpose of a docking station is to turn the laptop or notebook computer into a desktop machine and allow users the convenience of using such peripherals as a monitor and a full-sized keyboard. See the illustration. *See also* expansion slot, laptop, peripheral, portable computer.

Docking station.

DOCSIS *n.* Acronym for **D**ata **O**ver **C**able **S**ervice **I**nter-face **S**pecification. The International Telecommunications Union standard (ITU Recommendation J.112) that specifies functions and internal and external interfaces for high-speed, bidirectional transfer of digital data between cable television networks and subscribers. DOCSIS-compliant equipment ensures interoperability between cable modems and the cable television infrastructure, regardless of manufacturer or provider. Initially developed by a group of cable television providers, including Time Warner and TCI, DOCSIS was designed to support data, video, and rapid Internet access. Data rates are 27 Mbps to 36 Mbps downstream (from the cable network) and 320 Kbps to 10 Mbps upstream (to the cable network). *See also* cable modem. *Compare* IEEE 802.14.

doctype *n.* A declaration at the beginning of an SGML document that gives a public or system identifier for the document type definition (DTD) of the document. *See also* SGML.

document[1] *n.* Any self-contained piece of work created with an application program and, if saved on disk, given a unique filename by which it can be retrieved. Documents are generally thought of as word-processed materials only. To a computer, however, data is nothing more than a collection of characters, so a spreadsheet or a graphic is as much a document as is a letter or report. In the Macintosh environment in particular, a document is any user-created work named and saved as a separate file.

document[2] *vb.* To explain or annotate something, such as a program or a procedure.

documentation *n.* The set of instructions shipped with a program or a piece of hardware. Documentation usually includes necessary information about the type of computer system required, setup instructions, and instructions on the use and maintenance of the product.

document-centric *adj.* Of, pertaining to, or characteristic of an operating system in which the user opens document files and thus automatically invokes the applications (such as word processors or spreadsheet programs) that process them. Many graphical user interfaces, such as the Macintosh Finder, as well as the World Wide Web, are document-centric. *Compare* application-centric.

Document Content Architecture *n. See* DCA (definition 1).

Document Content Description *n. See* DCD (definition 2).

document file *n.* A user-created file that represents the output of a program. *Also called:* data file. *Compare* program file.

document image processing *n.* A system for storing and retrieving information for an enterprise in the form of bitmapped images of paper documents input with a scanner rather than in the form of text and numeric files. Document image processing takes more memory than purely electronic data processing, but it more readily incorporates signatures, drawings, and photographs and can be more familiar to users without computer training. *See also* paperless office.

Document Interchange Architecture *n. See* DIA.

document management *n.* The full spectrum of electronic document creation and distribution within an organization.

document management system *n.* A server-based network facility designed for the storage and handling of an organization's documents. A document management system, or DMS, is built around a central library known as a repository and typically supports controlled access, version tracking, cataloging, search capabilities, and the ability to check documents in and out electronically. The open interface specification known as ODMA (Open Document Management API) enables desktop applications that support ODMA to interface with a DMS so that users can access and manage documents from within their client applications. *Acronym:* DMS. *Also called:* EDMS, electronic document management system.

Document Object Model *n.* A World Wide Web Consortium specification that describes the structure of dynamic HTML and XML documents in a way that allows them to be manipulated through a Web browser. In the Document Object Model, or DOM, a document is presented as a logical structure rather than as a collection of tagged words. In essence, DOM is a means of defining a document as a treelike hierarchy of nodes in which the document is an object containing other objects, such as images and forms. Through DOM, programs and scripts can access these objects in order to change aspects such as their appearance or behavior. DOM is a vehicle for adding depth and interactivity to what would otherwise be a static Web page. *Acronym:* DOM.

document processing *n.* The act of retrieving and manipulating a document. In terms of the way a computer works, document processing involves three main steps: creating or retrieving a data file, using a program to manipulate the data in some way, and storing the modified file.

document reader *n.* A device that scans printed text and uses character recognition to convert it to computer text files. *See also* character recognition.

document retrieval *n.* A capability built into some application programs that enables the user to search for specific documents by specifying items of information, such as date, author, or previously assigned keywords. Document retrieval depends on an indexing scheme that the program maintains and uses. Depending on the program's capabilities, document retrieval might allow the user to specify more than one condition to refine a search.

document source *n.* The plain-text HTML form of a World Wide Web document, with all tags and other markup displayed as such rather than being formatted. *Also called:* source, source document. *See also* HTML.

Document Style Semantics and Specification Language *n.* An ISO standard derived from SGML that addresses the semantics of high-quality composition in a manner independent of particular formatting systems or processes. Like CSS and XSL, it can be used to format XML documents. *Acronym:* DSSSL. *See also* ISO, SGML.

document type definition *n. See* DTD.

document window *n.* In windowing environments, such as the Apple Macintosh and Microsoft Windows, an on-screen window (enclosed work area) in which the user can create, view, or work on a document.

DoD *n. See* U.S. Department of Defense.

do-gooder virus *n.* A virus or worm that has been released with the intention of correcting problems caused by other, more malicious viruses. The do-gooder virus typically looks for computers that have been compromised

and then infects the system and fixes back doors and other vulnerabilities left behind by the malicious program. The do-gooder virus may then use the repaired computer as a platform to infect other computers. *See also* anti-worm, automatic patching.

DO loop *n.* A control statement used in programs that executes a section of code a number of times until a specified condition is met. DO loops are found in FORTRAN and Basic, among other languages. *See also* iterative statement. *Compare* FOR loop.

DOM *n. See* Document Object Model.

domain *n.* **1.** In database design and management, the set of valid values for a given attribute. For example, the domain for the attribute AREA-CODE might be the list of all valid three-digit numeric telephone area codes in the United States. *See also* attribute (definition 1). **2.** For Windows NT Advanced Server, a collection of computers that share a common domain database and security policy. Each domain has a unique name. **3.** In the Internet and other networks, the highest subdivision of a domain name in a network address, which identifies the type of entity owning the address (for example, .com for commercial users or .edu for educational institutions) or the geographical location of the address (for example, .fr for France or .sg for Singapore). The domain is the last part of the address (for example, www.acm.org). *See also* domain name.

domain controller *n.* In Windows NT, the master server that holds the directory services database that identifies all network users and resources.

domain name *n.* An address of a network connection that identifies the owner of that address in a hierarchical format: *server.organization.type.* For example, www.whitehouse.gov identifies the Web server at the White House, which is part of the U.S. government.

domain name address *n.* The address of a device connected to the Internet or any other TCP/IP network, in the hierarchical system that uses words to identify servers, organizations, and types, such as www.logos.net. *See also* TCP/IP.

Domain Name Server *n. See* DNS server.

Domain Name Service *n. See* DNS (definition 2).

Domain Name System *n. See* DNS (definition 1).

Domain Naming System *n. See* DNS (definition 1).

domain slamming *n.* The practice of transferring ownership of domain names from one customer to another without the permission of the first customer.

Domino *n. See* Lotus Domino.

dongle *n.* **1.** *See* hardware key. **2.** An adapter device or cable enabling a nonstandard interface between a computer and a peripheral device or between two disparate items of computer hardware.

do-nothing instruction *n. See* no-operation instruction.

doorway page *n.* A Web page that functions as a doorway into a Web site. Usually a doorway page contains keywords, which Internet search engines seek when they scan the Internet. Placing the correct keywords on a doorway page can increase the number of viewers visiting a site.

dopant *n.* An impurity that is added in small quantities to semiconductor material during the manufacture of diodes, transistors, and integrated circuits. The resistance of a semiconductor falls between the resistance of a conductor and the resistance of an insulator (hence its name); dopants are added to the semiconductor to increase its conductivity. The type and amount of dopant determine whether the semiconductor will be N-type (in which current is conducted by free electrons) or P-type (in which current is conducted by electron vacancies, called *holes*). Common dopants include arsenic, antimony, bismuth, and phosphorus. *See also* N-type semiconductor, P-type semiconductor.

DoS *n.* Acronym for **d**enial **of s**ervice attack. A computerized assault, usually planned, that seeks to disrupt Web access. A denial of service attack can occur in a number of forms. The most common form of attack is to overwhelm an Internet server with connection requests that cannot be completed. This causes the server to become so busy attempting to respond to the attack that it ignores legitimate requests for connections. One example of this type of attack, known as a SYN flood, inundates the server's entry ports with false connection messages. Another, known as the Ping of Death, sends a ping command with an oversized IP packet that causes the server to freeze, crash, or restart. Other forms of denial of service attacks include the destruction or alteration of a server's configuration data, such as router information; unauthorized access to physical components of a system; and the sending of large or invalid data that causes a system to crash or freeze. *See also* packet, Ping of Death, SYN flood.

DOS *n.* **1.** Acronym for **d**isk **o**perating **s**ystem. A generic term describing any operating system that is loaded from disk devices when the system is started or rebooted. The term originally differentiated between disk-based systems and primitive microcomputer operating systems that were memory-based or that supported only magnetic or paper tape. **2.** *See* MS-DOS.

DOS box *n.* **1.** An OS/2 process that supports the execution of MS-DOS programs. *Also called:* compatibility box. **2.** A computer that uses the MS-DOS or PC-DOS operating system, as opposed to one that runs some other operating system, such as UNIX.

DOS extender *n.* A program designed to extend the 640 KB of conventional memory available for use by DOS and DOS-based applications. A DOS extender works by claiming a portion of reserved memory (memory used by other parts of the system, such as the video adapter, the ROM BIOS, and the I/O ports).

DOS prompt *n.* The visual indication from the MS-DOS command processor that the operating system is ready to accept a new command. The default DOS prompt is a path followed by a greater-than sign (for example, C:>); the user can also design a custom prompt with the PROMPT command.

DOS Protected Mode Interface *n.* A software interface, originally developed for Microsoft Windows version 3, that enables MS-DOS-based application programs to run in the protected mode built into 80286 and later microprocessors. In protected mode, the microprocessor can support multitasking and use of memory beyond 1 MB— capabilities otherwise unavailable to programs designed to run under MS-DOS. *See also* protected mode, real mode, Virtual Control Program Interface.

dot *n.* **1.** In the UNIX, MS-DOS, OS/2, and other operating systems, the character that separates a filename from an extension as in TEXT.DOC (pronounced "text-dot-doc"). **2.** In computer graphics and printing, a small spot combined with others in a matrix of rows and columns to form a character or a graphic element in a drawing or design. The dots forming an image on the screen are called pixels. The resolution of a display or printing device is often expressed in dots per inch (dpi). Dots are not the same as spots, which are groups of dots used in the halftoning process. *See also* pixel, resolution (definition 1). *Compare* spot. **3.** In an Internet address, the character that separates the different parts of the domain name, such as

D

the entity name from the domain. *See also* domain (definition 3), domain name.

dot address *n.* An IP address in dotted quad form. *See also* IP address.

dot-addressable mode *n.* A mode of operation in which a computer program can address ("point to") individual dots on the screen or in a printed character. *See also* all points addressable.

dot-bomb *n.* An Internet-based company or organization that has failed or downsized significantly. *See also* dot-commed.

dot-com *n.* A company doing business primarily or entirely on the Internet. The term is derived from the top-level domain, .com, at the end of the Web addresses of commercial Web sites.

dot command *n.* A formatting command typed into a document and preceded by a period (dot) to distinguish it from printable text. Text formatting programs such as the XENIX nroff editor and word processing programs such as WordStar use dot commands for formatting.

dot-commed *adj.* Losing a job because of the downsizing or failure of an Internet-based company or organization. *See also* dot-bomb.

dot file *n.* A file under UNIX whose name begins with a period. Dot files do not appear in ordinary listings of the files in a directory. Dot files are often used to store program setup information for the particular user; for example, .newsrc in a user's account indicates to a newsreader which newsgroups the user subscribes to.

dot-matrix[1] *adj.* Referring to video and print hardware that forms character and graphic images as patterns of dots.

dot matrix[2] *n.* The rectangular grid, or matrix, of tiny "cells" in which dots are displayed or printed in the patterns required to form text characters, circles, squares, and other graphical images. Depending on the frame of reference, the size of a dot matrix varies from a few rows and columns to an invisible grid covering an entire display screen or printed page. *See also* dot-matrix printer, raster.

dot-matrix printer *n.* Any printer that produces characters made up of dots using a wire-pin print head. The quality of output from a dot-matrix printer depends largely on the number of dots in the matrix, which might be low enough to show individual dots or might be high enough to approach the look of fully formed characters. Dot-matrix printers are often categorized by the number of pins

in the print head—typically 9, 18, or 24. *Compare* daisy-wheel printer, laser printer.

dot pitch *n.* **1.** In printers, the distance between dots in a dot-matrix. *See also* dot matrix[2]. **2.** In video displays or CRTs, a measure of image clarity. A video display's dot pitch is the vertical distance, expressed in millimeters, between like-colored pixels. A smaller dot pitch generally means a crisper image, although the difference between two displays can vary because some manufacturers use different methods to determine the dot pitch of their products. A display's dot pitch is an integral part of the product and so cannot be altered. *See also* CRT, display.

dots per inch *n.* A measure of screen and printer resolution that is expressed as the number of dots that a device can print or display per linear inch. *Acronym:* dpi.

dotted decimal notation *n.* The process of formatting an IP address as a 32-bit identifier made up of four groups of numbers, with each group separated by a period. For example, 123.432.154.12.

double buffering *n.* The use of two temporary storage areas (buffers) rather than one to hold information coming from and going to a particular input/output device. Because one buffer can be filled while the other is being emptied, double buffering increases transfer speed. *Also called:* ping-pong buffer.

double-byte characters *n.* A set of characters in which each character is represented by two bytes. Some languages, such as Japanese, Chinese, and Korean, require double-byte character sets.

double-click *vb.* To press and release a mouse button twice without moving the mouse. Double-clicking is a means of rapidly selecting and activating a program or program feature. *Compare* click, drag.

double dabble *n.* A method of converting binary numbers to decimals by a process of doubling sums and adding successive bits: doubling the bit farthest to the left, adding the next bit and doubling the sum, adding the next bit and doubling the sum, and so on until the rightmost bit has been included in the total.

Double Data Rate SDRAM *n. See* DDR SDRAM.

Double Data Rate Synchronous Dynamic RAM *n. See* DDR SDRAM.

double-density disk *n.* A disk created to hold data at twice the density (bits per inch) of a previous generation of disks. Early IBM PC floppy disks held 180 KB of data. Double-density disks increased that capacity to 360 KB. Double-density disks use modified frequency modulation encoding for storing data. *See also* floppy disk, microfloppy disk, modified frequency modulation encoding. *Compare* high-density disk.

double-dereference *vb.* To dereference a pointer that is pointed to by another pointer; in other words, to access the information pointed to by a handle. *See also* dereference, handle (definition 1), pointer (definition 1).

double leap year *n.* The mistaken idea that the year 2000 would have two leap days—February 29 and February 30—instead of one. In actuality, there was a potential leap year problem in 2000, but it was based on three rules for calculating leap years: (1) A year is a leap year if it is divisible by 4, *but* (2) not if it is divisible by 100, *unless* (3) it is also divisible by 400. Thus, 1900 was not a leap year, but 2000 is, although systems based on incorrect algorithms may not recognize it as a leap year and so may have difficulties functioning correctly after February 28, 2000.

double posting *n.* In newsgroup discussions, the practice of replying to one's own posts. Because it may be seen as the digital equivalent to talking to one's self, double posting is considered an undesirable practice.

double-precision *adj.* Of, pertaining to, or characteristic of a number stored in twice the amount (two words—typically 8 bytes) of computer memory that is required for storing a less precise (single-precision) number. Double-precision numbers are commonly handled by a computer in floating-point form. *See also* floating-point number. *Compare* single-precision.

double-sided disk *n.* A floppy disk that can hold data on both its top and bottom surfaces.

double slash *n. See //.*

double-strike *n.* On an impact printer, such as a daisy-wheel printer, the process of printing twice over a word, producing text that appears darker and heavier, or bolder, than it normally appears. On dot-matrix printers, double striking with a slight offset can be used to fill in the space between the dots, producing smoother and darker characters.

double supertwist nematic display *n. See* supertwist display.

double word *n.* A unit of data consisting of two contiguous words (connected bytes, not text) that are handled together by a computer's microprocessor.

doubly linked list *n.* A series of nodes (items representing discrete segments of information) in which each node refers to both the next node and the preceding node. Because of these two-way references, a doubly linked list can be traversed both forward and backward, rather than in a forward direction only, as with a singly linked list.

down *adj.* Not functioning, in reference to computers, printers, communications lines on networks, and other such hardware.

downflow *n.* One of the four stages of the data warehousing process, during which stored information is delivered and archived. *See also* data warehouse[2]. *Compare* inflow, metaflow, upflow.

downlink *n.* The transmission of data from a communications satellite to an earth station.

download *vb.* **1.** In communications, to transfer a copy of a file from a remote computer to the requesting computer by means of a modem or network. **2.** To send a block of data, such as a PostScript file, to a dependent device, such as a PostScript printer. *Compare* upload.

downloadable font *n.* A set of characters stored on disk and sent (downloaded) to a printer's memory when needed for printing a document. Downloadable fonts are most commonly used with laser printers and other page printers, although many dot-matrix printers can accept some of them. *Also called:* soft font.

Downloadable Sounds *n.* A standard for synthesizing wave sounds from digital samples stored in software. The DLS level 1 and level 2 standards are published by the MIDI Manufacturers Association. *Acronym:* DLS.

downsample *n.* To decrease the number of audio samples or pixels, by applying an operation such as averaging. Popular internet music formats, such as MP3, use downsampling to reduce file size.

downsizing *n.* In computing, the practice of moving from larger computer systems, such as mainframes and minicomputers, to smaller systems in an organization, generally to save costs and to update to newer software. The smaller systems are usually client/server systems composed of a combination of PCs, workstations, and some legacy system such as a mainframe, connected in one or more local area networks or wide area networks. *See also* client/server architecture, legacy system.

downstream[1] *n.* The direction in which information, such as a news feed for a newsgroup or data from an http

(Web) server, is passed from one server to the next. *See also* news feed, newsgroup, server.

downstream² *adv.* **1.** The location of a client computer in relation to a server. **2.** The direction in which data moves from the server to the client.

downstream³ *adj.* Refers to data that moves *from* a remote network *to* an individual computer. In some Internet-related communications technologies, data flows more quickly downstream than upstream; cable modems, for example, can transfer data as fast as 30 Mbps downstream but support much slower rates, from 128 Kbps to around 2 Mbps, upstream. *Compare* upstream.

downtime *n.* The amount or percentage of time a computer system or associated hardware remains nonfunctional. Although downtime can occur because hardware fails unexpectedly, it can also be a scheduled event, as when a network is shut down to allow time for maintenance.

downward compatibility *n.* The capability of source code or programs developed on a more advanced system or compiler version to be executed or compiled by a less advanced (older) version. *Compare* upward-compatible.

DP *n. See* data processing.

dpi *n. See* dots per inch.

DPMA *n.* Acronym for **D**ata **P**rocessing **M**anagement **A**ssociation. A trade organization of information systems (IS) professionals. DPMA was founded in 1951 as the National Machine Accountants Association.

DPMI *n. See* DOS Protected Mode Interface.

DPMS *n.* Acronym for VESA **D**isplay **P**ower **M**anagement **S**ignaling. A VESA standard for signals that put a video monitor into "standby" or suspend mode to reduce power consumption. *See also* green PC, VESA².

DPOF *n.* Short for **D**igital **P**rint **O**rder **F**ormat. A printing specification developed by Canon Computer Systems, Inc., Eastman Kodak Company, Fuji Photo Film Co., Ltd., and Matsushita Electric Industrial Co., Ltd. DPOF is intended to ease the process of printing images stored on digital camera memory cards by enabling users to select the images to print, as well as specify the number of copies desired, on the card. The images ordered can then be printed by a professional photofinishing service or on a home printer.

DPSK *n.* Acronym for **d**ifferential **p**hase-**s**hift **k**eying. *See* phase-shift keying.

draft mode *n.* A high-speed, relatively low-quality print mode offered by most dot-matrix printers. *See also* dot-matrix printer, draft quality, print quality.

draft quality *n.* A low grade of printing generated by the draft mode on dot-matrix printers. Draft quality varies among printers, ranging from suitable for most purposes to nearly useless. *See also* draft mode, print quality.

drag *vb.* In graphical user interface environments, to move an image or a window from one place on the screen to another by "grabbing" it and pulling it to its new location using the mouse. The mouse pointer is positioned over the object, and the mouse button is pressed and held while the mouse is moved to the new location.

drag-and-drop *vb.* **1.** In general, to delve into something in increasing detail. **2.** More specifically, to perform operations in a graphical user interface by dragging objects on the screen with the mouse. For example, to delete a document, a user can drag the document icon across the screen and drop it on the trashcan icon (Macintosh OS) or in the Recycle Bin (Windows). *See also* drag, graphical user interface.

drain *n.* **1.** In an FET, the electrode toward which charge carriers (electrons or holes) move from the source under control of the gate. *See also* FET, gate (definition 2), MOSFET, source (definition 2). **2.** *See* current drain.

DRAM *n. See* dynamic RAM.

DRAW *n.* Acronym for **d**irect **r**ead **a**fter **w**rite. A technique used with optical discs to verify the accuracy of information immediately after it has been recorded (written) on the disc. *Compare* DRDW.

drawer *n.* In the Mac OS X Aqua interface, small child windows containing extra information that slide out of the side of main parent windows. Drawers are intended to reduce clutter on the computer desktop by enabling more information to be displayed without opening additional full-sized windows. *Also called:* Drop Drawer.

drawing interchange format *n. See* DXF.

drawing program *n.* A program for manipulating object-oriented graphics, as opposed to manipulating pixel images. In a drawing program, for example, the user can manipulate an element, such as a line, a circle, or a block of text, as an independent object simply by selecting the object and moving it. *See also* object-oriented graphics, pixel image, vector graphics.

DRDW *n.* Acronym for **d**irect **r**ead **d**uring **w**rite. A technique used with optical discs to verify the accuracy of information at the time it is being recorded on the disc. *Compare* DRAW.

Dreamcast *n.* A console game system designed by the Sega corporation. It features a Hitachi 128-bit graphics engine with an on-board SH-4 RISC processor (operating frequency of 200 MHz 360 MIPS/1.4 GFLOPS) and a customized OS using Windows CE as its base (supporting DirectX). Game developers for the Dreamcast platform use an environment supported by Microsoft Visual Studio and refined Visual C++. *See also* computer game, console game, DirectX, gigaflops, MIPS, OS, RISC, Visual C++. *Compare* GameCube, PlayStation, Xbox.

dribbleware *n.* Updates, patches, and new drivers for a software product that are released one at a time, as they become available, rather than being issued together in a new version of the product. A company using the dribbleware technique might distribute new and replacement files on diskette or CD-ROM, or make them available for download through the Internet or a private network. *See also* driver, patch[1].

drift *n.* The movement of charge carriers in a semiconductor caused by an applied voltage. The term is also used to refer to any slow, unwanted change in a parameter; for example, the value of a resistor might change, or drift, slightly as the resistor warms or cools.

drill down *vb.* To start at a top-level menu, directory, or Web page and pass through several intermediate menus, directories, or linked pages, until the file, page, menu command, or other item being sought is reached. Drilling down is common practice in searching for files or information on the Internet, where high-level Gopher menus and World Wide Web pages are frequently very general and become more specific at each lower level. *See also* Gopher, menu, Web page.

drive *n. See* disk drive.

drive bay *n.* A hollow, rectangular area in a computer chassis designed to hold a disk drive. A drive bay always has side walls, usually made of metal, that generally contain holes to facilitate installation of a disk drive. Some drive bays, such as those intended to hold hard disks, are not visible to the user. Most drives are located on the front of the chassis so that the user can interact with the drive.

drive letter *n.* The naming convention for disk drives on IBM and compatible computers. Drives are named by letter, beginning with A, followed by a colon.

drive mapping *n.* The assignment of a letter or name to a disk drive so that the operating system or network server can identify and locate it. For example, in PCs, the primary drive mappings are A: and B: for floppy disk drives and C: for the hard disk. *See also* A:, disk drive, hard disk.

drive number *n.* The naming convention for Macintosh disk drives. For example, a two-drive system calls its drives 0 and 1.

driver *n.* A hardware device or a program that controls or regulates another device. A line driver, for example, boosts signals transmitted over a communications line. A software driver is a device-specific control program that enables a computer to work with a particular device, such as a printer or a disk drive. Because the driver handles device-specific features, the operating system is freed from the burden of having to understand—and support—the needs of individual hardware devices. *See also* device driver.

Driver Development Kit *n. See* DDK.

DRM *n.* Acronym for **D**igital **R**ights **M**anagement. A group of technologies developed to protect intellectual property from online piracy by controlling who can view protected content and in what form. A DRM package may allow the purchaser to view protected content, but prevent printing or forwarding. Content may also be set to expire after a set amount of time or if distributed to multiple users. DRM technology is meant to protect multiple forms of digital and analog content, and includes encryption, digital watermarking, and content tracking software.

DRO *n.* Acronym for **d**estructive **r**ead **o**ut. *See* destructive read.

drop cable *n.* A cable, also known as a transceiver cable, that is used to connect a network interface card (NIC) to a Thick Ethernet network.

drop cap *n.* A large capital letter at the beginning of a text block that occupies the vertical depth of two or more lines of regular text. See the illustration.

Asectetuer adipsicing elite in sed utm diam nonummy nibh wisi tincidunt eusismond ut laoreet dolore

Drop cap.

drop-dead halt *n. See* dead halt.

drop-down menu *n.* A menu that drops from the menu bar when requested and remains open without further action until the user closes it or chooses a menu item. *Compare* pull-down menu.

drop in *vb.* To read a spurious signal during a data read/write operation, producing erroneous data.

droplet *n.* **1.** An extension for Quark XPress that allows files to be dragged onto a page from the finder. **2.** A feature from Frontier that allows scripts to be embedded within an application and run when the application is double-clicked. **3.** A general name for any AppleScript program that allows files to be dragged and dropped into it for processing. *See also* AppleScript.

drop out *vb.* To lose the signal momentarily during a data read/write operation, thus producing erroneous data.

drum *n.* A rotating cylinder used with some printers and plotters and (in the early days of mainframe computing) as a magnetic storage medium for data. In laser printers, a rotating drum is coated with a photoelectric material that retains a charge when struck by a laser beam. The electrically charged spots on the drum then attract toner particles that the drum transfers to the paper as the paper passes by.

drum plotter *n.* A plotter in which paper is wrapped around a large revolving drum, with a pen that moves back and forth at the uppermost point on the drum. The paper is rolled with the drum to align the correct point on the paper with the pen. Drums take up a fraction of the space required by flatbed plotters that can handle the same paper size. They also effectively have no limit on the length of the paper they can handle, which can be an advantage in some applications. *See also* plotter. *Compare* flatbed plotter, pinch-roller plotter.

drum scanner *n.* A type of scanner where the medium being scanned, such as a sheet of paper, is rotated around a stationary scan head. *See also* scanner. *Compare* feed scanner, flatbed scanner, handheld scanner.

.drv *n.* The file extension for a driver file. *See also* driver.

dry run *n.* Running a program intended to have a dramatic effect, such as formatting a disk or printing a book, with the effect disabled, thus avoiding formatting a disk with data on it or wasting paper.

DS *n.* Acronym for **D**igital **S**ervices or **D**igital **S**ignal, a category used in referencing the speed, number of channels, and transmission characteristics of T1, T2, T3, and T4 communications lines. The basic DS unit, or level, is known as DS-0, which corresponds to the 64 Kbps speed of a single T1 channel. Higher levels are made up of multiple DS-0 levels. DS-1 represents a single T1 line that transmits at 1.544 Mbps. For higher rates, T1 lines are multiplexed to create DS-2 (a T2 line consisting of four T1 channels that transmits at 6.312 Mbps), DS-3 (a T3 line consisting of 28 T1 channels that transmits at 44.736 Mbps), and DS-4 (a T4 line consisting of 168 T1 channels that transmits at 274.176 Mbps).

DSA *n.* **1.** Acronym for **D**irectory **S**ystem **A**gent or **D**irectory **S**erver **A**gent. An X.500 server program that looks up the address of a user on the network when requested by a DUA (Directory User Agent). *See also* agent (definition 3), CCITT X series, DUA. **2.** *See* Digital Signature Algorithm.

DSL *n.* Acronym for **D**igital **S**ubscriber **L**ine, a recently developed (late 1990s) digital communications technology that can provide high-speed transmissions over standard copper telephone wiring. DSL is often referred to as xDSL, where the *x* stands for one or two characters that define variations of the basic DSL technology. Currently, ADSL (Asymmetric DSL) is the form most likely to be provided, but even it is, as yet, available only to limited groups of subscribers. *See also* ADSL, DSL Lite, HDSL, RADSL, SDSL, VDSL.

DSLAM *n.* Acronym for **D**igital **S**ubscriber **L**ine **A**ccess **M**ultiplexer. A device in a telephone company central office that splits DSL subscriber lines and connects them to Internet network hosts and to the public telephone network. The use of a DSLAM makes it possible to provide both voice and data service through a single pair of copper wires.

DSL Lite *n.* Short for **D**igital **S**ubscriber **L**ine **Lite**. A variation of ADSL currently under development that simplifies installation but transmits more slowly, at 1.544 Mbps. *See also* ADSL, DSL.

DSO *n.* Acronym for **D**ynamic **S**hared **O**bject. An Apache HTTP server module that supports all UNIX-based platforms. DSO uses a dynamically linked shared library of resources that are loaded and executed only at run time when necessary. DSO is most commonly used with Linux and is included in most Linux distributions.

DSOM *n.* *See* Distributed System Object Model.

DSP *n.* *See* digital signal processor.

DSR *n.* Acronym for **D**ata **S**et **R**eady. A signal used in serial communications sent, for example, by a modem to the computer to which it is attached, to indicate that it is

D

ready to operate. DSR is a hardware signal sent over line 6 in RS-232-C connections. *See also* RS-232-C standard. *Compare* CTS.

DSS *n. See* decision support system, digital satellite system, Digital Signature Standard.

DSSSL *n. See* Document Style Semantics and Specification Language.

DSTN display *n.* Acronym for **d**ouble **s**upertwist **n**ematic **display**. *See* supertwist display.

DSU *n. See* DDS.

DSVD *n. See* Digital Simultaneous Voice and Data.

DTD *n.* Acronym for **d**ocument **t**ype **d**efinition. A separate document that contains formal definitions of all of the data elements in a particular type of HTML, SGML, or XML document, such as a report or a book. By consulting the DTD for a document, a program called a parser can work with the markup codes that the document contains. *See also* HTML, SGML.

DTE *n.* Acronym for **D**ata **T**erminal **E**quipment. In the RS-232-C and X.25 specifications, a device, such as a PC, that has the ability to transmit information in digital form over a cable or a communications line to a mediating device (known as the DCE). *See also* RS-232-C standard. *Compare* DCE (definition 1).

DTL *n. See* diode-transistor logic.

DTMF *n.* Acronym for **D**ual **T**one **M**ultiple **F**requency. *See* touch tone dialing.

DTP *n. See* desktop publishing, distributed transaction processing.

DTR *n.* Acronym for **D**ata **T**erminal **R**eady. A signal used in serial communications sent, for example, by a computer to its modem to indicate that the computer is ready to accept an incoming transmission. *See also* RS-232-C standard.

DTV *n.* Acronym for **d**esk **t**op **v**ideo. The use of digital cameras over a network for video conferencing. *See also* video conferencing.

DUA *n.* Acronym for **D**irectory **U**ser **A**gent. An X.500 client program that sends a request to a DSA for the address of a user on the network. *Also called:* DCA, Directory Client Agent. *See also* agent (definition 3), DSA.

dual attachment station *n.* An FDDI node with two connections to the network—either through a node and a concentrator or through two concentrators. *Compare* single attachment station.

dual-band phone *n.* Wireless phone that broadcasts and receives signals on both 800-MHz (digital cellular) and 1900-MHz (personal communications service, or PCS) networks.

dual boot *n.* A computer configuration in which two different operating systems are installed and either can be loaded at start-up. A user might set up a dual boot system to take advantage of specific applications and functions in each operating system. A dual boot system might also be set up with each operating system in a different language. A dual boot system is not limited to only two operating systems, and when more than two are installed, it may be called a multi-boot system. *See also* boot[1].

dual channel controller *n.* A circuit or device that governs signal access to two pathways.

dual density *adj.* Of, pertaining to, or characteristic of floppy disk drives that can read from and write to disks in more than one density format.

dual disk drive *n.* A computer that has two floppy disk drives.

dual homing *n.* A form of fault tolerance used with critical network devices on FDDI networks, in which such devices are attached to both the primary and secondary (backup) rings through two concentrators to provide the maximum possible security in case the primary ring fails.

dual inline memory module *n. See* DIMM.

dual inline package or **dual in-line package** *n. See* DIP.

dual-mode phone *n.* Wireless phone that broadcasts and receives signals on both analog and digital networks. Dual-mode phones allow wireless phone users with digital service to send and receive calls on analog networks in areas where wireless carriers do not provide digital service.

dual processors *n.* Two processors used in a computer to speed its operation—one processor to control memory and the bus, and another to manage input/output. Many personal computers use a second processor to perform floating-point mathematical operations. *See also* coprocessor, floating-point notation.

dual-ring topology *n.* A token-passing ring topology implemented in FDDI networks that consists of two rings in which information travels in opposite directions. One

D

ring, the primary ring, carries information; the second ring is used for backup. *See also* FDDI.

dual-scan display *n.* A passive matrix LCD-type display used in laptop computers. The screen refresh rate is twice as fast in dual-scan displays as in standard passive matrix displays. Compared with active matrix displays, dual-scan displays are more economical in terms of power consumption but have less clarity and a smaller viewing angle. *See also* passive matrix display.

dual-sided disk drive *n.* A disk drive that can read or write information to both the top and bottom sides of a double-sided disk. Dual-sided disk drives have two read/ write heads, one for each disk surface.

Dual Tone Multiple Frequency *n. See* touch tone dialing.

DUB *n. See* dial-up boot loader.

dumb quotes *n.* Quotation marks that have the same appearance (usually upright like the apostrophe ' and quotation marks " on a typewriter) whether they stand before or after the material being quoted. *Compare* smart quotes.

dumb terminal *n.* A terminal that does not contain an internal microprocessor. Dumb terminals are typically capable of displaying only characters and numbers and responding to simple control codes. *Compare* smart terminal.

dummy *n.* A placeholder, usually a character, a record, or a variable, that is used to reserve space until the intended item is available. *See also* stub.

dummy argument *n.* In programming, an argument that does not convey any information into or out of the called routine and is usually used to hold a place for an argument that will be used in a future revision of the routine. *See also* argument.

dummy instruction *n. See* no-operation instruction.

dummy module *n.* A module, or group of routines, that performs no function but will do so in some future revision—essentially, a collection of dummy routines. *See also* dummy routine.

dummy routine *n.* A routine that performs no action but that can be rewritten to do so at some future time. Top-down program development usually involves the creation of dummy routines that are turned into functional routines as development proceeds. *Also called:* stub. *See also* dummy argument, dummy module, top-down programming.

DUN *n. See* dial-up networking.

duplex[1] *adj.* Capable of carrying information in both directions over a communications channel. A system is full-duplex if it can carry information in both directions at once; it is half-duplex if it can carry information in only one direction at a time.

duplex[2] *n.* **1.** Simultaneous communications, in both directions, between the sender and receiver. *Also called:* duplex transmission, full-duplex transmission. *See also* half-duplex transmission. **2.** Photographic paper on which an image can be printed on both sides.

duplex channel *n.* A communications link that allows for duplex (two-way) transmission.

duplex printer *n.* A printer capable of printing on both sides of the page.

duplex system *n.* A system of two computers, one of which is active while the other remains on standby, ready to take over processing if the active machine malfunctions.

duplex transmission *n. See* duplex[2] (definition 1).

duplicate key *n.* A value assigned to an indexed field in one record in a database that duplicates a value assigned to the same field in another record in the database. For example, a key (or index) composed of ZIP-CODE would necessarily contain duplicate values if the file contained a number of addresses from a single ZIP Code. A field in which duplicate values are permitted cannot serve as a primary key because the primary key must be unique, but it can serve as a component of a composite primary key. *See also* field (definition 1), key (definition 2), primary key.

duplication check *n.* **1.** A survey made to determine whether duplicate records or keys exist in a file. *See also* key. **2.** The use of separate independent calculations to establish the accuracy of a result.

DV *n. See* digital video.

DVD *n. See* digital video disc.

DVD decoder *n.* A hardware or software component that allows a digital video disc (DVD) drive to display movies on your computer screen. *See also* digital video disc.

DVD-E *n. See* digital video disc–erasable.

DVD-R *n. See* digital video disc–recordable.

DVD-ROM *n. See* digital video disc–ROM.

DVI *n.* Acronym for **D**igital **V**ideo **I**nterface. A hardware-based compression/decompression technique for storing full-motion video, audio, graphics, and other data on a computer or on a CD-ROM. DVI technology was developed by RCA in 1987 and acquired by Intel in 1988. Intel has since developed a software version of DVI, called Indeo. *Also called:* digital video–interactive.

DV-I *n. See* digital video–interactive.

DVMRP *n. See* Distance Vector Multicast Routing Protocol.

Dvorak keyboard *n.* A keyboard layout developed by August Dvorak and William L. Dealey in 1936 as an alternative to the overwhelmingly popular QWERTY keyboard. The Dvorak keyboard was designed to speed typing by placing the characters on the keyboard for easiest access to the most frequently typed letters. In addition, pairs of letters that often occur sequentially were separated so that the hands could alternate typing them. See the illustration. *See also* ergonomic keyboard, keyboard. *Compare* QWERTY keyboard.

Dvorak keyboard.

DVR *n.* Acronym for **D**igital **V**ideo **R**ecording. Technology allowing broadcast television programming to be digitized and played back immediately. Television signals are routed through a hard drive, converted to a digital format and displayed in real-time or, at the viewer's option, on a delayed basis. DVR technology can be used like a VCR to record favorite programs in advance, with the user picking the programs to be recorded from an online programming guide. DVR capabilities can also be added to products that have related digital technologies and components, such as set-top boxes and digital TV converters.

DVST *n. See* direct view storage tube.

DWDM *n. See* dense wavelength division multiplexing.

DXF *n.* Short for **d**rawing interchange **f**ormat. A computer-aided design file format originally developed by Autodesk; for use with the AutoCAD program to facilitate transfer of graphics files between different applications

dyadic *adj.* Of, pertaining to, or characteristic of a pair—for example, a dyadic processor, which contains two processors controlled by the same operating system. The term is usually limited to describing a system with two microprocessors. Dyadic Boolean operations are those such as AND and OR in which the outcome depends on both values. *See also* Boolean algebra, operand. *Compare* unary.

dye-diffusion printer *n. See* continuous-tone printer.

dye-polymer recording *n.* A recording technology used with optical discs in which dye embedded in a plastic polymer coating on an optical disc is used to create minute bumps on the surface that can be read by a laser. Dye-polymer bumps can be flattened and re-created, thus making an optical disc rewritable.

dye-sublimation printer *n. See* continuous-tone printer.

Dylan *n.* Short for **Dy**namic **Lan**guage. An object-oriented programming language developed by Apple Computer in the mid-1990s for application and systems development. It includes garbage collection, type-safety, error recovery, a module system, and programmer control over runtime extensibility of programs.

dynalink *n.* Short for **dyna**mic **link.** *See* dynamic-link library.

Dynaload drivers *n.* Device drivers that are supported by Dynaload. Dynaload is a command that can be run from a DOS prompt under IBM's PC DOS 7 and will load compliant device drivers without modification of the CONFIG.SYS file. *See also* CONFIG.SYS.

dynamic *adj.* Occurring immediately and concurrently. The term is used in describing both hardware and software; in both cases it describes some action or event that occurs when and as needed. In dynamic memory management, a program is able to negotiate with the operating system when it needs more memory.

dynamic address translation *n.* On-the-fly conversion of memory-location references from relative addresses (such as "three units from the beginning of X") to absolute addresses (such as "location number 123") when a program is run. *Acronym:* DAT.

D

dynamic allocation *n.* The allocation of memory during program execution according to current needs. Dynamic allocation almost always implies that dynamic deallocation is possible too, so data structures can be created and destroyed as required. *See also* allocate, deallocate. *Compare* static allocation.

dynamic binding *n.* Binding (converting symbolic addresses in the program to storage-related addresses) that occurs during program execution. The term often refers to object-oriented applications that determine, during run time, which software routines to call for particular data objects. *Also called:* late binding. *Compare* static binding.

dynamic caching *n.* A technique for storing recently used data in memory where cache size is based on how much memory is available rather than how much memory is assigned to the application currently running.

Dynamic Data Exchange *n. See* DDE.

dynamic dump *n.* A listing, either stored on disk or sent to a printer, of memory contents generated at the time of a break in the execution of a program—a useful tool for programmers interested in knowing what is happening at a certain point in the execution of a program.

Dynamic Host Configuration Protocol *n. See* DHCP.

dynamic HTML *n.* A technology designed to add richness, interactivity, and graphical interest to Web pages by providing those pages with the ability to change and update themselves dynamically—that is, in response to user actions, without the need for repeated downloads from a server. This is done by enabling the interaction of HTML, cascading style sheets (CSS), and JavaScript. Examples of dynamic HTML actions include moving graphics on the page and displaying information, such as menus or tables, in response to mouse movements or clicks. Interoperability is governed by the World Wide Web Consortium (W3C) Document Object Model (DOM) specification, a platform- and language-neutral interface to ensure that programs and scripts can dynamically access and update the content, structure, and style of documents. *Acronym:* DHTML.

dynamic keys *n.* An encryption technique in which messages are encrypted differently for each transmission based on different keys so that if a key is captured and decrypted, it would never be useful again. *See also* encryption, key (definition 3).

dynamic-link library *n.* A feature of the Microsoft Windows family of operating systems and OS/2 that allows executable routines to be stored separately as files with DLL extensions and to be loaded only when needed by a program. A dynamic-link library has several advantages. First, it does not consume any memory until it is used. Second, because a dynamic-link library is a separate file, a programmer can make corrections or improvements to only that module without affecting the operation of the calling program or any other dynamic-link library. Finally, a programmer can use the same dynamic-link library with other programs. *Acronym:* DLL.

dynamic memory allocation *n.* The allocation of memory to a process or program at run time. Dynamic memory is allocated from the system heap by the operating system upon request from the program.

dynamic page *n.* An HTML document that contains animated GIFs, Java applets, or ActiveX controls. *See also* ActiveX control, GIF, HTML, Java applet.

dynamic RAM *n.* A form of semiconductor random access memory (RAM). Dynamic RAM stores information in integrated circuits containing capacitors. Because capacitors lose their charge over time, dynamic RAM boards must include logic to refresh (recharge) the RAM chips continuously. While a dynamic RAM is being refreshed, it cannot be read by the processor; if the processor must read the RAM while it is being refreshed, one or more wait states occur. Despite being slower, dynamic RAM is more commonly used than RAM because its circuitry is simpler and because it can hold up to four times as much data. *Acronym:* DRAM. *See also* RAM. *Compare* static RAM.

dynamic random access memory *n. See* dynamic RAM.

dynamic relocation *n.* The relocation in memory of data or of the code of a currently running program by an internal system routine. Dynamic relocation helps a computer use memory efficiently.

dynamic routing *n.* Routing that adjusts automatically to the current conditions of a network. Dynamic routing typically uses one of several dynamic-routing protocols such as Routing Information Protocol (RIP) and Border Gateway Protocol (BGP). *Compare* static routing.

dynamic scheduling *n.* The management of concurrently running processes (programs), usually by the operating system.

Dynamic Shared Object *n. See* DSO.

dynamic SLIP *n.* Short for **dynamic** **S**erial **L**ine **I**nternet **P**rotocol. Internet access under SLIP in which the user's IP address is not permanent but is reassigned from a pool each time the user connects. The number of IP addresses an Internet service provider needs to offer is reduced to the number of connections that can be in use at once, rather than the total number of subscribers. *See also* IP address, ISP, SLIP. *Compare* DHCP.

dynamic storage *n.* **1.** Information storage systems whose contents will be lost if power is removed from the system. RAM (random access memory) systems are the most common form of dynamic storage, and both dynamic RAM (DRAM) and static RAM (SRAM) are considered forms of dynamic storage. *See also* dynamic RAM, static RAM. *Compare* permanent storage. **2.** In programming, blocks of memory that can be allocated, deallocated, or freely changed in size.

dynamic Web page *n.* A Web page that has fixed form but variable content, allowing it to be tailored to a customer's search criteria.

D

e *n.* The symbol for the base of the natural logarithm 2.71828. Introduced by Leonhard Euler in the mid-eighteenth century, *e* is a fundamental mathematical constant used in calculus, science, engineering, and programming languages, as in logarithmic and exponential functions in C and Basic.

e- *prefix* Short for **e**lectronic. A prefix indicating that a word refers to the computer-based version of some traditionally nonelectronic term, as e-mail, e-commerce, and e-money.

E- *prefix* *See* exa-.

E3 *n.* Acronym for **E**lectronic **E**ntertainment **E**xpo. A major convention where game industry developers, manufacturers, and publishers demonstrate their latest wares.

EAI *n.* Acronym for **E**nterprise **A**pplication **I**ntegration. The process of coordinating the operation of the various programs, databases, and existing technologies of a business or enterprise so that they function as an efficient, business-wide system.

early binding *n.* *See* static binding.

EAROM *n.* Acronym for **e**lectrically **a**lterable **r**ead-**o**nly **m**emory. *See* EEPROM.

Easter egg *n.* A hidden feature of a computer program. It may be a hidden command, an animation, a humorous message, or a list of credits for the people who developed the program. In order to display an Easter egg, a user often must enter an obscure series of keystrokes.

eavesdropper *n.* *See* lurker.

EBCDIC *n.* Acronym for **E**xtended **B**inary **C**oded **D**ecimal **I**nterchange **C**ode. An IBM code that uses 8 bits to represent 256 possible characters, including text, numbers, punctuation marks, and transmission control characters. It is used primarily in IBM mainframes and minicomputers. *Compare* ASCII.

e-bomb *n.* Short for **e**-mail **bomb**. A technique used by some hackers in which a target is put on a large number of mailing lists so that network traffic and storage are tied up by e-mail sent by other mailing list subscribers to the lists' recipients.

e-book *n.* Format allowing books and other large texts to be downloaded from a Web site and viewed digitally. Typically, reading an e-book requires using a small computer appliance that is about the size of a paperback book and consists of a display screen and basic controls. Users can bookmark, highlight, or annotate text, but rights management features may prevent users from e-mailing, printing, or otherwise sharing e-book contents. *Also called:* electronic book.

e-cash *n.* *See* e-money.

ECC *n.* *See* error-correction coding.

echo¹ *n.* In communications, a signal transmitted back to the sender that is distinct from the original signal. Network connections can be tested by sending an echo back to the main computer.

echo² *vb.* To transmit a received signal back to the sender. Computer programs, such as MS-DOS and OS/2, can be commanded to echo input by displaying data on the screen as it is received from the keyboard. Data communications circuits may echo text back to the originating terminal to confirm that it has been received.

echo cancellation *n.* A technique for eliminating unwanted incoming transmissions in a modem that are echoes of the modem's own transmission. The modem sends a modified, reversed version of its transmission on its receiving path, thus erasing echoes while leaving incoming data intact. Echo cancellation is standard in V.32 modems.

echo check *n.* In communications, a method for verifying the accuracy of transmitted data by retransmitting it to the sender, which compares the echoed signal with the original.

echo loop attack *n.* A form of denial of service (DoS) attack in which a connection is established between User Datagram Protocol (UDP) services on two or more host machines that bounce an increasing volume of packets back and forth. The echo loop attack ties up the host machines and causes network congestion.

echoplex *n.* In communications, a technique for error detection. The receiving station retransmits data back to the sender's screen, where it can be displayed visually to check for accuracy.

echo suppressor *n.* In communications, a method for preventing echoes in telephone lines. Echo suppressors inhibit signals from the listener to the speaker, creating a one-way channel. For modems that send and receive on the same frequency, the echo suppressor must be disabled to allow two-way transmission. This disabling produces the high-pitched tone heard in modem-to-modem connections.

ECL *n. See* emitter-coupled logic.

ECMA *n.* Acronym for **E**uropean **C**omputer **M**anufacturers **A**ssociation. An organization based in Geneva, Switzerland, whose American counterpart is CBEMA (Computer and Business Equipment Manufacturers Association). Its standard, ECMA-101, is used for transmitting formatted text and graphical images while retaining their original formatting.

ECMAScript *n.* A standardized, object-oriented scripting language specification defined by the European Computer Manufacturers Association (ECMA) 262 specification. This language was originally designed to perform computations and manipulate objects within a Web environment. Microsoft implements ECMAScript as JScript, and Netscape implements ECMAScript as JavaScript.

ECML *n. See* Electronic Commerce Modeling Language.

e-commerce *n.* Short for **e**lectronic **commerce**. Commercial activity that takes place by means of computers connected through a network. Electronic commerce can occur between a user and a vendor through the Internet, an online information service, or a bulletin board system (BBS), or between vendor and customer computers through electronic data interchange (EDI). *Also called:* e-tail. *See also* EDI.

ECP *n.* Acronym for **E**nhanced **C**apabilities **P**ort. A protocol, developed by Microsoft and Hewlett Packard, for bidirectional, high-speed communication between a computer and a printer or scanner. ECP is part of the IEEE 1284 standard, which specifies enhanced parallel ports that are compatible with the older, de facto standard Centronics parallel ports. *See also* EPP, IEEE 1284.

e-credit *n. See* electronic credit.

e-currency *n. See* e-money.

edge *n.* **1.** In graphics, a border joining two polygons. **2.** In data structures, a link between two nodes on a tree or graph. *See also* graph, node (definition 3), tree.

EDGE *n.* Acronym for **E**nhanced **D**ata Rates for **G**lobal Evolution or **E**nhanced **D**ata Rates for GSM and TDMA Evolution. A third-generation enhancement to the Global System for Mobile Communications (GSM) wireless service, which allows data, multimedia services, and applications to be delivered on broadband at rates up to 384 Kbps.

edge connector *n.* The set of wide, flat, metallic contacts on an expansion board that is inserted into a personal computer's expansion slot or a ribbon cable's connector. It connects the board with the system's shared data pathway, or bus, by means of a series of printed lines that connect to the circuits on the board. The number and pattern of lines differ with the various types of connectors. *See also* expansion board, ribbon cable.

EDI *n.* Acronym for **E**lectronic **D**ata **I**nterchange. A standard for exchanging bundles of data between two companies via telephone lines or the Internet. EDI transmits much larger bundles of data than can be transmitted via e-mail. For EDI to be effective, users must agree on certain standards for formatting and exchanging information, such as the X.400 protocol. *See also* CCITT X series, standard (definition 1).

edit[1] *n.* A change made to a file or a document.

edit[2] *vb.* **1.** To make a change to an existing file or document. Changes to the existing document are saved in memory or in a temporary file but are not added to the document until the program is instructed to save them. Editing programs typically provide safeguards against inadvertent changes, such as by requesting confirmation before saving under an existing filename, by allowing the user to assign a password to a file, or by giving the option of setting the file to read-only status. **2.** To run software that makes extensive, predictable changes to a file automatically, such as a linker or a filter for graphics.

editing keys *n.* A set of keys on some keyboards that assists in editing. Located between the main keyboard and the numeric keypad, editing keys consist of three pairs: Insert and Delete, Home and End, and Page Up and Page Down.

edit key *n.* In a software application, a predefined key or combination of keys that, when pressed, causes the application to enter edit mode.

edit mode *n.* The mode of a program in which a user can make changes to a document, as by inserting or deleting data or text. *Compare* command mode.

editor *n.* A program that creates files or makes changes to existing files. An editor is usually less powerful than a word processor, lacking the latter's capability for text formatting, such as use of italics. Text or full-screen editors allow the user to move through the document using direction arrows. In contrast, line editors require the user to indicate the line number on which text is to be edited. *See also* Edlin.

Edlin *n.* An outdated line-by-line text editor used in MS-DOS through version 5. Its OS/2 counterpart is SSE. *See also* editor.

EDMS *n.* Acronym for **e**lectronic **d**ocument **m**anagement system. *See* document management system.

EDO DRAM *n.* Acronym for **e**xtended **d**ata **o**ut **d**ynamic **r**andom **a**ccess **m**emory. A type of memory that allows for faster read times than DRAM of comparable speed by allowing a new read cycle to begin while data is being read from a previous cycle. This allows for faster overall system performance. *Compare* dynamic RAM, EDO RAM.

EDO RAM *n.* Acronym for **e**xtended **d**ata **o**ut **r**andom **a**ccess **m**emory. A type of dynamic RAM that keeps data available for the CPU while the next memory access is being initialized, resulting in increased speed. Pentium-class computers using Intel's Triton chip set are designed to take advantage of EDO RAM. *See also* central processing unit, dynamic RAM. *Compare* EDO DRAM.

EDP *n.* **1.** Acronym for **e**lectronic **d**ata **p**rocessing. *See* data processing. **2.** Acronym for **E**nhanced **C**apabilities **P**ort. A protocol, developed by Microsoft and Hewlett Packard, for bidirectional, high-speed communication between a computer and a printer or scanner. ECP is part of the IEEE 1284 standard, which specifies enhanced parallel ports that are compatible with the older, de facto standard Centronics parallel ports. *See also* EPP, IEEE 1284.

.edu *n.* In the Internet's Domain Name System, the top-level domain that identifies addresses operated by four-year, degreed educational institutions. The domain name .edu appears as a suffix at the end of the address. In the United States, schools that offer kindergarten through high school classes use the top-level domain of .k12.us or just .us. *See also* DNS (definition 1), domain (definition 3), .k12.us, .us. *Compare* .com, .gov, .mil, .net, .org.

edutainment *n.* Multimedia content in software, on CD-ROM, or on a Web site that purports to educate the user as well as entertain. *See also* multimedia.

EEMS *n.* Acronym for **E**nhanced **E**xpanded **M**emory Specification. A superset of the original Expanded Memory Specification (EMS). Version 3.0 of EMS allowed only storage of data and supported 4-page frames. EEMS allowed up to 64 pages along with executable code to be stored in expanded memory. The features of EEMS were included in EMS version 4.0. *See also* EMS, page frame.

EEPROM *n.* Acronym for **e**lectrically **e**rasable **p**rogrammable **r**ead-**o**nly **m**emory. A type of EPROM that can be erased with an electrical signal. It is useful for stable storage for long periods without electricity while still allowing reprogramming. EEPROMs contain less memory than RAM, take longer to reprogram, and can be reprogrammed only a limited number of times before wearing out. *See also* EPROM, ROM.

EFF *n. See* Electronic Frontier Foundation.

e-form *n.* Short for **e**lectronic **form**. An online document that contains blank spaces for a user to fill in with requested information and that can be submitted through a network to the organization requesting the information. On the Web, e-forms are often coded in CGI script and secured via encryption. *See also* CGI (definition 1).

EGA *n.* Acronym for **E**nhanced **G**raphics **A**dapter. An IBM video display standard introduced in 1984. It emulates the Color/Graphics Adapter (CGA) and the Monochrome Display Adapter (MDA) and provides medium-resolution text and graphics. It was superseded by Video Graphics Display (VGA).

ego-surfing *n.* The practice of using a Web search engine to search for one's own name on the Internet.

EGP *n. See* exterior gateway protocol.

e-home *n. See* smart home.

EIA *n.* Acronym for **E**lectronic **I**ndustries **A**ssociation. An association based in Washington, D.C., with members from various electronics manufacturers. It sets standards for electronic components. RS-232-C, for example, is the EIA standard for connecting serial components. *See also* RS-232-C standard.

EIDE or **E-IDE** *n.* Acronym for **E**nhanced **I**ntegrated **D**rive **E**lectronics. An extension of the IDE standard, EIDE is a hardware interface standard for disk drive designs that house control circuits in the drives themselves. It allows for standardized interfaces to the system bus while providing for advanced features, such as burst data transfer and direct data access. EIDE accommodates drives as large as 8.4 gigabytes (IDE supports up to 528 megabytes). It supports the ATA-2 interface, which permits transfer rates up to 13.3 megabytes per second (IDE permits up to 3.3 megabytes per second), and the ATAPI interface, which connects drives for CD-ROMs, optical discs and tapes, and multiple channels. Most PCs have EIDE drives, which are cheaper than SCSI drives and provide much of the same functionality. *See also* IDE, SCSI.

Eiffel *n.* An advanced object-oriented programming language with a syntax similar to C, developed by Bertrand Meyer in 1988. Eiffel runs on MS-DOS, OS/2, and UNIX. Its major design features are the ability to use modules in multiple programs and software extensibility.

Eiffel# *n.* Pronounced "Eiffel Sharp." A subset language of Eiffel specifically designed to target the .NET Framework and embody the full extent of Design by Contract. *See also* Design by Contract.

eight dot three *n. See* 8.3.

EIP *n. See* enterprise information portal.

EIS *n. See* executive information system.

EISA *n.* Acronym for **E**xtended **I**ndustry **S**tandard **A**rchitecture. A bus standard for the connection of add-on cards to a PC motherboard, such as video cards, internal modems, sound cards, drive controllers, and cards that support other peripherals. EISA was introduced in 1988 by a consortium of nine computer industry companies. The companies—AST Research, Compaq, Epson, Hewlett-Packard, NEC, Olivetti, Tandy, Wyse, and Zenith—were referred to collectively as "the Gang of Nine." EISA maintains compatibility with the earlier Industry Standard Architecture (ISA) but provides for additional features introduced by IBM in its Micro Chan-

nel Architecture bus standard. EISA has a 32-bit data path, and it uses connectors that can accept ISA cards. However, EISA cards are compatible only with EISA systems. EISA can operate at much higher frequencies than the ISA bus and provides much faster data throughput than ISA. *See also* ISA, Micro Channel Architecture.

EJB *n. See* Enterprise JavaBeans.

electroluminescent *adj.* Giving off light when electric current is applied. Electroluminescent panels are used in portable computers to backlight the liquid crystal displays. A thin phosphor layer is sandwiched between two thin electrode panels, one of which is nearly transparent. *See also* liquid crystal display.

electroluminescent display *n.* A type of flat-panel display used in laptops in which a thin phosphor layer is set between vertical and horizontal electrodes. These electrodes form *xy*-coordinates; when a vertical and a horizontal electrode are charged, the phosphor at their intersection emits light. Electroluminescent displays provide a sharp, clear image and a wide viewing angle. They were replaced by active matrix LCD screens. *See also* flat-panel display, liquid crystal display, passive-matrix display. *Compare* active-matrix display.

electrolysis *n.* A process in which a chemical compound is broken down into its constituent parts by passing an electric current through it.

electromagnet *n.* A device that creates a magnetic field when electric current passes through it. An electromagnet typically contains an iron or steel core with wire wrapped around it. Current is passed through the wire, producing a magnetic field. Electromagnets are used in disk drives to record data onto the disk surface.

electromagnetic radiation *n.* The propagation of a magnetic field through space. Radio waves, light, and X rays are examples of electromagnetic radiation, all traveling at the speed of light.

electromagnetic spectrum *n.* The range of frequencies of electromagnetic radiation. In theory, the spectrum's range is infinite. See the illustration.

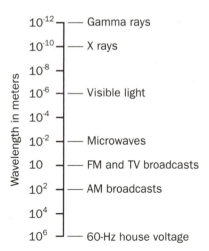

Electromagnetic spectrum.

electromotive force *n.* The force that causes movement in charge carriers (the electrons) in a conductor. *Acronym:* EMF. *Also called:* potential, voltage. *See also* ampere, coulomb.

electron beam *n.* A stream of electrons moving in one direction. An electron beam is used in a cathode-ray tube (CRT) to produce an image as it is passed across the phosphor coating inside the tube. *See also* CRT.

electron gun *n.* A device that produces an electron beam, typically found in television or computer monitors. *See also* CRT.

electronic bulletin board *n. See* BBS (definition 1).

electronic cash *n. See* e-money.

electronic circuit *n. See* circuit.

electronic commerce *n. See* e-commerce.

Electronic Commerce Modeling Language *n.* A computer language developed by leading e-commerce companies,as a standard for inputting e-wallet information into the payment fields of Web sites. This allows for one-click transfer of e-wallet information at compatible Web sites. *Acronym:* ECML.

electronic credit *n.* A form of electronic commerce involving credit card transactions carried out over the Internet. *Also called:* e-credit. *See also* e-commerce.

electronic data interchange *n. See* EDI.

electronic data processing *n. See* data processing.

electronic form *n. See* e-form.

Electronic Frontier Foundation *n.* A public advocacy organization dedicated to the defense of civil liberties for computer users. The organization was founded in 1990 by Mitchell Kapor and John Perry Barlow as a response to U.S. Secret Service raids on hackers. *Acronym:* EFF.

electronic funds transfer *n.* The transfer of money via automated teller machine, telephone lines, or Internet connection. Examples of electronic fund transfers include using a credit card to make purchases from an e-commerce site, or using an automated teller machine or automated telephone banking system to move funds between bank accounts. *Acronym:* EFT.

Electronic Industries Association *n. See* EIA.

electronic journal *n. See* journal.

electronic mail *n. See* e-mail[1].

electronic mail services *n.* Services that allow users, administrators, or daemons to send, receive, and process e-mail. *See also* daemon.

electronic mall *n.* A virtual collection of online businesses that affiliate with the intention of increasing the exposure of each business through the fellow businesses.

electronic money *n. See* e-money.

electronic music *n.* Music created with computers and electronic devices. *See also* MIDI, synthesizer.

electronic office *n.* A term used especially in the late 1970s to mid-1980s to refer to a hypothetical paperless work environment to be brought about by the use of computers and communications devices.

electronic paper *n.* Technology allowing a computer display to imitate the look and feel of traditional paper media. Electronic paper consists of thin, flexible sheets of plastic containing millions of small beads called microcapsules. Each microcapsule contains both a black and a white pigment and displays the proper color in response to an electrical charge. It retains this pattern until a new screen of text or images is requested.

electronic photography *n. See* digital photography.

Electronic Privacy Information Center *n. See* EPIC.

electronic publishing *n.* A general term for distributing information via electronic media, such as communications networks or CD-ROM.

electronics *n.* The branch of physics dealing with electrons, electronic devices, and electrical circuits.

Electronics Industries Association *n. See* EIA.

electronic software distribution *n.* A means of directly distributing software to users on line over the Internet. Electronic software distribution is analogous to direct-mail ordering. *Acronym:* ESD.

electronic spreadsheet *n. See* spreadsheet program.

electronic storefront *n.* A business that displays its merchandise on the Internet and has provisions for contact or online sales.

electronic text *n. See* e-text.

electron tube *n.* A device for switching and amplifying electronic signals. It consists of a sealed glass container with electronic elements, such as metallic plates and grids, inside. In most applications, tubes have been replaced by transistors, although they are still used in cathode-ray tubes and in some radio frequency circuits and audio amplifiers. *Also called:* vacuum tube, valve. *See also* CRT.

electrophotographic printers *n.* Printers in a category including laser, LED, LCD, and ion-deposition printers. In such a printer, a negative image is applied to an electrically charged, photosensitive drum. A photosensitive drum develops a pattern of electrostatic charge on its surface representing the photo negative of the image the drum will print. Powdered ink (toner) adheres to the charged areas of the drum, the drum presses the ink onto the paper, and then heat binds the toner to the paper. The printer types vary mainly in how they charge the drum. *See also* ion-deposition printer, laser printer, LCD printer, LED printer.

electrophotography *n.* The production of photographic images using electrostatic charges. This method is used in photocopiers and laser printers. *Also called:* xerography. *See also* electrophotographic printers.

electroplating *n.* The use of electrolysis for depositing a thin layer of one material onto another material. *See also* electrolysis.

electrostatic *adj.* Of or relating to electric charges that are not flowing along a conducting path. Electrostatic charges are used in copiers and laser printers to hold toner particles on a photoconducting drum and in flatbed plotters to hold the plot medium in place.

electrostatic discharge *n.* The discharge of static electricity from an outside source, such as human hands, into an integrated circuit, often resulting in damage to the circuit. *Acronym:* ESD.

electrostatic plotter *n.* A plotter that creates an image from a dot pattern on specially coated paper. The paper is electrostatically charged and exposed to toner, which adheres to the dots. Electrostatic plotters can be up to 50 times faster than pen plotters but are more costly. Color models produce images through multiple passes with cyan, magenta, yellow, and black. *See also* plotter. *Compare* electrophotographic printers, pen plotter.

electrostatic printer *n. See* electrostatic plotter.

elegant *adj.* Combining simplicity, terseness, efficiency, and subtlety. On the academic side of computer science, elegant design (say, of programs, algorithms, or hardware) is a priority, but in the frenetic pace of the computer industry, elegant design may be sacrificed for the sake of speeding a product's development, sometimes resulting in bugs that are difficult to correct.

element *n.* **1.** Any stand-alone item within a broader context. For example, a data element is an item of data with the characteristics or properties of a larger set; a picture element (pixel) is one single dot on a computer screen or in a computer graphic; a print element is the part of a daisy-wheel printer that contains the embossed characters. *See also* daisy-wheel printer, data element, graphics primitive, pixel, thimble. **2.** In markup languages such as HTML and SGML, the combination of a set of tags, any content contained between the tags, and any attributes the tags may have. Elements can be nested, one within the other. *See also* attribute (definition 3), HTML, markup language, SGML.

elevator *n.* The square box within a scroll bar that can be moved up and down to change the position of text or an image on the screen. See the illustration. *Also called:* scroll box, thumb. *See also* scroll bar.

Elevator.

elevator seeking *n.* A method of limiting hard disk access time in which multiple requests for data are prioritized based on the location of the data relative to the read/write head. This serves to minimize head movement. *See also* access time (definition 2), hard disk, read/write head.

elite *n.* **1.** A size of fixed-width type that prints 12 characters to the inch. **2.** A fixed-width font that may be available in various type sizes. *See also* monospace font.

ELIZA *n.* A program, modeled on Rogerian psychotherapy, that conducts simulated conversations with humans by echoing responses and posing questions based on key words in earlier comments. It was created by Dr. Joseph Weizenbaum, who considered it a bit of a joke and was alarmed that people took it seriously. *See also* artificial intelligence, Turing test.

ellipsis *n.* A set of three dots (...) used to convey incompleteness. In many windowing applications, selection of a command that is followed by an ellipsis will produce a submenu or a dialog box. In programming and software manuals, an ellipsis in a syntax line indicates the repetition of certain elements. *See also* dialog box, syntax.

elm *n.* Short for **el**ectronic **m**ail. A program for reading and composing e-mail on UNIX systems. The elm program has a full-screen editor, making it easier to use than the original mail program, but elm has largely been superseded by pine. *See also* e-mail[1]. *Compare* Eudora, pine.

e-mail[1] or **email** or **E-mail** *n.* **1.** Short for **e**lectronic **m**ail. The exchange of text messages and computer files over a communications network, such as a local area network or the Internet, usually between computers or terminals. **2.** An electronic text message.

e-mail[2] or **email** or **E-mail** *vb.* To send an e-mail message.

e-mail address *n.* A string that identifies a user so that the user can receive Internet e-mail. An e-mail address typically consists of a name that identifies the user to the mail server, followed by an at sign (@) and the host name and domain name of the mail server. For example, if Anne E. Oldhacker has an account on the machine called baz at Foo Enterprises, she might have an e-mail address aeo@baz.foo.com, which would be pronounced "A E O at baz dot foo dot com."

e-mail filter *n.* A feature in e-mail-reading software that automatically sorts incoming mail into different folders or mailboxes based on information contained in the message.

For example, all incoming mail from a user's Uncle Joe might be placed in a folder labeled "Uncle Joe." Filters may also be used either to block or accept e-mail from designated sources.

e-mail management system *n.* An automated e-mail response system used by an Internet-based business to sort incoming e-mail messages into predetermined categories and either reply to the sender with an appropriate response or direct the e-mail to a customer service representative. *Acronym:* EMS.

embed *vb.* To insert information created in one program, such as a chart or an equation, into another program. After the object is embedded, the information becomes part of the document. Any changes made to the object are reflected in the document.

embedded *adj.* In software, pertaining to code or a command that is built into its carrier. For example, application programs insert embedded printing commands into a document to control printing and formatting. Low-level assembly language is embedded in higher-level languages, such as C, to provide more capabilities or better efficiency.

embedded chip *n.* *See* embedded system.

embedded command *n.* A command placed in a text, graphics, or other document file, often used for printing or page-layout instructions. Such commands often do not appear on screen but can be displayed if needed. In transferring documents from one program to another, embedded commands can cause problems if the programs are incompatible.

embedded controller *n.* A processor-based controller circuit board that is built into the computer machinery. *See also* controller.

embedded hyperlink *n.* A link to a resource that is embedded within text or is associated with an image or an image map. *See also* hyperlink, image map.

embedded interface *n.* An interface built into a hardware device's drive and controller board so that the device can be directly connected to the computer's system bus. *See also* controller, interface (definition 3). *Compare* ESDI, SCSI, ST506 interface.

embedded system *n.* Microprocessors used to control devices such as appliances, automobiles, and machines used in business and manufacturing. An embedded system is created to manage a limited number of specific tasks within a larger device or system. An embedded system is often built onto a single chip or board and is used to control or monitor the host device—usually with little or no human intervention and often in real time. *See also* microprocessor.

em dash *n.* A punctuation mark (—) used to indicate a break or interruption in a sentence. It is named for the em, a typographical unit of measure that in some fonts equals the width of a capital M. *Compare* en dash, hyphen.

EMF *n. See* electromotive force.

emitter *n.* In transistors, the region that serves as a source of charge carriers. *Compare* base (definition 3), collector.

emitter-coupled logic *n.* A circuit design in which the emitters of two transistors are connected to a resistor so that only one of the transistors switches at a time. The advantage of this design is very high switching speed. Its drawbacks are the high number of components required and susceptibility to noise. *Acronym:* ECL.

EMM *n. See* Expanded Memory Manager.

e-money or **emoney** *n.* Short for **electronic money**. A generic name for the exchange of money through the Internet. *Also called:* cybercash, digicash, digital cash, e-cash, e-currency.

emotag *n.* In an e-mail message or newsgroup article, a letter, word, or phrase that is encased in angle brackets and that, like an emoticon, indicates the attitude the writer takes toward what he or she has written. Often emotags have opening and closing tags, similar to HTML tags, that enclose a phrase or one or more sentences. For example: <joke>You didn't think there would really be a joke here, did you?</joke>. Some emotags consist of a single tag, such as <grin>. *See also* emoticon, HTML.

emoticon *n.* A string of text characters that, when viewed sideways, form a face expressing a particular emotion. An emoticon is often used in an e-mail message or newsgroup post as a comment on the text that precedes it. Common emoticons include :-) or :) (meaning "I'm smiling at the joke here"), ;-) ("I'm winking and grinning at the joke here"), :-(("I'm sad about this"), :-7 ("I'm speaking with tongue in cheek"), :D or :-D (big smile; "I'm overjoyed"), and :-O (either a yawn of boredom or a mouth open in amazement). *Compare* emotag.

EMS *n.* Acronym for **E**xpanded **M**emory **S**pecification. A technique for adding memory to PCs that allows for increasing memory beyond the Intel 80x86 microproces-

sor real-mode limit of 1 megabyte (MB). In earlier versions of microprocessors, EMS bypassed this memory board limit with a number of 16-kilobyte banks of RAM that could be accessed by software. In later versions of Intel microprocessors, including the 80386 and 80486 models, EMS is converted from extended memory by software memory managers, such as EMM386 in MS-DOS 5. Now EMS is used mainly for older MS-DOS applications because Windows and other applications running in protected mode on 80386 and higher microprocessors are free of the 1-MB limit. *Also called:* LIM EMS. *See also* expanded memory, protected mode. *Compare* conventional memory, extended memory.

em space *n.* A typographical unit of measure that is equal in width to the point size of a particular font. For many fonts, this is equal to the width of a capital M, from which the em space takes its name. *Compare* en space, fixed space, thin space.

emulate *vb.* For a hardware or software system to behave in the same manner as another hardware or software system. In a network, for example, microcomputers might emulate terminals in order to communicate with mainframes.

emulation *n.* The process of a computer, device, or program imitating the function of another computer, device, or program.

emulator *n.* Hardware or software designed to make one type of computer or component act as if it were another. By means of an emulator, a computer can run software written for another machine. In a network, microcomputers might emulate terminals in order to communicate with mainframes.

emulsion laser storage *n.* A method for recording data in film by selective heating with a laser beam.

enable *vb.* To activate or turn on. *Compare* disable.

encapsulate *vb.* **1.** To treat a collection of structured information as a whole without affecting or taking notice of its internal structure. In communications, a message or packet constructed according to one protocol, such as a TCP/IP packet, may be taken with its formatting data as an undifferentiated stream of bits that is then broken up and packaged according to a lower-level protocol (for example, as ATM packets) to be sent over a particular network; at the destination, the lower-level packets are assembled, re-creating the message as formatted for the encapsulated protocol. *See also* ATM (definition 1). **2.** In object-oriented programming, to keep the implementation details of a class a separate file whose contents do not need to be known by a programmer using that class. *See also* object-oriented programming, TCP/IP.

Encapsulated PostScript *n. See* EPS.

encapsulated type *n. See* abstract data type.

encapsulation *n.* **1.** In object-oriented programming, the packaging of attributes (properties) and functionality (methods or behaviors) to create an object that is essentially a "black box"—one whose internal structure remains private and whose services can be accessed by other objects only through messages passed via a clearly defined interface (the programming equivalent of a mailbox or telephone line). Encapsulation ensures that the object providing service can prevent other objects from manipulating its data or procedures directly, and it enables the object requesting service to ignore the details of how that service is provided. *See also* information hiding. **2.** In terms of the Year 2000 problem, a method of dealing with dates that entails shifting either program logic (data encapsulation) or input (program encapsulation) backward into the past, to a parallel year that allows the system to avoid Year 2000 complications. Encapsulation thus allows processing to take place in a "time warp" created by shifting to an earlier time before processing and—for accuracy—shifting output forward by the same number of years to reflect the actual date. *See* data encapsulation, program encapsulation.

encipher *vb. See* encrypt.

encode *vb.* **1.** *See* encrypt. **2.** In programming, to put something into code, which frequently involves changing the form—for example, changing a decimal number to binary-coded form. *See also* binary-coded decimal, EBCDIC.

encoder *n.* **1.** In general, any hardware or software that encodes information—that is, converts the information to a particular form or format. For example, the Windows Media Encoder converts audio and video to a form that can be streamed to clients over a network. **2.** In reference to MP3 digital audio in particular, technology that converts a WAV audio file into an MP3 file. An MP3 encoder compresses a sound file to a much smaller size, about one-twelfth as large as the original, without a perceptible drop in quality. *Also called:* MP3 encoder. *See also* MP3, WAV. *Compare* rip, ripper.

encoding *n.* **1.** *See* Huffman coding. **2.** A method of dealing with computers with Year 2000 problems that entails storing a four-digit year in date fields designed to hold only two digits in a program or system. This can be accomplished by using the bits associated with the date field more efficiently—for example, by converting the date field from ASCII to binary or from decimal to hexadecimal, both of which allow storage of larger values.

encrypt *vb.* To encode (scramble) information in such a way that it is unreadable to all but those individuals possessing the key to the code. Encrypted information is known as cipher text. Also called: encipher, encode.

encryption *n.* The process of encoding data to prevent unauthorized access, especially during transmission. Encryption is usually based on one or more keys, or codes, that are essential for decoding, or returning the data to readable form. The U.S. National Bureau of Standards created a complex encryption standard, Data Encryption Standard (DES), which is based on a 56-bit variable that provides for more than 70 quadrillion unique keys to encrypt documents. *See also* DES.

encryption key *n.* A sequence of data that is used to encrypt other data and that, consequently, must be used for the data's decryption. *See also* decryption, encryption.

end-around carry *n.* A special type of end-around shift operation on a binary value that treats the carry bit as an extra bit; that is, the carry bit is moved from one end of the value to the other. *See also* carry, end-around shift, shift.

end-around shift *n.* An operation performed on a binary value in which a bit is shifted out of one end and into the other end. For example, a right-end shift on the value 00101001 yields 10010100. *See also* shift.

en dash *n.* A punctuation mark (–) used to show ranges of dates and numbers, as in 1990–92, and in compound adjectives where one part is hyphenated or consists of two words, as in pre–Civil War. The en dash is named after a typographical unit of measure, the en space, which is half the width of an em space. *See also* em space. *Compare* em dash, hyphen.

End key *n.* A cursor-control key that moves the cursor to a certain position, usually to the end of a line, the end of a screen, or the end of a file, depending on the program. See the illustration.

End key.

endless loop *n. See* infinite loop.

end mark *n.* A symbol that designates the end of some entity, such as a file or word processing document.

end-of-file *n.* **1.** A code placed by a program after the last byte of a file to tell the computer's operating system that no additional data follows. In ASCII, end-of-file is represented by the decimal value 26 (hexadecimal 1A) or the Ctrl+Z control character. *Acronym:* EOF. **2.** An indicator of some sort in a computer program or database that indicates that the end of a file has been reached. If older systems that have the capacity to store only two-digit years in the date field also use end-of-file markers such as 99, they can be susceptible to date-related problems. *See also* 99 or 9999.

end-of-text *n.* In data transmission, a character used to mark the end of a text file. End-of-text does not necessarily signify the end of transmission; other information, such as error-checking or transmission control characters, can be included at the end of the file. In ASCII, end-of-text is represented by the decimal value 3 (hexadecimal 03). *Acronym:* ETX.

end-of-transmission *n.* A character representing the end of a transmission. In ASCII, the end-of-transmission character has the decimal value 4 (hexadecimal 04). *Acronym:* EOT.

endpoint *n.* The beginning or end of a line segment.

end-to-end delivery *n.* A communications process in networks in which packets are delivered and then acknowledged by the receiving system.

end-to-end examination *n.* An inspection of all of the processes and systems in place at an organization that affect the computer systems. The examination begins with the data or information that flows into the system, continues with how the data is manipulated and stored, and ends with how the data is output. For example, end-to-end examination is one technique that was employed to ferret out Year 2000 problems in computer systems of an organization.

end user *n.* The ultimate user of a computer or computer application in its finished, marketable form.

End-User License Agreement *n.* A legal agreement between a software manufacturer and the software's purchaser with regard to terms of distribution, resale, and restricted use. *Acronym:* EULA.

Energy Star *n.* A symbol affixed to systems and components that denotes lower power-consumption design. Energy Star is the name of an Environmental Protection Agency program that encourages PC manufacturers to build systems that are energy efficient. Requirements dictate that systems or monitors be capable of automatically entering a "sleep state" or lower power-consumption state while the unit is inactive, where the low-power state is defined as 30 watts or less. Systems and monitors that comply with these guidelines are marked with an Energy Star sticker.

engine *n.* A processor or portion of a program that determines how the program manages and manipulates data. The term *engine* is most often used in relation to a specific use; for example, a database engine contains the tools for manipulating a database, and a Web search engine has the ability to search World Wide Web indexes for matches to one or more key words entered by the user. *Compare* back-end processor, front-end processor.

Enhanced Capabilities Port *n. See* ECP.

enhanced Category 5 cable *n. See* Cat 5e cable.

Enhanced Data Rates for Global Evolution *n. See* EDGE.

Enhanced Data Rates for GSM and TDMA Evolution *n. See* EDGE.

Enhanced Expanded Memory Specification *n. See* EEMS.

Enhanced Graphics Adapter *n. See* EGA.

Enhanced Graphics Display *n.* A PC video display capable of producing graphic images with resolutions ranging from 320 x 200 through 640 x 400 pixels, in color or in black and white. Resolution and color depth depend on the vertical and horizontal scanning frequencies of the display, the capabilities of the video display controller card, and available video RAM.

Enhanced IDE *n. See* EIDE.

Enhanced Integrated Device Electronics *n. See* EIDE.

enhanced keyboard *n.* An IBM 101/102-key keyboard that replaced the PC and AT keyboards. It features 12 function keys across the top (rather than 10 on the left side), extra Control and Alt keys, and a bank of cursor and editing keys between the main keyboard and number pad. It is similar to the Apple Extended Keyboard.

Enhanced Parallel Port *n. See* EPP.

enhanced serial port *n.* A connection port for peripheral devices, commonly used for mice and external modems. Enhanced serial ports utilize 16550-type or newer high-speed UART circuits for faster data throughput. Enhanced serial ports are capable of transferring data at speeds as high as 921.6 Kbps. *Acronym:* ESP. *See also* input/output port, UART.

Enhanced Small Device Interface *n. See* ESDI.

ENIAC *n.* An 1800-square-foot, 30-ton computer containing about 18,000 vacuum tubes and 6000 manual switches. Developed between 1942 and 1946 for the U.S. Army by J. Presper Eckert and John Mauchly at the University of Pennsylvania, ENIAC is considered to have been the first truly electronic computer. It remained in operation until 1955.

enlarge *vb.* In Windows and other graphical user interfaces, to increase the size of a window. *See also* maximize. *Compare* minimize, reduce.

E notation *n. See* floating-point notation.

ENQ *n. See* enquiry character.

enquiry character *n.* Abbreviated ENQ. In communications, a control code transmitted from one station to request a response from the receiving station. In ASCII, the enquiry character is designated by decimal value 5 (hexadecimal 05).

en space *n.* A typographical unit of measure that is equal in width to half the point size of a particular font. *Compare* em space, fixed space, thin space.

Enter key *n.* The key that is used at the end of a line or command to instruct the computer to process the command or text. In word processing programs, the Enter key is used at the end of a paragraph. *Also called:* Return key.

Enterprise Application Integration *n. See* EAI.

enterprise computing *n.* In a large enterprise such as a corporation, the use of computers in a network or series of interconnected networks that generally encompass a variety of different platforms, operating systems, protocols, and network architectures. *Also called:* enterprise networking.

enterprise information portal *n.* A portal or gateway that allows internal and external users in a business or enterprise to access information from intranets, extranets, and the Internet for business needs. An enterprise information portal provides a simple Web interface that is designed to help users sift through large amounts of data quickly to find the information they need. By organizing all internal information from company servers, databases, e-mail, and legacy systems, the enterprise information portal exercises control over the company's information availability and presentation. *Acronym:* EIP. *See also* portal.

Enterprise JavaBeans *n.* An application programming interface (API) designed to extend the JavaBean component model to cross-platform, server-side applications that can run on the various systems usually present in an enterprise environment. Enterprise JavaBeans are defined in the Enterprise JavaBean specification released by Sun Microsystems, Inc. The goal of the API is to provide developers with a means of applying Java technology to the creation of reusable server components for business applications, such as transaction processing. *Acronym:* EJB. *See also* Java, JavaBean.

enterprise network *n.* In a large enterprise such as a corporation, the network (or interconnected networks) of computer systems owned by the enterprise, which fills the enterprise's various computing needs. This network can span diverse geographical locations and usually encompasses a range of platforms, operating systems, protocols, and network architectures.

enterprise networking *n. See* enterprise computing.

Enterprise Resource Planning *n.* An approach to business information management that relies on integrated application software to provide data on all aspects of the enterprise, such as manufacturing, finance, inventory, human resources, sales, and so on. The objective of Enterprise Resource Planning software is to provide data, when and as needed, to enable a business to monitor and control its overall operation. *Acronym:* ERP. *Compare* Material Requirements Planning.

entity *n.* In computer-aided design and object-oriented design, an item that can be treated as a unit and, often, as a member of a particular category or type. *See also* CAD, object-oriented design.

E

entry *n.* **1.** A unit of information treated as a whole by a computer program. **2.** The process of inputting information.

entry point *n.* A place in a program where execution can begin.

enumerated data type *n.* A data type consisting of a sequence of named values given in a particular order.

envelope *n.* **1.** In communications, a single unit of information that is grouped with other items, such as error-checking bits. **2.** The shape of a sound wave, caused by changes in amplitude. See the illustration.

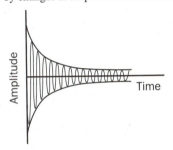

Envelope.

envelope delay *n.* In communications, the difference in travel times of different frequencies in a signal. If the frequencies reach their destination at different times, signal distortion and errors can result. *Also called:* delay distortion.

environment *n.* **1.** The configuration of resources available to the user. *Environment* refers to the hardware and the operating system running on it. For example, Windows and Macintosh are called windowing environments because they are based on screen regions called windows. **2.** In microcomputing, *environment* refers to a definition of the specifications, such as command path, that a program operates in.

EOF *n. See* end-of-file (definition 1).

EOL *n.* Acronym for **e**nd **o**f **l**ine. A control (nonprinting) character that signals the end of a data line in a data file.

EOT *n. See* end-of-transmission.

EPIC *n.* **1.** Short for **E**xplicitly **P**arallel **I**nstruction **C**omputing. A technology developed jointly by Intel and Hewlett-Packard as the foundation of the 64-bit instruction set architecture incorporated in IA-64, the basis of the Merced chip. EPIC technology is designed to enable IA-64 processors to execute instructions efficiently and extremely quickly. Core elements include explicit parallelism based on software identification of instructions that the processor

can execute concurrently; improved execution of branch paths; and earlier loads from memory. *See also* IA-64, Merced. **2.** Short for **E**lectronic **P**rivacy **I**nformation **C**enter. A public-interest research center based in Washington, D.C., dedicated to directing public attention toward civil liberties and online privacy related to electronic communication, cryptography, and related technologies.

epitaxial layer *n.* In semiconductors, a layer that has the same crystal orientation as the underlying layer.

EPP *n.* Acronym for **E**nhanced **P**arallel **P**ort, a high-speed port for peripheral devices other than printers and scanners—that is, for devices such as external drives. Specified in the IEEE 1284 standard, EPP describes bidirectional parallel ports that provide data throughput of 1 Mbps or more, as opposed to the 100 Kbps to 300 Kbps typical of the older, de facto standard Centronics ports. *See also* IEEE 1284, input/output port. *Compare* ECP.

EPP IEEE standard *n.* An IEEE standard relating to the Enhanced Parallel Port (EPP) protocol. This protocol was originally developed by Intel, Xircom, and Zenith Data Systems as a means to provide a high-performance parallel port link that would still be compatible with the standard parallel port. This protocol capability was implemented by Intel in the 386SL chip set (82360 I/O chip), prior to the establishment of the IEEE 1284 committee and the associated standards work. The EPP protocol offered many advantages to parallel port peripheral manufacturers and was quickly adopted by many as an optional data transfer method. A loose association of about 80 interested manufacturers was formed to develop and promote the EPP protocol. This association became the EPP Committee and was instrumental in helping to get this protocol adopted as one of the IEEE 1284 advanced modes. *See also* communications protocol, IEEE 1284, parallel port.

EPROM *n.* Acronym for **e**rasable **p**rogrammable **r**ead-**o**nly **m**emory. A nonvolatile memory chip that is programmed after it is manufactured. EPROMs can be reprogrammed by removing the protective cover from the top of the chip and exposing the chip to ultraviolet light. Though EPROMs are more expensive than PROM chips, they can be more cost-effective if many changes are required. *Also called:* reprogrammable read-only memory (RPROM). *See also* EEPROM, PROM, ROM.

.eps *n.* The file extension that identifies Encapsulated PostScript files. *See also* EPS.

EPS *n.* Acronym for **E**ncapsulated **P**ost**S**cript. A PostScript file format that can be used as an independent entity. The EPS image must be incorporated into the PostScript output of an application such as a desktop publisher. Many high-quality clip-art packages consist of such images. *See also* PostScript.

EPSF *n.* Acronym for **E**ncapsulated **P**ost**S**cript **f**ile. *See* EPS.

equality *n.* The property of being identical, used most often in reference to values and data structures.

equalization *n.* A form of conditioning used to compensate for signal distortion and delay on a communication channel. Equalization attempts to maintain the amplitude and phase characteristics of a signal so that it remains true to the original when it reaches the receiving device.

equation *n.* A mathematical statement that indicates equality with the use of an equal sign (=) between two expressions. In programming languages, assignment statements are written in equation form. *See also* assignment statement.

erasable programmable read-only memory *n.* *See* EPROM.

erasable storage *n.* Storage media that can be used repeatedly because the user has the ability to erase whatever data was previously there. Most forms of magnetic storage, such as tape and disk, are erasable.

erase *vb.* To remove data permanently from a storage medium. This is usually done by replacing existing data with zeros or meaningless text or, in magnetic media, by disturbing the magnetic particles' physical arrangement, either with the erase head or with a large magnet. *Erase* differs from *delete* in that *delete* merely tells the computer that data or a file is no longer needed; the data remains stored and is recoverable until the operating system reuses the space containing the deleted file. *Erase*, on the other hand, removes data permanently. *See also* erase head. *Compare* delete.

erase head *n.* The device in a magnetic tape machine that erases previously recorded information.

Eratosthenes' sieve *n.* *See* sieve of Eratosthenes.

ergonomic keyboard *n.* A keyboard designed to reduce the risk of wrist and hand injuries that result from prolonged use or repetitive movement. An ergonomic keyboard can include such features as alternative key layouts, palm rests, and shaping designed to minimize strain. *See*

also Dvorak keyboard, keyboard, Kinesis ergonomic keyboard.

ergonomics *n.* The study of people (their physical characteristics and the ways they function) in relation to their working environment (the furnishings and machines they use). The goal of ergonomics is to incorporate comfort, efficiency, and safety into the design of keyboards, computer desks, chairs, and other items in the workplace.

Erlang *n.* A concurrent functional programming language. Originally developed for controlling telephone exchanges, Erlang is a general-purpose language best suited for applications where rapid development of complex systems and robustness are essential. Erlang has built-in support for concurrency, distribution, and fault tolerance. The most widely implemented version of Erlang is the open source version.

ERP *n.* *See* Enterprise Resource Planning.

error *n.* A value or condition that is not consistent with the true, specified, or expected value or condition. In computers, an error results when an event does not occur as expected or when impossible or illegal maneuvers are attempted. In data communications, an error occurs when there is a discrepancy between the transmitted and received data. *See also* critical error, error message, error rate, error ratio, fatal error, hard error, inherent error, intermittent error, logic error, machine error, overflow error, parity error. *Compare* fault.

error analysis *n.* The art and science of detecting errors in numeric calculations, especially in long and involved computations, where the possibility of errors increases.

error checking *n.* A method for detecting discrepancies between transmitted and received data during file transfer.

error control *n.* **1.** The section of a program, procedure, or function that checks for errors such as type mismatches, overflows and underflows, dangling or illegal pointer references, and memory-use inconsistencies. **2.** The process of anticipating program errors during software development.

error-correcting code *n.* *See* error-correction coding.

error-correction coding *n.* A method for encoding that allows for detection and correction of errors that occur during transmission. Data is encoded in such a way that transmission errors may be detected and corrected by examination of the encoded data on the receiving end. Most error-correction codes are characterized by the maximum number of errors they can detect and by the maximum number of errors they can correct. Error-correction coding is used by most modems. *Also called:* error-correcting code. *See also* error detection and correction. *Compare* error-detection coding.

error detection and correction *n.* A method for discovering and resolving errors during file transfer. Some programs only detect errors; others detect and attempt to fix them.

error-detection coding *n.* A method of encoding data so that errors that occur during storage or transmission can be detected. Most error-detection codes are characterized by the maximum number of errors they can detect. *See also* checksum. *Compare* error-correction coding.

error file *n.* A file that records the time and type of data processing and transmission errors.

error handling *n.* The process of dealing with errors (or exceptions) as they arise during the running of a program. Some programming languages, such as C++, Ada, and Eiffel, have features that aid in error handling. *See also* bug (definition 1).

error message *n.* A message from the system or program indicating that an error requiring resolution has occurred.

error rate *n.* In communications, the ratio of the number of bits or other elements that arrive incorrectly during transmission. For a 1200-bps modem, a typical error rate would be 1 in every 200,000 bits. *See also* parity, parity bit, Xmodem, Ymodem.

error ratio *n.* The ratio of errors to the number of units of data processed. *See also* error rate.

error trapping *n.* **1.** The process by which a program checks for errors during execution. **2.** The process of writing a function, program, or procedure such that it is capable of continuing execution despite an error condition.

escape character *n. See* ESC character.

escape code *n.* A character or sequence of characters that indicates that a following character in a data stream is not to be processed in the ordinary way. In the C programming language, the escape code is the backslash \.

Escape key *n.* A key on a computer keyboard that sends the escape (ESC) character to the computer. In many applications, the Escape key moves the user back one level in the menu structure or exits the program. See the illustration. *See also* Clear key.

Escape key.

escape sequence *n.* A sequence of characters that usually begins with the ESC character (ASCII 27, hexadecimal 1B), which is followed by one or more additional characters. An escape sequence escapes from the normal sequence of characters (such as text) and issues an instruction or command to a device or program.

ESC character *n.* One of the 32 control codes defined in the ASCII character set. It usually indicates the beginning of an escape sequence (a string of characters that give instructions to a device such as a printer). It is represented internally as character code 27 (hexadecimal 1B). *Also called:* escape character.

Esc key *n. See* Escape key.

ESD *n. See* electronic software distribution, electrostatic discharge.

ESDI *n.* Acronym for **E**nhanced **S**mall **D**evice **I**nterface. A device that allows disks to communicate with computers at high speeds. ESDI drives typically transfer data at about 10 megabits per second, but they are capable of doubling that speed. Although fast, ESDI has been superseded by interfaces such as SCSI and EIDE. *See also* EIDE, SCSI.

ESP *n. See* enhanced serial port.

ESP IEEE standard *n.* Short for **E**ncapsulating **S**ecurity **P**ayload **IEEE standard**. A standard for providing integrity and confidentiality to IP (Internet Protocol) datagrams. In some circumstances, it can also provide authentication to IP datagrams. *See also* authentication, datagram, IEEE, IP.

ESRB *n.* Acronym for **E**ntertainment **S**oftware **R**ating **B**oard. An independent, self-regulatory body providing ratings to the public and support to companies in the interactive software entertainment industry. The ESRB provides

E

ratings for computer games and other interactive products such as Web sites, online games, and interactive chat.

e-tail *n. See* e-commerce.

e-text *n.* Short for **electronic text**. A book or other text-based work that is available on line in an electronic media format. An e-text can be read online or downloaded to a user's computer for offline reading. *See also* e-zine.

Ethernet *n.* **1.** The IEEE 802.3 standard for contention networks. Ethernet uses a bus or star topology and relies on the form of access known as Carrier Sense Multiple Access with Collision Detection (CSMA/CD) to regulate communication line traffic. Network nodes are linked by coaxial cable, by fiberoptic cable, or by twisted-pair wiring. Data is transmitted in variable-length frames containing delivery and control information and up to 1500 bytes of data. The Ethernet standard provides for baseband transmission at 10 megabits (10 million bits) per second and is available in various forms, including those known as Thin Ethernet, Thick Ethernet, 10Base2, 10Base5, 10Base-F, and 10Base-T. The IEEE standard dubbed 802.3z, or Gigabit Ethernet, operates at 10 times 100 Mbps speed. *See also* ALOHAnet, baseband, bus network, coaxial cable, contention, CSMA/CD, Gigabit Ethernet, IEEE 802 standards, twisted-pair cable. **2.** A widely used local area network system developed by Xerox in 1976, from which the IEEE 802.3 standard was developed.

Ethernet/802.3 *n.* The IEEE standard for 10- or 100-Mbps transmissions over an Ethernet network. Ethernet/802.3 defines both hardware and data packet construction specifications. *See also* Ethernet.

E-time *n. See* execution time.

etiquette *n. See* netiquette.

ETX *n. See* end-of-text.

Eudora *n.* An e-mail client program originally developed as freeware for Macintosh computers by Steve Dorner at the University of Illinois, now maintained in both freeware and commercial versions for both Macintosh and Windows by Qualcomm, Inc.

EULA *n. See* End-User License Agreement.

Euphoria *n.* Acronym for **E**nd **U**ser **P**rogramming with **H**ierarchical **O**bjects for **R**obust **I**nterpreted **A**pplications. An interpreted programming language intended for general application development and game programming on MS-DOS, Windows, and Linux platforms.

European Computer Manufacturers Association *n. See* ECMA.

European Laboratory for Particle Physics *n. See* CERN.

EUV lithography *n.* Acronym for **E**xtreme **U**ltra**V**iolet **lithography**. Manufacturing process allowing smaller circuits to be etched onto chips than is possible with traditional lithographic techniques. With this process, it is possible to economically produce chips that are much faster than those that are created using traditional processes. In EUV lithography, the image of a map of circuits to appear on a chip is bounced off a series of mirrors that condense the image. The condensed image is projected onto wafers containing layers of metal, silicon, and photosensitive material. Because EUV light has a short wavelength, extremely intricate circuit patterns can be created on the wafers.

evaluation *n.* The determination, by a program, of the value of an expression or the action that a program statement specifies. Evaluation can take place at compile time or at run time.

even parity *n. See* parity.

event *n.* An action or occurrence, often generated by the user, to which a program might respond—for example, key presses, button clicks, or mouse movements. *See also* event-driven programming.

event-driven *adj.* Of, pertaining to, or being software that accomplishes its purpose by responding to externally caused events, such as the user pressing a key or clicking a button on a mouse. For example, an event-driven data entry form will allow the user to click on and edit any field at any time rather than forcing the user to step through a fixed sequence of prompts.

event-driven processing *n.* A program feature belonging to more advanced operating-system architectures such as the Apple Macintosh operating system, Windows, and UNIX. In times past, programs were required to interrogate, and effectively anticipate, every device that was expected to interact with the program, such as the keyboard, mouse, printer, disk drive, and serial port. Often, unless sophisticated programming techniques were used, one of two events happening at the same instant would be lost. Event processing solves this problem through the creation and maintenance of an event queue. Most common events that occur are appended to the event queue for the program to process in turn; however, certain types of events can preempt others if they have a higher priority.

An event can be of several types, depending on the specific operating system considered: pressing a mouse button or keyboard key, inserting a disk, clicking on a window, or receiving information from a device driver (as for managing the transfer of data from the serial port or from a network connection). *See also* autopolling, event, interrupt.

event-driven programming *n.* A type of programming in which the program constantly evaluates and responds to sets of events, such as key presses or mouse movements. Event-driven programs are typical of Apple Macintosh computers, although most graphical interfaces, such as Windows or the X Window System, also use such an approach. *See also* event.

event handler *n.* 1. A method within a program that is called automatically whenever a particular event occurs. 2. A core function in JavaScript that handles client-side events. It is the mechanism that causes a script to react to an event. For example, common JavaScript event handlers coded in Web pages include onClick, onMouseOver, and onLoad. When the user initiates the action, such as a mouse over, the event handler executes, or carries out, the desired outcome. 3. In Java applets, rather than having a specific starting point, the applet has a main loop where it waits for an event or series of events (keystroke, mouse click, and so on). Upon occurrence of the event, the event handler carries out the instructions specified. *See also* applet, client, JavaScript.

event horizon *n.* The time at which hardware or software began to have the potential to encounter a Year 2000 problem. For instance, the event horizon in an accounting system in a company whose fiscal year ended on June 30, 1999, would be six months dating from January 1, 1999. *Also called:* time horizon to failure.

event log *n.* A file that contains information and error messages for all activities on the computer.

event logging *n.* The process of recording an audit entry in the audit trail whenever certain events occur, such as starting and stopping, or users logging on and off and accessing resources. *See also* event, service.

event procedure *n.* A procedure automatically executed in response to an event initiated by the user or program code, or triggered by the system.

event property *n.* A characteristic or parameter of an object that you can use to respond to an associated event.

You can run a procedure or macro when an event occurs by setting the related event property.

e-wallet *n.* A program used in e-commerce that stores a customer's shipping and billing information to facilitate Web-based financial transactions. An e-wallet allows customers to instantly enter encrypted shipping and billing information when placing an order, rather than manually typing the information into a form on a Web page.

exa- *prefix* A prefix meaning 1 quintillion (10^{18}). In computing, which is based on the binary (base-2) numbering system, exa- has a literal value of 1,152,921,504,606,846,976, which is the power of 2 (2^{60}) closest to one quintillion. *Abbreviation:* E.

exabyte *n.* Roughly one quintillion bytes, or a billion billion bytes, or 1,152,921,504,606,846,976 bytes. *Abbreviation:* EB.

Excel *n.* Microsoft's spreadsheet software for Windows PCs and Macintosh computers. Excel is part of the family of Office products. The most recent version, part of Office XP, includes the ability to access and analyze live data from the Web by simply copying and pasting Web pages into Excel. The first version of Excel was introduced for the Macintosh in 1985. Excel for Windows was released in 1987.

exception *n.* In programming, a problem or change in conditions that causes the microprocessor to stop what it is doing and handle the situation in a separate routine. An exception is similar to an interrupt; both refer the microprocessor to a separate set of instructions. *See also* interrupt.

exception handling *n. See* error handling.

exchangeable disk *n. See* removable disk.

exchange sort *n. See* bubble sort.

Excite *n.* A World Wide Web search engine developed by Excite, Inc. After conducting a search, Excite provides both a summary of each matching Web site it has located and a link to more information of the same type.

exclusive NOR *n.* A two-state digital electronic circuit in which the output is driven high only if the inputs are all high or all low.

exclusive OR *n.* A Boolean operation that yields "true" if and only if one of its operands is true and the other is false. See the table. *Acronym:* EOR. *Also called:* XOR. *See also* Boolean operator, truth table. *Compare* AND, OR.

Table E.1   Exclusive OR.

a	b	a XOR b
0	0	0
0	1	1
1	0	1
1	1	0

E

.exe *n.* In MS-DOS, a filename extension that indicates that a file is an executable program. To run an executable program, the user types the filename without the .exe extension at the prompt and presses Enter. *See also* executable program.

executable[1] *adj.* Of, pertaining to, or being a program file that can be run. Executable files have extensions such as .bat, .com, and .exe.

executable[2] *n.* A program file that can be run, such as file0.bat, file1.exe, or file2.com.

executable program *n.* A program that can be run. The term usually applies to a compiled program translated into machine code in a format that can be loaded into memory and run by a computer's processor. In interpreter languages, an executable program can be source code in the proper format. *See also* code (definition 1), compiler (definition 2), computer program, interpreter, source code.

execute *vb.* To perform an instruction. In programming, execution implies loading the machine code of the program into memory and then performing the instructions.

execute in place *n.* The process of executing code directly from ROM, rather than loading it from RAM first. Executing the code in place, instead of copying the code into RAM for execution, saves system resources. Applications in other file systems, such as on a PC Card storage device, cannot be executed in this way. *Acronym:* XIP.

execution time *n.* The time, measured in clock ticks (pulses of a computer's internal timer), required by a microprocessor to decode and carry out an instruction after it is fetched from memory. *Also called:* E-time. *See also* instruction time.

executive *n.* The set of kernel-mode components that form the base operating system for Microsoft Windows NT or later. *See also* operating system.

executive information system *n.* A set of tools designed to organize information into categories and reports. Because it emphasizes information, an executive information system differs from a decision support system

(DSS), which is designed for analysis and decision making. *Acronym:* EIS. *Compare* decision support system.

exerciser *n.* A program that exercises a piece of hardware or software by running it through a large set of operations.

exit *vb.* In a program, to move from the called routine back to the calling routine. A routine can have more than one exit point, thus allowing termination based on various conditions.

expanded *adj.* A font style that sets characters farther apart than the normal spacing. *Compare* condensed.

expanded memory *n.* A type of memory, up to 8 MB, that can be added to IBM PCs. Its use is defined by the Expanded Memory Specification (EMS). Expanded memory is not accessible to programs in MS-DOS, so the Expanded Memory Manager (EMM) maps pages (blocks) of bytes from expanded memory into page frames in accessible memory areas. Expanded memory is not needed in Windows 9x, all versions of Windows NT, and Windows 2000. *See also* EEMS, EMS, Expanded Memory Manager, page frame.

Expanded Memory Manager *n.* A driver that implements the software portion of the Expanded Memory Specification (EMS) to make expanded memory in IBM and compatible PCs accessible. *Acronym:* EMM. *See also* EMS, expanded memory, extended memory.

Expanded Memory Specification *n. See* EMS.

expansion *n.* A way of increasing a computer's capabilities by adding hardware that performs tasks that are not part of the basic system. Expansion is usually achieved by plugging printed circuit boards (expansion boards) into openings (expansion slots) inside the computer. *See also* expansion board, expansion slot, open architecture (definition 2), PC Card, PCMCIA slot.

expansion board *n.* A circuit board that is plugged into a computer's bus (main data transfer path) to add extra functions or resources to the computer. Typical expansion boards add memory, disk drive controllers, video support, parallel and serial ports, and internal modems. For laptops and other portable computers, expansion boards come in credit card-sized devices called PC Cards that plug into a slot in the side or back of the computer. *Also called:* expansion board, extender board. *See also* expansion slot, PC Card, PCMCIA slot.

expansion bus *n.* A group of control lines that provide a buffered interface to devices. These devices can be located either on the system board or on cards that are plugged into expansion connectors. Common expansion buses included on the system board are USB, PC Card, and PCI. *See also* AT bus.

expansion card *n. See* card (definition 1), expansion board.

expansion slot *n.* A socket in a computer, designed to hold expansion boards and connect them to the system bus (data pathway). Expansion slots are a means of adding or enhancing the computer's features and capabilities. In laptop and other portable computers, expansion slots come in the form of PCMCIA slots designed to accept PC Cards. *See also* expansion board, PC Card, PCMCIA slot.

experience points *n.* Often used in role-playing games (RPGs), experience points are a way of measuring how much a player has experienced or learned. As a player moves through a game, additional benefits, often in the form of increased statistics or skills, are earned. These points are frequently spent or used by the player to increase his or her score. *See also* computer game, role-playing game.

expert system *n.* An application program that makes decisions or solves problems in a particular field, such as finance or medicine, by using knowledge and analytical rules defined by experts in the field. It uses two components, a knowledge base and an inference engine, to form conclusions. Additional tools include user interfaces and explanation facilities, which enable the system to justify or explain its conclusions as well as allowing developers to run checks on the operating system. *See also* artificial intelligence, inference engine, intelligent database, knowledge base.

expiration date *n.* The date on which a shareware, beta, or trial version of a program stops functioning, pending purchase of the full version or the entry of an access code.

expire *vb.* To stop functioning in whole or in part. Beta versions of software are often programmed to expire when a new version is released. *See also* beta[2].

Explicitly Parallel Instruction Computing *n. See* EPIC.

exploded view *n.* A form of display that shows a structure with its parts separated but depicted in relation to each other. See the illustration.

Top shell
Woven liner
Hub
Magnetic disk
Woven liner
Write-protect tab
Bottom shell
Lifter presses liners against disk to trap dust
Shutter spring
Shutter

Exploded view.

Explorer *n. See* Internet Explorer, Windows Explorer.

ExploreZip *n.* A destructive virus that attacks computers running Windows, where it first appears as an e-mail attachment named zipped_files.exe. ExploreZip affects local drives, mapped drives, and accessible network machines and destroys both document and source-code files by opening and immediately closing them, leaving a zero-byte file. Described as both a Trojan horse (because it requires the victim to open the attachment) and a worm (because it can propagate itself in certain instances), ExploreZip spreads by mailing itself to the return address of every unread e-mail in the inbox of the computer's e-mail program, as well as by searching for—and copying itself to—the Windows directory on mapped drives and networked machines. *See also* Trojan horse, virus, worm.

exponent *n.* In mathematics, a number that shows how many times a number is used as a factor in a calculation; in other words, an exponent shows that number's power. Positive exponents, as in 2^3, indicate multiplication (2 times 2 times 2). Negative exponents, as in 2^{-3}, indicate division (1 divided by 2^3). Fractional exponents, as in $8^{1/3}$, indicate the root of a number (the cube root of 8).

exponential notation *n. See* floating-point notation.

exponentiation *n.* The operation in which a number is raised to a given power, as in 2^3. In computer programs and programming languages, exponentiation is often shown by a caret (^), as in 2^3.

export *vb.* To move information from one system or program to another. Files that consist only of text can be exported in ASCII (plain text format). For files with graphics, however, the receiving system or program must offer some support for the exported file's format. *See also* EPS, PICT, TIFF. *Compare* import.

export *n.* In NFS, a file or folder made available to other network computers using the NFS mount protocol. *See also* NFS.

expression *n.* A combination of symbols—identifiers, values, and operators—that yields a result upon evaluation. The resulting value can then be assigned to a variable, passed as an argument, tested in a control statement, or used in another expression.

extended ASCII *n.* Any set of characters assigned to ASCII values between decimal 128 and 255 (hexadecimal 80 through FF). The specific characters assigned to the extended ASCII codes vary between computers and between programs, fonts, or graphics characters. Extended ASCII adds capability by allowing for 128 additional characters, such as accented letters, graphics characters, and special symbols. *See also* ASCII.

Extended Binary Coded Decimal Interchange Code *n. See* EBCDIC.

extended characters *n.* Any of the 128 additional characters in the extended ASCII (8-bit) character set. These characters include those used in several foreign languages, such as accent marks, and special symbols used for creating pictures. *See also* extended ASCII.

extended data out random access memory *n. See* EDO RAM.

Extended Edition *n.* A version of OS/2 with built-in database and communications facilities, developed by IBM. *See also* OS/2.

eXtended Graphics Array *n.* An advanced standard for graphics controller and display mode design, introduced by IBM in 1990. This standard supports 640 x 480 resolution with 65,536 colors, or 1024 x 768 resolution with 256 colors, and is used mainly on workstation-level systems. *Acronym:* XGA.

Extended Industry Standard Architecture *n. See* EISA.

extended memory *n.* System memory beyond 1 megabyte in computers based on the Intel 80x86 processors. This memory is accessible only when an 80386 or higher-level processor is operating in protected mode or in emulation on the 80286. To use extended memory, MS-DOS programs need the aid of software that temporarily places the processor into protected mode or by the use of features in the 80386 or higher-level processors to remap portions of extended memory into conventional memory. Extended memory is not an issue in Windows 9x, all versions of Windows NT, Windows 2000, and Windows XP. *See also* EMS, extended memory specification, protected mode.

extended memory specification *n.* A specification developed by Lotus, Intel, Microsoft, and AST Research that defines a software interface allowing real-mode applications to use extended memory and areas of memory not managed by MS-DOS. Memory is managed by an installable device driver, the Expanded Memory Manager (EMM). The application must use the driver to access the additional memory. *Acronym:* XMS. *See also* Expanded Memory Manager, extended memory.

extended VGA *n.* An enhanced set of Video Graphics Array (VGA) standards that is capable of displaying an image of from 800 x 600 pixels to 1600 x 1200 pixels and that can support a palette of up to 16.7 million (2^{24}) colors. This palette approaches the 19 million colors that a normal person can distinguish, so it is considered a digital standard for color realism that parallels analog television. *Also called:* Super VGA, SVGA. *See also* analog-to-digital converter, CRT, VGA.

extender board *n. See* expansion board.

eXtensible Firmware Interface *n.* In computers with the Intel Itanium processor, the interface between the operating system and the computer's low-level booting and initialization firmware. The interface is made up of data tables that contain platform-related information, plus boot and run-time service calls that are available to the operating system and its loader to provide a standard environment for booting an operating system and running pre-boot applications. *Acronym:* EFI.

Extensible Forms Description Language or **eXtensible Forms Description Language** *n. See* XFDL.

Extensible Hypertext Markup Language *n. See* XHTML.

extensible language *n.* A computer language that allows the user to extend or modify the syntax and semantics of the language. In the strict sense, the term relates to only a few of the languages actually used that allow the programmer to change the language itself, such as Forth. *See also* computer language, semantics (definition 1), syntax.

Extensible Markup Language or **eXtensible Markup Language** *n. See* XML.

extensible style language *n. See* XSL.

eXtensible Stylesheet Language *n. See* XSL.

eXtensible Stylesheet Language Formatting Objects *n. See* XSL-FO.

Extensible Stylesheets Language-Transformations *n. See* XSLT.

extension *n.* **1.** A set of characters added to a filename that serves to extend or clarify its meaning or to identify a file as a member of a category. An extension may be assigned by the user or by a program, as, for example, .com or .exe for executable programs that MS-DOS can load and run. **2.** A supplemental set of codes used to include additional characters in a particular character set. **3.** A program or program module that adds functionality to or extends the effectiveness of a program. **4.** On the Macintosh, a program that alters or augments the functionality of the operating system. There are two types: system extensions, such as QuickTime, and Chooser extensions, such as printer drivers. When a Macintosh is turned on, the extensions in the Extensions folder within the System folder are loaded into memory. *See also* Chooser extension, QuickTime, System folder.

Extension Manager *n.* A Macintosh utility developed by Apple that allows the user to determine which extensions are loaded when the computer is turned on. *See also* extension (definition 4).

extent *n.* On a disk or other direct-access storage device, a continuous block of storage space reserved by the operating system for a particular file or program.

exterior gateway protocol *n.* A protocol used by routers (gateways) on separate, independent networks for distributing routing information between and among themselves—for example, between hosts on the Internet. *Acronym:* EGP. *Also called:* external gateway protocol. *Compare* interior gateway protocol.

external command *n.* A program included in an operating system such as MS-DOS that is loaded into memory and executed only when its name is entered at the system prompt. Although an external command is a program in its own right, it is called a command because it is included with the operating system. *See also* XCMD. *Compare* internal command.

external function *n. See* XFCN.

External Gateway Protocol *n.* A protocol for distributing information regarding availability to the routers and gateways that interconnect networks. *Acronym:* EGP. *See also* gateway, router.

external gateway protocol *n. See* exterior gateway protocol.

external hard disk *n.* A free-standing hard disk with its own case and power supply, connected to the computer with a data cable and used mainly as a portable unit. *See also* hard disk.

external interrupt *n.* A hardware interrupt generated by hardware elements external to the microprocessor. *See also* hardware interrupt, internal interrupt, interrupt.

external modem *n.* A stand-alone modem that is connected via cable to a computer's serial port. *See also* internal modem.

external reference *n.* A reference in a program or routine to some identifier, such as code or data, that is not declared within that program or routine. The term usually refers to an identifier declared in code that is separately compiled. *See also* compile.

external storage *n.* A storage medium for data, such as a disk or tape unit, that is external to a computer's memory.

external viewer *n.* A separate application used to view documents that are of a type that cannot be handled by the current application. *See also* helper program.

extract *vb.* **1.** To remove or duplicate items from a larger group in a systematic manner. **2.** In programming, to derive one set of characters from another by using a mask (pattern) that determines which characters to remove.

extra-high-density floppy disk *n.* A 3.5-inch floppy disk capable of holding 4 MB of data and requiring a special disk drive that has two heads rather than one. *See also* floppy disk.

extranet *n.* An extension of a corporate intranet using World Wide Web technology to facilitate communication with the corporation's suppliers and customers. An extranet allows customers and suppliers to gain limited access to a company's intranet in order to enhance the speed and efficiency of their business relationship. *See also* intranet.

extrinsic semiconductor *n.* A semiconductor that conducts electricity due to a P-type or N-type impurity that allows electrons to flow under certain conditions, such as heat application, by forcing them to move out of their standard state to create a new band of electrons or electron gaps. *See also* N-type semiconductor, P-type semiconductor, semiconductor.

eyeballs *n.* The individuals or the number of individuals who view a Web site or its advertising.

e-zine or **ezine** *n.* Short for **e**lectronic maga**zine**. A digital publication available on the Internet, a bulletin board system (BBS), or other online service, often free of charge.

F *n. See* farad.

F2F *adv.* Short for **f**ace-**to**-**f**ace. In person, rather than over the Internet. The term is used in e-mail.

face *n.* **1.** In geometry and computer graphics, one side of a solid object, such as a cube. **2.** In printing and typography, short for *typeface*.

face time *n.* Time spent dealing face-to-face with another person, rather than communicating electronically.

facsimile *n. See* fax.

factor *n.* In mathematics, an item that is multiplied in a multiplication problem; for example, 2 and 3 are factors in the problem 2 x 3. The prime factors of a number are a set of prime numbers that, when multiplied together, produce the number.

factorial *n.* Expressed as $n!$ (n factorial), the result of multiplying the successive integers from 1 through n; $n!$ equals n x $(n - 1)$ x $(n - 2)$ x ... x 1.

failback *n.* In a cluster network system (one with two or more interconnected servers), the process of restoring resources and services to their primary server after they have been temporarily relocated to a backup system while repairs were implemented on the original host. *See also* cluster, failover.

failover *vb.* In a cluster network system (one with two or more interconnected servers), to relocate an overloaded or failed resource, such as a server, a disk drive, or a network, to its redundant, or backup, component. For example, when one server in a two-server system stops processing because of a power outage or other malfunction, the system automatically fails over to the second server, with little or no disruption to the users. *See also* cluster, failback.

fail-safe system *n.* A computer system designed to continue operating without loss of or damage to programs and data when part of the system breaks down or seriously malfunctions. *Compare* fail-soft system.

fail-soft system *n.* A computer system designed to fail gracefully over a period of time when an element of hardware or software malfunctions. A fail-soft system terminates nonessential functions and remains operating at a diminished capacity until the problem has been corrected. *Compare* fail-safe system.

failure *n.* The inability of a computer system or related device to operate reliably or to operate at all. A common cause of system failure is loss of power, which can be minimized with a battery-powered backup source until all devices can be shut down. Within a system, electronic failures generally occur early in the life of a system or component and can often be produced by burning in the equipment (leaving it turned on constantly) for a few hours or days. Mechanical failures are difficult to predict but are most likely to affect devices, such as disk drives, that have moving parts.

failure rate *n.* The number of failures in a specified time period. Failure rate is a means of measuring the reliability of a device, such as a hard disk. *See also* MTBF.

fair queuing *n.* A technique used to improve quality of service that gives each session flow passing through a network device a fair share of network resources. With fair queuing, no prioritization occurs. *Acronym:* FQ. *See also* quality of service, queuing. *Compare* weighted fair queuing.

fair use *n.* A legal doctrine describing the boundaries of legitimate use of copyrighted software or other published material.

fallout *n.* Any failure of components that occurs while equipment is being burned in, especially when the test is done at the factory. *See also* burn in (definition 1).

family *n.* A series of hardware or software products that have some properties in common, such as a series of personal computers from the same company, a series of CPU chips from the same manufacturer that all use the same instruction set, a set of 32-bit operating systems based on the same API (for example, Windows 95 and Windows 98), or a set of fonts that are intended to be used together, such as Times New Roman. *See also* central processing unit, font, instruction set, operating system.

fan[1] *n.* The cooling mechanism built into computer cabinets, laser printers, and other such devices to prevent malfunction due to heat buildup. Fans are the main source of the continuous humming associated with computers and other hardware.

fan[2] *vb.* To flip through a stack of printer paper to ensure that the pages are loose and will not stick together or jam the printer.

fanfold paper *n.* Paper with pin-feed holes on both margins designed to be fed into the tractor-feed mechanism of a printer, page by page, in a continuous, unbroken stream. *Also called:* z-fold paper.

fan-in *n.* The maximum number of signals that can be fed to a given electronic device, such as a logic gate, at one time without risking signal corruption. The fan-in rating of a device depends on its type and method of construction. *Compare* fan-out.

fan-out *n.* The maximum number of electronic devices that can be fed by a given electronic device, such as a logic gate, at one time without the signal becoming too weak. The fan-out rating of a device depends on its type and method of construction. *Compare* fan-in.

fanzine *n.* A magazine, distributed on line or by mail, that is produced by and devoted to fans of a particular group, person, or activity. *See also* ezine.

FAQ *n.* Acronym for **f**requently **a**sked **q**uestions. A document listing common questions and answers on a particular subject. FAQs are often posted on Internet newsgroups where new participants tend to ask the same questions that regular readers have answered many times.

farad *n.* The unit of capacitance (the ability to hold a charge). A 1-farad capacitor holds a charge of 1 coulomb with a potential difference of 1 volt between its plates. In practical use, a farad is an extremely large amount of capacitance; capacitance is usually expressed in terms of microfarads (10^{-6}) or picofarads (10^{-12}). *Abbreviation:* F.

FARNET *n. See* Federation of American Research Networks.

Fast Ethernet *n. See* 100BaseX.

fast Fourier transform *n.* A set of algorithms used to compute the discrete Fourier transform of a function, which in turn is used for solving series of equations, performing spectral analysis, and carrying out other signal-processing and signal-generation tasks. *Acronym:* FFT. *See also* Fourier transform.

fast infrared port *n. See* FIR port.

fast packet *n.* A standard for high-speed network technology that utilizes fast switching of fixed-length cells or packets for real-time transmission of data. *Also called:* Asynchronous Transfer Mode, ATM. *See also* packet (definition 2), packet switching.

fast packet switching *adj.* Of, describing, or pertaining to high-speed packet-switching networks that perform little or no error checking. The term is often, however, restricted to high-speed networking technologies, such as ATM, that transmit fixed-length cells rather than including those, such as frame relay, that transmit variable-length packets.

fast page-mode RAM *n. See* page mode RAM.

Fast SCSI *n.* A form of the SCSI-2 interface that can transfer data 8 bits at a time at up to 10 megabytes per second. The Fast SCSI connector has 50 pins. *Also called:* Fast SCSI-2. *See also* SCSI, SCSI-2. Compare Fast/Wide SCSI, Wide SCSI.

Fast/Wide SCSI *n.* A form of the SCSI-2 interface that can transfer data 16 bits at a time at up to 20 megabytes per second. The Fast/Wide SCSI connector has 68 pins. *Also called:* Fast/Wide SCSI-2. *See also* SCSI, SCSI-2. Compare Fast SCSI, Wide SCSI.

FAT *n. See* file allocation table.

fatal error *n.* An error that causes the system or application program to crash—that is, to fail abruptly with no hope of recovery.

fatal exception error *n.* A Windows message signaling that an unrecoverable error, one that causes the system to halt, has occurred. Data being processed when the error occurs is usually lost, and the computer must be rebooted. *See also* error handling.

fat application *n.* An application that can be used on both PowerPC processor–based Macintosh computers and 68K-based Macintosh computers.

fat binary *n.* An application format that supports both PowerPC processor–based Macintosh computers and 68K-based Macintosh computers.

fatbits *n.* **1.** Originally (as FatBits), a feature of the Apple MacPaint program in which a small portion of a drawing can be enlarged and modified one pixel (FatBit) at a time. **2.** A similar feature in any program that allows pixel-by-pixel modification through a zoom feature.

fat client *n.* In a client/server architecture, a client machine that performs most or all of the processing, with little or none performed by the server. The client handles presentation and functions, and the server manages data and access to it. *See also* client (definition 3), client/server architecture, server (definition 2), thin server. *Compare* fat server, thin client.

FAT file system *n.* The system used by MS-DOS to organize and manage files. The FAT (file allocation table) is a data structure that MS-DOS creates on the disk when the disk is formatted. When MS-DOS stores a file on a formatted disk, the operating system places information about the stored file in the FAT so that MS-DOS can retrieve the file later when requested. The FAT is the only file system MS-DOS can use; OS/2, Windows NT, and Windows 9x operating systems can use the FAT file system in addition to their own file systems (HPFS, NTFS, and VFAT, respectively). *See also* file allocation table, HPFS, NTFS, OS/2, VFAT, Windows.

father *n. See* generation (definition 1).

father file *n.* A file that is the last previously valid set of a changing set of data. The father file is immediately preceded by a grandfather file and immediately succeeded by its son. The pairs *father* and *son*, *parent* and *child* (or *descendant*), and *independent* and *dependent* are synonymous. *See also* generation (definition 1).

fat server *n.* In a client/server architecture, a server machine that performs most of the processing, with little or none performed by the client. Applications logic and data reside on the server, and presentation services are handled by the client. *See also* client (definition 3), client/server architecture, server (definition 2), thin client. *Compare* fat client, thin server.

fatware *n.* Software that monopolizes hard disk space and power due to an overabundance of features or inefficient design. *Also called:* bloatware.

fault *n.* **1.** A physical defect, such as a loose connection, that prevents a system or device from operating as it should. **2.** A programming error that can cause the software to fail. **3.** As page fault, an attempt to access a page of virtual memory that is not mapped to a physical address. *See also* page fault.

fault resilience *n. See* high availability.

fault tolerance *n.* The ability of a computer or an operating system to respond to a catastrophic event or fault, such as a power outage or a hardware failure, in a way that ensures that no data is lost and any work in progress is not corrupted. This can be accomplished with a battery-backed power supply, backup hardware, provisions in the operating system, or any combination of these. In a fault-tolerant network, the system has the ability either to continue the system's operation without loss of data or to shut the system down and restart it, recovering all processing that was in progress when the fault occurred.

favorite *n.* In Microsoft Internet Explorer, a user-defined shortcut to a page on the World Wide Web, analogous to a bookmark in Netscape Navigator. *See also* Favorites folder, hotlist. *Compare* bookmark (definition 2).

Favorites folder *n.* In Microsoft Internet Explorer, a collection of shortcuts to Web sites that a user has selected for future reference. Other Web browsers refer to this collection by other names, such as bookmarks or hotlists. *See also* bookmark file (definition 1), Internet Explorer, URL. *Compare* bookmark (definition 2), hotlist.

fax *n.* Short for **facs**imile. The transmission of text or graphics over telephone lines in digitized form. Conventional fax machines scan an original document, transmit an image of the document as a bit map, and reproduce the received image on a printer. Resolution and encoding are standardized in the CCITT Groups 1–4 recommendations. Fax images can also be sent and received by microcomputers equipped with fax hardware and software. *See also* CCITT Groups 1–4.

fax machine *n.* Short for **facs**imile **machine**. A device that scans pages, converts the images of those pages to a digital format consistent with the international facsimile standard, and transmits the image through a telephone line. A fax machine also receives such images and prints them on paper. *See also* scan (definition 2).

fax modem *n.* A modem that sends (and possibly receives) data encoded in a fax format (typically CCITT fax format), which a fax machine or another modem decodes and converts to an image. The image must already have been encoded on the host computer. Text and graphic documents can be converted into fax format by special software usually provided with the modem; paper documents must first be scanned in. Fax modems may be internal or external and may combine fax and conventional modem capabilities. *See also* fax, modem.

fax on demand *n.* An automated system that makes information available for request by telephone. When a request is made, the system faxes the information to the telephone number given in the request. *Acronym:* FOD.

fax program *n.* A computer application that allows the user to send, receive, and print fax transmissions. *See also* fax.

fax server *n.* A computer on a network capable of sending and receiving fax transmissions to and from other computers on the network. *See also* fax, server (definition 1).

FCB *n. See* file control block.

FCC *n.* Acronym for **F**ederal **C**ommunications Commission. The U.S. agency created by the Communications Act of 1934, which regulates interstate and international wire, radio, and other broadcast transmissions, including telephone, telegraph, and telecommunications.

F connector *n.* A coaxial connector, used primarily in video applications, that requires a screw-on attachment. See the illustration.

F connector.

FDDI *n.* Acronym for **F**iber **D**istributed **D**ata **I**nterface. A standard developed by the American National Standards Institute (ANSI) for high-speed fiber-optic LANs (local area networks). FDDI provides specifications for transmission rates of 100 megabits (100 million bits) per second on networks based on the token ring standard. *See also* token ring network.

FDDI II *n.* Acronym for **F**iber **D**istributed **D**ata **I**nterface. An extension of the FDDI standard, FDDI II contains additional specifications for the real-time transmission of analog data in digitized form for high-speed fiber-optic LANs (local area networks). *See also* FDDI.

FDHP *n.* Acronym for **F**ull **D**uplex **H**andshaking Protocol. A protocol used by duplex modems to determine the source type of the transmission and match it. *See also* duplex[1], handshake.

FDM *n.* Acronym for **F**requency **D**ivision **M**ultiplexing. A means of loading multiple transmission signals onto separate bands of a single communications channel so that all signals can be carried simultaneously. FDM is used in analog transmissions, as on a baseband network or in communications over a telephone line. In FDM the frequency

range of the channel is divided into narrower bands, each of which can carry a different transmission signal. For example, FDM might divide a voice channel with a frequency range of 1400 hertz (Hz) into four subchannels—820–990 Hz, 1230–1400 Hz, 1640–1810 Hz, and 2050–2220 Hz—with adjacent subchannels separated by a 240-Hz guard band to minimize interference.

FDMA *n.* Acronym for **F**requency **D**ivision **M**ultiple **A**ccess. A method of multiplexing in which the set of frequencies assigned to cellular phone service is divided into 30 separate channels, each of which can be used by a different caller. FDMA is the technology used in the AMPS phone service, which is widespread in North America and in other countries around the world. *See also* AMPS. *Compare* TDMA.

fear, uncertainty, and doubt *n. See* FUD.

feasibility study *n.* An evaluation of a prospective project for the purpose of determining whether or not the project should be undertaken. Feasibility studies normally consider the time, budget, and technology required for completion and are generally used in computing departments in large organizations.

feature *n.* A unique, attractive, or desirable property of a program or of a computer or other hardware.

feature extraction *n.* The selection of significant aspects of a computer image for use as guidelines in computerized pattern matching and image recognition. *See also* image processing.

featuritis *n.* Jargon for a tendency to add new features to a program at the expense of its original compact size or elegance. Creeping featuritis describes the accretion of feature upon feature over time, eventually resulting in a large, unwieldy, generally inelegant program that is, or appears to be, a collection of ad-hoc additions. The result of featuritis is a program condition known as software bloat. *Also called:* creeping featuritis, creeping featurism, feeping creaturism. *See also* bloatware.

February 30 *n. See* double leap year.

Federal Communications Commission *n. See* FCC.

Federal Information Processing Standards *n.* A system of standards, guidelines, and technical methods for information processing within the U.S. federal government. *Acronym:* FIPS.

Federal Internet Exchange *n. See* FIX.

federated database *n.* A database to which scientists contribute their findings and knowledge regarding a particular field or problem. A federated database is designed for scientific collaboration on problems of such scope that they are difficult or impossible for an individual to solve. *See also* database.

Federation of American Research Networks *n.* A nonprofit association of internetworking technology companies in the United States that serves as a national advocate for internetworking, with a primary focus on the education, research, and related communities. *Acronym:* FARNET. *See also* internetwork.

Federation on Computing in the United States *n.* The U.S. representative of the International Federation of Information Processing (IFIP). *Acronym:* FOCUS. *See also* IFIP.

feed[1] *n. See* news feed.

feed[2] *vb.* **1.** To advance paper through a printer. **2.** To supply media to a recording device, as by inserting disks into a disk drive.

feedback *n.* The return of a portion of system output as input to the same system. Often feedback is deliberately designed into a system, but sometimes it is unwanted. In electronics, feedback is used in monitoring, controlling, and amplifying circuitry.

feedback circuit *n.* Any circuit or system that returns (feeds back) a portion of its output to its input. A common example of a feedback system, although it is not completely electronic, is a thermostatically controlled household heating system. This self-limiting or self-correcting process is an example of negative feedback, in which changes in output are fed back to the source so that the change in the output is reversed. In positive feedback, an increase in output is fed back to the source, increasing the output further, which creates a snowballing effect. An example of unwanted positive feedback is the "screech" that occurs when the microphone of a public address system is brought too close to its loudspeaker.

feed scanner *n. See* sheet-fed scanner.

feeping creaturism *n. See* featuritis.

female connector *n.* A connector that has one or more receptacles for the insertion of pins. Female connector part

numbers often include an *F* (female), an *S* (socket), a *J* (jack), or an *R* (receptacle). For example, a female DB-25 connector might be labeled DB-25S or DB-25F. (Note that although the letter *F* can denote a female connector, it does not have that meaning in *F connector*, which is a type of coaxial cable connector.) See the illustration. *Compare* male connector.

Female connector.

femto- *prefix* Metric prefix meaning 10^{-15} (one quadrillionth).

femtosecond *n.* One quadrillionth (10^{-15}) of a second. *Abbreviation:* fs.

FEP *n. See* front-end processor.

ferric oxide *n.* The chemical substance $Fe2O3$, an oxide of iron used with a binding agent in the magnetic coating applied to disks and tapes for data storage.

ferric RAM *n. See* FRAM.

ferromagnetic domain *n. See* magnetic domain.

ferromagnetic material *n.* A substance that can become highly magnetized. Ferrite and powdered iron are ferromagnetic materials commonly used in electronics, for example, as cores for inductors to increase their inductance, and as part of the coating on floppy and hard disks and magnetic tape.

FET *n.* Acronym for field-effect transistor. A type of transistor in which the flow of current between the source and the drain is modulated by the electric field around the gate electrode. FETs are used as amplifiers, oscillators, and switches and are characterized by an extremely high input impedance (resistance) that makes them particularly suitable for amplification of very small signals. Types of FETs include the junction FET and the metal-oxide semiconductor FET (MOSFET). See the illustration. *See also* MOSFET.

FET. An N-channel junction field-effect transistor.

fetch *vb.* To retrieve an instruction or an item of data from memory and store it in a register. Fetching is part of the execution cycle of a microprocessor; first an instruction or item of data must be fetched from memory and loaded into a register, after which it can be executed (if it is an instruction) or acted upon (if it is data).

fetch time *n. See* instruction time.

FF *n. See* form feed.

FFT *n. See* fast Fourier transform.

FFTDCA *n. See* Final-Form-Text DCA.

Fiber Distributed Data Interface *n. See* FDDI.

fiberoptic cable or **fiber-optic cable** *n.* A form of cable used in networks that transmits signals optically, rather than electrically as do coaxial and twisted-pair cable. The light-conducting heart of a fiberoptic cable is a fine glass or plastic fiber called the core. This core is surrounded by a refractive layer called the cladding that effectively traps the light and keeps it bouncing along the central fiber. Outside both the core and the cladding is a final layer of plastic or plastic-like material called the coat, or jacket. Fiberoptic cable can transmit clean signals at speeds as high as 2 Gbps. Because it transmits light, not electricity, it is also immune to eavesdropping.

fiber optics *n.* A technology for the transmission of light beams along optical fibers. A light beam, such as that produced in a laser, can be modulated to carry information.

Because light has a higher frequency on the electromagnetic spectrum than other types of radiation, such as radio waves, a single fiber-optic channel can carry significantly more information than most other means of information transmission. Optical fibers are thin strands of glass or other transparent material, with dozens or hundreds of strands housed in a single cable. Optical fibers are essentially immune to electromagnetic interference. *See also* optical fiber.

fiber to the curb *n. See* FTTC.

fiber to the home *n. See* FTTH.

Fibonacci numbers *n.* In mathematics, an infinite series in which each successive integer is the sum of the two integers that precede it—for example, 1, 1, 2, 3, 5, 8, 13, 21, 34, ... Fibonacci numbers are named for the thirteenth-century mathematician Leonardo Fibonacci of Pisa. In computing, Fibonacci numbers are used to speed binary searches by repeatedly dividing a set of data into groups in accordance with successively smaller pairs of numbers in the Fibonacci sequence. For example, a data set of 34 items would be divided into one group of 21 and another of 13. If the item being sought is in the group of 13, the group of 21 is discarded, and the group of 13 is divided into groups of 5 and 8; the search would continue until the item was located. The ratio of two successive terms in the Fibonacci sequence converges on the Golden Ratio, a "magic number" that seems to represent the proportions of an ideal rectangle. The number describes many things, from the curve of a nautilus shell to the proportions of playing cards or, intentionally, the Parthenon, in Athens, Greece. *See also* binary search.

fiche *n. See* microfiche.

Fidonet *n.* **1.** A protocol for sending e-mail, newsgroup postings, and files over telephone lines. The protocol originated on the Fido BBS, initiated in 1984 by Tom Jennings, and maintaining low costs has been a factor in its subsequent development. Fidonet can exchange e-mail with the Internet. **2.** The network of BBSs, private companies, NGOs (nongovernment organizations), and individuals that use the Fidonet protocol.

field *n.* **1.** A location in a record in which a particular type of data is stored. For example, EMPLOYEE-RECORD might contain fields to store Last-Name, First-Name, Address, City, State, Zip-Code, Hire-Date, Current-Salary, Title, Department, and so on. Individual fields are characterized by their maximum length and the type of data (for example, alphabetic, numeric, or financial) that can be placed in them. The facility for creating these specifications usually is contained in the data definition language (DDL). In relational database management systems, fields are called *columns*. **2.** A space in an on-screen form where the user can enter a specific item of information.

field-effect transistor *n. See* FET.

field expansion *n. See* date expansion.

Field Programmable Gate Array *n. See* FPGA.

field-programmable logic array *n.* An integrated circuit containing an array of logic circuits in which the connections between the individual circuits, and thus the logic functions of the array, can be programmed after manufacture, typically at the time of installation in the field. Programming can be performed only once, typically by passing high current through fusible links on the chip. *Acronym:* FPLA. *Also called:* PLA, programmable logic array.

field separator *n.* Any character that separates one field of data from another. *See also* delimiter, field (definition 1).

FIFO *n. See* first in, first out.

fifth-generation computer *n. See* computer.

fifth normal form *n. See* normal form (definition 1).

file *n.* A complete, named collection of information, such as a program, a set of data used by a program, or a user-created document. A file is the basic unit of storage that enables a computer to distinguish one set of information from another. A file is the "glue" that binds a conglomeration of instructions, numbers, words, or images into a coherent unit that a user can retrieve, change, delete, save, or send to an output device.

file allocation table *n.* A table or list maintained by some operating systems to manage disk space used for file storage. Files on a disk are stored, as space allows, in fixed-size groups of bytes (characters) rather than from beginning to end as contiguous strings of text or numbers. A single file can thus be scattered in pieces over many separate storage areas. A file allocation table maps available disk storage space so that it can mark flawed segments that should not be used and can find and link the pieces of a file. In MS-DOS, the file allocation table is commonly known as the FAT. *See also* FAT file system.

file attribute *n.* A restrictive label attached to a file that describes and regulates its use—for example, hidden, sys-

tem, read-only, archive, and so forth. In MS-DOS, this information is stored as part of the file's directory entry.

file backup *n. See* backup.

file compression *n.* The process of reducing the size of a file for transmission or storage. *See also* data compression.

file control block *n.* A small block of memory temporarily assigned by a computer's operating system to hold information about an opened file. A file control block typically contains such information as the file's identification, its location on a disk, and a pointer that marks the user's current (or last) position in the file. *Acronym:* FCB.

file conversion *n.* The process of transforming the data in a file from one format to another without altering the data—for example, converting a file from a word processor's format to its ASCII equivalent. In some cases, information about the data, such as formatting, may be lost. Another, more detailed, type of file conversion involves changing character coding from one standard to another, as in converting EBCDIC characters (which are used primarily with mainframe computers) to ASCII characters. *See also* ASCII, EBCDIC.

file extension *n. See* extension (definition 1).

file extent *n. See* extent.

file format *n.* The structure of a file that defines the way it is stored and laid out on the screen or in print. The format can be fairly simple and common, as are files stored as "plain" ASCII text, or it can be quite complex and include various types of control instructions and codes used by programs, printers, and other devices. Examples include RTF (Rich Text Format), DCA (Document Content Architecture), PICT, DIF (Data Interchange Format), DXF (Data Exchange File), TIFF (Tagged Image File Format), and EPSF (Encapsulated PostScript Format).

file fragmentation *n.* **1.** The breaking apart of files as they are stored by the operating system into small, separate segments on disk. The condition is a natural consequence of enlarging files and saving them on a crowded disk that no longer contains contiguous blocks of free space large enough to hold them. File fragmentation is not an integrity problem, although it can eventually slow read and write access times if the disk is very full and storage is badly fragmented. Software products are available for redistributing (optimizing) file storage to reduce fragmentation. **2.** In a database, a situation in which records are not stored in their optimal access sequence because of accumulated additions and deletions of records. Most database

F

systems offer or contain utility programs that resequence records to improve efficiency of access and to aggregate free space occupied by deleted records.

file gap *n. See* block gap.

file handle *n.* In MS-DOS, OS/2, and Windows, a token (number) that the system uses to identify or refer to an open file or, sometimes, to a device.

file-handling routine *n.* Any routine designed to assist in creating, opening, accessing, and closing files. Most high-level languages have built-in file-handling routines, although more sophisticated or complex file-handling routines in an application are often created by the programmer.

file header *n. See* header (definition 2).

file layout *n.* In data storage, the organization of records within a file. Frequently, descriptions of the record structure are also included within the file layout.

file librarian *n.* A person or process responsible for maintaining, archiving, copying, and providing access to a collection of data.

file maintenance *n.* Broadly, the process of changing information in a file, altering a file's control information or structure, or copying and archiving files. A person using a terminal to enter data, the program accepting the data from the terminal and writing it to a data file, and a database administrator using a utility to alter the format of a database file are all forms of file maintenance.

file management system *n.* The organizational structure that an operating system or program uses to order and track files. For example, a hierarchical file system uses directories in a so-called tree structure. All operating systems have built-in file management systems. Commercially available products implement additional features that provide more sophisticated means of navigating, finding, and organizing files. *See also* file system, hierarchical file system.

file manager *n.* A module of an operating system or environment that controls the physical placement of and access to a group of program files.

file name *n.* The set of letters, numbers, and allowable symbols assigned to a file to distinguish it from all other files in a particular directory on a disk. A file name is the label under which a computer user saves and requests a block of information. Both programs and data have file names and often extensions that further identify the type or purpose of the file. Naming conventions, such as maxi-

mum length and allowable characters of a file name, vary from one operating system to another. *See also* directory, path (definition 5).

file name extension *n. See* extension (definition 1).

filename globbing *n.* A Linux command-line feature, available on most FTP servers, which allows a user to refer to sets of files without individually listing each file name. Filename globbing can be used to select or delete all files in a working directory with a single command. At the discretion of the user, globbing can match all files, or only those with filenames containing a specific character or range of characters. *See also* wildcard character.

file property *n.* A detail about a file that helps identify it, such as a descriptive title, the author name, the subject, or a keyword that identifies topics or other important information in the file.

file protection *n.* A process or device by which the existence and integrity of a file are maintained. Methods of file protection range from allowing read-only access and assigning passwords to covering the write-protect notch on a disk and locking away floppy disks holding sensitive files.

file recovery *n.* The process of reconstructing lost or unreadable files on disk. Files are lost when they are inadvertently deleted, when on-disk information about their storage is damaged, or when the disk is damaged. File recovery involves the use of utility programs that attempt to rebuild on-disk information about the storage locations of deleted files. Because deletion makes the file's disk space available but does not remove the data, data that has not yet been overwritten can be recovered. In the case of damaged files or disks, recovery programs read whatever raw data they can find, and save the data to a new disk or file in ASCII or numeric (binary or hexadecimal) form. In some instances, however, such reconstructed files contain so much extraneous or mixed information that they are unreadable. The best way to recover a file is to restore it from a backup copy.

file retrieval *n.* The act of accessing a data file and transferring it from a storage location to the machine where it is to be used.

file server *n.* A file-storage device on a local area network that is accessible to all users on the network. Unlike a disk server, which appears to the user as a remote disk drive, a file server is a sophisticated device that not only stores files but manages them and maintains order as network users request files and make changes to them. To deal with the tasks of handling multiple—sometimes simultaneous—requests for files, a file server contains a processor and controlling software as well as a disk drive for storage. On local area networks, a file server is often a computer with a large hard disk that is dedicated only to the task of managing shared files. *Compare* disk server.

File Server for Macintosh *n.* An AppleTalk network integration service that allows Macintosh clients and personal computers clients to share files. *Also called:* MacFile. *See also* Print Server for Macintosh, Services for Macintosh.

file sharing *n.* The use of computer files on networks, wherein files are stored on a central computer or a server and are requested, reviewed, and modified by more than one individual. When a file is used with different programs or different computers, file sharing can require conversion to a mutually acceptable format. When a single file is shared by many people, access can be regulated through such means as password protection, security clearances, or file locking to prohibit changes to a file by more than one person at a time.

file size *n.* The length of a file, typically given in bytes. A computer file stored on disk actually has two file sizes, logical size and physical size. The logical file size corresponds to the file's actual size—the number of bytes it contains. The physical size refers to the amount of storage space allotted to the file on disk. Because space is set aside for a file in blocks of bytes, the last characters in the file might not completely fill the block (allocation unit) reserved for them. When this happens, the physical size is larger than the logical size of the file.

filespec *n. See* file specification (definition 1).

file specification *n.* **1.** The path to a file, from a disk drive through a chain of directory files to the file name that serves to locate a particular file. Abbreviated filespec. **2.** A file name containing wildcard characters that indicate which files among a group of similarly named files are requested. **3.** A document that describes the organization of data within a file.

file structure *n.* A description of a file or group of files that are to be treated together for some purpose. Such a description includes file layout and location for each file under consideration.

file system *n.* In an operating system, the overall structure in which files are named, stored, and organized. A file system consists of files, directories, or folders, and the information needed to locate and access these items. The term can also refer to the portion of an operating system

that translates requests for file operations from an application program into low-level, sector-oriented tasks that can be understood by the drivers controlling the disk drives. *See also* driver.

file transfer *n.* The process of moving or transmitting a file from one location to another, as between two programs or over a network.

File Transfer Protocol *n. See* FTP[1] (definition 1).

file type *n.* A designation of the operational or structural characteristics of a file. A file's type is often identified in the file name, usually in the file name extension. *See also* file format.

fill[1] *n.* In computer graphics, the colored or patterned "paint" inside an enclosed figure, such as a circle. The portion of the shape that can be colored or patterned is the fill area. Drawing programs commonly offer tools for creating filled or nonfilled shapes; the user can specify color or pattern.

fill[2] *vb.* To add color or a pattern to the enclosed portion of a circle or other shape.

fill handle *n.* The small black square in the lower-right corner of a cell selection. When you point to the fill handle, the pointer changes to a black cross.

film at 11 *n.* A phrase sometimes seen in newsgroups. An allusion to a brief newsbreak on TV that refers to a top news story that will be covered in full on the 11 o'clock news, it is used sarcastically to ridicule a previous article's lack of timeliness or newsworthiness. *See also* newsgroup.

film recorder *n.* A device for capturing on 35-mm film the images displayed on a computer screen.

film ribbon *n. See* carbon ribbon.

filter *n.* **1.** A program or set of features within a program that reads its standard or designated input, transforms the input in some desired way, and then writes the output to its standard or designated output destination. A database filter, for example, might flag information of a certain age. **2.** In communications and electronics, hardware or software that selectively passes certain elements of a signal and eliminates or minimizes others. A filter on a communications network, for example, must be designed to transmit a certain frequency but attenuate (dampen) frequencies above it (a lowpass filter), those below it (a highpass filter), or those above and below it (a bandpass filter). **3.** A pattern or mask through which data is passed to weed out specified items. For instance, a filter used in e-mail or in retrieving newsgroup messages can allow users to filter out messages from other users. *See also* e-mail filter, mask. **4.** In computer graphics, a special effect or production effect that is applied to bitmapped images; for example, shifting pixels within an image, making elements of the image transparent, or distorting the image. Some filters are built into a graphics program, such as a paint program or an image editor. Others are separate software packages that plug into the graphics program. *See also* bitmapped graphics, image editor, paint program.

filtering program *n.* A program that filters information and presents only results that match the qualifications defined in the program.

FilterKeys *n.* A Windows 9x accessibility control panel feature that enables users with physical disabilities to use the keyboard. With FilterKeys, the system ignores brief and repeated keystrokes that result from slow or inaccurate finger movements. *See also* accessibility. *Compare* MouseKeys, ShowSounds, SoundSentry, StickyKeys, ToggleKeys.

Final-Form-Text DCA *n.* A standard in Document Content Architecture (DCA) for storing documents in ready-to-print form for interchange between dissimilar programs. A related standard is Revisable-Form-Text DCA (RFTDCA). *Acronym:* FFTDCA. *See also* DCA (definition 1). *Compare* Revisable-Form-Text DCA.

finally *n.* A keyword used in the Java programming language that executes a block of statements regardless of whether a Java exception, or run-time error, occurred in a previous block defined by the "try" keyword. *See also* block, exception, keyword, try.

find *vb. See* search[2].

Finder *n.* The standard interface to the Macintosh operating system. The Finder allows the user to view the contents of directories (folders); to move, copy, and delete files; and to launch applications. Items in the system are often represented as icons, and a mouse or similar pointing device is used to manipulate these items. The Finder was the first commercially successful graphical user interface, and it helped launch a wave of interest in icon-based systems. *See also* MultiFinder.

finger[1] *n.* An Internet utility, originally limited to UNIX but now available on many other platforms, that enables a user to obtain information on other users who may be at other sites (if those sites permit access by finger). Given an e-mail address, finger returns the user's full name, an indication of whether or not the user is currently logged

on, and any other information the user has chosen to supply as a profile. Given a first or last name, finger returns the logon names of users whose first or last names match.

finger[2] *vb.* To obtain information on a user by means of the finger program.

fingerprint[1] *vb.* To scan a computer system to discover what operating system (OS) the computer is running. By detecting a computer's OS through fingerprinting, a hacker is better able to specify attacks on system vulnerabilities and therefore better able to plan an attack on that system. A hacker may use several different fingerprinting schemes separately and in tandem to pinpoint the OS of a target computer.

fingerprint[2] *n.* Information embedded or attached to a file or image to uniquely identify it. *Compare* digital watermark.

fingerprint reader *n.* A scanner that reads human fingerprints for comparison to a database of stored fingerprint images.

fingerprint recognition *n.* A technology used to control access to a computer, network, or other device or to a secure area through a user's fingerprints. The patterns of an individual's fingers are scanned by a fingerprint reader or similar device and matched with stored images of fingerprints before access is granted. *See also* biometric.

FIPS *n. See* Federal Information Processing Standards.

FIPS 140-1 *n.* Acronym for **F**ederal **I**nformation **P**rocessing **S**tandard 140-1. A U.S. Government standard, issued by the National Institute of Standards and Technology (NIST), entitled Security Requirements for Cryptographic Modules. FIPS 140-1 defines four levels of security requirements related to cryptographic hardware and software modules within computer and telecommunications systems used for sensitive but unclassified data. The four security levels range from basic module design through increasingly stringent levels of physical security. The standard covers such security-related features as hardware and software security, cryptographic algorithms, and management of encryption keys. FIPS 140-1 products can be validated for federal use in both the United States and Canada after independent testing under the Cryptographic Module Validation (CMV) Program, developed and jointly adopted by NIST and the Canadian Communication Security Establishment. *See also* cryptography.

firewall *n.* A security system intended to protect an organization's network against external threats, such as hackers, coming from another network, such as the Internet.

Usually a combination of hardware and software, a firewall prevents computers in the organization's network from communicating directly with computers external to the network and vice versa. Instead, all communication is routed through a proxy server outside of the organization's network, and the proxy server decides whether it is safe to let a particular message or file pass through to the organization's network. *See also* proxy server.

firewall sandwich *n.* The use of load-balancing appliances on both sides of Internetworked firewalls to distribute both inbound and outbound traffic among the firewalls. The firewall sandwich architecture helps to prevent firewalls from degrading network performance and creating a single point of network failure. *See also* firewall, load balancing.

FireWire *n.* A high-speed serial bus from Apple that implements the IEEE 1394 standard. *See also* IEEE 1394.

firmware *n.* Software routines stored in read-only memory (ROM). Unlike random access memory (RAM), read-only memory stays intact even in the absence of electrical power. Startup routines and low-level input/output instructions are stored in firmware. It falls between software and hardware in terms of ease of modification. *See also* RAM, ROM.

FIR port *n.* Short for **f**ast **i**nfrared **port**. A wireless I/O port, most common on a portable computer, that exchanges data with an external device using infrared light. *See also* infrared, input/output port.

FIRST *n.* Acronym for **F**orum of **I**ncident **R**esponse and **S**ecurity **T**eams. An organization within the Internet Society (ISOC) that coordinates with CERT in order to encourage information sharing and a unified response to security threats. *See also* CERT, Internet Society.

first-generation computer *n. See* computer.

first in, first out *n.* A method of processing a queue, in which items are removed in the same order in which they were added—the first in is the first out. Such an order is typical of a list of documents waiting to be printed. *Acronym:* FIFO. *See also* queue. *Compare* last in, first out.

first normal *n. See* normal form (definition 1).

fishbowl *n.* A secure area within a computer system in which intruders can be contained and monitored. A fishbowl is typically set up by a security administrator to impersonate important applications or information so that the system administrator can learn more about hackers who have broken into the network without the hacker learning more about or damaging the system. *See also* honeypot.

fitting *n.* The calculation of a curve or other line that most closely approximates a set of data points or measurements. *See also* regression analysis.

five-nines availability *n.* The availability of a system 99.999 percent of the time. *See also* high availability.

FIX *n.* Acronym for **F**ederal **I**nternet **E**xchange. A connection point between the U.S. government's various internets and the Internet. There are two Federal Internet Exchanges: FIX West, in Mountain View, California; and FIX East, in College Park, Maryland. Together, they link the backbones of MILNET, ESnet (the TCP/IP network of the Department of Energy), and NSInet (NASA Sciences Internet) with NSFnet. *See also* backbone (definition 1), MILNET, NSFnet, TCP/IP.

fixed disk *n. See* hard disk.

fixed-length field *n.* In a record or in data storage, a field whose size in bytes is predetermined and constant. A fixed-length field always takes up the same amount of space on a disk, even when the amount of data stored in the field is small. *Compare* variable-length field.

fixed-pitch spacing *n. See* monospacing.

fixed-point arithmetic *n.* Arithmetic performed on fixed-point numbers. *See also* fixed-point notation.

fixed-point notation *n.* A numeric format in which the decimal point has a specified position. Fixed-point numbers are a compromise between integral formats, which are compact and efficient, and floating-point numeric formats, which have a great range of values. Like floating-point numbers, fixed-point numbers can have a fractional part, but operations on fixed-point numbers usually take less time than floating-point operations. *See also* floating-point notation, integer.

fixed space *n.* A set amount of horizontal space used to separate characters in text—often, the width of a numeral in a given font. *See also* em space, en space, thin space.

fixed spacing *n. See* monospacing.

fixed storage *n.* Any nonremovable storage, such as a large disk that is sealed permanently in its drive.

fixed-width font *n. See* monospace font.

fixed-width spacing *n. See* monospacing.

F

fixed-word-length computer *n.* A description that applies to almost all computers and refers to the uniform size of the data units, or words, that are processed by the microprocessor and shuttled through the system over the hardware lines composing the main data bus. Fixed-word-length computers, including IBM and Macintosh personal computers, commonly work with 2 or 4 bytes at a time.

F keys *n. See* function key.

flag *n.* **1.** Broadly, a marker of some type used by a computer in processing or interpreting information; a signal indicating the existence or status of a particular condition. Flags are used in such areas as communications, programming, and information processing. Depending on its use, a flag can be a code, embedded in data, that identifies some condition, or it can be one or more bits set internally by hardware or software to indicate an event of some type, such as an error or the result of comparing two values. **2.** In the HDLC communications protocol, a flag is the unique series of bits 01111110, used to start and end a transmission frame (message unit). *See also* HDLC.

flame[1] *n.* An abusive or personally insulting e-mail message or newsgroup posting.

flame[2] *vb.* **1.** To send an abusive or personally insulting e-mail message or newsgroup posting. **2.** To criticize personally by means of e-mail messages or newsgroup postings.

flame bait *n.* A posting to a mailing list, newsgroup, or other online conference that is likely to provoke flames, often because it expresses a controversial opinion on a highly emotional topic. *See also* flame[1], flame war. *Compare* troll.

flamefest *n.* A series of inflammatory messages or articles in a newsgroup or other online conference.

flamer *n.* A person who sends or posts abusive messages via e-mail, in newsgroups and other online forums, and in online chats. *See also* chat[1] (definition 1), newsgroup.

flame war *n.* A discussion in a mailing list, newsgroup, or other online conference that has turned into a protracted exchange of flames. *See also* flame[1].

Flash *n.* A vector graphics file format (extension .swf) developed by Macromedia to enable designers to add animation and interactivity to multimedia Web pages. Flash files can be played back with a downloadable Shockwave plug-in or a Java program. The file format has been released by Macromedia as an open standard for the Internet.

flash *vb. See* burn.

flash memory *n.* A type of nonvolatile memory. Flash memory is similar to EEPROM memory in function but it must be erased in blocks, whereas EEPROM can be erased one byte at a time. Because of its block-oriented nature, flash memory is commonly used as a supplement to or replacement for hard disks in portable computers. In this context, flash memory either is built into the unit or, more commonly, is available as a PC Card that can be plugged into a PCMCIA slot. A disadvantage of the block-oriented nature of flash memory is that it cannot be practically used as main memory (RAM) because a computer needs to be able to write to memory in single-byte increments. *See also* EEPROM, nonvolatile memory, PC Card, PCMCIA slot.

flash ROM *n. See* flash memory.

flat address space *n.* An address space in which each location in memory is specified by a unique number. (Memory addresses start at 0 and increase sequentially by 1.) The Macintosh operating system, OS/2, and Windows NT use a flat address space. MS-DOS uses a segmented address space, in which a location must be accessed with a segment number and an offset number. *See also* segmentation. *Compare* segmented address space.

flatbed plotter *n.* A plotter in which paper is held on a flat platform and a pen moves along both axes, traveling across the paper to draw an image. This method is slightly more accurate than that used by drum plotters, which move the paper under the pen, but requires more space. Flatbed plotters can also accept a wider variety of media, such as vellum and acetate, because the material does not need to be flexible. *See also* plotter. *Compare* drum plotter, pinch-roller plotter.

flatbed scanner *n.* A scanner with a flat, transparent surface that holds the image to be scanned, generally a book or other paper document. A scan head below the surface moves across the image. Some flatbed scanners can also reproduce transparent media, such as slides. See the illustration. *Compare* drum scanner, handheld scanner, sheet-fed scanner.

Flatbed scanner.

flat file *n.* A file consisting of records of a single record type in which there is no embedded structure information that governs relationships between records.

flat-file database *n.* A database that takes the form of a table, where only one table can be used for each database. A flat-file database can only work with one file at a time. *Compare* relational database.

flat file directory *n.* A directory that cannot contain subdirectories but simply contains a list of file names. *Compare* hierarchical file system.

flat file format *n.* An image file format in which individual objects cannot be edited. Files stored in JPEG, GIF, and BMP formats, for example, are all flat files.

flat file system *n.* A filing system with no hierarchical order in which no two files on a disk may have the same name, even if they exist in different directories. *Compare* hierarchical file system.

flat memory *n.* Memory that appears to a program as one large addressable space, whether consisting of RAM or virtual memory. The 68000 and VAX processors have flat memory; by contrast, 80x86 processors operating in real mode have segmented memory, although when these processors operate in protected mode, OS/2 and 32-bit versions of Windows access memory using a flat memory model. *Also called:* linear memory.

flat pack *n.* An integrated circuit housed in a flat rectangular package with connecting leads along the edges of the package. The flat pack was a precursor of surface-mounted chip packaging. *See also* surface-mount technology. *Compare* DIP (definition 1).

flat-panel display *n.* A video display with a shallow physical depth, based on technology other than the CRT (cathode-ray tube). Such displays are typically used in lap-top computers. Common types of flat-panel displays are the electroluminescent display, the gas discharge display, and the LCD display.

flat panel monitor *n.* A desktop computer monitor that uses a liquid crystal display (LCD) rather than a cathode ray tube (CRT) to display data. Flat panel monitors are not as deep as CRT monitors and so occupy much less physical space.

flat screen *n. See* flat-panel display.

flatten *vb.* In digital graphic creation and manipulation programs, to combine all layers of text, images, and other graphic elements into a single layer. Elements cannot be edited after the graphic is flattened, so a graphic is not usually flattened until the final step when all adjustments have been made to the individual layers. Flattening an image significantly reduces its file size and allows it to be saved in a wider range of formats. Flattening is similar to grouping in that both actions combine a set of objects. However, flattening is a permanent action, whereas a group of objects can be ungrouped. *See also* layering.

flavor *n.* One of several varieties of a system, having its own details of operation. UNIX in particular is found in distinct flavors, such as BSD UNIX or AT&T UNIX System V.

flex circuit *n.* A circuit printed on a thin sheet of flexible polymer film that can be used in applications requiring circuits to curve and bend. Flex circuits offer space and weight savings over traditional circuits, and are used extensively for medical, industrial, and telecommunications applications.

flexible disk *n. See* floppy disk.

flexible transistor *n. See* plastic transistor.

flicker *n.* Rapid, visible fluctuation in a screen image, as on a television or computer monitor. Flicker occurs when the image is refreshed (updated) too infrequently or too slowly for the eye to perceive a steady level of brightness. In television and raster-scan displays, flicker is not noticeable when the refresh rate is 50 to 60 times per second. Interlaced displays, in which the odd-numbered scan lines are refreshed on one sweep and even-numbered lines on the other, achieve a flicker-free effective refresh rate of 50 to 60 times per second because the lines appear to merge, even though each line is actually updated only 25 to 30 times per second.

F

flies *n.* In Web development and marketing, individuals who spend significant time on the Web and who are the targets of specific Web content or advertising.

flight simulator *n.* A computer-generated recreation of the experience of flying. Sophisticated flight simulators costing hundreds of thousands of dollars can provide pilot training, simulating emergency situations without putting human crews and planes at risk. Flight simulator software running on personal computers simulates flight in a less realistic fashion; it provides entertainment and practice in navigation and instrument reading.

flip-flop *n.* A circuit that alternates between two possible states when a pulse is received at the input. For example, if the output of a flip-flop is high and a pulse is received at the input, the output "flips" to low; a second input pulse "flops" the output back to high, and so on. *Also called:* bistable multivibrator.

flippy-floppy *n.* An outmoded 5.25-inch floppy disk that uses both sides for storage but is used in an older drive that can read only one side at a time. Thus, to access the opposite side, the disk must be physically removed from the drive and flipped over. *See also* double-sided disk.

float *n.* The data type name used in some programming languages, notably C, to declare variables that can store floating-point numbers. *See also* data type, floating-point number, variable.

floating-point arithmetic *n.* Arithmetic performed on floating-point numbers. *See also* floating-point notation, floating-point number.

floating-point constant *n.* A constant representing a real, or floating-point, value. *See also* constant, floating-point notation.

floating-point notation *n.* A numeric format that can be used to represent very large real numbers and very small real numbers. Floating-point numbers are stored in two parts, a mantissa and an exponent. The mantissa specifies the digits in the number, and the exponent specifies the magnitude of the number (the position of the decimal point). For example, the numbers 314,600,000 and 0.0000451 are expressed respectively as 3146E5 and 451E-7 in floating-point notation. Most microprocessors do not directly support floating-point arithmetic; consequently, floating-point calculations are performed either by using software or with a special floating-point processor. *Also called:* exponential notation. *See also* fixed-point notation, floating-point processor, integer.

floating-point number *n.* A number represented by a mantissa and an exponent according to a given base. The mantissa is usually a value between 0 and 1. To find the value of a floating-point number, the base is raised to the power of the exponent, and the mantissa is multiplied by the result. Ordinary scientific notation uses floating-point numbers with 10 as the base. In a computer, the base for floating-point numbers is usually 2.

floating-point operation *n.* An arithmetic operation performed on data stored in floating-point notation. Floating-point operations are used wherever numbers may have either fractional or irrational parts, as in spreadsheets and computer-aided design (CAD). Therefore, one measure of a computer's power is how many millions of floating-point operations per second (MFLOPS or megaflops) it can perform. *Acronym:* FLOP. *Also called:* floating-point operation. *See also* floating-point notation, MFLOPS.

floating-point processor *n.* A coprocessor for performing arithmetic on floating-point numbers. Adding a floating-point processor to a system can speed up the processing of math and graphics dramatically if the software is designed to recognize and use it. The i486DX and 68040 and higher microprocessors have built-in floating-point processors. *Also called:* math coprocessor, numeric coprocessor. *See also* floating-point notation, floating-point number.

floating-point register *n.* A register designed to store floating-point values. *See also* floating-point number, register.

flooding *n.* The networking technique of forwarding a frame onto all ports of a switch except the port on which it arrived. Flooding can be used for robust data distribution and route establishment. *Also called:* flood routing.

FLOP *n.* *See* floating-point operation.

floppy disk *n.* A round piece of flexible plastic film coated with ferric oxide particles that can hold a magnetic field. When placed inside a disk drive, the floppy disk rotates to bring different areas, or sectors, of the disk surface under the drive's read/write head, which can detect and alter the orientation of the particles' magnetic fields to represent binary 1s and 0s. A floppy disk 5.25 inches in diameter is encased in a flexible plastic jacket and has a large hole in the center, which fits around a spindle in the disk drive; such a disk can hold from a few hundred thousand to over one million bytes of data. A 3.5-inch disk encased in rigid plastic is also called a floppy disk or a microfloppy disk. In addition, 8-inch floppy disks were common in DEC and other minicomputer systems. *See also* microfloppy disk.

floppy disk controller *n. See* disk controller.

floppy disk drive *n.* An electromechanical device that reads data from and writes data to floppy or microfloppy disks. See the illustration. *See also* floppy disk.

Floppy disk drive

Floppy disk drive.

FLOPS *n.* Acronym for **fl**oating-point **o**perations **p**er second. A measure of the speed at which a computer can perform floating-point operations. *See also* floating-point operation, MFLOPS. *Compare* MIPS.

floptical *adj.* Using a combination of magnetic and optical technology to achieve a very high data density on special 3.5-inch disks. Data is written to and read from the disk magnetically, but the read/write head is positioned optically by means of a laser and grooves on the disk.

flow analysis *n.* A method of tracing the movement of different types of information through a computer system, especially with regard to security and the controls applied to ensure the integrity of the information. *See also* flowchart.

flowchart *n.* A graphic map of the path of control or data through the operations in a program or an information-handling system. Symbols such as squares, diamonds, and ovals represent various operations. These symbols are connected by lines and arrows to indicate the flow of data or control from one point to another. Flowcharts are used both as aids in showing the way a proposed program will work and as a means of understanding the operations of an existing program. See the illustration.

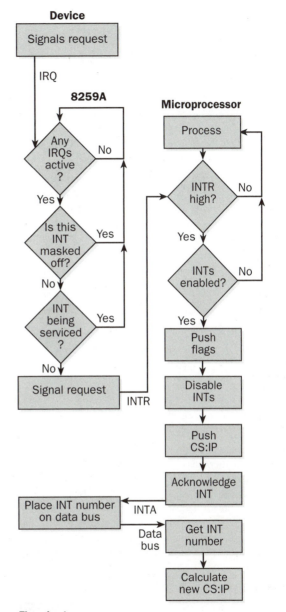

Flowchart.

flow control *n.* The management of data flow in a network to ensure that the receiver can handle all the incoming data. Flow-control mechanisms, implemented in both hardware and software, prevent a sender of traffic from sending it faster than the receiver can receive it.

F

flush[1] *adj.* Aligned in a certain way on the screen or on paper. Flush left, for example, means aligned on the left side; flush right means aligned on the right side. *See also* align (definition 1).

flush[2] *vb.* To clear a portion of memory. For example, to flush a disk file buffer is to save its contents on disk and then clear the buffer for filling again.

flux *n.* **1.** The total strength of a magnetic, electric, or radiation field over a given area. **2.** A chemical used to aid the binding of solder to electrical conductors.

flux reversal *n.* The change in orientation of the minute magnetic particles on the surface of a disk or tape toward one of two magnetic poles. The two different alignments are used to represent binary 1 and binary 0 for data storage: a flux reversal typically represents a binary 1, and no reversal represents a binary 0.

fly swapping *n. See* swap-on-the-fly.

FM *n. See* frequency modulation.

FM encoding *n. See* frequency modulation encoding.

focus *vb.* In television and raster-scan displays, to make an electron beam converge at a single point on the inner surface of the screen.

FOCUS *n. See* Federation on Computing in the United States.

FOD *n. See* fax on demand.

folder *n.* In the Mac OS, 32-bit versions of Windows, and other operating systems, a container for programs and files in graphical user interfaces, symbolized on the screen by a graphical image (icon) of a file folder. This container is called a directory in other systems, such as MS-DOS and UNIX. A folder is a means of organizing programs and documents on a disk and can hold both files and additional folders. It first appeared commercially in Apple Computer's Lisa in 1983 and in the Apple Macintosh in 1984. *See also* directory.

folio *n.* A printed page number.

follow-up *n.* A post to a newsgroup that replies to an article. The follow-up has the same subject line as the original article, with the prefix "Re:" attached. An article and all of its follow-ups, in the order they were received, constitute a thread, which a user can read together using a newsreader.

font *n.* A set of characters of the same typeface (such as Garamond), style (such as italic), and weight (such as bold).

A font consists of all the characters available in a particular style and weight for a particular design; a typeface consists of the design itself. Fonts are used by computers for on-screen displays and by printers for hard-copy output. In both cases, the fonts are stored either as bit maps (patterns of dots) or as outlines (defined by a set of mathematical formulas). Even if the system cannot simulate different typefaces on the screen, application programs may be able to send information about typeface and style to a printer, which can then reproduce the font if a font description is available. *See also* bit map, font generator.

font card *n. See* font cartridge, ROM card.

font cartridge *n.* A plug-in unit available for some printers that contains fonts in several different styles and sizes. Font cartridges, like downloadable fonts, enable a printer to produce characters in sizes and styles other than those created by the fonts built into it. *Also called:* font card. *See also* ROM cartridge.

Font/DA Mover *n.* An application for older Apple Macintosh systems that allows the user to install screen fonts and desk accessories.

font editor *n.* A utility program that enables the user to modify existing fonts or to create and save new ones. Such an application commonly works with a screen representation of the font, with a representation that can be downloaded to a PostScript or other printer, or with both. *See also* PostScript font, screen font.

font family *n.* The set of available fonts representing variations of a single typeface. For example, Times Roman and Times Roman Italic are members of the same font family. When the user indicates italic, the system selects the correct italic font for the font family, with its characteristic appearance. If there is no italic font in the family, the system simply slants, or "obliques," the corresponding roman character. *See also* italic, roman.

font generator *n.* A program that transforms built-in character outlines into bit maps (patterns of dots) of the style and size required for a printed document. Font generators work by scaling a character outline to size; often they can also expand or compress the characters they generate. Some font generators store the resultant characters on disk; others send them directly to the printer.

font number *n.* The number by which an application or operating system internally identifies a given font. On the Apple Macintosh, for example, fonts can be identified by their exact names as well as their font numbers, and a font number can be changed if the font is installed in a system already having a font with that number. *See also* font.

font page *n.* A portion of video memory reserved for holding programmer-specified character definition tables (sets of character patterns) used for displaying text on the screen on IBM Multi-Color Graphics Array video systems.

font size *n.* The point size of a set of characters in a particular typeface. *See also* point[1] (definition 1).

font suitcase *n.* A file on Macintosh computers that contains one or more fonts or desk accessories. Such files are indicated in early versions of the operating system with the icon of a suitcase marked with a capital A. From System 7.0 onward, this icon is used to denote individual fonts.

foo *n.* A string used by programmers in place of more specific information. Variables or functions in code examples intended to demonstrate syntax, as well as temporary scratch files, may all appear with the name *foo*. Likewise, a programmer may type *foo* to test a string input handler. If a second placeholder string is needed, it will often be *bar*, suggesting that the origin of both is the U.S. Army phrase FUBAR (an acronym which, in discreet language, represents Fouled Up Beyond All Recognition/Repair). However, other origins have been claimed. *Compare* fred (definition 2).

footer *n.* One or more identifying lines printed at the bottom of a page. A footer may contain a folio (page number), a date, the author's name, and the document title. *Also called:* running foot. *Compare* header (definition 1).

footprint *n.* The surface area occupied by a personal computer or other device.

force *vb.* In programming, to perform a particular action that would normally not occur. The term is most often used in the context of forcing data to be within a particular range of values—for example, forcing a divisor to be nonzero. *See also* cast.

force feedback *n.* A technology that generates push or resistance in an input/output device. Force feedback enables an input/output device, such as a joystick or a steering wheel, to react to the user's action in appropriate response to events displayed on the screen. For example, force feedback can be used with a computer game to react to a plane rising in a steep ascent or a race car turning a tight corner. *See also* input/output device.

foreground[1] *adj.* Currently having control of the system and responding to commands issued by the user. *See also* multitasking. *Compare* background[1].

foreground[2] *n.* **1.** The color of displayed characters and graphics. *Compare* background[2] (definition 1). **2.** The condition of the program or document currently in control and affected by commands and data entry in a windowing environment. *Compare* background[2] (definition 4).

forest *n.* A collection of one or more domains in Microsoft Windows that share a common schema, configuration, and global catalog and are linked with two-way transitive trusts. *See also* domain, global catalog, schema, transitive trust, two-way trust.

fork[1] *n.* One of the two parts of a file recognized by the Mac OS. A Macintosh file has a data fork and a resource fork. Most or all of a typical user-produced document is in the data fork; the resource fork usually contains application-oriented information, such as fonts, dialog boxes, and menus. *See also* data fork, resource fork.

fork[2] *vb.* To initiate a child process in a multitasking system after a parent process has been started. *See also* multitasking.

fork bomb *n.* In UNIX-based systems, a program or shell script that locks up the system by recursively spawning copies of itself using the Unix system call "fork(2)" until they occupy all the process table entries. *Also called:* logic bomb.

FOR loop *n.* A control statement that executes a section of code a specified number of times. Actual syntax and usage vary from language to language. In most cases, the value of an index variable moves through a range of values, being assigned a different (and usually consecutive) value each time the program moves through the section of code. *See also* iterative statement, loop[1] (definition 1). *Compare* DO loop.

form *n.* **1.** A structured document with spaces reserved for entering information and often containing special coding as well. **2.** In some applications (especially databases), a structured window, box, or other self-contained presentation element with predefined areas for entering or changing information. A form is a visual filter for the underlying data it is presenting, generally offering the advantages of better data organization and greater ease of viewing. **3.** In optical media, a data storage format used in compact disc technology. **4.** In programming, a metalanguage (such as Backus-Naur form) used to describe the syntax of a language. *See also* Backus-Naur form.

formal language *n.* A combination of syntax and semantics that completely defines a computer language. *See also* Backus-Naur form, semantics (definition 1), syntax.

formal logic *n.* A study of the logical expressions, sequences, and overall construction of a valid argument, without regard to the truth of the argument. Formal logic is used in proving program correctness.

format[1] *n.* **1.** In general, the structure or appearance of a unit of data. **2.** The arrangement of data within a document file that typically permits the document to be read or written by a certain application. Many applications can store a file in a more generic format, such as plain ASCII text. **3.** The layout of data storage areas (tracks and sectors) on a disk. **4.** The order and types of fields in a database. **5.** The attributes of a cell in a spreadsheet, such as its being alphabetic or numeric, the number of digits, the use of commas, and the use of currency signs. **6.** The specifications for the placement of text on a page or in a paragraph.

format[2] *vb.* **1.** To change the appearance of selected text or the contents of a selected cell in a spreadsheet. **2.** To prepare a disk for use by organizing its storage space into a collection of data "compartments," each of which can be located by the operating system so that data can be sorted and retrieved. When a previously used disk is formatted, any preexisting information on it is lost.

format bar *n.* A toolbar within an application used for modifying the format of the document being displayed, such as changing font size or type.

formatting *n.* **1.** The elements of style and presentation that are added to documents through the use of margins, indents, and different sizes, weights, and styles of type. **2.** The process of initializing a disk so that it can be used to store information. *See also* initialize.

form control *n.* On a Web site, an individual box or button with which you enter information on an electronic form.

form factor *n.* **1.** The size, shape, and configuration of a piece of computer hardware. The term is often applied to subcomponents such as disk drives, circuit boards, and small devices, such as handheld PCs. It can also be used more broadly to include the arrangement and positioning of external switches, plugs, and other components of the device, or it can refer to the footprint of an entire computer. **2.** A term used in computer graphics, specifically with reference to a method of rendering known as radiosity, which divides an image into small patches for calculating illumination. The form factor is a calculated value that represents the amount of energy radiated by one surface and received by another, taking into account such conditions as the distance between the surfaces, their orientation with respect to one another, and the presence of obstructions between them. **3.** When used to describe software, refers to the amount of memory required, the size of the program, and so on.

form feed *n.* A printer command that tells a printer to move to the top of the next page. In the ASCII character set, the form-feed character has the decimal value 12 (hexadecimal 0C). Because its purpose is to begin printing on a new page, form feed is also known as the page-eject character. *Acronym:* FF.

form letter *n.* A letter created for printing and distribution to a group of people whose names and addresses are taken from a database and inserted by a mail-merge program into a single basic document. *See also* mail merge.

formula *n.* A mathematical statement that describes the actions to be performed on numeric values. A formula sets up a calculation without regard to the actual values it is to act upon, such as $A + B$, with A and B representing whatever values the user designates. Thus, a formula is unlike an arithmetic problem, such as $1 + 2$, which includes values and must be restated if any value is changed. Through formulas, users of applications such as spreadsheets gain the power to perform "what-if" calculations simply by changing selected values and having the program recalculate the results. Sophisticated programs include many built-in formulas for performing standard business and mathematical calculations.

Forte *n.* Sun Microsystems integrated development environment (IDE) for Java developers. *See also* integrated development environment.

Fortezza *n.* A cryptographic technology developed by the United States National Security Agency (NSA) for enabling secure communication of sensitive information. Fortezza is based on encryption, authentication, and other technologies built into a personalized card known as the Fortezza Crypto Card that can be inserted into a PCMCIA slot on a computer. This card works with Fortezza-enabled hardware and software to secure applications such as e-mail, Web browsing, e-commerce, and file encryption. An RS-232 token can also be used with legacy systems that do not have card-reading capability. The technology is supported by a number of commercial vendors.

Forth *n.* A programming language originated by Charles Moore in the late 1960s. Moore chose the language's name, a shortened version of the word *fourth*, because he believed it was a fourth-generation language and his operating system would allow him to use only five letters for a program name. Forth is an interpreted, structured language that uses threading, which lets programmers easily extend the language and enables Forth to fit a great deal of functionality into limited space. Unlike most other programming languages, Forth uses postfix notation for its mathematical expressions and requires the programmer to work with the program stack directly. *See also* 4GL, interpreted language, postfix notation, stack, threading.

FORTRAN or **Fortran** *n.* Short for **for**mula **tran**slation. The first high-level computer language (developed over the period 1954–58 by John Backus) and the progenitor of many key high-level concepts, such as variables, expressions, statements, iterative and conditional statements, separately compiled subroutines, and formatted input/output. FORTRAN is a compiled, structured language. The name indicates its roots in science and engineering, where it is still used heavily, although the language itself has been expanded and improved vastly over the last 35 years to become a language that is useful in any field. *See also* compiled language, structured programming.

fortune cookie *n.* A proverb, prediction, joke, or other phrase chosen at random from a collection of such items and output to the screen by a program. Fortune cookies are sometimes displayed at logon and logoff times by UNIX systems.

forum *n.* A medium provided by an online service or BBS for users to carry on written discussions of a particular topic by posting messages and replying to them. On the Internet, the most widespread forums are the newsgroups in Usenet.

Forum of Incident Response and Security Teams *n. See* FIRST.

forward *vb.* In e-mail, to send a received message, either modified or in its entirety, to a new recipient.

forward chaining *n.* In expert systems, a form of problem solving that starts with a set of rules and a database of facts and works to a conclusion based on facts that match all the premises set forth in the rules. *See also* expert system. *Compare* backward chaining.

forward error correction *n.* In communications, a means of controlling errors by inserting extra (redundant) bits into a stream of data transmitted to another device. The redundant bits are used by the receiving device in detecting and, where possible, correcting errors in the data. *See also* error-correction coding.

forward pointer *n.* A pointer in a linked list that contains the address (location) of the next element in the list.

FOSDIC *n.* Acronym for **f**ilm **o**ptical **s**ensing **d**evice for **i**nput to **c**omputers. A device used by the U.S. government

to read documents on microfilm and store them digitally on magnetic tape or on a disk that can be accessed by a computer.

Fourier transform *n.* A mathematical method, developed by the French mathematician Jean-Baptiste-Joseph Fourier (1768–1830), for signal processing and signal generation tasks such as spectral analysis and image processing. The Fourier transform converts a signal value that is a function of time, space, or both into a function of frequency. The inverse Fourier transform converts a function of frequencies into a function of time, space, or both. *See also* fast Fourier transform.

four-nines availability *n.* The availability of a system 99.99 percent of the time. *See* high availability.

fourth-generation computer *n. See* computer.

fourth-generation language *n. See* 4GL.

fourth normal form *n. See* normal form (definition 1).

FPD *n. See* full-page display.

FPGA *n.* Acronym for **F**ield **P**rogrammable **G**ate **A**rray. A type of programmable logic chip that can be configured for a wide range of specialized applications after manufacture and delivery. FPGAs can be reprogrammed to incorporate innovations and upgrades. Because of their flexibility and adaptability, FPGAs are used in devices from microwave ovens to supercomputers.

FPLA *n. See* field-programmable logic array.

FPM RAM *n. See* page mode RAM.

FPU *n.* Acronym for **f**loating-**p**oint **u**nit. A circuit that performs floating-point calculations. *See also* circuit, floating-point operation.

FQ *n. See* fair queuing.

fractal *n.* A word coined by mathematician Benoit Mandelbrot in 1975 to describe a class of shapes characterized by irregularity, but in a way that evokes a pattern. Computer graphics technicians often use fractals to generate naturelike images such as landscapes, clouds, and forests. The distinguishing characteristic of fractals is that they are "self-similar"; any piece of a fractal, when magnified, has the same character as the whole. The standard analogy is that of a coastline, which has a similar structure whether viewed on a local or continental scale. Interestingly, it is often difficult to measure the length of the perimeter of such a shape exactly because the total distance measured depends on the size of the smallest element measured. For example, one could measure on a given coastline the

F

perimeter of every peninsula and inlet, or at a higher magnification the perimeter of every small promontory and jetty, and so on. In fact, a given fractal may have a finite area but an infinite perimeter; such shapes are considered to have a fractional dimension—for example, between 1 (a line) and 2 (a plane)—hence the name fractal. See the illustration. *See also* cellular automata, graftal.

Fractal.

fractional T1 *n.* A shared connection to a T1 line, in which only a fraction of the 24 T1 voice or data channels are used. *Acronym:* FT1. *See also* T1.

FRAD *n. See* frame relay assembler/disassembler.

fraggle attack *n. See* smurf attack.

fragmentation *n.* The scattering of parts of the same disk file over different areas of the disk. Fragmentation occurs as files on a disk are deleted and new files are added. Such fragmentation slows disk access and degrades the overall performance of disk operations, although usually not severely. Utility programs are available for rearranging file storage on fragmented disks.

FRAM *n.* Acronym for **f**erromagnetic **r**andom **a**ccess **m**emory. A form of data storage technology in which data is recorded semipermanently on small cards or strips of material coated with a ferric oxide (iron-based) magnetic film. As with tape or disk, the data persists without power; as with semiconductor RAM, a computer can access the data in any order.

frame *n.* **1.** In asynchronous serial communications, a unit of transmission that is sometimes measured in elapsed time and begins with the start bit that precedes a character and ends with the last stop bit that follows the character. **2.** In synchronous communications, a package of information transmitted as a single unit. Every frame follows the same basic organization and contains control information, such as synchronizing characters, station address, and an

error-checking value, as well as a variable amount of data. For example, a frame used in the widely accepted HDLC and related SDLC protocols begins and ends with a unique flag (01111110). See the illustration. *See also* HDLC, SDLC. **3.** A single screen-sized image that can be displayed in sequence with other, slightly different, images to create animated drawings. **4.** The storage required to hold one screen-sized image of text, graphics, or both. **5.** A rectangular space containing, and defining the proportions of, a graphic. **6.** The part of an on-screen window (title bar and other elements) that is controlled by the operating system rather than by the application running in the window. **7.** A rectangular section of the page displayed by a Web browser that is a separate HTML document from the rest of the page. Web pages can have multiple frames, each of which is a separate document. Associated with each frame are the same capabilities as for an unframed Web page, including scrolling and linking to another frame or Web site; these capabilities can be used independently of other frames on the page. Frames, which were introduced in Netscape Navigator 2.0, are often used as a table of contents for one or more HTML documents on a Web site. Most current Web browsers support frames, although older ones do not. *See also* HTML document, Web browser.

Flag	Address	Control	Data	Frame check sequence	Flag

Frame. The fields in an HDLC-SDLC frame.

frame buffer *n.* A portion of a computer's display memory that holds the contents of a single screen image. *See also* video buffer.

frame grabber *n. See* video digitizer.

frame rate *n.* **1.** The speed at which full, single-screen images are transmitted to and displayed by a raster-scan monitor. Frame rate is calculated as the number of times per second (hertz) the electron beam sweeps the screen. **2.** In animation, the number of times per second an image is updated. When the frame rate exceeds about 14 frames per second, animation seems to blend into smooth motion. *See also* animation.

frame relay *n.* A packet-switching protocol for use on WANs (wide area networks). Frame relay transmits variable-length packets at up to 2 Mbps over predetermined, set paths known as PVCs (permanent virtual circuits). It is a variant of X.25 but dispenses with some of

X.25's error detection for the sake of speed. *See also* ATM (definition 1), X.25.

frame relay access device *n. See* frame relay assembler/disassembler.

frame relay assembler/disassembler *n.* A combination channel service unit/digital service unit (CSU/DSU) and router that connects an internal network to a frame relay connection. The device converts data (which may be in the form of IP packets or conform to some other network protocol) into packets for transmission over the frame relay network and converts such packets back to the original data. Since this type of connection is direct—without a firewall—other network protection is necessary. *Acronym:* FRAD. *See also* firewall, frame relay, IP.

frame source *n.* In the HTML frames environment, a contents document that will look for the source document to display within a frame drawn by the local browser. *See also* HTML.

frames page *n.* A Web page that divides a Web browser window into different scrollable areas that can independently display several Web pages. One window can remain unchanged, while the other windows change based on hyperlinks that the user selects.

frames per second *n. See* frame rate.

framework *n.* In object-oriented programming, a reusable basic design structure, consisting of abstract and concrete classes, that assists in building applications. *See also* abstract class, object-oriented programming.

FRC *n. See* functional redundancy checking.

fred *n.* **1.** An interface utility for X.500. *See also* CCITT X series. **2.** A placeholder string used by programmers in syntax examples to stand for a variable name. If a programmer has used *fred*, the next placeholder needed is likely to be *barney*. *Compare* foo.

free block *n.* A region (block) of memory that is not currently being used.

FreeBSD *n.* A freely distributed version of BSD UNIX (Berkeley Software Distribution UNIX) for IBM and IBM-compatible PCs. *See also* BSD UNIX.

free-form language *n.* A language whose syntax is not constrained by the position of characters on a line. C and Pascal are free-form languages; FORTRAN is not.

freenet or **free-net** *n.* A community-based computer BBS and Internet service provider, usually operated by volunteers and providing free access to subscribers in the community or access for a very small fee. Many freenets are operated by public libraries or universities. *See also* ISP.

free software *n.* Software, complete with source code, that is distributed freely to users who are in turn free to use, modify, and distribute it, provided that all alterations are clearly marked and that the name and copyright notice of the original author are not deleted or modified in any way. Unlike freeware, which a user might or might not have permission to modify, free software is protected by a license agreement. Free software is a concept pioneered by the Free Software Foundation in Cambridge, Massachusetts. *Compare* freeware, open source, public-domain software, shareware.

Free Software Foundation *n.* An advocacy organization founded by Richard Stallman, dedicated to eliminating restrictions on people's right to use, copy, modify, and redistribute computer programs for noncommercial purposes. The Free Software Foundation is the maintainer of GNU software, which is UNIX-like software that can be freely distributed. *See also* GNU.

free space *n.* Space on a floppy disk or a hard drive not currently occupied by data. *See also* floppy disk, hard disk.

freeware *n.* A computer program given away free of charge and often made available on the Internet or through user groups. An independent program developer might offer a product as freeware either for personal satisfaction or to assess its reception among interested users. Freeware developers often retain all rights to their software, and users are not necessarily free to copy or distribute it further. *Compare* free software, public-domain software, shareware.

freeze-frame video *n.* Video in which the image changes only once every few seconds. *Compare* full-motion video.

frequency *n.* The measure of how often a periodic event occurs, such as a signal going through a complete cycle. Frequency is usually measured in hertz (Hz), with 1 Hz equaling 1 occurrence (cycle) per second. In the United States, household electricity is alternating current with a frequency of 60 Hz. Frequency is also measured in kilohertz (kHz, or 1000 Hz), megahertz (MHz, or 1000 kHz), gigahertz (GHz, or 1000 MHz), or terahertz (THz, or 1000 GHz). See the illustration. *Compare* wavelength.

F

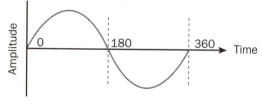

Frequency.

frequency counter *n.* **1.** An item of engineering test equipment that measures and displays the frequencies of electronic signals. **2.** An electronic circuit, often found embedded in process-control computers, that counts the frequency of occurrence of an activity.

Frequency Division Multiple Access *n. See* FDMA.

frequency-division multiplexing *n. See* FDM.

frequency hopping *n.* The switching of frequencies within a given bandwidth during a point-to-point transmission. Frequency hopping reduces the chance of unauthorized signal interception or the effects of single-frequency jamming.

frequency modulation *n.* A way of encoding information in an electrical signal by varying its frequency. The FM radio band uses frequency modulation, as does the audio portion of broadcast television. See the illustration. *Acronym:* FM. *Compare* amplitude modulation.

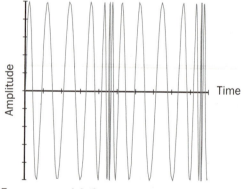

Frequency modulation.

frequency modulation encoding *n.* A method of storing information on a disk in which both data and additional synchronizing information, called clock pulses, are recorded on the surface. FM encoding is relatively inefficient because of the extra disk space required by the clock pulses. It has been generally superseded by a more efficient method called *modified* frequency modulation (MFM) encoding and by

the complex but extremely efficient technique called run-length limited (RLL) encoding. *Abbreviation:* FM encoding. *Compare* modified frequency modulation encoding, run-length limited encoding.

frequency response *n.* The range of frequencies an audio device can reproduce from its input signals. *See also* frequency.

frequency-shift keying *n. See* FSK.

frequently asked questions *n. See* FAQ.

friction feed *n.* A means of moving paper through a printer in which the paper is pinched either between the printer's platen and pressure rollers or (in printers that do not have a platen) between two sets of rollers. Friction feed is available on most printers, for use with paper that does not have pin-feed holes. In printers that have tractor feed as well as friction feed, the friction-feed mechanism should be left disengaged when the tractor is being used, to avoid unnecessary stress on the tractor gears. *See also* platen. *Compare* pin feed, tractor feed.

friendly *adj.* Referring to features built into hardware or software that make a computer or computer program easy to learn and easy to use. Friendliness is emphasized by most developers and sought after by most users. *See also* user-friendly.

fringeware *n.* Freeware whose reliability and value are questionable. *See also* freeware.

front end *n.* **1.** In a client/server application, the part of the program that runs on the client. *See also* client/server architecture. *Compare* back end (definition 1). **2.** In applications, software or a feature of software that provides an interface to another application or tool. Front ends are often used to supply a common interface for a range of tools produced by a software manufacturer. A front end generally offers a more user-friendly interface than that of the application running "behind" it. **3.** In networking, a client computer or the processing that takes place on it. *Compare* back end (definition 2).

front-end processor *n.* **1.** Generally, a computer or processing unit that produces and manipulates data before another processor receives it. *Compare* back-end processor (definition 2). **2.** In communications, a computer that is located between communications lines and a main (host) computer and is used to relieve the host of housekeeping chores related to communications; sometimes considered synonymous with communications controller.

A front-end processor is dedicated entirely to handling transmitted information, including error detection and control; receipt, transmission, and possibly encoding of messages; and management of the lines running to and from other devices. *See also* communications controller.

front panel *n.* The faceplate of a computer cabinet through which the control knobs, switches, and lights are available to an operator. *See also* console.

fry *vb.* To destroy a circuit board or another component of a computer by applying excessive voltage. Even when applied voltage is not excessive, an electronic component can become fried when it breaks down, conducting more current than its design permits.

fs *n. See* femtosecond.

FSK *n.* Acronym for **f**requency-**s**hift **k**eying. A simple form of modulation in which the digital values 0 and 1 are represented by two different frequencies. FSK was used by early modems running at 300 bits per second.

FT1 *n. See* fractional T1.

FTAM *n.* Acronym for **F**ile-**T**ransfer **A**ccess and **M**anagement. A communications standard for transferring files between different makes and models of computer.

FTP[1] *n.* **1.** Acronym for **F**ile **T**ransfer **P**rotocol, a fast, application-level protocol widely used for copying files to and from remote computer systems on a network using TCP/IP, such as the Internet. This protocol also allows users to use FTP commands to work with files, such as listing files and directories on the remote system. *See also* TCP/IP. **2.** A common logon ID for anonymous FTP.

FTP[2] *vb.* To download files from or upload files to remote computer systems, via the Internet's File Transfer Protocol. The user needs an FTP client to transfer files to and from the remote system, which must have an FTP server. Generally, the user also needs to establish an account on the remote system to FTP files, although many FTP sites permit the use of anonymous FTP. *See also* FTP client, FTP server.

FTP client or **ftp client** *n.* A program that enables the user to upload and download files to and from an FTP site over a network, such as the Internet, using the File Transfer Protocol. *See also* FTP[1] (definition 1). *Compare* FTP server.

FTP commands *n.* Commands that are part of the File Transfer Protocol. *See also* FTP[1] (definition 1).

FTP program or **ftp program** *n. See* FTP client.

FTP server *n.* A file server that uses the File Transfer Protocol to permit users to upload or download files through the Internet or any other TCP/IP network. *See also* file server, FTP[1] (definition 1), TCP/IP. *Compare* FTP client.

FTP site *n.* The collection of files and programs residing on an FTP server. *See also* FTP[1] (definition 1), FTP server.

FTTC *n.* Acronym for **f**iber **t**o **t**he **c**urb. The installation and use of fiber-optic cable from the central office (CO) to within a thousand feet of a user's home or office. With FTTC, coaxial cable or another medium carries the signals from the curb into the home or office. FTTC is a replacement for Plain Old Telephone Service (POTS) that enables the distribution of telephony, cable TV, Internet access, multimedia, and other communications over one line. *Compare* FTTH, POTS.

FTTH *n.* Acronym for **f**iber **t**o **t**he **h**ome. The installation and use of fiber-optic cable from the central office (CO) directly into a user's home or office. FTTH is a replacement for Plain Old Telephone Service (POTS) that enables the distribution of telephony, cable TV, Internet access, multimedia, and other communications over one line. *Compare* FTTC, POTS.

FUD *n.* Acronym for **f**ear, **u**ncertainty, and **d**oubt. Derogatory slang used to express disagreement or displeasure with a vendor's public statements, particularly when the vendor is speaking of a competitor's products. If a vendor is perceived as implying that buying from a competitor is obviously the wrong choice, that vendor is said to be using FUD as a marketing technique.

fuel cell *n.* An electrochemical device, similar to a battery in function, in which the chemical energy of a fuel, such as hydrogen, and an oxidant, usually oxygen, are converted directly into electrical energy. Unlike batteries, however, fuel cells do not store energy, and they never run down or need recharging as long as the fuel and oxidant are supplied continuously. The principle of fuel cell technology was discovered more than 100 years ago, but until recently it had found use only in laboratories and in space travel (the Apollo missions and the space shuttle). Today, large and small fuel cells are being developed that will power portable devices such as laptop computers and cellular phones, generate electricity and heat, and replace automotive combustion engines.

F

fulfillment *n.* The process of delivering goods and services ordered by a consumer. Fulfillment involves establishing a reliable procedure for tracking orders and delivering products.

fulfillment service provider *n.* A company that provides fulfillment services for an e-commerce Web site by tracking, packing, and shipping goods ordered via the e-commerce site. A fulfillment service provider allows an e-business to save time, costs, and labor by outsourcing order processing.

full adder *n.* A logic circuit used in a computer to add binary digits. A full adder accepts three digital inputs (bits): 2 bits to be added and a carry bit from another digit position. It produces two outputs: a sum and a carry bit. Full adders are combined with two-input circuits called *half adders* to enable computers to add 4 or more bits at a time. *See also* carry bit, half adder.

full-duplex *adj. See* duplex[1].

full-duplex transmission *n. See* duplex[2] (definition 1).

full justification *n.* In typesetting, word processing, and desktop publishing, the process of aligning text evenly along both the left and right margins of a column or page. *See also* justify (definition 2).

full mode *n.* The default operational state of Windows Media Player in which all of its features are displayed. The Player can also appear in skin mode. *See also* skin mode.

full-motion video *n.* Video reproduction at 30 frames per second (fps) for NTSC signals or 25 fps for PAL signals. *Also called:* continuous motion video. *See also* frame (definition 1). *Compare* freeze-frame video.

full-motion video adapter *n.* An expansion card for a computer that can convert motion video from devices such as a video cassette recorder to a digital format that a computer can use, such as AVI, MPEG, or Motion JPEG. *See also* AVI, Motion JPEG, MPEG.

full name *n.* A user's complete name, usually consisting of last name, first name, and middle initial. The full name is often maintained by the operating system as part of the information that identifies and defines a user account. *See also* user account.

full-page display *n.* A video display with sufficient size and resolution to show at least one 8$\frac{1}{2}$-by-11-inch image. Such displays are useful for desktop publishing applications. *Acronym:* FPD. *See also* portrait monitor.

full path *n.* In a hierarchical filing system, a pathname containing all the possible components of a pathname, including the network share or drive and root directory, as well as any subdirectories and the file or object name. For example, the MS-DOS full path c:\book\chapter\myfile.doc indicates that myfile.doc is located in a directory called *chapter*, which in turn is located in a directory called *book* in the root directory of the C: drive. *Also called:* full pathname. *See also* path (definition 2), root directory, subdirectory. *Compare* relative path.

full pathname *n. See* full path.

full-screen *adj.* Capable of using or being displayed on the full area of a display screen. Applications running in windowing environments, although they might use the entire area of the screen, commonly allocate different areas to different windows, any of which can be enlarged to fill the entire screen.

full-text search *n.* A search for one or more documents, records, or strings based on all of the actual text data rather than on an index containing a limited set of keywords. For example, a full-text search can locate a document containing the words "albatrosses are clumsy on land" by searching files for just those words without the need of an index containing the keyword "albatross." *See also* index.

fully formed character *n.* A character formed by striking an inked ribbon with a molded or cast piece of type in the manner of a typewriter. Impact printers that produce fully formed characters use letters attached to wheels (daisy wheels), balls, thimbles, bands, or chains, rather than dot-matrix wires. *See also* daisy wheel, near-letter-quality, thimble.

fully populated board *n.* A printed circuit board whose integrated circuit (IC) sockets are all occupied. Memory boards in particular may have fewer than the maximum possible number of memory chips, leaving some IC sockets empty. Such a board is said to be *partially populated.*

function *n.* **1.** The purpose of, or the action carried out by, a program or routine. **2.** A general term for a subroutine. **3.** In some languages, such as Pascal, a subroutine that returns a value. *See also* function call, procedure, routine, subroutine.

functional design *n.* The specification of the relationships between working parts of a computer system, including details of logical components and the way they work together. Functional design is shown graphically in a functional diagram, which uses special symbols to represent the elements of the system.

functional programming *n.* A style of programming in which all facilities are provided as functions (subroutines), usually without side effects. Pure functional programming languages lack a traditional assignment statement; assignment is usually implemented by copy and modify operations. Functional programming is thought to offer advantages for parallel-processing computers. *See also* side effect.

functional redundancy checking *n.* A method of preventing errors by having two processors execute the same instructions on the same data at the same time. If the results produced by the two processors do not agree, an error has occurred. The Intel Pentium and higher processors have built-in support for functional redundancy checking. *Acronym:* FRC.

functional specification *n.* A description of the scope, objectives, and types of operations that are to be considered in the development of an information-handling system.

function call *n.* A program's request for the services of a particular function. A function call is coded as the name of the function along with any parameters needed for the function to perform its task. The function itself can be a part of the program, be stored in another file and brought into the program when the program is compiled, or be a part of the operating system. *See also* function (definition 2).

function key *n.* Any of the 10 or more keys labeled F1, F2, F3, and so on, that are placed along the left side or across the top of a keyboard (or both) and are used for special tasks by different programs. The meaning of a function key is defined by a program or, in some instances, by the user. Function keys are used in application programs or the operating system to provide either a shortcut for a series of common instructions (such as calling up a program's on-screen help facility) or a feature that is not otherwise available. *See also* key (definition 1). *Compare* Command key, Control key, Escape key.

function library *n.* A collection of routines compiled together. *See also* function (definition 2), library (definition 1), toolbox.

function overloading *n.* The capability of having several routines in a program with the same name. The different functions are distinguished by their parameter types, return value types, or both; the compiler automatically selects the correct version, based on parameter types and return types. For example, a program might have one trigonometric sine function that uses a floating-point parameter to represent an angle in radians, and another that uses an integer parameter to represent an angle in degrees. In such a program, sin(3.14159/2.0) would return the value 1.0 (because the sine of p/2 radians is 1), but sin(30) would return the value 0.5 (because the sine of 30 degrees is 0.5). *See also* operator overloading.

Function procedure *n.* A procedure that returns a value and that can be used in an expression. You declare a function with the Function statement and end it with the End Function statement.

fuse *n.* A circuit element that burns out or breaks when the current passing through it exceeds a certain level. A fuse protects a circuit from damage caused by excess current. It performs the same function as a circuit breaker, but it cannot be reset, so it must be replaced if it breaks. A fuse consists of a short length of wire of a specific composition and thickness; the thicker the wire, the more current it can pass before the wire melts and breaks the circuit.

fusible link *n.* A circuit component, often part of an integrated circuit, that is designed to break, or burn like a fuse, when a relatively high current is applied. Rather than protecting against excessive current flow, fusible links allow intentional circuit modification in the field. Fusible links were used in PROM chips, and they form the foundation of a kind of integrated circuit known as a field-programmable logic array. One can customize such a circuit "in the field," after it has been made in the factory, by selectively programming high current through certain fusible links and breaking them. *See also* field-programmable logic array, PROM.

fuzzy computing *n.* **1.** A computing technique that deals with vague, incomplete, or ambiguous data in a precise mathematical way while providing solutions based on the human way of thinking. The term fuzzy relates to the type of data it processes, not to the technique itself, which is very exact. Fuzzy computing is also known as fuzzy set theory or fuzzy logic, and covers fuzzy control and fuzzy expert systems, for example. **2.** A computing technology in which the computer interprets data by looking for patterns in problems while completing tasks. Using fuzzy computing, the computer is able to examine patterns in the data it receives and to make inferences based on that data, and act accordingly.

fuzzy logic *n.* A form of logic used in some expert systems and other artificial-intelligence applications in which variables can have degrees of truthfulness or falsehood represented by a range of values between 1 (true) and 0 (false). With fuzzy logic, the outcome of an operation can be expressed as a probability rather than as a certainty. For example, an outcome might be probably true, possibly true, possibly false, or probably false. *See also* expert system.

fuzzy set *n.* A set constructed using the principles of fuzzy logic. It is used in artificial intelligence to deal with vague or continuous data that cannot be expressed by conventional set theory. In a fuzzy set, the membership function for the set of objects is not binary but continuous, such that an object may be a member of the set to a specific degree or arbitrary value. In computer programming, a fuzzy set is usually effectively represented by an array. *See also* array, artificial intelligence, fuzzy logic.

FWIW *adv.* Acronym for **f**or **w**hat **i**t's **w**orth. An expression used in e-mail and newsgroups.

FYI *n.* **1.** Acronym for **f**or **y**our **i**nformation. An expression used in e-mail and newsgroups to introduce information that is thought to be useful to the reader. **2.** An electronic document distributed through InterNIC like a request for comments (RFC), but intended to explain an Internet standard or feature for users rather than to define it for developers, as the RFC does. *See also* InterNIC. *Compare* RFC.

G *prefix* *See* giga-.

G3 *n.* *See* PowerPC 750.

G4 *n.* *See* Power Macintosh.

GaAs *n.* *See* gallium arsenide.

gain *n.* The increase in the amplitude of a signal, as of voltage, current, or power, that is produced by a circuit. Gain can be expressed as a factor or in decibels. *See also* decibel.

gallium arsenide *n.* A semiconductor compound used in place of silicon to make devices that perform faster, require less power, and are more tolerant of temperature changes and radiation than those made with silicon. *Also called:* GaAs.

game *n.* *See* computer game.

Game Boy *n.* Nintendo Corporation's popular battery-powered, portable handheld gaming system first introduced in 1990 and updated frequently. Games are supplied on cartridges. The latest Game Boy, Game Boy Advance, features a 32-bit ARM CPU with embedded memory and a 2.9-inch TFT reflective screen with 240x160 resolution. *See also* computer game, TFT.

game card *n.* *See* ROM card.

game cartridge *n.* *See* ROM cartridge.

game console *n.* *See* console game.

Game Control Adapter *n.* In IBM personal computers and compatibles, a circuit that processes input signals at a game port. Devices such as joysticks and game paddles use potentiometers to represent their positions as varying voltage levels; the Game Control Adapter converts these levels to numbers using an analog-to-digital converter (ADC). *See also* analog-to-digital converter, game port, potentiometer.

GameCube *n.* Nintendo Corporation's console gaming system. It features a developer-friendly format and introduces 1T-RAM technology, which reduces delays to the main memory and the graphics LSI mixed memory. The

microprocessor is a custom IBM Power PC "Gekko" featuring a secondary cache (Level One: Instruction 32 KB, Data 32 KB (8-way); Level Two: 256 KB (2-way)). Games are supplied on a GameCube game disc. *See also* computer game, console game. *Compare* Dreamcast, PlayStation, Xbox.

game pad *n.* An action-control input device used with arcade-type games played on PCs and game consoles such as Microsoft's Xbox, Nintendo's GameCube, Sega's Dreamcast, and Sony's PlayStation. A game pad, unlike a joystick, is meant to be held in a player's hands. Buttons on the game pad allow a player to control direction, speed, and other screen actions. *Also called:* joypad. *Compare* joystick.

game port *n.* In IBM personal computers and compatibles, an I/O port for devices such as joysticks and game paddles. The game port is often included with other I/O ports on a single expansion card. See the illustration. *See also* Game Control Adapter.

Game port

Game port.

gamer *n.* Refers to a person who plays games, sometimes role-playing games or trading card games; often a person who plays computer, console, arcade, or online games as a primary hobby or avocation.

game theory *n.* A mathematical theory, ascribed to John von Neumann, that considers strategy and probability in terms of competitive games in which all players have partial control and each seeks the most advantageous moves in relation to the others.

game tree *n.* A tree structure representing contingencies in a game and used by game developers for design purposes. Each node in a game tree represents a possible position (for example, the configuration of pieces on a chessboard) in the game, and each branching represents a possible move. *See also* computer game.

gamut *n.* The complete range of colors a display or printer is capable of producing. If a color falls outside the gamut of a device, it cannot be accurately displayed or printed from that device.

gamut alarm *n.* A feature in graphics programs that alerts the user if a chosen color will fall outside the currently selected gamut. *See also* gamut.

Gantt chart *n.* A bar chart that shows individual parts of a project as bars against a horizontal time scale. Gantt charts are used as a project-planning tool for developing schedules. Most project-planning software can produce Gantt charts.

gap *n.* *See* inter-record gap.

garbage *n.* **1.** Incorrect or corrupted data. **2.** Gibberish displayed on screen, either due to faulty hardware or software or because a program is unable to display a file's content. For example, an executable file is not meant to be displayed by a text editor and so is indecipherable on screen.

garbage collection *n.* A process for automatic recovery of heap memory. Blocks of memory that had been allocated but are no longer in use are freed, and blocks of memory still in use may be moved to consolidate the free memory into larger blocks. Some programming languages require the programmer to handle garbage collection. Others, such as Java, perform this task for the programmer. *See also* heap (definition 1).

garbage in, garbage out *n.* A computing axiom meaning that if the data put into a process is incorrect, the data output by the process will also be incorrect. *Acronym:* GIGO.

gas-discharge display *n.* A type of flat-panel display, used on some portable computers, containing neon between a horizontal and a vertical set of electrodes. When one electrode in each set is charged, the neon glows (as in a neon lamp) where the two electrodes intersect, representing a pixel. *Also called:* gas-plasma display. *See also* flat-panel display, pixel.

gas-plasma display *n.* *See* gas-discharge display.

gate *n.* **1.** An electronic switch that is the elementary component of a digital circuit. It produces an electrical output signal that represents a binary 1 or 0 and is related to the states of one or more input signals by an operation of Boolean logic, such as AND, OR, or NOT. *Also called:* logic gate. *See also* gate array. **2.** The input terminal of a field-effect transistor (FET). *Also called:* gate electrode. *See also* drain (definition 1), FET, MOSFET, source (definition 2). **3.** A data structure used by 80386 and higher microprocessors to control access to privileged functions, to change data segments, or to switch tasks.

gate array *n.* A special type of chip that starts out as a nonspecific collection of logic gates. Late in the manufacturing process, a layer is added to connect the gates for a specific function. By changing the pattern of connections, the manufacturer can make the chip suitable for many needs. This process is very popular because it saves both design and manufacturing time. The drawback is that much of the chip goes unused. *Also called:* application-specific integrated circuit, logic array.

gated *adj.* **1.** Transmitted through a gate to a subsequent electronic logic element. **2.** Transmitted through a gateway to a subsequent network or service. For example, a mailing list on BITNET may be gated to a newsgroup on the Internet.

gate electrode *n.* *See* gate (definition 2).

gateway *n.* A device that connects networks using different communications protocols so that information can be passed from one to the other. A gateway both transfers information and converts it to a form compatible with the protocols used by the receiving network. *Compare* bridge.

gateway page *n.* *See* doorway page.

gating circuit *n.* An electronic switch whose output is either on or off, depending on the state of two or more inputs. For example, a gating circuit may be used to pass or not pass an input signal, depending on the states of one or more control signals. A gating circuit can be constructed from one or more logic gates. *See also* gate (definition 1).

gatored *vb.* To have been the victim of a hijackware program that seized control of an Internet shopping or surfing experience and caused the victim's browser to display ads and Web sites chosen by the program. Users may be gatored when they have unknowingly installed a program or plug-in with a hidden marketing agenda, which intrudes on the user's Web shopping to display ads or Web sites promoting competing products. The term gatored comes from the name of a plug-in that was one of the first hijack-ware products to be used by Web marketers. *See also* hijackware.

GB *n. See* gigabyte.

Gbps *n. See* gigabits per second.

GDI *n.* Acronym for **G**raphical **D**evice **I**nterface. In Windows, a graphics display system used by applications to display or print bitmapped text (TrueType fonts), images, and other graphical elements. The GDI is responsible for drawing dialog boxes, buttons, and other elements in a consistent style on screen by calling the appropriate screen drivers and passing them the information on the item to be drawn. The GDI also works with GDI printers, which have limited ability to prepare a page for printing. Instead, the GDI handles that task by calling the appropriate printer drivers and moving the image or document directly to the printer, rather than reformatting the image or document in PostScript or another printer language. *See also* bitmapped font, dialog box, driver, PostScript.

Gecko *n.* A cross-platform Web browsing engine introduced by Netscape in 1998, distributed and developed as open-source software through Mozilla.org. Designed to be small, fast, and modular, the Gecko engine supports Internet standards including HTML, cascading style sheets (CSS), XML, and the Document Object Model (DOM). Gecko is the layout engine in Netscape's Communicator software.

geek *n.* **1.** Generally, a person who enjoys cerebral activities (such as wordplay or computer programming) more than the mainstream population does. Geeks in this sense increasingly claim the word with pride, but it may give offense when used by others, suggesting inadequacy in normal social relationships. **2.** A computer expert or specialist. For issues of etiquette, see definition 1. *Compare* guru, techie, wizard.

GENA *n.* Acronym for **G**eneral **E**vent **N**otification **A**rchitecture. An extension to HTTP defined by an Internet Engineering Task Force (IETF) Internet-Draft and used to communicate events over the Internet between HTTP resources. Universal Plug and Play (UPnP) services use GENA to send XML event messages to control points.

gender bender *n. See* gender changer.

gender changer *n.* A device for joining two connectors that are either both male (having pins) or both female (having sockets). See the illustration. *Also called:* gender bender.

Gender changer.

General Event Notification Architecture *n. See* GENA.

General Inter-ORB Protocol *n. See* IIOP.

General Packet Radio Service *n. See* GPRS.

General Protection Fault *n.* The error condition that occurs in an 80386 or higher processor running in protected mode (such as Windows 3.1) when an application attempts to access memory outside of its authorized memory space or when an invalid instruction is issued. *Acronym:* GPF. *See also* protected mode.

General Public License *n.* The agreement under which software, such as the GNU (GNU's Not UNIX) utilities, is distributed by the Free Software Foundation. Anyone who has a copy of such a program may redistribute it to another party and may charge for distribution and support services, but may not restrict the other party from doing the same. A user may modify the program, but if the modified version is distributed, it must be clearly identified as such and is also covered under the General Public License. A distributor must also either provide source code or indicate where source code can be obtained. *Acronym:* GPL. *Also called:* copyleft. *See also* free software, Free Software Foundation, GNU.

general-purpose computer *n.* A computer that can perform any computational task for which software is available. A PC is a general-purpose computer.

general-purpose controller *n.* A controller that is designed for multiple uses. *See also* controller.

General-Purpose Interface Bus *n.* A bus developed for the exchange of information between computers and industrial automation equipment. The electrical definition

G

of this bus has been incorporated into an IEEE standard. *Acronym:* GPIB. *See also* IEEE 488.

general-purpose language *n.* A programming language, such as Ada, Basic, C, or Pascal, designed for a variety of applications and uses. By contrast, SQL is a language designed to be used only with databases.

general-purpose register *n.* **1.** A register within a microprocessor that is available for any use rather than being reserved, like a segment selector or stack pointer, for a specific use by the processor design or operating system. **2.** Any digital circuit capable of storing binary data.

generation *n.* **1.** A concept used to distinguish stored versions of a set of files. The oldest is called the grandfather, the next oldest is the father, and the newest is the son. **2.** A concept used to distinguish among a process, another process that it initiates (its child), and the process that initiated it (its parent or the child's grandparent). *See also* process[1]. **3.** A category that distinguishes products, such as computers or programming languages, according to the technological advances they represent. *See also* computer.

generic icon *n.* An icon on a Macintosh screen that identifies a file only as a document or an application. Ordinarily the icon for an application will be specific to that application, and the icon for a document will be specific to the application that opens it. If a generic icon appears instead, the information that the Macintosh Finder uses to identify the application has been damaged. *See also* Finder, icon, Macintosh.

genetic algorithm *n.* A computational method for adapting problem solutions based on genetic aspects of evolution. Implementations typically use fixed-length text strings to represent information, together with a population of individuals that undergo crossover and mutation in order to find promising results. Genetic algorithms typically have three distinct stages: 1) Encoding of the potential solutions into bit strings that support the necessary variation, 2) mating and mutation algorithms that produce a new generation of individuals that recombine features of the parents, and 3) a fitness function that judges the results based on what is most appropriate for a potential solution to the problem. *See also* algorithm, genetic programming.

genetic programming *n.* A paradigm in which the principle of natural selection (whereby a biological entity whose structure is more fit for its environment than its peers produces descendants better able to survive) is applied to the creation of computer programs. Thus,

genetic programming seeks to find and develop, from the set of all possible programs, code that is highly fit to solve problems, but not necessarily explicitly designed for a specific task. This inductive discovery method aims to mimic the natural selection process by developing computer code based on its adaptability and suitability. *See also* artificial intelligence.

Genie *n.* An online information service originally developed by General Electric (GE) Information Services as GEnie (**G**eneral **E**lectric **n**etwork for **i**nformation **e**xchange); currently owned and provided by IDT Corporation as Genie (lowercase e). Genie provides business information, forums, home shopping, and news and can exchange e-mail with the Internet.

GEO *n. See* geostationary orbit satellite.

geographic information system *n.* An application or suite of applications for viewing and creating maps. Generally, geographic information systems contain a viewing system (sometimes allowing users to view maps with a Web browser), an environment for creating maps, and a server for managing maps and data for real-time online viewing. *Acronym:* GIS.

geometry *n.* The branch of mathematics that deals with the construction, properties, and relationships of points, lines, angles, curves, and shapes. Geometry is an essential part of computer-aided design and graphics programs.

GeoPort *n.* A fast serial input/output port on a range of Macintosh computers, including Macintosh Centris 660AV, Quadra 660AV, Quadra 840AV, or PowerMac. Any Macintosh-compatible serial device can be connected to a GeoPort, but with GeoPort-specific hardware and software the GeoPort can transmit data at up to 2 Mbps (megabits per second) and can handle voice, fax, data, and video transmission.

GEOS *n.* An operating system developed by Geoworks Corporation, used in some handheld devices. GEOS is designed to provide broad functionality in resource-constrained environments that have limited storage or memory capability, such as enhanced phones, some Internet access devices, and PDAs and other handheld computers.

geostationary *adj. See* geosynchronous.

geostationary orbit satellite *n.* A communications satellite that rotates with the earth and thus appears to remain fixed, or stationary, over a particular location. This travels in orbit 22,282 miles above the equator, where its period of rotation matches the earth's rotation. The service area, or *footprint,* of the satellite is approximately one-third of the earth's surface, so global satellite coverage can be achieved with three satellites in orbit. In a voice communication system, a round-trip to and from this satellite takes approximately 250 milliseconds. Satellite-based data communications are necessary for delivering high bandwidth options to rural areas. *Acronym:* GEO.

geosynchronous *adj.* Completing one revolution in the same time that the earth completes one rotation, as a communications satellite. *Also called:* geostationary.

germanium *n.* A semiconductor element (atomic number 32) that is used in some transistors, diodes, and solar cells but has been replaced by silicon in most applications. Germanium has a lower bias voltage than silicon but is more sensitive to heat (as in soldering).

get *n.* An FTP command that instructs the server to transfer a specified file to the client. *See also* FTP client, FTP commands, FTP server.

GFLOP *n. See* gigaflops.

GGA *n.* Acronym for **G**ood **G**ame **A**ll. GGA is often used in online and chat games at the conclusion of play. *See also* role-playing game.

ghost¹ *n.* **1.** A dim, secondary image that is displaced slightly from the primary image on a video display (due to signal reflection in transmission) or on a printout (due to unstable printing elements). **2.** An abandoned or no-longer-maintained Web site that remains accessible to visitors.

ghost² *vb.* **1.** To produce a duplicate, such as duplicating an application in memory. *See also* screen saver. **2.** To display an option on a menu or on a submenu in faint type to show that it cannot be selected at the present time.

ghosting *n. See* burn in (definition 2).

giant magnetoresistive head *n.* A type of hard-disk head developed by IBM and based on a physical property known as the giant magnetoresistive effect. Discovered by European scientists in the late 1980s, the giant magnetoresistive effect, or GMR, produces large resistance changes in magnetic fields when various metallic materials are "sandwiched" together in thin, alternating layers. When incorporated into disk heads, GMR technology allows for very dense data storage—currently, as much as 11.6 billion

bits per square inch, or the equivalent of more than 700,000 typewritten pages. *Acronym:* GMR. *See also* head.

.gif *n.* The file extension that identifies GIF bit map images. *See also* GIF.

GIF *n.* **1.** Acronym for **G**raphics **I**nterchange **F**ormat. A graphics file format developed by CompuServe and used for transmitting raster images on the Internet. An image may contain up to 256 colors, including a transparent color. The size of the file depends on the number of colors actually used. The LZW compression method is used to reduce the file size still further. *See also* LZW compression, raster graphics. **2.** A graphic stored as a file in the GIF format.

GIF animation *n.* A file containing a series of graphics that are displayed in rapid sequence in a Web browser to appear as though they are a moving picture.

giga- *prefix* **1.** One billion (1000 million, 10^9). **2.** In data storage, $1024 \times 1,048,576$ (2^{30}) or $1000 \times 1,048,576$. *See also* gigabyte, gigaflops, gigahertz, kilo-, mega-.

Gigabit Ethernet *n.* The IEEE standard dubbed 802.3z, which includes support for transmission rates of 1 Gbps (gigabit per second)—1000 Mbps (megabits per second)—over an Ethernet network. The usual Ethernet standard (802.3) supports only up to 100 Mbps. *Compare* Ethernet/802.3.

gigabit over copper *n. See* Cat 5 cable.

gigabits per second *n.* A measurement of data transfer speed, as on a network, in multiples of 1,073,741,824 (2^{30}) bits. *Acronym:* Gbps.

gigabyte *n.* **1.** 1024 megabytes (1024 x 1,048,576 [2^{30}] bytes). **2.** One thousand megabytes (1000 x 1,048,576 bytes). *Acronym:* GB.

gigaflops *n.* A measure of computing performance: one billion (1000 million) floating-point operations per second. *Acronym:* GFLOP. *See also* floating-point operation.

gigahertz *n.* A measure of frequency: one billion (1000 million) cycles per second. *Abbreviation:* GHz.

gigaPoP *n.* Short for **giga**bit **P**oint **of** **P**resence. A point of access for Internet2 (and possibly other high-speed networks) that supports data transfer speeds of at least 1 Gbps. Approximately 30 gigaPoPs are located at various points across the United States.

G

GIGO *n. See* garbage in, garbage out.

GIMP *n.* Acronym for **G**NU **I**mage **M**anipulation **P**rogram. A free and expandable graphics program for image creation and photo manipulation. GIMP is available for various UNIX-related platforms, including Linux and Mac OS X.

GIOP *n.* Short for **G**eneral **I**nter-ORB **P**rotocol. *See* IIOP.

GIS *n. See* geographic information system.

GKS *n. See* Graphical Kernel System.

glare filter *n.* A transparent mask placed over the screen of a video monitor to reduce or eliminate light reflected from its glass surface.

glitch *n.* **1.** A problem, usually minor. **2.** A brief surge in electrical power.

global *adj.* Pertaining to an entire document, file, or program rather than to a restricted segment of it. *Compare* local, local variable.

global assembly cache *n.* A machine-wide code cache, introduced with Microsoft's .NET systems, that stores assemblies specifically installed to be shared by many applications on the computer. Applications deployed in the global assembly cache must have a strong name. *Acronym:* GAC. *See also* assembly cache, strong name.

global catalog *n.* A directory Windows database that applications and clients can query to locate any object in a forest. The global catalog is hosted on one or more domain controllers in the forest. It contains a partial replica of every domain directory partition in the forest. These partial replicas include replicas of every object in the forest, as follows: the attributes most frequently used in search operations and the attributes required to locate a full replica of the object. *See also* Active Directory, attribute, domain controller, forest, replication.

globally unique identifier *n.* In the Component Object Model (COM), a 16-byte code that identifies an interface to an object across all computers and networks. Such an identifier is unique because it contains a time stamp and a code based on the network address hardwired on the host computer's LAN interface card. These identifiers are generated by a utility program. *Acronym:* GUID.

global operation *n.* An operation, such as a search and replace, that affects an entire document, program, or other object such as a disk.

Global Positioning System *n. See* GPS.

global search and replace *n.* A search-and-replace operation that finds and changes all instances of the selected string throughout a document. *See also* search and replace.

Global System for Mobile Communications *n. See* GSM.

global universal identification *n.* An identification scheme in which only one name is associated with a particular object; this name is accepted across platforms and applications. *Acronym:* GUID. *See also* globally unique identifier.

global variable *n.* A variable whose value can be accessed and modified by any statement in a program, not merely within a single routine in which it is defined. *See also* global. *Compare* local variable.

GMR *n. See* giant magnetoresistive head.

GNOME *n.* Acronym for **G**NU **N**etwork **O**bject **M**odel **E**nvironment. A popular open-source desktop environment for UNIX and UNIX-based operating systems such as Linux. GNOME provides a GUI desktop interface and basic applications that correspond to those found with Microsoft Windows or the Macintosh operating system. By providing a mainstream environment and familiar desktop appearance GNOME is intended to make UNIX easier for users. Development of GNOME is overseen by the GNOME Foundation, an association of computer industry companies and organizations with interests in the UNIX operating system. GNOME and KDE are leading contenders for consideration as a Linux desktop standard. *See also* KDE.

gnomon *n.* In computer graphics, a representation of the three-dimensional (*x-y-z*) axis system.

GNU *n.* Acronym for **G**NU's **N**ot **U**NIX. A collection of software based on the UNIX operating system maintained by the Free Software Foundation. GNU is distributed under the GNU General Public License, which requires that anyone who distributes GNU or a program based on GNU may charge only for distribution and support and must allow the user to modify and redistribute the code on the same terms. *See also* Free Software Foundation, General Public License. *Compare* Linux.

GNU Image Manipulation Program *n. See* GIMP.

Gnutella *n.* A file-sharing protocol that forms the basis of a number of peer-to-peer networking products. Gnutella forms a loose decentralized network with each user able to see and access all shared files of other Gnutella users. Unlike Napster, Gnutella does not require a central server, and any file type can be exchanged. Gnutella was originally developed by researchers at America Online's Nullsoft group but the original implementation of the protocol was never publicly released. An open-source Gnutella preview appeared that resulted in a number of variations becoming available. *See also* Napster.

Godwin's Law *n.* As originally proposed by Internet activist Michael Godwin, the theory that as an online discussion grows longer, a comparison involving Nazis or Hitler will inevitably be made. When a participant in an online discussion resorts to invoking such a comparison, other participants might cite Godwin's Law to indicate both that the person has lost the argument and that the discussion has continued too long.

Good Times virus *n.* A purported e-mail virus alluded to in a warning that has been propagated widely across the Internet, as well as by fax and standard mail. The letter claims that reading an e-mail message with the subject "Good Times" will cause damage to the user's system. In fact, it is currently impossible to harm a system by reading an e-mail message, although it is possible to include a virus in a file that is attached to an e-mail message. Some consider the chain letter itself to be the "virus" that wastes Internet bandwidth and the reader's time. Information on such hoaxes and on real viruses can be obtained from CERT (http://www.cert.org/). *See also* urban legend, virus.

Gopher or **gopher** *n.* An Internet utility for finding textual information and presenting it to the user in the form of hierarchical menus, from which the user selects submenus or files that can be downloaded and displayed. One Gopher client may access all available Gopher servers, so the user accesses a common "Gopherspace." The name of the program is a three-way pun: it is designed to go for desired information; it tunnels through the Internet and digs the information up; and it was developed at the University of Minnesota, whose athletic teams are named the Golden Gophers. Gopher is being subsumed by the World Wide Web.

Gopher server *n.* The software that provides menus and files to a Gopher user. *See also* Gopher.

Gopher site *n.* A computer on the Internet on which a Gopher server runs. *See also* Gopher, Gopher server.

Gopherspace *n.* The total set of information on the Internet that is accessible as menus and documents through Gopher. *See also* Gopher.

GOSIP *n.* Acronym for **G**overnment **O**pen **S**ystems **I**nterconnection **P**rofile. A U.S. government requirement that all of its new network purchases comply with the ISO/OSI standards. GOSIP went into effect on August 15, 1990, but was never fully implemented and was replaced by POSIT.

GOTO statement *n.* A control statement used in programs to transfer execution to some other statement; the high-level equivalent of a branch or jump instruction. Use of GOTO statements is generally discouraged because they make it difficult not only for a programmer to trace the logic of a program but also for a compiler to generate optimized code. *See also* branch instruction, jump instruction, spaghetti code.

.gov *n.* In the Internet's Domain Name System, the top-level domain that identifies addresses operated by government agencies. The domain name .gov appears as a suffix at the end of the address. In the United States, only non-military federal government agencies may use the .gov domain. State governments in the United States use the top-level domain of .state.us, with .us preceded by the two-letter abbreviation for the state, or just .us; other regional governments in the United States are registered under the .us domain. *See also* DNS (definition 1), domain (definition 3), .state.us, .us. *Compare* .com, .edu, .mil, .net, .org.

Government Open Systems Interconnection Profile *n. See* GOSIP.

GPF *n. See* General Protection Fault.

GPIB *n. See* General-Purpose Interface Bus.

GPL *n. See* General Public License.

GPRS *n.* Acronym for **G**eneral **P**acket **R**adio **S**ervice. A third-generation enhancement to the Global System for Mobile Communications (GSM), which supports non-voice applications such as Web browsing and other servicing requiring transfer of data packets without limits in message size. Systems using the service can be immediately connected when needed and therefore seem to the users to be always on. *See also* GSM, TDMA.

GPS *n.* Acronym for **G**lobal **P**ositioning **S**ystem. A radio navigation system developed by the U.S. Department of

Defense that uses a constellation of 24 earth satellites, which are monitored by ground-based control stations, to provide precise, continuous worldwide positioning and timing information. GPS offers two services: a public Standard Positioning Service that provides positioning data accurate to within 100 meters horizontally and 156 meters vertically and time accurate to within 340 nanoseconds; and a Precise Positioning Service, principally for government and military use, with positioning data accurate to within 22 meters horizontally and 27.7 meters vertically and time accurate to within 100 nanoseconds. *See also* GPS receiver.

GPS receiver *n.* A device that includes an antenna, a radio receiver, and a processor for use with the worldwide GPS (Global Positioning System). A GPS receiver uses position and time information from four GPS satellites to calculate precise information about its current location, its speed of travel, and the current time. A portable GPS receiver may be a stand-alone device or a plug-in unit for use with a portable computer. GPS receivers are used for scientific work, such as surveying, mapping, and studies of volcanoes, as well as for land, sea, and air navigation. On the consumer front, they are used in outdoor activities such as hiking and sailing and in cars to provide location, destination, and traffic information. *See also* GPS.

grabber *n.* **1.** A device for capturing graphical image data from a video camera or another full-motion video source and putting it into memory. *Also called:* frame grabber, video digitizer. **2.** Any device for capturing data. **3.** Software that takes a snapshot of the currently displayed screen image by transferring a portion of video memory to a file on disk. **4.** In some graphics-based applications, a special type of mouse pointer.

graceful exit *n.* The methodical termination of a process, even under error conditions, that allows the operating system or parent process to regain normal control, leaving the system in a state of equilibrium. This is expected behavior. *See also* fail-soft system.

grade *n.* In communications, the range of frequencies available for transmission on a single channel. For example, voice-grade telephone frequencies range from about 300 hertz (Hz) through 3400 Hz.

grade of service *n.* The probability that a user of a shared communications network, such as a public telephone system, will receive an "all channels busy" signal. The grade of service is used as a measure of the traffic-handling abil-

ity of the network and is usually applied to a specific period, such as the peak traffic hour. A grade of service of 0.002, for example, assumes that a user has a 99.8 percent chance that a call made during the specified period will reach its intended destination.

gradient *n.* A smooth progression of colors and shades, usually from one color to another color, or from one shade to another shade of the same color.

Graffiti *n.* A software application developed by Palm to allow handwriting recognition on personal digital assistants (PDAs). Graffiti contains preprogrammed shapes for each letter, which users of the application must match as closely as possible when writing. Text is written directly onto the PDA's display screen using a stylus. The Graffiti application then passes the translated letter to the PDA's application.

grafPort *n.* A structure used on the Apple Macintosh to define a graphics environment with its own pen size, font, fill patterns, and so on. Each window has a grafPort, and grafPorts can be used to send graphics to off-screen windows or files.

graftal *n.* One of a family of geometric forms, similar to fractals but easier to compute. Graftals are often used in the special-effects industry to create synthetic images of structures such as trees and plants. *See also* fractal.

grammar checker *n.* A software accessory that checks text for errors in grammatical construction.

Grammar Specification Language *n. See* GSL.

grandfather *n. See* generation (definition 1).

grandfather/father/son *adj. See* generation (definition 1).

grandparent *n. See* generation (definition 2).

granularity *n.* A description, from "coarse" to "fine," of a computer activity or feature (such as screen resolution, searching and sorting, or time slice allocation) in terms of the size of the units it handles (pixels, sets of data, or time slices). The larger the pieces, the coarser the granularity.

graph *n.* **1.** In programming, a data structure consisting of zero or more nodes and zero or more edges, which connect pairs of nodes. If any two nodes in a graph can be connected by a path along edges, the graph is said to be connected. A subgraph is a subset of the nodes and edges within a graph. A graph is directed (a digraph) if each edge links two nodes together only in one direction. A graph is weighted if each edge has some value associated with it. *See also* node (definition 3), tree. **2.** *See* chart.

Graphical Device Interface *n. See* GDI.

graphical interface *n. See* graphical user interface.

Graphical Kernel System *n.* A computer graphics standard, recognized by ANSI and ISO, that specifies methods of describing, manipulating, storing, and transferring graphical images. It functions at the application level rather than the hardware level and deals with logical workstations (combinations of input and output devices such as keyboard, mouse, and monitor) rather than with individual devices. Graphical Kernel System was developed in 1978 to handle two-dimensional graphics; the later modification, GKS-3D, extended the standard to three-dimensional graphics. *Acronym:* GKS. *See also* ANSI, ISO.

graphical user interface *n.* A visual computer environment that represents programs, files, and options with graphical images, such as icons, menus, and dialog boxes, on the screen. The user can select and activate these options by pointing and clicking with a mouse or, often, with the keyboard. A particular item (such as a scroll bar) works the same way for the user in all applications, because the graphical user interface provides standard software routines to handle these elements and report the user's actions (such as a mouse click on a particular icon or at a particular location in text, or a key press); applications call these routines with specific parameters rather than attempting to reproduce them from scratch. *Acronym:* GUI.

graphic character *n.* Any character that is represented by a visible symbol, such as an ASCII character. A graphic character is not the same as a graphics character. *Compare* graphics character.

graphic limits *n.* On a computer screen, the boundary of a graphical image in a graphics software program, including all the area enclosed within the graphic. In some graphics environments the limits of a graphic consist of the smallest rectangle that can completely enclose it, called its *bounding rectangle* or *bounding box.*

graphics accelerator *n.* A video adapter that contains a graphics coprocessor. A graphics accelerator can update the video display much more quickly than the CPU can, and it frees the CPU for other tasks. A graphics accelerator is a necessity for modern software such as graphical user interfaces and multimedia applications. *See also* graphics coprocessor, video adapter.

graphics adapter *n.* A video adapter capable of displaying graphics as well as alphanumeric characters. Almost all video adapters in common use today are graphics adapters.

graphics card *n. See* video adapter.

graphics character *n.* A character that can be combined with others to create simple graphics, such as lines, boxes, and shaded or solid blocks. See the illustration. *Compare* graphic character.

Graphics character. *Box built up from line graphics characters.*

graphics controller *n.* The part of the EGA and VGA video adapters that allows the computer to access the video buffer. *See also* EGA, VGA.

graphics coprocessor *n.* A specialized microprocessor, included in some video adapters, that can generate graphical images such as lines and filled areas in response to instructions from the CPU, freeing the CPU for other work.

graphics data structure *n.* A data structure that is designed specifically for representing one or more elements of a graphical image.

graphics engine *n.* **1.** A display adapter that handles high-speed graphics-related processing, freeing the CPU for other tasks. *Also called:* graphics accelerator, video accelerator. **2.** Software that, based on commands from an application, sends instructions for creating graphic images to the hardware that actually creates the images. Examples are Macintosh QuickDraw and Windows Graphics Device Interface (GDI).

graphics export component *n.* A technology developed by Apple for creating, editing, publishing, and viewing multimedia content. The graphics export component provides an application programming interface that enables a QuickTime player to export still images into a variety of file formats.

graphics import component *n.* A technology developed by Apple for creating, editing, publishing, and viewing multimedia content. The graphics import component provides an application programming interface that enables a QuickTime player to import still images from a variety of file formats.

G

Graphics Interchange Format *n. See* GIF.

graphics interface *n. See* graphical user interface.

graphics mode *n.* **1.** On computers such as the IBM PC, the display mode in which lines and characters on the screen are drawn pixel by pixel. Because graphics mode creates images from individual dots on the screen, programs have more flexibility in creating images than they do in text (or character) mode. Thus, the computer is able to display a mouse pointer as an arrowhead or other shape rather than as a blinking square or rectangle, and it can display character attributes, such as boldface and italics, as they will appear in print rather than using conventions such as highlighting, underlining, or alternate colors. *Compare* text mode. **2.** A particular set of color and resolution values, often related to a particular video adapter, such as VGA color with 16 colors and 640 x 480 pixels on the screen. *See also* high resolution, low resolution, resolution (definition 1).

graphics port *n. See* grafPort.

graphics primitive *n.* A drawing element, such as a text character, an arc, or a polygon, that is drawn and manipulated as a single unit and is combined with other primitives to create an image. *Compare* entity.

graphics printer *n.* A printer, such as a laser, ink-jet, or dot-matrix impact printer, that can produce graphics formed pixel by pixel and not merely text characters. Nearly all printers presently used with personal computers are graphics printers; daisy-wheel printers are the exception. *Compare* character printer.

graphics processor *n. See* graphics coprocessor.

graphics tablet *n.* A device used to input graphics position information in engineering, design, and illustration applications. A flat rectangular plastic board is equipped with a puck or a pen (also called a stylus) and sensing electronics that report the position of the puck or stylus to the computer, which translates that data into a cursor position on the screen. *Also called:* digitizing tablet. *See also* puck, stylus.

graphics terminal *n.* A terminal capable of displaying graphics as well as text. Such terminals usually interpret graphics control commands rather than receiving streams of already-processed pixels.

Graphite *n.* An alternate appearance option in Mac OS X that features a gray interface with more subtle highlights than the colorful standard Aqua appearance. *See also* Aqua.

Gray code *n. See* cyclic binary code.

gray market *n.* Resellers and other sources for hardware and software that obtain their inventory from distributors other than those authorized by the manufacturer. Gray market transactions may involve items that wholesalers purchase at discount and resell at higher prices, or they may refer to purchases made when sudden spikes in demand cannot be satisfied through normal distribution channels. On a more unsavory front, gray market transactions can also *illegally* involve stolen or counterfeit hardware, such as CPU chips and software packages.

gray scale *n.* A sequence of shades ranging from black through white, used in computer graphics to add detail to images or to represent a color image on a monochrome output device. Like the number of colors in a color image, the number of shades of gray depends on the number of bits stored per pixel. Grays may be represented by actual gray shades, by halftone dots, or by dithering. *See also* dithering, halftone.

greater than *adj. See* relational operator.

greater than or equal to *adj. See* relational operator.

Great Plains *n.* Microsoft Corporation's suite of business solution applications for finance, accounting, and management. Microsoft acquired the Great Plains applications in December 2000, when it purchased Great Plains Software, which had originally developed the suite of business accounting and management solutions. Great Plains Business Solutions include applications for accounting and finance, customer relations management, e-commerce, human resources, manufacturing, project accounting, and supply-chain management.

Great Renaming *n.* The changeover to the current system of Usenet hierarchies throughout the Internet. Before the Great Renaming, which took place in 1985, nonlocal newsgroup names had the form net.*; for example, a group that carried source code, formerly named net.sources, was renamed comp.sources.misc. *See also* local newsgroups, newsgroup, traditional newsgroup hierarchy, Usenet.

greeking *n.* **1.** The use of gray bars or other graphics to represent lines of characters too small to be drawn legibly on a screen at the chosen resolution, such as when viewing the layout of a whole page or pair of facing pages. **2.** The use of nonsense words to represent the text of a document in design samples. A garbled Latin text beginning "Lorem ipsum dolor sit amet" is traditionally used for this purpose.

Greeking does not involve substituting the Greek alphabet for the Roman one.

greek text *n. See* greeking.

Green Book *n.* A specifications book written by the Sony and Philips Corporations, covering the CD-I (compact disc-interactive) technology. *See also* CD-I. *Compare* Orange Book (definition 2), Red Book (definition 2).

green PC *n.* A computer system designed to conserve energy. For example, some computers shut off power to nonessential systems when no input has been detected for a certain amount of time, a condition known as *sleep mode*. Green PCs may also be distinguished by the use of minimal packaging materials and replaceable components, such as toner cartridges, that are recyclable.

Gregorian calendar *n.* The calendar used today in the Western world, introduced by Pope Gregory XIII in 1582 to replace the Julian calendar. To approximate better the length of the astronomical year (365.2422 days), years divisible by 100 are leap years only if they are also divisible by 400 (thus, 2000 was a leap year, but 1900 was not). To correct the error accumulated since A.D. 1, 10 days were dropped from October 1582; however, Britain and the American colonies did not adopt the Gregorian calendar until 1752 and had to remove 11 days then. Because the Gregorian calendar uses several rules for calculating leap years, systems based on algorithms that did not correctly determine that the year 2000 was a leap year might have encountered difficulties after February 28, 2000. *Compare* Julian calendar.

grep[1] *n.* Acronym for **g**lobal **r**egular **e**xpression **p**rint. A UNIX command used to search a file or files by keyword.

grep[2] *vb.* To search text, especially with the UNIX grep utility.

grid *n.* **1.** Two sets of lines or linear elements at right angles to each other. **2.** A spreadsheet is a grid of rows and columns; a graphics screen is a grid of horizontal and vertical lines of pixels. **3.** In optical character recognition, a grid is used for measuring or specifying characters. *See also* Cartesian coordinates.

gridlines *n.* **1.** Lines across a page in a graphics program that correspond to intervals on a ruler. **2.** In many word-processing and spreadsheet programs, thin lines that indicate the cell boundaries in a table. **3.** Lines you can add to a chart that make it easier to view and evaluate data. Grid-

lines extend from the tick marks on an axis across the plot area. Gridlines do not print when you print a document.

grok *vb.* To understand deeply and appreciatively. The term comes from Robert A. Heinlein's novel *Stranger in a Strange Land*, where it is also a Martian word for "to drink" and implies the kind of devoted interest that a Martian—native of a dry planet—would have in water. Hackers often use it (for example, in Internet discussions) in reference to computer expertise. *See also* cyberpunk.

ground *n.* A conducting path from an electric circuit to earth or to a conducting body serving in place of earth, usually used as a safety device. *See also* grounding.

grounding *n.* The connection of sections of an electrical circuit to a common conductor, called the *ground*, which serves as the reference for the other voltages in the circuit. The ground conductor on installed circuit boards is usually connected to the chassis, or metal frame, holding the electronic parts; the chassis is in turn usually connected to the third (round) prong on the power plug, which connects to a ground circuit that is, in fact, connected to the earth. This is important to avoid creating a shock hazard.

group[1] *n.* A collection of elements that can be treated as a whole, such as a collection of records in a database report, or a collection of objects that can be moved and transformed as a single object in a drawing program. In various multiuser operating systems, a group is a set of user accounts, sometimes called *members*; privileges can be specified for the group, and each member will then have those privileges. *See also* built-in groups, local group, user account.

group[2] *vb.* In a drawing program, to transform a number of objects into a group. *See also* drawing program.

Group Policy Object *n.* A collection of Group Policy settings that are essentially the documents created by the Group Policy snap-in, a utility in Microsoft Windows 2000. These settings are stored at the domain level and affect users and computers contained in sites, domains, and organizational units. *Acronym:* GPO.

groupware *n.* Software intended to enable a group of users on a network to collaborate on a particular project. Groupware may provide services for communication (such as e-mail), collaborative document development, scheduling, and tracking. Documents may include text, images, or other forms of information.

grovel *vb.* **1.** To search or do other work at great length without apparent progress. Some programs grovel over a whole input file before they begin to produce output. A programmer may have to grovel through manuals in search of documentation on a particular command, or through code in search of a bug. **2.** To post a plea for some favor to a newsgroup.

grunge *n. See* dead code.

GSL *n.* Acronym for **G**rammar **S**pecification **L**anguage. A grammar description format used by VoiceXML applications and other speech recognition systems. GSL was developed by Nuance and supports a number of XML-based speech editing and voice-browsing applications.

GSM *n.* Acronym for **G**lobal **S**ystem for **M**obile Communications. A digital cellular phone technology first deployed in 1992. In 2000, GSM was the predominant phone technology in Europe, and was used by 250 million subscribers worldwide. GSM phones offer a removable smart card containing subscriber account information. This card can be transferred from phone to phone quickly and easily, allowing the user to access his account from any phone in the system. Various enhancements to the GSM system allow increased Web browsing and data transfer options. *See also* GPRS, TDMA.

guest *n.* A common name for a login account that can be accessed without a password. BBSs and service providers often maintain such an account so that prospective subscribers can sample the services offered.

guest account *n.* An account used to log onto a system or domain where the user does not have access. Generally, resources and access are severely limited. On Windows NT technology, this account is built in to all domains. *See also* domain.

GUI *n. See* graphical user interface.

GUID *n. See* globally unique identifier, global universal identification.

GUID partition table *n.* A disk-partitioning scheme that is used by the eXtensible Firmware Interface (EFI) in Itanium-based computers. A GUID partition table offers more advantages than master boot record (MBR) partitioning because it allows up to 128 partitions per disk, provides support for volumes up to 18 exabytes in size, allows primary and backup partition tables for redundancy, and supports unique disk and partition IDs (GUIDs). *Acronym:* GPT. *See also* eXtensible Firmware Interface, Itanium, master boot record.

gunzip *n.* A GNU utility for decompressing files compressed with gzip. *See also* GNU, uncompress. *Compare* gzip.

guru *n.* A technical expert who is available to help solve problems and to answer questions in an intelligible way. *See also* techie, wizard (definition 1).

gutter *n.* The blank area between two or more columns of text or between two facing pages in a publication.

gzip *n.* A GNU utility for compressing files. *See also* compress[2], GNU. *Compare* gunzip.

H *n. See* henry.

H.320 *n.* An International Telecommunications Union (ITU) standard that enables interoperability among video-conferencing equipment from different manufacturers over circuit-switched services such as ISDN, thus making desktop video conferencing viable. H.320 establishes the common formats necessary to make audio and video inputs and outputs compatible and defines a protocol that makes it possible for a multimedia terminal to use audio/visual communications links and synchronization. *See also* International Telecommunications Union, ISDN, video conferencing.

H.323 *n.* An International Telecommunications Union (ITU) interoperability protocol enabling cross-communication of multimedia products and applications over packet-based networks. Under H.323, multimedia products offered by one vendor can work with those of another, regardless of hardware compatibility. For example, a PC can share audio and video streams over either an intranet or the Internet. Applications are thus network-, platform-, and application-independent. *See also* International Telecommunications Union, packet switching.

H.324 *n.* An International Telecommunications Union (ITU) standard for simultaneously transmitting video, data, and voice over POTS (Plain Old Telephone Service) modem connections. *See also* POTS.

hack[1] *n.* **1.** A modification to the code in a program, often made without taking the time to find an elegant solution. **2.** A sloppy job. *See also* kludge (definition 2), patch[2].

hack[2] *vb.* **1.** To apply creative ingenuity to a programming problem or project. **2.** To alter the behavior of an application or an operating system by modifying its code rather than by running the program and selecting options.

hacker *n.* **1.** A computerphile; a person who is totally engrossed in computer technology and computer programming or who likes to examine the code of operating systems and other programs to see how they work. **2.** A person, more commonly considered a cracker, who uses computer expertise for illicit ends, such as by gaining access to computer systems without permission and tam-pering with programs and data. *Also called:* cracker. *See also* hacktivist.

hacktivist *n.* An individual who furthers political or social agendas through hacking activity. Hacktivists may break into computer systems to disrupt traffic or cause confusion, and may alter Web pages or e-mail to display content sympathetic to a specific cause. *See also* hacker.

HAGO *n.* Acronym for **h**ave **a g**ood **o**ne. An expression used to conclude e-mail messages or in signing off from IRC.

HailStorm *n. See* .NET My Services.

hairline *n.* The smallest amount of visible space or the narrowest line that is displayable on a printed page. The size of a hairline depends on the materials, hardware, and software used or on the organizations involved. The United States Postal Service defines a hairline as 1/2 point (roughly 0.007 inch), whereas the Graphic Arts Technical Foundation (GATF) defines a hairline as 0.003 inch. *See also* point[1] (definition 1), rule (definition 1).

HAL *n.* **1.** *See* hardware abstraction layer. **2.** In the 1968 book and movie "2001: A Space Odyssey" by novelist Arthur C. Clarke, the intelligent but eventually psychotic computer, HAL 9000, that takes over a spaceship bound for Jupiter. The name HAL is an acronym for **H**euristic/**AL**gorithmic computer, but the letters H-A-L are also one letter removed from I-B-M in the alphabet.

half adder *n.* A logic circuit that can add two input data bits and produce a sum bit and a carry bit as output. A half adder cannot accept a carry bit from a previous addition; to add two input bits and a carry bit, a full adder is required. To add two multibit binary numbers, a computer uses a half adder and one or more full adders. *See also* carry bit, full adder.

half-card *n. See* short card.

half-duplex[1] *adj.* Of or pertaining to two-way communication that takes place in only one direction at a time. For example, transmission between half-duplex modems occurs when one modem waits to transmit until the other has finished sending. *Compare* duplex[1].

half-duplex[2] *n.* Two-way electronic communication that takes place in only one direction at a time. *Also called:* half-duplex transmission. *Compare* duplex[2] (definition 1), simplex transmission.

half-duplex transmission *n. See* half-duplex[2].

half-height drive *n.* Any of a generation of disk drives that are roughly one-half the height of the previous generation of drives.

half router *n.* A device that connects a local area network (LAN) to a communications line (such as one to the Internet) using a modem and that controls the routing of data to individual stations on the LAN.

halftone *n.* A printed reproduction of a photograph or other illustration, using evenly spaced spots of varying diameter to produce apparent shades of gray. The darker the shade at a particular point in the image, the larger the corresponding spot in the halftone. In traditional publishing, halftones are created by photographing an image through a screen. In desktop publishing, each halftone spot is represented by an area containing a number of dots printed by a laser printer or digital imagesetter. In both cases, the frequency of the halftone dots is measured in lines per inch. Higher printer resolution enables effective use of higher frequencies of halftone dots, enhancing image quality. *See also* dithering, gray scale, imagesetter, spot function.

half-word *n.* Half the number of bits considered to be a word in a particular computer; if a word is 32 bits, a half-word will be 16 bits or 2 bytes. *See also* word.

hammer *n.* The part of an impact printer that strikes or causes another component to strike the ribbon to print a character on the paper. In a dot-matrix printer, the pins or wires are the hammers; in a daisy-wheel printer, the hammer strikes the daisy wheel.

Hamming code *n.* A family of error-correction codes named for R. W. Hamming of Bell Labs. In one of the simplest Hamming codes, every 4 data bits are followed by 3 check bits, each computed from the 4 data bits. If any one of the 7 bits becomes altered, a simple computation can detect the error and determine which bit is altered. *See also* error-correction coding, forward error correction.

handheld computer *n.* A computer small enough to be held in one hand while being operated with the other hand.

Handheld computers are commonly used in transportation and other field service industries. They are usually built to perform specific tasks. They often have restricted specialized keyboards rather than the standard QWERTY layout, smaller displays, input devices such as bar code readers, and communications devices for sending their data to a central computer; they rarely have disk drives. Their software is usually proprietary and stored in ROM. *See also* QWERTY keyboard, ROM. Compare handheld PC, PDA.

Handheld Device Markup Language *n. See* HDML.

Handheld Device Transport Protocol *n. See* HDTP.

handheld PC *n.* A computer that is small enough to fit in a jacket pocket and can run, for example, Windows CE (an operating system for handheld PCs and embedded systems) and applications made for that operating system. See the illustration. *Acronym:* HPC. *Compare* handheld computer, PDA.

Handheld PC.

handheld scanner *n.* A type of scanner used as follows: the user passes the scan head, contained within a handheld unit, over the medium being scanned, such as a piece of paper. *See also* scan head, scanner. *Compare* drum scanner, feed scanner, flatbed scanner.

handle *n.* **1.** A pointer to a pointer; that is, a variable that contains the address of another variable, which in turn contains the address of the desired object. In certain operating systems, the handle points to a pointer stored in a fixed location in memory, whereas that pointer points to a movable block. If programs start from the handle whenever they access the block, the operating system can perform memory-management tasks such as garbage collection without affecting the programs. *See also* pointer. **2.** Any token that a program can use to identify and access an object such as a device, a file, a window, or a dialog box. **3.** One of several small squares displayed around a graphical object in a drawing program. The user can move or reshape the object by clicking on a handle and dragging. See the illustration. **4.** In online communication, such as chats and bulletin boards, the name a person uses to identify himself or herself. A handle is comparable to an alias or a nickname and is like those used with CB radio. **5.** A unique alphanumeric identifier of up to 10 characters assigned by InterNIC to the domain names, contacts, and network records in its domain name database. The NIC handle is used as a shorthand means of finding records and ensuring accuracy in the database. *Also called:* NIC handle.

 ——— Handle

Handle. *A computer graphic's handle.*

handler *n.* **1.** A routine that manages a common and relatively simple condition or operation, such as error recovery or data movement. **2.** In some object-oriented programming languages that support messages, a subroutine that processes a particular message for a particular class of objects. *See also* message, object-oriented programming.

handoff *n.* The process of transferring a wireless telephone signal between cell towers as a caller travels from one cell to another. A caller will not notice a smooth handoff, but an abrupt handoff can interfere with reception, with results ranging from momentary static to a disconnected call. *Also called:* handover. *See also* cell.

hands-free kit *n.* Wireless phone accessory that allows users to make calls without holding the phone. A basic kit includes a headset or an earpiece with a microphone. More elaborate sets for use in automobiles may include a power amplifier, dashboard microphone, phone cradle, and speakers.

handshake *n.* A series of signals acknowledging that communication or the transfer of information can take place between computers or other devices. A hardware handshake is an exchange of signals over specific wires (other than the data wires) in which each device indicates its readiness to send or receive data. A software handshake consists of signals transmitted over the same wires used to transfer data, as in modem-to-modem communications over telephone lines.

hands-on *adj.* Involving interactive work with a computer or a computer program. A hands-on tutorial, for example, would teach a skill (such as the use of a program) by means of practice sessions and question-and-answer dialogues.

handwriting input device *n.* A tool, such as a digital pen and tablet, used to enter text by writing instead of typing. Along with writing tablets, additional devices include 3-D drawing or computer-aided design (CAD) tablets, a tablet PC, or moving a mouse on the mouse pad.

handwriting recognition *n.* **1.** The ability of a computer to identify a user by recognizing features of handwriting, especially a signature. **2.** The ability of a computer to translate handwritten text into character data for input. This technology is still under considerable development, and most handwriting recognition programs require users to form letters and words in a very consistent and clear manner to work adequately. The development of handwriting recognition programs has been spurred by PDAs, which frequently have keyboards that are too small for data entry, and software designed for Asian markets that have languages with numerous characters, which makes keyboards a cumbersome method for entering text. *See also* PDA. *Compare* optical character recognition.

hang *vb.* To stop responding. A hung program or computer system does not respond to user input, but the screen looks as if everything is running normally. The program or system might be waiting for something—for example, information from a network—or it might have terminated abnormally. It might resume running normally on its own, or the user might need to terminate and restart the program or reboot the computer. A hung computer system is said to be locked up. *See also* crash[2] (definition 1).

hanging indent *n.* Placement of the beginning of the first line of a paragraph farther to the left than the subsequent lines. *Also called:* outdent. *Compare* indent.

haptics *n.* The study of the sense of touch. This study has extended to the study of human interaction with computer technology through tactile means. Haptics technology is central to virtual reality gaming settings, in which computers could sense and respond to finger, hand, body, or head movements. The computer could also re-create the sense of touch by altering texture, increasing resistance, or other simulations appropriate to the user's virtual reality experience. *See also* force feedback.

hard *adj.* **1.** Permanent, fixed, or physically defined; unchangeable by the ordinary operation of a computer system. *See also* hard copy, hard error, hard return, hard-sectored disk. *Compare* soft (definition 1). **2.** Retaining magnetization even in the absence of an external magnetic field. *Compare* soft (definition 2).

hard card *n.* A circuit board, carrying a hard disk and containing its controller, that plugs into an expansion slot and uses the expansion bus for power as well as for data and control signals. By contrast, a hard disk in a drive bay communicates with a separate controller card by a ribbon cable and has a direct cable to the computer's main power supply. *See also* controller, drive bay, expansion slot, ribbon cable.

hard-coded *adj.* **1.** Designed to handle a specific situation only. **2.** Depending on values embedded in the program code rather than on values that can be input and changed by the user.

hard copy *n.* Printed output on paper, film, or other permanent medium. *Compare* soft copy.

hard disk *n.* A device containing one or more inflexible platters coated with material in which data can be recorded magnetically, together with their read/write heads, the head-positioning mechanism, and the spindle motor in a sealed case that protects against outside contaminants. The protected environment allows the head to fly 10 to 25 millionths of an inch above the surface of a platter rotating typically at 3600 to 7200 rpm; therefore, much more data can be stored and accessed much more quickly than on a floppy disk. Most hard disks contain from two to eight platters. See the illustration. *Also called:* hard disk drive. *Compare* floppy disk.

Read/write head

Platter

Hard disk. *The cover of this hard disk has been removed to reveal the components within.*

hard disk drive *n. See* hard disk.

hard disk type *n.* One or more numbers that inform a computer about the characteristics of a hard disk, such as the number of read/write heads and the number of cylinders the hard disk contains. The hard disk type numbers are usually marked on a label attached to the disk and must be input to the computer when the hard disk is installed, often by means of the computer's CMOS setup program. *See also* CMOS setup.

hard error *n.* **1.** An error caused by a hardware failure or by accessing incompatible hardware. *See also* hard failure. *Compare* soft error. **2.** An error that prevents a program from returning to normal operation. *See also* fatal error.

hard failure *n.* A cessation of function from which no recovery is possible, usually requiring a call to a repair service to correct. *Also called:* hardware failure.

hard hyphen *n. See* hyphen.

hard return *n.* A character input by the user to indicate that the current line of text is to end and a new line is to begin. In word-processing programs that automatically break lines within the margins of a page, a hard return indicates the end of a paragraph. In text-entry programs that lack wordwrap, on the other hand, a hard return is required to end each line, and often two or more hard returns are needed to end a paragraph. *See also* wordwrap. *Compare* soft return.

hard-sectored disk *n.* A floppy disk whose data sectors have been physically marked with punched holes that are detected by sensors in the drive to locate the beginning of each sector. *Compare* soft-sectored disk.

hard space *n. See* nonbreaking space.

hardware *n.* The physical components of a computer system, including any peripheral equipment such as printers, modems, and mouse devices. *Compare* firmware, software.

hardware abstraction layer *n.* In advanced operating systems such as Windows NT, Windows 2000, and Windows XP a layer in which assembly language code is isolated. A hardware abstraction layer functions similarly to an application programming interface (API) and is used by programmers to write device-independent applications. *Acronym:* HAL. *See also* application programming interface, device independence.

hardware address *n. See* physical address.

hardware check *n.* **1.** An automatic check performed by hardware to detect internal errors or problems. **2.** On a PC, a check of system hardware performed by a PC's BIOS

(Basic Input/Output System) during the POST (Power On Self Test) portion of the startup process.

hardware conversion *n.* Changing all or part of a computer system to work with new or different devices.

hardware cryptographic module *n.* Hardware designed to handle the cryptographic functions necessary for data security. For example, a hardware cryptographic module, or HCM, can be used in an SSL-enabled Web server to reduce CPU processing time and improve overall performance by working to secure data during online transactions. Using an HCM allows the Web server to continue processing customer requests. *Acronym:* HCM. *See also* SSL.

hardware-dependent *adj.* Of or pertaining to programs, languages, or computer components and devices that are tied to a particular computer system or configuration. Assembly language, for example, is hardware-dependent because it is created for and works only with a particular make or model of microprocessor.

hardware emulation layer *n.* In advanced operating systems such as Windows NT, Windows 2000, and Windows XP a layer in which software drivers duplicate hardware functionality. This allows software programs to use hardware features even if the hardware is not present. *Acronym:* HEL. *Compare* hardware abstraction layer.

hardware failure *n.* A malfunction of a physical component in a computer system, such as a disk head crash or memory error. *See also* hard failure.

hardware handshake *n. See* handshake.

hardware interrupt *n.* A request for service from the central processing unit, generated either externally by a hardware device such as a disk drive or an input/output port, or internally by the CPU itself. External hardware interrupts are used for such situations as a character received from a port and needing to be processed, a disk drive ready to transfer a block of data, or a tick of the system timer. Internal hardware interrupts occur when a program attempts an impossible action such as accessing an unavailable address or dividing by zero. Hardware interrupts are assigned levels of importance or priority. The highest priority is given to a type of interrupt called a nonmaskable interrupt—one that indicates a serious error, such as a memory failure, that must be serviced immediately. *See also* external interrupt, interrupt.

hardware key *n.* **1.** A security device connected to an input/output port to permit the use of a particular software package on that computer. The use of the hardware key permits backup copying of software but prevents its unlicensed use on additional computers. *Also called:* dongle. **2.** Any physical device used to secure a computer system from unauthorized access, such as the lock on the front of the cabinet of some personal computers.

hardware monitor *n.* A separate board-level circuit used to oversee the performance of a hardware/software system. A hardware monitor can detect the cause of a fatal error such as a system crash, whereas a software monitor or debugger cannot. *Compare* debugger.

hardware profile *n.* A set of data that describes the configuration and characteristics of a given piece of computer equipment. Such data is typically used to configure computers for use with peripheral devices.

hardware tree *n.* In Windows 9x, a data structure containing information about the configuration and requirements of a system's hardware devices. Consisting of nodes that point to active devices, the hardware tree is dynamic and is reconstructed every time the operating system is started or refreshed. The hardware tree facilitates the Plug and Play capability of Windows 9x.

hardwired *adj.* **1.** Built into a system using hardware such as logic circuits, rather than accomplished through programming. **2.** Physically connected to a system or a network, as by means of a network connector board and cable.

Harvard architecture *n.* A processor architecture that uses separate address buses for code and for data. This increases throughput by allowing the system to fetch instructions at the same time that it reads and writes data. This architecture also allows optimization of memory system design because instructions tend to be fetched sequentially, whereas data reads and writes are more random.

Harvard Mark I *n. See* Mark I.

Harvest research project *n. See* ICP.

hash¹ *n.* In many FTP client programs, a command that instructs the FTP client to display a pound sign (#) each time it sends or receives a block of data. *See also* FTP client.

hash² *vb.* To be mapped to a numerical value by a transformation known as a hashing function. Hashing is used to convert an identifier or key, meaningful to a user, into a value for the location of the corresponding data in a structure, such as a table. For example, given the key MOUSE and a hashing function that added up the ASCII values of the characters, divided the total by 127, and took the remainder, MOUSE would hash to 12 and the data identified by

MOUSE would be found among the items in entry 12 in the table.

hash coding *n. See* hash².

hashing algorithm *n.* A formula used to generate hash values and digital signatures. *Also called:* hash function.

hash search *n.* A search algorithm that uses hashing to find an element of a list. Hash searches are highly efficient because the hashing enables direct or almost direct access to the target element. *See also* binary search, hash², linear search, search algorithm.

hash total *n.* An error-checking value derived from the addition of a set of numbers taken from data (not necessarily numeric data) that is to be processed or manipulated in some way. After processing, the hash total is recalculated and compared with the original total. If the two do not match, the original data has been changed in some way.

hash value *n.* A value used in creating digital signatures. This value is generated by imposing a hashing algorithm onto a message. This value is then transformed, or signed, by a private key to produce a digital signature. *Also called:* message digest.

Haskell *n.* A functional programming language based on lambda calculus and suitable for the creation of applications that need to be highly modifiable.

Hayes-compatible *adj.* Responding to the same set of commands as the modems manufactured by Hayes Microcomputer Products. This command set has become the de facto standard for microcomputer modems.

HCM *n. See* hardware cryptographic module.

HDBMS *n. See* hierarchical database management system.

HDCP *n.* Acronym for **H**igh-bandwidth **D**igital **C**ontent **P**rotection. An encryption and authentication specification created by Intel for Digital Video Interface (DVI) devices such as digital cameras, high-definition televisions, and video disk players. HDCP is designed to protect transmissions between DVI devices from being copied.

HDF *n. See* Hierarchical Data Format.

HDLC *n.* Acronym for **H**igh-level **D**ata **L**ink **C**ontrol. A protocol for information transfer adopted by the ISO. HDLC is a bit-oriented, synchronous protocol that applies to the data-link (message-packaging) layer (layer 2 of the ISO/OSI reference model) for computer-to-microcomputer communications. Messages are transmitted in units called frames, which can contain differing amounts of data but

which must be organized in a particular way. *See also* frame (definition 1), ISO/OSI reference model.

HDML *n.* Acronym for **H**andheld **D**evice **M**arkup Language. A simple, first-generation markup language used to define hypertext-like content and applications for wireless and other handheld devices with small displays. This language is used primarily to create Web sites viewed via wireless phones and personal digital assistants (PDAs). HDML provides content consisting mainly of text with limited graphics. *See also* WML.

HDSL *n.* Acronym for **H**igh-bit-rate **D**igital Subscriber Line. A form of DSL, HDSL is a protocol for digital transmission of data over standard copper telecommunications lines (as opposed to fiber-optic lines) at rates of 1.544 Mbps in both directions. *Also called:* High-data-rate Digital Subscriber Line. *See also* DSL.

HDTP *n.* Acronym for **H**andheld **D**evice **T**ransport **P**rotocol. Protocol that enables a handheld device, such as a wireless phone or personal digital assistant (PDA), to access the Internet. HDTP regulates the input and output of data interpreted by the device's microbrowser. *See also* WAP.

HDTV *n.* Acronym for **H**igh-**D**efinition **T**ele**V**ision. A new television display standard that doubles the existing screen resolution and increases the screen aspect ratio from 4:3 to 16:9. This aspect ratio creates a television screen that is shaped like a movie screen.

HDTV-over-IP *n.* An Internet-based delivery option for High Definition Television (HDTV). HDTV-over-IP provides options for new and expanded services to ISPs, cable companies, telecommunications carriers, and business intranets, with its most extensive use in education. Universities use high-speed networks such as Internet2 to provide the intensive bandwidth demanded by HDTV-over-IP. Because HDTV-over-IP offers extreme image fidelity and sharpness, it is seen as ideal for delivery of distance education courses requiring precise visuals for which conventional video cannot provide sufficient resolution. *Also called:* iHDTV.

head *n.* **1.** The read/write mechanism in a disk or tape drive. It converts changes in the magnetic field of the material on the disk or tape surface to changing electrical signals and vice versa. Disk drives usually contain one head for each surface that can be read from and written to. **2.** In relation to software or documents, the top or beginning of something. **3.** In HTML, a section of coding that precedes the body of a document and is used to describe the document itself (title, author, and so on) rather than the elements within the document.

head arm *n. See* access arm.

head-cleaning device *n.* An apparatus for applying a small amount of cleaning fluid to a magnetic head to remove accumulated debris.

head crash *n.* A hard disk failure in which a read/write head, normally supported on a cushion of air only millionths of an inch thick, comes into contact with the platter, damaging the magnetic coating in which data is recorded. Still more damage occurs when the head picks up material gouged out of the surface and pushes it. A head crash can be caused by mechanical failure or by heavy shaking of the disk drive. If the crash occurs on a directory track, the whole disk may become instantly unreadable.

header *n.* **1.** In word processing or printing, text that is to appear at the top of pages. A header might be specified for the first page, all pages after the first, even pages, or odd pages. It usually includes the page number and may also show the date, the title, or other information about a document. *Also called:* heading, running head. *Compare* footer. **2.** An information structure that precedes and identifies the information that follows, such as a block of bytes in communications, a file on a disk, a set of records in a database, or an executable program. **3.** One or more lines in a program that identify and describe for human readers the program, function, or procedure that follows.

header file *n.* A file that is identified to be included at the beginning of a program in a language such as C and that contains the definitions of data types and declarations of variables used by the functions in the program.

header label *n.* An initial structure, such as an opening record, in the linear organization of a file or communication that describes the length, type, and structure of the data that follows. *Compare* trailer label (definition 1).

header record *n.* The first record in a sequence of records.

heading *n. See* header (definition 1).

headless computer *n.* A computer system that does not have a keyboard, mouse, or video monitor during normal operation.

head-mounted device *n.* A headset or helmet used with virtual reality systems ranging from gaming to military, medical, educational, and industrial applications. A head-mounted device contains small screens that display images

in such a way that the headset allows the wearer to view and move about in a three-dimensional, virtual world. The simulated environment is generated by a controlling computer, which adjusts the images in accordance with the wearer's head and body movements. A head-mounted device can include audio capability and is often used with an interactive input device, such as a joystick or glove. *Acronym:* HMD. *See also* virtual reality, wearable computer.

head-per-track disk drive *n.* A disk drive that has one read/write head for every data track. Such a disk drive has a very low seek time because the heads do not have to move across the disk surface to the required track for reading and writing. Because read/write heads are expensive, this type of drive is uncommon.

head positioning *n.* The process of moving the read/write head of a disk drive to the proper track for reading and writing.

head slot *n.* The oblong opening in the jacket of a floppy disk that provides access to the magnetic surface of the disk for the read/write head. See the illustration.

Head slot.

head switching *n.* The process of electrically switching among multiple read/write heads in a disk drive.

heap *n.* **1.** A portion of memory reserved for a program to use for the temporary storage of data structures whose existence or size cannot be determined until the program is running. To build and use such elements, programming languages such as C and Pascal include functions and procedures for requesting free memory from the heap, accessing it, and freeing it when it is no longer needed. In contrast to stack memory, heap memory blocks are not freed in reverse of the order in which they were allocated, so free blocks may be interspersed with blocks that are in use. As the program continues running, the blocks may have to be moved around so that small free blocks can be merged together into larger ones to meet the program's needs. *See also* garbage collection. *Compare* stack. **2.** A complete binary tree in which the value of any node is not exceeded by the value of either of its children. *See also* binary tree.

heap sort or **heapsort** *n.* A space-efficient sorting method that first arranges the key fields into a heap structure; then repeatedly removes the root of the heap, which must, by definition, have the largest key; and re-forms the heap. *See also* heap (definition 1).

heat pipe *n.* A cooling device consisting of a sealed metal tube containing a liquid and a wick. The liquid evaporates at the hot end; the vapor spreads along the tube to the cold end, where it condenses onto the wick; the liquid flows back along the wick to the hot end by capillary action. Heat pipes have been used in Pentium-based laptop computers, which have high cooling requirements and little room for conventional heat sinks. *Compare* heat sink.

heat sink *n.* A device that absorbs and dissipates heat produced by an electrical component, such as an integrated circuit, to prevent overheating. Heat sinks are usually made of metal and often have fins that assist in transferring heat to the atmosphere. See the illustration. *Compare* heat pipe.

Heat sink.

hecto- *prefix* Metric prefix meaning 10^2 (one hundred).

HEL *n. See* hardware emulation layer.

hello, world *n.* The output of the first program in Brian Kernighan and Dennis Ritchie's *The C Programming Language.* The program is traditionally the first test a C programmer makes in a new environment.

help *n.* **1.** The capability of many programs and operating systems to display advice or instructions for using their features when so requested by the user, as by a screen button or a menu item or a function key. The user can access help without interrupting work in progress or leafing through a manual. Some help facilities are context-sensitive, meaning that the user receives information specific to the task or command being attempted. *Also called:* online help. **2.** In many applications, a command that displays an explanation of another command that follows it. For instance, in many FTP programs, the command *help* can be followed by other commands, such as *cd* (change directory) or *ls* (list files and directories), to discover the purpose of these other commands. **3.** In versions 5 and 6 of MS-DOS, the command used to request information about MS-DOS commands, command parameters, and switches.

Help *n.* An item on a menu bar in a graphical user interface that enables the user to access the help feature of the present application. *See also* graphical user interface, help (definition 1), menu bar.

help desk *n.* **1.** Technical support staff who help solve users' problems with hardware or software systems or refer such problems to those who can solve them. Help desks are typically run by larger organizations, such as corporations, universities, or vendors to corporations, to assist users in the organization. **2.** A software application for tracking problems with hardware and software and their solutions.

helper *n. See* helper application.

helper application *n.* An application intended to be launched by a Web browser when the browser downloads a file that it is not able to process itself. Examples of helper applications are sound and movie players. Helper applications generally must be obtained and installed by users; they usually are not included in the browser itself. Many current Web browsers no longer require helper applications for common multimedia file formats. *Also called:* helper program. *Compare* ActiveX controls, plug-in (definition 2).

helper program *n. See* helper application.

Help key *n.* A key on the keyboard that the user can press to request help. *See also* function key, help (definition 1).

help screen *n.* A screen of information that is displayed when the user requests help. *See also* help (definition 1).

henry *n.* The unit of inductance. A current changing at a rate of one ampere per second will generate one volt across an inductance of one henry. In practice, a henry is a very large unit; inductances measured in millihenries (mH $= 10^{-3}$ H), microhenries (<MU>H $= 10^{-6}$ H), or nanohenries (nH $= 10^{-9}$ H) are more commonly encountered. Abbreviated H. *See also* inductance.

Hercules Graphics Card *n. See* HGC.

hertz *n.* The unit of frequency measurement; one cycle (of a periodic event such as a waveform) per second. Frequencies of interest in computers and electronic devices are often measured in kilohertz (kHz = 1000 Hz = 10^3 Hz), megahertz (MHz = 1000 kHz = 10^6 Hz), gigahertz (GHz = 1000 MHz = 10^9 Hz), or terahertz (THz = 1000 GHz = 10^{12} Hz). Abbreviated Hz.

hertz time *n. See* clock rate.

heterogeneous environment *n.* A computing milieu, usually within an organization, in which hardware and software from two or more manufacturers are used. *Compare* homogeneous environment.

heuristic *n.* An approach or algorithm that leads to a correct solution of a programming task by nonrigorous or self-learning means. One approach to programming is first to develop a heuristic and then to improve on it. The term comes from Greek *heuriskein* ("to discover, find out") and is related to "eureka" ("I have found it").

Hewlett-Packard Graphics Language *n. See* HPGL.

Hewlett-Packard Printer Control Language *n. See* Printer Control Language.

hex *n. See* hexadecimal.

hexadecimal *adj.* Using 16 rather than 10 as the base for representing numbers. The hexadecimal system uses the digits 0 through 9 and the letters A through F (uppercase or lowercase) to represent the decimal numbers 0 through 15. One hexadecimal digit is equivalent to 4 bits, and 1 byte can be expressed by two hexadecimal digits. For example, binary 0101 0011 corresponds to hexadecimal 53. To prevent confusion with decimal numbers, hexadecimal numbers in programs or documentation are usually followed by *H* or preceded by *&*, *$*, or *0x*. Thus, 10H = decimal 16; 100H = decimal 16^2 = decimal 256. Equivalents and conversion tables for binary, decimal, hexadecimal, and octal numbers are given in Appendix E. *Also called:* hex.

hexadecimal conversion *n.* Conversion of a number to or from the hexadecimal system. See Appendix E.

HFS *n. See* Hierarchical File System.

HFS+ *n.* Acronym for **H**ierarchal **F**ile **S**ystem Plus. The primary file system format available on the Macintosh operating system. With Mac OS 8.1, HFS+ replaced the earlier HFS format, adding support for names longer than 31 characters and Unicode representation of file and directory names. *Also called:* Mac OS Extended format.

HGA *n.* Acronym for **H**ercules **G**raphics **A**dapter. *See* HGC.

HGC *n.* Acronym for **H**ercules **G**raphics **C**ard. A video adapter introduced in 1982 by Hercules Computer Technology for IBM personal computers and compatibles and now superseded by VGA and its successors. It offered a monochrome graphics mode with 720 x 348 pixels. *See also* VGA.

HGC Plus *n.* A video adapter, introduced in 1986 by Hercules Computer Technology, that offered additional video buffer space to store 12 fonts of 256 characters each, which could be used for graphics characters.

HHOK *n.* Acronym for **h**a, **h**a, **o**nly **k**idding. An indication of humor or facetiousness often used in e-mail and online communications.

hibernation *n.* A state in which a computer shuts down after saving everything in memory to the hard disk. When the computer is powered on, programs and documents that were open are restored to the desktop. *See also* standby.

hidden file *n.* A file that, in order to protect it from deletion or modification, is not shown in the normal listing of the files contained in a directory. Such a file is often used to store code or data critical to the operating system.

hidden line *n.* In any application, such as a CAD program, that represents solid three-dimensional objects, a line in a drawing that would (or should) be hidden if the object were perceived as a solid construction. The process of removing such lines in an application is called hidden-line removal. *See also* CAD, hidden surface.

hidden surface *n.* A surface of a solid three-dimensional object, such as one represented in a CAD program, that would not be visible when the object is viewed from a particular angle—for example, the underside of the wing of an airplane when viewed from above. *See also* CAD, hidden line.

hide *vb.* To temporarily remove the onscreen display of an application's active window while leaving the application running. Windows that have been hidden are returned to active display by issuing the appropriate command to the operating system.

H

hierarchical *adj.* Of, relating to, or organized as a hierarchy. *See also* hierarchy.

hierarchical computer network *n.* **1.** A network in which one host computer controls a number of smaller computers, which may in turn act as hosts to a group of PC workstations. **2.** A network in which control functions are organized according to a hierarchy and in which data processing tasks may be distributed.

hierarchical database *n.* A database in which records are grouped in such a way that their relationships form a branching, treelike structure. This type of database structure, most commonly used with databases for large computers, is well suited for organizing information that breaks down logically into successively greater levels of detail. The organization of records in a hierarchical database should reflect the most common or the most time-critical types of access expected.

hierarchical database management system *n.* A database management system that supports a hierarchical model. *Acronym:* HDBMS. *See also* hierarchical model.

Hierarchical Data Format *n.* A file format for storing multiple types of graphical and numerical data and transferring them between different types of machines, together with a library of functions for handling such files in a uniform way. NCSA developed and supports the file function and library and has placed them in the public domain. Hierarchical Data Format files are supported on most common types of computers. The format can easily be extended to accommodate additional data models. The library functions have both FORTRAN and C interfaces. *Acronym:* HDF. *See also* NCSA (definition 1).

hierarchical file system *n.* A system for organizing files on a disk in which files are contained in directories or folders, each of which can contain other directories as well as files. The main directory for the disk is called the root; the chain of directories from the root to a particular file is called the path. *See also* hierarchy, path (definition 2), root. *Compare* flat file system.

Hierarchical File System *n.* A tree-structured file system used on the Apple Macintosh in which folders can be nested within other folders. *Acronym:* HFS. *See also* hierarchy, path (definition 2), root. *Compare* flat file system.

hierarchical menu *n.* A menu that has one or more submenus. Such a menu/submenu arrangement is hierarchical because each level subsumes the next.

hierarchical model *n.* A model used in database management in which each record may be the "parent" of one or more child records, which may or may not have the same structure as the parent; a record can have no more than one parent. Conceptually, therefore, a hierarchical model can be, and usually is, regarded as a tree. The individual records are not necessarily contained in the same file. *See also* tree.

Hierarchical Storage Management *n. See* HSM.

hierarchy *n.* A type of organization that, like a tree, branches into more specific units, each of which is "owned" by the higher-level unit immediately above. Hierarchies are characteristic of several aspects of computing because they provide organizational frameworks that can reflect logical links, or relationships, between separate records, files, or pieces of equipment. For example, hierarchies are used in organizing related files on a disk, related records in a database, and related (interconnected) devices on a network. In applications such as spreadsheets, hierarchies of a sort are used to establish the order of precedence in which arithmetic operations are to be performed by the computer. *See also* hierarchical file system.

high availability *n.* The ability of a system or device to be usable when it is needed. When expressed as a percentage, high availability is the actual service time divided by the required service time. Although high availability does not guarantee that a system will have no downtime, a network often is considered highly available if it achieves 99.999 percent network uptime. *Also called:* RAS (reliability/availability/serviceability), fault resilience. *See also* five-nines availability, four-nines availability, three-nines availability, two-nines availability. *Compare* fault tolerance.

High-bit-rate Digital Subscriber Line *n. See* HDSL.

high byte *n.* The byte containing the most significant bits (bits 8 through 15) in a 2-byte grouping representing a 16-bit (bits 0 through 15) value. See the illustration. *See also* hexadecimal.

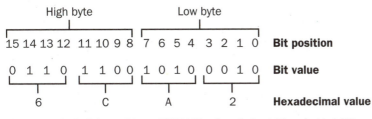

High byte. The high byte is binary 01101100 or hexadecimal 6C or decimal 108.

high-capacity CD-ROM *n. See* digital video disc.

High Contrast *n.* An accessibility display feature in Microsoft Windows that instructs programs to use the color scheme specified in the Settings dialog box and to increase legibility whenever possible.

High-data-rate Digital Subscriber Line *n. See* HDSL.

High-Definition Television *n. See* HDTV.

high-density disk *n.* **1.** A 3.5-inch floppy disk that can hold 1.44 MB. *Compare* double-density disk. **2.** A 5.25-inch floppy disk that can hold 1.2 MB. *Compare* double-density disk.

high DOS memory *n. See* high memory.

high-end *adj.* A descriptive term for something that uses the latest technology to maximize performance. There is usually a direct correlation between high-end technology and higher prices.

High-level Data Link Control *n. See* HDLC.

high-level language *n.* A computer language that provides a level of abstraction from the underlying machine language. Statements in a high-level language generally use keywords similar to English and translate into more than one machine-language instruction. In practice, every computer language above assembly language is a high-level language. *Acronym:* HLL. *Also called:* high-order language. *Compare* assembly language.

highlight *vb.* To alter the appearance of displayed characters as a means of calling attention to them, as by displaying them in reverse video (light on dark rather than dark on light, and vice versa) or with greater intensity. Highlighting is used to indicate an item, such as an option on a menu or text in a word processor, that is to be acted on in some way.

high memory *n.* **1.** Memory locations addressed by the largest numbers. **2.** In IBM PCs and compatibles, the range of addresses between 640 kilobytes and 1 megabyte,

used primarily for the ROM BIOS and control hardware such as the video adapter and input/output ports. *Compare* low memory.

high memory area *n.* In IBM PCs and compatibles, the 64-kilobyte range of addresses immediately above 1 megabyte. By means of the file HIMEM.SYS, MS-DOS (versions 5 and later) can move portions of itself into the high memory area, thereby increasing the amount of conventional memory available for applications. *Acronym:* HMA. *See also* conventional memory, expanded memory.

high-order *adj.* Having the most weight or significance. The high-order term usually appears first or leftmost in writing systems based on the Roman alphabet or Arabic numerals. For example, in the 2-byte hex value 6CA2, the high-order byte 6C has a value by itself of decimal 108 but counts for 108 x 256 = 27,648 in the group, whereas the low-order byte A2 counts only for decimal 162. *Compare* low-order.

high-order language *n. See* high-level language.

highpass filter *n.* An electronic circuit that passes all frequencies in a signal that are above a specified frequency. *Compare* bandpass filter, lowpass filter.

High-Performance File System *n. See* HPFS.

High-Performance Parallel Interface *n. See* HIPPI.

High-Performance Serial Bus *n. See* IEEE 1394.

high-persistence phosphor *n.* A phosphor that glows for a relatively long time after being struck by electrons. High-persistence phosphors are used in direct view storage tubes, but most CRTs (cathode-ray tubes) use phosphors of relatively low persistence so that their images can be changed quickly without "ghosts" of earlier images remaining on the screen. *See also* CRT, direct view storage tube.

high resolution *n.* The capability for reproducing text and graphics with relative clarity and fineness of detail.

High resolution is achieved by using a large number of pixels (dots) to create an image in a given area. For screen displays, the resolution is stated in terms of the total number of pixels in the horizontal and vertical dimensions. For example, the VGA video adapter has a resolution of 640 by 480 pixels. In printing, resolution refers to the number of dots per inch (dpi) produced by the printer, such as 300 to 600 dpi for a desktop laser or ink-jet printer or 1000 to 2000 dpi for a production-quality imagesetter. *Also called:* hi-res.

High Sierra specification *n.* An industry-wide format specification for the logical structure, file structure, and record structures on a CD-ROM. The specification is named after a meeting on CD-ROM held near Lake Tahoe in November 1985. It served as the basis for the international standard, ISO 9660.

high tech *n.* **1.** Cutting-edge applied science and engineering, usually involving computers and electronics. **2.** Sophisticated, often complex, specialized technical innovation.

hijackware *n.* Software that appears to be a useful plug-in or utility, but which will take over a user's Internet surfing or shopping activity by creating pop-up advertisements for competing products or redirecting the user to competitor's Web sites. Typically users will download and install a hijackware product believing it to be free browser enhancement software. Businesses pay the makers of hijackware products to push their shopping sites and product advertising onto Internet users, sometimes to the point of denying the user access to competing Web sites. *See also* gatored.

Hijiri calendar *n.* The lunar calendar used in Islamic countries. *Compare* Gregorian calendar, Julian calendar.

HIPPI *n.* Acronym for **Hi**gh-**P**erformance **P**arallel **I**nterface. An ANSI communications standard used with supercomputers.

hi-res *n. See* high resolution.

histogram *n.* A chart consisting of horizontal or vertical bars, the widths or heights of which represent the values of certain data.

history *n.* A list of the user's actions within a program, such as commands entered in an operating system shell, menus passed through using Gopher, or links followed using a Web browser.

hit *n.* **1.** A successful retrieval of data from a cache rather than from the slower hard disk or RAM. *See also* cache,

hard disk, RAM. **2.** A successful retrieval of a record matching a query in a database. *See also* query (definition 1), record[1]. **3.** Retrieval of a file from a Web site. Each separate file accessed on a Web page, including HTML documents and graphics, counts as a hit. **4.** In computer war and other games, when a character is successfully fired on, attacked, or otherwise taken out.

hit points *n.* Used in most computer and console war games to refer to the amount of times a player can be damaged before his or her character passes out or dies.

hive *n.* One of the top-level sets of keys, subkeys, and values in Windows 9x, Windows NT, Windows 2000, and Windows CE Registries. The term was created by a Microsoft programmer who thought the structure of the Registry resembled a beehive. Each hive is a permanent part of the Registry and is associated with a set of files containing information related to the configuration (applications, user preferences, devices, and so on) of the computer on which the operating system is installed. Registry hives include HKEY_LOCAL_MACHINE, HKEY_CURRENT_USER, and HKEY_CURRENT_CONFIG. *See also* Registry.

HKEY *n.* Short for **hkey** handle. In Windows 9x, Windows NT, and Windows 2000, a handle to a Registry key in which configuration information is stored. Each key leads to subkeys containing configuration information that, in earlier versions of Windows, was stored in .ini files. For example, the handle key HKEY_CURRENT_USERControl Panel leads to the subkey for the Windows Desktop. *See also* handle (definition 1).

HLL *n. See* high-level language.

HLS *n.* Acronym for **h**ue-**l**ightness-**s**aturation. *See* HSB.

HMA *n. See* high memory area.

HMD *n. See* head-mounted device.

Hollerith tabulating/recording machine *n.* An electromechanical machine invented by Herman Hollerith in the late 1800s for processing data supplied in the form of holes punched at predetermined locations in cards. Contacts made through the holes completed electrical circuits, allowing signals to be passed to counting and tabulating devices. This machine is considered to have reduced the time required to finish the 1890 U.S. census by two-thirds. Such machines were manufactured in the early 1900s by Hollerith's Tabulating Machine Company, which eventually became the International Business Machines Corporation (IBM).

hologram *n.* A three-dimensional image record created by holography. The hologram consists of a light interference pattern preserved in a medium such as photographic film. When suitably illuminated, it produces an image that changes its appearance as the viewer changes viewing angle. *See also* holography.

holography *n.* A method of reproducing three-dimensional visual images by recording light interference patterns on a medium such as photographic film, creating a hologram. *See also* hologram.

holy war *n.* **1.** A widespread and acrimonious debate among computer professionals over some aspect of the computer field, such as the debate over use of the GOTO statement in programming or that over big-endian versus little-endian data storage. **2.** An argument in a mailing list, newsgroup, or other forum over some emotional and controversial topic, such as abortion or Northern Ireland. Introducing a holy war that is off the purported topic of the forum is considered a violation of netiquette.

home *n.* A beginning position, such as the upper left corner of a character-based display, the left end of a line of text, cell A1 of a spreadsheet, or the top of a document.

home automation *n.* The process of programmatically controlling appliances, lighting, heating and cooling systems, and other devices in a home network. *See also* home network (definition 1).

homebrew *n.* Hardware or software developed by an individual at home or by a company for its own use rather than as a commercial product, such as hardware developed by electronics hobbyists when microcomputers first appeared in the 1970s.

home computer *n.* A personal computer designed and priced for use in the home.

home controller *n.* A software or hardware interface used to control the systems in a home network for home automation.

home directory *n.* A directory associated with a user account under UNIX. The home directory is the current directory when the user first logs in, and the user can return to it by entering the command *cd* (change directory) without a pathname. The user's files will ordinarily be stored in the home directory and its descendants.

homegrown software *n.* Software developed by an individual at home rather than in a professional environment.

Most public-domain and shareware programs are created this way.

Home key *n.* A key, found on most keyboards, whose function usually involves sending the cursor to some type of home position in an application. *See also* home.

home network *n.* **1.** A communications network in a home or building used for home automation. Home networks can use wiring (existing or new) or wireless connections. *See also* home automation, home controller. **2.** Two or more computers in a home that are interconnected to form a local area network (LAN).

home office *n.* **1.** An office set up within a residence. **2.** The main headquarters of a company.

home page *n.* **1.** A document intended to serve as a starting point in a hypertext system, especially the World Wide Web. A home page is called a *start page* in Microsoft Internet Explorer. **2.** An entry page for a set of Web pages and other files in a Web site. **3.** A personal Web page, usually for an individual.

Home Phoneline Networking Alliance *n. See* HomePNA.

HomePNA *n.* Short for **H**ome **P**honeline **N**etworking **A**lliance. An association of more than 100 companies working toward the adoption of a unified technology for setting up home networks over existing telephone wiring. Phoneline networking allows multiple PCs, printers, and peripheral devices to be connected for such purposes as multiplayer gaming, sharing printers and other peripherals, and rapid downloads over the Internet. The alliance was founded by a number of companies including IBM, Intel, AT&T, and Lucent Technologies.

Home Radio Frequency *n. See* HomeRF.

home record *n. See* header record.

HomeRF *n.* Acronym for **H**ome **R**adio **F**requency. A wireless home-networking specification that uses the 2.4-GHz frequency band to communicate between computers, peripherals, cordless phones, and other devices. HomeRF is supported by Siemens, Compaq, Motorola, National Semiconductor, Proxim, and other companies.

homogeneous environment *n.* A computing milieu, usually within an organization, in which only one manufacturer's hardware and one manufacturer's software are used. *Compare* heterogeneous environment.

homogeneous network *n.* A network on which all the hosts are similar and only one protocol is used.

Honeynet Project *n.* A nonprofit security research group created to collect and analyze data on hacking tools and methods by maintaining a decoy network of computers that is potentially attractive to hackers. The Honeynet Project sets up entire networks of computers in different combinations of operating systems and security to realistically simulate those used in businesses and organizations. Hackers are lured to the network where all inbound and outbound data is captured and contained to help researchers learn about hacker tactics and motives.

honeypot *n.* A security program designed to lure and distract a network attacker with decoy data. The honeypot appears to be a system that the intruder would like to crack but which, in reality, is safely separated from the actual network. This allows network administrators to observe attackers and study their activities without the intruders knowing they are being monitored. Honeypot programs get their name from the "like a bear to honey" metaphor.

honker *n.* A slang term for a hacker, the term originated in China. The Honker Union of China is an active group of Chinese hackers with nationalistic or hacktivist aims. The Honker Union of China has claimed patriotic motivation for defacing Japanese and U.S. Web sites, hacking U.S. networks, and releasing the Lion worm and other malicious programs. *See also* hacktivist, Lion worm.

hook *n.* A location in a routine or program in which the programmer can connect or insert other routines for the purpose of debugging or enhancing functionality.

hop *n.* In data communications, one segment of the path between routers on a geographically dispersed network. A hop is comparable to one "leg" of a journey that includes intervening stops between the starting point and the destination. The distance between each of those stops (routers) would be a communications hop.

horizontal blanking interval *n. See* blanking, horizontal retrace.

horizontal flyback *n. See* horizontal retrace.

horizontal market *n.* A broad category of business activity, such as accounting or inventory control, that carries across many types of business. *Compare* vertical market.

horizontal market software *n.* Application programs, such as word processors, that can be used in all types of business, as opposed to those geared for a certain industry.

horizontal retrace *n.* The movement of the electron beam in a raster-scan video display from the right end of one scan line to the left end (the beginning) of the next. During horizontal retrace, the electron beam is turned off, so the time required for the beam to move is called the horizontal blanking interval. *See also* blanking. *Compare* vertical retrace.

horizontal scrolling *n.* A feature of programs such as word processors and spreadsheets that enables the user to scroll left and right to display information beyond the horizontal limits of the screen (or window, in a graphical user interface).

horizontal synchronization *n.* On raster displays, the timing produced by a signal that controls the sweep of the display's electron beam as it moves from left to right and back again to form an image line by line. The horizontal synchronization signal is usually controlled by a circuit known as a phase-locked loop, which maintains a constant precise frequency so that a clear image is formed.

host[1] *n.* **1.** The main computer in a mainframe or minicomputer environment—that is, the computer to which terminals are connected. **2.** In PC-based networks, a computer that provides access to other computers. **3.** On the Internet or other large networks, a server computer that has access to other computers on the network. A host computer provides services, such as news, mail, or data, to computers that connect to it.

host[2] *vb.* To provide services to client computers that connect from remote locations—for example, to offer Internet access or to be the source for a news or mail service.

host adapter *n.* A device for connecting a peripheral to the main computer, typically in the form of an expansion card. *Also called:* controller, host bus adapter.

hosting *n.* The practice of providing computer and communication facilities to businesses or individuals, especially for use in creating Web and electronic commerce sites. A hosting service can provide high-speed access to the Internet, redundant power and data storage, and 24-hour maintenance at lower cost than implementing the same services independently. *See also* host[2], virtual hosting.

Host Integration Server *n.* A software application from Microsoft Corporation to allow businesses to integrate existing application, data, and network assets with new business applications and technologies. Host Integration Server preserves a company's existing legacy infrastructure and investments, while providing out-of-the-box development tools that enable integration with client/ server and Web networks.

host language *n.* **1.** The machine language of a CPU. **2.** A high-level language that is specifically supported by an operating system with its toolbox routines and native development systems.

host name *n.* The name of a specific server on a specific network within the Internet, leftmost in the complete host specification. For example, www.microsoft.com indicates the server called "www" within the network at Microsoft Corporation.

host not responding *n.* An error message issued by an Internet client indicating that the computer to which a request has been sent is refusing the connection or is otherwise unavailable to respond to the request.

host replacement *n. See* rehosting.

host timed out *n.* An error condition that occurs when a remote system fails to respond within a reasonable amount of time (a few minutes) during an exchange of data over a TCP connection. This condition may mean that the remote system has crashed or been disconnected from the network. The error message the user sees may or may not be phrased in this manner. *See also* TCP. *Compare* host not responding.

host unreachable *n.* An error condition that occurs when the particular computer to which the user wishes to connect over a TCP/IP network cannot be accessed on its LAN because it is either down or disconnected from the network. The error message the user sees may or may not be phrased in this manner. *See also* TCP/IP.

hot *adj.* Of special or urgent interest, or deemed popular.

HotBot *n.* An Internet search engine developed by Inktomi Corporation and HotWired, Inc. Using Slurp, a Web robot, this tool maintains a database of documents that can be matched to key words entered by the user, in a fashion similar to other search engines. HotBot incorporates many workstations in parallel to search and index Web pages. *See also* spider.

hot carrier diode *n. See* Schottky diode.

hot docking *n.* The process of attaching a laptop computer to a docking station while the computer is running, and automatically activating the docking station's video display and other functions. *See also* docking station, laptop.

hot insertion *n.* The insertion of a device or card while there is power to the system. Many newer laptops allow

for hot insertion of PCMCIA cards. High-end servers may also allow hot insertion to reduce downtimes.

HotJava *n.* A Web browser developed by Sun Microsystems, Inc., that is optimized to run Java applications and applets embedded in Web pages. *See also* applet, Java, Java applet.

hot key[1] *n.* A keystroke or combination of keystrokes that switches the user to a different program, often a terminate-and-stay-resident (TSR) program or the operating system user interface. *See also* TSR.

hot key[2] *vb.* To transfer to a different program by pressing a hot key.

hot link *n.* A connection between two programs that instructs the second program to make changes to data when changes occur in the first program. For example, a word processor or desktop publishing program could update a document based on information obtained from a database through a hot link. *See* hyperlink.

hotlist *n.* A list of frequently accessed items, such as Web pages in a Web browser, from which the user can select one. The hotlist of Web pages is called the bookmark list in Netscape Navigator and Lynx and is called the Favorites folder in Microsoft Internet Explorer.

Hotmail *n.* A Web-based e-mail service launched in 1996 and owned and operated by Microsoft since December 1997. Hotmail provides free e-mail accounts and can be used by anyone with Internet access and Web browsing software.

hot plugging *n.* A feature that allows equipment to be connected to an active device, such as a computer, while the device is powered on.

hot-potato routing *n.* A packet routing scheme that relies on keeping data moving, even if it may temporarily move away from its final destination. *Also called:* deflection routing.

hot spare *n.* In RAID (redundant array of independent disks) systems, a spare drive in the array that is configured as a backup on which data can be rebuilt in the event that another drive fails. Hot spares are kept on line and do not require operator intervention to be activated. *See also* RAID.

hot spot *n.* The position in a mouse pointer, such as the position at the tip of an arrow or the intersection of the lines in a cross, that marks the exact location that will be affected by a mouse action, such as a button press.

hot swapping *n. See* hot plugging.

HotSync *n.* Software application from Palm that permits data synchronization between a Palm handheld computing device and another computing device, such as a laptop or personal computer. The synchronization occurs via a cable connection or wirelessly (for example, via infrared signals).

HotWired *n.* A Web site affiliated with *Wired* magazine that contains news, gossip, and other information about the culture of the Internet.

housekeeping *n.* Any of various routines, such as updating the clock or performing garbage collection, designed to keep the system, the environment within which a program runs, or the data structures within a program in good working order.

hover button *n.* Text or an image on a Web page, usually in the form of a button, that changes appearance when a cursor passes over it. The hover button may change color, blink, display a pop-up with additional information, or produce other similar effects. Hover buttons are usually implemented through ActiveX objects and scripting, although hover behavior can also be set through HTML attributes.

HPC *n. See* handheld PC.

HPFS *n.* Acronym for **H**igh **P**erformance **F**ile **S**ystem. A file system available with OS/2 versions 1.2 and later. *See also* FAT file system, NTFS.

HPGL *n.* Acronym for **H**ewlett-**P**ackard **G**raphics **L**anguage. A language originally developed for images destined for plotters. An HPGL file consists of instructions that a program can use to reconstruct a graphical image.

HPIB *n.* Acronym for **H**ewlett-**P**ackard **I**nterface **B**us. *See* general-purpose interface bus.

HPPCL *n.* Acronym for **H**ewlett-**P**ackard **P**rinter **C**ontrol **L**anguage. *See* Printer Control Language.

HP/UX or **HP-UX** *n.* Acronym for **H**ewlett-**P**ackard **UNIX**. A version of the UNIX operating system specifically designed to be run on Hewlett-Packard's workstations. *See also* UNIX.

.hqx *n.* A file extension for a file encoded with BinHex. *See also* BinHex.

HREF *n.* Short for **h**ypertext **ref**erence. An attribute in an HTML document that defines a link to another document on the Web. *See also* HTML.

HSB *n.* Acronym for **h**ue-**s**aturation-**b**rightness. A color model in which hue is the color itself as placed on a color wheel, where 0° is red, 60° is yellow, 120° is green, 180° is cyan, 240° is blue, and 300° is magenta; saturation is the percentage of the specified hue in the color; and brightness is the percentage of white in the color. *Also called:* HLS, HSV, hue. *See also* color model. *Compare* CMY, RGB.

HSM *n.* Short for **H**ierarchical **S**torage **M**anagement. A technology for managing online data and data storage in which the medium on which the information resides is linked to the frequency with which the information is accessed. By migrating data to and from primary (rapidly accessed but expensive) and secondary (slower but less expensive) storage, HSM maintains often-used information on primary storage media and less frequently used data on secondary storage such as tape or an optical jukebox. Although information resides on different storage media, all of it appears to be on line and remains accessible to the user. When users request data residing on secondary storage, HSM moves the information back to the primary storage medium.

HSV *n.* Acronym for **h**ue-**s**aturation-**v**alue. *See* HSB.

H-sync *n. See* horizontal synchronization.

HTCPCP *n.* Acronym for **H**yper **T**ext **C**offee **P**ot **C**ontrol **P**rotocol. A protocol defined in jest as an April Fools' Day spoof of open Internet standards. HTCPCP/1.0 was proposed in RFC 2324 on April 1, 1998 by Larry Masinter of Xerox PARC. In this RFC, Masinter described a protocol for controlling, monitoring, and diagnosing coffee pots.

.htm *n.* The MS-DOS/Windows 3.*x* file extension that identifies Hypertext Markup Language (HTML) files, most commonly used as Web pages. Because MS-DOS and Windows 3.*x* cannot recognize file extensions longer than three letters, the .html extension is truncated to three letters in those environments. *See also* HTML.

.html *n.* The file extension that identifies Hypertext Markup Language (HTML) files, most commonly used as Web pages. *See also* HTML.

HTML *n.* Acronym for **H**ypertext **M**arkup **L**anguage. The markup language used for documents on the World Wide Web. A tag-based notation language used to format documents that can then be interpreted and rendered by an Internet browser. HTML is an application of SGML (Standard Generalized Markup Language) that uses tags to mark elements, such as text and graphics, in a document to indicate how Web browsers should display these elements to the user and should respond to user actions such as activation of a link by means of a key press or mouse click. HTML 2, defined by the Internet Engineering Task Force (IETF), included features of HTML common to all Web browsers as of 1994 and was the first version of HTML widely used on the World Wide Web. HTML+ was proposed for extending HTML 2 in 1994, but it was never implemented. HTML 3, which also was never standardized or fully implemented by a major browser developer, introduced tables. HTML 3.2 incorporated features widely implemented as of early 1996, including tables, applets, and the ability to flow text around images. HTML 4, the latest specification, supports style sheets and scripting languages and includes internationalization and accessibility features. Future HTML development will be carried out by the World Wide Web Consortium (W3C). Most Web browsers, notably Netscape Navigator and Internet Explorer, recognize HTML tags beyond those included in the present standard. *See also* .htm, .html, SGML, tag (definition 3), Web browser.

HTML attribute *n.* A value within an HTML tag that assigns additional properties to the object being defined. Some HTML editing software assigns some attributes automatically when you create an object such as a paragraph or table.

HTML code fragment *n.* HTML code that you add to a Web page to create features such as a script, a counter, or a scrolling marquee. Often used in the context of webrings to add a link and standard graphics or automation to an individual page to indicate membership.

HTML document *n.* A hypertext document that has been coded with HTML. *See* Web page.

HTML editor *n.* A software program used to create and modify HTML documents (Web pages). Most HTML editors include a method for inserting HTML tags without actually having to type out each tag. A number of HTML editors will also automatically reformat a document with HTML tags, based on formatting codes used by the word processing program in which the document was created. *See also* tag (definition 3), Web page.

HTML extensions *n.* A feature or setting that is an extension to the formal HTML specification. Extensions may not be supported by all Web browsers, but they may be used widely by Web authors. An example of an extension is marquee scrolling text.

HTML page *n. See* Web page.

HTML server control *n.* An ASP.NET server control that belongs to the System.Web.UI.HtmlControls namespace. An HTML server control maps directly to an HTML element and is declared on an ASP.NET page as an HTML element marked by a runat=server attribute. In contrast to Web server controls, HTML server controls do not have an <asp:ControlName> tag prefix. *See also* Web server control.

HTML source *n. See* source (definition 2).

HTML source file *n. See* source (definition 2).

HTML tag *n. See* tag (definition 3).

HTML validation service *n.* A service used to confirm that a Web page uses valid HTML according to the latest standard and/or that its hyperlinks are valid. An HTML validation service can catch small syntactical errors in HTML coding as well as deviations from the HTML standards. *See also* HTML.

HTTP *n.* Acronym for **H**yper**t**ext **T**ransfer **P**rotocol. The protocol used to carry requests from a browser to a Web server and to transport pages from Web servers back to the requesting browser. Although HTTP is almost universally used on the Web, it is not an especially secure protocol.

HTTPd *n.* Acronym for **H**yper**t**ext **T**ransfer **P**rotocol **Da**emon. A small, fast HTTP server that was available free from NCSA. HTTPd was the predecessor for Apache. *Also called:* HTTP Daemon. *See also* Apache, HTTP server, NCSA (definition 1).

HTTP Daemon *n. See* HTTPd.

HTTP Next Generation *n. See* HTTP-NG.

HTTP-NG *n.* Acronym for **H**yper**t**ext **T**ransfer **P**rotocol **N**ext **G**eneration. A standard under development by the World Wide Web Consortium (W3C) for improving performance and enabling the addition of features such as security. Whereas the current version of HTTP establishes a connection each time a request is made, HTTP-NG will set up one connection (which consists of separate channels for control information and data) for an entire session between a particular client and a particular server.

HTTPS *n.* **1.** Acronym for **H**yper**t**ext **T**ransfer **P**rotocol **S**ecure. A variation of HTTP that provides for encryption and transmission through a secure port. HTTPS was devised by Netscape and allows HTTP to run over a security mechanism known as SSL (Secure Sockets Layer). *See also* HTTP, SSL. **2.** Web server software for Windows NT. Developed by the European Microsoft Windows NT Academic Centre (EMWAC) at the University of Edinburgh,

H

Scotland, it offers such features as WAIS search capability. *See also* HTTP server, WAIS.

HTTP server *n.* **1.** Server software that uses HTTP to serve up HTML documents and any associated files and scripts when requested by a client, such as a Web browser. The connection between client and server is usually broken after the requested document or file has been served. HTTP servers are used on Web and Intranet sites. *Also called:* Web server. *See also* HTML, HTTP, server (definition 2). *Compare* application server. **2.** Any machine on which an HTTP server program is running.

HTTP status codes *n.* Three-digit codes sent by an HTTP server that indicate the results of a request for data. Codes beginning with 1 respond to requests that the client may not have finished sending; with 2, successful requests; with 3, further action that the client must take; with 4, requests that failed because of client error; and with 5, requests that failed because of server error. *See also* 400, 401, 402, 403, 404, HTTP.

HTTP streaming *n.* The process of downloading streaming digital media using an HTTP server (a standard Internet server) rather than a server designed specifically to transmit streaming media. HTTP streaming downloads the media file onto a computer, which plays the downloaded file as it becomes available. *See also* real-time streaming.

hub *n.* In a network, a device joining communication lines at a central location, providing a common connection to all devices on the network. The term is an analogy to the hub of a wheel. *See also* active hub, switching hub.

hue *n.* In the HSB color model, one of the three characteristics used to describe a color. Hue is the attribute that most readily distinguishes one color from other colors. It depends on the frequency of a light wave in the visible spectrum. *See also* color model, HSB. *Compare* brightness, saturation (definition 2).

Huffman coding *n.* A method of compressing a given set of data based on the relative frequency of the individual elements. The more often a given element, such as a letter, occurs, the shorter, in bits, is its corresponding code. It was one of the earliest data compression codes and, with modifications, remains one of the most widely used codes for a large variety of message types.

human engineering *n.* The designing of machines and associated products to suit the needs of humans. *See also* ergonomics.

human-machine interface *n.* The boundary at which people make contact with and use machines; when applied to programs and operating systems, it is more widely known as the user interface.

hung *adj. See* hang.

hybrid circuit *n.* A circuit in which fundamentally different types of components are used to perform similar functions, such as a stereo amplifier that uses both tubes and transistors.

hybrid computer *n.* A computer that contains both digital and analog circuits.

hybrid microcircuit *n.* A microelectronic circuit that combines individual microminiaturized components and integrated components.

hybrid network *n.* A network constructed of different topologies, such as ring and star. *See also* bus network, ring network, star network, Token-Ring network, topology.

Hybris virus *n.* A slow-spreading but persistent self-updating Internet worm first detected in late 2000. The Hybris virus is activated whenever an infected computer is connected to the Internet. It attaches itself to all outgoing e-mail messages, maintains a list of all e-mail addresses in the headers of incoming e-mail messages, and sends copies of itself to all e-mail addresses on the list. Hybris is difficult to eradicate because it updates itself regularly, accessing and downloading updates and plug-ins from anonymous postings to the alt.comp.virus newsgroup. Hybris incorporates downloaded extensions into its code, and it e-mails its modified form to additional potential victims. Hybris often includes a spiral plug-in which produces a spinning disk on top of any active windows on a user's screen.

HyperCard *n.* An information-management software tool, designed for the Apple Macintosh, that implements many hypertext concepts. A HyperCard document consists of a series of cards, collected into a stack. Each card can contain text, graphical images, sound, buttons that enable travel from card to card, and other controls. Programs and routines can be coded as scripts in an object-oriented language called HyperTalk or developed as external code resources (XCMDs and XFCNs). *See also* hypertext, object-oriented programming, XCMD, XFCN.

hyperlink *n.* A connection between an element in a hypertext document, such as a word, a phrase, a symbol, or an image, and a different element in the document, another document, a file, or a script. The user activates the link by clicking on the linked element, which is usually underlined or in a color different from the rest of the document to indicate that the element is linked. Hyperlinks are indicated in a hypertext document through tags in markup languages such as SGML and HTML. These tags are generally not visible to the user. *Also called:* hot link, hypertext link, link. *See also* anchor (definition 2), HTML, hypermedia, hypertext, URL.

hypermedia *n.* The combination of text, video, graphic images, sound, hyperlinks, and other elements in the form typical of Web documents. Essentially, hypermedia is the modern extension of hypertext, the hyperlinked, text-based documents of the original Internet. Hypermedia attempts to offer a working and learning environment that parallels human thinking—that is, one in which the user can make associations between topics, rather than move sequentially from one to the next, as in an alphabetic list. For example, a hypermedia presentation on navigation might include links to astronomy, bird migration, geography, satellites, and radar. *See also* hypertext.

hyperspace *n.* The set of all documents that can be accessed by following hyperlinks in the World Wide Web. *Compare* cyberspace (definition 2), Gopherspace.

HyperTalk *n.* A programming language used to manipulate HyperCard stacks developed by Apple Computer, Inc. *See also* HyperCard.

hypertext *n.* Text linked together in a complex, nonsequential web of associations in which the user can browse through related topics. For example, in an article with the word *iron*, traveling among the links to *iron* might lead the user to the periodic table of the elements or a map of the migration of metallurgy in Iron Age Europe. The term *hypertext* was coined in 1965 to describe documents presented by a computer that express the nonlinear structure of ideas as opposed to the linear format of books, film, and speech. The term *hypermedia*, more recently introduced, is nearly synonymous but emphasizes the nontextual element, such as animation, recorded sound, and video. *See also* HyperCard, hypermedia.

Hyper Text Coffee Pot Control Protocol *n. See* HTCPCP.

hypertext link *n. See* hyperlink.

Hypertext Markup Language *n. See* HTML.

Hypertext Transfer Protocol *n. See* HTTP.

Hypertext Transfer Protocol Daemon *n. See* HTTPd.

Hypertext Transfer Protocol Next Generation *n. See* HTTP-NG.

HyperWave *n.* A World Wide Web server that specializes in database manipulation and multimedia.

hyphen *n.* A punctuation mark (-) used to break a word between syllables at the end of a line or to separate the parts of a compound word. Word processing programs with sophisticated hyphenation capabilities recognize three types of hyphens: normal, optional, and nonbreaking. Normal hyphens, also called *required* or *hard hyphens*, are part of a word's spelling and are always visible, as in *long-term*. Optional hyphens, also called *discretionary* or *soft hyphens*, appear only when a word is broken between syllables at the end of a line; they are usually supplied by the word processing program itself. Nonbreaking hyphens are always visible, like normal hyphens, but they do not allow a line break. *See also* hyphenation program.

hyphenation program *n.* A program (often included as part of a word processing application) that introduces optional hyphens at line breaks. A good hyphenation program will avoid ending more than three lines in a row with hyphens and will prompt the user for confirmation or tag ambiguous breaks, as in the word *desert* (did the army de-sert in the des-ert?). *See also* hyphen.

hysteresis *n.* The tendency of a system, a device, or a circuit to behave differently depending on the direction of change of an input parameter. For example, a household thermostat might turn on at 68 degrees when the house is cooling down, but turn off at 72 degrees when the house is warming up. Hysteresis is important in many devices, especially those employing magnetic fields, such as transformers and read/write heads.

HYTELNET *n.* A menu-driven index of Internet resources that are accessible via telnet, including library catalogs, databases and bibliographies, bulletin boards, and network information services. HYTELNET can operate through a client program on a computer connected to the Internet, or through the World Wide Web.

HyTime *n.* Acronym for **H**ypermedia/**Time**-based Structuring Language. A markup language standard that describes links within and between documents and hypermedia objects. The standard defines structures and some semantic features, enabling description of traversal and presentation information of objects.

Hz *n. See* hertz.

I²L *n. See* integrated injection logic.

I2O *n.* Short for **I**ntelligent **I**nput/**O**utput. A specification for I/O device driver architecture that is independent of both the device being controlled and the host operating system. *See also* driver, input/output device.

i386 *n.* A family of 32-bit microprocessors developed by Intel. The i386 was introduced in 1985. *See also* 80386DX.

i486 *n.* A family of 32-bit microprocessors developed by Intel that extended and built upon the capabilities of the i386. The i486 was introduced in 1989. *See also* i486DX.

i486DX *n.* An Intel microprocessor introduced in 1989. In addition to the features of the 80386 (32-bit registers, 32-bit data bus, and 32-bit addressing), the i486DX has a built-in cache controller, a built-in floating-point coprocessor, provisions for multiprocessing, and a pipelined execution scheme. *Also called:* 486, 80486. *See also* pipelining (definition 1).

i486DX2 *n.* An Intel microprocessor introduced in 1992 as an upgrade to certain i486DX processors. The i486DX2 processes data and instructions at twice the system clock frequency. The increased operating speed leads to the generation of much more heat than in an i486DX, so a heat sink is often installed on the chip. *Also called:* 486DX, 80486. *See also* heat sink, i486DX, microprocessor. *Compare* OverDrive.

i486SL *n.* A low-power-consumption version of Intel's i486DX microprocessor designed primarily for laptop computers. The i486SL operates at a voltage of 3.3 volts rather than 5 volts, can shadow memory, and has a System Management Mode (SMM) in which the microprocessor can slow or halt some system components when the system is not performing CPU-intensive tasks, thus prolonging battery life. *See also* i486DX, shadow memory.

i486SX *n.* An Intel microprocessor introduced in 1991 as a lower-cost alternative to the i486DX. It runs at slower clock speeds and has no floating-point processor. *Also called:* 486, 80486. *See also* 80386DX, 80386SX. *Compare* i486DX.

IA-64 *n.* Short for **I**ntel **A**rchitecture **64**. Intel's 64-bit microprocessor architecture based on EPIC (Explicitly Parallel Instruction Computing) technology. IA-64 is the foundation for the 64-bit Merced chip, as well as future chips to be based on the same architecture. Unlike architectures based on the sequential execution of instructions, IA-64 is designed to implement the parallel execution defined by EPIC technology. It also provides for numerous registers (128 general registers for integer and multimedia operations and 128 floating-point registers) and for grouping instructions in threes as 128-bit bundles. IA-64 architecture also features inherent scalability and compatibility with 32-bit software. *See also* EPIC, Merced.

IAB *n. See* Internet Architecture Board.

IAC *n.* Acronym for **I**nformation **A**nalysis **C**enter. One of several organizations chartered by the U.S. Department of Defense to facilitate the use of existing scientific and technical information. IACs establish and maintain comprehensive knowledge bases, including historical, technical, and scientific data, and also develop and maintain analytical tools and techniques for their use.

IANA *n.* Acronym for **I**nternet **A**ssigned **N**umbers **A**uthority. The organization historically responsible for assigning IP (Internet Protocol) addresses and overseeing technical parameters, such as protocol numbers and port numbers, related to the Internet protocol suite. Under the direction of the late Dr. Jon Postel, IANA operated as an arm of the Internet Architecture Board (IAB) of the Internet Society (ISOC) under contract with the U.S. government. However, given the international nature of the Internet, IANA's functions, along with the domain name administration handled by U.S.-based Network Solutions, Inc. (NSI), were privatized in 1998 and turned over to a new, nonprofit organization known as ICANN (Internet Corporation for Assigned Names and Numbers). *See also* ICANN, NSI.

I-beam *n.* A mouse cursor used by many applications, such as word processors, when in text-editing mode. The I-beam cursor indicates sections of the document where text can be inserted, deleted, changed, or moved. The cursor is named for its I shape. *Also called:* I-beam pointer. *See also* cursor (definition 3), mouse.

I-beam pointer *n. See* I-beam.

IBG *n.* Acronym for **i**nter **b**lock **g**ap. *See* inter-record gap.

IBM AT *n.* A class of personal computers introduced in 1984 and conforming to IBM's PC/AT (Advanced Technology) specification. The first AT was based on the Intel 80286 processor and dramatically outperformed its predecessor, the XT, in speed. *See also* 80286.

IBM PC *n.* Short for **IBM P**ersonal **C**omputer. A class of personal computers introduced in 1981 and conforming to IBM's PC specification. The first PC was based on the Intel 8088 processor. For a number of years, the IBM PC was the de facto standard in the computing industry for PCs, and clones, or PCs that conformed to the IBM specification, have been called *PC-compatible. See also* PC-compatible, Wintel.

IBM PC/XT *n.* A class of personal computers released by IBM in 1983. XT, short for e**X**tended **T**echnology, enabled users to add a wider range of peripherals to their machines than was possible with the original IBM PC. Equipped with a 10-megabyte hard disk drive and one or two 5$\frac{1}{4}$-inch floppy drives, the PC/XT was expandable to 256K of RAM on the motherboard and was loaded with MS-DOS v2.1, which supported directories and subdirectories. The popularity of this machine contributed to the production of what came to be known in the industry as "clones," copies of its design by many manufacturers. *See also* IBM AT, IBM PC, XT.

IBM PC-compatible *adj. See* PC-compatible.

iBook *n.* A notebook computer introduced by Apple in July 1999. The iBook was intended as a portable version of the iMac and is easily distinguished by its rounded shape and the bright colors of its case. Initial iBook models were powered by a 300-MHz G3 (PowerPC 750) processor and had the capability for wireless networking. *See also* iMac, PowerPC 750.

IC[1] *adj.* Acronym for **I**n **C**haracter. Used to refer to events going on within a role-playing game, such as MUD, as opposed to events in real life. It is also used in the context of online chat, e-mail, and newsgroup postings. *See also* MUD, role-playing game.

IC[2] *n. See* integrated circuit.

ICANN *n.* Acronym for **I**nternet **C**orporation for **A**ssigned **N**ames and **N**umbers. The private, nonprofit corporation to which the U.S. government in 1998 delegated authority for administering IP (Internet Protocol) addresses, domain names, root servers, and Internet-related technical matters, such as management of protocol parameters (port numbers, protocol numbers, and so on). The successor to IANA (IP address administration) and NSI (domain name registration), ICANN was created to internationalize and privatize Internet management and administration. *See also* IANA, NSI.

I-CASE *n.* Acronym for **I**ntegrated **C**omputer-**A**ided **S**oftware **E**ngineering. Software that performs a wide variety of software engineering functions, such as program design, coding, and testing parts or all of the completed program.

ICE *n.* **1.** Acronym for **I**nformation and **C**ontent **E**xchange. A protocol based on XML (Extensible Markup Language) designed to automate the distribution of syndicated content over the World Wide Web. Based on the concept of content syndicators (distributors) and subscribers (receivers), ICE defines the responsibilities of the parties involved, as well as the format and means of exchanging content so that data can easily be transferred and reused. The protocol has been submitted to the World Wide Web Consortium by Adobe Systems, Inc., CNET, Microsoft, Sun Microsystems, and Vignette Corporation. It is intended to help in both publishing and inter-business exchanges of content. **2.** Acronym for **i**n **c**ircuit **e**mulator. A chip used as a stand-in for a microprocessor or a microcontroller. An in-circuit emulator is used to test and debug logic circuits. **3.** Acronym for **I**ntrusion **C**ountermeasure **E**lectronics. A fictional type of security software, popularized by science fiction novelist William Gibson, that responds to intruders by attempting to kill them. The origin of the term is attributed to a USENET subscriber, Tom Maddox. **4.** *See* Intelligent Concept Extraction.

ICM *n. See* image color matching.

ICMP *n.* Acronym for **I**nternet **C**ontrol **M**essage **P**rotocol. A network-layer (ISO/OSI level 3) Internet protocol that provides error correction and other information relevant to IP packet processing. For example, it can let the IP software on one machine inform another machine about an unreachable destination. *See also* communications protocol, IP, ISO/OSI reference model, packet (definition 1).

icon *n.* **1.** A small image displayed on the screen to represent an object that can be manipulated by the user. By serving as visual mnemonics and allowing the user to control certain computer actions without having to remember commands or type them at the keyboard, icons contribute significantly to the user-friendliness of graphical user interfaces and to PCs in general. *See also* graphical user interface. **2.** A high-level programming language designed to process non-numerical data structures and character strings using a Pascal-like syntax.

iconic interface *n.* A user interface that is based on icons rather than on typed commands. *See also* graphical user interface, icon.

icon parade *n.* The sequence of icons that appears during the boot-up of a Macintosh computer.

ICP *n.* Acronym for **I**nternet **C**ache **P**rotocol. A networking protocol used by cache servers to locate specific Web objects in neighboring caches. Typically implemented over UDP, ICP also can be used for cache selection. ICP was developed for the Harvest research project at the University of Southern California. It has been implemented in SQUID and other Web proxy caches.

ICQ *n.* A downloadable software program developed by Mirabilis, and now owned by AOL Time-Warner Inc., that notifies Internet users when friends, family, or other selected users are also on line and allows them to communicate with one another in real time. Through ICQ, users can chat, send e-mail, exchange messages on message boards, and transfer URLs and files, as well as launch third-party programs, such as games, in which multiple people can participate. Users compile a list of other users with whom they want to communicate. All users must register with the ICQ server and have ICQ software on their computer. The name is a reference to the phrase "I seek you." *See also* instant messaging.

ICSA *n.* Acronym for **I**nternational **C**omputer **S**ecurity **A**ssociation. An education and information organization concerned with Internet security issues. Known as the NCSA (National Computer Security Association) until 1997, the ICSA provides security assurance systems and product certification; disseminates computer security information in white papers, books, pamphlets, videos, and other publications; organizes consortiums devoted to various security issues; and maintains a Web site that provides updated information on viruses and other computer security topics. Founded in 1987, the ICSA is currently located in Reston, VA.

ID *n.* Acronym for **i**ntrusion **d**etection. *See* IDS.

IDE *n.* **1.** Acronym for **I**ntegrated **D**evice **E**lectronics. A type of disk-drive interface in which the controller electronics reside on the drive itself, eliminating the need for a separate adapter card. The IDE interface is compatible with the controller used by IBM in the PC/AT computer but offers advantages such as look-ahead caching. **2.** *See* integrated development environment.

identifier *n.* Any text string used as a label, such as the name of a procedure or a variable in a program or the name attached to a hard disk or floppy disk. *Compare* descriptor.

IDL *n.* Acronym for **I**nterface **D**efinition **L**anguage. In object-oriented programming, a language that lets a program or object written in one language communicate with another program written in an unknown language. An IDL is used to define interfaces between client and server programs. For example, an IDL can provide interfaces to remote CORBA objects. *See also* CORBA, MIDL, object-oriented programming.

idle *adj.* **1.** Operational but not in use. **2.** Waiting for a command.

idle character *n.* In communications, a control character transmitted when no other information is available or ready to be sent. *See also* SYN.

idle interrupt *n.* An interrupt that occurs when a device or process becomes idle.

idle state *n.* The condition in which a device is operating but is not being used.

IDS *n.* Acronym for **i**ntrusion-**d**etection **s**ystem. A type of security management system for computers and networks that gathers and analyzes information from various areas within a computer or a network to identify possible security breaches, both inside and outside the organization. An IDS can detect a wide range of hostile attack signatures, generate alarms, and, in some cases, cause routers to terminate communications from hostile sources. *Also called:* intrusion detection. *Compare* firewall.

IDSL *n.* Acronym for **I**nternet **d**igital **s**ubscriber **l**ine. A high-speed digital communications service that provides Internet access as fast as 1.1 Mbps (megabits per second) over standard telephone lines. IDSL uses a hybrid of ISDN and digital subscriber line technology. *See also* digital subscriber line, ISDN.

IE *n.* Acronym for **i**nformation **e**ngineering. A methodology for developing and maintaining information-processing systems, including computer systems and networks, within an organization.

IEEE *n.* Acronym for **I**nstitute of **E**lectrical and **E**lectronics **E**ngineers. A society of engineering and electronics professionals based in the United States but boasting membership from numerous other countries. The IEEE (pronounced "eye triple ee") focuses on electrical, electronics, computer engineering, and science-related matters.

IEEE 1284 *n.* The IEEE standard for high-speed signaling through a bidirectional parallel computer interface. A computer that is compliant with the IEEE 1284 standard can communicate through its parallel port in five modes: outbound data transfer to a printer or similar device ("Centronics" mode), inbound transfer 4 (nibble mode) or 8 (byte mode) bits at a time, bidirectional Enhanced Parallel Ports (EPP) used by storage devices and other nonprinter peripherals, and Enhanced Capabilities Ports (ECP) used for bidirectional communication with a printer. *See also* Centronics parallel interface, ECP, enhanced parallel port.

IEEE 1394 *n.* A nonproprietary, high-speed, serial bus input/output standard. IEEE 1394 provides a means of connecting digital devices, including personal computers and consumer electronics hardware. It is platform-independent, scalable (expandable), and flexible in supporting peer-to-peer (roughly, device-to-device) connections. IEEE 1394 preserves data integrity by eliminating the need to convert digital signals into analog signals. Created for desktop networks by Apple Computer and later developed by the IEEE 1394 working group, it is considered a low-cost interface for devices such as digital cameras, camcorders, and multimedia devices and is seen as a means of integrating personal computers and home electronics equipment. FireWire is the proprietary implementation of the standard by Apple Computer. *See also* analog data, IEEE.

IEEE 1394 connector *n.* A type of connector that enables you to connect and disconnect high-speed serial devices. An IEEE 1394 connector is usually on the back of your computer near the serial port or the parallel port. The IEEE 1394 bus is used primarily to connect high-end digital video and audio devices to your computer; however, some hard disks, printers, scanners, and DVD drives can also be connected to your computer using the IEEE 1394 connector.

IEEE 1394 port *n.* A 4- or 6-pin port that supports the IEEE 1394 standard and can provide direct connections between digital consumer electronics and computers. *See also* IEEE 1394.

IEEE 488 *n.* The electrical definition of the General-Purpose Interface Bus (GPIB), specifying the data and control lines and the voltage and current levels for the bus. *See also* General-Purpose Interface Bus.

IEEE 696/S-100 *n.* The electrical definition of the S-100 bus, used in early personal computer systems that used microprocessors such as the 8080, Z-80, and 6800. The S-100 bus, based on the architecture of the Altair 8800, was extremely popular with early computer enthusiasts because it permitted installation of a wide range of expansion boards. *See also* Altair 8800, S-100 bus.

IEEE 802.x *n.* A series of networking specifications developed by the IEEE. The x following 802 is a placeholder for individual specifications. The IEEE 802.x specifications correspond to the physical and data-link layers of the ISO/OSI reference model, but they divide the data-link layer into two sublayers. The logical link control (LLC) sublayer applies to all IEEE 802.x specifications and covers station-to-station connections, generation of message frames, and error control. The media access control (MAC) sublayer, dealing with network access and collision detection, differs from one IEEE 802 standard to another. IEEE 802.3 is used for bus networks that use CSMA/CD, both broadband and baseband, and the baseband version is based on the Ethernet standard. IEEE 802.4 is used for bus networks that use token passing, and IEEE 802.5 is used for ring networks that use token passing (token ring networks). IEEE 802.6 is an emerging standard for metropolitan area networks, which transmit data, voice, and video over distances of more than 5 kilometers. IEEE 802.14 is designed for bidirectional transmission to and from cable television networks over optical fiber and coaxial cable through transmission of fixed-length ATM cells to support television, data, voice, and Internet access. See the illustration. *See also* bus network, ISO/OSI reference model, ring network, token passing, token ring network.

ISO/OSI model

IEEE 802.x. ISO/OSI reference model with IEEE 802 LLC and MAC layers shown.

IEEE 802.11 *n.* The Institute of Electrical and Electronics Engineers' (IEEE) specifications for wireless networking. These specifications, which include 802.11, 802.11a, 802.11b, and 802.11g, allow computers, printers, and other devices to communicate over a wireless local area network (LAN).

IEEE printer cable *n.* A cable used to connect a printer to a PC's parallel port that adheres to the IEEE 1284. *See also* IEEE 1284.

IEPG *n.* Acronym for **I**nternet **E**ngineering and **P**lanning **G**roup. A collaborative group of Internet service providers whose goal is to promote the Internet and coordinate technical efforts on it.

IESG *n. See* Internet Engineering Steering Group.

IETF *n.* Acronym for **I**nternet **E**ngineering **T**ask **F**orce. A worldwide organization of individuals interested in networking and the Internet. Managed by the IESG (Internet Engineering Steering Group), the IETF is charged with studying technical problems facing the Internet and proposing solutions to the Internet Architecture Board (IAB). The work of the IETF is carried out by various Working Groups that concentrate on specific topics, such as routing and security. The IETF is the publisher of the specifications that led to the TCP/IP protocol standard. *See also* Internet Engineering Steering Group.

IFC *n. See* Internet Foundation Classes.

.iff *n.* The file extension that identifies files in the IFF (Interchange File Format) format. IFF was most commonly used on the Amiga platform, where it constituted almost any kind of data. On other platforms, IFF is mostly used to store image and sound files.

IFF *n.* Acronym for **I**nterchange **F**ile **F**ormat. *See* .iff.

IFIP *n.* Acronym for **I**nternational **F**ederation of Information **P**rocessing. An organization of societies, representing over 40 member nations, that serves information-processing professionals. The United States is represented by the Federation on Computing in the United States (FOCUS). *See also* AFIPS, FOCUS.

IFS *n. See* Installable File System Manager.

IF statement *n.* A control statement that executes a block of code if a Boolean expression evaluates to true. Most programming languages also support an ELSE clause, which specifies code that is to be executed only if the Boolean expression evaluates to false. *See also* conditional.

IGES *n. See* Initial Graphics Exchange Specification.

IGMP *n. See* Internet Group Membership Protocol.

IGP *n. See* Interior Gateway Protocol.

IGRP *n.* Acronym for **I**nterior **G**ateway **R**outing **P**rotocol. A protocol developed by Cisco Systems that allows coordination between the routing of a number of gateways. Goals of IGRP include stable routing in large networks, fast response to changes in network topology, and low overhead. *See also* communications protocol, gateway, topology.

IIA *n. See* SIIA.

IIL *n. See* integrated injection logic.

IIOP *n.* Acronym for **I**nternet **I**nter-**ORB** **P**rotocol. A networking protocol that enables distributed programs written in different programming languages to communicate over the Internet. IIOP, a specialized mapping in the General Inter-ORB Protocol (GIOP) based on a client/server model, is a critical part of CORBA. *See also* CORBA. *Compare* DCOM.

IIS *n. See* Internet Information Server.

ILEC *n.* Acronym for **I**ncumbent **L**ocal **E**xchange **C**arrier. A telephone company that provides local service to its customers. *Compare* CLEC.

illegal *adj.* Not allowed, or leading to invalid results. For example, an illegal character in a word processing program would be one that the program cannot recognize; an illegal operation might be impossible for a program or system because of built-in constraints. *Compare* invalid.

illuminance *n.* **1.** The amount of light falling on, or illuminating, a surface area. **2.** A measure of illumination (such as watts per square meter) used in reference to devices such as televisions and computer displays. *Compare* luminance.

IM *n.* *See* instant messaging.

iMac *n.* A family of Apple Macintosh computers introduced in 1998. Designed for nontechnical users, the iMac has a case that contains both the CPU and the monitor and is available in several bright colors. The "i" in iMac stands for Internet; the iMac was designed to make setting up an Internet connection extremely simple. The first version of the iMac included a 266-MHz PowerPC processor, a 66-MHz system bus, a hard drive, a CD-ROM drive, and a 15-inch monitor, with a translucent blue case. Later iMacs came with faster processors and a choice of case colors. See the illustration. *See also* Macintosh.

iMac.

.image *n.* A file extension for a Macintosh Disk Image, a storage type often used on Apple's FTP software download sites.

image *n.* **1.** A stored description of a graphic picture, either as a set of brightness and color values of pixels or as a set of instructions for reproducing the picture. *See also* bit map, pixel map. **2.** A duplicate, copy, or representation of all or part of a hard or floppy disk, a section of memory or hard drive, a file, a program, or data. For example, a RAM disk can hold an image of all or part of a disk in main memory; a virtual RAM program can create an image of some portion of the computer's main memory on disk. *See also* RAM disk.

image-based rendering *n.* *See* immersive imaging.

image color matching *n.* The process of image output correction to match the same colors that were scanned or input.

image compression *n.* The use of a data compression technique on a graphical image. Uncompressed graphics files tend to use up large amounts of storage, so image compression is useful to conserve space. *See also* compressed file, data compression, video compression.

image compression dialog component *n.* An application programming interface that sets parameters for compressing images and image sequences in QuickTime, a technology from Apple for creating, editing, publishing, and viewing multimedia content. The component displays a dialog box as a user interface, validates and stores the settings selected in the dialog box, and oversees the compression of the image or images based on the selected criteria.

Image Compression Manager *n.* A major software component used in QuickTime, a technology from Apple for creating, editing, publishing, and viewing multimedia content. The Image Compression Manager is an interface that provides image-compression and image-decompression services to applications and other managers. Because the Image Compression Manager is independent of specific compression algorithms and drivers, it can present a common application interface for software-based compressors and hardware-based compressors and offer compression options so that it or its application can use the appropriate tool for a particular situation. *See also* QuickTime.

image compressor component *n.* A software component used by the Image Compression Manager to compress image data in QuickTime, a technology from Apple for creating, editing, publishing, and viewing multimedia content. *See also* Image Compression Manager, QuickTime.

image decompressor component *n.* A software component used by the Image Compression Manager to decompress image data in QuickTime, a technology from Apple for creating, editing, publishing, and viewing multimedia content. *See also* Image Compression Manager, QuickTime.

image editing *n.* The process of changing or modifying a bitmapped image, usually with an image editor.

image editor *n.* An application program that allows users to modify the appearance of a bitmapped image, such as a scanned photo, by using filters and other functions. Creation of new images is generally accomplished in a paint or drawing program. *See also* bitmapped graphics, filter (definition 4), paint program.

image enhancement *n.* The process of improving the quality of a graphic image, either automatically by software or manually by a user through a paint or drawing program. *See also* anti-aliasing, image processing.

image map *n.* An image that contains more than one hyperlink on a Web page. Clicking different parts of the image links the user to other resources on another part of the Web page or a different Web page or in a file. Often an image map, which can be a photograph, drawing, or a composite of several different drawings or photographs, is used as a map to the resources found on a particular Web site. Older Web browsers support only server-side image maps, which are executed on a Web server through CGI script. However, most newer Web browsers (Netscape Navigator 2.0 and higher and Internet Explorer 3.0 and higher) support client-side image maps, which are executed in a user's Web browser. *Also called:* clickable maps. *See also* CGI script, hyperlink, Web page.

image processing *n.* The analysis, manipulation, storage, and display of graphical images from sources such as photographs, drawings, and video. Image processing spans a sequence of three steps. The input step (image capture and digitizing) converts the differences in coloring and shading in the picture into binary values that a computer can process. The processing step can include image enhancement and data compression. The output step consists of the display or printing of the processed image. Image processing is used in such applications as television and film, medicine, satellite weather mapping, machine vision, and computer-based pattern recognition. *See also* image enhancement, video digitizer.

image sensor *n.* A light-sensitive integrated circuit or group of integrated circuits used in scanners, digital cameras, and video cameras.

imagesetter *n.* A typesetting device that can transfer camera-ready text and artwork from computer files directly onto paper or film. Imagesetters print at high resolution (commonly above 1000 dpi) and are usually PostScript-compatible.

image transcoder component *n.* A component that transfers compressed images from one file format to another in QuickTime, a technology developed by Apple for creating, editing, publishing, and viewing multimedia content.

imaginary number *n.* A number that must be expressed as the product of a real number and i, where $i^2 = -1$. The sum of an imaginary number and a real number is a complex number. Although imaginary numbers are not directly encountered in the universe (as in "1.544 i megabits per second"), some pairs of quantities, especially in electrical engineering, behave mathematically like the real and imaginary parts of complex numbers. *Compare* complex number, real number.

imaging *n.* The processes involved in the capture, storage, display, and printing of graphical images.

IMAP4 *n.* Acronym for **I**nternet **M**essage **A**ccess **P**rotocol **4**. The latest version of IMAP, a method for an e-mail program to gain access to e-mail and bulletin board messages stored on a mail server. Unlike POP3, a similar protocol, IMAP allows a user to retrieve messages efficiently from more than one computer. *Compare* POP3.

IMC *n.* *See* Internet Mail Consortium.

IMHO *n.* Acronym for **i**n **m**y **h**umble **o**pinion. IMHO, used in e-mail and in online forums, flags a statement that the writer wants to present as a personal opinion rather than as a statement of fact. *See also* IMO.

Imitation Game *n.* *See* Turing test.

immediate access *n.* *See* direct access, random access.

immediate operand *n.* A data value, used in the execution of an assembly language instruction, that is contained in the instruction itself rather than pointed to by an address in the instruction.

immediate printing *n.* A process in which text and printing commands are sent directly to the printer without being stored as a printing file and without the use of an intermediate page-composition procedure or a file containing printer setup commands.

immersive imaging *n.* A method of presenting photographic images on a computer by using virtual reality techniques. A common immersive image technique puts the user in the center of the view. The user can pan 360 degrees within the image and can zoom in and out. Another technique puts an object in the center of the view and allows the user to rotate around the object to examine it from any perspective. Immersive imaging techniques can be used to provide virtual reality experiences without equipment such as a headpiece and goggles. *Also called:* image-based rendering. *See also* imaging, virtual reality.

IMO *n.* Acronym for **in m**y **o**pinion. A shorthand phrase used often in e-mail and Internet news and discussion groups to indicate an author's admission that a statement he or she has just made is a matter of judgment rather than fact. *See also* IMHO.

impact printer *n.* A printer, such as a wire-pin dot-matrix printer or a daisy-wheel printer, that drives an inked ribbon mechanically against the paper to form marks. *See also* daisy-wheel printer, dot-matrix printer. *Compare* nonimpact printer.

impedance *n.* Opposition to the flow of alternating current. Impedance has two aspects: resistance, which impedes both direct and alternating current and is always greater than zero; and reactance, which impedes alternating current only, varies with frequency, and can be positive or negative. *See also* resistance.

implementor *n.* In role-playing games, the administrator, coder, or developer of the game. *Also called:* Imp. *See also* role-playing game.

import *vb.* To bring information from one system or program into another. The system or program receiving the data must somehow support the internal format or structure of the data. Conventions such as the TIFF (Tagged Image File Format) and PICT formats (for graphics files) make importing easier. *See also* PICT, TIFF. *Compare* export.

IMT-2000 *n.* *See* International Mobile Telecommunications for the Year 2000.

inactive window *n.* In an environment capable of displaying multiple on-screen windows, any window other than the one currently being used for work. An inactive window can be partially or entirely hidden behind another window, and it remains inactive until the user selects it. *Compare* active window.

in-band signaling *n.* Transmission within the voice or data-handling frequencies of a communication channel.

in-betweening *n.* *See* tween.

Inbox *n.* In many e-mail applications, the default mailbox where the program stores incoming messages. *See also* e-mail, mailbox. *Compare* Outbox.

incident light *n.* The light that strikes a surface in computer graphics. *See also* illuminance.

in-circuit emulator *n.* *See* ICE (definition 2).

INCLUDE directive *n.* A statement within a source-code file that causes another source-code file to be read in at that spot, either during compilation or during execution. It enables a programmer to break up a program into smaller files and enables multiple programs to use the same files.

inclusive OR *n.* *See* OR.

increment[1] *n.* A scalar or unit amount by which the value of an object such as a number, a pointer within an array, or a screen position designation is increased. *Compare* decrement[1].

increment[2] *vb.* To increase a number by a given amount. For example, if a variable has the value 10 and is incremented successively by 2, it takes the values 12, 14, 16, 18, and so on. *Compare* decrement[2].

incumbent local exchange carrier *n.* *See* ILEC.

indent[1] *n.* **1.** Displacement of the left or right edge of a block of text in relation to the margin or to other blocks of text. **2.** Displacement of the beginning of the first line of a paragraph relative to the other lines in the paragraph. *Compare* hanging indent.

indent[2] *vb.* To displace the left or right edge of a text item, such as a block or a line, relative to the margin or to another text item.

Indeo *n.* A codec technology developed by Intel for compressing digital video files. *See also* codec. *Compare* MPEG.

independent content provider *n.* A business or organization that supplies information to an online information service, such as America Online, for resale to the information service's customers. *See also* online information service.

independent software vendor *n.* A third-party software developer; an individual or an organization that independently creates computer software. *Acronym:* ISV.

index[1] *n.* **1.** A listing of keywords and associated data that point to the location of more comprehensive information, such as files and records on a disk or record keys in a database. **2.** In programming, a scalar value that allows direct access into a multi-element data structure such as an array without the need for a sequential search through the collection of elements. *See also* array, element (definition 1), hash, list.

index[2] *vb.* **1.** In data storage and retrieval, to create and use a list or table that contains reference information pointing to stored data. **2.** In a database, to find data by using keys such as words or field names to locate records. **3.** In indexed file storage, to find files stored on disk by using an index of file locations (addresses). **4.** In programming and information processing, to locate information stored in a table by adding an offset amount, called the index, to the base address of the table.

indexed address *n.* The location in memory of a particular item of data within a collection of items, such as an entry in a table. An indexed address is calculated by starting with a base address and adding to it a value stored in a register called an index register.

indexed search *n.* A search for an item of data that uses an index to reduce the amount of time required.

indexed sequential access method *n.* A scheme for decreasing the time necessary to locate a data record within a large database, given a key value that identifies the record. A smaller index file is used to store the keys along with pointers that locate the corresponding records in the large main database file. Given a key, first the index file is searched for the key and then the associated pointer is used to access the remaining data of the record in the main file. *Acronym:* ISAM.

index hole *n.* The small, round hole near the large, round spindle opening at the center of a 5.25-inch floppy disk. The index hole marks the location of the first data sector, enabling a computer to synchronize its read/write operations with the disk's rotation.

Indexing Service Query Language *n.* A query language available in addition to SQL for the Indexing Service in Windows 2000. Formerly known as Index Server, its original function was to index the content of Internet Information Services (IIS) Web servers. Indexing Service now creates indexed catalogs for the contents and properties of both file systems and virtual Webs.

index mark *n.* **1.** A magnetic indicator signal placed on a soft-sectored disk during formatting to mark the logical start of each track. **2.** A visual information locator, such as a line, on a microfiche.

indicator *n.* A dial or light that displays information about the status of a device, such as a light connected to a disk drive that glows when the disk is being accessed.

indirect address *n. See* relative address.

inductance *n.* The ability to store energy in the form of a magnetic field. Any length of wire has some inductance, and coiling the wire, especially around a ferromagnetic

core, increases the inductance. The unit of inductance is the henry. *Compare* capacitance, induction.

induction *n.* The creation of a voltage or current in a material by means of electric or magnetic fields, as in the secondary winding of a transformer when exposed to the changing magnetic field caused by an alternating current in the primary winding. *See also* impedance. *Compare* inductance.

inductor *n.* A component designed to have a specific amount of inductance. An inductor passes direct current but impedes alternating current to a degree dependent on its frequency. An inductor usually consists of a length of wire coiled in a cylindrical or toroidal (doughnut-shaped) form, sometimes with a ferromagnetic core. See the illustration. *Also called:* choke.

Inductor. *One of several kinds of inductors.*

Industry Standard Architecture *n. See* ISA.

INET *n.* **1.** Short for **Internet**. **2.** An annual conference held by the Internet Society.

.inf *n.* The file extension for device information files, those files containing scripts used to control hardware operations.

infection *n.* The presence of a virus or Trojan horse in a computer system. *See also* Trojan horse, virus, worm.

infer *vb.* To formulate a conclusion based on specific information, either by applying the rules of formal logic or by generalizing from a set of observations. For example, from the facts that canaries are birds and birds have feathers, one can infer (draw the inference) that canaries have feathers.

inference engine *n.* The processing portion of an expert system. It matches input propositions with facts and rules contained in a knowledge base and then derives a conclusion, on which the expert system then acts.

inference programming *n.* A method of programming (as in Prolog) in which programs yield results based on logical inference from a set of facts and rules. *See also* Prolog.

infinite loop *n.* **1.** A loop that, because of semantic or logic errors, can never terminate through normal means. **2.** A loop that is intentionally written with no explicit termination condition but will terminate as a result of side effects or direct intervention. *See also* loop[1] (definition 1), side effect.

infix notation *n.* A notation, used for writing expressions, in which binary operators appear between their arguments, as in 2 + 4. Unary operators usually appear before their arguments, as in −1. *See also* operator precedence, postfix notation, prefix notation, unary operator.

.info *n.* One of seven new top-level domain names approved in 2001 by the Internet Corporation for Assigned Names and Numbers (ICANN). Unlike the other new domain names, which focus on specific types of Web sites, .info is meant for unrestricted use.

infobahn *n.* The Internet. *Infobahn* is a mixture of the terms *information* and *Autobahn*, a German highway known for the high speeds at which drivers can legally travel. *Also called:* Information Highway, Information Superhighway, the Net.

infomediary *n.* A term created from the phrase *information intermediary*. A service provider that positions itself between buyers and sellers, collecting, organizing, and distributing focused information that improves the interaction of consumer and online business.

information *n.* The meaning of data as it is intended to be interpreted by people. Data consists of facts, which become information when they are seen in context and convey meaning to people. Computers process data without any understanding of what the data represents.

Information Analysis Center *n. See* IAC.

Information and Content Exchange *n. See* ICE (definition 1).

information appliance *n.* A specialized computer designed to perform a limited number of functions and, especially, to provide access to the Internet. Although devices such as electronic address books or appointment calendars might be considered information appliances, the term is more typically used for devices that are less expensive and less capable than a fully functional personal computer. Set-top boxes are a current example; other devices, envisioned for the future, would include network-aware

microwaves, refrigerators, watches, and the like. *Also called:* appliance.

information center *n.* **1.** A large computer center and its associated offices; the hub of an information management and dispersal facility in an organization. **2.** A specialized type of computer system dedicated to information retrieval and decision-support functions. The information in such a system is usually read-only and consists of data extracted or downloaded from other production systems.

information engineering *n. See* IE (definition 1).

information explosion *n.* **1.** The current period in human history, in which the possession and dissemination of information has supplanted mechanization or industrialization as a driving force in society. **2.** The rapid growth in the amount of information available today. *Also called:* information revolution.

information hiding *n.* A design practice in which implementation details for both data structures and algorithms within a module or subroutine are hidden from routines using that module or subroutine, so as to ensure that those routines do not depend on some particular detail of the implementation. In theory, information hiding allows the module or subroutine to be changed without breaking the routines that use it. *See also* break, module, routine, subroutine.

Information Highway or **information highway** *n. See* Information Superhighway.

Information Industry Association *n. See* SIIA.

information kiosk *n. See* kiosk.

information management *n.* The process of defining, evaluating, safeguarding, and distributing data within an organization or a system.

information packet *n. See* packet (definition 1).

information processing *n.* The acquisition, storage, manipulation, and presentation of data, particularly by electronic means.

information resource management *n.* The process of managing the resources for the collection, storage, and manipulation of data within an organization or system.

information retrieval *n.* The process of finding, organizing, and displaying information, particularly by electronic means.

information revolution *n. See* information explosion.

information science *n.* The study of how information is collected, organized, handled, and communicated. *See also* information theory.

Information Services *n.* The formal name for a company's data processing department. *Acronym:* IS. *Also called:* Data Processing, Information Processing, Information Systems, Information Technology, Management Information Services, Management Information Systems.

Information Superhighway *n.* The existing Internet and its general infrastructure, including private networks, online services, and so on. *See also* National Information Infrastructure.

Information Systems *n. See* Information Services.

Information Technology *n. See* Information Services.

Information Technology Industry Council *n.* Trade organization of the information technology industry. The council promotes the interests of the information technology industry and compiles information on computers, software, telecommunications, business equipment, and other topics related to information technology. *Acronym:* ITIC.

information theory *n.* A mathematical discipline founded in 1948 that deals with the characteristics and the transmission of information. Information theory was originally applied to communications engineering but has proved relevant to other fields, including computing. It focuses on such aspects of communication as amount of data, transmission rate, channel capacity, and accuracy of transmission, whether over cables or within society.

information warehouse *n.* The total of an organization's data resources on all computers.

information warfare *n.* Attacks on the computer operations on which an enemy country's economic life or safety depends. Possible examples of information warfare include crashing air traffic control systems or massively corrupting stock exchange records.

Infoseek *n.* A Web search site that provides full-text results for user searches plus categorized lists of related sites. InfoSeek is powered by the Ultraseek search engine and searches Web pages, Usenet newsgroups, and FTP and Gopher sites.

infrared *adj.* Having a frequency in the electromagnetic spectrum in the range just below that of red light. Objects radiate infrared in proportion to their temperature. Infrared radiation is traditionally divided into four somewhat arbi-

trary categories based on its wavelength. See the table. *Acronym:* IR.

Table I.1 Infrared Radiation Categories.

near infrared	750–1500 nanometers (nm)
middle infrared	1500–6000 nm
far infrared	6000–40,000 nm
far-far infrared	40,000 nm–1 millimeter (mm)

Infrared Data Association *n. See* IrDA.

infrared device *n.* A computer, or a computer peripheral such as a printer, that can communicate by using infrared light. *See also* infrared.

infrared file transfer *n.* Wireless file transfer between a computer and another computer or device using infrared light. *See also* infrared.

infrared network connection *n.* A direct or incoming network connection to a remote access server using an infrared port. *See also* infrared port.

infrared port *n.* An optical port on a computer for interfacing with an infrared-capable device. Communication is achieved without physical connection through cables. Infrared ports can be found on some laptops, notebooks, and printers. *See also* cable, infrared, port.

inherent error *n.* An error in assumptions, design, logic, algorithms, or any combination thereof that causes a program to work improperly, regardless of how well written it is. For example, a serial communications program that is written to use a parallel port contains an inherent error. *See also* logic, semantics (definition 1), syntax.

inherit *vb.* To acquire the characteristics of another class, in object-oriented programming. The inherited characteristics may be enhanced, restricted, or modified. *See also* class.

inheritance *n.* **1.** The transfer of the characteristics of a class in object-oriented programming to other classes derived from it. For example, if "vegetable" is a class, the classes "legume" and "root" can be derived from it, and each will inherit the properties of the "vegetable" class: name, growing season, and so on. *See also* class, object-oriented programming. **2.** The transfer of certain properties, such as open files, from a parent program or process to another program or process that the parent causes to run. *See also* child (definition 1).

inheritance code *n.* A set of structural and procedural attributes belonging to an object that has been passed on to it by the class or object from which it was derived. *See also* object-oriented programming.

inhibit *vb.* To prevent an occurrence. For example, to inhibit interrupts from an external device means to prevent the external device from sending any interrupts. ˉ

.ini *n.* In MS-DOS and Windows 3.x, the file extension that identifies an initialization file, which contains user preferences and startup information about an application program.

ini file *n.* Short for **ini**tialization **file**, a text file containing information about the initial configuration of Windows and Windows-based applications, such as default settings for fonts, margins, and line spacing. Two ini files, win.ini and system.ini, are required to run the Windows operating system through version 3.1. In later versions of Windows, ini files are replaced by a database known as the registry. In addition to Windows itself, many older applications create their own ini files. Because they are composed only of text, ini files can be edited in any text editor or word processor to change information about the application or user preferences. All initialization files bear the extension .ini. *See also* configuration, configuration file, registry, system.ini, win.ini.

INIT *n.* On older Macintosh computers, a system extension that is loaded into memory at startup time. *See also* extension (definition 4). *Compare* cdev.

Initial Graphics Exchange Specification *n.* A standard file format for computer graphics, supported by the American National Standards Institute (ANSI), that is particularly suitable for describing models created with computer-aided design (CAD) programs. It includes a wide variety of basic geometric forms (primitives) and, in keeping with CAD objectives, offers methods for describing and annotating drawings and engineering diagrams. *Acronym:* IGES.*See also* ANSI.

initialization *n.* The process of assigning initial values to variables and data structures in a program.

initialization file *n. See* ini file.

initialization string *n.* A sequence of commands sent to a device, especially a modem, to configure it and prepare it for use. In the case of a modem, the initialization string consists of a string of characters.

initialize *vb.* **1.** To prepare a storage medium, such as a disk or a tape, for use. This may involve testing the medium's surface, writing startup information, and setting

up the file system's index to storage locations. **2.** To assign a beginning value to a variable. **3.** To start up a computer. *See also* cold boot, startup.

initializer *n.* An expression whose value is the first (initial) value of a variable. *See also* expression.

initial program load *n.* The process of copying an operating system into memory when a system is booted. *Acronym:* IPL. *See also* boot, startup.

initiator *n.* The device in a SCSI connection that issues commands. The device that receives the commands is the target. *See also* SCSI, target.

ink cartridge *n.* A disposable module that contains ink and is typically used in an ink-jet printer. *See also* ink-jet printer.

ink-jet printer or **inkjet printer** *n.* A nonimpact printer in which liquid ink is vibrated or heated into a mist and sprayed through tiny holes in the print head to form characters or graphics on the paper. Ink-jet printers are competitive with some laser printers in price and print quality if not in speed. However, the ink, which must be highly soluble to avoid clogging the nozzles in the print head, produces fuzzy-looking output on some papers and smears if touched or dampened shortly after printing. *See also* nonimpact printer, print head.

inline *adj.* **1.** In programming, referring to a function call replaced with an instance of the function's body. Actual arguments are substituted for formal parameters. An inline function is usually done as a compile-time transformation to increase the efficiency of the program. *Also called:* unfold, unroll. **2.** In HTML code, referring to graphics displayed along with HTML-formatted text. Inline images placed in the line of HTML text use the tag <IMG>. Text within an inline image can be aligned to the top, bottom, or middle of a specific image.

inline code *n.* Assembly language or machine language instructions embedded within high-level source code. The form it takes varies considerably from compiler to compiler, if it is supported at all.

inline discussion *n.* Discussion comments that are associated with a document as a whole or with a particular paragraph, image, or table of a document. In Web browsers, inline discussions are displayed in the body of the document; in word-processing programs, they are usually displayed in a separate discussion or comments pane.

inline graphics *n.* Graphics files that are embedded in an HTML document or Web page and viewable by a Web browser or other program that recognizes HTML. By avoiding the need for separate file opening operations, inline graphics can speed the access and loading of an HTML document. *Also called:* inline image.

inline image *n.* An image that is embedded within the text of a document. Inline images are common on Web pages. *See also* inline graphics.

inline processing *n.* Operation on a segment of low-level program code, called inline code, to optimize execution speed or storage requirements. *See also* inline code.

inline stylesheet *n.* A stylesheet included within an HTML document. Because an inline stylesheet is directly associated with an individual document, any changes made to that document's appearance will not affect the appearance of other Web site documents. *Compare* linked stylesheet.

inline subroutine *n.* A subroutine whose code is copied at each place in a program at which it is called, rather than kept in one place to which execution is transferred. Inline subroutines improve execution speed, but they also increase code size. Inline subroutines obey the same syntactical and semantic rules as ordinary subroutines.

Inmarsat *n.* Acronym for **In**ternational **Mar**itime **Sat**ellite. Organization based in London, England, that operates satellites for international mobile telecommunications services in more than 80 nations. Inmarsat provides services for maritime, aviation, and land use.

inner join *n.* An operator in relational algebra, often implemented in database management. The inner join produces a relation (table) that contains all possible ordered concatenations (joinings) of records from two existing tables that meet certain specified criteria on the data values. It is thus equivalent to a product followed by a select applied to the resulting table. *Compare* outer join.

inoculate *vb.* To protect a program against virus infection by recording characteristic information about it. For example, checksums on the code can be recomputed and compared with the stored original checksums each time the program is run; if any have changed, the program file is corrupt and may be infected. *See also* checksum, virus.

input[1] *n.* Information entered into a computer or program for processing, as from a keyboard or from a file stored on a disk drive.

input[2] *vb.* To enter information into a computer for processing.

input area *n. See* input buffer.

input-bound *adj. See* input/output-bound.

input buffer *n.* A portion of computer memory set aside for temporary storage of information arriving for processing. *See also* buffer[1].

input channel *n. See* input/output channel.

input device *n.* A peripheral device whose purpose is to allow the user to provide input to a computer system. Examples of input devices are keyboards, mice, joysticks, and styluses. *See also* peripheral.

input driver *n. See* device driver.

input language *n.* 1. A language to be inputted into the system through the keyboard, a speech-to-text converter, or an Input Method Editor (IME). 2. In Microsoft Windows XP, a Regional and Language Options setting that specifies the combination of the language being entered and the keyboard layout, IME, speech-to-text converter, or other device being used to enter it. This setting was formerly known as input locale.

Input Method Editor *n.* Programs used to enter the thousands of different characters in written Asian languages with a standard 101-key keyboard. An IME consists of both an engine that converts keystrokes into phonetic and ideograph characters and a dictionary of commonly used ideographic words. As the user enters keystrokes, the IME engine attempts to identify which character or characters the keystrokes should be converted into. *Acronym:* IME.

input/output *n.* The complementary tasks of gathering data for a computer or a program to work with, and of making the results of the computer's activities available to the user or to other computer processes. Gathering data is usually done with input devices such as the keyboard and the mouse, while the output is usually made available to the user via the display and the printer. Other data resources, such as disk files and communications ports for the computer, can serve as either input or output devices. *Acronym:* I/O.

input/output area *n. See* input/output buffer.

input/output-bound *adj.* Characterized by the need to spend lengthy amounts of time waiting for input and output of data that is processed much more rapidly. For example, if the processor is capable of making rapid changes to a large database stored on a disk faster than the drive mechanism can perform the read and write operations, the computer is input/output-bound. A computer may be just input-bound or just output-bound if only input or only output limits the speed at which the processor accepts and processes data. *Also called:* I/O-bound.

input/output buffer *n.* A portion of computer memory reserved for temporary storage of incoming and outgoing data. Because input/output devices can often write to a buffer without intervention from the CPU, a program can continue execution while the buffer fills, thus speeding program execution. *See also* buffer[1].

input/output bus *n.* A hardware path used inside a computer for transferring information to and from the processor and various input and output devices. *See also* bus.

input/output channel *n.* A hardware path from the CPU to the input/output bus. *See also* bus.

input/output controller *n.* Circuitry that monitors operations and performs tasks related to receiving input and transferring output at an input or output device or port, thus providing the processor with a consistent means of communication (input/output interface) with the device and also freeing the processor's time for other work. For example, when a read or write operation is performed on a disk, the drive's controller carries out the high-speed, electronically sophisticated tasks involved in positioning the read-write heads, locating specific storage areas on the spinning disk, reading from and writing to the disk surface, and even checking for errors. Most controllers require software that enables the computer to receive and process the data the controller makes available. *Also called:* device controller, I/O controller.

input/output device *n.* A piece of hardware that can be used both for providing data to a computer and for receiving data from it, depending on the current situation. A disk drive is an example of an input/output device. Some devices, such as a keyboard or a mouse, can be used only for input and are thus called input (input-only) devices. Other devices, such as printers, can be used only for output and are thus called output (output-only) devices. Most devices require installation of software routines called device drivers to enable the computer to transmit and receive data to and from them.

input/output interface *n. See* input/output controller.

input/output port *n. See* port.

input/output processor *n.* Hardware designed to handle input and output operations to relieve the burden on the main processing unit. For example, a digital signal processor can perform time-intensive, complicated analysis and synthesis of sound patterns without CPU overhead. *See also* digital signal processor, front-end processor (definition 1).

input/output statement *n.* A program instruction that causes data to be transferred between memory and an input or output device.

input port *n. See* port.

input stream *n.* A flow of information used in a program as a sequence of bytes that are associated with a particular task or destination. Input streams include series of characters read from the keyboard to memory and blocks of data read from disk files. *Compare* output stream.

inquiry *n.* A request for information. *See also* query.

INS *n. See* WINS.

insertion point *n.* A blinking vertical bar on the screen, such as in graphical user interfaces, that marks the location at which inserted text will appear. *See also* cursor (definition 1).

insertion sort *n.* A list-sorting algorithm that starts with a list that contains one item and builds an ever-larger sorted list by inserting the items to be sorted one at a time into their correct positions on that list. Insertion sorts are inefficient when used with arrays, because of constant shuffling of items, but are ideally suited for sorting linked lists. *See also* linked list, sort algorithm. *Compare* bubble sort, quicksort.

Insert key *n.* A key on the keyboard, labeled "Insert" or "Ins," whose usual function is to toggle a program's editing setting between an insert mode and an overwrite mode, although it may perform different functions in different applications. *Also called:* Ins key.

insert mode *n.* A mode of operation in which a character typed into a document or at a command line pushes subsequent existing characters farther to the right on the screen rather than overwriting them. Insert mode is the opposite of overwrite mode, in which new characters replace subsequent existing characters. The key or key combination used to change from one mode to the other varies among programs, but the Insert key is most often used. *Compare* overwrite mode.

insider attack *n.* An attack on a network or system carried out by an individual associated with the hacked system. Insider attacks are typically the work of current or former employees of a company or organization who have knowledge of passwords and network vulnerabilities. *Compare* intruder attack.

Ins key *n. See* Insert key.

install *vb.* To set in place and prepare for operation. Operating systems and application programs commonly include a disk-based installation, or setup, program that does most of the work of preparing the program to work with the computer, printer, and other devices. Often such a program can check for devices attached to the system, request the user to choose from sets of options, create a place for the program on the hard disk, and modify system startup files as necessary.

installable device driver *n.* A device driver that can be embedded within an operating system, usually in order to override an existing, less-functional service.

Installable File System Manager *n.* In Windows 9x and Windows 2000, the part of the file system architecture responsible for arbitrating access to the different file system components. *Acronym:* IFS.

installation program *n.* A program whose function is to install another program, either on a storage medium or in memory. An installation program, also called a setup program, might be used to guide a user through the often complex process of setting up an application for a particular combination of machine, printer, and monitor.

Installer *n.* A program, provided with the Apple Macintosh operating system, that allows the user to install system upgrades and make bootable (system) disks.

instance *n.* An object, in object-oriented programming, in relation to the class to which it belongs. For example, an object *myList* that belongs to a class *List* is an instance of the class *List*. *See also* class, instance variable, instantiate, object (definition 2).

instance variable *n.* A variable associated with an instance of a class (an object). If a class defines a certain variable, each instance of the class has its own copy of that variable. *See also* class, instance, object (definition 2), object-oriented programming.

instantiate *vb.* To create an instance of a class. *See also* class, instance, object (definition 2).

instant messaging *n.* A service that alerts users when friends or colleagues are on line and allows them to communicate with each other in real time through private online chat areas. With instant messaging, a user creates a list of other users with whom he or she wishes to communicate; when a user from his or her list is on line, the service alerts the user and enables immediate contact with the other user. While instant messaging has primarily been a proprietary service offered by Internet service providers such as AOL and MSN, businesses are starting to employ instant messaging to increase employee efficiency and make expertise more readily available to employees.

Institute of Electrical and Electronics Engineers *n. See* IEEE.

instruction *n.* An action statement in any computer language, most often in machine or assembly language. Most programs consist of two types of statements: declarations and instructions. *See also* declaration, statement.

instruction code *n. See* operation code.

instruction counter *n. See* instruction register.

instruction cycle *n.* The cycle in which a processor retrieves an instruction from memory, decodes it, and carries it out. The time required for an instruction cycle is the sum of the instruction (fetch) time and the execution (translate and execute) time and is measured by the number of clock ticks (pulses of a processor's internal timer) consumed.

instruction mix *n.* The assortment of types of instructions contained in a program, such as assignment instructions, mathematical instructions (floating-point or integer), control instructions, and indexing instructions. Knowledge of instruction mixes is important to designers of CPUs because it tells them which instructions should be shortened to yield the greatest speed, and to designers of benchmarks because it enables them to make the benchmarks relevant to real tasks.

instruction pointer *n. See* program counter.

instruction register *n.* A register in a central processing unit that holds the address of the next instruction to be executed.

instruction set *n.* The set of machine instructions that a processor recognizes and can execute. *See also* assembler, microcode.

instruction time *n.* The number of clock ticks (pulses of a computer's internal timer) required to retrieve an instruction from memory. Instruction time is the first part of an instruction cycle; the second part is the execution (translate and execute) time. *Also called:* I-time.

instruction word *n.* **1.** The length of a machine language instruction. **2.** A machine language instruction containing an operation code identifying the type of instruction, possibly one or more operands specifying data to be affected or its address, and possibly bits used for indexing or other purposes. *See also* assembler, machine code.

insulator *n.* **1.** Any material that is a very poor conductor of electricity, such as rubber, glass, or ceramic. *Also called:* nonconductor. *Compare* conductor, semiconductor. **2.** A device used to separate elements of electrical circuits and prevent current from taking unwanted paths, such as the stacks of ceramic disks that suspend high-voltage power lines from transmission towers.

integer *n.* **1.** A positive or negative "whole" number, such as 37, –50, or 764. **2.** A data type representing whole numbers. Calculations involving only integers are much faster than calculations involving floating-point numbers, so integers are widely used in programming for counting and numbering purposes. Integers can be signed (positive or negative) or unsigned (positive). They can also be described as long or short, depending on the number of bytes needed to store them. Short integers, stored in 2 bytes, cover a smaller range of numbers (for example, –32,768 through 32,767) than do long integers (for example, –2,147,483,648 through 2,147,483,647), which are stored in 4 bytes. *Also called:* integral number. *See also* floating-point notation.

integral modem *n.* A modem that is built into a computer, as opposed to an internal modem, which is a modem on an expansion card that can be removed. *See also* external modem, internal modem, modem.

integral number *n. See* integer (definition 2).

integrated circuit *n.* A device consisting of a number of connected circuit elements, such as transistors and resistors, fabricated on a single chip of silicon crystal or other semiconductor material. Integrated circuits are categorized by the number of elements they contain. See the table. *Acronym:* IC. *Also called:* chip. *See also* central processing unit.

Table I.2   *Types of Integrated Circuits.*

Category	Elements
small-scale integration (SSI)	in the 10s
medium-scale integration (MSI)	in the 100s
large-scale integration (LSI)	in the 1000s
very-large-scale integration (VLSI)	in the 100,000s
ultra-large-scale integration (ULSI)	1,000,000 or more

integrated development environment *n.* A set of integrated tools for developing software. The tools are generally run from one user interface and consist of a compiler, an editor, and a debugger, among others. *Acronym:* IDE.

Integrated Device Electronics *n. See* IDE (definition 1).

integrated injection logic *n.* A type of circuit design that uses both NPN and PNP transistors and does not require other components, such as resistors. Such circuits are moderately fast, consume little power, and can be manufactured in very small sizes. *Acronym:* I2L, IIL. *Also called:* merged transistor logic. *See also* NPN transistor, PNP transistor.

Integrated Services Digital Network *n. See* ISDN.

Integrated Services LAN *n. See* isochronous network.

integrated software *n.* A program that combines several applications, such as word processing, database management, and spreadsheets, in a single package. Such software is "integrated" in two ways: it can transfer data from one of its applications to another, helping users coordinate tasks and merge information created with the different software tools; and it provides the user with a consistent interface for choosing commands, managing files, and otherwise interacting with the programs so that the user will not have to master several, often very different, programs. The applications in an integrated software package are often not, however, designed to offer as much capability as single applications, nor does integrated software necessarily include all the applications needed in a particular environment.

integration *n.* **1.** In computing, the combining of different activities, programs, or hardware components into a functional unit. *See also* integral modem, integrated software, ISDN. **2.** In electronics, the process of packing multiple electronic circuit elements on a single chip. *See also* integrated circuit. **3.** In mathematics, specifically calculus, a procedure performed on an equation and related to finding the area under a given curve or the volume within a given shape.

integrator *n.* A circuit whose output represents the integral, with respect to time, of the input signal—that is, its total accumulated value over time. See the illustration. *Compare* differentiator.

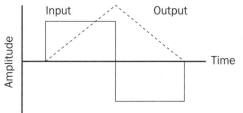

Integrator. *An example of the action of an integrator circuit.*

integrity *n.* The completeness and accuracy of data stored in a computer, especially after it has been manipulated in some way. *See also* data integrity.

Intel Architecture 64 *n. See* IA-64.

intellectual property *n.* Content of the human intellect deemed to be unique and original and to have marketplace value—and thus to warrant protection under the law. Intellectual property includes but is not limited to ideas; inventions; literary works; chemical, business, or computer processes; and company or product names and logos. Intellectual property protections fall into four categories: copyright (for literary works, art, and music), trademarks (for company and product names and logos), patents (for inventions and processes), and trade secrets (for recipes, code, and processes). Concern over defining and protecting intellectual property in cyberspace has brought this area of the law under intense scrutiny.

intelligence *n.* **1.** The ability of hardware to process information. A device without intelligence is said to be dumb; for example, a dumb terminal connected to a computer can receive input and display output but cannot process information independently. **2.** The ability of a program to monitor its environment and initiate appropriate actions to achieve a desired state. For example, a program waiting for data to be read from disk might switch to another task in the meantime. **3.** The ability of a program to simulate human thought. *See also* artificial intelligence. **4.** The ability of a machine such as a robot to respond appropriately to changing stimuli (input).

intelligent *adj.* Of, pertaining to, or characteristic of a device partially or totally controlled by one or more processors integral to the device.

intelligent agent *n. See* agent (definition 2).

intelligent cable *n.* A cable that incorporates circuitry to do more than simply pass signals from one end of the cable to the other, such as to determine the characteristics of the connector into which it is plugged. *Also called:* smart cable.

Intelligent Concept Extraction *n.* A technology owned by Excite, Inc., for searching indexed databases to retrieve documents from the World Wide Web. Intelligent Concept Extraction is like other search technologies in being able to locate indexed Web documents related to one or more key words entered by the user. Based on proprietary search technology, however, it also matches documents conceptually by finding relevant information even if the document found does not contain the key word or words specified by the user. Thus, the list of documents found by Intelligent Concept Extraction can include both documents containing the specified search term and those containing alternative words related to the search term. *Acronym:* ICE.

intelligent database *n.* A database that manipulates stored information in a way that people find logical, natural, and easy to use. An intelligent database conducts searches relying not only on traditional data-finding routines but also on predetermined rules governing associations, relationships, and even inferences regarding the data. *See also* database.

Intelligent hub *n.* A type of hub that, in addition to transmitting signals, has built-in capability for other network chores, such as monitoring or reporting on network status. Intelligent hubs are used in different types of networks, including ARCnet and 10Base-T Ethernet. *See also* hub.

Intelligent Input/Output *n. See* I2O.

intelligent terminal *n.* A terminal with its own memory, processor, and firmware that can perform certain functions independently of its host computer, most often the rerouting of incoming data to a printer or video screen.

Intelligent Transportation Infrastructure *n.* A system of automated urban and suburban highway and mass transit control and management services proposed in 1996 by U.S. Secretary of Transportation Federico Peña. *Acronym:* ITI.

IntelliSense *n.* A Microsoft technology used in various Microsoft products, including Internet Explorer, Visual Basic, Visual Basic C++, and Office that is designed to help users perform routine tasks. In Visual Basic, for example, information such as the properties and methods of an object is displayed as the developer types the name of the object in the Visual Basic code window.

Intensity Red Green Blue *n. See* IRGB.

interactive *adj.* Characterized by conversational exchange of input and output, as when a user enters a question or command and the system immediately responds. The interactivity of microcomputers is one of the features that makes them approachable and easy to use.

interactive fiction *n.* A type of computer game in which the user participates in a story by giving commands to the system. The commands given by the user determine, to some extent, the events that occur during the story. Typically the story involves a goal that must be achieved, and the puzzle is to determine the correct sequence of actions that will lead to the accomplishment of that goal. *See also* adventure game.

interactive graphics *n.* A form of user interface in which the user can change and control graphic displays, often with the help of a pointing device such as a mouse or a joystick. Interactive graphics interfaces occur in a range of computer products, from games to computer-aided design (CAD) systems.

interactive processing *n.* Processing that involves the more or less continuous participation of the user. Such a command/response mode is characteristic of microcomputers. *Compare* batch processing (definition 2).

interactive program *n.* A program that exchanges output and input with the user, who typically views a display of some sort and uses an input device, such as a keyboard, mouse, or joystick, to provide responses to the program. A computer game is an interactive program. *Compare* batch program.

interactive services *n. See* BISDN.

interactive session *n.* A processing session in which the user can more or less continuously intervene and control the activities of the computer. *Compare* batch processing (definition 2).

interactive television *n.* A video technology in which a viewer interacts with the television programming. Typical uses of interactive television include Internet access, video

on demand, and video conferencing. *See also* video conferencing.

interactive TV *n. See* iTV.

interactive video *n.* The use of computer-controlled video, in the form of a CD-ROM or videodisc, for interactive education or entertainment. *See also* CD-ROM, interactive, interactive television, videodisc.

interactive voice response *n.* A computer that operates through the telephone system, in which input commands and data are transmitted to the computer as spoken words and numbers or tones and dial pulses generated by a telephone instrument; and output instructions and data are received from the computer as prerecorded or synthesized speech. For example, a dial-in service that provides airline flight schedules when you press certain key codes on your telephone is an interactive voice response system. *Also called:* IVR.

interactive voice system *n. See* interactive voice response.

interapplication communication *n.* The process of one program sending messages to another program. For example, some e-mail programs allow users to click on a URL within the message. After the user clicks on the URL, browser software will automatically launch and access the URL.

interblock gap *n. See* inter-record gap.

Interchange File Format *n. See* .iff.

Interchange Format *n. See* Rich Text Format.

interconnect *n.* **1.** *See* System Area Network. **2.** An electrical or mechanical connection. Interconnect is the physical connection and communication between two components in a computer system.

interface *n.* **1.** The point at which a connection is made between two elements so that they can work with each other or exchange information. **2.** Software that enables a program to work with the user (the user interface, which can be a command-line interface, menu-driven interface, or a graphical user interface), with another program such as the operating system, or with the computer's hardware. *See also* application programming interface, graphical user interface. **3.** A card, plug, or other device that connects pieces of hardware with the computer so that information can be moved from place to place. For example, standardized interfaces such as RS-232-C standard and

SCSI enable communications between computers and printers or disks. *See also* RS-232-C standard, SCSI.

interface adapter *n. See* network adapter.

interface card *n. See* adapter.

Interface Definition Language *n. See* IDL.

interference *n.* **1.** Noise or other external signals that affect the performance of a communications channel. **2.** Electromagnetic signals that can disturb radio or television reception. The signals can be generated naturally, as in lightning, or by electronic devices, such as computers.

Interior Gateway Protocol *n.* A protocol used for distributing routing information among routers (gateways) in an autonomous network—that is, a network under the control of one administrative body. The two most often used interior gateway protocols are RIP (Routing Information Protocol) and OSPF (Open Shortest Path First). *Acronym:* IGP. *See also* autonomous system, OSPF, RIP. *Compare* exterior gateway protocol.

Interior Gateway Routing Protocol *n. See* IGRP.

Interix *n.* A software application from Microsoft that allows businesses to run existing UNIX-based legacy applications while adding applications based on the Microsoft Windows operating system. Interix serves as a single enterprise platform from which to run UNIX-based, Internet-based, and Windows-based applications.

interlaced *adj.* Pertaining to a display method on raster-scan monitors in which the electron beam refreshes or updates all odd-numbered scan lines in one vertical sweep of the screen and all even-numbered scan lines in the next sweep. *Compare* noninterlaced.

interlaced GIF *n.* A picture in GIF format that is gradually displayed in a Web browser, showing increasingly detailed versions of the picture until the entire file has finished downloading. Users of slower modems have a perceived shorter wait time for the image to appear, and they can sometimes get enough information about the image to decide whether to proceed with the download or move on. Users with faster connections will notice little difference in effect between an interlaced GIF and a noninterlaced GIF.

interlace scanning *n.* A display technique designed to reduce flicker and distortions in television transmissions; also used with some raster-scan monitors. In interlace scanning the electron beam in the television or monitor refreshes alternate sets of scan lines in successive top-to-bottom sweeps, refreshing all even lines on one pass, and

all odd lines on the other. Because of the screen phosphor's ability to maintain an image for a short time before fading and the tendency of the human eye to average or blend subtle differences in light intensity, the human viewer sees a complete display, but the amount of information carried by the display signal and the number of lines that must be displayed per sweep are halved. Interlaced images are not as clear as those produced by the progressive scanning typical of newer computer monitors. Interlace scanning is, however, the standard method of displaying analog broadcast television images. *Also called:* interlacing. *Compare* progressive scanning.

interlacing *n. See* interlace scanning.

interleave *vb.* To arrange the sectors on a hard disk in such a way that after one sector is read, the next sector in numeric sequence will arrive at the head when the computer is ready to accept it rather than before, which would make the computer wait a whole revolution of the platter for the sector to come back. Interleaving is set by the format utility that initializes a disk for use with a given computer.

interleaved memory *n.* A method of organizing the addresses in RAM memory in order to reduce wait states. In interleaved memory, adjacent locations are stored in different rows of chips so that after accessing a byte, the processor does not have to wait an entire memory cycle before accessing the next byte. *See also* access time (definition 1), wait state.

interlock *vb.* To prevent a device from acting while the current operation is in progress.

intermediate language *n.* **1.** A computer language used as an intermediate step between the original source language, usually a high-level language, and the target language, usually machine code. Some high-level compilers use assembly language as an intermediate language. *See also* compiler (definition 2), object code. **2.** *See* Microsoft intermediate language.

intermittent *adj.* Pertaining to something, such as a signal or connection, that is not unbroken but occurs at periodic or occasional intervals.

intermittent error *n.* An error that recurs at unpredictable times.

internal clock *n. See* clock/calendar.

internal command *n.* A routine that is loaded into memory along with the operating system and resides there for as long as the computer is on. *Compare* external command.

internal font *n.* A font that is already loaded in a printer's memory (ROM) when the printer is shipped. *Compare* downloadable font, font cartridge.

internal interrupt *n.* An interrupt generated by the processor itself in response to certain predefined situations, such as an attempt to divide by zero or an arithmetic value exceeding the number of bits allowed for it. *See also* interrupt. *Compare* external interrupt.

internal memory *n. See* primary storage.

internal modem *n.* A modem constructed on an expansion card to be installed in one of the expansion slots inside a computer. *Compare* external modem, integral modem.

internal schema *n.* A view of information about the physical files composing a database, including file names, file locations, accessing methodology, and actual or potential data derivations, in a database model such as that described by ANSI/X3/SPARC, that supports a three-schema architecture. The internal schema corresponds to the schema in systems based on CODASYL/DBTG. In a distributed database, there may be a different internal schema at each location. *See also* conceptual schema, schema.

internal sort *n.* **1.** A sorting operation that takes place on files completely or largely held in memory rather than on disk during the process. **2.** A sorting procedure that produces sorted subgroups of records that will be subsequently merged into one list.

International Computer Security Association *n. See* ICSA.

International Federation of Information Processing *n. See* IFIP.

International Maritime Satellite *n. See* Inmarsat.

International Mobile Telecommunications for the Year 2000 *n.* Specifications set forth by the International Telecommunications Union (ITU) to establish third-generation wireless telecommunication network architecture. The specifications include faster data transmission speeds and improved voice quality. *Acronym:* IMT-2000.

International Organization for Standardization *n. See* ISO.

International Telecommunication Union *n. See* ITU.

International Telecommunication Union-Telecommunication Standardization Sector *n. See* ITU-T.

International Telegraph and Telephone Consultative Committee *n.* English-language form of the name for the Comité Consultatif International Télégraphique et Télé-phonique, a standards organization that became part of the International Telecommunication Union in 1992. *See also* CCITT, ITU-T.

Internaut *n. See* cybernaut.

internet *n.* Short for **internet**work. A set of computer networks that may be dissimilar and are joined together by means of gateways that handle data transfer and conversion of messages from the sending networks' protocols to those of the receiving network.

Internet *n.* The worldwide collection of networks and gateways that use the TCP/IP suite of protocols to communicate with one another. At the heart of the Internet is a backbone of high-speed data communication lines between major nodes or host computers, consisting of thousands of commercial, government, educational, and other computer systems, that route data and messages. One or more Internet nodes can go off line without endangering the Internet as a whole or causing communications on the Internet to stop, because no single computer or network controls it. The genesis of the Internet was a decentralized network called ARPANET created by the U.S. Department of Defense in 1969 to facilitate communications in the event of a nuclear attack. Eventually other networks, including BITNET, Usenet, UUCP, and NSFnet, were connected to ARPANET. Currently the Internet offers a range of services to users, such as FTP, e-mail, the World Wide Web, Usenet news, Gopher, IRC, telnet, and others. *Also called:* the Net. *See also* BITNET, FTP[1] (definition 1), Gopher, IRC, NSFnet, telnet[1], Usenet, UUCP, World Wide Web.

Internet2 *n.* A computer-network development project launched in 1996 by a collaborative group of 120 universities under the auspices of the University Corporation for Advanced Internet Development (UCAID). The consortium is now being led by over 190 universities working with industry and government. The goal of Internet2, whose high-speed, fiberoptic backbone was brought on line in early 1999, is the development of advanced Internet technologies and applications for use in research and education at the university level. Though not open for public use, Internet2 and the technologies and applications developed by its members are intended to eventually benefit users of the commercial Internet as well. Some of the new technologies Internet2 and its members are developing and testing include IPv6, multicasting, and quality of service (QoS). Internet2 and the Next Generation Internet

(NGI) are complementary initiatives. *Compare* Internet, Next Generation Internet.

Internet access *n.* **1.** The capability of a user to connect to the Internet. This is generally accomplished through one of two ways. The first is through a dialing up of an Internet service provider or an online information services provider via a modem connected to the user's computer. This method is the one used by the majority of home computer users. The second way is through a dedicated line, such as a T1 carrier, that is connected to a local area network, to which, in turn, the user's computer is connected. The dedicated line solution is used by larger organizations, such as corporations, which either have their own node on the Internet or connect to an Internet service provider that is a node. A third way that is emerging is for users to use set-top boxes with their TVs. Generally, however, this will give a user access only to documents on the World Wide Web. *See also* dedicated line (definition 1), ISP, LAN, modem, node (definition 2), set-top box. **2.** The capability of an online information service to exchange data with the Internet, such as e-mail, or to offer Internet services to users, such as newsgroups, FTP, and the World Wide Web. Most online information services offer Internet access to their users. *See also* FTP[1] (definition 1), online information service.

Internet access device *n.* A communications and signal-routing mechanism, possibly incorporating usage tracking and billing features, for use in connecting multiple remote users to the Internet.

Internet access provider *n. See* ISP.

Internet account *n.* A generic term for a registered username at an Internet Service Provider (ISP). An Internet account is accessed via username and password. Services such as dial-in PPP Internet access and e-mail are provided by ISPs to Internet account owners.

Internet address *n. See* domain name address, e-mail address, IP address.

Internet appliance *n.* **1.** *See* set-top box. **2.** *See* server appliance.

Internet Architecture Board *n.* The body of the Internet Society (ISOC) responsible for overall architectural considerations regarding the Internet. The IAB also serves to adjudicate disputes in the standards process. *Acronym:* IAB. *See also* Internet Society.

Internet Assigned Numbers Authority *n. See* IANA, ICANN.

Internet backbone *n.* One of several high-speed networks connecting many local and regional networks, with at least one connection point where it exchanges packets with other Internet backbones. Historically, the NSFnet (predecessor to the modern Internet) was the backbone to the entire Internet in the United States. This backbone linked the supercomputing centers that the National Science Foundation (NSF) runs. Today, different providers have their own backbones so that the backbone for the supercomputing centers is independent of backbones for commercial Internet providers such as MCI and Sprint. *See also* backbone.

Internet broadcasting *n.* Broadcasting of audio, or audio plus video, signals across the Internet. Internet broadcasting includes conventional over-the-air broadcast stations that transmit their signals into the Internet as well as Internet-only stations. Listeners use audio Internet software, such as RealAudio. One method of Internet broadcasting is MBONE. *See also* MBONE, RealAudio.

Internet Cache Protocol *n. See* ICP.

Internet Control Message Protocol *n. See* ICMP.

Internet Corporation for Assigned Names and Numbers *n. See* ICANN.

Internet cramming *n. See* Web cramming.

Internet Directory *n.* **1.** Online database of sites organized by category where you can search for files and information by subject, keyword, or other criteria. **2.** Storage place for information such as names, Web addresses, organizations, departments, countries, and locations. Typically, Internet Directories are used to look up e-mail addresses that are not in a local address book or a corporate-wide directory.

Internet Draft *n.* A document produced by the Internet Engineering Task Force (IETF) for purposes of discussing a possible change in standards that govern the Internet. An Internet Draft is subject to revision or replacement at any time; if not replaced or revised, the Internet Draft is valid for no more than six months. An Internet Draft, if accepted, may be developed into an RFC. *See also* IETF, RFC.

Internet Engineering and Planning Group *n. See* IEPG.

Internet Engineering Steering Group *n.* The group within the Internet Society (ISOC) that, along with the Internet Architecture Board (IAB), reviews the standards proposed by the Internet Engineering Task Force (IETF). *Acronym:* IESG.

Internet Engineering Task Force *n. See* IETF.

Internet Explorer *n.* Microsoft's Web browsing software. Introduced in October 1995, the latest versions of Internet Explorer include many features that allow you to customize your experience on the Web. Internet Explorer is also available for the Macintosh and UNIX platforms. *See also* ActiveX control, Java applet, Web browser.

Internet Foundation Classes *n.* A Java class library developed by Netscape to facilitate the creation of full-feature, mission-critical Java applications. Internet Foundation Classes (IFC) comprises user-interface objects and frameworks intended to extend Java's Abstract Window Toolkit (AWT) and includes a multifont text editor; essential application controls; and drag-and-drop, drawing/event, windowing, animation, object persistence, single-thread, and localization frameworks. *See also* Abstract Window Toolkit, Application Foundation Classes, Java Foundation Classes, Microsoft Foundation Classes.

Internet gateway *n.* A device that provides the connection between the Internet backbone and another network, such as a LAN (local area network). Usually the device is a computer dedicated to the task or a router. The gateway generally performs protocol conversion between the Internet backbone and the network, data translation or conversion, and message handling. A gateway is considered a node on the Internet. *See also* gateway, Internet backbone, node (definition 2), router.

Internet Group Membership Protocol *n.* A protocol used by IP hosts to report their host group memberships to any immediately neighboring multicast routers. *Acronym:* IGMP.

Internet home *n. See* smart home.

Internet Information Server *n.* Microsoft's brand of Web server software, utilizing HTTP (Hypertext Transfer Protocol) to deliver World Wide Web documents. It incorporates various functions for security, allows for CGI programs, and also provides for Gopher and FTP services.

Internet Inter-ORB Protocol *n. See* IIOP.

Internet Mail Consortium *n.* An international membership organization of businesses and vendors involved in

activities related to e-mail transmission over the Internet. The goals of the Internet Mail Consortium are related to the promotion and expansion of Internet mail. The group's interests range from making Internet mail easier for new users to advancing new mail technologies and expanding the role played by Internet mail into areas such as electronic commerce and entertainment. For example, the Internet Mail Consortium supports two companion specifications, vCalendar and vCard, designed to facilitate electronic exchange of scheduling and personal information. *Acronym:* IMC.

Internet Naming Service *n. See* WINS.

Internet Printing Protocol *n.* A specification for transmission of documents to printers through the Internet. Development of the Internet Printing Protocol (IPP) was proposed in 1997 by members of the Internet Engineering Task Force (IETF). Intended to provide a standard protocol for Internet-based printing, IPP covers both printing and printer management (printer status, job cancellation, and so on). It is applicable to print servers and to network-capable printers.

Internet Protocol *n. See* IP.

Internet Protocol address *n. See* IP address.

Internet Protocol next generation *n. See* IPng.

Internet Protocol number *n. See* IP address.

Internet Protocol Security *n. See* IPSec.

Internet Protocol version 4 *n. See* IPv4.

Internet Protocol version 6 *n. See* IPv6.

Internet reference model *n. See* TCP/IP reference model.

Internet Relay Chat *n. See* IRC.

Internet Research Steering Group *n.* The governing body of the Internet Research Task Force (IRTF). *Acronym:* IRSG.

Internet Research Task Force *n.* A volunteer organization that is an arm of the Internet Society (ISOC) focused on making long-term recommendations concerning the Internet to the Internet Architecture Board (IAB). *Acronym:* IRTF. *See also* Internet Society.

Internet robot *n. See* spider.

Internet security *n.* A broad topic dealing with all aspects of data authentication, privacy, integrity, and verification for transactions over the Internet. For example, credit card purchases made via a World Wide Web browser require attention to Internet security issues to ensure that the credit card number is not intercepted by an intruder or copied from the server where the number is stored, and to verify that the credit card number is actually sent by the person who claims to be sending it.

Internet Security and Acceleration Server *n.* A software application from Microsoft Corporation to increase the security and performance of Internet access for businesses. Internet Security and Acceleration Server provides an enterprise firewall and high-performance Web cache server to securely manage the flow of information from the Internet through the enterprise's internal network. *Acronym:* ISA Server.

Internet Server Application Programming Interface *n. See* ISAPI.

Internet service provider *n. See* ISP.

Internet Society *n.* An international, nonprofit organization based in Reston, Virginia, comprising individuals, companies, foundations, and government agencies, that promotes the use, maintenance, and development of the Internet. The Internet Architecture Board (IAB) is a body within the Internet Society. In addition, the Internet Society publishes the *Internet Society News* and produces the annual INET conference. *Acronym:* ISOC. *See also* INET, Internet Architecture Board.

Internet Software Consortium *n.* A nonprofit organization that develops software that is available for free, via the World Wide Web or FTP, and engages in development of Internet standards such as the Dynamic Host Configuration Protocol (DHCP). *Acronym:* ISC. *See also* DHCP.

Internet SSE *n. See* SSE.

Internet Streaming Media Alliance *n. See* ISMA.

Internet synchronization *n.* **1.** The process of synchronizing data between computing and communication devices that are connected to the Internet. **2.** A feature in Microsoft Jet and Microsoft Access that allows replicated information to be synchronized in an environment in which an Internet server is configured with Microsoft Replication Manager, a tool included with Microsoft Office 2000 Developer.

Internet Talk Radio *n.* Audio programs similar to radio broadcasts but distributed over the Internet in the form of files that can be downloaded via FTP. Internet Talk Radio programs, prepared at the National Press Building in Washington, D.C., are 30 minutes to 1 hour in length; a 30-minute program requires about 15 MB of disk space. *Acronym:* ITR.

Internet telephone *n.* Point-to-point voice communication that uses the Internet instead of the public-switched telecommunications network to connect the calling and called parties. Both the sending and the receiving party need a computer, a modem, an Internet connection, and an Internet telephone software package to make and receive calls.

Internet Telephony Service Provider *n. See* ITSP.

Internet telephony *n. See* VoIP.

Internet television *n.* The transmission of television audio and video signals over the Internet.

Internet traffic distribution *n. See* ITM.

Internet traffic management *n. See* ITM.

internetwork[1] *adj.* Of or pertaining to communications between connected networks. It is often used to refer to communication between one LAN (local area network) and another over the Internet or another WAN (wide-area network). *See also* LAN, WAN.

internetwork[2] *n.* A network made up of smaller, interconnected networks.

Internetwork Packet Exchange *n. See* IPX.

Internetwork Packet Exchange/Sequenced Packet Exchange *n. See* IPX/SPX.

Internet World *n.* Series of international conferences and exhibitions on e-commerce and Internet technology sponsored by *Internet World* magazine. Major conferences include the world's largest Internet conferences, Internet World Spring and Internet World Fall.

Internet Worm *n.* A string of self-replicating computer code that was distributed through the Internet in November 1988. In a single night, it overloaded and shut down a large portion of the computers connected to the Internet at that time by replicating itself over and over on each computer it accessed, exploiting a bug in UNIX systems. Intended as a prank, the Internet Worm was written by a student at Cornell University. *See also* back door, worm.

InterNIC *n.* Short for NSFnet (**Inter**net) **N**etwork **I**nformation **C**enter. The organization that has traditionally registered domain names and IP addresses as well as distributed information about the Internet. InterNIC was formed in 1993 as a consortium involving the U.S. National Science Foundation, AT&T, General Atomics, and Network Solutions, Inc. (Herndon, Va.). The latter partner administers InterNIC Registration Services, which assigns Internet names and addresses.

interoperability *n.* Referring to components of computer systems that are able to function in different environments. For example, Microsoft's NT operating system is interoperable on Intel, DEC Alpha, and other CPUs. Another example is the SCSI standard for disk drives and other peripheral devices that allows them to interoperate with different operating systems. With software, interoperability occurs when programs are able to share data and resources. Microsoft Word, for example, is able to read files created by Microsoft Excel.

interpolate *vb.* To estimate intermediate values between two known values in a sequence.

interpret *vb.* **1.** To translate a statement or instruction into executable form and then execute it. **2.** To execute a program by translating one statement at a time into executable form and executing it before translating the next statement, rather than by translating the program completely into executable code (compiling it) before executing it separately. *See also* interpreter. *Compare* compile.

interpreted language *n.* A language in which programs are translated into executable form and executed one statement at a time rather than being translated completely (compiled) before execution. Basic, LISP, and APL are generally interpreted languages, although Basic can also be compiled. *See also* compiler. *Compare* compiled language.

interpreter *n.* A program that translates and then executes each statement in a program written in an interpreted language. *See also* compiler, interpreted language, language processor.

interprocess communication *n.* The ability of one task or process to communicate with another in a multitasking operating system. Common methods include pipes, semaphores, shared memory, queues, signals, and mailboxes. *Acronym:* IPC.

inter-record gap *n.* An unused space between data blocks stored on a disk or tape. Because the speed of disks and tapes fluctuates slightly during operation of the drives, a new data block may not occupy the exact space occupied by the old block it overwrites. The inter-record gap prevents the new block from overwriting part of adjacent blocks in such a case. *Acronym:* IRG. *Also called:* gap, interblock gap.

interrogate *vb.* To query with the expectation of an immediate response. For example, a computer may interrogate an attached terminal to determine the terminal's status (readiness to transmit or receive).

interrupt *n.* A signal from a device to a computer's processor requesting attention from the processor. When the processor receives an interrupt, it suspends its current operations, saves the status of its work, and transfers control to a special routine known as an interrupt handler, which contains the instructions for dealing with the particular situation that caused the interrupt. Interrupts can be generated by various hardware devices to request service or report problems, or by the processor itself in response to program errors or requests for operating-system services. Interrupts are the processor's way of communicating with the other elements that make up a computer system. A hierarchy of interrupt priorities determines which interrupt request will be handled first if more than one request is made. A program can temporarily disable some interrupts if it needs the full attention of the processor to complete a particular task. *See also* exception, external interrupt, hardware interrupt, internal interrupt, software interrupt.

interrupt-driven processing *n.* Processing that takes place only when requested by means of an interrupt. After the required task has been completed, the CPU is free to perform other tasks until the next interrupt occurs. Interrupt-driven processing is usually employed for responding to events such as a key pressed by the user or a floppy disk drive that has become ready to transfer data. *See also* interrupt. *Compare* autopolling.

interrupt handler *n.* A special routine that is executed when a specific interrupt occurs. Interrupts from different causes have different handlers to carry out the corresponding tasks, such as updating the system clock or reading the keyboard. A table stored in low memory contains pointers, sometimes called vectors, that direct the processor to the various interrupt handlers. Programmers can create interrupt handlers to replace or supplement existing handlers, such as by making a clicking sound each time the keyboard is pressed.

interrupt priority *n. See* interrupt.

interrupt request line *n.* A hardware line over which a device such as an input/output port, the keyboard, or a disk drive can send interrupts (requests for service) to the CPU. Interrupt request lines are built into the computer's internal hardware and are assigned different levels of priority so that the CPU can determine the sources and relative importance of incoming service requests. They are of concern mainly to programmers dealing with low-level operations close to the hardware. *Acronym:* IRQ.

interrupt vector *n.* A memory location that contains the address of the interrupt handler routine that is to be called when a specific interrupt occurs. *See also* interrupt.

interrupt vector table *n. See* dispatch table.

intersect *n.* An operator in relational algebra, used in database management. Given two relations (tables), A and B, that have corresponding fields (columns) containing the same types of values (that is, they are union-compatible), then INTERSECT A, B builds a third relation containing only those tuples (rows) that appear in both A and B. *See also* tuple.

interstitial *n.* An Internet ad format that appears in a pop-up window between Web pages. Interstitial ads download completely before appearing, usually while a Web page the user has chosen is loading. Because interstitial pop-up windows don't appear until the entire ad has downloaded, they often use animated graphics, audio, and other attention-getting multimedia technology that require longer download time.

in the wild *adj.* Currently affecting the computing public, particularly in regard to computer viruses. A virus that is not yet contained or controlled by antivirus software or that keeps reappearing despite virus detection measures is considered to be in the wild. *See also* virus.

intranet *n.* A private network based on Internet protocols such as TCP/IP but designed for information management within a company or organization. Its uses include such services as document distribution, software distribution, access to databases, and training. An intranet is so called because it looks like a World Wide Web site and is based on the same technologies, yet is strictly internal to the organization and is not connected to the Internet proper. Some intranets also offer access to the Internet, but such

connections are directed through a firewall that protects the internal network from the external Web. *Compare* extranet.

intraware *n.* Groupware or middleware for use on a company's private intranet. Intraware packages typically contain e-mail, database, workflow, and browser applications. *See also* groupware, intranet, middleware.

intrinsic font *n.* A font (type size and design) for which a bit image (an exact pattern) exists that can be used as is, without such modification as scaling. *Compare* derived font.

intruder *n.* An unauthorized user or unauthorized program, generally considered to have malicious intent, on a computer or computer network. *See also* bacterium, cracker, Trojan horse, virus.

intruder attack *n.* A form of hacker attack in which the hacker enters the system without prior knowledge or access to the system. The intruder will typically use a combination of probing tools and techniques to learn about the network to be hacked. *Compare* insider attack.

Intrusion Countermeasure Electronics *n. See* ICE (definition 3).

intrusion detection *n. See* IDS.

intrusion-detection system *n. See* IDS.

invalid *adj.* Erroneous or unrecognizable because of a flaw in reasoning or an error in input. Invalid results, for example, might occur if the logic in a program is faulty. *Compare* illegal.

inverse video *n. See* reverse video.

invert *vb.* **1.** To reverse something or change it to its opposite. For example, to invert the colors on a monochrome display means to change light to dark and dark to light. See the illustration. **2.** In a digital electrical signal, to replace a high level by a low level and vice versa. This type of operation is the electronic equivalent of a Boolean NOT operation.

Normal   Inverted

Invert. *An example showing the effects of inverting the colors on a monochrome display.*

inverted file *n. See* inverted list.

inverted list *n.* A method for creating alternative locators for sets of information. For example, in a file containing data about cars, records 3, 7, 19, 24, and 32 might contain the value "Red" in the field COLOR. An inverted list (or index) on the field COLOR would contain a record for "Red" followed by the locator numbers 3, 7, 19, 24, and 32. *See also* field, record. *Compare* linked list.

inverted-list database *n.* A database similar to a relational database but with several differences that make it much more difficult for the database management system to ensure data consistency, integrity, and security than with a relational system. The rows (records or tuples) of an inverted-list table are ordered in a specific physical sequence, independent of any orderings that may be imposed by means of indexes. The total database can also be ordered, with specified logical merge criteria being imposed between tables. Any number of search keys, either simple or composite, can be defined. Unlike the keys of a relational system, these search keys are arbitrary fields or combinations of fields. No integrity or uniqueness constraints are enforced; neither the indexes nor the tables are transparent to the user. *Compare* relational database.

inverted structure *n.* A file structure in which record keys are stored and manipulated separately from the records themselves.

inverter *n.* **1.** A logic circuit that inverts (reverses) the signal input to it—for example, inverting a high input to a low output. **2.** A device that converts direct current (DC) to alternating current (AC).

invoke *vb.* To call or activate; used in reference to commands and subroutines.

I/O *n. See* input/output.

I/O-bound *adj. See* input/output-bound.

I/O controller *n. See* input/output controller.

I/O device *n. See* input/output device.

ion-deposition printer *n.* A page printer in which the image is formed in electrostatic charges on a drum that picks up toner and transfers it to the paper, as in a laser, LED, or LCD printer, but the drum is charged using a beam of ions rather than light. These printers, used mainly in high-volume data-processing environments, typically operate at speeds from 30 to 90 pages per minute. In ion-deposition printers, toner is typically fused to paper by a method that is fast and does not require heat but leaves the paper a little glossy, making it unsuitable for business cor-respondence. In addition, ion-deposition printers tend to produce thick, slightly fuzzy characters; the technology is also more expensive than that of a laser printer. *See also* electrophotographic printers, nonimpact printer, page printer. *Compare* laser printer, LCD printer, LED printer.

I/O port *n. See* port[1] (definition 1).

I/O processor *n. See* input/output processor.

IO.SYS *n.* One of two hidden system files installed on an MS-DOS startup disk. IO.SYS in IBM releases of MS-DOS (called IBMBIO.COM) contains device drivers for peripherals such as the display, keyboard, floppy disk drive, hard disk drive, serial port, and real-time clock. *See also* MSDOS.SYS.

IP *n.* Acronym for **I**nternet **P**rotocol. The protocol within TCP/IP that governs the breakup of data messages into packets, the routing of the packets from sender to destination network and station, and the reassembly of the packets into the original data messages at the destination. IP runs at the internetwork layer in the TCP/IP model—equivalent to the network layer in the ISO/OSI reference model. *See also* ISO/OSI reference model, TCP/IP. *Compare* TCP.

IP address *n.* Short for **I**nternet **P**rotocol **address**. A 32-bit (4-byte) binary number that uniquely identifies a host (computer) connected to the Internet to other Internet hosts, for the purposes of communication through the transfer of packets. An IP address is expressed in "dotted quad" format, consisting of the decimal values of its 4 bytes, separated with periods; for example, 127.0.0.1. The first 1, 2, or 3 bytes of the IP address identify the network the host is connected to; the remaining bits identify the host itself. The 32 bits of all 4 bytes together can signify almost 2^{32}, or roughly 4 billion, hosts. (A few small ranges within that set of numbers are not used.) *Also called:* Internet Protocol number, IP number. *See also* host, IANA, ICANN, InterNIC, IP, IP address classes, packet (definition 2). *Compare* domain name.

IP address classes *n.* Short for **I**nternet **P**rotocol **address classes**. The classes into which IP addresses were divided to accommodate different network sizes. Each class is associated with a range of possible IP addresses and is limited to a specific number of networks per class and hosts per network. See the table. *See also* Class A IP address, Class B IP address, Class C IP address, IP address.

I

Address Class	Range of IP Addresses	Networks per Class	Hosts per Network (maximum number)
Class A (/8)	1.x.x.x to 126.x.x.x	126	16,777,214
Class B (/16)	128.0.x.x to 191.255.x.x	16,384	65,534
Class C (/24)	192.0.0.x to 223.255.255.x	2,097,152	254

IP address classes. *Each x represents the host-number field assigned by the network administrator.*

IP aliasing *n. See* NAT.

IPC *n. See* interprocess communication.

ipchains *n. See* iptables.

IP Filter *n.* Short for **I**nternet **P**rotocol **Filter**. A TCP/IP packet filter for UNIX, particularly BSD. Similar in functionality to netfilter and iptables in Linux, IP Filter can be used to provide network address translation (NAT) or firewall services. *See also* firewall. *Compare* netfilter, iptables.

IPL *n. See* initial program load.

IP masquerading *n. See* NAT.

IP multicasting *n.* Short for **I**nternet **P**rotocol **multicasting**. The extension of local area network multicasting technology to a TCP/IP network. Hosts send and receive multicast datagrams, the destination fields of which specify IP host group addresses rather than individual IP addresses. A host indicates that it is a member of a group by means of the Internet Group Management Protocol. *See also* datagram, Internet Group Membership Protocol, IP, MBONE, multicasting.

IPng *n.* Acronym for **I**nternet **P**rotocol **n**ext generation. A revised version of the Internet Protocol (IP) designed primarily to address growth on the Internet. IPng is compatible with, but an evolutionary successor to, the current version of IP, IPv4 (IP version 4), and was approved as a draft standard in 1998 by the IETF (Internet Engineering Task Force). It offers several improvements over IPv4 including a quadrupled IP address size (from 32 bits to 128 bits), expanded routing capabilities, simplified header formats, improved support for options, and support for quality of service, authentication, and privacy. *Also called:* IPv6. *See also* IETF, IP, IP address.

IP number *n. See* IP address.

IPP *n. See* Internet Printing Protocol.

IPSec *n.* Short for **I**nternet **P**rotocol **Sec**urity. A security mechanism under development by the IETF (Internet Engineering Task Force) designed to ensure secure packet exchanges at the IP (Internet Protocol) layer. IPSec is based on two levels of security: AH (Authentication Header), which authenticates the sender and assures the recipient that the information has not been altered during transmission, and ESP (Encapsulating Security Protocol), which provides data encryption in addition to authentication and integrity assurance. IPSec protects all protocols in the TCP/IP protocol suite and Internet communications by using Layer Two Tunneling Protocol (L2TP) and is expected to ensure secure transmissions over virtual private networks (VPNs). *See also* anti-replay, communications protocol, Diffie-Hellman, ESP, IETF, IP, IPv6, Layer L2TP, TCP/IP, packet, virtual private network.

IP Security *n. See* IPSec.

IP/SoC Conference and Exhibition *n.* Acronym for **I**ntellectual **P**roperty/**S**ystem **on** a **C**hip **Conference and Exhibition**. Leading conference and exhibition for executives, architects, and engineers using intellectual property in the design and production of system-on-a-chip semiconductors. The event features product exhibits and forums for the exchange of information.

IP splicing *n. See* IP spoofing.

IP spoofing *n.* The act of inserting a false sender IP address into an Internet transmission in order to gain unauthorized access to a computer system. *Also called:* IP splicing. *See also* IP address, spoofing.

IP switching *n.* A technology developed by Ipsilon Networks (Sunnyvale, Calif.) that enables a sequence of IP packets with a common destination to be transmitted over a high-speed, high-bandwidth Asynchronous Transfer Mode (ATM) connection.

iptables *n.* A utility used to configure firewall settings and rules in Linux. Part of the netfilter framework in the Linux kernel, iptables replaces ipchains, a previous implementation. *See also* netfilter. *Compare* IP Filter.

IP telephony *n.* Telephone service including voice and fax, provided through an Internet or network connection. IP telephony requires two steps: conversion of analog voice to digital format by a coding/uncoding device (codec) and conversion of the digitized information to packets for IP transmission. *Also called:* Internet telephony, Voice over IP (VoIP). *See also* H.323, VoIP.

IP tunneling *n.* A technique used to encapsulate data inside a TCP/IP packet for transmission between IP addresses. IP tunneling provides a secure means for data from different networks to be shared over the Internet.

IPv4 *n.* Short for **I**nternet **P**rotocol **v**ersion **4**. The current version of the Internet Protocol (IP), as compared with the next-generation IP, which is known familiarly as IPng and more formally as IPv6 (IP version 6). *See also* IP. *Compare* IPng.

IPv6 *n.* Short for **I**nternet **P**rotocol **v**ersion **6**. The next-generation Internet Protocol from the Internet Engineering Task Force (IETF), IPv6 is now included as part of IP support in many products and in the major operating systems. IPv6 offers several improvements from IPv4, most significantly an increase of available address space from 32 to 128 bits, which makes the number of available addresses effectively unlimited. Usually called IPng (next generation), IPv6 also includes support for multicast and anycast addressing. *See also* anycasting, IP, IPng.

ipvs *n.* Acronym for **IP** **V**irtual **S**erver. *See* LVS.

IPX *n.* Acronym for **I**nternetwork **P**acket **E**xchange. The protocol in Novell NetWare that governs addressing and routing of packets within and between LANs. IPX packets can be encapsulated in Ethernet packets or Token Ring frames. IPX operates at ISO/OSI levels 3 and 4 but does not perform all the functions at those levels. In particular, IPX does not guarantee that a message will be complete (no lost packets); SPX has that job. *See also* Ethernet (definition 1), packet, Token Ring network. *Compare* SPX (definition 1).

IPX/SPX *n.* Acronym for **I**nternetwork **P**acket **E**xchange/**S**equenced **P**acket **E**xchange. The network and transport level protocols used by Novell NetWare, which together correspond to the combination of TCP and IP in the TCP/IP protocol suite. IPX is a connectionless protocol that handles addressing and routing of packets. SPX, which runs above IPX, ensures correct delivery. *See also* IPX, SPX (definition 1).

IR *n. See* infrared.

IRC *n.* Acronym for **I**nternet **R**elay **C**hat. A service that enables an Internet user to participate in a conversation on line in real time with other users. An IRC channel, main-

tained by an IRC server, transmits the text typed by each user who has joined the channel to all other users who have joined the channel. Generally, a channel is dedicated to a particular topic, which may be reflected in the channel's name. An IRC client shows the names of currently active channels, enables the user to join a channel, and then displays the other participants' words on individual lines so that the user can respond. IRC was invented in 1988 by Jarkko Oikarinen of Finland. *See also* channel (definition 2), server (definition 2).

IrDA *n.* Acronym for **I**nfrared **D**ata **A**ssociation. The industry organization of computer, component, and telecommunications vendors who have established the standards for infrared communication between computers and peripheral devices such as printers.

IRE scale *n.* Short for **I**nstitute of **R**adio Engineers **scale**. Scale to determine video signal amplitudes as devised by the Institute of Radio Engineers, which is now part of the Institute of Electrical and Electronic Engineers (IEEE). The IRE scale includes a total of 140 units, with 100 up and 40 down from zero.

IRG *n. See* inter-record gap.

IRGB *n.* Acronym for **I**ntensity **R**ed **G**reen **B**lue. A type of color encoding originally used in IBM's Color/Graphics Adapter (CGA) and continued in the EGA (Enhanced Graphics Adapter) and VGA (Video Graphics Array). The standard 3-bit RGB color encoding (specifying eight colors) is supplemented by a fourth bit (called Intensity) that uniformly increases the intensity of the red, green, and blue signals, resulting in a total of 16 colors. *See also* RGB.

IRL *n.* Acronym for **i**n **r**eal **l**ife. An expression used by many online users to denote life outside the computer realm, especially in conjunction with virtual worlds such as online talkers, IRC, MUDs, and virtual reality. *See also* IRC, MUD, talker, virtual reality.

IRQ *n.* Acronym for **i**nterrupt **req**uest. One of a set of possible hardware interrupts, identified by a number, on a Wintel computer. The number of the IRQ determines which interrupt handler will be used. In the AT bus, ISA, and EISA, 15 IRQs are available; in Micro Channel Architecture, 255 IRQs are available. Each device's IRQ is hardwired or set by a jumper or DIP switch. The VL bus and the PCI local bus have their own interrupt systems, which they translate to IRQ numbers. *See also* AT bus, DIP switch, EISA, interrupt, IRQ conflict, ISA, jumper, Micro Channel Architecture, PCI local bus, VL bus.

IRQ conflict *n.* The condition on a Wintel computer in which two different peripheral devices use the same IRQ to request service from the central processing unit (CPU). An IRQ conflict will prevent the system from working correctly; for example, the CPU may respond to an interrupt from a serial mouse by executing an interrupt handler for interrupts generated by a modem. IRQ conflicts can be prevented by the use of Plug and Play hardware and software. *See also* interrupt handler, IRQ, Plug and Play.

irrational number *n.* A real number that cannot be expressed as the ratio of two integers. Examples of irrational numbers are the square root of 3, pi, and *e*. *See also* integer, real number.

IRSG *n. See* Internet Research Steering Group.

IRTF *n. See* Internet Research Task Force.

IS *n. See* Information Services.

ISA *n.* Acronym for **I**ndustry **S**tandard **A**rchitecture. A bus design specification that allows components to be added as cards plugged into standard expansion slots in IBM Personal Computers and compatibles. Originally introduced in the IBM PC/XT with an 8-bit data path, ISA was expanded in 1984, when IBM introduced the PC/AT, to permit a 16-bit data path. A 16-bit ISA slot actually consists of two separate 8-bit slots mounted end-to-end so that a single 16-bit card plugs into both slots. An 8-bit expansion card can be inserted and used in a 16-bit slot (it occupies only one of the two slots), but a 16-bit expansion card cannot be used in an 8-bit slot. *See also* EISA, Micro Channel Architecture.

ISAM *n. See* indexed sequential access method.

ISAPI *n.* Acronym for **I**nternet **S**erver **A**pplication **P**rogramming **I**nterface. An easy-to-use, high-performance interface for back-end applications for Microsoft's Internet Information Server (IIS). ISAPI has its own dynamic-link library, which offers significant performance advantages over the CGI (Common Gateway Interface) specification. *See also* API, dynamic-link library, Internet Information Server. *Compare* CGI.

ISAPI filter *n.* A DLL file used by Microsoft Internet Information Server (IIS) to verify and authenticate ISAPI requests received by the IIS.

ISA Server *n. See* Internet Security and Acceleration Server.

ISA slot *n.* A connection socket for a peripheral designed according to the ISA (Industry Standard Architecture) standard, which applies to the bus developed for use in the 80286 (IBM PC/AT) motherboard. *See also* ISA.

ISC *n. See* Internet Software Consortium.

ISDN *n.* Acronym for **I**ntegrated **S**ervices **D**igital Network. A high-speed digital communications network evolving from existing telephone services. The goal in developing ISDN was to replace the current telephone network, which requires digital-to-analog conversions, with facilities totally devoted to digital switching and transmission, yet advanced enough to replace traditionally analog forms of data, ranging from voice to computer transmissions, music, and video. ISDN is available in two forms, known as BRI (Basic Rate Interface) and PRI (Primary Rate Interface). BRI consists of two B (bearer) channels that carry data at 64 Kbps and one D (data) channel that carries control and signal information at 16 Kbps. In North America and Japan, PRI consists of 23 B channels and 1 D channel, all operating at 64 Kbps; elsewhere in the world, PRI consists of 30 B channels and 1 D channel. Computers and other devices connect to ISDN lines through simple, standardized interfaces. *See also* BRI, channel (definition 2), PRI.

ISDN terminal adapter *n.* The hardware interface between a computer and an ISDN line. *See also* ISDN.

I seek you *n. See* ICQ.

ISIS or **IS-IS** *n.* Acronym for **I**ntelligent **S**cheduling and **I**nformation **S**ystem. A toolkit designed to help prevent and eliminate faults in manufacturing systems. Developed in 1980 at Cornell University, ISIS is now available commercially.

ISLAN *n. See* isochronous network.

ISMA *n.* Acronym for **I**nternet **S**treaming **M**edia Alliance. A nonprofit organization promoting the adoption of open standards for the streaming of rich media over Internet Protocol (IP) networks. ISMA membership consists of a number of technology companies and groups including Apple Computer, Cisco Systems, IBM, Kasenna, Philips, and Sun Microsystems. *See also* Windows Metafile Format.

ISO *n.* Short for **I**nternational **O**rganization for Standardization (often incorrectly identified as an acronym for International Standards Organization), an international association of 130 countries, each of which is represented by its leading standard-setting organization—for example, ANSI (American National Standards Institute) for the United States. The ISO works to establish global standards for communications and information exchange. Primary among its accomplishments is the widely accepted ISO/OSI reference model, which defines standards for the interaction of computers connected by communications networks. *ISO* is not an acronym; rather, it is derived from the Greek word *isos*, which means "equal" and is the root of the prefix "iso-."

ISO 8601:1988 *n.* A standard entitled "Data elements and interchange formats" from the International Organization for Standardization (ISO) that covers a number of date formats.

ISO 9660 *n.* An international format standard for CD-ROM adopted by the International Organization for Standardization (ISO) that follows the recommendations embodied in the High Sierra specification, with some modifications. *See also* High Sierra specification.

ISOC *n. See* Internet Society.

isochronous network *n.* A type of network defined in the IEEE 802.9 specification that combines ISDN and LAN technologies to enable networks to carry multimedia. *Also called:* Integrated Services LAN, ISLAN.

isometric view *n.* A display method for three-dimensional objects in which every edge has the correct length for the scale of the drawing and in which all parallel lines appear parallel. An isometric view of a cube, for example, shows the faces in symmetrical relation to one another and the height and width of each face evenly proportioned; the faces do not appear to taper with distance as they do when the cube is drawn in perspective. See the illustration. *Compare* perspective view.

Isometric   Perspective
view   view

Isometric view. *A cube in isometric view and in perspective view.*

ISO/OSI reference model *n.* Short for International Organization for Standardization Open Systems Interconnection **reference model**. A layered architecture (plan)

that standardizes levels of service and types of interaction for computers exchanging information through a communications network. The ISO/OSI reference model separates computer-to-computer communications into seven protocol layers, or levels, each building—and relying—upon the standards contained in the levels below it. The lowest of the seven layers deals solely with hardware links; the highest deals with software interactions at the application-program level. It is a fundamental blueprint designed to help guide the creation of networking hardware and software. See the illustration. *Also called:* OSI reference model.

ISO/OSI MODEL	
ISO/OSI Layer	**Focus**
Application (highest level)	Program-to-program transfer of information
Presentation	Text formatting and display, code conversion
Session	Establishing, maintaining, and coordinating communication
Transport	Accurate delivery, service quality
Network	Transport routes, message handling and transfer
Data-link	Coding, addressing, and transmitting information
Physical	Hardware connections

ISO/OSI reference model.

ISP *n.* Acronym for **I**nternet **s**ervice **p**rovider. A business that supplies Internet connectivity services to individuals, businesses, and other organizations. Some ISPs are large national or multinational corporations that offer access in many locations, while others are limited to a single city or region. *Also called:* access provider, service provider.

ISSE *n. See* SSE.

ISV *n. See* independent software vendor.

IT *n.* Acronym for **I**nformation **T**echnology. *See* Information Services.

italic *n.* A type style in which the characters are evenly slanted toward the right. *This sentence is in italics.* Italics are commonly used for emphasis, foreign-language words and phrases, titles of literary and other works, technical terms, and citations. *See also* font family. *Compare* roman.

Itanium *n.* An Intel microprocessor that uses explicitly parallel instruction set computing and 64-bit memory addressing.

iterate *vb.* To execute one or more statements or instructions repeatedly. Statements or instructions so executed are said to be in a loop. *See also* iterative statement, loop.

iterative statement *n.* A statement in a program that causes the program to repeat one or more statements. Examples of iterative statements in Basic are FOR, DO, REPEAT..UNTIL, and DO..WHILE. *See also* control statement.

ITI *n. See* Intelligent Transportation Infrastructure.

I-time *n. See* instruction time.

ITM *n.* Short for **I**nternet **t**raffic **m**anagement. The analysis and control of Internet traffic to improve efficiency and optimize for high availability. With ITM, Web traffic is distributed among multiple servers using load balancers and other devices. *See also* load balancing.

ITR *n. See* Internet Talk Radio.

ITSP *n.* Acronym for **I**nternet **T**elephony **S**ervice **P**rovider. A business that supplies PC-to-telephone calling capabilities to individuals, businesses, and organizations. Through an ITSP, calls initiated on a PC travel over the Internet to a gateway that, in turn, sends the call to the standard public switched phone network and, eventually, to the receiving telephone. *See also* ISP, telephony.

ITU *n.* Acronym for **I**nternational **T**elecommunication Union. An international organization based in Geneva, Switzerland, that is responsible for making recommendations and establishing standards governing telephone and data communications systems for public and private telecommunications organizations. Founded in 1865 under the name International Telegraph Union, it was renamed the International Telecommunication Union in 1934 to signify the full scope of its responsibilities. ITU became an agency of the United Nations in 1947. A reorganization in 1992 aligned the ITU into three governing bodies: the Radiocommunication Sector, the Telecommunication Standardization Sector (ITU-TSS, ITU-T, for short; formerly the CCITT), and the Telecommunication Development Sector. *See also* ITU-T.

ITU-T *n.* The standardization division of the International Telecommunication Union, formerly called Comité Consultatif International Télégraphique et Téléphonique (CCITT). The ITU-T develops communications recommendations for all analog and digital communications. *Also called:* ITU-TSS. *See also* CCITT Groups 1-4, ITU.

ITU-TSS *n. See* ITU-T.

ITU-T V series *n. See* V series.

ITU-T X series *n. See* X series.

iTV *n.* Acronym for **I**nteractive **t**elevision. A communications medium combining television with interactive services. iTV offers two-way communications between users and communications providers. From their televisions, users can order special programming, respond to programming options, and access the Internet and additional services such as instant messaging and telephone functions.

IVR *n. See* interactive voice response.

IVUE *n.* A proprietary image format (from Live Pictures) that allows files to be adjusted to screen resolution at any zoom level.

i-way *n. See* Information Superhighway.

J2EE *n.* Acronym for **J**ava **2** Platform **E**nterprise **E**dition. An application server framework from Sun Microsystems, Inc., for the development of distributed applications. It includes all the previous Java APIs targeted for multi-tiered distributed enterprise information systems. The J2EE platform consists of a set of services, application programming interfaces (APIs), and protocols that provide the functionality for developing multitiered, Web-based applications. *See also* application programming interface, Enterprise Java Beans, IDL, Java, JDBC, Jini, JMS, JNDI, JSP, JTA, JTS, RMI-IIOP.

J *n.* A high-level programming language created by Kenneth Iverson, developer of APL, and Roger Hui. J is a successor language to APL that may be run on many platforms, including Windows 95, Windows NT, Macintosh, Linux, RS/6000, and Sun Sparc. Like APL, J is used primarily by mathematicians. *See also* APL.

jabber *n.* A continuous stream of random data transmitted over a network as the result of some malfunction.

Jabber *n.* An XML-based instant messaging system. Jabber software is available for most operating systems and allows user access to other instant messaging services. Jabber is an open source application overseen by Jabber.org.

jack *n.* A connector designed to receive a plug. A jack is commonly used in making audio and video connections.

jacket *n. See* disk jacket.

jack in *vb.* **1.** To log on to a computer. **2.** To connect to a network or BBS, especially for purposes of entering an IRC or a virtual reality simulation, such as a MUD. (To leave is to *jack out*.) *See also* IRC, MUD.

jack out *vb.* **1.** To log off a computer. **2.** To disconnect from a network or online bulletin board system. *See also* jack in, log on.

Jacquard loom *n.* The first machine that used punched cards to control its operation. In this loom, developed in 1801 by French inventor Joseph-Marie Jacquard, up to 24,000 cards were placed on a rolling drum. Where a hole was punched on a card, one of a set of rods could pass through and select a particular thread to be woven into the pattern. Jacquard was awarded a medal by the Emperor Napoleon for his invention. Later in the nineteenth century, punched cards were used in Charles Babbage's computerlike Analytical Engine and in Herman Hollerith's statistical tabulating machine. *See also* Analytical Engine, Hollerith tabulating/recording machine.

jaggies *n.* The "stairsteps" that appear in diagonal lines and curves drawn at low resolutions in computer graphics. *Also called:* aliasing.

Janet *n.* Short for the **J**oint **A**cademic **Net**work. A wide area network in the United Kingdom that serves as the principal backbone for the Internet in that country. *See also* backbone (definition 1).

.jar *n.* A file name extension that identifies a compressed JAR (**J**ava **Ar**chive) file. Note: By changing the .jar extension to .zip, you can use popular extraction tools such as PKZIP or WINZIP to look at a .jar file's contents. *See also* compressed file, JAR, PKZIP, .zip.

JAR *n.* Acronym for **J**ava **Ar**chive file. JAR files allow Java developers to efficiently deploy Java classes and their associated resources. The elements in a JAR file are compressed just as in a standard zip file. JAR files include a security mechanism and a special META-INF directory that contains administrative information about the contents of the files. Using a combination of a digital signature and the META-INF data, JAR files can be signed to ensure authenticity and security. *See also* .jar.

Java *n.* An object-oriented programming language developed by Sun Microsystems, Inc. Similar to C++, Java is smaller, more portable, and easier to use than C++ because it is more robust and it manages memory on its own. Java was also designed to be secure and platform-neutral (meaning that it can be run on any platform) through the fact that Java programs are compiled into bytecode, which is not refined to the point of relying on platform-specific instructions and runs on a computer in a special software environment known as a virtual machine. This characteristic of Java makes it a useful language for programming

Web applications, since users access the Web from many types of computers. Java is used in programming small applications, or applets, for the World Wide Web, as well as in creating distributed network applications. *See also* bytecode, Java applet, Jini, object-oriented programming.

Java applet *n.* A Java class that is loaded and run by an already-running Java application such as a Web browser or an applet viewer. Java applets can be downloaded and run by any Web browser capable of interpreting Java, such as Internet Explorer, Netscape Navigator, and HotJava. Java applets are frequently used to add multimedia effects and interactivity to Web pages, such as background music, real-time video displays, animations, calculators, and interactive games. Applets can be activated automatically when a user views a page, or they may require some action on the part of the user, such as clicking on an icon in the Web page. *See also* applet, Java.

JavaBean *n.* A Java component architecture defined in the JavaBeans specification developed by Sun Microsystems. A JavaBean, or Bean, is a reusable application component—an independent code segment—that can be combined with other JavaBean components to create a Java applet or application. The JavaBean concept emphasizes the platform-independence of the Java language, in which ideally a program, once written, can run on any computing platform. JavaBeans are similar to Microsoft's ActiveX controls. ActiveX controls, however, can be developed in different programming languages but executed only on a Windows platform. JavaBeans can be developed only in the Java programming language but ideally can run on any platform. *See also* ActiveX, Java.

Java Card *n.* An application programming interface (API) from Sun Microsystems, Inc., that allows Java applets and programs to run on smart cards and other devices with limited memory. Java Card uses a Java Card Virtual Machine designed for severely memory-constrained devices. *See also* applets, Java Card Virtual Machine, smart card (definition 2).

Java Card Virtual Machine *n.* An ultra-small-footprint, highly optimized foundation of a runtime environment within the Java 2 Platform Micro Edition. Derived from the Java Virtual Machine (JVM), it is targeted at smart cards and other severely memory-constrained devices. The Java Card Virtual Machine can run in devices with memory as small as 24 KB of ROM, 16 KB of EEPROM, and 512 bytes of RAM. *See also* EEPROM, Java Card, RAM, ROM.

Java chip *n.* An implementation on a single integrated circuit of the virtual machine specified for execution of the Java programming language. Such chips, which are being developed by Sun Microsystems, Inc., could be used in very small devices and as controllers for appliances. *See also* integrated circuit, Java, virtual machine.

Java-compliant browser *n.* A Web browser with support for the Java programming language built into it. Most current Web browsers are Java-compliant. *See also* Java, Web browser.

Java Developer's Kit *n.* A set of software tools developed by Sun Microsystems, Inc., for writing Java applets or applications. The kit, which is distributed free, includes a Java compiler, interpreter, debugger, viewer for applets, and documentation. *Acronym:* JDK. *See also* applet, Java, Java applet.

Java Foundation Classes *n.* A Java-based set of class libraries developed by Sun Microsystems, Inc. Encompassing fundamentals of the Internet Foundation Classes created by Netscape Communications Corp., the Java Foundation Classes extend the Java Abstract Window Toolkit (AWT) by providing graphical user interface components for use in developing commercial and Internet-related Java applications. *See also* Abstract Window Toolkit, Application Foundation Classes, Internet Foundation Classes, Java, JavaBean, Microsoft Foundation Classes.

Java HotSpot *n.* A Java performance engine introduced by Sun Microsystems, Inc., in 1999 that is designed to run Java applications faster than just-in-time (JIT) compilers. The core of Java HotSpot, and the feature for which it is named, is its ability to perform adaptive optimization—the identification and optimization of "hot spots," or sections of performance-critical code. Improved garbage collection (freeing of memory occupied by objects no longer in use) and better multithreading are additional features designed to contribute to increased performance. *See also* Java.

Java IDL *n.* Short for **Java I**nterface **D**efinition **L**anguage. A Java technology that provides CORBA interoperability and connectivity capabilities for the Java platform. These capabilities enable Java applications to invoke operations on remote network services using the Object Management Group Interface Definition Language and Internet Inter-ORB Protocol. *See also* CORBA, IDL, J2EE, RMI-IIOP.

JavaMail *n.* An API in the Sun Microsystems, Inc., Java platform for sending and receiving mail. A set of abstract APIs that model a mail system, JavaMail provides a platform-independent and protocol-independent framework to build Java-based e-mail client applications. *See also* application programming interface, e-mail, J2EE.

Java Management Application Programming Interface *n.* A set of application programming interface specifications, proposed by Sun Microsystems, Inc., to enable the Java language to be used for network management. *Acronym:* JMAPI. *See also* application programming interface, Java.

JavaOS *n.* An operating system designed to run applications written in the Java programming language. JavaOS was created by JavaSoft, an operating company of Sun Microsystems, Inc., to run the Java Virtual Machine (JVM) directly on microprocessors, and thus eliminate the need for a resident operating system. JavaOS is small and designed for network computers, as well as devices ranging from game machines to pagers and cellular telephones. *See also* Java.

JavaScript *n.* A scripting language developed by Netscape Communications and Sun Microsystems that is loosely related to Java. JavaScript, however, is not a true object-oriented language, and it is limited in performance compared with Java because it is not compiled. Basic online applications and functions can be added to Web pages with JavaScript, but the number and complexity of available application programming interface functions are fewer than those available with Java. JavaScript code, which is included in a Web page along with the HTML code, is generally considered easier to write than Java, especially for novice programmers. A JavaScript-compliant Web browser, such as Netscape Navigator or Internet Explorer, is necessary to run JavaScript code. *See also* application programming interface, HTML, scripting language. *Compare* Java.

JavaServer Pages *n. See* JSP.

Java Speech Grammar Format *n.* A platform-independent grammar description format developed for use with speech recognition systems. Java Speech Grammar Format is used extensively with Voice XML and can be used with most speech recognition systems and related applications. *Acronym:* JSGF.

Java Virtual Machine *n.* The environment in which Java programs run. The Java Virtual Machine gives Java programs a software-based "computer" they can interact with. (Programs, even the most seemingly unchallenging ones designed for children or entertainment, must run within an environment from which they can use memory, display

information, gather input, and so on.) Because the Java Virtual Machine is not a real computer but exists in software, a Java program can run on any physical computing platform, such as a Windows 9x computer or a Macintosh, equipped with an interpreter—usually an Internet browser—that can carry out the program's instructions and a Java Virtual Machine that provides the "hardware" on which the program can run. *Acronym:* JVM.

JCL *n.* Acronym for **J**ob **C**ontrol **L**anguage. A command language used in IBM OS/360 mainframe systems. JCL is used to launch applications and specifies information on running time, program size, and the program files used for each application. *See also* command language.

JDBC *n.* A Java API designed to provide access to relational databases and other tabular material, such as spreadsheets and flat files. Using JDBC, a developer can create a cross-platform Java application that can connect with, and send SQL statements to, a number of different relational databases. Although it is commonly thought to stand for Java Database Connectivity, JDBC is the name of the technology; it is not an acronym.

JDK *n. See* Java Developer's Kit.

jDoc *n.* A cross-platform, interactive format for display, distribution, and interaction with live Web pages. jDoc documents are small in size and can be embedded in HTML documents to offer client-side interactivity. jDoc was created by EarthStones and is an extension to Sun's Java platform.

JetSend Protocol *n.* A platform-independent communications protocol developed by Hewlett-Packard to enable direct device-to-device communication. The JetSend protocol is designed to provide JetSend-enabled devices with the ability to exchange information and data without the need for device drivers or reliance on servers or user intervention. The protocol is intended for use with printers, scanners, fax machines, and other such information "appliances" and was developed to simplify and improve interoperability between and among a wide range of devices.

Jet SQL *n.* A query language. Jet SQL is a dialect used by the Microsoft Access application, specifically by the Microsoft Jet database engine, to extract, manipulate, and structure data that resides in a relational database management system (RDBMS). Jet SQL is based largely on the ANSI SQL-92 standard, with additional extensions.

jewel box *n.* A clear plastic container used to package and store a compact disc. *Also called:* jewel case.

JFC *n. See* Java Foundation Classes.

JFIF *n.* Acronym for **J**PEG **F**ile **I**nterchange **F**ormat. A means of saving photographic images stored according to the Joint Photographic Experts Group image compression technique. JFIF represents a "common language" file format in that it is designed specifically to allow users to transfer JPEG images easily between different computers and applications. *See also* JPEG, TIFF JPEG.

Jini *n.* A technical specification developed by Sun Micro-systems that uses a small piece (48 KB) of Java code to allow any network device with a Java Virtual Machine (JVM) to announce its availability and provide its services to any other device connected to the same network. Jini is based on the concept of creating a "federation" of self-configuring devices capable of transparently exchanging code when necessary to simplify interactions between network devices. *See also* Java.

JIT *adj. See* just-in-time.

jitter *n.* **1.** Small vibrations or fluctuations in a displayed video image caused by irregularities in the display signal. Jitter is often visible in the form of horizontal lines that are of the same thickness as scan lines. **2.** A rough appearance in a fax caused by dots that are incorrectly recorded during the scanning process and thus wrongly positioned in the output. **3.** In digital communication, distortion caused by lack of synchronization of signals.

JMAPI *n. See* Java Management Application Programming Interface.

JMS *n.* Acronym for **J**ava **M**essaging **S**ervice. In the J2EE network platform, JMS is an API for using enterprise messaging systems such as IBM MQ Series, TIBCO Rendezvous, and others. *See also* application programming interface, J2EE.

JNDI *n.* Acronym for **J**ava **N**aming and **D**irectory Interface. A set of APIs in the J2EE platform from Sun Microsystems, Inc., that assists with the interfacing to multiple naming and directory services. *See also* application programming interface, J2EE.

job *n.* A specified amount of processing performed as a unit by a computer. On early mainframe computers, data was submitted in batches, often on punched cards, for processing by different programs; work was therefore scheduled and carried out in separate jobs, or operations.

Job Control Language *n. See* JCL.

job processing *n.* A computing method in which a series of jobs, each consisting of one or more tasks grouped together as a computationally coherent whole, is processed sequentially. *See also* batch processing (definition 2).

job queue *n.* A list of programs or tasks waiting for execution by a computer. Jobs in the queue are often ordered according to some basis of priority. *See also* queue.

join *n.* **1.** A database table operation that creates a resultant entry in another table for each entry in the one table whose key field matches that of an entry in the other. *See also* inner join. **2.** A multiprocessing command that causes a child process to return control to its parent. *See also* child (definition 1), multiprocessing.

join line *n.* In a database query, a line that connects fields between two tables and shows how the data is related. Generally, a join line starts with an arrow just beyond the boundary of the table window pointing at the field in one table and ends just beyond the boundary of another table with an arrow pointing at the related field. The type of join indicates which records are selected for the query's result set.

Joint Photographic Experts Group *n. See* JPEG (definition 1).

Joliet *n.* An extension to the ISO 9660 (1988) standard developed to include long filenames or filenames outside the 8.3 convention. This format is used in some new CD-ROMs for operating systems, such as Windows 9x, that can handle such filenames. *See also* 8.3, ISO 9660, long filenames.

Josephson junction *n.* A cryoelectronic device that can attain extremely high circuit-switching speeds. In the Josephson effect, when two superconducting materials are in close proximity but are separated by an insulator, electric current can jump or tunnel through the gap.

journal *n.* A computer-based log or record of transactions that takes place in a computer or across a network. A journal could be used, for example, to record message transfers on a communications network, to keep track of system activities that alter the contents of a database, or to maintain a record of files that have been archived for storage or deleted from the system. A journal is often kept as a means of reconstructing events or sets of data should they become lost or damaged. *See also* audit trail.

journaled file system *n.* A fault-resilient file system that includes backup and recovery capabilities. When file server indexes are updated, all changes and related information are recorded and stored in a separate log. If a system failure or other abnormal interruption occurs, the system will use stored backup files to repair files corrupted in the crash. Journaled file systems are widely used for business and intranet file servers. In 2001, IBM contributed journaled file system technology to the open source community to allow development of similar file systems for Linux servers.

joystick *n.* A pointing device used mainly but not exclusively for computer games. A joystick has a base, on which control buttons can be mounted, and a vertical stem, which the user can move in any direction to control the movement of an object on the screen; the stem may also have control buttons. The buttons activate various software features, generally producing on-screen events. A joystick is usually used as a relative pointing device, moving an object on the screen when the stem is moved and stopping the movement when the stem is released. In industrial control applications, the joystick can also be used as an absolute pointing device, with each position of the stem mapped to a specific location on the screen. See the illustration. *See also* absolute pointing device, relative pointing device. *Compare* game pad.

Joystick.

.jpeg *n.* The file extension that identifies graphic image files in the JPEG format. *See also* JPEG.

JPEG *n.* **1.** Acronym for **J**oint **P**hotographic **E**xperts **G**roup. An ISO/ITU standard for storing images in compressed form using a discrete cosine transform. JPEG trades off compression against loss; it can achieve a compression ratio of 100:1 with significant loss and possibly

20:1 with little noticeable loss. **2.** A graphic stored as a file in the JPEG format.

JPEG File Interchange Format *n. See* JFIF.

.jpg *n.* The file extension that identifies graphic images encoded in the JPEG File Interchange Format, as originally specified by the Joint Photographic Experts Group (JPEG). Inline graphics on World Wide Web pages are often .jpg files, such as coolgraphic.jpg. *See also* JPEG (definition 2).

JScript *n.* An interpreted, object-based scripting language that borrows from C, C++, and Java. It is Microsoft's implementation of the ECMA 262 language specification (ECMAScript Edition 3). The latest versions of JavaScript and JScript are compliant with the European Computer Manufacturing Association's ECMAScript Language Specification (ECMA 262 standard, for short).

JSGF *n. See* Java Speech Grammar Format.

JSP *n.* Short for **J**ava**S**erver **P**ages. A technology created by Sun Microsystems to enable development of platform-independent Web-based applications. Using HTML and XML tags and Java scriptlets, JSP helps Web site developers create cross-platform programs. JSP scriptlets run on the server, not in a Web browser, and generate dynamic content on Web pages, with the ability to integrate content from a variety of data sources, such as databases, files, and JavaBean components. Web site developers can concentrate on design and display of a Web site without the need for application development expertise. *See also* Java, JavaBean. *Compare* Active Server Pages.

JSP container *n.* Short for **J**ava**S**erver **P**ages **container.** In the J2EE platform, a JSP container provides the same services as a servlet container, such as providing network services over which requests and responses are sent, decoding requests, and formatting responses. All servlet containers must support HTTP as a protocol for requests and responses, but they may also support additional request-response protocols such as HTTPS. The JSP container is also an engine that interprets and processes JSP pages into a servlet. *See also* container, HTTP, HTTPS, J2EE, servlet, servlet container.

JTA *n.* Acronym for **J**ava **T**ransaction API. In the J2EE platform, JTA specifies transactions, comments, and rollbacks used by EJBs (Enterprise JavaBeans). It is a high-level, implementation-independent protocol API that allows applications and application servers to access transactions. *See also* application programming interface, J2EE, JTS, rollback.

JTS *n.* Acronym for **J**ava **T**ransaction **S**ervices. In the J2EE platform, JTS specifies the implementation of a transaction manager that supports JTA and implements the Java mapping of the OMG Object Transaction Service specification at a level below the API. JTS propagates transactions using the Internet Inter-ORB Protocol (IIOP). *See also* application programming interface, J2EE, JTA, rollback.

JUG *n.* Acronym for **J**ava **U**ser **G**roup. A user group that meets to discuss the Java programming language and the Java platform. *See also* user group.

Jughead *n.* Acronym for **J**onzy's **U**niversal **G**opher **H**ierarchy **E**xcavation **and** **D**isplay. An Internet service that enables a user to locate directories in Gopherspace through a keyword search. A Jughead server indexes keywords appearing in directory titles in top-level Gopher menus but does not index the files within the directories. To access Jughead, users must point their Gopher clients to a Jughead server. *See also* Gopher, Gopherspace. *Compare* Archie, Veronica.

jukebox *n.* Software that is designed to play a list of sound files in a user-specified order reminiscent of jukeboxes used to play vinyl records. *See also* CD-ROM jukebox.

Julian calendar *n.* The calendar introduced by Julius Caesar in 46 B.C. to replace the lunar calendar. The Julian calendar provided for a year of 365 days with a leap year every 4 years, or an average year length of 365.25 days. Because the solar year is slightly shorter, the Julian calendar gradually moved out of phase with the seasons and was superseded by the Gregorian calendar, introduced by Pope Gregory XIII. *Compare* Gregorian calendar, Hijiri calendar.

Julian date *n.* **1.** A date expressed as the number of days elapsed since January 1, 4713 B.C. (on the Julian calendar)—for example, 2,450,000 for October 9, 1995 (Gregorian). Julian dates are useful for finding elapsed times between events that may be many years apart, as in astronomy. The starting point is the beginning of the Julian Period, defined in 1583 by Joseph Scaliger as the coincidence of several cycles based on the Julian calendar. *See also* Gregorian calendar, Julian calendar. **2.** Often (but incorrectly), a date expressed as the year and the number of days elapsed since the beginning of the year—for example, 91.13 for January 13, 1991. *Acronym:* JD.

jumper *n.* A small plug or wire that can be connected between different points in an electronic circuit in order to alter an aspect of a hardware configuration. *Compare* DIP switch.

jump instruction *n.* An instruction that transfers the flow of execution from one statement or instruction to another. *See also* GOTO statement, transfer statement.

jump page *n. See* doorway page.

jump table *n. See* dispatch table.

Jump to .NET *n.* Acronym for **J**ava **U**ser **M**igration **P**ath to Microsoft **.NET.** A set of Microsoft technologies and services that enable Java programmers to preserve, enhance, and migrate Java language projects onto the Microsoft .NET platform. It includes tools for interoperability of existing code, Java language syntax support, and automated conversion of Java source code to C#. JUMP to .NET enables programmers using the Java language to move existing code to the Microsoft .NET platform. *See also* C#, .NET.

junction *n.* **1.** Any point at which two or more electrical components are connected. **2.** The contact between two types of semiconductors, such as N-type and P-type semiconductors. *See also* N-type semiconductor, P-type semiconductor, semiconductor.

justify *vb.* **1.** To align vertically. **2.** To align lines of text evenly along both the left and right margins of a column by inserting extra space between the words in each line. If the spacing is excessive, it can be reduced by rewriting or by hyphenating words at the ends of lines. *See also* align (definition 1). *Compare* rag.

just-in-time *adj.* **1.** Describing a system of inventory control and industrial production management based on the Japanese *kanban* system. Under a just-in-time system, workers receive materials from suppliers "just in time" for scheduled manufacturing to take place. Line workers generally signal that they require materials by means of a card or a computerized request system. **2.** Describing an action that is taken only when it becomes necessary, such as just-in-time compilation or just-in-time object activation. **3.** Describing a compiler that compiles Java on the fly. *Acronym:* JIT. *See also* Java, on the fly.

JVM *n. See* Java Virtual Machine.

K

K¹ *n.* Short for **k**ilobyte.

K² *prefix* *See* kilo-.

K&R C *n.* Short for (Brian W.) **K**ernighan and (Dennis M.) **R**itchie **C**. The version of the C programming language, defined by those two authors, that was the informal C standard until a more formal standard was developed by an ANSI committee. *See also* C.

Kalman filter *n.* An adaptive filter used to estimate the state of a system from measurements that contain random errors. This recursive adaptive filter determines the correct parameters of a process model. Each new measurement allows the parameters of a model to be predicted and adjusted, thus providing an estimate of error at each update. The Kalman filter's computational structure and its ability to incorporate the effects of noise (from both measurement and modeling) recommends itself for use in computer vision tracking applications. *See also* active vision, distortion, modeling, noise.

kamikaze packet *n.* *See* Chernobyl packet.

kashidas *n.* Special characters that are used to extend the joiner between two Arabic characters. Kashidas are used to improve the appearance of justified text by visually lengthening words rather than increasing the spacing between words. See the illustration.

Kashidas.

Kb *n.* *See* kilobit.

KB *n.* **1.** *See* kilobyte. **2.** Short for **K**nowledge **B**ase. Primary source of product information for Microsoft support engineers and customers. This comprehensive collection of articles, updated daily, contains detailed how-to information, answers to technical-support questions, and known issues. *Also called:* Microsoft Knowledge Base.

Kbit *n.* *See* kilobit.

Kbps *n.* *See* kilobits per second.

Kbyte *n.* *See* kilobyte.

kc *n.* *See* kilocycle.

KDE *n.* Acronym for **K** **D**esktop **E**nvironment. A popular open-source desktop environment originally intended for UNIX workstations and now developed for the Linux operating system. KDE provides a graphical user interface (GUI) and basic applications that correspond to those found with Microsoft Windows or the Macintosh operating system. By providing a mainstream environment and familiar desktop appearance, KDE is intended to make Linux easier for users. KDE and GNOME are leading contenders for consideration as a Linux desktop standard. *See also* GNOME, GUI.

Kerberos *n.* A network authentication protocol developed by MIT. Kerberos authenticates the identity of users attempting to log on to a network and encrypts their communications through secret-key cryptography. A free implementation of Kerberos is available from MIT, although it is also available in many commercial products. *Also called:* Kerberos v5 authentication protocol. *See also* authentication, cryptography, IPSec.

Kermit *n.* A file transfer protocol used in asynchronous communications between computers. Kermit is a very flexible protocol used in many software packages designed for communications over telephone lines. *Compare* Xmodem, Ymodem, Zmodem.

kern *vb.* To alter selectively the distance between pairs of letters for readability and to make the type spacing more balanced and proportional. See the illustration.

A W A KE
AWAKE

Kern. The first three letters of the second example are kerned.

kernel *n.* The core of an operating system—the portion of the system that manages memory, files, and peripheral devices; maintains the time and date; launches applications; and allocates system resources.

Kernel Extension *n.* See KEXT.

kernel panic *n.* In Mac OS X and UNIX-based systems, a type of error that occurs when the core level of the operating system is unable to properly handle an instruction. A kernel panic appears to the user as a text screen containing information about the nature of the error, which often can be corrected with a system reboot.

KEXT *n.* Acronym for **Ke**rnel **Ex**tension. In Mac OS X, an extension mechanism created to expand the functionality of the operating system kernel. KEXTs are modular and dynamic loading, and they may be created for any service that requires access to kernel internal interfaces. Creation of a KEXT allows the loading of pieces of code into the kernel without the need to recompile.

key *n.* **1.** On a keyboard, the combination of a plastic keycap, a tension mechanism that suspends the keycap but allows it to be pressed down, and an electronic mechanism that records the key press and key release. **2.** In database management, an identifier for a record or group of records in a datafile. *See also* B-tree, hash[2], index[1] (definition 1), inverted list, key field. **3.** In encryption and digital signatures, a string of bits used for encrypting and decrypting information to be transmitted. Encryption commonly relies on two different types of keys, a public key known to more than one person (say, both the sender and the receiver) and a private key known only to one person (typically, the sender). **4.** A metal object used with a physical lock to disable a computer system.

key binary large object *n.* A key binary large object (BLOB) provides a way to store keys outside of the cryptographic service provider (CSP) and is used to transfer

keys securely from one CSP to another. A key BLOB consists of a standard header followed by data representing the key. *Acronym:* key BLOB.

key BLOB *n. See* key binary large object.

keyboard *n.* A hardware unit with a set of switches that resembles a typewriter keyboard and that conveys information from a user to a computer or data communications circuit. *See also* Alt key, Apple key, arrow key, Backspace key, Break key, Caps Lock key, character code, Clear key, Command key, control character, Control key, Delete key, Dvorak keyboard, End key, enhanced keyboard, Enter key, ergonomic keyboard, Escape key, function key, Help key, Home key, Insert key, keyboard buffer, keyboard controller, keyboard enhancer, keycap, key code, numeric keypad, Num Lock key, Option key, original Macintosh keyboard, Page Down key, Page Up key, Pause key, PC/XT keyboard, Power-on key, Print Screen key, QWERTY keyboard, Return key, scan code, Scroll Lock key, Shift key, Sys Req key, Tab key.

keyboard buffer *n.* A small amount of system memory that stores the most recently typed characters. This buffer is used to store typed characters that have not yet been processed. *Also called:* type-ahead buffer.

keyboard controller *n.* A microprocessor installed in a keyboard whose primary function is to wait for and report on keystrokes.

keyboard enhancer *n.* A program that monitors keystrokes as they are typed and that can be used to redefine the meaning of certain keys or key combinations. Keyboard enhancers are used to create and store macros—sets of keystrokes, mouse actions, menu selections, or other instructions—that are then assigned to keys. *Also called:* macro program.

keyboard layout *n.* The key arrangement used for a particular keyboard, including such factors as the number of keys (101 is the current standard) and the configuration of the keys (QWERTY is the United States standard). Some proprietary systems use different layouts, and many allow you to map the keys to characters according to your preferences.

keyboard port *n.* The connector on a computer that receives data from the keyboard. *See also* port[1] (definition 1).

keyboard processor *n. See* keyboard controller.

keyboard repeat *n. See* typematic.

keyboard shortcut *n. See* application shortcut key.

keyboard template *n.* A piece of plastic or heavy paper that fits over or around part of the keyboard, such as the function keys, and has information printed on it about the meanings of the keys.

keycap *n.* The plastic piece identifying a key on a keyboard.

key code *n.* A unique code number assigned to a particular key on a computer keyboard, used to tell the computer which key has been pressed or released. A key code is a special identifier for the key itself and is always the same for a particular key, regardless of the letter, number, or symbol on the key or the character generated by the key. *Compare* character code, scan code.

key escrow *n.* An approach to key recovery in which an encryption key is provided to a third party approved by a government agency so that any encrypted message can, if necessary, be decrypted and read by the government. *See also* encryption, key recovery.

key field *n.* A field in a record structure or an attribute of a relational table that has been designated to be part of a key. Any field can be keyed, or indexed, to improve or simplify the performance of retrieval and/or update operations. *See also* attribute (definition 1), field (definition 1), primary key.

key-frame *adj.* Describing animation in which starting and ending positions of an object are given, and all frames in between are interpolated by a computer to produce smooth automated animation. Most ray-traced computer animation is created using this technique. *See also* ray tracing.

key in *vb.* To enter information into a computer by typing it on the computer's keyboard.

keymaster *n.* A common host name assigned by network administrators to a gateway or router. Popularized in part by the Keymaster character in the 1984 movie "Ghostbusters." *See also* gatekeeper.

keypad *n. See* numeric keypad.

key pair *n.* A widely used encryption scheme that allows secure use of digital certificate identification. A key pair consists of a public key and a private key. The public key is shared with other individuals; the private key is known only to its owner. The public and private key form an asymmetric pair, meaning the keys on either end of a transmission are different. A message encrypted with the public key can be decrypted only with the private key, and a message encrypted with the private key can be decrypted only with the public key.

keypunch *n.* An archaic keyboard-activated device used to punch holes in predetermined locations on paper cards roughly the size of a business envelope. It was used to provide programs and data to early computing systems.

key recovery *n.* General term referring to the ability to retrieve a cryptographic key in order to decode encrypted information. Key recovery can be used to regain a lost key or, as has been publicized in recent years, can be used as a means of enabling government agencies to decode encrypted information. One method of providing for key recovery is known as key escrow. *See also* encryption, key escrow, private key.

key sort *n. See* tag sort.

keystroke *n.* The act of pressing a key on a keyboard to enter a character or initiate a command in a program. The efficiency and ease of use of certain applications is often measured in terms of how many keystrokes it takes to perform common operations. *See also* command, key (definition 1), keyboard.

keyword *n.* **1.** A characteristic word, phrase, or code that is stored in a key field and is used to conduct sorting or searching operations on records in a database. *See also* key field. **2.** Any of the set of words that composes a given programming language or set of operating-system routines. *See also* reserved word.

keyword density *n.* A measurement of the keywords on a Web page as a percentage of total text. High keyword density can increase a Web site's probability of being found by search engines, some of which use keyword density to rank a Web page's relevance to an Internet search. *See also* keyword (definition 1).

keyword-in-context *n.* An automatic search methodology that creates indexes of document text or titles. Each keyword is stored in the resulting index along with some surrounding text, usually the word or phrase that precedes or follows the keyword in the text or title. *Acronym:* KWIC.

keyword stuffing *vb. See* spamdexter.

Khornerstone *n.* A benchmark of floating-point calculation performance used to test UNIX workstations. *See also* benchmark[1], Dhrystone, floating-point operation, Whetstone.

kHz *n. See* kilohertz.

K

kiddie script *n.* A simple and easy-to-use executable script used to hack into a computer or network. Unlike the traditional hacker's techniques, which require detailed networking and programming knowledge, a kiddie script does not require any specialized skills or knowledge. *See also* script, script kiddie.

kill *vb.* **1.** To stop or abort a process in a program or operating system. **2.** In file management, to erase a file, often without hope of reversing the action.

killer app *n.* **1.** An application of such popularity and widespread standardization that it fuels sales of the hardware platform or operating system for which it was written. *See also* application. **2.** An application that supplants its competition. *See also* application.

kill file *n. See* bozo filter.

kilo- *prefix* **1.** Metric prefix meaning 10^3 (one thousand). **2.** In computer-related terms, a prefix meaning 2^{10} (1024).

kilobaud *n.* A unit of measure of the transmission capacity of a communications channel, equal to 2^{10} (1024) baud. *See also* baud.

kilobit *n.* A data unit equal to 1024 bits. Abbreviated Kb or Kbit.

kilobits per second *n.* Data transfer speed, as through a modem or on a network, measured in multiples of 1024 bits per second. Abbreviated Kbps.

kilobyte *n.* A data unit of 1024 bytes. Abbreviated K, KB, or Kbyte. *See also* kilo-.

kilocycle *n.* A unit of measurement representing 1000 cycles, generally meaning 1000 cycles per second. Abbreviated kc. *See also* kilohertz.

kilohertz *n.* A measure of frequency equivalent to 1000 hertz, or 1000 cycles per second. Abbreviated kHz. *See also* hertz.

Kinesis ergonomic keyboard *n.* A keyboard designed ergonomically to eliminate repetitive strain injuries. *See also* ergonomic keyboard, repetitive strain injury.

kiosk *n.* A freestanding computer or terminal that provides information to the public, usually through a multimedia display.

kludge *n.* **1.** A short-term or makeshift hardware construction. **2.** A program characterized by a lack of design or forethought, as if written in a hurry to satisfy an immediate need. A kludge basically operates properly, but its construction or design is severely lacking in elegance or logical efficiency. *See also* braindamaged, hack[1] (definition 1), spaghetti code.

knockout *n.* **1.** In multicolor printing, the process of removing from one image the overlapping parts of a graphic or text that are to be printed in a different color so that ink colors will not mix. See the illustration. *See also* spot color. *Compare* overprint. **2.** In hardware, a section of a panel that can be removed to make space for a switch or other component.

Overprint

Knockout

Knockout. *A knockout allows an overlapping image to print in the correct color.*

knowbot *n.* Short for **know**ledge ro**bot**. An artificial-intelligence program that follows a set of predetermined rules to perform work, such as searching for files or looking for documents that contain specific pieces of information on a network, such as the Internet. *See also* bot (definition 2).

knowledge acquisition *n.* The process of translating knowledge from one or more human experts into a form of representation usable by a computer, for the purpose of developing an expert system. *See also* expert system.

knowledge base *n.* A form of database used in expert systems that contains the accumulated body of knowledge of human specialists in a particular field. The reasoning ability or problem-solving approach that a specialist would use is contained in the inference engine, which forms another crucial part of an expert system. *See also* expert system, inference engine.

knowledge-based system *n. See* expert system.

knowledge domain *n.* The specific area of expertise to which an expert system is devoted. *See also* expert system.

knowledge engineer *n.* A computer scientist who builds an expert system by acquiring the needed knowledge and translating it into a program. *See also* expert system.

knowledge representation *n.* The methodology that forms the basis for the decision-making structure in an expert system, usually taking the form of if-then rules. *See also* expert system.

knowledge worker *n.* Term invented by a management consultant, Peter Drucker, for an individual whose job centers on the collection, processing, and application of information, especially when meaningful value is added to purely factual information. A knowledge worker is someone with both formal education and the ability to apply that education—knowledge—in a work situation. *See also* information explosion.

Korn shell *n.* A command-line interface, available under UNIX, that combines features of the Bourne and C shells. The Korn shell is fully compatible with the Bourne shell but also offers the history and command-line editing capabilities of the C shell. *See also* command-line interface, shell[1], UNIX. *Compare* Bourne shell, C shell.

KSR terminal *n.* Short for **k**eyboard **s**end/**r**eceive **terminal**. A type of terminal that accepts input from a keyboard only and uses an internal printer rather than a screen to display the keyboard input and the output received from the sending terminal. *See also* TTY.

KWIC *n. See* keyword-in-context.

K

L1 cache *n.* A memory cache built into i486 and higher-level processors to help improve processing speed. The L1 cache, typically containing 8 KB, can be read in a single clock cycle, so it is tried first. The i486 contains one L1 cache; the Pentium contains two, one for code and one for data. *Also called:* level 1 cache, on-chip cache. *See also* cache, i486DX, Pentium. *Compare* L2 cache.

L2 cache *n.* A memory cache consisting of static RAM on a motherboard that uses an i486 or higher-level processor. The L2 cache, which typically contains 128 KB to 1 MB, is faster than the system DRAM but slower than the L1 cache built into the CPU chip. *Also called:* level 2 cache. *See also* cache, dynamic RAM, i486DX, static RAM. *Compare* L1 cache.

L2TP *n. See* Layer Two Tunneling Protocol.

L8R *adv.* Abbreviation for later, as in "See you later," an expression often used in e-mail or Usenet groups as a closing remark.

label *n.* An identifier. A label can be a physical item, such as a stick-on tag used to identify disks and other computer equipment, or an electronic label added to floppy disks or hard disks. It can also be a word, symbol, or other group of characters used to identify a file, a storage medium, an element defined in a computer program, or a specific item in a document such as a spreadsheet or a chart. *See also* identifier.

label edge router *n. See* MPLS.

label prefix *n.* In a spreadsheet, a character at the beginning of a cell entry that identifies the entry to the program as a label.

label switching *n. See* MPLS.

label switch path *n. See* MPLS.

label switch router *n. See* MPLS.

LACP *n.* Acronym for **L**ink **A**ggregation **C**ontrol **P**rotocol. *See* link aggregation.

lag *n.* The time difference between two events. In electronics, a lag is a delay between a change in input and a change in output. On computer displays, a lag is a fading brightness left on the phosphor coating of the screen after an image changes. *See also* persistence.

LAN *n.* Acronym for **l**ocal **a**rea **n**etwork. A group of computers and other devices dispersed over a relatively limited area and connected by a communications link that enables any device to interact with any other on the network. LANs commonly include PCs and shared resources such as laser printers and large hard disks. The devices on a LAN are known as nodes, and the nodes are connected by cables through which messages are transmitted. *See also* baseband network, broadband network, bus network, client/server architecture, collision detection, communications protocol, contention, CSMA/CD, network, peer-to-peer architecture, ring network, star network. *Compare* WAN.

landscape mode *n.* A horizontal print orientation in which text or images are printed "sideways"—that is, the width of the image on the page is greater than the height. *Compare* portrait mode.

landscape monitor *n.* A monitor that is wider than it is high. Landscape monitors are usually about 33 percent wider than they are high—roughly the same proportion as a television screen. *Compare* full-page display, portrait monitor.

LANE *n.* Acronym for **LAN E**mulation. *See* ATM (definition 1), communications protocol, LAN.

LANGID *n. See* language identifier.

language *n. See* programming language.

language-description language *n. See* metalanguage.

language identifier *n.* A standard international numeric abbreviation for a country or geographical region. A language identifier is a 16-bit value that consists of a primary language identifier and a secondary language identifier. *Acronym:* LANGID. *See also* locale identifier.

language processor *n.* A hardware device or a software program designed to accept instructions written in a particular language and translate them into machine code. *See also* compiler (definition 2), interpreter.

language translation program *n.* A program that translates statements written in one programming language into another programming language (usually from one high-level language into another). *See also* high-level language.

LAN Manager *n.* An older LAN (local area network) technology developed by Microsoft and distributed by Microsoft, IBM (as IBM LAN Server), and other original equipment manufacturers. Superseded by TCP/IP networking protocols in Windows 9x, LAN Manager implemented the NetBEUI protocol and was notable for its small stack size. It was used to connect computers running the MS-DOS, OS/2, or UNIX operating systems to allow users to share files and system resources and to run distributed applications using a client/server architecture. *See also* client/server architecture, LAN, NetBEUI.

LANtastic *n.* A network operating system from Artisoft designed to support both peer-to-peer and client/server networks consisting of PCs running a mix of MS-DOS and Windows operating systems.

laptop *n.* A small, portable personal computer that runs on either batteries or AC power, designed for use during travel. Laptops have flat LCD or plasma screens and small keyboards. Most can run the same software as their desktop counterparts and can accept similar peripherals, such as sound cards, internal or external modems, floppy disks, and CD-ROM drives. Some laptops are designed to be plugged into a docking station, effectively making them desktop computers. Most have connectors for plugging in external keyboards and full-sized monitors. Older laptops weighed as much as 15 pounds; current laptops can weigh as little as 5 pounds without peripherals. While *notebook* is the current term for ultralight portable computers, these machines are also commonly referred to as laptops. *See also* portable computer. *Compare* subnotebook computer.

large model *n.* A memory model of the Intel 80x86 processor family. The large model allows both code and data to exceed 64 kilobytes, but the total of both must generally be less than 1 megabyte. Each data structure must be less than 64 kilobytes in size. *See also* memory model.

large-scale integration *n.* A term describing a chip on which circuit elements number in the thousands. *Acronym:* LSI. *See also* integrated circuit. *Compare* medium-scale integration, small-scale integration, super-large-scale integration, ultra-large-scale integration, very-large-scale integration.

laser or **LASER** *n.* Acronym for **l**ight **a**mplification by **s**timulated **e**mission of **r**adiation. A device that uses certain quantum effects to produce coherent light, which travels with greater efficiency than noncoherent light because the beam diverges only slightly as it travels. Lasers are used in computer technology to transmit data through fiberoptic cables, to read and write data on CD-ROMs, and to place an image on a photosensitive drum in laser printers.

laser engine *n. See* printer engine.

laser printer *n.* An electrophotographic printer that is based on the technology used by photocopiers. A focused laser beam and a rotating mirror are used to draw an image of the desired page on a photosensitive drum. This image is converted on the drum into an electrostatic charge, which attracts and holds toner. A piece of electrostatically charged paper is rolled against the drum, which pulls the toner away from the drum and onto the paper. Heat is then applied to fuse the toner to the paper. Finally, the electrical charge is removed from the drum, and the excess toner is collected. By omitting the final step and repeating only the toner-application and paper-handling steps, the printer can make multiple copies. The only serious drawback of a laser printer is that it offers less paper-handling flexibility than do dot-matrix printers. Both multipart forms and wide-carriage printing, for example, are better handled by line printers or dot-matrix printers. *See also* electrophotographic printers, nonimpact printer, page printer. *Compare* dot-matrix printer, ion-deposition printer, LCD printer, LED printer.

laser storage *n.* The use of optical read/write technology with metallic discs for information storage. *See also* compact disc.

LaserWriter 35 *n.* The standard set of 35 PostScript fonts for the Apple LaserWriter family of laser printers. *See also* laser printer, PostScript font.

last in, first out *n.* A method of processing a queue in which items are removed in inverse order relative to the order in which they were added—that is, the last in is the first out. *Acronym:* LIFO. *See also* stack. *Compare* first in, first out.

last mile *n.* The connection (which may in fact be more or less than one mile) between an end user's system and that of a service provider, such as a telephone company. The "last mile" connection historically has referred to the twisted-pair copper wires used between a home and the

L

telephone company. While this definition remains accurate, "last mile" is now often used more broadly to refer to the link between an end user's system and the high-speed Internet access technology of a service provider, such as an ISP (Internet service provider). Thus, for modem users accessing the Internet through voice-grade lines, the last mile is still equivalent to the phone company's twisted-pair copper wiring. However, because standard modem transmission over voice-grade lines is sometimes frustratingly slow, other last mile solutions have been designed to provide greater speed and bandwidth. These include coaxial cable (used in cable TV), fiber optics, or a radio link (such as a cellular telephone or a point-to-point link). DSL and ISDN are methods for providing high-speed last-mile data service through twisted-pair copper wires. *See also* DSL, ISDN, twisted-pair wiring. *Compare* local loop.

latch *n.* A circuit or circuit element used to maintain a particular state, such as on or off, or logical true or false. A latch changes state only in response to a particular input. *See also* flip-flop.

late binding *n. See* dynamic binding.

latency *n.* The time required for a signal to travel from one point on a network to another. *See also* ping[1] (definition 1).

LaTeX[1] or **L^AT_EX** *n.* A document preparation system based on TeX, developed by Leslie Lamport. By using simple, intuitive commands for text elements such as headers, LaTeX lets the user focus more on document content than document appearance. *See also* header (definition 1), TeX.

LaTeX[2] *vb.* To process a LaTeX file. *See also* LaTeX[1].

launch *vb.* To activate an application program (especially on the Macintosh) from the operating system's user interface.

Launcher *n.* In Mac OS, a program that organizes frequently used applications and programs and that allows the user to execute them with a single mouse click.

layer *n.* **1.** The protocol or protocols operating at a particular level within a protocol suite, such as IP within the TCP/IP suite. Each layer is responsible for providing specific services or functions for computers exchanging information over a communications network (such as the layers in the ISO/OSI reference model) and information is

passed from one layer to the next. Although different suites have varying numbers of levels, generally the highest layer deals with software interactions at the application level, and the lowest governs hardware-level connections between different computers. See the table. *See also* ISO/OSI reference model, protocol stack, TCP/IP. **2.** In communications and distributed processing, a set of rules and standards that handles a particular class of events.

Table L.1   Layers in the ISO/OSI reference model.

ISO/OSI layer	*Focus*
Application (highest level)	Program-to-program transfer of information
Presentation	Text formatting and display, code conversion
Session	Establishing, maintaining, and coordinating communication
Transport	Accurate delivery, service quality
Network	Transport routes, message handling and transfer
Data-link	Coding, addressing, and transmitting information
Physical	Hardware connections

layer 4 switching *n.* In Network Address Translation (NAT), a function that handles incoming packets and changes the IP address and destination port to transfer them to the proper server within the private network, and then readdresses return packets leaving the private network. Because layer 4 switching controls the address on packets moving in both directions, the internal network remains transparent to the client. *See also* LVS, NAT.

layered architecture *n.* The division of a network model into multiple discrete layers, or levels, through which messages pass as they are prepared for transmission. In a layered architecture, protocols at each layer provide specific services or functions and rely on protocols in the layers above and below them for other needed services. *See also* protocol.

layered interface *n.* In programming, one or more levels of routines lying between an application and the computing hardware and separating activities according to the type of task the activities are designed to carry out. Ultimately, such an interface makes it easier to adapt a program to different types of equipment. See the illustration.

Layered interface.

layering *n.* In computer graphics, the grouping of logically related elements in a drawing. Layering enables a program user to view, and work on independently, portions of a graphic instead of the entire drawing.

Layer Two Tunneling Protocol *n.* An industry-standard Internet tunneling protocol that provides encapsulation for sending Point-to-Point Protocol (PPP) frames across packet-oriented media. For IP networks, Layer Two Tunneling Protocol traffic is sent as User Datagram Protocol (UDP) messages. In Microsoft operating systems, this protocol is used in conjunction with Internet Protocol security (IPSec) as a virtual private network (VPN) technology to provide remote access or router-to-router VPN connections. Layer Two Tunneling Protocol is described in RFC 2661. *Acronym:* L2TP. *See also* IPSec, Point-to-Point Protocol, tunnel, User Datagram Protocol.

layout *n.* **1.** The overall plan or design of a document system. *See also* page layout. **2.** In programming, the order and sequence of input and output. **3.** In computer design, the arrangement of circuits and other components of the system.

lazy evaluation *n.* A programming mechanism that allows an evaluation action to be performed only when needed and only to a certain extent. Lazy evaluation

allows a program to handle data objects such as extremely large tables and lists in a timely and effective manner.

LBA *n. See* logical block addressing.

LCC *n. See* leaded chip carrier, leadless chip carrier.

lcd *n.* In some FTP clients, the command that changes the current directory on the local system. *See also* FTP client.

LCD *n. See* liquid crystal display.

LCD printer *n.* Short for **l**iquid **c**rystal **d**isplay **printer**. An electrophotographic printer similar to a laser printer and often incorrectly labeled as one. LCD printers use a bright light source, typically a halogen lamp. *Also called:* liquid crystal shutter printer. *See also* electrophotographic printers, nonimpact printer, page printer. *Compare* ion-deposition printer, laser printer, LED printer.

LCD projector *n.* Short for **l**iquid **c**rystal **d**isplay **projector**. A type of data projector that uses electricity to turn the pixels representing a projected image off or on. Unlike the newer DLP projectors, LCD projectors are able to display shades of color (gray scale) by controlling the amount of electricity used to turn a particular pixel on or off. *See also* gray scale, liquid crystal display. *Compare* DLP projector.

LCP *n. See* Point-to-Point Protocol.

LDAP *n. See* Lightweight Directory Access Protocol.

lead¹ *n.* In electronics, the metallic connector of certain components such as resistors and capacitors.

lead² *n.* In typography, the amount of vertical space between two lines of text.

leaded chip carrier *n.* A method of mounting chips on boards. A leaded chip carrier has leglike pins for connecting it to the board. The chip makes contact with the board through surface mount technology in which the leads are soldered to the surface rather than into predrilled holes. Somewhat confusingly, a leaded chip carrier goes by the same acronym (LCC) as a lead*less* chip carrier. *Acronym:* LCC. *Compare* leadless chip carrier.

leader *n.* A row of dots, hyphens, or other such characters used to lead the eye across a printed page to related information. Leaders can be created by many word processors and other programs.

leading *n.* The space, expressed in points, between lines of type, measured from the baseline (bottom) of one line to the baseline of the next. The term is derived from the traditional typesetting practice of inserting a thin bar of

L

lead between lines of metal type. See the illustration. *See also* point[1].

Leading →‡ A generous amount of space between lines of type is called open leading.

Baselines ┘

Leading. *Ordinary text is typically set with leading one or two points greater than the point size of the type.*

leading edge *n.* The initial part of an electronic signal. If a digital signal switches from off to on and then back to off, the transition from off to on is the leading edge of the signal.

leading zero *n.* A zero that precedes the most significant (leftmost) digit of a number. One or more leading zeros may be used as fill characters in a field containing numeric input. Leading zeros have no significance in the value of a number.

lead ion battery *n.* An energy storage device that is based on the conversion of chemical to electrical energy as ions flow from one terminal to another through an acid medium in which lead and copper are suspended. This type of battery is used in laptop and notebook computers.

leadless chip carrier *n.* A method of mounting chips on boards. A leadless chip carrier has contacts, rather than leglike pins, for connecting it to the board. The chip simply rests in a socket that has contacts on its base for completing the connection, and the chip is clamped in place so that the contacts are secure. *Acronym:* LCC. *See also* PLCC. *Compare* DIP (definition 1), pin grid array.

leaf *n.* Any node (location) in a tree structure that is at the farthest distance from the root (primary node), no matter which path is followed. Thus, in any tree, a leaf is a node at the end of a branch—one that has no descendants. *See also* root, subtree, tree.

leapfrog attack *n.* A method used by hackers to make an attack difficult to trace back to the source. In a leapfrog attack the hacker uses a User ID stolen from another source or routes information through a series of hosts to hide their identity and obscure the origin of the attack. *Also called:* network weaving.

leapfrog test *n.* A diagnostic routine, used for testing disk or tape storage, that repeatedly copies itself onto the storage medium.

leap year *n.* A potential problem for some systems that follow an erroneous algorithm for calculating leap years.

There are three rules for calculating leap years: (1) A year is a leap year if it is divisible by 4, *but* (2) not if it is divisible by 100, *unless* (3) it is also divisible by 400. Thus, 1900 was not a leap year, but 2000 was.

leased line *n. See* dedicated line (definition 1).

least significant bit *n.* In a sequence of one or more bytes, the low-order (usually rightmost) bit of a binary number. *Acronym:* LSB. *See also* low-order. *Compare* most significant bit.

least significant character *n.* The low-order, or rightmost, character in a string. *Acronym:* LSC. *See also* low-order. *Compare* most significant character.

least significant digit *n.* The low-order, or rightmost, digit in the normal representation of a number. *Acronym:* LSD. *See also* low-order. *Compare* most significant digit.

LED *n. See* light-emitting diode.

LED printer *n.* Short for light-emitting diode printer. An electrophotographic printer similar to LCD and laser printers. The significant difference between LED and laser or LCD printers is in the light source; LED printers use an array of light-emitting diodes. *See also* electrophotographic printers, light-emitting diode, nonimpact printer, page printer. *Compare* ion-deposition printer, laser printer, LCD printer.

left justification *n.* In typesetting, word processing, and desktop publishing, the process of aligning text evenly along the left margin of a column or page. The right edge of the text is ragged. *See also* justify (definition 1), rag. *Compare* full justification, right justification.

left-justify *vb.* To justify, as text, along the left. *See also* justify (definition 1), rag. *Compare* right-justify.

legacy *adj.* Of or pertaining to documents, data, or hardware that existed prior to a certain time. The designation refers particularly to a change in process or technique that requires translating old data files to a new system.

legacy data *n.* Data acquired by an organization that was compiled by another organization. The acquiring organization thus receives the existing information as a "legacy" from the information's prior owner.

legacy system *n.* A computer, software program, network, or other computer equipment that remains in use after a business or organization installs new systems. Compatibility with legacy systems is an important consideration when a new version is installed. For example, will

L

a new spreadsheet software release be able to read the existing business records without expensive and time-consuming conversion to a new format? Legacy systems in many organizations are based on mainframe computers, which may be either augmented or slowly replaced by client/server architectures. *See also* mainframe computer. *Compare* client/server architecture.

legend *n.* Text that describes or explains a graphic, usually printed below the graphic. On a graph or map, the legend is the key to the patterns or the symbols used.

Lempel Ziv compression *n.* A data compression method designed by Abraham Lempel and Jakob Ziv in 1977 and 1978. Lempel Ziv compression is based on the substitution of certain values for repeated data. It is implemented in two basic forms: LZ77, which is based on values that point to the positions of repeating data, and LZ78, which builds a dictionary and uses the dictionary index to point to repeating data. An enhanced version of LZ78, known as LZW, is implemented in well-known file formats, such as GIF and TIF. *See also* .lzh, LZW compression.

length *n.* The number of linear units of storage space occupied by an object, such as a file on disk or a data structure in a program, typically measured in bits, bytes, or blocks.

LEO *n. See* low-Earth-orbit satellite.

LER *n. See* MPLS.

less than *adj. See* relational operator.

less than or equal to *adj. See* relational operator.

letterbomb *n.* An e-mail message that is intended to impair the recipient's computer use. Some sequences of control characters can lock up a terminal, files attached to the message may contain viruses or Trojan horses, and a sufficiently large message can overflow a mailbox or crash a system. *See also* control character, e-mail[1] (definition 1), mailbox, Trojan horse, virus.

letter quality *adj.* Pertaining to or being a level of print quality on dot-matrix printers that is better than draft quality. As the name implies, letter quality is supposed to be crisp and dark enough for use in business letters. *See also* print quality. *Compare* draft quality, near-letter-quality.

letter-quality printer *n.* Any printer that produces output high enough in quality to be acceptable for business letters. *See also* daisy-wheel printer, laser printer.

level 1 cache *n. See* L1 cache.

level 2 cache *n. See* L2 cache.

lexicographic sort *n.* A sort that arranges items in the order in which they would appear if listed in a dictionary. A lexicographic sort puts numbers, for instance, where they would be if they were spelled out; for example, 567 would fall in the Fs. *Compare* alphanumeric sort.

lexicon *n.* **1.** The words of a language and their definitions. **2.** In programming, the identifiers, keywords, constants, and other elements of a language that make up its "vocabulary." The ways in which these vocabulary elements can be put together is the syntax of the language. *Compare* syntax.

LF *n. See* linefeed.

LHARC *n.* A freeware file-compression utility program developed by Haruyasu Yoshizaki and introduced in 1988. With LHARC, the contents of one or more files can be compressed into a singular, smaller file, with the extension .lha. A copy of the program is required to uncompress these files. LHARC can also embed a small program with the compressed information and save everything in a single file, called a self-extracting archive, with an .exe extension. As a result, the recipient of the compressed file does not need a separate utility program to uncompress the file. *See also* freeware, PKZIP, utility program.

library *n.* **1.** In programming, a collection of routines stored in a file. Each set of instructions in a library has a name, and each performs a different task. **2.** A collection of software or data files.

library routine *n.* In programming, a routine stored in a collection of routines (a library) that can be used by any program that can link into the library. *See also* function library, library (definition 1).

license agreement *n.* A legal contract between a software provider and a user specifying the rights of the user regarding the software. Usually the license agreement is in effect with retail software once the user opens the software package. *See also* End-User License Agreement.

licensing key *n.* A short character string that serves as a password during the installation of licensed commercial software. The use of licensing keys is a security device aimed at reducing illegal duplication of licensed software.

LIFO *n. See* last in, first out.

ligature *n.* In typography, a single character created from two joined letters that replaces the two separate letters. Because ligatures are not included with all digital

L

fonts, their use may cause text problems in font substitution situations.

light-emitting diode *n.* A semiconductor device that converts electrical energy into light, used, for example, for the activity lights on computer disk drives. Light-emitting diodes work on the principle of electroluminescence and are highly efficient, producing little heat for the amount of light output. *Acronym:* LED.

light guide *n.* A structure, such as a fiberoptic filament, designed to transmit light over distances with minimal attenuation or loss.

lightmap *n.* A basic lighting scheme used in 3D computer game rendering and other digital animation applications. A lightmap generates a precalculated 3D grid for lighting all objects in a game but cannot be adjusted for player-initiated changes within the scene.

light pen *n.* An input device consisting of a stylus that is connected to a computer's monitor. The user points at the screen with the stylus and selects items or chooses commands either by pressing a clip on the side of the light pen or by pressing the light pen against the surface of the screen (the equivalent of performing a mouse click). *See also* absolute pointing device. *Compare* touch screen.

light source *n.* **1.** The device that provides the luminescence (for example, a bulb or laser) in any technology based on the use and interpretation of light, such as a scanner or CRT. **2.** In computer graphics, the imaginary location of a source of light, which determines the shading in an image.

lightwave system *n.* A system that transmits information by means of light.

Lightweight Directory Access Protocol *n.* A network protocol designed to work on TCP/IP stacks to extract information from a hierarchical directory such as X.500. This gives users a single tool to comb through data to find a particular piece of information, such as a user name, an e-mail address, a security certificate, or other contact information. *Acronym:* LDAP. *See also* CCITT X series.

Lightweight Internet Person Schema *n.* In Lightweight Directory Access Protocol directories, a specification for the retrieval of such information as names and e-mail addresses. *Acronym:* LIPS. *See also* Lightweight Directory Access Protocol.

LIM EMS *n.* Acronym for **L**otus/**I**ntel/**M**icrosoft **E**xpanded **M**emory **S**pecification. *See* EMS.

limit check *n.* In programming, a test that checks specified information to verify that it is within acceptable limits. *See also* array.

limiting operation *n.* Any routine or operation that constrains the performance of a larger process in which it is included; a bottleneck.

line *n.* **1.** Any wire or wires, such as power lines and telephone lines, used to transmit electrical power or signals. **2.** In communications, a connection, usually a physical wire or other cable, between sending and receiving (or calling and called) devices, including telephones, computers, and terminals. **3.** In a SONET network, a segment that runs between two multiplexers. *See also* SONET. **4.** In word processing, a string of characters displayed or printed in a single horizontal row. **5.** In programming, a statement (instruction) that occupies one line of the program. In this context, the common reference is to a "program line" or a "line of code."

line adapter *n.* A device, such as a modem or network card, that connects a computer to a communications line and converts a signal to an acceptable form for transmission.

line analyzer *n.* A monitoring device used to verify the integrity of a communications line and to assist in troubleshooting.

linear *adj.* **1.** Having the characteristics of a line. **2.** Proceeding sequentially. For example, a linear search is one that moves from A to B to C. **3.** In mathematics and electronics, having a direct and proportional relationship among characteristics or variables. For example, the output of a linear amplifier is directly proportional to the input. *See also* linear programming.

linear addressing architecture *n.* An architecture that allows a microprocessor to access any individual memory location by means of a single address value. Thus, each memory location within the entire range of addressable memory has a unique, specified address. *See also* flat address space, segmented address space.

linear bus *n. See* bus network.

linear inferences per second *n. See* LIPS (definition 2).

linear list *n.* A simple ordered list of elements in which each element except the first immediately succeeds one other element, and each except the last immediately precedes one other. *Compare* linked list.

linear memory *n. See* flat memory.

linear programming *n.* The process of creating programs that find optimal solutions for systems of equations (composed of linear functions) in which the terms given are not sufficient to derive a straightforward solution.

linear search *n.* A simple, though inefficient, search algorithm that operates by sequentially examining each element in a list until the target element is found or the last item has been completely processed. Linear searches are primarily used for very short lists. *Also called:* sequential search. *See also* search algorithm. *Compare* binary search, hash search.

linear structure *n.* A structure in which items are organized according to strict rules of precedence. In a linear structure, two conditions apply: if X precedes Y and Y precedes Z, then X precedes Z; and if X precedes Y and X precedes Z, then either Y precedes Z or Z precedes Y.

line-based browser *n.* A Web browser whose display is based on text rather than graphics. A popular line-based browser is Lynx. *See also* Lynx, Web browser.

line cap *n.* The way in which a line segment is terminated when the segment is printed, especially on a PostScript-compatible printer. See the illustration. *See also* line join.

Butt cap

Square cap

Round cap

Line cap. *The dots represent the mathematical endpoints of a specified line.*

line chart *n.* A business graphic in which values from one or more sets of data are connected by lines. See the illustration.

Line chart.

line concentration *n.* The funneling of multiple input channels into a smaller number of output channels. *See also* concentrator.

line conditioner *n.* A device for filtering electrical power to compensate for brownouts, suppress power surges, and act as a buffer between a power line and the computer (or other piece of equipment). Line conditioners contain transformers, capacitors, and other circuitry that help regulate the quality of power to ensure that electrical flow is constant. *See also* brownout, UPS.

line conditioning *n. See* conditioning, line conditioner.

line drawing *n.* A drawing made up of solid lines without shading or other features that suggest mass or contouring.

line driver *n.* A device used to increase transmission distance by amplifying a signal before placing it on the line or passing it along the line. *See also* short-haul.

line editor *n.* A text-editing program that numbers each line of text, working with the document on a line-by-line rather than on a word-by-word basis. *See also* editor.

linefeed *n.* A control character that tells a computer or printer to advance one line below the current line without moving the position of the cursor or print head. *Acronym:* LF.

line join *n.* The way in which two line segments are connected when they are printed, especially on a PostScript-compatible printer. See the illustration. *See also* line cap.

Miter join

Round join

Beveled join

Line join. *Three styles of line join.*

line level *n.* The strength of a communications signal at a given point on the line, measured in decibels (a multiple of the base-10 logarithm of the ratio between two values) or nepers (the natural logarithm of the ratio between two values).

line load *n.* **1.** In communications, a measure of the usage of a communications line expressed as a percentage of the maximum capacity of the circuit. **2.** In electronics, the amount of current carried by a line.

line noise *n.* Spurious signals in a communications channel that interfere with the exchange of information. In an analog circuit, line noise may take the form of a pure audio tone, static, or signals leaked from another circuit. In a digital circuit, line noise is any signal that makes it difficult or impossible for the device at the receiving end of the circuit to interpret the transmitted signal accurately. *See also* channel.

line number *n.* **1.** A number assigned by a line editor to a line of text and used to refer to that line for purposes of viewing, editing, or printing. The line numbers are sequential. *See also* line editor. **2.** In communications, an identifying number assigned to a communications channel.

line printer *n.* Any printer that prints one line at a time as opposed to one character at a time (as with many dot-matrix printers) or one page at a time (as with some dot-matrix and most laser printers). Line printers typically produce the familiar 11-by-17-inch fanfold "computer" printouts. They are high-speed devices and are often used with mainframes, minicomputers, or networked machines rather than with single-user systems.

line regulator *n. See* voltage regulator.

line segment *n.* A portion of a line, defined by its beginning and ending points.

lines of code *n.* A measure of program length. Depending on circumstances, a line of code can be each line in the program (including blank lines and comments), each line containing actual code, or each statement. *See also* statement.

line spacing *n. See* leading.

line speed *n. See* baud rate, data rate.

lines per minute *n.* A measurement of printer speed, the number of lines of characters printed in one minute. *Acronym:* LPM.

line style *n.* In desktop publishing, printing, and high-end word processing, the form and quality of a line, such as a dotted line, a double line, or a hairline. *See also* hairline.

line surge *n.* A sudden, transient increase in the voltage or current carried by a line. A nearby lightning strike, for example, can cause a surge in power lines that can damage electrical equipment. Delicate types of equipment such as computers are often protected from line surges by surge suppressors placed in the power lines.

line voltage *n.* The voltage present in a power line. In North America, line voltage is approximately 115 volts alternating current (VAC).

line width *n.* The length of a line of type measured from the left margin to the right margin on a piece of paper or on a computer screen. On a typewriter, line width is usually measured in terms of the number of monospace alphanumeric characters that can fit on the line; on a computer monitor or printer, line width is normally measured in inches, centimeters, points, or picas. *See also* pica (definition 2), point[1] (definition 1).

linguistics *n.* The analytic study of human language. Close ties exist between linguistics and computer science because of the mutual interest in grammar, syntax, semantics, formal language theory, and natural-language processing.

link[1] *vb.* **1.** To produce an executable program from compiled modules (programs, routines, or libraries) by merging the object code (assembly language object code, executable machine code, or a variation of machine code) of the program and resolving interconnecting references (such as a library routine called by a program). *See also* linker. **2.** To connect two elements in a data structure by using index variables or pointer variables. *See also* index (definition 1), pointer (definition 1).

link[2] *n. See* hyperlink.

linkage editor *n. See* linker.

link aggregation *n.* A technique for combining two or more Ethernet connections into one logical link, or trunk, between two devices. It is used to increase the bandwidth capacity of connections and to make these connections more resilient. The IEEE 802.3ad specification standardizes this process among different vendors using the Link Aggregation Control Protocol (LACP). *Also called:* bonding, trunking. *See also* IEEE 802.x.

Link Aggregation Control Protocol *n. See* link aggregation.

Link Control Protocol *n. See* Point-to-Point Protocol.

link edit *vb. See* link[1] (definition 1).

linked list *n.* In programming, a list of nodes or elements of a data structure connected by pointers. A singly linked list has one pointer in each node pointing to the next node in the list; a doubly linked list has two pointers in each node that point to the next and previous nodes. In a circular list, the first and last nodes of the list are linked together. *See also* array, key (definition 2), list, node (definition 1), pointer (definition 1). *Compare* linear list.

linked object *n.* An object that is inserted into a document but still exists in the source file. When information is linked, the new document is updated automatically if the information in the original document changes. If you want to edit the linked information, double-click it and the toolbars and menus from the original program appear, allowing you to edit it in its native format. If the original document is on your computer, changes that you make to the linked information will also appear in the original document. *See also* OLE, package, source document.

linked stylesheet *n.* A stylesheet existing separately from the HTML documents to which it is linked. A linked stylesheet may be used for sets of Web pages or entire Web sites requiring a uniform appearance. Since the style is defined once and linked to associated Web pages, the entire site can be changed by modifying a single stylesheet file. *Compare* inline stylesheet.

linker *n.* A program that links compiled modules and data files to create an executable program. A linker can also have other functions, such as creating libraries. *See also* library, link[1] (definition 1), program creation.

linkrot *n.* A condition affecting inadequately maintained Web pages that results in outdated, inoperative links to other Web pages.

link time *n.* **1.** The length of time required to link a program. *See also* link[1] (definition 1). **2.** The period during which a program is being linked. *See also* compile time (definition 2), link[1] (definition 1), run time (definition 1).

link-time binding *n.* Assignment of a meaning to an identifier (such as a subroutine label) in a program at the time that various files of compiled code are linked together to form an executable program, rather than when the source code is compiled or when the program is run. *Compare* compile-time binding, run-time binding.

Linotronic *n.* Any in the series of high-quality typesetting devices known as Linotronic laser imagesetters, which can print at resolutions such as 1270 and 2540 dots per inch (dpi). These devices are commonly attached to PostScript raster image processors (RIPs) so that desktop publishing applications can typeset directly from a microcomputer. *See also* imagesetter, PostScript, raster image processor.

Linpack *n.* A benchmarking routine that solves 100 simultaneous equations in a test of CPU, floating-point processor, and memory access speeds. *See also* benchmark[2], central processing unit, floating-point processor.

Linux *n.* A version of the UNIX System V Release 3.0 kernel developed for PCs with 80386 and higher-level microprocessors. Developed by Linus Torvalds (for whom it is named) along with numerous collaborators worldwide, Linux is distributed free, and its source code is open to modification by anyone who chooses to work on it, although some companies distribute it as part of a commercial package with Linux-compatible utilities. The Linux kernel works with the GNU utilities developed by the Free Software Foundation, which did not produce a kernel. It is used by some as an operating system for network servers and in the 1998/1999 timeframe began to gain increased visibility through support from vendors such as IBM and Compaq. *See also* free software, GNU, kernel, UNIX.

Linux Virtual Server *n. See* LVS.

Linux World Expo *n.* The world's largest trade show for designers, engineers, and businesses using the Linux operating system.

Lion worm *n.* A UNIX shellscript worm first detected in early 2001 that infects Linux servers using Berkeley Internet Name Domain (BIND) tools. After it has used a BIND exploit to infect a machine, Lion steals password files and other critical information and transmits them to the hacker. Lion then installs hacking tools and replaces critical files, hiding itself and opening multiple back doors for further compromise. The Lion worm was apparently launched in early 2001 by a group of Chinese hackers with a specific political agenda. In references to this worm, "Lion" may also be spelled as "1i0n".

LIPS *n.* **1.** Acronym for **L**anguage **I**ndependent **P**rogram **S**ubtitling. A system developed by the GIST group (C-DAC, India) and used by Indian Television for nationwide broadcast of programs with multilingual subtitles in teletext mode. This system was judged the best design in the VLSI (Very Large Scale Integration) design contest in the VLSI '93 International Conference. Three versions of this application-specific integrated circuit (ASIC) with different features were implemented in Xilinx 3K and 4K series FPLAs (field programmable logic arrays). *See also* field-programmable logic array, gate array, very-large-scale integration. **2.** Acronym for **l**inear **i**nferences **p**er **s**econd. A measure of speed for some types of artificial-intelligence

L

machines and expert systems. *See also* artificial intelligence, expert system. **3.** *See* Lightweight Internet Person Schema.

liquid crystal display *n.* A type of display that uses a liquid compound having a polar molecular structure, sandwiched between two transparent electrodes. When an electric field is applied, the molecules align with the field, forming a crystalline arrangement that polarizes the light passing through it. A polarized filter laminated over the electrodes blocks polarized light. In this way, a grid of electrodes can selectively "turn on" a cell, or a pixel, containing the liquid crystal material, turning it dark. In some types of liquid crystal displays, an electroluminescent panel is placed behind the screen to illuminate it. Other types of liquid crystal displays are capable of reproducing color. *Acronym:* LCD. *See also* supertwist display, twisted nematic display.

liquid crystal display printer *n. See* LCD printer.

liquid crystal shutter printer *n. See* LCD printer.

LISP *n.* Short for **Li**st **P**rocessing. A list-oriented programming language developed in 1959–60 by John McCarthy and used primarily to manipulate lists of data. LISP is heavily used in research and academic circles and is considered the standard language for artificial-intelligence research. *See also* artificial intelligence. *Compare* Prolog.

list *n.* A multielement data structure that has a linear (first, second, third, . . .) organization but that allows elements to be added or removed in any order. Queues, deques, and stacks are simply lists with restrictions on adding and removing elements. *See also* deque, element (definition 1), linked list, queue, stack.

list box *n.* A control in Windows that enables the user to choose one option from a list of possibilities. The list box appears as a box, displaying the currently selected option, next to a button marked with a down arrow. When the user clicks the button, the list appears. The list has a scroll bar if there are more options than the list has room to show.

listing *n.* A printed copy of program source code. Some compilers and assemblers produce optional assembly listings during compilation or assembly. Such listings of code often have additional information such as line numbers, nested block depth, and cross-reference tables. *See also* assembly listing.

list processing *n.* The maintenance and manipulation of multielement data structures. This involves adding and deleting elements, writing data into elements, and traversing the list. List processing is the basis of the artificial-intelligence programming language LISP. *See also* LISP, list, node (definition 1).

LISTSERV *n.* One of the most popular commercial mailing list managers, marketed by L-SOFT International in versions for BITNET, UNIX, and Windows. *See also* mailing list, mailing list manager.

literal *n.* A value, used in a program, that is expressed as itself rather than as a variable's value or the result of an expression. Examples are the numbers 25 and 32.1, the character *a*, the string *Hello*, and the Boolean value TRUE. *See also* constant, variable.

lithium ion battery *n.* An energy storage device based on the conversion of chemical to electrical energy in "dry" chemical cells. Despite the higher cost, the laptop industry is quickly adopting lithium ion batteries because of their increased storage capacity over both nickel cadmium and nickel metal hydride batteries, in response to the demand for greater power brought on by higher processor speeds and the use of devices such as CD-ROM drives. *Compare* nickel cadmium battery, nickel metal hydride battery.

little endian *adj.* Of, pertaining to, or being a method of storing a number so that the least significant byte appears first in the number. For example, given the hexadecimal number A02B, the little endian method would cause the number to be stored as 2BA0. The little endian method is used by Intel microprocessors. *Also called:* reverse byte ordering. *Compare* big endian.

live[1] *adj.* **1.** Of or relating to real-world data or a program working with it, as opposed to test data. **2.** Of or relating to audio or video that is transmitted from one site to another as it is being produced, as opposed to being recorded before broadcast time. *See also* synchronous transmission. **3.** Capable of being manipulated by a user to cause changes in a document or part of a document.

live[2] *n.* Used to identify a Web site that has been published to a Web server and can be browsed by site visitors. *Also called:* going live.

Live3D *n.* A Netscape proprietary Virtual Reality Modeling Language (VRML) plug-in for Web browsers that allows users to view and interact with a virtual-reality world. *See also* VRML.

liveware *n.* A slang term for people, to distinguish them from hardware, software, and firmware. *Also called:* wetware.

LLC *n.* Acronym for **L**ogical **L**ink **C**ontrol. In the IEEE 802.x specifications, the higher of two sublayers that make up the ISO/OSI data link layer. The LLC is responsible for managing communications links and handling frame traffic. *See also* IEEE 802.x, MAC.

Lmhosts file *n.* A local text file that lists the names of network hosts (sometimes called NetBIOS names) to IP addresses for hosts that are not located on the local subnet. *See also* IP address, systemroot.

load[1] *n.* **1.** The total computing burden a system carries at one time. **2.** In electronics, the amount of current drawn by a device. **3.** In communications, the amount of traffic on a line.

load[2] *vb.* To place information from storage into memory for processing, if it is data, or for execution, if it is program code.

load-and-go *adj.* In reference to a routine, able to begin execution immediately, once loaded. The term is commonly used in reference to compilers and the machine code they generate.

load balancing *n.* **1.** In distributed processing, the distribution of activity across two or more servers in order to avoid overloading any one with too many requests from users. Load balancing can be either static or dynamic. In the former, the load is balanced ahead of time by assigning different groups of users to different servers. In the latter, software refers incoming requests at runtime to whichever server is most capable of handling them. **2.** In client/server network administration, the process of reducing heavy traffic flows either by dividing a busy network segment into multiple smaller segments or by using software to distribute traffic among multiple network interface cards working simultaneously to transfer information to a server. **3.** In communications, the process of routing traffic over two or more routes rather than one. Such load balancing results in faster, more reliable transmissions.

loaded line *n.* A transmission cable fitted with loading coils, usually spaced about a mile apart, that reduce amplitude distortion in a signal by adding inductance (resistance to changes in current flow) to the line. Loaded lines minimize distortion within the range of frequencies affected by the loading coils, but the coils also reduce the bandwidth available for transmission.

loader *n.* A utility that loads the executable code of a program into memory for execution. On most microcomputers, the loader is an invisible part of the operating system

and is automatically invoked when a program is run. *See also* loader routine, load module.

loader routine *n.* A routine that loads executable code into memory and executes it. A loader routine can be part of an operating system or it can be part of the program itself. *See also* loader, overlay[1] (definition 1).

load module *n.* An executable unit of code loaded into memory by the loader. A program consists of one or more load modules, each of which can be loaded and executed independently. *See also* loader.

load point *n.* The beginning of the valid data area on a magnetic tape.

load sharing *n.* A method of managing one or more tasks, jobs, or processes by scheduling and simultaneously executing portions of them on two or more microprocessors.

load shedding *n.* In electrical systems, the process of turning off power to some electronic equipment in order to maintain the integrity of the power supply to other connected devices. *See also* UPS.

lobby page *n.* A page of information about the broadcast that is displayed in the viewer's browser before the broadcast begins. It can contain a title, subject, host's name, information about the broadcast, and a countdown to the time of the broadcast.

local *adj.* **1.** In general, close at hand or restricted to a particular area. **2.** In communications, a device that can be accessed directly rather than by means of a communications line. **3.** In information processing, an operation performed by the computer at hand rather than by a remote computer. **4.** In programming, a variable that is restricted in scope, that is, used in only one part (subprogram, procedure, or function) of a program. *Compare* remote.

local area network *n. See* LAN.

local bus *n.* A PC architecture designed to speed up system performance by allowing some expansion boards to communicate directly with the microprocessor, bypassing the normal system bus entirely. *See also* PCI local bus, VL bus.

local bypass *n.* A telephone connection used by some businesses that links separate buildings but bypasses the telephone company.

locale identifier *n.* A 32-bit value that consists of a language identifier and a sort identifier. In code, a locale

L

identifier (LCID) identifies the primary language and any secondary language of a specific locale. *Acronym:* LCID. *See also* language identifier.

localhost *n.* The name that is used to represent the same computer on which a TCP/IP message originates. An IP packet sent to localhost has the IP address 127.0.0.1 and does not actually go out to the Internet. *See also* IP address, packet (definition 1), TCP/IP.

localization *n.* The process of altering a program so that it is appropriate for the geographic area in which it is to be used. Localization involves the customization or translation of the separated data and resources required for a specific region or language. For example, the developers of a word processing program must localize the sorting tables in the program for different countries or languages because the correct order of characters in one language might be incorrect in another. L10N is a common abbreviation for Localization, where the "L" in Localization is followed by 10 letters and ends with the letter "N."

localized version *n.* A version of a program that has been translated into another language. *Also called:* international version.

local loop *n.* The (end) portion of a telephone connection that runs from the subscriber to the local telephone exchange. *See also* last mile.

local memory *n.* In multiprocessor systems, the memory on the same card or high-speed bus as a particular processor. Typically, memory that is local to one processor cannot be accessed by another without some form of permission.

local newsgroups *n.* Newsgroups that are targeted toward a geographically limited area such as a city or educational institution. Posts to these newsgroups contain information that is specific to the area, concerning such topics as events, meetings, and sales. *See also* newsgroup.

local reboot *n.* A reboot of the machine that one is directly working on, rather than of a remote host. *See also* reboot.

LocalTalk *n.* An inexpensive cabling scheme used by AppleTalk networks to connect Apple Macintosh computers, printers, and other peripheral devices. *See also* AppleTalk.

local user profile *n.* A user profile that is created automatically on the computer the first time a user logs on to a computer. *See also* mandatory user profile, roaming user profile, user profile.

local variable *n.* A program variable whose scope is limited to a given block of code, usually a subroutine. *See also* scope (definition 1). *Compare* global variable.

location *n. See* address[1] (definition 1).

location-based service *n.* A service provided to a wireless mobile device based on the device's location. Location-based services can range from simple services, such as listing nearby restaurants, to more complex features, such as connecting to the Internet to monitor traffic conditions and find the least congested route to a destination.

lock *n.* **1.** A software security feature that requires a key or dongle in order for the application to run correctly. *See also* dongle. **2.** A mechanical device on some removable storage medium (for example, the write-protect notch on a floppy disk) that prevents the contents from being overwritten. *See also* write-protect notch.

locked file *n.* **1.** A file on which one or more of the usual types of manipulative operation cannot be performed—typically, one that cannot be altered by additions or deletions. **2.** A file that cannot be deleted or moved or whose name cannot be changed.

locked volume *n.* On the Apple Macintosh, a volume (storage device, such as a disk) that cannot be written to. The volume can be locked either physically or through software.

lockout *n.* The act of denying access to a given resource (file, memory location, I/O port), usually to ensure that only one program at a time uses that resource.

lock up *n.* A condition in which processing appears to be completely suspended and in which the program in control of the system will accept no input. *See also* crash[1].

log *n.* A record of transactions or activities that take place on a computer system. *See* logarithm.

logarithm *n.* Abbreviated log. In mathematics, the power to which a base must be raised to equal a given number. For example, for the base 10, the logarithm of 16 is (approximately) 1.2041 because $10^{1.2041}$ equals (approximately) 16. Both natural logarithms (to the base e, which is approximately 2.71828) and common logarithms (to the base 10) are used in programming. Languages such as C and Basic include functions for calculating natural logarithms.

log files *n.* A computer file that records requests received by online applications or the number of hits a Web page receives. Log files are useful in analyzing the technical performance of a Web site, redesigning Web site navigation, and revising marketing strategies used by e-businesses.

logic *n.* In programming, the assertions, assumptions, and operations that define what a given program does. Defining the logic of a program is often the first step in developing the program's source code. *See also* formal logic.

logical *adj.* **1.** Based on true and false alternatives as opposed to arithmetic calculation of numeric values. For example, a logical expression is one that, when evaluated, has a single outcome, either true or false. *See also* Boolean algebra. *Compare* fuzzy logic. **2.** Conceptually true to a particular design or idea—for example, network transmissions travel in a circle around a logical ring, even though the ring shape itself is not physically apparent. *Compare* physical.

logical block addressing *n.* A technique in which the cylinder, head, and sector locations on a hard disk are converted to 24-bit addresses for data storage and retrieval. Logical block addressing is used with SCSI drives and is also a feature of Enhanced IDE (EIDE) disk drives, on which it breaks through the earlier 528-MB IDE limit and allows support for drives up to 8.4 GB in capacity if 24-bit logical address space is used. Address conversion is performed by an EIDE drive's disk controller, but also requires support from the BIOS and the computer's operating system. *Acronym:* LBA. *See also* EIDE, SCSI.

logical decision *n.* Any decision that can have one of two outcomes (true/false, yes/no, and so on). *Compare* fuzzy logic.

logical device *n.* A device named by the logic of a software system, regardless of its physical relationship to the system. For example, a single floppy disk drive can simultaneously be, to the MS-DOS operating system, both logical drive A and drive B.

logical drive *n. See* logical device.

logical error *n. See* logic error.

logical expression *n. See* Boolean expression.

logical file *n.* A file as seen from a conceptual standpoint, without reference to and as distinct from its physical realization in memory or storage. For example, a logical file might consist of a contiguous series of records, whereas the file might be physically stored in small pieces scat-tered over the surface of a disk or even on several disks. A logical file might also consist of some subset of columns (fields) and rows (records) extracted from a database. In this case, the logical file (or view) is only that information required by a particular application program or user.

Logical Link Control *n. See* LLC.

logical memory *n.* A correlation between physical memory of the computer system and an address range that is accessible to devices. The hardware abstraction layer (HAL) provides this correlation (or mapping). *See also* map.

logical network *n.* A way to describe the topology, or layout, of a computer network. Referring to a logical (rather than physical) topology describes the way information moves through the network—for example, in a straight line (bus topology) or in a circle (ring topology). The difference between describing a network as logical or physical is sometimes subtle because the physical network (the actual layout of hardware and cabling) doesn't necessarily resemble the logical network (the path followed by transmissions). A logical ring, for example, might include groups of computers cabled octopus-like to hardware "collection points" which, in turn, are cabled to one another. In such a network, even though the physical layout of computers and connecting hardware might not visually resemble a ring, the logical layout followed by network transmissions would, indeed, be circular. *See also* bus network, ring network, star network, token ring network, topology. *Compare* physical network.

logical operator *n.* An operator that manipulates binary values at the bit level. In some programming languages, logical operators are identical to Boolean operators, which manipulate true and false values. *See also* Boolean operator, mask.

logical record *n.* Any unit of information that can be handled by an application program. A logical record can be a collection of distinct fields or columns from a database file or a single line in a text file. *See also* logical file.

logical schema *n. See* conceptual schema.

logic analyzer *n.* A hardware device that facilitates sophisticated low-level debugging of programs. Typical features include the ability to monitor bus signals during execution, to halt execution when a given memory location is read or written to, and to trace back through some number of instructions when execution is halted for any reason. *See also* debugger.

L

logic array *n. See* gate array.

logic board *n.* Another name for motherboard or processor board. The term was used in conjunction with older computers to distinguish the video board (*analog board*) from the motherboard. *See also* motherboard.

logic bomb *n.* **1.** A logic error in a program that manifests itself only under certain conditions, usually when least expected or desired. The term *bomb* implies an error that causes the program to fail spectacularly. *See also* logic error. **2.** A type of Trojan horse that executes when certain conditions are met, such as when a user performs a specific action. **3.** *See* Year 2000 problem. **4.** *See* fork bomb.

logic chip *n.* An integrated circuit that processes information, as opposed to simply storing it. A logic chip is made up of logic circuits.

logic circuit *n.* An electronic circuit that processes information by performing a logical operation on it. A logic circuit is a combination of logic gates. It produces output based on the rules of logic it is designed to follow for the electrical signals it receives as input. *See also* gate (definition 1).

logic diagram *n.* A schematic that shows the connections between computer logic circuits and specifies the expected outputs resulting from a specific set of inputs.

logic error *n.* An error, such as a faulty algorithm, that causes a program to produce incorrect results but does not prevent the program from running. Consequently, a logic error is often very difficult to find. *See also* logic, semantics, syntax.

logic gate *n. See* gate (definition 1).

logic operation *n.* **1.** An expression that uses logical values and operators. **2.** A bit-level manipulation of binary values. *See also* Boolean operator.

logic programming *n.* A style of programming, best exemplified by Prolog, in which a program consists of facts and relationships from which the programming language is expected to draw conclusions. *See also* Prolog.

logic-seeking printer *n.* Any printer with built-in intelligence that lets it look ahead of the current print position and move the print head directly to the next area to be printed, thus saving time in printing pages that are filled with spaces.

logic symbol *n.* A symbol that represents a logical operator such as AND or OR. For example, the symbol + in Boolean algebra represents logical OR, as in A + B (read, "A or B," not "A plus B").

logic tree *n.* A logic specification method that uses a branching representation. Each of the tree's forks represents a decision point; the ends of the branches denote actions to be taken.

login *n. See* logon.

log in *vb. See* log on.

Logo *n.* A programming language with features that are heavily drawn from LISP. Logo is often used to teach programming to children and was developed originally by Seymour Papert at MIT in 1968. Logo is considered an educational language, although some firms have sought to make it more widely accepted in the programming community. *See also* LISP, turtle, turtle graphics.

logoff *n.* The process of terminating a session with a computer accessed through a communications line. *Also called:* logout.

log off *vb.* To terminate a session with a computer accessed through a communications line—usually a computer that is both distant and open to many users. *Also called:* log out. *Compare* log on.

logon *n.* The process of identifying oneself to a computer after connecting to it over a communications line. *Also called:* login.

log on *vb.* To gain access to a specific computer, a program, or a network by identifying oneself with a username and a password. *Also called:* log in. *Compare* log off.

logon script *n.* A file assigned to certain user accounts on a network system. A logon script runs automatically every time the user logs on. It can be used to configure a user's working environment at every logon, and it allows an administrator to influence a user's environment without managing all aspects of it. A logon script can be assigned to one or more user accounts. *Also called:* login script. *See also* user account.

logout *n. See* logoff.

log out *vb. See* log off.

LOL *n.* Acronym for laughing out loud. An interjection used in e-mail, online forums, and chat services to express appreciation of a joke or other humorous occurrence. *See also* ROFL.

Long data type *n.* A fundamental data type that holds large integers. A Long variable is stored as a 32-bit number ranging in value from –2,147,483,648 to 2,147,483,647.

long filenames *n.* A feature of most current PC operating systems, including the Macintosh, Windows 9x, Windows NT, Windows 2000, and OS/2. Long filenames allow a user to assign a plain-text name to a file, rather than limiting possible names to just a few characters. Names can be over 200 characters long, include uppercase and lowercase letters, and have spaces between characters. *Compare* 8.3.

long-haul *adj.* Of, pertaining to, or being a type of modem that is able to transmit over long distances. *Compare* short-haul.

longitudinal redundancy check *n. See* LRC.

LonWorks *n.* An open standard for network automation created by the Echelon Corporation and supported by the LonMark Interoperability Association. LonWorks, introduced in 1991, can be used in building, transportation, industrial, and home applications to implement a distributed control network.

lookup *n.* A function, often built into spreadsheet programs, in which a previously constructed table of values called a lookup table is searched for a desired item of information. A lookup table consists of rows and columns of data. A lookup function examines the table either horizontally or vertically and then retrieves the data that corresponds to the argument specified as part of the lookup function.

loop¹ *n.* **1.** A set of statements in a program executed repeatedly, either a fixed number of times or until some condition is true or false. *See also* DO loop, FOR loop, infinite loop, iterative statement. **2.** A pair of wires that runs between a telephone central office and customer premises.

loop² *vb.* To execute a group of statements repeatedly.

loop check *n. See* echo check.

loop configuration *n.* A communications link in which multiple stations are joined to a communications line that runs in a closed loop. Generally, data sent by one station is received and retransmitted in turn by each station on the

loop. The process continues until the data reaches its final destination. See the illustration. *See also* ring network.

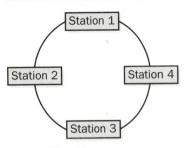

Loop configuration.

loophole *n.* In programming, a logical failure to account for all possible situations. *See also* bug (definition 1), logic error.

loop invariant *n.* A condition that remains true while a loop iterates.

loop structure *n. See* iterative statement.

lo-res *adj. See* low resolution.

loss balancing *n.* Amplification of a signal or value to compensate for loss during a transmission or translation of a value.

lossless compression *n.* The process of compressing a file such that, after being compressed and decompressed, it matches its original format bit for bit. Text, code, and numeric data files must be compressed using a lossless method; such methods can typically reduce a file to 40 percent of its original size. *Compare* lossy compression.

lossy compression *n.* The process of compressing a file such that some data is lost after the file is compressed and decompressed. Video and sound files often contain more information than is apparent to the viewer or listener; a lossy compression method, which does not preserve that excess information, can reduce such data to as little as 5 percent of its original size. *Compare* lossless compression.

lost cluster *n.* A cluster (disk storage unit) marked by the operating system as being in use but not representing any part of any chain of stored segments of a file. A lost cluster usually represents debris resulting from incomplete data "housekeeping," as might result from the ungraceful exit (messy or abrupt termination) of an application program.

Lotus 1-2-3 *n.* An electronic spreadsheet product introduced in 1983 by Lotus Development Corporation. Notable for its inclusion of graphing and data-management (database) capabilities in addition to spreadsheet functionality, Lotus 1-2-3 is important in the history of the personal computer because it was one of the first "killer apps" that convinced businesses to buy and use a PC. Lotus Development was purchased by IBM in 1995. *See also* killer app.

Lotus cc:Mail *n. See* cc:Mail.

Lotus Domino *n.* A groupware application that transforms Lotus Notes into an application and messaging server. *See also* Lotus Notes.

Lotus Notes *n.* A groupware application introduced in 1988 by Lotus Development Corporation and now owned by IBM. Lotus Notes combines e-mail, calendar management, group scheduling, contact and task management, newsgroup access, and Web browsing capability (through the integration of Microsoft Internet Explorer) in one client application. Lotus Notes also offers search capabilities across multiple formats and file types on a network or the Web.

low-Earth-orbit satellite *n.* A communications satellite put into orbit no higher than 500 miles above the earth's surface. A low-Earth-orbit satellite, or LEO, circles the planet in 90 minutes to 2 hours. LEOs allow for use of smaller dishes and handheld devices, so they are well-suited for interactive conferencing. However, because a LEO remains above the local horizon for about only 20 minutes, large numbers of these satellites, in several different orbits, are required to maintain service. *Acronym:* LEO. *Compare* geostationary orbit satellite.

lowercase *adj.* In reference to letters, not capital—for example, *a, b, c. Compare* uppercase.

low frequency *n.* The portion of the electromagnetic spectrum between 30 kilohertz (kHz) and 300 kHz. This range of frequencies is used for several types of radio communication, including the longwave broadcast band in Europe and Asia.

low-level language *n.* A language that is machine dependent or that offers few control instructions and data types. Each statement in a program written in a low-level language usually corresponds to one machine instruction. *See also* assembly language. *Compare* high-level language.

low memory *n.* On computers running MS-DOS, the first 640 kilobytes of RAM. This RAM is shared by MS-DOS, device drivers, data, and application programs. *Also called:* conventional memory. *Compare* high memory.

low-order *adj.* Carrying the least weight or significance; typically, the rightmost element in a group. For example, the rightmost bit in a group of bits is the low-order bit. *Compare* high-order.

lowpass filter *n.* An electronic circuit that allows all frequencies below a specified frequency to pass through it. *Compare* bandpass filter, highpass filter.

low resolution *adj.* Abbreviated lo-res. Appearing in relatively coarse detail, used in reference to text and graphics in raster-oriented computer displays and printing. Low-resolution printing is comparable to draft-quality dot-matrix output printed at 125 dots per inch or less. *See also* resolution. *Compare* high resolution.

LPM *n. See* lines per minute.

LPMUD *n.* A type of multiuser dungeon (MUD), typically combat related, that contains its own object-oriented programming language for the creation of new areas and objects in the virtual world. *See also* MUD.

LPT *n.* Logical device name for a line printer, a name reserved by the MS-DOS operating system for up to three parallel printer ports designated LPT1, LPT2, and LPT3. The first port, LPT1, is usually the same as the primary MS-DOS hard-copy output device PRN (the logical device name for the printer). The letters LPT were originally used to stand for *line print terminal.*

LRC *n.* Acronym for **l**ongitudinal **r**edundancy **c**heck. A procedure used to check the accuracy of data stored on magnetic tape or transmitted over a communications line. *See also* parity bit. *Compare* VRC.

ls *n.* A UNIX command that instructs the server to return a list of files and subdirectories in the current directory or the directory specified in the command. Because many FTP sites are built on UNIX systems, this command can also be used on those sites. *See also* FTP site, UNIX.

LS-120 *n.* Acronym for **L**aser **St**orage-**120**. A floppy disk drive developed by Imation Corporation that uses proprietary laser storage 120-megabyte (MB) media as well as standard 1.44 MB 3.5-inch floppy media. The LS-120 disk drive is capable of storing 120 MB of data on a single 3.5-inch floppy disk and is compatible with other floppy disk formats. LS-120 drives are ATAPI (AT Attachment Packet Interface) compliant so several different drives can use the same EIDE controller. *Also called:* Super Disk.

LSB *n.* **1.** *See* least significant bit. **2.** Acronym for **L**inux **S**tandard **B**ase. A standard developed to aid in Linux software development by providing a uniform foundation for all versions of the operating system. The Linux model provided by the LSB provides a stable platform for developers to create software that may be used with any version of the operating system, while leaving companies the ability to add other features on top of the base.

LSC *n.* *See* least significant character.

LSD *n.* *See* least significant digit.

LSI *n.* *See* large-scale integration.

LSP *n.* *See* MPLS.

LSR *n.* *See* MPLS.

LU *n.* Acronym for **l**ogical **u**nit. In an IBM SNA network, a point denoting the beginning or end of a communications session. *See also* SNA.

Luddite *n.* A person opposed to technological advances, especially those designed to replace human skill and experience with automated machinery. The first Luddites were bands of textile workers in Nottinghamshire, England, who protested the use of new large-scale machinery, which they blamed for low wages and high unemployment. The origin of the term has never been verified, but the most popular theory is that the name derives from Ned Ludd, an apprentice knitter who destroyed his knitting frame with a hammer to protest beatings by his master. *See also* technophobe. *Compare* technophile.

LUG *n.* Acronym for **L**inux **U**sers **G**roup. *See* user group.

luggable computer *n.* The first portable computers, produced in the early to mid-1980s. These early units, all of which had built-in CRT-based displays, weighed over 20 pounds and were the size of a medium suitcase—hence their name. *See also* portable computer.

luminance *n.* **1.** A measure of the amount of light radiated by a given source, such as a computer display screen. **2.** The perceived brightness component of a given color, as opposed to its hue or its saturation. *See also* HSB. *Compare* illuminance.

luminance decay *n.* *See* persistence.

luminosity *n.* The brightness of a color based on a scale from black to white on your monitor.

Lunar calendar *n.* Predominant calendar type used in Israel among Hebrew speakers, in Islamic cultures, and in most of Asia. Lunar calendars calculate months based on lunar phases.

lurk *vb.* To receive and read articles or messages in a newsgroup or other online conference without contributing to the ongoing exchange.

lurker *n.* A person who lurks in a newsgroup or other online conference. *See also* lurk. *Compare* netizen.

LVS *n.* Acronym for **L**inux **V**irtual **S**erver. A high-performance open source server that handles connections from clients and passes them on to a cluster of real servers. LVS receives incoming packets and forwards them to the proper back-end server. LVS is typically used to build scalable Web, mail, or other network services. *Also called:* ipvs. *See also* layer 4 switching.

Lycos *n.* A Web search engine and directory that provides summaries of pages matching search requests. In addition, the Lycos site offers categorized directories of sites, reviews of selected sites, and services for finding names, viewing maps, and so on.

Lynx *n.* A text-only Web browser program for UNIX platforms.

.lzh *n.* The file extension that identifies archive files compressed with the Lempel Ziv and Haruyasu algorithm. *See also* compressed file, Lempel Ziv compression, LHARC.

LZW compression *n.* A compression algorithm named after Abraham Lempel and Jakob Ziv (creators of Lempel Ziv compression) and LZW designer Terry Welch that makes use of repeating strings of data in its compression of character streams into code streams. It is also the basis of GIF compression. *See also* GIF, Lempel Ziv compression.

L

m *prefix* See milli-.

M *prefix* See mega-.

Mac- *prefix* A prefix used to indicate a software product's applicability for the Macintosh computer, as in MacDraw.

Mac *n.* See Macintosh.

MAC *n.* Acronym for **M**edia **A**ccess **C**ontrol. In the IEEE 802.x specifications, the lower of two sublayers that make up the ISO/OSI data link layer. The MAC manages access to the physical network, delimits frames, and handles error control. *See also* IEEE 802.x, LLC.

MacBinary *n.* A file transfer protocol used to preserve coding for Macintosh-produced files stored in non-Macintosh computers, containing the file's resource fork, data fork, and Finder information block. *See also* data fork, Finder, resource fork.

Mach *n.* A variant of the UNIX operating system developed at Carnegie-Mellon University. Mach was designed to support advanced features such as multitasking, multiprocessing, and distributed systems. *See also* UNIX.

Mach 3.0 *n.* The microkernel forming the lowest level of the Mac OS X operating system. Mach 3.0 provides basic services such as memory management, thread-handling, virtual memory, and address space management to the operating system kernel.

mach 3 kernel *n.* See Mach 3.0.

machine address *n.* See absolute address.

machine code *n.* The ultimate result of the compilation of assembly language or any high-level language such as C or Pascal: sequences of 1s and 0s that are loaded and executed by a microprocessor. Machine code is the only language computers understand; all other programming languages represent ways of structuring human language so that humans can get computers to perform specific tasks. *Also called:* machine language. *See also* compiler (definition 2).

machine cycle *n.* **1.** The time required for the fastest operation (usually a NOP, or no-op, which does nothing) a

microprocessor can perform. **2.** The steps taken for each machine instruction. These steps are, typically, fetch the instruction, decode it, execute it, and perform any necessary storing.

machine-dependent *adj.* Of, pertaining to, or being a program or a piece of hardware that is linked to a particular type of computer because it makes use of specific or unique features of the equipment and that cannot easily be used with another computer, if at all. *Compare* machine-independent.

machine error *n.* A hardware error. Probably the most common type of machine error involves media, such as an error in reading a hard disk.

machine identification *n.* A code by which an executing program can determine the identity and characteristics of the computer and other devices with which it is operating.

machine-independent *adj.* Of, pertaining to, or being a program or piece of hardware that can be used on more than one type of computer with little or no modification. *Compare* machine-dependent.

machine instruction *n.* An instruction (action statement) in machine code that can be directly executed by a processor or microprocessor. *See also* instruction, statement.

machine language *n.* See machine code.

machine-readable *adj.* **1.** Presented in a form that a computer can interpret and use as input. For example, bar codes that can be scanned and used directly as computer input contain machine-readable information. **2.** Coded in the binary form used by computers and stored on a suitable medium such as magnetic tape. *See also* optical character recognition.

machine translation *n.* The use of computer software to translate large amounts of text from one natural language into another. Machine translation is usually used by corporations, publishers, and government agencies that need large amounts of documentation, news stories, or business data translated quickly. *See also* natural-language processing.

Macintosh *n.* A popular series of personal computers introduced by the Apple Computer Corporation in January 1984. The Macintosh was one of the earliest personal computers to incorporate a graphical user interface and the first to use 3.5-inch floppy disks. It was also the first to use the 32-bit Motorola 68000 microprocessor. Despite its user-friendly features, the Macintosh lost market share to PC-compatible computers during the 1990s, but it still enjoys widespread use in desktop publishing and graphics-related applications. In late 1998, both Apple Computer and Macintosh gained increased visibility with release of the home-oriented iMac computer. See the illustration. *Also called:* Mac. *See also* graphical user interface, iMac, PC-compatible.

Macintosh.

Macintosh Application Environment *n.* A system shell for open RISC-based systems that provides a Macintosh interface within an X Window System window. The Macintosh Application Environment is compatible with both Mac and UNIX and will support all off-the-shelf products for the Macintosh. *Acronym:* MAE. *See also* RISC, X Window System.

Macintosh File System *n.* The early, flat file system used on the Macintosh before the Hierarchical File System was introduced. *Acronym:* MFS. *See also* flat file system. *Compare* Hierarchical File System.

Mac OS *n.* Short for **Mac**intosh **o**perating **s**ystem. The name given to the Macintosh operating system, beginning with version 7.5 in September 1994, when Apple started

licensing the software to other computer manufacturers. *See also* Macintosh.

Mac OS X *n.* The first complete revision of the Macintosh operating system. Mac OS X is BSD 4.4 UNIX-based, uses the Mach 3.0 microkernel, and is built around Apple's open-source Darwin. Mac OS X adds symmetric multiprocessing, multithreading, preemptive multitasking, advanced memory management, and protected memory to the Macintosh. The UNIX foundation of Mac OS X allows greater options for software development, networking, and update and expansion of the operating system. Mac OS X includes a graphical user interface and a command-line interface.

macro *n.* **1.** In applications, a set of keystrokes and instructions recorded and saved under a short key code or macro name. When the key code is typed or the macro name is used, the program carries out the instructions of the macro. Users can create a macro to save time by replacing an often-used, sometimes lengthy, series of strokes with a shorter version. **2.** In programming languages, such as C or assembly language, a name that defines a set of instructions that are substituted for the macro name wherever the name appears in a program (a process called *macro expansion*) when the program is compiled or assembled. Macros are similar to functions in that they can take arguments and in that they are calls to lengthier sets of instructions. Unlike functions, macros are replaced by the actual instructions they represent when the program is prepared for execution; function instructions are copied into a program only once. *Compare* function (definition 2).

macro assembler *n.* An assembler that can perform macro substitution and expansion. The programmer can define a macro that consists of several statements and then use the macro name later in the program, thus avoiding having to rewrite the statements. For example, a macro called *swap* exchanges the values of two variables: After defining swap, the programmer can then insert an instruction such as "swap a, b" in the assembly language program. While assembling, the assembler replaces the instruction with the statements within the macro that swap the values of the variables *a* and *b*.

M

macrocontent *n.* The primary text or other content of a Web page. *Compare* microcontent.

macro expansion *n.* The act of replacing a macro with its defined equivalent. *Also called:* macro substitution. *See also* macro (definition 2), macro assembler, macro processor.

macro instruction *n.* An instruction used to manage macro definitions. *See also* macro language.

macro language *n.* The collection of macro instructions recognized by a given macro processor. *See also* macro instruction, macro processor.

macro processor *n.* A program that performs macro expansion. All programs that support macros have some form of macro processor, but macro processors differ from program to program and in the macro language they support. *See also* macro (definition 2), macro expansion, macro instruction.

macro program *n.* *See* keyboard enhancer.

macro recorder *n.* A program that records and stores keyboard macros. *See also* macro (definition 1).

macro substitution *n.* *See* macro expansion.

macro virus *n.* A virus that is written in a macro language associated with an application. The macro virus is carried by a document file used with that application and executes when the document is opened.

MacTCP *n.* A Macintosh extension that allows Macintosh computers to use TCP/IP. *See also* TCP/IP.

MADCAP *n.* *See* multicast address dynamic client allocation protocol.

MAE *n.* **1.** *See* Macintosh Application Environment. **2.** Acronym for **M**etropolitan **A**rea **E**xchange. One of the Internet exchange points operated by MCI WorldCom, through which Internet service providers (ISPs) connect in order to exchange data. The two largest MAEs, MAE East (outside Washington, D.C.) and MAE West (near San Jose, California) are major national and international network interconnect points; more than half of all traffic through the Internet travels through one or both of these points. MCI WorldCom also operates smaller, regional MAEs in Chicago, Dallas, Houston, Los Angeles, New York, Paris, and Frankfurt. *See also* backbone (definition 1), ISP.

Magellan *n.* A Web directory. Named for the Portuguese explorer, Magellan reviews and rates all Web sites it lists.

Published by the McKinley Group, Magellan is now owned by Excite, Inc.

magic date *n.* A date or dates that in some computer systems resembles a reserved number or flag with a special significance. Examples are the numbers 00 and 99, which have been used in some systems or programs based on two-digit years. Magic dates indicate some special status—for example, that a system component or resource should never expire or should never be purged. Because 99 in particular has been used in this way in many systems, dates in the year 1999 had the potential to cause problems in those systems.

magnetic bubble *n.* A movable magnetic domain in a thin-film substrate. In bubble memory, magnetic bubbles representing bits circulate past circuits that can read and write them. High costs and relatively long access times have relegated magnetic bubbles to specialized applications. *See also* bubble memory, magnetic domain. *Compare* core, RAM.

magnetic disk *n.* A computer disk enclosed in a protective case (hard disk) or jacket (floppy disk) and coated with a magnetic material that enables data to be stored in the form of changes in magnetic polarity (with one polarity representing a binary 1 and the other a 0) on many small sections (magnetic domains) of the disk surface. Magnetic disks should be protected from exposure to sources of magnetism, which can damage or destroy the information they hold. *See also* disk, floppy disk, hard disk. *Compare* compact disc, magneto-optic disc.

magnetic domain *n.* A region of a ferromagnetic material in which the individual atomic or molecular magnetic particles are aligned in the same direction. *Also called:* ferromagnetic domain.

magnetic field *n.* The space around a magnetic object in which magnetic force acts. A magnetic field is conceived of as consisting of flux lines that originate at the north magnetic pole and terminate at the south magnetic pole.

magnetic head *n.* *See* head.

magnetic-ink character recognition *n.* A form of character recognition that reads text printed with magnetically charged ink, determining the shapes of characters by sensing the magnetic charge in the ink. Once the shapes have been determined, character recognition methods are used to translate the shapes into computer text. A familiar use of this form of character recognition is to identify bank checks. *Acronym:* MICR. *See also* character recognition. *Compare* optical character recognition.

magnetic oxide *n. See* ferric oxide.

magnetic storage *n.* A generic term for non-internal-memory computer data storage involving a magnetic medium, such as disk or tape.

magnetic tape *n. See* tape (definition 1).

magneto-optical recording *n.* A type of recording technology used with optical discs in which a laser beam heats a small portion of the magnetic material covering the disc. The heating enables a weak magnetic field to change the orientation of the portion, thus recording onto the disc. This technique can also be used to erase the disc, making the disc rewritable.

magneto-optic disc *n.* An erasable or semi-erasable storage disc, similar to a CD-ROM disc and of very high capacity, in which a laser beam is used to heat the recording surface to a point at which tiny regions on the surface can be magnetically aligned to store bits of data. *See also* CD-ROM, magneto-optical recording.

magnitude *n.* The size of a number, regardless of its sign (+ or –). For example, 16 and –16 have the same magnitude. *See also* absolute value.

mailbomb[1] *n.* An excessively large amount of e-mail data (a very large number of messages or one very large message) sent to a user's e-mail address in an attempt to make the user's mailer program crash or to prevent the user from receiving further legitimate messages. *See also* e-mail[1] (definition 1). *Compare* letterbomb.

mailbomb[2] *vb.* To send a mailbomb to a user. One person might mailbomb a user with a single enormous message; a large number of users might mailbomb an unpopular person by simultaneously sending messages of normal size.

mailbot *n.* A program that automatically responds to e-mail messages or performs actions based on commands within the messages. A mailing list manager is one example. *See also* mailing list manager.

mailbox *n.* A disk storage area assigned to a network user for receipt of e-mail messages. *See also* e-mail[1] (definition 1).

mail digest *n. See* digest (definition 2).

mailer-daemon *n.* A program used to transport e-mail between hosts on a network. *See also* daemon.

mail filter *n. See* e-mail filter.

mail header *n.* A block of text at the top of an e-mail message containing such information as the addresses of the sender and recipients, the date and time sent, the address to which a reply is to be sent, and the subject. The mail header is used by an e-mail client or program. *See also* e-mail[1] (definition 1).

mailing list *n.* A list of names and e-mail addresses that are grouped under a single name. When a user places the name of the mailing list in a mail client's To: field, the client sends the message to the machine where the mailing list resides, and that machine automatically sends the message to all the addresses on the list (possibly allowing a moderator to edit it first). *See also* LISTSERV, mailing list manager, Majordomo, moderator.

mailing list manager *n.* Software that maintains an Internet or intranet mailing list. The mailing list manager accepts messages posted by subscribers; sends copies of the messages (which may be edited by a moderator) to all the subscribers; and accepts and processes user requests, such as to subscribe or to unsubscribe to the mailing list. The most commonly used mailing list managers are LISTSERV and Majordomo. *See also* LISTSERV, mailing list, Majordomo, moderator.

mail merge *n.* A mass-mail facility that takes names, addresses, and sometimes pertinent facts about recipients and merges the information into a form letter or another such basic document.

mail reflector *n.* A newsgroup that consists simply of the messages posted to a mailing list translated into newsgroup format.

mailto *n.* A protocol designator used in the HREF of a hyperlink that enables a user to send e-mail to someone. For instance, Anne E. Oldhacker has the e-mail address aeo@baz.foo.com and an HTML document contains the code <A HREF="mailto:aeo@baz.foo.com">E-mail Anne!</A>. If a user clicks on the hyperlink "E-mail Anne!", the user's e-mail application is launched and the user can send e-mail to her without knowing her actual e-mail address. *See also* e-mail[1] (definition 1), HTML, hyperlink.

mainboard *n. See* motherboard.

main body *n.* The set of statements in a computer program at which execution of the program begins and that invokes the subroutines of the program.

M

mainframe *n.* A type of large computer system (in the past often water-cooled), the primary data processing resource for many large businesses and organizations. Some mainframe operating systems and solutions are over 40 years old and have the capacity to store year values only as two digits.

mainframe computer *n.* A high-level, typically large and expensive computer designed to handle intensive computational tasks. Mainframe computers are characterized by their ability to simultaneously support many users connected to the computer by terminals. The name is derived from "main frame," the cabinet originally used to house the processing unit of such computers. *See also* computer, supercomputer.

main function *n.* The main body of a program written in a computer language that uses sets of functions to create an entire program. For example, the C language requires each program to contain a function called *main*, which C uses as the starting point of execution. *See also* main body.

main loop *n.* A loop in the main body of a program that performs the principal function of the program over and over until termination is somehow signaled. In event-driven programs, this loop checks for events received from the operating system and handles them appropriately. *See also* event-driven programming, main body.

main memory *n. See* primary storage.

main segment *n.* On the Macintosh, the principal code segment of a program, which must remain loaded throughout the execution of the program.

maintenance *n.* The process of taking measures to ensure that a hardware, software, or database system is functioning properly and is up to date.

Majordomo *n.* The name of a popular software program that manages and supports Internet mailing lists. *See also* mailing list, mailing list manager.

major geographic domain *n.* A two-character sequence in an Internet domain name address that indicates the country/region in which a host is located. The major geographic domain is the last part of the domain name address, following the subdomain and domain codes; for example, uiuc.edu.us indicates a host at the University of Illinois in the United States, whereas cam.ac.uk indicates a host at the University of Cambridge in the United Kingdom. The code .us, which indicates a domain in the United

States, is usually omitted. *Also called:* country code. *See also* DNS (definition 1), domain name address.

major key *n. See* primary key.

Make Changes *n.* The Macintosh-style permission that gives users the right to make changes to a folder's contents; for example, modifying, renaming, moving, creating, and deleting files. When AppleTalk network integration translates access privileges into permissions, a user who has the Make Changes privilege is given Write and Delete permissions. *See also* permission.

make-table query *n.* In Microsoft Office, an action query that moves the resulting data to a new table in either the current database or another database.

male connector *n.* A type of connector that has pins for insertion into receptacles. Male connector part numbers often include an *M* (male) or *P* (plug). For example, a male DB-25 connector might be labeled *DB-25M* or *DB-25P*. See the illustration. *Compare* female connector.

Male connector.

malicious mobile code *n.* A virus or other destructive program that takes advantage of security weaknesses in wireless transmission systems. Malicious mobile code may affect computers, PDAs, Internet-capable digital phones, and other wireless networking devices.

malware *n.* Software created and distributed for malicious purposes, such as invading computer systems in the form of viruses, worms, or innocent-seeming plug-ins and extensions that mask other destructive capabilities. *Also called:* malicious software.

MAME *n.* Acronym for **M**ultiple **A**rcade **M**achine **E**mulator. MAME is software written in C that emulates the hardware and software of original arcade games, allowing them to run on PCs. *See also* arcade game, C.

MAN *n.* Acronym for **m**etropolitan **a**rea **n**etwork. A high-speed network that can carry voice, data, and images at up to 200 Mbps or faster over distances of up to 75 km. Based on the network architecture, the transmission speed can be higher for shorter distances. A MAN, which can include one or more LANs as well as telecommunications equipment such as microwave and satellite relay stations, is smaller than a wide area network but generally operates at a higher speed. *Compare* LAN, WAN.

managed code *n.* Code that is executed by the common language runtime environment rather than directly by the operating system. Managed code applications gain common language runtime services such as automatic garbage collection, runtime type checking and security support, and so on. These services provide uniform platform- and language-independent behavior of managed-code applications. *See also* unmanaged code.

managed service provider *n.* A business that supplies remote access services to individuals and enterprises. Managed service providers offer remote connections, network management, user support, security, and applications hosting. *Acronym:* MSP. *Compare* ISP.

Management and Monitoring Tools *n.* Software components that include utilities for network management and monitoring, along with services that support client dialing and the updating of client phone books. Also included is the Simple Network Management Protocol (SNMP). *See also* SNMP.

Management Information Base *n.* A set of objects that represents various types of information about a device, used by a network management protocol (for example, SNMP) to manage the device. Because different network management services are used for different types of devices and protocols, each service has its own set of objects. *Acronym:* MIB. *See also* service, SNMP.

Management Information Services *n. See* Information Services.

management information system *n.* A computer-based system for processing and organizing information so as to provide various levels of management within an organization with accurate and timely information needed for supervising activities, tracking progress, making decisions, and isolating and solving problems. *Acronym:* MIS.

Management Information Systems *n. See* Information Services.

manager *n.* Any program that is designed to perform a certain set of housekeeping tasks related to computer operation, such as the maintenance of files. On the Macintosh, Manager (with a capital M) is used in the names of various separate portions of the computer's operating system that handle input, output, and internal functions (for example, File Manager and Memory Manager).

Manchester coding *n.* A method of encoding data used in communications, such as on some LANs, that combines both data and timing signals in a stream of transmitted bits. *See also* phase encoding.

mandatory user profile *n.* A user profile that is not updated when the user logs off. It is downloaded to the user's desktop each time the user logs on, and it is created by an administrator and assigned to one or more users to create consistent or job-specific user profiles. *See also* local user profile, roaming user profile, user profile.

Mandelbrot set *n. See* fractal.

man-in-the-middle attack *n.* A form of attack in which the intruder intercepts messages between parties in a public key exchange. Each party's messages are diverted to the intruder, who may alter them before sending them on. The parties on each end of the exchange remain unaware that their messages are being intercepted and modified. *Also called:* bucket brigade attack.

man-machine interface *n.* The set of commands, displays, controls, and hardware devices enabling the human user and the computer system to exchange information. *See also* user interface.

man pages *n.* **1.** Online documentation for UNIX commands and programs and the UNIX library routines available for use in C programs. These documents, also found in the UNIX Programmer's Manual, can be displayed on a user's terminal or printed using the command *man*. **2.** Short for **man**ual **pages**. A set of help files included with a Linux distribution. Man pages may come with the Linux distribution and be installed along with the operating system or may be available from online sources.

mantissa *n.* **1.** In calculations that have logarithms, the positive decimal fraction of a common (base-10) logarithm. For example, the common logarithm of 16 is 1.2041; the characteristic, or whole-number portion, of the logarithm is 1 (the logarithm of 10); and the mantissa, or fractional portion, is .2041 (the logarithm of 1.6). *See also* characteristic, logarithm. **2.** In floating-point notation, the portion expressing the significant digits of a number. For example, the floating-point representation of 640,000 is 6.4E+05. The mantissa is 6.4;

M

the exponent (E+05) shows the power of 10 to which 6.4 is raised. *Also called:* significand. *See also* floating-point notation.

manual link *n.* A link that requires you to take action to update your data after the data in the source document changes.

many-to-many relationship *n.* A complex association between two sets of parameters in which many parameters of each set can relate to many others in the second set. A many-to-many relationship is most commonly used to describe an association between two tables in which one record in either table can relate to many records in the other table.

many-to-one relationship *n.* **1.** A server configuration in which several small servers replicate the abilities of one larger, more powerful server. *See also* key pair. **2.** In reference to asymmetric key encryption, the idea that many individuals in possession of the public key can decrypt the digital signature of one individual in possession of the private key.

map¹ *n.* Any representation of the structure of an object. For example, a memory map describes the layout of objects in an area of memory, and a symbol map lists the associations between symbol names and memory addresses in a program. *See also* image map.

map² *vb.* To translate one value into another. For example, in computer graphics one might map a three-dimensional image onto a sphere. In reference to virtual memory systems, a computer might translate (map) a virtual address into a physical address. *See also* virtual memory.

MAPI *n.* Acronym for **M**essaging **A**pplication **P**rogramming **I**nterface. The Microsoft interface specification that allows different messaging and workgroup applications (including e-mail, voice mail, and fax) to work through a single client, such as the Exchange client included with Windows 95 and Windows NT. *See also* application programming interface.

mapped data field *n.* A field that represents commonly used information, such as "First Name." If a data source contains a "First Name" field or variation, such as "FName," the data source field automatically maps to the corresponding mapped data field.

mapped drives *n.* **1.** In the Windows environment, network drives that have been assigned local drive letters and are locally accessible. **2.** Under UNIX, disk drives that have been defined to the system and can be made active.

MapPoint *n.* Business mapping software introduced by Microsoft as an Office-compatible product in 1999. Designed for use by business people, MapPoint consists of a database of United States maps showing detail down to the level of individual streets and demographic data broken out by state, county, zip code, and other regions. *See also* Office.

margin *n.* In printing, those portions of a page—top, bottom, and sides—outside the main body of text.

mark *n.* **1.** In applications and data storage, a symbol or other device used to distinguish one item from others like it. **2.** In digital transmission, the state of a communications line (positive or negative) corresponding to a binary 1. In asynchronous serial communications, a mark condition is the continuous transmission of binary 1s to indicate when the line is idle (not carrying information). In asynchronous error checking, setting the parity bit to 1 in each group of transmitted bits is known as mark parity. *See also* parity. *Compare* space. **3.** In optical sensing, a pencil line, as on a voting form or an IQ test, that can be recognized by an optical reader.

marker *n.* **1.** Part of a data communications signal that enables the communications equipment to recognize the structure of the message. Examples are the start and stop bits that frame a byte in asynchronous serial communications. **2.** A symbol that indicates a particular location on a display surface.

Mark I *n.* **1.** An electromechanical calculating machine designed in the late 1930s and early 1940s by Howard Aiken of Harvard University and built by IBM. *Also called:* Automatic Sequence Controlled Calculator, Harvard Mark I. **2.** The first fully electronic stored-program computer, designed and built at Manchester University in England. It successfully executed its first program in June 1948. **3.** The first commercial computer, which was based on the Manchester Mark I and released in 1951.

markup *n.* Comments and tracked changes such as insertions, deletions, and formatting changes that you can view or print.

markup language *n.* A set of codes in a text file that instructs a computer how to format the file on a printer or video display or how to index and link its contents. Examples of markup languages are Hypertext Markup Language (HTML) and Extensible Markup Language (XML), which are used in Web pages, and Standard Generalized Markup Language (SGML), which is used for typesetting and desktop publishing purposes and in electronic documents. Markup languages of this sort are designed to enable documents and other files to be platform-independent and highly portable between applications. *See also* HTML, SGML, XML.

marquee *n.* A nonstandard HTML extension that causes scrolling text to appear as part of a Web page. Currently, marquees are viewable only with Internet Explorer. *See also* HTML, Internet Explorer, Web page.

marquee component *n.* A region on a page that displays a horizontally scrolling text message.

mask *n.* **1.** A binary value used to selectively screen out or let through certain bits in a data value. Masking is performed by using a logical operator (AND, OR, XOR, or NOT) to combine the mask and the data value. For example, the mask 00111111, when used with the AND operator, removes (masks off) the two uppermost bits in a data value but does not affect the rest of the value. See the illustration. *See also* logical operator, mask bit. **2.** In television and display technology, a thin perforated sheet of metal or a close-set series of metal strips on the surface of the screen that helps create a clear, sharp image by ensuring that the electron beam for a particular color (red, blue, or green) strikes only the phosphor it is intended to illuminate, while the phosphors for the other colors are shadowed by the mask. Three types of masks are in use: a shadow mask, with round perforations; an aperture grill, with vertical stripes; and a slot mask, with elliptical openings. *See also* aperture mask, shadow mask, slot mask.

```
      11010101   Data value
AND   00111111   Mask
      _____
      00010101   Resulting value
```

Mask.

maskable interrupt *n.* A hardware interrupt that can be temporarily disabled (masked) during periods when a program needs the full attention of the microprocessor. *See also* external interrupt, hardware interrupt, interrupt. *Compare* nonmaskable interrupt.

mask bit *n.* A given bit within a binary mask whose function is to screen out or let through the corresponding bit in a data value when the mask is used in an expression with a logical operator. *See also* mask (definition 1).

masking *n.* The process of using the *mask* operation to perform operations on bits, bytes, or words of data. *See also* mask (definition 1).

mask off *vb.* To use a mask to remove bits from a byte of data. *See also* mask (definition 1).

massively parallel processing *n.* A computer architecture in which each of a large number of processors has its own RAM, which contains a copy of the operating system, a copy of the application code, and its own part of the data, on which that processor works independently of the others. *Acronym:* MPP. *Compare* SMP.

massively parallel processor *n.* A computer designed to perform massively parallel processing.

mass storage *n.* A generic term for disk, tape, or optical disc storage of computer data, so called for the large masses of data that can be stored in comparison with computer memory capacity. *Compare* memory.

Master Boot Record *n.* The first sector of the first hard disk; a physically small but critical element in the startup process on an x86-based computer. When a computer is booted, it processes a series of self-tests and then reads the Master Boot Record, or MBR, into memory. The MBR contains instructions that locate the disk's system (startup) partition, read the contents of the first sector of the system partition into memory, and then carry out the instructions contained in that sector. If the sector represents what is known as a Partition Boot Sector, the instructions found there begin the process of loading and starting the operating system. In other words, the startup process on an x86-based computer is as follows: self-test to Master Boot Record; MBR to system partition and Partition Boot Sector; Partition Boot Sector to operating system; and, finally, a computer ready to go to work. *Acronym:* MBR. *See also* Partition Boot Sector.

master file *n.* In a set of database files, the file containing more or less permanent descriptive information about the principal subjects of the database, summary data, and one or more critical key fields. For example, customers' names, account numbers, addresses, and credit terms might be stored in a master file. *See also* master record. *Compare* transaction file.

master key *n.* The server-based component of software or data protection. In some systems, data or applications are stored on a server and must be downloaded to the local machine for use. When a client requests the data, it presents a session key. If the session key supplied matches the master key, the key server sends the requested packet. *See also* client (definition 3), server (definition 2).

master record *n.* A record in a master file; typically, the descriptive and summary data related to the item that is the subject of the record. *See also* master file.

master reseller *n.* A status assigned by computer equipment manufacturers to dealers and distributors who meet certain qualifications, usually related to the number of pieces the reseller expects to sell.

master/slave arrangement *n.* A system in which one device, called the master, controls another device, called the slave. For example, a computer can control devices connected to it.

matching *n.* The process of testing whether two data items are identical or of finding a data item that is identical to a key. *See also* pattern recognition.

Material Requirements Planning *n.* An approach to information management in a manufacturing environment that makes use of software to help monitor and control processes related to manufacturing—for example, managing schedules and determining when and in what quantities to order materials. *Acronym:* MRP. *Also called:* Material Resource Planning. *See also* Enterprise Resource Planning.

math coprocessor *n. See* floating-point processor.

mathematical expression *n.* An expression that uses numeric values, such as integers, fixed-point numbers, and floating-point numbers, and operators, such as addition, subtraction, multiplication, and division. *See also* expression.

mathematical function *n.* A function in a program that performs a set of mathematical operations on one or more values or expressions and that returns a numeric value.

mathematical model *n.* The mathematical assumptions, expressions, and equations that underlie a given program. Mathematical models are used to model "real-world" physical systems such as planets in orbit around a star or resource production and consumption within a closed system.

MathML *n.* Acronym for **Math**ematical **M**arkup **L**anguage. An XML application for describing mathematical notation and capturing both its structure and content. The goal of MathML is to enable mathematics to be served, received, and processed on the Web, just as HTML has enabled this functionality for text.

matrix *n.* An arrangement of rows and columns used for organizing related items, such as numbers, dots, spreadsheet cells, or circuit elements. Matrices are used in mathematics for manipulating rectangular sets of numbers. In computing and computer applications, matrices are used for the similar purpose of arranging sets of data in table form, as in spreadsheets and lookup tables. In hardware, matrices of dots are used in creating characters on the screen as well as in print (as by dot-matrix printers). In electronics, matrices of diodes or transistors are used to create networks of logic circuits for such purposes as encoding, decoding, or converting information. *See also* grid.

matrix line printer *n. See* line printer.

MAU *n.* Acronym for **M**ultistation **A**ccess **U**nit. A hub device in a token-ring network that connects computers in a physical hub-and-spokes arrangement but uses the logical ring required in token ring networks. *Also called:* MSAU. *See also* hub, token-ring network.

maximize *vb.* In a graphical user interface, to cause a window to expand to fill all the space available within a larger window or on the screen. *See also* enlarge, graphical user interface, Maximize button, window. *Compare* minimize, reduce.

Maximize button *n.* In Windows 3.*x*, Windows 9x, Windows NT, and Windows 2000, a button in the upper right-hand corner of a window that, when clicked, maximizes a window to fill all the space available within a larger window or on the screen. *See also* graphical user interface, window. *Compare* Minimize button, zoom box.

Maximum Transmission Unit *n. See* MTU.

Mb *n. See* megabit.

MB *n. See* megabyte.

MBONE or **Mbone** *n.* Short for **m**ulticast back**bone**. A small set of Internet sites, each of which can transmit real-time audio and video simultaneously to all the others. MBONE sites are equipped with special software to send and receive packets at high speed using the IP one-to-many multicasting protocol. The MBONE has been used for video conferencing and even for a Rolling Stones concert in 1994. *See also* RealAudio.

Mbps *n.* Short for **m**ega **b**its **p**er **s**econd. One million bits per second.

MBR *n. See* Master Boot Record.

MC *n. See* megacycle.

MC68000 *n. See* 68000.

MC68020 *n. See* 68020.

MC68030 *n. See* 68030.

MC68040 *n. See* 68040.

MC68881 *n. See* 68881.

MCF *n. See* Meta-Content Format.

MCGA *n.* Acronym for **Multi-Color Graphics Array.** An older video adapter included in the IBM PS/2 Models 25 and 30. The MCGA was capable of emulating the CGA (Color/Graphics Adapter) and provided two additional graphics modes: the first mode had 640 horizontal pixels by 480 vertical pixels with 2 colors chosen from a palette of 262,144 colors; the second had 320 horizontal pixels by 200 vertical pixels with 256 colors chosen from a palette of 262,144 colors. *See also* graphics mode (definition 2).

MCI *n.* **1.** Acronym for **Media Control Interface.** Part of the Windows application programming interface that enables a program to control multimedia devices. **2.** A major long-distance telephone service carrier, originally Microwave Communications, Inc.

m-commerce *n.* Short for **mobile commerce.** M-commerce involves the use of personal digital assistants (PDAs), digital phones, and other wireless handheld devices equipped with microbrowsers for the online buying and selling of goods. M-commerce is distinguished from other electronic commerce by the level of portability. Wireless Application Protocol (WAP) standards form the foundation of m-commerce technology, which takes advantage of smart phone capabilities with e-mail, fax, Internet, and phone in one mobile unit. *See also* microbrowser, Wireless Application Protocol.

MCP *n.* Acronym for **Microsoft Certified Professional.** A basic certification from Microsoft that verifies an individual's ability to successfully implement a Microsoft product or technology as part of a solution for an organization. The MCP certification is often used as a building block for acquiring additional certifications in specialized skill areas such as databases, programming languages, and Web development.

MCSA *n.* Acronym for **Microsoft Certified Systems Administrator.** A certification from Microsoft that verifies an individual's ability to implement, manage, and troubleshoot existing Microsoft Windows and Windows .NET network and system environments. *See also* MCP.

MCSD *n.* Acronym for **Microsoft Certified Solution Developer.** A certification from Microsoft that verifies an individual's ability to use Microsoft development tools, technologies, and platforms to design and develop business solutions. *See also* MCP.

MCSE *n.* Acronym for **Microsoft Certified System Engineer.** A certification from Microsoft that verifies an individual's ability to analyze business requirements and then design and implement business solutions with Microsoft Windows platforms and server software. *See also* MCP.

MD2 *n.* A hashing algorithm that creates a 128-bit hash value used to verify data integrity. MD2 is an earlier, 8-bit version of the more common MD5. *See also* hashing algorithm.

MD4 *n.* A hashing algorithm that creates a 128-bit hash value used to verify data integrity. Like the latest version, MD5, MD4 is optimized for 32-bit machines. *See also* hashing algorithm.

MD5 *n.* An industry-standard, one-way, 128-bit hashing scheme, developed by MIT Laboratory for Computer Science and RSA Data Security, Inc., and used by various Point-to-Point Protocol (PPP) vendors for encrypted authentication. An extension of MD4, MD5 is slightly slower than the earlier version but offers improved data security. *See also* hashing algorithm.

MDA *n.* Acronym for **Monochrome Display Adapter.** The video adapter introduced with the earliest model of the IBM PC in 1981. MDA was capable of only one video mode: a character mode with 25 lines of 80 characters each, with underlining, blinking, and high-intensity characters. IBM did not use the name *Monochrome Display Adapter* or the acronym *MDA*.

MDI *n.* Acronym for **multiple-document interface.** A user interface in an application that allows the user to have more than one document open at the same time. *See also* user interface.

MDIS *n. See* Metadata Interchange Specification.

mean time between failures *n. See* MTBF.

mean time to repair *n. See* MTTR.

mechanical mouse *n.* A type of mouse in which the motion of a ball on the bottom of the mouse is translated into directional signals. As the user moves the mouse, the ball rolls, turning a pair of wheels mounted at right angles inside the mouse that have conductive markings on their

M

surfaces. Because the markings permit an electric current to flow, a set of conductive brushes that ride on the surface of the conductive wheels can detect these conductive markings. The electronics in the mouse translate these electrical movement signals into mouse-movement information that can be used by the computer. *See also* mouse, trackball. *Compare* optical mouse, optomechanical mouse.

mechatronics *n.* A term derived from the words *mechanical* and *electronics* to describe a field of engineering that applies mechanical, electrical, and electronic engineering concepts to product design and manufacture. A relatively new discipline, mechatronics is applicable to products in fields as diverse as medicine, robotics, manufacturing, and consumer electronics.

media *n.* The physical material, such as paper, disk, and tape, used for storing computer-based information. *Media* is plural; *medium* is singular.

Media Access Control *n. See* MAC.

Media Control Interface *n. See* MCI (definition 1).

media conversion *n.* Transferring data from one storage medium to another—for example, from disk to tape.

media eraser *n.* A device that removes or obliterates data from a storage medium on a wholesale basis, usually by writing meaningless data (such as zeros) over it. *See also* bulk eraser.

media filter *n.* **1.** A device used with local area networks (LANs) as an adapter between two different types of media. For example, an RJ-45 connector might be used between coaxial cable and unshielded twisted pair (UTP) cables. Media filters are similar in function to transceivers. As with many components to LANs, manufacturers often choose different names for similar products, so a LAN expert is needed to decide which media filters are required for a particular LAN. *See also* coaxial cable, connector (definition 1), LAN, transceiver, UTP. **2.** A device added to data networks to filter out electronic noise from the environment. For example, a media filter might be added to an Ethernet network based on coaxial cabling to prevent data loss from interference by nearby electronic equipment. *See also* coaxial cable, Ethernet (definition 1).

media stream *n.* A continuous sequence of audio or audio-and-video through a network.

medium[1] *adj.* Of or relating to the middle part of a range of possible values.

medium[2] *n.* A substance in which signals can be transmitted, such as a wire or fiber-optic cable. *See* media.

medium model *n.* A memory model of the Intel 80x86 processor family. The medium model allows only 64 kilobytes for data but generally up to 1 megabyte for code. *See also* memory model.

medium-scale integration *n.* A concentration of circuit elements in the hundreds on a single chip. *Acronym:* MSI. *See also* integrated circuit.

meg *n. See* megabyte.

mega- *prefix* One million (10^6). In computing, which is based on the binary (base-2) numbering system, *mega-* has a literal value of 1,048,576, which is the power of 2 (2^{20}) closest to one million. *Abbreviation:* M.

megabit *n.* Usually 1,048,576 bits (2^{20}); sometimes interpreted as 1 million bits. *Abbreviation:* Mb, Mbit.

megabyte *n.* Usually 1,048,576 bytes (2^{20}); sometimes interpreted as 1 million bytes. *Abbreviation:* MB.

megacycle *n.* A term for 1 million cycles—usually used to mean 1 million cycles per second. *Abbreviation:* MC. *See also* megahertz.

megaflops *n. See* MFLOPS.

megahertz *n.* A measure of frequency equivalent to 1 million cycles per second. *Abbreviation:* MHz.

megapel display *n. See* megapixel display.

megapixel *adj.* A reference to image resolution of one million pixels or more. The term is used in reference to devices such as digital cameras, scanners, and computer monitors and display adapters.

megapixel display *n.* A video display capable of displaying at least 1 million pixels. For example, a video display with a screen size of 1024 horizontal pixels and 1024 vertical pixels is a megapixel display. *Also called:* megapel display.

Melissa *n.* A macro virus that affects Word files in Microsoft Office 97 and Office 2000 and first appeared in the spring of 1999. Melissa is delivered as an attachment to an e-mail with the subject line "An Important Message From *<user name>*," a message beginning "Here is that document you asked for…," or both. When the attachment is opened, the virus propagates (if Microsoft Outlook is installed) by sending itself to the first 50 e-mail addresses in the user's Outlook address book. On the infected machine,

M

the virus also changes the registry, infects the Normal.dot Word template (which, in turn, infects new documents), and, in Office 2000, disables the Word macro virus warning. Although the Melissa virus does not destroy data, it can affect e-mail performance through the increased volume of messages. If an infected document is open at a time when the day of the month is the same as the minute value of the current time, the virus inserts the text "Twenty-two points, plus triple-word-score, plus fifty points for using all my letters. Game's over. I'm outta here" at the current location of the cursor. The virus was named after an acquaintance of the hacker who developed it.

meltdown *n.* **1.** The complete collapse of a computer network caused by a higher level of traffic than the network can support. The term refers, by analogy, to the accidental melting down of a nuclear reactor core. **2.** Colloquially, the breakdown of a person, usually in a job situation, caused by overwork, stress, or failure.

member *n.* **1.** In object-oriented programming, a variable or routine that is part of a class. *See also* C++, class. **2.** A value that is part of a set data structure. *See also* set[2] (definition 1).

membrane keyboard *n.* A keyboard in which an unbroken plastic or rubber shell (a membrane) covers keys that have little or no travel (movement). Rather than use normal, full-travel keys, membrane keyboards use pressure-sensitive areas that are sometimes, but not always, defined by small bumps under the membrane.

memo field *n.* A field in a database file that can contain unstructured text.

memo pad *n.* A note-taking feature offered by many personal digital assistants and other handheld computing devices. Memo pad allows for the entry of short notes via typing or handwriting recognition applications. The notes can be categorized, organized, and edited later.

memory *n.* A device where information can be stored and retrieved. In the most general sense, memory can refer to external storage such as disk drives or tape drives; in common usage, it refers only to a computer's main memory, the fast semiconductor storage (RAM) directly connected to the processor. *See also* core, EEPROM, EPROM, flash memory, PROM, RAM, ROM. *Compare* bubble memory, mass storage.

memory bank *n.* The physical location on a motherboard where a memory module can be inserted. *See also* bank (definition 1).

memory board *n.* A plug-in printed circuit board that contains one or more memory chips. *See also* memory chip.

memory cache *n. See* CPU cache.

memory card *n.* A memory module that is used to extend RAM storage capacity or in place of a hard disk in a portable computer, such as a laptop, notebook, or handheld PC. The module is usually the size of a credit card and can be plugged into a PCMCIA-compliant portable computer. The module can be composed of EPROM, RAM, or ROM chips or flash memory. *Also called:* RAM card, ROM card. *See also* EPROM, flash memory, handheld PC, hard disk, memory cartridge, module (definition 2), PCMCIA, RAM, ROM.

memory cartridge *n.* A plug-in module containing RAM (random access memory) chips that can be used to store data or programs. Memory cartridges are used primarily in portable computers as smaller, lighter (but more expensive) substitutes for disk drives. Memory cartridges typically use either a nonvolatile form of RAM, which does not lose its contents when power is turned off, or battery-backed RAM, which maintains its contents by drawing current from a rechargeable battery within the cartridge. *Also called:* RAM cartridge. *See also* memory card, RAM. *Compare* ROM cartridge.

memory cell *n.* An electronic circuit that stores one bit of data. *See also* bit.

memory chip *n.* An integrated circuit devoted to memory storage. The memory storage can be *volatile* and hold data temporarily, such as RAM, or *nonvolatile* and hold data permanently, such as ROM, EPROM, EEPROM, or PROM. *See also* EEPROM, EPROM, integrated circuit, memory board, nonvolatile memory, PROM, RAM, volatile memory.

memory management *n.* **1.** In operating systems for personal computers, procedures for optimizing the use of RAM (random access memory). These procedures include selectively storing data, monitoring it carefully, and freeing memory when the data is no longer needed. Most current operating systems optimize RAM usage on their own; some older operating systems, such as early versions of MS-DOS, required the use of third-party utilities to optimize RAM usage and necessitated that the user be more

M

knowledgeable about how the operating system and applications used memory. *See also* memory management unit, RAM. **2.** In programming, the process of ensuring that a program releases each chunk of memory when it is no longer needed. In some languages, such as C and C++, the programmer must keep track of memory usage by the program. Java, a newer language, automatically frees any chunk of memory that is not in use. *See also* C, C++, garbage collection, Java.

memory management program *n.* **1.** A program used to store data and programs in system memory, monitor their use, and reassign the freed space following their execution. **2.** A program that uses hard disk space as an extension of the random access memory (RAM).

memory management unit *n.* The hardware that supports the mapping of virtual memory addresses to physical memory addresses. In some systems, such as those based on the 68020, the memory management unit is separate from the processor. In most modern microcomputers, however, the memory management unit is built into the CPU chip. In some systems, the memory management unit provides interfacing between the microprocessor and memory. This type of memory management unit is typically responsible for address multiplexing and, in the case of DRAMs, the refresh cycle. *Acronym:* MMU. *See also* physical address, refresh cycle, virtual address.

memory model *n.* The approach used to address the code and the data that are used in a computer program. The memory model dictates how much memory can be used in a program for code and how much for data. Most computers with a flat address space support only a single memory model. Computers with a segmented address space usually support multiple memory models. *See also* compact model, flat address space, large model, medium model, segmented address space, small model, tiny model.

memory module *n.* A removable circuit board, cartridge, or other carrier that contains one or more RAM memory chips. *See also* memory card, memory cartridge, RAM.

memory-resident *adj.* Permanently located in a computer's memory, rather than swapped in and out of memory as needed. *See also* memory, TSR.

memory scrubbing *n.* **1.** In mainframe computers, the process of a computer reading its own memory during idle periods in order to find and fix errors. **2.** The process of

examining and correcting errors as data is transferred from memory to the CPU of a computer.

memory size *n.* The memory capacity of a computer, usually measured in megabytes. *See also* megabyte, memory.

memory typewriter *n.* An electric typewriter with internal memory and typically a one-line liquid crystal display for viewing the contents of that memory. Memory typewriters can usually hold one page of text at a time, to which small modifications can be made. Memory typewriters usually do not retain the contents of memory when power is turned off.

MEMS *n.* Acronym for **m**icro-**e**lectro**m**echanical **s**ystems. A technology combining computers with extremely tiny mechanical devices. MEMS devices contain microcircuitry on a tiny silicon chip onto which a mechanical device such as a sensor or an actuator is attached. MEMS devices are used in switches, pacemakers, games, GPS tracking, data storage, and for accelerometers in air bags. Because MEMS devices have the potential to be manufactured in large quantities for little cost, many additional MEMS products are being planned or studied.

menu *n.* A list of options from which a user can make a selection in order to perform a desired action, such as choosing a command or applying a particular format to part of a document. Many application programs, especially those that offer a graphical interface, use menus as a means of providing the user with an easily learned, easy-to-use alternative to memorizing program commands and their appropriate usage.

menu bar *n.* A rectangular bar displayed in an application program's on-screen window, often at the top, from which menus can be selected by the user. Names of available menus are displayed in the menu bar; choosing one with the keyboard or with a mouse causes the list of options in that menu to be displayed.

menu-driven *adj.* Using menus to present choices of commands and available options. Menu-driven programs are usually considered friendlier and easier to learn than programs with a command-line interface. *Compare* command-line interface.

menu item *n.* A choice on a menu, selectable by either the keyboard or a mouse. In some instances, a menu item that is not available (that is, not appropriate) for a given situation is "grayed" (dimmed in comparison to the valid menu choices).

Merced *n.* Former code name for the next-generation 64-bit microprocessor designed by Intel and Hewlett-Packard and released in 2000. Based on the IA-64 architecture, the 64-bit microprocessor contains upwards of 10 million transistors and is used primarily in servers and high-performance workstations. *See also* IA-64.

Mercury *n.* A logic/functional programming language that combines the clarity and expressiveness of declarative programming with advanced static analysis and error-detection features.

merge *vb.* To combine two or more items, such as lists, in an ordered way and without changing the basic structure of either. *Compare* concatenate.

merged transistor logic *n. See* integrated injection logic.

merge sort *n.* A sorting technique that combines several sorted (input) lists into a single sorted (output) list. *See also* bubble sort, insertion sort, quicksort, sort algorithm.

mesa *n.* An area of a germanium or silicon wafer that was protected during the etching process and is therefore higher than the surrounding etched areas. *See also* photolithography.

mesh network *n.* A communications network having two or more paths to any node.

message *n.* **1.** In communications, a unit of information transmitted electronically from one device to another. A message can contain one or more blocks of text as well as beginning and ending characters, control characters, a software-generated header (destination address, type of message, and other such information), and error-checking or synchronizing information. A message can be routed directly from sender to receiver through a physical link, or it can be passed, either whole or in parts, through a switching system that routes it from one intermediate station to another. *See also* asynchronous transmission, block (definition 4), control character (definition 1), frame (definition 1), frame (definition 2), header (definition 2), message switching, network, packet (definition 1), packet switching, synchronous transmission. **2.** In software, a piece of information passed from the application or operating system to the user to suggest an action, indicate a condition, or inform that an event has occurred. **3.** In message-based

operating environments, such as Windows, a unit of information passed among running programs, certain devices in the system, and the operating environment itself.

message header *n.* A sequence of bits or bytes at the beginning of a message that usually provides a timing sequence and specifies such aspects of the message structure as its length, data format, and block identification number. *See also* header (definition 2).

message of the day *n.* A daily bulletin for users of a network, multiuser computer, or other shared system. In most cases, users are shown the message of the day when they log into the system. *Acronym:* MOTD.

Message Passing Interface *n. See* MPI.

message queue *n.* An ordered list of messages awaiting transmission, from which they are taken up on a first in, first out (FIFO) basis.

Message Queuing *n.* A message queuing and routing system for Microsoft Windows that enables distributed applications running at different times to communicate across heterogeneous networks and with computers that may be off line. Message Queuing provides guaranteed message delivery, efficient routing, security, and priority-based messaging. Message Queuing was formerly known as MSMQ.

message reflection *n.* In object-oriented programming environments, such as Visual C++, OLE, and ActiveX, a function that allows a control to handle its own message. *See also* ActiveX controls, control (definition 2), OCX, VBX.

Message Security Protocol *n.* A protocol for Internet messages that is based on the use of encryption and verification to ensure security. It also allows for permissions at the server level for delivery or rejection of e-mail. *Acronym:* MSP.

message switching *n.* A technique used on some communications networks in which a message, with appropriate address information, is routed through one or more intermediate switching stations before being sent to its destination. On a typical message-switching network, a central computer receives messages, stores them (usually briefly), determines their destination addresses, and then delivers them. Message switching enables a network both to regulate traffic and to use communications lines efficiently. *Compare* circuit switching, packet switching.

M

message transfer agent *n. See* MTA.

messaging *n.* The use of computers and data communication equipment to convey messages from one person to another, as by e-mail, voice mail, or fax.

messaging application *n.* An application that enables users to send messages (such as e-mail or fax) to each other.

Messaging Application Programming Interface *n. See* MAPI.

messaging client *n.* An application program that enables its user to send or receive messages (such as e-mail or fax) to and from other users with the help of a remote server.

messaging-oriented middleware *n. See* MOM.

meta- *prefix* Literally, a prefix that describes a process or characteristic beyond the normal meaning of the word without the prefix. For example, metaphysics is "beyond physics." In computing, meta- is usually attached to a word to indicate that the "metaterm" describes, defines, or acts upon objects or concepts of the same type as itself. So, for example, metadata is data about data and a meta-tool is a tool for working on tools.

metacharacter *n.* A character embedded in a program source or a data stream that conveys information about other characters, rather than itself representing a character. A simple example is the backslash (\) character, which, when used in strings in the C programming language, indicates that the letter following the backslash is part of an escape sequence that enables C to display a nongraphic character. *See also* escape character.

metacompiler *n.* A compiler that produces compilers. The UNIX utility *yacc* (Yet Another Compiler-Compiler) is a metacompiler. If it is given a language specification, yacc produces a compiler for that language. *See also* compiler (definition 2).

Meta-Content Format *n.* An open format for describing information about content of a structured body of data such as a Web page, a set of files on a Windows desktop, or a relational database. Meta-Content Format might be used for indexes, data dictionaries, or price lists. *Acronym:* MCF.

metadata or **meta data** *n.***1.** Data about data. For example, the title, subject, author, and size of a file constitute metadata about the file. *See also* data dictionary, repository. **2.** In the Microsoft .NET Framework, information that describes every element managed by the runtime: an assembly, loadable file, type, method, and so on. This can include information required for debugging and garbage collection, as well as security attributes, marshaling data, extended class and member definitions, version binding, and other information required by the runtime.

Metadata Interchange Specification *n.* A set of specifications dealing with the exchanging, sharing, and managing of metadata. *Acronym:* MDIS. *See also* metadata (definition 1).

metafile *n.* A file that contains or defines other files. Many operating systems use metafiles to contain directory information about other files on a given storage device.

metaflow *n.* One of the four stages of the data warehousing process, during which metadata (data about data) is tracked and managed; the business modeling stage. During metaflow, the operational environment is mapped to the data warehouse environment. *See also* data warehouse (definition 2), downflow, inflow, metadata (definition 1), upflow.

metalanguage *n.* A language used to describe other languages. Backus-Naur form (BNF) is a metalanguage commonly used to define programming languages. *Also called:* language-description language. *See also* Backus-Naur form.

metal-oxide semiconductor *n. See* MOS.

metal-oxide semiconductor field-effect transistor *n. See* MOSFET.

metaoperating system *n.* An operating system under which several other operating systems are active. *Also called:* supervisor.

metatag or **meta tag** *n.* A tag in an HTML or XML document that allows a Web-page creator to include such information as the author's name, keywords identifying content, and descriptive details (for example, non-text objects on the page). The information that is marked with metatags does not appear on the Web page when a user views it in a browser, but it can be viewed in the HTML or XML source. Metatags are included in the head of a document and are often used to assist search engines in indexing the page. *See also* HTML, source, tag, XML.

method *n.* In object-oriented programming, a process performed by an object when it receives a message. *See also* object (definition 2), object-oriented programming.

Metropolitan Area Exchange *n. See* MAE (definition 2).

metropolitan area network *n. See* MAN.

MFC *n. See* Microsoft Foundation Classes.

MFLOPS *n.* Acronym for **m**illion **fl**oating-point **o**perations **per second**. A measure of computing speed. *Also called:* megaflops.

MFM encoding *n. See* modified frequency modulation encoding.

MFP *n. See* multifunction peripheral.

MFS *n. See* Macintosh File System.

mget *n.* Short for **m**ultiple **get**. A command in most FTP clients with which a user can request the transfer of several files at once. *See also* FTP[1] (definition 1).

MHTML *n.* Acronym for **M**ultipurpose Internet Mail Extension **H**ypertext **M**arkup **L**anguage, or MIME HTML. A standard method for sending an HTML document encapsulated with inline graphics, applets, linked documents, and other items referred to in the HTML document. *See also* HTML, MIME.

MHz *n. See* megahertz.

MI *n. See* multiple inheritance.

MIB *n. See* Management Information Base.

mickey *n.* A unit of measure for mouse movement. One mickey is typically equal to 1/200th of an inch.

MICR *n. See* magnetic-ink character recognition.

micro- *prefix* **1.** In nonexact measurements, small or compact, as in *microprocessor* or *microcomputer*. **2.** Metric prefix meaning 10^{-6} (one millionth).

microbrowser *n.* An application for mobile phones that allows users to access the Internet to send and receive e-mail and browse the Web. Microbrowsers don't have the full functionality of a Web browser on a PC. For instance, microbrowsers are capable of loading only stripped-down text versions of Web pages. Most microbrowser products are built to utilize the Wireless Application Protocol (WAP) standard. *See also* Wireless Application Protocol.

microcapsule *n.* In an electronic paper display, millions of tiny beads filled with dark dye and light pigment that, in response to an electrical charge, change color to create images and text. *See also* electronic paper.

Micro Channel Architecture *n.* The design of the bus in IBM PS/2 cosmputers (except Models 25 and 30). The Micro Channel is electrically and physically incompatible with the IBM PC/AT bus. Unlike the PC/AT bus, the Micro Channel functions as either a 16-bit or a 32-bit bus.

The Micro Channel also can be driven independently by multiple bus master processors.

microchip *n. See* integrated circuit.

microcircuit *n.* A miniaturized electronic circuit etched on a semiconductor chip. A microcircuit is made up of interconnected transistors, resistors, and other components. However, it is fabricated as a unit, rather than as a set of vacuum tubes, discrete transistors, or other elements that have to be wired together. *See also* integrated circuit.

microcode *n.* Very low-level code that defines how a processor operates. Microcode is even lower in level than machine code; it specifies what the processor does when it executes a machine-code instruction. *See also* machine code, microprogramming.

microcomputer *n.* A computer built around a single-chip microprocessor. Less powerful than minicomputers and mainframes, microcomputers have nevertheless evolved into very powerful machines capable of complex tasks. Technology has progressed so quickly that state-of-the-art microcomputers—essentially, in today's terms, a desktop PC—are as powerful as mainframe computers of only a few years ago, at a fraction of the cost. *See also* computer.

microcontent *n.* Short pieces of text on a Web page that help provide an overview of the page's contents. Microcontent introduces, summarizes, or enhances the macrocontent of a Web page, and includes headings, page titles, ALT text, links, and subheads. *Compare* macrocontent.

microcontroller *n.* A special-purpose, single-chip computer designed and built to handle a particular, narrowly defined task. In addition to the central processing unit (CPU), a microcontroller usually contains its own memory, input/output channels (ports), and timers. When part of a larger piece of equipment, such as a car or a home appliance, a microcontroller is an embedded system. *See also* embedded system.

microdisplay *n.* A tiny monitor screen that provides a full-size view when magnified. Microdisplays work by magnifying a screen as small as one-tenth of an inch to fill the user's field of vision. Microdisplays may be used with computers, DVD players, or handheld devices, in headsets and viewfinders, or anywhere a full-size monitor is impractical or undesirable.

Microdrive *n.* A 1-inch disk drive, introduced in 1998 by IBM. The Microdrive is designed for use in handheld computers and special-purpose devices such as digital cameras and cellular telephones.

micro-electromechanical systems *n. See* MEMS.

microelectronics *n.* The technology of constructing electronic circuits and devices in very small packages. The most significant advance in microelectronics technology has been the integrated circuit. Circuits that 40 years ago required a roomful of power-hungry vacuum tubes can now be fabricated on a silicon chip smaller than a postage stamp and require only a few milliwatts of power. *See also* integrated circuit.

microfiche *n.* A small sheet of film, about 4 by 6 inches, used for recording photographically reduced images, such as document pages, in rows and columns forming a grid pattern. The resulting images are too small to read with the naked eye, and a microfiche reader is required to view the documents. *Compare* microfilm.

microfilm *n.* A thin strip of film stored on a roll and used to record sequential data images. As with microfiche, a special device magnifies the images so that they can be read. *See also* CIM (definition 2), COM (definition 4). *Compare* microfiche.

microfloppy disk *n.* A 3.5-inch floppy disk of the type used with the Macintosh and with IBM and compatible microcomputers. A microfloppy disk is a round piece of polyester film coated with ferric oxide and encased in a rigid plastic shell equipped with a sliding metal cover. On the Macintosh, a single-sided microfloppy disk can hold 400 kilobytes (KB); a double-sided (standard) disk can hold 800 KB; and a double-sided high-density disk can hold 1.44 megabytes (MB). On IBM and compatible machines, a microfloppy can hold either 720 KB or 1.44 MB of information. *See also* floppy disk.

microfluidics *n.* Technology for control and manipulation of fluids on a microscopic scale using microscopic pumps and valves placed on a chip. Microfluidics devices have implications for a number of medical, pharmaceutical, genomics, and other biotechnology applications.

microform *n.* The medium, such as microfilm or microfiche, on which a photographically reduced image, called a *microimage*, is stored. A microimage usually represents text, such as archived documents. *See also* microfiche, microfilm, micrographics.

micrographics *n.* The techniques and methods for recording data on microfilm. *See also* microform.

microimage *n.* A photographically reduced image, usually stored on microfilm or microfiche, that is too small to be read without magnification. *See also* microform, micrographics.

microinstruction *n.* An instruction that is part of the microcode. *See also* microcode.

microjustification *n. See* microspace justification.

microkernel *n.* **1.** In programming, the strictly hardware-dependent part of an operating system that is intended to be portable from one type of computer to another. The microkernel provides a hardware-independent interface to the rest of the operating system, so only the microkernel needs to be rewritten to port the operating system to a different platform. *See also* kernel, operating system. **2.** A kernel that has been designed with only the basic features and typically in a modular fashion.

micrologic *n.* A set of instructions, stored in binary form, or a set of electronic logic circuits that defines and governs the operation within a microprocessor.

microminiature *n.* An extremely small circuit or other electronic component, especially one that is a refinement of an already miniaturized element.

microphone *n.* **1.** A device that converts sound waves into analog electrical signals. Additional hardware can convert the microphone's output into digital data that a computer can process; for example, to record multimedia documents or analyze the sound signal. **2.** A communications program that runs on the Macintosh computer.

microphotonics *n.* Technology for directing light on a microscopic scale. Microphotonics employs tiny mirrors or photonic crystals to reflect and transmit specific wavelengths of light, which can carry digital signals. Microphotonics technology has implications for optical networks under development for the telecommunications industry. *See also* MEMS, optical switching.

microprocessor *n.* A central processing unit (CPU) on a single chip. A modern microprocessor can have several million transistors in an integrated-circuit package that can easily fit into the palm of one's hand. Microprocessors are at the heart of all personal computers. When memory and power are added to a microprocessor, all the pieces, excluding peripherals, required for a computer are present.

The most popular lines of microprocessors today are the 680x0 family from Motorola, which powers the Apple Macintosh line, and the 80x86 family from Intel, which is at the core of all IBM PC–compatible computers. *See also* 6502, 65816, 6800, 68000, 68020, 68030, 68040, 80286, 80386DX, 80386SX, 8080, 8086

microprogramming *n.* The writing of microcode for a processor. Some systems, chiefly minicomputers and mainframes, allow modification of microcode for an installed processor. *See also* microcode.

microsecond *n.* One millionth (10^{-6}) of a second. *Abbreviation:* μs.

microsite *n.* **1.** A small Web site targeted to a single message or topic and nested within a larger site. Microsites geared to promotional and sales of specific products and services may be integrated into popular Web sites by advertisers. **2.** A small Web site with a single focus. *Also called:* minisite.

Microsoft Access *n. See* Access.

Microsoft Active Accessibility *n. See* Active Accessibility.

Microsoft DOS *n. See* MS-DOS.

Microsoft Excel *n. See* Excel.

Microsoft Foundation Classes *n.* A C++ class library developed by Microsoft. The Microsoft Foundation Class library, or MFC, provides the framework and classes that make it easier and faster for programmers to build Windows applications. MFC supports ActiveX and is bundled with several C++ compilers, including Microsoft Visual C++, Borland C++, and Symantec C++. *Acronym:* MFC. *See also* ActiveX, C++. *Compare* Application Foundation Classes.

Microsoft FrontPage *n.* A program you can use to create and manage Internet and intranet sites without programming; FrontPage is available as part of one of the Microsoft Office suites or as a stand-alone product.

Microsoft intermediate language *n.* The CPU-independent instruction set into which .NET Framework programs are compiled. It contains instructions for loading, storing, initializing, and calling methods on objects.

Combined with metadata and the common type system, Microsoft intermediate language allows for true cross-language integration. Prior to execution, MSIL is converted to machine code. It is not interpreted. *Acronym:* MSIL.

Microsoft Internet Explorer *n. See* Internet Explorer.

Microsoft Knowledge Base *n. See* KB (definition 2).

Microsoft Management Console *n. See* MMC.

Microsoft MapPoint *n. See* MapPoint.

Microsoft Money *n. See* Money.

Microsoft MSN Explorer *n. See* MSN Explorer.

Microsoft MSN Messenger Service *n. See* .NET Messenger Service.

Microsoft .NET Messenger Service *n. See* .NET Messenger Service.

Microsoft Network *n. See* MSN.

Microsoft Office *n. See* Office.

Microsoft Operations Manager *n.* A server and application management solution developed by Microsoft Corporation to deliver event and performance management for the Windows 2000–based environment and .NET Enterprise Server applications. Operations management features include enterprise event log reports from across the corporate network, proactive monitoring and alert messaging, and reporting and trend analysis for problem tracking. Microsoft Operations Manager provides flexibility through sophisticated management rules, which can be customized to meet the needs of individual businesses. Microsoft Operations Manager support for management technology standards permits easy integration with other enterprise management systems.

Microsoft Outlook *n. See* Outlook.

Microsoft PowerPoint *n. See* PowerPoint.

Microsoft Project *n.* A software application developed by Microsoft Corporation to simplify the planning and management of projects. Microsoft Project includes features that help you build and manage projects, set schedules and milestones, and communicate and share ideas with team members.

M

M

Microsoft Reader *n.* A software application developed by Microsoft for downloading electronic books and other publications onto any personal computer, laptop computer, or Pocket PC handheld device. Additional features allow users to bookmark pages, highlight text, write notes, and look up definitions.

Microsoft Tech•Ed *n.* An annual training conference held by Microsoft Corporation to educate engineers and businesses using Microsoft technology. The conference provides attendees with access to information, experts, and training labs on Microsoft's latest technologies.

Microsoft Visual InterDev *n. See* Visual InterDev.

Microsoft Visual Studio *n. See* Visual Studio.

Microsoft Visual Studio .NET *n.* A complete development environment for building on the Microsoft .NET technology. Using Visual Studio .NET, developers can create secure, scalable applications and Web services quickly in the language of their choice, leveraging existing systems and skills.

Microsoft Windows *n. See* Windows.

Microsoft Windows 2000 *n. See* Windows 2000.

Microsoft Windows 95 *n. See* Windows 95.

Microsoft Windows 98 *n. See* Windows 98.

Microsoft Windows CE *n. See* Windows CE.

Microsoft Windows Messenger *n. See* .NET Messenger Service.

Microsoft Windows NT *n. See* Windows NT.

Microsoft Word *n. See* Word.

Microsoft XML *n. See* MSXML.

microspace justification *n.* The addition of thin spaces between characters within words to fill out a line for justification, instead of relying only on adding space between words. Good microspace justification gives justified text a more polished, professional look; excessive microspace justification causes words to lose visual coherence. *Also called:* microjustification. *See also* justify (definition 2), microspacing.

microspacing *n.* In printing, the process of adjusting character placement by very small increments.

microtransaction *n.* A business transaction that involves a very small amount of money, typically under about $5. *See also* millicent technology.

microwave relay *n.* A communications link that uses point-to-point radio transmissions at frequencies higher than approximately 1 gigahertz (1000 megahertz).

middleware *n.* **1.** Software that sits between two or more types of software and translates information between them. Middleware can cover a broad spectrum of software and generally sits between an application and an operating system, a network operating system, or a database management system. Examples of middleware include CORBA and other object broker programs and network control programs. *See also* CORBA. **2.** Software that provides a common application programming interface (API). Applications written using that API will run in the same computer systems as the middleware. An example of this type of middleware is ODBC, which has a common API for many types of databases. *See also* application programming interface, ODBC. **3.** Software development tools that enable users to create simple programs by selecting existing services and linking them with a scripting language. *See also* scripting language.

MIDI *n.* Acronym for **M**usical **I**nstrument **D**igital Interface. A serial interface standard that allows for the connection of music synthesizers, musical instruments, and computers. The MIDI standard is based partly on hardware and partly on a description of the way in which music and sound are encoded and communicated between MIDI devices. The information transmitted between MIDI devices is in a form called a *MIDI message*, which encodes aspects of sound such as pitch and volume as 8-bit bytes of digital information. MIDI devices can be used for creating, recording, and playing back music. Using MIDI, computers, synthesizers, and sequencers can communicate with each other, either keeping time or actually controlling the music created by other connected equipment. *See also* synthesizer.

MIDL *n.* Acronym for **M**icrosoft **I**nterface **D**efinition Language. Microsoft implementation and extension of the Interface Definition Language (IDL). *See also* IDL.

midrange computer *n.* A medium-size computer. The term is used interchangeably with *minicomputer*, except midrange computers do not include single-user workstations. *See also* minicomputer.

migration *n.* The process of making existing applications and data work on a different computer or operating system.

.mil *n.* In the Internet's Domain Name System, the top-level domain that identifies addresses operated by U.S. military organizations. The designation .mil appears at the end of the address. *See also* DNS (definition 1), domain (definition 3). *Compare* .com, .edu, .gov, .net, .org.

Military Network *n.* *See* MILNET.

millennium bug *n.* *See* Year 2000 problem.

millennium-compliant *adj.* *See* Year 2000-compliant.

millennium computer bug *n.* *See* Year 2000 problem.

millennium transition *n.* *See* Year 2000 rollover.

milli- *prefix* Metric prefix meaning 10^{-3} (one thousandth). *Abbreviation:* m.

millicent technology *n.* A set of protocols for small-scale commercial transactions over the Internet, developed by Digital Equipment Corporation. Millicent technology is intended to handle purchases of items of information at prices less than a cent.

millions of instructions per second *n.* *See* MIPS.

millisecond *n.* One thousandth of a second. *Abbreviation:* ms or msec.

millivolt *n.* One thousandth of a volt. *Abbreviation:* mV.

MILNET *n.* Short for **Mil**itary **Net**work. A wide area network that represents the military side of the original ARPANET. MILNET carries nonclassified U.S. military traffic. *See also* ARPANET. *Compare* NSFnet.

MIMD *n.* Acronym for **m**ultiple **i**nstruction, **m**ultiple **d**ata stream processing. A category of computer architecture engaged in parallel processing in which central processing units independently fetch instructions and operate on data. *See also* architecture (definition 1), central processing unit, instruction, parallel processing. *Compare* SIMD.

MIME or **mime** *n.* Acronym for **M**ultipurpose **I**nternet **M**ail **E**xtensions. A protocol widely used on the Internet that extends the SMTP (Simple Mail Transfer Protocol) to permit data, such as video, sound, and binary files, to be transmitted by Internet e-mail without having to be translated into ASCII format first. This is accomplished by the use of MIME types, which describe the contents of a document. A MIME-compliant application sending a file, such as some e-mail programs, assigns a MIME type to the file. The receiving application, which must also be

MIME-compliant, refers to a standardized list of documents that are organized into MIME types and subtypes to interpret the content of the file. For instance, one MIME type is *text*, and it has a number of subtypes, including *plain* and *html*. A MIME type of *text/html* refers to a file that contains text written in HTML. MIME is part of HTTP, and both Web browsers and HTTP servers use MIME to interpret e-mail files they send and receive. *See also* HTTP, HTTP server, Simple Mail Transfer Protocol, Web browser. *Compare* BinHex[1] (definition 1).

mindshare *n.* The presence and familiarity of a product, service, or company in the minds of users or consumers. Unlike *market share*, which is the percentage of the market won by a particular product, service, or company, mindshare is a less quantifiable but still important factor in engaging customer attention and generating sales. The term is used frequently by, but is not limited to, the computer industry.

miniaturization *n.* In the development of integrated circuits, the process of reducing the size and increasing the density of transistors and other elements on a semiconductor chip. In addition to providing the benefits of small size, miniaturization of electronic circuits also lowers power requirements, reduces heat, and shortens delays in the propagation of signals from one circuit element to the next. *See also* integrated circuit, integration (definition 2).

minicomputer *n.* A mid-level computer built to perform complex computations while dealing efficiently with a high level of input and output from users connected via terminals. Minicomputers also frequently connect to other minicomputers on a network and distribute processing among all the attached machines. Minicomputers are used heavily in transaction-processing applications and as interfaces between mainframe computer systems and wide area networks. *See also* computer, mainframe computer, microcomputer, supercomputer, wide area network. *Compare* midrange computer, workstation (definition 2).

mini-driver architecture *n.* An architecture in Windows 3.1, Windows 95, Windows 98, Windows NT, and Windows 2000 that uses a relatively small and simple driver, containing any additional instructions needed by a specific hardware device, to interface with the universal driver for that class of devices. *See also* driver.

minifloppy *n.* A 5.25-inch floppy disk. *See also* floppy disk.

M

minimize *vb.* In a graphical user interface, to hide a window without shutting down the program responsible for the window. Usually an icon, a button, or a name for the window is placed on the desktop; when the user clicks on the button, icon, or name, the window is restored to its previous size. *See also* graphical user interface, Minimize button, taskbar, window. *Compare* maximize.

Minimize button *n.* In Windows 3.*x*, Windows 9x, Windows NT, and Windows 2000, a button in the upper right-hand corner of a window that when clicked hides the window. In Windows 3.*x* and Windows NT 3.5 and earlier, an icon appears on the desktop that represents the window; in Windows 95, Windows NT 4, and later versions, the name of the window appears on the taskbar at the bottom of the desktop screen. When the icon or the name is clicked, the window is restored to its previous size. *See also* graphical user interface, taskbar, window.

mini-notebook *n.* A portable computer in a case smaller than that of a standard laptop computer. Most mini-notebook computers have small keyboards, LCD screens built into folding cases, Pentium processors, and built-in hard drives. They are designed to run on standard operating systems, such as Windows 98, rather than on the Windows CE operating system used by the even smaller handheld computers.

miniport driver *n.* A kernel-mode driver that is specific to a device. A miniport driver is linked to a port driver that provides an interface between the port driver and the operating system. This is typically implemented as a dynamic-link library.

minisite *n. See* microsite.

minitower *n.* A vertical floor-standing computer cabinet that is about half the height (13 inches) of a tower case (24 inches). *See also* tower.

minor key *n. See* alternate key (definition 1).

MIP mapping *n.* Short for **m**ultum **i**n **p**arvo (Latin, "much in little") **mapping**. A form of mapping in which the appearance of a bitmapped image is precalculated from a distance and used in a texture mapper. This allows for smoother texture-mapped images calculated in the distance, since pixel conversion may alter colors relative to human perception.

MIPS *n.* Acronym for **m**illions of **i**nstructions **p**er **s**econd. A common measure of processor speed. *See also* central processing unit, MFLOPS.

mirror image *n.* An image that is an exact duplicate of the original with the exception that one dimension is reversed. For example, a right-pointing arrow and a left-pointing arrow of the same size and shape are mirror images.

mirroring *n.* **1.** In computer graphics, the ability to display a mirror image of a graphic—a duplicate rotated or reflected relative to some reference such as an axis of symmetry. See the illustration. **2.** In a network, a means of protecting data on a network by duplicating it, in its entirety, on a second disk. Mirroring is one strategy implemented in RAID security. **3.** On the Internet, replicating a Web site or an FTP site on another server. A site is often mirrored if it is frequently visited by multiple users. This eases the network traffic to the site, making it easier for users to gain access to the information or files on it. A site may also be mirrored in different geographic locations to facilitate downloading by users in various areas. *See also* RAID.

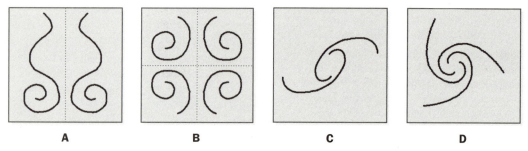

Mirroring. *(A) twofold symmetry with vertical axis; (B) fourfold symmetry with vertical and horizontal axes; (C) twofold radial symmetry; (D) threefold radial symmetry.*

mirror site *n.* A file server that contains a duplicate set of files to the set on a popular server. Mirror sites exist to spread the distribution burden over more than one server or to eliminate the need to use high-demand international circuits.

MIS *n. See* IS.

misc. newsgroups *n.* Usenet newsgroups that are part of the misc. hierarchy and have the prefix *misc.* These newsgroups cover topics that do not fit into the other standard Usenet hierarchies (comp., news., rec., sci., soc., talk.). *See also* newsgroup, traditional newsgroup hierarchy, Usenet.

mission critical *adj.* Pertaining to information, equipment, or other assets of a business or project that are essential to the successful operation of the organization. For example, accounting data and customer records are often considered mission critical information.

misuse detection *n. See* IDS.

mixed cell reference *n.* In spreadsheets, a cell reference (the address of a cell needed to solve a formula) in which either the row or the column is relative (automatically changed when the formula is copied or moved to another cell) and the other is absolute (not changed when the formula is copied or moved). *See also* cell (definition 1).

MMC *n.* Acronym for Microsoft Management Console. A framework for hosting administrative tools called snap-ins. A console might contain tools, folders or other containers, World Wide Web pages, and other administrative items. These items are displayed in the left pane of the console, called a console tree. A console has one or more windows that can provide views of the console tree. The main MMC window provides commands and tools for authoring consoles. The authoring features of MMC and the console tree itself might be hidden when a console is in User Mode. *See also* snap-in.

MMDS *n.* Short for multichannel multipoint distribution service. A fixed wireless service proposed for use as an alternative when DSL or cable modem options are not practical or desirable. The MMDS spectrum was originally used for distance learning and wireless cable video services before attracting interest for fixed broadband wireless services. *See also* broadband.

MMU *n. See* memory management unit.

MMX *n.* Short for Multimedia Extensions. An enhancement to the architecture of Intel Pentium processors that improves the performance of multimedia and communications applications.

mnemonic *n.* A word, rhyme, or other memory aid used to associate a complex or lengthy set of information with something that is simple and easy to remember. Mnemonics are widely used in computing. Programming languages other than machine language, for example, are known as *symbolic languages* because they use short mnemonics, such as *ADD* (for *addition*) and *def* (for *define*) to represent instructions and operations. Similarly, operating systems and applications based on typed commands use mnemonics to represent instructions to the program. MS-DOS, for example, uses *dir* (for *directory*) to request a list of files.

MNP10 *n.* Short for Microcom Networking Protocol, Class **10**. An industry-standard communication protocol used for modem connections over analog cellular telephone connections. The most recent version of MNP10 is MNP 10EC (EC stands for Enhanced Cellular). *See also* communications protocol.

mobile computing *n.* The process of using a computer while traveling. Mobile computing usually requires a portable computer that is battery powered, rather than a desktop system.

Mobile Explorer *n.* A modular wireless applications and services platform designed by Microsoft to power Web-enabled wireless telephones. When connected to a wireless network, Mobile Explorer provides secure mobile access to corporate or personal e-mail, corporate networks, and the Internet. It includes a multimode microbrowser, which can display Web content coded in a variety of markup languages used for small, handheld devices, including cHTML, HTML, WAP 1.1, and WML. *See also* microbrowser.

Mobile Information Server *n.* A software application developed by Microsoft to allow telecommunications carriers, enterprise customers, and business partners to securely extend Microsoft Exchange Server information, corporate intranet applications, and services to users of wireless handheld computing devices. Microsoft Information Server provides mobile users with access to personal services and data stored on the intranet, such as e-mail, document files, appointment calendars, and contacts.

mobile IP *n.* Acronym for **mobile** Internet Protocol. An Internet protocol designed to support host mobility. Mobile IP enables a host to remain connected to the Internet with the same IP address (called the home address)

M

while moving to different locations. Mobile IP tracks a moving host by registering the presence of the host with a foreign agent; the home agent then forwards packets to the remote network. *See also* IP.

mobile telephone switching office *n.* Computer that controls wireless phone calls. The mobile telephone switching office controls the operation of wireless cell sites, tracks calls, and transfers signals between wireless networks and traditional wired telephone systems. *Acronym:* MTSO.

mode *n.* The operational state of a computer or a program. For example, edit mode is the state in which a program accepts changes to a file. *See also* address mode, compatibility mode, safe mode, video mode, virtual real mode.

modec *n.* In telecommunications, a device that generates analog modem signals digitally. The term *modec* is a combination of the terms *modem* and *codec. See also* codec (definition 1), modem (definition 2).

model *n.* A mathematical or graphical representation of a real-world situation or object—for example, a mathematical model of the distribution of matter in the universe, a spreadsheet (numeric) model of business operations, or a graphical model of a molecule. Models can generally be changed or manipulated so that their creators can see how the real version might be affected by modifications or varying conditions. *See also* modeling, simulation.

modeling *n.* **1.** The use of computers to describe the behavior of a system. Spreadsheet programs, for example, can be used to manipulate financial data representing the health and activity of a company, to develop business plans and projections, or to evaluate the impact of proposed changes on the company's operations and financial status. *See also* simulation, spreadsheet program. **2.** The use of computers to describe physical objects and the spatial relationships among them mathematically. CAD programs, for example, are used to create on-screen representations of such physical objects as tools, office buildings, complex molecules, and automobiles. These models use equations to create lines, curves, and other shapes and to place those shapes accurately in relation to each other and to the two-dimensional or three-dimensional space in which they are drawn. *See also* CAD, rendering, solid model, surface modeling, three-dimensional model, two-dimensional model, wire-frame model.

modem *n.* **1.** Short for **mo**dulator/**dem**odulator. A communications device that converts between digital data from a computer or terminal and analog audio signals that can pass through a standard telephone line. Because the telephone system was designed to handle voice and other audio signals and a computer processes signals as discrete units of digital information, a modem is necessary at both ends of the telephone line to exchange data between computers. At the transmit end, the modem converts from digital to analog audio; at the receiving end, a second modem converts the analog audio back to its original digital form. In order to move a high volume of data, high-speed modems rely on sophisticated methods for "loading" information onto the audio carrier—for example, they may combine frequency shift keying, phase modulation, and amplitude modulation to enable a single change in the carrier's state to represent multiple bits of data. In addition to the basic modulation and demodulation functions, most modems also include firmware that allows them to originate and answer telephone calls. International standards for modems are specified by the International Telecommunications Union, or ITU. Despite their capabilities, modems do require communications software in order to function. *See also* amplitude modulation, frequency modulation, quadrature amplitude modulation. *Compare* digital modem. **2.** Any communications device that acts as an interface between a computer or terminal and a communications channel. Although such a device may not actually modulate or demodulate analog signals, it may be described as a modem because a modem is perceived by many users to be a black box that connects a computer to a communications line (such as a high-speed network or a cable TV system). *See also* digital modem.

modem bank *n.* A collection of modems connected to a server maintained by an ISP or the operator of a BBS or remote-access LAN. Most modem banks are configured to allow a remote user to dial a single phone number that routes calls to an available phone number on the bank. *See also* BBS (definition 1), ISP, LAN.

modem eliminator *n.* A device that enables two computers to communicate without modems. *See also* null modem.

modem port *n.* A serial port used for connecting an external modem to a personal computer. *See also* modem (definition 1), serial port.

modem ready *n. See* MR.

moderated *adj.* Subjected to review by a moderator, who may remove irrelevant or inflammatory articles or messages before redistributing them through a newsgroup, mailing list, or other messaging system.

moderated discussion *n.* Communication taking place on a mailing list, newsgroup, or other online forum that is edited by a moderator. When a user submits a message to a moderated discussion, the moderator decides if the message is relevant to the discussion topic. If so, it is forwarded to the discussion group. The content of a moderated discussion is often perceived as more valuable than that of an unmoderated one because the information has been read and approved by a "gatekeeper," who has (presumably) filtered out irrelevant submissions. Some moderators also filter submissions for obscene or pornographic material or material that is potentially offensive. *See also* mailing list, moderator, newsgroup.

moderator *n.* In some Internet newsgroups and mailing lists, a person through whom all messages are filtered before they are distributed to the members of the newsgroup or list. The moderator discards or edits any messages that are not considered appropriate. *See also* mailing list, newsgroup.

modified frequency modulation encoding *n.* An older method of storing data on disks. Modified frequency modulation encoding is based on an earlier technique called frequency modulation encoding but improves on its efficiency by reducing the need for synchronizing information and by basing the magnetic coding of each bit on the status of the previously recorded bit. This method of encoding stores more information on a disk than does frequency modulation encoding. It is not, however, as efficient a space saver as the technique known as *run-length limited encoding*, or RLL. *Abbreviation:* MFM encoding. *Compare* frequency modulation encoding, run-length limited encoding.

modifier key *n.* A key on the keyboard that, when held down while another key is pressed, changes the meaning of the keystroke. *See also* Alt key, Command key, Control key, Shift key.

modify structure *n.* An operator available in some database management systems that permits fields (columns) to be added or deleted without the need to rebuild the entire database.

MO disk *n. See* magneto-optic disc.

MO disk drive *n. See* magneto-optic disc.

Modula-2 *n.* A modular high-level language designed in 1980 by Niklaus Wirth. Derived from Pascal, Modula-2 is noted for its emphasis on modular programming, its early support for data abstraction, and its lack of standard functions and procedures. *See also* modular programming.

modular design *n.* An approach to designing hardware or software in which a project is broken into smaller units, or modules, each of which can be developed, tested, and finished independently before being combined with the others in the final product. Each unit is designed to perform a particular task or function and can thus become part of a library of modules that can often be reused in other products having similar requirements. In programming, for example, one module might consist of instructions for moving the cursor in a window on the screen. Because it is deliberately designed as a stand-alone unit that can work with other sections of the program, the same module might be able to perform the same task in another program as well, thus saving time in development and testing.

modular jack *n. See* phone connector.

modular programming *n.* An approach to programming in which the program is broken into several independently compiled modules. Each module exports specified elements (such as constants, data types, variables, functions, and procedures); all other elements remain private to the module. Other modules can use only the exported elements. Modules clarify and regularize the interfaces among the major parts of a program. Thus, they facilitate group programming efforts and promote reliable programming practices. Modular programming is a precursor of object-oriented programming. *See also* module (definition 1), object-oriented programming.

modular software *n.* A program created from multiple stand-alone software components. Modular components can work together to perform the work for which the larger program is designed while still remaining individually usable—and reusable—in other programs. Modular software is, in effect, made up of recyclable parts. Because each component is functionally autonomous and self-contained, other components can call on its services without having to "know" how it works. Thus, a programmer can change or modify the way one component performs its work without adversely affecting other components in the same program. *See also* component software, integrated software, modular design.

modulate *vb.* To change some aspect of a signal intentionally, usually for the purpose of transmitting information.

M

modulation *n.* **1.** The process of changing or regulating the characteristics of a carrier wave vibrating at a certain amplitude (height) and frequency (timing) so that the variations represent meaningful information. **2.** In computer communications, the means by which a modem converts digital information sent by a computer to the audio form that it sends over a telephone line.

modulation standards *n.* Protocols that determine how modems convert digital data into analog signals that can be transmitted over telephone lines. Initially, Bell created modulation standards used in the United States, and the CCITT created international recommendations. The ITU-T (formerly called the CCITT) now makes recommendations generally adopted by modem manufacturers both internationally and in the United States. The ITU-TV series recommendations (such as V.34 and V.90) define data communication over the telephone network. The suffixes -bis and -ter (for example, V.32bis) indicate later versions. *See also* V.34, V.90.

module *n.* **1.** In programming, a collection of routines and data structures that performs a particular task or implements a particular abstract data type. Modules usually consist of two parts: an interface, which lists the constants, data types, variables, and routines that can be accessed by other modules or routines; and an implementation, which is private (accessible only to the module) and which contains the source code that actually implements the routines in the module. *See also* abstract data type, information hiding, Modula-2, modular programming. **2.** In hardware, a self-contained component that can provide a complete function to a system and can be interchanged with other modules that provide similar functions. *See also* memory card, SIMM.

modulo *n.* An arithmetic operation whose result is the remainder of a division operation. For example, 17 *modulo* 3 = 2 because 17 divided by 3 yields a remainder of 2. Modulo operations are used in programming.

moiré *n.* A visible wavy distortion or flickering in an image that is displayed or printed with an inappropriate resolution. Several parameters affect moiré patterns, including the size and resolution of the image, resolution of the output device, and halftone screen angle.

molecular beam epitaxy *n.* A process used in the fabrication of semiconductor devices, such as integrated circuits. A device employing molecular beam epitaxy creates thin layers of semiconducting material by vaporizing the material and then directing a beam of molecules at the substrate on which the layer is to be formed. This technique allows very precise and very thin layers to be created.

MOM *n.* Acronym for **m**essaging-**o**riented **m**iddleware. A class of programs that translates data and messages between applications that use one format and communications services (such as NetBIOS and TCP/IP) that expect a different format.

monadic *adj. See* unary.

Money *n.* Microsoft's Windows-based financial-management software for individuals, families, and small businesses. Money includes tools for managing bank accounts and investments, budgeting, tax estimating and financial planning, and paying bills.

monitor *n.* The device on which images generated by the computer's video adapter are displayed. The term *monitor* usually refers to a video display and its housing. The monitor is attached to the video adapter by a cable. *See also* CRT.

monitoring software *n.* A program or set of programs used to oversee computer-based systems and networks for the purpose of tracking usage or identifying, reporting on, and solving problems at the earliest possible stage. Monitoring software is used in a variety of areas ranging from hardware platforms and their components to operating systems, databases, Internet/intranet access, and business applications. Typically, different tools are used to monitor individual system components, though the individual monitors might feed information to a higher-level monitor in order to encompass an entire computing environment.

monitor port *n. See* display port.

monochrome *adj.* Of, pertaining to, or being a monitor that displays images in only one color—black on white (as on early monochrome Macintosh screens) or amber or green on black (as on early IBM and other monochrome monitors). The term is also applied to a monitor that displays only variable levels of a single color, such as a gray-scale monitor.

monochrome adapter *n.* A video adapter capable of generating a video signal for one foreground color or sometimes for a range of intensities in a single color, as for a gray-scale monitor.

monochrome display *n.* **1.** A video display capable of rendering only one color. The color displayed depends on the phosphor of the display (often green or amber). **2.** A display capable of rendering a range of intensities in only one color, as in a gray-scale monitor.

Monochrome Display Adapter *n. See* MDA.

monochrome graphics adapter *n. See* HGC.

monochrome monitor *n. See* monochrome display.

monographics adapter *n.* Any video adapter that can display only monochrome text and graphics; any video adapter functionally compatible with the Hercules Graphics Card (HGC). *See also* HGC.

monospace font *n.* A font (set of characters in a particular style and size), similar to that used on a typewriter, in which each character occupies the same amount of horizontal space regardless of its width—an *i*, for example, taking as much room as an *m*. See the illustration. *Also called:* fixed-width font. *See also* monospacing. *Compare* proportional font.

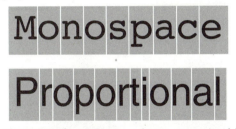

Monospace font. *Monospace font vs. proportional font.*

monospacing *n.* A form of print and display spacing in which each character occupies the same amount of horizontal space on the line, regardless of whether the character is wide (such as *m*) or narrow (such as *I*). *Also called:* fixed-pitch spacing, fixed spacing, fixed-width spacing. *See also* monospace font. *Compare* proportional spacing.

Monte Carlo method *n.* A mathematical technique that uses repeated calculations and random numbers to find an approximate solution to a complex problem. The Monte Carlo method, named for its relationship to games of chance played in the casinos at Monte Carlo, Monaco, can be used in situations in which it is possible to calculate the probability of a particular event occurring but not to factor in the complex effects of many other contributing factors.

MOO *n.* Short for MUD, object-oriented. A type of virtual environment on the Internet, similar to a game-oriented MUD but based on an object-oriented language and generally focused more on programming than on games. *See also* MUD.

Moore's Law *n.* A prediction by Intel cofounder Gordon Moore in the early days of the computer revolution regarding the growth of semiconductor technology. Moore predicted that the number of transistors that could be put on a chip would double every year, and it did. Ten years later, Moore predicted that chip capacity would double every two years, and capacity has actually doubled every 18 months since then. The doubling of capacity every 18 months is popularly referred to as a "law."

.moov *n.* A file extension indicating a QuickTime MooV video file for a Macintosh computer. *See also* MooV.

MooV *n.* The file format for QuickTime movies that stores synchronized tracks for control, video, audio, and text. *See also* QuickTime.

morphing *n.* Short for meta**morph**o**sing**. A process by which one image is gradually transformed into another, creating the illusion of a metamorphosis occurring in a short time. A common motion picture special-effects technique, morphing is available in many advanced computer animation packages. *See also* tween.

MOS *n.* Acronym for **m**etal-**o**xide **s**emiconductor. An integrated-circuit technology in which field-effect transistors (FETs) are made with an insulating layer of silicon dioxide between a metal gate electrode and a semiconductor channel. MOS designs are widely used both in discrete components and in integrated circuits. MOS integrated circuits have the advantages of high component density, high speed, and low power consumption. MOS devices are easily damaged by static electricity, so before they are inserted in a circuit, they should be kept with their connectors embedded in conducting foam to prevent the buildup of static charges. *See also* FET, MOSFET.

Mosaic *n.* The first popular graphical World Wide Web browser. Released on the Internet in early 1993 by the National Center for Supercomputing Applications (NCSA) at the University of Illinois at Urbana-Champaign, Mosaic is available as freeware and shareware for Windows, Macintosh, and X Window systems. Mosaic is distinguished from other early Web browsers by its ease of use and its addition of inline images to Web documents. *Also called:* NCSA Mosaic.

MOSFET *n.* Acronym for **m**etal-**o**xide **s**emiconductor **f**ield-**e**ffect **t**ransistor. A common type of field-effect transistor in which a layer of silicon dioxide insulates the

M

metal gate from the semiconductor current channel. MOS-FETs have extremely high input impedance and therefore require almost no driving power. They are used in many audio applications, including high-gain amplifier circuits. Like all metal-oxide semiconductor (MOS) devices, MOSFETs are easily damaged by static electricity. See the illustration. *See also* FET, MOS.

MOSFET.

most significant bit *n.* In a sequence of one or more bytes, the highest-order bit of a binary number, not including the sign bit. *Acronym:* MSB. *See also* high-order. *Compare* least significant bit.

most significant character *n.* The high-order, or left-most, character in a string. *Acronym:* MSC. *See also* high-order. *Compare* least significant character.

most significant digit *n.* In a sequence of one or more digits, the highest-order digit, which is the leftmost digit. In *456.78, 4* is the most significant digit. *Acronym:* MSD. *Compare* least significant digit.

MOTD *n. See* message of the day.

motherboard *n.* The main circuit board containing the primary components of a computer system. This board contains the processor, main memory, support circuitry, and bus controller and connector. Other boards, including expansion memory and input/output boards, may attach to the motherboard via the bus connector. *See also* expansion slot. *Compare* daughterboard.

Motion JPEG *n.* A standard for storing motion video, proposed by the Joint Photographic Experts Group (JPEG), that uses JPEG image compression for each frame. *See also* JPEG (definition 1). *Compare* MPEG (definition 1).

motion path *n.* The path that a specified object or text will follow as part of an animation sequence for a slide.

mount *vb.* To make a physical disk or tape accessible to a computer's file system. The term is most commonly used to describe accessing disks in Macintosh and UNIX-based computers.

mount *n.* In NFS, a folder or file retrieved from elsewhere on the network and accessed locally. *See also* NFS.

MOUS *n.* Acronym for **M**icrosoft **O**ffice **U**ser **S**pecialist. A certification from Microsoft that verifies an individual's skills with the Microsoft Office desktop programs. *See also* MCP.

mouse *n.* A common pointing device. The basic features of a mouse are a flat-bottomed casing designed to be gripped by one hand, one or more buttons on the top, a multidirectional detection device (usually a ball) on the bottom, and a cable connecting the mouse to the computer. By moving the mouse on a surface (such as a desk top), the user typically controls an on-screen cursor. A mouse is a relative pointing device because there are no defined limits to the mouse's movement and because its placement on a surface does not map directly to a specific screen location. To select items or choose commands on the screen, the user presses one of the mouse's buttons, producing a "mouse click." See the illustration. *See also* bus mouse, mechanical mouse, optical mouse, optomechanical mouse, relative pointing device, serial mouse. *Compare* trackball.

Mouse. *Two types of mouse: for the Macintosh (left) and for the PC (right).*

MouseKeys *n.* A feature in Windows that allows a user to use the numeric keyboard to move the mouse pointer. MouseKeys is primarily intended for people who may have physical limitations that make it difficult to move a conventional mouse. *See also* mouse.

mouse pad *n.* A surface on which a mouse can be moved, typically a rectangular rubber pad covered with fabric, providing more traction than a wooden or glass desktop or tabletop. *See also* mouse.

mouse pointer *n.* An on-screen element whose location changes as the user moves the mouse. Depending on the location of the mouse pointer and the operation of the program with which it is working, the area of the screen where the mouse pointer appears serves as the target for an action when the user presses one of the mouse buttons. *See also* block cursor, cursor (definition 3).

mouse port *n.* **1.** In many PC-compatible computers, a dedicated connector where a mouse or other pointing device plugs into the computer. If a mouse port is not available, a serial port can be used to connect the mouse to the computer. See the illustration. *See also* connector, mouse, pointing device, serial port. **2.** In a Macintosh, the Apple Desktop Bus port. *See also* Apple Desktop Bus.

— Mouse port

Mouse port.

mouse scaling *n. See* mouse sensitivity.

mouse sensitivity *n.* The relationship of mouse movement to screen cursor movement. A more sensitive mouse signals to the computer more "mouse moves" per inch of physical mouse movement than does a less sensitive mouse. Increasing the sensitivity of the program or mouse driver can result in smaller cursor moves for a given mouse move, making it easier for the user to position the cursor precisely. High sensitivity is good for exacting work, such as CAD/CAM and graphic art; low sensitivity is good for tasks in which getting around the screen quickly is important and for applications such as Web browsers, word processors, and spreadsheets, in which the cursor is used mostly to select buttons or text. *Also called:* mouse scaling, mouse tracking.

mouse tracking *n. See* mouse sensitivity.

mouse trails *n.* The creation of a shadowlike trail following the mouse pointer on screen in order to make it easier to see. Mouse trails are useful for laptops and notebooks, particularly ones with passive matrix displays or older models with monochrome screens. The relatively low resolution and contrast of these screens made it easy to lose sight of a small mouse pointer. *See also* mouse pointer, submarining.

mousetrapping *n.* A practice employed by some Web sites in which the back and exit buttons of a visitor's Web browser are disabled and attempts to leave the site are redirected to other pages on the site or to other sites against the visitor's will. Mousetrapping is most often associated with adult-oriented Web sites. *Compare* page-jacking.

.mov *n.* A filename extension for a movie file in Apple's QuickTime format. *See also* QuickTime.

move *n.* A command or an instruction to transfer information from one location to another. Depending on the operation involved, a move can affect data in a computer's memory or it can affect text or a graphical image in a data file. In programming, for example, a move instruction might transfer a single value from one memory location to another. In applications, on the other hand, a move command might relocate a paragraph of text or all or part of a graphic from one place in a document to another. Unlike a copy procedure, which duplicates information, a move indicates that information either is or can be deleted from its original location. *Compare* copy.

.movie *n. See* .mov.

Moving Picture Experts Group *n. See* MPEG (definition 1).

Mozilla *n.* **1.** A nickname for the Netscape Navigator (later, Netscape Communicator) Web browser, coined by the Netscape Corporation. *See also* Mosaic, Netscape Navigator. **2.** Since 1998, when the Communicator source code was released for free, for use by any interested parties, the name Mozilla has been extended as a generic reference to any Web browser based on Navigator source code.

mozilla.org *n.* The name of the group charged by the Netscape Corporation to act as a clearinghouse for Mozilla-related matters, such as questions, changes to code, bug reporting, forums, and so on.

MP3 *n.* Acronym for **MPEG** Audio Layer-**3**. A digital audio coding scheme used in distributing recorded music over the Internet. MP3 shrinks the size of an audio file by a factor of 10 to 12 without seriously degrading the quality (CD-recording level) of the sound. MP3 files are given the file extension .mp3. Although MP3 is part of the MPEG family, it is audio-only and is not the same as the now-defunct MPEG-3 standard. *See also* MPEG-3.

MP3 encoder *n. See* encoder.

M

MPC *n. See* Multimedia PC.

.mpeg *n.* The file extension that identifies video and sound files compressed in the MPEG format specified by the Moving Pictures Experts Group. *See also* MPEG.

MPEG *n.* **1.** Acronym for **M**oving **P**icture **E**xperts **G**roup. A set of standards for audio and video compression established by the Joint ISO/IEC Technical Committee on Information Technology. The MPEG standard has different types that have been designed to work in different situations. *Compare* Motion JPEG. **2.** A video/audio file in the MPEG format. Such files generally have the extension .mpg. *See also* JPEG. *Compare* Motion JPEG.

MPEG-1 *n.* The original MPEG standard for storing and retrieving video and audio information, designed for CD-ROM technology. MPEG-1 defines a medium bandwidth of up to 1.5 Mbps, two audio channels, and noninterlaced video. *See also* MPEG (definition 1). *Compare* MPEG-2, MPEG-3, MPEG-4.

MPEG-2 *n.* An extension of the MPEG-1 standard designed for broadcast television, including HDTV. MPEG-2 defines a higher bandwidth of up to 40 Mbps, five audio channels, a wider range of frame sizes, and interlaced video. *See also* HDTV, MPEG (definition 1). *Compare* MPEG-1, MPEG-3, MPEG-4.

MPEG-3 *n.* Initially an MPEG standard designed for HDTV (high-definition television), but it was found that MPEG-2 could be used instead. Therefore, this standard no longer exists. *See also* HDTV, MPEG (definition 1). *Compare* MP3, MPEG-1, MPEG-2, MPEG-4.

MPEG-4 *n.* A standard currently under development designed for videophones and multimedia applications. MPEG-4 provides a lower bandwidth of up to 64 Kbps. *See also* MPEG (definition 1). *Compare* MPEG-1, MPEG-2, MPEG-3.

.mpg *n. See* .mpeg.

MPI *n.* Acronym for **M**essage **P**assing **I**nterface. A specification for message passing on workstation clusters and massively parallel processing (MPP) architectures. MPI was designed as a proposed standard by the MPI Forum, a committee of vendors and users.

MPLS *n.* Acronym for **M**ulti**p**rotocol **L**abel **S**witching. A standards-based technique used to manage and optimize traffic flow for large-scale networks. In an MPLS network, incoming packets are assigned a label by a label edge router (LER). Label switch routers (LSRs) use these labels to forward the packets through the network along a label switch path (LSP). Each LSR removes the existing label and assigns a new one. MPLS combines the advantages of bridges (Layer 2 switching, which is used in ATM and frame relay) and routers (Layer 3 switching, which is used in IP). MPLS serves to create faster and more scalable networks to facilitate quality of service, class of service, and the use of VPNs.

MP/M *n.* Acronym for **M**ultitasking **P**rogram for **M**icrocomputers. A multitasking, multiuser version of the CP/M operating system. *See also* CP/M.

MPOA *n.* Acronym for **M**ulti-**P**rotocol **O**ver **A**TM. A specification established by the ATM Forum (an industry group of Asynchronous Transfer Mode users and vendors) to integrate ATM into existing Ethernet, token ring, and TCP/IP networks. *See also* ATM (definition 1).

MPP *n. See* massively parallel processing, massively parallel processor.

MPPP *n. See* Multilink Point-to-Point Protocol.

MPR II *n.* A standard for limiting magnetic and electric field emissions from video monitors, including VLF radiation. MPR II is a voluntary standard developed by the Swedish Board for Measurement and Testing in 1987 and updated in 1990. *See also* VLF radiation.

mput *n.* In many FTP clients, the command that instructs the local client to transmit multiple files to the remote server.

MR *n.* Acronym for **m**odem **r**eady. A light on the front panel of a modem indicating that the modem is ready.

MRP *n. See* Material Requirements Planning.

ms *n. See* millisecond.

MSAA *n.* Short for **M**icrosoft **A**ctive **A**ccessibility. *See* Active Accessibility.

MSAU *n. See* MAU.

MS Audion. *n.* The code name, or working name, of Windows Media Audio, before the technology was released by Microsoft. *See also* Windows Media Audio.

MSB *n. See* most significant bit.

MSC *n. See* most significant character.

MSD *n. See* most significant digit.

MSDN *n.* Acronym for the **M**icrosoft **D**eveloper **N**etwork. An online, print, and CD-DVD resource for developers that features content and programs focused on development trends and Microsoft technologies. Some features of MSDN include technical articles and reference material; information on upcoming conferences and events; developer support through peer-to-peer interaction, information sharing, and direct interaction with Microsoft; and software subscription programs.

MS-DOS *n.* Short for **M**icrosoft **D**isk **O**perating **S**ystem. A single-tasking, single-user operating system with a command-line interface, released in 1981, for IBM PCs and compatibles. MS-DOS, like other operating systems, oversees operations such as disk input and output, video support, keyboard control, and many internal functions related to program execution and file maintenance.

MS-DOS mode *n.* A shell in which the MS-DOS environment is emulated in 32-bit systems such as Windows 95. *See also* MS-DOS, shell[1].

MS-DOS shell *n.* A shell environment based on a command-line prompt that allows a user to interact with MS-DOS or an MS-DOS-emulating operating system.

MSDOS.SYS *n.* One of two hidden system files installed on an MS-DOS startup disk. MSDOS.SYS, called IBM-DOS.SYS in IBM releases of MS-DOS, contains the software that makes up the heart (kernel) of the operating system. *See also* IO.SYS.

msec *n. See* millisecond.

MSI *n. See* medium-scale integration.

MSIL *n. See* Microsoft intermediate language.

MSN *n.* Acronym for **M**icrosoft **N**etwork. An online service and Internet portal, launched with the introduction of Windows 95 in August 1995.

MSN Explorer *n.* Microsoft software that integrates the functionality of Internet Explorer, Windows Media Player, Hotmail, MSN Messenger, MSN Communities, Music Central, and other MSN content and services. *See also* MSN.

MSN Messenger Service *n. See* .NET Messenger Service.

MSP *n. See* Message Security Protocol, managed service provider.

MS-Windows *n. See* Windows.

MSXML *n.* Acronym for **M**icrosoft **XML**. A Java-based XML parser from Microsoft that provides support for World Wide Web Consortium (W3C) standards for XML documents and applications.

MTA *n.* Acronym for **m**essage **t**ransfer **a**gent. An application process, as described in the X.400 message-handling system, responsible for delivering e-mail messages. After receiving a message, an MTA stores it temporarily and either delivers it or forwards it to another MTA. During this process, the MTA can change the message headers. *See also* X series.

MTBF *n.* Acronym for **m**ean **t**ime **b**etween **f**ailures. The average time interval, usually expressed in thousands or tens of thousands of hours (sometimes called *power-on hours* or *POH*), that will elapse before a hardware component fails and requires service.

MTTR *n.* Acronym for **m**ean **t**ime **t**o **r**epair. The average time interval, usually expressed in hours, that it takes to repair a failed component.

MTU *n.* Acronym for **M**aximum **T**ransmission **U**nit. The largest packet of data that can be transmitted on a network. MTU size varies, depending on the network—576 bytes on X.25 networks, for example, 1500 bytes on Ethernet, and 17,914 bytes on 16 Mbps Token Ring. Responsibility for determining the size of the MTU lies with the link layer of the network. When packets are transmitted across networks, the path MTU, or PMTU, represents the smallest packet size (the one that all networks can transmit without breaking up the packet) among the networks involved.

MUD *n.* Acronym for **m**ultiuser **d**ungeon. A virtual environment on the Internet in which multiple users simultaneously participate in a role-playing game—generally a medieval fantasy, hence the "dungeon"—and interact with each other in real time. *Also called:* multiuser simulation environment.

MUD, object-oriented *n. See* MOO.

multiband phone *n.* Wireless phone that operates on two or more broadcast frequencies.

multiboot *n.* **1.** Startup capability of some operating systems, such as Windows NT, OS/2, UNIX, and some Power Macs, that allows users to choose which of two or more installed operating systems—for example, Windows NT or UNIX—they want to use for the current session. *See also* boot. **2.** A computer configuration that runs two or more operating systems. *See also* dual boot, startup.

Multibus *n.* A computer expansion bus designed by Intel Corporation that is used extensively by designers of high-performance workstations. A high-bandwidth bus

M

(capable of extremely fast data transmission), Multibus also allows multiple bus masters. *See also* bus.

multicast address dynamic client allocation protocol *n.* An extension to the DHCP protocol standard used to support dynamic assignment and configuration of IP multicast addresses on TCP/IP-based networks. *Acronym:* MADCAP.

multicast backbone *n. See* MBONE.

multicasting *n.* The process of sending a message simultaneously to more than one destination on a network. *Compare* anycasting.

multichannel multipoint distribution service *n. See* MMDS.

Multi-Color Graphics Array *n. See* MCGA.

multi-element *adj.* Consisting of multiple data elements that all have the same format for storing the same kind of information. The data elements may be simple variables, as in an array of integer variables, or they may be more complicated data structures, as in an array of employee records each of which contains fields for an employee's name, Social Security number, pay rate, and so on.

multifile sorting *n.* The process of sorting a body of data that resides in more than one file.

MultiFinder *n.* A version of the Macintosh Finder that provides support for multitasking. The primary use of MultiFinder is to allow multiple applications to be simultaneously resident in memory. A single mouse click switches between applications, and information from one application can be copied to another. If the active application allows true multitasking, background tasks can be processed. *See also* Finder.

multifunction board *n.* A computer add-in board that provides more than one function. Multifunction boards for personal computers frequently offer additional memory, serial/parallel ports, and a clock/calendar.

multifunction peripheral *n.* A multipurpose device that combines printing with faxing, scanning (color or black and white), and copying (color or black and white) in a single unit. Multifunction peripherals are especially popular with the SOHO (small office, home office) market, where cost-effectiveness and space limitations can be significant considerations. *Acronym:* MFP. *Also called:* multifunction printer.

multifunction printer *n. See* multifunction peripheral.

multihoming *n.* **1.** In Mac OS X, an automatic network selection feature that allows one computer to maintain multiple network addresses. Multihoming may be used with a computer that is used from multiple locations, such as home and office, or to create special connection settings, such as separate systems for communication inside and outside of an intranet. **2.** The use of multiple addresses and/or multiple interfaces for a single node. A multihomed host has either multiple network interfaces connected to two or more networks, or a single network interface that has been assigned multiple IP addresses. Multihoming can be used to provide redundancy to achieve quality of service.

multilayer *adj.* **1.** In board design, of or pertaining to a printed circuit board consisting of two or more layers of board material. Each separate layer has its own metallic tracings to provide electrical connections between various electronic components and to provide connections to the other layers. The layers are laminated together to produce a single circuit board to which the components, such as integrated circuits, resistors, and capacitors, are attached. Multilayer design allows many more discrete paths between components than single-layer boards do. **2.** In computer-aided design (CAD), of or pertaining to drawings, such as electronic circuits, that are built up using multiple layers, each with a different level of detail or a different object, so that distinct parts of the drawing can easily be manipulated, overlaid, or peeled off.

multilayer switch *n.* A network switch that uses information from more than one ISO/OSI layer (Layer 2, Layer 3, Layer 4, and/or Layer 7) to forward traffic. *See also* ISO/OSI reference model, switch (definition 4).

Multilink Point-to-Point Protocol *n.* An Internet protocol that allows computers to establish multiple physical links to combine their bandwidths. This technology creates a virtual link with more capacity than a single physical link. *Acronym:* MPPP. *See also* PPP.

multimedia *n.* The combination of sound, graphics, animation, and video. In the world of computers, multimedia is a subset of hypermedia, which combines the aforementioned elements with hypertext. *See also* hypermedia, hypertext.

Multimedia Extensions *n. See* MMX.

Multimedia PC *n.* Software and hardware standards set forth by the Multimedia PC Marketing Council, which

M

sets minimum standards for a PC's sound, video, and CD-ROM playing capabilities. *Acronym:* MPC.

Multimedia Personal Computer *n. See* Multimedia PC.

multimode phone *n.* Wireless phone that operates on both analog and digital networks. A multimode phone may be dual-mode (analog and one digital network) or tri-mode (analog and two digital networks).

multinode computer *n.* A computer that uses multiple processors to share in the computation of a complex task. *See also* central processing unit, parallel processing.

multipart forms *n.* Computer printer paper arranged in sets with carbon paper between the sheets (or with a chemical coating that emulates carbon on the back of each sheet except the last) to produce copies of output from impact printers. Multipart forms are designated by the number of copies in a set, such as two-part, three-part, and so on.

multipartite virus *n.* A type of virus that combines characteristics and techniques of both boot sector and file viruses. Multipartite viruses first infect either system sectors or files and then spread quickly to infect the entire system. Because of their multiple capabilities, multipartite viruses are difficult to remove from an infected system. *Also called:* bimodal virus, bipartite virus. *See also* boot.

multipass sort *n.* A sorting operation that, usually because of the sorting algorithm being used, requires two or more passes through the data before completion. *See also* bubble sort, insertion sort, Shell sort, sort algorithm.

multiple-document interface *n. See* MDI.

multiple inheritance *n.* A feature of some object-oriented programming languages that allows a new class to be derived from several existing classes. Multiple inheritance both extends and combines existing types. *Acronym:* MI. *See also* class, inherit, type.

multiple instruction, multiple data streams *n. See* MIMD.

multiple master font *n.* An advanced font creation and management classification developed by Adobe. A multiple master font contains two or more sets of font outlines or master designs that determine the dynamic range of each design axis in a typeface. Multiple master fonts include one or more design axes—weight, width, style, and optical size—that allow the user to create thousands of variations on a single typeface.

multiple-pass printing *n.* A form of dot-matrix printing in which the print head makes more than one pass across the page for each printed line, printing each line a second time exactly on top of the first pass. Multiple-pass printing can be used with dot-matrix printers to darken the print and smooth out errors in alignment. On better printers, a second pass might occur after the paper is moved up slightly, so that the dots in the characters overlap to create a crisper, darker image.

multiple recipients *n.* **1.** The capability of sending e-mail to more than one user at a time by listing more than one e-mail address on a line. Delimiters such as commas or semicolons are used to separate the e-mail addresses. *See also* e-mail[1] (definition 1), mailing list. **2.** The subscribers on a mailing list. A message sent to the list is addressed to the "multiple recipients of" the list.

multiple regression *n.* A statistical technique that seeks to describe the behavior of a so-called "dependent" variable in terms of the observed behavior of numerous other, "independent" variables thought to affect it. For each independent variable, a regression analysis can determine the correlation coefficient of the independent variable—that is, the degree to which variations in the independent variable cause changes in the dependent variable. *See also* dependent variable.

multiple-user system *n. See* multiuser system.

multiplexer *n.* A device for funneling several different streams of data over a common communications line. Multiplexers are used either to attach many communications lines to a smaller number of communications ports or to attach a large number of communications ports to a smaller number of communications lines. *Acronym:* MUX.

multiplexer channel *n.* One of the inputs to a multiplexer. *See also* multiplexer.

multiplexing *n.* A technique used in communications and input/output operations for transmitting a number of separate signals simultaneously over a single channel or line. To maintain the integrity of each signal on the channel, multiplexing can separate the signals by time, space, or frequency. The device used to combine the signals is a *multiplexer. See also* FDM, space-division multiplexing, time-division multiplexing.

multiplicand *n.* In arithmetic, the number that is multiplied by another number (the multiplier). In mathematics, the multiplicand and the multiplier are interchangeable, depending on how the problem is stated, because the result

M

is the same if the two are reversed—for example, 2 x 3 and 3 x 2. In arithmetic performed by computers, however, the multiplicand is different from the multiplier because computer multiplication is usually performed as addition. Therefore, 2 x 3 means "add 2 three times," whereas 3 x 2 means "add 3 two times." *See also* factor. *Compare* multiplier (definition 1).

multiplier *n.* **1.** In arithmetic, the number that indicates how many times another number (the multiplicand) is multiplied. *See also* factor. *Compare* multiplicand. **2.** In computing, an electronic device independent of the central processing unit (CPU) that performs multiplication by adding the multiplicand according to the value of the digits in the multiplier.

multipoint configuration *n.* A communications link in which multiple stations are connected sequentially to the same communications line. Typically, the communications line is controlled by a primary station, such as a computer, and the stations attached to the line are secondary. See the illustration.

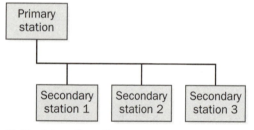

Multipoint configuration.

multiport repeater *n. See* active hub.

multiprocessing *n.* A mode of operation in which two or more connected and roughly equal processing units each carry out one or more processes (programs or sets of instructions) in tandem. In multiprocessing, each processing unit works on a different set of instructions or on different parts of the same process. The objective is increased speed or computing power, the same as in parallel processing and in the use of special units called *coprocessors*. *Compare* coprocessor, parallel processing.

multiprogramming *n.* A form of processing in which a computer holds more than one program in memory and works on them in round-robin fashion—that is, by sharing out the processor's time so that each program receives some

attention some of the time. This way of working is in contrast to using the processor to run one program at a time.

Multiprotocol Label Switching *n. See* MPLS.

Multi-Protocol Over ATM *n. See* MPOA.

Multipurpose Internet Mail Extensions *n. See* MIME.

Multipurpose Internet Mail Extensions HTML *n. See* MHTML.

multiscan monitor *n.* A computer monitor capable of adapting to different video frequencies to accommodate multiple screen resolutions and to support different video adapters and graphics display methods.

Multistation Access Unit *n. See* MAU.

multisystem network *n.* A communications network in which two or more host computers can be accessed by network users.

multitasking *n.* A form of processing supported by most current operating systems in which a computer works on multiple tasks—roughly, separate "pieces" of work—seemingly at the same time by parceling out the processor's time among the different tasks. Multitasking can be either cooperative or preemptive. In the former, the operating system relies on the task to voluntarily cede control to another task; in the latter, the operating system decides which task receives priority. *See also* background[1], context switching, cooperative multitasking, foreground[1], time slice.

multithreaded application *n.* A program capable of running more than one program thread simultaneously. *See also* multithreading (definition 1), thread (definition 1).

multithreading *n.* **1.** The running of several processes in rapid sequence (multitasking) within a single program. *See also* thread (definition 1). **2.** In data manipulation, a technique in which nodes in a tree data structure contain pointers to higher nodes to make traversal of the structure more efficient. *See also* thread (definition 2).

multi-tier *n. See* three-tier.

multiuser *n. See* multiuser system.

multiuser dungeon *n. See* MUD.

multiuser simulation environment *n. See* MUD.

multiuser system *n.* Any computer system that can be used by more than one person. Although a microcomputer shared by several people can be considered a multiuser system, the term is generally reserved for machines that can be accessed simultaneously by several people through communications facilities or via network terminals. *Compare* single-user computer.

multum in parvo mapping *n. See* MIP mapping.

MUMPS *n.* Acronym for **M**ass(achusetts) **U**tility **M**ulti **P**rogramming **S**ystem. An advanced, high-level programming language and integrated database developed in 1966 at Massachusetts General Hospital and used widely by health care businesses. A unique feature of MUMPS is its ability to store both data and program fragments in its database.

munging *n. See* address munging.

MUSE *n.* Short for **m**ultiuser **s**imulation environment. *See* MUD.

.museum *n.* One of seven new top-level domain names approved in 2000 by the Internet Corporation for Assigned Names and Numbers (ICANN), .museum is meant for use by museum Web sites.

Musical Instrument Digital Interface *n. See* MIDI.

mutual exclusion *n.* A programming technique that ensures that only one program or routine at a time can access some resource, such as a memory location, an I/O port, or a file, often through the use of semaphores, which are flags used in programs to coordinate the activities of more than one program or routine. *See also* semaphore.

MUX *n. See* multiplexer.

My Briefcase *n.* A Windows 9x utility, helpful for workers away from the office, that manages the updating of modified files once the remote user's computer is connected back on the office network.

Mylar *n.* A polyester film product created by DuPont, often used as the base for magnetically coated storage media (disks and tape) and for carbon ribbons used with impact printers.

Mylar ribbon *n. See* carbon ribbon.

MYOB *n.* Acronym for **M**ind **y**our **o**wn **b**usiness. An expression used in e-mail and newsgroups.

my two cents *n.* An expression used informally in newsgroup articles and, less frequently, e-mail messages or mailing lists, to indicate that the message is the writer's contribution to an ongoing discussion. *Also called:* $0.02. *See also* mailing list, newsgroup.

M

n *prefix* *See* nano-.

NACN *n.* *See* North American Cellular Network.

nagware *n.* Slang for computer shareware that, on starting or before closing, displays a prominent reminder to pay for the program. *See also* shareware.

NAK *n.* Acronym for **n**egative **ack**nowledgement. A control code, ASCII character 21 (hexadecimal 15), transmitted to a sending station or computer by the receiving unit as a signal that transmitted information has arrived incorrectly. *Compare* ACK.

NAK attack *n.* Acronym for **n**egative **ack**nowledgement **attack**. A hacker attack that uses the negative acknowledgement control code character to enter a seemingly secure system. A NAK attack uses weaknesses in the system handling NAK replies that may leave it temporarily unprotected. *See also* NAK.

naked PC *n.* A personal computer sold without an operating system (OS) installed. The purchaser of a naked PC must then choose and install an OS before the computer can be used. Naked PCs are chiefly purchased by users with some degree of expertise with computer equipment who may want to install a version of Linux or an offshoot OS. Computer and software manufacturers have expressed concern over the possibility of software piracy with the sale of naked PCs.

.name *n.* One of seven new top-level domain names approved in 2000 by the Internet Corporation for Assigned Names and Numbers (ICANN), .name is meant for registration by individuals for personal Web sites. The seven new domain names became available for use in the spring of 2001.

Name Binding Protocol *n.* *See* NBP.

named anchor *n.* In HTML, a tag within a document that can act as a destination for a hyperlink. Named anchors are useful because they allow a link to a specific location within a document. *Also called:* named target. *See also* anchor (definition 2), HTML, hyperlink.

named entity *n.* *See* character entity.

named pipes *n.* In programming, one-way (simplex) or two-way (duplex) connections used to transfer data between processes. Named pipes are portions of memory set aside for temporary data storage. They are created by server processes and can be used simultaneously by more than one client process, each accessing a separate instance with its own buffers and handles. Named pipes can be used to transfer data either locally or on a network.

named target *n.* *See* named anchor.

name server *n.* *See* CSO name server, DNS server.

namespace *n.* **1.** A grouping of one or more names that represent individual objects within the group in a shared computing environment, such as a network. The names within a namespace are unique, are created according to the same rules, and can be resolved into a particular identifying item of information, such as an IP address or a network device. A namespace can be either flat—a single collection of unique names—or hierarchical, as is the Internet's DNS (Domain Name System), which is based on a treelike structure that is refined through successive levels beginning with the root server and the Internet's top-level domains (.com, .net, .org, and so on). In everyday terms, a namespace is comparable to a telephone book, in which each name is unique and resolves to the phone number and address of a particular individual, business, or other entity. **2.** A means of identifying elements and attributes in an XML document by assigning them a two-part name with the first part being the namespace and the second part being the functional name. A namespace identifies a set of names to prevent confusion when multiple objects with identical functional names are taken from different sources and brought together in the same XML document. Namespaces typically reference a Uniform Resource Identifier (URI) because each URI will be unique.

name-value pair *n.* **1.** In the Perl programming language, a data set in which the data is associated with a name. *See also* Perl. **2.** In CGI programming, one of the data items collected from an HTML form by the browser and passed through the server to a CGI script for processing. *See also* CGI, CGI script, HTML.

naming container *n.* Any ASP.NET control that implements the INamingContainer interface. This is a marker interface that enables a control to create a new naming scope under itself so that ID attributes assigned to its child controls are unique within the entire ASP.NET page that contains the control.

NAMPS *n.* Acronym for **N**arrow-band **A**nalog **M**obile **P**hone Service. A standard proposed by Motorola Corporation that combines the current AMPS cellular telephone standard with digital signaling information, resulting in higher performance and increased capabilities. *See also* AMPS.

NAND *n.* Short for **NOT AND**. A logical operation that combines the values of two bits (0,1) or two Boolean values (false, true) that returns a value of 1 (or true) if one input value is 0 (or false), and returns a 0 (false) only if both inputs are true.

NAND gate *n.* Short for **NOT AND gate**. A digital circuit whose output is true (1) if any input is false (0). A NAND gate is an AND circuit (output with the value of 1 when all input values are 1) followed by a NOT circuit (output that is the logical complement of the input). Thus, NAND gate output is high if any of its inputs are low. *See also* AND gate, gate (definition 1), NOT gate.

nano- *prefix* Abbreviated n. Metric prefix meaning 10^{-9} (one billionth).

nanosecond *n.* One billionth of a second. A nanosecond is a time measure used to represent computing speed, particularly the speed at which electrical signals travel through circuits within the computer. *Acronym:* ns.

NAP *n. See* Network Access Point.

Napster *n.* An Internet music search application that allows users to search for and swap MP3 files over the Web. In response to a user request for a song or an artist, Napster searches the hard drives of all other Napster users on line. When the requested item is found, the file is downloaded to the computer making the request. Napster also includes a chat room and a library of most popular items. The introduction of Napster in 1999 sparked heated debate over copyright and digital distribution issues. *See also* MP3.

narrowband *n.* A bandwidth set aside by the FCC for mobile or portable radio services, such as advanced two-way paging systems, including transmission rates between 50 bps and 64 Kbps. Narrowband formerly referred to the bandwidth from 50 to 150 bps. *See also* bandwidth, FCC. *Compare* broadband.

narrowband ISDN *n.* Name used to distinguish current ISDN lines from the developing broadband ISDN technology. *See also* broadband ISDN, ISDN.

narrowcast *vb.* To transmit data or programming to a defined or limited area or audience. A cable television company narrowcasts its programs only to subscribers, whereas network television stations *broadcast* to everyone with reception equipment in their transmission range. On the Web, content delivered to users via push technology represents a form of narrowcasting. *See also* unicast. *Compare* broadcast (definition 2), multicasting.

Narrow SCSI *n.* A SCSI or SCSI-2 interface that can transfer data only 8 bits at a time. *See also* SCSI, SCSI-2. *Compare* Fast/Wide SCSI, Wide SCSI.

NAS *n.* Acronym for **N**etwork-**A**ttached **S**torage. A platform-independent storage appliance connected to a network. NAS uses a storage unit with a built-in server that can communicate with clients over a network. NAS devices are popular for ease of maintenance, manageability, and scalability. *Compare* SAN.

NAT *n.* Acronym for **N**etwork **A**ddress **T**ranslation. The process of converting between IP addresses used within an intranet or other private network and Internet IP addresses. This approach makes it possible to use a large number of addresses within the private network without depleting the limited number of available numeric Internet IP addresses. Variations of NAT displaying similar functions include IP aliasing, IP masquerading, and Port Address Translation.

national attachment point *n. See* Network Access Point.

National Center for Supercomputing Applications *n. See* NCSA (definition 1).

National Committee for Information Technology Standards *n.* A committee formed by the Information Technology Industry Council to develop national standards for use in the information technology industry and to promote those standards for international use. *Acronym:* NCITS.

National Computer Security Association *n. See* ICSA.

N

357

National Information Infrastructure *n.* A U.S. government program to extend and oversee the development of the Information Superhighway. The National Information Infrastructure is made up of a high-bandwidth, wide area network that can carry data, fax, video, and voice transmissions to users throughout the United States. The network is being developed mostly by private carriers. Many of the services, which are aimed at enabling the efficient creation and dissemination of information, are already available on the Internet itself, including increased accessibility to quality education through distance learning and increased access to government services. *Acronym:* NII. *See also* Information Superhighway, Internet2, Next Generation Internet. *Compare* Internet.

National Institute of Standards and Technology *n.* A branch of the U.S. Commerce Department that works to develop and encourage standards for measurement, science, and technology in order to promote commerce and improve productivity in the marketplace. Prior to 1988, the National Institute of Standards and Technology was known as the National Bureau of Standards. *Acronym:* NIST.

national language support *n.* **1.** The practice of creating programs that can display text in any language necessary. **2.** A function in Windows that enables you to specify system and user locale information. *Acronym:* NLS.

National Science Foundation *n.* A U.S. government agency intended to promote scientific research by funding both research projects and projects that facilitate scientific communication, such as NSFnet, the former backbone of the Internet. *Acronym:* NSF. *See also* backbone (definition 1), NSFnet.

National Television System Committee *n. See* NTSC.

native *adj.* Of, pertaining to, or characteristic of something that is in its original form. For example, many applications are able to work with files in a number of formats; the format the application uses internally is its native file format. Files in other formats must be converted to the application's native format before they can be processed by the application.

native application *n.* A program that is designed specifically for a particular type of microprocessor, that is, a program that is binary compatible with a processor. A native application generally will run much faster than a nonnative application, which must be run with the help of an emulator program. *See also* binary compatibility, emulator.

native code *n.* Code that has been compiled to processor-specific machine code.

native compiler *n.* A compiler that produces machine code for the computer on which it is running, as opposed to a cross-compiler, which produces code for another type of computer. Most compilers are native compilers. *See also* compiler (definition 2), cross-compiler.

native file format *n.* The format an application uses internally to process data. The application must convert files in other formats to the native format before it can work with them. For example, a word processor might recognize text files in ASCII text format, but it will convert them to its own native format before it displays them.

native language *n. See* host language.

natural language *n.* A language spoken or written by humans, as opposed to a programming language or a machine language. Understanding natural language and approximating it in a computer environment is one goal of research in artificial intelligence.

natural-language processing *n.* A field of computer science and linguistics that studies computer systems that can recognize and react to human language, either spoken or written. *See also* artificial intelligence. *Compare* speech recognition.

natural language query *n.* A query to a database system that is composed in a subset of a natural language, such as English or Japanese. The query must conform to some restrictive syntax rules so that the system can parse it. *See also* parse, syntax.

natural-language recognition *n. See* speech recognition.

natural language support *n.* A voice recognition system that allows the user to use verbal commands in his or her own language to direct a computer's actions. *Acronym:* NLS.

natural number *n.* An integer, or whole number, that is equal to or greater than zero. *See also* integer.

navigation bar *n.* On a Web page, a grouping of hyperlinks for getting around in that particular Web site. *See also* hyperlink.

navigation keys *n.* The keys on a keyboard controlling cursor movement, including the four arrow keys and the Backspace, End, Home, Page Down, and Page Up keys. *See also* arrow key, Backspace key, End key, Home key, Page Down key, Page Up key.

Navigator *n. See* Netscape Navigator.

NBP *n.* Acronym for **N**ame **B**inding **P**rotocol. A protocol used on AppleTalk local area networks to translate between node names (known to users) and numeric Apple-Talk addresses. NBP operates at the transport level (level 4 of the ISO/OSI reference model). *See also* AppleTalk, communications protocol, ISO/OSI reference model.

NC *n. See* network computer.

NCC *n. See* network-centric computing.

N-channel MOS *n. See* NMOS.

NCITS *n. See* National Committee for Information Technology Standards.

NCP *n. See* Point-to-Point Protocol.

NCR paper *n.* Short for **n**o **c**arbon **r**equired **paper**. A special paper used for multipart forms. NCR paper is impregnated with a chemical that darkens it when pressure is applied. *See also* multipart forms.

NCSA *n.* **1.** Acronym for **N**ational **C**enter for **S**upercomputing **A**pplications. A research center located at the University of Illinois at Urbana-Champaign. NCSA was founded in 1985 as a part of the National Science Foundation, specializing in scientific visualization tasks, but is best known as the home of NCSA Mosaic, the first graphical Web browser, and of NCSA Telnet. *See also* Mosaic, NCSA Telnet. **2.** *See* ICSA.

NCSA Mosaic *n. See* Mosaic.

NCSA server *n.* The HTTP server developed by the National Center for Supercomputing Applications of the University of Illinois. This server and the CERN server were the first HTTP servers developed for the World Wide Web and are available free through downloading. *See also* HTTP server (definition 1), NCSA (definition 1). *Compare* CERN server.

NCSA Telnet *n.* A freeware telnet client program developed and distributed by the National Center for Supercomputing Applications. *See also* client (definition 2), NCSA (definition 1).

NDIS *n.* Acronym for **N**etwork **D**river **I**nterface **S**pecification, a software interface, or set of rules, designed to enable different network protocols to communicate with a variety of network adapters. Providing a standard—a common "language"—for the drivers used by network adapters, NDIS enables a single network adapter to support multiple protocols and, conversely, also enables a single

protocol to work with network adapters from different vendors. *See also* device driver.

NDMP *n.* Acronym for **N**etwork **D**ata **M**anagement **Pro**tocol. An open protocol for network-based backups of file servers that allows platform-independent data storage. *See also* backup, communications protocol, file server.

NDR *n. See* nondestructive readout.

NDRO *n. See* nondestructive readout.

NDS *n.* Acronym for **N**ovell **D**irectory **S**ervices. A feature introduced in Novell Netware 4.0 that provides access to directories that may be located on one or more servers.

near-letter-quality *adj.* A print mode on high-end dot-matrix printers that produces clearer, darker characters than normal (draft-quality) printing. Near-letter-quality printing, although it is sharper than plain dot-matrix printing, is not as legible as output from a fully-formed-character printer, such as a daisy-wheel printer. *Acronym:* NLQ. *See also* print quality. *Compare* draft quality, letter quality.

negation *n.* The conversion of a two-state (binary) signal or bit pattern to its opposite state—for example, the conversion of 1001 to 0110.

negative acknowledgement *n. See* NAK.

negative entry *n.* The act of assigning a negative sign to a number that has been entered into a calculator, thereby transforming the number to a negative number.

nest *vb.* To embed one construct inside another. For example, a database may contain a nested table (a table within a table), a program may contain a nested procedure (a procedure declared within a procedure), and a data structure may include a nested record (a record containing a field that is itself a record).

nested transaction *n.* In programming, an operation or sequence of operations taking place within a larger transaction. A nested transaction can be aborted without requiring abortion of the larger transaction. *Also called:* subtransaction. *See also* nest.

.net *n.* In the Internet's Domain Name System, the top-level domain that identifies addresses of network providers. The designation .net appears at the end of the address. *See also* DNS (definition 1), domain (definition 3). *Compare* .com, .edu, .gov, .mil, .org.

net.- *prefix* A prefix used to describe people and institutions on the Internet. For example, a very well respected person might be described as a net.god.

N

Net *n.* **1.** Short for Inter**net**. **2.** Short for Use**net**.

.NET *n.* The set of Microsoft technologies that provides tools for connecting information, people, systems, and devices. The technologies provide individuals and organizations with the ability to build, host, deploy, and use XML Web service connected solutions.

net address *n.* **1.** A World Wide Web address (URL). *See also* URL. **2.** An e-mail address. **3.** The DNS name or IP address of a machine. *See also* DNS (definition 1), IP address. **4.** The address, burned into a network adapter, that is used to uniquely identify a node on a network. *See also* network interface card.

NetBEUI *n.* Short for **NetB**IOS **E**xtended **U**ser **I**nterface. NetBEUI is a network protocol created by IBM and now used by Microsoft, HP, and Compaq. It is usually used in small, department-size local area networks (LANs) of 1 to 200 clients. It can use Token Ring source routing as its only method of routing. It is the extended version of the NetBIOS standard. *See also* CCP, communications protocol, LAN, NetBIOS.

NetBIOS *n.* An application programming interface (API) that can be used by application programs on a local area network consisting of IBM and compatible microcomputers running MS-DOS, OS/2, or some version of UNIX. Primarily of interest to programmers, NetBIOS provides application programs with a uniform set of commands for requesting the lower-level network services required to conduct sessions between nodes on a network and to transmit information back and forth. *See also* application programming interface.

NetBIOS Extended User Interface *n. See* NetBEUI.

net boot *n. See* PXE boot.

NetBSD *n.* A free version of the BSD UNIX operating system developed as a result of a volunteer effort. NetBSD is highly interoperable, runs on many hardware platforms, and is nearly POSIX compliant. *See also* BSD UNIX, POSIX.

Netcaster *n. See* netcasting (definition 2).

netcasting *n.* **1.** Synonym for webcasting. **2.** A Netscape technology used in Netscape Netcaster that enabled a user to subscribe to channels that pushed Web content to the user's desktop without actively retrieving the information. Netscape Netcaster, which was part of previous versions of Netscape Navigator, competed with Microsoft Active Desktop. Unlike Active Desktop, which uses Microsoft's

Channel Definition Format (CDF), the Netcaster push client was based on existing open standards (HTML, Java, and JavaScript). See also push (definition 2). *Compare* Active Desktop.

.NET Compact Framework *n.* A hardware-independent environment for running programs on resource-constrained computing devices. It inherits the full .NET Framework architecture of the common language runtime, supports a subset of the .NET Framework class library, and contains classes designed exclusively for the .NET Compact Framework. Supported devices include personal data assistants (PDAs) (such as the Pocket PC), mobile phones, set-top boxes, automotive computing devices, and custom-designed embedded devices built with the Microsoft Windows CE operating system.

.NET data provider *n.* A component of ADO.NET that provides access to data from a relational database.

netfilter *n.* The packet-filtering system for Linux introduced in the 2.4 kernel. Netfilter is the first stateful firewall implemented in Linux. *See also* firewall, iptables. *Compare* IP Filter.

NetFind *n. See* AOL NetFind.

.NET Framework *n.* A platform for building, deploying, and running XML Web services and applications. It provides a highly productive, standards-based, multilanguage environment for integrating existing investments with next generation applications and services, as well as the agility to solve the challenges of deployment and operation of Internet-scale applications. The .NET Framework consists of three main parts: the common language runtime, a hierarchical set of unified class libraries, and a componentized version of ASP called ASP.NET. *See also* ASP.NET, common language runtime, .NET Framework class library.

.NET Framework class library *n.* A Common Language Specification (CLS)–compliant library of classes, interfaces, and value types that are included in the Microsoft .NET Framework SDK. This library provides access to system functionality and is designed to be the foundation on which .NET Framework applications, components, and controls are built.

.NET Framework data provider *n.* A component of ADO.NET that provides access to data from a relational data source. A .NET Framework data provider contains classes to connect to a data source, execute commands at the data source, and return query results from the data source, including the ability to execute commands within transactions. A .NET Framework data provider also contains classes to populate a DataSet with results from a data source and propagate changes in a DataSet back to the data source.

net.god *n.* A highly respected person within the Internet community.

nethead *n.* **1.** A person who uses the Internet as if addicted to it. **2.** A Grateful Dead fan who participates in the rec.music.gdead newsgroup or some other forum dedicated to that band.

netiquette *n.* Short for **net**work e**tiquette**. Principles of courtesy observed in sending electronic messages, such as e-mail and Usenet postings. The consequences of violating netiquette include being flamed and having one's name placed in the bozo filter of one's intended audience. Disapproved behavior includes gratuitous personal insults; posting of large amounts of irrelevant material; giving away the plot of a movie, television show, or novel without warning; posting offensive material without encrypting it; and excessive cross-posting of a message to multiple groups without regard to whether the group members are likely to find it interesting. *See also* bozo filter, flame[2].

netizen *n.* A person who participates in online communication through the Internet and other networks, especially conference and chat services, such as Internet news or Fidonet. *Compare* lurker.

NetMeeting *n.* A software application developed by Microsoft Corporation to allow video conferencing among parties using personal computers connected via the Internet. NetMeeting allows participants in different locations to view each other, engage in text chat conversations, send and receive videos, exchange information graphically via an electronic whiteboard, share Windows-based applications, and transfer files.

.NET Messenger Service *n.* A popular instant-messaging service provided by Microsoft as part of the .NET strategy. With .NET Messenger Service, formerly called MSN Messenger Service, users can communicate using the Windows Messenger, included in Windows XP, or MSN Messenger applications. *See also* instant messaging. *Compare* AIM, ICQ, Yahoo! Messenger.

.NET My Services *n.* A suite of XML Web services for managing and protecting personal information and interactions across applications, devices, and services. Formerly code-named HailStorm, .NET My Services is based on the Microsoft .NET Passport user-authentication system. The suite of .NET My Services includes services such as .NET ApplicationSettings, .NET Calendar, .NET Contacts, .NET Devices, .NET Documents, .NET Inbox, .NET Locations, .NET Profile, and .NET Wallet. *See also* .NET, Passport.

NetPC *n.* Short for **Net**work **PC**. An industry-defined, Windows-based PC system that is small and meant to act as simply an access point. These PCs generally have very small hard drives, no disk drives, and are built to have a very low cost. Some older NetPCs can boot through remote access to a server and user server-based resources for most computing actions.

net.personality *n.* A slang term for a person who has attained some degree of celebrity on the Internet.

net.police *n.* Persons (usually self-appointed) who try to enforce their understanding of the "rules" that apply to conduct on the Internet. Their activities may be directed toward users who violate the rules of netiquette, spammers who send unsolicited advertising as e-mail or to newsgroups, or even people who post "politically incorrect" comments to newsgroups or mailing lists. *See also* netiquette, spam.

Netscape Navigator *n.* The widely used family of Web browser programs, made by Netscape Corporation. Versions of Netscape Navigator are available for the Windows and Macintosh platforms, and for many varieties of UNIX. Netscape Navigator, which is based on NCSA's Mosaic Web browser, was one of the first commercially available Web browsers. In 1999, Netscape Corporation was purchased by America Online. *See also* Mosaic, Web browser.

Netscape Netcaster *n. See* netcasting (definition 2).

Netscape Server Application Programming Interface *n. See* NSAPI.

Netspeak *n.* The set of conventions for writing English in e-mail, IRCs, and newsgroups. Netspeak is characterized by acronyms (such as IMHO or ROFL) and clarifying devices such as emotags and emoticons. Use of Netspeak should be governed by netiquette. *See also* emotag, emoticon, IMHO, IRC, netiquette, ROFL.

netspionage *n.* Corporate-sponsored hacking of a competitor's digital information for the theft of trade secrets.

Net surfing *n.* The practice of exploring the Internet without a specific goal in mind. The concept of Net surfing is similar to (and probably derived from) "channel surfing" in reference to watching television.

Net TV *n. See* Internet television.

NetWare *n.* A family of LAN (local area network) operating system products developed by Novell, Inc. Designed to run on PCs and Macintoshes, Novell NetWare allows users to share files and system resources such as hard disks and printers. *See also* network operating system.

network *n.* A group of computers and associated devices that are connected by communications facilities. A network can involve permanent connections, such as cables, or temporary connections made through telephone or other communication links. A network can be as small as a LAN (local area network) consisting of a few computers, printers, and other devices, or it can consist of many small and large computers distributed over a vast geographic area (WAN, or wide area network). *See also* ALOHAnet, Ethernet (definition 1), LAN, WAN.

Network Access Point *n.* One of the interchange points for Internet traffic, where various Internet network carriers and major ISPs exchange data. When Internet traffic originates on one network and goes to another network, it almost always passes through at least one Network Access Point, or NAP. In the United States, major NAPs include MAE East, in Vienna, Virginia, and MAE West, in San Jose, California (both operated by MCI WorldCom); the Chicago NAP (operated by Ameritech); the Pacific Bell NAP (with multiple locations in California); the Digital Internet Exchange in Palo Alto, California (operated by Digital/Compaq); and the Sprint NAP in Pennsauken, New Jersey. Additional local and regional exchange points are located in many other locations around the world. *Acronym:* NAP. *Also called:* National Attachment Point.

network adapter *n. See* network interface card.

Network Address Translation *n. See* NAT.

network administrator *n.* The person in charge of operations on a computer network. The duties of a network administrator can be broad and might include such tasks as installing new workstations and other devices, adding and removing individuals from the list of authorized users, archiving files, overseeing password protection and other security measures, monitoring usage of shared resources, and handling malfunctioning equipment. *See also* system administrator.

network architecture *n.* The underlying structure of a computer network, including hardware, functional layers, interfaces, and protocols, used to establish communication and ensure the reliable transfer of information. Network architectures are designed to provide both philosophical and physical standards for the complexities of establishing communications links and transferring information without conflict. Various network architectures exist, including the internationally accepted seven-layer ISO Open Systems Interconnection (OSI) model and IBM's Systems Network Architecture (SNA). *See also* ISO/OSI reference model, SNA.

Network-Attached Storage *n. See* NAS.

network boot *n. See* PXE boot.

network card *n. See* network interface card.

network-centric computing *n.* A computing environment in which a network server or servers represent the hub of activity. Considered the "third wave" in large-system computing after mainframe and desktop developments, network-centric computing establishes servers as the main source of computing power, to give users direct access to network-based applications and information. In network-centric computing systems, applications are not preinstalled or uninstalled locally, that is, on the desktop; they are accessed on an as-needed, "on-the-fly" basis. Thus, individual desktop computers do not have to maintain large amounts of disk storage or load and manage application programs. *See also* server.

network computer *n.* A computer designed for use on a network in which programs and storage are provided by servers. Network computers, unlike dumb terminals, have their own processing power, but their design does not include local storage and they depend on network servers for applications. *Acronym:* NC.

network congestion *n. See* congestion.

network connection *n. See* Ethernet.

network control program *n.* In a communications network that includes a mainframe computer, a program that usually resides in a communications controller and takes over communications tasks such as routing, error control, line control, and polling (checking terminals for transmissions), leaving the main computer free for other functions. *See also* communications controller.

Network Control Protocol *n. See* Point-to-Point Protocol.

network database *n.* **1.** A database that runs in a network. **2.** A database containing the address of other users in the network. **3.** In information management, a type of database in which data records can be related to one another in more than one way. A network database is similar to a hierarchical database in the sense that it contains a progression from one record to another. It differs in being less rigidly structured: any single record can point to more than one other record and, conversely, can be pointed to by one or more records. In effect, a network database allows more than one path between any two records, whereas a hierarchical database allows only one, from parent (higher-level record) to child (lower-level record). *Compare* hierarchical database, relational database.

Network Data Management Protocol *n. See* NDMP.

network device driver *n.* Software that coordinates communication between the network adapter card and the computer's hardware and other software, controlling the physical function of the network adapter card.

network directory *n.* On a local area network, a directory on a disk that is located on a computer other than the one the user is operating. A network directory differs from a network drive in that the user has access to only that directory. Whether the rest of the disk is accessible to the user depends on whether he or she has been granted access rights by the network administrator. On the Macintosh, a network directory is referred to as a shared folder. *Also called:* networked directory, shared directory. *See also* network drive, shared folder.

network drive *n.* On a local area network, a disk drive whose disk is available to other computers on the network. Access to a network drive might not be allowed to all users of the network; many operating systems contain security provisions that enable a network administrator to grant or deny access to part or all of a network drive. *Also called:* networked drive. *See also* network directory.

Network Driver Interface Specification *n. See* NDIS.

networked directory *n. See* network directory.

networked drive *n. See* network drive.

networked home *n. See* smart home.

Network File System *n. See* NFS.

network information center *n. See* NIC (definition 2).

network interface card *n.* An expansion card or other device used to provide network access to a computer or other device, such as a printer. Network interface cards

mediate between the computer and the physical media, such as cabling, over which transmissions travel. *Acronym:* NIC. *Also called:* network adapter, network card.

Network Kernel Extension *n. See* NKE.

network latency *n.* The time it takes for information to be transferred between computers in a network.

network layer *n.* The third of the seven layers in the ISO/OSI reference model for standardizing computer-to-computer communications. The network layer is one level above the data-link layer and ensures that information arrives at its intended destination. It is the middle of the three layers (data-link, network, and transport) concerned with the actual movement of information from one device to another. See the illustration. *See also* ISO/OSI reference model.

ISO/OSI MODEL	
ISO/OSI Layer	**Focus**
Application (*highest level*)	Program-to-program transfer of information
Presentation	Text formatting and display, code conversion
Session	Establishing, maintaining, and coordinating communication
Transport	Accurate delivery, service quality
Network	Transport routes, message handling and transfer
Data-link	Coding, addressing, and transmitting information
Physical	Hardware connections

Network layer.

network meltdown *n. See* broadcast storm, meltdown.

network model *n.* A database structure, or layout, similar to a hierarchical model, except that records can have multiple parent records as well as multiple child records. A database management system that supports a network model can be used to simulate a hierarchical model. *See also* CODASYL, network database (definition 3). *Compare* hierarchical model.

network modem *n.* A modem that is shared by users of a network for calling an online service provider, an ISP, a service bureau, or other online source. *See also* ISP, modem online information service, service bureau (definition 2).

network news *n.* The newsgroups on the Internet, especially those in the Usenet hierarchy.

Network News Transfer Protocol *n. See* NNTP.

network operating system *n.* An operating system specifically designed to support networking. A server-based network operating system provides networking support for multiple simultaneous users as well as administrative, security, and management functions. On the desktop, a network-aware operating system provides users with the ability to access network resources. Unlike a single-user operating system, a network operating system must acknowledge and respond to requests from many workstations, managing such details as network access and communications, resource allocation and sharing, data protection, and error control. *Acronym:* NOS. *Also called:* network OS.

network operation center *n.* The office in an enterprise that is responsible for maintaining network integrity and improving network efficiency while reducing system downtime. *Acronym:* NOC.

network OS *n. See* network operating system.

network protocol *n.* A set of rules and parameters that defines and enables communication through a network.

Network Query Language *n.* A scripting language for controlling intelligent agents for Web applications. *Acronym:* NQL.

network server *n. See* server.

network services *n.* **1.** In a corporate environment, the division that maintains the network and the computers. **2.** In a Windows environment, extensions to the operating system that allow it to perform network functions such as network printing and file sharing.

network software *n.* Software including a component that facilitates connection to or participation in a network.

Network Solutions, Inc. *n. See* NSI.

network structure *n.* The record organization used in a particular network model.

Network Terminator 1 *n.* An ISDN device that acts as an interface between an ISDN telephone line and one or more terminal adapters or terminal devices, such as an ISDN telephone. *Acronym:* NT-1. *See also* ISDN, ISDN terminal adapter.

Network Time Protocol *n.* An Internet protocol used to synchronize the clocks in computers connected to the Internet. *Acronym:* NTP. *See also* communications protocol.

network topology *n. See* topology.

network weaving *n. See* leapfrog attack.

NetWorld+Interop *n.* International conference and exhibition for the networking and information technology industry. NetWorld+Interop draws attendees from a variety of industries, including telecommunications, Internet services, and e-commerce. NetWorld+Interop features product exhibits, educational conferences, tutorials, and workshops.

NeuralCast Technology *n.* Technology developed by RealNetworks to improve the transmission of digital media over RealNetworks servers. NeuralCast Technology uses a variety of protocols, introduces new techniques to correct errors in streaming signals, and uses telephone and satellite transmissions to coordinate server networks to optimize digital media transmission.

neural network *n.* A type of artificial-intelligence system modeled after the neurons (nerve cells) in a biological nervous system and intended to simulate the way a brain processes information, learns, and remembers. A neural network is designed as an interconnected system of processing elements, each with a limited number of inputs and an output. These processing elements are able to "learn" by receiving weighted inputs that, with adjustment, time, and repetition, can be made to produce appropriate outputs. Neural networks are used in areas such as pattern recognition, speech analysis, and speech synthesis. *See also* artificial intelligence (definition 1), pattern recognition.

newbie *n.* **1.** An inexperienced user on the Internet. **2.** In a particularly derogatory sense, an inexperienced Usenet user who asks for information that is readily available in the FAQ. *See also* FAQ.

newline character *n.* A control character that causes the cursor on a display or the printing mechanism on a printer to move to the beginning of the next line. It is functionally equivalent to a combination of the carriage return (CR) and linefeed (LF) characters. *Acronym:* NL. *See also* carriage return, linefeed.

news *n.* The Internet protocol for retrieving files from an Internet newsgroup. You can create hyperlinks to newsgroups using news://.

news.announce.newusers *n.* A newsgroup that contains general information for new users about using Internet newsgroups.

newsfeed or **news feed** *n.* Deliveries, exchanges, or distributions of newsgroup articles to and from news servers. Newsfeeds are accomplished through cooperating news servers, which communicate via NNTP through network connections. *Also called:* feed. *See also* newsgroup, news server, NNTP.

newsgroup *n.* A forum on the Internet for threaded discussions on a specified range of subjects. A newsgroup consists of articles and follow-up posts. An article with all of its follow-up posts—which are (supposed to be) related to the specific subject named in the original article's subject line—constitutes a thread. Each newsgroup has a name that consists of a series of words, separated by periods, indicating the newsgroup's subject in terms of increasingly narrow categories, such as rec.crafts.textiles.needlework. Some newsgroups can be read and posted to only on one site; others, such as those in the seven Usenet hierarchies or those in ClariNet, circulate throughout the Internet. *See also* article, bit. newsgroups, ClariNet, follow-up, Great Renaming, local newsgroups, mail reflector, threaded discussion, traditional newsgroup hierarchy, Usenet. *Compare* mailing list.

newsmaster *n.* The person in charge of maintaining the Internet news server at a particular host. Sending e-mail to "newsmaster@domain.name" is the standard way to reach a given newsmaster.

news. newsgroups *n.* Usenet newsgroups that are part of the news. hierarchy and begin with "news." These newsgroups cover topics that deal with Usenet itself, such as Usenet policy and the creation of new Usenet newsgroups. *See also* newsgroup, traditional newsgroup hierarchy, Usenet. *Compare* comp. newsgroups, misc. newsgroups, rec. newsgroups, sci. newsgroups, soc. newsgroups, talk. newsgroups.

.newsrc *n.* The file extension that identifies a setup file for UNIX-based newsreaders. The setup file typically contains a current list of newsgroups that the user subscribes to and the articles in each newsgroup that the user has already read. *See also* newsreader, setup (definition 2).

newsreader *n.* A Usenet client program that enables a user to subscribe to Usenet newsgroups, read articles, post follow-ups, reply by e-mail, and post articles. Many Web browsers also provide these functions. *See also* article, e-mail (definition 1), follow-up, newsgroup, Usenet, Web browser.

news server *n.* A computer or program that exchanges Internet newsgroups with newsreader clients and other servers. *See also* newsgroup, newsreader.

Newton *n.* A personal digital assistant (PDA) developed by Apple Computer, Inc. *See also* PDA.

Newton OS *n.* The operating system that controls the Newton MessagePad personal digital assistant (PDA). *See also* PDA.

NeXT *n.* A computer designed and produced by NeXT Computer, Inc. (later NeXT Software, Inc.), a computer manufacturer and software developer founded in 1985 by Steven Jobs. NeXT was purchased by Apple Computer in 1997.

Next Generation Internet *n.* An initiative funded by the U.S. federal government designed to develop faster, more powerful networking technologies than are available on the current global Internet. The Next Generation Internet, or NGI, was begun in 1997 under the auspices of a number of government agencies, including DARPA (Defense Advanced Research Projects Agency), NASA (National Aeronautics & Space Administration), and the NSF (National Science Foundation). Its objective is to develop advanced networking technologies and to demonstrate them on university and government test networks running 100 to 1000 times faster than the current Internet. The technologies developed are intended for eventual use by schools, businesses, and the general public. *Acronym:* NGI. *Compare* Internet, Internet2.

NFS *n.* Acronym for **N**etwork **F**ile **S**ystem. A distributed file system that allows users to access remote files and directories on a network as if they were local. NFS is compatible with Microsoft Windows and UNIX-based systems, including Linux and Mac OS X.

NGI *n. See* Next Generation Internet.

nibble or **nybble** *n.* Half a byte (4 bits). *Compare* quadbit.

NIC *n.* **1.** *See* network interface card. **2.** Acronym for **n**etwork **i**nformation **c**enter. An organization that provides information about a network and other support to users of the network. The principal NIC for the Internet is Inter-NIC. Intranets and other private networks may have their own NICs. *See also* InterNIC.

NiCad battery *n. See* nickel cadmium battery.

N

NIC handle *n. See* handle.

nickel cadmium battery *n.* A rechargeable battery that uses an alkaline electrolyte. Nickel cadmium batteries typically have a longer operating life and storage life than similar lead-acid batteries. *Also called:* NiCad battery. *Compare* lead ion battery, lithium ion battery, nickel metal hydride battery.

nickel metal hydride battery *n.* A rechargeable battery that offers longer life and superior performance compared with similar nickel cadmium or other alkaline batteries. *Also called:* NiMH battery. *Compare* lead ion battery, lithium ion battery, nickel cadmium battery.

nickname *n.* A name used in the destination field of an e-mail editor in place of one or more complete network addresses. For example "Fred" might be a nickname for fred@history.washington.edu. If the nickname has been established within the program, a user need only type "Fred" instead of the entire address, or perhaps "history faculty" instead of all the individual faculty addresses. *See also* alias (definition 2).

NIDS *n.* Acronym for **n**etwork-based **i**ntrusion-**d**etection **S**ystem. A type of intrusion detection system (IDS) that analyzes the individual packets moving across a network. NIDS can detect packets that a firewall might not catch. *See also* IDS.

NII *n. See* National Information Infrastructure.

nil pointer *n. See* null pointer.

Nimda worm *n.* A persistent worm that can slow or freeze mail servers, take control of Web pages, and infect systems through several different means. The Nimda worm spreads as an attached file through e-mail, through an Internet scan for vulnerable Web servers, through a JavaScript on an infected Web page, or through network sharing. The Nimda worm first appeared in 2001, with several variants following the original version.

NiMH battery *n. See* nickel metal hydride battery.

nine's complement *n.* A number in the base-10 (decimal) system that is the complement of another number. It is derived by subtracting each digit of the number to be complemented from 1 less than the base. For example, the nine's complement of 64 is 35—the number derived by subtracting 6 from 9 and 4 from 9. *See also* complement.

NIS *n.* Acronym for **N**etwork **I**nformation **S**ervice. *See* Yellow Pages (definition 1).

NIST *n. See* National Institute of Standards and Technology.

*NIX *n.* Slang for any UNIX-related operating system, or all UNIX-related operating systems. *NIX typically refers to UNIX and Linux, and may also include Mac OS X.

nixpub *n.* A list of ISPs (Internet service providers) available in the newsgroups comp.bbs.misc and alt.bbs. *See also* ISP.

NKE *n.* Acronym for **N**etwork **K**ernel **E**xtension. A modification or extension of the Mac OS X networking infrastructure. NKEs may be loaded or unloaded dynamically, without recompiling the kernel or without the need to reboot the system. NKEs allow the creation and configuration of protocol stacks and modules that may monitor or modify network traffic or add other networking features to the kernel.

NL *n. See* newline character.

NLQ *n. See* near-letter-quality.

NLS *n. See* natural language support.

NMI *n. See* nonmaskable interrupt.

NMOS or **N-MOS** *n.* Acronym for **N**-channel **m**etal-**o**xide **s**emiconductor. A semiconductor technology in which the conduction channel in MOSFETs is formed by the movement of electrons rather than holes (electron "vacancies" created as electrons move from atom to atom). Because electrons move faster than holes, NMOS is faster than PMOS, although it is more difficult and more expensive to fabricate. *See also* MOS, MOSFET, N-type semiconductor. *Compare* CMOS, PMOS.

NNTP *n.* Acronym for **N**etwork **N**ews **T**ransfer **P**rotocol. A de facto protocol standard on the Internet used to distribute news articles and query news servers.

NOC *n. See* network operation center.

node *n.* **1.** A junction of some type. **2.** In networking, a device, such as a client computer, a server, or a shared printer, that is connected to the network and is capable of communicating with other network devices. **3.** In tree structures, a location on the tree that can have links to one or more nodes below it. Some authors make a distinction between node and element, with an element being a given data type and a node comprising one or more elements as well as any supporting data structures. *See also* element (definition 1), graph, pointer (definition 1), queue, stack, tree.

noise *n.* **1.** Any interference that affects the operation of a device. **2.** Unwanted electrical signals, produced either naturally or by the circuitry, that distort or degrade the quality or performance of a communications channel. *See also* distortion.

nonbreaking space *n.* A character that replaces the standard space character in order to keep two words together on one line rather than allowing a line to break between them.

noncompetes *n.* An agreement between employer and employee that states that the employee will not accept work with a competing company for a specified length of time after leaving the employer's company. Noncompete agreements are common in high-tech companies and are typically requested to help maintain company secrets and retain valuable employees.

nonconductor *n. See* insulator.

noncontiguous data structure *n.* In programming, a data structure whose elements are not stored contiguously in memory. Data structures such as graphs and trees, whose elements are connected by pointers, are noncontiguous data structures. *Compare* contiguous data structure.

nondedicated server *n.* A computer on a network that can function as both a client and a server; typically, a desktop machine on a peer-to-peer network. *Compare* dedicated server.

nondestructive readout *n.* A reading operation that does not destroy the data read, either because the storage technology is capable of retaining the data or because the reading operation is accompanied by a data refresh (update) function. *Acronym:* NDR, NDRO. *Compare* destructive read.

nonexecutable statement *n.* **1.** A program statement that cannot be executed because it lies outside the flow of execution through the program. For example, a statement immediately following a *return( )* statement but before the end of the block in C is nonexecutable. **2.** A type definition, variable declaration, preprocessor command, comment, or other statement in a program that is not translated into executable machine code.

nonimpact printer *n.* Any printer that makes marks on the paper without striking it mechanically. The most common types are ink-jet, thermal, and laser printers. *See also* ink-jet printer, laser printer, thermal printer. *Compare* impact printer.

noninterlaced *adj.* Pertaining to a display method on raster-scan monitors in which the electron beam scans each line of the screen once during each refresh cycle. *Compare* interlaced.

nonmaskable interrupt *n.* A hardware interrupt that bypasses and takes priority over interrupt requests generated by software and by the keyboard and other such devices. A nonmaskable interrupt cannot be overruled (masked) by another service request and is issued to the microprocessor only in disastrous circumstances, such as severe memory errors or impending power failures. *Acronym:* NMI. *Compare* maskable interrupt.

nonprocedural language *n.* A programming language that does not follow the procedural paradigm of executing statements, subroutine calls, and control structures sequentially but instead describes a set of facts and relationships and then is queried for specific results. *Compare* procedural language.

nonreturn to zero *n.* **1.** In data transmission, a method of encoding data in which the signal representing binary digits alternates between positive and negative voltage when there is a change in digits from 1 to 0 or vice versa. In other words, the signal does not return to a zero, or neutral, level after transmission of each bit. Timing is used to distinguish one bit from the next. **2.** In the recording of data on a magnetic surface, a method in which one magnetic state represents a 1 and, usually, the opposite state represents a 0. *Acronym:* NRZ.

nontrivial *adj.* Being either difficult or particularly meaningful. For example, a complicated programmed procedure to handle a difficult problem would represent a nontrivial solution.

Non-Uniform Memory Access *n. See* NUMA.

nonuniform memory architecture *n.* A system architecture designed for Sequent's Non-Uniform Access Memory, a type of distributed shared memory using a number of shared memory segments instead of a single centralized physical memory. *Acronym:* NUMA.

nonvolatile memory *n.* A storage system that does not lose data when power is removed from it. Intended to refer to core memory, ROM, EPROM, flash memory, bubble memory, or battery-backed CMOS RAM, the term is occasionally used in reference to disk subsystems as well. *See also* bubble memory, CMOS RAM, core, EPROM, flash memory, ROM.

NO-OP *n. See* no-operation instruction.

N

no-operation instruction *n.* A machine instruction that has no results other than to cause the processor to use up clock cycles. Such instructions are useful in certain situations, such as padding out timing loops or forcing subsequent instructions to align on certain memory boundaries. *Acronym:* NO-OP, NOP. *See also* machine instruction.

NOP *n. See* no-operation instruction.

NOR gate *n.* Short for **NOT OR gate**. A digital circuit whose output is true (1) only if all inputs are false (0). A NOR gate is an OR circuit (output with the value of 1 if any input value is 1) followed by a NOT circuit (output that is the logical complement of the input). *See also* gate (definition 1), NOT gate, OR gate.

normal distribution *n.* In statistics, a type of function that describes the probabilities of the possible values of a random variable. The function, whose graph is the familiar bell-shaped curve, can be used to determine the probability that the value of the variable will fall within a particular interval of values.

normal form *n.* **1.** In a relational database, an approach to structuring (organizing) information in order to avoid redundancy and inconsistency and to promote efficient maintenance, storage, and updating. Several "rules" or levels of normalization are accepted, each a refinement of the preceding one. Of these, three forms are commonly used: first normal (1NF), second normal (2NF), and third normal (3NF). First normal forms, the least structured, are groups of records (such as employee lists) in which each field (column) contains unique and nonrepeating information. Second and third normal forms break down first normal forms, separating them into different tables by defining successively finer interrelationships between fields. Second normal forms do not include fields that are subsets of fields other than the primary (key) field; for example, a second normal form keyed to employee name would not include both job grade and hourly rate if pay were dependent on job grade. Third normal forms do not include fields that provide information about fields other than the key field; for example, a third normal form keyed to employee name would not include project name, crew number, and supervisor unless the crew number and supervisor were assigned only to the project the employee was working on. Further normalization refinements include Boyce-Codd Normal Form (BCNF), fourth normal form (4NF), and projection-join (or fifth) normal form (PJ/NF or 5NF). These levels, however, are not as commonly used as the first, second, and third normal forms. **2.** In program-

ming, the metalanguage sometimes called the Backus normal form (Backus-Naur form)—a language used for describing the syntax of other languages, specifically ALGOL 60, for which it was invented. *See also* Backus-Naur form.

normal hyphen *n. See* hyphen.

normalize *vb.* **1.** In programming, to adjust the fixed-point and exponent portions of a floating-point number to bring the fixed-point portions within a specific range. **2.** In database management, to apply a body of techniques to a relational database in order to minimize the inclusion of duplicate information. Normalization greatly simplifies query and update management, including security and integrity considerations, although it does so at the expense of creating a larger number of tables. *See also* normal form (definition 1).

North American Cellular Network *n.* Telecommunications network that enables wireless phone users in North America to send and receive calls when roaming outside their service area. *Acronym:* NACN.

NOS *n. See* network operating system.

NOT *n.* An operator that performs Boolean or logical negation. *See also* Boolean operator, logical operator.

NOT AND *n. See* NAND.

notation *n.* In programming, the set of symbols and formats used to describe the elements of programming, mathematics, or a scientific field. A language's syntax is defined in part by notation. *See also* syntax.

notebook computer *n. See* portable computer.

NOT gate *n.* One of the three basic logic gates (with AND and OR) from which all digital systems can be built. The NOT circuit, also referred to as an *inverter*, has output that is the reverse of its input—that is, the output is true (1) if the input is false (0) and false (0) if the input is true (1). *See also* AND gate, gate (definition 1), OR gate.

notification *n.* A signal from the operating system that an event has occurred.

Novell Directory Services *n. See* NDS.

Novell NetWare *n. See* NetWare.

NPN transistor *n.* A type of transistor in which a base of P-type material is sandwiched between an emitter and a collector of N-type material. The base, emitter, and collector are the three terminals through which current flows. In an NPN transistor, electrons represent the majority of the charge carriers, and they flow from the emitter to the collector. See the illustration. *See also* N-type semiconductor, P-type semiconductor. *Compare* PNP transistor.

Internal diagram

Schematic diagram

NPN transistor.

NQL *n. See* Network Query Language.

NRZ *n. See* nonreturn to zero.

ns *n. See* nanosecond.

NSAPI *n.* Acronym for **N**etscape **S**erver **A**pplication **P**rogramming **I**nterface. A specification for interfaces between the Netscape HTTP server and other application programs. NSAPI can be used to provide access to application programs from a Web browser through a Web server. *See also* HTTP server (definition 1), Web browser.

NSF *n. See* National Science Foundation.

NSFnet *n.* Short for the **N**ational **S**cience **F**oundation **Net**work. A WAN (wide area network), developed by the National Science Foundation to replace ARPANET for civilian purposes. NSFnet served as a major backbone for the Internet until mid-1995. Backbone services in the United States for the Internet are now provided by commercial carriers. *See also* ARPANET, backbone (definition 1).

NSFnet Network Information Center *n. See* InterNIC.

NSI *n.* Acronym for **N**etwork **S**olutions, **I**nc. The organization responsible, since 1992, for registering top-level

Internet domain names and maintaining the authoritative ("A") database of top-level domains replicated daily on 12 other root servers on the Internet. In 1998, with the privatization of Internet administration, the functions performed by NSI (under cooperative agreement with the U.S. National Science Foundation) became the responsibility of ICANN, a new, nonprofit organization. NSI remains active, but its association with the U.S. government entered the "ramping down" phase in 1998/1999. *See also* IANA, ICANN.

NT *n. See* Windows NT.

NT-1 *n. See* Network Terminator 1.

NT file system *n. See* NTFS.

NTFS *n.* Acronym for **NT f**ile **s**ystem. An advanced file system designed for use specifically with the Windows NT operating system. It supports long filenames, full security access control, file system recovery, extremely large storage media, and various features for the Windows NT POSIX subsystem. It also supports object-oriented applications by treating all files as objects with user-defined and system-defined attributes. *See also* FAT file system, HPFS, POSIX.

NTLM authentication protocol *n.* A challenge/response authentication protocol. The NTLM authentication protocol was the default for network authentication in Windows NT version 4.0 and earlier and Windows Millennium Edition (Windows Me) and earlier. The protocol continues to be supported in Windows 2000 and Windows XP but no longer is the default. *See also* Kerberos.

NTP *n.* Acronym for **N**etwork **T**ime **P**rotocol. A protocol used for synchronizing the system time on a computer to that of a server or other reference source such as a radio, satellite receiver, or modem. NTP provides time accuracy within a millisecond on local area networks and a few tens of milliseconds on wide area networks. NTP configurations may utilize redundant servers, diverse network paths, and cryptographic authentication to achieve high accuracy and reliability.

NTSC *n.* Acronym for **N**ational **T**elevision **S**ystem (later changed to Standards) **C**ommittee. The standards-setting body for television and video in the United States. It is the sponsor of the NTSC standard for encoding color, a coding system compatible with black-and-white signals and the system used for color broadcasting in the United States.

N

N-type semiconductor *n.* Semiconductor material in which electrical conduction is carried by electrons, in contrast to P-type semiconductors, in which conduction is carried by holes—that is, electron "vacancies." N-type semiconductors are created by adding a dopant with an excess of electrons during the manufacturing process. *See also* semiconductor. *Compare* P-type semiconductor.

NuBus *n.* A high-performance expansion bus used in Macintosh computers, offering high bandwidth and multiple bus controllers. Invented at the Massachusetts Institute of Technology (MIT), NuBus was eventually licensed to Texas Instruments and other companies. *See also* bus.

nudge *vb.* To move an object one pixel at a time.

nuke *vb.* **1.** To erase a file, directory, or entire hard disk. **2.** To stop a process in an operating system, an application, or a program. *Also called:* kill.

NUL *n.* **1.** A character code with a null value; literally, a character meaning "nothing." Although it is real in the sense of being recognizable, occupying space internally in the computer, and being sent or received as a character, a NUL character displays nothing, takes no space on the screen or on paper, and causes no specific action when sent to a printer. In ASCII, NUL is represented by the character code 0. *See also* ASCII. **2.** A "device," recognized by the operating system, that can be addressed like a physical output device (such as a printer) but that discards any information sent to it.

null character *n. See* NUL.

null cycle *n.* The shortest amount of time required for execution of a program; the time needed to cycle through the program without requiring it to process new data or loop through sets of instructions.

null modem *n.* A way of connecting two computers via a cable that enables them to communicate without the use of modems. A null modem cable accomplishes this by crossing the sending and receiving wires so that the wire used for transmitting by one device is used for receiving by the other and vice versa. See the illustration.

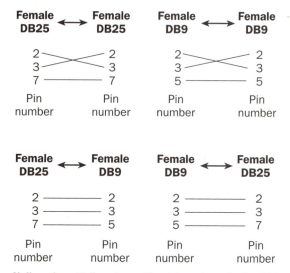

Null modem. *Null modem cable-wiring schematics for IBM PC-compatible computers.*

null modem cable *n.* A serial data cable used to connect two personal computers, without a modem or other DCE device in between, through the computers' serial ports. Because both computers use the same pins to send data, a null modem cable connects the output pins in one computer's serial port to the input pins in the other. A null modem cable is used to transfer data between two personal computers in close proximity. *See also* serial port.

null pointer *n.* A pointer to nothing—usually a standardized memory address, such as 0. A null pointer usually marks the last of a linear sequence of pointers or indicates that a data search operation has come up empty. *Also called:* nil pointer. *See also* pointer (definition 1).

null string *n.* A string containing no characters; a string whose length is zero. *See also* string.

null-terminated string *n. See* ASCIIZ string.

NUMA *n.* Acronym for **N**on-**U**niform **M**emory **A**ccess. A multiprocessing architecture that manages memory according to its distance from the processor. Banks of memory at various distances require different amounts of access time, with local memory accessed faster than remote memory. *See also* SMP.

number cruncher *n.* **1.** A computer that is able to quickly perform large amounts of mathematical computations. **2.** A powerful workstation. **3.** A program whose main task is to perform mathematical computations—for example, a statistical program. **4.** A person who uses a computer to analyze numbers.

number crunching *vb.* The calculation of large amounts of numeric data. Number crunching can be repetitive, mathematically complex, or both, and it generally involves far more internal processing than input or output functions. Numeric coprocessors greatly enhance the ability of computers to perform these tasks.

numerical analysis *n.* The branch of mathematics devoted to finding ways to solve abstract mathematical problems and finding concrete or approximate solutions for them.

numeric coprocessor *n.* *See* floating-point processor.

numeric keypad *n.* A calculator-style block of keys, usually at the right side of a keyboard, that can be used to enter numbers. In addition to keys for the digits 0 through 9 and keys for indicating addition, subtraction, multiplication, and division, a numeric keypad often includes an Enter key (usually not the same as the Enter or Return key on the main part of the keyboard). On Apple keyboards, the numeric keypad also includes a Clear key that usually functions like the Backspace key for deleting characters. In addition, many of the keys can serve dual purposes, such as cursor movement, scrolling, or editing tasks, depending on the status of the Num Lock key. See the illustration. *See also* Num Lock key.

numeric messaging *n.* Service that enables wireless phones and pagers to receive messages consisting only of numeric information, such as phone numbers.

numeric paging *n.* *See* numeric messaging.

Num Lock key *n.* Short for **Num**eric **Lock key**. A toggle key that, when turned on, activates the numeric keypad so that its keys can be used for calculator-style data entry. When the Num Lock key is toggled off, most of the numeric keypad keys are used for cursor movement and on-screen scrolling. *See also* numeric keypad.

NVM *n.* Acronym for **N**on-**V**olatile **M**emory. Memory that persists in its state when the power is removed. *Also called:* Flash memory.

NVRAM *n.* Acronym for **N**on-**V**olatile **R**andom **A**ccess **M**emory. Non-volatile read/write memory or normally volatile memory that has been fitted with a battery backup to retain data. *See also* NVM.

NWLink *n.* An implementation of the Internetwork Packet Exchange (IPX), Sequenced Packet Exchange (SPX), and NetBIOS protocols used in Novell networks. NWLink is a standard network protocol that supports routing and can support NetWare client-server applications, where NetWare-aware Sockets-based applications communicate with IPX/SPX Sockets-based applications. *See also* IPX/SPX, NetBIOS, RIPX.

nybble *n.* *See* nibble.

N

Numeric Keypad

Numeric keypad.

OAGI *n.* Acronym for **O**pen **A**pplications **G**roup, **I**nc. A nonprofit consortium of software vendors and businesses created to develop and define XML-based interoperability specifications and standards among enterprise-scale applications. The OAGI was formed in 1995 by a small number of business enterprise software companies and organizations and has grown to more than sixty member companies.

OAGIS *n.* Acronym for **O**pen **A**pplications **G**roup Integration **S**pecification. A set of XML-based specifications and standards designed to promote B2B e-commerce by providing interoperability between enterprise-scale applications and between companies. OAGIS includes business document specifications and definitions, business process scenarios, and templates for business forms such as invoices and requisitions. OAGIS is overseen by the Open Applications Group, Inc., a nonprofit consortium of software vendors and customers. *See also* OAGI.

OASIS *n.* Acronym for **O**rganization for the **A**dvancement of **S**tructured **I**nformation **S**tandards. A consortium of technology companies formed to develop guidelines for use of XML (Extensible Markup Language) and related information standards.

Oberon *n.* An extensible object-oriented language based on Modula-2, whose later versions support the .NET Framework. *Also called:* Active Oberon for .NET.

object *n.* **1.** Short for object code (machine-readable code). **2.** In object-oriented programming, a variable comprising both routines and data that is treated as a discrete entity. *See also* abstract data type, module (definition 1), object-oriented programming. **3.** In graphics, a distinct entity. For example, a bouncing ball might be an object in a graphics program. **4.** A single, runtime instance of object type that the operating system defines. Objects visible in user mode include event, file, I/O completion port, key, object directory, port, process, section, semaphore, symbolic link, thread, timer, and token objects. Many user-mode objects are implemented through the use of a corresponding kernel-mode object. Kernel-mode-only objects include adapter, APC, controller, device, device queue, DPC, driver, interrupt, mutex, and stream file objects.

object code *n.* The code, generated by a compiler or an assembler, that was translated from the source code of a program. The term most commonly refers to machine code that can be directly executed by the system's central processing unit (CPU), but it can also be assembly language source code or a variation of machine code. *See also* central processing unit.

object computer *n.* The computer that is the target of a specific communications attempt.

object database *n.* *See* object-oriented database.

Object Database Management Group *n.* An organization that promotes standards for object databases and defines interfaces to object databases. *Acronym:* ODMG. *See also* OMG.

object file *n.* A file containing object code, usually the output of a compiler or an assembler and the input for a linker. *See also* assembler, compiler (definition 2), linker, object code.

Objective-C *n.* An object-oriented version of the C language developed in 1984 by Brad Cox. It is most widely known for being the standard development language for the NeXT operating system. *See also* object-oriented programming.

object linking and embedding *n.* *See* OLE.

Object Management Architecture *n.* *See* OMA.

Object Management Group *n.* *See* OMG.

object model *n.* **1.** The structural foundation for an object-oriented language, such as C++. This foundation includes such principles as abstraction, concurrency, encapsulation, hierarchy, persistence, polymorphism, and typing. *See also* abstract data type, object (definition 2), object-oriented programming, polymorphism. **2.** The structural foundation for an object-oriented design. *See also* object-oriented design. **3.** The structural foundation for an object-oriented application.

object module *n.* In programming, the object-code (compiled) version of a source-code file that is usually a collection of routines and is ready to be linked with other object modules. *See also* linker, module (definition 1), object code.

object-oriented *adj.* Of, pertaining to, or being a system or language that supports the use of objects. *See also* object (definition 2).

object-oriented analysis *n.* A procedure that identifies the component objects and system requirements of a system or process that involves computers and describes how they interact to perform specific tasks. The reuse of existing solutions is an objective of this sort of analysis. Object-oriented analysis generally precedes object-oriented design or object-oriented programming when a new object-oriented computer system or new software is developed. *See also* object (definition 2), object-oriented design, object-oriented programming.

object-oriented database *n.* A flexible database that supports the use of abstract data types, objects, and classes and that can store a wide range of data, often including sound, video, and graphics, in addition to text and numbers. Some object-oriented databases allow data retrieval procedures and rules for processing data to be stored along with the data or in place of the data. This allows the data to be stored in areas other than in the physical database, which is often desirable when the data files are large, such as those for video files. *Acronym:* OODB. *See also* abstract data type, class, object (definition 2). *Compare* relational database.

object-oriented design *n.* A modular approach to creating a software product or computer system, in which the modules (objects) can be easily and affordably adapted to meet new needs. Object-oriented design generally comes after object-oriented analysis of the product or system and before any actual programming. *See also* object (definition 2), object-oriented analysis.

object-oriented graphics *n.* Computer graphics that are based on the use of graphics primitives, such as lines, curves, circles, and squares. Object-oriented graphics, used in applications such as computer-aided design and drawing and illustration programs, describe an image mathematically as a set of instructions for creating the objects in the image. This approach contrasts with the use of bitmapped graphics, in which a graphic is represented as a group of black-and-white or colored dots arranged in a certain pattern. Object-oriented graphics enable the user to manipulate objects as units. Because objects are

described mathematically, object-oriented graphics can be layered, rotated, and magnified relatively easily. *Also called:* structured graphics. *See also* graphics primitive. *Compare* bitmapped graphics, paint program.

object-oriented interface *n.* A user interface in which elements of the system are represented by visible screen entities, such as icons, that are used to manipulate the system elements. Object-oriented display interfaces do not necessarily imply any relation to object-oriented programming. *See also* object-oriented graphics.

object-oriented operating system *n.* An operating system based on objects and designed in a way that facilitates software development by third parties, using an object-oriented design. *See also* object (definition 2), object-oriented design.

object-oriented programming *n.* A programming paradigm in which a program is viewed as a collection of discrete objects that are self-contained collections of data structures and routines that interact with other objects. *Acronym:* OOP. *See also* C++, object (definition 2), Objective-C.

Object Pascal *n.* An object-oriented derivative of Pascal. *See also* Pascal.

object-relational server *n.* A database server that supports object-oriented management of complex data types in a relational database. *See also* database server, relational database.

object request broker *n. See* ORB.

object wrapper *n.* In object-oriented applications, a means of encapsulating a set of services provided by a non-object-oriented application so that the encapsulated services can be treated as an object. *See also* object (definition 2).

oblique *adj.* Describing a style of text created by slanting a roman font to simulate italics when a true italic font isn't available on the computer or printer. *See also* font, italic, roman.

OC3 *n.* Short for **o**ptical **c**arrier **3**. One of several optical signal circuits used in the SONET high-speed fiberoptic data transmission system. OC3 carries a signal of 155.52 Mbps, the minimum transmission speed for which SONET and the European standard, SDH, are fully interoperable. *See also* SONET.

OCR *n. See* optical character recognition.

octal *n.* The base-8 number system consisting of the digits 0 through 7, from the Latin *octo*, meaning "eight." The octal system is used in programming as a compact means of representing binary numbers. *See also* base (definition 2).

octet *n.* A unit of data that consists of exactly 8 bits, regardless of the number of bits a computer uses to represent a small amount of information such as a character. *Compare* byte.

OCX *n.* Short for **OLE c**ustom control. A software module based on OLE and COM technologies that, when called by an application, produces a control that adds some desired feature to the application. OCX technology is portable across platforms, works on both 16-bit and 32-bit operating systems, and can be used with many applications. It is the successor to VBX (Visual Basic custom control) technology, which supported only Visual Basic applications, and is the basis for ActiveX controls. OCXs have, in fact, been superseded by ActiveX controls, which are much smaller and therefore work much better over the Internet. *See also* ActiveX control, COM (definition 2), control (definition 2), OLE, VBX, Visual Basic.

ODBC *n.* Acronym for **O**pen **D**ata**b**ase **C**onnectivity. In the Microsoft WOSA (Windows Open System Architecture) structure, an interface providing a common language for Windows applications to gain access to a database on a network. *See also* WOSA.

ODBC driver *n.* Short for **O**pen **D**ata**b**ase **C**onnectivity **driver**. A program file used to connect to a particular database. Each database program, such as Access or dBASE, or database management system, such as SQL Server, requires a different driver.

ODBMG *n.* *See* Object Database Management Group.

odd parity *n.* *See* parity.

ODI *n.* Acronym for **O**pen **D**ata-link **I**nterface. A specification developed by Novell to enable a network interface card (NIC) to support multiple protocols, such as TCP/IP and IPX/SPX. ODI also simplifies development of device drivers by eliminating concern about the particular protocol to be used in transferring information over the network. ODI is comparable in some ways to the Network Driver Interface Specification, or NDIS. *See also* NDIS, network adapter.

ODMA *n.* Acronym for **O**pen **D**ocument **M**anagement API. A specification for a standard application program interface that enables desktop applications, such as

Microsoft Word, to interact seamlessly with specialized document management systems (DMS) installed on network servers. The ODMA specification is the property of the Association for Information & Image Management (AIIM). *See also* API, document management system.

OEM *n.* *See* original equipment manufacturer.

OFC *n.* *See* Open Financial Connectivity.

Office *n.* Microsoft's family of individual and business application software suites for the Windows and Macintosh platforms. Office is built around three core products: Word for word processing, Excel for spreadsheets, and Outlook for e-mail and collaboration. Office XP, the most recent version for the Windows platform, is available in several versions: the Office XP Standard or Standard for Students and Teachers version, which includes Word, Excel, Outlook, and PowerPoint; the Office XP Professional version, which adds Access; Office XP Developer, which includes Word, Excel, Outlook, PowerPoint, Access, FrontPage, Microsoft's new SharePoint Team Services collaboration and team Web solution, and Developer Tools; and finally, Office XP Professional Special Edition, which offers all the programs in Office XP Professional plus FrontPage, SharePoint Team Services, Publisher, and IntelliMouse Explorer. Office v. X for Mac is the most recent version for the Macintosh and includes Word, Entourage (for e-mail and collaboration), Excel, and PowerPoint. See the table.

Table O.1   Application Specifications

Product	Function	Platform
Word	Word processing	Windows, Macintosh
Excel	Spreadsheets	Windows, Macintosh
Outlook	E-mail, collaboration	Windows
Entourage	E-mail, collaboration	Macintosh
Publisher	Desktop publishing	Windows
Access	Database management	Windows
PowerPoint	Presentation graphics	Windows, Macintosh
FrontPage	Web site creation	Windows
SharePoint Team Services	Team Web solution	Windows

office automation *n.* The use of electronic and communications devices, such as computers, modems, and fax machines and any associated software, to perform office functions mechanically rather than manually.

offline *adj.* **1.** In reference to a computing device or a program, unable to communicate with or be controlled by a computer. *Compare* online (definition 1). **2.** In reference to one or more computers, being disconnected from a network. *Compare* online (definition 2). **3.** Colloquially, a reference to moving a discussion between interested parties to a later, more appropriate, time. For example, "We can talk about this offline. Let's get back on topic now."

offline navigator *n.* Software designed to download e-mail, Web pages, or newsgroup articles or postings from other online forums and save them locally to a disk, where they can be browsed without the user paying the cost of idle time while being connected to the Internet or an online information service. *Also called:* offline reader.

offline reader *n. See* offline navigator.

offline storage *n.* A storage resource, such as a disk, that is not currently available to the system.

offload *vb.* To assume part of the processing demand from another device. For example, some LAN-attached gateways can offload TCP/IP processing from the host machine, thereby freeing up significant processing capacity in the CPU. *See also* central processing unit, gateway, host, TCP/IP.

offset *n.* In relative addressing methods, a number that tells how far from a starting point a particular item is located. *See also* relative address.

off-the-shelf *adj.* Ready-to-use; packaged. The term can refer to hardware or software.

ohm *n.* The unit of measure for electrical resistance. A resistance of 1 ohm will pass 1 ampere of current when a voltage of 1 volt is applied.

OLAP *n. See* OLAP database.

OLAP database *n.* Short for **on**line **a**nalytical **p**rocessing **database.** A relational database system capable of handling queries more complex than those handled by standard relational databases, through multidimensional access to data (viewing the data by several different criteria), intensive calculation capability, and specialized indexing techniques. *See also* database, query (definition 1), relational database.

OLAP provider *n.* A set of software that provides access to a particular type of OLAP database. This software can include a data source driver and other client software that is necessary to connect to a database. *See also* OLAP database.

OLE *n.* Acronym for **o**bject **l**inking and **e**mbedding. A technology for transferring and sharing information among applications. When an object, such as an image file created with a paint program, is linked to a compound document, such as a spreadsheet or a document created with a word processing program, the document contains only a reference to the object; any changes made to the contents of a linked object will be seen in the compound document. When an object is embedded in a compound document, the document contains a copy of the object; any changes made to the contents of the original object will not be seen in the compound document unless the embedded object is updated.

OLED *n.* Acronym for **O**rganic **L**ight-**E**mitting **D**evice. Technology developed for the production of thin, lightweight digital displays. An OLED features a series of thin organic films between two conductors. When current is applied, bright light is emitted. OLED displays are lightweight, durable, and power-efficient.

OLE Database *n.* An application programming interface developed by Microsoft for accessing databases. OLE Database is an open specification that can interface with all types of data files on a computer network. *Acronym:* OLE DB.

OLTP *n.* Acronym for **on**line **t**ransaction **p**rocessing. A system for processing transactions as soon as the computer receives them and updating master files immediately in a database management system. OLTP is useful in financial record keeping and inventory tracking. *See also* database management system, transaction processing. *Compare* batch processing (definition 3).

OM-1 *n. See* OpenMPEG Consortium.

OMA *n.* Acronym for **O**bject **M**anagement **A**rchitecture. A definition developed by the Object Management Group (OMG) for object-oriented distributed processing. OMA includes the Common Object Request Broker Architecture (CORBA). *See also* CORBA, OMG.

OMG *n.* Acronym for **O**bject **M**anagement **G**roup. A nonprofit organization that provides a framework of standards for object-oriented interfaces. The open and nonproprietary architecture developed and managed by the OMG allows developers to work with a large toolkit of standard components in building applications with a solid common foundation. The OMG was formed in 1989 by a group of software developers and system vendors and now has more than six hundred member companies.

on-board computer *n.* A computer that resides within another device.

on-chip cache *n. See* L1 cache.

on-demand publishing point *n.* A type of publishing point that streams content in such a way that the client can control (start, stop, pause, fast-forward, or rewind) the content. Typically, the on-demand content is a Windows Media file or a directory of files. Content streamed from an on-demand publishing point is always delivered as a unicast stream. Formerly called a station.

one-off *n.* **1.** A product that is produced one at a time, instead of being mass produced. **2.** A CD-ROM created on a CD-R machine, which can create only one copy of a CD-ROM at a time.

one-pass compiler *n.* A compiler that needs to read through a source file only once to produce the object code. The syntax of some languages makes it impossible to write a one-pass compiler for those languages. *See also* compiler (definition 2).

one's complement *n.* A number in the binary (base-2) system that is the complement of another number. *See also* complement.

one-to-many relationship *n.* An association between two tables in which the primary key value of each record in the primary table corresponds to the value in the matching field or fields of many records in the related table.

one-to-many replication *n.* A server configuration allowing replication of data from one or more large servers to a greater number of smaller servers.

one-to-one relationship *n.* An association between two tables in which the primary key value of each record in the primary table corresponds to the value in the matching field or fields of one and only one record in the related table.

one-way trust *n.* A type of trust relationship in which only one of the two domains trusts the other domain. For example, domain A trusts domain B and domain B does not trust domain A. All one-way trusts are nontransitive. *See also* transitive trust, two-way trust.

onion routing *n.* An anonymous communication technique first developed by the U.S. Navy, in which a message is wrapped in layers of encryption and passed through several intermediate stations to obscure its point of origin. In onion routing, data packets are sent through a complex network of routers, each of which opens an anon-

ymous connection to the next, until it reaches its destination. When the packet is received by the first onion router, it is encrypted once for each additional router it will pass through. Each subsequent onion router unwraps one layer of encryption until the message reaches its destination as plain text.

online *adj.* **1.** In reference to a computing device or a program, activated and ready for operation; capable of communicating with or being controlled by a computer. *Compare* offline (definition 1). **2.** In reference to one or more computers, connected to a network. *Compare* offline (definition 2). **3.** In reference to a user, currently connected to the Internet, an online service, or a BBS or using a modem to connect to another modem. **4.** In reference to a user, being able to connect to the Internet, an online service, or a BBS by virtue of having an account that gives one access.

online analytical processing *n. See* OLAP database.

online community *n.* **1.** All users of the Internet and World Wide Web collectively. **2.** A local community that places political forums on line for the discussion of local government or issues of public concern. **3.** Members of a specific newsgroup, mailing list, MUD, BBS, or other online forum or group. *See also* BBS (definition 1), mailing list, MUD, newsgroup.

online game *n.* A game that is meant to be played while connected to the Internet, intranet, or other network, with one or more other people simultaneously connected. Online games allow gamers to interact with other players without having their physical presence necessary. *See also* computer game.

online help *n. See* help.

online information service *n.* A business that provides access to databases, file archives, conferences, chat groups, and other forms of information through dial-up, or dedicated communications links, or through the Internet. Most online information services also offer access to the Internet connections along with their own proprietary services. The largest consumer online information services in the U.S. are America Online, CompuServe, and MSN.

Online Privacy Alliance *n. See* OPA.

online service *n. See* online information service.

online state *n.* The state of a modem when it is communicating with another modem. *Compare* command state.

online transaction processing *n. See* OLTP.

on-screen keyboard *n.* An interactive keyboard that appears as a graphical image on the display screen of a computing device. A user spells words by tapping the letters on the screen with a stylus. On-screen keyboards appear primarily on personal digital assistants (PDAs) and other handheld computing devices that are too small to contain a traditional keyboard.

on the fly *adv.* Doing a task or process as needed without suspending or disturbing normal operations. For example, it is often said that an HTML document can be edited on the fly because its content can be revised without the need to completely shut down or re-create the Web site on which it resides. *See also* HTML document, Web site.

OO *adj. See* object-oriented.

OOP *n. See* object-oriented programming.

OPA *n.* Acronym for **O**nline **P**rivacy **A**lliance. An organization of over eighty Internet companies and trade associations created to be the voice of the industry on digital privacy issues. The OPA stresses the need for consumer trust and encourages online businesses to post privacy policies. The OPA created a set of guidelines for privacy policies that have become the industry standard.

opacity *n.* The quality that defines how much light passes through an object's pixels. If an object is 100 percent opaque, no light passes through it.

opcode *n. See* operation code.

open¹ *adj.* Of, pertaining to, or providing accessibility. For example, an open file is one that can be used because a program has issued an open file command to the operating system.

open² *vb.* To make an object, such as a file, accessible.

Open Applications Group, Inc. *n. See* OAGI.

open architecture *n.* **1.** Any computer or peripheral design that has published specifications. A published specification lets third parties develop add-on hardware for a computer or device. *Compare* closed architecture (definition 1). **2.** A design that provides for expansion slots on the motherboard, thereby allowing the addition of boards to enhance or customize a system. *Compare* closed architecture (definition 2).

OpenCyc *n.* An open source artificial intelligence platform. OpenCyc forms the foundation of knowledge-dependent applications such as speech understanding,

database integration, and e-mail routing and prioritizing. OpenCyc development is administered through Open-Cyc.org.

Open Data-link Interface *n. See* ODI.

OpenDoc *n.* An object-oriented application programming interface (API) that enables multiple independent programs (component software) on several platforms to work together on a single document (compound document). Similar to OLE, OpenDoc allows images, sound, video, other documents, and other files to be embedded or linked to the document. OpenDoc is supported by an alliance that includes Apple, IBM, the Object Management Group, and the X Consortium. *See also* application programming interface, component software. *Compare* ActiveX, OLE.

Open Document Management API *n. See* ODMA.

open file *n.* A file that can be read from, written to, or both. A program must first open a file before the file's contents can be used, and it must close the file when done. *See also* open².

Open Financial Connectivity *n.* The Microsoft specification for an interface between electronic banking services and Microsoft Money personal finance software. *Acronym:* OFC.

OpenGL *n.* An industry standard application programming interface (API) for 3D graphics rendering and 3D hardware acceleration. OpenGL is cross-platform and is available for all major operating systems.

Open Group *n.* A consortium of computer hardware and software manufacturers and users from industry, government, and academia that is dedicated to the advancement of multi-vendor information systems. The Open Group was formed in 1996 as a consolidation of the Open Software Foundation and X/Open Company Limited.

OpenMPEG Consortium *n.* An international organization of hardware and software developers for promoting the use of the MPEG standards. *Acronym:* OM-1. *See also* MPEG.

Open Prepress Interface *n. See* OPI.

Open Profiling Standard *n.* An Internet personalization and privacy specification submitted for consideration to the World Wide Web Consortium by Netscape Communications Corporation, Firefly Network, Inc., and VeriSign, Inc. Open Profiling Standard (OPS) enables users to customize online services while protecting their privacy. To

O

achieve personalization and privacy concomitantly, OPS is based on the concept of a Personal Profile, which is stored on the individual's computer and contains the user's unique identification, demographic and contact data, and possibly content preferences. This information remains under the user's control and can be released wholly or in part to the requesting site. *Acronym:* OPS. *See also* cookie, digital certificate.

open shop *n.* A computer facility that is open to users and not restricted to programmers or other personnel. An open shop is one in which people can work on or attempt to solve computer problems on their own rather than handing them over to a specialist.

Open Shortest Path First *n. See* OSPF.

Open Software Foundation *n. See* OSF.

open source *n.* The practice of making the source code (program instructions) for a software product freely available, at no cost, to interested users and developers, even though they were not involved in creating the original product. The distributors of open source software expect and encourage users and outside programmers to examine the code in order to identify problems, and to modify the code with suggested improvements and enhancements. Widely used open source products include the Linux operating system and the Apache Web server.

open standard *n.* A publicly available set of specifications describing the characteristics of a hardware device or software program. Open standards are published to encourage interoperability and thereby help popularize new technologies. *See also* standard (definition 2).

open system *n.* **1.** In communications, a computer network designed to incorporate all devices—regardless of the manufacturer or model—that can use the same communications facilities and protocols. **2.** In reference to computer hardware or software, a system that can accept add-ons produced by third-party suppliers. *See also* open architecture (definition 1).

Open Systems Interconnection reference model *n. See* ISO/OSI reference model.

OpenType *n.* A collaborative initiative by Microsoft and Adobe to unify support for Microsoft TrueType and Adobe PostScript Type 1 fonts. The OpenType font format enables font creators and users to work with the font type that best suits their needs without having to worry about

whether the font is based on TrueType or PostScript technology. *Also called:* TrueType Open version 2. *See also* PostScript font, TrueType.

Opera *n.* A Web browser developed by Opera Software S/A. Opera is notable for its strict W3C standards support. Opera is often chosen by Web developers to test Web sites for W3C compliance. *See also* W3C, Web browser.

operand *n.* The object of a mathematical operation or a computer instruction.

operating system *n.* The software that controls the allocation and usage of hardware resources such as memory, central processing unit (CPU) time, disk space, and peripheral devices. The operating system is the foundation software on which applications depend. Popular operating systems include Windows 98, Windows NT, Mac OS, and UNIX. *Acronym:* OS. *Also called:* executive.

operation *n.* **1.** A specific action carried out by a computer in the process of executing a program. **2.** In mathematics, an action performed on a set of entities that produces a new entity. Examples of mathematical operations are addition and subtraction.

operation code *n.* The portion of a machine language or assembly language instruction that specifies the type of instruction and the structure of the data on which it operates. *Also called:* opcode. *See also* assembly language, machine code.

operations research *n.* The use of mathematical and scientific approaches to analyze and improve efficiency in business, management, government, and other areas. Developed around the beginning of World War II, operations research was initially used to improve military operations during the war. The practice later spread to business and industry as a means of breaking down systems and procedures and studying their parts and interactions to improve overall performance. Operations research involves use of the critical path method, statistics, probability, and information theory.

operator *n.* **1.** In mathematics and in programming and computer applications, a symbol or other character indicating an operation that acts on one or more elements. *See also* binary[1], unary. **2.** A person who controls a machine or system such as a computer or telephone switchboard.

operator associativity *n.* A characteristic of operators that determines the order of evaluation in an expression

O

when adjacent operators have equal precedence. The two possibilities are left to right and right to left. The associativity for most operators is left to right. *See also* expression, operator (definition 1), operator precedence.

operator overloading *n.* The assignment of more than one function to a particular operator, with the implication that the operation performed will vary depending on the data type (operands) involved. Some languages, such as Ada and C++, specifically allow for operator overloading. *See also* Ada, C++, function overloading, operator (definition 1).

operator precedence *n.* The priority of the various operators when more than one is used in an expression. In the absence of parentheses, operations with higher precedence are performed first. *See also* expression, operator (definition 1), operator associativity.

OPI *n.* Acronym for **O**pen **P**repress **I**nterface. A format for preparing digital publication text and graphics for printing, introduced by Aldus (now Adobe), creating a low-resolution graphic for layout and a high-resolution graphic for print. Depending on the method used, the OPI process creates a single file that allows for color layer extraction though a desktop color separation program or creates multiple color-separated files when using DCS (Desktop Color Separation). *Compare* DCS.

OPS *n. See* Open Profiling Standard.

optical character recognition *n.* The process in which an electronic device examines printed characters on paper and determines their shapes by detecting patterns of dark and light. Once the scanner or reader has determined the shapes, character recognition methods—pattern matching with stored sets of characters—are used to translate the shapes into computer text. *Acronym:* OCR. *See also* character recognition. *Compare* magnetic-ink character recognition.

optical communications *n.* The use of light and of light-transmitting technology, such as optical fibers and lasers, in sending and receiving data, images, or sound.

optical disc *n. See* compact disc.

optical drive *n.* A disk drive that reads and often can write data on optical (compact) discs. Examples of optical drives include CD-ROM drives and WORM disk drives. *See also* CD-ROM drive, compact disc, WORM.

optical fiber *n.* A thin strand of transparent material used to carry optical signals. Optical fibers are constructed from special kinds of glass and plastic, and they are designed so that a beam of light introduced at one end will remain within the fiber, reflecting off the inner surfaces as it travels down the length of the fiber. Optical fibers are inexpensive, compact, and lightweight and are often packaged many hundred to a single cable. *See also* fiber optics.

optical mouse *n.* **1.** A type of mouse that uses a CMOS digital camera and a digital signal processor to detect motion. The camera photographs the surface over which the mouse moves 1500 times per second, and the digital signal processor uses the photographs to convert the mouse movement into onscreen movements of the cursor. IntelliMouse Explorer and IntelliMouse with IntelliEye, two optical mouse models with no moving parts and requiring no special mouse pad, were introduced by Microsoft in 1999. *See also* mouse. **2.** A type of mouse that uses a pair of light-emitting diodes (LEDs) and a special reflective grid pad to detect motion. The two lights are of different colors, and the special mouse pad has a grid of lines in the same colors, one color for vertical lines and another for horizontal lines. Light detectors paired with the LEDs sense when a colored light passes over a line of the same color, indicating the direction of movement. *See also* mouse. *Compare* mechanical mouse, optomechanical mouse.

optical reader *n.* A device that reads text from printed paper by detecting the pattern of light and dark on a page and then applying optical character recognition methods to identify the characters. *See also* optical character recognition.

optical recognition *n. See* optical character recognition.

optical scanner *n.* An input device that uses light-sensing equipment to scan paper or another medium, translating the pattern of light and dark or color into a digital signal that can be manipulated by either optical character recognition software or graphics software. Scanners have different methods for holding the input medium, including flatbed, whereby the medium is held on a piece of glass; sheet-fed, whereby sheets of paper are pulled over a stationary scanning mechanism; handheld, whereby the user moves the device over the document to be scanned; and overhead, whereby the document is placed face up on a stationary bed below a small tower, which moves across

O

the page. *Compare* magnetic-ink character recognition, spatial digitizer.

optical switching *n.* A technology in which transmissions are sent as light from origin to destination. With optical switching, transmissions are switched through banks of adjustable, circular millimeter mirrors at cross connections, meaning signals don't need to be converted from light to electronic and back during transmission. When used with wave-division multiplexing (WDM), all-optical traffic may be 100 times faster than electrical transmission. *See also* photonics.

optimization *n.* **1.** In programming, the process of producing more efficient (smaller or faster) programs through selection and design of data structures, algorithms, and instruction sequences. **2.** The process of a compiler or assembler in producing efficient executable code. *See also* optimizing compiler.

optimize *vb.* **1.** In Web design functions, to reduce the file size of a photo or graphic to allow faster loading. Files are typically optimized through a combination of means such as reducing overall image quality and fine-tuning color information. **2.** To fine-tune an application for improved performance. *See also* optimization.

optimizer *n.* A program or device that improves the performance of a computer, network, or other device or system. For example, a disk optimizer program reduces file access time.

optimizing compiler *n.* A compiler that analyzes its output (assembly language or machine code) to produce more efficient (smaller or faster) instruction sequences.

opt-in *vb.* To choose to receive certain services or features offered by an e-business. With the opt-in process, a user is not automatically enrolled in services or features. The user must choose to enroll in a service or feature.

optional hyphen *n. See* hyphen.

Option key *n.* A key on Apple Macintosh keyboards that, when pressed in combination with another key, produces special characters—graphics, such as boxes; international characters, such as currency symbols; and special punctuation marks, such as en dashes and em dashes. The Option key serves a purpose similar to that of the Control key or the Alt key on IBM and compatible keyboards in that it changes the meaning of the key with which it is used.

Options *n. See* Preferences.

optoelectronics *n.* The branch of electronics in which the properties and behavior of light are studied. Optoelec-

tronics deals with electronic devices that generate, sense, transmit, and modulate electromagnetic radiation in the infrared, visible, and ultraviolet portions of the electromagnetic spectrum.

optomechanical mouse *n.* A type of mouse in which motion is translated into directional signals through a combination of optical and mechanical means. The optical portion includes pairs of light-emitting diodes (LEDs) and matching sensors; the mechanical portion consists of rotating wheels with cutout slits. When the mouse is moved, the wheels turn and the light from the LEDs either passes through the slits and strikes a light sensor or is blocked by the solid portions of the wheels. These changes in light contact are detected by the pairs of sensors and interpreted as indications of movement. Because the sensors are slightly out of phase with one another, the direction of movement is determined based on which sensor is the first to regain light contact. Because it uses optical equipment instead of mechanical parts, an optomechanical mouse eliminates the need for many of the wear-related repairs and maintenance necessary with purely mechanical mice, but it does not require the special operating surfaces associated with optical mice. See the illustration. *See also* mouse. *Compare* mechanical mouse, optical mouse.

LED

Phototransistor

Optomechanical mouse.

opt-out *vb.* To choose not to receive certain services or features offered by an e-business. Some e-businesses automatically enroll users in a predetermined range of services, but allow users to opt-out of features in which they do not choose to participate.

OR *n.* A logical operation for combining two bits (0 or 1) or two Boolean values (false or true). If one or both values are 1 (true), it returns the value 1 (true). See the table.

Table O.2 The results of the OR logical operation.

a	b	a OR b
0	0	0
0	1	1
1	0	1
1	1	1

Orange Book *n.* **1.** A U.S. Department of Defense standards document entitled "Trusted Computer System Evaluation Criteria, DOD standard 5200.28-STD, December, 1985," which defines a system of ratings from A1 (most secure) to D (least secure), indicating the ability of a computer system to protect sensitive information. *Compare* Red Book (definition 1). **2.** A specifications book written by the Sony and Philips Corporations, covering the compact disc write-once formats (CD-R, PhotoCD). *See also* CD-R, ISO 9660, PhotoCD. *Compare* Green Book, Red Book (definition 2).

ORB *n.* Acronym for **o**bject **r**equest **b**roker. In client/server applications, an interface to which the client makes a request for an object. The ORB directs the request to the server containing the object and then returns the resulting values to the client. *See also* client (definition 1), CORBA.

order[1] *n.* **1.** In computing, the relative significance of a digit or byte. *High-order* refers to the most significant (usually leftmost) digit or byte; *low-order* refers to the least significant (usually rightmost) digit or byte. **2.** The magnitude of a database in terms of the number of fields it contains. **3.** The sequence in which arithmetic operations are performed.

order[2] *vb.* To arrange in a sequence, such as alphabetic or numeric.

ordinal number *n.* A number whose form indicates position in an ordered sequence of items, such as first, third, or twentieth. *Compare* cardinal number.

.org *n.* In the Internet's Domain Name System, the top-level domain that identifies addresses operated by organizations that do not fit any of the other standard domains. For instance, the Public Broadcasting System (PBS) is neither a commercial, for-profit corporation (.com) nor an educational institution with enrolled students (.edu), so it has the Internet address pbs.org. The designation .org appears at the end of the address. *See also* DNS (definition 1), domain (definition 3). *Compare* .com, .edu, .gov, .mil, .net.

Organic Light-Emitting Device *n. See* OLED.

Organization for the Advancement of Structured Information Standards *n. See* OASIS.

OR gate *n.* One of the three basic logic gates (with AND and NOT) from which all digital systems can be built. The output of an OR circuit is true (1) if any input is true. *See also* AND gate, gate (definition 1), NOT gate.

orientation *n. See* landscape mode, portrait mode.

original equipment manufacturer *n.* The maker of a piece of equipment. In making computers and related equipment, manufacturers of original equipment typically purchase components from other manufacturers of original equipment, integrate them into their own products, and then sell the products to the public. *Acronym:* OEM. *Compare* value-added reseller.

original Macintosh keyboard *n.* The keyboard supplied as standard equipment with the 128-KB Apple Macintosh and the Mac 512K. The original Macintosh keyboard is small and has no numeric keypad or function keys. Also, because the overall design goal was that the Macintosh should feel familiar, the only elements of this 58-key keyboard that differ from a typewriter keyboard are the Option keys at both ends of the bottom row, the Command key to the left of the Spacebar, and the Enter key to the right of the Spacebar.

orphan *n.* The first line of a paragraph printed alone at the bottom of a page or column of text, or the last line of a paragraph printed alone at the top of a page or column. Orphans are visually unattractive and thus undesirable in printed materials. *Compare* widow.

orphan file *n.* A file that remains on a system after it has ceased to be of use. For example, a file may be created to support a particular application but may remain after the application has been removed.

OS *n. See* operating system.

OS/2 *n.* Short for **O**perating **S**ystem/**2**. A protected-mode, virtual-memory, multitasking operating system for personal computers based on the Intel 80286, 80386, i486, and Pentium processors. OS/2 can run most MS-DOS applications and can read all MS-DOS disks. OS/2's Presentation Manager provides a graphical user interface. The latest version, known as OS/2 Warp 4, is a 32-bit operating system that provides networking, Internet, and Java support, as well as speech recognition technology. OS/2 was initially developed as a joint project of Microsoft and IBM but later became an IBM product. *See also* protected mode, virtual memory.

oscillation *n.* A periodic change or alternation. In electronics, oscillation refers to a periodic change in an electrical signal.

oscillator *n.* An electronic circuit that produces a periodically varying output at a controlled frequency. Oscillators, an important type of electronic circuit, can be designed to provide a constant or an adjustable output. Some oscillator circuits use a quartz crystal to generate a stable frequency. Personal computers use an oscillator circuit to provide the clock frequency—typically 1 to 200 megahertz (MHz)—that drives the processor and other circuits.

oscilloscope *n.* A test and measurement instrument that provides a visual display for an electrical signal. Most commonly, oscilloscopes are used to create a display of voltage over time. *Also called:* cathode-ray oscilloscope.

OSF *n.* Acronym for **O**pen **S**oftware **F**oundation. A nonprofit consortium of firms (including DEC, Hewlett-Packard, and IBM), formed in 1988, that promotes standards and specifications for programs operating under UNIX and licenses software (as source code) to its members. OSF's products include the Distributed Computing Environment, the graphical user interface Motif, and the OSF/1 operating system (a variant of UNIX).

OSI *n. See* ISO/OSI reference model.

OSI protocol stack *n.* The set of protocols based on—and corresponding to—the ISO/OSI reference model.

OSI reference model *n. See* ISO/OSI reference model.

OSPF *n.* Acronym for **O**pen **S**hortest **P**ath **F**irst. A routing protocol for IP networks, such as the Internet, that allows a router to calculate the shortest path to each node for sending messages. The router sends information on the nodes it is linked to, called link-state advertisements, to other routers on the network to accumulate link-state information to make its calculations. *See also* communications protocol, node (definition 2), path (definition 1), router.

OS X *n. See* Mac OS X.

OTOH *n.* Acronym for **o**n **t**he **o**ther **h**and. A shorthand expression often used in e-mail, Internet news, and discussion groups.

Outbox *n.* In many e-mail applications, the default mailbox where the program stores outgoing messages. *See also* e-mail[1] (definition 1), mailbox. *Compare* Inbox.

outdent *n. See* hanging indent.

outer join *n.* In database management, an operator in relational algebra. An outer join performs an extended join operation in which the tuples (rows) in one relation (table) that have no counterpart in the second relation appear in the resulting relation concatenated with all null values. *Compare* inner join.

outline font *n.* A font (type design) stored in a computer or printer as a set of outlines for drawing each of the alphabetic and other characters in a character set. Outline fonts are templates rather than actual patterns of dots and are scaled up or down to match a particular type size. Such fonts are most often used for printing, as is the case with most PostScript fonts on a PostScript-compatible laser printer and TrueType fonts. *Compare* bitmapped font, screen font, stroke font.

Outlook *n.* Microsoft's messaging and collaboration application software. A member of the Microsoft Office suite, Outlook includes e-mail, an integrated calendar, and contact-management and task-management features, and it also provides support for building customized tools, such as special-purpose forms, for collaborative functions.

out-of-band signaling *n.* Transmission of some signals, such as control information, on frequencies outside the bandwidth available for voice or data transfer on a communications channel. *Compare* in-band signaling.

output[1] *n.* The results of processing, whether sent to the screen or printer, stored on disk as a file, or sent to another computer in a network.

output[2] *vb.* To send out data by a computer or sound by a speaker.

output area *n. See* output buffer.

output-bound *n. See* input/output-bound.

output buffer *n.* A portion of memory set aside for temporary storage of information, leaving main memory for storage, display, printing, or transmission. *See also* buffer[1].

output channel *n. See* channel (definition 1), input/output channel.

output simulation *n.* A feature of color management applications in which a computer display is calibrated to help predict the results of printing a graphics file on a specific device. *Also called:* soft proofing.

output stream *n.* A flow of information that leaves a computer system and is associated with a particular task or destination. In programming, an output stream can be a series of characters sent from the computer's memory to a display or to a disk file. *Compare* input stream.

outsourcing *n.* The assignment of tasks to independent contractors, such as individual consultants or service bureaus. Tasks such as data entry and programming are often performed via outsourcing.

OverDrive *n.* A type of microprocessor from Intel designed to replace a computer's existing i486SX or i486DX microprocessor. The OverDrive is functionally identical to Intel's i486DX2 microprocessor, but it is an end-user product, whereas the i486DX2 is sold only to computer manufacturers who build it into their own systems. Upgrading a system with an OverDrive processor differs from system to system, and some systems might not be able to support an OverDrive processor. *See also* i486DX, i486SL, i486SX, microprocessor. *Compare* i486DX2.

overflow *n.* **1.** Generally, the condition that occurs when data resulting from input or processing requires more bits than have been provided in hardware or software to store the data. Examples of overflow include a floating-point operation whose result is too large for the number of bits allowed for the exponent, a string that exceeds the bounds of the array allocated for it, and an integer operation whose result contains too many bits for the register into which it is to be stored. *See also* overflow error. *Compare* underflow. **2.** The part of a data item that cannot be stored because the data exceeds the capacity of the available data structure.

overflow error *n.* An error that arises when a number, often the result of an arithmetic operation, is too large to be contained in the data structure that a program provides for it.

overhead *n.* Work or information that provides support—possibly critical support—for a computing process but is not an intrinsic part of the operation or data. Overhead often adds to processing time but is generally necessary.

overlaid windows *n.* *See* cascading windows.

overlapped communication operation *n.* The performance of two distinct communication operations simultaneously; for example, a simultaneous read/write operation. Windows CE does not support overlapped communication operation, but it does support multiple read/writes pending on a device.

overlay[1] *n.* **1.** A section of a program designed to reside on a designated storage device, such as a disk, and to be loaded into memory when needed, usually overwriting one or more overlays already in memory. Use of overlays allows large programs to fit into a limited amount of memory, but at the cost of speed. **2.** A printed form positioned over a screen, tablet, or keyboard for identification of particular features. *See also* keyboard template.

overlay[2] *vb.* **1.** In computer graphics, to superimpose one graphic image over another. **2.** In video, to superimpose a graphic image generated on a computer over video signals, either live or recorded.

overprint *vb.* The process of printing an element of one color over one of another color without removing, or knocking out, the material underneath. *Compare* knockout (definition 1).

override *vb.* To prevent something from happening in a program or in an operating system or to initiate another response. For example, a user can often override and thus abort a lengthy sorting procedure in a database program by pressing the Escape key.

overrun *n.* In information transfer, an error that occurs when a device receiving data cannot handle or make use of the information as rapidly as it arrives. *See also* input/output-bound.

overscan *n.* The part of a video signal sent to a raster display that controls the area outside the rectangle containing visual information. The overscan area is sometimes colored to form a border around the screen.

overshoot *n.* The phenomenon in which a system suffers from a time delay in responding to input and continues to change state even after it has reached the desired state. This situation requires that correcting input be made so that the system reaches the desired state. For example, the arm carrying the heads in a hard disk drive might move slightly past the desired track before it stops, requiring another signal to pull it back.

overstrike *vb.* To type or print one character directly over another so that the two occupy the same space on the page or screen.

O

overtype mode *n. See* overwrite mode.

overwrite mode *n.* A text-entry mode in which newly typed characters replace existing characters under or to the left of the cursor insertion point. *Also called:* overtype mode, typeover mode. *Compare* insert mode.

overwriting virus *n.* A type of virus that overwrites the host file it has infected, destroying the original data. *Also called:* overwrite virus.

Oz *n.* A concurrent, object-oriented programming language.

O

p *prefix* *See* pico-.

P *prefix* *See* peta-.

P2P or P-to-P *n.* An Internet-based networking option in which two or more computers connect directly to each other to communicate and share files without use of a central server. Interest in P2P networking blossomed with the introduction of Napster and Gnutella. Short for Peer-to-Peer. *See also* peer-to-peer architecture, peer-to-peer communications.

P3P *n.* Acronym for **P**latform for **P**rivacy **P**references. An open W3C protocol that allows Internet users to control the type of personal information that is collected by the Web sites they visit. P3P uses User Agents built into browsers and Web applications to allow P3P-enabled Web sites to communicate privacy practices to users before they log on to the Web site. P3P compares the Web site's privacy policies with the user's personal set of privacy preferences, and it reports any disagreements to the user.

P5 *n.* Intel's internal working name for the Pentium microprocessor. Although it was not intended to be used publicly, the name P5 leaked out to the computer-industry trade press and was commonly used to reference the microprocessor before it was released. *See also* 586, Pentium.

pack *vb.* To store information in a more compact form. Packing eliminates unnecessary spaces and other such characters and may use other special methods of compressing data as well. It is used by some programs to minimize storage requirements.

package *n.* **1.** A computer application consisting of one or more programs created to perform a particular type of work—for example, an accounting package or a spreadsheet package. **2.** In electronics, the housing in which an electronic component is packaged. *See also* DIP. **3.** A group of classes or interfaces and a keyword in the Java programming language. Packages are declared in Java by using the "package" keyword. *See also* class, declare, interface (definition 1), keyword.

packaged software *n.* A software program sold through a retail distributor, as opposed to custom software. *See also* canned software.

packed decimal *adj.* A method of encoding decimal numbers in binary form that maximizes storage space by using each byte to represent two decimal digits. When signed decimal numbers are stored in packed decimal format, the sign appears in the rightmost four bits of the rightmost (least significant) byte.

packet *n.* **1.** A unit of information transmitted as a whole from one device to another on a network. **2.** In packet-switching networks, a transmission unit of fixed maximum size that consists of binary digits representing both data and a header containing an identification number, source and destination addresses, and sometimes error-control data. *See also* packet switching.

packet assembler and disassembler *n.* *See* packet assembler/disassembler.

packet assembler/disassembler *n.* An interface between non-packet-switching equipment and a packet-switching network. *Acronym:* PAD.

packet filtering *n.* The process of controlling network access based on IP addresses. Firewalls will often incorporate filters that allow or deny users the ability to enter or leave a local area network. Packet filtering is also used to accept or reject packets such as e-mail, based on the origin of the packet, to ensure security on a private network. *See also* firewall, IP address, packet (definition 1).

packet flooding *n.* A technique employed in a number of DoS (denial of service) attacks in which a flood of packets of data are sent to a target server, overwhelming the computer and rendering it unable to respond to legitimate network requests. Examples of specific types of packet flooding include smurf attacks and SYN flood attacks. *See also* DoS, packet, smurf attack, SYN flood.

packet header *n.* The portion of a data packet that precedes the body (data). The header contains data, such as source and destination addresses and control and timing information, that is needed for successful transmission.

Packet Internet Groper *n. See* ping[1] (definition 1).

packet sniffer *n.* A hardware and/or software device that examines every packet sent across a network. To work, a packet sniffer must be installed in the same network block as the network it is intended to sniff. Designed as a problem-solving tool to isolate problems degrading network performance, packet sniffers have become security risks on some networks because crackers can use them to capture nonencrypted user IDs, passwords, credit card numbers, e-mail addresses, and other confidential information. *See also* cracker, packet. *Compare* monitoring software.

packet switching *n.* A message-delivery technique in which small units of information (packets) are relayed through stations in a computer network along the best route available between the source and the destination. A packet-switching network handles information in small units, breaking long messages into multiple packets before routing. Although each packet may travel along a different path, and the packets composing a message may arrive at different times or out of sequence, the receiving computer reassembles the original message correctly. Packet-switching networks are considered to be fast and efficient. To manage the tasks of routing traffic and assembling/disassembling packets, such a network requires some intelligence from the computers and software that control delivery. The Internet is an example of a packet-switching network. Standards for packet switching on networks are documented in the International Telecommunication Union (ITU) recommendation X.25. *Compare* circuit switching.

Packet Switching Exchange *n.* An intermediary switching station in a packet-switching network.

packet trailer *n.* The portion of a data packet that follows the body (data). The trailer typically contains information related to error checking and correction. *See also* packet.

packing density *n.* The number of storage units per length or area of a storage device. Bits per inch is one measure of packing density.

PackIT *n.* A file format used on the Apple Macintosh to represent collections of Mac files, possibly Huffman compressed. *See also* Huffman coding, Macintosh.

PAD *n. See* packet assembler/disassembler.

pad character *n.* In data input and storage, an extra character inserted as filler to use up surplus space in a predefined block of a specified length, such as a fixed-length field.

padding *n.* In data storage, the addition of one or more bits, usually zeros, to a block of data to fill it, to force the actual data bits into a certain position, or to prevent the data from duplicating a bit pattern that has an established meaning, such as an embedded command.

paddle *n.* An early type of input device often used with computer games especially for side-to-side or up-and-down movements of an on-screen object. A paddle is less sophisticated than a joystick because it permits the user, by turning a dial, to specify movement along only a single axis. The paddle got its name because its most popular use was to control the on-screen paddles in the simple early video games, such as Pong. See the illustration.

Paddle.

paddle switch *n.* Any switch that has a wide handle. The large on/off switch on many IBM personal computers is one type of paddle switch.

page *n.* **1.** In word processing, the text and display elements to be printed on one side of a sheet of paper, subject to formatting specifications such as depth, margin size, and number of columns. **2.** A fixed-size block of memory. When used in the context of a paging memory system, a page is a block of memory whose physical address can be changed via mapping hardware. *See also* EMS, memory management unit, virtual memory. **3.** In computer graphics, a portion of display memory that contains one complete full-screen image; the internal representation of a screenful of information. **4.** *See* Web page.

page banner *n.* A section of a Web page containing a graphic element and text, such as the page title. Page banners are usually displayed at the top of a Web page. Page banners can also be used to link to other Web sites for advertising purposes. *Also called:* banner.

P

page break *n.* The point at which the flow of text in a document moves to the top of a new page. Most word processors automatically place page breaks when the material on the page reaches a specified maximum. By contrast, a "hard" or "manual" page break is a command or a code inserted by the user to force a page break at a specific place in the text. *See also* form feed.

paged address *n.* In the 80386, i486, and Pentium paged memory architecture, an address in memory created by combining the processes of segment translation and page translation. In the paged-memory scheme, which requires that the microprocessor's paging feature be enabled, logical addresses are transformed into physical addresses in two steps: segment translation and page translation. The first step, segment translation, converts a logical to a linear address—an address that refers indirectly to a physical address. After the linear address is obtained, the microprocessor's paging hardware converts the linear address to a physical address by specifying a page table (an array of 32-bit page specifiers), a page (a 4-KB unit of contiguous addresses within physical memory) within that table, and an offset within that page. This information collectively refers to a physical address.

page-description language *n.* A programming language, such as PostScript, that is used to describe output to a printer or a display device, which then uses the instructions from the page-description language to construct text and graphics to create the required page image. Page-description languages are like other computer languages, with logical program flow allowing for sophisticated manipulation of the output. A page-description language, like a blueprint, sets out specifications (as for fonts and type sizes) but leaves the work of drawing characters and graphics to the output device itself. Because this approach delegates the detail work to the device that produces the output, a page-description language is machine-independent. These abilities come at a price, however. Page-description languages require printers with processing power and memory comparable to, and often exceeding, that of personal computers. *Acronym:* PDL. *See also* PostScript.

paged memory management unit *n.* A hardware unit that performs tasks related to accessing and managing memory used by different applications or by virtual-memory operating systems. *Acronym:* PMMU.

Page Down key *n.* A standard key (often labeled "PgDn") on most computer keyboards whose specific meaning is different in different programs. In many cases, it moves the cursor down to the top of the next page or a specific number of lines.

page fault *n.* The interrupt that occurs when software attempts to read from or write to a virtual memory location that is marked "not present." The mapping hardware of a virtual memory system maintains status information about every page in the virtual address space. A page either is mapped onto a physical address or is not present in physical memory. When a read or write to an unmapped virtual address is detected, the memory management hardware generates the page fault interrupt. The operating system must respond to the page fault by swapping in the data for the page and updating the status information in the memory management unit. *See also* page (definition 2), swap (definition 2), virtual memory.

page frame *n.* A physical address to which a page of virtual memory may be mapped. In a system with 4096-byte pages, page frame 0 corresponds to physical addresses 0 through 4095. *See also* paging, virtual memory.

page-image buffer *n.* Memory in a page printer used to hold the bit map (image) of a page as the printer's raster image processor builds the page and as the printer produces the page. *See also* page printer, raster image processor.

page-image file *n.* A file containing the necessary code for a printer or other display device to create the page or screen image. *See also* PostScript.

page-jacking *n.* A deceptive practice that detours Web visitors from legitimate sites generated as search engine results to copycat Web pages, from which they will be redirected to pornographic or other unwanted sites. Page-jacking is accomplished by copying the contents and metatags of a Web page, altering its title and content so that, on search results, it displays before the original, and then submitting the copied page to search engines. When clicking on the link to the copied site, the visitor will instead be redirected to an unwanted and unrelated site. *See also* metatag. *Compare* mousetrapping.

P

page layout *n.* In desktop publishing, the process of arranging text and graphics on the pages of a document. Page-layout programs excel in text placement and management of special effects applied to text. Although page-layout programs are generally slower than word-processing programs, they can perform such advanced tasks as flowing text into complex multicolumn page designs, printing documents in signatures, managing color separations, and supporting sophisticated kerning and hyphenation.

page makeup *n.* The assembling of graphics and text on a page in preparation for printing.

page mode RAM *n.* A specially designed dynamic RAM that supports access to sequential memory locations with a reduced cycle time. This is especially attractive in video RAM, in which each location is accessed in ascending order to create the screen image. Page mode RAM can also improve the execution speed of code because code tends to execute sequentially through memory. *See also* cycle time, dynamic RAM.

page orientation *n. See* landscape mode, portrait mode.

page printer *n.* Any printer, such as a laser printer, that prints an entire page at once. Because page printers must store the entire page in memory before printing, they require relatively large amounts of memory. *Compare* line printer.

pager *n.* Pocket-sized wireless electronic device that uses radio signals to record incoming phone numbers or short text messages. Some pagers allow users to send messages as well. *Also called:* beeper.

page reader *n. See* document reader.

page setup *n.* A set of choices that affect how a file is printed on the page. Page setup might reflect the size of paper going into the printer, the page margins, the specific pages in the document to be printed, whether the image is to be reduced or enlarged when printed, and whether another file is to be printed immediately after the first file is printed.

pages per minute *n. See* PPM.

Page Up key *n.* A standard key (often labeled "PgUp") on most computer keyboards whose specific meaning is different in different programs. In many cases, it moves the cursor up to the top of the previous page or a specific number of lines.

pagination *n.* **1.** The process of dividing a document into pages for printing. **2.** The process of adding page numbers, as in a running head.

paging *n.* A technique for implementing virtual memory. The virtual address space is divided into a number of fixed-size blocks called pages, each of which can be mapped onto any of the physical addresses available on the system. Special memory management hardware (MMU or PMMU) performs the address translation from virtual addresses to physical addresses. *See also* memory management unit, paged memory management unit, virtual memory.

paging file *n.* A hidden file on the hard disk that operating systems (such as Windows, Mac OS X, and UNIX) use to hold parts of programs and data files that do not fit in memory. The paging file and physical memory, or RAM, make up virtual memory. Data is moved from the paging file to memory as needed and moved from memory to the paging file to make room for new data in memory. *Also called:* swap file. *See also* virtual memory.

paint[1] *n.* A color and pattern used with graphics programs to fill areas of a drawing, applied with tools such as a paintbrush or a spraycan.

paint[2] *vb.* To fill a portion of a drawing with paint (color or a pattern).

paintbrush *n.* An artist's tool in a paint program or another graphics application for applying a streak of solid color to an image. The user can usually select the width of the streak. *See also* paint program. *Compare* spraycan.

paint program *n.* An application program that creates graphics as bit maps. A paint program, because it treats a drawing as a group of dots, is particularly appropriate for freehand drawing. Such a program commonly provides tools for images requiring lines, curves, and geometric shapes but does not treat any shape as an entity that can be moved or modified as a discrete object without losing its identity. *Compare* drawing program.

palette *n.* **1.** In paint programs, a collection of drawing tools, such as patterns, colors, brush shapes, and different line widths, from which the user can choose. **2.** A subset of the color look-up table that establishes the colors that can be displayed on the screen at a particular time. The number of colors in a palette is determined by the number of bits used to represent a pixel. *See also* color bits, color look-up table, pixel.

palmtop *n.* A portable personal computer whose size enables it to be held in one hand while it is operated with the other hand. A major difference between palmtop computers and laptop computers is that palmtops are usually powered by off-the-shelf batteries such as AA cells. Palmtop computers typically do not have disk drives; rather, their programs are stored in ROM and are loaded into RAM when they are switched on. More recent palmtop computers are equipped with PCMCIA slots to provide wider flexibility and greater capability. *See also* handheld PC, PCMCIA slot, portable computer. *Compare* laptop.

PAM *n. See* pulse amplitude modulation.

panning *n.* In computer graphics, a display method in which a viewing window on the screen scans horizontally or vertically, like a camera, to bring offscreen extensions of the current image smoothly into view.

PANTONE MATCHING SYSTEM *n.* In graphic arts and printing, a standard system of ink color specification consisting of a swatch book in which each of about 500 colors is assigned a number. *Acronym:* PMS. *See also* color model.

PAP *n.* **1.** Acronym for **P**assword **A**uthentication **P**rotocol. A method for verifying the identity of a user attempting to log on to a Point-to-Point Protocol (PPP) server. PAP is used if a more rigorous method, such as the Challenge Handshake Authentication Protocol (CHAP), is not available or if the user name and password that the user submitted to PAP must be sent to another program without encryption. **2.** Acronym for **P**rinter **A**ccess **P**rotocol. The protocol in AppleTalk networks that governs communication between computers and printers.

paper feed *n.* A mechanism that moves paper through a printer. In laser printers and other page printers, the paper feed is usually a series of rollers that firmly grip and align the paper. In dot-matrix printers, the paper feed is usually a pin feed or tractor feed, in which small pins drag or push paper that has detachable edges punched with sprocket holes. Friction feed is another type of paper feed, in which the paper is gripped between the platen and pressure rollers and pulled by rotation of the platen.

paperless office *n.* The idealized office in which information is entirely stored, manipulated, and transferred electronically rather than on paper.

paper-white *adj.* Of, pertaining to, or being a type of monochrome computer monitor whose default operating colors are black text on a white background. Paper-white monitors are popular in desktop publishing and word processing environments because the monitor most closely resembles a white sheet of paper printed with black characters.

paper-white monitor *n.* A display monitor in which text and graphics characters are displayed in black against a white background to resemble the appearance of a printed page. Some manufacturers use the name to refer to a background that is tinted in a manner corresponding to bonded paper.

paradigm *n.* An archetypal example or pattern that provides a model for a process or system.

paragraph *n.* **1.** In word processing, any part of a document preceded by one paragraph mark and ending with another. To the program, a paragraph represents a unit of information that can be selected as a whole or given formatting distinct from the surrounding paragraphs. **2.** On IBM and other computers built around the Intel 8088 or 8086 microprocessor, a 16-byte section of memory beginning at a location (address) that can be divided evenly by 16 (hexadecimal 10).

parallel *adj.* **1.** Of or relating to electronic circuits in which the corresponding terminals of two or more components are connected. **2.** In geometry and graphics, of, relating to, or being lines that run side by side in the same direction in the same plane without intersecting. **3.** In data communications, of, relating to, or being information that is sent in groups of bits over multiple wires, one wire for each bit in a group. *See also* parallel interface. *Compare* serial. **4.** In data handling, of or relating to handling more than one event at a time, with each event having its own portion of the system's resources. *See also* parallel processing.

parallel access *n.* The ability to store or retrieve all of the bits composing a single unit of information, such as a byte or a word (usually two bytes), at the same time. *Also called:* simultaneous access.

parallel adder *n.* A logic device that processes the addition of several (typically 4, 8, or 16) binary inputs simultaneously rather than sequentially, as is the case with half adders and full adders. Parallel adders speed processing

P

because they require fewer steps to produce the result. *Compare* full adder, half adder.

parallel algorithm *n.* An algorithm in which more than one portion of the algorithm can be followed at one time. Parallel algorithms are usually used in multiprocessing environments. *Compare* sequential algorithm.

parallel circuit *n.* A circuit in which the corresponding leads of two or more of the circuit components are connected. In a parallel circuit, there are two or more separate pathways between points. The individual components in a parallel circuit all receive the same voltage but share the current load. See the illustration. *Compare* series circuit.

Parallel circuit.

parallel computer *n.* A computer that uses several processors that work concurrently. Software written for parallel computers can increase the amount of work done in a specific amount of time by dividing a computing task among several simultaneously functioning processors. *See also* parallel processing.

parallel computing *n.* The use of multiple computers or processors to solve a problem or perform a function. *See also* array processor, massively parallel processing, pipeline processing, SMP.

parallel connection *n. See* parallel interface.

parallel database *n.* A database system involving the concurrent use of two or more processors or operating system processes to service database management requests such as SQL queries and updates, transaction logging, I/O handling, and data buffering. A parallel database is capable of performing a large number of simultaneous tasks across multiple processors and storage devices, providing quick access to databases containing many gigabytes of data.

Parallel Data Structure *n. See* PDS (definition 2).

parallel execution *n. See* concurrent execution.

parallel interface *n.* The specification of a data transmission scheme that sends multiple data and control bits simultaneously over wires connected in parallel. The most common parallel interface is the Centronics interface. *See also* Centronics parallel interface. *Compare* serial interface.

parallel port *n.* An input/output connector that sends and receives data 8 bits at a time, in parallel, between a computer and a peripheral device such as a printer, scanner, CD-ROM, or other storage device. The parallel port, often called a Centronics interface after the original design standard, uses a 25-pin connector called a DB-25 connector that includes three groups of lines: four for control signals, five for status signals, and eight for data. *See also* Centronics parallel interface, ECP, EPP, IEEE 1284, input/output port. *Compare* serial port.

Parallel port

Parallel port.

parallel printer *n.* A printer that is connected to the computer via a parallel interface. In general, a parallel connection can move data between devices faster than a serial connection can. The parallel interface is preferred in the IBM PC world because its cabling is more standardized than that of the serial interface and because the computer's operating system assumes that the system printer is attached to the parallel port. *See also* parallel interface. *Compare* serial printer.

parallel processing *n.* A method of processing that can run only on a computer that contains two or more processors running simultaneously. Parallel processing differs from multiprocessing in the way a task is distributed over the available processors. In multiprocessing, a process might be divided up into sequential blocks, with one processor managing access to a database, another analyzing the data, and a third handling graphical output to the screen. Programmers working with systems that perform parallel processing must find ways to divide a task so that it is more or less evenly distributed among the processors available. *Compare* coprocessor, multiprocessing.

parallel server *n.* A computer system that implements some form of parallel processing to improve its performance as a server. *See also* SMP server.

parallel transmission *n.* The simultaneous transmission of a group of bits over separate wires. With microcomputers, parallel transmission refers to the transmission of 1 byte (8 bits). The standard connection for parallel transmission is known as the Centronics interface. *See also* Centronics parallel interface. *Compare* serial transmission.

parameter *n.* In programming, a value that is given to a variable, either at the beginning of an operation or before an expression is evaluated by a program. Until the operation is completed, a parameter is effectively treated as a constant value by the program. A parameter can be text, a number, or an argument name assigned to a value that is passed from one routine to another. Parameters are used as a means of customizing program operation. *See also* argument, pass by address, pass by value, routine.

parameter-driven *adj.* Of, pertaining to, or being a program or an operation whose character or outcome is determined by the values of the parameters that are assigned to it.

parameter passing *n.* In programming, the substitution of an actual parameter value for a formal parameter when a procedure or function call is processed.

parameter RAM *n.* A few bytes of battery-backed CMOS RAM on the motherboards of Apple Macintosh computers. Information about the configuration of the system is stored in parameter RAM. *Acronym:* PRAM. *See also* CMOS RAM. *Compare* CMOS (definition 2).

PARC *n. See* Xerox PARC.

parent/child *adj.* **1.** Pertaining to or constituting a relationship between processes in a multitasking environment in which the parent process calls the child process and most often suspends its own operation until the child process aborts or is completed. **2.** Pertaining to or constituting a relationship between nodes in a tree data structure in which the parent is one step closer to the root (that is, one level higher) than the child.

parity *n.* The quality of sameness or equivalence, in the case of computers usually referring to an error-checking procedure in which the number of 1s must always be the same—either even or odd—for each group of bits trans-

mitted without error. If parity is checked on a per-character basis, the method is called vertical redundancy checking, or VRC; if checked on a block-by-block basis, the method is called longitudinal redundancy checking, or LRC. In typical modem-to-modem communications, parity is one of the parameters that must be agreed upon by sending and receiving parties before transmission can take place. See the table. *See also* parity bit, parity check, parity error.

Table P.1   Types of Parity.

Type	Description
Even parity	The number of 1s in each successfully transmitted set of bits must be an even number.
Odd parity	The number of 1s in each successfully transmitted set of bits must be an odd number.
No parity	No parity bit is used.
Space parity	A parity bit is used and is always set to 0.
Mark parity	A parity bit is used and is always set to 1.

parity bit *n.* An extra bit used in checking for errors in groups of data bits transferred within or between computer systems. With PCs, the term is frequently encountered in modem-to-modem communications, in which a parity bit is often used to check the accuracy with which each character is transmitted, and in RAM, where a parity bit is often used to check the accuracy with which each byte is stored.

parity check *n.* The use of parity to check the accuracy of transmitted data. *See also* parity, parity bit.

parity error *n.* An error in parity that indicates an error in transmitted data or in data stored in memory. If a parity error occurs in communications, all or part of a message must be retransmitted; if a parity error occurs in RAM, the computer usually halts. *See also* parity, parity bit.

park *vb.* To position the read/write head over a portion of a disk that stores no data (and therefore can never be damaged) or beyond the surface of the disk, prior to shutting down the drive, especially in preparation for moving it. Parking can be performed manually, automatically, or by a disk utility program.

P

parrallaxing *n.* A 3-D animation technique, often used by computer game developers, where backgrounds are displayed using different levels of speed to achieve realism. For example, distant levels move at a slower speed than closer levels, thereby giving the illusion of depth. *See also* animation.

parse *vb.* To break input into smaller chunks so that a program can act upon the information.

parser *n.* An application or device that breaks data into smaller chunks so that an application can act on the information. *See also* parse.

partition *n.* **1.** A logically distinct portion of memory or a storage device that functions as though it were a physically separate unit. **2.** In database programming, a subset of a database table or file.

Partition Boot Sector *n.* The first sector in the system (startup) partition of a computer's bootable hard disk, or the first sector of a bootable floppy disk. On an x86-based computer, the Partition Boot Sector is read into memory at startup by the Master Boot Record. It is the Partition Boot Sector that contains the instructions required to begin the process of loading and starting the computer's operating system. *See also* Master Boot Record, partition table.

partition table *n.* A table of information in the first sector of a computer's hard disk that tells where each partition (discrete portion of storage) on the disk begins and ends. The physical locations are given as the beginning and ending head, sector, and cylinder numbers. In addition to these "addresses," the partition table identifies the type of file system used for each partition and identifies whether the partition is bootable—whether it can be used to start the computer. Although it is a small data structure, the partition table is a critical element on the hard disk.

partnership *n.* The settings on a desktop computer and Windows CE device that allow information to be synchronized, as well as copied or moved between the computer and device. The mobile device can have partnerships with up to two desktop computers. *See also* synchronization (definition 6).

Pascal *n.* A concise procedural language designed between 1967 and 1971 by Niklaus Wirth. Pascal, a compiled, structured language built upon ALGOL, simplifies syntax while adding data types and structures such as subranges, enumerated data types, files, records, and sets. *See also* ALGOL, compiled language. *Compare* C.

pASP *n. See* pocket Active Server Pages.

pass[1] *n.* In programming, the carrying out of one complete sequence of events.

pass[2] *vb.* To forward a piece of data from one part of a program to another. *See also* pass by address, pass by value.

pass by address *n.* A means of passing an argument or parameter to a subroutine. The calling routine passes the address (memory location) of the parameter to the called routine, which can then use the address to retrieve or modify the value of the parameter. *Also called:* pass by reference. *See also* argument, call[1]. *Compare* pass by value.

pass by reference *n. See* pass by address.

pass by value *n.* A means of passing an argument or a parameter to a subroutine. A copy of the value of the argument is created and passed to the called routine. When this method is used, the called routine can modify the copy of the argument, but it cannot modify the original argument. *See also* argument, call[1]. *Compare* pass by address.

passivation *n.* In Sun Microsystems's J2EE network platform, the process of "turning off" an enterprise java bean (EJB) by caching it from memory to secondary storage. *See also* Enterprise JavaBeans, J2EE. *Compare* activation.

passive hub *n.* A type of hub used on ARCnet networks that passes signals along but has no additional capability. *See also* ARCnet. *Compare* active hub, Intelligent hub.

passive-matrix display *n.* An inexpensive, low-resolution liquid crystal display (LCD) made from a large array of liquid crystal cells that are controlled by transistors outside of the display screen. One transistor controls an entire row or column of pixels. Passive-matrix displays are commonly used in portable computers, such as laptops and notebooks, because of their thin width. While these displays have good contrast for monochrome screens, the resolution is weaker for color screens. These displays are also difficult to view from any angle other than straight on, unlike active-matrix displays. However, computers with passive-matrix displays are considerably cheaper than those with active-matrix screens. See the illustration. *Also called:* dual-scan display. *See also* liquid crystal display, supertwist display, transistor, twisted nematic display. *Compare* active-matrix display.

P

ITO electrodes in columns on opposite side of the LCD panel

LCD panel matrix

Pixel element

Indium Tin Oxide (ITO) electrodes in rows on one side of the LCD panel

Passive-matrix display.

passive node *n.* A network node that "listens" for transmissions but is not actively involved in passing them along the network; typical of a node on a bus network. *See also* bus network, node (definition 2).

Passport *n.* A suite of personal identification services from Microsoft that consolidates user names, passwords, and other information. With the Passport single sign-in service, a user enters one name and password at any Passport site on the Internet; after signing in to one Passport site, a user can sign in to others without reentering the information. Passport also provides a server-based wallet service that stores credit card and billing information, a Kids Passport service, and a public-profile service. Passport is one of the foundation services of the Microsoft .NET initiative. *See also* .NET, .NET My Services, single sign-on, wallet.

pass-through *adj.* **1.** In general, a reference to something that acts as an intermediary between other entities. For example, a pass-through proxy server allows external access to an internal (protected) server by passing requests from the requesting client to the server without allowing direct access. **2.** Pertaining to a device or connector that

moves a signal or set of signals from the input to the output without making any changes. For example, a peripheral device such as a SCSI adapter might have a pass-through parallel I/O port for connecting a printer through the same connector.

password *n.* The string of characters entered by a user to verify his or her identity to the network. The system compares the code against a stored list of authorized passwords and users. If the code is legitimate, the system allows the user access at whatever security level has been approved for the owner of the password. Ideally a password is a combination of text, numbers, and punctuation or other characters that cannot be guessed at or easily cracked by intruders.

password attack *n.* An attack on a computer or network in which a password is stolen and decrypted or is revealed by a password dictionary program. The compromised password opens the network to the hacker and may also be used to reveal additional network passwords. *See also* password sniffing.

Password Authentication Protocol *n. See* PAP (definition 1).

password protection *n.* The use of passwords as a means of allowing only authorized users access to a computer system or its files.

password shadowing *n.* A security system in which an encrypted password is stored in a separate "shadow" file, and its place is taken by a token representing the password. Password shadowing is used as protection from password attacks. *See also* password attack, password sniffing.

password sniffing *n.* A technique employed by hackers to capture passwords by intercepting data packets and searching them for passwords. *Also called:* packet sniffing.

paste *vb.* To insert text or a graphic that has been cut or copied from one document into a different location in the same or a different document. *See also* cut, cut and paste.

patch[1] *n.* A piece of object code that is inserted in an executable program as a temporary fix for a bug.

patch[2] *vb.* In programming, to repair a deficiency in the functionality of an existing routine or program, generally in response to an unforeseen need or set of operating

P

circumstances. Patching is a common means of adding a feature or a function to a program until the next version of the software is released. *Compare* hack (definition 2), kludge (definition 2).

path *n.* **1.** In communications, a link between two nodes in a network. **2.** A route through a structured collection of information, as in a database, a program, or files stored on disk. **3.** In programming, the sequence of instructions a computer carries out in executing a routine. **4.** In information processing, such as the theory underlying expert (deductive) systems, a logical course through the branches of a tree of inferences leading to a conclusion. **5.** In file storage, the route followed by the operating system through the directories in finding, sorting, and retrieving files on a disk. **6.** In graphics, an accumulation of line segments or curves to be filled or drawn.

path menu *n.* In windowed environments, the menu or drop box used to enter the universal naming convention path to a shared network resource.

pathname *n.* In a hierarchical filing system, a listing of the directories or folders that lead from the current directory to a file. *Also called:* directory path.

pattern recognition *n.* **1.** A broad technology describing the ability of a computer to identify patterns. The term usually refers to computer recognition of visual images or sound patterns that have been converted to arrays of numbers. **2.** The recognition of purely mathematical or textual patterns.

Pause key *n.* **1.** A key on a keyboard that temporarily stops the operation of a program or a command. The Pause key is used, for example, to halt scrolling so that a multiscreen listing or document can be read. **2.** Any key that creates a pause in an operation. For example, many game programs have a Pause key, often simply the P key, that temporarily suspends the game.

payload *n.* The effects caused by a virus or other malicious code. The payload of a virus may include moving, altering, overwriting, and deleting files, or other destructive activity. A virus or worm may contain more than one payload, each with a separate trigger.

PB *n. See* petabyte.

PB SRAM *n. See* pipeline burst static RAM.

PBX *n.* Acronym for **P**rivate **B**ranch **E**xchange. An automatic telephone switching system that enables users within an organization to place calls to each other without going through the public telephone network. Users can also place calls to outside numbers.

PC *n.* **1.** A microcomputer that conforms to the standard developed by IBM for personal computers, which uses a microprocessor in the Intel 80x86 family (or compatible) and can execute the BIOS. See the illustration. *See also* 8086, BIOS, clone, IBM PC. **2.** A computer in IBM's Personal Computer line. *Also called:* IBM PC. *See also* PC-compatible (definition 1), personal computer.

PC.

PCB *n. See* printed circuit board.

PC board *n. See* printed circuit board.

PC Card *n.* An add-in card that conforms to the PCMCIA specification. A PC Card is a removable device, approximately the same size as a credit card, that is designed to plug into a PCMCIA slot. Release 1 of the PCMCIA specification, introduced in June 1990, specified a Type I card that is 3.3 millimeters thick and is intended to be used primarily as a memory-related peripheral. Release 2 of the PCMCIA specification, introduced in September 1991, specifies both a 5-millimeter-thick Type II card and a 10.5-millimeter-thick Type III card. Type II cards accommodate devices such as modem, fax, and network cards. Type III cards accommodate devices that require more space, such as wireless communications devices and rotating storage media (such as hard disks). *See also* PCMCIA, PCMCIA slot.

PC Card slot *n. See* PCMCIA slot.

PC-compatible *adj.* Conforming to IBM PC/XT and PC/ AT hardware and software specifications, which have been the de facto standard in the computing industry for personal computers that use the Intel 80x86 family or compatible chips. Most PC-compatible computers today are developed outside of IBM; they are still sometimes referred to as clones. *Also called:* IBM PC. *See also* 8086, clone, de facto standard, IBM AT, Wintel.

PC-DOS *n.* Acronym for **P**ersonal **C**omputer **D**isk **O**perating **S**ystem. The version of MS-DOS sold by IBM. MS-DOS and PC-DOS are virtually identical, although filenames of utility programs sometimes differ in the two versions. *See also* MS-DOS.

PC Expo *n.* Annual exposition centering on issues relating to the personal computer industry. PC Expo encompasses product exhibitions and educational events covering a wide range of topics affecting personal computing.

P-channel MOS *n. See* PMOS.

PCI *n. See* PCI local bus.

PCI card *n.* Short for **P**eripheral **C**omponent **I**nterconnect **card**. A card that fits into a PCI local bus to add functionality to a PC. Examples of the types of PCI cards available include TV tuner cards, video adapters, and network interface cards. *See also* card, PCI local bus.

PCI expansion slot *n.* A connection socket for a peripheral designed for the Peripheral Component Interconnect (PCI) local bus on a computer motherboard.

PCI Industrial Computer Manufacturers Group *n. See* PICMG.

PCI local bus *n.* Short for **P**eripheral **C**omponent **I**nterconnect **local bus**. A specification introduced by Intel Corporation that defines a local bus system that allows up to 10 PCI-compliant expansion cards to be installed in the computer. A PCI local bus system requires the presence of a PCI controller card, which must be installed in one of the PCI-compliant slots. Optionally, an expansion bus controller for the system's ISA, EISA, or Micro Channel Architecture slots can be installed as well, providing increased synchronization over all the system's bus-installed resources. The PCI controller can exchange data with the system's CPU

either 32 bits or 64 bits at a time, depending on the implementation, and it allows intelligent, PCI-compliant adapters to perform tasks concurrently with the CPU using a technique called bus mastering. The PCI specification allows for multiplexing, a technique that permits more than one electrical signal to be present on the bus at one time. *See also* local bus. *Compare* VL bus.

PCIX *n.* **1.** Acronym for **P**eripheral **C**omponent **I**nterconnect **E**xtended. A computer bus technology developed by IBM, Compaq, and Hewlett-Packard that allows data to be transferred at greater speeds. PCIX increases the speed of data from 66 MHz to 133 MHz, but it will not run faster than the connected peripherals or computer processor will allow. PCI and PCIX peripherals are compatible with one another. *Also called:* PCI-X. **2.** Acronym for **P**ermission-based **C**ustomer **I**nformation **E**xchange. A framework for the organization and exchange of information between customer and vendor. PCIX allows different companies to map information into a customer-friendly, permission-based format without changing internal database structures.

PCL *n. See* Printer Control Language.

PCM *n. See* pulse code modulation.

PCMCIA *n.* Acronym for **P**ersonal **C**omputer **M**emory **C**ard **I**nternational **A**ssociation. A group of manufacturers and vendors formed to promote a common standard for PC Card–based peripherals and the slot designed to hold them, primarily on laptop, palmtop, and other portable computers, as well as for intelligent electronic devices. PCMCIA is also the name of the standard for PC Cards, first introduced in 1990 as release 1. *See also* PC Card, PCMCIA slot.

PCMCIA card *n. See* PC Card.

PCMCIA connector *n.* The 68-pin female connector inside a PCMCIA slot designed to hold the 68-pin male connector on a PC Card. *See also* PC Card, PCMCIA slot.

PCMCIA slot *n.* An opening in the housing of a computer, peripheral, or other intelligent electronic device designed to hold a PC Card. *Also called:* PC Card slot. *See also* PC Card, PCMCIA connector.

PC memory card *n.* **1.** An add-in circuit card that increases the amount of RAM in a system. *See also* memory card. **2.** A Type I PC Card as specified by PCMCIA. In

P

this context, such a card consists of conventional static RAM chips powered by a small battery and is designed to provide additional RAM to the system. *See also* PC Card. *Compare* flash memory.

PCMIA device *n. See* PC Card.

p-code *n. See* pseudocode.

PCS *n. See* Personal Communications Services.

PCT *n.* **1.** Acronym for **p**rogram **c**omprehension **t**ool. A software engineering tool that facilitates the process of understanding the structure and/or functionality of computer programs. **2.** Acronym for **P**rivate **C**ommunications **T**echnology, a protocol standard drafted by Microsoft and submitted to the IETF for consideration. PCT, like the Netscape-designed SSL (Secure Sockets Layer), supports authentication and encryption for securing privacy in Internet communications. **3.** Acronym for **P**ersonal **C**ommunications **T**echnology. An enhanced version of Secure Sockets Layer (SSL).

.pcx *n.* The file extension that identifies bitmapped images in the PC Paintbrush file format.

PC/XT *n.* The second-generation of the original IBM Personal Computer. The IBM PC/XT was introduced in 1983 and was the first of the PC computers to support hard disks. *See also* IBM PC.

PC/XT keyboard *n.* The keyboard for the PC/XT. Strong, reliable, and equipped with 83 keys, the PC/XT keyboard offers a typist an audible click. *See also* IBM PC, PC/XT.

PDA *n.* Acronym for **P**ersonal **D**igital **A**ssistant. A lightweight palmtop computer designed to provide specific functions like personal organization (calendar, note taking, database, calculator, and so on) as well as communications. More advanced models also offer multimedia features. Many PDA devices rely on a pen or other pointing device for input instead of a keyboard or mouse, although some offer a keyboard too small for touch typing to use in conjunction with a pen or pointing device. For data storage, a PDA relies on flash memory instead of power-hungry disk drives. *See also* firmware, flash memory, handheld PC, PC Card, pen computer.

PDC *n. See* Primary Domain Controller.

PD-CD drive *n.* Short for **p**hase change rewritable **d**isc– compact **d**isc **drive**. A storage device that combines a CD-ROM drive and a phase change rewritable disc (PD) drive, which can store up to 650 megabytes of data on cartridges of rewritable optical discs. *See also* phase-change recording.

PDD *n.* Acronym for **P**ortable **D**igital **D**ocument. A graphics file created from a document by QuickDraw GX under Mac OS. PDDs are stored in a form that is independent of printer resolution; they print at the highest resolution available on the printer used; and they can contain the original fonts used in the document. Therefore, a PDD can be printed by a computer other than the one on which it was created.

.pdf *n.* The file extension that identifies documents encoded in the Portable Document Format developed by Adobe Systems. To display or print a .pdf file, the user should obtain the freeware Adobe Acrobat Reader. *See also* Acrobat, Portable Document Format.

PDL *n. See* page-description language.

PDM *n. See* pulse duration modulation.

PDO *n. See* Portable Distributed Objects.

PDS *n.* **1.** Acronym for **P**rocessor **D**irect **S**lot. An expansion slot in Macintosh computers that is connected directly to the CPU signals. There are several kinds of PDS slots with different numbers of pins and different sets of signals, depending on which CPU is used in a particular computer. **2.** Acronym for **P**arallel **D**ata **S**tructure. A hidden file, located in the root directory of a disk that is shared under AppleShare, that contains access privilege information for folders.

Peachy virus *n.* A virus, first detected in 2001, that was the first to attempt to spread itself through PDF files. The Peachy virus takes advantage of an Adobe Acrobat feature that enables users to embed files in PDF documents. The embedded Peachy virus file infects the computer of a user who downloads the PDF file and then opens the file in Adobe Acrobat.

peek *vb*. **1.** To read a byte from an absolute memory location. Peek commands are often found in programming languages such as Basic that do not normally allow access to specific memory locations. **2.** To look at the next character in a buffer associated with an input device without actually removing the character from the buffer.

peer *n*. Any of the devices on a layered communications network that operate on the same protocol level. *See also* network architecture.

peer-to-peer architecture *n*. A network of two or more computers that use the same program or type of program to communicate and share data. Each computer, or *peer*, is considered equal in terms of responsibilities and each acts as a server to the others in the network. Unlike a client/server architecture, a dedicated file server is not required. However, network performance is generally not as good as under client/server, especially under heavy loads. *Also called:* peer-to-peer network. *See also* peer, peer-to-peer communications, server. *Compare* client/server architecture.

peer-to-peer communications *n*. Interaction between devices that operate on the same communications level on a network based on a layered architecture. *See also* network architecture.

peer-to-peer network *n*. *See* peer-to-peer architecture.

PE file *n*. *See* portable executable file.

pel *n*. Short for **p**icture **el**ement. *See* pixel.

PEM *n*. *See* Privacy Enhanced Mail.

pen *n*. *See* light pen, stylus.

pen-based computing *n*. The process of entering handwritten symbols into a computer via a stylus and pressure-sensitive pad. *See also* pen computer.

pen computer *n*. Any of a class of computers whose primary input device is a pen (stylus) instead of a keyboard. A pen computer is usually a smaller, handheld device and has a flat semiconductor-based display such as an LCD display. It requires either a special operating system designed to work with the pen input device or a proprietary operating system designed to work with a specific-purpose device. The pen computer is the primary model for an emerging class of computers known as personal digital assistants (PDAs). *See also* clipboard computer, PC Card, PDA.

Penguin *n*. Slang for the Linux operating system or a Linux user. The name comes from the penguin character used as the Linux mascot. *See also* Tux.

pen plotter *n*. A traditional graphics plotter that uses pens to draw on paper. Pen plotters use one or more colored pens, either fiber-tipped pens or, for highest-quality output, drafting pens. *See also* plotter. *Compare* electrostatic plotter.

Pentium *n*. A family of 32-bit microprocessors introduced by Intel in March 1993 as the successor to the i486. The Pentium family is composed of superscalar, CISC-based microprocessors containing between 3 million (earlier models) and 28 million transistors. They have a 32-bit address bus, a 64-bit data bus, a built-in floating-point unit and memory management unit, built-in caches, and a System Management Mode (SMM), which provides the microprocessor with the ability to slow or halt some system components when the system is idle or performing non-CPU-intensive tasks, thereby lessening power consumption. The Pentium also employs *branch prediction*, resulting in faster system performance. In addition, the Pentium has built-in features to ensure data integrity, and it supports functional redundancy checking (FRC). The Pentium II introduced MMX media enhancement support. *See also* branch prediction, CISC, functional redundancy checking, i486DX, L1 cache, L2 cache, microprocessor, MMX, P5, SIMD, superscalar.

Pentium upgradable *n*. **1.** An i486 motherboard capable of being adapted to run a Pentium-class processor. *See also* i486DX, microprocessor, motherboard, Pentium.

2. A 486 PC that can be upgraded to Pentium class by adding a Pentium processor. *See also* i486DX.

perfboard *n.* Short for **perf**orated fiber **board**. *See* breadboard.

performance monitor *n.* A process or program that appraises and records status information about various system devices and other processes.

period *n.* The length of time required for an oscillation to complete one full cycle. For an oscillating electrical signal, the period is the time between waveform repetitions. If f is the frequency of oscillation in hertz, and t is the period in seconds, then $t = 1/f$. See the illustration.

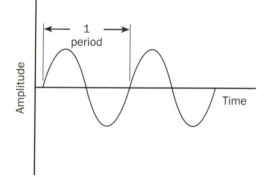

Period. *The period of an oscillating signal.*

peripheral *n.* In computing, a device, such as a disk drive, printer, modem, or joystick, that is connected to a computer and is controlled by the computer's microprocessor. *Also called:* peripheral device. *See also* console.

Peripheral Component Interconnect *n. See* PCI local bus.

peripheral device *n. See* peripheral.

peripheral power supply *n.* An auxiliary source of electricity used by a computer or a device as a backup in case of a power failure. *Acronym:* PPS.

Perl *n.* Acronym for **P**ractical **E**xtraction and **R**eport **L**anguage. An interpreted language, based on C and several UNIX utilities. Perl has powerful string-handling features for extracting information from text files. Perl can assemble a string and send it to the shell as a command; hence, it

is often used for system administration tasks. A program in Perl is known as a script. Perl was devised by Larry Wall at NASA's Jet Propulsion Laboratory.

permanent storage *n.* A recording medium that retains the data recorded on it for long periods of time without power. Ink on paper is by far the most widely used permanent storage, but data can be transferred from paper to a computer only with difficulty. Typically, some form of magnetic medium, such as floppy disk or tape, is preferable. Magnetic media are generally accepted as permanent, even though the magnetic fields that encode data in the media tend to fade eventually (in five years or more). *See also* nonvolatile memory.

permanent swap file *n.* In Windows, a file composed of contiguous disk sectors used for virtual memory operations. *See also* swap file, virtual memory.

permanent virtual circuit *n. See* PVC.

permission *n.* In a networked or multiuser computer environment, the ability of a particular user to access a particular resource by means of his or her user account. Permissions are granted by the system administrator or other authorized person. Several levels of access can be given: read only, read and write (view and change), or read, write, and delete. *Also called:* Access permission.

permission class *n.* A class that defines access to a resource or defines an identity by supporting authorization checks.

permission object *n.* An instance of a permission class that represents access rights to resources or identity. A permission object can be used to specify a request, a demand, or a grant of permission.

permissions log *n.* A file on a network or multiuser computer environment where permissions for users are stored. When a user attempts to access a resource on the system, the permissions log is checked to see whether the user has permission to use it.

perpendicular recording *n.* A method of increasing storage capacity on magnetic media by aligning the magnetic dipoles, whose orientation determines bit values, in a direction that is perpendicular to the recording surface. *Also called:* vertical recording.

per-pixel lighting *n.* A lighting scheme used in 3D computer game rendering and other digital animation applications that calculates proper lighting for every pixel displayed. Per-pixel lighting allows highly realistic lighting effects but requires significant video card capabilities to display properly. *Also called:* Phong shading.

Per Seat Licensing *n.* A licensing mode that requires a separate Client Access License for each client computer, regardless of whether all the clients access the server at the same time. *See also* client. *Compare* Per Server Licensing.

Per Server Licensing *n.* A licensing mode that requires a separate Client Access License for each concurrent connection to the server, regardless of whether there are other client computers on the network that do not happen to connect concurrently. *Compare* Per Seat Licensing.

persistence *n.* A characteristic of some light-emitting materials, such as the phosphors used in CRTs, that causes an image to be retained for a short while after being irradiated, as by an electron beam in a CRT. The decay in persistence is sometimes called *luminance decay*.

persistent client connection *n. See* persistent connection.

persistent connection *n.* A connection to a client that remains open after a server sends a response. Included in HTTP 1.1 and similar to the Netscape HTTP 1.0 Keep-Alive extension, persistent connections are used to improve Internet efficiency and performance by eliminating the overhead associated with multiple connections. *Also called:* persistent client connection. *See also* pipelining (definition 1).

persistent data *n.* Data that is stored in a database or on tape so that it is retained by the computer between sessions.

persistent link *n. See* hot link (definition 1).

persistent storage *n.* Memory that remains intact when the power to a device is turned off, such as ROM. *See also* memory.

Personal Communications Services *n.* Term used by the United States Federal Communications Commission (FCC) to cover a range of wireless, all-digital communications technologies and services, including cordless phones, voice mail, paging, faxing, and personal digital assistants (PDAs). Personal Communications Services, or PCS, is

divided into narrowband and broadband categories. Narrowband, which operates in the 900 MHz band of frequencies, provides paging, data messaging, faxing, and one- and two-way electronic messaging capabilities. Broadband, which operates in the 1850 MHz to 1990 MHz range and is considered the next-generation PCS, enables two-way voice, data, and video communications. The cellular phone technologies known as GSM (Global System for Mobile Communications), CDMA (Code Division Multiple Access), and TDMA (Time Division Multiple Access) are included in the PCS category. *Acronym:* PCS. *Compare* Code Division Multiple Access, Global Systems for Mobile Communications, Time Division Multiple Access.

personal computer *n.* A computer designed for use by one person at a time. Personal computers do not need to share the processing, disk, and printer resources of another computer. IBM PC–compatible computers and Apple Macintoshes are both examples of personal computers. *Acronym:* PC.

Personal Computer *n. See* IBM PC.

Personal Computer Memory Card International Association *n. See* PCMCIA.

personal digital assistant *n. See* PDA.

personal finance manager *n.* A software application designed to assist the user in performing simple financial accounting tasks, such as balancing checkbooks and paying bills.

Personal Handyphone System *n.* A device developed in Japan to act as a cellular phone that can handle phone, FAX, and voice. *Acronym:* PHS.

personal identification number *n. See* PIN.

personal information manager *n. See* PIM.

personalization technology *n.* An e-commerce marketing technique in which Web sites and services analyze the interests of individual customers. The e-business then uses this information to deliver services, product offerings, and advertising that match each customer's personal interests.

Personal Web Server *n.* Microsoft applications that allow a computer running the Windows family of operating systems to function as a Web server for publishing personal Web pages and intranet sites. Personal Web

P

Server is available as part of Microsoft Windows NT 4.0 Option Pack (NTOP), Windows 98, and Windows 95 OEM Service Release 2. FrontPage Personal Web Server is available as part of FrontPage 1.1, FrontPage 97, FrontPage 98, and FrontPage 2000.

perspective view *n.* In computer graphics, a display method that shows objects in three dimensions (height, width, and depth), with the depth aspect rendered according to the desired perspective. An advantage of perspective view is that it presents a more accurate representation of what the human eye perceives. *Compare* isometric view.

peta- *prefix* Denotes 1 quadrillion (10^{15}). In computing, which is based on the binary (base 2) numbering system, *peta-* has a literal value of 1,125,899,906,842,624, which is the power of 2 (2^{50}) closest to 1 quadrillion. *Abbreviation:* P.

petabyte *n.* Either 1 quadrillion bytes or 1,125,899,906,842,624 bytes. *Abbreviation:* PB.

PGA *n. See* pin grid array, Professional Graphics Adapter.

PgDn key *n. See* Page Down key.

PGP *n.* Acronym for **P**retty **G**ood **P**rivacy. A program for public key encryption, using the RSA algorithm, developed by Philip Zimmermann. PGP software is available in unsupported free versions and supported commercial versions. *See also* privacy, public key encryption, RSA encryption.

PgUp key *n. See* Page Up key.

phage virus *n.* A destructive virus that affects the Palm operating system (OS). Phage copies itself, overwriting application files and destroying them. Once the first host file is infected, Phage will spread to all available files. Phage may be spread from one Palm device to another by beaming or connection with a docking station. Phage was one of the first viruses created specifically to affect handheld wireless devices and the first to impact the Palm OS.

phase *n.* A relative measurement that describes the temporal relationship between two signals that have the same frequency. Phase is measured in degrees, with one full oscillation cycle having 360 degrees. The phase of one signal can lead or follow the other by 0 through 180 degrees. See the illustration.

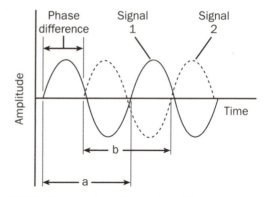

Phase. *The ratio of a to b is the phase difference, expressed in degrees.*

phase-change recording *n.* In optical media, a recording technique that uses a laser beam focused on a microscopic portion of metallic crystal to alter the reflectiveness of its structure in such a way that the change can be read as a 0 bit or 1 bit, depending on whether the resulting structure reflects or absorbs the laser light. *See also* PD-CD drive.

phase encoding *n.* **1.** The process of placing digital information on an analog carrier wave while periodically changing the phase of the carrier to increase the bit density of the transmission. *See also* Manchester coding, phase. **2.** A recording technique used with magnetic storage devices in which each data-holding unit is divided into two parts, each of which is magnetized so that it is opposite in polarity to the other.

phase-locked *adj.* Of, pertaining to, or characteristic of the relationship between two signals whose phases relative to each other are kept constant by a controlling mechanism, such as an electronic device.

phase modulation *n.* A method of imposing information onto a waveform signal by shifting the phase of the wave to represent information, such as the binary digits 0 and 1. See the illustration. *See also* phase-shift keying.

P

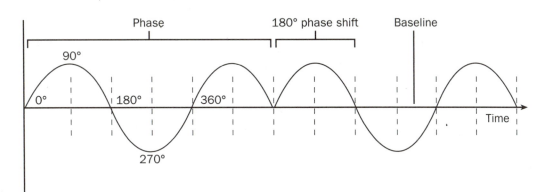

Phase modulation. *A phase shift of 180 degrees.*

phase-shift keying *n.* A communications method used by modems to encode data that relies on phase shifts in a carrier wave to represent digital information. In its simplest form, phase-shift keying allows the phase of the carrier wave to be in either of two states: shifted 0 degrees or shifted 180 degrees, effectively reversing the phase of the wave. This straightforward phase-shift keying, however, is useful only when each phase can be measured against an unchanging reference value, so a more sophisticated technique called *differential phase-shift keying*, or *DPSK*, is used in many modems. In differential phase-shift keying, the phase of the carrier wave is shifted to represent more than two possible states, and each state is interpreted as a relative change from the state preceding it. No reference values or timing considerations are required and because more than two states are possible, more than one binary digit can represent each state. *Acronym: PSK. See also* phase modulation.

Phoenix BIOS *n.* An IBM-compatible ROM BIOS manufactured by Phoenix Technologies, Ltd. A popular ROM BIOS in many so-called PC clone computers, the Phoenix BIOS was an early leader among the IBM-compatible computers shortly after they began to appear in the marketplace. *See also* BIOS, ROM BIOS. *Compare* AMI BIOS.

phone connector *n.* An attachment, usually an RJ-11 connector, used to join a telephone line to a device such as a modem. See the illustration.

Phone connector.

phoneline networking *n.* The use of telephone wiring for connecting computers and other devices in a small network, such as a home network. *See also* HomePNA.

phoneme *n.* In linguistics, the smallest unit of speech that distinguishes one word sound from another. Phonemes are the elements on which computer speech is based.

phono connector *n.* An attachment used to connect a device, such as a microphone or a pair of headphones, to a piece of audio equipment or to a computer peripheral or adapter with audio capability. See the illustration.

Phono connector.

phosphor *n.* Any substance capable of emitting light when struck by radiation. The inside surface of a CRT screen is coated with a phosphor that, when excited by an electron beam, displays an image on the screen. *See also* persistence.

P

PhotoCD *n.* A digitizing system from Kodak that allows 35mm film pictures, negatives, slides, and scanned images to be stored on a compact disc. Images are stored in a file format called Kodak PhotoCD IMAGE PAC File Format, or PCD. Many photography or film development businesses offer this service. Images stored on a PhotoCD can usually be viewed by any computer with CD-ROM capabilities and the software required to read PCD. Such images can also be viewed using one of a variety of players designed to display images stored on CDs.

photo cell *n.* *See* photoelectric device.

photocomposition *n.* In traditional typesetting, the use of photographic and electronic equipment in laying out and producing a printed page. In desktop publishing, phototypesetters are used to accomplish the same ends. *See also* phototypesetter. *Compare* imagesetter.

photoconductor *n.* A material that exhibits increased conductivity when it is exposed to a source of light. Photoconductors are used in photodetectors, which are used in fiber optics to register light and convert it into electrical pulses. *See also* fiber optics.

photo editor *n.* A graphics application used to manipulate an image, such as a scanned photograph, digitally.

photoelectric device *n.* A device that uses light to create or modulate an electric signal. A photoelectric device uses semiconductor material and falls in one of two categories. In one type (photocell), light falling on the semiconductor generates an electrical current. In another type of device (photosensor), light changes the resistance of the semiconductor material, modulating an applied voltage.

photolithography *n.* A technique used in the fabrication of integrated circuits. The circuit pattern is drawn, photographed, and reduced to a negative having the desired final size. This negative is called the *photomask*. Light is passed through the photomask onto a wafer made of semiconductor material that has been coated with a photoresistive material. Where light strikes the photoresistive material, its composition is changed. In the next step, the photoresistive material not affected by light is washed off. Finally, the semiconductor material is exposed to an etching solution that eats away the surface not protected by the photoresistive material, creating the desired circuit pattern on the surface of the wafer. *See also* photomask, photoresist.

photomask *n.* A photographic negative image of a circuit pattern used in fabrication of integrated circuits. *See also* photolithography.

photonics *n.* Optoelectronic systems that transmit visible light or infrared energy. Photonic systems are used with fiber optic networks and optical circuits. Photonic networks offer dramatic increases in speed and bandwidth, allowing significantly greater amounts of information to be encoded and transmitted than with traditional cabling solutions.

photorealism *n.* The process of creating images that are as close to photographic or "real-life" quality as possible. In computer graphics, photorealism requires powerful computers and highly sophisticated software and is heavily mathematical. *See also* ray tracing.

photoresist *n.* A compound that is used in photolithographic fabrication of integrated circuits and printed circuit boards. When exposed to ultraviolet light through a photomask, the photoresistive material exposed to the light polymerizes (hardens); the areas not exposed can be washed away, leaving the pattern of traces on the substrate. Subsequent etching removes areas not protected by the polymerized photoresist.

photosensor *n.* *See* photoelectric device.

Photoshop *n.* Adobe software product for digital image editing and enhancement, photo retouching, and color management of graphic images. Photoshop includes such features as multiple undo, text editing with formatting control, and enhanced color management and controls. The program supports numerous Web and graphics file formats and runs on both the Windows and Power Macintosh platforms.

phototypesetter *n.* A printer similar to a laser printer but capable of resolutions over 2,000 dots per inch. Phototypesetters apply light directly to a photographic film or photosensitive paper. *See also* photocomposition. *Compare* imagesetter.

photovoltaic cell *n.* *See* solar cell.

PHP *n.* Acronym for **PHP: H**ypertext **P**reprocessor. An open source scripting language used with HTML documents to execute server-side interactive functions. PHP runs on all major operating systems and is primarily used with Linux and UNIX Web servers or on Windows servers with add-on software. PHP may be embedded in a Web

P

page and used to access and present database information. An HTML document that contains a PHP script usually has a .php filename extension. Originally PHP stood for "Personal Home Page," with later versions standing for "PHP Hypertext Preprocessor" or simply PHP. The syntax of PHP is fairly simple and very similar to that of Perl, with some aspects of Bourne shell, JavaScript, and C. It can also be regarded as a technology (server-side environment for ported script engines, like ASP).

phreak[1] *n.* A person who breaks into, or *cracks*, telephone networks or other secured systems. In the 1970s, the telephone system used audible tones as switching signals, and *phone phreaks* used homebrew hardware to match the tones and steal long-distance service. *See also* homebrew. *Compare* cracker, hacker (definition 2).

phreak[2] *vb.* To break into, or *crack*, phone networks or computer systems. *See also* homebrew. *Compare* hack.

PHS *n. See* Personal Handyphone System.

physical *adj.* In computing, of, pertaining to, or characteristic of a real, as opposed to a conceptual, piece of equipment or frame of reference. *Compare* logical (definition 2).

physical address *n.* An address that corresponds to a hardware memory location. In simple processors such as the 8088 and the 68000, every address is a physical address. In processors supporting virtual memory, programs reference virtual addresses, which are then mapped by memory management hardware onto physical addresses. *Also called:* hardware address. *See also* memory management unit, paging, virtual memory.

physical-image file *n.* A hard disk copy of the material to be recorded onto a CD-ROM. Creating a complete copy precludes problems in writing the CD-ROM because of delays in assembling the material from a scattered group of files. *See also* CD-ROM. *Compare* virtual-image file.

physical layer *n.* The first, or lowest, of the seven layers in the ISO/OSI reference model for standardizing computer-to-computer communications. The physical layer is totally hardware-oriented and deals with all aspects of establishing and maintaining a physical link between communicating computers. Among specifications covered on the physical layer are cabling, electrical signals, and mechanical connections. See the illustration. *See also* ISO/OSI reference model.

ISO/OSI MODEL	
ISO/OSI Layer	**Focus**
Application (highest level)	Program-to-program transfer of information
Presentation	Text formatting and display, code conversion
Session	Establishing, maintaining, and coordinating communication
Transport	Accurate delivery, service quality
Network	Transport routes, message handling and transfer
Data-link	Coding, addressing, and transmitting information
Physical	Hardware connections

Physical layer. *Lowest layer in the ISO/OSI reference model.*

physical memory *n.* Memory actually present in the system, as opposed to virtual memory. A computer might have 64 megabytes of physical RAM but support a virtual memory capacity of 1 gigabyte or more. *Compare* virtual memory.

physical network *n.* One of two ways of describing the topology, or layout, of a computer network; the other is logical network. A physical network refers to the actual configuration of the hardware forming a network—that is, to the computers, connecting hardware, and especially the cabling patterns that give the network its shape. Basic physical layouts include the bus, ring, and star topologies. *See also* bus network, logical network, ring network, star network.

physical storage *n. See* real storage.

pi *n.* A mathematical constant equal to approximately 3.1415926535897932, describing the ratio of the circumference of a circle to its diameter.

PIC *n. See* programmable interrupt controller.

pica *n.* **1.** With reference to typewriters, a fixed-width type font that fits 10 characters to the linear inch. *See also* pitch. **2.** As used by typographers, a unit of measure equal to 12 points or approximately 1/6 inch. *See also* point[1] (definition 1).

P

PICMG *n.* Acronym for the **P**CI **I**ndustrial **C**omputer **M**anufacturers **G**roup. A consortium of more than 350 computer product vendors, this non-profit organization develops specifications for PCI-based devices, such as the CompactPCI specification. *See also* CompactPCI.

pico- *prefix* Denotes one trillionth (10^{-12}), or, in the British numbering system, one million millionth. *Abbreviation:* p.

picoJava *n.* A microprocessor developed by Sun Microsystems, Inc., that executes Java code. *See also* Java.

picosecond *n.* One trillionth of a second. *Abbreviation:* psec.

PICS *n. See* Platform for Internet Content Selection.

.pict *n.* The file extension that identifies graphic images in the Macintosh PICT format. *See also* PICT.

PICT *n.* A file-format standard for encoding graphical images, both object-oriented and bitmapped. The PICT file format was first used in Macintosh applications, but many PC applications can read the format too. *See also* bitmapped graphics, object-oriented graphics.

picture element *n. See* pixel.

pie chart *n.* A type of graph that presents values as percentages (slices) of a whole (a pie).

piezoelectric *adj.* Of, pertaining to, or characteristic of crystals that can convert between mechanical and electrical energy. An electric potential applied to a piezoelectric crystal causes a small change in the shape of the crystal. Likewise, physical pressure applied to the crystal creates an electrical potential difference between the surfaces of the crystal.

piggyback board *n.* A printed circuit board that plugs into another circuit board to enhance its capabilities. A piggyback board is sometimes used to replace a single chip, in which case the chip is removed and the piggyback board is inserted into the empty socket. *See also* daughterboard.

Pilot *n.* A series of popular handheld personal digital assistants (PDAs) designed by Palm and based on the Palm OS operating system. Palm introduced its first Pilot model in 1996, followed in 1997 by the PalmPilot, and thereafter by a series of other Palm handheld models.

PILOT *n.* Acronym for **P**rogrammed **I**nquiry, **L**earning **o**r **T**eaching. A programming language developed in 1976 by John A. Starkweather and designed primarily for creating applications for computer-aided instruction.

PIM *n.* Acronym for **p**ersonal **i**nformation **m**anager. An application that usually includes an address book and organizes unrelated information, such as notes, appointments, and names, in a useful way.

pin *n.* A slender prong. Pins are commonly encountered as the contacts protruding from a male connector. Connectors are often identified by the number of pins they have. Other types of pins are the spidery, leglike metal appendages that connect computer chips to sockets on a circuit board or directly to the circuit board. See the illustration.

Pins

Pin. *A 16-pin DIP (top) and a 6-pin DIN (bottom).*

PIN *n.* Acronym for **p**ersonal **i**dentification **n**umber. A unique code number used to gain access to personal information or assets via an electronic device. PINs are used by a variety of electronic services such as automated bank tellers, Internet sites, and wireless phone services.

pinch roller *n.* A small cylindrical pulley that presses magnetic tape against the drive's capstan to move the tape over the tape machine's heads. *See also* capstan.

pinch-roller plotter *n.* A type of plotter, intermediate between drum and flatbed types, that uses hard rubber or metal wheels to hold the paper against the main roller. *See also* plotter. *Compare* drum plotter, flatbed plotter.

pin-compatible *adj.* Having pins that are equivalent to the pins on another chip or device. A chip, for example, might have different internal circuitry from that used in another chip, but if the two chips use the same pins for input and output of identical signals, they are pin-compatible. *Compare* plug-compatible.

P

pine *n.* Acronym for **p**ine **i**s **n**ot **e**lm, or for **P**rogram for **I**nternet **N**ews and **E**-mail. One of the most commonly encountered programs for reading and composing e-mail on character-based UNIX systems. The pine program was developed as an improved version of elm at the University of Washington. *Compare* elm.

pin feed *n.* A method of feeding paper through a printer in which small pins, mounted on rollers on the ends of the platen, engage holes near the edges of continuous-form paper. *See also* continuous-form paper, paper feed. *Compare* tractor feed.

ping[1] *n.* **1.** Acronym for **P**acket **I**nternet **G**roper. A protocol for testing whether a particular computer is connected to the Internet by sending a packet to its IP address and waiting for a response. The name actually comes from submarine active sonar, where a sound signal—called a "ping"—is broadcast, and surrounding objects are revealed by their reflections of the sound. **2.** A UNIX utility that implements the ping protocol.

ping[2] *vb.* **1.** To test whether a computer is connected to the Internet using the ping utility. **2.** To test which users on a mailing list are current by sending e-mail to the list asking for a response.

Ping of Death *n.* A form of Internet vandalism that entails sending a packet that is substantially larger than the usual 64 bytes over the Internet via the ping protocol to a remote computer. The size of the packet causes the computer to crash or reboot. *See also* packet (definition 2), ping[1] (definition 1).

ping packet *n.* An "are you there" message transmitted by a Packet Internet Groper program. A ping packet is sent from one node to the IP (Internet Protocol) address of a network computer to determine whether that node is able to send and receive transmissions. Many shareware and freeware ping utilities for PCs are available for download from the Internet. *See also* ping[1] (definition 1), packet[1] (definition 1).

ping pong *n.* **1.** In communications, a technique that changes the direction of transmission so that the sender becomes the receiver and vice versa. **2.** In information processing and transfer, the technique of using two temporary storage areas (buffers) rather than one to hold both input and output.

ping-pong buffer *n.* A double buffer in which each part is alternately filled and flushed, resulting in a more or less continuous stream of input and output data. *See also* ping pong (definition 2).

pin grid array *n.* A method of mounting chips on boards, preferred for chips with a very large number of pins. Pin grid array packages have pins protruding from the bottom surface of the chip, as opposed to dual in-line packages and leaderless chip carrier packages, which have pins protruding from the edges. *Acronym:* PGA. *Compare* DIP, leadless chip carrier.

pink contract *n.* A non-standard addendum to a contract with an Internet service provider (ISP), specifically offering the client the opportunity to send unsolicited commercial e-mail and put up spam-related Web sites. *See also* spam.

pinout *n.* A description or diagram of the pins of a chip or connector. *See also* pin.

PIO *n.* Acronym for **P**rogrammed **I**nput/**O**utput (or, less frequently, Processor Input/Output). One of two transfer methods used in moving data between a disk drive and memory. With PIO, the disk controller moves a block of data into the CPU's registers, and the CPU then moves the data to its intended destination. PIO is characteristic of IDE drives. The alternative data-transfer method, direct memory access (DMA), bypasses the CPU and moves data directly between disk and memory. *See also* Bus, bus mastering, controller. *Compare* direct memory access.

pipe *n.* **1.** A portion of memory that can be used by one process to pass information along to another. Essentially, a pipe works like its namesake: it connects two processes so that the output of one can be used as the input to the other. *See also* input stream, output stream. **2.** The vertical line character (|) that appears on a PC keyboard as the shift character on the backslash (\) key. **3.** In MS-DOS and UNIX, a command function that transfers the output of one command to the input of a second command.

pipeline burst static RAM *n.* A type of static RAM that uses burst and pipelining technologies to increase the speed at which information can be provided to a computer's CPU. By pipelining requests so that one is being acted upon at the same time the next is getting underway, pipeline burst static RAM, or PB SRAM, can provide information to the CPU at high speed. PB SRAM is used in L2 caches (rapid-response memory dedicated to storing

P

frequently requested data) on computers running at bus speeds of 75 MHz or higher. *Acronym:* PB SRAM. *See also* burst (definition 2), L2 cache, pipelining, static RAM. *Compare* asynchronous static RAM, dynamic RAM, synchronous burst static RAM.

pipeline processing *n.* A method of processing on a computer that allows fast parallel processing of data. This is accomplished by overlapping operations using a *pipe*, or a portion of memory that passes information from one process to another. *See also* parallel processing, pipe (definition 1), pipelining (definition 3).

pipelining *n.* **1.** A method of fetching and decoding instructions (preprocessing) in which, at any given time, several program instructions are in various stages of being fetched or decoded. Ideally, pipelining speeds execution time by ensuring that the microprocessor does not have to wait for instructions; when it completes execution of one instruction, the next is ready and waiting. *See also* superpipelining. **2.** In parallel processing, a method in which instructions are passed from one processing unit to another, as on an assembly line, and each unit is specialized for performing a particular type of operation. **3.** The use of pipes in passing the output of one task as input to another until a desired sequence of tasks has been carried out. *See also* pipe (definition 1), pour.

piracy *n.* **1.** The theft of a computer design or program. **2.** Unauthorized distribution and use of a computer program.

.pit *n.* A file extension for an archive file compressed with PackIT. *See also* PackIT.

pitch *n.* A measure, generally used with monospace fonts, that describes the number of characters that fit in a horizontal inch. *See also* characters per inch, screen pitch. *Compare* point[1] (definition 1).

PivotChart *adj.* A graphical tool in Microsoft Excel or Access that can be used to display data from a list or database in chart form. Based on user-selected information incorporated in an Excel PivotTable report or list, a PivotChart report provides the ability to chart the data interactively—for example, to "pivot" the chart's point of view from product sales by category to product sales by region or by salesperson. *See also* PivotTable.

PivotTable *adj.* An interactive table in Microsoft Excel or Access that can show the same data from a list or a database in more than one arrangement. A user can manipulate the rows and columns in a PivotTable to view or summarize the information in different ways for purposes of analysis. In Excel, a PivotTable report is the basis for creating a PivotChart report that displays the same data in chart form. *See also* PivotChart.

pivot year *n.* In Year 2000 windowing, a date in a 100-year period that serves as the point from which correct dates can be calculated in systems or software that can store only 2-digit years. For example, a pivot year of 1970 means that the numbers 70 through 99 are interpreted as the years 1970 to 1999, and the numbers 00 through 69 as the years 2000 through 2069. *See also* windowing.

pixel *n.* Short for picture (**pix**) **el**ement. One spot in a rectilinear grid of thousands of such spots that are individually "painted" to form an image produced on the screen by a computer or on paper by a printer. A pixel is the smallest element that display or print hardware and software can manipulate in creating letters, numbers, or graphics. See the illustration. *Also called:* pel.

Pixel. *The letter A is actually made up of a pattern of pixels in a grid, as is the cat's eye.*

pixel image *n.* The representation of a color graphic in a computer's memory. A pixel image is similar to a bit image, which also describes a screen graphic, but a pixel image has an added dimension, sometimes called depth, that describes the number of bits in memory assigned to each on-screen pixel.

pixel map *n.* A data structure that describes the pixel image of a graphic, including such features as color, image, resolution, dimensions, storage format, and number of bits used to describe each pixel. *See also* pixel, pixel image.

PJL *n. See* Printer Job Language.

PJ/NF *n.* Acronym for **p**rojection-**j**oin **n**ormal **f**orm. *See* normal form (definition 1).

PKUNZIP *n.* A shareware utility program that uncompresses files compressed by the PKZIP shareware utility program. PKUNZIP is generally made available with PKZIP; distribution of PKUNZIP for commercial purposes is not permitted without obtaining permission from its publisher, PKware, Inc. *See also* PKZIP.

PKZIP *n.* A widely used shareware utility program for compressing files. Developed by PKware, Inc., in 1989 and available from a wide variety of sources, PKZIP can combine one or more files into a compressed output file having the extension .zip. A companion utility program, PKUNZIP, is required to uncompress the compressed files. *See also* PKUNZIP, shareware, utility program.

PLA *n.* Acronym for **p**rogrammable **l**ogic **a**rray. *See* field-programmable logic array.

placeholder *n.* **1.** A character that masks or hides another character for security reasons. For example, when a user types a password, an asterisk is displayed on the screen to take the place of each character typed. **2.** Text or some other element used in an application as an indicator that the user should enter in his or her own text.

Plain Old Telephone Service *n. See* POTS.

plaintext *n.* **1.** Nonencrypted or decrypted text. *See also* decryption, encryption. **2.** A file that is stored as plain ASCII data. *Compare* ciphertext.

plain vanilla *adj.* Ordinary; the standard version of hardware or software without any enhancements. For example, a plain vanilla modem might have data transfer capability but no fax or voice features.

.plan *n.* A file in a UNIX user's home directory that is displayed when other users finger that account. Users can enter information into .plan files at their discretion to provide information in addition to that normally displayed by the finger command. *See also* finger.

planar *adj.* **1.** In computer graphics, lying within a plane. **2.** In the fabrication of semiconductor materials, maintaining the original flat surface of the silicon wafer throughout processing, while the chemicals that make up the elements that control the flow of current are diffused into (and beneath) the surface.

planar transistor *n.* A special form of transistor that is fabricated with all three elements (collector, emitter, and base) on a single layer of semiconductor material. The structure of a planar transistor permits it to dissipate relatively large amounts of heat, making this design suitable for power transistors. See the illustration.

Planar transistor.

plasma display *n. See* gas-discharge display.

plastic leadless chip carrier *n. See* PLCC.

plastic transistor *n.* A transistor produced entirely from plastic rather than the traditional silicon. A plastic transistor is flexible enough to be embedded in curved surfaces or folded. Production of plastic transistors begins with a thin piece of clear plastic, onto which layers of plastic are printed or sprayed through a mesh. The result is a lightweight, flexible and transparent transistor that can be manufactured in high volumes for a fraction of the cost of silicon transistors. The flexibility and low-cost of plastic transistors make them useful in applications from transparent foldable displays to one-use product containers. *See also* electronic paper.

platen *n.* The cylinder in most impact printers and typewriters, around which the paper wraps and against which the print mechanism strikes the paper. The paper bail, a spring-loaded bar with small rollers, holds the paper smoothly against the platen just above the print mechanism.

platform *n.* **1.** The foundation technology of a computer system. Because computers are layered devices composed

P

of a chip-level hardware layer, a firmware and operating-system layer, and an applications program layer, the bottommost layer of a machine is often called a platform. **2.** In everyday usage, the type of computer or operating system being used.

Platform for Internet Content Selection *n.* A specification for rating and labeling Internet content. Originally developed by the World Wide Web Consortium to enable parents, teachers, administrators, and other caretakers to control the material to which children have online access, its use has expanded to include the protection of privacy and intellectual property. PICS is not itself a system for rating Internet content. Rather, it specifies the format conventions to be used by rating systems in devising labels that can be read by PICS-compatible software. *Acronym:* PICS.

Platform for Privacy Preference Project *n. See* P3P.

Platform for Privacy Preferences *n. See* P3P.

platform invoke *n.* The functionality provided by the run time to enable managed code to call unmanaged native DLL entry points.

platter *n.* One of the individual metal data storage disks within a hard disk drive. Most hard disks have from two to eight platters. See the illustration. *See also* hard disk.

Platters

Platter.

player *n.* In relation to digital audio, a program that plays music and other audio files that have been ripped (transferred from a compact disc to a hard disk) and then encoded in a playable format, such as MP3. *See also* encoder, MP3, ripper.

PlayStation *n.* Sony Corporation's console computer entertainment gaming system. PlayStation 2, the latest version, is a 128-bit system that features a 300-Mhz pro-

cessor, 32 MB of Direct RDRAM main memory, and a floating-point performance of 6.2 GFLOPS. PlayStation 2 also offers the capability to play CDs and DVDs. *See also* computer game, console game. *Compare* Dreamcast, GameCube, Xbox.

PL/C *n.* A version of the PL/I programming language developed at Cornell University and used on mainframe computers. *See also* PL/I.

PLCC *n.* Acronym for **p**lastic **l**eadless **c**hip **c**arrier. An inexpensive variation of the leadless chip carrier (LCC) method of mounting chips on boards. Although the two carriers are similar in appearance, PLCCs are physically incompatible with leadless chip carriers, which are made from a ceramic material. *See also* leadless chip carrier.

PLD *n. See* programmable logic device.

PL/I *n.* Acronym for **P**rogramming **L**anguage **I** (One). A programming language developed by IBM (1964–1969), designed to bring together the key features of FORTRAN, COBOL, and ALGOL while introducing such new concepts as condition-based error handling and multitasking. The result of this effort was a compiled, structured language that was so complex that it never gained widespread acceptance. Nevertheless, PL/I is still used in some academic and research environments. *See also* ALGOL, COBOL, compiled language, FORTRAN.

PL/M *n.* Acronym for **P**rogramming **L**anguage for **M**icrocomputers. A programming language derived from PL/I and developed in the early 1970s by Intel Corporation for microprocessors. PL/M was used primarily for the creation of operating systems. *See also* PL/I.

plot *vb.* To create a graphic or a diagram by connecting points representing variables (values) that are defined by their positions in relation to a horizontal (x) axis and a vertical (y) axis (and sometimes a depth, or z, axis).

plotter *n.* Any device used to draw charts, diagrams, and other line-based graphics. Plotters use either pens or electrostatic charges and toner. Pen plotters draw on paper or transparencies with one or more colored pens. Electrostatic plotters "draw" a pattern of electrostatically charged dots on the paper and then apply toner and fuse it in place. Plotters use three basic types of paper handling: flatbed, drum, and pinch roller. Flatbed plotters hold the paper still and move the pen along both *x* and *y* axes. Drum plotters roll the paper over a cylinder. The pen moves along one axis while the drum, with the paper attached, moves along the other. Pinch-roller plotters are a hybrid of the two, in which the pen moves only along one axis while the paper is moved back and forth by small rollers.

PL/SQL *n.* Short for **P**rocedural **L**anguage Extension to **SQL**. Oracle's data manipulation language that allows sequenced or grouped execution of SQL statements and is commonly used to manipulate data in an Oracle database. The syntax is similar to the Ada programming language.

plug *n.* A connector, especially a male connector, one that fits into a socket. *See also* male connector.

plug and play *n.* **1.** Generally, a reference to the ability of a computer system to automatically configure a device added to it. Plug and play capability exists in Macintoshes based on the NuBus and, since Windows 95, on PC-compatible computers. **2.** When capitalized and, especially, when abbreviated PnP, a set of specifications developed by Intel and Microsoft that allows a PC to configure itself automatically to work with peripherals such as monitors, modems, and printers. A user can plug in a peripheral and "play" it without manually configuring the system. A Plug and Play PC requires both a BIOS that supports Plug and Play and a Plug and Play expansion card. *Abbreviation:* PnP. *See also* BIOS, expansion board, peripheral.

plugboard *n.* A board that permits users to control the operation of a device by plugging cables into sockets.

plug-compatible *adj.* Equipped with connectors that are equivalent both in structure and in usage. For example, most modems having DB-25 connectors on their rear panels are plug-compatible—that is, one can be replaced by another without the cable having to be rewired. *Compare* pin-compatible.

plug-in *n.* **1.** A small software program that plugs into a larger application to provide added functionality. **2.** A software component that plugs into the Netscape Navigator. Plug-ins permit the Web browser to access and execute files embedded in HTML documents that are in formats the browser normally would not recognize, such as many animation, video, and audio files. Most plug-ins are developed by software companies who have proprietary software in which the embedded files are created. *Compare* helper application.

p-machine *n. See* pseudomachine.

PMML *n.* Acronym for **P**redictive **M**odel **M**arkup **L**anguage. An XML-based language that enables sharing of defined predictive models between compliant vendor applications.

PMMU *n. See* paged memory management unit.

PMOS *n.* Acronym for **P**-channel **m**etal-**o**xide **s**emiconductor. A MOSFET semiconductor technology in which the conduction channel is formed by the movement of holes (electron "vacancies" created as electrons move from atom to atom) rather than electrons. Because holes move more slowly than electrons do, PMOS is slower than NMOS, but it is also easier and less expensive to fabricate. *See also* MOS, MOSFET, P-type semiconductor. *Compare* CMOS, NMOS.

PMS *n. See* PANTONE MATCHING SYSTEM.

PNG *n.* Acronym for **P**ortable **N**etwork **G**raphics. A file format for bitmapped graphic images, designed to be a replacement for the GIF format, without the legal restrictions associated with GIF. *See also* GIF.

PNNI *n.* Short for **P**rivate **N**etwork-to-**N**etwork **I**nterface. A routing protocol used in ATM networks that provides switches with the ability to communicate changes in the network. Through PNNI, switches can be informed of changes to the network as they occur and can then use the information to make appropriate routing decisions. *See also* ATM.

PnP *n. See* plug and play (definition 2).

PNP *n. See* PNP transistor.

PNP transistor *n.* A type of bipolar transistor in which a base of N-type material is sandwiched between an emitter and a collector of P-type material. The base, emitter, and collector are the three terminals of the transistor through which current flows. In a PNP transistor, holes (electron "vacancies") are the majority of the charge carriers, and they flow from the emitter to the collector. See the illustration. *See also* N-type semiconductor, P-type semiconductor. *Compare* NPN transistor.

Internal diagram

Schematic diagram

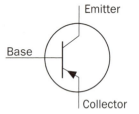

PNP transistor.

pocket Active Server Pages *n.* A scaled-down version of the Active Server Pages optimized for server-side Mobile Channels scripting. *Acronym:* pASP.

pocket Excel *n.* A scaled-down version of Microsoft Excel for the Pocket PC. *See also* Microsoft Excel.

Pocket PC *n.* A personal handheld computing device based on specifications designed by Microsoft and running the Microsoft Windows for Pocket PC operating system. Pocket PCs maintain the look of a Windows operating system display screen and offer compact versions of many of the applications that run on Windows-powered personal computers. A number of manufacturers produce Pocket PCs, including Hewlett-Packard, Compaq, and Casio.

pocket Word *n.* A scaled-down version of Microsoft Word for the Pocket PC. *See also* Microsoft Word.

point[1] *n.* **1.** A unit of measure used in printing, equal to approximately $1/72$ of an inch. Character height and the amount of space (leading) between lines of text are usually specified in points. **2.** A single pixel on the screen, identified by its row and column numbers. **3.** A location in

a geometric form, represented by two or more numbers that constitute its coordinates.

point[2] *vb.* To move an arrow or other such indicator to a particular item or position on the screen by using direction keys or by maneuvering a pointing device such as a mouse.

point-and-click *adj.* Enabling a user to select data and activate programs by using a mouse or other pointing device to move a cursor to a desired location ("point") and pressing a button on the mouse or other pointing device ("click").

PointCast *n.* An Internet service that delivers and displays a personalized set of news articles to individual users. Unlike the World Wide Web and other Internet applications, PointCast is a *push* technology, where the server automatically uploads data without a specific command from the client. *See also* server (definition 2).

point chart *n. See* scatter diagram.

point diagram *n. See* scatter diagram.

pointer *n.* In programming and information processing, a variable that contains the memory location (address) of some data rather than the data itself. *See also* address[1] (definition 1), handle (definition 1), mouse pointer, reference[1].

pointing device *n.* An input device used to control an on-screen cursor for such actions as "pressing" on-screen buttons in dialog boxes, choosing menu items, and selecting ranges of cells in spreadsheets or groups of words in a document. A pointing device is often used to create drawings or graphical shapes. The most common pointing device is the mouse, which was popularized by its use with the Apple Macintosh. Other pointing devices include graphics tablets, styluses, light pens, joysticks, pucks, and trackballs. *See also* graphics tablet, joystick, light pen, mouse, puck, stylus, trackball.

point listing *n.* A database of popular Web sites categorized by topics of interest and often rated by design and content.

point of presence *n.* **1.** A point in a wide area network to which a user can connect with a local telephone call. **2.** A point at which a long distance telephone carrier connects to a local telephone exchange or to an individual user. *Acronym:* POP.

point of sale *n.* See POS.

point-to-point configuration *n.* A communications link in which dedicated links exist between individual origins and destinations, as opposed to a point-to-multipoint configuration, in which the same signal goes to many destinations (such as a cable TV system), or a switched configuration, in which the signal moves from the origin to a switch that routes the signal to one of several possible destinations. *Also called:* point-to-point connection.

point-to-point connection *n.* See point-to-point configuration.

point-to-point message system *n.* In Sun Microsystems's J2EE network platform, a messaging system that uses message queues to store asynchronous, formatted data for coordinating enterprise applications. Each message is addressed to a specific queue, and client applications retrieve messages from the queues. *See also* asynchronous, J2EE.

Point-to-Point Protocol *n.* See PPP.

point-to-point tunneling *n.* A means of setting up secure communications over an open, public network such as the Internet. *See also* PPTP.

Point-to-Point Tunneling Protocol *n.* See PPTP.

Poisson distribution *n.* A mathematical curve often used in statistics and simulation to represent the likelihood of some event occurring, such as the arrival of a customer in a queue, when the average likelihood is known. This distribution, named after the French mathematician S. D. Poisson, is simpler to calculate than the normal and binomial distributions. *See also* binomial distribution, normal distribution.

poke *vb.* To store a byte into an absolute memory location. PEEK (read a byte from memory) and POKE commands are often found in programming languages, such as Basic, that do not normally allow access to specific memory locations.

polar coordinates *n.* Coordinates of the form (r, q) used to locate a point in two dimensions (on a plane). The polar coordinate r is the length of the line that starts at the origin and ends at the point, and q (Greek theta) is the angle between that line and the positive x-axis. *Compare* Cartesian coordinates.

polarity *n.* The sign of the potential (voltage) difference between two points in a circuit. When a potential difference exists between two points, one point has a positive polarity and the other a negative polarity. Electrons flow from negative to positive; by convention, however, current is considered to flow from positive to negative.

polarized component *n.* A circuit component that must be installed with its leads in a particular orientation with respect to the polarity of the circuit. Diodes, rectifiers, and some capacitors are examples of polarized components.

polarizing filter *n.* A transparent piece of glass or plastic that polarizes the light passing through it; that is, it allows only waves vibrating in a certain direction to pass through. Polarizing filters are often used to reduce glare on monitor screens. *See also* glare filter.

Polish notation *n.* See prefix notation.

polling *n.* See autopolling.

polling cycle *n.* The time and sequence required for a program to poll each of its devices or network nodes. *See also* autopolling.

polygon *n.* Any two-dimensional closed shape composed of three or more line segments, such as a hexagon, an octagon, or a triangle. Computer users encounter polygons in graphics programs.

polyline *n.* An open shape consisting of multiple connected segments. Polylines are used in CAD and other graphics programs. *See also* CAD.

polymorphism *n.* In an object-oriented programming language, the ability to redefine a routine in a derived class (a class that inherited its data structures and routines from another class). Polymorphism allows the programmer to define a base class that includes routines that perform standard operations on groups of related objects, without regard to the exact type of each object. The programmer then redefines the routines in the derived class for each type, taking into account the characteristics of the object. *See also* class, derived class, object (definition 2), object-oriented programming.

Pong *n.* The first commercial video game, a table tennis simulation, created by Nolan Bushnell of Atari in 1972.

P

pop *vb.* To fetch the top (most recently added) element of a stack, removing that element from the stack in the process. *Compare* push[2] (definition 1).

POP *n. See* point of presence, Post Office Protocol.

POP3 *n.* Acronym for **P**ost **O**ffice **P**rotocol **3**. This is the current version of the Post Office Protocol standard in common use on TCP/IP networks. *See also* Post Office Protocol, TCP/IP.

populate *vb.* **1.** To put chips in the sockets of a circuit board. **2.** To import prepared data into a database from a file using a software procedure rather than by having a human operator enter individual records.

pop-under ad *n.* An advertisement on the Internet that appears in a new window in the background, behind the Web site content. Users may be unaware of the presence of pop-under ads until they close foreground windows at the end of a Web session. Pop-under ads may appear in response to a mouse click, a rollover, or after a user has spent a predetermined amount of time at a Web site. *See also* pop-up ad.

pop-up ad *n.* An advertisement on the Internet that appears in a new window in the foreground, often whenever a new page is opened within a site. Pop-up ads may appear in response to a mouse click, a rollover, or after a user has spent a predetermined amount of time at a Web site. *See also* pop-under ad.

pop-up Help *n.* An online help system whose messages appear as pop-up windows when the user clicks on a topic or area of the screen about which help is desired. Typically, a special form of click, such as clicking the right mouse button or Option-clicking, will activate pop-up Help, if it is available. *See also* Balloon Help.

pop-up menu or **popup menu** *n.* In a graphical user interface, a menu that appears on-screen when a user selects a certain item. Pop-up menus can appear anywhere on the screen and generally disappear when the user selects an item in the menu. *Also called:* popup. *Compare* drop-down menu, pull-down menu.

pop-up messages *n.* The messages that appear when pop-up Help is used.

pop-up window *n.* A window that appears when an option is selected. Typically, the window remains visible until the mouse button is released.

port[1] *n.* **1.** An interface through which data is transferred between a computer and other devices (such as a printer, mouse, keyboard, or monitor), a network, or a direct connection to another computer. The port appears to the CPU as one or more memory addresses that it can use to send or receive data. Specialized hardware, such as in an add-on circuit board, places data from the device in the memory addresses and sends data from the memory addresses to the device. Ports may also be dedicated solely to input or to output. Ports typically accept a particular type of plug used for a specific purpose. For example, a serial data port, a keyboard, and a high-speed network port all use different connectors, so it's not possible to plug a cable into the wrong port. *Also called:* input/output port. **2.** port number.

port[2] *vb.* **1.** To change a program in order to be able to run it on a different computer. **2.** To move documents, graphics, and other files from one computer to another.

port 25 blocking *n.* An anti-spam technique adopted by many ISPs to prevent bulk mailings of unsolicited commercial e-mail. Spammers may try to use SMTP servers to relay a single commercial e-mail to multiple recipients. Port 25 blocking filters prevent this spam distribution method. Although it is a popular remedy for some spam problems, port 25 blocking may cause problems for legitimate users of non-compatible e-mail programs.

portable *adj.* **1.** Capable of running on more than one computer system or under more than one operating system. Highly portable software can be moved to other systems with little effort, moderately portable software can be moved only with substantial effort, and nonportable software can be moved only with effort similar to or greater than the effort of writing the original program. **2.** Light enough, rugged enough, and free enough of encumbering external connections to be carried by a user.

portable computer *n.* Any computer designed to be moved easily. Portable computers can be characterized by size and weight. See the table.

P

Table P.2   Portable Computers.

Type	Approximate weight	Power source	Comments
Transportable	15–30 lb.	House current	Sometimes called luggable; usually has floppy and hard-drives; standard CRT screen.
Laptop	8–15 lb.	House current or batteries	Can be held on the lap; usually has a floppy drive; uses flat LCD or plasma screen.
Ultralight	2–8 lb.	Batteries or trans-former pack	Easy to carry in a briefcase; sometimes uses RAM drive or EPROM instead of floppy or hard drive; thinner models are known as notebook computers.
Handheld	Less than 2 lb.	Batteries or trans-former pack	Also called palmtop or palm-sized; can be held in one hand.

Portable Digital Document *n. See* PDD.

Portable Distributed Objects *n.* Software from NeXT, running under UNIX, that supports an object model in which objects to be stored at various locations on a network can be accessed as though they were at a single location. *Acronym:* PDO.

Portable Document Format *n.* The Adobe specification for electronic documents that use the Adobe Acrobat family of servers and readers. *Acronym:* PDF. *See also* Acrobat, .pdf.

portable executable file *n.* The file format used for executable programs as well as for files that are linked together to form executable programs.

portable keyboard *n.* A portable keyboard for use with personal digital assistants (PDAs), wireless phones with advanced digital features, and other handheld mobile devices. Light, compact, and easy to carry, most portable keyboards fold for convenient storage and connect to the handheld device via a built-in cradle.

portable language *n.* A language that runs in the same way on different systems and therefore can be used for developing software for all of them. C, FORTRAN, and Ada are portable languages because their implementations on different systems are highly uniform; assembly language is extremely nonportable.

Portable Network Graphics *n. See* PNG.

portal *n.* A Web site that serves as a gateway to the Internet. A portal is a collection of links, content, and services designed to guide users to information they are likely to find interesting—news, weather, entertainment, commerce sites, chat rooms, and so on. Yahoo!, Excite, MSN.com, and Netscape NetCenter are examples of portals. *See also* home page (definition 1), Web site.

port enumerator *n.* In Windows, part of the Plug and Play system that detects I/O ports and reports them to the configuration manager. *See also* plug and play (definition 2).

port expander *n.* A hardware mechanism used for connecting several devices to a single port. Although several devices might be connected, only one can use the port at any given moment.

portmapper *n.* A service used by Remote Procedure Call (RPC) to assign port numbers. RPC doesn't follow the Well-Known Ports port designations, and only Portmapper is assigned a permanent port number. Because hackers may gain access to portmapper communication, various portmapper security tools are often used to prevent theft of information. *See also* remote procedure call.

port number *n.* A number that enables IP packets to be sent to a particular process on a computer connected to the Internet. Some port numbers, called "well-known" port numbers, are permanently assigned; for example, e-mail data under SMTP goes to port number 25. A process such as a telnet session receives an "ephemeral" port number

P

when it starts; data for that session goes to that port number, and the port number goes out of use when the session ends. A total of 65,535 port numbers are available for use with TCP, and the same number are available for UDP. *See also* IP, Simple Mail Transfer Protocol, socket (definition 1), TCP, UDP. *Compare* IP address.

portrait mode *n.* A vertical print orientation in which a document is printed across the narrower dimension of a rectangular sheet of paper. This is the print mode typical of most letters, reports, and other such documents. *Compare* landscape mode.

portrait monitor *n.* A monitor with a screen shape higher than it is wide. The proportions (but not necessarily the size) of the screen are usually the same as for a sheet of $8^1/_2$-by-11-inch paper. *Compare* landscape monitor.

port replicator *n.* A device that enables easy connection of portable computers to less portable devices, such as printers, monitors, and full-sized keyboards. Instead of having to connect each such device individually to a portable computer, a user can plug it permanently into a port replicator and use it simply by plugging the computer into a single socket, also on the port replicator. Port replicators are comparable to docking stations, but without the same capability for expansion and storage. *Also called:* convenience adapter. *See also* docking station, port.

POS *n.* Acronym for **p**oint **o**f **s**ale. The place in a store at which goods are paid for. Computerized transaction systems, such as those in use at automated supermarkets, use scanners for reading tags and bar codes, electronic cash registers, and other special devices to record purchases at this point.

POSIT *n.* Acronym for **P**rofiles for **O**pen **S**ystems **I**nternetworking **T**echnology. A set of nonmandatory standards for U.S. government network equipment. POSIT, which recognizes the prevalence of TCP/IP, is the successor to GOSIP. *See also* GOSIP, TCP/IP.

positional notation *n.* In mathematics, a form of notation whose meaning relies in part on the relative location of the elements involved. For example, common numeric notation is positional notation. In the decimal number 34, the position of the numeral 3 signifies three 10s and the position of the numeral 4 signifies four 1s.

POSIX *n.* Acronym for **P**ortable **O**perating **S**ystem **I**nterface for UNI**X**. An Institute of Electrical and Electronics Engineers (IEEE) standard that defines a set of operating-system services. Programs that adhere to the POSIX standard can be easily ported from one system to another. POSIX was based on UNIX system services, but it was created in a way that allows it to be implemented by other operating systems. *See also* service (definition 2).

post¹ *n. See* article.

post² *vb.* **1.** To submit an article in a newsgroup or other online conference or forum. The term is derived from the "posting" of a notice on a physical bulletin board. *See also* newsgroup. **2.** To place a file on a server on a network or on a Web site.

POST *n. See* power-on self test.

posterization *n. See* contouring.

postfix notation *n.* A form of algebraic notation in which the operators appear after the operands. *Also called:* reverse Polish notation. *Compare* infix notation, prefix notation.

postmaster *n.* The logon name (and therefore the e-mail address) of an account that is responsible for maintaining e-mail services on a mail server. When an account holder is having trouble with e-mail, a message to postmaster or "postmaster@machine.org.domain.name" will usually reach a human who can solve the problem.

post office *n.* The server and associated storage and mail handling services that provide the centralized location for collection and distribution of e-mail over a network.

Post Office Protocol *n.* A protocol for servers on the Internet that receive, store, and transmit e-mail and for clients on computers that connect to the servers to download and upload e-mail. *Acronym:* POP.

postprocessor *n.* A device or a software routine, such as a linker, that operates on data manipulated first by another processor. *See also* back-end processor (definition 2). *Compare* preprocessor.

PostScript *n.* A page-description language from Adobe Systems that offers flexible font capability and high-quality graphics. The most well-known page-description lan-

P

guage, PostScript uses English-like commands to control page layout and to load and scale outline fonts. Adobe Systems is also responsible for Display PostScript, a graphics language for computer displays that gives users of both PostScript and Display PostScript absolute WYSI-WYG (what-you-see-is-what-you-get), which is difficult when different methods are used for displaying and printing. *See also* outline font, page-description language.

PostScript font *n.* A font defined in terms of the Post-Script page-description language rules and intended to be printed on a PostScript-compatible printer. PostScript fonts are distinguished from bitmapped fonts by their smoothness, detail, and faithfulness to standards of quality established in the typographic industry. *See also* Post-Script. *Compare* screen font.

pot *n. See* potentiometer.

potential *n. See* electromotive force.

potentiometer *n.* A circuit element that can be adjusted to provide varying amounts of resistance. The twist-knob and slider-type volume controls on many radios and television sets are potentiometers. *Also called:* pot.

POTS *n.* Acronym for **P**lain **O**ld **T**elephone **S**ervice. Basic dialup telephone connections to the public switched network without any added features or functions. A POTS line is nothing but a phone line connected to a simple, single-line telephone instrument.

pour *vb.* To send a file or the output from a program to another file or to a device using a pipe. *See also* pipe (definition 1).

power *n.* **1.** In mathematics, the number of times a value is multiplied by itself—for example, 10 to the third power means 10 times 10 times 10. **2.** In computing, the electricity used to run a computer. **3.** The speed at which a computer performs and the availability of various features. *See also* computer power.

PowerBook *n.* Any of several computers in the family of portable Macintosh computers made by Apple.

power conditioning *n.* A feature of uninterruptible power supply (UPS) that removes spikes, surges, sags, and

noise from the power supply. *Also called:* line conditioning. *See also* UPS.

power down *vb.* To shut down (a computer); to turn off the power.

power failure *n.* Loss of electricity, which causes a loss of unsaved data in a computer's random access memory (RAM) if no backup power supply is connected to the machine. *Compare* surge.

Power Mac *n. See* Power Macintosh.

Power Macintosh *n.* A Macintosh computer based on the PowerPC processor. The first Power Macintoshes, 6100/60, 7100/66, and 8100/80, were unveiled in 1994. Several upgraded versions followed, and in early 1999 the G3, a PowerPC 750, was released. This was followed later in the year with the unveiling of the Power Macintosh G4. The Power Mac G4 uses the PowerPC 7400 processor and features significant boosts in processing speed. The Power Mac G4 uses Apple's Velocity Engine to process information in 128-bit chunks, allowing sustained performance in excess of one gigaflop. *Also called:* Power Mac. *See also* PowerPC.

power management *n.* The regulation of power consumption on a computer, especially a portable battery-operated device such as a laptop. Power management reduces power to certain components, such as the screen and CPU, to use power efficiently and extend battery life. *See also* ACPI, Advanced Power Management.

Power-on key *n.* A special key on the Apple ADB and Extended keyboards used for turning on a Macintosh II. The Power-on key is marked with a left-pointing triangle and is used in lieu of the on/off switch. There is no Power-off key; the system is shut down by choosing the Shut Down command from the Special menu.

power-on self test *n.* A set of routines stored in a computer's read-only memory (ROM) that tests various system components such as RAM, the disk drives, and the keyboard to see whether they are properly connected and operating. If problems are found, these routines alert the user by sounding a series of beeps or displaying a message, often accompanied by a diagnostic numeric value, to

P

the standard output or standard error device (usually the screen). If the power-on self test is successful, it passes control to the system's bootstrap loader. *Acronym:* POST. *See also* bootstrap loader.

PowerPC *n.* A microprocessor architecture developed in 1992 by Motorola and IBM, with some participation by Apple. A PowerPC microprocessor is RISC-based and superscalar, with a 64-bit data bus and 32-bit address bus. It also has separate data and instruction caches, although the size of each varies by implementation. All PowerPC microprocessors have multiple integer and floating-point units. The voltage and operating speed varies with the implementation. Starting with the PowerPC 740, the microprocessors were manufactured with copper, instead of aluminum, for better performance and reliability. *See also* L1 cache, L2 cache, microprocessor, RISC, superscalar.

PowerPC Platform *n.* A platform developed by IBM, Apple, and Motorola based on the 601 and later chips. This platform supports the use of multiple operating systems such as Mac OS, Windows NT, and AIX as well as software designed for those individual operating systems. *Acronym:* PPCP.

PowerPC Reference Platform *n.* An open system standard developed by IBM. IBM's goal in designing the PowerPC Reference Platform was to ensure compatibility among PowerPC systems built by different companies. Apple's PowerPC Macintoshes are not yet compliant with the PowerPC Reference Platform, but future versions are expected to be. *Acronym:* PReP. *See also* Common Hardware Reference Platform, open system, PowerPC.

PowerPoint *n.* Microsoft's presentation software. PowerPoint includes text-editing and graphics tools that can create slides for public presentations. The presentations can be printed, projected, displayed on a monitor, or, in the version included with Office 2000, saved and published as Web pages.

power supply *n.* An electrical device that transforms standard wall outlet electricity (115–120 VAC in the United States) into the lower voltages (typically 5 to 12 volts DC) required by computer systems. Personal computer power supplies are rated by wattage; they usually range from about 90 watts at the low end to 250 watts at the high end.

power surge *n. See* surge.

power up *vb.* To start up a computer; to begin a cold boot procedure; to turn on the power.

power user *n.* A person adept with computers, particularly on an applications-oriented level rather than on a programming level. A power user is someone who knows a considerable amount about computers and is comfortable enough with applications to be able to work with their most sophisticated features.

PPCP *n. See* PowerPC Platform.

PPM or **ppm** *n.* **1.** Acronym for **p**ages **p**er **m**inute. A rating of a printer's output capacity—that is, the number of printed pages the printer can produce in one minute. A printer's PPM rating is usually provided by the manufacturer and is based on a "normal" page. Pages with excessive graphics or fonts may reduce a printer's PPM rate dramatically. **2.** *See* pulse position modulation.

PPP *n.* Acronym for **P**oint-to-**P**oint **P**rotocol. A widely used data link protocol for transmitting TCP/IP packets over dial-up telephone connections, such as between a computer and the Internet. PPP, which supports dynamic allocation of IP addresses, provides greater protection for data integrity and security and is easier to use than SLIP, at a cost of greater overhead. PPP itself is based on a Link Control Protocol (LCP) responsible for setting up a computer-to-computer link over telephone lines and a Network Control Protocol (NCP) responsible for negotiating network-layer details related to the transmission. It was developed by the Internet Engineering Task Force in 1991. *Compare* SLIP.

PPPoE *n.* Acronym for **P**oint-to-**P**oint **P**rotocol **o**ver Ethernet. A specification for connecting users on an Ethernet network to the Internet through a broadband connection, such as a single DSL line, wireless device, or cable modem. Using PPPoE and a broadband modem, LAN users can gain individual authenticated access to high-speed data networks. By combining Ethernet and Point-to-Point Protocol (PPP), PPPoE provides Internet Service Providers (ISPs) with the ability to manipulate a limited number of IP addresses by assigning an address only when the user is connected to the Internet. PPPoE is an efficient way to create a separate connection for each user to a remote server. When the Internet connection is broken, the IP address becomes available to be assigned to another user.

PPS *n. See* peripheral power supply.

PPTP *n.* Acronym for **P**oint-to-**P**oint **T**unneling **P**rotocol. An extension of the Point-to-Point Protocol used for communications on the Internet. PPTP was developed by Microsoft to support virtual private networks (VPNs), which allow individuals and organizations to use the Internet as a secure means of communication. PPTP supports encapsulation of encrypted packets in secure wrappers that can be transmitted over a TCP/IP connection. *See also* virtual network.

PRAM *n.* Short for **p**arameter **RAM**. A portion of RAM in Macintosh computers that contains configuration information such as the date and time, desktop pattern, and other control panel settings. *See also* RAM.

P-rating *n.* Short for **p**erformance **rating**. A microprocessor rating system by IBM, Cyrix, and others, based on throughput in realistic applications. Formerly, microprocessor clock speed was widely used as a method of rating, but it does not account for differing chip architectures or different types of work people do with computers. *See also* central processing unit, clock (definition 1), microprocessor.

precedence *n.* In applications, the order in which values in a mathematical expression are calculated. In general, application programs perform multiplication and division first, followed by addition and subtraction. Sets of parentheses can be placed around expressions to control the order in which they are calculated. *See also* operator associativity, operator precedence.

precision *n.* **1.** The extent of detail used in expressing a number. For example, 3.14159265 gives more precision—more detail—about the value of pi than does 3.14. Precision is related to, but different from, accuracy. Precision indicates degree of detail; accuracy indicates correctness. The number 2.83845 is also more precise than 3.14, but it is less accurate for pi. *Compare* accuracy. **2.** In program-

ming, numeric values are often referred to as single-precision or double-precision values. The difference between the two is in the amount of storage space allotted to the value. *See also* double-precision, single-precision.

precompiler *n.* A program that reads in a source file and makes certain changes to prepare the source file for compilation. *Also called:* preprocessor. *See also* compiler (definition 2).

preemptive multitasking *n.* A form of multitasking in which the operating system periodically interrupts the execution of a program and passes control of the system to another waiting program. Preemptive multitasking prevents any one program from monopolizing the system. *Also called:* time-slice multitasking. *See also* multitasking. *Compare* cooperative multitasking.

Preferences *n.* A menu choice in many graphical user interface applications that allows the user to specify how the application will act each time it is used. For example, in a word processing application the user may be allowed to specify whether the ruler will appear, whether the document will appear in the same way as it will print (including margins), and other choices. *Also called:* Options, Prefs.

prefetch *vb.* Preloading buffering data for a streaming video clip before the clip begins playing. When prefetched data is stored on a computer, the video clip can be played without waiting for the initial buffering that usually occurs with streaming media. *See also* preroll.

prefix notation *n.* A form of algebraic notation, developed in 1929 by Jan Lukasiewicz, a Polish logician, in which the operators appear before the operands. For example, the expression $(a + b)$ x $(c - d)$ would be written in prefix notation as x + a b – c d. *Also called:* Polish notation. *See also* infix notation, postfix notation.

Prefs *n. See* Preferences.

Premiere *n.* Digital video editing software developed by Adobe Systems. The Premiere user interface uses command menus, windows, and floating pallets to make modifications to video clips. A timeline feature presents a graphic presentation of the length of the individual scenes and the order in which they appear. The editor can modify

P

the edits and preview the results before exporting the file into one of several video formats.

PReP *n. See* PowerPC Reference Platform.

preprocessor *n.* A device or routine that performs preliminary operations on input before passing it on for further processing. *See also* front-end processor (definition 1). *Compare* postprocessor.

preroll *vb.* Data buffering that occurs before a streaming media clip plays. Preroll time varies depending on available bandwidth and the size of the file being buffered.

presence technology *n.* An application, such as instant messaging, which finds specific users when they are connected to the network and which may alert interested users to each other's presence. Third-generation wireless networks will integrate presence technology with digital cell phones, PDAs, pagers, and other communications and entertainment devices.

presentation broadcast *n.* A PowerPoint feature that allows you to run a presentation over the Web. The presentation is saved in HTML format and can contain audio and video. It can also be recorded and saved to be viewed later.

presentation graphics *n.* The representation of business information, such as sales figures and stock prices, in chart form rather than as lists of numbers. Presentation graphics are used to give viewers an immediate grasp of business statistics and their significance. Common examples are area charts, bar charts, line charts, and pie charts. *Also called:* business graphics.

presentation layer *n.* The sixth of the seven layers in the ISO/OSI reference model for standardizing computer-to-computer communications. The presentation layer is responsible for formatting information so that it can be displayed or printed. This task generally includes interpreting codes (such as tabs) related to presentation, but it can also include converting encryption and other codes and translating different character sets. See the illustration. *See also* ISO/OSI reference model.

ISO/OSI MODEL	
ISO/OSI Layer	*Focus*
Application (highest level)	Program-to-program transfer of information
Presentation	Text formatting and display, code conversion
Session	Establishing, maintaining, and coordinating communication
Transport	Accurate delivery, service quality
Network	Transport routes, message handling and transfer
Data-link	Coding, addressing, and transmitting information
Physical	Hardware connections

Presentation layer.

Presentation Manager *n.* The graphical user interface provided with OS/2 versions 1.1 and later. The Presentation Manager derives from the MS-DOS–based Windows environment and provides similar capabilities. The user sees a graphical, window-oriented interface, and the programmer uses a standard set of routines for handling screen, keyboard, mouse, and printer input and output, no matter what hardware is attached to the system. *See also* OS/2, Windows.

pressure-sensitive *adj.* Of or pertaining to a device in which pressing on a thin surface produces an electrical connection and causes an event to be registered by the computer. Pressure-sensitive devices include touch-sensitive drawing pens, membrane keyboards, and some touch screens. *See also* touch screen.

Pretty Good Privacy *n. See* PGP.

pretty print *n.* A feature of some editors used in programming that formats code so that it is easier to read and understand when printed. For example, a pretty-print feature might insert blank lines to set off modules or indent nested routines to make them easier to spot. *See also* code[1] (definition 1), editor, module (definition 1), routine.

preventive maintenance *n.* Routine servicing of hardware intended to keep equipment in good operating condition and to find and correct problems before they develop into severe malfunctions.

preview *n.* In word processors and other applications, the feature that formats a document for printing but displays it on the video monitor rather than sending it directly to the printer.

PRI *n.* Acronym for **P**rimary **R**ate **I**nterface. One of two ISDN transmission rate services (the other is the basic rate interface, BRI). PRI has two variations. The first, which operates at 1.536 Mbps, transmits data over 23 B channels and sends signaling information at 64 Kbps over one D channel in the United States, Canada, and Japan. The second, which operates at 1.984 Mbps, transmits data over 30 B channels and sends signaling information at 64 Kbps over one D channel in Europe and Australia. *See also* BRI, ISDN.

primary channel *n.* The data-transmission channel in a communications device, such as a modem. *Compare* secondary channel.

Primary Domain Controller *n.* **1.** In Windows NT, a database providing a centralized administration site for resources and user accounts. The database allows users to log onto the domain, rather than onto a specific host machine. A separate account database keeps track of the machines in the domain and allocates the domain's resources to users. **2.** In any local area network, the server that maintains the master copy of the domain's user accounts database and that validates logon requests. *Acronym:* PDC.

primary key *n.* In databases, the key field that serves as the unique identifier of a specific tuple (row) in a relation (database table). *Also called:* major key. *See also* alternate key (definition 1), candidate key. *Compare* secondary key.

Primary Rate Interface *n.* *See* PRI.

primary storage *n.* Random access memory (RAM); the main general-purpose storage region to which the microprocessor has direct access. A computer's other storage options, such as disks and tape, are called *secondary storage* or (sometimes) *backing storage*.

primitive *n.* **1.** In computer graphics, a shape, such as a line, circle, curve, or polygon, that can be drawn, stored, and manipulated as a discrete entity by a graphics program. A primitive is one of the elements from which a large graphic design is created. **2.** In programming, a fundamen-

tal element in a language that can be used to create larger procedures that do the work a programmer wants to do.

print *vb.* In computing, to send information to a printer. The word is also sometimes used in the sense of "show me" or "copy this." For example, the PRINT statement in Basic causes output to be displayed (printed) on the screen. Similarly, an application program that can be told to print a file to disk interprets the command as an instruction to route output to a disk file instead of to a printer.

print buffer *n.* A section of memory to which print output can be sent for temporary storage until the printer is ready to handle it. A print buffer can exist in a computer's random access memory (RAM), in the printer, in a separate unit between the computer and the printer, or on disk. Regardless of its location, the function of a print buffer is to free the computer for other tasks by taking print output at high speed from the computer and passing it along at the much slower rate required by the printer. Print buffers vary in sophistication: some simply hold the next few characters to be printed, and others can queue, reprint, or delete documents sent for printing.

printed circuit board *n.* A flat board made of nonconducting material, such as plastic or fiberglass, on which chips and other electronic components are mounted, usually in predrilled holes designed to hold them. The component holes are connected electrically by predefined conductive metal pathways that are printed on the surface of the board. The metal leads protruding from the electronic components are soldered to the conductive metal pathways to form a connection. A printed circuit board should be held by the edges and protected from dirt and static electricity to avoid damage. See the illustration. *Acronym:* PCB.

Printed circuit board.

printer *n.* A computer peripheral that puts text or a computer-generated image on paper or on another medium, such as a transparency film. Printers can be categorized in any of several ways: impact versus nonimpact; print technology; character formation; method of transmission; method of printing; print capability; and print quality.

- **Impact versus nonimpact** The most common distinction is impact versus nonimpact. Impact printers physically strike the paper and are exemplified by pin dot-matrix printers and daisy-wheel printers; nonimpact printers include every other type of print mechanism, including laser, ink-jet, and thermal printers.

- **Print technology** Chief among types of print technology are pin dot-matrix, ink-jet, laser, thermal, and (although somewhat outdated) daisy-wheel or thimble printers. Pin dot-matrix printers can be further classified by the number of pins in the print head: 9, 18, 24, and so on.

- **Character formation** Fully formed characters made of continuous lines (such as those produced by a daisy-wheel printer) versus dot-matrix characters composed of patterns of dots (such as those produced by standard dot-matrix, ink-jet, and thermal printers). Laser printers, while technically dot-matrix, are generally considered to produce fully formed characters because their output is very clear and the dots are extremely small and closely spaced.

- **Method of transmission** Parallel (byte-by-byte transmission) versus serial (bit-by-bit transmission). These categories refer to the means by which output is sent to the printer rather than to any mechanical distinctions. Many printers are available in either parallel or serial versions, and still other printers offer both choices, yielding greater flexibility in installation options.

- **Method of printing** Character by character, line by line, or page by page. Character printers include standard dot-matrix, ink-jet, thermal, and daisy-wheel printers. Line printers include the band, chain, and drum printers that are commonly associated with large computer installations or networks. Page printers include the electrophotographic printers, such as laser printers.

- **Print capability** Text-only versus text-and-graphics. Text-only printers, including most daisy-wheel and thimble printers and some dot-matrix and laser printers, can reproduce only characters for which they have matching patterns, such as embossed type or internal character maps. Text-and-graphics printers—dot-matrix, ink-jet, laser, and others—can reproduce all manner of images by "drawing" each as a pattern of dots.

- **Print quality** Draft versus near-letter quality versus letter quality.

Printer Access Protocol *n. See* PAP (definition 2).

Printer Control Language *n.* A printer control language from Hewlett-Packard, used in its LaserJet, DeskJet, and RuggedWriter printer lines. Because of the LaserJet's dominance in the laser printer market, Printer Control Language has become a de facto standard. *Acronym:* PCL. Also called: Hewlett-Packard Printer Control Language.

printer controller *n.* The processing hardware in a printer, especially in a page printer. It includes the raster image processor, the memory, and any general-purpose microprocessors. A printer controller can also reside in a personal computer, attached via a high-speed cable to a printer that simply carries out its instructions. *Compare* printer engine.

printer driver *n.* A software program designed to enable other programs to work with a particular printer without concerning themselves with the specifics of the printer's hardware and internal language. Application programs can communicate properly with a variety of printers by using printer drivers, which handle all of the subtleties of each printer so that the application program doesn't have to. Today graphical user interfaces offer their own printer drivers, eliminating the need for an application that runs under the interface to have its own printer driver.

printer engine *n.* The part of a page printer, such as a laser printer, that actually performs the printing. Most printer engines are self-contained, replaceable cartridges. The engine is distinct from the printer controller, which includes all the processing hardware in the printer. The most widely used printer engines are manufactured by Canon. *Compare* printer controller.

printer file *n.* Output that would normally be destined for the printer but has been diverted to a computer file instead. A printer file is created for any of several reasons. For example, it allows output to be transferred to another program or to another computer. It also allows additional copies to be made at any time by simply copying the print image to the printer. Occasionally, the term *printer file* is used, incorrectly, to refer to the printer driver.

printer font *n.* A font residing in or intended for a printer. A printer font can be internal, downloaded, or on a font cartridge. *Compare* screen font.

Printer Job Language *n.* The printer command language developed by Hewlett-Packard that provides printer control at the print-job level. Using PJL commands, you can change default printer settings such as the number of copies to print. PJL commands also permit switching printer languages between print jobs without action by the user. If bi-directional communication is supported, a PJL-compatible printer can send information such as printer model and job status to the print server. *Also called:* Hewlett-Packard Printer Job Language. *Acronym:* PJL. *See also* page-description language, PostScript, Printer Control Language.

printer port *n.* A port through which a printer can be connected to a personal computer. On PC-compatible machines, printer ports are usually parallel ports and are identified in the operating system by the logical device name LPT. On many newer PCs, the parallel port on the case of the CPU has a printer icon beside it to identify it as a printer port. Serial ports can also be used for some printers (logical device name COM), although configuration is generally required. On Macintoshes, printer ports are usually serial ports and are also used to connect Macs to an AppleTalk network. *See also* AppleTalk, central processing unit, logical device, parallel port, serial port.

printer server *n. See* print server.

print head or **printhead** *n.* A component of an impact printer that contains the pins or other components that force ink from a ribbon onto paper.

printing pool *n.* Two or more identical printers that are connected to one print server and act as a single printer. In this case, when you print a document, the print job will be sent to the first available printer in the pool. *See also* print job, printer.

print job *n.* A single batch of characters printed as a unit. A print job usually consists of a single document, which can be one page or hundreds of pages long. To avoid having to print individual documents separately, some software can group multiple documents into a single print job. *See also* print spooler.

print mode *n.* A general term for the format of print output by a printer. Print modes range from portrait or landscape orientation of the paper to letter quality and size of the print. Dot-matrix printers support two print modes: draft and letter quality (LQ) or near-letter-quality (NLQ). Some printers can interpret both plain text (ASCII) and a page definition language such as PostScript. *See also* PostScript, printer.

printout *n. See* hard copy.

print quality *n.* The quality and clarity of characters produced by a printer. Print quality varies with the type of printer; in general, dot-matrix printers produce lower-quality output than laser printers. The printer mode can also affect quality. *See also* resolution (definition 1).

print queue *n.* A buffer for documents and images waiting to be printed. When an application places a document in a print queue, it is held in a special part of the computer's memory, where it waits until the printer is ready to receive it.

Print Screen key *n.* A key on IBM PC and compatible keyboards that normally causes the computer to send a character-based "picture" of the screen contents to the printer. The print screen feature works only when the display is in text mode or CGA graphics mode (the lowest-resolution color and graphics mode available on IBM compatibles). It will not work properly in other graphics modes. Some programs use the Print Screen key to capture a screen image and record it as a file on disk. These programs can typically work in any graphics mode and record the file as a graphics image. When the user is working directly with the MS-DOS operating system, and with some programs, the combination Control-Print Screen toggles the printer on or off. With printing turned on, the system sends every character to the printer as well as to the screen. The Print Screen key on the Apple Extended Keyboard is included for compatibility with operating systems such as MS-DOS. *Also called:* PrtSc key.

print server *n.* A workstation that is dedicated to managing printers on a network. The print server can be any station on the network. *Also called:* printer server.

Print Server for Macintosh *n.* An AppleTalk network integration service that enables computers running the Macintosh and Windows operating systems to share printers. *Also called:* MacPrint.

print spooler *n.* Computer software that intercepts a print job on its way to the printer and sends it to disk or memory instead, where the print job is held until the printer is

P

ready for it. The term *spooler* is an acronym created from "simultaneous peripheral operations on line."

print to file *n*. A command in many applications that instructs the program to format a document for printing and store the formatted document as a file rather than sending it to a printer.

print wheel *n*. *See* daisy wheel.

priority *n*. Precedence in receiving the attention of the microprocessor and the use of system resources. Within a computer, unseen and unnoticed levels of priority are the means by which many different types of potential clashes and disruptions are avoided. Similarly, tasks running on a computer can be assigned priorities that determine when and for how long they receive time from the microprocessor. On networks, stations can be assigned priorities that determine when and how often they can control the communications line, and messages can be assigned priorities that indicate how soon they must be transmitted. *See also* interrupt.

Priority Frame *n*. A telecommunications protocol developed by Infonet and Northern Telecom, Inc., designed to carry data, facsimile, and voice information.

privacy *n*. The concept that a user's data, such as stored files and e-mail, is not to be examined by anyone else without that user's permission. A right to privacy is not generally recognized on the Internet. Federal law protects only e-mail in transit or in temporary storage, and only against access by Federal agencies. Employers often claim a right to inspect any data on their systems. To obtain privacy, the user must take active measures such as encryption. *See also* encryption, PGP, Privacy Enhanced Mail. *Compare* security.

Privacy Enhanced Mail *n*. An Internet standard for e-mail systems that use encryption techniques to ensure the privacy and security of messages. *Acronym:* PEM. *See also* encryption, standard. *Compare* PGP.

privacy policy *n*. Public statement delineating how a Web site uses the information it gathers from visitors to the site. Some Web sites sell this information to third parties or use the information for marketing purposes. Other sites have strict policies limiting how that information may be used.

private *adj*. A keyword used in some programming languages to signify that methods or variables can be accessed only by elements residing in the same class or module. *See also* class, keyword (definition 2), local variable, reserved word, scope. *Compare* public.

private assembly *n*. An assembly that is used by only one application. A private assembly is deployed into the directory structure of the application that uses it. *Also called:* private side-by-side assembly. *See also* shared assembly.

Private Branch Exchange *n*. *See* PBX.

private channel *n*. In Internet relay chat (IRC), a channel reserved for the use of a certain group of people. Private channel names are hidden from view by the public at large. *Also called:* secret channel. *See also* IRC.

Private Communications Technology *n*. *See* PCT (definition 2).

private folders *n*. In a shared network environment, those folders on a user's computer that are not accessible by other users on the network. *Compare* public folders.

private key *n*. One of two keys in public key encryption. The user keeps the private key secret and uses it to encrypt digital signatures and to decrypt received messages. *See also* public key encryption. *Compare* public key.

private line *n*. *See* dedicated line (definition 1).

Private Network-to-Network Interface *n*. *See* PNNI.

privatization *n*. Generally, the process of turning something over from government to commercial industry control. In the context of computer science and the Internet, the term refers to the government's turning over of various Internet backbones to private industry—for example, control of NSFnet was passed from the government to private business in 1992—and to the government's more recent (1998) privatization of responsibility for domain names and addresses, which was shifted from IANA and NSI/InterNIC to a new organization known as ICANN. *See also* IANA, ICANN, InterNIC.

privileged instruction *n*. An instruction (usually a machine instruction) that can be executed only by the operating system. Privileged instructions exist because the operating system needs to perform certain operations that applications should not be allowed to perform; therefore, only the operating-system routines have the necessary privilege to execute these particular instructions.

privileged mode *n.* A mode of execution, supported by the protected mode of the Intel 80286 and higher microprocessors, in which software can carry out restricted operations that manipulate critical components of the system, such as memory and input/output ports (channels). Application programs cannot be executed in privileged mode; the heart (kernel) of the OS/2 operating system can be, as can the programs (device drivers) that control devices attached to the system.

privileges *n. See* access privileges.

PRN *n.* The logical device name for *printer*. A name reserved by the MS-DOS operating system for the standard print device. PRN usually refers to a system's first parallel port, also known as LPT1.

.pro *n.* One of seven new top-level domain names approved in 2000 by the Internet Corporation for Assigned Names and Numbers (ICANN), .pro is meant for use in Web sites relating to professions such as physicians, accountants, and lawyers. Six of the new domains became available for use in the spring of 2001; negotiations are still underway for the final registry agreement for the .pro domain.

probability *n.* The likelihood that an event will happen, which can often be estimated mathematically. In mathematics, statistics and probability theory are related fields. In computing, probability is used to determine the likelihood of failure or error in a system or device.

problem solving *n.* **1.** The process of devising and implementing a strategy for finding a solution or for transforming a less desirable condition into a more desirable one. **2.** An aspect of artificial intelligence wherein the task of problem solving is performed solely by a program. *See also* artificial intelligence.

procedural language *n.* A programming language in which the basic programming element is the procedure (a named sequence of statements, such as a routine, subroutine, or function). The most widely used high-level languages (C, Pascal, Basic, FORTRAN, COBOL, Ada) are all procedural languages. *See also* procedure. *Compare* nonprocedural language.

procedural rendering *n.* The rendering of a two-dimensional image from three-dimensional coordinates with texturing according to user-specified conditions, such as direction and degree of lighting.

procedure *n.* In a program, a named sequence of statements, often with associated constants, data types, and variables, that usually performs a single task. A procedure can usually be called (executed) by other procedures, as well as by the main body of the program. Some languages distinguish between a procedure and a function, with the latter (the function) returning a value. *See also* function, parameter, procedural language, routine, subroutine.

procedure call *n.* In programming, an instruction that causes a procedure to be executed. A procedure call can be located in another procedure or in the main body of the program. *See also* procedure.

process[1] *n.* A program or part of a program; a coherent sequence of steps undertaken by a program.

process[2] *vb.* To manipulate data with a program.

process-bound *adj.* Limited in performance by processing requirements. *See also* computation-bound.

process color *n.* A method of handling color in a document in which each block of color is separated into its subtractive primary color components for printing: cyan, magenta, and yellow (as well as black). All other colors are created by blending layers of various sizes of halftone spots printed in cyan, magenta, and yellow to create the image. *See also* color model, color separation (definition 1). *Compare* spot color.

processing *n.* The manipulation of data within a computer system. Processing is the vital step between receiving data (input) and producing results (output)—the task for which computers are designed.

processor *n. See* central processing unit, microprocessor.

Processor Direct Slot *n. See* PDS (definition 1).

Processor Input/Output *n. See* PIO.

Procmail *n.* An open-source e-mail-processing utility for Linux and other UNIX-based computers and networks. Procmail can be used to create mail servers and mailing lists, filter mail, sort incoming mail, preprocess mail, and perform other mail-related functions.

Prodigy *n.* An Internet service provider (ISP) that offers Internet access and a wide range of related services. Prodigy was founded by IBM and Sears as a proprietary online service, was acquired by International Wireless in 1996, and in 1999 entered into a partnership with SBC Commu-

P

nications. The addition of SBC's Internet customer base made Prodigy the third largest ISP in the United States.

Prodigy Information Service *n.* An online information service founded by IBM and Sears. Like its competitors America Online and CompuServe, Prodigy offers access to databases and file libraries, online chat, special interest groups, e-mail, and Internet connectivity. *Also called:* Prodigy.

product *n.* **1.** An operator in the relational algebra used in database management that, when applied to two existing relations (tables), results in the creation of a new table containing all possible ordered concatenations (combinations) of tuples (rows) from the first relation with tuples from the second. The number of rows in the resulting relation is the product of the number of rows in the two source relations. *Also called:* Cartesian product. *Compare* inner join. **2.** In mathematics, the result of multiplying two or more numbers. **3.** In the most general sense, an entity conceived and developed for the purpose of competing in a commercial market. Although computers are products, the term is more commonly applied to software, peripherals, and accessories in the computing arena.

production system *n.* In expert systems, an approach to problem solving based on an "IF this, THEN that" approach that uses a set of rules, a database of information, and a "rule interpreter" to match premises with facts and form a conclusion. Production systems are also known as rule-based systems or inference systems. *See also* expert system.

Professional Graphics Adapter *n.* A video adapter introduced by IBM, primarily for CAD applications. The Professional Graphics Adapter is capable of displaying 256 colors, with a horizontal resolution of 640 pixels and a vertical resolution of 480 pixels. *Acronym:* PGA.

Professional Graphics Display *n.* An analog display introduced by IBM, intended for use with their Professional Graphics Adapter. *See also* Professional Graphics Adapter.

profile[1] *n. See* user profile.

profile[2] *vb.* To analyze a program to determine how much time is spent in different parts of the program during execution.

profiler *n.* A diagnostic tool for analyzing the run-time behavior of programs.

Profiles for Open Systems Internetworking Technology *n. See* POSIT.

program[1] *n.* A sequence of instructions that can be executed by a computer. The term can refer to the original source code or to the executable (machine language) version. *Also called:* software. *See also* program creation, routine, statement.

program[2] *vb.* To create a computer program, a set of instructions that a computer or other device executes to perform a series of actions or a particular type of work.

program button *n.* On a handheld device, a navigation control that is pressed to launch an application. *Also called:* application button.

program card *n. See* PC Card, ROM card.

program cartridge *n. See* ROM cartridge.

program comprehension tool *n.* A software engineering tool that facilitates the process of understanding the structure and/or functionality of computer applications. *Acronym:* PCT. *Also called:* software exploration tool.

program counter *n.* A register (small, high-speed memory circuit within a microprocessor) that contains the address (location) of the instruction to be executed next in the program sequence.

program creation *n.* The process of producing an executable file. Traditionally, program creation comprises three steps: (1) compiling the high-level source code into assembly language source code; (2) assembling the assembly language source code into machine-code object files; and (3) linking the machine-code object files with various data files, run-time files, and library files into an executable file. Some compilers go directly from high-level source to machine-code object, and some integrated development environments compress all three steps into a single command. *See also* assembler, compiler (definition 2), linker, program.

program encapsulation *n.* A method of dealing with programs with Year 2000 problems that entailed modifying the data with which a program worked. The input data is modified to reflect a parallel date in the past that the program can handle. When output is generated, that data is changed again, to reflect the correct date. The program itself remains unchanged.

program file *n.* A disk file that contains the executable portions of a computer program. Depending on its size and complexity, an application or other program, such as an operating system, can be stored in several different files, each containing the instructions necessary for some part of the program's overall functioning. *Compare* document file.

program generator *n.* A program that creates other programs (usually in source code) based on a set of specifications and relationships given by the user. Program generators are often used to simplify the task of creating an application. *See also* 4GL, application generator.

program listing *n.* A copy, usually on paper, of the source code of a program. Some compilers can generate program listings with line numbers, cross-references, and so on.

program logic *n.* The logic behind the design and construction of a program—that is, the reasons it works the way it does. *See also* logic error.

programmable *adj.* Capable of accepting instructions for performing a task or an operation. Being programmable is a characteristic of computers.

programmable function key *n.* Any of several, sometimes unlabeled, keys on some third-party keyboards that allow the user to "play back" previously stored key combinations or sequences of keystrokes called *macros*. The same effect can be achieved with a standard keyboard and a keyboard enhancer, the latter of which intercepts the keyboard codes and substitutes modified values; but programmable function keys accomplish this without requiring RAM-resident software. *Compare* keyboard enhancer.

programmable interrupt controller *n.* An Intel chip that handles interrupt requests (IRQs). IBM AT machines use two programmable interrupt controllers to accommodate a maximum of 15 IRQs. The programmable interrupt controller has been replaced by the advanced programmable interrupt controller (APIC), which supports multiprocessing. *Acronym:* PIC. *See also* IBM AT, IRQ.

programmable logic array *n. See* field-programmable logic array.

programmable logic device *n.* A logic chip that is programmed by the customer rather than by the manufacturer. Like a gate array, a programmable logic device consists of a collection of logic gates; unlike a gate array, a programmable logic device need not have its programming completed as part of the manufacturing process. *Acronym:* PLD. *See also* logic chip. *Compare* gate array.

programmable read-only memory *n. See* PROM.

program maintenance *n.* The process of supporting, debugging, and upgrading a program in response to feedback from individual or corporate users or the marketplace in general.

programmatic interface *n.* **1.** A user interface dependent on user commands or on a special programming language, as contrasted with a graphical user interface. UNIX and MS-DOS have programmatic interfaces; the Apple Macintosh and Microsoft Windows have graphical user interfaces. *See also* command-line interface, graphical user interface, iconic interface. **2.** The set of functions any operating system makes available to a programmer developing an application. *See also* application programming interface.

Programmed Input/Output *n. See* PIO.

Programmed Inquiry, Learning or Teaching *n. See* PILOT.

programmer *n.* **1.** An individual who writes and debugs computer programs. Depending on the size of the project and the work environment, a programmer might work alone or as part of a team, be involved in part or all of the process from design through completion, or write all or a portion of the program. *See also* program. **2.** In hardware, a device used to program read-only memory chips. *See also* PROM, ROM (definition 2).

programmer's switch *n.* A pair of buttons on Macintosh computers that enable the user to reboot the system or to enter a command-line interface at a low level of the operating system. Originally, only programmers testing software were expected to need those functions, so early models of the Macintosh hid the buttons inside the cabinet and supplied a plastic clip that could be attached so that the programmer could push them. In many later models the buttons are built into the cabinet; the button to reboot the system is marked with a triangle pointing leftward, and the other button is marked with a circle.

programming *n.* The art and science of creating computer programs. Programming begins with knowledge of one or more programming languages, such as Basic, C, Pascal, or assembly language. Knowledge of a language alone does not make a good program. Much more can be involved, such as expertise in the theory of algorithms, user interface design, and characteristics of hardware devices. Computers are rigorously logical machines, and

P

programming requires a similarly logical approach to designing, writing (coding), testing, and debugging a program. Low-level languages, such as assembly language, also require familiarity with the capabilities of a microprocessor and the basic instructions built into it. In the modular approach advocated by many programmers, a project is broken into smaller, more manageable modules—stand-alone functional units that can be designed, written, tested, and debugged separately before being incorporated into the larger program. *See also* algorithm, kludge (definition 2), modular design, object-oriented programming, spaghetti code, structured programming.

programming language *n.* Any artificial language that can be used to define a sequence of instructions that can ultimately be processed and executed by the computer. Defining what is or is not a programming language can be tricky, but general usage implies that the translation process—from the source code expressed using the programming language to the machine code that the computer needs to work with—be automated by means of another program, such as a compiler. Thus, English and other natural languages are ruled out, although some subsets of English are used and understood by some fourth-generation languages. *See also* 4GL, compiler (definition 2), natural language, program.

Programming Language I *n. See* PL/I.

program specification *n.* In software development, a statement of the goals and requirements of a project, as well as the relation of the project to other projects.

program state *n.* The condition of a program (stack contents, memory contents, instruction being executed) at a given moment.

program statement *n.* The statement defining the name, briefly describing the operation, and possibly giving other information about a program. Some languages, such as Pascal, have an explicit program statement; others do not, or they use other forms (such as the main( ) function in C).

progressive JPEG *n.* An enhancement to the JPEG graphics file format that gradually displays a photo-realistic picture in a Web browser, showing increasingly detailed versions of the picture until the entire file has finished downloading.

progressive scanning *n.* **1.** A display technique used on computer monitors in which the image is created, line by line, in a single top-to-bottom sweep of the electron gun.

The resulting image is of higher quality than is possible with the interlace scanning used for television sets. Progressive scanning might be used on next-generation digital television equipment. It does, however, require twice the signal bandwidth of interlace scanning. *Compare* interlace scanning. **2.** A line-by-line (rather than every-other-line) technique used with some video cameras to capture images of moving objects. Such cameras are used primarily for tasks such as monitoring assembly lines and traffic flow.

project *n.* An operator in the relational algebra used in database management. Given relation (table) A, the *project* operator builds a new relation containing only a specified set of attributes (columns) of A.

Project 802 *n.* The IEEE project to define networking standards that resulted in the 802.x specifications. *See also* IEEE, IEEE 802.x.

Project Gutenberg *n.* A project that makes the texts of books that are in the public domain available over the Internet. The files for the books are in plain ASCII, to make them accessible to as many people as possible. Project Gutenberg, based at the University of Illinois at Urbana-Champaign, can be reached at mrcnext.cso.uiuc.edu via FTP or through the Web page http://www.promo.net/pg/. *See also* ASCII.

projection-join normal form *n. See* normal form (definition 1).

project life cycle *n.* A sequence of preplanned stages for taking a project from beginning to end.

project management *n.* The process of planning, monitoring, and controlling the course and development of a particular undertaking.

Prolog *n.* Short for **Pro**gramming in **Log**ic. A language designed for logic programming. Prolog evolved during the 1970s in Europe (primarily France and Scotland), and the first Prolog compiler was developed in 1972 by Philippe Roussel, at the University of Marseilles. The language has subsequently attained wide use in the field of artificial intelligence. Prolog is a compiled language that works with the logical relationship between pieces of data rather than mathematical relationships. *See also* artificial intelligence.

PROM *n.* Acronym for **p**rogrammable **r**ead-**o**nly **mem**ory. A type of read-only memory (ROM) that allows data to be written into the device with hardware called a PROM programmer. After a PROM has been programmed, it is dedicated to that data, and it cannot be reprogrammed. *See also* EEPROM, EPROM, ROM (definition 2).

PROM blaster *n. See* PROM programmer.

PROM blower *n. See* PROM programmer.

promiscuous-mode transfer *n.* In network communications, a transfer of data in which a node accepts all packets regardless of their destination address.

PROM programmer *n.* A hardware device that records instructions or data on a PROM (programmable read-only memory) chip or an EPROM (erasable programmable read-only memory) chip. *Also called:* PROM blaster, PROM blower. *See also* EPROM, PROM.

prompt *n.* **1.** In command-driven systems, one or more symbols that indicate where users are to enter commands. For instance, in MS-DOS, the prompt is generally a drive letter followed by a greater than symbol (C>). In UNIX, it is usually %. *See also* command-driven system, DOS prompt. **2.** Displayed text indicating that a computer program is waiting for input from the user.

propagated error *n.* An error used as input to another operation, thus producing another error.

propagation *n.* Travel of a signal, such as an Internet packet, from its source to one or more destinations. Propagation of messages over different paths with different lengths can cause messages to appear at a user's computer with varying delivery times. *See also* propagation delay.

propagation delay *n.* The time needed by a communications signal to travel between two points; in satellite links, a noticeable delay of between one-quarter second and one-half second, caused by the signal traveling through space.

propeller head *n.* Slang for a person who is obsessed with computers or other technology; a geek. The name refers to a child's beanie cap topped by a spinning propeller.

property *n.* In Windows 9x, a characteristic or parameter of an object or device. Properties of a file, for example, include type, size, and creation date and can be identified by accessing the file's property sheet. *See also* property sheet.

property sheet *n.* A type of dialog box in Windows 9x, accessed by choosing Properties in the File menu or by right-clicking on an object and selecting Properties, that lists the attributes or settings of an object such as a file, application, or hardware device. A property sheet presents the user with a tabbed, index-card-like selection of prop-

erty pages, each of which features standard dialog-style controls for customizing parameters.

proportional font *n.* A set of characters in a particular style and size in which a variable amount of horizontal space is allotted to each letter or number. In a proportional font, the letter *i*, for example, is allowed less space than the letter *m*. *Compare* monospace font.

proportional spacing *n.* A form of character spacing in which the horizontal space each character occupies is proportional to the width of the character. The letter *w*, for example, takes up more space than the letter *i*. *Compare* monospacing.

proprietary *adj.* Of, pertaining to, or characteristic of something that is privately owned. Generally, the term refers to technology that has been developed by a particular corporation or entity, with specifications that are considered by the owner to be trade secrets. Proprietary technology may be legally used only by a person or entity purchasing an explicit license. Also, other companies are unable to duplicate the technology, both legally and because its specifications have not been divulged by the owner. *Compare* public domain.

proprietary software *n.* A program owned or copyrighted by an individual or a business and available for use only through purchase or by permission of the owner. *Compare* open source, public-domain software.

protected *n.* A keyword in a programming language (such as Java or C++) used in a method or variable declaration. It signifies that the method or variable can be accessed only by elements residing in its class, subclasses, or classes in the same package. *See also* class, declaration, method, package, variable.

protected mode *n.* An operating mode of the Intel 80286 and higher microprocessors that supports larger address spaces and more advanced features than real mode. When started in protected mode, these CPUs provide hardware support for multitasking, data security, and virtual memory. The Windows (version 3.0 and later) and OS/2 operating systems run in protected mode, as do most versions of UNIX for these microprocessors. *Compare* real mode.

protocol *n. See* communications protocol.

protocol analyzer *n.* A management tool designed to identify and diagnose computer network problems. A protocol analyzer looks at LAN (local area network) or WAN (wide area network) traffic and finds protocol errors, connection delays, and other network faults. The protocol

P

analyzer can filter and decode traffic, suggest solutions to problems, provide graphical reports, and show traffic by protocol and percent utilization. *See also* communications protocol.

protocol layer *n. See* layer.

protocol stack *n.* The set of protocols that work together on different levels to enable communication on a network. For example, TCP/IP, the protocol stack on the Internet, incorporates more than 100 standards including FTP, IP, SMTP, TCP, and Telnet. *See also* ISO/OSI reference model. *Compare* protocol suite.

protocol suite *n.* A set of protocols designed, usually by one vendor, as complementary parts of a protocol stack. *Compare* protocol stack.

prototyping *n.* The creation of a working model of a new computer system or program for testing and refinement. Prototyping is used in the development of both new hardware and software systems and new systems of information management. Tools used in the former include both hardware and support software; tools used in the latter can include databases, screen mockups, and simulations that, in some cases, can be developed into a final product.

proxy *n.* A computer (or the software that runs on it) that acts as a barrier between a network and the Internet by presenting only a single network address to external sites. By acting as a go-between representing all internal computers, the proxy protects network identities while still providing access to the Internet. *See also* proxy server.

proxy server *n.* A firewall component that manages Internet traffic to and from a local area network (LAN) and can provide other features, such as document caching and access control. A proxy server can improve performance by supplying frequently requested data, such as a popular Web page, and can filter and discard requests that the owner does not consider appropriate, such as requests for unauthorized access to proprietary files. *See also* firewall.

PrtSc key *n. See* Print Screen key.

.ps *n.* The file extension that identifies PostScript printer files. *See also* PostScript.

PS/2 bus *n. See* Micro Channel Architecture.

PSD *n.* A graphics file format used to create, modify, and display still images in Photoshop, a software application designed by Adobe Systems. PSD files have a file extension of .psd.

PSE *n. See* Packet Switching Exchange.

psec *n. See* picosecond.

pseudocode *n.* **1.** A machine language for a nonexistent processor (a pseudomachine). Such code is executed by a software interpreter. The major advantage of p-code is that it is portable to all computers for which a p-code interpreter exists. The p-code approach has been tried several times in the microcomputer industry, with mixed success. The best known attempt was the UCSD p-System. *Abbreviation*: p-code. *See also* pseudomachine, UCSD p-System. **2.** Any informal, transparent notation in which a program or algorithm description is written. Many programmers write their programs first in a pseudocode that looks much like a mixture of English and their favorite programming language, such as C or Pascal, and then translate it line by line into the actual language being used.

pseudo compiler *n.* A compiler that generates a pseudolanguage. *See also* pseudolanguage.

pseudocomputer *n. See* pseudomachine.

pseudolanguage *n.* A nonexistent programming language—that is, one for which no implementation exists. The term can refer either to the machine language for a nonexistent processor or to a high-level language for which no compiler exists. *See also* pseudocode.

pseudomachine *n.* A processor that doesn't actually exist in hardware but that is emulated in software. A program written for the pseudomachine can run on several platforms without having to be recompiled. *Abbreviation:* p-machine. *See also* pseudocode, UCSD p-System.

pseudo-op *n. See* pseudo-operation.

pseudo-operation *n.* In programming, a program instruction that conveys information to an assembler or compiler but is not translated into a machine language instruction—for example, an instruction that establishes the value of a constant or the manner in which Boolean (logical) expressions are to be evaluated. *Abbreviation:* pseudo-op.

pseudo-streaming *n.* A method used for real-time display of audio and video over the Web. Unlike sound or video files that are downloaded to a computer in their entirety before they can be played back, pseudo-streaming enables playback after only a portion of the file—enough to fill a buffer on the receiving computer—has been downloaded. Pseudo-streaming, unlike "true," or Web, streaming, does not depend on server software to dynamically monitor the transmission. It can, however, play back only from the beginning of the file, rather than from any point, as can be the case with true streaming. *See also* stream.

PSK *n. See* phase-shift keying.

PSN *n.* Acronym for **p**acket-**s**witching **n**etwork. *See* packet switching.

PSTN *n. See* Public Switched Telephone Network.

p-system *n.* An operating system based on a pseudomachine implemented in software. A program written for the p-system is more portable than one written for a machine-dependent operating system. *See also* UCSD p-System.

P-type semiconductor *n.* Semiconductor material in which electrical conduction is carried by holes ("vacancies" left by electrons). Whether a semiconductor is N-type or P-type depends on the kind of dopant added during manufacture. A dopant with a shortage of electrons results in a P-type semiconductor. *Compare* N-type semiconductor.

pub *n. See* /pub.

/pub *n.* Short for **pub**lic. A directory in an anonymous FTP archive that is accessible by the public and that generally contains files available for free download. *See also* anonymous FTP.

public *adj.* A keyword in some programming languages to signify that methods or variables can be accessed by elements residing in other classes or modules. *See also* class., keyword (definition 2), global variable, reserved word, scope. *Compare* private.

public directory *n.* A directory on an FTP server that is accessible by anonymous users for the purpose of retrieving or storing files. Often the directory is called /pub. *See also* anonymous FTP, FTP (definition 1), FTP server /pub.

public domain *n.* The set of all creative works, such as books, music, or software, that are not covered by copyright or other property protection. Works in the public domain can be freely copied, modified, and otherwise used in any manner for any purpose. Much of the information, texts, and software on the Internet is in the public domain, but putting a copyrighted work on the Internet does not put it in the public domain. *Compare* proprietary.

public-domain software *n.* A program donated for public use by its owner or developer and freely available for copying and distribution. *Compare* free software, freeware, proprietary software, shareware.

public files *n.* Files with no access restrictions.

public folders *n.* The folders that are made accessible on a particular machine or by a particular user in a shared networking environment. *Compare* private folders.

public key *n.* One of two keys in public key encryption. The user releases this key to the public, who can use it for encrypting messages to be sent to the user and for decrypting the user's digital signature. *See also* public key encryption. *Compare* private key.

public key cryptography *n. See* public key encryption.

public key encryption *n.* An asymmetric scheme that uses a pair of keys for encryption: the public key encrypts data, and a corresponding secret key decrypts it. For digital signatures, the process is reversed: the sender uses the secret key to create a unique electronic number that can be read by anyone possessing the corresponding public key, which verifies that the message is truly from the sender. *See also* private key, public key.

public rights *n.* In the context of the Internet, the extent to which members of the public are permitted to use (and to place) information on the Internet under intellectual property law. *See also* fair use, public domain, public-domain software.

Public Switched Telephone Network *n.* The public telephone system.

Publisher *n.* A software application developed by Microsoft Corporation to help businesses create high-quality marketing and business material. A part of the Office product family, Publisher provides business users with design options for a variety of publications, such as newsletters, flyers, brochures, and Web pages.

publishing point *n.* A publishing point is a virtual directory used for storing content or delivering a live stream. End users reach a publishing point through its URL. There are two types of unicast publishing points: on-demand for stored content and broadcast for live streams. *See also* on-demand publishing point, broadcast publishing point. *Compare* unicast.

puck *n.* A pointing device used with a graphics tablet. A puck, which is often used in engineering applications, is a mouselike device with buttons for selecting items or choosing commands and a clear plastic section extending from one end with cross hairs printed on it. The intersection of the cross hairs on the puck points to a location on the graphics tablet, which in turn is mapped to a specific location on the screen. Because the puck's cross hairs are on a transparent surface, a user can easily trace a drawing by placing it between the graphics tablet and the puck and moving the cross hairs over the lines of the drawing. *See also* graphics tablet, stylus.

Puck.

puff and sip device *n.* An assistive computer technology for people with mobility impairments. A puff and sip device is a head-mounted alternative to using a mouse or keyboard. For mouse functionality, the device allows a user to move the mouse pointer without using his or her hands by puffing air into a tube.

pull *vb.* The process of retrieving data from a network server. *Compare* push (definition 2). *See* pop.

pull-down menu *n.* A menu that is pulled down from the menu bar and that remains available as long as the user holds it open. *Compare* drop-down menu.

pulse *n.* A transient signal, usually brief and with a discrete onset and offset.

pulse amplitude modulation *n.* A method of encoding information in a signal by varying the amplitude of pulses. The unmodulated signal consists of a continuous train of pulses of constant frequency, duration, and amplitude. During modulation the pulse amplitudes are changed to reflect the information being encoded. See the illustration. *Acronym:* PAM. *Compare* pulse code modulation, pulse duration modulation, pulse position modulation.

Pulse amplitude modulation.

pulse code modulation *n.* A method of encoding information in a signal by varying the amplitude of pulses. Unlike pulse amplitude modulation (PAM), in which pulse amplitude can vary continuously, pulse code modulation limits pulse amplitudes to several predefined values. Because the signal is discrete, or digital, rather than analog, pulse code modulation is more immune to noise than PAM. *Acronym:* PCM. *Compare* pulse amplitude modulation, pulse duration modulation, pulse position modulation.

pulse dialing *n. See* rotary dialing.

pulse duration modulation *n.* A method of encoding information in a signal by varying the duration of pulses. The unmodulated signal consists of a continuous train of pulses of constant frequency, duration, and amplitude. During modulation, the pulse durations are changed to reflect the information being encoded. See the illustration. *Acronym:* PDM. *Also called:* pulse length modulation, pulse width modulation.

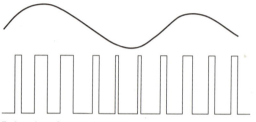

Pulse duration modulation.

pulse length modulation *n. See* pulse duration modulation.

pulse position modulation *n.* A method of encoding information in a signal by varying the position of pulses. The unmodulated signal consists of a continuous train of pulses of constant frequency, duration, and amplitude. During modulation, the pulse positions are changed to reflect the information being encoded. See the illustration. *Acronym:* PPM. *Compare* pulse amplitude modulation, pulse code modulation, pulse duration modulation.

Pulse position modulation.

pulse width modulation *n. See* pulse duration modulation.

punched card *n.* An outdated computer-input medium made of stiff paper that stores data bits in columns containing patterns of punched holes. The method for creating the patterns used for different byte values is called Hollerith coding. *See also* Hollerith tabulating/recording machine.

punched-card reader *n. See* card reader.

pure procedure *n.* Any procedure that modifies only data that is dynamically allocated (usually on the stack). A pure procedure cannot modify either global data or its own code. This restriction allows a pure procedure to be called simultaneously by separate tasks. *See also* reentrant code.

purge *vb.* To eliminate old or unneeded information systematically; to clean up, as files.

push[1] *n.* A technology developed in relation to the World Wide Web, designed to provide end users with personalized Web access by having a site actively "push" requested information to the user's desktop, either automatically or at specified intervals. Push was developed as a means of relieving users from having to actively retrieve ("pull") information from the Web. It is not, as yet, especially popular.

push[2] *vb.* **1.** To add a new element to a stack, a data structure generally used to temporarily hold pieces of data being transferred or the partial result of an arithmetic operation. *See also* stack. *Compare* pop. **2.** In networks and the Internet, to send data or a program from a server to a client at the instigation of the server. *See also* push[2]. *Compare* pull.

put *vb.* In programming, to write data, typically to a file; in particular, to write a very small unit of data, such as a character.

PVC *n.* Acronym for **p**ermanent **v**irtual **c**ircuit. A permanent logical connection between two nodes on a packet-switching network. The PVC appears as a dedicated line to the nodes, but the data can be transmitted on a common carrier. *See also* common carrier, node (definition 2), packet switching, virtual private network. *Compare* SVC.

pwd *n.* Acronym for **p**rint **w**orking **d**irectory. The UNIX command for displaying the current directory.

PWM *n.* Acronym for **p**ulse **w**idth **m**odulation. *See* pulse duration modulation.

PXE boot *n.* Acronym for **P**reboot **E**xecution **E**nvironment **boot**. A BIOS-supported technology used to boot a PC remotely. To power on a PC and boot it from the network, PXE must be enabled in the BIOS, and the NIC in the PC must be PXE compliant. PXE boot is specified in the Intel Wired for Management (WfM) standard. *Also called:* network boot.

pyramid diagram *n.* A diagram that is used to show foundation-based relationships.

Python *n.* A portable, interpreted, object-oriented programming language developed and freely distributed by its developer. Python runs on many platforms, including UNIX, Windows, OS/2, and Macintosh, and is used for writing TCP/IP applications.

P

QAM *n.* *See* quadrature amplitude modulation, queued access method.

QBasic *n.* An interpreted language. QBasic is a dialect of Basic created by Microsoft for the MS-DOS platform. This language is no longer supported.

QBE *n.* *See* query by example.

QIC *n.* **1.** Acronym for **q**uarter-**i**nch **c**artridge. A storage technology used with tape backup drives and cartridges. A means of backing up data on computer systems, QIC represents a set of standards devised to enable tapes to be used with drives from different manufacturers. The QIC standards specify the length of tape, the number of recording tracks, and the magnetic strength of the tape coating, all of which determine the amount of information that can be written to the tape. Older QIC-80 drives can hold up to 340 MB of compressed data. Newer versions can hold more than 1 GB of information. **2.** A consortium of quarter-inch tape manufacturers. Quarter-Inch Cartridge Drive Standards Inc. (QIC) establishes standards for the production of quarter-inch tapes. For example, QIC-40 and QIC-80, designed to use a PC's floppy disk drive controller, are called the "floppy tape standards."

QOS or **QoS** *n.* *See* quality of service.

quadbit *n.* A set of 4 bits representing one of 16 possible combinations. In communications, quadbits are a means of increasing transmission rates by encoding 4 bits at a time, instead of 1 or 2. The 16 quadbits are 0000, 0001, 0010, 0011, 0100, 0101, 0110, 0111, 1000, 1001, 1010, 1011, 1100, 1101, 1110, and 1111. *Compare* nibble.

quadrature amplitude modulation *n.* In communications, an encoding method that combines amplitude modulation and phase modulation to create a constellation of signal points, each representing one unique combination of bits that can be identified with one possible state that the carrier wave can be in. *Acronym:* QAM. *See also* amplitude modulation, constellation, phase-shift keying, trellis-coded modulation.

quadrature encoding *n.* The most common method used to determine in which direction a mouse is moving. In mechanical mice, movement of the mouse ball is translated into horizontal or vertical movement by a pair of turning disks, one disk for horizontal movement and one disk for vertical movement, each of which makes and breaks contact with two sensors located on it. The two sensors are placed out of phase with each other, and the mouse notes which sensor receives contact first. The phrase *quadrature encoding* comes from the fact that each sensor sends a square-wave signal 90 degrees out of phase with the other. If the first signal occurs before the second, the mouse is assumed to have been moved in one direction; if the second signal occurs before the first, the mouse is assumed to have been moved in the opposite direction. *See also* mechanical mouse, mouse, optomechanical mouse.

quality assurance *n.* A system of procedures carried out to ensure that a product or a system adheres or conforms to established standards. *Also called:* quality control.

quality of service *n.* **1.** Generally, the handling capacity of a system or service; the time interval between request and delivery of a product or service to the client or customer. **2.** In computer technology, the guaranteed throughput (data transfer rate) level.

quantity *n.* A number—positive or negative, whole or fractional—that is used to indicate a value.

quantize *vb.* To divide an element into separate, distinct units (quanta) and to assign a value to each resulting unit, especially in the domain of time. *Compare* digitize.

quantum *n.* **1.** In communications, the unit resulting from division of a signal by quantization. **2.** A portion of time allotted on a time-sharing system. *Compare* time slice. **3.** An amount of something; for example, in physics, a unit of radiant energy.

quantum bit *n.* *See* qubit.

quantum computing *n.* A theoretical design for computers based on quantum mechanics. Unlike classic (current) digital computers, which calculate sets of values sequentially because a single bit can represent only 1 or 0 at any given time, a quantum computer is based on the ability of each bit to represent more than one value at the same time.

Because each quantum bit—called a qubit—represents multiple values, a quantum computer can be in multiple states simultaneously and can thus work on numerous problems at the same time to offer far more computing power than is currently available. Quantum computing is under investigation by the United States Defense Advanced Research Projects Agency (DARPA) and other groups. Although atoms of hydrogen and carbon have been used to create the rudiments of a quantum computer, the technology is still in its infancy.

quarter-inch cartridge *n. See* QIC (definition 1).

Quartz *n.* The 2-D drawing engine that forms the imaging foundation of the Mac OS X Aqua interface. The Quartz graphics application programming interface (API) is based on Adobe's Portable Document Format (PDF) standard.

quartz crystal *n.* A precisely shaped and precisely sized piece of the mineral quartz, used for its piezoelectric properties. When a voltage is applied to a quartz crystal, it vibrates at a frequency determined by its size and shape. Quartz crystals are commonly used to control the frequency of oscillator circuits such as the clocks in microcomputers. *See also* piezoelectric.

quasi-language *n.* A derogatory term for any programming language that, because of deficiencies, is not suitable for any serious work.

qubit *n.* Short for **qu**antum **bit**. The bits (currently, atomic particles) that make up the theoretical machines known as quantum computers. Qubits are unlike bits in current computers in that they exist in more than one state at the same time. They can, therefore, represent both 0 and 1 simultaneously. Qubits, like quantum computers, are based on the science of quantum mechanics.

query[1] *n.* A specific set of instructions for extracting particular data.

query[2] *vb.* To extract data from a database and present it for use.

query by example *n.* A simple-to-use query language implemented on several relational database management systems. Using query by example, the user specifies fields to be displayed, intertable linkages, and retrieval criteria directly onto forms displayed on the screen. These forms are a direct pictorial representation of the table and row structures that make up the database. Thus, the construction of a query becomes a simple "checkoff" procedure from the viewpoint of the user. *Acronym:* QBE.

query language *n.* A subset of the data manipulation language; specifically, that portion relating to the retrieval and display of data from a database. It is sometimes used loosely to refer to the entire data manipulation language. *See also* data manipulation language.

question mark *n. See* ?.

queue[1] *n.* A multi-element data structure from which (by strict definition) elements can be removed only in the same order in which they were inserted; that is, it follows a first in, first out (FIFO) constraint. There are also several types of queues in which removal is based on factors other than order of insertion—for example, some priority value assigned to each element. *See also* deque, element (definition 1). *Compare* stack.

queue[2] *vb.* To place (an item) in a queue.

queued access method *n.* A programming technique that minimizes input/output delays by synchronizing the transfer of information between the program and the computer's input and output devices. *Acronym:* QAM.

queuing *n.* In networking, the process of buffering data in preparation for transmission. *See also* fair queuing; first in, first out; last in, first out; weighted fair queuing.

QuickDraw *n.* On the Apple Macintosh, the built-in group of routines within the operating system that controls the display of graphics and text. Application programs call QuickDraw for on-screen displays. *See also* Toolbox.

QuickDraw 3-D *n.* A version of the Macintosh QuickDraw library that includes routines for doing 3-D graphics calculations. *See also* QuickDraw.

Quicken *n.* Financial-management software from Intuit, Inc. The personal-finance version, introduced by Intuit in 1984, includes tools for balancing and tracking bank accounts and investments, budgeting, paying bills, planning and preparing tax returns, financial planning, and estate planning. A small-business version, Quicken Home & Business, adds tools for business-related matters, such as invoicing and accounts receivable and payable.

quicksort *n.* An efficient sort algorithm, described by C.A.R. Hoare in 1962, in which the essential strategy is to "divide and conquer." A quicksort begins by scanning the list to be sorted for a median value. This value, called the *pivot*, is then moved to its final position in the list. Next, all items in the list whose values are less than the pivot value are moved to one side of the list, and the items with values greater than the pivot value are moved to the other

Q

side. Each resulting side is sorted the same way, until a fully sorted list results. *See also* sort algorithm. *Compare* bubble sort, insertion sort, merge sort.

QuickTime *n.* Software components developed by Apple for creating, editing, publishing, and viewing multimedia content. QuickTime, which supports video, animation, graphics, 3-D, VR (virtual reality), MIDI, music, sound, and text, has been part of the Mac OS since version 7 of the operating system and is used in many Macintosh applications. Windows applications can also run QuickTime files but require the installation of special player software. QuickTime is often used on the Web to provide Web pages with video and animation. Most Web browsers support plug-ins for running these types of files. QuickTime is also part of the new MPEG-4 specification. *See also* MPEG-4.

Quick View *n.* A feature, optionally installed as part of Windows 9x, that provides a set of file viewers for previewing the contents of files without having to start the application(s) that created them. The feature is accessed through the Quick View command, available either from the File menu or by right-clicking a filename. If the feature has been installed but the file type is not supported by a viewer, the Quick View command does not appear.

quiet answer *n.* A telephone-answering protocol in which incoming calls are answered with silence instead of a tone signal. Some telephone-switching systems use quiet answering. These switching systems expect the caller to provide another phone number, code, or extension after the quiet answer.

quit[1] *n.* **1.** An FTP command that instructs the server to drop the current connection with the client from which it received the command. **2.** A command in many applications for exiting the program.

quit[2] *vb.* **1.** To stop in an orderly manner. **2.** To execute the normal shutdown of a program and return control to the operating system. *Compare* abort, bomb[2], crash[2] (definition 1), hang.

QWERTY keyboard *n.* A keyboard layout named for the six leftmost characters in the top row of alphabetic characters on most keyboards—the standard layout of most typewriters and computer keyboards. *Compare* Dvorak keyboard.

Q

R&D *n.* Acronym for **r**esearch and **d**evelopment.

race condition *n.* **1.** A condition in which a feedback circuit interacts with internal circuit processes in a way that produces chaotic output behavior. **2.** A condition in which data propagates rapidly through a logic circuit far ahead of the clock signal intended to control its passage.

rack-mounted *adj.* Built for installation in a metal frame or cabinet of standard width (typically 19 inches or 23 inches) and mounting arrangements.

RAD *n.* Acronym for **r**apid **a**pplication **d**evelopment. A method of building computer systems in which the system is programmed and implemented in segments, rather than waiting until the entire project is completed for implementation. Developed by programmer James Martin, RAD uses such tools as CASE and visual programming. *See also* CASE, visual programming.

radian *n.* The angle between two radii of a circle such that the length of the arc between them is equal to the radius. The circumference of a circle is equal to 2p times the radius, so one radian contains 360/(2p) = 180/p = approximately 57.2958 degrees. Conversely, multiplying the number of degrees by p/180 gives the number of radians; 360 degrees equals 2p radians. See the illustration.

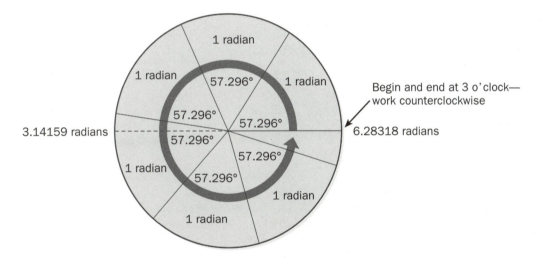

Radians = (3.14159 x (angle of degree)) ÷ 180
1 degree = 0.017453 radian

Radian.

radio *n.* **1.** Electromagnetic waves longer than about 0.3 mm (frequencies lower than about 1 THz). Radio is used to transmit a wide variety of signals, using various frequency ranges and types of modulation, such as AM and FM broadcasts, microwave relays, and television broadcasts. *See also* hertz, radio frequency. **2.** Audio signals transmitted over the Internet of quality comparable to those broadcast by commercial radio stations. *See also* Internet Talk Radio, MBONE, RealAudio.

radio button *n.* In graphical user interfaces, a means of selecting one of several options, usually within a dialog box. A radio button appears as a small circle that, when selected, has a smaller, filled circle inside it. Radio buttons act like the station selector buttons on a car radio. Selecting one button in a set deselects the previously selected button, so one and only one of the options in the set can be selected at any given time. In contrast, check boxes are used when more than one option in the set can be selected at the same time. *Compare* check box.

radio clock *n.* A device that receives a broadcast containing a standard time signal. Radio clocks are used in network communications to synchronize the host's hardware clock to the Universal Time Coordinate format in accordance with the Network Time Protocol (NTP). *See also* NTP, Universal Time Coordinate.

radio frequency *n.* The portion of the electromagnetic spectrum with frequencies between 3 kilohertz and 300 gigahertz. This corresponds to wavelengths between 30 kilometers and 0.3 millimeter. *Acronym:* RF. *See also* radio (definition 1).

radio frequency interference *n. See* RFI.

radiosity *n.* A method used in computer graphics to render photographic-quality, realistic images. Radiosity is based on dividing an image into smaller polygons, or patches, for purposes of calculating the global illumination emitted by sources of light and reflected from surfaces. Unlike ray tracing, which follows rays of light between a light source and the objects it illuminates, radiosity takes into account both the light emitted from a light source and the light reflected by all objects in the image environment. Radiosity thus accounts not only for a source of illumination (such as a lightbulb) but also for the effects of that illumination as it is absorbed by, and reflected from, every object in the "picture." *See also* form factor. *Compare* ray tracing.

RADIUS *n.* Acronym for **R**emote **A**uthentication **D**ial-**I**n **U**ser **S**ervice protocol. A proposed Internet protocol in which an authentication server provides authorization and authentication information to a network server to which a user is attempting to link. *See also* authentication, communications protocol, server (definition 2).

radix *n.* The base of a number system—for example, 2 in the binary system, 10 in the decimal system, 8 in the octal system, and 16 in the hexadecimal system. *See also* base (definition 2).

radix-minus-1 complement *n.* In a system for representing numbers using a fixed number of possible digits (radix) and a fixed number of positions for them, the number obtained from another number by subtracting each of the digits of the other number from the largest possible digit (equal to the radix minus 1). For example, in a system of five-digit decimal numbers, the radix-minus-1 complement of 1,234 is 98,765. Adding any number to its radix-minus-1 complement produces the largest possible number in the system (in the example, 99,999). Adding another 1 to this number produces, in our example, 100,000—but since only the lower five digits are used, the result is zero. Thus, the negative of any number in the system is its radix-minus-1 complement plus 1, because $-a + a = 0$. In the binary system, the radix-minus-1 complement is the one's complement, which is easily formed electronically by inverting all bits.

radix point *n.* The period or other character that separates the integer portion of a number from the fractional portion. In the decimal system, the radix point is the decimal point, as in the number 1.33.

radix sort *n. See* digital sort.

radix sorting algorithm *n.* A sorting algorithm that sorts by grouping elements according to successive parts of their keys. A simple example is sorting a list of numbers in the range 0–999. First the list is sorted by the hundreds digit into a set of (up to) 10 lists; then each list, one at a time, is sorted into a set of (up to) 10 lists based on the tens digit; and finally each of those lists is sorted by the ones digit. This algorithm is usually most efficient when the sorting is done using binary values, which simplifies comparisons (is a given bit on or off?) and reduces the number of lists (each pass produces at most two lists).

RADSL *n.* Acronym for **r**ate-**a**daptive **a**symmetric **d**igital **s**ubscriber **l**ine. A flexible, high-speed version of ADSL (asymmetric digital subscriber line) that is capable of adjusting transmission speed (bandwidth) based on signal quality and length of the transmission line. As the signal quality improves or deteriorates while a transmission line is being used, the transmission speed is adjusted accordingly. *See also* ADSL, xDSL.

rag *n.* Irregularity along the left or right edge of a set of lines of text on a printed page. Rag complements justification, in which one or both edges of the text form a straight vertical line. See the illustration. *See also* justify, ragged left, ragged right.

Ragged right	Justified	Ragged left

Rag.

ragged left *adj.* Of, relating to, or being lines of text whose left ends are not vertically aligned but form an irregular edge. Text may be right-justified and have a ragged left margin. Ragged-left text is used infrequently—typically, for visual effect in advertisements. *See also* rag, right-justify.

ragged right *adj.* Of, relating to, or being lines of text whose right ends are not vertically aligned but form an irregular edge. Letters and other word-processed documents are commonly left-justified, with ragged-right margins. *See also* left-justify, rag.

RAID *n.* Acronym for **r**edundant **a**rray of **i**ndependent (or inexpensive) **d**isks. A data storage method in which data is distributed across a group of computer disk drives that function as a single storage unit. All the information stored on each of the disks is duplicated on other disks in the array. This redundancy ensures that no information will be lost if one of the disks fails. RAID is generally used on network servers where data accessibility is critical and fault tolerance is required. There are various defined levels of RAID, each offering differing trade-offs among access speed, reliability, and cost. *See also* disk controller, error-correction coding, Hamming code, hard disk, parity bit, server (definition 1).

RAID array *n. See* RAID.

RAM *n.* Acronym for **r**andom **a**ccess **m**emory. Semiconductor-based memory that can be read and written by the central processing unit (CPU) or other hardware devices. The storage locations can be accessed in any order. Note that the various types of ROM memory are capable of random access but cannot be written to. The term *RAM*, however, is generally understood to refer to volatile memory that can be written to as well as read. *Compare* core, EPROM, flash memory, PROM, ROM (definition 2).

RAMAC *n.* **1.** Acronym for **R**andom **A**ccess **M**ethod of **A**ccounting **C**ontrol. Developed by an IBM team led by Reynold B. Johnson, RAMAC was the first computer disk drive. It was introduced in 1956. The original RAMAC consisted of a stack of 50 24-inch platters, with a storage capacity of 5 megabytes and an average access time of 1 second. **2.** A high-speed, high-capacity disk storage system introduced by IBM in 1994. Based on the original RAMAC storage device, it was designed to fulfill enterprise requirements for efficient and fault-tolerant storage.

Rambus DRAM *n. See* RDRAM.

Rambus dynamic random access memory *n. See* RDRAM.

RAM cache *n.* Short for **r**andom **a**ccess **m**emory **cache**. Cache memory that is used by the system to store and retrieve data from the RAM. Frequently accessed segments of data may be stored in the cache for quicker access compared with secondary storage devices such as disks. *See also* cache, RAM.

RAM card *n.* Short for **r**andom **a**ccess **m**emory **card**. An add-in circuit board containing RAM memory and the interface logic necessary to decode memory addresses.

RAM cartridge *n. See* memory cartridge.

RAM chip *n.* Short for **r**andom **a**ccess **m**emory **chip**. A semiconductor storage device. RAM chips can be either dynamic or static memory. *See also* dynamic RAM, RAM, static RAM.

RAM compression *n.* Short for **r**andom **a**ccess **m**emory **compression**. This technology was an attempt by a number of software vendors to solve the problem of running out of global memory under Windows 3.*x*. Compression of the usual contents of RAM may lessen the system's need to read or write to virtual (hard disk–based) memory and thus speed up the system, as virtual memory is much slower than physical RAM. Because of the falling prices of RAM and the introduction of operating systems that handle RAM

R

more efficiently, such as Windows 9x, Windows NT, and OS/2, RAM compression is generally used only on older PCs. *See also* compression, RAM, Windows.

RAMDAC *n.* Acronym for **r**andom **a**ccess **m**emory **d**igital-to-**a**nalog **c**onverter. A chip built into some VGA and SVGA video adapters that translates the digital representation of a pixel into the analog information needed by the monitor to display it. The presence of a RAMDAC chip generally enhances overall video performance. *See also* SVGA, VGA.

RAM disk *n.* Short for **r**andom **a**ccess **m**emory **disk.** A simulated disk drive whose data is actually stored in RAM memory. A special program allows the operating system to read from and write to the simulated device as if it were a disk drive. RAM disks are extremely fast, but they require that system memory be given up for their use. Also, RAM disks usually use volatile memory, so the data stored on them disappears when power is turned off. Many portables offer RAM disks that use battery-backed CMOS RAM to avoid this problem. *See also* CMOS RAM. *Compare* disk cache.

RAM refresh *n. See* refresh (definition 2).

RAM resident *adj. See* memory-resident.

RAM-resident program *n. See* terminate-and-stay-resident program.

random *adj.* Specifically, a reference to an arbitrary or unpredictable situation or event. The term is also given an extended, pejorative or semi-pejorative meaning, however, in which it is used in the sense of *nonspecific*, *incoherent*, *poorly organized*, *loser*, and so on.

random access *n.* The ability of a computer to find and go directly to a particular storage location without having to search sequentially from the beginning location. The human equivalent of random access would be the ability to find a desired address in an address book without having to proceed sequentially through all the addresses. A computer's semiconductor memory (both RAM and ROM) provides random access. Certain types of files stored on disk under some operating systems also allow random access. Such files are best used for data in which each record has no intrinsic relationship to what comes physically before or after it, as in a client list or an inventory. *Also called:* direct access. *See also* RAM, ROM (definition 2). *Compare* indexed sequential access method, sequential access.

random access memory *n. See* RAM.

random noise *n.* A signal in which there is no relationship between amplitude and time and in which many frequencies occur randomly, without pattern or predictability.

random number generation *n.* Production of an unpredictable sequence of numbers in which no number is any more likely to occur at a given time or place in the sequence than any other. Truly random number generation is generally viewed as impossible. The process used in computers would be more properly called "pseudorandom number generation."

range *n.* **1.** A block of cells selected for similar treatment in a spreadsheet. A range of cells can extend across a row, down a column, or over a combination of the two, but all cells in the range must be contiguous, sharing at least one common border. Ranges allow the user to affect many cells with a single command—for example, to format them similarly, enter the same data into all of them, give them a name in common and treat them as a unit, or select and incorporate them into a formula. **2.** In more general usage, the spread between specified low and high values. Range checking is an important method of validating data entered into an application.

range check *n.* In programming, a limit check of both the upper and lower limits of a value, thus determining whether the value lies within an acceptable range. *See also* limit check.

RAPI *n. See* Remote Application Programming Interface.

RARP *n.* Acronym for **R**everse **A**ddress **R**esolution **P**rotocol. A TCP/IP protocol for determining the IP address (or logical address) of a node on a local area network connected to the Internet, when only the hardware address (or physical address) is known. While RARP refers only to finding the IP address and ARP technically refers to the opposite procedure, ARP is commonly used for both senses. *See also* ARP.

RAS *n.* **1.** *See* remote access server, Remote Access Service. **2.** Acronym for **r**eliability, **a**vailability, **s**erviceability. *See* high availability.

raster *n.* A rectangular pattern of lines; on a video display, the horizontal scan lines from which the term *raster scan* is derived.

raster display *n.* A video monitor (typically a CRT) that displays an image on the screen as a series of horizontal scan lines from top to bottom. Each scan line consists of pixels that can be illuminated and colored individually. Television screens and most computer monitors are raster displays. *See also* CRT, pixel. *Compare* vector display.

raster fonts *n.* Fonts that are stored as bitmaps. Raster fonts are designed with a specific size and resolution for a specific printer and cannot be scaled or rotated. If a printer does not support raster fonts, it will not print them. The five raster fonts are Courier, MS Sans Serif, MS Serif, Small, and Symbol. *Also called:* bitmapped fonts. *See also* font, printer.

raster graphics *n.* A method of generating graphics that treats an image as a collection of small, independently controlled dots (pixels) arranged in rows and columns. *Compare* vector graphics.

raster image *n.* A display image formed by patterns of light and dark or differently colored pixels in a rectangular array. *See also* raster graphics.

raster image processor *n.* A device, consisting of hardware and software, that converts vector graphics or text into a raster (bitmapped) image. Raster image processors are used in page printers, phototypesetters, and electrostatic plotters. They compute the brightness and color value of each pixel on the page so that the resulting pattern of pixels re-creates the vector graphics and text originally described. *Acronym:* RIP.

rasterization *n.* The conversion of vector graphics (images described in terms of mathematical elements, such as points and lines) to equivalent images composed of pixel patterns that can be stored and manipulated as sets of bits. *See also* pixel.

raster-scan display *n. See* raster display.

rate-adaptive asymmetric digital subscriber line *n. See* RADSL.

raw data *n.* **1.** Unprocessed, typically unformatted, data, such as a stream of bits that has not been filtered for commands or special characters. *See also* raw mode. *Compare* cooked mode. **2.** Information that has been collected but not evaluated.

raw infrared *n.* A method of receiving data through an infrared (IR) transceiver. Raw infrared treats the IR transceiver like a serial cable and does not process data in any way. The application is responsible for handling collision detection and other potential problems.

raw mode *n.* A way in which the UNIX and MS-DOS operating systems "see" a character-based device. If the identifier for the device indicates raw mode, the operating system does not filter input characters or give special treatment to carriage returns, end-of-file markers, and linefeed and tab characters. *Compare* cooked mode.

ray tracing *n.* A sophisticated and complex method of producing high-quality computer graphics. Ray tracing calculates the color and intensity of each pixel in an image by tracing single rays of light backward and determining how they were affected on their way from a defined source of light illuminating the objects in the image. Ray tracing is demanding in terms of processing capability because the computer must account for reflection, refraction, and absorption of individual rays, as well as for the brightness, transparency level, and reflectivity of each object and the positions of the viewer and the light source. *Compare* radiosity.

RCA connector *n.* A connector used for attaching audio and video devices, such as stereo equipment or a composite video monitor, to a computer's video adapter. See the illustration. *See also* composite video display. *Compare* phono connector.

RCA connector. *A female version (left) and a male version (right).*

RDBMS *n.* Acronym for **r**elational **d**ata **b**ase **m**anagement **s**ystem. *See* relational database.

RDF *n. See* Resource Description Framework.

RDO *n. See* Remote Data Objects.

RDRAM *n.* Acronym for **R**ambus **d**ynamic **r**andom **a**ccess **m**emory. A type of DRAM designed by Rambus, Inc. In its fastest form, known as Direct RDRAM, this technology provides a 16-bit data path and a peak bandwidth of 1.6 GB per second (approximately eight to ten times faster than synchronous DRAM, or SDRAM). RDRAM has been used in graphics and video chips; Direct RDRAM is expected to replace DRAM and SDRAM in personal computers. *Also called:* Rambus DRAM. *See also* dynamic RAM, SDRAM.

R

read[1] *n.* The action of transferring data from an input source into a computer's memory or from memory into the CPU (central processing unit). *Compare* write[1].

read[2] *vb.* To transfer data from an external source, such as from a disk or the keyboard, into memory or from memory into the central processing unit (CPU). *Compare* write[2].

read-after-write *n.* A feature of certain data storage devices, such as tape drives, in which the device reads data immediately after it is written as a means of verifying data integrity.

reader *n. See* card reader.

Reader *n. See* Microsoft Reader.

read error *n.* An error encountered while a computer is in the process of obtaining information from storage or from another source of input. *Compare* write error.

README *n.* A file containing information that the user either needs or will find informative and that might not have been included in the documentation. README files are placed on disk in plain-text form (without extraneous or program-specific characters) so that they can be read easily by a variety of word processing programs.

read notification *n.* An e-mail feature providing feedback to the sender that a message has been read by the recipient.

read-only *adj.* Capable of being retrieved (read) but not changed (written). A read-only file or document can be displayed or printed but not altered in any way. Read-only memory (ROM) holds programs that cannot be changed; a read-only storage medium, such as CD-ROM, can be played back but cannot be used for recording information. *Compare* read/write.

read-only attribute *n.* A file attribute, stored with a file's directory entry, indicating whether or not a file may be changed or erased. When the read-only attribute is off, the file can be modified or deleted; when it is on, the file can only be displayed.

read-only memory *n. See* ROM.

read-only terminal *n. See* RO terminal.

read/write *adj.* Able to be both read from and written to. *Abbreviation:* R/W. *Compare* read-only.

read/write channel *n. See* input/output channel.

read/write head *n. See* head.

read/write memory *n.* Memory that can be both read from and written to (modified). Semiconductor RAM and core memory are typical read/write memory systems. *Compare* ROM (definition 2).

real address *n.* An absolute (machine) address specifying a physical location in memory. *See also* physical address. *Compare* relative address, virtual address.

RealAudio *n.* Streaming audio technology developed by RealNetworks, Inc., for distributing radio and FM-quality sound files over the Internet in real time. RealAudio is based on two components: client software for decompressing the sound on the fly and server software for delivering it. The client software is free, distributed either as a downloadable program or as part of browser software. *See also* RealPlayer, RealVideo, stream, streaming.

reallocate *n.* A function in C that allows the programmer to request a larger portion of heap memory than was previously assigned to a particular pointer. *See also* dynamic memory allocation, heap (definition 1).

reallysafe palette *n.* A color look-up table (CLUT) consisting of 22 colors from the 216-color websafe palette that are completely consistent when viewed with all Web browsers on all major computer platforms. The reallysafe palette arose from an experiment that indicated that most of the colors of the websafe palette shift to some degree in different viewing environments. *See also* browser CLUT, websafe palette.

real mode *n.* An operating mode in the Intel 80x86 family of microprocessors. In real mode, the processor can execute only one program at a time. It can access no more than about 1 MB of memory, but it can freely access system memory and input/output devices. Real mode is the only mode possible in the 8086 processor and is the only operating mode supported by MS-DOS. In contrast, the protected mode offered in the 80286 and higher microprocessors provides the memory management and memory protection needed for multitasking environments such as Windows. *See also* 8086, privileged mode. *Compare* protected mode, virtual real mode.

real-mode mapper *n.* An enhancement for Windows 3.*x* systems that allows 32-bit file system access. The real-mode mapper provides a 32-bit disk access interface to the DOS device driver chain. *Acronym:* RMM.

real number *n.* **1.** A number that can be represented in a number system with a given base, such as the decimal system, by a finite or infinite sequence of digits and a radix point. For example, 1.1 is a real number, as is 0.33333.... *See also* irrational number. *Compare* complex number, imaginary number. **2.** A data type, in a programming language such as Pascal, that is used for storing, to some limit of precision, values that include both integer and fractional parts. *See also* double-precision, single-precision. *Compare* floating-point number, integer.

RealPlayer *n.* An Internet media player and browser plug-in developed by RealNetworks, Inc., that supports playback of RealAudio and RealVideo, as well as certain other formats, after installation of appropriate plug-ins. The current version allows RealPlayer users to surf for media content directly from the player or through a Web browser. *See also* RealAudio, RealVideo.

Real Soon Now *adv.* Soon, but not really expected to be as soon as claimed. One might say, for example, that a commercial program will have some desired feature Real Soon Now if several versions ago the vendor knew of the need for the feature and has done nothing. *Acronym:* RSN.

real storage *n.* The amount of RAM memory in a system, as distinguished from virtual memory. *Also called:* physical memory, physical storage. *See also* virtual memory.

RealSystem G2 *n.* An open, standards-based platform for delivery of streaming audio and video over the Internet and other TCP/IP networks developed by RealNetworks, Inc. RealSystem G2 was introduced by RealNetworks in its audio and video players, servers, and development tools in 1998. Among other features, RealSystem G2 scales to different bandwidths, includes streaming that adjusts delivery to available bandwidth, and supports SMIL (Synchronized Multimedia Integration Language) for multimedia presentations. *See also* RealPlayer, RealVideo, SMIL, streaming.

RealSystem Producer *n.* A software application developed by RealNetworks that converts most types of video and sound files into RealMedia formats for use as streaming media over the Internet or within a corporate intranet.

RealSystem Server *n.* Software developed by RealNetworks to enable a server to broadcast streaming media. Several versions of RealSystem Server are available, designed to meet needs ranging from small intranet servers to large proxy servers.

real-time *adj.* Of, or relating to, a time frame imposed by external constraints. Real-time operations are those in which the machine's activities match the human perception of time or those in which computer operations proceed at the same rate as a physical or external process. Real-time operations are characteristic of aircraft guidance systems, transaction-processing systems, scientific applications, and other areas in which a computer must respond to situations as they occur (for example, animating a graphic in a flight simulator or making corrections based on measurements).

real-time animation *n.* Computer animation in which images are computed and updated on the screen at the same rate at which the objects simulated might move in the real world. Real-time animation allows dynamic involvement by the user because the computer can accept and incorporate keystrokes or controller movements as it is drawing the next image in the animation sequence. Arcade-style animation (such as in a flight simulator program) makes use of real-time animation in translating game plays into on-screen actions. In contrast, in animation done in virtual time, image frames are first calculated and stored and later replayed at a higher rate to achieve smoother movement. *See also* animation, bit block.

real-time clock *n.* In PCs, a circuit or other hardware element that provides the system with real-world time. Upon startup of the system, the real-time clock puts the date and time in memory, where it can then be systematically incremented by the BIOS. A real-time clock generally has a battery that is separate from the rest of the system, so it's not dependent upon the system's power source. This is not the same thing as a system clock, which synchronizes the processor. *Acronym:* RTC. *See also* clock (definition 2).

real-time conferencing *n. See* teleconferencing.

R

Real-Time Control Protocol *n.* A scalable transport control protocol that works with the Real-Time Protocol (RTP) to monitor real-time transmissions to multiple participants over a network—for example, during videoconferencing. The Real-Time Control Protocol, or RTCP, transmits packets of control information at regular intervals and is used to determine how well information is being delivered to recipients. *Acronym:* RTCP. *See also* Real-Time Protocol, Real-Time Streaming Protocol, Resource Reservation Setup Protocol.

real-time operating system *n.* An operating system designed for the needs of a process-controlled environment. A real-time operating system recognizes that responses must be made and tasks handled instantly, with no lag time. Real-time operating systems are typically used as embedded systems in devices and applications requiring time-critical reaction, such as telecommunications, air traffic control, and robotic functions. *Acronym:* RTOS. *See also* real-time system.

Real-Time Protocol *n.* An Internet-standard network transport protocol used in delivering real-time data, including audio and video. The Real-Time Protocol, or RTP, works with both unicast (single sender, single recipient) and multicast (single sender, multiple recipients) services. RTP is often used in conjunction with the Real-Time Control Protocol (RTCP), which monitors delivery. *Acronym:* RTP. *See also* Real-Time Control Protocol, Real-Time Streaming Protocol, stream.

real-time streaming *n.* The process of delivering a streaming media file via a specialized streaming media server using real-time streaming protocol (RTSP). With real-time streaming, the file itself actually plays on the streaming media server, even though it is viewed on the computer that opened the file. Real-time streaming transmits at a higher bandwidth than HTTP streaming. It is often used to broadcast live events, such as concerts or keynote conference addresses. *See also* HTTP streaming.

Real-Time Streaming Protocol *n.* A control protocol for the delivery of streamed multimedia data over Internet Protocol (IP) networks. The Real-Time Streaming Protocol, or RTSP, was developed by Columbia University, Progressive Networks, and Netscape and has been submitted as a proposed standard to the IETF (Internet Engineering Task Force). RTSP is designed to deliver real-time, live, or stored audio and video efficiently over a network. It can be used either for groups of recipients or for on-demand

delivery to a single recipient. *Acronym:* RTSP. *See also* Advanced Streaming Format, Real-Time Protocol, Resource Reservation Setup Protocol, stream.

real-time system *n.* A computer and/or a software system that reacts to events before the events become obsolete. For example, airline collision avoidance systems must process radar input, detect a possible collision, and warn air traffic controllers or pilots while they still have time to react.

RealVideo *n.* The streaming technology developed by RealNetworks, Inc., for distributing video over intranets and the Internet. RealVideo transmits video from a server in encoded (compressed) form. The video and accompanying sound are viewed on the client end with the help of a software player. RealVideo works with both IP and IP multicasting and, as with RealAudio, does not require transmission of complete files before playback can begin. *See also* RealAudio, RealPlayer, streaming.

reboot *vb.* To restart a computer by reloading the operating system. *See also* boot[2], cold boot, warm boot.

receipt notification *n.* An e-mail feature providing feedback to the sender that a message has been received by the recipient.

receive *vb.* To accept data from an external communications system, such as a local area network (LAN) or a telephone line, and store the data as a file.

Receive Data *n. See* RXD.

rec. newsgroups *n.* Usenet newsgroups that are part of the rec. hierarchy and whose names have the prefix *rec*. These newsgroups cover topics devoted to discussions of recreational activities, hobbies, and the arts. *See also* newsgroup, traditional newsgroup hierarchy, Usenet. *Compare* comp. newsgroups, misc. newsgroups, news. newsgroups, sci. newsgroups, soc. newsgroups, talk. newsgroups.

recompile *vb.* To compile a program again, usually because of changes that needed to be made in the source code in response to error messages generated by the compiler. *See also* compile.

record[1] *n.* A data structure that is a collection of fields (elements), each with its own name and type. Unlike an array, whose elements all represent the same type of information and are accessed using an index, the elements of a record represent different types of information and are accessed by name. A record can be accessed as a collective

R

unit of elements, or the elements can be accessed individually. *See also* array, data structure, type[1] (definition 1).

record[2] *vb.* To retain information, usually in a file.

record format *n. See* record structure.

record head *n.* The device in a tape machine that places data on the tape. In some tape machines, the record head is combined with the read head.

record layout *n.* The organization of data fields within a record. *See also* record[1].

record length *n.* The amount of storage space required to contain a record, typically given in bytes. *See also* record[1].

record locking *n.* A strategy employed in distributed processing and other multiuser situations to prevent more than one user at a time from writing data to a record. *See also* record[1].

record number *n.* A unique number assigned to a record in a database in order to identify it. A record number can identify an existing record by its position (for example, the tenth record from the beginning of a database), or it can be assigned to the record to serve as a key (for example, the number 00742 assigned to the tenth record from the beginning of the database). *See also* record[1].

record structure *n.* An ordered list of the fields that compose a record, together with a definition of the domain (acceptable values) of each field. *See also* record[1].

recover *vb.* **1.** To return to a stable condition after some error has occurred. A program recovers from an error by stabilizing itself and resuming execution of instructions without user intervention. **2.** To put back into a stable condition. A computer user may be able to recover lost or damaged data by using a program to search for and salvage whatever information remains in storage. A database may be recovered by restoring its integrity after some problem has damaged it, such as abnormal termination of the database management program.

recoverable error *n.* An error that can be successfully managed by software. For example, when the user enters a number when a letter is required, the program can simply display an error message and prompt the user again.

recovery *n.* The restoration of lost data or the reconciliation of conflicting or erroneous data after a system failure. Recovery is often achieved using a disk or tape backup and system logs. *See also* backup.

Recreational Software Advisory Council *n.* An independent, nonprofit organization established in the fall of 1994 by a group of six trade organizations, led by the Software Publishers Association. The Council's goal was to create a new, objective content-labeling rating system for recreational software and other media such as the Internet. *Acronym:* RSAC.

rectangle ad *n.* An Internet ad format that is larger than a traditional banner ad and is generally inserted directly into page content for greater visibility.

rectifier *n.* A circuit component that passes current flowing in one direction but stops current flowing in the other direction. Rectifiers are used to convert alternating current to direct current.

recto *n.* The right-hand page of two facing pages. A recto is characteristically an odd-numbered page. *Compare* verso.

recursion *n.* The ability of a routine to call itself. Recursion enables certain algorithms to be implemented with small, simple routines, but it does not guarantee speed or efficiency. Erroneous use of recursion can cause a program to run out of stack space during execution, causing the program, and sometimes the entire system, to crash. *See also* call[1] (definition 2), routine.

Recycle Bin *n.* A folder in Windows 9x, Windows CE, Windows NT, Windows 2000, and Windows XP represented by an icon on the screen resembling a basket decorated with the recycling logo. To remove a file, the user drags its icon to the Recycle Bin. However, a file in the Recycle Bin is not actually deleted from the disk until the user opens the Recycle Bin, selects the file, and presses the Delete key; until then, the user can retrieve it. *Compare* Trash.

Red Book *n.* **1.** The standards documents of the U.S. National Security Agency entitled "Trusted Network Interpretation of the Trusted Computer System Evaluation Criteria (NCSC-TG-005)" and "Trusted Network Interpretation (NCS-TG-011)." These documents define a system of ratings from A1 (most secure) to D (nonsecure), indicating the ability of a computer network to protect sensitive information. *Compare* Orange Book (definition 1). **2.** A specifications book written by the Sony Corporation and Philips Corporation and endorsed by ISO, covering audio compact discs. *Compare* Green Book, Orange Book (definition 2). **3.** Telecommunications standards published by the CCITT.

red-green-blue *n. See* RGB.

redirection *n.* The process of writing to or reading from a file or device different from the one that would normally be the target or the source. For example, the MS-DOS or OS/2 command *dir >prn* redirects a directory listing from the screen to the printer. *Compare* pipe.

redirector *n.* Software on a client computer that intercepts requests for information and, when appropriate, directs them to the network. Redirectors can either be built into the client operating system or be part of an added networking package.

redlining *n.* A feature of a word processing application that marks changes, additions, or deletions made to a document by a coauthor or editor. The purpose of redlining is to produce a record of the changes made to a document during the course of its development.

redraw *n. See* refresh (definition 1).

reduce *vb.* In a graphical user interface, to decrease the size of a window. A user can reduce a window either by clicking the appropriate button in the title bar or by clicking the mouse on the border of the window and dragging the border toward the middle of the window. *See also* maximize, minimize.

Reduced Instruction Set Computing *n. See* RISC.

redundancy *n.* Using one or more servers on a Web site to perform identical tasks. If one of the servers crashes, another server assumes its tasks. Redundancy ensures that the Web site will continue to function if one of the servers stops working.

redundancy check *n. See* CRC, LRC.

redundant code *n.* Code that duplicates a function performed elsewhere—for example, code to sort a list that has already been sorted.

reengineer *vb.* To rethink and redefine processes and procedures. In the context of computer systems, to reengineer means to change the way work is done in order to maximize the benefits of new technology.

reengineering *vb.* **1.** With regard to software, changing existing software to strengthen desirable characteristics and remove weaknesses. **2.** With regard to corporate management, using information technology principles to address the challenges posed by a global economy and to consolidate management of a rapidly expanding work force.

reentrant code *n.* Code written so that it can be shared by several programs at the same time. When a program is executing reentrant code, another program can interrupt

the execution and can then start or continue execution of that same code. Many operating-system routines are written to be reentrant so that only one copy needs to reside in memory to serve all executing applications. *See also* relocatable code.

refactoring *n.* An optimization process in object-oriented programming intended to improve the design or structure of a program without changing its functionality. The goal of refactoring is to make the program clearer and easier to work with—in part by removing duplication, abstracting common behaviors, and refining class hierarchies—and to improve the extensibility and reusability of existing code.

reference[1] *n.* A data type in the C++ programming language. A reference must be initialized with a variable name. The reference then becomes an alias for that variable but actually stores the address of the variable.

reference[2] *vb.* To access a variable, such as an element in an array or a field in a record.

reference parameter *n.* A parameter in which the address of a variable, rather than the explicit value, is passed to the called routine. *See also* parameter.

reference type *n.* A data type that is represented by a reference (similar to a pointer) to the type's actual value. If a reference type is assigned to a variable, that variable references (or "points to") the original value. No copy is made. Reference types comprise classes, interfaces, delegates, and boxed value types. *See also* data type, value type.

reflecting software *n. See* reflector.

reflective liquid-crystal display *n.* A liquid crystal display that is not equipped with edge light or backlight to enhance readability but rather depends on reflecting ambient light, making it difficult to read in brightly lit environments such as the outdoors. *Also called:* reflective LCD.

reflective routing *n.* In wide area networks, the process of using a reflector to distribute data, thereby reducing the load of the network server. *See also* reflector.

reflector *n.* A program that sends messages to a number of users upon receipt of a signal from a single user. A common type of reflector is an e-mail reflector, which forwards any e-mail sent to it to the multiple recipients currently on its list. *See also* multiple recipients. *Compare* mail reflector.

reformat *vb.* **1.** In applications, to change the look of a document by altering stylistic details, such as font, layout, indention, and alignment. **2.** In data storage, to prepare for

R

reuse a disk that already contains programs or data, effectively destroying the existing contents.

refresh *vb.* **1.** To retrace a video screen at frequent intervals, even if the image does not change, so as to keep the phosphors irradiated. **2.** To recharge dynamic random access memory chips (DRAMs) so that they continue to retain the information stored in them. Circuitry on the memory board automatically performs this function. *See also* refresh cycle.

refreshable *adj.* In programming, referring to a program module capable of being replaced in memory without affecting processing of the program or the information being used by the program.

refresh cycle *n.* The process in which controller circuitry provides repeated electric pulses to dynamic random access memory chips in order to renew the stored electric charges in those locations that contain binary 1. Each pulse is one refresh cycle. Without constant refreshing, dynamic semiconductor RAM loses any information stored in it—as it does when the computer is turned off or when the power fails. *See also* dynamic RAM, static RAM.

refresh rate *n.* In reference to video hardware, the frequency with which the entire screen is redrawn to maintain a constant, flicker-free image. On TV screens and raster-scan monitors, the electron beam that lights the phosphor coating on the inner surface of the screen typically refreshes the entire image area at a rate of about 60 hertz, or 60 times per second. Interlaced monitors, which redraw alternate lines during each sweep of the electron beam, actually refresh any particular line only 30 times per second. Because odd and even lines are refreshed on successive sweeps, however, the effective refresh rate is 60 times per second. *See also* refresh (definition 1).

REGEDIT *n. See* Registry Editor.

regenerate *vb. See* rewrite.

regeneration buffer *n. See* video buffer.

regenerator *n. See* repeater.

region *n.* **1.** An area dedicated to or reserved for a particular purpose. **2.** In video programming, a contiguous group of pixels that are treated as a unit. On the Apple Macintosh, for example, a region is an area in a grafPort that can be defined and manipulated as an entity. The visible working area within a window is an example of a region. *See also* grafPort.

region code *n.* Codes on DVD movie titles and DVD-ROM drives that prevent playback of certain DVDs in certain geographical regions. Region codes are part of the DVD specification. *See also* CSS, DeCSS.

region fill *n.* In computer graphics, the technique of filling a defined region on the screen with a selected color, pattern, or other attribute. *See also* region (definition 2).

register *n.* A set of bits of high-speed memory within a microprocessor or other electronic device, used to hold data for a particular purpose. Each register in a central processing unit is referred to in assembly language programs by a name such as *AX* (the register that contains the results of arithmetic operations in an Intel 80x86 processor) or *SP* (the register that contains the memory address of the top of the stack in various processors).

registered file type *n.* File types that are tracked by the system registry and are recognized by the programs you have installed on your computer. *See also* file type.

registration *n.* The process of precisely aligning elements or superimposing layers in a document or a graphic so that everything will print in the correct relative position. *See also* registration marks.

registration marks *n.* Marks placed on a page so that in printing, the elements or layers in a document can be arranged correctly with respect to each other. Each element to be assembled contains its own registration marks; when the marks are precisely superimposed, the elements are in the correct position. See the illustration.

Registration marks.

registry *n.* A central hierarchical database in Windows 9x, Windows CE, Windows NT, and Windows 2000 used to store information necessary to configure the system for one or more users, applications, and hardware devices. The Registry contains information that Windows continually references during operation, such as profiles for each user, the applications installed on the computer and the types of documents each can create, property sheet settings for folders and application icons, what hardware exists on the system, and which ports are being used. The Registry replaces most of the text-based .ini files used in Windows 3.*x* and MS-DOS configuration files, such as AUTOEXEC.BAT and CONFIG.SYS. Although the Registry is common to the several Windows platforms, there

R

are some differences among them. *Also called:* system registry. *See also* hierarchical database, *.ini,* input/output port, property sheet, Registry Editor.

Registry Editor *n.* An application under Windows that allows the user to edit the entries in the registry. *Acronym:* REGEDIT. *See also* registry.

regression analysis *n.* In statistics, an analysis of the degree to which variations in an independent variable affect a dependent variable (a variable whose value depends on the value of another variable). *See also* multiple regression.

regression testing *n.* Complete retesting of a modified program, rather than a test of only the modified routines, to ensure that no errors have been introduced with the modifications.

relation *n.* A structure composed of attributes (individual characteristics, such as name or address, corresponding to the columns in a table) and tuples (sets of attribute values describing particular entities, such as customers, corresponding to the rows in a table). Within a relation, tuples cannot be repeated; each must be unique. Further, tuples are unordered within a relation; interchanging two tuples does not change the relation. Finally, if relational theory is to be applicable, the domain of each attribute must be atomic—that is, a simple value, rather than a structure such as an array or a record. A relation in which the domains of all attributes are atomic is said to be normalized or in first normal form. *See also* normal form (definition 1).

relational algebra *n.* A collection of rules and operators that permits relations (tables) to be manipulated. Relational algebra is usually described as having the following operators: SELECT, PROJECT, PRODUCT, UNION, INTERSECT, DIFFERENCE, JOIN (or INNER JOIN), and DIVIDE. In a relational database, relational algebra is used to develop procedures to build new relations based on the existing relations.

relational calculus *n.* In database management, a non-procedural method for manipulating relations (tables). There are two families of relational calculus: domain calculus and tuple calculus. The two families of relational calculus are mathematically equivalent to each other and to relational algebra. Using either family, one can formulate a description of a desired relation, based on the existing relations in the database.

relational database *n.* A database or database management system that stores information in tables—rows and columns of data—and conducts searches by using data in specified columns of one table to find additional data in another table. In a relational database, the rows of a table represent records (collections of information about separate items) and the columns represent fields (particular attributes of a record). In conducting searches, a relational database matches information from a field in one table with information in a corresponding field of another table to produce a third table that combines requested data from both tables. For example, if one table contains the fields EMPLOYEE-ID, LAST-NAME, FIRST-NAME, and HIRE-DATE, and another contains the fields DEPT, EMPLOYEE-ID, and SALARY, a relational database can match the EMPLOYEE-ID fields in the two tables to find such information as the names of all employees earning a certain salary or the departments of all employees hired after a certain date. In other words, a relational database uses matching values in two tables to relate information in one to information in the other. Microcomputer database products typically are relational databases. *Compare* flat-file database, inverted-list database.

relational database management system *n. See* relational database.

relational expression *n.* An expression that uses a relational operator such as "less than" or "greater than" to compare two or more expressions. A relational expression resolves to a Boolean (true/false) value. *See also* Boolean, relational operator.

relational model *n.* A data model in which the data is organized in relations (tables). This is the model implemented in most modern database management systems.

relational operator *n.* An operator that allows the programmer to compare two (or more) values or expressions. Typical relational operators are greater than (>), equal to (=), less than (<), not equal to (<>), greater than or equal to (>=), and less than or equal to (<=). *See also* relational expression.

relational structure *n.* The record organization used in the implementation of a relational model.

relative address *n.* A location, as in a computer's memory, that is specified in terms of its distance (displacement or offset) from a starting point (base address). A relative address is typically computed by adding an offset to the base. In everyday terms, this is similar to creating the address 2001 Main Street, in which the base is the 2000 block of Main Street and the offset is 1, which specifies the first house from the beginning of the block. *Also called:* indirect address.

relative coordinates *n.* Coordinates that are defined in terms of their distance from a given starting point, rather than from the origin (intersection of two axes). For example, from a starting point on the screen, a square defined by relative coordinates can be drawn as a series of lines, each representing a displacement in distance and direction from the end of the preceding point. The entire square can be redrawn at another location simply by changing the coordinates of the starting point rather than by recalculating the coordinates of each corner with reference to the origin. See the illustration. *Compare* absolute coordinates.

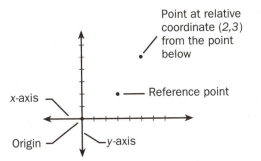

Point at relative coordinate (2,3) from the point below

Reference point

x-axis

Origin

y-axis

Relative coordinates.

relative movement *n.* **1.** Motion whose distance and direction are relative to a starting point. For example, when a mouse pointer is moved on the screen, the coordinates of its new position are relative to the previous location of the pointer. *See also* relative coordinates, relative pointing device. **2.** In computer graphics and cinematography, the movement of one object in relation to another, such as the movement of horse A from the perspective of horse B on a racetrack.

relative path *n.* A path that is implied by the current working directory. When a user enters a command that refers to a file, if the full pathname is not entered the current working directory becomes the relative path of the file referred to. *Compare* full path.

relative pointing device *n.* A cursor-control device, such as a mouse or a trackball, in which the movement of an on-screen cursor is linked to the movement of the device but not to the position of the device. For example, if a user picks

up a mouse and puts it down in a different location on a desk, the position of the on-screen cursor does not change because no movement (rolling) is detected. When the user rolls the mouse again, the cursor moves to reflect the mouse movement against the surface of the desk. Relative pointing devices differ from absolute pointing devices, such as graphics tablets, in which the device's location within a defined area is always associated with a predefined on-screen position. *See also* relative coordinates, relative movement (definition 1). *Compare* absolute pointing device.

relative URL *n.* Short for **relative u**niform **r**esource **loca**tor. A form of URL in which the domain and some or all directory names are omitted, leaving only the document name and extension (and perhaps a partial list of directory names). The indicated file is found in a location relative to the pathname of the current document. *Acronym:* RELURL. *See also* file extension, URL.

RELAX NG *n.* An XML schema language based on Tree Regular Expressions for XML (TREX) and Regular Language Description for XML (RELAX). RELAX NG supports XML namespaces, uses XML syntax, maintains the information set of the XML document, and provides unrestricted support for mixed or unordered content.

relay *n.* A switch activated by an electrical signal. A relay allows another signal to be controlled without the need for human action to route the other signal to the control point, and it also allows a relatively low-power signal to control a high-power signal.

release[1] *n.* **1.** A particular version of a piece of software, most commonly associated with the most recent version (as in "the latest release"). Some companies use the term *release* as an integral part of the product name (as in Lotus 1-2-3 Release 2.2). **2.** A version of a product that is available in general distribution. *Compare* alpha[2], beta[2].

release[2] *vb.* **1.** To relinquish control of a block of memory, a device, or another system resource to the operating system. **2.** To formally make a product available to the marketplace.

reliability *n.* The likelihood of a computer system or device continuing to function over a given period of time and under specified conditions. Reliability is measured by different performance indexes. For example, the reliability of a hard disk is often given as mean time between failures (MTBF): the average length of time the disk can be expected to function without failing. *See also* MTBF, MTTR.

R

reliability, availability, serviceability *n. Acronym:* RAS. *See* high availability.

reload *vb.* **1.** To load a program into memory from a storage device again in order to run it, because the system has crashed or the program's operation was otherwise interrupted. **2.** To retrieve a new copy of the Web page currently visible in a Web browser.

relocatable address *n.* In programming, an address that is to be adjusted to reflect the actual place in memory into which a program is loaded for execution. In "Get the byte located 12 bytes from this instruction," the address is relocatable; in "Get the byte located at address 255," the address is not relocatable. This convention is comparable to describing the "address" of a parked car as "level 2, row G" on one day and "level 5, row B" on another.

relocatable code *n.* A program written in such a way that it can be loaded into any part of available memory rather than having to be placed in one specific location. In relocatable code, address references that depend on the program's physical location in memory are calculated at run time so that program instructions can be carried out correctly. *See also* reentrant code.

relocate *n.* To move programs and blocks of memory about within available space so as to use memory resources flexibly and efficiently. A relocatable program can be loaded by the operating system into any part of available memory rather than into only one specific area. A relocatable block of memory is a portion of memory that can be moved around by the operating system as required; for example, the system might collect several available, relocatable blocks of memory to form one larger block of the size requested for use by a program.

RELURL *n. See* relative URL.

remailer *n.* A service that will forward e-mail while concealing the e-mail address of the originator of the message. Remailers may be used by individuals who wish to retain their privacy or avoid unsolicited commercial e-mail (UCE). Remailers may also be used to hide the identities of individuals and businesses sending spam or malicious or fraudulent e-mail.

remark *n. See* comment, REM statement.

remote *adj.* Not in the immediate vicinity, as a computer or other device located in another place (room, building, or city) and accessible through some type of cable or communications link.

remote access *n.* The use of a remote computer.

remote access server *n.* A host on a LAN (local area network) that is equipped with modems to enable users to connect to the network over telephone lines. *Acronym:* RAS.

Remote Access Service *n.* Windows software that allows a user to gain remote access to the network server via a modem. *Acronym:* RAS. *See also* remote access.

remote administration *n.* The performance of system administration–related tasks via access from another machine in a network.

Remote Application Programming Interface *n.* A Remote Procedure Call (RPC) mechanism that enables an application running on a desktop computer to make function calls on a Windows CE–based device. The desktop computer is known as the Remote Application Programming Interface (RAPI) client, and the Windows CE device is known as the RAPI server. RAPI runs over Winsock and TCP/IP. *Acronym:* RAPI. *See also* remote procedure call.

Remote Authentication Dial-In User Service *n. See* RADIUS.

remote communications *n.* Interaction with a remote computer through a telephone connection or another communications line.

remote computer system *n. See* remote system.

Remote Data Objects *n.* An object-oriented data access tool featured in Visual Basic 4 and later. Remote Data Objects have no native file format of their own; they can be used only with databases complying with the most recent ODBC standards. This feature is popular for its speed and minimal coding requirements. *Acronym:* RDO. *See also* ODBC, Visual Basic.

Remote Installation Services *n.* Software services that allow an administrator to set up new client computers remotely, without having to visit each client. The target clients must support remote booting. *Acronym:* RIS.

remote login *n.* The action of logging in to a computer at a distant location by means of a data communications connection with the computer that one is presently using. After remote login, the user's own computer behaves like a terminal connected to the remote system. On the Internet, remote login is done primarily by rlogin and telnet. *See also* rlogin[1] (definition 1), telnet[1].

remote monitoring *n. See* RMON.

remote network monitoring *n. See* RMON.

Remote PC *n. See* remote system.

remote procedure call *n.* In programming, a call by one program to a second program on a remote system. The second program generally performs a task and returns the results of that task to the first program. *Acronym:* RPC.

remote system *n.* The computer or network that a remote user is accessing via a modem. *See also* remote access. *Compare* remote terminal.

remote terminal *n.* A terminal that is located at a site removed from the computer to which it is attached. Remote terminals rely on modems and telephone lines to communicate with the host computer. *See also* remote access. *Compare* remote system.

removable disk *n.* A disk that can be removed from a disk drive. Floppy disks are removable; hard disks usually are not. *Also called:* exchangeable disk.

REM statement *n.* Short for **rem**ark **statement**. A statement in the Basic programming language and the MS-DOS and OS/2 batch file languages that is used to add comments to a program or batch file. Any statement beginning with the word *REM* is ignored by the interpreter or compiler or the command processor. *See also* comment.

rename *n.* A command in most file transfer protocol (FTP) clients and in many other systems that allows the user to assign a new name to a file or files.

render *vb.* To produce a graphic image from a data file on an output device such as a video display or printer.

rendering *n.* The creation of an image containing geometric models, using color and shading to give the image a realistic look. Usually part of a geometric modeling package such as a CAD program, rendering uses mathematics to describe the location of a light source in relation to the object and to calculate the way in which the light would create highlights, shading, and variations in color. The degree of realism can range from opaque, shaded polygons to images approximating photographs in their complexity. *See also* ray tracing.

RenderMan Shading Language *n.* A C-like graphics and rendering language developed by Pixar.

repaginate *vb.* To recalculate the page breaks in a document.

Repeat *n.* A command in Microsoft Word that causes all information contained in either the last command dialog box or the last uninterrupted editing session to be repeated.

repeat counter *n.* A loop counter; typically, a register that holds a number representing how many times a repetitive process has been or is to be executed.

Repeat delay *n.* A delay for the amount of time that elapses before a character begins repeating when you hold down a key.

repeater *n.* A device used on communications circuits that decreases distortion by amplifying or regenerating a signal so that it can be transmitted onward in its original strength and form. On a network, a repeater connects two networks or two network segments at the physical layer of the ISO/OSI reference model and regenerates the signal.

repeating Ethernet *n. See* repeater.

repeat key *n.* On some keyboards, a key that must be held down at the same time as a character key to cause the character key's key code to be sent repeatedly. On most computer keyboards, however, a repeat key is not needed because a key automatically repeats if held down for longer than a brief delay. *Compare* typematic.

RepeatKeys *n.* A feature of Windows 9x and Windows NT that allows a user to adjust or disable the typematic keyboard feature so as to accommodate users with restricted mobility, who may activate typematic by accident because they have trouble lifting their fingers from the keys. *See also* typematic. *Compare* BounceKeys, FilterKeys, MouseKeys, ShowSounds, SoundSentry, StickyKeys, ToggleKeys.

repetitive strain injury *n.* An occupational disorder of the tendons, ligaments, and nerves caused by the cumulative effects of prolonged repetitious movements. Repetitive strain injuries are appearing with increasing frequency among office workers who spend long hours typing at computerized workstations that are not equipped with safeguards such as wrist supports. *Acronym:* RSI. *See also* carpal tunnel syndrome, ergonomic keyboard, wrist support.

replace *vb.* To put new data in the place of other data, usually after conducting a search for the data to be replaced. Text-based applications such as word processors typically include search-and-replace commands. In such

R

operations, both old and new data must be specified, and search-and-replace procedures may or may not be sensitive to uppercase and lowercase, depending on the application program. *See also* search[1], search and replace.

replay attack *n.* An attack in which a valid message is intercepted and then repeatedly retransmitted, either for fraudulent purposes or as part of a larger attack scheme.

replication *n.* In a distributed database management system, the process of copying the database (or parts of it) to the other parts of the network. Replication allows distributed database systems to remain synchronized. *See also* distributed database, distributed database management system.

report *n.* The presentation of information about a given topic, typically in printed form. Reports prepared with computers and appropriate software can include text, graphics, and charts. Database programs can include special software for creating report forms and generating reports. Desktop publishing software and laser printers or typesetting equipment can be used to produce publication-quality output.

report generator *n.* An application, commonly part of a database management program, that uses a report "form" created by the user to lay out and print the contents of a database. A report generator is used to select specific record fields or ranges of records, to make the output attractive by including such features as headings, running heads, page numbers, and fonts.

Report Program Generator *n. See* RPG (definition 2).

report writer *n. See* report generator.

repository *n.* **1.** A collection of information about a computing system. **2.** A superset of a data dictionary. *See also* data dictionary.

reprogrammable PROM *n. See* EPROM.

reprogrammable read-only memory *n. See* EPROM.

requested permissions *n.* Optionally specified permissions in an assembly that represent the minimum required, optionally desired, and always refused permissions for all code in the assembly. If there is no request, the code is granted the maximum that policy allows.

Request for Comments *n. See* RFC.

Request for Discussion *n.* A formal proposal for a discussion concerning the addition of a newsgroup to the

Usenet hierarchy, the first step in a process that ends with a call for votes. *Acronym:* RFD. *See also* traditional newsgroup hierarchy, Usenet.

Request to Send *n. See* RTS.

required hyphen *n. See* hyphen.

Research Libraries Information Network *n.* The combined online catalog of the Research Libraries Group, which includes many of the major research libraries in the United States. *Acronym:* RLIN.

reserve *n.* A command that allocates contiguous disk space for the device instance's workspace. Digital video devices recognize this command.

reserve accumulator *n.* An auxiliary storage register generally used to store the intermediate results of an extended calculation.

reserved character *n.* A keyboard character that has a special meaning to a program and, as a result, normally cannot be used in assigning names to files, documents, and other user-generated tools, such as macros. Characters commonly reserved for special uses include the asterisk (*), forward slash (/), backslash (\), question mark (?), and vertical bar (|).

reserved date *n.* A date with a special meaning, rather than the date on the calendar. For example, some programs use 9999 to indicate an account or a database listing that does not expire. *See also* magic dates.

reserved memory *n. See* UMA.

reserved word *n.* A word that has special meaning to a program or in a programming language. Reserved words usually include those used for control statements (IF, FOR, END), data declarations, and the like. A reserved word can be used only in certain predefined circumstances; it cannot be used in naming documents, files, labels, variables, or user-generated tools such as macros.

reset button *n.* A device that restarts a computer without turning off its power. *Compare* big red switch.

resident font *n. See* internal font.

resident program *n. See* TSR.

resistance *n.* The ability to impede (resist) the flow of electric current. With the exception of superconductors, all substances have a greater or lesser degree of resistance. Substances with very low resistance, such as metals, conduct electricity well and are called *conductors*. Substances with very high resistance, such as glass and rubber, conduct electricity poorly and are called *nonconductors* or *insulators*.

resistor *n.* A circuit component designed to provide a specific amount of resistance to current flow.

resize *vb.* To make an object or space larger or smaller. *Also called:* scale.

resolution *n.* **1.** The fineness of detail attained by a printer or a monitor in producing an image. For printers that form characters from small, closely spaced dots, resolution is measured in dots per inch, or dpi, and ranges from about 125 dpi for low-quality dot-matrix printers to about 600 dpi for some laser and ink-jet printers (typesetting equipment can print at resolutions of over 1000 dpi). For a video display, the number of pixels is determined by the graphics mode and video adapter, but the size of the display depends on the size and adjustment of the monitor; hence the resolution of a video display is taken as the total number of pixels displayed horizontally and vertically. *See also* high resolution, low resolution. **2.** The process of translation between a domain name address and an IP address. *See also* DNS, IP address.

resolve *vb.* **1.** To match one piece of information to another in a database or lookup table. **2.** To find a setting in which no hardware conflicts occur. **3.** To convert a logical address to a physical address or vice versa. **4.** To convert an Internet domain name to its corresponding IP address. *See also* DNS, IP address.

resource *n.* **1.** Any part of a computer system or a network, such as a disk drive, printer, or memory, that can be allotted to a program or a process while it is running. **2.** An item of data or code that can be used by more than one program or in more than one place in a program, such as a dialog box, a sound effect, or a font in a windowing environment. Many features in a program can be altered by adding or replacing resources without the necessity of recompiling the program from source code. Resources can also be copied and pasted from one program into another, typically by a specialized utility program called a *resource editor*. **3.** Any nonexecutable data that is logically deployed with an application. A resource might be displayed in an application as error messages or as part of the user interface. Resources can contain data in a number of forms, including strings, images, and persisted objects.

resource allocation *n.* The process of distributing a computer system's facilities to different components of a job in order to perform the job.

resource data *n.* The data structures, templates, definition procedures, management routines, icon maps, and so forth associated with a particular resource, such as a menu, window, or dialog box. *See also* resource (definition 2), resource fork.

Resource Description Framework *n.* A specification developed by the World Wide Web Consortium (W3C) to define a flexible infrastructure for organizing and managing metadata (data about data) across the Web and the Internet. The Resource Description Framework is intended to provide a framework based on XML (eXtensible Markup Language) that can standardize the way applications exchange metadata (or metacontent). Possible uses include search engines, content rating systems, and other areas in which exchange of information about data is valuable. *Acronym:* RDF. *See also* XML.

resource file *n.* A file that consists of resource data and the resource map that indexes it. *See also* resource (definition 2), resource fork.

resource fork *n.* One of the two forks of an Apple Macintosh file (the other being the *data fork*). The resource fork of a program file contains reusable items of information that the program can use during the course of execution, such as fonts, icons, windows, dialog boxes, menus, and the program code itself. A user-created document typically stores its data in the data fork, but it can also use its resource fork for storing items that might be used more than once in the document. For example, in a HyperCard stack, the data that constitutes each card, or record, in the stack is stored in the data fork; digitized sounds and icons that might be used more than once are stored in the resource fork. The use of such resources makes program development easier because resources can be developed and altered independently of the program code. *See also* HyperCard, resource (definition 2). *Compare* data fork.

resource ID *n.* A number that identifies a particular resource within a given resource type on the Apple Macintosh—for example, a particular menu among many resources of type MENU that a program might use. *See also* resource (definition 2).

Resource Reservation Setup Protocol *n.* A communications protocol designed to allow for "bandwidth on demand." A remote receiver requests that a certain amount

R

of bandwidth be reserved by the server for a data stream; the server sends back a message (similar to the RSVP sent in reply to an invitation) indicating whether or not the request has been granted. *Acronym:* RSVP (Resource **Res**ervation Setup **P**rotocol).

resource sharing *n.* The act of making files, printers, and other network resources available for use by others.

resource type *n.* One of numerous classes of structural and procedural resources in the Macintosh operating system, such as code, fonts, windows, dialog boxes, templates, icons, patterns, strings, drivers, cursors, color tables, and menus. Resource types have characteristic identifying labels, such as CODE for blocks of program instructions, FONT for fonts, and CURS for mouse cursors. *See also* resource (definition 2), resource fork.

response time *n.* **1.** The time, often an average, that elapses between the issuance of a request and the provision of the data requested (or notification of inability to provide it). **2.** The time required for a memory circuit or storage device to furnish data requested by the central processing unit (CPU).

restart *vb. See* reboot.

restore[1] *n.* The act of restoring a file or files. *See also* backup, recovery.

restore[2] *vb.* To copy files from a backup storage device to their normal location, especially if the files are being copied to replace files that were accidentally lost or deleted.

restricted function *n.* A function or an operation that can be executed only under certain circumstances, especially when the central processing unit (CPU) is in privileged mode. *See also* privileged mode.

Restructured Extended Executor *n. See* REXX.

retrace *n.* The path followed by the electron beam in a raster-scan computer monitor as it returns either from the right to the left edge of the screen or from the bottom to the top of the screen. The retrace positions the electron beam for its next sweep across or down the screen; during this interval, the beam is briefly turned off to avoid drawing an unwanted line on the screen. Retracing occurs many times each second and uses tightly synchronized signals to ensure that the electron beam is turned off and on during the retrace. *See also* blanking, horizontal retrace, raster display, vertical retrace.

retrieve *vb.* To obtain a specific requested item or set of data by locating it and returning it to a program or to the user. Computers can retrieve information from any source of storage—disks, tapes, or memory.

retro virus *n.* A type of virus that avoids detection by attacking or disabling antivirus programs. *Also called:* anti-anti-virus.

return *vb.* **1.** To transfer control of the system from a called routine or program back to the calling routine or program. Some languages support an explicit *return* or *exit* statement; others allow return only at the end (last statement) of the called routine or program. *See also* call[2] (definition 2). **2.** To report the outcome of a called routine to the calling routine or program.

return code *n.* In programming, a code that is used to report the outcome of a procedure or to influence subsequent events when a routine or process terminates (returns) and passes control of the system to another routine. Return codes can, for example, indicate whether an operation was successful or not and can thus be used to determine what is to be done next.

return from the dead *vb.* To regain access to the Internet after having been disconnected.

Return key *n.* A key on a keyboard that is used to terminate input of a field or record or to execute the default action of a dialog box. On IBM PCs and compatibles, this key is called ENTER. The corresponding key on a typewriter causes the carriage holding the paper to return to the starting position to begin a new line; hence the name. *See also* Enter key.

return to zero *n.* A method of recording on magnetic media in which the reference condition, or "neutral state," is the absence of magnetization. *Abbreviation:* RZ. *Compare* nonreturn to zero.

reusability *n.* The ability of code or a design to be usable again in another application or system.

Reverse Address Resolution Protocol *n. See* RARP.

Reverse ARP *n. See* RARP.

reverse byte ordering *n. See* little endian.

reverse engineering *n.* A method of analyzing a product in which the finished item is studied to determine its makeup or component parts—for example, studying a completed ROM chip to determine its programming or studying a new computer system to learn about its design. For computer software, reverse engineering typically involves decompilation of a substantial portion of the object code and studying the resulting decompiled code.

reverse path forwarding *n.* A technique that makes routing decisions through a TCP/IP network by using the source address of a datagram rather than the destination address. Reverse path forwarding is used in broadcast and multicast applications because it reduces redundant transmissions to multiple recipients. *Acronym:* RPF. *See also* datagram, TCP/IP.

reverse Polish notation *n. See* postfix notation.

reverse video *n.* The reversal of light and dark in the display of selected characters on a video screen. For example, if text is normally displayed as white characters on a black background, reverse video presents text as black letters on a white background. Programmers commonly use reverse video as a means of highlighting text or special items (such as menu choices or the cursor) on the screen.

revert *vb.* To return to the last saved version of a document. Choosing this command tells the application to abandon all changes made in a document since the last time it was saved.

Revisable-Form-Text DCA *n.* A standard within Document Content Architecture (DCA) for storing documents in such a way that the formatting can be changed by the receiver. A related standard is Final-Form-Text DCA. *Acronym:* RFTDCA. *See also* DCA. *Compare* Final-Form-Text DCA.

revision mark *n.* A mark that shows where a deletion, insertion, or other editing change has been made in a document.

rewind *vb.* To wind a magnetic tape spool or cassette to its beginning.

rewritable digital video disc *n.* Technology for recording data on disks that have the same storage capacity as digital video discs (DVDs) but can be rewritten like the compact disc–rewritable (CD-RW) devices. *See also* digital video disc, PD-CD drive.

rewrite *vb.* To write again, especially in situations where information is not permanently recorded, such as RAM or a video display. *Also called:* refresh, regenerate. *See also* dynamic RAM.

REXX *n.* Acronym for **R**estructured **Ex**tended **E**xecutor. A structured programming language used on IBM mainframes and with OS/2 Version 2.0. REXX programs invoke application programs and operating system commands.

RF *n. See* radio frequency.

RFC *n.* Acronym for **R**equest **f**or **C**omments. A document in which a standard, a protocol, or other information pertaining to the operation of the Internet is published. The RFC is actually issued, under the control of the IAB, *after* discussion and serves as the standard. RFCs can be obtained from sources such as InterNIC.

RFD *n. See* Request for Discussion.

RFI *n.* Acronym for **r**adio **f**requency **i**nterference. Noise introduced into an electronic circuit, such as a radio or television, by electromagnetic radiation produced by another circuit, such as a computer.

RF shielding *n.* A structure, generally sheet metal or metallic foil, designed to prevent the passage of radio frequency (RF) electromagnetic radiation. RF shielding is intended to keep RF radiation either inside a device or out of a device. Without proper RF shielding, devices that use or emit RF radiation can interfere with each other; for example, running an electric mixer might cause interference on a television. Computers generate RF radiation and, to meet Federal Communications Commission (FCC) standards, must be properly shielded to prevent this RF radiation from leaking out. The metal case of a PC provides most of the needed RF shielding. Devices meeting FCC type A standards are suitable for business use. Devices meeting the more stringent FCC type B standards are suitable for home use. *See also* radio frequency, RFI.

RFTDCA *n. See* Revisable-Form-Text DCA.

RGB *n.* Acronym for **r**ed-**g**reen-**b**lue. A model for describing colors that are produced by emitting light, as on a video monitor, rather than by absorbing it, as with ink on paper. The three kinds of cone cells in the eye respond to red, green, and blue light, respectively, so percentages of these additive primary colors can be mixed to get the appearance of any desired color. Adding no color produces black; adding 100 percent of all three colors results in white. *See also* CMYK, RGB monitor. *Compare* CMY.

RGB display *n. See* RGB monitor.

RGB monitor *n.* A color monitor that receives its signals for red, green, and blue levels over separate lines. An RGB monitor generally produces sharper and cleaner images

R

than those produced by a composite monitor, which receives levels for all three colors over a single line. *See also* RGB. *Compare* composite video display.

ribbon cable *n.* A flat cable containing up to 100 parallel wires for data and control lines. For example, ribbon cables are used inside a computer's case to connect the disk drives to their controllers.

ribbon cartridge *n.* A disposable module containing an inked fabric ribbon or a carbon-coated plastic film ribbon. Many impact printers use ribbon cartridges to make ribbon changing easier and cleaner.

Rich Text Format *n.* An adaptation of DCA (Document Content Architecture) that is used for transferring formatted text documents between applications, even those applications running on different platforms, such as between IBM and compatibles and Macintoshes. *Acronym:* RTF. *See also* DCA.

RIFF *n.* Acronym for **R**esource **I**nterchange **F**ile **F**ormat. Developed jointly by IBM and Microsoft, RIFF is a broad-based specification designed to be used in defining standard formats for different types of multimedia files. A tagged-file specification, RIFF relies on headers that "tag" individual data elements in a file, identifying them by type and length. Because tags identify data elements, the RIFF specification can be extended to cover new types of elements while continuing to support older applications, which can simply ignore new, unrecognized elements they encounter in a file. *See also* AVI, MCI.

right click *vb.* To make a selection using the button on the right side of a mouse or other pointing device. Doing so in Windows 9x and Windows NT 4.0 and later typically brings up a pop-up menu with options applicable to the object over which the cursor is positioned. *See also* mouse, pointing device.

right click disabler *n.* A program or script that prevents a user from employing any functions controlled by clicking the right mouse button. A right click disabler script may be run when a user visits a Web site to control the user's actions and options.

right justification *n.* In typesetting, word processing, and desktop publishing, the process of aligning text evenly along the right margins of a column or page. The left edge of the text is ragged. *See also* justify (definition 1), rag. *Compare* full justification, left justification.

right-justify *vb.* To align lines of text and other display elements so that the right edges form a smooth line. *See also* align (definition 1), rag. *Compare* left-justify.

rigid disk *n.* *See* hard disk.

RIMM *n.* A plug-in module jointly developed by Rambus and Intel for the high-bandwidth computer memory known as Direct RDRAM. A RIMM is comparable to a DIMM in size and shape, but the two are not pin-compatible. *See also* DIMM, RDRAM.

ring network *n.* A LAN (local area network) in which devices (nodes) are connected in a closed loop, or ring. Messages in a ring network pass around the ring from node to node in one direction. When a node receives a message, it examines the destination address attached to the message. If the address is the same as the node's, the node accepts the message; otherwise, it regenerates the signal and passes the message along to the next node in the ring. Such regeneration allows a ring network to cover larger distances than star and bus networks. The ring can also be designed to bypass any malfunctioning or failed node. Because of the closed loop, however, adding new nodes can be difficult. See the illustration. *Also called:* ring topology. *See also* token passing, token ring network. *Compare* bus network, star network.

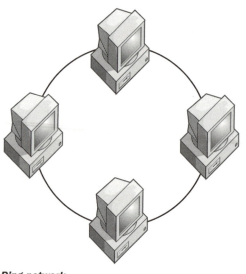

Ring network.

ring topology *n.* *See* ring network.

rip *vb.* To convert audio data from a compact disc into a WAV file or other digital format, typically in preparation for further encoding as an MP3 file. *See also* MP3.

RIP *n.* **1.** Acronym for **R**outing **I**nformation **P**rotocol. An Internet protocol, defined in RFC 1058, that defines the exchange of routing table information. Through RIP, each router on a network sends its routing table to its nearest neighbor every 30 seconds. Under RIP, routing is determined by the number of hops between source and destination. RIP is an interior gateway protocol (a protocol used by gateways for exchanging routing information). Because it is not the most efficient of routing protocols, it is being replaced by the more efficient Open Shortest Path First (OSPF) protocol. *See also* Bellman-Ford distance-vector routing algorithm, communications protocol, interior gateway protocol, OSPF. **2.** *See* raster image processor.

RIPE *n.* Acronym for **R**eseaux **IP** **E**uropéens. A voluntary organization of ISPs (Internet service providers) dedicated to the goal of a smoothly functioning, pan-European Internet network. Most of the work performed by RIPE is handled by discrete working groups that deal with issues such as management of the RIPE database and technical networking questions. RIPE also provides services that include registering domain names within top-level Internet domains and assigning IP (Internet Protocol) addresses. Member organizations of RIPE are supported by the RIPE NCC (Network Coordination Centre), based in Amsterdam, The Netherlands. *See also* American Registry for Internet Numbers.

ripper *n.* Digital audio technology that converts audio data from a compact disc into a WAV file or other digital format. An encoder then converts this file into a file (typically an MP3 file) that can be played back by software known as a player. *See also* encoder, MP3.

RIPX *n.* A protocol used by routers to exchange information between routers on an IPX network and by hosts to determine the best routers to use when forwarding IPX traffic to a remote IPX network. *Also called:* RIP for IPX. *See also* communications protocol, IPX, NWLink, router.

RIS *n.* *See* Remote Installation Services.

RISC *n.* Acronym for **R**educed **I**nstruction **S**et **C**omputing. A microprocessor design that focuses on rapid and efficient processing of a relatively small set of simple instructions that comprises most of the instructions a computer decodes and executes. RISC architecture optimizes each of these instructions so that it can be carried out very rapidly—usually within a single clock cycle. RISC chips thus execute simple instructions more quickly than general-purpose CISC (Complex Instruction Set Computing) microprocessors, which are designed to handle a much wider array of instructions. They are, however, slower than CISC chips at executing complex instructions, which must be broken down into many machine instructions that RISC microprocessors can perform. Families of RISC chips include Sun Microsystems' SPARC, Motorola's 88000, Intel's i860, and the PowerPC developed by Apple, IBM, and Motorola. *See also* architecture, SPARC. *Compare* CISC.

RISC86 *n.* A "hybrid" microprocessor technology in which CISC (Complex Instruction Set Computing) instructions are translated into RISC (Reduced Instruction Set Computing) instructions for processing. RISC86 is designed to support the 80x86 CISC architecture while providing the speed gains characteristic of RISC technology. RISC86 was developed by NexGen and is implemented in AMD's K6 microprocessor.

Rivest-Shamir-Adleman encryption *n.* *See* RSA encryption.

RJ-11 connector *n.* *See* phone connector.

RJ-11 jack *n.* *See* phone connector.

RJ-45 connector *n.* Short for **R**egistered **J**ack-**45 connector**. An eight-wire connector used to attach devices to cables. The eight wires are encased in a plastic sheath and color-coded to match corresponding slots in jacks. RJ-45 jacks are used to connect computers to LANs (local area networks) and to link ISDN (Integrated Services Digital Network) devices to NT-1 (Network Terminator 1) devices. *Also called:* RJ-45 jack. *See also* ISDN.

RJ-45 jack *n.* *See* RJ-45 connector.

RLE *n.* Short for **R**un **L**ength **E**ncoding. A data compression format in which only the first of a series of consecutive identical pixels is saved, along with the total number of pixels in the run. When the file is decompressed, each representative pixel is copied the correct number of times to replace those not saved. RLE compression works best with simple black and white or flat color graphics.

RLIN *n.* *See* Research Libraries Information Network.

RLL encoding *n.* *See* run-length limited encoding.

rlogin[1] *n.* **1.** A protocol used to log in to a networked computer in which the local system automatically supplies the user's login name. *See also* communications protocol, logon. *Compare* telnet1. **2.** A UNIX command in BSD UNIX that enables a user to log in to a remote computer on a network using the rlogin protocol. *See also* BSD UNIX.

rlogin[2] *vb.* To connect to a networked computer using the rlogin protocol.

RLSD *n.* Acronym for **R**eceived **L**ine **S**ignal **D**etect. *See* DCD.

RMI-IIOP *n.* Acronym for **R**emote **M**ethod **I**nvocation over **I**nternet **I**nter-**ORB** **P**rotocol. A subsystem of the Java 2 Platform, Enterprise Edition (J2EE). It provides the ability to write CORBA applications for the Java platform without learning the CORBA Interface Definition Language (IDL). RMI-IIOP includes the full functionality of a CORBA Object Request Broker and allows the programming of CORBA servers and applications via the RMI application programming interface (API). RMI-IIOP is useful for developers using Enterprise Java Beans (EJBs), since the remote object model for an EJB is RMI-based. *Also called:* RMI over IIOP. *See also* CORBA, Enterprise JavaBeans, J2EE.

RMM *n. See* real-mode mapper.

RMON *n.* Acronym for **r**emote **mon**itoring or **r**emote network **mon**itoring. A protocol that enables network information to be monitored and analyzed at a central site. The nine management information bases (MIBs) defined by RMON provide statistics about network traffic. *See also* MIB. *Compare* SNMP.

roaming user profile *n.* A server-based user profile that is downloaded to the local computer when a user logs on; it is updated both locally and on the server when the user logs off. A roaming user profile is available from the server when logging on to a workstation or server computer. When logging on, the user can use the local user profile if it is more current than the copy on the server. *See also* local user profile, mandatory user profile, user profile.

robopost *vb.* To post articles to newsgroups automatically, usually by means of a bot. *See also* bot (definition 3), newsgroup, post.

robot *n.* **1.** A machine that can sense and react to input and cause changes in its surroundings with some degree of intelligence, ideally without human supervision. Although robots are often designed to mimic human movements in carrying out their work, they are seldom humanlike in appearance. Robots are commonly used in manufacturing products such as automobiles and computers. *See also* robotics. **2.** *See* bot, spider.

robotics *n.* The branch of engineering devoted to the creation and training of robots. Roboticists work within a wide range of fields, such as mechanical and electronic engineering, cybernetics, bionics, and artificial intelligence, all toward the end of endowing their creations with as much sensory awareness, physical dexterity, independence, and flexibility as possible. *See also* artificial intelligence, bionics, cybernetics.

robust *adj.* Able to function or to continue functioning well in unexpected situations.

ROFL *n.* Acronym for **r**olling **o**n the **f**loor, **l**aughing. An expression, used mostly in newsgroups and online conferences, to indicate one's appreciation of a joke or other humorous circumstance. *Also called:* ROTFL.

role-playing game *n.* A game that is played on line, such as MUD, in which participants take on the identities of characters who interact with each other. These games often have a fantasy or science fiction setting and a set of rules that all players need to follow. Role-playing games may be similar to adventure games in terms of story line, but also feature management and decision making for the character assumed during the course of the game. *Acronym:* RPG. *See also* MUD. *Compare* adventure game.

rollback *n.* **1.** A return to a previous stable condition, as when the contents of a hard disk are restored from a backup after a destructive hard disk error. **2.** The point in an online transaction when all updates to any databases involved in the transaction are reversed.

rollover *n. See* Year 2000 rollover.

ROM *n.* **1.** Acronym for **r**ead-**o**nly **m**emory. A semiconductor circuit into which code or data is permanently installed by the manufacturing process. The use of this technology is economically viable only if the chips are produced in large quantities; experimental designs or small volumes are best handled using PROM or EPROM. **2.** Acronym for **r**ead-**o**nly **m**emory. Any semiconductor circuit serving as a memory that contains instructions or data that can be read but not modified (whether placed there by manufacturing or by a programming process, as in PROM and EPROM). *See also* EEPROM, EPROM, PROM.

roman *adj.* Having upright rather than slanted characters in a typeface. *See also* font family. *Compare* italic.

ROM Basic *n.* Short for **r**ead-**o**nly **m**emory **B**eginner's **A**ll-purpose **S**ymbolic **I**nstruction **C**ode. A Basic interpreter stored in ROM (read-only memory) so that the user can start programming after simply turning on the machine, without having to load Basic from a disk or tape. ROM Basic was a feature of many early home computers.

ROM BIOS *n.* Acronym for **r**ead-**o**nly **m**emory **b**asic **i**nput/**o**utput **s**ystem. *See* BIOS.

ROM card *n.* Short for **r**ead-**o**nly **m**emory **card**. A plug-in module that contains one or more printer fonts, programs, or games or other information stored in ROM (read-only memory). A typical ROM card is about the size of a credit card and several times thicker. It stores information directly in integrated circuit boards. *Also called:* font card, game card. *See also* ROM (definition 1), ROM cartridge.

ROM cartridge *n.* Short for **r**ead-**o**nly **m**emory **cartridge**. A plug-in module that contains one or more printer fonts, programs, games, or other information stored in ROM (read-only memory) chips on a board enclosed in a plastic case with a connector exposed at one end so that it can easily plug into a printer, computer, game system, or other device. For example, a cartridge that plugs into a game system is a ROM cartridge. *Also called:* game cartridge. *See also* ROM (definition 1), ROM card.

ROM emulator *n.* Short for **r**ead-**o**nly **m**emory **emulator**. A special circuit containing RAM memory that is connected to a target computer in place of the target computer's ROM chips. A separate computer writes the contents into the RAM, and then the target computer reads the RAM as if it were ROM. ROM emulators are used to debug ROM-resident software without the high cost and delay of manufacturing chips. Even though the use of a ROM emulator is more expensive than programming an EPROM, it is often preferred today because its contents can be changed much more quickly than those of an EPROM. *Also called:* ROM simulator. *See also* EEPROM, EPROM, ROM (definition 1).

ROM simulator *n.* *See* ROM emulator.

root *n.* The main or uppermost level in a hierarchically organized set of information. The root is the point from which subsets branch in a logical sequence that moves from a broad focus to narrower perspectives. *See also* leaf, tree.

root account *n.* On UNIX systems, the account having control over the operation of a computer. The system administrator uses this account for system maintenance. *Also called:* superuser. *See also* system administrator.

root directory *n.* The point of entry into the directory tree in a disk-based hierarchical directory structure. Branching from this root are various directories and subdirectories, each of which can contain one or more files and subdirectories of its own. For example, in the MS-DOS operating system the root directory is identified by a name consisting of a single backslash character (\). Beneath the root are other directories, which may contain further directories, and so on. See the illustration.

Root directory.

root folder *n.* The folder on a drive from which all other folders branch. The root folder's name consists of a single backslash character (\). For example, on drive C, this folder would be represented in the file system as C:\.

rootless *n.* A mode in which an application belonging to a different user interface can run on top of a computer's underlying operating system without affecting that desktop or applications it may be running. For example, programs belonging to a rootless version of the X Window System can be run on a Mac OS X computer without disturbing the Aqua desktop. *See also* Mac OS X, X Window System.

root name *n.* In MS-DOS and Windows, the first part of a filename. In MS-DOS and earlier versions of Windows, the maximum length of the root name was eight characters; in Windows NT and later versions of Windows, the root name may be as long as 255 characters. *See also* 8.3, extension (definition 1), filename, long filenames.

root name server *n.* *See* root server.

root server *n.* A computer with the ability to locate DNS servers containing information about top-level Internet domains, such as com, org, uk, it, jp, and other country domains, in the Internet's Domain Name System (DNS) hierarchy. Beginning with the root server and

R

continuing through referrals to name servers at lower levels of the hierarchy, the DNS is able to match a "friendly" Internet address, such as microsoft.com, with its numerical counterpart, the IP address. Root servers thus contain the data needed for referrals to name servers at the highest level of the hierarchy. There are 13 root servers in the world, located in the United States, the United Kingdom, Sweden, and Japan. *Also called:* root name server. *See also* DNS (definition 1), DNS server, top-level domain.

root web *n.* The default, top-level web provided by a Web server. To access the root web, you supply the URL of the server without specifying a page name or subweb.

ROT13 encryption *n.* A simple encryption method in which each letter is replaced with the letter of the alphabet 13 letters after the original letter, so that A is replaced by N, and so forth; N, in turn, is replaced by A, and Z is replaced by M. ROT13 encryption is not used to protect messages against unauthorized readers; rather, it is used in newsgroups to encode messages that a user may not want to read, such as sexual jokes or spoilers. Some newsreaders can automatically perform ROT13 encryption and decryption at the touch of a key.

rotary dialing *n.* The signaling system used in telephones with rotary dials, in which each digit is associated with a set number of pulses. During dialing, these pulses, which are audible as series of clicks, momentarily turn the current in the telephone wires on and off. *Also called:* pulse dialing. *Compare* touch tone dialing.

rotate *vb.* **1.** To turn a model or other graphical image so that it is viewed at a different angle. **2.** To move bits in a register to the left or to the right. The bit that moves out of the end position rotates to the newly vacated position at the opposite end of the register. *Compare* shift.

rotational delay *n.* The time required for a desired disk sector to rotate to the read/write head. *Also called:* rotational latency.

rotational latency *n. See* rotational delay.

RO terminal *n.* Short for read-only **terminal**. A terminal that can receive data but cannot send data. Nearly all printers can be classified as RO terminals.

ROTFL *n. See* ROFL.

round *vb.* To shorten the fractional part of a number, increasing the last remaining (rightmost) digit or not, according to whether the deleted portion was over or under five. For example, 0.3333 rounded to two decimal places is 0.33, and 0.6666 is 0.67. Computer programs often round numbers, sometimes causing confusion when the resulting values do not add up "correctly." Percentages in a spreadsheet can thus total 99 percent or 101 percent because of rounding.

round robin *n.* A sequential, cyclical allocation of resources to more than one process or device.

roundtripping *n.* The process of converting files from one format to another for viewing or editing and then converting the files back to the original format again. In some cases, roundtripping can involve repeated conversions of the file from one format to another and back. Frequent roundtripping may be a concern because each conversion has the potential to introduce unwanted changes to the file.

routable protocol *n.* A communications protocol that is used to route data from one network to another by means of a network address and a device address. TCP/IP is an example of a routable protocol.

router *n.* An intermediary device on a communications network that expedites message delivery. On a single network linking many computers through a mesh of possible connections, a router receives transmitted messages and forwards them to their correct destinations over the most efficient available route. On an interconnected set of LANs (local area networks)—including those based on differing architectures and protocols—using the same communications protocols, a router serves the somewhat different function of acting as a link between LANs, enabling messages to be sent from one to another. *See also* bridge, gateway.

routine *n.* Any section of code that can be invoked (executed) within a program. A routine usually has a name (identifier) associated with it and is executed by referencing that name. Related terms (which may or may not be exact synonyms, depending on the context) are *function*, *procedure*, and *subroutine*. *See also* function (definition 3), procedure, subroutine.

routing *n.* The process of forwarding packets between networks from source to destination. *See also* dynamic routing, static routing.

Routing Information Protocol *n. See* RIP (definition 1).

routing table *n.* In data communications, a table of information that provides network hardware (bridges and routers) with the directions needed to forward packets of data to locations on other networks. The information contained in a routing table differs according to whether it is used by a bridge or a router. A bridge relies on both the source (originating) and destination addresses to determine where and how to forward a packet. A router relies on the destination address and on information in the table that gives the possible routes—in hops or in number of jumps—between itself, intervening routers, and the destination. Routing tables are updated frequently as new or more current information becomes available. *See also* bridge, hop, internetwork, router.

row *n.* A series of items arranged horizontally within some type of framework—for example, a continuous series of cells running from left to right in a spreadsheet; a horizontal line of pixels on a video screen; or a set of data values aligned horizontally in a table. *Compare* column.

royalty-free *n.* The absence of a requirement to pay the original owner of music, images, software, or other content for the right to use, edit, or distribute their content.

RPC *n. See* remote procedure call.

RPF *n. See* reverse path forwarding.

RPG *n.* **1.** *See* role-playing game. **2.** Acronym for **R**eport **P**rogram **G**enerator. An IBM programming platform introduced in 1964. The earliest version of RPG was not a language but a program generator intended to aid in producing business reports. Versions of RPG have been developed for various platforms, including IBM's AS/400 server, UNIX, MS-DOS, and Windows.

RPN *n.* Acronym for **r**everse **P**olish **n**otation. *See* postfix notation.

RPROM *n.* Short for **r**eprogrammable **PROM**. *See* EPROM.

RS-232-C standard *n.* An accepted industry standard for serial communications connections. Adopted by the Electrical Industries Association, this Recommended Standard (RS) defines the specific lines and signal characteristics used by serial communications controllers to standardize the transmission of serial data between devices. The letter *C* denotes that the current version of the standard is the third in a series. *See also* CTS, DSR, DTR, RTS, RXD, TXD.

RS-422/423/449 *n.* Standards for serial communications with transmission distances over 50 feet. RS-449 incorporates RS-422 and RS-423. Macintosh serial ports are RS-422 ports. *See also* RS-232-C standard.

RSA *n.* A widely used public/private key algorithm. It is the default cryptographic service provider (CSP) for

Microsoft Windows. It was patented by RSA Data Security, Inc., in 1977. *See also* cryptographic service provider.

RSAC *n. See* Recreational Software Advisory Council.

RSA encryption *n.* Short for **R**ivest-**S**hamir-**A**dleman **encryption**. The public key encryption algorithm, introduced by Ronald Rivest, Adi Shamir, and Leonard Adleman in 1978, on which the PGP (Pretty Good Privacy) encryption program is based. *See also* PGP, public key encryption.

RSI *n. See* repetitive strain injury.

RSN *adv. See* Real Soon Now.

R-squared value *n.* An indicator from 0 to 1 that reveals how closely the estimated values for the trendline correspond to your actual data. A trendline is most reliable when its R-squared value is at or near 1. *Also called:* the coefficient of determination.

RSVP *n. See* Resource Reservation Setup Protocol.

RTC *n. See* clock (definition 2).

RTCP *n. See* Real-Time Control Protocol.

RTF *n. See* Rich Text Format.

RTFM *n.* Acronym for **r**ead **t**he **f**laming (or friendly) **m**anual. A common answer to a question in an Internet newsgroup or product support conference that is adequately explained in the instruction manual. (The F in this acronym is not necessarily assumed to represent polite language.) *Also called:* RTM.

RTM *n.* Acronym for **r**ead **t**he **m**anual. *See* RTFM.

RTOS *n. See* real-time operating system.

RTP *n. See* Real-Time Protocol.

RTS *n.* Acronym for **R**equest **t**o **S**end. A signal sent, as from a computer to its modem, to request permission to transmit; the signal is often used in serial communications. RTS is a hardware signal sent over pin 4 in RS-232-C connections. *See also* RS-232-C standard. *Compare* CTS.

RTSP *n. See* Real-Time Streaming Protocol.

rubber banding *n.* In computer graphics, changing the shape of an object made up of connected lines by "grabbing" a point on an anchored line and "pulling" it to the new location.

Ruby *n.* An interpreted open source scripting language for object-oriented programming. Its simple syntax is partially based on the syntax of Eiffel and Ada. Considered to

R

be similar to Perl, it has many features to process text files and perform system management tasks.

rudder control *n.* A device, consisting of a pair of pedals, that enables a user to input rudder movements in a flight simulation program. The rudder control is used along with a joystick (which controls the simulated ailerons and elevators) and possibly a throttle control.

rule *n.* **1.** A line printed above, below, or to the side of some element, either to set that item off from the remainder of the page or to improve the look of the page. Footnotes, for example, often appear below a short rule that sets them off from the main text on the page. The thickness of a rule is typically measured in points. (A point is approximately $1/72$ inch.) *See also* point[1] (definition 1). **2.** In expert systems, a statement that can be used to verify premises and to enable a conclusion to be drawn. *See also* expert system.

rule-based system *n. See* expert system, production system.

ruler *n.* In some application programs, such as word processors, an on-screen scale marked off in inches or other units of measure and used to show line widths, tab settings, paragraph indents, and so on. In programs in which the ruler is "live," the on-screen ruler can be used with the mouse or with the keyboard to set, adjust, or remove tab stops and other settings.

run *vb.* To execute a program.

run around *vb.* In page composition, to position text so that it flows around an illustration or other display.

run-length encoding *n.* A simple compression method that replaces a contiguous series (run) of identical values in a data stream with a pair of values that represent the length of the series and the value itself. For example, a data stream that contains 57 consecutive entries with the value 10 could replace them all with the much shorter pair of values 57, 10. *Acronym:* RLE.

Run Length Encoding *n. See* RLE.

run-length limited encoding *n.* A fast and highly efficient method of storing data on a disk (usually a hard disk) in which patterns in the bits representing information are translated into codes rather than being stored literally bit by bit and character by character. In RLL encoding, changes in magnetic flux are based on the number of zeros

that occur in sequence. This scheme allows data to be stored with fewer changes in magnetic flux than would otherwise be needed for the number of data bits involved and results in considerably higher storage capacity than is possible with older technologies, such as frequency modulation (FM) and modified frequency modulation (MFM) encoding. *Abbreviation:* RLL encoding. *Compare* frequency modulation encoding, modified frequency modulation encoding.

running foot *n.* One or more lines of text in the bottom margin area of a page, composed of one or more elements such as the page number, the name of the chapter, and the date. *Also called:* footer.

running head *n.* One or more lines of text in the top margin area of a page, composed of one or more elements such as the page number, the name of the chapter, and the date. *Also called:* header.

RUNOFF *n.* A very early text editor/text formatting program, developed by J. E. Saltzer at M.I.T. for the CTSS (Compatible Time-Sharing System) operating system in the mid-1960s, in order to format his Ph.D. thesis. RUNOFF was the ancestor of many other text processors, including TeX, and the UNIX programs roff, nroff, and troff.

run-time *adj.* Occurring after a program has begun to be executed, such as evaluation of variable expressions and dynamic allocation of memory.

run time *n.* **1.** The time period during which a program is running. *See also* compile time, dynamic allocation, dynamic binding, link time. **2.** The amount of time needed to execute a given program.

runtime *n. See* common language runtime.

run-time binding *n.* Assignment of a meaning to an identifier (such as a variable) in a program at the time the program is executed rather than at the time the program is compiled. *Compare* compile-time binding, link-time binding.

run-time error *n.* A software error that occurs while a program is being executed, as detected by a compiler or other supervisory program.

run-time library *n.* A file containing one or more prewritten routines to perform specific, commonly used functions. A run-time library, used primarily in high-level languages such as C, saves the programmer from having to rewrite those routines.

run-time version *n.* **1.** Program code that is ready to be executed. Generally, this code has been compiled and can operate without error under most user command sequences and over most ranges of data sets. **2.** A special release that provides the computer user with some, but not all, of the capabilities available in the full-fledged software package.

R/W *adj. See* read/write.

RXD *n.* Short for Receive (**rx**) **D**ata. A line used to carry received serial data from one device to another, such as from a modem to a computer. Pin 3 is the RXD line in RS-232-C connections. *See also* RS-232-C standard. *Compare* TXD.

RZ *n. See* return to zero.

R

S-100 bus *n.* A 100-pin bus specification used in the design of computers built around the Intel 8080 and Zilog Z-80 microprocessors. System designs using the Motorola 6800, 68000, and Intel iAPx86 family of microprocessors have also been built around the S-100 bus. S-100 computers were extremely popular with early computer enthusiasts. They had an open architecture, which permitted the configuration of systems with a wide range of add-on expansion boards.

SA *n.* Identifier for Intel's line of RISC-based microprocessors for portable and embedded devices. *See also* StrongARM.

SAA *n.* Acronym for **S**ystems **A**pplication **A**rchitecture. An IBM-developed standard for the appearance and operation of application software that will give programs written for all IBM computers—mainframe computers, minicomputers, and personal computers—a similar look and feel. SAA defines how an application interfaces with both the user and the supporting operating system. True SAA-compliant applications are compatible at the source level (before being compiled) with any SAA-compliant operating system—provided the system is capable of furnishing all the services required by the application.

Sad Mac *n.* An error indication that occurs on Apple Macintosh computers when the system fails the initial diagnostic test. A Sad Mac is a picture of a Macintosh with a frowning face and X's for eyes, with an error code beneath the picture.

safe mode *n.* In some versions of Windows, such as Windows 95, a boot mode that bypasses startup files and loads only the most basic drivers. Safe mode allows the user to correct some problem with the system—for example, if the system fails to boot or the registry has become corrupted. *See also* boot[1].

salt *n.* Random data used to supplement encryption schemes. A salt value allows two identical packets of data to be encrypted into two different packets of ciphertext using the same key by changing the salt value with each packet. *Also called:* salt string, salt value.

Samba *n.* A popular freeware program that provides file and print services, authentication and authorization, name resolution, and service announcement (browsing). As a file server, Samba enables the sharing of files, printers, and other resources on a UNIX Samba server with Windows clients over a network. Based on the Server Message Block (SMB) protocol, Samba originally was developed as a Network File System (NFS) for UNIX by Andrew Tridgell. *See also* NFS, SMB.

sampling *vb.* **1.** In statistics, gathering data from a representative subset of a larger group (called a population)—for example, determining a country's presumed voting pattern by polling a demographic cross section of voters. Other uses of this type of sampling might include checking the accuracy and efficiency of computerized transactions by reviewing every hundredth transaction or predicting traffic volumes by measuring traffic flow in a few strategic streets. There are many statistical procedures for estimating how accurately a given sample reflects the behavior of a group as a whole. **2.** The conversion of analog signals to a digital format; samples are taken at periodic intervals to measure and record some parameter, such as a signal from a temperature sensor or a microphone. Analog-to-digital converters are used in computers to sample analog signals as voltages and convert them to the binary form a computer can process. The two primary characteristics of this type of sampling are the sampling rate (usually expressed in samples per second) and the sampling precision (expressed in bits; 8-bit samples, for instance, can measure an input voltage accurate to 1/256 of the measured range).

sampling rate *n.* The frequency with which samples of a physical variable, such as sound, are taken. The higher the sampling rate (that is, the more samples taken per unit of time), the more closely the digitized result resembles the original. *See also* sampling (definition 2).

sampling synthesizer *n.* A device designed to reproduce sounds, at differing frequencies, based on a digitized sound stored in read-only memory. For example, a recorded piano note, digitized and stored in memory, is used by the synthesizer to create other piano-like notes.

samurai *n.* A hacker employed by a company or organization to manage network security or conduct legal cracking operations. A samurai uses the skills of a hacker to meet the legitimate needs of an employer.

SAN *n. See* storage area network.

sandbox *n.* **1.** Java Virtual Machine security area for downloaded (remote or untrusted) applets, an area in which such applets are confined and prevented from accessing system resources. Confinement to the sandbox prevents downloaded applets from carrying out potentially dangerous operations, maliciously or otherwise. They have to "play" inside the sandbox, and any attempt to "escape" is thwarted by the Java Security Manager. **2.** Slang for the research and development department at many software and computer companies. *See also* applet, Java Virtual Machine.

sans serif *adj.* Literally, "without stroke"; describes any typeface in which the characters have no serifs (the short lines or ornaments at the upper and lower ends of the strokes). A sans serif typeface usually possesses a more straightforward, geometric appearance than a typeface with serifs and typically lacks the contrast between thick and thin strokes found in serif faces. Sans serif typefaces are used more frequently in display type, such as headlines, than in blocks of text. *Compare* serif[1].

SAOL *n.* Acronym for **S**tructured **A**udio **O**rchestra Language. Part of the MPEG-4 standard, SAOL describes a set of tools for producing computer music, audio for computer games, streaming Internet sound or music, and other multimedia applications. SAOL is a flexible computer language for describing music synthesis and integrating synthetic sound with recorded sound in an MPEG-4 bit stream. *See also* bit stream, MPEG-4, streaming (definition 1).

SAP *n. See* Service Advertising Protocol.

SAPI *n.* Acronym for **S**peech **A**pplication **P**rogramming **I**nterface. A feature in Windows 9x and Windows NT that allows applications to include speech recognition or convert text to speech. *Also called:* Speech API. *See also* voice recognition.

SAS *n. See* single attachment station.

SASL *n.* Acronym for **S**imple **A**uthentication and **S**ecurity **L**ayer. An authentication support mechanism for use with connection-based protocols. SASL allows a client to request identification from a server and negotiate use of an added security layer for authentication during subsequent client/server interaction.

satellite *n. See* communications satellite.

satellite computer *n.* A computer that is connected to another computer, with which it interacts over a communications link. As its name indicates, a satellite computer is of lesser "stature" than the main, or host, computer; the host controls either the satellite itself or the tasks the satellite performs. *See also* remote communications.

satellite dish *n.* A parabolic (dish-shaped) reflector and antenna that is used for transmitting and receiving signals between the ground and earth satellites. Satellite dishes are commonly used for receiving television transmissions.

saturated mode *n.* The state in which a switching device or amplifier is passing the maximum possible current. A device is in saturated mode when increasing the control signal does not result in output of additional current.

saturation *n.* **1.** In a switching device or amplifier, the fully conducting state. At saturation, the device is passing the maximum possible current. The term is most commonly used with reference to circuits containing bipolar or field-effect transistors. **2.** In color graphics and printing, the amount of color in a specified hue, often specified as a percentage. *See also* HSB.

save *vb.* To write data (typically a file) to a storage medium, such as a disk or tape.

SAX *n.* Acronym for **S**imple **API** for **XML**. An event-driven application program interface (API) used to interpret an XML file. SAX works with an XML parser, providing an interface between the parser and an XML application. SAX is used as an alternative to the more complex object-based Document Object Model (DOM) interface. *See also* DOM.

scalability *n.* A measure of how well a computer, service, or application can grow to meet increasing performance demands. For server clusters, it is the ability to incrementally add one or more systems to an existing cluster when the overall load of the cluster exceeds its capabilities. *See also* server cluster.

S

scalable *adj.* Of or relating to the characteristic of a piece of hardware or software or a network that makes it possible for it to expand—or shrink—to meet future needs and circumstances. For example, a scalable network allows the network administrator to add many additional nodes without the need to redesign the basic system.

scalable font *n.* Any font that can be scaled to produce characters in varying sizes. Examples of scalable fonts are screen fonts in a graphical user interface, stroke fonts (such as Courier) and outline fonts common to most PostScript printers, TrueType fonts, and the method for screen font definition used in Macintosh System 7. In contrast, most text-based interfaces and printing devices (such as daisy-wheel printers) offer text in only one size. *See also* outline font, PostScript font, screen font, stroke font, TrueType.

scalable parallel processing *n.* Multiprocessing architectures in which additional processors and additional users can easily be added without excessive increases in complexity and loss of performance. *Acronym:* SPP.

Scalable Processor Architecture *n. See* SPARC.

Scalable Vector Graphics *n. See* SVG.

scalar *n.* A factor, coefficient, or variable consisting of a single value (as opposed to a record, an array, or some other complex data structure). *Compare* vector.

scalar data type *n.* A data type defined as having a predictable and enumerable sequence of values that can be compared for greater-than/less-than relationships. Scalar data types include integers, characters, user-defined enumerated data types, and (in most implementations) Boolean values. Some debate exists as to whether or not floating-point numbers can be considered a scalar data type; although they can be ordered, enumeration is often questionable because of rounding and conversion errors. *See also* Boolean expression, enumerated data type, floating-point number.

scalar processor *n.* A processor designed for high-speed computation of scalar values. A scalar value can be represented by a single number.

scalar variable *n. See* scalar.

scale[1] *n.* A horizontal or vertical line on a graph that shows minimum, maximum, and interval values for the data plotted.

scale[2] *vb.* **1.** To enlarge or reduce a graphic display, such as a drawing or a proportional character font, by adjusting its size proportionally. **2.** To alter the way in which values are represented so as to bring them into a different range—for example, to change linear feet to quarter inches on a blueprint drawing of a house. **3.** In programming, to determine the number of digits occupied by fixed-point or floating-point numbers. *See also* fixed-point notation, floating-point number.

scaling *n.* In computer graphics, the process of enlarging or reducing a graphical image—scaling a font to a desired size or scaling a model created with a CAD program, for example. *See also* CAD.

scan *vb.* **1.** In television and computer display technologies, to move an electron beam across the inner surface of the screen, one line at a time, to light the phosphors that create a displayed image. **2.** In facsimile and other optical technologies, to move a light-sensitive device across an image-bearing surface such as a page of text, converting the light and dark areas on the surface to binary digits that can be interpreted by a computer.

scan code *n.* A code number transmitted to an IBM or compatible computer whenever a key is pressed or released. Each key on the keyboard has a unique scan code. This code is not the same as the ASCII code for the letter, number, or symbol shown on the key; it is a special identifier for the key itself and is always the same for a particular key. When a key is pressed, the scan code is transmitted to the computer, where a portion of the ROM BIOS (read-only memory basic input/output system) dedicated to the keyboard translates the scan code into its ASCII equivalent. Because a single key can generate more than one character (lowercase *a* and uppercase *A*, for example), the ROM BIOS also keeps track of the status of keys that change the keyboard state, such as the Shift key, and takes them into account when translating a scan code. *Compare* key code.

scan head *n.* An optical device found in scanners and fax machines that moves across the subject being scanned, converts light and dark areas to electrical signals, and sends those signals to the scanning system for processing.

scan line *n.* **1.** One of many horizontal lines of a graphics display screen, such as a television or raster-scan monitor. **2.** A single row of pixels read by a scanning device.

scanner *n.* An optical input device that uses light-sensing equipment to capture an image on paper or some other subject. The image is translated into a digital signal that can then be manipulated by optical character recognition

(OCR) software or graphics software. Scanners come in a number of types, including flatbed (scan head passes over a stationary subject), feed (subject is pulled across a stationary scan head), drum (subject is rotated around a stationary scan head), and handheld (user passes device over a stationary subject).

scan rate *n. See* refresh rate.

scatter diagram *n.* A graph consisting of points whose coordinates represent values of data, often used to illustrate a correlation between one or more variables and a test group. See the illustration. *Also called:* point chart, point diagram.

Scatter diagram.

schedule *vb.* To program a computer to perform a specified action at a specified time and date.

scheduler *n.* An operating-system process that starts and ends tasks (programs), manages concurrently running processes, and allocates system resources. *Also called:* dispatcher.

scheduling algorithm *n.* An algorithm that governs the proper timing of a sequence of events in an operating system or application. For example, an effective motion graphics scheduling algorithm would be able to retrieve the graphic objects, process them, and display them without causing stutter or disruptions. *See also* algorithm.

schema *n.* A description of a database to a database management system (DBMS) in the language provided by the DBMS. A schema defines aspects of the database, such as attributes (fields) and domains and parameters of the attributes.

schematic *n.* A diagram that shows a circuit's components and the connections between them using lines and a set of standard symbols to represent various electronic components. See the illustration.

Schematic.

Schottky diode *n.* A type of diode (device that passes current in one direction) in which a semiconductor layer and a metal layer are brought into contact. It is characterized by very fast switching speeds. *Also called:* hot carrier diode, Schottky barrier diode.

scientific notation *n.* A floating-point method of representing a number, especially a very large or very small one, in which numbers are expressed as products consisting of a number between 1 and 10 multiplied by a power of 10. Scientific notation commonly uses the letter E in place of "times 10," as in 5.0E3, meaning 5.0 times 10 to the third power, or 10^3. *See also* floating-point notation.

sci. newsgroups *n.* Usenet newsgroups that are part of the sci. hierarchy and begin with "sci." These newsgroups are devoted to discussions of scientific research and applications, except for computer science, which is discussed in the comp. newsgroups. *See also* newsgroup, traditional newsgroup hierarchy, Usenet. *Compare* comp. newsgroups, misc. newsgroups, news. newsgroups, rec. newsgroups, soc. newsgroups, talk. newsgroups.

scissoring *n. See* clip.

scope *n.* **1.** In programming, the extent to which an identifier, such as a constant, data type, variable, or routine, can be referenced within a program. Scope can be global

S

or local. Scope can also be affected by redefining identifiers, such as by giving the same name to both a global variable and a local variable. *See also* block[1](definition 3), global, local. **2.** In electronics, slang for oscilloscope. *See also* oscilloscope.

score *n.* When referring to a spelling checker, a score is a number that indicates how much a replacement word differs from the original misspelled word. A low score indicates that the misspelled word was changed slightly, while a high score indicates that the word was changed a great deal.

SCP *n.* Acronym for **S**imple **C**ontrol **P**rotocol. A lightweight peer-to-peer networking protocol for devices that have limited processing and memory resources and operate over limited-bandwidth networks such as powerline carrier (PLC) systems. Products using SCP can interoperate with products using the Universal Plug and Play (UPnP), CEBus, and Home Plug & Play (HPnP) standards. Developed by a team of companies including Microsoft and General Electric, SCP enables the interaction between UPnP devices, devices based on Internet Protocol (IP), and non-IP-capable devices such as coffeemakers and alarm clocks. SCP, which was designed as a stand-alone protocol, can be used in residential, commercial, industrial, and utility applications. *See also* UPnP networking.

SCR *n. See* silicon-controlled rectifier.

scrambler *n.* A device or program that reorders a signal sequence in order to render it indecipherable. *See also* encryption.

scrap *n.* An application or system file maintained for storing data that has been marked for movement, copying, or deletion. *See also* clipboard (definition 1).

scrapbook *n.* **1.** A file in which a series of text and graphical images can be saved for subsequent use. **2.** A Macintosh system file that can hold a number of text and graphical images for later use. *Compare* clipboard (definition 1).

scratch[1] *n.* A memory region or file used by a program or operating system to hold work in progress temporarily. Created and maintained usually without the end user's knowledge, the scratch is needed only until the current session is terminated, at which time the data is saved or discarded. *Also called:* scratch file. *See also* temporary file. *Compare* scrap.

scratch[2] *vb.* To erase or discard data.

scratch file *n. See* scratch[1].

scratchpad *n.* **1.** A temporary storage area used by a program or operating system for calculations, data, and other work in progress. *See also* scratch[1], temporary file. **2.** A high-speed memory circuit used to hold small items of data for rapid retrieval. *See also* cache.

scratchpad memory *n. See* cache.

scratchpad RAM *n.* Memory used by a central processing unit (CPU) for temporary data storage. *Also called:* scratchpad, scratchpad memory. *See also* central processing unit, register.

scream *vb.* To operate at very high speed. For example, a modem that can transfer data several times faster than the one it replaced or a computer with a very high clock speed could be said to "scream."

screamer *n.* Slang for a piece of computer equipment that operates at a very high speed. Generally, "screamers" are the newest versions of a particular piece of equipment, such as a PC with the latest, fastest microprocessor, or are comprised of multiple components that increase the operating speed over standard models, such as a PC that has a huge amount of RAM (Random Access Memory), a high-performance video board, a superfast CD-ROM drive, and the latest microprocessor. However, as technology evolves and new, faster devices are introduced, yesterday's screamer rapidly becomes today's snail.

screen angle *n.* The angle at which the dots in a halftone screen are printed. A correct angle will minimize blur and other undesirable effects, such as moiré patterns. *See also* color separation (definition 1), halftone, moiré.

screen buffer *n. See* video buffer.

screen dump *n.* A duplicate of a screen image; essentially, a snapshot of the screen that is either sent to a printer or saved as a file.

screen flicker *n. See* flicker.

screen font *n.* A typeface designed for display on a computer monitor screen. Screen fonts often have accompanying PostScript fonts for printing to PostScript-compatible printers. *See also* derived font, intrinsic font. *Compare* PostScript font, printer font.

screen frequency *n. See* halftone.

screen grabber *n. See* grabber (definition 3).

screen name *n.* A name under which an America Online user is known. The screen name may be the same as the user's real name. *See also* America Online.

screen phone *n.* A type of Internet appliance combining a telephone with an LCD display screen, a digital fax modem, and a computer keyboard, with ports for a mouse, printer, and other peripheral devices. Screen phones can be used as regular telephones for voice communications and can also be used as terminals to gain access to the Internet and other online services.

screen pitch *n.* A measurement of a computer monitor's screen density, representing the distance between phosphors on the display. The lower the number, the more detail can be displayed clearly. For example, a .28-dot-pitch screen has better resolution than one with .32. See the illustration. *See also* phosphor.

.28-mm screen pitch

Screen pitch.

screen saver *n.* A utility that causes a monitor to blank out or display a certain image after a specified amount of time passes without the keyboard being touched or the mouse being moved. Touching a key or moving the mouse deactivates the screen saver. Screen savers were originally used to prevent images from becoming permanently etched on a monitor's screen. Although modern monitors are not susceptible to this problem, screen savers remain popular for their decorative and entertainment value. See the illustration.

Screen saver.

screen shot *n.* An image that shows all or part of a computer display.

ScreenTips *n.* Notes that appear on the screen to provide information about a toolbar button, tracked change, or comment or to display a footnote or an endnote. Screen-Tips also display the text that will appear if you choose to insert a date or AutoText entry.

script *n.* A program consisting of a set of instructions to an application or a utility program. The instructions usually use the rules and syntax of the application or utility. On the World Wide Web, scripts are commonly used to customize or add interactivity to Web pages. *See also* macro.

scripting language *n.* A simple programming language designed to perform special or limited tasks, sometimes associated with a particular application or function. An example of a scripting language is Perl. *See also* Perl, script.

script kiddie *n.* A would-be hacker who does not have the technical skills or knowledge needed for traditional hacking methods; one who relies on easy-to-use kiddie scripts. *See also* hacker, kiddie script.

scriptlet *n.* A reusable Web page based on the features of Dynamic HTML (DHTML) that can be created with HTML text and a scripting language and then inserted as a control in another Web page or in an application. Developed by Microsoft and introduced in Internet Explorer version 4, scriptlets are implemented as .htm files that give developers a relatively easy, object-based means of creating components that reflect the Web metaphor and that can be used to add interactivity and functionality—for example, animation, color changes, pop-up menus, or drag-and-drop capability—to Web pages without requiring repeated trips to the server. *Also called:* Microsoft Scripting Component. *See also* dynamic HTML. *Compare* applet.

scroll *vb.* To move a document or other data in a window in order to view a particular portion of the document. Scrolling may be controlled by the mouse, arrow keys, or other keys on the keyboard. *See also* scroll bar.

scroll arrow *n. See* scroll bar.

scroll bar *n.* In some graphical user interfaces, a vertical or horizontal bar at the side or bottom of a display area that can be used with a mouse for moving around in that area. Scroll bars often have four active areas: two scroll arrows for moving line by line, a sliding scroll box for moving to an arbitrary location in the display area, and gray areas for moving in increments of one window at a time.

scroll box *n. See* elevator.

S

Scroll Lock key *n.* On the IBM PC/XT and AT and compatible keyboards, a key on the top row of the numeric keypad that controls the effect of the cursor control keys and sometimes prevents the screen from scrolling. On the enhanced and Macintosh keyboards, this key is to the right of the function keys on the top row. Many modern applications ignore the Scroll Lock setting.

scroll wheel *n.* A thumbwheel on a mouse that, when turned, enables the user to scroll or zoom without clicking the scroll bar or using the keyboard. Depending on the mouse, a scroll wheel can also double as a third mouse button. *See also* scroll bar.

SCSI *n.* Acronym for **S**mall **C**omputer **S**ystem **I**nterface, a standard high-speed parallel interface defined by the X3T9.2 committee of the American National Standards Institute (ANSI). A SCSI (pronounced "scuzzy") interface is used to connect microcomputers to SCSI peripheral devices, such as many hard disks and printers, and to other computers and local area networks. *Also called:* SCSI-1, SCSI I. *Compare* ESDI, IDE.

SCSI-1 *n. See* SCSI.

SCSI-2 *n.* An enhanced ANSI standard for SCSI (Small Computer System Interface) buses. Compared with the original SCSI standard (now called SCSI-1), which can transfer data 8 bits at a time at up to 5 MB per second, SCSI-2 offers increased data width, increased speed, or both. A SCSI-2 disk drive or host adapter can work with SCSI-1 equipment at the older equipment's maximum speed. *Also called:* SCSI II. *See also* Fast SCSI, Fast/Wide SCSI, SCSI, Wide SCSI. *Compare* UltraSCSI.

SCSI bus *n.* A parallel bus that carries data and control signals from SCSI devices to a SCSI controller. *See also* bus, controller, SCSI device.

SCSI chain *n.* A set of devices on a SCSI bus. Each device (except the host adapter and the last device) is connected to two other devices by two cables, forming a daisy chain. *See also* daisy chain, SCSI.

SCSI connector *n.* A cable connector used to connect a SCSI device to a SCSI bus. See the illustration. *See also* bus, connector (definition 1), SCSI device.

SCSI connector.

SCSI device *n.* A peripheral device that uses the SCSI standard to exchange data and control signals with a computer's CPU. *See also* peripheral, SCSI.

SCSI I *n. See* SCSI.

SCSI II *n. See* SCSI-2.

SCSI ID *n.* The unique identity of a SCSI device. Each device connected to a SCSI bus must have a different SCSI ID. A maximum of eight SCSI IDs can be used on the same SCSI bus. *See also* bus, SCSI device.

SCSI network *n.* A set of devices on a SCSI bus, which acts like a local area network. *See also* SCSI.

SCSI port *n.* **1.** A SCSI host adapter within a computer, which provides a logical connection between the computer and all of the devices on the SCSI bus. *See also* SCSI. **2.** A connector on a device for a SCSI bus cable. *See also* SCSI.

SDH *n. See* Synchronous Digital Hierarchy.

SDK *n.* Acronym for **s**oftware **d**evelopment **k**it. *See* developer's toolkit.

SDLC *n.* Acronym for **S**ynchronous **D**ata **L**ink **C**ontrol, the data transmission protocol most widely used by networks conforming to IBM's Systems Network Architecture (SNA). SDLC is similar to the HDLC (High-level Data Link Control) protocol developed by the International Organization for Standardization (ISO). *See also* HDLC.

SDM *n. See* space-division multiplexing.

S

SDMI *n. See* Secure Digital Music Initiative.

SDRAM *n.* Acronym for **s**ynchronous **DRAM**. A form of dynamic random access memory (DRAM) that can run at higher clock speeds than conventional DRAM by employing a bursting technique in which the DRAM predicts the address of the next memory location to be accessed. *See also* dynamic RAM.

SDSL *n.* Acronym for **s**ymmetric (or single-line) **d**igital **s**ubscriber **l**ine, a digital telecommunications technology that is a variation of HDSL. SDSL uses one pair of copper wires rather than two pairs of wires and transmits at 1.544 Mbps. *Compare* ADSL.

.sea *n.* A file extension for a self-extracting Macintosh archive compressed with StuffIt. *See also* self-extracting file.

seamless integration *n.* The favorable result that occurs when a new hardware component or program blends smoothly into the overall operation of the system. It is usually the result of thoughtful design and programming.

search¹ *n.* The process of seeking a particular file or specific data. A search is carried out by a program through comparison or calculation to determine whether a match to some pattern exists or whether some other criteria have been met. *See also* binary search, hash search, linear search, search and replace, wildcard character.

search² *vb.* **1.** To look for the location of a file. **2.** To seek specific data within a file or data structure. *See also* replace.

search algorithm *n.* An algorithm designed to locate a certain element, called the target, in a data structure. *See also* algorithm, binary search, hash search, linear search.

search and replace *n.* A common process in applications such as word processors in which the user specifies two strings of characters. The process finds instances of the first string and replaces them with the second string.

search criteria *n.* The terms or conditions that a search engine uses to find items in a database. *See also* search engine.

search engine *n.* **1.** A program that searches for keywords in documents or in a database. **2.** On the Internet, a program that searches for keywords in files and documents found on the World Wide Web, newsgroups, Gopher menus, and FTP archives. Some search engines are used for a single Internet site, such as a dedicated search engine for a Web site. Others search across many sites, using such agents as spiders to gather lists of avail-able files and documents and store these lists in databases that users can search by keyword. Examples of the latter type of search engine are Lycos and Excite. Most search engines reside on a server. *See also* agent (definition 2), FTP, Gopher or gopher, newsgroup, spider, World Wide Web.

search key *n.* **1.** The particular field (or column) of the records to be searched in a database. *See also* primary key, secondary key. **2.** The value that is to be searched for in a document or any collection of data.

search path *n.* The route followed by an operating system to find the location of a stored file. The search path begins with a drive or volume (disk) designator or a network share, continues through a chain of directories and subdirectories, if any, and ends with the file name. C:\books\diction\start.exe is an example of a search path. *Also called:* access path.

search string *n.* The string of characters to be matched in a search—typically (but not necessarily) a text string.

seat¹ *n.* One workstation or computer, in the context of software licensing on a per-seat basis. *See also* license agreement, workstation (definition 1).

seat² *vb.* To insert a piece of hardware fully and position it correctly in a computer or affiliated equipment, as in seating a single inline memory module (SIMM) in its socket.

secondary channel *n.* A transmission channel in a communications system that carries testing and diagnostic information rather than actual data. *Compare* primary channel.

secondary key *n.* A field that is to be sorted or searched within a subset of the records having identical primary key values. *See also* alternate key (definition 1), candidate key. *Compare* primary key.

secondary service provider *n.* An Internet service provider that provides a Web presence but not direct connectivity. *See also* ISP.

secondary storage *n.* Any data storage medium other than a computer's random access memory (RAM)—typically tape or disk. *Compare* primary storage.

Second Generation *n. See* 2G.

second-level domain *n.* The level immediately beneath the top-level domain in the Internet's DNS hierarchy. *See also* domain (definition 3).

second normal form *n. See* normal form (definition 1).

secret channel *n. See* private channel.

section *n.* A length of fiberoptic cable in a SONET network. *See also* line, path.

sector *n.* A portion of the data storage area on a disk. A disk is divided into sides (top and bottom), tracks (rings on each surface), and sectors (sections of each ring). Sectors are the smallest physical storage units on a disk and are of fixed size; typically, they are capable of holding 512 bytes of information apiece. See the illustration.

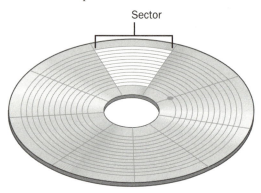

Sector

Sector.

sector interleave *n. See* interleave.

sector map *n.* **1.** A map that indicates the unusable sectors on a disk. **2.** A table used to translate the sector numbers that are requested by the operating system into physical sector numbers. The sector map represents a different method of performing sector interleaving. When a sector map is used, the sectors are formatted on the disk in sequential order. The mapping enables the system to read sectors in a nonsequential order. For example, using a 3-to-1 sector interleaving map, a system request for sectors 1 through 4 will result in the disk driver reading physical sectors 1, 4, 7, and 10. *See also* interleave.

secure channel *n.* A communications link that has been protected against unauthorized access, operation, or use by means of isolation from the public network, encryption, or other forms of control. *See also* encryption.

Secure Digital Music Initiative *n.* A coalition of companies from the recording, electronics, and information technology industries founded in February 1999 for the purpose of developing an open standard for the secure distribution of music in digital form. The Secure Digital Music Initiative specification is designed to provide consumers with flexibility and convenient access to electroni-

cally distributed music (that is, over the Internet) while also protecting the rights of artists. *Acronym:* SDMI. *See also* MP3, Windows Media Technologies.

Secure Electronics Transactions protocol *n.* Protocol for conducting secure transactions over the Internet, the result of a joint effort by GTE, IBM, MasterCard, Microsoft, Netscape, SAIC, Terisa Systems, VeriSign, and Visa. *Acronym:* SET.

Secure Hash Algorithm *n. See* SHA.

Secure HTTP *n. See* S-HTTP, HTTPS.

Secure Hypertext Transfer Protocol *n. See* S-HTTP.

Secure/Multipurpose Internet Mail Extensions *n. See* S/MIME.

Secure Password Authentication *n.* A feature that allows a server to confirm the identity of the person logging on. *Acronym:* SPA.

secure site *n.* A Web site having the capability of providing secure transactions, ensuring that credit card numbers and other personal information will not be accessible to unauthorized parties.

Secure Sockets Layer *n. See* SSL.

Secure Transaction Technology *n.* The use of the SSL (Secure Sockets Layer), S-HTTP (Secure HTTP), or both in online transactions, such as form transmission or credit card purchases. *Acronym:* STT. *See also* S-HTTP, SSL.

secure wide area network *n.* A set of computers that communicate over a public network, such as the Internet, but use security measures, such as encryption, authentication, and authorization, to prevent their communications from being intercepted and understood by unauthorized users. *Acronym:* S/WAN. *See also* authentication, authorization, encryption, virtual private network (definition 1).

security *n.* The technologies used to make a service resistant to unauthorized access to the data that it holds or for which it is responsible. A major focus of computer security, especially on systems that are accessed by many people or through communications lines, is the prevention of system access by unauthorized individuals.

security kernel *n.* An operating-system kernel that is protected from unauthorized use. *See also* kernel.

security log *n.* A log, generated by a firewall or other security device, that lists events that could affect security, such as access attempts or commands, and the names of the users involved. *See also* firewall, log (definition 1).

seed *n.* A starting value used in generating a sequence of random or pseudorandom numbers. *See also* random number generation.

seek *n.* The process of moving the read/write head in a disk drive to the proper site, typically for a read or write operation.

seek time *n.* The time required to move a disk drive's read/write head to a specific location on a disk. *See also* access time (definition 2).

segment *n.* A section of a program that, when compiled, occupies a contiguous address space and that is usually position independent; that is, it can be loaded anywhere in memory. With Intel-based microcomputers, a native-mode segment is a logical reference to a 64-KB contiguous portion of RAM in which the individual bytes are accessed by means of an offset value. Collectively, the segment:offset values reference a single physical location in RAM. *See also* overlay[1] (definition 1), real mode, segmentation.

segmentation *n.* The act of breaking up a program into several sections, or segments. *See also* segment.

segmented addressing architecture *n.* A memory-access technique typified by Intel 80x86 processors. Memory is divided into 64-KB segments in this architecture for addressing locations under the 16-bit address scheme; 32-bit schemes can address memory in segments as large as 4 GB. *Also called:* segmented instruction addressing, segmented memory architecture. *Compare* linear addressing architecture.

segmented address space *n.* An address space that is logically divided into chunks called segments. To address a given location, a program must specify both a segment and an offset within that segment. (The offset is a value that references a specific point within the segment, based on the beginning of the segment.) Because segments may overlap, addresses are not unique; there are many logical ways to access a given physical location. The Intel 80x86 real-mode architecture is segmented; most other microprocessor architectures are flat. *See also* segment. *Compare* flat address space.

segmented instruction addressing *n. See* segmented addressing architecture.

segmented memory architecture *n. See* segmented addressing architecture.

select *vb.* **1.** In general computer use, to specify a block of data or text on screen by highlighting it or otherwise marking it with the intent of performing some operation on it. **2.** In database management, to choose records according to a specified set of criteria. *See also* sort. **3.** In information processing, to choose from a number of options or alternatives, such as subroutines or input/output channels.

selected cell *n. See* active cell.

selection *n.* **1.** In applications, the highlighted portion of an on-screen document. **2.** In communications, the initial contact made between a computer and a remote station receiving a message. **3.** In programming, a conditional branch. *See also* conditional branch.

selective calling *n.* The capability of a station on a communications line to designate the station that is to receive a transmission.

selector channel *n.* An input/output data transfer line used by one high-speed device at a time.

selector pen *n. See* light pen.

select query *n.* A query that asks a question about the data stored in your tables and returns a result set in the form of a datasheet, all without changing the data.

self-adapting *adj.* The ability of systems, devices, or processes to adjust their operational behavior to environmental conditions.

self-checking digit *n.* A digit, appended to a number during its encoding, whose function is to confirm the accuracy of the encoding. *See also* checksum, parity bit.

self-clocking *n.* A process in which timing signals are inserted into a data stream rather than being provided by an external source, such as in phase encoding.

self-documenting code *n.* Program source code that, through its use of a high-level language and descriptive identifiers, can be understood by other programmers without the need for additional comments.

self-extracting archive *n. See* self-extracting file.

self-extracting file *n.* An executable program file that contains one or more compressed text or data files. When a user runs the program, it uncompresses the compressed files and stores them on the user's hard drive. See the illustration.

S

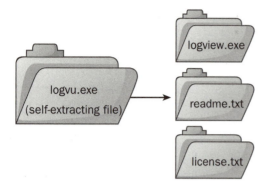

Self-extracting file.

self-modifying code *n.* Program code, usually object code generated by a compiler or an assembler, that modifies itself during instruction by writing new operation codes, addresses, or data values over existing instructions. *See also* pure procedure.

self-monitoring analysis and reporting technology system *n. See* SMART system.

self-organizing map *n. See* SOM (definition 2).

self-test *n.* A set of one or more diagnostic tests that a computer or peripheral device (such as a printer) performs on itself. *See also* power-on self test.

self-validating code *n.* Program code that can test itself to verify that it behaves correctly, usually by feeding itself a set of standard input values and testing the results against a set of expected output values.

semantic error *n.* An error in meaning; a statement in a program that is syntactically correct (legal) but functionally incorrect. *See also* logic, semantics (definition 1), syntax.

semantics *n.* **1.** In programming, the relationship between words or symbols and their intended meanings. Programming languages are subject to certain semantic rules; thus, a program statement can be syntactically correct but semantically incorrect; that is, a statement can be written in an acceptable form and still convey the wrong meaning. See the illustration. *See also* syntax. **2.** In artificial-intelligence research, the capacity of a network to represent relationships among objects, ideas, or situations in a humanlike way. *Compare* syntax.

```
CANARY — is a — BIRD
                |
               has
                |
            FEATHERS
```

Semantics.

semaphore *n.* In programming, a signal—a flag variable—used to govern access to shared system resources. A semaphore indicates to other potential users that a file or other resource is in use and prevents access by more than one user. *See also* flag (definition 1).

Semicon *n.* Short for **S**emiconductors **E**quipment and **M**aterial **I**nternational **Con**ference. A series of international conferences sponsored by the Semiconductors Equipment and Material International (SEMI), a trade group for the international semiconductor industry. The conference provides members with up-to-date information on issues affecting the semiconductor industry and provides SEMI members with a forum for showcasing products and services.

semiconductor *n.* A substance, commonly silicon or germanium, whose ability to conduct electricity falls between that of a conductor and that of a nonconductor (insulator). The term is used loosely to refer to electronic components made from semiconductor materials.

send *vb.* To transmit a message or file through a communications channel.

sendmail *n.* A popular open-source UNIX-based implementation of the Simple Mail Transfer Protocol (SMTP) for delivering e-mail. Written in 1981 by Eric Allman at the University of California at Berkeley, sendmail was the first Internet message transfer agent (MTA).

send statement *n.* In SLIP and PPP scripting languages, a statement that tells the program that dials an Internet service provider's number (a *dialer program*) to send certain characters. *See also* ISP, PPP, scripting language, SLIP.

sensor *n.* A device that detects or measures something by converting nonelectrical energy to electrical energy. A photocell, for example, detects or measures light by converting it to electrical energy. *See also* transducer.

sensor glove *n.* A hand-worn computer input device for virtual-reality environments. The glove translates finger movements by the user to commands for manipulating objects in the environment. *Also called:* data glove. *See also* virtual reality.

SEPP *n.* Acronym for **S**oftware **E**ngineering for **P**arallel **P**rocessing. A project of nine European universities and research institutions to develop tools for the development of parallel application programs for distributed memory multiprocessors.

sequence *n.* An ordered arrangement, as in a set of numbers, such as the Fibonacci sequence. *See also* Fibonacci numbers.

sequence check *n.* A process that verifies that data or records conform to a particular order. *Compare* completeness check, consistency check, duplication check.

Sequenced Packet Exchange *n. See* SPX (definition 1).

sequential access *n.* A method of storing or retrieving information that requires the program to start reading at the beginning and continue until it finds the desired data. Sequential access is best used for files in which each piece of information is related to the information that comes before it, such as mailing list files and word processing documents. *Also called:* serial access. *See also* indexed sequential access method. *Compare* random access.

sequential algorithm *n.* An algorithm in which each step must occur in a particular order. *See also* algorithm. *Compare* parallel algorithm.

sequential execution *n.* The act of executing routines or programs in a linear sequence. *Compare* concurrent execution.

sequential logic element *n.* A logic circuit element that has at least one input and one output and in which the output signal depends on the present and past states of the input signal or signals.

sequential processing *n.* **1.** The processing of items of information in the order in which they are stored or input. **2.** The execution of one instruction, routine, or task followed by the execution of the next in line. *Compare* multiprocessing, parallel processing, pipelining (definition 1).

sequential search *n. See* linear search.

serial *adj.* One by one. For example, in serial transmission, information is transferred one bit at a time; a serial computer has only one arithmetic logic unit, which must execute the whole program one step at a time. *Compare* parallel (definition 3).

serial access *n. See* sequential access.

serial adder *n.* A circuit that adds two numbers one bit position (one digit place) at a time.

serial communication *n.* The exchange of information between computers or between computers and peripheral devices one bit at a time over a single channel. Serial communications can be synchronous or asynchronous. Both sender and receiver must use the same baud rate, parity, and control information. *See also* baud rate, parity, start bit, stop bit.

Serial Infrared *n.* A system developed by Hewlett-Packard for transmitting data between two devices up to 1 meter apart using an infrared light beam. Infrared ports on the receiving and the sending devices must be aligned. Generally, Serial Infrared is used with laptops and many notebook computers, as well as with peripherals such as printers. *Acronym:* SIR. *See also* infrared port.

serial interface *n.* A data transmission scheme in which data and control bits are sent sequentially over a single channel. In reference to a serial input/output connection, the term usually implies the use of an RS-232 or RS-422 interface. *See also* RS-232-C standard, RS-422/423/449. *Compare* parallel interface.

serialize *vb.* To change from parallel transmission (byte by byte) to serial transmission (bit by bit). *Compare* deserialize.

SerialKey device *n.* Enables you to attach an alternative input device (also called an augmentative communication device) to your computer's serial port. This feature is designed for people who are unable to use the computer's standard keyboard and mouse.

SerialKeys *n.* A feature of Windows 9x, Windows NT, Windows 2000, and Windows XP that, in conjunction with a communications aid interface device, allows keystrokes and mouse controls to be accepted through a computer's serial port.

Serial Line Internet Protocol *n. See* SLIP.

serial mouse *n.* A pointing device that attaches to the computer through a standard serial port. *See also* mouse. *Compare* bus mouse.

serial port *n.* An input/output location (channel) that sends and receives data to and from a computer's central processing unit or a communications device one bit at a time. Serial ports are used for serial data communication and as interfaces with some peripheral devices, such as mice and printers.

S

serial port adapter *n.* An interface card or device that either provides a serial port or converts a serial port to another use. *See also* adapter, serial port.

serial printer *n.* A printer connected to the computer via a serial interface (commonly RS-232-C or compatible). Connectors for this type of printer vary widely, which is one reason they are less popular than parallel printers among those who use IBM and IBM-compatible PCs. Serial printers are standard for Apple computers. *See also* DB connector, serial, serial transmission. *Compare* parallel printer.

serial processing *n. See* sequential processing (definition 2).

Serial Storage Architecture *n. See* SSA.

serial transmission *n.* The transfer of discrete signals one after another. In communications and data transfer, serial transmission involves sending information over a single line one bit at a time, as in modem-to-modem connections. *Compare* parallel transmission.

series circuit *n.* A circuit in which two or more components are linked in series. All the current passes through each component in a series circuit, but the voltage is divided among the components. See the illustration. *Compare* parallel circuit.

Series circuit.

serif[1] *adj.* Marked by the use of serifs. For example, Goudy is a serif typeface, whereas Helvetica is a sans serif typeface. See the illustration. *See also* serif[2]. *Compare* sans serif.

ABC

Serifs

ABC

Serif. A serif typeface (top) and a sans serif typeface (bottom).

serif[2] *n.* Any of the short lines or ornaments at the ends of the strokes that form a typeface character.

server *n.* **1.** On a local area network (LAN), a computer running administrative software that controls access to the network and its resources, such as printers and disk drives, and provides resources to computers functioning as workstations on the network. **2.** On the Internet or other network, a computer or program that responds to commands from a client. For example, a file server may contain an archive of data or program files; when a client submits a request for a file, the server transfers a copy of the file to the client. *See also* application server (definitions 1 and 2), client/server architecture. *Compare* client (definition 3).

server appliance *n.* A device designed to deliver one or more specific network services in a single turnkey package that includes both hardware and software. All necessary programs are preinstalled on a server appliance, which has minimal, simplified options and controls. Server appliances can be used to complement or replace traditional servers on a network and can provide such services as file and printer sharing and Internet connectivity. *Also called:* appliance. *See also* information appliance.

server-based application *n.* A program that is shared over a network. The program is stored on the network server and can be used at more than one client machine at a time.

server cluster *n.* A group of independent computer systems, known as nodes, working together as a single system to ensure that mission-critical applications and resources remain available to clients. A server cluster is the type of cluster that Cluster service implements. *See also* cluster.

server control *n. See* ASP.NET server control.

server error *n.* A failure to complete a request for information through HTTP that results from an error at the server rather than an error by the client or the user. Server errors are indicated by HTTP status codes beginning with 5. *See also* HTTP, HTTP status codes.

server farm *n.* A centralized grouping of network servers maintained by an enterprise or, often, an Internet service provider (ISP). A server farm provides a network with load balancing, scalability, and fault tolerance. Individual servers may be connected in such a way that they appear to represent a single resource.

serverlet *n. See* servlet.

Server Message Block *n. See* SMB.

server push-pull *n.* A combination of Web client/server techniques individually called "server push" and "client pull." In server push, the server loads data to the client, but the data connection stays open. This allows the server to continue sending data to the browser as necessary. In client pull, the server loads data to the client, but the data connection does not stay open. The server sends an HTML directive to the browser telling it to reopen the connection after a certain interval to get more data or possibly to open a new URL. See the illustration. *See also* HTML, server (definition 2), URL.

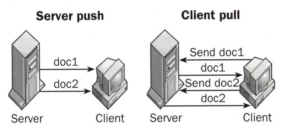

Server push-pull.

server-side include *n.* A mechanism for including dynamic text in World Wide Web documents. Server-side includes are special command codes that are recognized and interpreted by the server; their output is placed in the document body before the document is sent to the browser. Server-side includes can be used, for example, to include the date/time stamp in the text of the file. *Acronym:* SSI. *See also* server (definition 2).

service *n.* **1.** A customer-based or user-oriented function, such as technical support or network provision. **2.** In reference to programming and software, a program or routine that provides support to other programs, particularly at a low (close to the hardware) level. **3.** In networking, specialized, software-based functionality provided by network servers—for example, directory services that provide the network equivalent of "phone books" needed for locating users and resources. *See also* utility.

Service Advertising Protocol *n.* A method used by a service-providing node in a network (such as a file server or application server) to notify other nodes on the network that it is available for access. When a server boots, it uses the protocol to advertise its service; when the same server goes off line, it uses the protocol to announce that it is no longer available. *Acronym:* SAP. *See also* server (definition 1).

service bureau *n.* **1.** A company that provides various services related to publishing, such as prepress production, desktop publishing, typesetting, imagesetting, and optical scanning of graphics. **2.** An organization that provides data processing services and access to software packages for a fee.

service provider *n. See* ISP.

servlet or **servelet** *n.* A small Java program that runs on a server. The term is a companion to applet, a Java program that usually runs on the client. Servlets perform lightweight Web services, such as redirecting a Web user from an outdated address to the correct page—tasks traditionally handled by CGI (Common Gateway Interface) applications. Because servlets are automatically threaded and highly responsive, they execute quickly, thereby reducing system overhead. *Also called:* serverlet. *See also* applet, CGI.

servlet container *n.* In Sun Microsystems's J2EE network platform, a container that decodes requests, formats responses, and provides the network services over which requests and responses are sent. All servlet containers must support HTTP as a protocol for requests and responses, but they may also support additional request-response protocols such as HTTPS. *See also* container, HTTP, HTTPS, J2EE.

servo *n.* The part of a servomechanism, controlled by the servomechanism's feedback circuit, that produces the final mechanical output. *Also called:* servomotor. *See also* servomechanism.

servomechanism *n.* A control system in which the final output is mechanical movement. A servomechanism uses feedback to control the position, velocity, or acceleration of a mechanical component. *Also called:* servo system.

servomotor *n. See* servo.

servo system *n. See* servomechanism.

session *n.* **1.** The time during which a program is running. In most interactive programs, a session is the time during which the program accepts input and processes information. **2.** In communications, the time during which two computers maintain a connection. **3.** A specific protocol layer in the ISO/OSI reference model that manages communication between remote users or processes. *See also* ISO/OSI reference model, session layer.

session bean *n.* In the Java programming language and J2EE network platform, an enterprise bean that is created

S

by a client and usually exists only for the duration of a single client/server session. It performs operations, such as calculations or accessing a database, for the client. While a session bean may be transactional, it is not recoverable should a system crash occur. Session bean objects can either be stateless or can maintain conversational state across methods and transactions. If a session bean maintains state, the Enterprise JavaBean (EJB) container manages this state if the object must be removed from memory. However, the session bean object itself must manage its own persistent data. *See also* EJB, stateless.

session layer *n.* The fifth of seven layers in the ISO/OSI reference model. The session layer handles the details that must be agreed on by the two communicating devices. See the illustration. *See also* ISO/OSI reference model.

ISO/OSI MODEL

ISO/OSI Layer	Focus
Application (highest level)	Program-to-program transfer of information
Presentation	Text formatting and display, code conversion
Session	Establishing, maintaining, and coordinating communication
Transport	Accurate delivery, service quality
Network	Transport routes, message handling and transfer
Data-link	Coding, addressing, and transmitting information
Physical	Hardware connections

Session layer.

set[1] *n.* In printing and display, a group of related characters, such as a character set. *See also* character set.

set[2] *vb.* **1.** To change the value of a bit to 1. **2.** To establish a particular condition, such as setting tab stops, setting a counter to 0, or setting a breakpoint. *See also* breakpoint.

SET protocol *n. See* Secure Electronics Transactions protocol.

settling time *n.* The time required for a disk drive's read/write head to stabilize over a new location on the disk after being moved.

set-top box *n.* A device that converts a cable TV signal to an input signal to the TV set. Set-top boxes can be used to access the World Wide Web and are a type of information appliance. *See also* information appliance.

setup *n.* **1.** A computer along with all its devices. **2.** The procedures involved in preparing a software program or application to operate within a computer.

setup program *n.* **1.** A built-in BIOS program for reconfiguring system parameters to accommodate a new disk drive. *See also* BIOS. **2.** *See* installation program.

setup string *n. See* control code.

setup wizard *n.* In Windows, a utility that asks users a structured series of questions and gives them options to aid the process of installing a new program.

seven-segment display *n.* A light-emitting diode (LED) display or liquid crystal display (LCD) that can show any of the 10 decimal digits. The seven segments are the seven bars that form a numeral 8 as in a calculator display.

sex changer *n. See* gender changer.

sfx *n.* A computer language used to generate digital audio effects and synthesizer instrument audio. It is a superset of the MPEG-4 standard SAOL audio compiler language. Sfx provides professional-quality audio synthesis, real-time MIDI and audio generation, and fully customizable instruments and effects. Because the sfx compiler is a C++ front-end compiler, code is converted to C++ and then compiled into executable orchestras that are used to generate real-time audio. As a result, the current release of sfx requires that Microsoft Visual C++ be installed on the system on which sfx is running. *See also* C++, compiler, MIDI, MPEG-4, SAOL, Visual C++.

.sgm *n.* The MS-DOS/Windows 3.*x* file extension that identifies files encoded in Standard Generalized Markup Language (SGML). Because MS-DOS and Windows 3.*x* cannot recognize file extensions longer than three letters, the .sgml extension is truncated to three letters in those environments. *See also* SGML.

.sgml *n.* The file extension that identifies files encoded in Standard Generalized Markup Language. *See also* SGML.

SGML *n.* Acronym for **S**tandard **G**eneralized **M**arkup **L**anguage. An information management standard adopted by the International Organization for Standardization (ISO) in 1986 as a means of providing platform- and application-independent documents that retain formatting, indexing, and linked information. SGML provides a grammarlike mechanism for users to define the structure of their documents and the tags they will use to denote the structure in individual documents. *See also* ISO.

SGRAM *n. See* synchronous graphics RAM.

sh *n. See* Bourne shell.

SHA *n.* Acronym for **S**ecure **H**ash **A**lgorithm. A technique that computes a 160-bit condensed representation of a message or data file, called a *message digest*. The SHA is used by the sender and the receiver of a message in computing and verifying a digital signature, for security purposes. *See also* algorithm, digital signature.

shade[1] *n.* A particular color variation produced by mixing black with a pure color. *See also* brightness, IRGB.

shade[2] *vb.* To give added dimension to an image by including changes in appearance caused by light and shadow. *See also* color model.

shadow mask *n.* A type of mask used in cathode ray tube (CRT) monitors in which an opaque sheet perforated by tiny pinholes ensures that the electron beam for a particular color strikes only the phosphor it is supposed to illuminate. Like the aperture grill, which relies on vertical stripes, and the slot mask, which is based on elliptical openings, a shadow mask helps create a clear, sharp image by narrowly focusing the electron beam. *See also* CRT, mask (definition 2). *Compare* aperture grill, slot mask.

shadow memory *n.* A technique employed by the BIOS in some 80x86-based computers to copy the system's ROM BIOS routines into an unused section of RAM during the computer's startup process. This helps boost system performance by diverting system requests for the BIOS routines to their "shadow" copies. *Also called:* shadow RAM, shadow ROM.

shadow print *n.* A style applied to text in which a duplicate of each character is shifted, typically down and to the right, to create a shadow effect. See the illustration.

Shadow print.

shadow RAM *n. See* shadow memory.

shadow ROM *n. See* shadow memory.

share *vb.* To make files, directories, or folders accessible to other users over a network.

shared assembly *n.* An assembly that can be referenced by more than one application. An assembly must be explicitly built to be shared by giving it a cryptographically strong name. *See also* private assembly, strong name.

shared directory *n. See* network directory.

shared folder *n.* On a Macintosh computer connected to a network and running System 6.0 or higher, a folder that a user has made available to others on the network. A shared folder is analogous to a network directory on a PC. *See also* network directory.

shared logic *n.* The use, by multiple circuits or software routines, of common circuits or routines to implement an operation.

shared medium *n.* The communications medium shared by network nodes; essentially, the network bandwidth.

shared memory *n.* **1.** Memory accessed by more than one program in a multitasking environment. **2.** A portion of memory used by parallel-processor computer systems to exchange information. *See also* parallel processing.

shared name *n. See* strong name.

shared network directory *n. See* network directory.

shared printer *n.* A printer that receives input from more than one computer.

shared resource *n.* **1.** Any device, data, or program used by more than one device or program. **2.** On a network, any resource made available to network users, such as directories, files, and printers.

SharePoint team Web site *n.* A customizable Web site with features that help a team work together. The default site has pages for document libraries, announcements, and team events. Only members, specified by the site creator, can use the site.

shareware *n.* Copyrighted software that is distributed on a try-before-you-buy basis. Users who want to continue using the program after the trial period are encouraged to send a payment to the program's author. *Compare* free software, freeware, public-domain software.

sharpness *n. See* resolution (definition 1).

sheet *n.* A feature for handling dialog boxes included in the Mac OS X Aqua interface. When the user chooses to

S

save or print a document, a translucent sheet emerges from the window title bar and remains attached to that window even if it is moved to the background. The sheet allows the user to continue working in the window, or in other windows, without closing the sheet.

sheet-fed scanner *n.* A scanner with a single-sheet feed mechanism, in which sheets of paper are pulled in by the scanner and scanned as they pass over a stationary scanning mechanism. Sheet-fed scanners allow for automatic scanning of multiple-sheet documents. *See also* scanner. *Compare* drum scanner, flatbed scanner, handheld scanner.

sheet feeder *n.* A device that accepts a stack of paper and feeds it to a printer one page at a time.

shelfware *n.* Software that has been unsold or unused for a long time, and so has remained on a retailer's or user's shelf.

shell¹ *n.* A piece of software, usually a separate program, that provides direct communication between the user and the operating system. Examples of shells are Macintosh Finder and the MS-DOS command interface program COMMAND.COM. *See also* Bourne shell, C shell, Finder, Korn shell. *Compare* kernel.

shell² *vb. See* shell out.

shell account *n.* A computer service that permits a user to enter operating-system commands on the service provider's system through a command-line interface (usually one of the UNIX shells) rather than having to access the Internet through a graphical user interface. Shell accounts can provide Internet access through character-based tools such as Lynx for browsing the World Wide Web. *See also* shell¹.

shell archive *n.* In UNIX and GNU, a collection of compressed files that has been prepared for transmission by an e-mail service using the shar command.

shell out *vb.* To obtain temporary access to the operating-system shell without having to shut down the current application and return to that application after performing the desired shell function. Many UNIX programs allow the user to shell out; the user can do the same in windowing environments by switching to the main system window.

shell script *n.* A script executed by the command interpreter (shell) of an operating system. The term generally refers to scripts executed by the Bourne, C, and Korn shells on UNIX platforms. *Also called:* batch file. *See also* batch file, script, shell¹.

Shell sort *n.* A programming algorithm used for ordering data in which data are sorted in subsets so that the process works its way from unsorted to progressively more sorted. Named after its inventor, Donald Shell, it is faster than the bubble sort and the insertion sort. *See also* algorithm. *Compare* bubble sort, insertion sort.

Sherlock *n.* An advanced search mechanism included with the Macintosh OS. Sherlock provides the ability to search multiple Internet search engines simultaneously and incorporates the Macintosh Find File interface for searches of local volumes. Additional plug-ins can expand the number of search engines available for access and increase search options.

shielded twisted-pair wiring *n. See* twisted-pair wiring.

shift *vb.* In programming, to move the bit values one position to the left or right in a register or memory location. *See also* end-around shift. *Compare* rotate (definition 2).

Shift+click or **Shift click** *vb.* To click the mouse button while holding down the Shift key. Shift+clicking performs different operations in different applications, but its most common use in Windows is to allow users to select multiple items in a list, for example, to select a number of files for deletion or copying.

Shift key *n.* A keyboard key that, when pressed in combination with another key, gives that key an alternative meaning; for example, producing an uppercase character when a letter key is pressed. The Shift key is also used in various key combinations to create nonstandard characters or to perform special operations. The term is adapted from usage in relation to manual typewriters, in which the key physically shifted the carriage to print an alternative character. *See also* Caps Lock key.

Shift-PrtSc *n. See* Print Screen key.

shift register *n.* A circuit in which all bits are shifted one position at each clock cycle. It can be either linear (a bit is inserted at one end and "lost" at the other during each cycle) or it can be cyclic or looped (the "lost" bit is inserted back at the beginning). *See also* register, shift.

Shockwave *n.* A format for multimedia audio and video files within HTML documents, created by Macromedia, which markets a family of Shockwave servers and plug-in programs for Web browsers. *See also* HTML.

shopping cart *n.* In e-commerce programs, a file in which an online customer stores information on potential purchases until ready to order. Usually represented on screen with a drawing of a shopping cart, the virtual shopping cart provides a recognizable point of reference to users new to the e-commerce experience. *See also* e-commerce.

short card *n.* A printed circuit board that is half as long as a standard-size circuit board. *Also called:* half-card. *See also* printed circuit board.

short-circuit evaluation *n.* A form of expression evaluation that guarantees that Boolean expressions will be evaluated only far enough to determine their value. *See also* AND, Boolean operator, OR.

shortcut *n.* In Windows 9x, Windows XP, Windows NT 4, and Windows 2000, an icon on the desktop that a user can double-click to immediately access a program, a text or data file, or a Web page. *See also* symbolic link.

shortcut key *n. See* accelerator.

short-haul *adj.* Of or pertaining to a communications device that transmits a signal over a communications line for a distance less than approximately 20 miles. *Compare* long-haul.

short message service *n.* Service for wireless phones that allows users to send and receive brief messages consisting of text and numbers. *Acronym:* SMS.

shout *vb.* To use ALL CAPITAL LETTERS for emphasis in e-mail or a newsgroup article. Excessive shouting is considered a violation of netiquette. A word can be more acceptably emphasized by placing it between *asterisks* or _underscores_. *See also* netiquette.

shovelware *n.* A commercially sold CD-ROM containing a miscellaneous assortment of software, graphic images, text, or other data that could otherwise be obtained at little or no cost, such as freeware or shareware from the Internet and BBSs or public-domain clip art. *See also* BBS (definition 1), freeware, shareware.

ShowSounds *n.* In Windows 9x and Windows NT 4, a global flag that instructs application programs to provide some kind of visual indication that the program is generating a sound in order to alert users with hearing impairments or those in a noisy location such as a factory floor.

shredder *n.* An application designed to completely destroy digital data so it cannot be reconstructed with file recovery software.

shrinkwrap agreement *n.* A contract or license in or on a software box or package that sets forth conditions for use of the software. Typically, a shrinkwrap agreement

states that a user accepts the terms of the agreement when he or she opens the box. A shrinkwrap agreement is a print version of an End-User License Agreement. *Also called:* box-top license. *See also* End-User License Agreement. *Compare* clickwrap agreement.

shrink-wrapped *adj.* Boxed and sealed in clear plastic film for commercial distribution. Use of the term implies a final version of a product as opposed to a beta version. *See also* beta[1].

SHS virus *n.* Any of a class of viruses that infect a user's system by hiding in files with an .shs extension. These viruses typically spread through e-mail attachments. A widely distributed e-mail warning cautions readers to beware of the "SHS virus," but no one specific virus by that name exists.

SHTML *n.* Short for **s**erver-parsed **HTML**. Hypertext Markup Language (HTML) text that contains embedded server-side include commands. SHTML documents are fully read, parsed, and modified by the server before being passed to the browser. *See also* HTML, server-side include.

S-HTTP or **SHTTP** *n.* Acronym for **S**ecure **H**ypertext **T**ransfer **P**rotocol. An extension to HTTP that supports various encryption and authentication measures to keep all transactions secure from end to end. S-HTTP is designed to ensure the security of individual transmissions over the Internet and has been approved as a standard by the Internet Engineering Task Force (IETF). S-HTTP should not be confused with HTTPS, a Netscape-developed technology based on SSL (Secure Sockets Layer). HTTPS is also designed to ensure secure transmissions, but does so between communicating computers rather than on a message-by-message basis. *Also called:* Secure HTTP. *See also* SSL.

shut down *vb.* To close a program or an operating system in a manner ensuring that no data is lost.

sibling *n.* A process or node in a data tree that is descended from the same immediate ancestor(s) as other processes or nodes. *See also* generation (definition 2), node (definition 3).

sideband *n.* The upper or lower portion of a modulated carrier wave. One portion can be processed while the other is used to carry separate data, a technique that doubles the amount of information that can be carried over a single line. See the illustration.

S

Sideband.

sidebar *n.* A block of text placed to the side of the main body of text in a document, often set off by a border or other graphic element.

side-by-side execution *n.* The ability to install and use multiple versions of an assembly in isolation at the same time. This can occur on the same machine, or in the same process or application domain. Side-by-side execution can apply to applications and components as well as the components of the .NET Framework. Allowing assemblies to run side-by-side is essential to support robust versioning in the common language runtime.

side effect *n.* Any change of state caused by a subroutine, such as a routine that reads a value from a file and advances the current file position.

side head *n.* A heading placed in the margin of a printed document and top-aligned with the body text, rather than being vertically aligned with text, as is a normal head.

sieve of Eratosthenes *n.* An algorithm for finding prime numbers. It is often used as a benchmark in testing the speed of a computer or programming language. *See also* benchmark[1].

.sig *n.* A file extension for a signature file for e-mail or Internet newsgroup use. The contents of this file are automatically appended to e-mail correspondence or newsgroup articles by their respective client software. *See also* signature file (definition 1).

SIG *n.* Acronym for **s**pecial **i**nterest **g**roup. An e-mail online discussion group or a group of users who meet and share information, especially one of the groups supported by the Association for Computing Machinery (ACM), such as SIGGRAPH for computer graphics.

SIGGRAPH *n.* Short for **S**pecial **I**nterest **G**roup on Computer **Graph**ics, a part of the Association for Computing Machinery (ACM).

sigmoid function *n.* A kind of S-shaped mathematical function arising in many dynamical systems, including neural networks, because it is the solution to a first-order differential equation. It typically maps a real value, which may be arbitrarily large in magnitude (positive or nega-

tive), to another real value, which lies within some narrow range. The sigmoid function, in neural network computation literature, is also sometimes referred to as the logistic function. The reason for its prevalence is that it is thought to resemble the probability that a true neuron generates as an action potential in response to particular input and output. *See also* artificial intelligence, neural network.

sign *n.* The character used to indicate a positive or negative number. In assembly-level programming, the sign is indicated by the sign bit accompanying the number. *See also* sign bit.

signal *n.* **1.** Any electrical quantity, such as voltage, current, or frequency, that can be used to transmit information. **2.** A beep or tone from a computer's speaker or a prompt displayed on screen that tells a user that the computer is ready to receive input.

signal converter *n.* A device or circuit that converts a signal from one form to another, such as analog to digital, or pulse code modulation to frequency modulation.

signal-to-noise ratio *n.* The amount of power, measured in decibels, by which the signal exceeds the amount of channel noise at the same point in transmission. *Abbreviation:* S/N. *See also* noise (definition 2).

signature *n.* **1.** A sequence of data used for identification, such as text appended to an e-mail message or a fax. **2.** A unique number built into hardware or software for authentication purposes.

signature block *n.* A block of text that an e-mail client or a newsreader automatically places at the end of every message or article before the message or article is transmitted. Signature blocks typically contain the name, e-mail address, and affiliation of the person who created the message or article.

signature file *n.* **1.** A file that contains information inserted by a user and automatically appended to e-mail correspondence or newsgroup articles by client software. A signature file typically contains the name or nickname of the user and might include such information as the user's e-mail address, Web page, company, or job title. **2.** A file that updates an antivirus program so that the program recognizes signatures of new viruses and removes the viruses from the user's computer. *See also* antivirus program, virus signature.

sign bit *n.* The most significant, or leftmost, bit of a number field, usually set to 1 if the number is negative.

S

sign extension *n. See* sign bit.

significand *n. See* mantissa.

significant digits *n.* The sequence from the first nonzero digit to the last digit in a number (the last nonzero digit in an integer), used to express the number's precision (for example, 12,300 has three significant digits, and 0.000120300 has six). *See also* floating-point notation.

sign off *vb. See* log off.

sign on *vb. See* log on.

sign propagation *n. See* sign bit.

SIIA *n.* Acronym for **S**oftware & **I**nformation **I**ndustry **A**ssociation. A nonprofit trade association representing over 1200 high-tech companies worldwide and charged with watching over the interests of the software and digital content industry. The SIIA was formed in 1999 when the Software Publishers Association (SPA) merged with the Information Industry Association (IIA). The SIIA focuses on three areas: providing information and forums in which to distribute information to the high-tech industry; protection in the form of an antipiracy program geared to help members enforce their copyrights; and promotion and education.

silica gel *n.* A desiccant (moisture-absorbing substance) often packaged with optical or electronic equipment.

silicon *n.* A semiconductor used in many devices, especially microchips. Silicon, with atomic number 14 and atomic weight 28, is the second most common element in nature. *Compare* silicone.

Silicon Alley *n.* The Manhattan, New York, metropolitan area. Originally the term referred to the area of Manhattan below 41st Street, which had a heavy concentration of technology companies, but it now includes the entire island, reflecting the number of businesses involved in computer technology in that area. The name was inspired by Silicon Valley, the area of northern California that is home to many technology firms. *See also* Silicon Valley.

silicon chip *n.* An integrated circuit that uses silicon as its semiconductor material.

silicon-controlled rectifier *n.* A semiconductor rectifier whose conductance can be controlled by a gate signal. *Acronym:* SCR. *See also* gate (definition 1), rectifier.

silicon dioxide *n.* An insulator used to form thin insulating layers in some types of semiconductors; also the primary component of glass.

silicone *n.* A polymer in which silicon and oxygen are major components. Silicone is an excellent electrical insulator and conducts heat well. *Compare* silicon.

silicon foundry *n.* A factory or machine used to create wafers of crystalline silicon.

silicon on insulator *n. See* SOI.

silicon-on-sapphire *n.* A method of fabricating semiconductors in which the semiconductor devices are formed in a thin single layer of silicon that has been grown on an insulating substrate of synthetic sapphire. *Acronym:* SOS.

Silicon Valley *n.* The region of California south of San Francisco Bay, otherwise known as the Santa Clara Valley, roughly extending from Palo Alto to San Jose. Silicon Valley is a major center of electronics and computer research, development, and manufacturing. See the illustration.

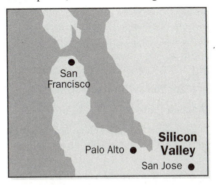

Silicon Valley.

Silicorn Valley *n.* Clusters of high-tech companies headquartered in small cities in the Midwestern United States, particularly in areas of rural Iowa.

SIM *n. See* Society for Information Management.

SIM card *n.* Short for **S**ubscriber **I**dentity **M**odule **card**. A smart card designed for use with GSM (Global System for Mobile Communications) mobile phones. SIM cards contain chips that store a subscriber's personal identifier (SIM PIN), billing information, and data (names, phone numbers). *See also* Global System for Mobile Communications, smart card (definition 2).

SIMD *n.* Acronym for **s**ingle-**i**nstruction, **m**ultiple-**d**ata stream processing. A category of parallel-processor computer architecture in which one instruction processor fetches instructions and distributes orders to several other processors. See the illustration. *See also* parallel processing. *Compare* MIMD.

S

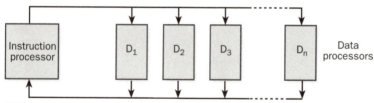

SIMD.

SIMM *n.* Acronym for single inline memory module. A small circuit board designed to accommodate surface-mount memory chips.

Simple API for XML *n. See* SAX.

Simple Authentication and Security Layer *n. See* SASL.

Simple Control Protocol *n. See* SCP.

Simple Mail Transfer Protocol *n.* A TCP/IP protocol for sending messages from one computer to another on a network. This protocol is used on the Internet to route e-mail. *Acronym:* SMTP. *See also* communications protocol, TCP/IP. *Compare* CCITT X series, Post Office Protocol.

Simple Network Management Protocol *n. See* SNMP.

Simple Object Access Protocol *n. See* SOAP.

simplex *n.* Communication that takes place only from sender to receiver. *Compare* duplex^2 (definition 1), half-duplex^2.

simplex transmission *n. See* simplex.

SIMULA *n.* Short for **simu**lation **la**nguage. A general-purpose programming language based on ALGOL 60, with special features designed to aid the description and simulation of active processes. Visual C++ is based on aspects of this language.

simulation *n.* The imitation of a physical process or an object by a program that causes a computer to respond mathematically to data and changing conditions as though it were the process or object itself. *See also* emulator, modeling (definition 1).

simultaneous access *n. See* parallel access.

simultaneous processing *n.* **1.** True multiple-processor operation in which more than one task can be processed at a time. *See also* multiprocessing, parallel processing. **2.** Loosely, concurrent operation in which more than one task is processed by dividing processor time among the tasks. *See also* concurrent, multitasking.

sine wave *n.* A uniform, periodic wave often generated by an object that vibrates at a single frequency. See the illustration. *Compare* square wave.

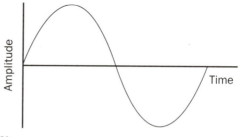

Sine wave.

single attachment station *n.* An FDDI node that connects to the primary ring through a concentrator. *Compare* dual attachment station.

single-board *adj.* Of or pertaining to a computer that occupies only one circuit board, usually with no capacity for additional boards.

single-density *adj.* Of or pertaining to a disk that is certified only for use with frequency modulation (FM) recording. A single-density disk can store much less data than a disk using modified FM encoding or run-length limited encoding. *See also* modified frequency modulation encoding, run-length limited encoding.

Single Image Random Dot Stereogram *n. See* autostereogram.

Single Image Stereograms *n. See* autostereogram.

single inline memory module *n. See* SIMM.

single inline package *n. See* SIP.

single inline pinned package *n. See* SIP.

single-instruction, multiple-data stream processing *n. See* SIMD.

single-line digital subscriber line *n. See* SDSL.

single-precision *adj.* Of or pertaining to a floating-point number having the least precision among two or more options commonly offered by a programming language, such as single-precision versus double-precision. *See also* floating-point notation, precision (definition 2). *Compare* double-precision.

single-sided *adj.* Of or pertaining to a floppy disk in which data can be stored on only one side.

single sign-on *n.* A system enabling a user to enter one name and password to log on to different computer systems or Web sites. Single sign-on is also available for enterprise systems so a user with a domain account can log on to a network once, using a password or smart card, and thereby gain access to any computer in the domain. *See also* domain, smart card (definition 1).

single step *vb.* To execute a program one step at a time, usually within the context of a debugger. *See also* debugger.

single switch device *n.* An assistive computer technology for people with mobility impairments. A single switch device allows users to interact with a computer by using slight body movements.

single threading *n.* **1.** Within a program, the running of a single process at a time. **2.** A condition in which each leaf node of a tree data structure contains a pointer to its parent. *See also* node (definition 3), pointer (definition 1), threading.

single-user computer *n.* A computer designed for use by a single individual; a personal computer. *Compare* multi-user system.

sink *n.* A device or part of a device that receives something from another device. *See also* data sink, heat sink.

SIP *n.* Acronym for **s**ingle **i**nline **p**ackage. A type of housing for an electronic component in which all leads (connections) protrude from one side of the package. *Also called:* single inline pinned package. *Compare* DIP.

SIPP *n.* Acronym for **s**ingle **i**nline **p**inned **p**ackage. *See* SIP.

SIR *n.* *See* Serial Infrared.

SirCam worm *n.* A malicious worm that combines fast infection with the potential to deliver multiple malicious payloads. SirCam spreads through multiple means, both by mailing infected personal files from a compromised disk to other potential victims and through Windows network shares on unprotected machines. One time in 20 Sir-Cam deletes the contents of the infected drive, and one time in 50 it fills all free space on the disk with trash data.

SirCam was discovered in mid-2001 and has reappeared regularly since that time.

SIRDS *n.* Acronym for **S**ingle **I**mage **R**andom **D**ot **S**tereogram. *See* autostereogram.

SIS *n.* Acronym for **S**ingle **I**mage **S**tereogram. *See* autostereogram.

.sit *n.* The file extension for a Macintosh file compressed with StuffIt. *See also* StuffIt.

site *n.* *See* Web site.

site license *n.* A purchase agreement for using multiple copies of the same software at a business or an institution, usually at a volume discount.

size box *n.* A control in the upper right corner of the frame of a window on the Macintosh screen. When the user clicks the size box, the window toggles between the size the user has set for it by dragging and the maximum size. *Compare* Maximize button.

skew *n.* The difference between what is and what should be—for example, the misalignment of a page that prevents accurate reproduction, or the difference between input and output when circuits do not respond evenly to a propagated signal.

skin *n.* An alternative graphical interface for an operating system (OS) or a software program. A skin customizes the look of the OS or program but does not affect its functionality. Programs that allow the use of skins usually make standards available for the creation and distribution of new skins. *See also* graphical user interface.

skin mode *n.* An operational state of various media players, including RealPlayer, Winamp, and Windows Media Player, in which the user interface is customized and displayed as a skin. Often some features of the player are not accessible in skin mode. Skin mode was called compact mode in Windows Media Player 7. *See also* full mode.

Skutch box *n.* A slang term for a device manufactured by Skutch Electronics, Inc., that simulates the functioning of a telephone line with a good connection. Telephone line simulators are used to test telecommunications systems and devices.

skyscraper *n.* One of several larger formats for online ads developed to replace traditional banner ads on the Internet. *See* avalanche ad.

S

slave *n.* Any device, including a computer, that is controlled by another computer, referred to as the master. *See also* master/slave arrangement.

sleep[1] *n.* **1.** In a multiprocessing environment, a temporary state of suspension during which a process remains in memory so that some event, such as an interrupt or a call from another process, can "awaken" it. **2.** In programming, a state of suspension caused by a loop statement that creates an intentional delay.

sleep[2] *vb.* To suspend operation without terminating.

sleep mode *n.* A power management mode that shuts down all unnecessary computer operations to save energy after it has received no input or other activity for a specified period of time. A computer in sleep mode usually awakens when it receives an input signal from a user or a network, such as a keyboard entry or an incoming call through a modem. Many battery-powered devices, including portable computers, support sleep mode. *See also* green PC, sleep[1] (definition 1), Suspend command.

sleeve *n. See* disk envelope.

slice *n. See* time slice.

SLIP *n.* Acronym for **S**erial **L**ine **I**nternet **P**rotocol. A data link protocol that allows transmission of TCP/IP data packets over dial-up telephone connections, thus enabling a computer or a LAN (local area network) to be connected to the Internet or some other network. It is an older, less secure protocol than the PPP (Point-to-Point Protocol) and does not support dynamic allocation of IP addresses. A newer form of SLIP, known as CSLIP (Compressed SLIP), optimizes transmission of long documents by compressing header information. *See also* data link, IP. *Compare* PPP.

SLIP emulator *n.* Software that mimics a SLIP connection in UNIX shell accounts that do not offer a direct SLIP connection. Many Internet service providers (ISPs) are UNIX based and offer shell accounts to users for Internet access. Like a SLIP connection, the SLIP emulator allows the user to avoid dealing with the ISP's UNIX environment directly when accessing the Internet and to use Internet applications such as graphical Web browsers. *See also* ISP, shell account, SLIP.

slot *n.* **1.** *See* expansion slot. **2.** An integrated circuit mounting connector designed to connect a microprocessor with a PC's data bus. Currently, only newer models of

Intel's Pentium family employ this. *See also* Pentium, Slot 1, Slot 2.

Slot 1 *n.* A receptacle on a PC motherboard designed to hold a Pentium II microprocessor. The microprocessor, which is encased in Intel's Single Edge Contact (SEC) packaging, slides into the slot on the motherboard. Slot 1 includes 242 electrical contact points and communicates with the chip's L2 cache at half of the PC's clock speed. Slot 1 replaced socket 7 and socket 8 in Intel architectures, but has been superceded by Slot 2 in newer model Pentiums. *See also* L2 cache, motherboard, Pentium. *Compare* Slot 2, socket 7, socket 8.

Slot 2 *n.* A receptacle on a PC motherboard designed to hold Intel microprocessors beginning with the Pentium II Xeon and including the Pentium III microprocessor. Like Slot 1, Slot 2 is encased in Intel's Single Edge Contact packaging, so it slides easily into the slot on the motherboard. It includes 330 electrical contact points and is slightly wider than Slot 1. It also supports communication between the CPU and the L2 cache at the full clock speed of the PC. *See also* L2 cache, motherboard, Pentium. *Compare* Slot 1.

slot mask *n.* A type of mask used in cathode ray tube (CRT) monitors in which a thin sheet of metal perforated with elliptical holes is used to ensure that the electron beam for a particular color (red, green, or blue) strikes only the phosphor (of the corresponding color) that it is intended to illuminate. The elliptical—lozenge-shaped—holes in a slot mask place it between a shadow mask, which is based on round openings, and an aperture grill, which is based on vertical strips of metal. Slot masks were introduced by NEC in its CromaClear technology. *See also* CRT, mask (definition 2). *Compare* aperture grill, shadow mask.

slot pitch *n.* The distance, measured horizontally, between phosphor dots of the same color on a cathode ray tube (CRT) display based on slot mask technology. Although the measurements are based on different methods of applying phosphor to the screen surface, slot pitch is comparable to dot pitch, the measurement used with CRTs based on shadow mask technology. *See also* CRT, mask (definition 2), slot mask. *Compare* dot pitch, stripe pitch.

slotted-ring network *n.* A ring network allowing data to be transmitted between data stations in one direction. A slotted-ring network transfers data in predefined time slots (fixed-length portions of a data frame) in the transmission stream over one transmission medium. *See also* data frame, ring network. *Compare* token ring network.

SlowKeys *n.* An accessibility feature built into Macintosh computers and available for DOS and Windows that allows the user to add a delay to the keyboard so that a key must be held down for a certain amount of time before it is accepted. This feature facilitates the use of the keyboard by individuals with poor motor control who might accidentally bump keys when moving around the keyboard.

SLSI *n. See* super-large-scale integration.

Small Business Server *n.* A software application developed by Microsoft Corporation to increase the efficiency of Web-based services for small businesses with 50 or fewer personal computers. Small Business Server provides shared Internet access, features for building Web-based customer management and customer communications tools, and additional features that increase productivity by streamlining employee access to files and applications over the Web.

small caps *n.* A font of capital letters that are smaller than the standard capital letters in that typeface.

Small Computer System Interface *n. See* SCSI.

small model *n.* A memory model of the Intel 80x86 processor family that allows only 64 kilobytes (KB) for code and 64 KB for data. *See also* memory model.

Small Office/Home Office *n. See* SOHO.

small-scale integration *n.* A concentration of fewer than 10 components on a single chip. *Acronym:* SSI. *See also* integrated circuit.

Smalltalk *n.* An object-oriented language and development system developed at Xerox Palo Alto Research Center (PARC) in 1980. Smalltalk pioneered many language and user interface concepts that are now widely used in other environments, such as the concept of an object that contains data and routines and on-screen icons that the user can choose to make the computer perform certain tasks. *See also* object-oriented programming.

smart *adj.* A synonym for intelligent. *See* intelligence.

smart cable *n. See* intelligent cable.

smart card *n.* **1.** In computers and electronics, a circuit board with built-in logic or firmware that gives it some kind of independent decision-making ability. **2.** In banking and finance, a credit card that contains an integrated cir-

cuit that gives it a limited amount of intelligence and memory.

smart card reader *n.* A device that is installed in computers to enable the use of smart cards for enhanced security features. *See also* smart card (definition 2).

smart device *n.* An electronic device capable of being networked and remotely controlled in a smart home. Smart devices can include appliances, lighting, heating and cooling systems, entertainment systems, and security systems. *See also* home automation, home network (definition 1), smart home.

smart home *n.* A home or building wired for networking and home automation. In a smart home, occupants control smart devices programmatically or on command using a home-networking communications protocol. *Also called:* automated home, digital home, e-home, Internet home, networked home, smart house, wired home. *See also* home automation, home network (definition 1).

smart house *n. See* smart home.

smart linkage *n.* A feature of programming languages that guarantees that routines will always be called with correct parameter types. *See also* link (definition 1).

smartphone *n.* A hybrid between a wireless telephone and a personal digital assistant (PDA). Smartphones integrate wireless telephones with many of the personal organizational functions of PDAs, such as calendar, calculator, database, e-mail, wireless Web access, note taking, and other programs common to lightweight palm-style computers. Smartphones may rely on a stylus, keypad, or both for data entry or may use voice recognition technology. *See also* cell, palmtop, PDA, pen computer, wireless phone.

smart quotes *n.* In word processors, a function that automatically converts the ditto marks (") produced by most computer keyboards to the inverted commas (" and ") used in typeset text.

SmartSuite *n.* A suite of business application programs sold by Lotus Development. Lotus SmartSuite includes six programs: Lotus 1-2-3 spreadsheet, Lotus WordPro word processor, Lotus Approach database, Lotus Freelance Graphics presentation software, Lotus Organizer time-management software, and Lotus FastSite Internet/intranet publishing tool. SmartSuite Millennium Edition 9.7 supports collaboration, Web publishing, use of Internet/intranet resources, and customizable document and project organizers. SmartSuite competes with Microsoft Office and WordPerfect Office.

S

SMART system *n.* Short for **s**elf-**m**onitoring **a**nalysis and **r**eporting **t**echnology **system**. A system by which technology is used to monitor and predict device performance and reliability. A SMART system employs various diagnostic tests to detect problems with devices, with the object of increasing productivity and protecting data.

smart terminal *n.* A terminal that contains a microprocessor and random access memory (RAM) and that does some rudimentary processing without intervention from the host computer. *Compare* dumb terminal.

SMB *n.* Acronym for **S**erver **M**essage **B**lock. A file-sharing protocol designed to allow networked computers to transparently access files that reside on remote systems over a variety of networks. The SMB protocol defines a series of commands that pass information between computers. SMB uses four message types: session control, file, printer, and message. *See also* LAN Manager, NetBIOS, Samba.

SMDS *n.* Acronym for **S**witched **M**ultimegabit **D**ata Services. A very high-speed, connectionless, packet-switched data transport service that connects LANs (local area networks) and WANs (wide area networks).

SMIL *n.* Acronym for **S**ynchronized **M**ultimedia **I**ntegration **L**anguage. A markup language that enables separate elements, including audio, video, text, and still images, to be accessed separately and then integrated and played back as a synchronized multimedia presentation. Based on XML (eXtensible Markup Language), SMIL allows Web authors to define the objects in the presentation, describe their locations onscreen, and determine when they will be played back. The language is based on statements that can be entered with a text editor and was developed under the auspices of the World Wide Web Consortium (W3C). *See also* markup language, XML.

smiley *n. See* emoticon.

S/MIME *n.* Acronym for **S**ecure/**M**ultipurpose **I**nternet **M**ail **E**xtensions. An Internet e-mail security-oriented protocol that adds public key encryption and support for digital signatures to the widely used MIME e-mail protocol. *See also* public key encryption.

SMIS *n.* Acronym for **S**ociety for **M**anagement Information **S**ystems. *See* Society for Information Management.

smoke test *n.* The testing of a piece of hardware after assembly or repairs by turning it on. The device fails the test if it produces smoke, explodes, or has some other unexpected violent or dramatic reaction, even if it appears to work.

smooth *vb.* **1.** To eliminate irregularities in statistical data by some process such as continuous averaging or by removing random (irrelevant) values. **2.** In graphics, to remove jagged edges from a figure or line. *See also* anti-aliasing.

SMP *n.* Acronym for **s**ymmetric **m**ulti**p**rocessing. A computer architecture in which multiple processors share the same memory, which contains one copy of the operating system, one copy of any applications that are in use, and one copy of the data. Because the operating system divides the workload into tasks and assigns those tasks to whichever processors are free, SMP reduces transaction time. *See also* architecture, multiprocessing.

SMP server *n.* Short for **s**ymmetric **m**ulti**p**rocessing **server**. A computer that is designed with the SMP architecture to improve its performance as a server in client/server applications. *See also* SMP.

SMS *n. See* Systems Management Server.

SMS *n. See* short message service.

SMT *n. See* surface-mount technology.

SMTP *n. See* Simple Mail Transfer Protocol.

smurf attack *n.* A form of denial-of-service attack on an Internet server that sends simultaneous echo request packets ("ping" packets) to one or more broadcast IP addresses (such as an IRC server), each of which in turn relays the request to as many as 255 individual host computers, with the address of the attack's victim as the forged (spoofed) source address. When the hosts return echo packets to the apparent source of the request, the volume of the responses is enough to disable the network. *See also* denial of service attack, spoofing.

SNA *n.* Acronym for **S**ystems **N**etwork **A**rchitecture. A network model devised by IBM to enable IBM products, including mainframes, terminals, and peripherals, to communicate and exchange data. SNA started out as a five-layer model and was later extended with two additional layers to correspond more closely to the ISO/OSI reference model. More recently, the SNA model was modified to include minicomputers and microcomputers in a specification known as APPC (Advanced Program to Program Communications). See the illustration. *See also* APPC. *Compare* ISO/OSI reference model.

ISO Open Systems Interconnection

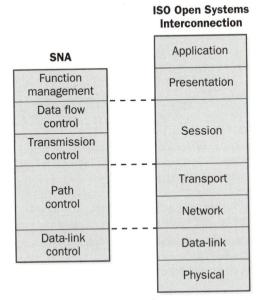

SNA. *Comparable (not compatible) layers in the SNA and ISO/OSI architechures.*

snail mail *n.* A popular phrase on the Internet for referring to mail services provided by the U.S. Postal Service and similar agencies in other countries. The term has its origins in the fact that regular postal mail is slow compared with e-mail.

snap-in *n.* **1.** *See* plug-in. **2.** A software component that provides system administration and system management capability within the framework of the Microsoft Management Console (MMC) for Windows NT, Windows 2000, and Windows XP. A snap-in (also capitalized as Snap-In) is a COM object that represents one unit of management behavior, the smallest extension available through the MMC. There are two types of snap-ins: stand-alone (not reliant on any other snap-in) and extension (invoked by a parent snap-in). Multiple snap-ins can be combined to create larger management tools.

snapshot *n.* A copy of main memory or video memory at a given instant, sent to the printer or hard disk. *Also called:* snapshot dump. *See also* screen dump.

snapshot program *n.* A program that performs a trace by taking a snapshot of certain chunks of memory at specified times.

.snd *n.* A file extension for a type of interchangeable sound file format used on Sun, NeXT, and Silicon Graphics computers, consisting of raw audio data preceded by a text identifier.

sneaker *n.* An individual employed by a company or organization to test their security by breaking into the employer's network. Information gathered by the sneaker can be used to repair network security weaknesses. *See also* tiger team.

sneakernet *n.* Transfer of data between computers that are not networked together. The files must be written onto floppy disks on the source machine, and a person must physically transport the disks to the destination machine.

sniffer *n. See* packet sniffer.

SNMP *n.* Acronym for **S**imple **N**etwork **M**anagement **P**rotocol. The network management protocol of TCP/IP. In SNMP, agents, which can be hardware as well as software, monitor the activity in the various devices on the network and report to the network console workstation. Control information about each device is maintained in a structure known as a management information block. *See also* agent (definition 4), TCP/IP.

SNOBOL *n.* Acronym for **S**tring-**O**riented **S**ym**bol**ic Language. A string- and text-processing language developed between 1962 and 1967 by Ralph Griswold, David Farber, and I. Polonsky at AT&T Bell Laboratories. *See also* string.

snow *n.* **1.** In television, temporary distortion of a displayed image caused by interference, usually in a weak signal, that takes the form of random white spots. **2.** In computer displays, a specific type of distortion characterized by the blinking on and off of random pixels that occurs when the microprocessor and the display hardware interfere with each other by attempting to use the computer's video memory at the same time.

SOAP *n.* Acronym for **S**imple **O**bject **A**ccess **P**rotocol. A simple, XML-based protocol for exchanging structured and type information on the Web. The protocol contains

S

no application or transport semantics, which makes it highly modular and extensible.

SOC *n.* Acronym for **s**ystem **o**n a **c**hip. A chip integrating computer, microprocessors, and all necessary support components in a single unit. SOC technology is used in firewalls, gateways, specialized servers, and interactive devices like Web pads and vending machines.

social engineering *n.* The practice of penetrating system security by tricking individuals into divulging passwords and information about network vulnerabilities. Often done by calling the individual on phone and pretending to be another employee of company with a computer-related question.

Society for Information Management *n.* A professional society based in Chicago for information systems executives, formerly the Society for Management Information Systems. *Acronym:* SIM.

Society for Management Information Systems *n. See* Society for Information Management.

socket *n.* **1.** An identifier for a particular service on a particular node on a network. The socket consists of a node address and a port number, which identifies the service. For example, port 80 on an Internet node indicates a Web server. *See also* port number, sockets API. **2.** The receptacle part of a connector, which receives a plug. *See also* female connector. **3.** A receptacle on a PC motherboard into which a microprocessor is plugged. A socket-mounted microprocessor, such as the Pentium, connects to the motherboard through numerous pins on the underside. Newer Intel microprocessors, such as the Pentium II and later, plug into the motherboard through an edge connector along the side of the chip. *See also* socket 4, socket 5, socket 7, socket 8. *Compare* Slot 1, Slot 2.

socket 4 *n.* A 5-volt mounting socket on a PC motherboard designed to hold a Pentium microprocessor operating at 60 MHz or 66 MHz. Socket 4 includes openings for 273 pins. *See also* Pentium, socket (definition 3). *Compare* Slot 1, Slot 2, socket 5, socket 7, socket 8.

socket 5 *n.* A 3.3-volt mounting socket on a PC motherboard designed to hold a Pentium microprocessor operating at the following speeds: 75, 90, 100, 120, 133, 150, 166, 180, and 200 MHz. Socket 5 includes openings for 320 pins. It has been superceded by socket 7, socket 8, slot 1, and slot 2. *See also* Pentium, socket (definition 3). *Compare* Slot 1, Slot 2, socket 4, socket 7, socket 8.

socket 7 *n.* A mounting socket on a PC motherboard designed to hold a microprocessor operating at the following speeds: 150, 166, 180, 200, 210, and 233 MHz. Socket 7 includes openings for 321 pins and operates at two voltages, 2.5 volts at the core and 3.3 volts input/output. It is used with the Pentium MMX chip and competitive microprocessor chips from other manufacturers, such as AMD and Cyrix. *See also* MMX, Pentium, socket (definition 3). *Compare* Slot 1, Slot 2, socket 4, socket 5, socket 8.

socket 8 *n.* A 2.5-volt mounting socket on a PC motherboard designed to hold a Pentium Pro microprocessor. Socket 8 has openings for 387 pins. *See also* Pentium, socket (definition 3). *Compare* Slot 1, Slot 2, socket 4, socket 5, socket 7.

sockets API *n.* An application programming interface implemented to create and use sockets in client/server networking. The most common sockets API is the University of California at Berkeley UNIX/BSD implementation (Berkeley Sockets API), which is the basis for Winsock. *See also* socket (definition 1).

soc. newsgroups *n.* Usenet newsgroups that are part of the soc. hierarchy and have the prefix soc. These newsgroups are devoted to discussions of current events and social issues. Soc. newsgroups are one of the seven original Usenet newsgroup hierarchies. The other six are comp., misc., news., rec., sci., and talk. *See also* newsgroup, traditional newsgroup hierarchy, Usenet.

soft *adj.* **1.** In computing, temporary or changeable. For example, a soft error is a problem from which the system can recover, and a soft patch is a temporary program fix that holds only while the program is running. *Compare* hard (definition 1). **2.** In electronics, characterized by magnetic materials that do not retain their magnetism when a magnetic field is removed. *Compare* hard (definition 2).

soft boot *n. See* warm boot.

soft copy *n.* The temporary images presented on a computer display screen. *Compare* hard copy.

soft error *n.* An error from which a program or operating system is able to recover. *Compare* hard error.

soft font *n. See* downloadable font.

soft hyphen *n. See* hyphen.

soft link *n. See* symbolic link.

softmodem *n. See* software-based modem.

soft patch *n.* A fix or modification performed only while the code being patched is loaded into memory, so that the executable or object file is not modified in any way. *See also* patch[1].

soft return *n.* A line break inserted in a document by a word processor when the next word in the current line of text would cause the line to overflow into the margin—a movable line break. *See also* wordwrap. *Compare* hard return.

soft-sectored disk *n.* A disk, especially a floppy disk, whose sectors have been marked with recorded data marks rather than punched holes. *See also* index hole. *Compare* hard-sectored disk.

software *n.* Computer programs; instructions that make hardware work. Two main types of software are system software (operating systems), which controls the workings of the computer, and applications, such as word processing programs, spreadsheets, and databases, which perform the tasks for which people use computers. Two additional categories, which are neither system nor application software but contain elements of both, are network software, which enables groups of computers to communicate, and language software, which provides programmers with the tools they need to write programs. In addition to these task-based categories, several types of software are described based on their method of distribution. These include packaged software (canned programs), sold primarily through retail outlets; freeware and public domain software, which are distributed free of charge; shareware, which is also distributed free of charge, although users are requested to pay a small registration fee for continued use of the program; and vaporware, software that is announced by a company or individuals but either never makes it to market or is very late. *See also* application, canned software, freeware, network software, operating system, shareware, system software, vaporware. *Compare* firmware, hardware, liveware.

Software & Information Industry Association *n.* See SIIA.

software-based modem *n.* A modem that uses a general-purpose, reprogrammable digital signal processor chip and RAM-based program memory rather than a dedicated chip with the modem functions burned into the silicon. A software-based modem can be reconfigured to update and change the modem's features and functions.

software bloat *n.* A software condition caused by the addition of excessive number of possibly unnecessary features and functions as new versions of the software are released. Software bloat is generally assumed to result in long loading times and inordinate resource (memory and storage) requirements. *See also* bloatware, creeping featurism.

software conversion *n.* Changing or moving a program designed to run on one computer to run on another. Usually this involves detailed (professional) work on the program itself.

software-dependent *adj.* Of, pertaining to, or being a computer or device that is tied to a particular program or set of programs developed for it.

software development kit *n. See* developer's kit.

software engineer *n.* **1.** In general, one who works at the code level with software. Although such engineering can be considered to encompass everything from software design to management and testing, the term is generally considered more or less synonymous with *programmer*— one who actually writes the code. **2.** *See* developer.

software engineering *n.* The design and development of software. *See also* programming.

software handshake *n.* A handshake that consists of signals transmitted over the same wires used to transfer the data, as in modem-to-modem communications over telephone lines, rather than signals transmitted over special wires. *See also* handshake.

software house *n.* An organization that develops and supports software for its customers.

software IC *n. See* software integrated circuit.

software integrated circuit *n.* An existing software module that can be designed into a program, much as an integrated circuit can be designed into a logic board. *Abbreviation:* software IC. *See also* abstract data type, module (definition 1), object-oriented programming.

software interrupt *n.* A program-generated interrupt that stops current processing in order to request a service provided by an interrupt handler (a separate set of instructions designed to perform the task required). *Also called:* trap.

software package *n.* A program sold to the public, ready to run and containing all necessary components and documentation.

software piracy *n. See* piracy.

S

software portability *n. See* portable (definition 1).

software program *n. See* application.

software protection *n. See* copy protection.

software publisher *n.* A business engaged in the development and distribution of computer software.

Software Publishers Association *n. See* SIIA.

software publishing *n.* The design, development, and distribution of noncustom software packages.

software rot *n. See* dead code.

software stack *n. See* stack.

software suite *n. See* suite (definition 1).

software tools *n.* Programs, utilities, libraries, and other aids, such as editors, compilers, and debuggers, that can be used to develop programs.

SOHO *n.* Acronym for **S**mall **O**ffice/**H**ome **O**ffice, a term used for home-based and small businesses. The fast-growing SOHO market has sparked a concomitant expansion in computer software and hardware products designed specifically to meet the needs of self-employed individuals or small businesses. *See also* distributed workplace, telecommuter.

SOI *n.* Acronym for **s**ilicon **o**n **i**nsulator. A method used in the construction of microprocessors in which the chip's transistors—the tiny circuits that conduct electrical charges—are built on a layer of silicon placed on top of a layer of insulating material, such as glass. SOI construction improves speed at the same time it reduces the amount of power required by the microprocessor.

solar cell *n.* A photoelectric device that produces electrical power when exposed to light. *Also called:* photovoltaic cell.

Solaris *n.* A distributed UNIX-based computing environment created by Sun Microsystems, Inc., widely used as a server operating system. Versions of Solaris exist for SPARC computers, 386 and higher Intel platforms, and the PowerPC.

solenoid *n.* An electromagnetic device that converts electrical energy to mechanical movement, typically consisting of an electromagnet with a movable rod through the center.

solid ink *n.* Ink manufactured in the form of solid sticks resembling crayons, for use in solid-ink printers. *See also* solid-ink printer.

solid-ink printer *n.* A computer printer using solid ink sticks. The ink sticks are heated until they melt, and the molten ink is sprayed onto the page, where it cools and solidifies. *See also* solid ink.

solid model *n.* A geometric shape or construction that has continuity in length, width, and depth and is treated by a program as if it had both surface and internal substance. *Compare* surface modeling, wire-frame model.

solid-state device *n.* A circuit component whose properties depend on the electrical or magnetic characteristics of a solid substance (as opposed to a gas or vacuum). Transistors, diodes, and integrated circuits are solid-state devices.

solid-state disk drive *n.* A mass storage device that holds data in RAM rather than in magnetic storage. *See also* magnetic storage, RAM.

solid-state memory *n.* Computer memory that stores information in solid-state devices.

solid-state relay *n.* A relay that depends on solid-state components, rather than mechanical components, to open and close a circuit.

SOM *n.* **1.** Acronym for **S**ystem **O**bject **M**odel. A language-independent architecture from IBM that implements the CORBA standard. *See also* CORBA, OMA. **2.** Acronym for **s**elf-**o**rganizing **m**ap. A form of neural network in which neurons and their connections are added automatically as needed to develop the desired mapping from input to output.

SONET *n.* Acronym for **S**ynchronous **O**ptical **Net**work. A high-speed network that provides a standard interface for communications carriers to connect networks based on fiberoptic cable. SONET is designed to handle multiple data types (voice, video, and so on). It transmits at a base rate of 51.84 Mbps, but multiples of this base rate go as high as 2.488 Gbps (gigabits per second).

sort *vb.* To organize data, typically a set of records, in a particular order. Programs and programming algorithms for sorting vary in performance and application. *See also* bubble sort, distributive sort, insertion sort, merge sort, quicksort, Shell sort.

sort algorithm *n.* An algorithm that puts a collection of data elements into some sequenced order, sometimes based on one or more key values in each element. *See also* algorithm, bubble sort, distributive sort, insertion sort, merge sort, quicksort, Shell sort.

sorter *n.* A program or routine that sorts data. *See also* sort.

sort field *n. See* sort key.

sort key *n.* A field (commonly called a key) whose entries are sorted to produce a desired arrangement of the records containing the field. *See also* field (definition 1), primary key, secondary key.

SOS *n. See* silicon-on-sapphire.

Sound Blaster *n.* **1.** A family of sound cards manufactured by Creative Technology or its subsidiary, Creative Labs. *See also* sound card. **2.** A de facto standard set by the family of sound cards developed by Creative Technologies and its subsidiaries. Many other manufacturers also make Sound Blaster–compatible products.

sound board *n. See* sound card.

sound buffer *n.* A region of memory used to store the bit image of a sequence of sounds to be sent to a computer's speaker(s).

sound card *n.* A type of expansion board on PC-compatible computers that allows the playback and recording of sound, such as from a WAV or MIDI file or a music CD-ROM. Most PCs sold at retail include a sound card. *Also called:* sound board. *See also* expansion board, MIDI, WAV.

sound clip *n.* A file that contains a short audio item, usually an excerpt from a longer recording.

sound editor *n.* A program that allows the user to create and manipulate sound files.

sound generator *n.* A chip or chip-level circuit that can produce electronic signals that can drive a speaker and synthesize sound.

sound hood *n.* A five-sided box, lined with soundproofing material, that is placed over a loud printer to muffle its noise.

SoundSentry *n.* An optional Windows feature that instructs Windows to produce a visual cue such as a screen flash or a blinking title bar whenever a system beep occurs. SoundSentry is designed for users with hearing impairments or users who operate a computer in a noisy environment.

source *n.* **1.** In information processing, a disk, file, document, or other collection of information from which data is taken or moved. *Compare* destination. **2.** In a FET, the electrode toward which charge carriers (electrons or holes) move from the source under control of the gate. *See also*

CMOS (definition 1), drain (definition 1), FET, gate (definition 2), MOSFET, NMOS, PMOS.

source code *n.* Human-readable program statements written by a programmer or developer in a high-level or assembly language that are not directly readable by a computer. Source code needs to be compiled into object code before it can be executed by a computer. *Compare* object code.

source code control system *n.* A tool designed to track changes made to source code files. Changes are documented in such a way that previous versions of the files can be retrieved. Source code control is used in software development, particularly in situations involving concurrent development and multiple user access to source code files.

source computer *n.* **1.** A computer on which a program is compiled. *Compare* object computer. **2.** A computer from which data is transferred to another computer.

source data *n.* The original data on which a computer application is based.

source data acquisition *n.* The process of sensing, as with a bar code reader or other scanning device, or receiving source data. *See also* source data.

source data capture *n. See* source data acquisition.

source directory *n.* During a file copy operation, the directory in which the original versions of the files are located.

source disk *n.* Any disk from which data will be read, as during a copy operation or when an application is loaded from a disk into memory. *Compare* target disk.

source document *n.* The original document from which data is taken.

source drive *n.* The disk drive from which files are being copied during a copy operation.

source file *n.* **1.** A file that contains source code. *See also* source code. **2.** A file that contains the data that a program will process and store in a destination file. **3.** In MS-DOS and Windows commands that involve the copying of data or program instructions, the file containing the data or instructions that are copied.

source language *n.* The programming language in which the source code for a program is written. *See also* programming language, source code.

source program *n.* The source code version of a program. *See also* source code. *Compare* executable program.

S

source statement *n.* A single statement in the source code of a program. *See also* source code, statement.

SPA *n. See* SIIA.

spacebar *n.* The long key occupying much of the bottom row of most keyboards that sends a space character to the computer.

space character *n.* A character that is entered by pressing the Spacebar on the keyboard and that typically appears on the screen as a blank space.

space-division multiplexing *n.* The first automated form of communications multiplexing, which replaced the human-operated switchboard. Space-division multiplexing was replaced by frequency-division multiplexing (FDM), which was in turn replaced by time-division multiplexing (TDM). *Acronym:* SDM. *See also* FDM, multiplexing, time-division multiplexing.

spaghetti code *n.* Code that results in convoluted program flow, usually because of excessive or inappropriate use of GOTO or JUMP statements. *See also* GOTO statement, jump instruction.

spam¹ *vb.* To distribute unwanted, unrequested mail widely on the Internet by posting a message to too many recipients or too many newsgroups. The act of distributing such mail, known as spamming, angers most Internet users and has been known to invite retaliation, often in the form of return spamming that can flood and possibly disable the electronic mailbox of the original spammer.

spam² *n.* **1.** An unsolicited e-mail message sent to many recipients at one time, or a news article posted simultaneously to many newsgroups. Spam is the electronic equivalent of junk mail. In most cases, the content of a spam message or article is not relevant to the topic of the newsgroup or the interests of the recipient; spam is an abuse of the Internet in order to distribute a message to a huge number of people at minimal cost. **2.** An unsolicited e-mail message from a business or individual that seeks to sell the recipient something. *Also called:* UCE, unsolicited commercial e-mail.

spam blocking *n. See* address munging.

spambot *n.* A program or device that automatically posts large amounts of repetitive or otherwise inappropriate material to newsgroups on the Internet. *See also* bot (definition 3), robopost, spam¹.

spamdexter *n.* An individual who lures users to spam-related Web sites by loading the site with hundreds of hid-

den copies of popular keywords, even if those words have no relation to the Web site. Because the keywords appear so many times, the spamdexter's site will appear near the top of search result and indexing lists. The term spamdexter was created by combining the words *spam* and *index*. *Also called:* keyword stuffing.

span *n. See* range.

SPARC *n.* Short for Scalable Processor Architecture. A RISC (reduced instruction set computing) microprocessor specification from Sun Microsystems, Inc. *See also* RISC.

sparse array *n.* An array (arrangement of items) in which many of the entries are identical, commonly zero. It is not possible to define precisely when an array is sparse, but it is clear that at some point, usually when about one-third of the array consists of identical entries, it becomes worthwhile to redefine the array. *See also* array.

sparse infector *n.* A type of virus or other malicious code that delivers its payload only when certain predetermined conditions are met. A sparse infector might hide on an infected computer until a certain date or until a certain number of files or applications have been run. By restricting their active phases to only certain situations, sparse infectors are more likely to avoid detection.

spatial data management *n.* The representation of data as a collection of objects in space, particularly as icons on a screen, in order to make the data easier to comprehend and manipulate.

spatial digitizer *n.* A three-dimensional scanner most often used in medical and geographical work. *Compare* optical scanner.

speaker dependent recognition *n.* A type of automatic speech recognition (ASR) in which the computer system becomes accustomed to the voice and accent of a specific speaker, allowing a larger vocabulary can be recognized. *See also* ASR, speaker independent recognition.

speaker independent recognition *n.* A type of automatic speech recognition (ASR) in which the computer system will respond to commands from any speaker. Because the system does not adjust to the nuances of a specific voice, only a limited vocabulary is possible. *See also* ASR, speaker dependent recognition.

spec *n. See* specification.

special character *n.* Any character that is not alphabetic, numeric, or the space character (for example, a

S

punctuation character). *See also* reserved character, wild-card character.

special interest group *n. See* SIG.

special-purpose language *n.* A programming language whose syntax and semantics are best suited for a given field or approach. *See also* Prolog.

specification *n.* **1.** A detailed description of something. **2.** In relation to computer hardware, an item of information about the computer's components, capabilities, and features. **3.** In relation to software, a description of the operating environment and proposed features of a new program. **4.** In information processing, a description of the data records, programs, and procedures involved in a particular task. *Also called:* spec.

spectral color *n.* In video, the hue represented by a single wavelength in the visible spectrum. *See also* color model.

spectral response *n.* In relation to sensing devices, the relationship between the device's sensitivity and the frequency of the detected energy.

spectrum *n.* The range of frequencies of a particular type of radiation. *See also* electromagnetic spectrum.

Speech API *n. See* SAPI.

Speech Application Programming Interface *n. See* SAPI.

speech recognition *n. See* voice recognition.

Speech Recognition API *n. See* SRAPI.

Speech Recognition Application Programming Interface *n. See* SRAPI.

speech synthesis *n.* The ability of a computer to produce "spoken" words. Speech synthesis is produced either by splicing together prerecorded words or by programming the computer to produce the sounds that make up spoken words. *See also* artificial intelligence, neural network, synthesizer.

spelling checker *n.* An application that employs a disk-based dictionary to check for misspellings in a document. *Also called:* spell checker.

spew *vb.* On the Internet, to post an excessive number of e-mail messages or newsgroup articles.

spider *n.* An automated program that searches the Internet for new Web documents and indexes their addresses and content-related information in a database, which can be examined for matches by a search engine. Spiders are generally considered to be a type of bot, or Internet robot.

Also called: crawler. *See also* bot (definition 3), search engine (definition 2).

spike *n.* A transient electrical signal of very short duration and usually high amplitude. *Compare* surge.

spindle *n.* **1.** An axle for mounting a disk or reel of magnetic tape. **2.** Any drive included within the chassis of a laptop or other portable computer. A laptop including a floppy disk drive and a hard drive would be considered a two-spindle machine.

spintronics *n.* An emerging field of study in electronics and physics that is based on the ability to detect and control the spin of electrons in magnetic materials. Using spintronics, it might eventually be possible to produce small, fast electronic devices, including transistors, memory devices, and quantum computers.

Spirale virus *n. See* Hybris virus.

splash screen *n.* A screen containing graphics, animation, or other attention-getting elements that appears while a program is loading or as an introductory page to a Web site. A splash screen used with an application typically contains a logo, version information, author credits, or a copyright notice, and it appears when a user opens a program and disappears when loading is complete. A splash screen used on a Web site serves as a front door, typically loading before any content-related pages.

spline *n.* In computer graphics, a curve calculated by a mathematical function that connects separate points with a high degree of smoothness. See the illustration. *See also* Bézier curve.

Spline.

split screen *n.* A display method in which a program can divide the display area into two or more sections, which can contain different files or show different parts of the same file.

spoiler *n.* A post to a newsgroup or mailing list that reveals what is intended to be a surprise, such as a plot twist in a film or television episode or the solution to a

S

game. The subject line should contain the word *spoiler*, but netiquette requires that the sender further protect readers who do not or cannot scan posts for subject lines in advance by encrypting the post, putting one or more screenfuls of white space above the text, or both. *See also* netiquette.

spoofing *n.* The practice of making a transmission appear to come from an authorized user. For example, in IP spoofing, a transmission is given the IP address of an authorized user in order to obtain access to a computer or network. *See also* IP address.

spool *vb.* To store a data document in a queue, where it awaits its turn to be printed. *See also* print spooler.

spot *n.* A "composite dot" produced through the halftone creation process on a PostScript printer that consists of a group of dots arranged in a pattern reflecting the gray level of a particular pixel. *See also* gray scale, halftone. *Compare* dot (definition 2).

spot color *n.* A method of handling color in a document in which a particular color of ink is specified and each page having elements in that color is printed as a separate layer. The printer then prints one layer for each spot color in the document. *See also* color model, color separation (definition 1), PANTONE MATCHING SYSTEM. *Compare* process color.

spot function *n.* The PostScript procedure used to create a given type of screen in a halftone. *See also* halftone, PostScript, spot.

SPP *n. See* scalable parallel processing.

spraycan *n.* An artist's tool in Paintbrush or another graphics application for applying a pattern of dots to an image.

spreadsheet program *n.* An application commonly used for budgets, forecasting, and other finance-related tasks that organizes data values using cells, where the relationships between cells are defined by formulas. A change to one cell produces changes to related cells. Spreadsheet programs usually provide graphing capabilities for output and a variety of formatting options for text, numeric values, and graph features. *See also* cell (definition 1).

spread spectrum *adj.* Of or pertaining to a system of secure radio communication in which the content of a transmission is broken into split-second pieces, which are transmitted over separate frequencies. When a receiver identifies a spread spectrum signal, it reassembles it to its original form. Spread spectrum was invented

by the actress Hedy Lamarr in 1940, but it was not used until 1962.

Springboard *n.* Handspring Inc.'s expansion platform for its line of Visor handheld personal digital assistants. The term describes both the 68-pin Springboard socket incorporated into the Visor, as well as a series of add-on Springboard modules that fit into the socket. Add-on modules include features such as multimedia, games, e-books, additional memory storage, and a wireless phone module. *See also* Visor.

sprite *n.* In computer graphics, a small image that can be moved on the screen independently of other images in the background. Sprites are widely used in animation sequences and video games. *See also* object (definition 3).

sprocket feed *n.* A paper feed in which pins engage holes in the paper to move it through a printer. Pin feed and tractor feed are both sprocket feeds. *See also* paper feed, pin feed, tractor feed.

SPX *n.* **1.** Acronym for Sequenced Packet Exchange. The transport level (ISO/OSI level 4) protocol used by Novell NetWare. SPX uses IPX to transfer the packets, but SPX ensures that messages are complete. *See also* ISO/OSI reference model. *Compare* IPX. **2.** Acronym for **simplex**. *See* simplex.

SQL *n. See* structured query language.

square wave *n.* A blocklike waveform that is generated by a source that changes instantly between alternate states, usually at a single frequency. See the illustration. *Compare* sine wave.

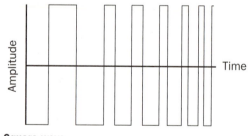

Square wave.

SRAM *n. See* static RAM.

SRAPI *n.* Acronym for Speech Recognition Application Programming Interface. A cross-platform application programming interface for speech recognition and text-to-speech functions supported by a consortium of developers including Novell, IBM, Intel, and Philips Dictation Systems. *See also* application programming interface, speech recognition.

SSA *n.* Acronym for **S**erial **S**torage **A**rchitecture. An interface specification from IBM in which devices are arranged in a ring topology. In SSA, which is compatible with SCSI devices, data can be transferred at up to 20 megabytes per second in each direction. *See also* SCSI device.

SSD *n.* Acronym for **s**olid-**s**tate **d**isk. *See* solid-state disk drive.

SSE *n.* Short for **S**treaming **SIMD** **E**xtensions. A set of 70 new instructions implemented in Intel's Pentium III microprocessor. SSE, more formally called Internet SSE (ISSE), uses SIMD (single-instruction, multiple-data) operations to accelerate floating point calculations. Designed to improve performance in visual areas such as real-time 3-D and graphics rendering, SSE also provides support for development of such applications as real-time video and speech recognition. *See also* SIMD.

SSI *n.* **1.** *See* small-scale integration. **2.** *See* server-side include.

SSL *n.* Acronym for **S**ecure **S**ockets **L**ayer. A protocol developed by Netscape Communications Corporation for ensuring security and privacy in Internet communications. SSL supports authentication of client, server, or both, as well as encryption during a communications session. While primary purpose of SSL is to enable secure electronic financial transactions on the World Wide Web, it is designed to work with other Internet services as well. This technology, which uses public key encryption, is incorporated into the Netscape Navigator Web browser and Netscape's commerce servers. *See also* commerce server, open standard, public key encryption, PCT. *Compare* S-HTTP.

SSO *n.* *See* single sign-on.

ST506 interface *n.* The hardware signal specification developed by Seagate Technologies for hard-disk-drive controllers and connectors. The ST506/412 version of this interface has become a de facto standard.

stack *n.* A region of reserved memory in which programs store status data such as procedure and function call addresses, passed parameters, and sometimes local variables. *See also* pop, push (definition 1). *Compare* heap (definition 1).

stacking order *n.* The order in which layers in a digital graphic file are arranged. Foreground elements are typically stacked on top of background elements. Changes in stacking order can affect the way the final graphic is seen by the viewer. *See also* layering.

stack pointer *n.* A register that contains the current address of the top element of the stack. *See also* pointer (definition 1), stack.

stackware *n.* A HyperCard application consisting of a HyperCard data stack and HyperCard programming. *See also* HyperCard.

staging web *n.* A local Web site maintained on a file system or local Web server that currently cannot be browsed by site visitors. These Web sites allow authors and workgroups to make changes or updates to Web sites before they are published.

staging Web server *n.* A Web server where you publish and test your Web site before putting it on a production server. A staging Web server cannot be browsed by an Internet or intranet audience.

stairstepping *n.* A rough outline like the steps of a stair in a graphic line or curve that should be smooth. *Also called:* aliasing, jaggies.

stale link *n.* A hyperlink to an HTML document that has been deleted or moved, rendering the hyperlink useless. *See also* HTML document, hyperlink.

stale pointer bug *n.* *See* aliasing bug.

stand-alone or **standalone** *adj.* Of, pertaining to, or being a device that does not require support from another device or system, for example, a computer that is not connected to a network.

standard *n.* **1.** A de jure technical guideline advocated by a recognized noncommercial or government organization that is used to establish uniformity in an area of hardware or software development. The standard is the result of a formal process, based on specifications drafted by a cooperative group or committee after an intensive study of existing methods, approaches, and technological trends and developments. The proposed standard is later ratified or approved by a recognized organization and adopted over time by consensus as products based on the standard become increasingly prevalent in the market. Standards of this type are numerous, including the ASCII character set, the RS-232-C standard, the SCSI interface, and ANSI-standard programming languages, such as C and FORTRAN. *See also* ANSI, convention, RS-232-C standard,

S

SCSI. **2.** A de facto technical guideline for hardware or software development that occurs when a product or philosophy is developed by a single company and, through success and imitation, becomes so widely used that deviation from the norm causes compatibility problems or limits marketability. This type of highly informal standard setting is exemplified by Hayes-compatible modems and IBM PC–compatible computers. *See also* compatibility (definition 3).

standard ASCII *n.* The set of characters assigned to ASCII (American Standard Code for Information Interchange) values between decimal 0 and 127 (hexadecimal 00 through 7F). These characters include most found on a standard keyboard, including the letters A–Z (uppercase and lowercase), numerals (0 through 9), and some special characters, such as colons and parentheses. Standard ASCII has for years been used as a near-universal "common language" in the PC environment for enabling different programs to exchange information reliably. *See also* ASCII. *Compare* Extended ASCII.

standard deviation *n.* In statistics, a measure of the dispersion of a group of measurements relative to the mean (average) of that group. Each score's difference from the mean is squared, and the standard deviation is defined as the square root of the average of these squared values.

standard disclaimer *n.* A phrase placed in an e-mail message or news article that is intended to replace the statement required by some businesses and institutions that the contents of the message or article do not necessarily represent the opinions or policies of the organization from whose e-mail system the message originated.

standard function *n.* A function that is always available within a particular programming language. *See also* function (definition 1).

Standard Generalized Markup Language *n. See* SGML.

standby *n.* A state in which your computer consumes less power when it is idle but remains available for immediate use. While your computer is on standby, information in computer memory is not saved on your hard disk. If there is an interruption in power, the information in memory is lost.

star *n. See* *.

star bus *n.* A network topology in which nodes connect to hubs in a star pattern, but the hubs are connected by a bus trunk. Star bus is a combination of star and bus topologies.

star-dot-star or **star dot star** *n.* A file specification (*.*) using the asterisk wildcard, which means "any combination of file name and extension" in operating systems such as MS-DOS. *See also* *.*, asterisk, wildcard character.

star network *n.* A LAN (local area network) in which each device (node) is connected to a central computer in a star-shaped configuration (topology); commonly, a network consisting of a central computer (the hub) surrounded by terminals. See the illustration. *Compare* bus network, ring network.

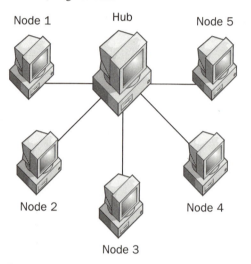

Node 1   Hub   Node 5

Node 2   Node 4

Node 3

Star network.

start bit *n.* In asynchronous transmission, the bit (actually, a timing signal) that represents the beginning of a character. *See also* asynchronous transmission. *Compare* parity bit, stop bit.

Start button *n.* In Microsoft Windows 9x and Windows NT 4 and later, the control on the desktop task bar that opens the main menu.

starting point *n.* A World Wide Web document designed to help users begin navigating the Web. A starting point often contains tools such as search engines and hyperlinks to selected Web sites. *See also* hyperlink, search engine (definition 2), World Wide Web.

star topology *n.* A network configuration based on a central hub, from which nodes radiate in a star-shaped pattern. *See also* topology.

start page *n. See* home page (definition 2).

start/stop transmission *n. See* asynchronous transmission.

startup *n. See* boot[1].

startup application *n.* On the Macintosh, the application that takes control of the system when the computer is turned on.

STARTUP.CMD *n.* A special-purpose batch file stored in the root directory of the startup disk in OS/2—the OS/2 equivalent of an MS-DOS AUTOEXEC.BAT file.

startup disk *n. See* system disk.

startup ROM *n.* The bootstrap instructions coded into a computer's ROM (read-only memory) and executed at startup. The startup ROM routines enable a computer to check itself and its devices (such as the keyboard and disk drives), prepare itself for operation, and run a short program to load an operating-system loader program. *See also* boot[1], power-on self test.

startup screen *n.* A text or graphics display that appears on the screen when a program is started (run). Startup screens usually contain information about the software's version and often contain a product or corporate logo.

star-wired ring *n.* A network topology in which hubs and nodes connect to a central hub in typical star fashion, but the connections within the central hub form a ring. Star-wired ring is a combination of star and ring topologies.

state *n. See* status.

stateful *adj.* Of or pertaining to a system or process that monitors all details of the state of an activity in which it participates. For example, stateful handling of messages takes account of their content. *Compare* stateless.

stateless *adj.* Of or pertaining to a system or process that participates in an activity without monitoring all details of its state. For example, stateless handling of messages might take account of only their sources and destinations but not their content. *Compare* stateful.

statement *n.* The smallest executable entity within a programming language.

state-of-the-art *adj.* Up to date; at the forefront of current hardware or software technology.

static[1] *adj.* In information processing, fixed or predetermined. For example, a static memory buffer remains invariant in size throughout program execution. The opposite condition is *dynamic*, or ever-changing.

static[2] *n.* In communications, a crackling noise caused by electrical interference with a transmitted signal. *See also* noise (definition 2).

static allocation *n.* Apportionment of memory that occurs once, usually when the program starts. The memory remains allocated during the program's execution and is not deallocated until the program is finished. *See also* allocate, deallocate. *Compare* dynamic allocation.

static binding *n.* Binding (converting symbolic addresses in the program to storage-related addresses) that occurs during program compilation or linkage. *Also called:* early binding. *Compare* dynamic binding.

static buffer *n.* A secondary sound buffer that contains an entire sound; these buffers are convenient because the entire sound can be written once to the buffer. *See also* streaming buffer.

static electricity *n.* An electrical charge accumulated in an object. Although generally harmless to humans, the discharge of static electricity through an electronic circuit can cause severe damage to the circuit.

static RAM *n.* A form of semiconductor memory (RAM) based on the logic circuit known as a flip-flop, which retains information as long as there is enough power to run the device. Static RAMs are usually reserved for use in caches. *Acronym:* SRAM. *See also* cache, RAM, synchronous burst static RAM. *Compare* dynamic RAM.

static routing *n.* Routing based on a fixed forwarding path. Unlike dynamic routing, static routing does not adjust to changing network conditions. *Compare* dynamic routing.

static Web page *n.* Web page that displays the same content to all viewers. Usually written in hypertext markup language (HTML), a static Web page displays content that changes only if the HTML code is altered. *See also* dynamic Web page.

station *n.* **1.** In the IEEE 802.11 wireless LAN specification, a single, often mobile, node. **2.** *See* workstation.

stationery[1] *adj.* Describing a type of document that, when opened by the user, is duplicated by the system; the copy is opened for the user's modification while the original document remains intact. Stationery documents can be used as document templates or boilerplates. *See also* boilerplate, template (definition 5).

stationery[2] *n.* A stationery document. *See also* stationery[1].

S

statistical multiplexer *n.* A multiplexing device that adds intelligence to time-division multiplexing by using buffering (temporary storage) and a microprocessor to combine transmission streams into a single signal and to allocate available bandwidth dynamically. *Also called:* stat mux. *See also* dynamic allocation, multiplexing, time-division multiplexing.

statistics *n.* The branch of mathematics that deals with the relationships among groups of measurements and with the relevance of similarities and differences in those relationships. *See also* binomial distribution, Monte Carlo method, probability, regression analysis, standard deviation, stochastic.

stat mux *n. See* statistical multiplexer.

status *n.* The condition at a particular time of any of numerous elements of computing—a device, a communications channel, a network station, a program, a bit, or other element—used to report on or to control computer operations.

status bar *n.* In Windows 9x and Windows NT 4 and later, a space at the bottom of many program windows that contains a short text message about the current condition of the program. Some programs also display an explanation of the currently selected menu command in the status bar. See the illustration.

| Page 2 | Sec 1 | 2/46 | At 4" | Ln 19 | Col 9 | |

Status bar.

status codes *n.* Strings of digits or other characters that indicate the success or failure of some attempted action. Status codes were commonly used to report the results of early computer programs, but most software today uses words or graphics. Internet users, especially those with UNIX shell accounts, are likely to encounter status codes while using the Web or FTP. *See also* HTTP status codes.

steganography *n.* A "hide-in-plain-sight" technique for concealing information by embedding a message within an innocuous cover message. In steganography, bits of unnecessary data within an image, sound, text, or even a blank file are replaced with bits of invisible information. The term steganography comes from the Greek for "covered writing" and has traditionally included any method of secret communication that conceals the existence of the message. Because steganography cannot be detected by decryption software, it is often used to replace or supplement encryption.

step-frame *n.* The process of capturing video images one frame at a time. This process is used by computers that are too slow to capture analog video images in real time.

stepper motor *n.* A mechanical device that rotates only a fixed distance each time it receives an electrical pulse. A stepper motor is part of a disk drive.

step-rate time *n.* The time required to move a disk actuator arm from one track to the next. *See also* actuator, stepper motor.

stereogram *n. See* autostereogram.

sticky *adj.* In reference to a Web site, properties such as targeted content or services that increase the amount of time users choose to spend at the site and increase user's desire to return to the site repeatedly.

StickyKeys *n.* An accessibility feature built into Macintosh and Windows computers that causes modifier keys such as Shift, Control, or Alt to "stay on" after they are pressed, eliminating the need to press multiple keys simultaneously. This feature facilitates the use of modifier keys by users who are unable to hold down one key while pressing another.

stochastic *adj.* Based on random occurrences. For example, a stochastic model describes a system by taking into account chance events as well as planned events.

stop bit *n.* In asynchronous transmission, a bit that signals the end of a character. In early electromechanical teleprinters, the stop bit provided time for the receiving mechanism to coast back to the idle position and, depending on the mechanism, had a duration of 1, 1.5, or 2 data bits. *See also* asynchronous transmission. *Compare* parity bit, start bit.

Stop error *n.* A serious error that affects the operating system and that could place data at risk. The operating system generates an obvious message, a screen with the Stop error, rather than continuing on and possibly corrupting data. *Also called:* blue screen error, fatal system error. *See also* Blue Screen of Death.

storage *n.* In computing, any device in or on which information can be kept. Microcomputers have two main types of storage: random access memory (RAM) and disk drives and other external storage media. Other types of storage include read-only memory (ROM) and buffers.

storage area network *n.* A high-speed network that provides a direct connection between servers and storage, including shared storage, clusters, and disaster-recovery devices. A storage area network, or SAN, includes components such as hubs and routers that are also used in local area networks (LANs), but it differs in being something of a "subnetwork" dedicated to providing a high-speed connection between storage elements and servers. Most SANs rely on fiber-channel connections that deliver speeds up to 1000 Mbps and can support up to 128 devices. SANs are implemented to provide the scalability, speed, and manageability required in environments that demand high data availability. *Acronym:* SAN. *Also called:* system area network.

storage device *n.* An apparatus for recording computer data in permanent or semipermanent form. When a distinction is made between primary (main) storage devices and secondary (auxiliary) storage devices, the former refers to random access memory (RAM) and the latter refers to disk drives and other external devices.

storage location *n.* The position at which a particular item can be found—either an addressed location or a uniquely identified location on a disk, tape, or similar medium.

storage media *n.* The various types of physical material on which data bits are written and stored, such as floppy disks, hard disks, tape, and optical discs.

storage tube *n. See* direct view storage tube.

store-and-forward *n.* A method of delivering transmissions in which messages are held temporarily by an intermediary before being sent on to their destination. Store and forward is used by some switches in delivering packets to their destinations. *Compare* cut-through switch.

stored procedure *n.* A precompiled collection of SQL statements and optional control-of-flow statements stored under a name and processed as a unit. They are stored in an SQL database and can be run with one call from an application.

stored program concept *n.* A system architecture scheme, credited largely to the mathematician John von Neumann, in which both programs and data are in direct-access storage (random access memory, or RAM), thereby allowing code and data to be treated interchangeably. *See also* von Neumann architecture.

storefront *n. See* virtual storefront.

storm *n.* On a network, a sudden, excessive burst of traffic. Storms are often responsible for network outages.

STP *n.* Acronym for **s**hielded **t**wisted **p**air. A cable consisting of one or more twisted pairs of wires and a sheath of foil and copper braid. The twists protect the pairs from interference by each other, and the shielding protects the pairs from interference from outside. Therefore, STP cable can be used for high-speed transmission over long distances. *See also* twisted-pair cable. *Compare* UTP.

straight-line code *n.* Program code that follows a direct sequence of statements rather than skipping ahead or jumping back via transfer statements such as GOTO and JUMP. *See also* GOTO statement, jump instruction. *Compare* spaghetti code.

stream[1] *n.* Any data transmission, such as the movement of a file between disk and memory, that occurs in a continuous flow. Manipulating a data stream is a programming task. Consumers, however, are likely to encounter references to streams and streaming in connection to the Internet, which has increased reliance on stream techniques to enable users (even those with slower equipment) to access large multimedia files—especially those containing audio and video components—and to display or play them before all the data has been transferred.

stream[2] *vb.* To transfer data continuously, beginning to end, in a steady flow. Many aspects of computing rely on the ability to stream data: file input and output, for example, and communications. If necessary, an application receiving a stream must be able to save the information to a buffer in order to prevent loss of data. On the Internet, streaming enables users to begin accessing and using a file before it has been transmitted in its entirety.

stream cipher *n.* A method for encrypting a data sequence of unlimited length using a key of fixed length. *See also* key (definition 3). *Compare* block cipher.

streaming *n.* **1.** On the Internet, the process of delivering information, especially multimedia sound or video, in a steady flow that the recipient can access as the file is being transmitted. **2.** In magnetic tape storage devices, a low-cost technique to control the motion of the tape by removing tape buffers. Although streaming tape compromises start/stop performance, it achieves highly reliable storage and retrieval of data, and is useful when a steady supply of data is required by a particular application or computer.

streaming buffer *n.* A small sound buffer that can play lengthy sounds because the application dynamically loads audio data into the buffer as it plays. For example, an application could use a buffer that can hold 3 seconds of audio data to play a 2-minute sound. A streaming buffer requires much less memory than a static buffer. *See also* static buffer.

S

Streaming Server *n.* A server technology designed by Apple Computer to send streaming QuickTime media files over the Internet. Built on RTP and RTSP standard Internet protocols, Streaming Server can set up a QuickTime streaming media Web broadcasting station capable of streaming digital videos and music files to more than 3000 users via the Internet. Streaming Server may be used with Mac OS X and other UNIX-based operating systems. *Also called:* Darwin Streaming Server, QuickTime Streaming Server.

streaming tape *n. See* tape (definition 1).

stream interface device driver *n.* A user-level DLL that controls devices connected to a Windows CE–based platform. A stream interface device driver presents the services of a hardware device to applications by exposing Win32 stream interface functions. Stream interface drivers also can control devices built into a Windows CE–based platform, depending on the software architecture for the drivers. *Also called:* installable device driver.

stream-oriented file *n.* A file used to store a fairly continuous series of bits, bytes, or other small, structurally uniform units.

street price *n.* The actual retail or mail-order price of a consumer hardware or software product. In most cases, the street price is somewhat lower than the "suggested retail price."

stress test *n.* A test of a software or hardware system's functional limits, performed by subjecting the system to extreme conditions, such as peak volumes of data or extremes in temperature.

strikethrough *n.* One or more lines drawn through a selected range of text, usually to show deletion or the intent to delete. See the illustration.

Strikethrough.

string *n.* A data structure composed of a sequence of characters usually representing human-readable text.

string variable *n.* An arbitrary name assigned by the programmer to a string of alphanumeric characters and used to reference that entire string. *See also* string.

stripe *vb. See* disk striping.

stripe pitch *n.* The distance, measured horizontally, between bands of phosphor that are the same color on a cathode ray tube (CRT) display based on aperture grill technology. Although the measurements are based on different methods of applying phosphor to the screen surface, stripe pitch is comparable to dot pitch, the measurement used with CRTs based on shadow mask technology. *See also* aperture grill, CRT, mask (definition 2). *Compare* dot pitch, slot pitch.

striping *n.* A means of protecting data on a network by spreading it across multiple disks. In the most commonly used approach, striping is combined with parity (error-correcting information) to ensure that if some portion of the data is lost, it can be reconstructed. Striping is implemented in RAID security. *See also* RAID. *Compare* disk mirroring.

strobe *n.* A timing signal that initiates and coordinates the passage of data, typically through an input/output (I/O) device interface, such as a keyboard or printer.

stroke *n.* **1.** In data entry, a keystroke—a signal to the computer that a key has been pressed. **2.** In typography, a line representing part of a letter. **3.** In paint programs, a "swipe" of the brush made with the mouse or keyboard in creating a graphic. **4.** In display technology, a line created as a vector (a path between two coordinates) on a vector graphics display (as opposed to a line of pixels drawn dot by dot on a raster graphics display).

stroke font *n.* A font printed by drawing a combination of lines rather than by filling a shape, as with an outline font. *Compare* outline font.

stroke weight *n.* The width, or thickness, of the lines (strokes) that make up a character. *See also* font.

stroke writer *n.* In video, a display unit that draws characters and graphic images as sets of strokes—lines or curves connecting points—rather than as sets of dots, as on a typical raster-scan monitor. *See also* vector graphics.

StrongARM *n.* The architecture underlying Intel's low-power, high-performance SA microprocessors. StrongARM is based on the 32-bit RISC architecture licensed by ARM Limited. StrongARM-based SA microprocessors support a number of platforms, including Windows CE and Java, and are designed for use in four primary areas:

smart portable devices, such as cellular phones and hand-held computers; Internet access devices, such as set-top boxes; networking devices, such as switches and routers; and embedded controls, such as entertainment devices and automation equipment. *See also* ARM.

strong name *n.* A name that consists of an assembly's identity: its simple text name, version number, and often the culture information strengthened by a public key and a digital signature generated over the assembly. Assemblies with the same strong name are expected to be identical.

strong typing *n.* A characteristic of a programming language that does not allow the program to change the data type of a variable during program execution. *See also* data type, variable. *Compare* weak typing.

structure *n.* **1.** The design and composition of a program, including program flow, hierarchy, and modularity. **2.** A collection of data elements. *See also* data structure.

structured graphics *n. See* object-oriented graphics.

structured programming *n.* Programming that produces programs with clean flow, clear design, and a degree of modularity or hierarchical structure. *See also* modular programming, object-oriented programming. *Compare* spaghetti code.

structured query language *n.* A database sublanguage used in querying, updating, and managing relational databases—the de facto standard for database products. *Acronym:* SQL.

structured walkthrough *n.* **1.** A meeting of programmers working on different aspects of a software development project, in which the programmers attempt to coordinate the various segments of the overall project. The goals, requirements, and components of the project are systematically reviewed in order to minimize the error rate of the software under development. **2.** A method for examining a computer system, including its design and implementation, in a systematic fashion.

STT *n. See* Secure Transaction Technology.

stub *n.* A routine that contains no executable code and that generally consists of comments describing what will eventually be there; it is used as a placeholder for a routine to be written later. *Also called:* dummy routine. *See also* top-down programming.

StuffIt *n.* A file compression program originally written for the Apple Macintosh, used for storing a file on one or more disks. Originally shareware, StuffIt is now a commercial product for Macs and PCs that supports multiple compression techniques and allows file viewing. StuffIt files can be uncompressed using a freeware program, StuffIt Expander.

style sheet *n.* **1.** A file of instructions used to apply character, paragraph, and page layout formats in word processing and desktop publishing. **2.** A text file containing code to apply semantics such as page layout specifications to an HTML document. *See also* HTML document, semantics (definition 1).

stylus *n.* A pointing device, similar to a pen, used to make selections, usually by tapping, and to enter information on the touch-sensitive surface.

subclass *n.* A class in object-oriented programming that is derived from, and inherits its attributes and methods from, another class known as a superclass. *Compare* superclass.

subcommand *n.* A command in a submenu (a menu that appears when a user selects an option in a higher-level menu).

subdirectory *n.* A directory (logical grouping of related files) within another directory.

subdomain *n.* A domain, often representing an administrative or other organizational subgroup within a second-level domain. *See also* domain.

subform *n.* A form contained within another form or a report.

subject drift *n. See* topic drift.

subject tree *n.* A type of World Wide Web index that is organized by subject categories, many of which are broken down into subcategories, or "branches." An example of a World Wide Web subject tree is Yahoo! *See also* Yahoo!

submarining *n.* A phenomenon that occurs when some part of a screen display moves more quickly than the screen can show. The object (such as the mouse pointer) disappears from the screen and reappears where it comes to rest, just as a submarine resurfaces after a dive. Submarining is especially a problem with the slowly responding passive-matrix LCD displays on many laptop computers.

submenu *n.* A menu that appears as the result of the selection of an item on another, higher-level menu.

S

subnet *n.* **1.** In general, a network that forms part of a larger network. **2.** In terms of the ISO/OSI reference model, the subnet comprises the layers below the transport layer—that is, the network, data link, and physical layers.

subnet mask *n. See* address mask.

subnetting *n.* The division of a network into subnets to improve network security and performance. *See also* subnet (definition 1). *Compare* supernetting.

subnetwork *n.* A network that is part of another, larger network.

subnotebook *n.* A class of portable computer that is smaller in size and lighter in weight than a full-sized laptop. Subnotebooks feature a reduced-sized keyboard and screen and often use an external floppy drive to save space and weight. Despite their size, subnotebooks retain all the functions of a full-sized portable computer.

subportable *n. See* subnotebook.

subprogram *n.* A term used in some languages for *routine* (procedure or function) because the structure and syntax of a subprogram closely model those of a program. *See also* program, routine.

subreport *n.* A report contained within another report.

subroutine *n.* A common term for *routine*, likely to be used in reference to shorter, general, frequently called routines. *See also* procedure, routine.

subschema *n.* The definition of a user view of the database (in CODASYL/DBTG systems only), roughly equivalent to the external schema of an ANSI/X3/SPARC database management system or to a view in a relational database management system. *See also* schema.

subscribe *vb.* **1.** To add a newsgroup to the list of such groups from which a user receives all new articles. **2.** To add a name to a LISTSERV distribution list. *See also* LISTSERV.

Subscriber Identity Module card *n. See* SIM card.

subscript *n.* **1.** One or more characters printed slightly below the baseline of surrounding text. *See also* baseline. *Compare* superscript. **2.** In programming, one or more numbers or variables that identify the location of an element in an array. *See also* array, index (definition 2).

subscription site *n.* E-commerce Web site that provides information or services to customers who pay a subscription fee.

substrate *n.* The inactive supporting material used in a manufacturing process. In circuit boards, it is the base to which the traces (foil areas) are attached. In tapes and disks, it is the material on which the magnetic particles are fused.

substring *n.* A sequential section of a string. *See also* string.

subtransaction *n. See* nested transaction.

subtree *n.* Any node within a tree, along with any selection of connected descendant nodes. *See also* node (definition 3), tree.

subweb *n.* A named subdirectory of the root Web site that is a complete FrontPage-based Web site. Each subweb can have independent administration, authoring, and browsing permissions from the root Web site and other subwebs.

suitcase *n.* A file on Macintosh computers that contains one or more fonts or desk accessories. In early versions of the operating system, such files are indicated with the icon of a suitcase. *See also* font suitcase.

suite *n.* **1.** A set of application programs sold as a package, usually at a lower price than that of the individual applications sold separately. A suite for office work, for example, might contain a word processing program, a spreadsheet, a database management program, and a communications program. **2.** *See* protocol suite.

summarize *vb.* To post the results of a survey or vote in short form to a newsgroup or mailing list after collecting the results by e-mail.

SunOS *n.* Short for **Sun O**perating **S**ystem. A variety of the UNIX operating system used on workstations from Sun Microsystems, Inc.

superclass *n.* A class in object-oriented programming from which another class—a subclass—is derived. The subclass inherits its attributes and methods from the superclass. *Compare* subclass.

supercomputer *n.* A large, extremely fast, and expensive computer used for complex or sophisticated calculations. *See also* computer.

superconductor *n.* A substance that has no resistance to the flow of electricity.

SuperDrive *n.* An Apple 3.5-inch disk drive that can read and write in both Apple Macintosh (400K and 800K) and MS-DOS/Windows (720K and 1.44-MB) formats.

super-large-scale integration *n.* A reference to the density with which components (transistors and other elements) are packed onto an integrated circuit and to the fineness of the connections between them. The actual number of components is nonspecific, but generally considered to be in of 50,000 to 100,000 range. *Acronym:* SLSI. *See also* integrated circuit. *Compare* large-scale integration, medium-scale integration, small-scale integration, ultra-large-scale integration, very-large-scale integration.

superminicomputer *n. See* computer.

supernetting *n.* The aggregation of multiple network addresses of the same class into a single block. *See also* classless interdomain routing, IP address classes. *Compare* subnetting.

superpipelining *n.* A method of preprocessing used by some microprocessors in which two or more of a microprocessor's execution stages (fetch, decode, execute, and write-back) are divided into two or more pipelined stages, resulting in higher performance. *See also* DECchip 21064, pipelining (definition 1).

superscalar *adj.* Of, pertaining to, or being a microprocessor architecture that enables the microprocessor to execute multiple instructions per clock cycle. *See also* CISC, RISC.

superscript *n.* A character printed slightly above the surrounding text, usually in smaller type. *Compare* subscript (definition 1).

superserver *n.* A network server with especially high capabilities for speed and data storage. *See also* server (definition 1).

superstitial *n.* An Internet ad format that downloads in the background while a user is viewing a Web page and then plays in a pop-up window when triggered by a mouse click or a break in surfing. Because the superstitial doesn't appear until it has completely downloaded and temporarily cached itself on the user's system, attention-getting effects like animation, sound, and large graphics can be used without slowing down the ad. Unicast developed the "polite cache and play" technology used with the superstitial ad format.

supertwist display *n.* A form of passive-matrix liquid crystal displays (LCDs) that rotates polarized light as it passes through liquid crystal molecules in which the top and bottom orientations of the molecules causes them to twist 180 to 270 degrees. This technology is used to improve contrast and widen the screen's viewing angle. Supertwist displays, also known as supertwist nematic displays, are widely used and are less expensive than active-matrix displays. Different forms of supertwist displays include DSTN (double supertwist nematic), which is based on two supertwist layers with opposite twist directions, and CSTN (color supertwist nematic), which produces wide-angle, high-quality color. *Nematic* refers to microscopic threadlike bodies characteristic of the liquid crystals used in these displays. Supertwist displays are widely used in cellular telephones and other devices that may be used in low-light environments. *Also called:* color supertwist nematic display, CSTN, double supertwist nematic, DSTN, twisted nematic display. *See also* twisted nematic display.

superuser *n.* A UNIX user account with root (i.e., unrestricted) access privileges, usually that of a system administrator. *See also* root account, system administrator, user account.

super VAR *n.* Short for **super v**alue-**a**dded **r**eseller. A large value-added reseller. *See also* value-added reseller.

Super VGA *n. See* SVGA.

supervisor *n.* **1.** *See* operating system. **2.** A metaoperating system under which several operating systems are active. *See also* metaoperating system.

supervisor state *n.* The most privileged of the modes in which a Motorola 680x0 microprocessor can operate. Every operation of which the microprocessor is capable can be executed in the supervisor state. *See also* privileged mode. *Compare* user state.

support[1] *n.* Assistance, such as technical advice provided to customers.

support[2] *vb.* To work with another program or product; for example, an application might support file transfers from another program.

surf *vb.* To browse among collections of information on the Internet, in newsgroups, in Gopherspace, and especially on the World Wide Web. As in channel surfing while watching television, users ride the wave of what interests them, jumping from topic to topic or from one Internet site to another. *Also called:* cruise.

surface modeling *n.* A display method used by some CAD programs that gives on-screen constructions the appearance of solidity. *See also* CAD. *Compare* solid model, wire-frame model.

S

surface-mount technology *n.* A method of manufacturing printed circuit boards in which chips are fixed directly to the surface of the board instead of being soldered into holes predrilled to hold them. Its advantages are compactness, resistance to vibration, and the capacity for dense interconnections on both sides of the board. *Acronym:* SMT. *Compare* DIP, leadless chip carrier, pin grid array.

surge *n.* A sudden—and possibly damaging—increase in line voltage. *See also* surge protector, voltage regulator. *Compare* power failure, spike.

surge protector *n.* A device that prevents surges from reaching a computer or other kinds of electronic equipment. *Also called:* surge suppressor. *See also* surge, transient suppressor.

surge suppressor *n. See* surge protector.

suspend *vb.* To halt a process temporarily. *See also* sleep[2].

Suspend command *n.* A power management feature of Windows 9x and Windows NT 4 and later for portable computers. Clicking on the Suspend command in the Start menu allows the user to temporarily suspend operations of the machine (enter "Suspend mode") without turning the power off, saving battery power without having to restart applications or reload data.

suspend mode *n. See* sleep mode.

sustained transfer rate *n.* A measure of the speed at which data can be transferred to a storage device such as a disk or a tape. The sustained transfer rate is the data transfer speed that can be kept up by the device for an extended period of time.

SVC *n.* Acronym for **s**witched **v**irtual **c**ircuit. A logical connection between two nodes on a packet-switching network that is established only when data is to be transmitted. *See also* node (definition 1), packet switching. *Compare* PVC.

SVG *n.* Acronym for **S**calable **V**ector **G**raphics. An XML-based language for device-independent description of two-dimensional graphics. SVG images maintain their appearance when printed or when viewed with different screen sizes and resolutions. SVG is a recommendation of the World Wide Web Consortium (W3C).

SVGA *n.* Acronym for **S**uper **V**ideo **G**raphics **A**rray. A video standard established by the Video Electronics Standards Association (VESA) in 1989 to provide high-resolution color display on IBM-compatible computers.

Although SVGA is a standard, compatibility problems can occur with the video BIOS. *See also* BIOS, video adapter.

S-video connector *n.* A hardware interface for video devices that handles chrominance (color) and luminance (black and white) separately. An S-video connector is capable of providing a sharper image than those achieved with systems using RCA-type, or composite, connectors.

S/WAN *n. See* secure wide area network.

swap *vb.* **1.** To exchange one item for another, as in swapping floppy disks in and out of a single drive. **2.** To move segments of programs or data between memory and disk storage. *See also* virtual memory.

swap file *n.* A hidden file on the hard drive that Windows uses to hold parts of programs and data files that do not fit in memory. The operating system moves data from the swap file to memory as needed and moves data out of memory to the swap file to make room for new data. The swap file is a form of virtual memory. *See also* memory, virtual memory.

swap-on-the-fly *n.* In Linux, a process which allows swap space to be added as needed. Swap-on-the-fly allows a swap file to be created at any time on any available disk, and active only until the system is shut down.

swapping *n.* **1.** A technique for enabling an operating system, and therefore a computer, to address—roughly, have available—more memory than is physically present in the system. Swapping in this sense (as opposed to swapping disks in and out of a drive, for example) involves moving blocks of information in units known as pages between memory and disk as they are needed during the execution of the application. Swapping is supported by operating systems such as Windows NT and later, Windows 9x and later, OS/2, and Linux. **2.** A technique for moving entire processes in and out of main memory. **3.** In programming, the process of exchanging two values—for example, exchanging values between two variables. *See also* page (definition 2), swap, swap file, virtual memory.

swap space *n. See* swap file.

swarm intelligence *n.* An emerging subfield of artificial intelligence that relies on the collective knowledge of relatively simple particles or agents. Based loosely on the principles of social insect colonies, it seeks to apply the collective intelligence of fragmented agents or groups. It emphasizes distributedness, direct or indirect interactions, flexibility, and robustness. Successful applications of its principles have been evidenced in communications networks, and robotics. *See also* artificial intelligence, robotics.

Swatch *n.* Short for **S**imple **Watch**er. A UNIX log monitoring and alarm program. Swatch filters system log data as specified by the user, forwarding only important data. Swatch also looks for patterns of changes made in the log file and alerts the user to system problems as they occur.

swim *n.* A condition in which images slowly move about the positions they are supposed to occupy on screen.

SWING set *n.* A library of Java GUIs that run uniformly on any native platform that supports the Java Virtual Machine (JVM). Swing Set components have largely supplanted Sun Microsystems's Abstract Window Toolkit. *See also* Abstract Window Toolkit, graphical user interface, Java Virtual Machine.

switch *n.* **1.** A circuit element that has two states: on and off. **2.** A control device that allows the user to choose one of two or more possible states. **3.** In communications, a computer or electromechanical device that controls routing and operation of a signal path. **4.** In networking, a device capable of forwarding packets directly to the ports associated with particular network addresses. *See also* bridge, multilayer, router. **5.** In operating systems such as MS-DOS, an argument used to control the execution of a command or an application, typically starting with a slash character (/).

switch box *n.* An enclosure that contains a selector switch. When a user selects a switch setting, the signal passing through the box may be directed either from a single input to one of multiple outputs, or from the selected input to a single output. Switch boxes are often used to connect multiple peripherals, such as printers, to a single port.

switched configuration *n.* A communications link in which a signal moves from the origin to a switch that routes the signal to one of several possible destinations. *Compare* point-to-point configuration.

switched Ethernet *n.* An Ethernet network run through a high-speed switch instead of an Ethernet hub. A switched Ethernet involves dedicated bandwidth of 10 Mbps between stations rather than a shared medium. *See also* Ethernet (definition 1), switch (definition 3).

switched line *n.* A standard dial-up telephone connection; the type of line established when a call is routed through a switching station. *Compare* leased line.

Switched Multimegabit Data Services *n. See* SMDS.

switched network *n.* A communications network that uses switching to establish a connection between parties, such as the dial-up telephone system.

Switched T1 *n.* A circuit-switched form of T1 communications. *See also* T1.

switched virtual circuit *n. See* SVC.

Switcher *n.* A special Macintosh utility that allowed more than one program to be resident in memory at one time. Switcher was made obsolete by MultiFinder. *See also* MultiFinder.

switching *n.* A communications method that uses temporary rather than permanent connections to establish a link or to route information between two parties. In the dial-up telephone network, for example, a caller's line goes to a switching center, where the actual connection is made to the called party. In computer networks, message switching and packet switching allow any two parties to exchange information. In both instances, messages are routed (switched) through intermediary stations that together serve to connect the sender and the receiver.

switching hub *n.* A central device (switch) that connects separate communication lines in a network and routes messages and packets among the computers on the network. The switch functions as a hub, or PBX, for the network. *See also* hub, packet (definition 1), PBX, switch (definition 3), switched Ethernet, switched network.

switching speed *n.* In a packet-switching telecommunications technology, such as ATM, the speed at which data packets are sent through the network. Switching speed is generally measured in kilobits or megabits per second. *See also* ATM (definition 1), packet switching.

SYLK file *n.* Short for **sy**mbolic **l**in**k** file. A file constructed with a proprietary Microsoft format, used primarily for exchanging spreadsheet data in such a way that formatting information and intercellular data value relationships are preserved.

symbol *n.* In programming, a name that represents a register, an absolute value, or a memory address (relative or absolute). *See also* identifier, operator (definition 1).

symbol font *n.* A special font or typeface that replaces the characters normally accessible from the keyboard with alternative characters used as symbols, such as scientific, linguistic, or foreign-alphabet characters.

S

symbolic address *n.* A memory address that can be referred to in a program by name rather than by number.

symbolic coding *n.* The expression of an algorithm in words, decimal numbers, and symbols rather than in binary numbers, so that a person can read and understand it. Symbolic coding is used in high-level programming languages. *See also* algorithm, high-level language.

symbolic language *n.* A computer language that uses symbols such as keywords, variables, and operators to form instructions. All computer languages except machine language are symbolic.

symbolic link *n.* A disk directory entry that takes the place of a directory entry for a file but is actually a reference to a file in a different directory. *Also called:* alias, shortcut, soft link, symlink.

symbolic logic *n.* A representation of the laws of reasoning, so named because symbols rather than natural-language expressions are used to state propositions and relationships. *See also* logic.

symbol set *n.* Any collection of symbols legitimized by a data-coding system, such as extended ASCII, or a programming language.

symbol table *n.* A list of all identifiers encountered when a program is compiled (or assembled), their locations in the program, and their attributes, such as variable, routine, and so on. *See also* compile, identifier, linker, module (definition 1), object code.

symlink *n. See* symbolic link.

symmetric digital subscriber line *n. See* SDSL.

symmetric multiprocessing *n. See* SMP.

symmetric multiprocessing server *n. See* SMP server.

SYN *n.* Short for **syn**chronous idle character. A character used in synchronous (timed) communications that enables the sending and receiving devices to maintain the same timing. *Also called:* sync character.

sync character *n. See* SYN.

syncDRAM *n. See* SDRAM.

synchronization *n.* **1.** In networking, a communications transmission in which multibyte packets of data are sent and received at a fixed rate. *See also* packet (definition 1). **2.** In networking, the matching of timing between computers on the network. All of the computers are generally assigned identical times to facilitate and coordinate com-

munications. **3.** In a computer, the matching of timing between components of the computer so that all are coordinated. For instance, operations performed by the operating system are generally synchronized with the signals of the machine's internal clock. *See also* clock (definition 1), operating system. **4.** In application or database files, version comparisons of copies of the files to ensure they contain the same data. **5.** In multimedia, precise real-time processing. Audio and video are transmitted over a network in synchronization so that they can be played back together without delayed responses. *See also* real-time. **6.** In handheld computing, the process of updating or backing up the data on a handheld computer to the linked software applications on a desktop computer. Data changes made on the desktop computer may also be copied to the handheld during synchronization. *See also* partnership.

synchronization signal *n. See* sync signal.

synchronize *vb.* To cause to occur at the same time.

Synchronized Multimedia Integration Language *n. See* SMIL.

synchronous *adj.* Occurring at the same time. In computer transmissions, a reference to activity governed by a clock or by synchronized timing.

synchronous burst static RAM *n.* A type of static RAM that is synchronized with the system clock. Synchronous burst static RAM is used in a computer's L2 cache, where frequently accessed information is stored for fast retrieval by the CPU. Synchronous burst static RAM is faster than asynchronous static RAM but is limited to a maximum bus speed of 66 MHz. Computers running at faster speeds can use another form of cache memory known as pipeline burst static RAM. *Also called:* sync SRAM. *See also* L2 cache, static RAM. *Compare* asynchronous static RAM, dynamic RAM, pipeline burst static RAM.

synchronous communications *n.* Computer-to-computer communications in which transmissions are synchronized by timing between the sending and receiving machines.

Synchronous Data Link Control *n. See* SDLC.

Synchronous Digital Hierarchy *n.* An ITU recommendation implemented in Europe and similar in most respects to the SONET standard used in North America and Japan. *See also* SONET.

S

synchronous DRAM *n. See* SDRAM.

synchronous graphics RAM *n.* A form of dynamic RAM optimized for the high-speed, high-volume data transfers required by 3D graphics, video, and other memory-intensive applications. Used primarily on video accelerator cards, synchronous graphics RAM makes use of burst operations and includes features such as block writes that increase efficiency in retrieving and writing graphics data to the screen. *Acronym:* SGRAM. *See also* block, mask.

synchronous idle character *n. See* SYN.

synchronous operation *n.* **1.** Any procedure under the control of a clock or timing mechanism. *Compare* asynchronous operation. **2.** In communications and bus operation, data transfer accompanied by clock pulses either embedded in the data stream or provided simultaneously on a separate line.

synchronous operation *n.* **1.** Two or more processes that depend on the occurrences of specific events such as common timing signals. **2.** A data transmission method in which there is constant time between successive bits, characters, or events. The timing is achieved by the sharing of a single clock. Each end of the transmission synchronizes itself with the use of clocks and information sent along with the transmitted data. Characters are spaced by time and not by start and stop bits. **3.** A function call that blocks execution of a process until it returns. *See also* asynchronous operation.

Synchronous Optical Network *n. See* SONET.

synchronous protocol *n.* A set of guidelines developed to standardize synchronous communications between computers, usually based on either bit stream transmission or recognized character codes. Examples include the character-oriented binary synchronous (BISYNC) protocol and the bit-oriented High-level Data Link Control (HDLC) and Synchronous Data Link Control (SDLC) protocols. *See also* BISYNC, HDLC, SDLC.

synchronous transmission *n.* Data transfer in which information is transmitted in blocks (frames) of bits separated by equal time intervals. *Compare* asynchronous transmission.

synchronous UART *n.* A universal asynchronous receiver/transmitter (UART) that supports synchronous serial transmission, where the sender and receiver share a timing signal. *See also* UART.

sync signal *n.* Short for **sync**hronization **signal**. The part of a raster-display video signal that denotes the end of each scan line (the horizontal sync signal) and the end of the last scan line (the vertical sync signal).

sync SRAM *n. See* synchronous burst static RAM.

SYN flood *n.* A method of overwhelming a host computer on a network, especially the Internet, by sending the host a high volume of SYN (synchronization) packets requesting a connection, but never responding to the acknowledgement packets returned by the host. A SYN flood is a form of denial of service attack. *See also* denial of service attack. *Compare* Ping of Death.

synonym *n.* **1.** A word that is an equivalent of another word. When used in reference to data input, for example, the verbs *type* and *keyboard* are synonyms. **2.** In hashing, one of two distinct keys that produce the same hash address. *See also* hash[2].

syntax *n.* The grammar of a language; the rules governing the structure and content of statements. *See also* logic, programming language, syntax error. *Compare* semantics (definition 1).

syntax checker *n.* A program for identifying errors in syntax for a programming language. *See also* syntax, syntax error.

syntax error *n.* An error resulting from a statement that violates one or more of the grammatical rules of a language and is thus not "legal." *See also* logic, semantics (definition 1), syntax.

synthesis *n.* The combining of separate elements to form a coherent whole, or the result of such a combining (for example, combining digital pulses to replicate a sound, or combining digitized words to synthesize human speech). *See also* speech synthesis.

synthesizer *n.* A computer peripheral, chip, or stand-alone system that generates sound from digital instructions rather than through manipulation of physical equipment or recorded sound. *See also* MIDI.

.sys *n.* A file extension for system configuration files.

sysadmin *n.* The usual logon name or e-mail address for the system administrator of a UNIX-based system. *See also* system administrator.

sysgen *n. See* system generation.

sysop *n.* Short for **sys**tem **op**erator. The overseer of a bulletin board system (BBS) or a small multiuser computer system.

S

Sys Req key *n.* Short for **Sys**tem **Req**uest **key**. A key on some IBM and compatible keyboards that is intended to provide the same function as the Sys Req key on an IBM mainframe computer terminal: to reset the keyboard or to change from one session to another.

system *n.* Any collection of component elements that work together to perform a task. Examples are a hardware system consisting of a microprocessor, its allied chips and circuitry, input and output devices, and peripheral devices; an operating system consisting of a set of programs and data files; or a database management system used to process specific kinds of information.

system administrator *n.* The person responsible for administering use of a multiuser computer system, communications system, or both. A system administrator performs such duties as assigning user accounts and passwords, establishing security access levels, allocating storage space, and watching for unauthorized access to prevent virus or Trojan horse programs from entering the system. *Also called:* sysadmin. *See also* superuser, Trojan horse, virus. *Compare* sysop.

system area network *n. See* storage area network.

system board *n. See* motherboard.

system clock *n. See* clock (definition 1).

system console *n.* The control center of a computer system, primarily with reference to mainframe and minicomputers. In networked or distributed systems, one workstation is designated as the system administrator's; this workstation is analogous to the LAN system console. *See also* console, LAN.

system conversion *n.* Changing from one operating system to another—for example, from Windows 98 to Windows 2000, UNIX, or OS/2.

system development *n.* The process of defining, designing, testing, and implementing a new system.

system disk *n.* A disk that contains an operating system and can be used to boot a computer. *Also called:* startup disk. *See also* boot[2], operating system.

system error *n.* A software condition that renders the operating system incapable of continuing to function normally. This type of error usually requires rebooting the system.

system failure *n.* The inability of a computer to continue functioning, usually caused by software rather than hardware.

System file *n.* A resource file on the Macintosh that contains the resources needed by the operating system, such as fonts, icons, and default dialog boxes.

System folder *n.* The Macintosh file folder (directory) that contains the System file and other vital files, such as Finder, device drivers, INIT files, and control panel files. *See also* control panel, Finder, INIT, System file.

system font *n.* On the Macintosh and in some PC applications, the font used by the computer for on-screen text, such as menu titles and items (but not on-screen text within a word processor or other application). *See also* font.

system generation *n.* The process of configuring and installing system software for a particular set of hardware components. Complex operating systems such as UNIX are shipped with device drivers and utilities that are often not relevant to a particular hardware configuration; putting together only the necessary components, as well as specifying important system characteristics, is part of the system generation process. *Also called:* sysgen.

system heap *n. See* heap (definition 1).

system.ini *n.* In Windows 3.x, the initialization file used to store the hardware configuration information necessary to run the Windows operating environment. The system.ini file was replaced by the registry database in Windows 9x and in Windows NT. *See also* ini file.

system life cycle *n.* An information system's useful life. At the end of a system's life cycle it is not feasible to repair or expand it, so it must be replaced.

system memory *n. See* memory.

System Object Model *n. See* SOM (definition 1).

system on a chip *n. See* SOC.

system operator *n. See* sysop.

system prompt *n. See* prompt (definition 1).

system recovery *n.* Processing that takes place after a system failure in order to restore a system to normal operation. System recovery takes place after the operating system is initiated. It sometimes requires that tasks in process during the failure be backed out of and that structures in memory during the failure be reconstructed.

System Registry *n. See* registry.

system replacement *n. See* replacement strategy.

System Request key *n. See* Sys Req key.

system resource *n.* On the Macintosh, any of numerous routines, definitions, and data fragments that are stored in the Macintosh System file, such as floating-point arithmetic routines, font definitions, and peripheral drivers. *See also* resource (definition 2).

systems analysis *n.* The examination of a system or problem with the goal of either improving an existing system or designing and implementing a new one. As a science, systems analysis is related to cybernetics, a branch of engineering that studies the behavior of systems.

systems analyst *n.* A person who works on designing and developing systems. Systems analysts generally combine technical, managerial, and human-relations activities in order to complete their analyses.

Systems Application Architecture *n. See* SAA.

systems integration *n.* The development of a computer system for a particular customer by combining products from different original equipment manufacturers (OEMs).

Systems Management Server *n.* A Microsoft Back-Office component that provides services for centralized network management. *Acronym:* SMS.

Systems Network Architecture *n. See* SNA.

system software *n.* The collection of programs and data that make up and relate to the operating system. *Compare* application.

systems programming *n.* The development or maintenance of programs designed to execute as part of an operating system, such as I/O routines, user interfaces, command-line interpreters, and task-scheduling and memory management routines.

system support *n.* The provision of services and material resources for the use, maintenance, and improvement of an implemented system.

system timer *n. See* clock (definition 1).

system unit *n. See* console.

System V *n.* A version of the UNIX system provided by AT&T and others. It is both a standard (principally controlled by AT&T) and a set of commercial products. *See also* UNIX.

S

T *prefix* *See* tera-.

T1 or **T-1** *n.* A high-speed communications line that can handle digital communications and Internet access at the rate 1.544 Mbps (megabits per second). Although originally designed by AT&T to carry multiple voice calls over standard twisted-pair telephone wiring, this high-bandwidth telephone line can also transmit text and images. T1 speed is attained through multiplexing 24 separate 64 Kbps channels into a single data stream. T1 lines are commonly used by larger organizations for Internet connectivity. *Also called:* T-1 carrier. *See also* T-carrier. *Compare* fractional T1, T2, T3, T4.

T.120 standard *n.* A family of International Telecommunications Union (ITU) specifications for multipoint data communications services within computer applications, such as conferencing and multipoint file transfer.

T2 or **T-2** *n.* A T-carrier that can handle 6.312 Mbps (megabits per second) or 96 voice channels. *See also* T-carrier. *Compare* T1, T3, T4.

T3 or **T-3** *n.* A T-carrier that can handle 44.736 Mbps (megabits per second) or 672 voice channels. *See also* T-carrier. *Compare* T1, T2, T4.

T4 or **T-4** *n.* A T-carrier that can handle 274.176 Mbps (megabits per second) or 4032 voice channels. *See also* T-carrier. *Compare* T1, T2, T3.

TA *n.* *See* terminal adapter.

tab character *n.* A character used to align lines and columns on screen and in print. Although a tab is visually indistinguishable from a series of blank spaces in most programs, the tab character and the space character are different to a computer. A tab is a single character and therefore can be added, deleted, or overtyped with a single keystroke. The ASCII coding scheme includes two codes for tab characters: a horizontal tab for spacing across the screen or page and a vertical tab for spacing down the screen or page. *See also* Tab key.

Tab key *n.* A key, often labeled with both a left-pointing and a right-pointing arrow, that traditionally (as in word processing) is used to insert tab characters into a docu-

ment. In other applications, such as menu-driven programs, the Tab key is often used to move the on-screen highlight from place to place. Many database and spreadsheet programs allow the user to press the Tab key to move around within a record or between cells. The word *tab* is short for "tabulator," which was the name given to this key on typewriters, where it was used in creating tables. *See also* tab character.

table *n.* **1.** In programming, a data structure usually consisting of a list of entries, each entry being identified by a unique key and containing a set of related values. A table is often implemented as an array of records, a linked list, or (in more primitive languages) several arrays of different data types, all using a common indexing scheme. *See also* array, list, record[1]. **2.** In relational databases, a data structure characterized by rows and columns, with data occupying or potentially occupying each cell formed by a row-column intersection. The table is the underlying structure of a relation. *See also* relational database. **3.** In word processing, desktop publishing, and in HTML documents, a block of text formatted in aligned rows and columns.

table lookup *n.* The process of using a known value to search for data in a previously constructed table of values—for example, using a purchase price to search a tax table for the appropriate sales tax. *See also* lookup.

tablet *n.* *See* graphics tablet.

Tablet PC *n.* A touch-sensitive computer screen tablet designed by Microsoft for the entry of handwritten text using a stylus or digital pen. The Tablet PC runs Windows applications and can function as a primary personal computer as well as a note-taking device.

tabulate *vb.* **1.** To total a row or column of numbers. **2.** To arrange information in table form.

TACACS *n.* Acronym for **T**erminal **A**ccess **C**ontroller **A**ccess **C**ontrol **S**ystem. A network access technique in which users log into a single centralized server that contains a database of authorized accounts. After the access server authenticates the user, it forwards the login information to the data server requested by the user. *See also* authentication, server (definition 2).

tag *n.* **1.** In programming, one or more characters containing information about a file, record type, or other structure. **2.** In certain types of data files, a key or an address that identifies a record and its storage location in another file. *See also* tag sort. **3.** In markup languages such as SGML and HTML, a code that identifies an element in a document, such as a heading or a paragraph, for the purposes of formatting, indexing, and linking information in the document. In both SGML and HTML, a tag is generally a pair of angle brackets that contain one or more letters and numbers. Usually one pair of angle brackets is placed before an element, and another pair is placed after, to indicate where the element begins and ends. For example, in HTML, <I>hello world</I> indicates that the phrase "hello world" should be italicized. *See also* <>, element, emotag, HTML, SGML. **4.** An early-generation raster graphics format used for Macintosh Ready, Set, Go programs and Letraset's ImageStudio. *See also* raster graphics.

Tagged Image File Format *n. See* TIFF.

tag sort *n.* A sort performed on one or several key fields for the purpose of establishing the order of their associated records. *Also called:* key sort.

tag switching *n.* A multilayer Internet switching technology developed by Cisco Systems that integrates routing and switching.

talk[1] *n.* The UNIX command that, when followed by another user's name and address, is used to generate a request for a synchronous chat session on the Internet. *See also* chat[1] (definition 1).

talk[2] *vb. See* chat[2].

talker *n.* An Internet-based synchronous communication mechanism most commonly used to support multiuser chat functions. Such systems typically provide specific commands for movement through separate *rooms*, or chat areas, and allow users to communicate with other users in real time through text messages, indicate simple gestures, use a bulletin board system (BBS) for posting comments, and send internal e-mail. *See also* BBS (definition 1), chat[1] (definition 1).

talk. newsgroups *n.* Usenet newsgroups that are part of the talk. hierarchy and have the prefix talk. as part of their names. These newsgroups are devoted to debate and discussion of controversial topics. Talk. newsgroups are one of the seven original Usenet newsgroup hierarchies. The other six are comp., misc., news., rec., sci., and soc. *See also* newsgroup, traditional newsgroup hierarchy, Usenet.

tandem processors *n.* Multiple processors wired so that the failure of one processor transfers central processing unit (CPU) operation to another processor. Using tandem processors is part of the strategy for implementing fault-tolerant computer systems. *See also* central processing unit.

TANSTAAFL *n.* Acronym for **T**here **a**in't **n**o **s**uch **t**hing **a**s **a f**ree **l**unch. An expression used on the Internet in e-mail, chat sessions, mailing lists, newsgroups, and other online forums; derived from *The Moon Is a Harsh Mistress*, a science-fiction classic by Robert A. Heinlein. *See also* chat[1] (definition 1), e-mail[1] (definition 1), mailing list, newsgroup.

tap[1] *n.* A device that can be attached to an Ethernet bus to enable a computer to be connected.

tap[2] *vb.* To use a stylus to quickly touch a device screen to perform an activity. Tapping is analogous to clicking with a mouse.

tap and hold *vb.* To hold a stylus on a device screen to open a pop-up or shortcut menu. Analogous to right-clicking with a mouse.

tape *n.* **1.** A thin strip of polyester film coated with magnetic material that permits the recording of data. Because tape is a continuous length of data storage material and because the read/write head cannot "jump" to a desired point on the tape without the tape first being advanced to that point, tape must be read or written sequentially, not randomly (as can be done on a floppy disk or a hard disk). **2.** A storage medium consisting of a thin strip of paper used to store information in the form of sequences of punched holes, chemical impregnation, or magnetic ink imprinting.

tape cartridge *n.* A module that resembles an audio cassette and contains magnetic tape that can be written on and read from by a tape drive. Tape cartridges are primarily used to back up hard disks. *See also* tape (definition 1).

tape drive *n.* A device for reading and writing tapes. *See also* tape (definition 1).

tape dump *n.* The process of simply printing the data contained on a tape cartridge without performing any report formatting. *See also* tape cartridge.

tape tree *n.* A means of audiotape distribution, used in Usenet music newsgroups and mailing lists, in which a

T

recording is copied and sent to a number of *branch* participants, who in turn send copies to their *children*, or *leaves*. *See also* branch (definition 1), child (definition 2), leaf, tree structure. *Compare* vine.

TAPI *n.* Acronym for **T**elephony **A**pplication **P**rogramming **I**nterface. In the Windows Open Systems Architecture (WOSA), a programming interface that gives Windows client applications access to a server's voice services. TAPI facilitates interoperability between personal computers and telephone equipment. *Also called:* Telephony API. *See also* application programming interface, WOSA. *Compare* TSAPI.

.tar *n.* The file extension that identifies uncompressed UNIX archives in the format produced by the tar program.

tar¹ *n.* Acronym for **t**ape **ar**chive. A UNIX utility for making a single file out of a set of files that a user wishes to store together. The resulting file has the extension .tar. Unlike PKZIP, tar does not compress files, so compress or gzip is usually run on the .tar file to produce a file with extensions .tar.gz or .tar.Z. *See also* compress¹, gzip, PKZIP. *Compare* untar¹.

tar² *vb.* To make a single file out of a set of files using the tar utility. *See also* compress², PKZIP. *Compare* untar².

target *n.* Loosely, the objective of a computer command or operation. Examples are a computer that is to run a program translated for its use, a "foreign" language (for another computer) into which a program is to be translated, or a group of people for whom a particular product is designed. In MS-DOS usage, the target is often the disk referred to by prompts in a copy operation (for example, "insert *target* diskette"). In terms of the SCSI (small computer system interface) connection, the target is the device that receives commands. *See also* SCSI, target computer, target disk, target language.

target computer *n.* The computer that receives data from a communications device, a hardware add-in, or a software package.

target disk *n.* The disk to which data is to be written, as in a copy operation. *See also* target. *Compare* source disk.

target language *n.* The language into which source code is compiled or assembled. *See also* assembler, compiler (definition 2), cross-compiler.

task *n.* A stand-alone application or a subprogram that is run as an independent entity.

taskbar *n.* A graphic toolbar used in Windows 9x, Windows CE, Windows NT, and Windows 2000 to select, via the mouse, one of a number of active applications. *See also* task button, toolbar.

task button *n.* In Windows 9x, Windows CE, Windows NT, and Windows 2000, a button that appears on the taskbar on the screen when an application is run. By clicking on the button, the user can switch from another application to the application corresponding to the button. *See also* taskbar.

task management *n.* The operating-system process of tracking the progress of and providing necessary resources for separate tasks that are running on a computer, especially in a multitasking environment.

task swapping *n.* The process of switching from one application to another by saving the data for the application presently running in the foreground to a storage device and loading the other application. *See also* foreground² (definition 2), task, task switching.

task switching *n.* The act of moving from one program to another without shutting down the first program. Task switching is a single act, as compared to multitasking, in which the central processing unit rapidly switches back and forth between two or more programs. *See also* task, task swapping. *Compare* multitasking.

TB *n. See* terabyte.

T-carrier *n.* A long-distance, digital communications line provided by a common carrier. Multiplexers at either end merge several voice channels and digital data streams for transmission and separate them when received. T-carrier service, introduced by AT&T in 1993, is defined at several capacity levels: T1, T2, T3, and T4. In addition to voice communication, T-carriers are used for Internet connectivity. *See also* T1, T2, T3, T4.

TCB *n.* Acronym for **T**rusted **C**omputing **B**ase. The complete set of security mechanisms that create security on a network. The TCB includes all the hardware, software, and firmware components that are responsible for system security.

Tcl/Tk *n.* Acronym for **T**ool **C**ommand **L**anguage/**T**ool **K**it. A programming system that includes a scripting language (Tcl) and a graphical user interface toolkit (Tk). The Tcl language issues commands to interactive programs, such as text editors, debuggers, and shells, which tie together complex data structures into scripts. *See also* graphical user interface, script, scripting language.

TCM *n. See* trellis-coded modulation.

TCO *n. See* total cost of ownership.

TCP *n.* Acronym for **T**ransmission **C**ontrol **P**rotocol. The protocol within TCP/IP that governs the breakup of data messages into packets to be sent via IP (Internet Protocol), and the reassembly and verification of the complete messages from packets received by IP. A connection-oriented, reliable protocol (reliable in the sense of ensuring error-free delivery), TCP corresponds to the transport layer in the ISO/OSI reference model. *See also* ISO/OSI reference model, packet, TCP/IP. *Compare* UDP.

TCP/IP *n.* Acronym for **T**ransmission **C**ontrol **P**rotocol/ **I**nternet **P**rotocol. A protocol suite (or set of protocols) developed by the U.S. Department of Defense for communications over interconnected, sometimes dissimilar, networks. It is built into the UNIX system and has become the de facto standard for data transmission over networks, including the Internet.

TCP/IP reference model *n.* A networking model designed around the concept of internetworking—the exchange of information among different networks, often built on different architectures. The TCP/IP reference model, often called the Internet reference model, consists of four layers, the most distinctive of which is the internetwork that deals with routing messages and that has no equivalent in the ISO/OSI reference model or the SNA model. *Compare* ISO/OSI reference model, SNA.

TCP/IP stack *n.* The set of TCP/IP protocols. *See also* protocol stack, TCP/IP.

TDM *n. See* time-division multiplexing.

TDMA *n.* Short for **T**ime **D**ivision **M**ultiple **A**ccess. A multiplexing technology used to divide a single cellular phone channel into multiple subchannels. TDMA works by allocating separate time slots to each user. It is implemented in D-AMPS (Digital Advanced Mobile Phone Service), which relies on TDMA to divide each of the 30 analog AMPS channels into 3 separate subchannels, and GSM (Global System for Mobile Communications). *See also* D-AMPS, Global System for Mobile Communications. *Compare* AMPS, FDMA.

team Web site *n. See* SharePoint team Web site.

Teardrop attack *n.* An Internet-based attack that breaks a message into a series of IP fragments with overlapping offset fields. When these fragments are reassembled at their destination, the fields don't match, causing the system to hang, reboot, or crash.

tearing *n.* A visual artifact produced when the screen refresh rate is out of sync with an application's frame rate. The top portion of one frame is displayed at the same time as the bottom portion of another frame, with a discernible tear between the two partial images.

tear-off *adj.* Capable of being dragged from an original position in a graphical user interface and placed where the user desires. For example, many graphics applications feature tear-off menus of tool palettes that can be dragged to locations other than the menu bar.

techie *n.* A technically oriented person. Typically, a techie is the person on whom a user calls when something breaks or the user cannot understand a technical problem. A techie may be an engineer or a technician, but not all engineers are techies. *See also* guru.

technical author *n. See* tech writer.

technobabble *n.* Language that includes incomprehensible technical terms and jargon. In ordinary conversation, many of the words in this dictionary might be considered technobabble.

technology *n.* The application of science and engineering to the development of machines and procedures in order to enhance or improve human conditions, or at least to improve human efficiency in some respect. *See also* high tech.

technophile *n.* Someone who is enthusiastic about emerging technology. *Compare* computerphile.

technophobe *n.* A person who is afraid of or dislikes technological advances, especially computers. *See also* Luddite. *Compare* technophile.

tech writer *n.* Short for technical writer. One who writes the documentation material for a hardware or software product. *Also called:* technical author. *See also* documentation.

telco *n.* Short for **tele**phone **co**mpany. A term generally used in reference to a telephone company's provision of Internet services.

telecom closet *n. See* wiring closet.

telecommunications *n.* The transmission and reception of information of any type, including data, television pictures, sound, and facsimiles, using electrical or optical signals sent over wires or fibers or through the air.

telecommunications closet *n. See* wiring closet.

T

telecommute *vb.* To work in one location (often at home) and communicate with a main office at a different location through a personal computer equipped with a modem and communications software.

telecommuter *n.* A member of the workforce who conducts business outside the traditional office setting, collaborating with business associates and colleagues through communications and computer technologies. Some workers telecommute full-time; others part-time. The telecommuting ranks include self-employed home workers, small-business entrepreneurs, and employees of large corporations or organizations. *See also* distributed workplace, SOHO.

teleconferencing *n.* The use of audio, video, or computer equipment linked through a communications system to enable geographically separated individuals to participate in a meeting or discussion. *See also* video conferencing.

telecopy *vb. See* fax.

telematics *n.* In communications technology, the linking of computers and telecommunications. Telematics technology is becoming standard in the automotive industry, with dashboard navigation systems, roadside assistance, entertainment, Internet, and cellular services available in vehicles.

telephony *n.* Telephone technology—voice, fax, or modem transmissions based on either the conversion of sound into electrical signals or wireless communication via radio waves.

Telephony API *n. See* TAPI.

telephony device *n.* A mechanism designed to translate sound into electrical signals, transmit them, and then convert them back to sound.

Telephony Service Provider *n.* A modem driver that enables access to vendor-specific equipment through a standard device driver interface. *Acronym:* TSP. *See also* Telephony Service Provider Interface.

Telephony Service Provider Interface *n.* The external interface of a service provider to be implemented by vendors of telephony equipment. A telephony service provider accesses vendor-specific equipment through a standard device driver interface. Installing a service provider allows Windows CE–based applications that use elements of telephony to access the corresponding telephony equipment. *Acronym:* TSPI. *See also* Telephony Service Provider.

teleprocess *vb.* To use a terminal or computer and communications equipment to access computers and computer files located elsewhere. *Teleprocess* is a term originated by IBM. *See also* distributed processing, remote access.

teleprocessing monitor *n. See* TP monitor.

Telescript *n.* A communications-oriented programming language, released in 1994 by General Magic, that was designed to address the need for cross-platform, network-independent messaging and abstraction of complex network protocols. *See also* communications protocol.

teletext *n.* All-text information broadcast by a television station to a subscriber's television set.

Teletype *n.* The Teletype Corporation, developer of the teletypewriter (TTY) and various other printers used with computers and communications systems. *See also* TTY.

teletype mode *n.* A mode of operation in which a computer or an application limits its actions to those characteristic of a teletypewriter (TTY). On the display, for example, teletype mode means that only alphanumeric characters can be shown, and they are simply "typed" on the screen, one letter after the other, and cannot be placed in any desired position. *See also* Teletype, TTY.

teletypewriter *n. See* TTY.

teleworker *n.* A businessperson who substitutes information technologies for work-related travel. Teleworkers include home-based and small business workers who use computer and communications technologies to interact with customers and/or colleagues. *See also* distributed workplace, SOHO.

telnet[1] *n.* **1.** A client program that implements the Telnet protocol. **2.** A protocol in the TCP/IP suite that enables individuals to log on to and use a remote computer as if they were sitting at a terminal directly connected to the machine.

telnet[2] *vb.* To access a remote computer over the Internet using the Telnet protocol. *See also* telnet[1].

Telnet *n.* A protocol that enables an Internet user to log on to and enter commands on a remote computer linked to the Internet, as if the user were using a text-based terminal directly attached to that computer. Telnet is part of the TCP/IP suite of protocols.

template *n.* **1.** In an application package, an overlay for the keyboard that identifies special keys and key combinations. **2.** In image processing, a pattern that can be used to identify or match a scanned image. **3.** In spreadsheet programs, a predesigned spreadsheet that contains formulas, labels, and other elements. **4.** In MS-DOS, a small portion of memory that holds the most recently typed MS-DOS command. **5.** In word processing and desktop publishing programs, a predesigned document that contains formatting and, in many cases, generic text.

temporary file *n.* A file created either in memory or on disk, by the operating system or some other program, to be used during a session and then discarded. *Also called:* temp file. *See also* scratch[1].

temporary storage *n.* A region in memory or on a storage device that is temporarily allocated for use in storing intermediate data in a computational, sorting, or transfer operation.

ten's complement *n.* A number in the base-10 system that is the true complement of another number and is derived either by subtracting each digit from 1 less than the base and adding 1 to the result or by subtracting each number from the next higher power of the base. For example, the ten's complement of 25 is 75, and it can be derived either by subtracting each digit from 9, which is 1 less than the base ($9 - 2 = 7, 9 - 5 = 4$) and then adding 1 ($74 + 1 = 75$) or by subtracting 25 from the next higher power of 10, which is 100 ($100 - 25 = 75$). *See also* complement. *Compare* nine's complement.

tera- *prefix* A prefix meaning 10^{12}: 1 trillion in the American numbering system, 1 million million in British numbering. *Abbreviation:* T. *See also* terabyte.

terabyte *n.* A measurement used for high-capacity data storage. One terabyte equals 2^{40}, or 1,099,511,627,776, bytes, although it is commonly interpreted as simply one trillion bytes. *Abbreviation:* TB.

teraflops *n.* One trillion floating-point operations (FLOPS) per second. Teraflops serves as a benchmark for larger computers that measures the number of floating-point operations they can perform in a set amount of time. *Also called:* TFLOPS. *See also* FLOPS.

terminal *n.* **1.** In networking, a device consisting of a video adapter, a monitor, and a keyboard. The adapter and monitor and, sometimes, the keyboard are typically combined in a single unit. A terminal does little or no computer processing on its own; instead, it is connected to a computer with a communications link over a cable. Terminals are used primarily in multiuser systems and today are not often found on single-user personal computers. *See also* dumb terminal, smart terminal, terminal emulation. **2.** In electronics, a point that can be physically linked to something else, usually by a wire, to form an electrical connection.

Terminal *n.* An application that provides command-line access to the Mac OS X UNIX core. The Terminal command-line environment allows UNIX functions from within Mac OS X.

Terminal Access Controller Access Control System *n. See* TACACS.

terminal adapter *n.* The correct name for an ISDN modem, which connects a PC to an ISDN line but does not modulate or demodulate signals as a typical modem does.

terminal emulation *n.* The imitation of a terminal by using software that conforms to a standard, such as the ANSI standard for terminal emulation. Terminal-emulation software is used to make a microcomputer act as if it were a particular type of terminal while it is communicating with another computer, such as a mainframe. *See also* VT-52, VT-100, VT-200.

terminal server *n.* In a LAN (local area network), a computer or a controller that allows terminals, microcomputers, and other devices to connect to a network or host computer, or to devices attached to that particular computer. See the illustration. *See also* controller, LAN, microcomputer, terminal.

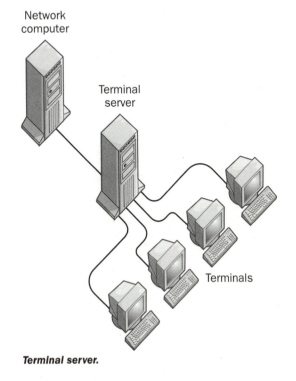

Terminal server.

terminal session *n.* The period of time spent actively using a terminal. *See also* session.

terminal strip *n.* A usually long and narrow assembly containing one or more electrical connectors. Commonly, terminal strips consist of screws on which bare wires are wrapped before the screws are tightened; for example, some consumer-grade stereo receiver/amplifiers incorporate a set of terminal strips on the rear panel for attaching speaker wires to the unit.

terminate *vb.* **1.** With reference to software, to end a process or program. Abnormal termination occurs in response to user intervention or because of a hardware or software error. **2.** With reference to hardware, to install a plug, jack, or other connector at the end of a wire or cable.

terminate-and-stay-resident program *n. See* TSR.

terminator *n.* **1.** A character that indicates the end of a string, such as the null character in an ASCIIZ string. *See also* ASCII, ASCIIZ string. **2.** An item of hardware that must be installed in the last device in a daisy chain or bus network, such as Ethernet or SCSI. The terminator caps the end of a cable in a bus network in order to keep signals from bouncing back along the line. *See also* terminator cap.

terminator cap *n.* A special connector that must be attached to each end of an Ethernet bus. If one or both terminator caps are missing, the Ethernet network will not work.

ternary *adj.* In programming, of, pertaining to, or characteristic of an element with three possible values, a condition that has three possible states, or a base-3 number system. *Compare* binary[1], unary.

tessellate *vb.* To break an image into small, square regions for processing or output.

test *vb.* To check program correctness by trying out various sequences and input values. *See also* debug, test data.

test automation software *n.* A program that automatically enters a predetermined set of characters or user commands in order to test new or modified versions of software applications.

test data *n.* A set of values used to test proper functioning of a program. Reasons for choosing particular test data include verifying known output (anticipated output) and pushing boundary conditions that might cause the program to fail.

test post *n.* A newsgroup article that contains no actual message but is used simply as a means of checking the connection. *See also* article, newsgroup.

TeX or **T$_E$X** *n.* A text-formatting software system created by mathematician and computer scientist Donald Knuth for producing typeset-quality scientific, mathematical, or other complex technical documents from plain ASCII text input. Implementations of TeX for UNIX systems, MS-DOS and Windows, and the Apple Macintosh are available free over the Internet (ftp://ftp.tex.ac.uk/tex-archive/) or in commercial distributions (which often include enhancements). Commands in the input file produce format elements and special symbols; for example, ${\pi}r^2$ produces the expression pr^2. TeX is extensible through macros, and macro files are available for a wide variety of applications. *See also* LaTeX[1].

Texas Instruments Graphics Architecture *n. See* TIGA.

texel *n.* A single element in a texture. When a texture has been applied to an object, the texels rarely correspond to pixels on the screen. Applications can use texture filtering to control how texels are sampled and interpolated to pixels.

text *n.* **1.** Data that consists of characters representing the words and symbols of human speech; usually, characters coded according to the ASCII standard, which assigns numeric values to numbers, letters, and certain symbols. **2.** In word processing and desktop publishing, the main portion of a document, as opposed to headlines, tables, figures, footnotes, and other elements.

text box *n.* In a dialog box or HTML form, a box in which the user may enter text.

TextEdit *n.* A standard set of routines in the Macintosh operating system that are available to programs for controlling the way text is displayed. *See also* Toolbox.

text editor *n. See* editor.

text entry *n.* The inputting of text characters by means of a keyboard.

text file *n.* A file composed of text characters. A text file can be a word-processing file or a "plain" ASCII file encoded in a format practically all computers can use. *See also* ASCII file, text (definition 1).

text mode *n.* A display mode in which the monitor can display letters, numbers, and other text characters but no graphical images or WYSIWYG ("what-you-see-is-what-you-get") character formatting (italics, superscript, and so on). *Also called:* alphanumeric mode, character mode. *Compare* graphics mode.

text-only file *n. See* ASCII file.

text-to-speech *n.* The conversion of text-based data into voice output by speech synthesis devices to allow users to gain access to information by telephone or to allow blind or illiterate people to use computers.

Text-to-Speech *n.* *See* TTS (definition 1).

texture *n.* In computer graphics, shading or other attributes added to the "surface" of a graphical image to give it the illusion of a physical substance. For example, a surface could be made to appear reflective to simulate metal or glass, or a scanned image of wood grain could be applied to a shape intended to simulate an object made of wood.

texture mapping *n.* In 3-D graphics, the process of adding detail to an object by creating a picture or a pattern that can be "wrapped" around the object. For example, a texture map of stones might be wrapped around a pyramid shape to create a realistic image. Texture mapping can also account for changes in perspective as the picture is wrapped around the shape. The technique is valued in 3-D graphics because it enables creation of detailed images without the performance degradation that can result from the computation required to manipulate images created with large numbers of polygons.

TFLOPS *n.* *See* teraflops.

TFT *n.* Acronym for **t**hin **f**ilm **t**ransistor. A transistor created using thin film methodology. *See also* active matrix display, thin film, transistor.

TFT display *n.* *See* active matrix display.

TFT LCD *n.* Acronym for **t**hin **f**ilm **t**ransistor **l**iquid **c**rystal **d**isplay. *See* active matrix display.

TFTP *n.* *See* Trivial File Transfer Protocol.

TGA *n.* **1.** Short for **T**arga. A raster graphics file format from Truevision, Inc., that handles 16-, 24-, and 32-bit color. *See also* 16-bit color, 24-bit color, 32-bit color, raster graphics, video graphics board. **2.** The brand name of a series of high-resolution video graphics boards.

theme *n.* **1.** A set of visual elements that provide a unified look for your computer desktop. A theme determines the look of the various graphic elements of your desktop, such as the windows, icons, fonts, colors, and the background and screen saver pictures. It can also define sounds associated with events, such as opening or closing a program. **2.** A set of coordinated graphic elements applied to a document or Web page, or across all pages in a Web site. Themes can consist of designs and color schemes for fonts, link bars, and other page elements.

The Microsoft Network *n.* *See* MSN.

thermal printer *n.* A nonimpact printer that uses heat to generate an image on specially treated paper. The printer uses pins to produce an image, but rather than striking the pins against a ribbon to mark the paper as does a wire-pin dot-matrix printer, it heats the pins and brings them into gentle contact with the paper. The special coating on the paper discolors when it is heated.

thermal transfer printer *n.* *See* thermal wax-transfer printer.

thermal wax printer *n.* *See* thermal wax-transfer printer.

thermal wax-transfer printer *n.* A special type of non-impact printer that uses heat to melt colored wax onto paper to create an image. Like a standard thermal printer, it uses pins to apply the heat. Rather than making contact with coated paper, however, the pins touch a wide ribbon saturated with different colored waxes. The wax melts under the pins and adheres to the paper.

thesaurus *n.* **1.** A book of words and their synonyms. **2.** In microcomputer applications, both a file of synonyms stored on disk and the program used to search the file.

The World—Public Access UNIX *n.* One of the oldest public access Internet service providers, based in Boston. In 1990, The World began offering full dial-up Internet access to the public. Other services include World Wide Web access, Usenet, SLIP/PPP support, telnet, FTP, IRC, Gopher, and e-mail. In 1995, The World began supporting local dial-up access via UUNET. *See also* ISP.

thick Ethernet *n.* *See* 10Base5.

thick film *adj.* A term describing a method used in the manufacture of integrated circuits. Thick film technology uses a stencil-like technique called *photosilkscreening* to deposit multiple layers of special inks or pastes on a ceramic substrate. The inks or pastes can be conducting, insulating, or resistive. The passive components (wires, resistors, and capacitors) of the integrated circuits are formed by depositing a series of films of different characteristics and patterns. *Compare* thin film.

ThickNet *n.* *See* 10Base5.

ThickWire *n.* *See* 10Base5.

thimble *n.* A type element, similar to a daisy wheel, that bears a full character set, with each character on a separate type bar. As with a daisy wheel, the spokes, or type bars, radiate out from a central hub. On a thimble print element,

T

however, each type bar is bent 90 degrees at its halfway point, so the type bars stick straight up with the type facing away from the hub. *See also* thimble printer. *Compare* daisy wheel, daisy-wheel printer.

thimble printer *n.* A printer that uses a thimble print element, best known in a line of printers from NEC. Because these printers use fully formed characters like those on a typewriter, they generate letter-quality output that is indistinguishable from that of a typewriter. This includes the slight impression created by the type hitting the paper hard through the ribbon, which distinguishes this type of printout from that of laser printers. *See also* thimble. *Compare* daisy-wheel printer.

thin client *n.* A software layer of a small client for a centrally managed, network terminal. The thin client allows the user access to server-hosted applications and data.

thin Ethernet *n. See* 10Base2.

thin film *adj.* A method used in the fabrication of integrated circuits. Thin film technology operates on the same basic principles as thick film technology. Rather than using inks or pastes, however, thin film technology uses metals and metal oxides that are "evaporated" and then deposited on the substrate in the desired pattern to form the integrated circuit's passive components (wires, resistors, and capacitors). *See also* molecular beam epitaxy. *Compare* thick film.

thin film transistor *n. See* TFT.

ThinNet *n. See* 10Base2.

thin server *n.* A client/server architecture in which most of an application is run on the client machine, which is called a fat client, with occasional data operations on a remote server. Such a configuration yields good client performance, but complicates administrative tasks, such as software upgrades. *See also* client/server architecture, fat client, thin client. *Compare* fat server.

thin space *n.* An amount of horizontal space in a font, equal to one-quarter the point size of the font. For example, a thin space in a 12-point font is 3 points wide. *See also* point[1] (definition 1). *Compare* em space, en space, fixed space.

thin system *n. See* thin server.

ThinWire *n. See* 10Base2.

Third Generation *n. See* 3G.

third-generation computer *n.* Any of the computers produced from the mid-1960s to the 1970s that were based on integrated circuits rather than on separately wired transistors. *See also* computer.

third-generation language *n. See* 3GL.

third normal form *n. See* normal form (definition 1).

third-party[1] *adj.* In computer console games, a game made for a specific console by a company other than the console manufacturer.

third party[2] *n.* A company that manufactures and sells accessories or peripherals for use with a major manufacturer's computer or peripheral, usually without any involvement from the major manufacturer.

thrashing *n.* The state of a virtual memory system that is spending almost all its time swapping pages in and out of memory rather than executing applications. *See also* swap (definition 2), virtual memory.

thread *n.* **1.** In programming, a process that is part of a larger process or program. **2.** In a tree data structure, a pointer that identifies the parent node and is used to facilitate traversal of the tree. **3.** In electronic mail and Internet newsgroups, a series of messages and replies related to a specific topic.

threaded discussion *n.* In a newsgroup or other online forum, a series of messages or articles in which replies to an article are nested directly under it, instead of the articles being arranged in chronological or alphabetical order. *See also* newsgroup, thread (definition 3).

threaded newsreader *n.* A newsreader that displays posts in newsgroups as threads. Replies to a post appear directly after the original post, rather than in chronological or any other order. *See also* newsreader, post, thread (definition 3).

threaded tree *n.* A tree in which the leaf (end) nodes contain pointers to some of the nodes from which they arise. The pointers facilitate searching the tree for information. *See also* thread (definition 2).

threading *n.* A technique used by certain interpretive languages, such as many Forth implementations, to speed execution. The references to other support routines in each threaded support routine, such as a predefined word in Forth, are replaced by pointers to those routines. *See also* Forth, thread (definition 1).

three-dimensional array *n.* An ordered arrangement of information in which three numbers (integers) are used to locate a particular item. A three-dimensional array treats data as if it were laid out in rows, columns, and layers. *See also* 3-D array, array, two-dimensional array.

three-dimensional model *n.* A computer simulation of a physical object in which length, width, and depth are real attributes—a model, with x-, y-, and z-axes, that can be rotated for viewing from different angles.

three-finger salute *n.* Slang term for a warm, or soft, boot, in which the Ctrl, Alt, and Delete keys are pressed simultaneously to restart a computer without first turning off the power. *Also called:* Vulcan death grip. *See also* warm boot.

three-nines availability *n.* The availability of a system 99.9% of the time. Three-nines availability equates to approximately 526 minutes of downtime in a standard 365-day year. *See also* high availability.

three-point editing *n.* In digital video editing, a feature that simplifies the process of placing new video within a sequence by assisting in calculating edit points. To make an edit, in and out points must be defined in the video clip to be added and in the sequence into which the clip is to be inserted. The user provides any three of these edit points and the editing software determines the fourth.

three-tier client/server *n.* A client/server architecture in which software systems are structured into three tiers or layers: the user interface layer, the business logic layer, and the database layer. Layers may have one or more components. For example, there can be one or more user interfaces in the top tier, each user interface may communicate with more than one application in the middle tier at the same time, and the applications in the middle tier may use more than one database at a time. Components in a tier may run on a computer that is separate from the other tiers, communicating with the other components over a network. *See also* client/server architecture. *Compare* two-tier client/server.

throbber *n.* An animated icon that moves while an application is completing a task, such as a browser loading a Web page. Throbbers serve to reassure the user that the application is still working on the task and has not frozen. Web browsers and some other applications come with a throbber icon. In some cases, the user can replace the original throbber with a customized icon of the user's choice.

throttle control *n.* A device that enables the user of a flight simulator or game to control simulated engine power. The throttle control is used along with a joystick

(which controls the simulated ailerons and elevators) and possibly a rudder control.

throughput *n.* **1.** The data transfer rate of a network, measured as the number of bits per second transmitted. **2.** A measure of the data processing rate in a computer system.

throughput test *n. See* bandwidth test.

thumb *n. See* elevator.

thumbnail *n.* A miniature version of an image or electronic version of a page that is generally used to allow quick browsing through multiple images or pages. For example, Web pages often contain thumbnails of images (which can be loaded much more quickly by the Web browser than the full-size image). Many of these thumbnails can be clicked on to load the complete version of the image.

thumbwheel *n.* A wheel embedded in a case so that only a portion of the outside rim is revealed. When rolled with the thumb, the wheel can control an on-screen element such as a pointer or a cursor. Thumbwheels are used with three-dimensional joysticks and trackballs to control the depth aspect of the pointer or cursor. *See also* joystick, relative pointing device, trackball.

thunk¹ *n.* Code that enables 16-bit code to call 32-bit code, and vice versa. There are three different types of thunk: a flat thunk relies on a thunk compiler to allow 32-bit code to call a 16-bit DLL and 16-bit code to call a 32-bit DLL; a generic thunk enables a 16-bit application to load and call a 32-bit DLL; and a universal thunk allows 32-bit code to load and call a 16-bit DLL. All thunks are Windows-based, but the type of thunk used depends on the Windows version.

thunk² *vb.* To call 32-bit code from 16-bit code, or vice versa. Thunking involves, in large part, the translation to and from 16-bit segment offset memory addressing and 32-bit flat, or linear, memory addressing. *See also* address space, flat address space, segmented address space.

TIA *n.* Acronym for **t**hanks **i**n **a**dvance. On the Internet, a popular sign-off to a request of some sort. *Also called:* aTdHvAaNnKcSe.

tick *n.* **1.** A regular, rapidly recurring signal emitted by a clocking circuit; also, the interrupt generated by this signal. **2.** In some microcomputer systems, notably Macintosh, one sixtieth of a second, the basic time unit used by the internal clock that is accessible by programs.

T

tiebreaker *n.* A circuit that arbitrates competing circuits and resolves bottlenecks by giving priority to one circuit at a time.

tie line *n.* A private line leased from a communications carrier and often used to link two or more points in an organization.

Tier 1 *n.* An Internet Network Access Point that provides access to and interconnection among major national and international network backbone providers, such as MCI WorldCom, Sprint, BBN, and IBM. *See also* Network Access Point. *Compare* Tier 2.

Tier 2 *n.* A regional Internet Network interchange location where local ISPs exchange data. By using a Tier 2 exchange point, ISPs in the same area can move data between their users without the need to transport that data over long distances. For example, if a user in Singapore connects to a Web site in the same city through a local Tier 2 exchange point, it is not necessary to move the data through a major Network Access Point, or NAP, in Japan or North America. Tier 2 locations generally have much smaller capacities than the national and international Tier 1 NAPs. *See also* Network Access Point. *Compare* Tier 1.

.tif or **.tiff** *n.* The file extension that identifies bitmap images in Tagged Image File Format (TIFF). *See also* TIFF.

TIFF or **TIF** *n.* Acronym for **T**agged **I**mage **F**ile **F**ormat or **T**ag **I**mage **F**ile **F**ormat. A standard file format commonly used for scanning, storage, and interchange of gray-scale graphic images. TIFF may be the only format available for older programs (such as older versions of MacPaint), but most modern programs are able to save images in a variety of other formats, such as GIF or JPEG. *See also* gray scale. *Compare* GIF, JPEG.

TIFF JPEG *n.* Acronym for **T**agged **I**mage **F**ile Format **JPEG**. A means of saving photographic images compressed according to the JPEG (Joint Photographic Experts Group) standard. TIFF JPEG saves more information about an image than does the lower-end JFIF (JPEG File Interchange Format), but TIFF JPEG files are limited in portability because of differences in implementation among applications. *See also* JFIF, JPEG.

TIGA *n.* Acronym for **T**exas **I**nstruments **G**raphics Architecture. A video adapter architecture based on the Texas Instruments 340x0 graphics processor.

tiger team *n.* A group of users, programmers, or hackers who are charged with finding flaws in networks, applica-

tions, or security procedures. Tiger teams may be hired or may be composed of volunteers, and may have a single, short-term goal or may be used for a number of investigative purposes over a longer period of time. The term "tiger team" was originally used by the military to describe infiltration groups, and was first used in the computer industry to refer to hackers hired to expose flaws in network security.

tightly coupled *adj.* **1.** Refers to two computing processes whose successful completion and individual performance rates are highly interdependent. **2.** Of, pertaining to, or characteristic of a relationship of interdependency between computers, as in multiprocessing.

tile *vb.* **1.** In computer-graphics programming, to fill adjacent blocks of pixels on the screen with a design or pattern without allowing any blocks to overlap. **2.** To fill the space on a monitor or within a smaller area with multiple copies of the same graphic image. **3.** In an environment with multiple windows, to rearrange and resize all open windows so that they appear fully on the screen without any overlap.

time and date *n.* In computing, the timekeeping and datekeeping functions maintained by the computer's operating system, used most visibly as a means of "stamping" files with the date and time of creation or last revision.

time and date stamp *n. See* time stamp.

time bomb *n.* **1.** A feature often built into evaluation or beta versions of software that renders the software unusable after a certain period of time. With some evaluation versions of software containing time bombs, users are given codes or registration numbers after purchasing the software that will deactivate the time bomb. **2.** *See* logic bomb. **3.** *See* Year 2000 problem.

Time Division Multiple Access *n. See* TDMA.

time-division multiplexing *n.* A form of multiplexing in which transmission time is broken into segments, each of which carries one element of one signal. *Acronym:* TDM. *See also* statistical multiplexer. *Compare* FDM.

time horizon to failure *n. See* event horizon.

time out or **timeout** or **time-out** *n.* An event that indicates that a predetermined amount of time has elapsed without some other expected event taking place. The time-out event is used to interrupt the process that had been waiting for the other expected event. For example, a dial-up remote system might allow the user 60 seconds to log in after making a connection. If the user fails to enter a

T

valid login name and password within this time, the computer breaks the connection, thus protecting itself against crackers as well as freeing a phone line that may have gone dead.

timer *n.* A register (high-speed memory circuit) or a special circuit, chip, or software routine used to measure time intervals. A timer is not the same as the system clock, although its pulses can be derived from the system clock frequency. *See also* time and date. *Compare* clock (definition 1), clock/calendar.

time server *n.* A computer that periodically synchronizes the time on all computers within a network. This ensures that the time used by network services and local functions remains accurate.

time-sharing or **timesharing** *n.* **1.** The use of a computer system by more than one individual at the same time. Time-sharing runs separate programs concurrently by interleaving portions of processing time allotted to each program (user). *See also* quantum (definition 2), time slice. **2.** A method, used primarily in the 1960s and 1970s, for sharing the capabilities (and cost) of a computer, such as a mainframe. Time-sharing allowed different clients to "rent" time on a large computer and pay for only the portion of time they used.

time shifting *n.* A method of dealing with programs with Year 2000 problems that entails modifying the date either in data with which a program works (program encapsulation) or in the input/output logic of the program (data encapsulation). In both cases, the date is moved back in time to process the input, and forward in time to the correct date to produce output. *See also* encapsulation.

time slice *n.* A brief period of time during which a particular task is given control of the microprocessor in a time-sharing multitasking environment. *See also* multitasking, preemptive multitasking. *Compare* quantum (definition 2).

time-slice multitasking *n. See* preemptive multitasking.

timestamp *n.* A certification by a trusted third party specifying that a particular message existed at a specific time and date. In a digital context, trusted third parties generate a trusted timestamp for a particular message by having a timestamping service append a time value to a message and then digitally signing the result. *See also* digital signature, service.

time stamp *n.* A time signature that is added by a program or system to files, e-mail messages, or Web pages. A time stamp indicates the time and usually the date when a file or Web page was created or last modified or when an e-mail message was sent or received. Most time stamps are created by programs and are based on the time kept by the system clock of a computer on which the program resides. Commercial time stamp services are available on the Web or by e-mail, and offer proof of posting certificates to corroborate the time and date a message was sent. *Also called:* date and time stamp, date stamp, time and date stamp.

time-synchronization service *n.* A program used to ensure that all systems on a network use a common time. Time-synchronization services on the Internet typically update real-time clocks to Universal Time Coordinate (UTC) using Network Time Protocol (NTP). Windows Time Synchronization Service (Win32Time) is a time-synchronization service. *See also* clock (definition 2), Network Time Protocol, Universal Time Coordinate.

Time to Live *n.* A header field for a packet sent over the Internet indicating how long the packet should be held. *Acronym:* TTL. *See also* header (definition 2), packet (definition 1).

timing attack *n.* An attack on a cryptographic system that exploits the fact that different cryptographic operations take slightly different amounts of time to process. The attacker exploits these slight time differences by carefully measuring the amount of time required to perform private key operations. Taking these measurements from a vulnerable system can reveal the entire secret key. Cryptographic tokens, network-based cryptosystems, and other applications where attackers can make reasonably accurate timing measurements are potentially at risk from this form of attack.

timing signals *n.* **1.** Any of several types of signals used to coordinate activities within a computer system. **2.** A signal used to coordinate data transfer operations.

Tinkerbell program *n.* A program used to monitor network traffic and alert security administrators when connections are made from a predetermined list of sites and individuals. A Tinkerbell program acts as a low-level security reporting feature.

tiny model *n.* A memory model in the Intel 80x86 processor family. The tiny model allows a combined total of only 64 kilobytes (KB) for code and for data. *See also* 8086, memory model.

T

title bar *n.* In a graphical user interface, a horizontal space at the top of a window that contains the name of the window. Most title bars also contain boxes or buttons for closing and resizing the window. Clicking on the title bar allows the user to move the entire window.

TLA *n.* Acronym for **t**hree-**l**etter **a**cronym. An ironic term, usually used in jest on the Internet in e-mail, newsgroups, and other online forums, referring to the large number of acronyms in computer terminology, particularly those consisting of three letters.

TLD *n. See* top-level domain.

TLS *n.* Acronym for **T**ransport **L**ayer **S**ecurity. A standard protocol that is used to provide secure Web communications on the Internet or intranets. It enables clients to authenticate servers or, optionally, servers to authenticate clients. It also provides a secure channel by encrypting communications. TLS is the latest and a more secure version of the SSL protocol. *See also* authentication, communications protocol, SSL.

TMS34010 *n. See* 34010, 34020.

TN display *n. See* twisted nematic display.

TOF *n. See* top-of-file.

toggle[1] *n.* An electronic device with two states or a program option that can be turned on or off using the same action, such as a mouse click.

toggle[2] *vb.* To switch back and forth between two states. For example, the Num Lock key on an IBM-style keyboard toggles the numeric keypad between numbers and cursor movement.

ToggleKeys *n.* A feature of Windows 9x and Windows NT 4 that sounds high and low beeps when one of the toggle keys (Caps Lock, Num Lock, or Scroll Lock) is turned on or off. *See also* typematic. *Compare* BounceKeys, FilterKeys, MouseKeys, ShowSounds, SoundSentry, StickyKeys.

token *n.* **1.** A unique structured data object or message that circulates continuously among the nodes of a token ring and describes the current state of the network. Before any node can send a message, it must first wait to control the token. *See also* token bus network, token passing, token ring network. **2.** Any nonreducible textual element in data that is being parsed—for example, the use in a program of a variable name, a reserved word, or an operator. Storing tokens as short codes shortens program files and speeds execution. *See also* Basic, parse.

token bus *n.* The IEEE 802.4 specification for token-passing networks based on a bus or tree topology. Token bus networks were designed primarily for manufacturing but the specification also corresponds to the ARCnet architecture used for LANs.

token bus network *n.* A LAN (local area network) formed in a bus topology (stations connected to a single, shared data highway) that uses token passing as a means of regulating traffic on the line. On a token bus network, a token governing the right to transmit is passed from one station to another, and each station holds the token for a brief time, during which it alone can transmit information. The token is transferred in order of priority from an "upstream" station to the next "downstream" station, which might or might not be the next station on the bus. In essence, the token "circles" through the network in a logical ring rather than a physical one. Token bus networks are defined in the IEEE 802.4 standards. *See also* bus network, IEEE 802 standards, token passing. *Compare* token ring network.

token passing *n.* A method of controlling network access through the use of a special signal, called a *token*, that determines which station is allowed to transmit. The token, which is actually a short message or a small packet, is passed from station to station around the network. Only the station with the token can transmit information. *See also* token bus network, token ring network. *Compare* collision detection, contention, CSMA/CD.

token ring *n.* Spelled with lowercase *t* and *r*, the IEEE specification 802.5 for token ring networks. *See also* token ring network.

Token Ring *n. See* Token Ring network.

token ring network *n.* A LAN (local area network) formed in a ring (closed loop) topology that uses token passing as a means of regulating traffic on the line. On a token ring network, a token governing the right to transmit is passed from one station to the next in a physical circle. If a station has information to transmit, it "seizes" the token, marks it as being in use, and inserts the information. The "busy" token, plus message, is then passed around the circle, copied when it arrives at its destination, and eventually returned to the sender. The sender removes the attached message and then passes the freed token to the next station in line. Token ring networks are defined in the IEEE 802.5 standards. *See also* IEEE 802 standards, ring network, token passing. *Compare* token bus network.

522

Token Ring network *n.* A token-passing, ring-shaped local area network (LAN) developed by IBM that operates at 4 megabits (4 million bits) per second. With standard telephone wiring, the Token Ring network can connect up to 72 devices; with shielded twisted-pair (STP) wiring, the network supports up to 260 devices. Although it is based on a ring (closed loop) topology, the Token Ring network uses star-shaped clusters of up to eight workstations connected to a wiring concentrator (Multistation Access Unit, or MSAU), which, in turn, is connected to the main ring. The Token Ring network is designed to accommodate microcomputers, minicomputers, and mainframes; it follows the IEEE 802.5 standards for token ring networks. See the illustration. *See also* ring network, STP, token passing.

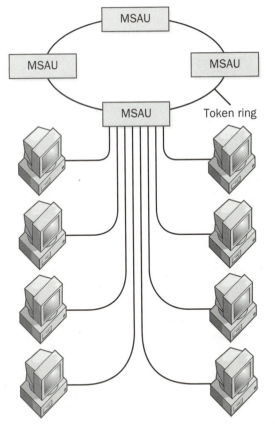

Token Ring network. *An IBM Token Ring configuration with MSAUs.*

tone *n.* **1.** A particular tint of a color. *Also called:* shade, value. *See also* brightness, color model. **2.** One sound or signal of a particular frequency.

tone compression *n.* In digital graphics, the compression of the complete color range of an image to the narrower range of the chosen output device. Allowing for tone compression in scanning and graphics editing may improve the quality of the final printed image.

toner *n.* Powdered pigment that is used in office copiers and in laser, LED, and LCD printers. *See also* electrophotographic printers.

toner cartridge *n.* A disposable container that holds toner for a laser printer or other page printer. Some types of toner cartridge contain toner only; however, the most popular printer engines pack all expendables, including toner and the photosensitive drum, in a single cartridge. Toner cartridges are interchangeable among printers that use the same engine.

toolbar *n.* In an application in a graphical user interface, a row, column, or block of on-screen buttons or icons. When these buttons or icons are clicked on with the mouse, macros or certain functions of the application are activated. For example, word processors often feature toolbars with buttons for changing text to italic, boldface, and other styles. Toolbars often can be customized by the user and usually can be moved around on the screen according to the user's preference. See the illustration. *See also* graphical user interface. *Compare* menu bar, palette (definition 1), taskbar, title bar.

Toolbar.

toolbox *n.* A set of predefined (and usually precompiled) routines a programmer can use in writing a program for a particular machine, environment, or application. *Also called:* toolkit. *See also* library (definition 1).

Toolbox *n.* A set of routines stored mostly in the read-only memory of a Macintosh that provides application programmers with the tools needed to support the graphical interface characteristic of the computer. *Also called:* User Interface Toolbox.

Tool Command Language/Tool Kit *n. See* Tcl/Tk.

toolkit *n. See* toolbox.

ToolTips *n.* Brief descriptions of the names of buttons and boxes on toolbars and in the toolbox. A ToolTip is displayed when the mouse pointer rests on the button or combo box. *See also* ScreenTips.

top-down design *n.* A program design methodology that starts with defining program functionality at the highest level (a series of tasks) and then breaks down each task into lower-level tasks, and so on. *See also* bottom-up programming, top-down programming. *Compare* bottom-up design.

top-down programming *n.* An approach to programming that implements a program in top-down fashion. Typically, this is done by writing a main body with calls to several major routines (implemented as stubs). Each routine is then coded, calling other, lower-level, routines (also done initially as stubs). *See also* bottom-up design, stub, top-down design. *Compare* bottom-up programming.

topic drift *n.* The tendency of an online discussion to move from its original subject to other related or unrelated subjects. For example, someone in a conference devoted to television may ask about a news program; then somebody else may say something about a story on that program about food poisoning, which leads somebody else to start a general discussion on the advantages of organic fruits and vegetables.

topic group *n.* An online discussion area for participants with a common interest in a particular subject.

top-level domain *n.* In the domain-name system of Internet addresses or DNS hierarchy, any of the broadest category of names, under which all domain names fit. Top-level domains for sites in the United States include .com, .edu, .gov, .net, and .org. *See also* DNS (definition 1), major geographic domain.

top-of-file *n.* **1.** The beginning of a file. **2.** A symbol used by a program to mark the beginning of a file—the first character in the file or, in an indexed (ordered) database, the first indexed record. *Acronym:* TOF. *See also* beginning-of-file.

topology *n.* The configuration or layout of a network formed by the connections between devices on a LAN (local area network) or between two or more LANs. *See also* bus network, LAN, ring network, star network, token ring network, tree network.

top posting *n.* In e-mail and newsgroup discussions, placing new material before material quoted from earlier posts rather than after. Because top-posted messages are read out of chronological order, top-posting is considered an undesirable practice.

total bypass *n.* A communications network that uses satellite transmission to bypass both local and long-distance telephone links.

total cost of ownership *n.* Specifically, the cost of owning, operating, and maintaining a single PC; more generally, the cost to businesses and organizations of setting up and maintaining complex and far-reaching networked computer systems. Total cost of ownership includes the up-front costs of hardware and software added to later costs of installation, personnel training, technical support, upgrades, and repairs. Industry initiatives designed to lower the total cost of ownership include centralized network management and administration, as well as hardware solutions in the form of network-based computers with or without local storage and expansion capability. *Acronym:* TCO.

touch pad *n.* A variety of graphics tablet that uses pressure sensors, rather than the electromagnetics used in more expensive high-resolution tablets, to track the position of a device on its surface. *See also* absolute pointing device, graphics tablet.

touch screen *n.* A computer screen designed or modified to recognize the location of a touch on its surface. By touching the screen, the user can make a selection or move a cursor. The simplest type of touch screen is made up of a grid of sensing lines, which determine the location of a touch by matching vertical and horizontal contacts. Another, more accurate type uses an electrically charged surface and sensors around the outer edges of the screen to detect the amount of electrical disruption and pinpoint exactly where contact has been made. A third type has infrared light-emitting diodes (LEDs) and sensors around the outer edges of the screen. These LEDs and sensors create an invisible infrared grid, which the user's finger interrupts, in front of the screen. *Compare* light pen.

touch-sensitive display *n.* *See* touch screen.

touch-sensitive tablet *n.* *See* touch pad.

touch tone dialing *n.* The signaling system used in telephones with touch-tone keypads, in which each digit is associated with two specific frequencies. During dialing, these frequencies—for example, 1336 Hz and 697 Hz for the number 2—are transmitted to the telephone company. *Also called:* DTMF, Dual Tone Multiple Frequency.

tower *n.* A microcomputer system in which the cabinet for the central processing unit (CPU) is tall, narrow, and deep rather than short, wide, and deep. The motherboard is usually vertical, and the disk drives are often perpendicular to the motherboard. A tower cabinet is at least 24 inches tall. See the illustration. *See also* cabinet, microcomputer, motherboard. *Compare* minitower.

Tower.

TP *n. See* transaction processing.

TPC *n. See* Transaction Processing Council.

TPC-D *n.* Acronym for **T**ransaction **P**rocessing **C**ouncil Benchmark **D**. A benchmark standard that addresses a broad range of decision support applications working with complex data structures. *See also* Transaction Processing Council.

TPI *n. See* tracks per inch.

TP monitor *n.* Short for **te**leprocessing **monitor** or trans-action **processing monitor**. A program that controls the transfer of data between terminals (or clients) and a mainframe (or one or more servers) so as to provide a consistent environment for one or more online transaction processing (OLTP) applications. A TP monitor may also control the appearance of the screen displays and check input data for proper format. *See also* client (definition 3), mainframe computer, OLTP, server (definition 1).

trace *vb.* To execute a program in such a way that the sequence of statements being executed can be observed. *See also* debugger, single step.

traceroute *n.* A utility that shows the route a packet takes through a network to arrive at a remote host. A traceroute also reports the IP addresses of all intermediate hosts or routers and the time required for the packet to reach each of them. *See also* IP address, packet.

track[1] *n.* One of numerous circular data storage areas on a floppy disk or a hard drive, comparable to a groove on a record but not spiral. Tracks, composed of sectors, are recorded on a disk by an operating system during a disk format operation. On other storage media, such as tape, a track runs parallel to the edge of the medium. See the illustration.

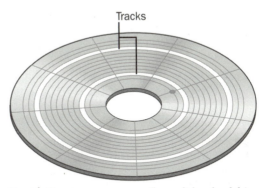

Track[1]. *The storage areas on a floppy disk or hard drive.*

track[2] *vb.* **1.** To follow a path. **2.** In data management, to follow the flow of information through a manual or an automated system. **3.** In data storage and retrieval, to follow and read from a recording channel on a disk or a magnetic tape. **4.** In computer graphics, to cause a displayed symbol, such as a pointer, to match on the screen the movements of a mouse or another pointing device.

trackball *n.* A pointing device that consists of a ball resting on two rollers at right angles to each other, which translate the ball's motion into vertical and horizontal movement on the screen. A trackball also typically has one or more buttons to initiate other actions. A trackball's housing is stationary; its ball is rolled with the hand. See the illustration. *Compare* mechanical mouse.

Trackball.

tracked change *n.* A mark that shows where a deletion, insertion, or other editing change has been made in a document.

trackpad *n.* A pointing device consisting of a small, flat pad that is sensitive to touch. Users move the mouse cursor on screen by touching the trackpad and moving their fingers across the trackpad's surface. Such devices are most commonly installed on laptop computers. *See also* pointing device.

tracks per inch *n.* The density with which concentric tracks (data storage rings) are recorded or can be recorded in an inch of radius on a disk. The greater the density (the more tracks per inch), the more information a disk can hold. *Acronym:* TPI.

tractor feed *n.* A method of feeding paper through a printer using pins mounted on rotating belts. The pins engage holes near the edges of continuous-form paper and either push or pull the paper through. *See also* continuous-form paper. *Compare* pin feed.

trademark *n.* A word, phrase, symbol, or design (or some combination thereof) used to identify a proprietary product, often accompanied by the symbol ™ or ®.

trade show *n.* A multivendor sales event or exposition that showcases companies' products. The computer industry has a number of trade shows every year, including COMDEX.

traditional newsgroup hierarchy *n.* The seven standard newsgroup categories in Usenet: comp., misc., news., rec., sci., soc., and talk. Newsgroups can be added within the traditional hierarchy only following a formal voting process. *See also* comp. newsgroups, misc. newsgroups, newsgroup, news. newsgroups, rec. newsgroups, Request for Discussion, sci. newsgroups, soc. newsgroups, talk. newsgroups, Usenet. *Compare* alt. newsgroups.

traffic *n.* The load carried by a communications link or channel.

traffic management *n. See* ITM.

traffic shaping *n.* A technique for allocating bandwidth and preventing packet loss by enforcing prioritization policies on the transmission of data over a network. *Also called:* bandwidth shaping. *See also* bandwidth management, bandwidth reservation, token passing.

trailer *n.* Information, typically occupying several bytes, at the tail end of a block (section) of transmitted data and often containing a checksum or other error-checking data useful for confirming the accuracy and status of the transmission. *See also* checksum. *Compare* header (definition 2).

trailer label *n.* **1.** A small block of information used in tape processing that marks the end of a file or the end of the tape and that can contain other information, such as the number of records in the file or files on the tape. *Compare* header label. **2.** A label used in communications data frames that follows the data and might contain an end-of-message mark, a checksum, and some synchronization bits.

trailing edge *n.* The latter part of an electronic signal. When a digital signal switches from on to off, the transition is the trailing edge of the signal.

train¹ *n.* A sequence of items or events, such as a digital pulse train consisting of transmitted binary signals.

train² *vb.* To teach an end user how to use a software or hardware product.

transaction *n.* A discrete activity within a computer system, such as an entry of a customer order or an update of an inventory item. Transactions are usually associated with database management, order entry, and other online systems.

transactional e-mail *n.* A form of Web-based marketing in which goods and services are sold to consumers directly from an e-mail message. Unlike traditional e-mail marketing that requires the e-mail recipient to visit the seller's Web site, transactional e-mail allows an entire sales transaction to be completed from within the marketing e-mail. To take advantage of transactional e-mail buying options, the recipient must view the e-mail message in HTML format.

transaction file *n.* A file that contains the details of transactions, such as items and prices on invoices. It is used to update a master database file. *See also* transaction. *Compare* master file.

transaction log *n. See* change file.

transaction processing *n.* A processing method in which transactions are executed immediately after they are received by the system. *Acronym:* TP. *See also* transaction. *Compare* batch processing (definition 3).

Transaction Processing Council *n.* A group of hardware and software vendors with the goal of publishing benchmark standards. *Acronym:* TPC.

transaction processing monitor *n. See* TP monitor.

Transaction Tracking System *n. See* TTS (definition 2).

Transact-SQL *n.* A query language. Transact-SQL is sophisticated SQL dialect loaded with additional features beyond what is defined in the ANSI SQL 92 Standard. *Also called:* T-SQL, TSQL.

transceiver *n.* Short for **trans**mitter/re**ceiver**. A device that can both transmit and receive signals. On LANs (local area networks), a transceiver is the device that connects a computer to the network and that converts signals to and from parallel and serial form.

transceiver cable *n.* A cable that is used to connect a host adapter within a computer to a LAN (local area network). *See also* AUI cable, LAN.

transducer *n.* A device that converts one form of energy into another. Electronic transducers either convert electric energy to another form of energy or convert nonelectric to electric energy.

transfer[1] *n.* **1.** The movement of data from one location to another. **2.** The passing of program control from one portion of code to another.

transfer[2] *vb.* To move data from one place to another, especially within a single computer. *Compare* transmit.

transfer rate *n.* The rate at which a circuit or a communications channel transfers information from source to destination, as over a network or to and from a disk drive. Transfer rate is measured in units of information per unit of time—for example, bits per second or characters per second—and can be measured either as a raw rate, which is the maximum transfer speed, or as an average rate, which includes gaps between blocks of data as part of the transmission time.

transfer statement *n.* A statement in a programming language that transfers the flow of execution to another location in the program. *See also* branch instruction, CALL statement, GOTO statement, jump instruction.

transfer time *n.* The time elapsed between the start of a data transfer operation and its completion.

transform *vb.* **1.** To change the appearance or format of data without altering its content; that is, to encode information according to predefined rules. **2.** In mathematics and computer graphics, to alter the position, size, or nature of an object by moving it to another location (translation), making it larger or smaller (scaling), turning it (rotation), changing its description from one type of coordinate system to another, and so on.

transformer *n.* A device used to change the voltage of an alternating current signal or to change the impedance of an alternating current circuit.

transient *adj.* **1.** Fleeting, temporary, or unpredictable. **2.** Of or pertaining to the region of memory used for programs, such as applications, that are read from disk storage and that reside in memory temporarily until they are replaced by other programs. In this context, *transient* can also refer to the programs themselves. **3.** In electronics, of or pertaining to a short-lived, abnormal, and unpredictable increase in power supply, such as a voltage spike or surge. *Transient time* is the interval during which a change in current or voltage is building up or decaying.

transient suppressor *n.* A circuit designed to reduce or eliminate unwanted electrical signals or voltages.

transistor *n.* Short for **tran**sfer re**sistor**. A solid-state circuit component, usually with three leads, in which a voltage or a current controls the flow of another current. The transistor can serve many functions, including those of amplifier, switch, and oscillator, and is a fundamental component of almost all modern electronics. See the illustration. *See also* base (definition 3), FET, NPN transistor, PNP transistor.

Transistor.

transistor-transistor logic *n.* A type of bipolar circuit design that utilizes transistors connected to each other either directly or through resistors. Transistor-transistor logic offers high speed and good noise immunity and is used in many digital circuits. A large number of transistor-transistor logic gates can be fabricated on a single integrated circuit. *Acronym:* TTL.

transitive trust *n.* The standard type of trust relationship between Windows domains in a domain tree or forest. When a domain joins an existing forest or domain tree, a transitive trust is automatically established. Transitive trusts are always two-way relationships. This series of trusts, between parent and child domains in a domain tree and between root domains of domain trees in a forest, allows all domains in a forest to trust each other for the purposes of authentication. For example, if domain A trusts domain B and domain B trusts domain C, then domain A trusts domain C. *See also* domain, forest, one-way trust, two-way trust.

translate *vb.* **1.** In programming, to convert a program from one language to another. Translation is performed by special programs such as compilers, assemblers, and interpreters. **2.** In computer graphics, to move an image in the "space" represented on the display, without turning (rotating) the image.

translated file *n.* A file containing data that has been changed from binary (8-bit) format to ASCII (7-bit) format. BinHex and uuencode both translate binary files into ASCII. Such translation is necessary to transmit data through systems (such as e-mail) that may not preserve the eighth bit of each byte. A translated file must be decoded to its binary form before being used. *See also* BinHex, uuencode.

translator *n.* A program that translates one language or data format into another.

transmission channel *n. See* channel.

Transmission Control Protocol *n. See* TCP.

Transmission Control Protocol/Internet Protocol *n. See* TCP/IP.

transmit *vb.* To send information over a communications line or a circuit. Computer transmissions can take place in the following ways: asynchronous (variable timing) or synchronous (exact timing); serial (essentially, bit by bit) or parallel (byte by byte; a group of bits at once); duplex or full-duplex (simultaneous two-way communication), half-duplex (two-way communication in one direction at a time), or simplex (one-way communication only); and burst (intermittent transmission of blocks of information). *Compare* transfer[2].

Transmit Data *n. See* TXD.

transmitter *n.* Any circuit or electronic device designed to send electrically encoded data to another location.

transparency *n.* The quality that defines how much light passes through an object's pixels. If an object is 100 percent transparent, light passes through it completely and renders the object invisible; in other words, you can see through the object.

transparency scanner *n. See* scanner.

transparent *adj.* **1.** In computer use, of, pertaining to, or characteristic of a device, function, or part of a program that works so smoothly and easily that it is invisible to the user. For example, the ability of one application to use files created by another is transparent if the user encounters no difficulty in opening, reading, or using the second program's files or does not even know the use is occurring. **2.** In communications, of, pertaining to, or characteristic of a mode of transmission in which data can include any characters, including device-control characters, without the possibility of misinterpretation by the receiving station. For example, the receiving station will not end a transparent transmission until it receives a character in the data that indicates end of transmission. Thus, there is no danger of the receiving station ending communications prematurely. **3.** In computer graphics, of, pertaining to, or characteristic of the lack of color in a particular region of an image so that the background color of the display shows through.

transponder *n.* A transceiver in a communications satellite that receives a signal from an earth station and retransmits it on a different frequency to one or more other earth stations.

transportable computer *n. See* portable computer.

transport layer *n.* The fourth of the seven layers in the International Organization for Standardization's Open Systems Interconnection (OSI) reference model for standardizing computer-to-computer communications. The transport layer is one level above the network layer and is responsible for both quality of service and accurate delivery of information. Among the tasks performed on this layer are error detection and correction. See the illustration. *See also* ISO/OSI reference model.

ISO/OSI MODEL	
ISO/OSI Layer	**Focus**
Application (highest level)	Program-to-program transfer of information
Presentation	Text formatting and display, code conversion
Session	Establishing, maintaining, and coordinating communication
Transport	Accurate delivery, service quality
Network	Transport routes, message handling and transfer
Data-link	Coding, addressing, and transmitting information
Physical	Hardware connections

Transport layer.

Transport Layer Security *n. See* TLS.

transpose[1] *n.* The result of rotating a matrix.

transpose[2] *vb.* **1.** To reverse, as the order of the letters *h* and *t* in *hte*, in correcting the spelling of *the*; or reversing two wires in a circuit. **2.** In mathematics and spreadsheets, to rotate a matrix (a rectangular array of numbers) about a diagonal axis.

transputer *n.* Short for **trans**istor com**puter**. A complete computer on a single chip, including RAM and an FPU, designed as a building block for parallel computing systems.

trap[1] *n. See* interrupt.

trap[2] *vb.* **1.** To intercept an action or event before it occurs, usually in order to do something else. Trapping is commonly used by debuggers to allow interruption of program execution at a given spot. *See also* interrupt, interrupt handler. **2.** To slightly overlap adjacent colors in preparing material for printing. Page layout and prepress programs trap color to prevent gaps between colors caused by minor variations in registration during printing.

trapdoor *n. See* back door.

trap handler *n. See* interrupt handler.

Trash *n.* An icon on the screen in the Macintosh Finder, resembling a garbage can. To delete a file or eject a diskette, the user drags the icon for the file or diskette to the Trash. However, until the user shuts down the system or

chooses the menu option "Empty Trash," a file in the Trash is not actually deleted; the user can retrieve it by double-clicking the Trash icon and dragging the file's icon out of the resulting window. *Compare* Recycle Bin.

traverse *vb.* In programming, to access in a particular order all of the nodes of a tree or similar data structure.

tree *n.* A data structure containing zero or more nodes that are linked together in a hierarchical fashion. If there are any nodes, one node is the root; each node except the root is the child of one and only one other node; and each node has zero or more nodes as children. *See also* child (definition 2), graph, leaf, node (definition 3), parent/child (definition 2), root.

tree network *n.* A topology for a local area network (LAN) in which one machine is connected to one or more other machines, each of which is connected to one or more others, and so on, so that the structure formed by the network resembles that of a tree. See the illustration. *See also* bus network, distributed network, ring network, star network, token ring network, topology.

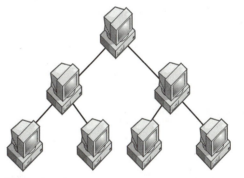

Tree network.

tree search *n.* A search procedure performed on a tree data structure. At each step of the search, a tree search is able to determine, by the value in a particular node, which branches of the tree to eliminate, without searching those branches themselves. *See also* branch (definition 1), tree structure.

tree structure *n.* Any structure that has the essential organizational properties of a tree. *See also* tree.

tree view *n.* A hierarchical representation of the folders, files, disk drives, and other resources connected to a computer or network. For example, Windows Explorer uses a tree view to display the resources that are attached to a computer or a network. *See also* resource.

T

trellis-coded modulation *n.* An enhanced form of quadrature amplitude modulation that is used by modems that operate at or above 9,600 bps (bits per second). Trellis-coded modulation encodes information as unique sets of bits associated with changes in both the phase and amplitude of the carrier, as well as using extra signal points for error-checking bits. *Acronym:* TCM. *See also* quadrature amplitude modulation.

trendline *n.* A graphic representation of trends in data series, such as a line sloping upward to represent increased sales over a period of months. Trendlines are used for the study of problems of prediction. *Also called:* regression analysis.

triage[1] *n.* The process of prioritizing projects or elements of a project (such as bug fixes) to ensure that available resources are assigned in the most effective, time-efficient, and cost-efficient manner. Traditionally, triage has referred to the prioritization of treatment to the wounded during wartime or medical disaster situations. More recently, the term also refers to anticipating and preventing computer system crashes brought on by the Year 2000 (Y2K) problem. *See also* Year 2000 Problem.

triage[2] *vb.* To identify and prioritize the elements of a project or problem to order them in a way that makes best use of labor, funds, and other resources.

tri-band phone *n.* A wireless phone designed for international travel. Tri-band phones broadcast on the personal communication service (PCS) frequency used in North America as well as PCS frequencies used in other regions of the world.

trichromatic *adj.* Of, pertaining to, or characteristic of a system that uses three colors (red, green, and blue in computer graphics) to create all other colors. *See also* color model.

trigger[1] *n.* **1.** In a database, an action that causes a procedure to be carried out automatically when a user attempts to modify data. A trigger can instruct the database system to take a specific action, depending on the particular change attempted. Incorrect, unwanted, or unauthorized changes can thereby be prevented, helping to maintain the integrity of the database. **2.** A function built into a virus or worm that controls the release of a malicious payload or similar event. The trigger may be activated at a predetermined time or date or in response to a user-initiated event, such as opening a specific program or file. In some cases,

the trigger may reset itself repeatedly until the virus is neutralized.

trigger[2] *vb.* To activate a function or program, such as the release of a virus payload, in response to a specific event, date, or time.

trigonometry *n.* The branch of mathematics dealing with arcs and angles, expressed in functions (for example, sine and cosine) that show relationships—for example, between two sides of a right triangle or between two complementary angles.

trilinear filtering *n.* A technique used in 3-D computer game rendering and other digital animation applications that produces the illusion of depth of field by making distant objects less distinct and detailed than nearer objects.

tri-mode phone *n.* A wireless phone that broadcasts on 1900 MHz personal communication service (PCS), 800 MHz digital cellular networks, and 800 MHz analog networks.

triple-pass scanner *n.* A color scanner that performs one scanning pass on an image for each of the three primary colors of light (red, green, and blue). *See also* color scanner.

tristimulus values *n.* In color graphics, the varying amounts of three colors, such as red, blue, and green, that are combined to produce another color. *See also* color, color model.

Trivial File Transfer Protocol *n.* A simplified version of File Transfer Protocol (FTP) that provides basic file transfer with no user authentication and is often used to download the initial files needed to begin an installation process. *Acronym:* TFTP. *See also* communications protocol.

troff *n.* Short for **t**ypesetting **r**un **off**. A UNIX text formatter often used to format man pages. *See also* man pages, RUNOFF. *Compare* TeX.

Trojan horse *n.* A destructive program disguised as a game, utility, or application. When run, a Trojan horse does something harmful to the computer system while appearing to do something useful. *See also* virus, worm.

troll *vb.* To post a message in a newsgroup or other online conference in the hopes that somebody else will consider the original message so outrageous that it demands a heated reply. A classic example of trolling is an article in favor of torturing cats posted in a pet lovers' newsgroup. *See also* YHBT.

troubleshoot *vb.* To isolate the source of a problem in a program, computer system, or network and remedy it.

troubleshooter *n.* A person trained and hired to find and resolve problems or breakdowns in machinery and technical equipment or systems. Troubleshooters often work as short-term consultants or freelancers because many organizations and businesses regard troubleshooting as a short-term effort or possibly an exceptional—unplanned—part of a project or system. *See also* troubleshoot.

trouble ticket *n.* A report of a problem with a particular device or system that is tracked through the workflow process. Originally written on paper, electronic trouble tickets are featured by many workflow and help-desk applications. *See also* help desk (definition 2), workflow application.

True BASIC *n.* A version of Basic created in 1983 by John Kemeny and Thomas Kurtz, the creators of the original Basic, to standardize and modernize the language. True BASIC is a compiled, structured version of Basic that does not require line numbers. True BASIC includes advanced control structures that make structured programming possible. *See also* Basic, structured programming.

true color *n. See* 24-bit color.

true complement *n. See* complement.

TrueType *n.* An outline font technology introduced by Apple Computer, Inc., in 1991 and by Microsoft Corporation in 1992 as a means of including high-grade fonts within the Macintosh and Windows operating systems. TrueType is a WYSIWYG font technology, which means that the printed output of TrueType fonts is identical to what appears on the screen. *See also* bitmapped font, outline font, PostScript.

TrueType Open version 2 *n. See* OpenType.

truncate *vb.* To cut off the beginning or end of a series of characters or numbers; specifically, to eliminate one or more of the least significant (typically rightmost) digits. In truncation, numbers are simply eliminated, unlike rounding, in which the rightmost digit might be incremented to preserve accuracy. *Compare* round.

trunk *n.* **1.** In communications, a channel connecting two switching stations. A trunk usually carries a large number of calls at the same time. **2.** In networking, the cable forming the main communications path on a network. On a bus network, the single cable to which all nodes connect. *See also* backbone.

trunking *n. See* link aggregation.

Trusted Computing Base *n. See* TCB.

trust relationship *n.* A logical relationship established between domains to allow pass-through authentication, in which a trusting domain honors the logon authentications of a trusted domain. User accounts and global groups defined in a trusted domain can be given rights and permissions in a trusting domain, even though the user accounts or groups don't exist in the trusting domain's directory. *See also* authentication, domain, group, permission, user account.

truth table *n.* A table showing the value of a Boolean expression for each of the possible combinations of variable values in the expression. *See also* AND, Boolean operator, exclusive OR, NOT, OR.

try *n.* A keyword used in the Java programming language to define a block of statements that may throw a Java language exception. If an exception is thrown, an optional "catch" block can handle specific exceptions thrown within the "try" block. Also, an optional "finally" block will be executed regardless of whether an exception is thrown. *See also* block, catch, exception, finally.

TSAPI *n.* Acronym for **T**elephony **S**ervices **A**pplication **P**rogramming **I**nterface. The set of standards for the interface between a large telephone system and a computer network server, developed by Novell and AT&T and supported by many telephone equipment manufacturers and software developers. *Compare* TAPI.

TSP *n. See* Telephony Service Provider.

TSPI *n. See* Telephony Service Provider Interface.

T-SQL or **TSQL** *n. See* Transact-SQL.

TSR *n.* Acronym for **t**erminate-and-**s**tay-**r**esident. A program that remains loaded in memory even when it is not running, so that it can be quickly invoked for a specific task performed while another program is operating. Typically, these programs are used with operating systems that are not multitasking, such as MS-DOS. *See also* hot key.

TSV *n.* Filename extension, short for **t**ab **s**eparated **v**alues, assigned to text files containing tabular (row and column) data of the type stored in database fields. As the name indicates, individual data entries are separated by tabs. *Compare* CSV (definition 3).

TTFN *n.* Acronym for **T**a **t**a **f**or **n**ow. An expression sometimes used in Internet discussion groups, such as Internet Relay Chat (IRC), to signal a participant's temporary departure from the group. *See also* IRC.

T

TTL *n. See* Time to Live, transistor-transistor logic.

TTS *n.* **1.** Acronym for **T**ext-**t**o-**S**peech. The process of converting digital text into speech output. TTS is used extensively in fax, e-mail, and other services for the blind, and for telephone-based informational and financial services. **2.** Acronym for **T**ransaction **T**racking **S**ystem. A feature developed to protect databases from corruption caused by incomplete transactions. TTS monitors attempted transactions and in the event of a hardware or software failure, TTS will cancel the update and back out to maintain database integrity.

TTY *n.* Acronym for **t**ele**t**ypewriter. A device for low-speed communications over a telephone line, consisting of a keyboard that sends a character code for each keystroke and a printer that prints characters as their codes are received. The simplest video display interface behaves like a TTY. *See also* KSR terminal, teletype mode.

tunnel *vb.* To encapsulate or wrap a packet or a message from one protocol in the packet for another. The wrapped packet is then transmitted over a network via the protocol of the wrapper. This method of packet transmission is used to avoid protocol restrictions. *See also* communications protocol, packet (definition 2).

tunneling *n.* A method of transmission over internetworks based on differing protocols. In tunneling, a packet based on one protocol is wrapped, or encapsulated, in a second packet based on whatever differing protocol is needed in order for it to travel over an intermediary network. In effect, the second wrapper "insulates" the original packet and creates the illusion of a tunnel through which the wrapped packet travels across the intermediary network. In real-life terms, tunneling is comparable to "encapsulating" a present (the original packet) in a box (the secondary wrapper) for delivery through the postal system.

tunnel server *n.* A server or router that terminates tunnels and forwards traffic to the hosts on the target network. *See also* host, router, server, tunnel.

tuple *n.* In a database table (relation), a set of related values, one for each attribute (column). A tuple is stored as a row in a relational database management system. It is the analog of a record in a nonrelational file. *See also* relation.

Turing machine *n.* **1.** A theoretical model created by British mathematician Alan Turing in 1936 that is considered the prototype for digital computers. Described in a paper ("On Computable Numbers with an Application to

the Entscheidungsproblem") published in the *Proceedings of the London Mathematical Society*, the Turing machine was a logical device that could scan one square at a time (either blank or containing a symbol) on a paper tape. Depending on the symbol read from a particular square, the machine would change its status and/or move the tape backward or forward to erase a symbol or to print a new one. *See also* status. **2.** A computer that can successfully mimic human intelligence in the Turing test.

Turing test *n.* A test of machine intelligence proposed by Alan Turing, British mathematician and developer of the Turing machine. In the Turing test, also known as the Imitation Game, a person uses any series of questions to interrogate two unseen respondents, a human and a computer, to try to determine which is the computer.

turnaround time *n.* **1.** The elapsed time between submission and completion of a job. **2.** In communications, the time required to reverse the direction of transmission in half-duplex communication mode. *See also* half-duplex transmission.

turnkey system *n.* A finished system, complete with all necessary hardware and documentation and with software installed and ready to be used.

turnpike effect *n.* The communications equivalent of gridlock; a reference to bottlenecks caused by heavy traffic over a communications system or network.

turtle *n.* A small on-screen shape, usually a triangle or a turtle shape, that acts as a drawing tool in graphics. A turtle is a friendly, easily manipulated tool designed for children learning to use computers. It takes its name from a mechanical, dome-shaped turtle that was developed for the Logo language and moved about the floor in response to Logo commands, raising and lowering a pen to draw lines.

turtle graphics *n.* A simple graphics environment, present in Logo and other languages, in which a turtle is manipulated by simple commands. Some versions display the turtle and its track on screen; others use electromechanical turtles that write on paper.

tutorial *n.* A teaching aid designed to help people learn to use a product or procedure. In computer applications, a tutorial might be presented in either a book or a manual or as an interactive disk-based series of lessons provided with the program package.

Tux *n.* The mascot of the Linux operating system. Tux is a rotund cartoonish penguin and the Tux image is available for use by any provider of Linux products or services. The name Tux is both short for tuxedo, in reference to a penguin's appearance, and an acronym for **T**orvalds's Uni**X**, after Linus Torvalds, the creator of the Linux operating system.

TV tuner card *n.* A PCI card that allows a computer to receive television programming and display it on the computer's monitor. *See also* PCI card.

TWAIN *n.* The de facto standard interface between software applications and image-capturing devices such as scanners. Nearly all scanners contain a TWAIN driver, but only TWAIN-compatible software can use the technology. The TWAIN specification was developed by the TWAIN Working Group, a consortium of industry vendors formed in 1992. The name is thought by some to be an acronym for the phrase "technology without an interesting name," although the TWAIN Working Group maintains the name is not an acronym. Others attribute the name to the quote "Ne'er the twain shall meet," because the TWAIN driver and the application receiving the image are separated. *See also* scanner.

tweak *vb.* To make final small changes to improve hardware or software performance; to fine-tune a nearly complete product.

tween *vb.* In a graphics program, to calculate intermediary shapes during the metamorphosis of one shape into another.

twinaxial *adj.* Having two coaxial cables contained in a single insulated jacket. *See also* coaxial cable.

twip *n.* A unit of measure used in typesetting and desktop publishing, equal to one-twentieth of a printer's point, or 1/1440th of an inch. *See also* point[1] (definition 1).

twisted nematic display *n.* A type of passive-matrix liquid crystal display (LCD) in which the glass sheets enclosing nematic liquid crystal material are treated in such a way that the crystal molecules twist 90 degrees between top and bottom—in other words, the orientation at the bottom of the crystal is perpendicular to the orientation at the top. When an electrical charge is applied selectively to these crystals, they become temporarily untwisted and block the passage of polarized light. This blockage is what produces the dark pixels on an LCD display. The *nematic* part of the description refers to microscopic threadlike bodies that characterize the type of liquid crystals used in these displays. *Also called:* TN display.

twisted-pair cable *n.* A cable made of two separately insulated strands of wire twisted together. It is used to

reduce signal interference introduced by a strong radio source such as a nearby cable. One of the wires in the pair carries the sensitive signal, and the other wire is grounded.

twisted-pair wiring *n.* Wiring consisting of two insulated strands of copper twisted around one another to form a cable. Twisted-pair wiring comes in two forms, unshielded twisted pair (UTP) and shielded twisted pair (STP), the latter named for an extra protective sheath wrapped around each insulated pair of wires. Twisted-pair wiring can consist of a single pair of wires or, in thicker cables, two, four, or more pairs of wires. Twisted-pair wiring is typical of telephone cabling. *Compare* coaxial cable, fiberoptic cable.

two-digit date storage *n.* A limitation in many computer systems and programs that store the year portion of a date as two digits instead of four. This practice in programming dates from the earliest days of computers when space on punch cards and memory in the computer were very limited, and many programmers used a two-digit year in date fields to economize on space or memory requirements.

two-digit shortcut *n.* The practice of using two digits to indicate the year in a program, particularly those written in programming languages or running on systems that have the capability to work with a four-digit year (hence the term shortcut).

two-dimensional *adj.* Existing in reference to two measures, such as height and width—for example, a two-dimensional model drawn with reference to an *x*-axis and a *y*-axis, or a two-dimensional array of numbers placed in rows and columns. *See also* Cartesian coordinates.

two-dimensional array *n.* An ordered arrangement of information in which the location of any item is described by two numbers (integers) identifying its position in a particular row and column of a matrix.

two-dimensional model *n.* A computer simulation of a physical object in which length and width are real attributes but depth is not; a model with *x*- and *y*-axes. *Compare* three-dimensional model.

two-nines availability *n.* The availability of a system 99% of the time. Two-nines availability equates to approximately 87.6 hours of downtime in a standard 365-day year. *See also* high availability.

two-out-of-five code *n.* An error-sensitive code for data transmission that stores each of the ten decimal digits (0 through 9) as a set of five binary digits: either two of the

T

digits are 1s and the other three digits are 0s or two of the digits are 0s and the other three digits are 1s.

two's complement *n.* A number in the base-2 system (binary system) that is the true complement of another number. A two's complement is usually derived by reversing the digits in a binary number (changing 1s to 0s and 0s to 1s) and adding 1 to the result. When two's complements are used to represent negative numbers, the most significant (leftmost) digit is always 1. *See also* complement.

two-tier client/server *n.* A client/business logic layer and the database layer. Fourth-generation languages (4GL) have helped to popularize the two-tier client/server architecture. *Compare* three-tier client/server.

two-way trust *n.* A type of trust relationship in which both of the domains in the relationship trust each other. In a two-way trust relationship, each domain has established a one-way trust with the other domain. For example, domain A trusts domain B and domain B trusts domain A. Two-way trusts can be transitive or nontransitive. All two-way trusts between Windows domains in the same domain tree or forest are transitive. *See also* domain, forest, one-way trust, transitive trust.

TXD *n.* Short for Transmit (**tx**) **D**ata. A line used to carry transmitted data from one device to another, as from computer to modem; in RS-232-C connections, pin 2. *See also* RS-232-C standard. *Compare* RXD.

.txt *n.* A file extension that identifies ASCII text files. In most cases, a document with a .txt extension does not include any formatting commands, so it is readable in any text editor or word processing program. *See also* ASCII.

Tymnet *n.* A public data network available in over 100 countries, with links to some online services and Internet service providers.

type[1] *n.* **1.** In programming, the nature of a variable—for example, integer, real number, text character, or floating-point number. Data types in programs are declared by the programmer and determine the range of values a variable can take as well as the operations that can be performed on it. *See also* data type. **2.** In printing, the characters that make up printed text, the design of a set of characters (typeface), or, more loosely, the complete set of characters in a given size and style (font). *See also* font, typeface.

type[2] *vb.* To enter information by means of the keyboard.

Type I PC Card *n. See* PC Card.

Type II PC Card *n. See* PC Card.

Type III PC Card *n. See* PC Card.

type-ahead buffer *n. See* keyboard buffer.

type-ahead capability *n.* The ability of a computer program to gather incoming keystrokes in a temporary memory reservoir (buffer) before displaying them on the screen. This capability ensures that keystrokes are not lost if they are typed faster than the program can display them.

type ball *n.* A small ball mounted on the print head of a printer or a typewriter (for example, the IBM Selectric) that bears all the characters in the character set on its surface. The ball rotates to align the correct character with the paper and with an inked or carbon ribbon before striking against the paper. See the illustration.

Type ball.

type checking *n.* The process performed by a compiler or interpreter to make sure that when a variable is used, it is treated as having the same data type as it was declared to have. *See also* compiler (definition 2), data type, interpreter.

type declaration *n.* A declaration in a program that specifies the characteristics of a new data type, usually by combining more primitive existing data types.

typeface *n.* A specific, named design of a set of printed characters, such as Helvetica Bold Oblique, that has a specified obliqueness (degree of slant) and stroke weight (thickness of line). A typeface is not the same as a *font*, which is a specific size of a specific typeface, such as 12-point Helvetica Bold Oblique. Nor is a typeface the same as a *typeface family*, which is a group of related typefaces, such as the Helvetica family including Helvetica, Helvetica Bold, Helvetica Oblique, and Helvetica Bold Oblique. *See also* font.

type font *n. See* font.

typematic *adj.* The keyboard feature that repeats a keystroke when a key is held down longer than usual. *Also called:* auto-key, auto-repeat. *See also* repeat key, Repeat-Keys.

typeover mode *n. See* overwrite mode.

type size *n.* The size of printed characters, usually measured in points (a point is approximately $1/72$ inch). *See also* point[1] (definition 1).

type style *n.* **1.** The obliqueness, or degree of slant, of a typeface. **2.** Loosely, the overall design of a typeface or a typeface family. **3.** One of the variant forms of a type character, including roman, bold, italic, and bold italic.

typography *n.* **1.** The art of font design and typesetting. *See also* computer typesetting, font. **2.** The conversion of unformatted text into camera-ready type, suitable for printing. *See also* camera-ready.

typosquatter *n.* A form of cybersquatter that takes advantage of typographical errors to snare Web surfers. The typosquatter registers variations of popular trademarked domain names that contain the most likely spelling errors (for example: JCPenny). A user who makes a mistake typing in a Web site address will be taken to the typosquatter's site, which typically is loaded with banner and pop-up ads. The typosquatter is paid by the number of users who see the ads. *See also* cybersquatter.

T

u- *prefix* A letter sometimes substituted for the Greek letter μ (mu), meaning micro, used as a prefix in measurements denoting one millionth, or 10^{-6}. *See also* micro- (definition 2).

UA *n. See* user agent.

UART *n.* Acronym for **u**niversal **a**synchronous **r**eceiver-**t**ransmitter. A module, usually composed of a single integrated circuit, that contains both the receiving and transmitting circuits required for asynchronous serial communication. A UART is the most common type of circuit used in personal computer modems. *Compare* USRT.

ubiquitous computing *n.* A term coined by Mark Wieser (1988) at the Xerox PARC Computer Science Lab to describe a computing environment so pervasive in daily life that it's invisible to the user. Household appliances such as VCRs and microwave ovens are contemporary low-level examples of ubiquitous computing. In the future, prognosticators say, computers will be so embedded in all facets of life—so ubiquitous—that their presence will fade into the background. Ubiquitous computing is considered to be the third stage in the evolution of computing technology, after the mainframe and the personal computer. *Acronym*: UC.

UC *n. See* ubiquitous computing.

UCAID *n.* Acronym for **U**niversity **C**orporation for **A**dvanced **I**nternet **D**evelopment. An organization created to provide guidance in advanced networking development within the university community. UCAID is responsible for the development of the Abilene fiber-optic backbone network that will interconnect over 150 universities into the Internet2 project.

UCE *n.* Acronym for **u**nsolicited **c**ommercial **e**-mail. *See* spam.

UCITA *n.* Acronym for **U**niform **C**omputer **I**nformation **T**ransactions **A**ct. Legislation proposed or enacted in several states that will set legal standards and control systems for dealing with computer information. UCITA is a model law intended as an amendment to the Uniform Commercial Code to cover new technology-related issues. One of

UCITA's main provisions is a standard for mass market software shrinkwrap and clickwrap agreements. *See also* clickwrap agreement, shrinkwrap agreement.

UCSD p-system *n.* A portable operating system and development environment that was developed by Kenneth Bowles at the University of California at San Diego. The system was based on a simulated, 16-bit, stack-oriented "pseudomachine." The development environment included a text editor and compilers for several languages, such as FORTRAN and Pascal. Programs written for a p-system were more portable than programs compiled to machine language. *See also* bytecode, pseudomachine, p-system, virtual machine.

UDDI *n.* Acronym for **U**niversal **D**escription, **D**iscovery, and **I**ntegration. A platform-independent framework functioning like a directory (similar to a telephone book) that provides a way to locate and register Web services on the Internet. The UDDI specification calls for three elements: white pages, which provide business contact information; yellow pages, which organize Web services into categories (for example, credit card authorization services); and green pages, which provide detailed technical information about individual services. The UDDI also contains an operational registry, which is available today.

UDP *n.* Acronym for **U**ser **D**atagram **P**rotocol. The connectionless protocol within TCP/IP that corresponds to the transport layer in the ISO/OSI reference model. UDP converts data messages generated by an application into packets to be sent via IP, but it is "unreliable" because it does not establish a path between sender and receiver before transmitting and does not verify that messages have been delivered correctly. UDP is more efficient than TCP, so it is used for various purposes, including SNMP; the reliability depends on the application that generates the message. *See also* communications protocol, ISO/OSI reference model, packet, SNMP, TCP/IP. *Compare* IP, TCP.

UDT *n.* Acronym for **u**niform **d**ata **t**ransfer. The service used in the OLE extensions to Windows that allows two applications to exchange data without either program knowing the internal structure of the other.

UI *n. See* user interface.

UKnet *n.* **1.** The University of Kentucky's campus network. **2.** In the United Kingdom, an Internet service provider (ISP) based at the University of Kent. *See also* ISP.

ULSI *n. See* ultra-large-scale integration.

UltimateTV *n.* A television digital recording technology developed by Microsoft. UltimateTV can record up to 35 hours of DIRECTV broadcasts. Because the television signal is recording on UltimateTV's hard drive, viewers can pause a live show, rewind scenes, and watch previously shown parts of the show in slow or fast motion while UltimateTV records the remainder of the show live.

Ultra DMA/33 *n.* A data transfer protocol, based on direct memory access, for transferring data between a hard drive and a computer's RAM. Ultra DMA/33 improves ATA/IDE performance, doubles burst transfer rates to 33 megabytes per second, and increases data transfer integrity. *See also* ATA, direct memory access, IDE (definition 1).

ultrafiche *n.* Microfiche with very high density. The image in ultrafiche is reduced at least 90 times from its original size. *See also* microfiche.

ultra-large-scale integration *n.* The highest currently possible density at which components (transistors and other elements) are packed onto an integrated circuit. "Ultra-large-scale" is generally applied to component densities of 1,000,000 or greater. *Acronym:* ULSI. *See also* integrated circuit. *Compare* large-scale integration, medium-scale integration, small-scale integration, super-large-scale integration, very-large-scale integration.

ultralight computer *n. See* portable computer.

UltraSCSI *n.* An extension of the SCSI-2 standard that doubles the transfer speed of Fast-SCSI to allow a transfer rate of 20 megabytes per second (MBps) on an 8-bit connection and 40 MBps on a 16-bit connection. *See also* SCSI, SCSI-2.

Ultra Wide SCSI *n. See* UltraSCSI.

UMA *n.* **1.** Acronym for **u**pper **m**emory **a**rea. The portion of DOS memory between the first 640K and 1 MB. *Compare* high memory area. **2.** Acronym for **U**niform **M**emory **A**rchitecture. *See* SMP.

UMB *n.* Acronym for **u**pper **m**emory **b**lock. A block of memory in the UMA (upper memory area) that can be used for device drivers or TSRs. A UMB is allocated and managed by special memory manager programs such as EMM386.EXE. *See also* device driver, TSR, UMA (definition 1).

UML *n.* Acronym for **U**nified **M**odeling **L**anguage. A language developed by Grady Booch, Ivar Jacobson, and Jim Rumbaugh of Rational Software that can be used for specifying, building, and documenting software and non-software systems, such as business models. UML notation provides a common foundation for object-oriented design by providing descriptions of modeling concepts including object class, associations, interface, and responsibility. The UML standard is supported by software developers and vendors and overseen by the Object Management Group (OMG).

UMTS *n.* Acronym for **U**niversal **M**obile **T**elecommunications **S**ystem. Third-generation wireless communications standard developed to provide a consistent set of packet-based voice, text, video, and multimedia capabilities to users in any communications environment worldwide. When UMTS reaches full implementation, users will be able maintain computer and phone Internet connections from anywhere in the world.

unary *adj.* Of, pertaining to, or characteristic of a mathematical operation with a single operand (object); monadic. *Compare* dyadic.

unary operator *n.* An operator that takes only one operand —for example, unary minus (as in –2.5). *See also* operator. *Compare* binary operator.

unbuffered *adj.* Of, pertaining to, or characteristic of something that does not store data characters in memory but instead processes them as they are received. *See also* buffer[2].

unbundle *vb.* To separate the items of a composite sales package; for example, to sell components of a software package separately rather than as a package. *Compare* bundle.

unbundled *adj.* Not included as part of a complete hardware/software package; the term particularly applies to a product that was previously bundled, as opposed to one that has always been sold separately.

UNC *n.* Acronym for **U**niversal **N**aming **C**onvention or, sometimes, **U**niform **N**aming **C**onvention. The system of naming files among computers on a network so that a file on a given computer will have the same pathname when accessed from any of the other computers on the network.

U

For example, if the directory *c:\path1\path2\..pathn* on computer *servern* is shared under the name *pathdirs*, a user on another computer would open *servern\pathdirs\filename.ext* to access the file *c:\path1\path2\..pathn\ filename.ext* on *servern*. *See also* URL, virtual path.

uncompress *vb.* To restore the contents of a compressed file to its original form. *Also called:* decompress. *Compare* compress[2].

unconditional branch *n.* A transfer of execution to another line of code in a program without a check for some condition being true or false. The transfer always takes place whenever such an instruction is encountered. *See also* branch (definition 2). *Compare* conditional branch.

undelete[1] *n.* The act of restoring deleted information. An undelete is comparable to (and usually included as part of) an undo command; it is more restricted, however, in that "undo" reverses any previous act, but *undelete* reverses only a deletion. *Undelete* generally refers only to excised text or deleted files. *See also* undo.

undelete[2] *vb.* **1.** To restore deleted information, usually the last item deleted. **2.** In file storage, to restore a file's storage information so that a deleted file becomes available for access again. *Also called:* unerase. *See also* file recovery.

undeliverable *adj.* Not able to be delivered to an intended recipient. If an e-mail message is undeliverable, it is returned to the sender with information added by the mail server explaining the problem; for example, the e-mail address may be incorrect, or the recipient's mailbox may be full.

undercolor separation *n.* In the CMYK color model, the process of converting equal quantities of cyan, magenta, and yellow to equivalent gray levels, which are then printed in black ink. This produces grays that are clearer and sharper than those produced by mixing colored inks. *See also* CMY, CMYK, color model.

underflow *n.* A condition in which a mathematical calculation produces a result too near to zero to be represented by the range of binary digits available to the computer for holding that value in the specified precision. *See also* precision (definition 2), single-precision.

underline *vb.* To format a selection of text so that the text is printed with a line slightly below it.

Undernet *n.* An international network of Internet Relay Chat (IRC) servers created in 1992 as an alternative to the larger and more chaotic main IRC network. For information about connecting to Undernet, see http://www.undernet.org. *See also* IRC.

underscore *n.* An underline character often used to emphasize a letter or a word; on nongraphics displays, generally used to indicate italic characters.

undo *vb.* To reverse the last action—for example, to undo a deletion, thus restoring deleted text to a document. Many application programs enable the user both to undo and to redo an action. *See also* undelete (definition 1).

undock *vb.* **1.** To detach a laptop or other portable computer from a docking station. *See also* docking station, laptop. **2.** To move a toolbar from the edge of a window so that the toolbar becomes its own free-floating window. *See also* toolbar.

unerase *n. See* undelete[1].

unfold *adj. See* inline (definition 1).

unhandled exception *n.* An error condition that an application does not internally resolve. When an unhandled exception occurs, the operating system terminates the application that caused the error.

Unibus *n.* A bus architecture introduced by Digital Equipment Corporation in 1970.

unicast *vb.* To transmit between a single sender and a single receiver over a network. A two-way, point-to-point transmission, unicast is typical of network communications. *Compare* anycasting, narrowcast.

Unicode *n.* A 16-bit character encoding standard developed by the Unicode Consortium between 1988 and 1991. By using 2 bytes to represent each character, Unicode enables almost all the written languages of the world to be represented using a single character set. (By contrast, 8-bit ASCII is not capable of representing all the combinations of letters and diacritical marks that are used just with the Roman alphabet.) Approximately 39,000 of the 65,536 possible Unicode character codes have been assigned to date, 21,000 of them being used for Chinese ideographs. The remaining combinations are open for expansion. *Compare* ASCII.

unified messaging *n.* The integration of various communications technologies such as voicemail, fax, and e-mail into a single service. Unified messaging is designed to be a time-saving tool to provide users with a single package with which they can receive, organize, and respond to messages in a variety of media.

Unified Modeling Language *n. See* UML.

Uniform Computer Information Transactions Act *n. See* UCITA.

Uniform Data Transfer *n. See* UDT.

Uniform Memory Access *n. See* SMP.

Uniform Naming Convention *n. See* UNC.

Uniform Resource Citation *n.* A description of an object on the World Wide Web, consisting of pairs of attributes and their values, such as the Uniform Resource Identifiers (URIs) of associated resources, author names, publisher names, dates, and prices. *Acronym:* URC.

Uniform Resource Identifier *n.* A character string used to identify a resource (such as a file) from anywhere on the Internet by type and location. The set of Uniform Resource Identifiers includes Uniform Resource Names (URNs) and Uniform Resource Locators (URLs). *Acronym:* URI. *See also* relative URL, Uniform Resource Name, URL.

Uniform Resource Locator *n. See* URL.

Uniform Resource Name *n.* A scheme for uniquely identifying resources that might be available on the Internet by name, without regard to where they are located. The specifications for the format of Uniform Resource Names are still under development by the Internet Engineering Task Force (IETF). They include all Uniform Resource Identifiers (URIs) having the schemes urn:, fpi:, and path:; that is, those that are not Uniform Resource Locators (URLs). *Acronym:* URN. *See also* IETF, Uniform Resource Identifier, URL.

UniForum *n.* **1.** The International Association of Open System Professionals, an organization of UNIX users and administrators. **2.** A series of UNIX trade shows sponsored by UniForum and managed by Softbank COMDEX, Inc. *See also* COMDEX.

Unimodem *n.* **1.** The universal modem driver, provided with Windows CE, that translates Telephony Service Provider Interface (TSPI) calls into AT commands and sends the commands to a virtual device driver that talks to the modem. **2.** A universal modem that supports standard modem AT commands. Windows CE currently supports only PCMCIA modems.

uninstall *vb.* To remove software completely from a system, including the elimination of files and components residing in system locations such as the registry in Windows 9x, Windows NT, or Windows 2000. Some applications have built-in uninstall utilities, and in other cases a separate uninstall program can be used. *Also called:* deinstall.

uninterruptible power supply *n. See* UPS.

union *n.* **1.** In set theory, the smallest combination of two sets that contains all elements of both sets. **2.** In logic, an inclusive OR operation—that is, the result, C, of any union of A and B is true (1) except when A and B are both false (0). See the table. **3.** In programming, a structure that can be used to store different types of variables (such as integer, character, or Boolean). **4.** In database management, a relational operator. Given two relations (tables), A and B, that are union-compatible (contain the same number of fields, with corresponding fields containing the same types of values), A UNION B builds a new relation containing those tuples (records) that appear either in A or in B or in both. *Compare* difference, intersect.

Table U.1   A Truth Table Showing the Results of Unions.

A	OR	B	=	C
1		1		1
1		0		1
0		1		1
0		0		0

union-compatible *adj.* In database management, of, pertaining to, or characteristic of two relations (tables) that are of the same order (have the same number of attributes) and whose corresponding attributes are based on the same domain (the set of acceptable values).

unipolar *adj.* Having one state. In electronics, a unipolar device or signal is one in which the same voltage polarity (positive or negative) is used to represent binary states—on/off or true/false. *Compare* bipolar.

unique user *n.* An individual visitor to a Web site. Tracking unique users is important in ascertaining the success of a given Web site because it indicates how many different visitors access the site, as opposed to the number of hits—visits by the same or different individuals—the site receives. *Also called:* unique visitor.

unique visitor *n. See* unique user.

United States of America Standards Institute *n.* The former name of the American National Standards Institute. *See also* ANSI.

U

unit position *n.* The "one's place" in a multiple-digit number—for example, the 3 in the number 473.

UNIVAC I *n.* Short for **Uni**versal **A**utomatic **C**alculator **I**. The first commercially available electronic computer, designed by J. Presper Eckert and John Mauchly, also the inventors of ENIAC (generally considered the first fully electronic computer). UNIVAC I was the first computer to handle both numeric and textual information.

universal asynchronous receiver-transmitter *n. See* UART.

Universal Description, Discovery, and Integration *n. See* UDDI.

Universal Mobile Telecommunications System *n. See* UMTS.

Universal Naming Convention *n. See* UNC.

Universal Plug and Play *n. See* UPnP.

Universal Plug and Play Forum *n. See* UPnP Forum.

Universal Plug and Play networking *n. See* UPnP networking.

Universal Product Code *n. See* UPC.

Universal Resource Locator *n. See* URL.

universal serial bus *n. See* USB.

Universal Server *n.* **1.** Software from Oracle Corporation that supplies information from its database in a variety of forms, such as text, sound, and video, in response to HTTP requests. **2.** Database software from Informix that works with snap-in software modules to handle user needs for specific data types and ways of processing.

universal synchronous receiver-transmitter *n. See* USRT.

Universal Time Coordinate *n.* For all practical purposes, the same as Greenwich Mean Time, which is used for the synchronization of computers on the Internet. *Acronym:* UTC. *Also called:* coordinated universal time format.

University Corporation for Advanced Internet Development *n. See* UCAID.

UNIX *n.* A multiuser, multitasking operating system. Originally developed by Ken Thompson and Dennis Ritchie at AT&T Bell Laboratories from 1969 through 1973 for use on minicomputers, UNIX has evolved into a complex, powerful operating system that, because it is

written in the C language, is more portable—that is, less machine-specific—than many other operating systems. UNIX has been released in a wide variety of versions, or flavors, including System V (developed by AT&T for commercial release; many current flavors on based on it), BSD UNIX (freeware developed at the University of California Berkeley, which has spun off many related flavors), AIX (a version of System V adapted by IBM to run on RISC-based workstations), A/UX (a graphical version for the Macintosh), Linux (a newer version that runs on the Intel chip), and SunOS (based on BSD UNIX and available on Sun workstations). Many flavors of UNIX are available free. With some flavors, the source code is also free, making it an instrumental part of the open source movement. UNIX is widely used as a network operating system, especially in conjunction with the Internet. *See also* BSD UNIX, Linux, open source, System V.

UNIX shell account *n.* A shell account providing command-line access to a UNIX system. *See also* shell account.

UNIX shell scripts *n.* Sequences of UNIX commands stored as files that can be run as programs. In MS-DOS, batch (.bat) files provide similar capabilities. *See also* batch file, shell[1], shell script.

UNIX-to-UNIX Copy *n. See* UUCP.

UNIX wizard *n.* A particularly expert and helpful UNIX programmer. Some companies actually use this phrase as a job title. The newsgroup comp.unix.wizards provides answers to many user questions.

unknown host *n.* A response to a request for a connection to a server that indicates that the network is unable to find the specified address. *See also* server (definition 1).

unknown recipients *n.* A response to an e-mail message that indicates that the mail server is unable to identify one or more of the destination addresses.

unload *vb.* **1.** To remove a storage medium, such as a tape or disk, from its drive. **2.** To remove software from system memory. *See also* memory.

unmanaged code *n.* Code that is executed directly by the operating system, outside of the common language runtime environment. Unmanaged code must provide its own garbage collection, type checking, security support, and so on, unlike managed code, which receives these services

U

from the common language runtime. *See also* managed code.

unmoderated *adj.* Of, pertaining to, or characteristic of a newsgroup or mailing list in which all articles or messages received by the server are automatically available or distributed to all subscribers. *Compare* moderated.

unmount *vb.* To remove a disk or tape from active use. *Compare* mount.

unpack *vb.* To restore packed data to its original format. *Compare* pack.

unpopulated board *n.* A circuit board whose sockets are empty. *Compare* fully populated board.

unread *adj.* **1.** Of, pertaining to, or being an article in a newsgroup that a user has not yet received. Newsreader client programs distinguish between "read" and "unread" articles for each user and download only unread articles from the server. **2.** Of, pertaining to, or being an e-mail message that a user has received but has not yet opened in an e-mail program.

unrecoverable error *n.* A fatal error—one that a program is unable to recover from without the use of external recovery techniques. *Compare* recoverable error.

unreliable protocol *n.* A communications protocol that makes a "best effort" attempt to deliver a transmission but does not provide for verifying that the transmission arrives without error.

unroll *adj. See* inline (definition 1).

unset *vb.* To make the value of a bit position equal to 0. *Compare* set (definition 1).

unshielded cable *n.* Cable that is not surrounded with a metal shield. If the wires in an unshielded cable are not at least twisted around each other in pairs, the signals they carry have no protection from interference by external electromagnetic fields. Consequently, unshielded cable should be used only over very short distances. *Compare* coaxial cable, ribbon cable, twisted-pair cable, UTP.

unshielded twisted pair *n. See* UTP.

unshielded twisted-pair wiring *n. See* UTP.

unsolicited commercial e-mail *n. See* spam.

unsubscribe *vb.* **1.** In a newsreader client program, to remove a newsgroup from the list of newsgroups to which

one subscribes. *See also* newsgroup. **2.** To remove oneself as a recipient on a mailing list. *See also* mailing list.

untar[1] *n.* A utility, available for systems in addition to UNIX, for separating the individual files out of an archive assembled using the UNIX *tar* program. *Compare* tar[1].

untar[2] *vb.* To separate the individual files out of an archive assembled with the UNIX *tar* program. *Compare* tar[2].

unzip *vb.* To uncompress an archive file that has been compressed by a program such as compress, gzip, or PKZIP.

up *adj.* Functioning and available for use; used in describing computers, printers, communications lines on networks, and other such hardware.

UPC *n.* Acronym for Universal Product Code. A system of numbering commercial products using bar codes. A UPC consists of 12 digits: a number system character, a five-digit number assigned to the manufacturer, a five-digit product code assigned by the manufacturer, and a modulo 10 check digit. *See also* bar code.

update[1] *n.* A new release of an existing software product. A software update usually adds relatively minor new features to a product or corrects errors (bugs) found after the program was released. Updates are generally indicated by small changes in software version numbers, such as *4.0b* from *4.0. See also* version number. *Compare* release[1].

update[2] *vb.* To change a system or a data file to make it more current.

update query *n.* A database query that changes a set of records according to search conditions or criteria.

upflow *n.* In the data warehousing process, the stage during which stored information is checked for completeness, summarized, and readied for distribution. *See also* data warehouse[2]. *Compare* downflow, inflow, metaflow.

upgrade[1] *n.* The new or enhanced version of a product.

upgrade[2] *vb.* To change to a newer, usually more powerful or sophisticated version.

uplink *n.* The transmission link from an earth station to a communications satellite.

upload[1] *n.* **1.** In communications, the process of transferring a copy of a file from a local computer to a remote computer by means of a modem or network. **2.** The copy of the file that is being or has been transferred.

U

upload² *vb.* To transfer a copy of a file from a local computer to a remote computer. *Compare* download.

UPnP *n.* Acronym for **U**niversal **P**lug a**n**d **P**lay. A Microsoft initiative which prompted the creation of the UPnP Forum for interconnecting computers, appliances, networks, and services. UPnP extends conventional Plug and Play to include devices connected to networks. It allows peripheral devices to discover and connect to other devices and to enumerate the characteristics of those devices. UPnP is intended to be an element of home networking, in which PCs, appliances, and the services they provide are linked together.

UPnP Device Architecture *n.* A specification developed by the Universal Plug and Play (UPnP) Forum that defines the structure of UPnP networking. The UPnP Device Architecture, formerly known as the DCP Framework, provides information about discovery, description, control, eventing, and presentation in a UPnP network. *See also* UPnP networking.

UPnP Forum *n.* A consortium of companies and individuals that oversees Universal Plug and Play (UPnP) specifications, protocols, logos, sample implementations, test suites, white papers, and other UPnP-related efforts. *See also* UPnP, UPnP Device Architecture, UPnP networking.

UPnP networking *n.* The peer-to-peer networking of intelligent machines, appliances, wireless devices, computers, and other devices according to the Universal Plug and Play (UPnP) Device Architecture. UPnP networking uses control points, devices, services, and protocols including GENA, SOAP, SSDP, standard TCP/IP, and other Internet protocols. *See also* UPnP Device Architecture.

uppercase *adj.* Of, pertaining to, or characterized by capital letters. *Compare* lowercase.

upper memory area *n. See* UMA (definition 1).

upper memory block *n. See* UMB.

UPS *n.* Acronym for **u**ninterruptible **p**ower **s**upply. A device, connected between a computer (or other electronic equipment) and a power source (usually an outlet receptacle), that ensures that electrical flow to the computer is not interrupted because of a blackout and, in most cases, protects the computer against potentially damaging events, such as power surges and brownouts. All UPS units are equipped with a battery and a loss-of-power sensor; if the sensor detects a loss of power, it switches over to the battery so that the user has time to save his or her work and shut off the computer. *See also* blackout, brownout.

upstream¹ *n.* The direction in which information is delivered from a client to a (Web) server. *Compare* downstream¹.

upstream² *adj.* **1.** The location of a server in relation to another server. *Compare* downstream² (definition 1). **2.** The direction in which data moves *from* an individual computer *to* the remote network. With certain communications technologies, such as ADSL, cable modems, and high-speed 56-Kbps modems, data flows upstream more slowly than downstream. For example, a 56-Kbps modem can deliver data at a 56-Kbps maximum only downstream; upstream, it delivers data at either 28.8 or 33.6 Kbps. *Compare* downstream² (definition 2).

uptime *n.* The amount or percentage of time a computer system or associated hardware is functioning and available for use. *Compare* downtime.

upward-compatible *adj.* Of, pertaining to, or characteristic of a computer product, especially software, designed to perform adequately with other products that are expected to become widely used in the foreseeable future. The use of standards and conventions makes upward compatibility easier to achieve.

urban legend *n.* A widely distributed story that remains in circulation in spite of the fact that it is not true. Many urban legends have been floating around the Internet and other online services for years, including the request for cards for the sick boy in England (he's long since recovered and grown up), the cookie or cake recipe that cost $250 (it's a myth), and the Good Times or Penpal Greetings virus, which will infect your computer when you read an e-mail message (it does not exist). *See also* Good Times virus.

URC *n. See* Uniform Resource Citation.

URI *n. See* Uniform Resource Identifier.

URL *n.* Acronym for **U**niform **R**esource **L**ocator. An address for a resource on the Internet. URLs are used by Web browsers to locate Internet resources. A URL specifies the protocol to be used in accessing the resource (such as http: for a World Wide Web page or ftp: for an FTP site), the name of the server on which the resource resides (such as //www.whitehouse.gov), and, optionally, the path to a resource (such as an HTML document or a file on that server). *See also* FTP¹ (definition 1), HTML, HTTP, path (definition 1), server (definition 2), virtual path (definition 1), Web browser.

URN *n. See* Uniform Resource Name.

usable *adj.* Of, pertaining to, or characteristic of the ease and adaptability with which a product can be applied to the performance of the work for which it is designed. A high degree of usability implies ease of learning, flexibility, freedom from bugs, and good design that does not involve unnecessarily complicated procedures.

usage analysis *n.* Data collected to evaluate how a Web site is being used, such as visitor user names, how often each page was visited, and the types of Web browsers used.

USB *n.* Acronym for **u**niversal **s**erial **b**us. A serial bus with a data transfer rate of 12 megabits per second (Mbps) for connecting peripherals to a microcomputer. USB can connect up to 127 peripherals, such as external CD-ROM drives, printers, modems, mice, and keyboards, to the system through a single, general-purpose port. This is accomplished by daisy chaining peripherals together. USB is designed to support the ability to automatically add and configure new devices and the ability to add such devices without having to shut down and restart the system (hot plugging). USB was developed by Intel, Compaq, DEC, IBM, Microsoft, NEC, and Northern Telecom. It competes with DEC's ACCESS.bus for lower-speed applications. *See also* bus, daisy chain, hot plugging, input/output port, peripheral. *Compare* ACCESS.bus.

U.S. Department of Defense *n.* The military branch of the United States government. The Department of Defense developed ARPANET, the origin of today's Internet and MILNET, through its Advanced Research Projects Agency (ARPA). *See also* ARPANET, Internet, MILNET.

Usenet or **UseNet** or **USENET** *n.* A worldwide network of UNIX systems that has a decentralized administration and is used as a bulletin board system by special-interest discussion groups. Usenet, which is considered part of the Internet (although Usenet predates it), is comprised of thousands of newsgroups, each devoted to a particular topic. Users can post messages and read messages from others in these newsgroups in a manner similar to users on dial-in BBSs. Usenet was originally implemented using UUCP (UNIX-to-UNIX Copy) software and telephone connections; that method remains important, although more modern methods, such as NNTP and network connections, are more commonly used. *See also* BBS (definition 1), newsgroup, newsreader, NNTP, UUCP.

Usenet User List *n.* A list maintained by the Massachusetts Institute of Technology that contains the name and e-mail address of everyone who has posted to the Usenet. *See also* Usenet.

user account *n.* On a secure or multiuser computer system, an established means for an individual to gain access to the system and its resources. Usually created by the system's administrator, a user account consists of information about the user, such as password, rights, and permissions. *See also* group[1], logon, user profile.

user agent *n.* In the terminology established by the ISO/OSI reference model for LANs (local area networks), a program that helps a client connect with a server. *Acronym:* UA. *See also* agent (definition 3), ISO/OSI reference model, LAN.

user control *n.* In ASP.NET: A server control that is authored declaratively using the same syntax as an ASP.NET page and is saved as a text file with an .ascx extension. User controls allow page functionality to be partitioned and reused. Upon first request, the page framework parses a user control into a class that derives from System.Web.UI.UserControl and compiles that class into an assembly, which it reuses on subsequent requests. User controls are easy to develop due to their page-style authoring and deployment without prior compilation. In Windows Forms: A composite control that provides consistent behavior and user interface within or across applications. The user control can be local to one application or added to a library and compiled into a DLL for use by multiple applications.

User Datagram Protocol *n. See* UDP.

user-defined data type *n.* A data type defined in a program. User-defined data types are usually combinations of data types defined by the programming language being used and are often used to create data structures. *See also* data structure, data type.

user-defined function key *n. See* keyboard enhancer, programmable function key.

user-friendly *adj.* Easy to learn and easy to use.

user group *n.* A group of people drawn together by interest in the same computer system or software. User groups, some of which are large and influential organizations, provide support for newcomers and a forum where members can exchange ideas and information.

user-initiated update *n.* An operating system update mechanism, provided by the dial-up boot loader, which is designed to be used by remote users and field technicians. The operating system image is downloaded using a modem connection. *See also* automatic update, factory update.

U

user interface *n.* The portion of a program with which a user interacts. Types of user interfaces, or UIs, include command-line interfaces, menu-driven interfaces, and graphical user interfaces. *Acronym:* UI.

User Interface Toolbox *n. See* Toolbox.

username *n.* The name by which a user is identified to a computer system or network. During the logon process, the user must enter the username and the correct password. If the system or network is connected to the Internet, the username generally corresponds to the leftmost part of the user's e-mail address (the portion preceding the @ sign, as in username@company.com). *See also* e-mail address, logon.

user name *n.* The name by which a person is known and addressed on a communications network. *See also* alias (definition 2).

user profile *n.* A computer-based record maintained about an authorized user of a multiuser computer system. A user profile is needed for security and other reasons; it can contain such information as the person's access restrictions, mailbox location, type of terminal, and so on. *See also* user account.

user state *n.* The least privileged of the modes in which a Motorola 680x0 microprocessor can operate. This is the mode in which application programs are run. *See also* 68000. *Compare* supervisor state.

USnail *n.* **1.** Slang for the United States Postal Service. USnail, a term used on the Internet, is a reference to how slow the postal service is in comparison to e-mail. **2.** Mail delivered by the United States Postal Service. *See also* snail mail.

/usr *n.* A directory in a computer system that contains subdirectories owned or maintained by individual users of the computer system. These subdirectories can contain files and additional subdirectories. Typically, /usr directories are used in UNIX systems and can be found on many FTP sites. *See also* FTP site.

USRT *n.* Acronym for **u**niversal **s**ynchronous **r**eceiver-transmitter. A module, usually composed of a single integrated circuit, that contains both the receiving and transmitting circuits required for synchronous serial communication. *Compare* UART.

UTC *n. See* Universal Time Coordinate.

UTF-8 *n.* Acronym for **U**CS **T**ransformation **F**ormat **8**. A character set for protocols evolving beyond the use of ASCII. The UTF-8 protocol provides for support of extended ASCII characters and translation of UCS-2, an international 16-bit Unicode character set. UTF-8 enables a far greater range of names than can be achieved using ASCII or extended ASCII encoding for character data. *See also* ASCII, Unicode.

utility *n.* A program designed to perform a particular function; the term usually refers to software that solves narrowly focused problems or those related to computer system management. *See also* application.

utility program *n.* A program designed to perform maintenance work on the system or on system components (for example, a storage backup program, disk and file recovery program, or resource editor).

UTP *n.* Acronym for **u**nshielded **t**wisted **p**air. A cable containing one or more twisted pairs of wires without additional shielding. UTP is more flexible and takes up less space than shielded twisted-pair (STP) cable but has less bandwidth. See the illustration. *See also* twisted-pair cable. *Compare* STP.

UTP.

.uu *n.* The file extension for a binary file that has been translated into ASCII format using uuencode. *Also called:* .uud. *See also* ASCII, binary file, uuencode[1]. *Compare* .uue.

UUCP *n.* Acronym for **UNIX-to-UNIX Copy**. A set of software programs that facilitates transmission of information between UNIX systems using serial data connections, primarily the public switched telephone network. *See also* uupc.

.uud *n. See* .uu.

uudecode[1] *n.* A UNIX program that converts a uuen-coded file back into its original binary format. This pro-gram (along with uuencode) allows binary data, such as images or executable code, to be disseminated through e-mail or newsgroups. *Compare* uuencode[1].

uudecode[2] *vb.* To transform a uuencoded file back into its binary original using the uudecode program. *Compare* uuencode[2].

.uue *n.* The file extension for a file that has been decoded from ASCII format back into binary format using uude-code. *See also* ASCII, binary file, uudecode[1].

uuencode[1] *n.* A UNIX program that converts a binary file, in which all 8 bits of every byte are significant, into printable 7-bit ASCII characters without loss of informa-tion. This program (along with uudecode) allows binary data, such as images or executable code, to be dissemi-nated through e-mail or newsgroups. A file thus encoded

is one-third again as long as the original. *Compare* uudecode[1].

uuencode[2] *vb.* To transform a binary file into printable 7-bit ASCII text using the uuencode program. *Compare* uudecode[2].

UUID *n.* Acronym for **u**niversally **u**nique **id**entifier. A 128-bit value that uniquely identifies objects such as OLE servers, interfaces, manager entry-point vectors, and client objects. Universally unique identifiers are used in cross-process communication, such as remote procedure calling (RPC) and OLE. *Also called:* GUID.

uupc *n.* The version of UUCP for IBM PCs and PC-compatibles running DOS, Windows, or OS/2. This ver-sion is a collection of programs for copying files to, log-ging in to, and running programs on remote networked computers. *See also* UUCP.

U

V.120 *n.* The ITU-T (formerly CCITT) standard that governs serial communications over ISDN lines. Data is encapsulated using a protocol similar to the Lightweight Directory Access Protocol (LDAP), and more than one connection may be multiplexed on a communications channel. *See also* communications channel, communications protocol, International Telecommunications Union, ISDN, Lightweight Directory Access Protocol, multiplexing, standard (definition 1), V series.

V20, V30 *n.* NEC microprocessors that were slight improvements on Intel's 8088 and 8086, using the same command sets but different microcode.

V.2x, V.3x, V.4x, V.5x series *n. See* V series.

V.32terbo *n.* A modem protocol developed by AT&T for 19,200-bps modems, with fallback to the speeds supported by the ITU-T (formerly CCITT) V.32 standard. This protocol is proprietary to AT&T and was not adopted by CCITT or ITU-T. In the V series, V.34 takes the place of V.32terbo. *See also* International Telecommunications Union, V series.

V.34 *n.* Data transmission standard that provides for up to 28,800 bits per second (bps) communications over telephone lines. It defines a full-duplex (two-way) modulation technique and includes error-correcting and negotiation. *See also* bits per second, full-duplex, modulation standards, V.90.

V.42 *n.* The ITU-T (formerly CCITT) recommendation specifying procedures for error correction in data communications equipment (DCEs) designed for asynchronous-to-synchronous conversion. *See also* V series.

V.42bis *n.* The ITU-T (formerly CCITT) recommendation specifying procedures for data compression in data-circuit terminating equipment utilizing error-correction operations. *See also* V series.

V86 mode *n. See* virtual real mode.

V.90 *n.* Data transmission standard that provides for up to 56,000 bits per second (bps) communications over telephone lines. The transmission speed from the client-side modem for uploads is 33,600 bps. The transmission speed for downloads from the host-side modem such as an Internet service provider (ISP) or a corporate network is up to 56,000 bps, with an average speed of 40,000 to 50,000 bps. When the host-side modem does not support this standard, the alternative is V.34. *See also* bits per second, client, host, ISP, modem, modulation standards, V.34.

VAB *n. See* voice answer back.

VAC *n. See* volts alternating current.

vacuum tube *n.* A set of metal electrodes and intervening metal grids, contained in a glass or metal tube from which all gas has been removed. Voltages on the grids control electrical currents between the electrodes. Formerly used for amplification and switching in electronic circuits, vacuum tubes are now used in applications such as cathode-ray tubes and those requiring very high power levels. A vacuum tube is known as a *valve* in Great Britain.

validation server controls *n.* A set of server controls, included with ASP.NET, that verify user input. The input is checked as it comes from HTML server controls and Web server controls (for example, a Web page form) against programmer-defined requirements. Validation controls perform input checking in server code. If the user is working with a browser that supports DHTML, the validation controls can also perform validation using client script. *See also* ASP.NET server control, HTML server control, Web server control.

validation suite *n.* A set of tests that measures compliance with a standard, especially a standard definition of a programming language. *See also* standard (definition 1).

valid date interval *n.* A span of time during which a computer will maintain the correct date. For many PCs, the valid date interval is 1980 forward.

validity check *n.* The process of analyzing data to determine whether it conforms to predetermined completeness and consistency parameters.

value *n.* A quantity assigned to an element such as a variable, symbol, or label. *See* tone (definition 1).

value-added network *n.* A communications network that offers additional services, such as message routing, resource management, and conversion facilities, for computers communicating at different speeds or using different protocols. *Acronym:* VAN.

value-added reseller *n.* A company that buys hardware and software and resells it to the public with added services, such as user support. *Acronym:* VAR.

value list *n.* A list of values used by some application, such as a database, as a search string or as values for a filtered query. *See also* filter (definition 1), query (definition 1), search string.

value type *n.* A data type that is represented by the type's actual value. If a value type is assigned to a variable, that variable is given a fresh copy of the value. (This is in contrast to a reference type, where assignment does not create a copy.) Value types are usually created on a method's stack frame, rather than in the garbage-collected heap. A value type can be boxed, which is a process that creates a corresponding reference type. *See also* reference type.

valve *n. See* electron tube, vacuum tube.

vampire tap *n.* A type of transceiver used on Ethernet networks that is equipped with sharp metal prongs that pierce the insulation on thicknet cable to make contact with the copper core over which signals travel.

VAN *n. See* value-added network.

vanilla *adj. See* plain vanilla.

vaporware *n.* Software that has been announced but not released to customers. The term implies sarcastically that the product exists only in the minds of the marketing department. *Compare* freeware, shareware.

VAR *n. See* value-added reseller.

variable *n.* In programming, a named storage location capable of containing data that can be modified during program execution. *See also* data structure, data type, global variable, local variable. *Compare* constant.

variable expression *n.* An expression that depends on the value of at least one variable and, hence, must be evaluated during program execution. *See also* run time (definition 1), variable. *Compare* constant expression.

variable-length field *n.* In a record, a field that can vary in length according to how much data it contains. *See also* field (definition 1).

variable-length record *n.* A record that can vary in length because it contains variable-length fields, certain fields only under certain conditions, or both of these. *See also* variable-length field.

VAX *n.* Acronym for **v**irtual **a**ddress e**x**tension. A family of 32-bit minicomputers introduced by Digital Equipment Corporation in 1978. The VAX, like the later 68000 microprocessor, has a flat address space and a large instruction set. The VAX was highly favored within the hacker community but has been superseded by microprocessors and RISC workstations. *See also* flat address space, instruction set, microprocessor, minicomputer, RISC.

VBA *n. See* Visual Basic for Applications.

vBNS *n.* Short for **v**ery high-speed **B**ackbone **N**etwork **S**ervice. A network connecting several supercomputer centers and reserved for high-performance, high-bandwidth scientific applications requiring massive computing power. The vBNS was developed by the National Science Foundation and MCI Telecommunications. It began operation in 1995, reaching speeds of 2.4 Gbps, using MCI's network of advanced switching and fiberoptic transmission technologies. Later, vBNS expanded to provide backbone services for Internet2.

VBScript *n. See* Visual Basic, Scripting Edition.

VBS/VBSWG virus *n.* Acronym for **V**isual **B**asic **S**cript/ **V**isual **B**asic **S**cript **W**orm **G**enerator **virus**. Any virus created using the VBSWG virus creation toolkit. The tools available in VBSWG worm kit allow individuals to write viruses without having significant computer knowledge. Homepage and the Anna Kournikova virus are examples of VBS/VBSWG viruses.

VBX *n.* Short for **V**isual **B**asic custom control. A software module that, when called by a Visual Basic application, produces a control that adds some desired feature to the application. A VBX is a separate executable file, usually written in C, that is dynamically linked to the application at run time and can be used by other applications, including some applications not developed in Visual Basic. Although VBX technology was developed by Microsoft, most VBXs have been written by third-party developers. VBXs are still in use, but the technology has been superseded by OCXs and ActiveX controls. *See also* control (definition 2), Visual Basic. *Compare* ActiveX controls, dynamic-link library, OCX.

VCACHE *n.* The disk caching software used with VFAT driver in Windows 9x. VCACHE uses 32-bit code, runs in

V

protected mode, and automatically allocates space in RAM rather than requiring the user to reserve space for the cache. *See also* cache, driver, protected mode, RAM, VFAT.

vCalendar *n.* A specification defining the format for applications to exchange scheduling information. The vCalendar specification is based on existing industry standards, including international standards for representing dates and times, and permits the exchange of schedules and "to-do" lists of the sort users commonly enter into personal calendars. Like the companion vCard specification for electronic business cards, it was created by the versit consortium founded by Apple, AT&T, IBM, and Siemens. Handed off to the Internet Mail Consortium (IMC) in 1996, vCalendar is supported by numerous hardware and software vendors. *See also* vCard.

vCard *n.* A specification for creating an electronic business card (or personal-information card) and for the card itself. Designed to be exchanged through applications such as e-mail and teleconferencing, a vCard includes information such as name, address, telephone and fax number(s), and e-mail address. It can also include timezone, geographic location, and multimedia data such as photographs, company logos, and sound clips. Based on the ITU's X.500 directory services specification, vCard was developed by versit, a consortium whose principal members include Apple, AT&T, IBM, and Siemens. The specification is under the guidance of the Internet Mail consortium Version 3.0 of the vCard specification has been approved as a proposed standard by the IETF. A companion specification known as vCalendar supports electronic exchange of scheduling information. *See also* vCalendar, X series.

V-chip *n.* Electronic chip for installation in a television, VCR, cable box, or stand-alone device to provide adults with the ability to block programming they deem inappropriate. Intended to provide parents with a means of controlling the programming viewed by children, the V-chip allows adults to screen programs based on a rating level transmitted in the portion of the TV signal known as the vertical blanking interval (the same portion that carries closed captioning information). When programs exceed the chosen level, the V-chip signals the television, which then displays an "unauthorized to receive" message on a blank screen.

VCOMM *n.* The communications device driver in Windows 9x that provides the interface between Windows-based applications and drivers on one side, and port drivers and modems on the other. *See also* driver.

VCPI *n. See* Virtual Control Program Interface.

VCR-style mechanism *n.* **1.** A user interface for playing movie files that has controls similar to those on a video-cassette recorder (VCR). **2.** A type of motorized docking mechanism in which a laptop or notebook computer is physically locked into place by the docking station. The advantage to a VCR-style mechanism is that it provides an electrically consistent, secure bus connection. *See also* docking mechanism, docking station, laptop, portable computer.

VDD *n.* Acronym for **v**irtual **d**isplay **d**evice driver. *See* virtual device driver.

VDL *n.* Acronym for **V**ienna **D**efinition **L**anguage. A metalanguage, containing both a syntactic and a semantic metalanguage, used to define other languages. *See also* metalanguage.

VDM *n. See* video display metafile.

VDSL *n.* Short for **v**ery-high-speed **d**igital **s**ubscriber **l**ine. The high-speed version of the xDSL (digital subscriber line) communication technologies, all of which operate over existing phone lines. VDSL can deliver up to 52 Mbps downstream, but it is effective only within about 4500 to 5000 feet of the central exchange. The data delivery rate is, in fact, related to the distance the signal must travel. To attain a rate of 52 Mbps, for example, the subscriber must be within 1000 feet of the exchange office. At a distance of 3000 feet, the data rate drops to about 26 Mbps; and at 5000 feet, the data rate drops to about 13 Mbps. *See also* central office, xDSL.

VDT *n.* Acronym for **v**ideo **d**isplay **t**erminal. A terminal that includes a CRT (cathode-ray tube) and keyboard. *See also* CRT.

VDU *n.* Acronym for **v**ideo **d**isplay **u**nit. A computer monitor. *See also* monitor.

vector *n.* **1.** In mathematics and physics, a variable that has both distance and direction. *Compare* scalar. **2.** In computer graphics, a line drawn in a certain direction from a starting point to an endpoint, both of whose locations are identified by the computer using x-y-coordinates on a grid. Vectors are used in the output of some graphics programs instead of groups of dots (on paper) or pixels (on screen). *See also* vector graphics. **3.** In data structures, a one-dimensional array—a set of items arranged in a single column or row. *See also* array, matrix.

vector display *n.* A CRT (cathode-ray tube), commonly used in oscilloscopes and DVST (direct view storage tube) displays, that allows the electron beam to be arbitrarily deflected, based on x-y-coordinate signals. For example, to draw a line on a vector display, the video adapter sends signals to the X and Y yokes to move the electron beam over the path of the line; there is no background composed of scan lines, so the line drawn on the screen is not constructed of pixels. *See also* CRT, yoke. *Compare* raster display.

vector font *n.* A font in which the characters are drawn using arrangements of line segments rather than arrangements of bits. *See also* font. *Compare* bitmapped font.

vector graphics *n.* Images generated from mathematical descriptions that determine the position, length, and direction in which lines are drawn. Objects are created as collections of lines rather than as patterns of individual dots or pixels. *Compare* raster graphics.

Vector Markup Language *n. See* VML.

vector table *n. See* dispatch table.

Velocity Engine *n.* A component of Apple's Macintosh G4 processor that processes data in 128-bit chunks. The Velocity Engine is capable of over one gigaflop of floating-point operations per second.

Venn diagram *n.* A type of diagram, used to express the result of operations on sets, in which a rectangle represents the universe and circles inside the rectangle represent sets of objects. Relationships between sets are indicated by the positions of the circles in relation to one another. The Venn diagram is named after John Venn (1834–1923), an English logician at Cambridge University. See the illustration.

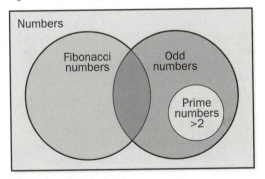

Venn diagram.

verbose *adj.* Displaying messages as English text rather than as concise (but cryptic) codes.

verify *vb.* To confirm either that a result is correct or that a procedure or sequence of operations has been performed.

Veronica *n.* Acronym for **v**ery **e**asy **r**odent-**o**riented **Net**-wide **i**ndex to **c**omputerized **a**rchives. An Internet service developed at the University of Nevada that searches for Gopher archives by keywords. Users can enter Boolean operators, such as AND, OR, and XOR, to help narrow or expand their search. If any matching archives are found, they are listed on a new Gopher menu. *See also* Boolean operator, Gopher. *Compare* Archie, Jughead.

version *n.* A particular issue or release of a hardware product or software title.

version control *n.* The process of maintaining a database of all the source code and related files in a software development project to keep track of changes made during the project.

version number *n.* A number assigned by a software developer to identify a particular program at a particular stage, before and after public release. Successive public releases of a program are assigned increasingly higher numbers. Version numbers usually include decimal fractions. Major changes are generally marked by a change in the whole number, whereas for minor changes only the number after the decimal point increases.

verso *adj.* The publishing term for a left-hand page, which is always even-numbered. *Compare* recto.

vertex *n.* The highest point of a curve, the point where a curve ends, or the point where two line segments meet in a polygon or freeform.

vertical application *n.* A specialized application designed to meet the unique needs of a particular business or industry—for example, an application to keep track of billing, tips, and inventory in a restaurant.

vertical bandwidth *n.* The rate at which a display screen is refreshed entirely, expressed in hertz (Hz). The vertical bandwidth of display systems ranges from 45 Hz to over 100 Hz. *Also called:* vertical scan rate, vertical sync, V-sync.

vertical blanking interval *n.* The time required for the electron beam in a raster-scan display to perform a vertical retrace. *See also* blanking, vertical retrace.

vertical recording *n. See* perpendicular recording.

vertical redundancy check *n. See* VRC.

vertical retrace *n.* On raster-scan displays, the movement of the electron beam from the lower right corner back to the upper left corner of the screen after the beam has completed a full sweep of the screen. *See also* blanking, vertical blanking interval. *Compare* horizontal retrace.

V

vertical scan rate *n. See* vertical bandwidth.

vertical scrolling *n.* Movement up or down in a displayed document. *See also* scroll bar.

vertical sync *n. See* vertical bandwidth.

vertical sync signal *n.* The part of a video signal to a raster display that denotes the end of the last scan line at the bottom of the display.

very-high-level language *n. See* 4GL.

very-high-rate digital subscriber line *n. See* VDSL.

very-high-speed integrated circuit *n.* An integrated circuit that performs operations, usually logic operations, at a very high speed. *Acronym:* VHSIC.

Very Large Database *n.* A database system containing volumes of data hundreds of gigabytes, or even terabytes, in size. A Very Large Database must often support thousands of users and tables with billions of rows of data, must often be able to operate across several different platforms and operating systems, and must often be able to work with many different software applications. *Acronym:* VLDB. *See also* data warehouse.

Very Large Memory *n.* A memory system designed to handle the huge data blocks associated with a Very Large Database. Very Large Memory uses 64-bit RISC technology to allow the use of addressable main memory and file sizes larger than 2 gigabytes (GB) and to cache as much as 14 GB of memory. *Acronym:* VLM. *See also* RISC, Very Large Database.

very-large-scale integration *n.* A reference to the density with which transistors and other elements are packed in an integrated circuit and to the thinness of the connections between them. Very-large-scale integration is generally considered to encompass the range from 5000 to 50,000 components. *Acronym:* VLSI. *See also* integrated circuit. *Compare* large-scale integration, medium-scale integration, small-scale integration, super-large-scale integration, ultra-large-scale integration.

Very Long Instruction Word *n. See* VLIW.

very-low-frequency electromagnetic radiation *n. See* VLF radiation.

VESA[1] *adj.* Having VL bus expansion slots. *Also called:* VLB. *See also* expansion slot, VL bus. *Compare* VESA/EISA, VESA/ISA.

VESA[2] *n.* Acronym for **V**ideo **E**lectronics **S**tandards **A**ssociation. An organization of hardware manufacturers and vendors dedicated to drafting and improving standards for video and multimedia devices. Standards developed by VESA include the Display Data Channel (DDC), Display Power Management Signaling (DPMS), and VESA local bus (VL bus). *See also* DDC, DPMS, VL bus.

VESA DDC *n. See* DDC.

VESA Display Data Channel *n. See* DDC.

VESA Display Power Management Signaling *n. See* DPMS.

VESA/EISA *adj.* Having both EISA and VL bus expansion slots. *See also* EISA, expansion slot, VESA[2], VL bus. *Compare* VESA[1], VESA/ISA.

VESA/ISA *adj.* Having both ISA and VL bus expansion slots. *See also* expansion slot, ISA, VESA[2], VL bus. *Compare* VESA[1], VESA/EISA.

VESA local bus *n. See* VL bus.

vesicular film *n.* A coating for optical discs that facilitates erasing and rewriting. The surface is marked by small bumps, which can be flattened and thereby erased, rather than by the pits used in standard CD-ROM discs.

V.everything *n.* A marketing term used by some modem manufacturers to describe modems that comply with both the ITU-T (formerly CCITT) V.34 standard and the various proprietary protocols that were used before the standard was adopted, such as V.Fast Class. A V.everything modem should be compatible with any other modem that operates at the same speed. *See also* V.Fast Class, V series.

V.Fast Class *n.* A de facto modulation standard for modems implemented by Rockwell International prior to approval of the V.34 protocol, which is the standard. Although both V.Fast Class and V.34 are capable of 28.8-Kbps transmission, V.Fast Class modems cannot communicate with V.34 modems without an upgrade. *Acronym:* V.FC. *See also* V series.

VFAT *n.* Acronym for **V**irtual **F**ile **A**llocation **T**able. The file system driver software used under the Windows 9x Installable File System Manager (IFS) for accessing disks. VFAT is compatible with MS-DOS disks but runs more efficiently. VFAT uses 32-bit code, runs in protected mode, uses VCACHE for disk caching, and supports long filenames. *See also* Installable File System Manager, long filenames, protected mode, VCACHE, Windows. *Compare* file allocation table.

V.FC *n. See* V.Fast Class.

VGA *n.* Acronym for **V**ideo **G**raphics **A**dapter. A video adapter that duplicates all the video modes of the EGA (Enhanced Graphics Adapter) and adds several more. *See also* video adapter. *Compare* EGA.

VHLL *n.* Acronym for very-high-level language. *See* 4GL.

VHSIC *n. See* very-high-speed integrated circuit.

vi¹ *n.* Short for **vi**sual. The first full-screen text editor under UNIX. The vi editor offers many powerful but not very intuitive keyboard commands. It is still in use on UNIX systems, despite the existence of other editors such as Emacs. *See also* editor, UNIX.

vi² *vb.* To edit a file using the vi editor. *See also* vi¹.

VIA *n. See* Virtual Interface Architecture.

VI Architecture *n. See* Virtual Interface Architecture.

video *adj.* Of or pertaining to the visual component of a television signal. In relation to computers, *video* refers to the rendering of text and graphics images on displays. *Compare* audio.

video accelerator *n. See* graphics engine (definition 1).

video adapter *n.* The electronic components that generate the video signal sent through a cable to a video display. The video adapter is usually located on the computer's main system board or on an expansion board, but it is sometimes built into the terminal. *Also called:* video adapter board, video board, video card, video controller, video display adapter.

video adapter board *n. See* video adapter.

video board *n. See* video adapter.

video buffer *n.* The memory on a video adapter that is used to store data to be shown on the display. When the video adapter is in a character mode, this data is in the form of ASCII character and attribute codes; when it is in a graphics mode, the data defines each pixel. *See also* bit image, bit plane, color bits, pixel image.

video capture board *n. See* video capture device.

video capture card *n. See* video capture device.

video capture device *n.* An expansion board that converts analog video signals to digital form and stores them in a computer's hard disk or other mass storage device. Some video capture devices are also capable of converting digital video to analog video for use in a VCR. *Also called:* video capture board, video capture card. *See also* expansion board.

video card *n. See* video adapter.

video clip *n.* A file that contains a short video item, usually an excerpt from a longer recording.

video compression *n.* Reduction of the size of files containing video images stored in digital form. If no compression were done, 24-bit color video at 640 x 480 pixels would occupy almost one megabyte per frame, or over a gigabyte per minute. Video compression can, however, be lossy without affecting the perceived quality of the image. *See also* lossy compression, Motion JPEG, MPEG.

video conferencing *n.* Teleconferencing in which video images are transmitted among the various geographically separated participants in a meeting. Originally done using analog video and satellite links, today video conferencing uses compressed digital images transmitted over wide area networks or the Internet. A 56K communications channel supports freeze-frame video; with a 1.544-Mbps (T1) channel, full-motion video can be used. *See also* 56K, desktop conferencing, freeze-frame video, full-motion video, T1, teleconferencing. *Compare* data conferencing.

video controller *n. See* video adapter.

video digitizer *n.* A device used in computer graphics that uses a video camera, rather than a scan head, to capture a video image and then stores it in memory with the aid of a special-purpose circuit board. *See also* digitize. *Compare* digital camera.

videodisc *n.* An optical disc used to store video images and associated audio information. *See also* CD-ROM.

video display *n.* Any device capable of displaying, but not printing, text or graphics output from a computer.

video display adapter *n. See* video adapter.

video display board *n.* A video adapter implementation using an expansion board rather than the computer's main system board. *See also* video adapter.

video display card *n. See* video display board.

video display metafile *n.* A file containing video display information for the transport of images from one system to another. *Acronym:* VDM.

video display page *n.* A portion of a computer's video buffer that holds one complete screen image. If the buffer can hold more than one page, or frame, screen updates can be completed more rapidly because an unseen page can be filled while another is being displayed.

video display terminal *n. See* VDT.

video display tube *n. See* CRT.

video display unit *n. See* monitor.

video DRAM *n. See* video RAM.

video driver *n.* Software that provides the interface between the video adapter hardware and other programs, including the operating system. The user can access the video driver to specify the resolution and color-bit depth of images on the monitor during the setup process. *See also* driver, monitor, video adapter.

video editor *n.* A device or program used to modify the contents of a video file.

Video Electronics Standards Association *n. See* VESA[2].

video game *n. See* computer game.

Video Graphics Adapter or **Video Graphics Array** *n. See* VGA.

video graphics board *n.* A video adapter that generates video signals for displaying graphical images on a video screen.

video look-up table *n. See* color look-up table.

video memory *n.* Memory from which a display image is created, located in the video adapter or video subsystem. If both the video processor and the central processing unit (CPU) have access to video memory, images are produced by the CPU's modification of video memory. Video circuitry normally has priority over the processor when both attempt to read or write to a video memory location, so updating video memory is often slower than accessing main memory. *See also* video RAM.

video mode *n.* The manner in which a computer's video adapter and monitor display on-screen images. The most common modes are text (character) mode and graphics mode. In text mode, characters include letters, numbers, and some symbols, none of which are "drawn" on screen dot by dot. In contrast, graphics mode produces all screen images, whether text or art, as patterns of pixels (dots) that are drawn one pixel at a time.

videophone *n.* A device equipped with camera and screen, as well as a microphone and speaker, capable of transmitting and receiving video signals as well as voice over a telephone line. Using conventional telephone lines, a videophone can transmit only freeze-frame video. *See also* freeze-frame video.

video port *n.* A cable connector or port on a computer that outputs video signals to a monitor.

video RAM *n.* A special type of dynamic RAM (DRAM) used in high-speed video applications. Video RAM uses separate pins for the processor and the video circuitry, providing the video circuitry with a back door to the video RAM. The video circuitry can access the video RAM serially (bit by bit), which is more appropriate for transferring pixels to the screen than is the parallel access provided by conventional DRAM. *Acronym:* VRAM. *See also* dynamic RAM.

video server *n.* A server designed to deliver digital video-on-demand and other broadband interactive services to the public over a wide area network.

video signal *n.* The signal sent from a video adapter or other video source to a raster display. The signal can include horizontal and vertical synchronization signals, as well as image information. *See also* composite video display, RGB monitor.

video terminal *n. See* terminal (definition 1).

videotex *n.* An interactive information retrieval service designed to be accessed by subscribers over telephone lines. Information can be displayed on a home television screen or a videotex terminal. Subscribers use keypads to choose from menus and to request specific screens, or pages. *Also called:* videotext.

videotext *n. See* videotex.

Vienna Definition Language *n. See* VDL.

view[1] *n.* **1.** The display of data or an image from a given perspective or location. **2.** In relational database management systems, a logical table created through the specification of one or more relational operations on one or more tables. A view is equivalent to a divided relation in the relational model. *See also* relational database, relational model.

view[2] *vb.* To cause an application to display information on a computer screen.

viewer *n.* An application that displays or otherwise outputs a file in the same way as the application that created the file. An example of a viewer is a program to display the images stored in GIF or JPEG files. *See also* GIF, JPEG.

viewport *n.* In computer graphics, a view of a document or an image. A viewport is similar to the view in a window, but usually only part of the document or graphical image is visible. *Compare* window.

vine *n.* A means of distributing audiotape copies that is similar to a tape tree. Because vine tapes are digital in format, there is no degradation of sound quality as tapes are copied down the vine from one participant to the next. *Compare* tape tree.

Vines *n.* A UNIX-based networking operating system from Banyan Systems.

viral marketing *n.* A marketing concept that relies on computer users to distribute marketing materials, possibly without even being aware of their participation. Viral marketing is often tied in with free e-mail accounts or other free online services, from which users pass along advertisements with every message they send.

virgule *n.* The forward slash (/) character. *Compare* backslash.

virtual *adj.* Of or pertaining to a device, service, or sensory input that is perceived to be what it is not in actuality, usually as more "real" or concrete than it actually is.

virtual 8086 mode *n. See* virtual real mode.

virtual 86 mode *n. See* virtual real mode.

virtual address *n.* In a virtual memory system, the address that the application uses to reference memory. The memory management unit (MMU) translates this address into a physical address before the memory is actually read or written to. *See also* physical address, virtual memory. *Compare* real address.

virtual channel *n.* In Asynchronous Transfer Mode (ATM), the path taken by data sent from one sender to one receiver. *See also* ATM (definition 1), virtual path (definition 2).

virtual circuit *n.* A connection between communicating computers that provides the computers with what appears to be a direct link but can actually involve routing data over a defined but longer path.

virtual community *n. See* online community.

Virtual Control Program Interface *n.* A specification for MS-DOS programs to allow access to extended memory under a multitasking environment (for example, Windows) for 386 and higher-level processors. *Acronym:* VCPI. *See also* 80386DX, extended memory, multitasking. *Compare* protected mode.

virtual desktop *n.* A desktop enhancement tool that provides access to the desktop when it is covered by open windows or that expands the size of the working desktop. *See also* desktop.

virtual device *n.* A device that can be referenced but that does not physically exist. Virtual-memory addressing, for example, uses magnetic disk storage to simulate memory larger than that physically available.

virtual device driver *n.* Software in Windows 9x that manages a hardware or software system resource. If a resource retains information from one access to the next that affects the way it behaves when accessed (for example, a disk controller with its status information and buffers), a virtual device driver must exist for it. Virtual device drivers are described using three-letter abbreviations beginning with V and ending with D; the middle letter indicates the type of device, such as D for a display, P for a printer, T for a timer, and *x* when the type of device is not under discussion. *Acronym:* VxD. *See also* device driver.

virtual disk *n. See* RAM disk.

virtual display device driver *n. See* virtual device driver.

Virtual File Allocation Table *n. See* VFAT.

virtual hosting *n.* A form of hosting that provides a Web server, communication, and other services to customers for their own Web sites. In addition to hardware, software, and communication, virtual hosting can include assistance with domain name registration, e-mail addresses, and other Web-related issues. *See also* host, hosting.

virtual image *n.* An image that is stored in computer memory but is too large to be shown in its entirety on the screen. Scrolling and panning are used to bring unseen portions of the image into view. *See also* virtual screen.

virtual-image file *n.* A file that specifies the material to be recorded onto a CD-ROM. A virtual-image file generally contains pointers to files that are distributed across a hard disk rather than gathered in one area. Since a complete copy of the material is not assembled, problems may occur in writing the CD-ROM due to delays in assembling the material from a scattered group of files. *See also* CD-ROM. *Compare* physical-image file.

Virtual Interface Architecture *n.* An interface specification that defines a standard low-latency, high-bandwidth means of communication between clusters of servers in a System Area Network (SAN). Developed by Compaq, Intel, Microsoft, and more than 100 industry groups, the Virtual Interface Architecture is processor and operating system independent. By reducing the time required for message-passing between applications and the network, it seeks to reduce overhead and thus deliver enterprise-level scalability for mission-critical applications. *Acronym:* VIA. *Also called:* VI Architecture. *See also* cluster, System Area Network.

virtual LAN *n.* Short for **virtual l**ocal **a**rea **n**etwork. A local area network consisting of groups of hosts that are on physically different segments but that communicate as though they were on the same wire. *See also* LAN.

virtual machine *n.* Software that mimics the performance of a hardware device, such as a program that allows applications written for an Intel processor to be run on a Motorola chip. *Acronym:* VM.

virtual memory *n.* Memory that appears to an application to be larger and more uniform than it is. Virtual memory may be partially simulated by secondary storage such as a hard disk. Applications access memory through virtual addresses, which are translated (mapped) by special hardware and software onto physical addresses. *Acronym:* VM. *Also called:* disk memory. *See also* paging, segmentation.

virtual monitor *n.* An enhanced monitor viewing system for visually impaired users that uses a virtual-reality headset to move enlarged text across the screen in a direction opposite to head motion. *See also* virtual reality.

virtual name space *n.* The set of all hierarchical sequences of names that can be used by an application to locate objects. One such sequence of names defines a path through the virtual name space, regardless of whether the hierarchy of names reflects the actual arrangement of objects around the system. For example, the virtual name space of a Web server consists of all possible URLs on the network on which it runs. *See also* URL.

virtual network *n.* A part of a network that appears to a user to be a network of its own. For example, an Internet service provider can set up multiple domains on a single HTTP server so that each one can be addressed with its company's registered domain name. *See also* domain name, HTTP server (definition 1), ISP.

virtual path *n.* **1.** A sequence of names that is used to locate a file and that has the same form as a pathname in the file system but is not necessarily the actual sequence of directory names under which the file is located. The part of a URL that follows the server name is a virtual path. For example, if the directory *c:\bar\sinister\forces\distance* on the server *miles* is shared on the local area network at *foo.com* under the name *\\miles\baz* and contains the file *elena.html*, that file may be returned by a Web request for *http://miles.foo.com/baz/elena.html.* **2.** In Asynchronous Transfer Mode (ATM), a set of virtual channels that are switched together as a unit through the network. *See also* ATM (definition 1), virtual channel.

virtual peripheral *n.* A peripheral that can be referenced but does not physically exist. For example, an application might treat a serial port through which data is being transmitted as a printer, but the device receiving the data might be another computer instead.

virtual printer *n.* A feature in many operating systems that allows printer output to be saved to a file until a printer becomes available.

virtual printer device driver *n. See* virtual device driver.

virtual private network *n.* **1.** Nodes on a public network such as the Internet that communicate among themselves using encryption technology so that their messages are as safe from being intercepted and understood by unauthorized users as if the nodes were connected by private lines. **2.** A WAN (wide area network) formed of permanent virtual circuits (PVCs) on another network, especially a network using technologies such as ATM or frame relay. *Acronym:* VPN. *See also* ATM (definition 1), frame relay, PVC.

virtual reality *n.* A simulated 3-D environment that a user can experience and manipulate as if it were physical. The user sees the environment on display screens, possibly mounted in a special pair of goggles. Special input devices, such as gloves or suits fitted with motion sensors, detect the user's actions. *Acronym:* VR.

Virtual Reality Modeling Language *n. See* VRML.

virtual real mode *n.* A feature of the Intel 80386 (SX and DX) and later microprocessors that allows them to emulate several 8086 (real-mode) environments at the same time. The microprocessor provides a set of virtual registers and virtual memory space to each virtual 8086 environment. A program running in a virtual 8086 environment is completely protected from other virtual 8086 environments in the system and behaves as if it had control of the entire system. *Also called:* V86 mode, virtual 8086 mode, virtual 86 mode. *See also* real mode.

virtual root *n.* The root directory that a user sees when connected to an Internet server, such as an HTTP or FTP server. The virtual root is actually a pointer to the physical root directory, which may be in a different location, such as on another server. The advantages of using a virtual root include being able to create a simple URL for the Internet site and to move the root directory without affecting the URL. *Also called:* v-root. *See also* pointer (definition 1), root directory, server (definition 2), URL.

virtual route *n. See* virtual circuit.

virtual screen *n.* An image area that extends beyond the dimensions of the physical screen on the monitor, allowing manipulation of large documents or of multiple documents that lie partially outside the normal screen view. *See also* monitor.

virtual server *n.* A virtual machine that resides on an HTTP server but has the appearance to the user of being a separate HTTP server. Several virtual servers can reside on one HTTP server, each capable of running its own programs and each with individualized access to input and peripheral devices. Each virtual server has its own domain name and IP address and appears to the user as an individual Web site. Some Internet service providers use virtual servers for those clients who want to use their own domain names. *See also* domain name, HTTP server (definition 2), IP address.

virtual storefront *n.* A company's point of presence on the Web, providing opportunities for online sales. *Also called:* electronic storefront.

virtual terminal *n.* *See* terminal emulation.

virtual timer device driver *n.* *See* virtual device driver.

virtual world *n.* **1.** A 3-D modeled environment, often created in VRML, where a user can interact with the viewer to change variables. *See also* viewer, VRML. **2.** An electronic environment that has no basis in the physical world. Multiuser dungeons (MUDs), talkers, and chat rooms are often considered virtual worlds. *See also* chat[1] (definition 1), MUD, talker.

virus *n.* An intrusive program that infects computer files by inserting in those files copies of itself. The copies are usually executed when the file is loaded into memory, allowing the virus to infect still other files, and so on. Viruses often have damaging side effects—sometimes intentionally, sometimes not. For example, some viruses can destroy a computer's hard disk or take up memory space that could otherwise be used by programs. *See also* Good Times virus, Trojan horse, worm.

virus signature *n.* A portion of unique computer code contained in a virus. Antivirus programs search for known virus signatures to identify infected programs and files. *See also* virus.

visible page *n.* In computer graphics, the image that is being displayed on the screen. Screen images are written into display memory in sections called pages, each of which contains one screen display.

Visio *n.* A software application offered by Microsoft that allows users to create diagrams and visual presentations in electronic form. Visio enables users to share ideas and concepts visually by using diagrams to augment written material in documents or by expanding visual elements in a public presentation. Microsoft acquired the Visio application in 1999, when it purchased Visio Corporation.

visit *n.* A session during which a person views one or more pages in a particular Web site.

visitor *n.* A person who views a Web page or Web site.

Visor *n.* A product line of handheld personal digital assistants (PDAs) developed by Handspring Corporation. Features include an address list, an appointments calendar, a to-do list, and memos. Visor also features a 68-pin Springboard socket that allows plug-ins of additional devices offered by Handspring. *See also* Springboard.

Visual Basic *n.* A trademarked name owned by Microsoft Corporation for a high-level, visual-programming version of Basic. Visual Basic was designed for building Windows-based applications. *See also* Basic, Visual Basic for Applications, Visual Basic, Scripting Edition, visual programming.

Visual Basic Editor *n.* An environment in which you write new and edit existing Visual Basic for Applications code and procedures. The Visual Basic Editor contains a complete debugging toolset for finding syntax, run-time, and logic problems in your code.

Visual Basic for Applications *n.* A macro-language version of Visual Basic that is used to program many Windows 9x applications and is included with several Microsoft applications. *Acronym:* VBA. *See also* macro language, Visual Basic.

Visual Basic Script *n.* *See* Visual Basic, Scripting Edition.

Visual Basic, Scripting Edition *n.* A subset of the Visual Basic programming language, optimized for Web-related programming. As with JavaScript, code for Visual Basic, Scripting Edition is embedded in HTML documents. This version is included with the Internet Explorer Web browser. *Also called:* VBScript, Visual Basic Script. *See also* Visual Basic for Applications.

Visual C++ *n.* A Microsoft application development system for the programming language C++ that runs under MS-DOS and Windows. Visual C++ is a visual programming environment. *See also* visual programming. *Compare* Visual Basic, Visual J++.

V

Visual Café *n.* The Java-based suite of software development tools from Symantec Corporation. Visual Café is available in several product packages. The Standard Edition, intended for beginning Java programmers, includes an integrated editor, debugger, and compiler, as well as a JavaBean library, wizards, and utilities. The Professional Edition provides a larger library of JavaBeans and more sophisticated tools for development and debugging. The Database Edition, as the name indicates, adds support for database functionality. The Enterprise Suite provides a high-end environment for development of enterprise applications. *See also* Java.

Visual FoxPro Database and Command Language *n.* A Microsoft product for developing database applications that includes a rich object-oriented programming language derived from the Xbase language.

Visual InterDev *n.* Microsoft's integrated development environment for Web applications. Visual InterDev includes tools for end-to-end (design through deployment) development, as well as integrated tools for database programming and design. The first version of Microsoft Visual InterDev was released in 1997.

visual interface *n. See* graphical user interface.

visualization *n.* A feature of an application that displays data in the form of a video image. For example, some databases can interpret and show data in the form of a two- or three-dimensional model.

Visual J++ *n.* Microsoft's Java visual programming environment, which can be used to create applets and applications in the Java language. *See also* applet, Java, Java applet, visual programming.

visual programming *n.* A method of programming using a programming environment or language in which basic program components can be selected through menu choices, buttons, icons, and other predetermined methods.

Visual SourceSafe *n.* A project-oriented version control system designed by Microsoft to manage software and Web site development. Visual SourceSafe stores files in a secure repository that provides easy access to authorized users and tracks all changes made to files. Visual Source-Safe works with any type of file produced by any development language, authoring tool, or application.

Visual Studio *n.* Microsoft's suite of software development tools for rapid development of business applications and components. Visual Studio is provided in two editions. The Professional Edition, for professional programmers, includes the Visual Basic and Visual C++

languages, Visual FoxPro for database development, Visual InterDev for Web development, and Visual J++ for Java development. The Enterprise Edition, for enterprise-level development, also includes Visual SourceSafe (a team-based source code control system) and the Developer Edition of Microsoft BackOffice Server.

Visual Studio .NET *n.* A development environment for creating XML Web services and applications on the Microsoft .NET platform. *See also* .NET, .NET My Services.

VLAN *n. See* virtual LAN.

VLB[1] *adj. See* VESA[1].

VLB[2] *n. See* VL bus.

VL bus *n.* Short for **VESA local bus**. A type of local bus architecture introduced by the Video Electronics Standards Association. The VL bus specification allows up to three VL bus slots to be built into a PC motherboard and allows for bus mastering (wherein intelligent adapter cards can do some processing independently of the CPU). A VL bus slot consists of a standard connector plus an additional 16-bit Micro Channel Architecture connector and must be built into the motherboard by the manufacturer. Standard connectors cannot simply be converted to VL bus slots. A non–VL bus adapter card can be used in a VL bus slot, but it cannot use the local bus and so performs as it normally would in a non–VL bus slot. *Also called:* VL local bus. *See also* local bus, PCI local bus.

VLF radiation *n.* Short for **very-low-frequency radiation**. Electromagnetic radiation (radio) at frequencies within the range of approximately 300 Hz to 30,000 Hz (30 kHz). Computer monitors emit this type of radiation. A voluntary standard, MPR II, regulates the amount of VLF radiation that a monitor can emit. *See also* MPR II.

VLIW *n.* Acronym for **Very Long Instruction Word**. An architecture that combines many simple instructions into a single long instruction word that uses different registers.

VL local bus *n. See* VL bus.

VLSI *n. See* very-large-scale integration.

VM *n.* Acronym for **Virtual Machine**. An operating system for IBM mainframes that provides virtual-machine capability. VM was developed by IBM customers and later taken over by IBM itself under the name OS/VM. *See also* virtual machine, virtual memory.

VML *n.* Acronym for **Vector Markup Language**. An XML-based specification for the exchange, editing, and delivery of 2-D vector graphics on the Web. An application of XML (Extensible Markup Language), VML uses XML tags and Cascading Style Sheets to create and place vector graphics, such as circles and squares, in an XML or HTML document, such as a Web page. These graphics, which are rendered in the native operating system, can include color and are editable in a variety of graphics programs. *See also* Cascading Style Sheets, XML.

VoATM *n.* Short for **V**oice **o**ver **A**synchronous **T**ransfer **M**ode. The transmission of voice and other telephony over an ATM network. *See also* ATM, VoFR, VoIP.

VoFR *n.* Short for **V**oice **o**ver **F**rame **R**elay. Voice transmission over a frame relay network. *See also* frame relay, VoATM, VoIP.

voice answer back *n.* The use of sound-recorded messages by a computer in responding to commands or queries. *Acronym:* VAB.

voice-capable modem *n.* A modem that can support voice messaging applications along with its data-handling functions.

voice chat *n.* A feature offered by Internet service providers (ISPs) that allows users to converse with each other directly through an Internet connection. *See also* Internet telephone.

voice coil *n.* A device that moves a disk drive actuator arm using electromagnetism. It works more quickly than a stepper motor. *See also* actuator. *Compare* stepper motor.

voice-grade channel *n.* A communications channel, such as a telephone line, with an audio bandwidth of 300 to 3000 Hz, suitable for carrying speech. A voice-grade channel can also be used for transmitting facsimile, analog, and digital information at rates up to 33 kilobits per second (Kbps).

voice input *n.* Spoken instructions that a computer translates into executable commands using speech recognition technology or that are embedded into documents with the aid of a microphone. *See also* speech recognition.

voice mail *n.* A system that records and stores telephone messages in a computer's memory. Unlike a simple answering machine, a voice mail system has separate mailboxes for multiple users, each of whom can copy, store, or redistribute messages.

voice messaging *n.* A system that sends and receives messages in the form of sound recordings.

voice modem *n.* A modulation/demodulation device that supports a switch to change between telephony and data transmission modes. Such a device might contain a built-in loudspeaker and microphone for voice communication, but more often it uses the computer's sound card. *See also* modem, sound card, telephony.

voice navigation *n.* The use of spoken commands to control a Web browser. Voice navigation is a feature of some plug-in applications that embellish Web browsers to allow the user to navigate the Web by means of his or her voice. *See also* Web browser.

voice-net *n.* A term used on the Internet to refer to the telephone system, often preceding the user's telephone number in an e-mail signature.

voice output *n. See* speech synthesis.

Voice over Asynchronous Transfer Mode *n. See* VoATM.

Voice over Frame Relay *n. See* VoFR.

Voice over IP *n. See* VoIP.

voice recognition *n.* The capability of a computer to understand the spoken word for the purpose of receiving commands and data input from the speaker. Systems that can recognize limited vocabularies as spoken by specific individuals have been developed, but developing a system that deals with a variety of speech patterns and accents, as well as with the various ways in which a request or a statement can be made, is more difficult, although advances are being made in this area. *Also called:* speech recognition. *See also* artificial intelligence, dictation software, neural network.

voice synthesis *n. See* speech synthesis.

VoIP *n.* Acronym for **V**oice **o**ver **IP**. The use of the Internet Protocol (IP) for transmitting voice communications. VoIP delivers digitized audio in packet form and can be used for transmitting over intranets, extranets, and the Internet. It is essentially an inexpensive alternative to traditional telephone communication over the circuit-switched Public Switched Telephone Network (PSTN). VoIP covers computer-to-computer, computer-to-telephone, and telephone-based communications. For the sake of compatibility and interoperability, a group called the VoIP Forum promotes product development based on the ITU-T H.323 standard for transmission of multimedia over the Internet. *Also called:* Internet telephony. *See also* H.323.

V

volatile memory *n.* **1.** Memory, such as RAM, that loses its data when the power is shut off. *Compare* nonvolatile memory. **2.** Memory used by a program that can change independently of the program, such as memory shared by another program or by an interrupt service routine.

volt *n.* The unit used to measure potential difference or electromotive force. One volt is defined as the potential across which 1 coulomb of charge will do 1 joule of work, or the potential generated by 1 ampere of current flowing through 1 ohm of resistance. *See also* electromotive force.

voltage *n. See* electromotive force.

voltage regulator *n.* A circuit or circuit component that maintains a constant output voltage despite variations in input voltage.

volts alternating current *n.* The measure of the peak-to-peak voltage swing of an electrical signal. *Acronym:* VAC.

volume *n.* **1.** A disk or tape that stores computer data. Sometimes, large hard disks are divided into several volumes, each of which is treated as a separate disk. **2.** The loudness of an audio signal.

volume label *n.* A name for a disk or tape. MS-DOS systems, which seldom use disk names except in directory listings, use the term *volume label*. Apple Macintosh systems, which often refer to disks by name, use the term *volume name*.

volume name *n. See* volume label.

volume reference number *n. See* volume serial number.

volume serial number *n.* The optional identifying volume number of a disk or tape. MS-DOS systems use the term *volume serial number*. Apple Macintosh systems use the term *volume reference number*. A volume serial number is not the same as a volume label or volume name. *Compare* volume label.

VON *n.* Acronym for **v**oice **o**n the **n**et. A broad category of hardware and software technology for real-time voice and video transmission over the Internet. The term was coined by Jeff Pulver, who formed a group called the VON Coalition, which opposes regulation of VON technology and promotes VON to the public.

von Neumann architecture *n.* The most common structure for computer systems, attributed to the mathematician John von Neumann. It uses the concept of a program that can be permanently stored in a computer and manipulated or made self-modifying through machine-based instructions. Sequential processing is characteristic of von Neu-mann architecture. Parallel architectures have evolved to improve on the encumbrances of sequential instructions. *See also* parallel computer.

von Neumann bottleneck *n.* Competition between data and instructions for CPU time. Mathematician John von Neumann was the first to show that a computer based on architecture linking a single processor with memory will actually spend more time retrieving data from memory than processing it. The bottleneck arises when the processor has to trade off between executing a large number of instructions per second and reading in a large amount of data in the same time. *See also* CPU.

VPD *n.* Acronym for **v**irtual **p**rinter **d**evice driver. *See* virtual device driver.

VPN *n. See* virtual private network.

VR *n. See* virtual reality.

VRAM *n. See* video RAM.

VRC *n.* Acronym for **v**ertical **r**edundancy **c**heck. A method for checking the accuracy of transmitted data. VRC generates an extra bit (parity bit) for each character transmitted. The parity bit indicates whether the character contains an odd or an even number of 1 bits. If its value does not match the type of the character, that character is assumed to be incorrectly transmitted. *See also* parity. *Compare* LRC.

VRML *n.* Acronym for **V**irtual **R**eality **M**odeling **L**anguage. A scene description language for creating 3-D interactive Web graphics similar to those found in some video games, allowing the user to "move around" within a graphic image and interact with objects. VRML, a subset of Silicon Graphics' Inventor File Format (ASCII), was created by Mark Pesce and Tony Parisi in 1994. VRML files can be created in a text editor, although CAD packages, modeling and animation packages, and VRML authoring software are the tools preferred by most VRML authors. VRML files reside on an HTTP server; links to these files can be embedded in HTML documents, or users can access the VRML files directly. To view VRML Web pages, users need a VRML-enabled browser or a VRML plug-in for Internet Explorer or Netscape Navigator. *See also* 3-D graphic, HTML document, HTTP server (definition 1).

v-root *n. See* virtual root.

V series *n.* The series of ITU-T (formerly CCITT) recommendations relating to modems and modem communications over the public phone system, including signaling, coding, and circuit characteristics. See the table.

V

Table V.1   Recommendations in the V Series for Modem Communications.

Recommendation Number	What It Covers
V.17	14,000-bps two-wire modems used for facsimile applications
V.21	300-bps modems used with dial-up lines; full-duplex transmission; not the same as Bell 103 (in North America)
V.22	1200-bps modems used with dial-up and leased lines; full-duplex transmission; not the same as Bell 212A (in North America)
V.22bis	2400-bps modems used with dial-up and leased lines; full-duplex transmission
V.23	600/1200-bps synchronous or asynchronous modems used with dial-up and leased lines; half-duplex transmission
V.26	2400-bps modems used with four-wire leased lines; full-duplex transmission
V.26bis	1200/2400-bps modems used with dial-up lines; full-duplex transmission
V.26ter	2400-bps modems used with dial-up and two-wire leased lines; DPSK modulation; fallback to 1200 bps; echo canceling to remove phone-line echo; full-duplex transmission
V.27	4800-bps modems used with leased lines; manual equalizer; full-duplex transmission
V.27bis	2400/4800-bps modems used with leased lines; automatic equalizer; full-duplex transmission
V.27ter	2400/4800-bps modems used with dial-up lines; full-duplex transmission
V.29	9600-bps modems used with point-to-point leased circuits; half-duplex transmission or full-duplex transmission
V.32	9600-bps modems used with dial-up lines; echo canceling to remove phone-line echo; full-duplex transmission
V.32bis	4800/7200/9600/12,000/14,400-bps modems used with dial-up lines; echo canceling; full-duplex transmission
V.33	12,000/14,400-bps modems used with four-wire leased lines; synchronous; QAM modulation; time-division multiplexing; full-duplex transmission
V.34	28,800-bps modems; full-duplex transmission
V.35	Group band modems, which combine the bandwidth of more than one telephone circuit
V.54	Operation of loop test devices in modems
V.56	Network transmission model for evaluating modem performance over standard voice-grade telephone connections
V.56bis	Network transmission model for evaluating modem performance over two-wire voice-grade connections
V.56ter	Network transmission model for evaluating modem performance over two-wire, 4-kilohertz duplex modems
V.61	4800-bps modems operating at voice plus data rate or 14,000-bps modems operating at data-only rate over standard switched telephone circuits or on point-to-point, two-wire phone circuits

V-sync *n. See* vertical bandwidth.

VT-52, VT-100, VT-200 *n.* A popular set of control codes used in terminals with those model numbers that were originally manufactured by Digital Equipment Corporation. Appropriate software can enable a microcomputer to use these codes to emulate such terminals.

VTD *n.* Acronym for **v**irtual **t**imer **d**evice driver. *See* virtual device driver.

Vulcan death grip *n.* A warm boot by pressing the Alt+Crl+Delete keys. The name is a reference from *Star Trek. See also* three-finger salute, warm boot.

VxD *n. See* virtual device driver.

w³ *n. See* World Wide Web.

W3 *n. See* World Wide Web.

W3C *n.* Abbreviation for the World Wide Web Consortium, a standards body based in the United States, Europe, and Japan. The W3C is dedicated (in part) to encouraging the development of open Web standards, such as the HTML and XML document markup languages, to promote interoperability and assist the Web in achieving its potential.

wafer *n.* A thin, flat piece of semiconductor crystal used in the fabrication of integrated circuits. Various etching, doping, and layering techniques are used to create the circuit components on the surface of the wafer. Usually multiple identical circuits are formed on a single wafer, which is then cut into sections. Each integrated circuit then has leads attached and is packaged in a holder. *See also* integrated circuit, semiconductor.

wafer-scale integration *n.* The fabrication on a single wafer of different microcircuits that are then connected to form a single circuit the full size of the wafer. *See also* wafer.

WAI *n.* Acronym for **W**eb **A**ccessibility **I**nitiative. A set of guidelines released by the World Wide Web Consortium (W3C) in May 1999. The WAI is intended to promote Web accessibility for users with disabilities by setting Web design and compatibility guidelines that help assure Web access and usability for all users. *See also* accessibility.

WAIS *n.* Acronym for **W**ide **A**rea **I**nformation **S**erver. A UNIX-based document search and retrieval system on the Internet that can be used to search over 400 WAIS libraries, such as Project Gutenberg, for indexed files that match keywords entered by the user. WAIS can also be used on an individual Web site such as a search engine. WAIS, developed by Thinking Machines Corporation, Apple Computer, and Dow Jones, uses the Z39.50 standard to process natural language queries. The list of documents returned by WAIS often contains numerous false matches. Users need a WAIS client to use a WAIS server. *See also* natural language query, Project Gutenberg, search engine, Z39.50 standard.

WAIS client *n.* The program needed for accessing the WAIS (Wide Area Information Server) system to search

its databases. A WAIS client program must be installed on a user's own machine or accessed from a computer with such a program already installed. Many freeware and shareware WAIS programs for various operating systems, including UNIX, MS-DOS, OS/2, and Windows, are available for download on the Internet. To look for documents in a WAIS database, the user selects the database(s) to search and types a query containing keywords to search for. The WAIS client sends this query to the server, communicating with the server via the Z39.50 protocol. The server processes the request using indexes and returns a list of document headlines matching the query to the client. The user can then choose which document to retrieve, send that request to the server, and receive the complete document in return. *See also* WAIS.

WAIS database *n. See* WAIS.

waisindex *n.* **1.** A UNIX utility for building an index to text files for access using WAIS (Wide Area Information Server) query software. **2.** A URL for accessing WAIS. The URL takes the form wais://*hostport*/*database*[? *search*].

WAIS library *n.* A WAIS (Wide Area Information Server) database. A WAIS library is a comprehensive collection of online documents on a specific topic—for example, Project Gutenberg's collection of public-domain literary and historical texts available over the Internet, and the Dow Jones Information Service collection of business and financial information products. Because the hundreds of WAIS free libraries currently accessible are updated and maintained by volunteers, the quality of topic coverage is uneven. *See also* WAIS, WAIS client, Project Gutenberg.

WAIS server or **waisserver** *n. See* WAIS.

wait state *n.* A processing cycle of the microprocessor during which it only waits for data from an input/output device or from memory. While a single wait state is not humanly perceptible, the cumulative effect of wait states is to slow system performance. *See also* zero wait state.

wallet *n.* In electronic commerce, a software program that contains a user's address and credit card information for use in paying for online purchases. When the wallet is opened at the electronic checkout, it identifies the user to the merchant's server and allows the user to authorize the appropriate debit to a credit card.

wallpaper *n.* In a graphical user interface such as Windows, a pattern or picture in the screen background that can be chosen by the user. *See also* graphical user interface.

WAN *n.* Acronym for **w**ide **a**rea **n**etwork. A geographically widespread network, one that relies on communications capabilities to link the various network segments. A WAN can be one large network, or it can consist of a number of linked LANs (local area networks).

wand *n.* Any pen-shaped device used for data entry, such as a graphics tablet's stylus or, most commonly, the scanning instrument used with many bar code readers. *See also* optical scanner, scan head. *Compare* stylus.

wanderer *n.* A person who frequently uses the World Wide Web. Many of these people make indexes of what they find.

WAP *n. See* Wireless Application Protocol.

war dialer *n.* A computer program that calls a range of phone numbers to identify those numbers that make a connection to a computer modem. War dialers are typically used by hackers to search for vulnerable computers and, once a connection is made, the war dialers may automatically probe the computer for potential weaknesses. Early war dialer programs called demon dialers were used to crack telephone systems in the 1970s and 1980s.

warez *n.* Illegal copies of computer software distributed through the Internet and other online channels, such as bulletin boards and FTP servers. The spelling is part of the tendency among some online groups to use odd symbols and intentional misspellings. *Compare* freeware, shareware.

warm boot *n.* The restarting of a running computer without first turning off the power. *Also called:* soft boot, three-finger salute, vulcan death grip, warm start.

warm start *n. See* warm boot.

warp *vb.* Sometimes used by computer game developers to describe the need to completely redraw a screen within a game. For example, moving through a door or advancing to a higher level would require a complete screen overhaul. *See also* computer game.

watchdog *n.* A hardware device (usually a timer or driver) used to monitor continuing system health and functionality through communications with the system software using a dedicated device driver.

watermark *n.* A semitransparent image often used for letters and business cards. In currency, a watermark is visible when you hold a bill up to the light.

watt *n.* The unit of power equal to the expenditure of 1 joule of energy in 1 second. The power of an electrical circuit is a function of the potential across the circuit and the current flowing through the circuit. If E = potential, I = current, and R = resistance, power in watts can be calculated as $I \times E$, $I^2 \times R$, or E^2/R.

.wav *n.* The file extension that identifies sound files stored in waveform (WAV) audio format. *See also* WAV.

WAV *n.* A file format in which Windows stores sounds as waveforms. Such files have the extension .wav. Depending on the sampling frequency, on whether the sound is monaural or stereo, and on whether 8 or 16 bits are used for each sample, one minute of sound can occupy as little as 644 kilobytes or as much as 27 megabytes of storage. *See also* sampling, waveform.

wave *n.* **1.** Any disturbance or change that has an oscillatory, periodic nature, for example, a light or sound wave. *See also* waveform. **2.** In electronics, the time-amplitude profile of an electrical signal.

wave division multiplexing *n. See* dense wavelength division multiplexing.

waveform *n.* The manner in which a wave's amplitude changes over time. *See also* period, phase, wavelength.

wavelength *n.* The distance between successive peaks or troughs in a periodic signal that is propagated through space. Wavelength is symbolized by the Greek letter lambda and can be calculated as speed divided by frequency.

wavelet *n.* A mathematical function that varies over a limited extent of time. Wavelets are coming into increasing use for analyzing signals (such as sound). They have limited duration and sudden changes in frequency and amplitude rather than the infinite duration and constant amplitude and frequency of the sine and cosine functions. *Compare* Fourier transform.

wave table synthesis or **wavetable synthesis** *n.* A method of producing sound, especially music, through a PC. Wave table synthesis is based on use of a wave table, which is a collection of digitized sound samples taken from recordings of actual instruments. These samples are typically stored on a sound card and are edited and mixed together to produce music. Wave table synthesis produces higher quality audio output than FM (frequency modulation) techniques.

WBEM *n.* Acronym for **W**eb-**B**ased **E**nterprise **M**anagement. A protocol that links a Web browser directly to a device or an application that monitors a network. *See also* communications protocol.

WDEF *n. See* window definition function.

WDL *n. See* Windows Driver Library.

WDM *n. See* dense wavelength division multiplexing, Windows Driver Model.

weak typing *n.* A characteristic of a programming language that allows the program to change the data type of a variable during program execution. *See also* data type, variable. *Compare* strong typing.

wearable computer *n.* A portable personal computer that its user wears like eyeglasses, clothing, or a wristwatch but which, unlike those items, is interactive, responds to commands, and carries out instructions. A wearable computer may be used like a conventional computer for data collection, storage, and retrieval, but without tying the user to a stationary location while operating the computer. The earliest wearable computers were clandestine devices used in the mid-1960s to predict the performance of roulette wheels. Today, wearable computers are used for such applications as inventory and express package tracking.

web *n.* A set of interlinked documents in a hypertext system. The user enters the web through a home page. *See also* World Wide Web.

Web *n. See* World Wide Web.

Web Accessibility Initiative *n. See* WAI.

Web address *n. See* URL.

Web application *n.* A set of clients and servers that cooperate to provide the solution to a problem.

Web architect *n.* An individual who analyzes the purpose of a Web site and forms a plan for assembling and integrating the hardware, software, and other technical resources necessary to make the site function properly.

Web author *n.* A person who creates content for the World Wide Web. A Web author might be a writer who produces text for a designer to include in a Web page, or a Web designer who writes the text and also adds graphic elements and prepares the HTML code.

Web-Based Enterprise Management *n. See* WBEM.

Web browser *n.* Software that lets a user view HTML documents and access files and software related to those documents. Originally developed to allow users to view or browse documents on the World Wide Web, Web browsers can blur the distinction between local and remote resources for the user by also providing access to documents on a network, an intranet, or the local hard drive. Web browser software is built on the concept of hyperlinks, which allow users to point and click with a mouse in order to jump from document to document in whatever order they desire. Most Web browsers are also capable of downloading and transferring files, providing access to newsgroups, displaying graphics embedded in the document, playing audio and video files associated with the document, and executing small programs, such as Java applets or ActiveX controls included by programmers in the documents. Helper applications or plug-ins are required by some Web browsers to accomplish one or more of these tasks. *Also called:* browser. *See also* ActiveX control, helper application, hyperlink, Internet Explorer, Java applet, Lynx, Mosaic, Netscape Navigator, plug-in.

Web bug *n.* A small, nearly undetectable graphic that links to a Web page and is embedded in a document for use as an eavesdropping device. A Web bug usually takes the form of a 1-by-1-pixel transparent GIF file, so it is nearly invisible. This file is placed in a Web page, Microsoft Word file, or other document that users will access. The application in which the document is opened immediately links to the Web to download and display the embedded graphic. Information about the user, including IP address, browser, referrer, and time viewed, is passed to the author of the file when the application retrieves the invisible graphic information.

Webby Award *n.* Award bestowed annually by the International Academy of Digital Arts and Sciences to Web sites. The academy bestows awards to Web sites in more than 20 categories, which include technical achievement, humor, and best community site.

Web cam or **webcam** *n.* A video camera whose output appears on a Web page, usually updated on a regular and frequent schedule. Web cams are used to display weather and traffic conditions, to allow customers and other users to observe current activities at the site owner's business or home (for example, at a day care center), for promotional purposes, and as a form of "gee whiz, look at this!" entertainment.

W

webcast[1] *n.* Live or delayed audio or video programming delivered to users over the Web. Downloading these broadcasts requires a user to have the appropriate video or audio application, such as RealPlayer. The necessary application is usually available from the webcaster without cost.

webcast[2] *vb.* To produce and disseminate Web-based audio, video, and text programming.

webcaster *n.* A company or organization that produces and disseminates Web-based audio, video, and text programming.

webcasting *n.* Popular term for broadcasting information via the World Wide Web, using push and pull technologies to move selected information from a server to a client. An emergent technology in 1997, webcasting was developed to provide users with customized content—for example, sports, news, stocks, and weather—that can be updated both regularly and automatically. Webcasting gives users the ability to specify the type of content they want to see, and it gives content providers a means of delivering such information directly to the user's desktop. *Also called:* netcasting. *See also* pull, push (definition 2).

Web clipping *n.* A Web service that delivers brief snippets of information to handheld Web-enabled devices, such as wireless phones and personal digital assistants. Rather than opening a Web site and browsing for information, Web clipping allows a customer to request specific types of information from a service. The Web clipping service then downloads the information to the handheld device.

web CLUT *n. See* browser CLUT.

Web container *n.* A container that implements the Web component contract of Sun Microsystems's Java 2 Platform Enterprise Edition (J2EE) network architecture. This contract specifies a run time environment for Web components that includes security, concurrency, life cycle management, transaction, deployment, and other services. Provided by a Web or J2EE server, a Web container provides the same services as a JavaServer Pages (JSP) container and provides a federated view of the J2EE platform APIs. *See also* API, container, J2EE, JSP container, servlet container.

Web cramming *n.* A common form of fraud in which Internet Service Providers (ISPs) add charges to the monthly bill for fictitious services or for services the customer had been told were free.

WebCrawler *n.* A World Wide Web search engine operated by America Online. *See also* search engine.

WebDAV *n.* Short for **Web D**istributed **A**uthoring and **V**ersioning. A set of extensions to the HTTP protocol that allows users to collaboratively edit, publish, and manage resources on the World Wide Web. WebDAV-enabled additions to HTTP include document writing, editing, and publishing tools and search, storage, and file sharing options.

Web development *n.* The design and coding of World Wide Web pages.

Web directory *n.* A list of Web sites, giving the URL and a description of each. *See also* URL.

Web Distributed Authoring and Versioning *n. See* WebDAV.

Web Forms *n.* The ASP.NET page framework, which consists of programmable Web pages (called Web Forms pages) that contain reusable server controls. *See also* ASP.NET server control.

Web hosting *n. See* hosting.

Web index *n.* A Web site intended to enable a user to locate other resources on the Web. The Web index may include a search facility or may merely contain individual hyperlinks to the resources indexed.

Weblication *n.* Slang for Web application. *See* Web application.

Weblog or **weblog** or **web log** *n.* A Web site that has regularly updated content reflecting the interests of the site's host. Often, but not always, the content is in journal form, has highlights of news and information from other Web sites, and is presented from a personal point of view. On some sites, the Weblog is a collaboration between visitors to the site. The high-tech-oriented Slashdot.org is frequently cited as being among the best-known Weblogs.

Webmaster or **webmaster** *n.* A person responsible for creating and maintaining a World Wide Web site. A Webmaster is often responsible for responding to e-mail, ensuring the site is operating properly, creating and updating Web pages, and maintaining the overall structure and design of the site. *Also called:* webmistress, webweaver.

webmistress *n. See* Webmaster.

webographics *n.* Demographics of Web users specifically focusing on surfing and online shopping habits and on other related information, such as connection method, browser, and platform.

WebPad *n.* A class of wireless Internet appliances offering full Internet and personal digital assistant (PDA) functions. A WebPad features a larger LCD screen than other hand-held communications devices and resembles a tablet.

Web page *n.* A document on the World Wide Web. A Web page consists of an HTML file, with associated files for graphics and scripts, in a particular directory on a particular machine (and thus identifiable by a URL). Usually a Web page contains links to other Web pages. *See also* URL.

Web page embedding *n.* Embedding a digital streaming media player directly onto a Web page using HTML code. Rather than displaying a hyperlink to the media file, Web page embedding uses browser plug-ins to present the media player as a visual element in the layout of the Web page.

Web phone *n. See* Internet telephone.

Web Presence Provider *n.* A Web hosting and Internet service provider who manages the Web server hardware and software required to make a Web site available on the Internet. *Acronym:* WPP.

Web rage *n.* **1.** Anger or frustration related to the use or operation of the Internet. **2.** An intemperate, rude, or angry posting on the Internet; a flame. **3.** The latest fad to gain popularity among Web users.

websafe palette *n. See* browser CLUT.

Web server *n. See* HTTP server.

Web server control *n.* An ASP.NET server control that belongs to the System.Web.UI.WebControls namespace. Web server controls are richer and more abstract than HTML server controls. A Web server control has an <asp:ControlName> prefix on an ASP.NET page. *See also* ASP.NET server control, HTML server control, namespace.

Web services *n.* A modular collection of Web protocol–based applications that can be mixed and matched to provide business functionality through an Internet connection. Web services can be used over the Internet or an intranet to create products, business processes, and B2B interactions. Web services use standard Internet protocols such as HTTP, XML, and SOAP to provide connectivity and interoperability between companies.

Web Services Description Language *n. See* WSDL.

Web site *n.* A group of related HTML documents and associated files, scripts, and databases that is served up by an HTTP server on the World Wide Web. The HTML documents in a Web site generally cover one or more related topics and are interconnected through hyperlinks. Most Web sites have a home page as their starting point, which frequently functions as a table of contents for the site. Many large organizations, such as corporations, will have one or more HTTP servers dedicated to a single Web site. However, an HTTP server can also serve several small Web sites, such as those owned by individuals. Users need a Web browser and an Internet connection to access a Web site. *See also* home page, HTML, HTTP server (definition 1), Web browser.

Web Storage System *n.* The storage component of Exchange 2000 Server and SharePoint Portal servers, which integrates Web server, database, file system, and workgroup functionality. The Web Storage System lets you store and share many types of data in a single integrated system. *Acronym:* WSS.

Web switch *n.* A network device—a switch—designed to optimize Web traffic routing by using the information embedded in HTTP requests to route the requests to the most appropriate servers, no matter where they are located. Web switches are intended to address issues of speed, scalability, and performance for high-volume Web sites. *See also* switch.

Web terminal *n.* A system containing a central processing unit (CPU), RAM, a high-speed modem or other means of connecting to the Internet, and powerful video graphics, but no hard disk, intended to be used solely as a client to the World Wide Web rather than as a general-purpose computer. *Also called:* network computer.

Web-to-host *n.* A service that allows remote users to access programs and data on legacy or mainframe systems through a Web browser. Web-to-host packages typically include a combination of services such as emulation support, legacy access, centralized management, host services, and security options, with some degree of customization possible. *See also* legacy system, mainframe computer.

WebTV *n.* A system that provides consumers with the ability to access the Web as well as send and receive e-mail on a television by means of a set-top box equipped with a modem. Users must have an ISP (Internet service provider) and subscribe to the WebTV Network. Developed by WebTV Networks, WebTV was purchased by Microsoft in 1996.

W

webweaver *n. See* Webmaster.

webzine *n.* An electronic publication distributed primarily through the World Wide Web, rather than as an ink-on-paper magazine. *See also* e-zine.

weighted code *n.* A data representation code in which each bit position has a specified inherent value, which might or might not be included in the interpretation of the data, depending on whether the bit is on or off.

weighted fair queuing *n.* A technique used to improve quality of service that prioritizes each session flow passing through a network device. With weighted fair queuing, high-bandwidth traffic is given a smaller proportion of network capacity than low-bandwidth traffic. *Acronym:* WFQ. *Compare* fair queuing.

welcome page *n. See* home page.

WELL *n.* Acronym for **W**hole **E**arth 'Lectronic **L**ink. A conferencing system based in San Francisco, California, that is accessible through the Internet and through dial-up access points in many major cities. The WELL attracts many computer professionals, along with other people who enjoy participating in one of the Internet's most successful virtual communities. Because of the number of journalists and other prominent people who participate in the WELL, it has substantial influence beyond its own relatively small number of subscribers.

well-behaved *adj.* **1.** Of, pertaining to, or characteristic of a program that performs properly even when given extreme or erroneous input values. **2.** Obeying the rules of a particular programming environment.

well-formed *n.* An XML or HTML document that follows all the rules of syntax outlined in the protocol's specification. A well-formed XML or HTML document can be read by all Web browsers without difficulty.

well-mannered *adj. See* well-behaved.

WEP *n.* Acronym for **W**ired **E**quivalent **P**rivacy. An encryption algorithm system included as part of the 802.11 standard, developed by the Institute of Electrical and Electronics Engineers as a security measure to protect wireless LANs from casual eavesdropping. WEP uses a shared secret key to encrypt packets before transmission between wireless LAN devices and monitors packets in transit to detect attempts at modification. WEP offers both 40-bit and 128-bit hardware-based encryption options.

wetware *n.* Slang for human beings—part of the environment that also includes hardware and software. *Also called:* liveware.

WFC *n. See* Windows Foundation Classes.

WFQ *n. See* weighted fair queuing.

whatis *n.* **1.** A UNIX utility for obtaining a summary of a keyword's documentation. *See also* man pages. **2.** An Archie command for locating software whose description contains desired words.

What You See Before You Get It *adj. See* WYSBYGI.

What You See Is What You Get *adj. See* WYSIWYG.

wheel printer *n. See* daisy-wheel printer.

Whetstone *n.* A benchmark test that attempts to measure the speed and efficiency with which a computer carries out floating-point operations. The result of the test is given in units called *whetstones*. The Whetstone benchmark has fallen out of favor because it produces inconsistent results compared with other benchmarks such as the Dhrystone and the sieve of Eratosthenes. *See also* benchmark[1], Dhrystone, sieve of Eratosthenes.

WHIRLWIND *n.* A digital computer using vacuum tubes, developed at the Massachusetts Institute of Technology in the 1940s and used during the 1950s. The innovations introduced with WHIRLWIND included CRT displays and real-time processing. WHIRLWIND project members included Kenneth H. Olsen, who founded Digital Equipment Corporation in 1957. *See also* CRT, real-time, vacuum tube.

Whistler *n.* The code name for Microsoft Windows XP that was used during its development cycle. New visual and operational features are designed to make Windows XP easy for the home user to operate. Features include real-time voice, video and application sharing, enhanced mobility, added support for digital photos and video, and download and playback of high-quality audio and video content. Like Microsoft Windows 2000, Windows XP was developed from Windows NT, consolidating consumer and business operating systems into a single code base.

W

whiteboard *n.* Software that allows multiple users across a network to work together on a document that is simultaneously displayed on all the users' screens, as though they are all gathered around a physical whiteboard.

Whiteboard *n.* Microsoft NetMeeting feature that opens a separate window in which multiple users can simultaneously review, create, and update graphic information. The Whiteboard is object-oriented, not pixel-oriented, allowing participants to manipulate the contents by clicking and dragging with the mouse. In addition, they can use a remote pointer or highlighting tool to point out specific contents or sections of shared pages. The NetMeeting Whiteboard is T.126 compliant and is interoperable with other T.126-compatible whiteboards.

white box *n.* A nonbranded PC assembled by a reseller, potentially including components from a number of manufacturers. The name refers to the typical color of the shipping carton, a box unadorned by brand name or logo.

white box testing *n.* A method of testing software that is based on knowledge of how the software is intended to function. Unlike black box testing, which focuses on how the software functions without reference to how it is designed, white box testing relies on detailed knowledge of the program code itself and is intended to find flaws and/or errors in its design and specification. *Also called:* glass box testing. *Compare* black box testing.

white hat *n.* A hacker who operates without malicious intent. A white hat will not break into a system with the intention of doing damage. White hats may be employed to provide security against other hackers. *See also* hacker. *Compare* black hat.

white noise *n.* Noise that contains components at all frequencies, at least within the frequency band of interest. It is called "white" by analogy to white light, which contains light at all the visible frequencies. In the audible spectrum, white noise is a hiss or a roar, such as that produced when a television set is tuned to a channel over which no station is broadcasting.

white pages *n.* *See* DIB (definition 2).

white space *n.* The areas of blank space on a page that can be used in a design for balance, contrast, and visual appeal.

whois *n.* **1.** An Internet service, provided by some domains, that enables a user to find e-mail addresses and other information for users listed in a database at that domain. **2.** A UNIX command to access the whois service. **3.** A command that displays a list of all users logged onto a Novell network.

whois client *n.* A program (such as the UNIX whois command) that enables a user to access databases of usernames, e-mail addresses, and other information. *See also* whois (definition 1).

whois server *n.* Software that provides the usernames and e-mail addresses from a database (often listing people who have accounts at an Internet domain) to users who request the information using whois clients. *See also* whois (definition 1).

Whole Earth 'Lectronic Link *n.* *See* WELL.

whole number *n.* A number without a fractional component—for example, 1 or 173; an integer.

WID *n.* Acronym for **W**ireless **I**nformation **D**evice. Smart phone or other handheld wireless device capable of multiple communications functions, including e-mail and Internet access.

Wide Area Information Server *n.* *See* WAIS.

wide area network *n.* *See* WAN.

wideband transmission *n.* *See* broadband network.

Wide SCSI *n.* A form of the SCSI-2 interface that can transfer data 16 bits at a time at up to 20 megabytes per second. The Wide SCSI connector has 68 pins. *Also called:* Wide SCSI-2. *See also* SCSI, SCSI-2. *Compare* Fast SCSI, Fast/Wide SCSI.

Wide SCSI-2 *n.* *See* Wide SCSI.

widow *n.* A last line of a paragraph, shorter than a full line, appearing at the top of a page. A widow is considered visually undesirable on the printed page. *Compare* orphan.

wildcard character *n.* A keyboard character that can be used to represent one or many characters. The asterisk (*), for example, typically represents one or more characters, and the question mark (?) typically represents a single character. Wildcard characters are often used in operating systems as a means of specifying more than one file by name.

W

WIMP *n.* Acronym for **W**indows, **I**cons, **M**ouse, and **P**ointers. A graphical user interface (GUI) such as those provided by the Apple Macintosh and Microsoft Windows operating systems. WIMP is usually said to stand for Windows, Icons, Mouse, and Pointers, but the acronym is sometimes spelled out as either Windows, Icons, Menus, and Pointers or Windows, Icons, Mouse, and Pull-down menus. The WIMP interface was invented at the Xerox Palo Alto Research Center (PARC), where it was first used in the Alto computer in the early 1970s. *See also* graphical user interface.

Win32 *n.* The application programming interface in Windows 95 and Windows NT that enables applications to use the 32-bit instructions available on 80386 and higher processors. Although Windows 95 and Windows NT support 16-bit 80x86 instructions as well, Win32 offers greatly improved performance. *See also* 16-bit machine, 32-bit machine, 80386DX, 8086, application programming interface, central processing unit, Win32s.

Win32 Driver Model *n. See* Windows Driver Model.

Win32s *n.* A subset of the Win32 application programming interface that works under Windows 3.*x*. By including the Win32s software, which is distributed as freeware, an application can gain in performance from using the 32-bit instructions available on 80386 and higher processors while running on Windows 3.x. *See also* 32-bit machine, 80386DX, central processing unit, Win32.

Winchester disk *n.* An early IBM name for a hard disk. The term is derived from IBM's internal code name for its first hard disk, which stored 30 megabytes (MB) and had a 30-millisecond access time, reminding its inventors of a Winchester .30-caliber rifle known as a ".30-.30."

window *n.* In applications and graphical interfaces, a portion of the screen that can contain its own document or message. In window-based programs, the screen can be divided into several windows, each of which has its own boundaries and can contain a different document (or another view into the same document).

window definition function *n.* A resource associated with a window in a Macintosh application. The Macintosh Window Manager calls this function to perform such actions as drawing and resizing the window. *Also called:* WDEF.

windowing *n.* An approach to remediation (correction of problems) or simply user convenience in which two-digit years are interpreted in relation to a window of time. Logical procedures based on windowing thus enable software to correctly produce accurate four-digit years. In windowing, the century is determined by presuming that the year falls within a 100-year span. So if the window ranges from 1995 to 2094, any year that is 95 or greater is presumed to be in the twentieth century (19xx), while any number less than 95 is presumed to be in the twenty-first century (20xx). *Fixed windowing* presupposes that a window always starts with the same date, or pivot year. *Moving windowing* permits a user or another system to specify the pivot year when the program is installed or started. *Sliding windowing* is calculated every time a program runs and can be based on a predetermined span of time, called a slider, that can be added to the current date to produce the pivot year for the window. Potential differences in windows require analysis whenever importing or exporting data between systems. *Also called:* logic fix. *See also* pivot year.

windowing environment *n.* An operating system or shell that presents the user with specially delineated areas of the screen called *windows*. Windowing environments typically allow windows to be resized and moved around on the display. The Macintosh Finder, Windows, and the OS/2 Presentation Manager are all examples of windowing environments. *See also* graphical user interface, window.

window random access memory *n. See* WRAM.

Windows *n.* An operating system introduced by Microsoft Corporation in 1983. Windows is a multitasking graphical user interface environment that runs on MS-DOS–based computers (Windows 3.x. and Windows for Workgroups), and as a self-contained operating system for desktop computers (Windows 9x and Windows Me), workstations (Windows NT Workstation, Windows 2000 Professional), and network servers (Windows NT Server, Windows NT Enterprise Edition, Windows 2000 Server, and Windows 2000 Advanced Server). The most recent

W

versions of Windows are Windows XP Home (home and entertainment use) and Professional (advanced computing, businesses, and large organizations). The next generation of Windows server products will be the Windows .NET Server family. Windows provides a standard graphical interface based on drop-down menus, windowed regions on the screen, and a pointing device such as a mouse.

Windows 95 *n.* An operating system with a graphical user interface for 80386 and higher processors, released by Microsoft Corporation in 1995. Intended to replace Windows 3.11, Windows for Workgroups 3.11, and MS-DOS, Windows 95 is a complete operating system, rather than a shell that requires MS-DOS, as does Windows 3.*x*. For backward compatibility, Windows 95 can run MS-DOS software. Under Windows 95, filenames can be up to 255 characters long and may include dots and spaces. Windows 95 supports the Plug and Play method for installing and configuring hardware and can access Windows, NetWare, and UNIX networks. The minimum configuration for Windows 95 is an 80386 processor with 4 MB of RAM, but an i486 or higher processor with at least 8 MB of RAM is recommended. Internet functionality is provided in large part in Windows 95 by Microsoft Internet Explorer. *See also* MS-DOS, NetWare, Plug and Play, Windows.

Windows 98 *n.* An operating system with a graphical user interface for i486 and higher processors, released by Microsoft Corporation in 1998. Building upon Windows 95, Windows 98 features an improved interface and more robust functionality. With the Active Desktop, Windows 98 integrates Internet connectivity even more closely, allowing users to access remote files in the same way they would access files on their hard drives. Hardware support includes USB, IEEE 1394, AGP ports, television tuner cards, DVD drives, multiple modems, and multiple monitors. Windows 98, Second Edition, released in 1999, builds on the features in the initial release and offers home networking and improved maintenance features. *See also* Windows, Windows 95.

Windows 9x *n.* The architecture upon which Windows 95 and Windows 98 were built. *See also* Windows 95, Windows 98.

Windows 2000 *n.* A Microsoft operating system, the successor to Windows NT, designed for business rather than consumer use. Like its predecessor, Windows 2000 is a multithreaded, multitasking 32-bit operating system.

Implemented in desktop and several server versions, Windows 2000 focuses overall on improved ease of use, networking, management, reliability, scalability, and security. See the table.

Table W.1   ATA Specifications.

Version	Designed For	Features
Windows 2000 Professional	Business desktop	Improvements in: Ease of use; security, performance, and reliability; support for mobile computing
Windows 2000 Server	Small to medium-sized deployments— workgroups, branch offices, departmental application, file, print servers	Two-way symmetric multiprocessing (SMP); ActiveDirectory; management tools; Kerberos and PKI security; COM+; Windows Terminal Support; improved Internet services
Windows 2000 Advanced Server	Mid-range departmental and application deployments	Windows 2000 Server features, plus four-way SMP; load balancing; clustering; high-performance sorting; 64-GB physical memory
Windows 2000 Datacenter Server	Large operations— data warehouses, online transaction-processing (OLTP), science and engineering simulations, enterprise solutions	Windows 2000 Advanced Server features, plus 16-way SMP

Windows 2000 Advanced Server *n.* Microsoft's network server for larger organizations. Designed to replace Windows NT 4 Enterprise Edition, it supports up to four-way SMP, large physical memories, and database-intensive work. It integrates clustering and load balancing support. *See also* SMP, Windows.

Windows 2000 Datacenter Server *n.* Microsoft's network server for larger organizations. Considered the most

W

powerful and functional server operating system ever offered by Microsoft, it supports up to 16-way SMP and up to 64 GB of physical memory (depending on system architecture). Like Windows 2000 Advanced Server, it provides both clustering and load balancing services as standard features. It is optimized for large data ware-houses, econometric analysis, large-scale simulations in science and engineering, OLTP, and server consolidation projects. *See also* OLTP, SMP, Windows.

Windows 2000 Professional *n.* Microsoft's mainstream desktop operating system for businesses of all sizes. Designed to replace Windows NT Workstation 4, which many people are using today as the standard business desktop, Windows 2000 Professional builds upon the interface and kernel in NT 4. It also includes improved security, state-of-the-art features for mobile users, indus-trial-strength reliability, and better performance.

Windows 2000 Server *n.* Microsoft's network server for small to medium businesses. Designed to replace Windows NT 4 Server, Windows 2000 Server offers improved functionality and supports new systems with up to two-way symmetric multiprocessing (SMP).

Windows application *n.* A software application designed for use with the Microsoft Windows environment.

Windows-based accelerator *n.* A type of super VGA (SVGA) video adapter designed specifically to run Win-dows and Windows-based applications more quickly. A Windows-based accelerator achieves performance improvements over a standard SVGA video adapter with the help of special routines built into the adapter's read-only memory. These routines relieve the Windows operat-ing system of some of the video-related duties it must per-form on a nonaccelerated system. *Also called:* Windows-based accelerator card. *See also* SVGA.

Windows CE *n.* A small operating system from Microsoft designed for use with handheld and palm-size PCs and in embedded systems, such as the AutoPC. Windows CE, which has a user interface that is similar to Windows 9x and Windows NT, includes scaled-down versions of sev-eral Microsoft applications, including Excel, Word, Inter-net Explorer, Schedule+, and an e-mail client. *See also* handheld PC.

Windows CE Services *n.* A set of technologies that makes Windows CE–based devices Web enabled. It pro-vides the functionality to deliver Web content information to Windows CE–based devices from a wireless network or by desktop synchronization.

Windows Distributed interNet Applications Architecture *n. See* Windows DNA.

Windows DNA *n.* Short for Microsoft **Windows D**istrib-uted inter**N**et **A**pplications Architecture. A framework introduced in 1997 as a means of integrating client/server and Web technologies in the creation of scalable, multitier applications delivered over an enterprise network. Win-dows DNA is based on a number of technologies, among them COM (Component Object Model), ActiveX, and dynamic HTML.

Windows Driver Library *n.* A collection of hardware device drivers for a Microsoft Windows operating system that were not included in the original Windows package. *Acronym:* WDL. *See also* driver.

Windows Driver Model *n.* A 32-bit layered architecture for device and bus drivers that allows for drivers that can be used by both Windows NT and Windows 98. It pro-vides common input/output services understood by both operating systems and supports Plug and Play, USB (Uni-versal Serial Bus), IEEE 1394 bus, and various devices, including input, communication, imaging, and DVD. *Acronym:* WDM. *Also called:* Win32 Driver Model.

Windows Explorer *n.* A utility in Windows that enables the user to locate and open files and folders. Windows Explorer resembles the File Manager of Windows 3.1. The user can select folders from a list displayed on the left side of the screen and access files in a selected folder from a list displayed on the right side of the screen.

Windows Forms *n.* A rich Windows client library for building Windows client applications.

Windows Foundation Classes *n.* A Java class library for developing Java applications to run in the Windows environment. Designed by Microsoft to make it easy to write code for the Windows platform using the powerful Java programming language, the Windows Foundation Classes represent an object-oriented framework that encapsulates and unifies the Microsoft Win32 API and Dynamic HTML programming models. This framework enables developers to link Java code directly to Windows APIs. *Acronym:* WFC. *See also* Java, Java Foundation Classes.

Windows Image Acquisition *n.* A device-driver inter-face that supports still digital cameras and low-end and high-end scanners and allows retrieving of still images from IEEE 1394-based DV camcorders and USB-based Web cams. *Acronym:* WIA.

Windows IP Configuration *n. See* Winipcfg.

Windows Management Instrumentation *n.* A management infrastructure in Windows that supports monitoring and controlling system resources through a common set of interfaces and provides a logically organized, consistent model of Windows operation, configuration, and status. *Acronym:* WMI. *See also* resource.

Windows Me *n.* Released in 2000, the Windows Millennium Edition (Windows Me) operating system designed for home users as an upgrade from Windows 95 or Windows 98. Windows Me offers an improved home user experience including making it easier for users to share and manipulate digital photos, music, and videos, enhanced home networking capabilities, a rich Internet experience with support for broadband connections, different Internet communication tools, and online gaming.

Windows Media Audio *n.* A digital audio coding scheme developed by Microsoft that is used in distributing recorded music, usually over the Internet. Windows Media Audio shrinks the size of the audio file by a factor of 20 to 24 without seriously degrading the quality (CD-recording level) of the sound. Windows Media Audio files are given the file extension .wma and can be created with Windows Media Tools and played with the Windows Media Player. *Acronym:* WMA. *See also* Windows Media Technologies. *Compare* MP3, RealAudio, Secure Digital Music Initiative.

Windows Media Encoder *n.* A Windows Media technology that compresses live or prerecorded audio and video into a Windows Media stream, which can either be distributed immediately or saved as a Windows Media file for later distribution. The technology allows content developers to convert both live and prerecorded audio, video, and computer screen images to Windows Media Format for live and on-demand delivery. Windows Media Encoder also can save a stream as a Windows Media file and convert a file into Windows Media Format. Windows Media Encoder can distribute a stream via HTTP protocol. *Also called:* (if context is clear) Encoder, the encoder, the encoder engine.

Windows Media Player *n.* A client/control that receives a stream from a Windows Media server or local content for playback. It can run as a stand-alone client executable program. Windows Media Player can also be embedded in a Web page, a C++ program, or a Microsoft Visual Basic program that uses the client ActiveX control.

Windows Media server *n.* A server on which Windows Media Services has been installed.

Windows Media Services *n.* A digital media platform that runs on a server, such as Windows 2000, to support streaming media, such as video and audio.

Windows Media Technologies *n.* Microsoft technologies for the creation, delivery, and playing of streaming audio and video over a network, including both intranets and the Internet. Windows Media Technologies, downloadable from the Microsoft Web site, support both live and on-demand (delivered from storage) content and are based on files delivered in Advanced Streaming Format (ASF). Three major components—Windows Media Tools, Windows Media Services, and Windows Media Player—comprise Windows Media Technologies. See the table. *See also* Advanced Streaming Format. *Compare* RealSystem G2.

Table W.2   ATA Specifications.

Component	Purpose	Features
Windows Media Tools	Content creation	ASF authoring and editing tools, including tools for converting files from other formats (WAV, AVI, MPEG, and MP3) to ASF.
Windows Media Services	Content delivery	Tools for real-time and on-demand content delivery, administration tools, and Windows Media Rights Manager for piracy control.
Windows Media Player for PC platforms, Windows Media Player for Macintosh, Windows Media Player for UNIX	Content playback	ASF player for audio, audio plus still images, and full-motion video. Also supports other multimedia data, including RealAudio.

Windows Media Tools *n. See* Windows Media Technologies.

Windows Messenger *n. See* .NET Messenger Service.

Windows Metafile Format *n.* A graphics file format used by Windows to store vector graphics in order to exchange graphics information between applications and to store information between sessions. *Acronym:* WMF. *See also* vector graphics.

Windows Movie Maker *n.* Software from Microsoft for capturing, editing, and arranging audio and video source material to create movies. *Acronym:* WMM.

Windows .NET Server *n.* The next generation of Windows servers. Built on Windows 2000, the Windows .NET Server family includes the functionality, dependability, scalability, and security options to serve as the computing foundation for businesses of all sizes. The flexible computing architecture, built on industry standards, allows businesses to create robust and innovative applications, improve collaboration across the organization, and connect securely with customers.

Windows NT *n.* An operating system released by Microsoft Corporation in 1993. The Windows NT operating system, sometimes referred to as simply NT, is the high-end member of a family of operating systems from Microsoft. It is a completely self-contained operating system with a built-in graphical user interface. Windows NT is a 32-bit, preemptive multitasking operating system that features networking, symmetric multiprocessing, multithreading, and security. It is a portable operating system that can run on a variety of hardware platforms including those based on the Intel 80386, i486, and Pentium microprocessors and MIPS microprocessors; it can also run on multiprocessor computers. Windows NT supports up to 4 gigabytes of virtual memory and can run MS-DOS, POSIX, and OS/2 (character-mode) applications. *See also* MS-DOS, operating system, OS/2, POSIX, Windows.

Windows NT Advanced Server *n.* A superset of Windows NT that provides centralized, domain-based network management and security. Windows NT Advanced Server also offers advanced hard disk fault-tolerance features, such as mirroring and additional connectivity. *See also* Windows NT.

Windows NT Embedded *n.* A version of the Microsoft Windows NT operating system designed for devices and other products that have embedded systems. Windows NT Embedded, released in 1999, targets devices in the midrange to high end of the embedded device industry, including high-speed copiers, patient monitors, private branch exchanges (PBXs), and point-of-sale terminals. Windows NT Embedded features include headless operation (with no keyboard, mouse, or display devices needed), diskless operation, and remote management infrastructure. *See also* embedded system, Windows NT.

Windows Open Services Architecture *n. See* WOSA.

Windows Open System Architecture *n. See* WOSA.

Windows Script Host *n.* The language-independent scripting host for Microsoft Windows platforms. Windows Script Host is a tool that allows users to run VBScript, JScript, or any other scripting language to automate common tasks and to create macros and logon scripts.

Windows Sockets *n. See* Winsock.

Windows terminal *n.* A thin-client solution from Microsoft, designed to enable terminals and minimally configured computers to display Windows applications even if they are not, in themselves, capable of running Windows software. Windows terminals work in conjunction with Windows NT Server, Terminal Server edition. *See also* thin client.

Windows XP *n.* A member of the Microsoft Windows family of operating systems. Windows XP was released in 2001 in two versions: Windows XP Home Edition for home use and Windows XP Professional for advanced home computing, businesses, and larger organizations. Windows XP features a new visual design that simplifies navigation and search capabilities, improved file management, additional media and Web publishing capabilities, an improved system for device discovery and installation, and advanced features for mobile computing.

WinG *n.* Short for **Win**dows **G**ames. An application programming interface for games in the Windows 9x environment. Under WinG, games can access the video frame buffer directly for increased speed. *See also* application programming interface, buffer[1], frame buffer.

WinHEC *n.* Short for Microsoft **Win**dows **H**ardware **E**ngineering **C**onference. Annual meeting of the computer hardware industry featuring forums, seminars, exhibits, and educational sessions for developers, technical managers, engineers, and product planners who use the Microsoft Windows family of operating systems.

win.ini *n.* In Windows 3.x and MS-DOS, the initialization file used to pass the program configuration information necessary to run the Windows operating environment. The win.ini file has been supplanted by the registry database in Windows 95 and later and Windows NT and later. *See also* configuration file, ini file, registry.

Winipcfg *n.* Short for **Win**dows **IP** **C**onfiguration. A Windows 9x utility that enables users to access information about their TCP/IP (Transmission Control Protocol/Internet Protocol) and network adapter card settings. Running the Winipcfg program (winipcfg.exe) opens the IP Configuration window, which reveals the physical address, IP address, subnet mask, and default gateway settings of the primary TCP/IP adapter (or settings of multiple adapters if more than one is installed). This information is also helpful for troubleshooting. *See also* TCP/IP.

WINS *n.* Acronym for **W**indows **I**nternet **N**aming **S**ervice. A Windows NT Server method for associating a computer's host name with its address. *Also called:* INS, Internet Naming Service. *Compare* DNS (definition 1).

Winsock *n.* Short for **Win**dows **Sock**ets. An application programming interface standard for software that provides a TCP/IP interface under Windows. The Winsock standard developed out of a Birds of a Feather (BOF) discussion that arose among software vendors at a UNIX conference in 1991; it has gained the general support of software developers, including Microsoft. *See also* application programming interface, BOF, socket (definition 1), sockets API, TCP/IP.

Wintel *adj.* Of, pertaining to, or characteristic of a computer that uses the Microsoft Windows operating system and an Intel central processing unit (CPU). *See also* Windows.

wired *adj.* **1.** Of, pertaining to, or characteristic of an electronic circuit or hardware grouping in which the configuration is determined by the physical interconnection of the components (as opposed to being programmable in software or alterable by a switch). *See also* hardwired (definition 1). **2.** Knowledgeable about Internet resources, systems, and culture. **3.** Having access to the Internet.

Wired Equivalent Privacy *n. See* WEP.

wired home *n. See* smart home.

wire-frame model *n.* In computer graphics applications such as CAD programs, a representation of a three-dimensional object using separate lines that resemble strands of wire joined to create a model. *Compare* solid model, surface modeling.

wireless *adj.* Of, pertaining to, or characteristic of communications that take place without the use of interconnecting wires or cables, such as by radio, microwave, or infrared light.

Wireless Application Protocol *n.* A specification for a global standard for enabling digital cellular phones and other wireless devices to access Internet and other information services. The Wireless Application Protocol, or WAP, is supported by an organization known as WAP Forum, which includes such members as Motorola, Nokia, L. M. Ericsson, and Unwired Planet. The goal of the forum is to create an open standard that works with different wireless technologies. *Acronym:* WAP.

wireless communication *n.* Communication between a computer and another computer or device without wires. The form of wireless communication provided as part of the Windows operating system uses infrared light to transmit files. Radio frequencies, as used by cellular and cordless telephones, are another form of wireless communication. *See also* infrared, infrared device, infrared port.

Wireless Information Device *n. See* WID.

wireless Internet *n.* Version of the Internet designed for use on wireless phones and handheld devices with small display screens, limited memory, and slower data transmission speeds than a personal computer. Most wireless Internet sites offer content as basic text with limited graphics.

wireless LAN *n.* A LAN (local area network) that sends and receives data via radio, infrared optical signaling, or some other technology that does not require a physical connection between individual nodes and the hub. Wireless LANs are often used in office or factory settings where a user must carry a portable computer from place to place. *Also called:* WLAN.

Wireless Markup Language *n. See* WML.

Wireless Multimedia Forum *n. See* WMF (definition 2).

wireless phone *n.* Telephone that operates by means of radio waves without a wire connection. A base station (cell tower) relays the phone's signal to a wireless carrier's network, where it is transmitted to another wireless phone or to a wired telephone network.

Wireless Services server component *n.* A component that allows a content provider or carrier to configure and schedule any number of information acquisition/encoding/ transmission components to create a data stream to be transmitted by a carrier to a device. The server component builds

W

on an open architecture to allow new server components to be installed in any part of the stream at any time.

Wireless Transaction Protocol *n.* A lightweight request/reply transaction protocol for devices with limited resources over networks with low to medium bandwidth. It is not called the Wireless Transport Protocol or the Wireless Transfer Protocol. *Acronym:* WTP.

Wireless Transport Layer Security *n. See* WTLS.

wire-pin printer *n. See* dot-matrix printer.

wire-wrapped circuits *n.* Circuits constructed on perforated boards using wire instead of the metal traces found on printed circuit boards. The stripped ends of insulated wires are wrapped around the long pins of special wire-wrapped integrated circuit sockets. Wire-wrapped circuits are generally handmade, one-of-a-kind devices used for prototyping and research in electrical engineering. *Compare* printed circuit board.

wiring closet *n.* A room or location in a building where telecommunications and/or networking equipment such as hubs, switches, and routers are installed. *Also called:* data closet, telecom closet, telecommunications closet.

wizard *n.* **1.** Someone who is adept at making computers perform their "magic." A wizard is an outstanding and creative programmer or a power user. *Compare* guru, UNIX wizard. **2.** A participant in a multiuser dungeon (MUD) who has permission to control the domain, even to delete other players' characters. *See also* MUD. **3.** An interactive help utility within an application that guides the user through each step of a particular task, such as starting up a word processing document in the correct format for a business letter.

wizzywig *n. See* WYSIWYG.

WLAN *n. See* wireless LAN.

WMA *n.* Acronym for **W**indows **M**edia **A**udio. *See* Windows Media Audio.

.wmf *n.* A file extension that identifies a vector image encoded as a Microsoft Windows Metafile.

WMF *n.* **1.** *See* Windows Metafile Format. **2.** Acronym for **W**ireless **M**ultimedia **F**orum. A consortium of technology companies formed to promote open standards for wireless streaming products. WMF members include Cisco Systems, Intel, and the Walt Disney Internet Group. *See also* ISMA.

WMI *n. See* Windows Management Instrumentation.

WML *n.* Acronym for **W**ireless **M**arkup **L**anguage. A markup language developed for Web sites that are accessed with microbrowsers on Wireless Application Protocol (WAP)–enabled devices. A Web site written with WML would be viewable on handheld devices with small screens, such as cell phones. *See also* markup language, microbrowser, Wireless Application Protocol.

WMLScript *n.* A scripting language derived from the JavaScript language for use in the development of Wireless Markup Language (WML).

WMM *n. See* Windows Movie Maker.

word *n.* The native unit of storage on a particular machine. A word is the largest amount of data that can be handled by the microprocessor in one operation and also, as a rule, is the width of the main data bus. Word sizes of 16 bits and 32 bits are the most common. *Compare* byte, octet.

Word *n.* Microsoft's word processing software, available for the Windows and Macintosh platforms. In addition to extensive editing, formatting, and customization features, Word provides such tools as automatic text completion and correction. The most recent version, Word 2002 (part of Office XP) adds Web functionality—for example, the ability to save documents in HTML format. The first version, Microsoft Word for MS-DOS 1.00, was introduced in 1983.

word-addressable processor *n.* A processor that cannot access an individual byte of memory but can access a larger unit. In order to perform operations on an individual byte, the processor must read and write memory in the larger unit. *See also* central processing unit.

WordPerfect Office *n.* A suite of business application programs from Corel Corporation. The basic (Standard Edition) WordPerfect Office suite includes the WordPerfect word processor, Quattro Pro spreadsheet, Corel Presentations presentation software, CorelCENTRAL personal information manager, Microsoft Visual Basic for Applications scripting tools, and Trellix Web publisher. A home and small-business package, the Voice-Powered Edition, adds speech recognition and publishing products; a business and corporate package, the Professional Edition, adds database and Internet tools to all of the preceding.

word processing *n.* The act of entering and editing text with a word processor. *Acronym:* WP.

word processor *n.* An application program for creating and manipulating text-based documents. A word processor is the electronic equivalent of paper, pen, typewriter, eraser, and, most likely, dictionary and thesaurus. Depending on

W

the program and the equipment in use, word processors can display documents either in text mode (using highlighting, underlining, or color to represent italics, boldfacing, and other such formatting) or in graphics mode (in which formatting and, sometimes, a variety of fonts appear on the screen as they will on the printed page). All word processors offer at least limited facilities for document formatting, such as font changes, page layout, paragraph indentation, and the like. Some word processors can also check spelling, find synonyms, incorporate graphics created with another program, align mathematical formulas, create and print form letters, perform calculations, display documents in multiple on-screen windows, and enable users to record macros that simplify difficult or repetitive operations. *Compare* editor, line editor.

wordwrap or **word wrap** *n.* The ability of a word processing program or a text-editing program to break lines of text automatically to stay within the page margins or window boundaries of a document without the user having to do so with carriage returns, as is typically necessary when using a typewriter. *See also* hard return, soft return.

workaround *n.* A tactic for accomplishing a task despite a bug or other inadequacy in software or hardware without actually fixing the underlying problem. *See also* kludge.

workbook *n.* In a spreadsheet program, a file containing a number of related worksheets. *See also* worksheet.

workflow application *n.* A set of programs that aids in the tracking and management of all the activities in a project from start to finish.

workgroup *n.* A group of users working on a common project and sharing computer files, typically over a LAN (local area network). *See also* groupware.

workgroup computing *n.* A method of working electronically in which various individuals on the same project share resources and access to files using a network arrangement, such as a local area network, enabling them to coordinate their separate tasks. This is accomplished through using software designed for workgroup computing. *See also* groupware.

Workplace Shell *n.* The graphical user interface of OS/2. Like the Mac OS and Windows 95, the Workplace Shell is document-centric. Document files are displayed as icons; clicking an icon starts the corresponding application, and the user can print a document by dragging the document's icon to a printer icon. The Workplace Shell uses the graphical functions of Presentation Manager. *Acronym:* WPS.

worksheet *n.* In a spreadsheet program, a page organized into rows and columns appearing on screen and used for constructing a single table.

workstation *n.* **1.** A combination of input, output, and computing hardware that can be used for work by an individual. **2.** A powerful stand-alone computer of the sort used in computer-aided design and other applications requiring a high-end, usually expensive, machine with considerable calculating or graphics capability. **3.** A microcomputer or terminal connected to a network.

World Wide Web *n.* The total set of interlinked hypertext documents residing on HTTP servers all around the world. Documents on the World Wide Web, called pages or Web pages, are written in HTML (Hypertext Markup Language), identified by URLs (Uniform Resource Locators) that specify the particular machine and pathname by which a file can be accessed, and transmitted from server to end user under HTTP (Hypertext Transfer Protocol). Codes, called tags, embedded in an HTML document associate particular words and images in the document with URLs so that a user can access another file, which may be halfway around the world, at the press of a key or the click of a mouse. These files may contain text (in a variety of fonts and styles), graphics images, movie files, and sounds as well as Java applets, ActiveX controls, or other small embedded software programs that execute when the user activates them by clicking a link. A user visiting a Web page also may be able to download files from an FTP site and send messages to other users via e-mail by using links on the Web page. The World Wide Web was developed by Timothy Berners-Lee in 1989 for the European Laboratory for Particle Physics, or Conseil Européen pour le Recherche Nucléaire, in French (CERN). *Acronym:* WWW. *Also called:* w^3, W3, Web. *See also* ActiveX controls, HTML, HTTP, HTTP server (definition 2), Java applet, URL.

World Wide Web Consortium *n. See* W3C.

worm *n.* A program that propagates itself across computers, usually by creating copies of itself in each computer's memory. A worm might duplicate itself in one computer so often that it causes the computer to crash. Sometimes written in separate segments, a worm is introduced surreptitiously into a host system either as a prank or with the intent of damaging or destroying information. *See also* bacterium, Internet Worm, Trojan horse, virus.

WORM *n.* Acronym for write once, read many. A type of optical disc that can be read and reread but cannot be

W

altered after it has been recorded. WORMs are high-capacity storage devices. Because they cannot be erased and rerecorded, they are suited to storing archives and other large bodies of unchanging information. *See also* compact disc.

WOSA *n.* Acronym for **W**indows **O**pen **S**ervices Architecture, also known as **W**indows **O**pen **S**ystem **A**rchitecture. A set of application programming interfaces from Microsoft that is intended to enable Windows-based applications from different vendors to communicate with each other, such as over a network. The interfaces within the WOSA standard include Open Database Connectivity (ODBC), the Messaging Application Programming Interface (MAPI), the Telephony Application Programming Interface (TAPI), Windows Sockets (Winsock), and Microsoft Remote Procedure Calls (RPC). *See also* MAPI, ODBC, remote procedure call, TAPI, Winsock.

.wp *n.* A file extension used to identify files formatted for the WordPerfect word processor.

WP *n. See* word processing.

WPS *n. See* Workplace Shell.

WRAM *n.* Acronym for **w**indow **r**andom **a**ccess **m**emory. A type of RAM used in video adapters. Like video RAM (VRAM), WRAM allows the screen to be repainted while a graphical image is being written, but WRAM is faster. *Compare* video RAM.

wrap around *vb.* To continue movement, as with the cursor or a search operation, to the beginning or to a new starting point rather than stopping when the end of a series is reached. For example, the screen cursor might wrap around to the first column of the next line rather than stopping when it reaches the last column of the current line. Likewise, a program starting a search or replace operation in the middle of a document might be instructed to wrap around to the beginning rather than stop when it reaches the end of the document.

wrapper *n.* In the Java programming language, an object that encapsulates and delegates to another object with the aim of altering its behavior or interface. *See also* Java, object.

.wri *n.* The file format that identifies document files in the Microsoft Write format.

wrist support *n.* A device placed in front of a computer keyboard to support the wrists in an ergonomically neutral position, thereby safeguarding against repetitive strain inju-

ries, such as carpal tunnel syndrome. *Also called:* wrist rest. *See also* carpal tunnel syndrome, repetitive strain injury.

write[1] *n.* A transfer of information to a storage device, such as a disk, or to an output device, such as a monitor or a printer. For example, a disk write means that information is transferred from memory to storage on disk. *See also* output[1]. *Compare* read[1].

write[2] *vb.* To transfer information either to a storage device, such as a disk, or to an output device, such as a monitor or a printer. Writing is the means by which a computer provides the results of processing. A computer can also be said to write to the screen when it displays information on the monitor. *See also* output[1]. *Compare* read[1].

write access *n.* A privilege on a computer system that allows a user to save, change, or delete stored data. Write access is usually set by the system administrator for a networked or server system and by the owner of the computer for a stand-alone machine. *See also* access privileges.

write-back cache *n.* A type of cache with the following feature: when changes are made to cached data, they are not simultaneously made to the original data as well. Instead, the changed data is marked, and the original data is updated when the cached data is deallocated. A write-back cache can perform more quickly than a write-through cache. But in some contexts, differences between cached and original data could lead to problems, and write-through caches must be used. *See also* cache. *Compare* write-through cache.

write-behind cache *n.* A form of temporary storage in which data is held, or cached, for a short time in memory before being written on disk for permanent storage. Caching improves system performance in general by reducing the number of times the computer must go through the relatively slow process of reading from and writing to disk. *See also* CPU cache, disk cache.

write cache *n. See* write-behind cache.

write error *n.* An error encountered while a computer is in the process of transferring information from memory to storage or to another output device. *Compare* read error.

write mode *n.* In computer operation, the state in which a program can write (record) information in a file. In write mode, the program is permitted to make changes to existing information. *Compare* read-only.

write protect *vb.* To prevent the writing (recording) of information, usually on a disk. Either a floppy disk or an individual file on a floppy disk or a hard disk can be write protected (though not necessarily infallibly). *See also* write-protect notch.

write-protect notch *n.* A small opening in the jacket of a floppy disk that can be used to make the disk unwritable. On a 5.25-inch floppy disk, the write-protect notch is a rectangular hole on the edge of the disk jacket. When this notch is covered, a computer can read from the disk but cannot record new information on it. On 3.5-inch micro-floppy disks that are enclosed in plastic shells, the write-protect notch is an opening in a corner. When the sliding tab in this opening is moved to uncover a small hole, the disk is protected and cannot be written to. *Also called:* write-protect tab. *See also* write[2].

write-protect tab *n. See* write-protect notch.

write-through cache *n.* A type of cache in which changes made to cached data are simultaneously made in the original copy, rather than being marked for later updating. A write-through cache, though not as fast as a write-back cache, is needed in situations where problems would occur if both the original and cached data did not match. *Compare* write-back cache.

.wrl *n.* File extension required for saving all Virtual Reality Modeling Language (VRML) documents; for example, cube.wrl. *See also* VRML.

WSDL *n.* Acronym for **W**eb **S**ervices **D**escription Language. An XML format developed to allow for better interoperability among Web services and development tools. WSDL describes network services as collections of communication endpoints capable of exchanging messages and is extensible to allow description of endpoints and their messages regardless of what message formats or network protocols are used to communicate.

WSS *n. See* Web Storage System.

WTLS *n.* Acronym for **W**ireless **T**ransport **L**ayer **S**ecurity. A security protocol that provides encryption and authentication services for the Wireless Application Protocol (WAP). The WTLS layer uses data integrity, authentication, and encryption mechanisms to provide end-to-end security and privacy for wireless transactions. WTLS is based on Transport Layer Security (TLS), a Secure Socket Layer equivalent used with Internet applications. *See also* Wireless Application Protocol.

WWW *n. See* World Wide Web.

WYSBYGI *adj.* Acronym for **W**hat **Y**ou **S**ee **B**efore **Y**ou **G**et **I**t. Providing a preview of the effects of the changes the user has selected before the changes are finally applied. For example, a dialog box in a word processing program might display a sample of the font a user has chosen before the font is actually changed in the document. The user can cancel any changes after previewing them, and the document will be unaffected. *See also* WYSIWYG.

WYSIWYG *adj.* Acronym for **W**hat **Y**ou **S**ee **I**s **W**hat **Y**ou **G**et, pronounced "wizzywig." Allowing a user to view a document as it will appear in the final product, and to directly edit the text, graphics, or other elements within that view. A WYSIWYG language is often easier to use than a markup language, which provides no immediate visual feedback regarding the changes being made. *Compare* markup language.

W

X10 *n.* A popular communications protocol for powerline carrier (PLC) systems that uses existing electrical wiring in a home or building for home networking. X10 uses RF signals to communicate between transmitters and receivers. *See also* home automation, home network, powerline carrier system.

X.200 *n. See* X series.

X.25 *n.* A recommendation published by the ITU-T (formerly CCITT) international communications standards organization that defines the connection between a terminal and a packet-switching network. X.25 incorporates three definitions: the electrical connection between the terminal and the network, the transmission or link-access protocol, and the implementation of virtual circuits between network users. Taken together, these definitions specify a synchronous, full-duplex terminal-to-network connection. Packet format, error control, and other features are equivalent to portions of the HDLC (High-level Data Link Control) protocol defined by the International Organization for Standardization (ISO). *See also* CCITT X series, HDLC, packet switching, virtual circuit.

X3D *n.* Acronym for **3D XML.** An XML-based 3-D graphics specification incorporating the behavior capabilities of the Virtual Reality Modeling Language (VRML). X3D is compatible with existing VRML content and tools and supports full integration with other XML-based technologies. The X3D specification was developed and administered by the Web 3D Consortium.

X.400 *n. See* X series.

X.445 *n. See* X series.

X.500 *n. See* X series.

X.509 *n. See* X series.

X.75 *n. See* X series.

x86 *n.* Any computer based on an 8086, 80286, 80386, 80486, or Pentium microprocessor.

x-axis *n.* The horizontal reference line on a grid, chart, or graph that has horizontal and vertical dimensions. *See also* Cartesian coordinates.

Xbase *n.* A generic name for a family of database languages based on dBASE, a copyrighted product of the Ashton-Tate Corporation. Xbase languages have since developed characteristics of their own and are now only partly compatible with the dBASE family. Xbase primarily refers to three different file types (.dbf, .dbt, and .ndx). *Also called:* xBase, xbase, XBase.

Xbox *n.* A video game console developed by Microsoft Corporation and released in 2001. Powered by an Intel 733-MHz processor, the Xbox delivers increased graphics capability over previously released game consoles and provides extensive storage capacity for gaming information. Peripherals plug into four game controller ports. An Ethernet port enables online gaming via a broadband connection. *See also* computer game, console game, GameCube, PlayStation. *Compare* Dreamcast.

X button *n. See* close button.

XCMD *n.* Short for **external command.** An external code resource used in HyperCard, a hypermedia program developed for the Macintosh. See also HyperCard, XFCN.

X Consortium *n.* The body, composed of several hardware firms, that governed the standards for the X Window System. The Open Group's X Project Team now has responsibility for the X Window System. *See also* X Window System.

xDSL *n.* An umbrella term for all of the digital subscriber line (DSL) technologies, which use a variety of modulation schemes to pack data onto copper wires. The *x* is a placeholder for the first or first two letters of a member technology, which might be ADSL, HDSL, IDSL, RADSL, or SDSL. *See also* DSL.

XENIX *n.* A version of UNIX that was originally adapted by Microsoft for Intel-based personal computers. Although it has been sold by many vendors, including Microsoft, Intel, and the Santa Cruz Operation (SCO), it has become principally identified with SCO. *See also* UNIX.

xerography *n. See* electrophotography.

Xerox Network System *n. See* XNS.

Xerox PARC *n.* Short for **Xerox P**alo **A**lto **R**esearch Center. Xerox's research and development facility in Palo Alto, California. Xerox PARC is the birthplace of such innovations as the local area network (LAN), the laser printer, and the graphical user interface (GUI).

XFCN *n.* Short for **ex**ternal **fun**ction. An external code resource that returns a value after it has completed executing. XFCNs are used in HyperCard, a hypermedia program developed for the Macintosh. *See also* HyperCard, XCMD.

XFDL *n.* Short for **Ex**tensible **F**orms **D**escription **L**anguage, a document description language introduced and submitted to the World Wide Web Committee in 1998 by the Canadian Internet forms company UWI.Com. XFDL is an XML-based language for describing complex forms, such as legal and government documents. It is designed to allow for interactivity yet remain consistent with Internet standards.

XGA *n. See* Extended Graphics Array.

x-height *n.* In typography, the height of the lowercase letter x in a particular font. The x-height thus represents the height of the body only of a lowercase letter, excluding ascenders (such as the top of the letter b) and descenders (such as the tail on the letter g). *See also* ascender, descender.

XHTML *n.* Short for **Ex**tensible **H**ypertext **M**arkup **L**anguage. A markup language incorporating elements of HTML and XML. Web sites designed using XHTML can be more readily displayed on handheld computers and digital phones equipped with microbrowsers. XHTML was released for comments by the World Wide Web Consortium (W3C) in September 1999. *See also* HTML, microbrowser, XML.

XIP *n. See* execute in place.

XLANG *n.* A derivative XML language that describes the logical sequencing of business processes, as well as the implementation of the business process by using various application services.

XLink *n.* An XML language that provides a set of attributes that are used to create links between resources. XLink provides complex extended linking, link behavior, and management capabilities. XLink is able to describe links that connect sets of resources, point to multiple targets, or serve multiple roles within an XML document.

XLL *n.* Acronym for **eX**tensible **L**inking **L**anguage. Broad term intended to denote the family of XML linking/pointing/addressing languages, which include XLink, XPointer, and XPath.

XMI *n.* **1.** Acronym for **XML M**etadata **I**nterchange Format. An object-based model for exchanging program data across the Internet. XMI is sponsored by IBM, Unisys, and others and was submitted as a proposed standard to the Object Management Group (OMG); it is now one of OMG's recommended technologies. XMI is designed to allow for storing and sharing programming information and exchanging data among tools, applications, and storage locations through a network or the Internet so that software developers can collaborate on applications, even if they are not all using the same development tools. **2.** As XMI *bus*, a 64-bit parallel bus supported on certain DEC and Alpha-Server processors. An XMI bus is capable of transferring data, exclusive of addressing overhead, at 100 Mbps.

XML *n.* Acronym for **eX**tensible **M**arkup **L**anguage, a condensed form of SGML (Standard Generalized Markup Language). XML lets Web developers and designers create customized tags that offer greater flexibility in organizing and presenting information than is possible with the older HTML document coding system. XML is defined as a language standard published by the W3C and supported by the industry. *See also* SGML.

XML attribute *n.* Information added to a tag to provide more information about the tag, such as <ingredient quantity="2"units="cups">flour</ingredient>.

XML element *n.* Information delimited by a start tag and an end tag in an eXtensible Markup Language (XML) document. An example would be <Lastname> Davalio</LastName>.

XML entities *n.* Combinations of characters and symbols that replace other characters when an XML document is parsed, usually those that have other meanings in XML. For example, &lt represents the < symbol, which is also the opening bracket for a tag.

XML Metadata Interchange Format *n. See* XMI (definition 1).

XML-RPC *n.* Acronym for **eX**tensible **M**arkup **L**anguage-**R**emote **P**rocedure **C**all. A set of XML-based implementations that allows cross-platform and cross-programming language procedure calls over the Internet. XML-RPC

X

permits complex data structures to be transmitted, processed, and returned between different operating systems running in different environments.

XML Schema *n.* A specification providing a common base for data description and validation in XML environments. XML schema replaces Document Type Definition (DTD) by defining a greater set of data types with more explicit data descriptions. XML schema has been developed as an open, vendor-neutral format to enhance information exchange and e-commerce over the Internet. It is also a standard for the description and encoding of data.

XML Schema Description Language *n. See* XSDL.

XML stylesheet *n.* Contains formatting rules that are applied to an XML file referencing the stylesheet. The standard set of rules for XML stylesheets is the Extensible Stylesheet Language (XSL). *See also* XSL.

XML Web services *n.* Units of application logic providing data and services to other applications. Applications access XML Web services via standard Web protocols and data formats such as HTTP, XML, and SOAP, independent of how each XML Web service is implemented. XML Web services combine the best aspects of component-based development and the Web and are a cornerstone of the Microsoft .NET programming model.

Xmodem *n.* A file transfer protocol used in asynchronous communications that transfers information in blocks of 128 bytes.

Xmodem 1K *n.* A version of the Xmodem file transfer protocol designed for larger, longer-distance file transfers. Xmodem 1K transmits information in 1-kilobyte (1024-byte) blocks and uses a more reliable form of error checking. *See also* Xmodem.

Xmodem-CRC *n.* An enhanced version of the Xmodem file transfer protocol that incorporates a 2-byte cyclical redundancy check (CRC) to detect transmission errors. *See also* CRC.

XMS *n. See* extended memory specification.

XMT *n.* Short for **trans**mit. A signal used in serial communications.

XNS *n.* Acronym for **X**erox **N**etwork **S**ystem. A set of protocols assigned to five numbered layers (0 through 4) that form a suite designed to handle packaging and delivery of network transmissions.

XON/XOFF *n.* An asynchronous communications protocol in which the receiving device or computer uses special characters to control the flow of data from the transmitting device or computer. When the receiving computer cannot continue to receive data, it transmits an XOFF control character that tells the sender to stop transmitting; when transmission can resume, the computer signals the sender with an XON character. *Also called:* software handshake. *See also* handshake.

XOR *n. See* exclusive OR.

XOR encryption *n.* Short for E**x**clusive-**OR encryption**. A simple encryption scheme using the "exclusive-or" concept, in which a decision is based on only one of two conditions being met. Using a provided key, XOR encryption performs an exclusive-or process on each byte of data to be encrypted. Because XOR encryption is not a strong security tool used alone, it is typically used as an additional level of security for Internet transmission of sensitive information.

XPath *n.* An XML language for addressing items in an XML document by specifying a path through the document structure. XPath is used by XPointer and XSLT to locate and identify XML document data. XPath is also considered a query language complement to XQuery. XPath is more supported than XQuery even though there is no approved standard yet for either. *See also* XPointer.

XPointer *n.* An XML language used to locate data within an XML document based on data property descriptions, such as attributes, location, and content. XPointer references the internal structure of a document, allowing links to be made to occurrences of a word, character set, content attribute, or other element, rather than to a specific point within the document. *See also* XPath.

XQuery *n.* Short for e**X**tensible **Query** Language. Designed to be a functional query language that is broadly applicable to a variety of XML data types derived from Quilt, XPath, and XQL. Both Ipedo and Software AG implement their own versions of the W3C's proposed specification for the XQuery language. *Also called:* XML Query, XQL.

XSD *n.* Acronym for e**X**tensible **S**chema **D**efinition. A prefix used by convention to indicate a W3C schema namespace.

X

XSDL *n.* Acronym for **XML S**chema **D**escription Language. A World Wide Web Consortium (W3C) recommendation for representing XML structure. XSDL is capable of describing complex XML-based data structures, and provides options not available with Document Type Definitions (DTDs), including namespace support, XML datatypes, and improved extensibility and data type support.

X series *n.* A set of recommendations adopted by the International Telecommunication Union Telecommunication Standardization Sector (ITU-T), formerly the CCITT, and International Organization for Standardization (ISO) for standardizing equipment and protocols used in both public access and private computer networks. See the table.

Table X.1   *Recommendations in X Series for Network Communications.*

Recommendation Number	What It Covers
X.25	Interface required to connect a computer to a packet-switched network such as the Internet
X.75	Protocols for connecting two public data networks
X.200	Seven-layer set of protocols known as the ISO/OSI reference model for standardizing computer-to-computer connections
X.400	Format at the ISO/OSI application layer for e-mail messages over various network transports, including Ethernet, X.25, and TCP/IP. Gateways must be used to translate e-mail messages between the X.400 and Internet formats
X.445	Asynchronous Protocol Specification, which governs the transmission of X.400 messages over dial-up telephone lines
X.500	Protocols for client/server systems that maintain and access directories of users and resources in X.400 form
X.509	Digital certificates

XSL *n.* Acronym for **Ex**tensible **S**tylesheet **L**anguage. A World Wide Web Consortium (W3C) standard stylesheet language for XML documents. XSL determines how data in an XML document is displayed on the Web. XSL controls what data will be displayed, in what format, and in what type size and style. XSL contains two major extensions: XSL Transformations (XSLT), a language used to convert XML documents to HTML or other document types, and XSL Formatting Objects (XSL-FO), a language for specifying formatting semantics. *See also* XSL-FO, XSLT.

XSL-FO *n.* Acronym for **Ex**tensible **S**tylesheet **L**anguage **F**ormatting **O**bjects. An XML-based markup language for specifying formatting semantics. XSL-FO allows format and style information to be applied to an XML document and can be used with XSLT to produce source documents. *See also* XSL.

XSLT *n.* Acronym for **Ex**tensible **S**tylesheet **L**anguage **T**ransformations. A language used in transforming an existing XML document into a restructured XML document. Formalized as a W3C Recommendation in 1999, XSLT is primarily intended for use as part of XSL. XSL describes the styling of a document in terms of XSLT transformations into an XML document. *See also* XML, XSL.

X terminal *n.* An intelligent display device, connected to an Ethernet network, that performs operations on request from client applications in an X Window System. *See also* Ethernet (definition 1), X Window System.

XT keyboard *n. See* PC/XT keyboard.

XUL *n.* A standards-based interface description language that provides a standard way to exchange data describing a program's user interface. XUL balances simplicity, flexibility, and ease of use with precise layout control. XUL was developed by Netscape and Mozilla and is used with XML, CSS, DOM, and HTML.

X Windows *n. See* X Window System.

X Window System *n.* A nonproprietary standardized set of display-handling routines, developed at MIT. Most often encountered on UNIX workstations, the X Window System is independent of hardware and operating system. An X Window System client calls on the server, which is located on the user's workstation, to provide a window in which the client can generate a display of text or graphics. *Also called:* X Windows. *See also* X Consortium.

X

X-Y display *n. See* vector display.

x-y **matrix** *n.* An arrangement of rows and columns with a horizontal (*x*) axis and a vertical (*y*) axis.

x-y **plotter** *n. See* plotter.

x-y-z **coordinate system** *n.* A three-dimensional system of Cartesian coordinates that includes a third (*z*) axis running perpendicular to the horizontal (*x*) and vertical (*y*) axes. The *x-y-z* coordinate system is used in computer graphics for creating models with length, breadth, and depth. See the illustration. *See also* Cartesian coordinates.

x-y-z **coordinate system.**

X

Y2K *n. See* Year 2000 problem.

Y2K BIOS patch card *n.* An ISA board that ensures that system calls to the BIOS return the correct year. The BIOS patch card checks the date the BIOS gets from the real-time clock and sends the correct date to whichever application or process requested it. While a BIOS patch card proved effective for most situations once the year 2000 was reached, some applications and processes that work directly with the real-time clock (not an advisable practice) actually received the wrong date on non-Year-2000-compliant PCs.

Y2K BIOS test *n. See* BIOS test.

Y2K bug *n. See* Year 2000 problem.

Y2K-compliant *adj. See* Year 2000 compliant.

Y2K computer bug *n. See* Year 2000 problem.

Y2K ready *adj. See* Year 2000 compliant.

Yahoo! *n.* The first major online Web-based directory and search engine for Internet resources, which can be found at http://www.yahoo.com. *See also* search engine (definition 2).

Yahoo! Mail *n.* A popular Web-based e-mail service provided for free by Yahoo! Inc. *Compare* Hotmail.

Yahoo! Messenger *n.* A popular instant-messaging application provided for free by Yahoo! Inc. on a variety of operating systems. *See also* instant messaging. *Compare* AIM, ICQ, .NET Messenger Service.

Yanoff list *n.* The informal name of the Internet services list created and maintained by Scott Yanoff. The Yanoff list was one of the earliest directories of Internet services and resources. It is located at http://www.spectracom.com/islist/.

y-axis *n.* The vertical reference line on a grid, chart, or graph that has horizontal and vertical dimensions. *See also* Cartesian coordinates.

YB *n. See* yottabyte.

Year 2000 compliant *adj.* The criteria for this varied among companies and organizations; however, a general theme was that software or hardware would make the transition from 1999 to 2000 without producing errors. For a PC, the general thinking was that if the real-time clock passed a Year 2000 BIOS test, it was Year 2000 compliant. However, testing the computing environment from end to end, considering the readiness of the operating systems, applications, custom code, data, and system interfaces, was also strongly recommended.

Year 2000 Information and Readiness Disclosure Act *n.* A U.S. statute enacted in October 1998 that required U.S. companies to publicly disclose how they were attempting to make their systems or products ready for the year 2000. Many companies made this information available on the World Wide Web.

Year 2000 problem *n.* Prior to January 1, 2000, a potential software problem stemming from the use of two digits (99) rather than four (1999) as year indicators in computer programs. Such programs assumed that 19 preceded every year value, and so could potentially fail or produce incorrect calculations by interpreting the year 2000 (00) as an earlier date than 19xx when the year rolled over into a new century. The use of two-digit year indicators was prevalent in, though not limited to, older programs that had been written when a saving of two bytes (digits) per year value was significant in terms of computer memory. Because the use of two-digit year indicators was widespread, companies, governments, and other organizations took measures on a large scale to prevent the Year 2000 problem from affecting their computing systems. In the end, however, the problem—luckily—proved largely uneventful.

Year 2000 ready *adj. See* Year 2000 compliant.

Year 2000 rollover *n.* The moment when the year in a computer system changed from 1999 to 2000. *Also called:* date rollover, millennium transition, rollover, Year 2000 transition.

Year 2000 time problem *n. See* Year 2000 problem.

Year 2000 transition *n. See* Year 2000 rollover.

Yellow Pages *n.* **1.** The former name of a UNIX utility, provided by SunSoft (Sun Microsystems system software), that maintains a central database of names and locations of the resources on a network. The Yellow Pages enables processes on any node to locate resources by name. This utility is now known formally as NIS (Network Information Service). **2.** InterNIC Registration Services' database of domain names and their IP addresses. *See also* domain name, IP address. **3.** Any of several Internet business directory services. Some are print publications, some are strictly electronic, and some are both.

Yes/No data type *n.* A data type used to define database fields that will contain only one of two values, such as Yes or No and True or False. Null values are not allowed. *See also* boolean.

Yettie *n.* Short for **Y**oung, **E**ntrepreneurial **T**ech-based **T**wenty-something or **Y**oung, **E**ntrepreneurial **T**echnocrat. A person who works in a technology or Internet-related field and who embraces technological change and opportunity. Yettie is intended to be a successor to the older term "yuppie."

YHBT *n.* Acronym for **y**ou **h**ave **b**een **t**rolled. An expression used in e-mail and newsgroups to indicate that the receiver has taken a deliberately set bait. *See also* troll.

YHL *n.* Acronym for **y**ou **h**ave **l**ost. An expression used in e-mail and newsgroups, often following YHBT. *See also* YHBT.

Ymodem *n.* A variation of the Xmodem file transfer protocol that includes the following enhancements: the ability to transfer information in 1-kilobyte (1024-byte) blocks, the ability to send multiple files (batch file transmission), cyclical redundancy checking (CRC), and the ability to abort transfer by transmitting two CAN (cancel) characters in a row. *See also* CRC, Xmodem.

yocto- *prefix* A metric prefix meaning 10^{-24} (one septillionth in the U.S. system).

yoke *n.* The part of a CRT (cathode-ray tube) that deflects the electron beam, causing it to strike a specific area on the screen. *Also called:* deflection coils. *See also* CRT.

yotta- *prefix* A metric prefix meaning 10^{24} (one septillion in the U.S. system).

yottabyte *n.* A unit of measure equal to 2^{80} bytes, or approximately 1 septillion (10^{24}) bytes. When calculated as a multiple of 1000 zettabytes (the next highest unit of measure), a yottabyte is 1,000,000,000,000,000,000,000,000 bytes; when calculated as 1024 zettabytes, a yottabyte is 1,208,925,819,614,629,174,706,176 bytes. The prefix *yotta-* is meant to sound like the Greek letter *iota*. *Abbreviation:* YB.

YY *n.* The form in which the year part of a date is stored in some, mostly older, computer systems. Before 2000, the possibility existed that computers that used a 2-digit date would incorrectly interpret the year 2000 (year 00) as the year 1900 and disrupt the computer's operation.

YYYY *n.* Symbolic of providing fully distinguished dates, including 4-digit years. Using 4-digit years was an important step in many Year 2000 remediation programs—especially those focused on data.

Y

.z *n.* The file extension identifying a UNIX file compressed using the gzip or compact utility. *See also* gzip.

.Z *n.* The file extension for UNIX files that have been compressed using the compress utility. *See also* compress[1].

Z39.50 standard *n.* A specification for a query language based on SQL (structured query language). It is used by WAIS, among other Internet services, to search for files through the use of keywords and is widely used for remote access to library catalogs. *See also* structured query language, WAIS.

Z80 *n.* An 8-bit microprocessor from Zilog, a company founded by former Intel engineers. The Z80 has a 16-bit address bus, yielding a 64-kilobyte addressable memory space, and an 8-bit data bus. A descendant of the Intel 8080, it was the favored processor in the days of the CP/M operating system. One of the most popular computers of the early 1980s, the Radio Shack TRS-80, was based on this chip. *See also* CP/M.

zap *vb.* **1.** To erase permanently. For example, to zap a file means to remove it without hope of retrieval. **2.** To damage a device, usually by discharging static electricity through it.

z-axis *n.* The third axis in a three-dimensional coordinate system, used in computer graphics to represent depth. *See also* Cartesian coordinates, *x-y-z* coordinate system.

ZB *n. See* zettabyte.

zepto- *prefix* A metric prefix meaning 10^{-21} (one sextillionth in the American system).

zero[1] *n.* The arithmetic symbol (0) representing no magnitude.

zero[2] *vb.* To fill or replace with zeros (for example, to zero a specified portion of memory, a field, or some other limited structure).

zero divide *n.* A division operation in which the divisor is zero. Division by zero is mathematically undefined, is not allowed in a program, and is considered a bug.

zero flag *n.* A flag (bit) in a microprocessor that is set (turned on), typically in a flag register, when the result of an operation is zero. *See also* flag (definition 1).

zero-insertion-force socket *n. See* ZIF socket.

zero-length string *n.* A string that contains no characters. You can use a zero-length string to indicate that you know there's no value for a field. You enter a zero-length string by typing two double quotation marks with no space between them ("").

zero out *vb.* To set a variable value or a series of bits to zero.

zero suppression *n.* The elimination of leading (nonsignificant) zeros in a number. For example, zero suppression would truncate 000123.456 to 123.456. *See also* significant digits.

zero wait state *n.* The condition of random access memory (RAM) that is fast enough to respond to the processor without requiring wait states. *See also* wait state.

zetta- *prefix* A metric prefix meaning 10^{21} (one sextillion in the American system).

zettabyte *n.* A unit of measure equal to 2^{70} bytes, or one sextillion (10^{21}) bytes. When calculated as a multiple of 1000 exabytes (the next highest unit of measure), a zettabyte is 1,000,000,000,000,000,000,000 bytes; when calculated as 1024 exabytes, a zettabyte is 1,180,591,620,717,411,303,424 bytes. The prefix (*zetta-*) is meant to sound like the Greek letter *zeta. Abbreviation:* ZB.

z-fold paper *n. See* fanfold paper.

ZIF socket *n.* Short for **z**ero-**i**nsertion-**f**orce **socket**. A kind of socket for integrated circuits that can be opened with a lever or screw, allowing the chip to be placed in the socket without the application of pressure. The lever or screw of the socket is then closed, causing the socket contacts to grip the chip's pins. ZIF sockets facilitate frequent insertion and removal of chips, but they take up more space and are more expensive than conventional sockets.

zinc-air battery *n.* Non rechargeable battery that is relatively inexpensive, offers extended battery life, and contains none of the harsh chemicals or metals found in conventional nickel metal cadmium (NiCad), nickel metal hydride (NiMH), or lithium ion (Li-ion) batteries.

.zip *n.* A file extension that identifies a compressed archive file encoded in ZIP format, as by PKZIP. *See also* compressed file, PKZIP.

Zip drive *n.* A disk drive developed by Iomega that uses 3.5-inch removable disks (Zip disks) capable of storing 100 megabytes of data. See the illustration. *See also* disk drive.

Zip drive.

Z

Zmodem *n.* An enhancement of the Xmodem file transfer protocol that handles larger data transfers with less error. Zmodem includes a feature called checkpoint restart, which resumes transmission at the point of interruption, rather than at the beginning, if the communications link is broken during data transfer. *See also* Xmodem.

zombie *n.* A computer that has become the unwilling host of a DDoS (distributed denial of services) attack program and that is controlled by remote signals from the attacker. To create a zombie, a hacker utilizes security vulnerabilities to crack a Web, mail, news, or application server and plant hidden DDoS tools such as Trinoo and Tribal Flood Network. Later, at a signal from the attacker, the server becomes a zombie that will participate in a coordinated attack on other servers. *See also* DDoS, hacker.

zone *n.* **1.** On a LAN (local area network), a subgroup of users within a larger group of interconnected networks. **2.** In Macintosh programming, a portion of memory that is allocated and reallocated by the memory manager facility as memory is requested and released by applications and by other parts of the operating system. *See also* heap (definition 1).

zone header *n.* On the Apple Macintosh, a header at the beginning of a block of memory that contains information needed by the memory management facility in order to use that memory block effectively. *See also* header (definition 2).

zone transfer *n.* The process whereby a secondary DNS server obtains information about a zone or domain from the primary server. *See also* zone (definition 1).

.zoo *n.* The file extension that identifies compressed archive files created with the zoo file compression utility. *See also* zoo210.

zoo210 *n.* Version 2.1 of zoo, a program for creating compressed archive files (whose names have the extension .zoo). The algorithm for zoo210 is based on that of LHARC. Implementations of zoo210 are available for UNIX and Intel systems. *See also* archive file, LHARC.

zoom *vb.* To enlarge a selected portion of a graphical image or document to fill a window or the screen. Zooming is a feature of many programs, including drawing, word processing, and spreadsheet programs, that allows the user to select a small part of the screen, zoom it, and make changes to the enlarged portion at a finer level of detail. *See also* window.

zoom box *n.* A control in the upper right corner of the frame of a window on the Macintosh screen. When the user clicks on the zoom box, the window toggles between the maximum size and the size the user has set for it by dragging. *See also* window. *Compare* Maximize button.

zoomed video port *n.* *See* ZV port.

zoo virus *n.* A virus that is kept in an isolated environment for the benefit of anti-virus research and training. Zoo viruses are not found outside the labs of anti-virus companies.

Zope *n.* An open source application server for publishing objects on the Internet. Zope provides tools to integrate data and content from multiple sources into complete Web applications and can be used in conjunction with XML-RPC to form a system for remotely scriptable Web objects. Zope runs on UNIX, Windows NT and later, and most other major operating systems. *See also* XML-RPC.

z-order *n.* **1.** The order in which objects are drawn on top of one another onscreen to simulate depth (the third dimension) in conjunction with the x and y (height and width) coordinates. **2.** The visual layering of windows or controls on a form along the z-axis (depth). The z-order determines which controls are in front of other controls. Each window or control has a unique position in the z-order.

Zulu time *n.* Slang for Greenwich Mean Time.

ZV port *n.* Short for **z**oomed **v**ideo **port**. Port available on many portable computers as an inexpensive multimedia alternative to traditional video input. The ZV port allows data to flow uninterrupted from source to destination without need for buffering. Zoomed video was adopted by the Personal Computer Memory Card International Association (PCMCIA) to enable high transfer rates for portable computers, connected video cameras, and other multimedia devices.

Appendix A

Common Character Sets

ANSI Character Set

Character	Unicode Value (Hex)	ANSI code (decimal)	Description
NUL	0000	0	Null
SOH	0001	1	Start of heading
STX	0002	2	Start of text
ETX	0003	3	End of text
EOT	0004	4	End of transmission
ENQ	0005	5	Enquiry
ACK	0006	6	Acknowledge
BEL	0007	7	Bell
BS	0008	8	Backspace
HT	0009	9	Horizontal tabulation
LF	000A	10	Line feed
VT	000B	11	Vertical tabulation
FF	000C	12	Form feed
CR	000D	13	Carriage return
SO	000E	14	Shift out
SI	000F	15	Shift in
DLE	0010	16	Data link escape
DC1	0011	17	Device control 1
DC2	0012	18	Device control 2
DC3	0013	19	Device control 3
DC4	0014	20	Device control 4
NAK	0015	21	Negative acknowledge
SYN	0016	22	Synchronous idle
ETB	0017	23	End of transmission block
CAN	0018	24	Cancel
EM	0019	25	End of medium
SUB	001A	26	Substitute
ESC	001B	27	Escape
FS	001C	28	File separator
GS	001D	29	Group separator
RS	001E	30	Record separator
US	001F	31	Unit separator
SP	0020	32	Space
!	0021	33	Exclamation point
"	0022	34	Quotation mark

ANSI Character Set *continued*

Character	Unicode Value (Hex)	ANSI code (decimal)	Description
#	0023	35	Number sign
$	0024	36	Dollar sign
%	0025	37	Percent
&	0026	38	Ampersand
'	0027	39	Apostrophe
(	0028	40	Left parenthesis
)	0029	41	Right parenthesis
*	002A	42	Asterisk
+	002B	43	Plus sign
,	002C	44	Comma
-	002D	45	Hyphen
.	002E	46	Full stop
/	002F	47	Solidus
0	0030	48	Digit zero
1	0031	49	Digit one
2	0032	50	Digit two
3	0033	51	Digit three
4	0034	52	Digit four
5	0035	53	Digit five
6	0036	54	Digit six
7	0037	55	Digit seven
8	0038	56	Digit eight
9	0039	57	Digit nine
:	003A	58	Colon
;	003B	59	Semicolon
<	003C	60	Less-than sign
=	003D	61	Equals sign
>	003E	62	Greater-than sign
?	003F	63	Question mark
@	0040	64	Commercial at
A	0041	65	Latin capital letter A
B	0042	66	Latin capital letter B
C	0043	67	Latin capital letter C
D	0044	68	Latin capital letter D
E	0045	69	Latin capital letter E
F	0046	70	Latin capital letter F
G	0047	71	Latin capital letter G
H	0048	72	Latin capital letter H
I	0049	73	Latin capital letter I
J	004A	74	Latin capital letter J
K	004B	75	Latin capital letter K
L	004C	76	Latin capital letter L
M	004D	77	Latin capital letter M
N	004E	78	Latin capital letter N
O	004F	79	Latin capital letter O

ANSI Character Set *continued*

Character	Unicode Value (Hex)	ANSI code (decimal)	Description
P	0050	80	Latin capital letter P
Q	0051	81	Latin capital letter Q
R	0052	82	Latin capital letter R
S	0053	83	Latin capital letter S
T	0054	84	Latin capital letter T
U	0055	85	Latin capital letter U
V	0056	86	Latin capital letter V
W	0057	87	Latin capital letter W
X	0058	88	Latin capital letter X
Y	0059	89	Latin capital letter Y
Z	005A	90	Latin capital letter Z
[	005B	91	Left square bracket
\	005C	92	Reverse solidus
]	005D	93	Right square bracket
^	005E	94	Circumflex accent
_	005F	95	Low line
`	0060	96	Grave accent
a	0061	97	Latin small letter a
b	0062	98	Latin small letter b
c	0063	99	Latin small letter c
d	0064	100	Latin small letter d
e	0065	101	Latin small letter e
f	0066	102	Latin small letter f
g	0067	103	Latin small letter g
h	0068	104	Latin small letter h
i	0069	105	Latin small letter i
j	006A	106	Latin small letter j
k	006B	107	Latin small letter k
l	006C	108	Latin small letter l
m	006D	109	Latin small letter m
n	006E	110	Latin small letter n
o	006F	111	Latin small letter o
p	0070	112	Latin small letter p
q	0071	113	Latin small letter q
r	0072	114	Latin small letter r
s	0073	115	Latin small letter s
t	0074	116	Latin small letter t
u	0075	117	Latin small letter u
v	0076	118	Latin small letter v
w	0077	119	Latin small letter w
x	0078	120	Latin small letter x
y	0079	121	Latin small letter y
z	007A	122	Latin small letter z
{	007B	123	Left curly bracket
		007C	124	Vertical line

ANSI Character Set *continued*

Character	Unicode Value (Hex)	ANSI code (decimal)	Description
}	007D	125	Right curly bracket
~	007E	126	Tilde
DEL	007F	127	Delete
	0080	128	Reserved
	0081	129	Reserved
	0082	130	Reserved
	0083	131	Reserved
IND	0084	132	Index
NEL	0085	133	Next line
SSA	0086	134	Start of selected area
ESA	0087	135	End of selected area
	0088	136	Character tabulation set
	0089	137	Character tabulation with justification
	008A	138	Line tabulation set
PLD	008B	139	Partial line down
PLU	008C	140	Partial line up
	008D	141	Reverse line feed
SS2	008E	142	Single shift two
SS3	008F	143	Single shift three
DCS	0090	144	Device control string
PU1	0091	145	Private use one
PU2	0092	146	Private use two
STS	0093	147	Set transmit state
CCH	0094	148	Cancel character
MW	0095	149	Message waiting
	0096	150	Start of guarded area
	0097	151	End of guarded area
	0098	152	Start of string
	0099	153	Reserved
	009A	154	Single character introducer
CSI	009B	155	Control sequence introducer
ST	009C	156	String terminator
OSC	009D	157	Operating system command
PM	009E	158	Privacy message
APC	009F	158	Application program command
	00A0	160	No-break space
¡	00A1	161	Inverted exclamation mark
¢	00A2	162	Cent sign
£	00A3	163	Pound sign
¤	00A4	164	Currency sign
¥	00A5	165	Yen sign
¦	00A6	166	Broken bar
§	00A7	167	Section sign
¨	00A8	168	Diaeresis

ANSI Character Set *continued*

Character	Unicode Value (Hex)	ANSI code (decimal)	Description
©	00A9	169	Copyright sign
ª	00AA	170	Feminine ordinal indicator
«	00AB	171	Left-pointing double angle quotation mark
¬	00AC	172	Not sign
-	00AD	173	Soft hyphen
®	00AE	174	Registered sign
¯	00AF	175	Macron
°	00B0	176	Degree sign
±	00B1	177	Plus-minus sign
²	00B2	178	Superscript two
³	00B3	179	Superscript three
´	00B4	180	Acute accent
µ	00B5	181	Micro sign
¶	00B6	182	Pilcrow sign
·	00B7	183	Middle dot
	00B8	184	Cedilla
¹	00B9	185	Superscript one
º	00BA	186	Masculine ordinal indicator
»	00BB	187	Right-pointing double angle quotation mark
¼	00BC	188	Vulgar fraction one quarter
½	00BD	189	Vulgar fraction one half
¾	00BE	190	Vulgar fraction three quarters
¿	00BF	191	Inverted question mark
À	00C0	192	Latin capital letter A with grave
Á	00C1	193	Latin capital letter A with acute
Â	00C2	194	Latin capital letter A with circumflex
Ã	00C3	195	Latin capital letter A with tilde
Ä	00C4	196	Latin capital letter A with diaeresis
Å	00C5	197	Latin capital letter A with ring above
Æ	00C6	198	Latin capital ligature AE
Ç	00C7	199	Latin capital letter C with cedilla
È	00C8	200	Latin capital letter E with grave
É	00C9	201	Latin capital letter E with acute
Ê	00CA	202	Latin capital letter E with circumflex
Ë	00CB	203	Latin capital letter E with diaeresis
Ì	00CC	204	Latin capital letter I with grave
Í	00CD	205	Latin capital letter I with acute
Î	00CE	206	Latin capital letter I with circumflex
Ï	00CF	207	Latin capital letter I with diaeresis
Ð	00D0	208	Latin capital letter ETH
Ñ	00D1	209	Latin capital letter N with tilde
Ò	00D2	210	Latin capital letter O with grave
Ó	00D3	211	Latin capital letter O with acute
Ô	00D4	212	Latin capital letter O with circumflex

ANSI Character Set *continued*

Character	Unicode Value (Hex)	ANSI code (decimal)	Description
Õ	00D5	213	Latin capital letter O with tilde
Ö	00D6	214	Latin capital letter O with diaeresis
×	00D7	215	Multiplication sign
Ø	00D8	216	Latin capital letter O with stroke
Ù	00D9	217	Latin capital letter U with grave
Ú	00DA	218	Latin capital letter U with acute
Û	00DB	219	Latin capital letter U with circumflex
Ü	00DC	220	Latin capital letter U with diaeresis
Ý	00DD	221	Latin capital letter Y with acute
Þ	00DE	222	Latin capital letter thorn
ß	00DF	223	Latin small letter sharp s
à	00E0	224	Latin small letter a with grave
á	00E1	225	Latin small letter a with acute
â	00E2	226	Latin small letter a with circumflex
ã	00E3	227	Latin small letter a with tilde
ä	00E4	228	Latin small letter a with diaeresis
å	00E5	229	Latin small letter a with ring above
æ	00E6	230	Latin small ligature ae
ç	00E7	231	Latin small letter c with cedilla
è	00E8	232	Latin small letter e with grave
é	00E9	233	Latin small letter e with acute
ê	00EA	234	Latin small letter e with circumflex
ë	00EB	235	Latin small letter e with diaeresis
ì	00EC	236	Latin small letter i with grave
í	00ED	237	Latin small letter i with acute
î	00EE	238	Latin small letter i with circumflex
ï	00EF	239	Latin small letter i with diaeresis
ð	00F0	240	Latin small letter eth
ñ	00F1	241	Latin small letter n with tilde
ò	00F2	242	Latin small letter o with grave
ó	00F3	243	Latin small letter o with acute
ô	00F4	244	Latin small letter o with circumflex
õ	00F5	245	Latin small letter o with tilde
ö	00F6	246	Latin small letter o with diaeresis
÷	00F7	247	Division sign
ø	00F8	248	Latin small letter o with stroke
ù	00F9	249	Latin small letter u with grave
ú	00FA	250	Latin small letter u with acute
û	00FB	251	Latin small letter u with circumflex
ü	00FC	252	Latin small letter u with diaeresis
ý	00FD	253	Latin small letter y with acute
þ	00FE	254	Latin small letter thorn
ÿ	00FF	255	Latin small letter y with diaeresis

Apple Macintosh Extended Character Set

ASCII	Hex	Times	New York	Courier	Zapf Dingbats	Symbol
128	80	Ä	Ä	Ä	❨	
129	81	Å	Å	Å	❩	
130	82	Ç	Ç	Ç	❪	
131	83	É	É	É	❫	
132	84	Ñ	Ñ	Ñ	❬	
133	85	Ö	Ö	Ö	❭	
134	86	Ü	Ü	Ü	❮	
135	87	á	á	á	❯	
136	88	à	à	à	❰	
137	89	â	â	â	❱	
138	8A	ä	ä	ä	❲	
139	8B	ã	ã	ã	❳	
140	8C	å	å	å	❴	
141	8D	ç	ç	ç	❵	
142	8E	é	é	é		
143	8F	è	è	è		
144	90	ê	ê	ê		
145	91	ë	ë	ë		
146	92	í	í	í		
147	93	ì	ì	ì		
148	94	î	î	î		
149	95	ï	ï	ï		
150	96	ñ	ñ	ñ		
151	97	ó	ó	ó		
152	98	ò	ò	ò		
153	99	ô	ô	ô		
154	9A	ö	ö	ö		
155	9B	õ	õ	õ		
156	9C	ú	ú	ú		
157	9D	ù	ù	ù		
158	9E	û	û	û		
159	9F	ü	ü	ü		
160	A0	†	†	†		

Apple Macintosh Extended Character Set *continued*

ASCII	Hex	Times	New York	Courier	Zapf Dingbats	Symbol
161	A1	°	°	°	❡	Υ
162	A2	¢	¢	¢	✒	′
163	A3	£	£	£	✣	≤
164	A4	§	§	§	♥	/
165	A5	•	•	•	♣	∞
166	A6	¶	¶	¶	✿	ƒ
167	A7	ß	ß	ß	❧	♣
168	A8	®	®	®	♣	♦
169	A9	©	©	©	♦	♥
170	AA	™	™	™	♥	♠
171	AB	´	´	´	♠	↔
172	AC	¨	¨	¨	①	←
173	AD	≠	≠	≠	②	↑
174	AE	Æ	Æ	Æ	③	→
175	AF	Ø	Ø	Ø	④	↓
176	B0	∞	∞	∞	⑤	°
177	B1	±	±	±	⑥	±
178	B2	≤	≤	≤	⑦	″
179	B3	≥	≥	≥	⑧	≥
180	B4	¥	¥	¥	⑨	×
181	B5	μ	μ	μ	⑩	∝
182	B6	∂	∂	∂	❶	∂
183	B7	Σ	Σ	Σ	❷	•
184	B8	Π	Π	Π	❸	÷
185	B9	π	π	π	❹	≠
186	BA	∫	∫	∫	❺	≡
187	BB	ª	ª	ª	❻	≈
188	BC	º	º	º	❼	…
189	BD	Ω	Ω	Ω	❽	|
190	BE	æ	æ	æ	❾	—
191	BF	ø	ø	ø	❿	↵
192	C0	¿	¿	¿	①	ℵ
193	C1	¡	¡	¡	②	ℑ

Apple Macintosh Extended Character Set *continued*

ASCII	Hex	Times	New York	Courier	Zapf Dingbats	Symbol
194	C2	¬	¬	¬	③	ℜ
195	C3	√	√	√	④	℘
196	C4	ƒ	ƒ	ƒ	⑤	⊗
197	C5	≈	≈	≈	⑥	⊕
198	C6	Δ	Δ	Δ	⑦	∅
199	C7	«	«	«	⑧	∩
200	C8	»	»	»	⑨	∪
201	C9	…	…	…	⑩	⊃
202	CA	——NBSP (nonbreaking space)——			❶	⊇
203	CB	À	À	À	❷	⊄
204	CC	Ã	Ã	Ã	❸	⊂
205	CD	Õ	Õ	Õ	❹	⊆
206	CE	Œ	Œ	Œ	❺	∈
207	CF	œ	œ	œ	❻	∉
208	D0	-	-	-	❼	∠
209	D1	—	—	—	❽	∇
210	D2	"	"	"	❾	®
211	D3	"	"	"	❿	©
212	D4	'	'	'	→	™
213	D5	'	'	'	→	∏
214	D6	÷	÷	÷	↔	√
215	D7	◊	◊	◊	↕	·
216	D8	ÿ	ÿ	ÿ	↘	¬
217	D9	Ÿ	Ÿ	Ÿ	→	∧
218	DA	/	/	/	↗	∨
219	DB	¤	¤	¤	→	⇔
220	DC	‹	‹	‹	➔	⇐
221	DD	›	›	›	→	⇑
222	DE	fi	fi	fi	→	⇒
223	DF	fl	fl	fl	→	⇓
224	E0	‡	‡	‡	→	◊
225	E1	·	·	·	➡	⟨
226	E2	‚	‚	‚	➢	®

Apple Macintosh Extended Character Set *continued*

ASCII	Hex	Times	New York	Courier	Zapf Dingbats	Symbol
227	E3	„	„	"	➢	©
228	E4	‰	‰	‰	➤	™
229	E5	Â	Â	Â	➡	∑
230	E6	Ê	Ê	Ê	➡	⌠
231	E7	Á	Á	Á	▶	⎮
232	E8	Ë	Ë	Ë	➡	⎝
233	E9	È	È	È	⇨	⎡
234	EA	Í	Í	Í	⇨	⎢
235	EB	Î	Î	Î	⇦	⎣
236	EC	Ï	Ï	Ï	⇦	⎧
237	ED	Ì	Ì	Ì	⇨	⎨
238	EE	Ó	Ó	Ó	⇨	⎩
239	EF	Ô	Ô	Ô	⇨	⎪
240	F0			———— Not Used ————		
241	F1	Ò	Ò	Ò	⇨	⎞
242	F2	Ú	Ú	Ú	↻	⌡
243	F3	Û	Û	Û	➻	⎛
244	F4	Ù	Ù	Ù	➘	⎜
245	F5	ı	ı	ı	➚	⎟
246	F6	ˆ	ˆ	ˆ	➹	⎠
247	F7	˜	˜	˜	➘	⎟
248	F8	¯	¯	¯	➽	⎞
249	F9	˘	˘	˘	➹	⎤
250	FA	˙	˙	˙	➞	⎥
251	FB	˚	˚	˚	➟	⎦
252	FC	¸	¸	¸	➠	⎫
253	FD	˝	˝	˝	➡	⎬
254	FE	˛	˛	˛	⇒	⎭
255	FF	ˇ	ˇ	ˇ		

IBM Extended Character Set

Dec	Hex	Char	Dec	Hex	Char	Dec	Hex	Char	Dec	Hex	Char
128	80	Ç	156	9C	£	184	B8	╕	212	D4	╘
129	81	ü	157	9D	¥	185	B9	╣	213	D5	╒
130	82	é	158	9E	₧	186	BA	║	214	D6	╓
131	83	â	159	9F	ƒ	187	BB	╗	215	D7	╫
132	84	ä	160	A0	á	188	BC	╝	216	D8	╪
133	85	à	161	A1	í	189	BD	╜	217	D9	┘
134	86	å	162	A2	ó	190	BE	╛	218	DA	┌
135	87	ç	163	A3	ú	191	BF	┐	219	DB	█
136	88	ê	164	A4	ñ	192	C0	└	220	DC	▄
137	89	ë	165	A5	Ñ	193	C1	┴	221	DD	▌
138	8A	è	166	A6	ª	194	C2	┬	222	DE	▐
139	8B	ï	167	A7	º	195	C3	├	223	DF	▀
140	8C	î	168	A8	¿	196	C4	─	224	E0	α
141	8D	ì	169	A9	⌐	197	C5	┼	225	E1	β
142	8E	Ä	170	AA	¬	198	C6	╞	226	E2	Γ
143	8F	Å	171	AB	½	199	C7	╟	227	E3	π
144	90	É	172	AC	¼	200	C8	╚	228	E4	Σ
145	91	æ	173	AD	¡	201	C9	╔	229	E5	σ
146	92	Æ	174	AE	«	202	CA	╩	230	E6	µ
147	93	ô	175	AF	»	203	CB	╦	231	E7	τ
148	94	ö	176	B0	░	204	CC	╠	232	E8	Φ
149	95	ò	177	B1	▒	205	CD	═	233	E9	Θ
150	96	û	178	B2	▓	206	CE	╬	234	EA	Ω
151	97	ù	179	B3	│	207	CF	╧	235	EB	δ
152	98	ÿ	180	B4	┤	208	D0	╨	236	EC	∞
153	99	Ö	181	B5	╡	209	D1	╤	237	ED	φ
154	9A	Ü	182	B6	╢	210	D2	╥	238	EE	ε
155	9B	¢	183	B7	╖	211	D3	╙	239	EF	∩

IBM Extended Character Set *continued*

Dec	Hex	Char	Dec	Hex	Char	Dec	Hex	Char	Dec	Hex	Char
240	F0	≡	244	F4	⌠	248	F8	°	252	FC	η
241	F1	±	245	F5	⌡	249	F9	●	253	FD	²
242	F2	≥	246	F6	÷	250	FA	·	254	FE	●
243	F3	≤	247	F7	≈	251	FB	√	255	FF	

EBCDIC Character Set

Dec	Hex	Name	Character	Meaning
0	00	NUL		Null
1	01	SOH		Start of heading
2	02	STX		Start of text
3	03	ETX		End of text
4	04	SEL		Select
5	05	HT		Horizontal tab
6	06	RNL		Required new line
7	07	DEL		Delete
8	08	GE		Graphic escape
9	09	SPS		Superscript
10	0A	RPT		Repeat
11	0B	VT		Vertical tab
12	0C	FF		Form feed
13	0D	CR		Carriage return
14	0E	SO		Shift out
15	0F	SI		Shift in
16	10	DLE		Data length escape
17	11	DC1		Device control 1
18	12	DC2		Device control 2
19	13	DC3		Device control 3
20	14	RES/ENP		Restore/enable presentation
21	15	NL		New line
22	16	BS		Backspace
23	17	POC		Program-operator communication
24	18	CAN		Cancel
25	19	EM		End of medium
26	1A	UBS		Unit backspace
27	1B	CU1		Customer use 1
28	1C	IFS		Interchange file separator
29	1D	IGS		Interchange group separator
30	1E	IRS		Interchange record separator
31	1F	IUS/ITB		Interchange unit separator/intermediate transmission block
32	20	DS		Digit select
33	21	SOS		Start of significance
34	22	FS		Field separator
35	23	WUS		Word underscore
36	24	BYP/INP		Bypass/inhibit presentation
37	25	LF		Line feed
38	26	ETB		End of transmission block
39	27	ESC		Escape
40	28	SA		Set attribute
41	29	SFE		Start field extended

EBCDIC Character Set *continued*

Dec	Hex	Name	Character	Meaning
42	2A	SM/SW		Set mode/switch
43	2B	CSP		Control sequence prefix
44	2C	MFA		Modify field attribute
45	2D	ENQ		Enquiry
46	2E	ACK		Acknowledge
47	2F	BEL		Bell
48	30			(not assigned)
49	31			(not assigned)
50	32	SYN		Synchronous idle
51	33	IR		Index return
52	34	PP		Presentation position
53	35	TRN		Transparent
54	36	NBS		Numeric backspace
55	37	EOT		End of transmission
56	38	SBS		Subscript
57	39	IT		Indent tab
58	3A	RFF		Required form feed
59	3B	CU3		Customer use 3
60	3C	DC4		Device control 4
61	3D	NAK		Negative acknowledge
62	3E			(not assigned)
63	3F	SUB		Substitute
64	40	SP		Space
65	41	RSP		Required space
66	42			(not assigned)
67	43			(not assigned)
68	44			(not assigned)
69	45			(not assigned)
70	46			(not assigned)
71	47			(not assigned)
72	48			(not assigned)
73	49			(not assigned)
74	4A		¢	
75	4B		.	
76	4C		<	
77	4D		(	
78	4E		+	
79	4F				Logical OR
80	50		&	
81	51			(not assigned)
82	52			(not assigned)
83	53			(not assigned)
84	54			(not assigned)
85	55			(not assigned)
86	56			(not assigned)

EBCDIC Character Set *continued*

Dec	Hex	Name	Character	Meaning
87	57			(not assigned)
88	58			(not assigned)
89	59			(not assigned)
90	5A		!	
91	5B		$	
92	5C		*	
93	5D		)	
94	5E		;	
95	5F		¬	Logical NOT
96	60		–	
97	61		/	
98	62			(not assigned)
99	63			(not assigned)
100	64			(not assigned)
101	65			(not assigned)
102	66			(not assigned)
103	67			(not assigned)
104	68			(not assigned)
105	69			(not assigned)
106	6A		¦	Broken pipe
107	6B		,	
108	6C		%	
109	6D		_	
110	6E		>	
111	6F		?	
112	70			(not assigned)
113	71			(not assigned)
114	72			(not assigned)
115	73			(not assigned)
116	74			(not assigned)
117	75			(not assigned)
118	76			(not assigned)
119	77			(not assigned)
120	78			(not assigned)
121	79		`	Grave accent
122	7A		:	
123	7B		#	
124	7C		@	
125	7D		'	
126	7E		=	
127	7F		"	
128	80			(not assigned)
129	81		a	
130	82		b	
131	83		c	

EBCDIC Character Set *continued*

Dec	Hex	Name	Character	Meaning
132	84		d	
133	85		e	
134	86		f	
135	87		g	
136	88		h	
137	89		i	
138	8A			(not assigned)
139	8B			(not assigned)
140	8C			(not assigned)
141	8D			(not assigned)
142	8E			(not assigned)
143	8F			(not assigned)
144	90			(not assigned)
145	91		j	
146	92		k	
147	93		l	
148	94		m	
149	95		n	
150	96		o	
151	97		p	
152	98		q	
153	99		r	
154	9A			(not assigned)
155	9B			(not assigned)
156	9C			(not assigned)
157	9D			(not assigned)
158	9E			(not assigned)
159	9F			(not assigned)
160	A0			(not assigned)
161	A1		~	
162	A2		s	
163	A3		t	
164	A4		u	
165	A5		v	
166	A6		w	
167	A7		x	
168	A8		y	
169	A9		z	
170	AA			(not assigned)
171	AB			(not assigned)
172	AC			(not assigned)
173	AD			(not assigned)
174	AE			(not assigned)
175	AF			(not assigned)

EBCDIC Character Set *continued*

Dec	Hex	Name	Character	Meaning
176	B0			(not assigned)
177	B1			(not assigned)
178	B2			(not assigned)
179	B3			(not assigned)
180	B4			(not assigned)
181	B5			(not assigned)
182	B6			(not assigned)
183	B7			(not assigned)
184	B8			(not assigned)
185	B9			(not assigned)
186	BA			(not assigned)
187	BB			(not assigned)
188	BC			(not assigned)
189	BD			(not assigned)
190	BE			(not assigned)
191	BF			(not assigned)
192	C0		{	Opening brace
193	C1		A	
194	C2		B	
195	C3		C	
196	C4		D	
197	C5		E	
198	C6		F	
199	C7		G	
200	C8		H	
201	C9		I	
202	CA	SHY		Syllable hyphen
203	CB			(not assigned)
204	CC			(not assigned)
205	CD			(not assigned)
206	CE			(not assigned)
207	CF			(not assigned)
208	D0		}	Closing brace
209	D1		J	
210	D2		K	
211	D3		L	
212	D4		M	
213	D5		N	
214	D6		O	
215	D7		P	
216	D8		Q	
217	D9		R	
218	DA			(not assigned)
219	DB			(not assigned)

EBCDIC Character Set *continued*

Dec	Hex	Name	Character	Meaning
220	DC			(not assigned)
221	DD			(not assigned)
222	DE			(not assigned)
223	DF			(not assigned)
224	E0		\	Reverse slash
225	E1	NSP		Numeric space
226	E2		S	
227	E3		T	
228	E4		U	
229	E5		V	
230	E6		W	
231	E7		X	
232	E8		Y	
233	E9		Z	
234	EA			(not assigned)
235	EB			(not assigned)
236	EC			(not assigned)
237	ED			(not assigned)
238	EE			(not assigned)
239	EF			(not assigned)
240	F0		0	
241	F1		1	
242	F2		2	
243	F3		3	
244	F4		4	
245	F5		5	
246	F6		6	
247	F7		7	
248	F8		8	
249	F9		9	
250	FA			(not assigned)
251	FB			(not assigned)
252	FC			(not assigned)
253	FD			(not assigned)
254	FE			(not assigned)
255	FF	EO		Eight ones

Appendix B

Common File Extensions

File Extension	Type of File
.0	File containing information on hard disk compressed with DoubleSpace.
.123	Spreadsheet file in Lotus 123.
.4th	Source file in Forth.
.a	Source file in Macintosh Assembly.
.ad	Screensaver file in After Dark.
.ada	Source file in Ada.
.ai	Vector graphic file in Adobe Illustrator.
.aif	*See* .aiff.
.aifc	*See* .aiff.
.aiff	Audio file in the Apple Audio Interchange Format originally used on Apple and Silicon Graphics (SGI) computers.
.ani	**1.** Animated cursor file in Microsoft Windows 9x and Windows NT. **2.** Animation file.
.aol	File related to America Online.
.aps	Source file in Microsoft Visual C++.
.arc	Archive file compressed with ARC.
.arj	Archive file compressed with ARJ.
.asc	**1.** ASCII text file. **2.** File encrypted with PGP (Pretty Good Privacy).
.asf	File in Microsoft Advanced Streaming Format.
.asm	Source file in Assembler.
.asp	File in Active Server Page format, generally found on the World Wide Web.
.atm	File in Adobe Type Manager.
.au	Sound file, generally on UNIX systems or the World Wide Web.
.avi	Audio visual interleaved data file in the Microsoft RIFF format.
.bac	*See* .bak.
.bak	Backup file.
.bas	Source file in Basic.
.bat	Batch program file.
.bfc	Briefcase file in Microsoft Windows 9x.
.bin	**1.** Archive file compressed with MacBinary. **2.** Binary file.
.bk	*See* .bak.

Common File Extensions *continued*

File Extension	Type of File
.bmk	Bookmarked file.
.bmp	Raster graphics file stored in bitmap format.
.box	Mailbox file in Lotus Notes.
.c	Source file in C.
.c++	Source file in C++.
.cab	Microsoft cabinet file—multiple files compressed into one and extractable with the extract.exe utility.
.cas	Comma-delimited ASCII text file.
.cb	Clean boot file in Microsoft Windows.
.cbl	Source file in Cobol.
.cca	E-mail message in Lotus cc:mail.
.cda	CD audio track.
.cdf	1. File in Microsoft Channel Definition Format. 2. File in Common Data Format.
.cdi	File in Phillips Compact Disk Interactive format.
.cdr	Vector graphics file in CorelDraw.
.cgi	File containing Common Gateway Interface scripts, generally for use on the World Wide Web.
.cgm	Vector graphics file in Computer Graphics Metafile format.
.chk	Portions of unidentifiable files saved in Windows by the Disk Defragmentor or ScanDisk utilities.
.chm	File containing compiled HTML.
.cil	Microsoft Clip Gallery download package.
.class	Class file in Java.
.clp	Temporary file created by Microsoft Windows Clipboard utility.
.cmd	Command file in Windows NT, OS/2, MS-DOS, and CP/M.
.cmf	File in Corel Metafile.
.cob	Source file in Cobol.
.com	Command file or program.
.cpl	Control Panel file in Microsoft Windows 9x.
.cpp	Source file in C++.
.crt	Certificate file.
.css	Cascading Style Sheet file, generally used in conjunction with Web sites.
.csv	Comma-delimited text file.
.ct	Graphics file in Paint Shop Pro.
.cur	Cursor file in Windows.
.cxx	Source file in C++.
.dat	Data file.
.dbf	Database in dBASE and FoxPro.
.dcr	Multimedia file in Macromedia Shockwave.
.dib	Graphics file in Device Independent Bitmap format.
.dif	File in Data Interchange Format.
.dll	Dynamic-link library file.

Common File Extensions *continued*

File Extension	Type of File
.doc	1. Document file in Microsoft Word. 2. In the past, document file in Adobe FrameMaker or WordStar. 3. Document file formatted for a word processor.
.dos	MS-DOS–related files in Microsoft Windows 9x.
.dot	Document template in Microsoft Word.
.drv	Device driver.
.dtd	Document Type Definition file in SGML or XML.
.dtp	Document file in Microsoft Publisher or PublishIt!
.dv	Video file.
.dvi	Document file in TEX Device Independent File format.
.emf	File in Enhanced Windows Metafile format.
.eml	Mail message in Microsoft Outlook Express.
.eps	Encapsulated PostScript file.
.exe	Executable program or file.
.F	Source file in Fortran.
.F77	Source file in Fortran 77.
.F90	Source file in Fortran 90.
.fax	Fax file in many Fax programs.
.fdf	File in Adobe Acrobat Forms.
.fla	Movie file in Macromedia Flash.
.fli	Animation file in AutoDesk FLIC file.
.flf	Device driver in OS/2.
.fm	Document file in Adobe FrameMaker.
.fon	System font file in Windows.
.for	Source file in Fortran.
.fp	File in FileMaker Pro.
.fpt	*See* .fp.
.frm	Document file in Adobe FrameMaker.
.gid	Index file in Windows 9x.
.gif	Raster image file in GIF format.
.giff	*See* .gif.
.gtar	UNIX archive file compressed in GNU tar utility.
.gz	UNIX archive file compressed by gzip.
.gzip	*See* .gz.
.h	Header file.
.hdf	File in Hierarchical Data Format.
.hex	File encoded with Macintosh BinHex utility.
.hlp	Help file in Microsoft Windows.
.hqx	File encoded with BinHex utility.
.htm	*See* .html.
.html	HTML file, most commonly used as a Web page.

Common File Extensions *continued*

File Extension	Type of File
.ico	Icon file in Microsoft Windows 9x.
.iff	1. Image or sound file in IFF format.
	2. Data file on Amiga systems.
.image	Image file in Macintosh Disk Image format.
.inf	Device information file, which contains scripts used to control hardware operations.
.ini	In MS-DOS and Windows 3.x, an initialization file, which contains user preferences and startup information about an application program.
.ins	File containing InstallShield install script.
.isu	File containing InstallShield uninstall script.
.jas	Image file in JAS format.
.jav	*See* .java.
.java	Source file in Java.
.jff	*See* .jpg.
.jfif	*See* .jpg.
.jpe	*See* .jpg.
.jpeg	*See* .jpg.
.jpg	Graphic image file encoded in the JPEG File Interchange Format.
.js	Source file in JavaScript.
.l	Source file in LISP.
.latex	Text file in LaTeX.
.lha	Archive file compressed with LZH.
.lib	Library file in many programming languages.
.lnk	Shortcut file in Windows 9x and Windows NT 4.
.log	Log file.
.lsp	Source file in LISP.
.lzh	*See* .lha.
.mac	Image file in MacPaint.
.mak	Project file in Microsoft Visual Basic or Microsoft Visual C++.
.man	Manual page in UNIX.
.mbox	Mailbox file in BSD UNIX.
.mbx	1. Address file in Microsoft Outlook.
	2. Mailbox file in Eudora.
.mcw	Document file in Microsoft Word for the Macintosh.
.mdb	Database in Microsoft Access.
.mic	Image file in Microsoft Image Composer.
.mid	Music file in MIDI format.
.midi	*See* .mid.
.mime	File encoded in MIME format.
.moov	Video file in Apple QuickTime.
.mov	*See* .moov.
.movie	*See* .moov.

Common File Extensions *continued*

File Extension	Type of File
.mp2	Audio file compressed and encoded according to the MPEG Audio Layer-2 standard.
.mp3	Audio file compressed and encoded according to the MPEG Audio Layer-3 standard.
.mpe	*See* .mpg.
.mpeg	*See* .mpg.
.mpg	Compressed video and audio file in MPEG format.
.mpp	1. Graphics file in CAD format.
	2. File in Microsoft Project.
.msg	E-mail message in Microsoft Outlook.
.ncb	File in Microsoft Developer Studio.
.ncf	Command file in Novell NetWare.
.ncf	Temporary file created by Microsoft Windows Clipboard utility.
.net	Network configuration file.
.newsrc	Setup file for UNIX-based newsreaders.
.nlb	Data file in Oracle 7.
.nlm	Module file in Novell NetWare.
.nsf	Database in Lotus Notes.
.nws	News message file in Microsoft Outlook Express.
.obd	File in Microsoft Office Binder.
.ocx	Microsoft OLE control.
.ole	Microsoft OLE object.
.opt	*See* .ncb.
.p	Source file in Pascal.
.p65	Document file in PageMaker 6.5.
.pab	Address book file in Microsoft Outlook.
.pcd	Image file in Kodak Photo-CD.
.pcl	File in Hewlett-Packard Printer Control Language.
.pcx	Bitmapped image file in PC Paintbrush.
.pdf	Document file encoded in Adobe Portable Document Format.
.pgp	File encrypted in PGP (Pretty Good Privacy).
.pic	1. Image file in PC Paint format.
	2. *See* .pict.
.pict	Image file in the Macintosh PICT.
.pl	1. Source file in Perl.
	2. Source file in Prolog.
.png	Bitmap image file in PNG format.
.pps	1. Image file in Paint Shop Pro.
	2. Slide show file in Microsoft PowerPoint.
.ppt	Presentation file in Microsoft PowerPoint.
.prc	Text or program file for 3Com PalmPilot.
.prg	File in Microsoft FoxPro, Ashton-Tate dBase, or CA Clipper.
.ps	PostScript printer file.

Common File Extensions *continued*

File Extension	Type of File
.psd	Image file in Adobe PhotoShop.
.pst	Personal File Folder file in Microsoft Outlook.
.pub	Document file in Ventura Publisher, Adobe PageMaker, or Microsoft Publisher.
.pwd	Document file in Microsoft Pocket Word for handheld and palm-size computers.
.pwl	Password file in Microsoft Windows 9x.
.pxl	Spreadsheet file in Microsoft Pocket Excel for handheld and palm-size computers.
.qic	Backup file in Microsoft Backup.
.qif	*See* .qti.
.qt	*See* .qtm.
.qti	Image file in Apple QuickTime.
.qtif	*See* .qti.
.qtm	Movie file in Apple QuickTime.
.qts	*See* .qti.
.qtx	*See* .qti.
.qxd	Document file in QuarkXPress.
.ra	Sound file in RealAudio.
.ram	Metafile in RealAudio.
.ras	Raster image bitmap on Sun systems.
.rast	*See* .ras.
.raw	Bitmap file in RAW format.
.rdf	Resource Description Framework file in XML.
.rgb	*See* .raw.
.rif	Bitmap file in RIFF format.
.riff	*See* .rif.
.rle	Bitmap file in RLE compression scheme.
.rm	Video file in RealAudio.
.rtf	Document file in Rich Text Format.
.s	1. Source file in Assembler. 2. Source file in Scheme.
.sam	Document file in Lotus Ami Professional.
.sav	1. Saved file in many games. 2. Saved backup file.
.scc	File in Microsoft SourceSafe.
.scd	File in Microsoft Schedule+.
.scr	Screensaver file in Microsoft Windows.
.sea	Self-extracting Macintosh archive file compressed with StuffIt.
.set	File set in Microsoft Backup.
.sgm	File in SGML.
.sgml	*See* .sgm.
.shtml	1. File in HTML format that has SSI (server side includes). 2. Secure file in HTML.

Common File Extensions *continued*

File Extension	Type of File
.sig	Signature file for e-mail or Internet newsgroup use.
.sit	Macintosh archive file compressed with StuffIt.
.sm	Source file in Smalltalk.
.snd	**1.** Interchangeable sound file format used on Sun, NeXT, and Silicon Graphics computers, consisting of raw audio data preceded by a text identifier.
	2. Sound resource file on the Macintosh.
.spl	File in Macromedia Shockwave Flash.
.sql	Query or report file in SQL.
.stm	*See* .shtml.
.sun	Raster graphics file in Sun systems.
.swa	Audio file in Macromedia Shockwave.
.swf	File in Macromedia Shockwave Flash.
.swp	Swap file in Microsoft Windows.
.sys	System configuration file.
.tar	Uncompressed UNIX archive in tar format.
.taz	UNIX archive file in Gzip or tar format.
.tcl	Source file in TCL.
.tga	Bitmap file in Targa format.
.tif	Bitmap images in TIFF format.
.tiff	*See* .tif.
.tmp	Temporary file in Windows.
.tsv	Tab separated values file.
.ttf	TrueType font file.
.txt	ASCII text file.
.udf	Database file in Microsoft Windows NT.
.uri	File containing list of URIs.
.url	Shortcut file on the Internet for a URL.
.uu	*See* .uud.
.uud	Binary file that has been translated into ASCII format using uuencode.
.uue	File that has been decoded from ASCII format back into binary format using uudecode.
.vbx	Custom control in Microsoft Visual Basic.
.vda	*See* .tga.
.vp	Document file in Ventura Publisher.
.vrm	**1.** *See* .vrml.
	2. Source file in Visual ReXX.
.vrml	A 3-D graphics file in VRML.
.vst	Bitmap image file in Targa.
.vxd	Virtual device driver in Microsoft Windows.
.wab	E-mail file in Microsoft Outlook Express.
.wav	Sound file stored in waveform (WAV) audio format.
.wmf	Vector image file encoded as a Microsoft Windows Metafile.

Common File Extensions *continued*

File Extension	*Type of File*
.wp	Document file in Corel WordPerfect.
.wp6	Document file in Corel WordPerfect 6.x.
.wpd	*See* .wp.
.wpg	Graphic file in Corel WordPerfect.
.wps	Document file in Microsoft Works.
.wri	Document file in Microsoft Write.
.xls	Spreadsheet file in Microsoft Excel.
.z	UNIX file archive compressed with gzip.
.Z	UNIX file archive compressed with compress utility.
.zip	Archive file compressed in ZIP format with PKZIP or WinZip.
.zoo	Archive file compressed with zoo.

Appendix C

Instant Messaging Emoticons and Acronyms

Instant messaging, chat, and other Internet communications formats have led to a variety of shorthand indicators and clarifiers meant to enhance the user experience.

Emotags

Emotags were first used in e-mail and newsgroups to clarify a message for the reader. Typically, emotags consist of a word or words in brackets or parentheses, such as *<joke>*, and appear right after or both before and after the text they refer to.

Smileys

The most common emoticons are faces and expressions composed of standard keyboard punctuation marks and symbols, and which are viewed sideways. These are known as "smileys" in reference to the first emoticons, which represented a smile, such as: : -). Smileys are indicators of the emotional "tone of voice" intended by the writer.

Smileys

Text	Meaning
:-)	smile
(-:	left-handed smile
:o)	smile with a large nose (or clown smiley)
:)	smile with no nose
:->	smirk (or wry smile)
:-}	wry smile (or leer)
:-t	unsmiley
:*)	just clowning around (or inebriated)
:-))))	extreme happiness (or sarcastic happiness)
:-D	very happy (or laughing)
(-D	laughing hard
:-) :-) :-)	loud guffaw
:'-)	laughing and crying
%-)	amused (and possibly confused)
:-/	chagrined (or skeptical)
:-I	indifferent
:~)	touched (or ill with a cold)

Smileys *continued*

Text	Meaning
(:-(	sad (or bald and sad)
:-(	frown (or unhappy)
:-c	very unhappy
:-((((	extremely unhappy (or sarcastic unhappiness)
:-<	forlorn
>:-(	annoyed
:-[	pouting
(:-& or %-(	angry
>:-<	very angry
~ :-(	very angry (or fuming mad)
%-(or :/)	not amused
:-|	expressionless
:-| or :-(	have an ordinary day
:-e	disappointed
:-X	lips are sealed (or not saying a word)
:-v	talking
:-I	hmmm
:-8(	condescending stare
:-O	shouting (or shocked)
:-@	screaming
:,-(or :'-(	crying
~:-o	baby
]:-)>	devilish
):-)	impish
;->	lewd
:-x	kiss
:-*	ready for a kiss (or just ate something sour)
8-]	wow
:-J	tongue-in-cheek
:-&	tongue-tied (or biting tongue)
:-p	no way! (or nyah nyah)
;-)	wink
'-)	one-eyed wink
:-7	wry statement (or tongue-in-cheek)
:-| :-|	déjà vu
?-(	sorry, I don't know what went wrong (or black eye)
:-C	that's unbelievable! (or incredible!)
B-D	serves you right
:-B	drooling
:-*)	drunk

Smileys *continued*

Text	Meaning
:-9	licking lips
l-p	yuck!
:-b	sticking out tongue
-]:-)[-	impressed
8-I or 8-l	in suspense
l:-l	excessively rigid
:-]	obnoxious
l-)	bored (or asleep)
l-I	asleep
I^o	snoring
l-O	yawning
:-"	whistling (or pursing lips)
:-s	incoherent statement
:-#	just said the wrong thing (or braces)
:-!	foot in mouth
:-() or :-D	big mouth
(:-$ or :-(*)	ill
(:~) or :-')	ill with a cold
:-R	ill with the flu
%+l or %+{	lost a fight
X-(	unconscious (or dead)
<:-)	dunce
*:o)	bozo
@;-)	flirt
X:-)	child
:>)	big nose
&:-)	curly hair (or girl smiley)
#:-)	matted hair
8-)	wearing glasses
8:-)	glasses on forehead (or little girl, or hair in curlers)
B-)	wearing horn-rimmed glasses (or sunglasses)
B-]	wearing cool sunglasses
O:-)	angel
&8-l	nerd
c:-) or (:-)	bald
:-{	has a moustache
:-)} or :-)#	has a beard
:-Q or :-I	smoker
:-d~	heavy smoker
:-?	pipe smoker

Smileys *continued*

Text	Meaning
:-/I	no smoking
:-) X	wearing a bow tie
{(:-)	wearing a toupee
:-{}	lipstick
[:-)	stereo headphones
d :-o	hats off
~:-(	has been flamed (or is on fire)
~~:-(	has been flamed repeatedly
)	Cheshire cat
(:-I	egghead
3:-o	cow
[: l]	robot
M-)	see no evil
:X)	hear no evil
:-M	speak no evil
*8((:	strange
O+	female
O->	male
ll*(	handshake offered
ll*)	handshake accepted
<{:-)}	message in a bottle
(-: :-)	putting heads together
[] or ()	hug given (name or initials can be included between the brackets)
((( )))	lots of hugs
((( ))):**	hugs and kisses
(::()::)	Band-Aid (or comfort)
@->–	a rose
@—>—	a long-stemmed rose
@==	atomic bomb
<')))))-<	a fish
^	giggles

Alternate (Japanese) Smileys

Alternate smileys, which do not require users to tilt their heads sideways, were developed by Internet users in Japan and are becoming more common worldwide. Some versions of these emoticons leave out the ( ) brackets around the faces.

Alternate Smileys

Text	Meaning
(^_^)	male smiley
(^.^)	female smiley
(^L^) or (^(^)	happy
(-_-)	secret smile
(^o^)	laughing out loud
(^_^;)	laughing to cover nervousness
(^_^)/	waving hello
(;_;)/	waving good-bye
(^_~) or (^_-)	winking
(*^o^*) or (*^.^*)	exciting
\(^_^)/	joyful
(;_;) or (~~>.<~~)	crying
(>.<) or (>_<)	angry
(v_v)	expressionless
(^o^;>	excuse me?
(*^_^*)	blushing (or shy)
(^_^;;;)	embarrassed (or in a cold sweat)
(?_?)	confused (or wondering)
(!_!) or (o_o)	shocked
(*_*)	frightened (or in love)
(=_=)~	sleepy
(u_u)	sleeping
(@_@)	stunned
'\=o-o=/'	wearing glasses
m(_)m	humble bow of thanks or apology

Acronyms and Shorthand

The first emotional indicators in newsgroups and e-mail were acronyms designed to give readers clues to the attitude and intent of the sender. Acronyms also quickly developed as keyboarding shortcuts. Use of acronyms is particularly prevalent in instant messaging, primarily to maintain the pace of real-time conversation.

Acronyms

Text	Meaning
AAMOF	as a matter of fact
AAR	at any rate
ADN	any day now
AFAIK	as far as I know
AFK	away from keyboard
AFKBRB	away from keyboard, be right back
ASAP	as soon as possible
A/S/L	age/sex/location
B2W	back to work
B4N (or BFN)	bye for now
BAK	back at keyboard
BBL	be back later
BBS	be back soon
BCNU	be seeing you
BF (or B/F)	boyfriend
BMN	but maybe not
BRB	be right back
BTDT	been there, done that
BTDTBTT	been there, done that, bought the tape
BTDTGTTS	been there, done that, got the t-shirt
BTDTGTTSAWIO	been there, done that, got the t-shirt, and wore it out
BTW	by the way
BYKT	but you knew that
CIO	cut it out
CMIIW	correct me if I'm wrong
CU (or CYA)	see you
CUL (or CUL8R)	see you later
DIY	do it yourself
DYJHIW	don't you just hate it when
EAK	eating at keyboard
EOL	end of lecture
EOM	end of message
F2F (or FTF)	face to face
FAPP	for all practical purposes

Acronyms *continued*

Text	Meaning
FOFL (or FOTFL)	falling on the floor laughing
FTR	for the record
FWIW	for what it's worth
FYA	for your amusement
FYEO	for your eyes only
FYI	for your information
g (or <g>)	grin
G (or <G>)	big grin
G2G (or GTG)	got to go
GAL	get a life
GD&H	grinning, ducking, and hiding
GD&R	grinning, ducking, and running
GD&RVVF	grinning, ducking, and running, very, very fast
GF (or G/F)	girlfriend
GG	gotta go (or good game)
GIWIST	gee, I wish I said that
GMTA	great minds think alike
GoAT	go away, troll
HAK	hugs and kisses
HAGD	have a great day
HAND	have a nice day
HEH	a courtesy laugh
HHOS	ha-ha, only serious
HTH	hope this helps (or hope that helps)
IAE	in any event
HW	homework (or hardware)
IANAL	I am not a lawyer
IC	I see
ICBW	I could be wrong (or it could be worse)
IDTS	I don't think so
IINM	if I'm not mistaken
IIRC	if I recall correctly
IIUC	if I understand correctly
IMCO	in my considered opinion
IME	in my experience
IMHO	in my humble opinion
IMNSHO	in my not-so-humble opinion
IMO	in my opinion

Acronyms *continued*

Text	Meaning
IOW	in other words
IRL	in real life
ISTM	it seems to me
ISWYM	I see what you mean
ITRW	in the real world
J (or <J>)	joking
JC	just chillin'
JIC	just in case
JK (or J/K)	just kidding (or that was a joke)
JTYWTK	just thought you wanted to know
JW	just wondering
K	okay
KWIM	know what I mean?
L (or <L>)	laughing
L8R	later
LJBF	let's just be friends
LOL	laughing out loud
LTNS	long time no see
MHBFY	my heart bleeds for you
MHOTY	my hat's off to you
MOTAS	member of the appropriate sex
MOTD	message of the day
MYOB	mind your own business
NBD	no big deal
NBIF	no basis in fact
NOYB	none of your business
NP	no problem
NRN	no response necessary (or no reply necessary)
OIC	oh, I see
OM	oh my (or old man, as in husband)
OOI	out of interest
OOTB	out of the box
OTL	out to lunch
OTOH	on the other hand
OTTH	on the third hand
PAW	parents are watching
PC	politically correct
PDA	public display of affection
PEST	please excuse slow typing

Acronyms *continued*

Text	Meaning
PI (or PIC)	politically incorrect
PKB (or P/K/B)	pot, kettle, black (or pot calling the kettle black)
PMBI	pardon my butting in
PMFJI	pardon me for jumping in
POS	parent over shoulder (or parents over shoulder)
POV	point of view
PPL	people
PTB	powers that be
R (or r)	are
REHI	re-hello (following a short time away) (or hi again)
RFC	request for comment
RL	real life
ROTFL	rolling on the floor laughing
ROTFLOL	rolling on the floor laughing out loud
RSN	real soon now
S (or <S>)	smile
SCNR	sorry, could not resist
SITD	still in the dark
SOP	standard operating procedure
SPMD	some people may differ
SUP	what's up?
TBE	to be expected
THX (or TX)	thanks
TIA	thanks in advance
TANJ	there ain't no justice
TIC	tongue-in-cheek
TPHB	the pointy-haired boss
TPTB	the powers that be
TTBOMK	to the best of my knowledge
TTFN	ta-ta for now
TTYL	talk to you later
TVM	thanks very much
TVMIA	thanks very much in advance
TYVMIA	thank you very much in advance
U	you
UW	you're welcome
VBG (or <VBG>)	very big grin
WB	welcome back
WCD	what's cookin' doc?

Acronyms *continued*

Text	Meaning
WHBT	we have been trolled
WOA	work of art
WRT	with regard to (or with respect to)
WTG	way to go
WTH	what the heck?
Y (or <Y>)	yawning
YHBT	you have been told (or you have been trolled)
YHBW	you have been warned
YHGMTPOTG	you have greatly misinterpreted the purpose of this group
YHM	you have mail
YMMV	your mileage may vary
YOYO	you're on your own
YWSYLS	you win some, you lose some

Appendix D

Internet Domains

Top-Level Domains: Organizational

Domain	Type of Organization
.aero	Air-transport industry
.biz	Businesses
.com	Commercial
.coop	Cooperatives
.edu	Educational
.gov	Nonmilitary agency, United States federal government
.info	Unrestricted use
.int	International organization
.mil	United States military
.museum	Museums
.name	Individuals
.net	Network provider
.org	Nonprofit organization
.pro	Professional workers

Top-Level Domains: Geographic

Domain	Country/Region
.ac	Ascension Island
.ad	Andorra
.ae	United Arab Emirates
.af	Afghanistan
.ag	Antigua and Barbuda
.ai	Anguilla
.al	Albania
.am	Armenia
.an	Netherlands Antilles
.ao	Angola
.aq	Antarctica
.ar	Argentina

Top-Level Domains: Geographic *continued*

Domain	Country/Region
.as	American Samoa
.at	Austria
.au	Australia
.aw	Aruba
.az	Azerbaijan
.ba	Bosnia and Herzegovina
.bb	Barbados
.bd	Bangladesh
.be	Belgium
.bf	Burkina Faso
.bg	Bulgaria
.bh	Bahrain
.bi	Burundi
.bj	Benin
.bm	Bermuda
.bn	Brunei
.bo	Bolivia
.br	Brazil
.bs	Bahamas, The
.bt	Bhutan
.bv	Bouvet Island
.bw	Botswana
.by	Belarus
.bz	Belize
.ca	Canada
.cc	Cocos (Keeling) Islands
.cd	Congo (DRC)
.cf	Central African Republic
.cg	Congo
.ch	Switzerland
.ci	Côte d'Ivoire
.ck	Cook Islands
.cl	Chile
.cm	Cameroon
.cn	China
.co	Colombia
.cr	Costa Rica
.cu	Cuba
.cv	Cape Verde
.cx	Christmas Island

Top-Level Domains: **Geographic** *continued*

Domain	Country/Region
.cy	Cyprus
.cz	Czech Republic
.de	Germany
.dj	Djibouti
.dk	Denmark
.dm	Dominica
.do	Dominican Republic
.dz	Algeria
.ec	Ecuador
.ee	Estonia
.eg	Egypt
.er	Eritrea
.es	Spain
.et	Ethiopia
.fi	Finland
.fj	Fiji Islands
.fk	Falkland Islands (Islas Malvinas)
.fm	Micronesia
.fo	Faroe Islands
.fr	France
.ga	Gabon
.gd	Grenada
.ge	Georgia
.gf	French Guiana
.gg	Guernsey
.gh	Ghana
.gi	Gibraltar
.gl	Greenland
.gm	Gambia, The
.gn	Guinea
.gp	Guadeloupe
.gq	Equatorial Guinea
.gr	Greece
.gs	South Georgia and the South Sandwich Islands
.gt	Guatemala
.gu	Guam
.gw	Guinea-Bissau
.gy	Guyana
.hk	Hong Kong SAR
.hm	Heard Island and McDonald Islands

Top-Level Domains: **Geographic** *continued*

Domain	*Country/Region*
.hn	Honduras
.hr	Croatia
.ht	Haiti
.hu	Hungary
.id	Indonesia
.ie	Ireland
.il	Israel
.im	Man, Isle of
.in	India
.io	British Indian Ocean Territory
.iq	Iraq
.ir	Iran
.is	Iceland
.it	Italy
.je	Jersey
.jm	Jamaica
.jo	Jordan
.jp	Japan
.ke	Kenya
.kg	Kyrgzstan
.kh	Cambodia
.ki	Kiribati
.km	Comoros
.kn	St. Kitts and Nevis
.kp	North Korea
.kr	Korea
.kw	Kuwait
.ky	Cayman Islands
.kz	Kazakhstan
.la	Laos
.lb	Lebanon
.lc	St. Lucia
.li	Liechtenstein
.lk	Sri Lanka
.lr	Liberia
.ls	Lesotho
.lt	Lithuania
.lu	Luxembourg
.lv	Latvia
.ly	Libya

Top-Level Domains: Geographic *continued*

Domain	Country/Region
.ma	Morocco
.mc	Monaco
.md	Moldova
.mg	Madagascar
.mh	Marshall Islands
.mk	Macedonia, Former Yugoslav Republic of
.ml	Mali
.mm	Myanmar
.mn	Mongolia
.mo	Macau SAR
.mp	Northern Mariana Islands
.mq	Martinique
.mr	Mauritania
.ms	Montserrat
.mt	Malta
.mu	Mauritius
.mv	Maldives
.mw	Malawi
.mx	Mexico
.my	Malaysia
.mz	Mozambique
.na	Namibia
.nc	New Caledonia
.ne	Niger
.nf	Norfolk Island
.ng	Nigeria
.ni	Nicaragua
.nl	Netherlands, The
.no	Norway
.np	Nepal
.nr	Nauru
.nu	Niue
.nz	New Zealand
.om	Oman
.pa	Panama
.pe	Peru
.pf	French Polynesia
.pg	Papua New Guinea
.ph	Philippines
.pk	Pakistan

Top-Level Domains: Geographic *continued*

Domain	Country/Region
.pl	Poland
.pm	St. Pierre and Miquelon
.pn	Pitcairn Islands
.pr	Puerto Rico
.ps	Palestinian Authority
.pt	Portugal
.pw	Palau
.py	Paraguay
.qa	Qatar
.re	Reunion
.ro	Romania
.ru	Russia
.rw	Rwanda
.sa	Saudi Arabia
.sb	Solomon Islands
.sc	Seychelles
.sd	Sudan
.se	Sweden
.sg	Singapore
.sh	St. Helena
.si	Slovenia
.sj	Svalbard and Jan Mayen
.sk	Slovakia
.sl	Sierra Leone
.sm	San Marino
.sn	Senegal
.so	Somalia
.sr	Suriname
.st	São Tomé and Príncipe
.sv	El Salvador
.sy	Syria
.sz	Swaziland
.tc	Turks and Caicos Islands
.td	Chad
.tf	French Southern and Antarctic Lands
.tg	Togo
.th	Thailand
.tj	Tajikistan
.tk	Tokelau

Top-Level Domains: **Geographic** *continued*

Domain	Country/Region
.tm	Turkmenistan
.tn	Tunisia
.to	Tonga
.tp	East Timor
.tr	Turkey
.tt	Trinidad and Tobago
.tv	Tuvalu
.tw	Taiwan
.tz	Tanzania
.ua	Ukraine
.ug	Uganda
.uk	United Kingdom
.um	U.S. Minor Outlying Islands
.us	United States
.uy	Uruguay
.uz	Uzbekistan
.va	Vatican City
.vc	St. Vincent and the Grenadines
.ve	Venezuela
.vg	Virgin Islands, British
.vi	Virgin Islands
.vn	Vietnam
.vu	Vanuatu
.wf	Wallis and Futuna
.ws	Samoa
.ye	Yemen
.yt	Mayotte
.yu	Yugoslavia
.za	South Africa
.zm	Zambia
.zw	Zimbabwe

Appendix E

Numeric Equivalents

Decimal (Base 10)	Hexadecimal (Base 16)	Octal (Base 8)	Binary (Base 2)
1	01	01	00000001
2	02	02	00000010
3	03	03	00000011
4	04	04	00000100
5	05	05	00000101
6	06	06	00000110
7	07	07	00000111
8	08	10	00001000
9	06	11	00001001
10	0A	12	00001010
11	0B	13	00001011
12	0C	14	00001100
13	0D	15	00001101
14	0E	16	00001110
15	0F	17	00001111
16	10	20	00010000
17	11	21	00010001
18	12	22	00010010
19	13	23	00010011
20	14	24	00010100
21	15	25	00010101
22	16	26	00010110
23	17	27	00010111
24	18	30	00011000
25	19	31	00011001
26	1A	32	00011010
27	1B	33	00011011
28	1C	34	00011100
29	1D	35	00011101
30	1E	36	00011110
31	1F	37	00011111
32	20	40	00100000

Numeric Equivalents *continued*

Decimal (Base 10)	Hexadecimal (Base 16)	Octal (Base 8)	Binary (Base 2)
33	21	41	00100001
34	22	42	00100010
35	23	43	00100011
36	24	44	00100100
37	25	45	00100101
38	26	46	00100110
39	27	47	00100111
40	28	50	00101000
41	29	51	00101001
42	2A	52	00101010
43	2B	53	00101011
44	2C	54	00101100
45	2D	55	00101101
46	2E	56	00101110
47	2F	57	00101111
48	30	60	00110000
49	31	61	00110001
50	32	62	00110010
51	33	63	00110011
52	34	64	00110100
53	35	65	00110101
54	36	66	00110110
55	37	67	00110111
56	38	70	00111001
57	39	71	00111000
58	3A	72	00111010
59	3B	73	00111011
60	3C	74	00111100
61	3D	75	00111101
62	3E	76	00111110
63	3F	77	00111111
64	40	100	01000000
65	41	101	01000001
66	42	102	01000010
67	43	103	01000011
68	44	104	01000100
69	45	105	01000101
70	46	106	01000110
71	47	107	01000111

Numeric Equivalents *continued*

Decimal (Base 10)	Hexadecimal (Base 16)	Octal (Base 8)	Binary (Base 2)
72	48	110	01001000
73	49	111	01001001
74	4A	112	01001010
75	4B	113	01001011
76	4C	114	01001100
77	4D	115	01001101
78	4E	116	01001110
79	4F	117	01001111
80	50	120	01010000
81	51	121	01010001
82	52	122	01010010
83	53	123	01010011
84	54	124	01010100
85	55	125	01010101
86	56	126	01010110
87	57	127	01010111
88	58	130	01011000
89	59	131	01011001
90	5A	132	01011010
91	5B	133	01011011
92	5C	134	01011100
93	5D	135	01011101
94	5E	136	01011110
95	5F	137	01011111
96	60	140	01100000
97	61	141	01100001
98	62	142	01100010
99	63	143	01100011
100	64	144	01100100
101	65	145	01100101
102	66	146	01100110
103	67	147	01100111
104	68	150	01101000
105	69	151	01101001
106	6A	152	01101010
107	6B	153	01101011
108	6C	154	01101100
109	6D	155	01101101
110	6E	156	01101110
111	6F	157	01101111

Numeric Equivalents *continued*

Decimal (Base 10)	Hexadecimal (Base 16)	Octal (Base 8)	Binary (Base 2)
112	70	160	01110000
113	71	161	01110001
114	72	162	01110010
115	73	163	01110011
116	74	164	01110100
117	75	165	01110101
118	76	166	01110110
119	77	167	01110111
120	78	170	01111000
121	79	171	01111001
122	7A	172	01111010
123	7B	173	01111011
124	7C	174	01111100
125	7D	175	01111101
126	7E	176	01111110
127	7F	177	01111111
128	80	200	10000000
129	81	201	10000001
130	82	202	10000010
131	83	203	10000011
132	84	204	10000100
133	85	205	10000101
134	86	206	10000110
135	87	207	10000111
136	88	210	10001000
137	89	211	10001001
138	8A	212	10001010
139	8B	213	10001011
140	8C	214	10001100
141	8D	215	10001101
142	8E	216	10001110
143	8F	217	10001111
144	90	220	10010000
145	91	221	10010001
146	92	222	10010010
147	93	223	10010011
148	94	224	10010100
149	95	225	10010101
150	96	226	10010110

Numeric Equivalents *continued*

Decimal (Base 10)	Hexadecimal (Base 16)	Octal (Base 8)	Binary (Base 2)
151	97	227	10010111
152	98	230	10011000
153	99	231	10011001
154	9A	232	10011010
155	9B	233	10011011
156	9C	234	10011100
157	9D	235	10011101
158	9E	236	10011110
159	9F	237	10011111
160	A0	240	10100000
161	A1	241	10100001
162	A2	242	10100010
163	A3	243	10100011
164	A4	244	10100100
165	A5	245	10100101
166	A6	246	10100110
167	A7	247	10100111
168	A8	250	10101000
169	A9	251	10101001
170	AA	252	10101010
171	AB	253	10101011
172	AC	254	10101100
173	AD	255	10101101
174	AE	256	10101110
175	AF	257	10101111
176	B0	260	10110000
177	B1	261	10110001
178	B2	262	10110010
179	B3	263	10110011
180	B4	264	10110100
181	B5	265	10110101
182	B6	266	10110110
183	B7	267	10110111
184	B8	270	10111000
185	B9	271	10111001
186	BA	272	10111010
187	BB	273	10111011
188	BC	274	10111100
189	BD	275	10111101
190	BE	276	10111110

Numeric Equivalents *continued*

Decimal (Base 10)	Hexadecimal (Base 16)	Octal (Base 8)	Binary (Base 2)
191	BF	277	10111111
192	C0	300	11000000
193	C1	301	11000001
194	C2	302	11000010
195	C3	303	11000011
196	C4	304	11000100
197	C5	305	11000101
198	C6	306	11000110
199	C7	307	11000111
200	C8	310	11001000
201	C9	311	11001001
202	CA	312	11001010
203	CB	313	11001011
204	CC	314	11001100
205	CD	315	11001101
206	CE	316	11001110
207	CF	317	11001111
208	D0	320	11010000
209	D1	321	11010001
210	D2	322	11010010
211	D3	323	11010011
212	D4	324	11010100
213	D5	325	11010101
214	D6	326	11010110
215	D7	327	11010111
216	D8	330	11011000
217	D9	331	11011001
218	DA	332	11011010
219	DB	333	11011011
220	DC	334	11011100
221	DD	335	11011101
222	DE	336	11011110
223	DF	337	11011111
224	E0	340	11100000
225	E1	341	11100001
226	E2	342	11100010
227	E3	343	11100011
228	E4	344	11100100
229	E5	345	11100101

Numeric Equivalents *continued*

Decimal (Base 10)	Hexadecimal (Base 16)	Octal (Base 8)	Binary (Base 2)
230	E6	346	11100110
231	E7	347	11100111
232	E8	350	11101000
233	E9	351	11101001
234	EA	352	11101010
235	EB	353	11101011
236	EC	354	11101100
237	ED	355	11101101
238	EE	356	11101110
239	EF	357	11101111
240	F0	360	11110000
241	F1	361	11110001
242	F2	362	11110010
243	F3	363	11110011
244	F4	364	11110100
245	F5	365	11110101
246	F6	366	11110110
247	F7	367	11110111
248	F8	370	11111000
249	F9	371	11111001
250	FA	372	11111010
251	FB	373	11111011
252	FC	374	11111100
253	FD	375	11111101
254	FE	376	11111110
255	FF	377	11111111

Work smarter—
conquer your software *from the inside out!*

Hey, you know your way around a desktop. Now dig into Office XP applications and the Windows XP operating system and *really* put your PC to work! These supremely organized software reference titles pack hundreds of timesaving solutions, troubleshooting tips and tricks, and handy workarounds in a concise, fast-answer format. They're all muscle and no fluff. All this comprehensive information goes deep into the nooks and crannies of each Office application and Windows XP feature. And every *Inside Out* includes a CD-ROM full of handy tools and utilities, sample files, links to related sites, and other help. Discover the best and fastest ways to perform everyday tasks, and challenge yourself to new levels of software mastery!

MICROSOFT WINDOWS® XP INSIDE OUT
ISBN 0-7356-1382-6

MICROSOFT® OFFICE XP INSIDE OUT
ISBN 0-7356-1277-3

MICROSOFT WORD VERSION 2002 INSIDE OUT
ISBN 0-7356-1278-1

MICROSOFT EXCEL VERSION 2002 INSIDE OUT
ISBN 0-7356-1281-1

MICROSOFT OUTLOOK® VERSION 2002 INSIDE OUT
ISBN 0-7356-1282-X

MICROSOFT ACCESS VERSION 2002 INSIDE OUT
ISBN 0-7356-1283-8

MICROSOFT FRONTPAGE® VERSION 2002 INSIDE OUT
ISBN 0-7356-1284-6

MICROSOFT VISIO® VERSION 2002 INSIDE OUT
ISBN 0-7356-1285-4

Microsoft
microsoft.com/mspress

Target your problem and
fix it yourself—
fast!

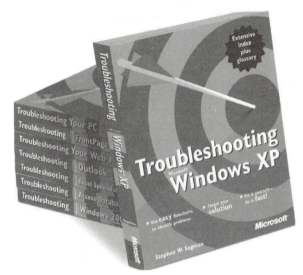

When you're stuck with a computer problem, you need answers right now. *Troubleshooting* books can help. They'll guide you to the source of the problem and show you how to solve it right away. Get ready solutions with clear, step-by-step instructions. Go to quick-access charts with *Top 20 Problems* and *Prevention Tips*. Find even more solutions with *Quick Fixes* and handy *Tips.* Walk through the remedy with plenty of screen shots. Find what you need with the extensive, easy-reference index. Get the answers you need to get back to business fast with *Troubleshooting* books.

Troubleshooting Microsoft® Office XP
ISBN 0-7356-1491-1

Troubleshooting Microsoft® Access Databases
(Covers Access 97 and Access 2000)
ISBN 0-7356-1160-2

Troubleshooting Microsoft® Access 2002
ISBN 0-7356-1488-1

Troubleshooting Microsoft Excel Spreadsheets
(Covers Excel 97 and Excel 2000)
ISBN 0-7356-1161-0

Troubleshooting Microsoft Excel 2002
ISBN 0-7356-1493-8

Troubleshooting Microsoft® Outlook®
(Covers Microsoft Outlook 2000 and Outlook Express)
ISBN 0-7356-1162-9

Troubleshooting Microsoft Outlook 2002
(Covers Microsoft Outlook 2002 and Outlook Express)
ISBN 0-7356-1487-3

Troubleshooting Your Web Page
(Covers Microsoft FrontPage® 2000)
ISBN 0-7356-1164-5

Troubleshooting Microsoft FrontPage 2002
ISBN 0-7356-1489-X

Troubleshooting Microsoft Windows®
(Covers Windows Me, Windows 98, and Windows 95)
ISBN 0-7356-1166-1

Troubleshooting Microsoft Windows 2000 Professional
ISBN 0-7356-1165-3

Troubleshooting Microsoft Windows XP
ISBN 0-7356-1492-X

Troubleshooting Your PC
ISBN 0-7356-1163-7

Microsoft Press® products are available worldwide wherever quality computer books are sold. For more information, contact your book or computer retailer, software reseller, or local Microsoft Sales Office, or visit our Web site at microsoft.com/mspress. To locate your nearest source for Microsoft Press products, or to order directly, call 1-800-MSPRESS in the U.S. (in Canada, call 1-800-268-2222).

Prices and availability dates are subject to change.

microsoft.com/mspress

Work smarter, add value, and get results!

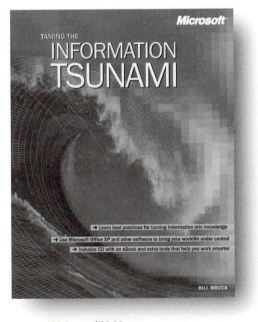

U.S.A. **$39.99**
Canada $57.99
ISBN: 0-7356-1434-2

For every business professional swamped with e-mail, drowning in paper, and wading through data, here are real-world solutions for turning all that information into business results! TAMING THE INFORMATION TSUNAMI demonstrates simple ways to change how you think about and use everyday technologies such as Microsoft® Office and Microsoft Internet Explorer—helping you match the right tool to the task, the right solution for your situation. Apply the skills, principles, and habits that empower you to work smarter and faster—and get out from under the deluge of too much work, too little time! Learn best practices for turning information into knowledge. Use Microsoft Office XP and other software to take control of your worklife. Work even smarter using the tools and eBook included on the CD-ROM!

microsoft.com/mspress

Work anywhere, anytime

with the Microsoft guide to mobile technology

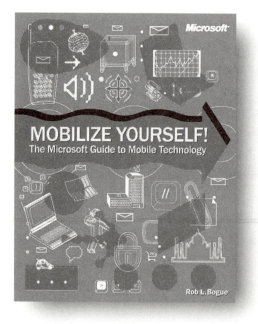

U.S.A. $29.99
Canada $43.99
ISBN: 0-7356-1502-0

Okay. You're at the airport but your flight has been delayed. For four hours. No worries—you've got your laptop so you're ready to work. Or are you? Can you connect to the Internet? What about reliable battery power? Here's the answer: MOBILIZE YOURSELF! THE MICROSOFT GUIDE TO MOBILE TECHNOLOGY. This comprehensive guide explains how to maximize the mobility of the technology you have today. And it provides smart answers about the mobile technologies and services you might be considering. From PDAs to the wireless Web, this book packs the insights and solutions that keep you—and your technology—up and running when you're out and about.

microsoft.com/mspress